Lecture Notes in Computer Science   12317

More information about this series at http://www.springer.com/series/7409

Xin Wang · Rui Zhang ·
Young-Koo Lee · Le Sun ·
Yang-Sae Moon (Eds.)

Web and Big Data

4th International Joint Conference, APWeb-WAIM 2020
Tianjin, China, September 18–20, 2020
Proceedings, Part I

 Springer

Editors
Xin Wang ⓘ
Tianjin University
Tianjin, China

Young-Koo Lee ⓘ
Kyung Hee University
Yongin, Democratic People's Republic
of Korea

Yang-Sae Moon ⓘ
Kangwon National University
Chunchon, Korea (Republic of)

Rui Zhang ⓘ
University of Melbourne
Melbourn, NSW, Australia

Le Sun
Nanjing University of Information Science
and Technology
Nanjing, China

ISSN 0302-9743   ISSN 1611-3349 (electronic)
Lecture Notes in Computer Science
ISBN 978-3-030-60258-1   ISBN 978-3-030-60259-8 (eBook)
https://doi.org/10.1007/978-3-030-60259-8

LNCS Sublibrary: SL3 – Information Systems and Applications, incl. Internet/Web, and HCI

This Springer imprint is published by the registered company Springer Nature Switzerland AG
The registered company address is: Gewerbestrasse 11, 6330 Cham, Switzerland

Preface

This volume (LNCS 12317) and its companion volume (LNCS 12318) contain the proceedings of the 4th Asia-Pacific Web (APWeb) and Web-Age Information Management (WAIM) Joint Conference on Web and Big Data (APWeb-WAIM 2020). This joint conference aims at attracting professionals from different communities related to Web and big data who have common interests in interdisciplinary research to share and exchange ideas, experiences, and the underlying techniques and applications, including Web technologies, database systems, information management, software engineering, and big data.

APWeb-WAIM 2020 was held in Tianjin, China, during September 18–20, 2020. APWeb and WAIM are two separate leading international conferences on research, development, and applications of Web technologies and database systems. Previous APWeb conferences were held in Beijing (1998), Hong Kong (1999), Xi'an (2000), Changsha (2001), Xi'an (2003), Hangzhou (2004), Shanghai (2005), Harbin (2006), Huangshan (2007), Shenyang (2008), Suzhou (2009), Busan (2010), Beijing (2011), Kunming (2012), Sydney (2013), Changsha (2014), Guangzhou (2015), and Suzhou (2016). Previous WAIM conferences were held in Shanghai (2000), Xi'an (2001), Beijing (2002), Chengdu (2003), Dalian (2004), Hangzhou (2005), Hong Kong (2006), Huangshan (2007), Zhangjiajie (2008), Suzhou (2009), Jiuzhaigou (2010), Wuhan (2011), Harbin (2012), Beidaihe (2013), Macau (2014), Qingdao (2015), and Nanchang (2016). Starting in 2017, the two conference committees agreed to launch a joint conference. The first APWeb-WAIM conference was held in Beijing (2017), the second APWeb-WAIM conference was held in Macau (2018), and the third APWeb-WAIM conference was held in Chengdu (2019). With the increased focus on big data, the new joint conference is expected to attract more professionals from different industrial and academic communities, not only from the Asia Pacific countries but also from other continents.

The high-quality program documented in these proceedings would not have been possible without the authors who chose APWeb-WAIM for disseminating their findings. After the double-blind review process (each paper received at least three review reports), out of 259 submissions, the conference accepted 68 regular papers (acceptance rate 26.25%), 29 short research papers, and 8 demonstrations. The contributed papers address a wide range of topics, such as big data analytics, data and information quality, data mining and application, graph data and social networks, information extraction and retrieval, knowledge graph, machine learning, recommender systems, storage, indexing and physical database design, text analysis, and mining. We are deeply thankful to the Program Committee members for lending their time and expertise to the conference. The technical program also included keynotes by Prof. James Hendler (Rensselaer Polytechnic Institute, USA), Prof. Masaru Kitsuregawa (The University of Tokyo, Japan), Prof. Xuemin Lin (University of New South Wales, Australia), and Prof. Xiaofang Zhou (The University of Queensland, Australia). We are grateful to these distinguished scientists for their invaluable contributions to the conference program.

We thank the honorary chairs (Masaru Kitsuregawa and Keqiu Li) and the general co-chairs (Xiaofang Zhou and Zhiyong Feng) for their guidance and support. Thanks also go to the workshop co-chairs (Qun Chen and Jianxin Li), panel co-chairs (Bin Cui and Weining Qian), tutorial co-chairs (Yunjun Gao and Leong Hou U), demo co-chairs (Xin Huang and Hongzhi Wang), industry co-chairs (Feifei Li and Guoliang Li), publication co-chairs (Le Sun and Yang-Sae Moon), and publicity co-chairs (Yi Cai, Yoshiharu Ishikawa, and Yueguo Chen).

We hope you enjoyed the exciting program of APWeb-WAIM 2020 as documented in these proceedings.

August 2020   Xin Wang
                                                                       Rui Zhang
                                                                  Young-Koo Lee

Organization

Honorary Chairs

Masaru Kitsuregawa	The University of Tokyo, Japan
Keqiu Li	Tianjin University, China

General Chairs

Xiaofang Zhou	The University of Queensland, Australia
Zhiyong Feng	Tianjing University, China

Program Committee Chairs

Xin Wang	Tianjin University, China
Rui Zhang	The University of Melbourne, Australia
Young-Koo Lee	Kyunghee University, South Korea

Panel Chairs

Bin Cui	Peking University, China
Weining Qian	East China Normal University, China

Workshop Chairs

Qun Chen	Northwestern Polytechnical University, China
Jianxin Li	Deakin University, Australia

Tutorial Chairs

Yunjun Gao	Zhejiang University, China
Leong Hou U.	University of Macau, Macau

Demo Chairs

Xin Huang	Hong Kong Baptist University, Hong Kong
Hongzhi Wang	Harbin Institue of Technology, China

Industry Chairs

Feifei Li	University of Utah, USA, and Alibaba, China
Guoliang Li	Tsinghua University and Huawei, China

Publication Chairs

Le Sun   Nanjing University of Information Science
                            and Technology, China
Yang-Sae Moon   Kangwon National University, South Korea

Publicity Chairs

Yi Cai   South China University of Technology, China
Yoshiharu Ishikawa   Nagoya University, Japan
Yueguo Chen   Renmin University of China, China

APWeb-WAIM Steering Committee Representative

Yanchun Zhang   Victoria University, Australia

Senior Program Committee

Wolf-Tilo Balke   TU Braunschweig, Germany
K. Selçuk Candan   Arizona State University, USA
Reynold Cheng   The University of Hong Kong, Hong Kong
Byron Choi   Hong Kong Baptist University, Hong Kong
Saiful Islam   Griffith University, Australia
Mizuho Iwaihara   Waseda University, Japan
Peer Kroger   Ludwig Maximilian University of Munich, Germany
Byung Suk Lee   University of Vermont, USA
Bohan Li   Nanjing University of Aeronautics and Astronautics,
                            China
Guoliang Li   Tsinghua University, China
Sebastian Link   The University of Auckland, New Zealand
Makoto Onizuka   Osaka University, Japan
Wookey Lee   Inha University, South Korea
Demetrios   University of Cyprus, Cyprus
   Zeinalipour-Yazti
Xiangliang Zhang   King Abdullah University of Science and Technology,
                            Saudi Arabia
Ying Zhang   University of Technology Sydney, Australia
Xiang Zhao   National University of Defence Technology, China
Shuigeng Zhou   Fudan University, China

Program Committee

Toshiyuki Amagasa   University of Tsukuba, Japan
Wolf-Tilo Balke   University of Hannover, Germany
Zhifeng Bao   RMIT University, Australia
Ilaria Bartolini   University of Bologna, Italy

Ladjel Bellatreche	ISAE-ENSMA, France
Zouhaier Brahmia	University of Sfax, Tunisia
Yi Cai	School of Software Engineering, China
Tru Hoang Cao	Ho Chi Minh City University of Technology, Vietnam
Xin Cao	University of New South Wales, Australia
Hong Chen	Renmin University of China, China
Lisi Chen	Hong Kong Baptist University, Hong Kong
Lu Chen	Aalborg University, Denmark
Qun Chen	Northwestern Polytechnical University, China
Shimin Chen	Chinese Academy of Sciences, China
Jiangtao Cui	Xidian University, China
Lizhen Cui	Shandong University, China
Maria Luisa Damiani	University of Milano, Italy
Alex Delis	University of Athens, Greece
Lei Duan	Sichuan University, China
Amr Ebaid	Purdue University, USA
Markus Endres	University of Augsburg, Germany
Ju Fan	Renmin University of China, China
Yaokai Feng	Kyushu University, Japan
Jun Gao	Peking University, China
Yunjun Gao	Zhejiang University, China
Tingjian Ge	University of Massachusetts, USA
Zhiguo Gong	University of Macau, Macau
Yu Gu	Northeastern University, China
Giovanna Guerrini	Universita di Genova, Italy
Jialong Han	Tencent AI Lab, China
Tanzima Hashem	Bangladesh University of Engineering and Technology, Bangladesh
Xiaofeng He	East China Normal University, China
Zhenying He	Fudan University, China
Liang Hong	Wuhan University, China
Haibo Hu	Hong Kong Polytechnic University, Hong Kong
Jilin Hu	Inception Institute of Artificial Intelligence, UAE
Jianbin Huang	Xidian University, China
Chih-Chieh Hung	Tamkang University, Taiwan
Dawei Jiang	Zhejiang University, China
Cheqing Jin	East China Normal University, China
Peiquan Jin	Universiity of Science and Technology of China, China
Tung Kieu	Aalborg University, Denmark
Carson K. Leung	University of Manitoba, Canada
Bohan Li	Nanjing University of Aeronautics and Astronautics, China
Cuiping Li	Renmin University of China, China
Feifei Li	The University of Utah, USA
Hui Li	Xiamen University, China
Jianxin Li	Deakin University, Australia

Jingjing Li	University of Electronic Science and Technology of China, China
Lin Li	Wuhan University of Technology, China
Ronghua Li	Shenzhen University, China
Tianrui Li	School of Information Science and Technology, China
Yafei Li	Zhengzhou University, China
Yu Li	Hangzhou Dianzi University, China
Zheng Li	Amazon, USA
Zhixu Li	Soochow University, China
Defu Lian	Big Data Research Center, China
Xiang Lian	Kent State University, USA
Guoqiong Liao	Jiangxi University of Finance and Economics, China
An Liu	Soochow University, China
Guanfeng Liu	Macquarie University, Australia
Hailong Liu	Northwestern Polytechnical University, China
Hongyan Liu	Tsinghua University, China
Yu Liu	Huazhong University of Science and Technology, China
Lizhen Wang	Yunnan University, China
Hua Lu	Aalborg University, Denmark
Wei Lu	Renmin University of China, China
Jizhou Luo	Harbin Institute of Technology, China
Mihai Lupu	Vienna University of Technology, Austria
Zakaria Maamar	Zayed University, UAE
Sanjay Kumar Madria	Missouri University of Science and Technology, USA
Yang-Sae Moon	Kangwon National University, South Korea
Mirco Nanni	ISTI-CNR, Italy
Wee Ng	Institute for Infocomm Research, Singapore
Baoning Niu	Taiyuan University of Technology, China
Hiroaki Ohshima	University of Hyogo, Japan
Vincent Oria	NJIT, USA
P. Krishna Reddy	International Institute of Information Technology, Hyderabad, India
Haiwei Pan	Harbin Engineering University, China
Sanghyun Park	Yonsei University, South Korea
Yuwei Peng	Wuhan University, China
Jianzhong Qi	The University of Melbourne, Australia
Tieyun Qian	Wuhan University, China
Lu Qin	University of Technology Sydney, Australia
Yanghui Rao	Sun Yat-sen University, China
Daniele Riboni	University of Cagliari, Italy
Chuitian Rong	Tiangong University, China
Dimitris Sacharidis	TU Wien, Austria
Aviv Segev	University of South Alabama, USA
Shuo Shang	University of Electronic Science and Technology of China, China

Junming Shao	University of Electronic Science and Technology of China, China
Yingxia Shao	Beijing University of Posts and Telecommunications, China
Derong Shen	Northeastern University, China
Wei Shen	Nankai University, China
Victor S. Sheng	Texas Tech University, USA
Yongpan Sheng	Tsinghua University, China
Kyuseok Shim	Seoul National University, South Korea
Lidan Shou	Zhejiang University, China
Shaoxu Song	Tsinghua University, China
Wei Song	Wuhan University, China
Han Su	Big Data Research Center, China
Le Sun	Nanjing University of Information Science and Technology, China
Weiwei Sun	Fudan University, China
Chih-Hua Tai	National Taipei University, Taiwan
Yong Tang	South China Normal University, China
Bo Tang	Southern University of Science and Technology, China
Xiaohui Tao	University of Southern Queensland, Australia
Yongxin Tong	Beihang University, China
Goce Trajcevski	Iowa State University, USA
Leong Hou U.	University of Macau, Macau
Kazutoshi Umemoto	The University of Tokyo, Japan
Hongzhi Wang	Harbin Institute of Technology, China
Hua Wang	Victoria University, Australia
Jianguo Wang	University of California San Diego, USA
Jin Wang	University of California Los Angeles, USA
Junhu Wang	Griffith University, Australia
Meng Wang	Southeast University, China
Peng Wang	Fudan University, China
Senzhang Wang	Nanjing University of Aeronautics and Astronautics, China
Sheng Wang	New York University, USA
Wei Wang	University of New South Wales, Australia
Xin Wang	Tianjin University, China
Yangtao Wang	Huazhong University of Science and Technology, China
Yijie Wang	National University of Defense Technology, China
Raymond Chi-Wing Wong	Hong Kong University of Science and Technology, Hong Kong
Shengli Wu	Jiangsu University, China
Xiaokui Xiao	National University of Singapore, Singapore
Yanghua Xiao	Fudan University, China
Qing Xie	Wuhan University of Technology, China
Xike Xie	University of Science and Technology of China, China

Jiajie Xu	Soochow University, China
Jianliang Xu	Hong Kong Baptist University, Hong Kong
Jianqiu Xu	Nanjing University of Aeronautics and Astronautics, China
Xinshun Xu	Shandong University, China
Zhouming Xu	Hohai University, China
Dingyu Yang	Shanghai Dianji University, China
Lianghuai Yang	Zhejiang University of Technology, China
Shiyu Yang	East China Normal University, China
Yajun Yang	Tianjin University, China
Junjie Yao	East China Normal University, China
Hongzhi Yin	The University of Queensland, Australia
Jian Yin	Sun Yat-sen University, China
Xiaohui Yu	Shandong University, China
Kai Zeng	Microsoft, USA
Dongyang Zhang	University of Electronic Science and Technology of China, China
Haiwei Zhang	Nankai University, China
Meihui Zhang	Beijing Institute of Technology, China
Wen Zhang	Wuhan University, China
Xiaowang Zhang	Tianjin University, China
Yong Zhang	Tsinghua University, China
Yongqing Zhang	Chengdu University of Information Technology, China
Yuxiang Zhang	Civil Aviation University of China, China
Zheng Zhang	Harbin Institute of Technology, China
Zhiqiang Zhang	Zhejiang University of Finance and Economics, China
Zhiwei Zhang	Hong Kong Baptist University, Hong Kong
Lei Zhao	Soochow University, China
Xiang Zhao	National University of Defence Technology, China
Xujian Zhao	Southwest University of Science and Technology, China
Bolong Zheng	Huazhong University of Science and Technology, China
Kai Zheng	University of Electronic Science and Technology of China, China
Weiguo Zheng	Fudan University, China
Xiangmin Zhou	RMIT University, Australia
Xuan Zhou	Renmin University of China, China
Feida Zhu	Singapore Management University, Singapore
Xingquan Zhu	Florida Atlantic University, USA
Lei Zou	Peking University, China
Zhaonian Zou	Harbin Institute of Technology, China

Contents – Part I

Big Data Analytic

Active Classification of Cold-Start Users in Large Sparse Datasets   3
Xiang Li, Xiao Li, and Tao Wang

Instance-Aware Evaluation of Sensitive Columns in Tabular Dataset   11
Zheng Gong, Kechun Zhao, Hui Li, and Yingxue Wang

EPUR: An Efficient Parallel Update System over Large-Scale RDF Data   20
Xiang Kang, Pingpeng Yuan, and Hai Jin

Graph Data and Social Networks

Multiple Local Community Detection via High-Quality
Seed Identification.   37
Jiaxu Liu, Yingxia Shao, and Sen Su

Partition-Oriented Subgraph Matching on GPU.   53
Jing Chen, Yu Gu, Qiange Wang, Chuanwen Li, and Ge Yu

An Index Method for the Shortest Path Query on Vertex Subset
for the Large Graphs   69
Zian Pan, Yajun Yang, and Qinghua Hu

Efficient Personalized Influential Community Search in Large Networks   86
Yanping Wu, Jun Zhao, Renjie Sun, Chen Chen, and Xiaoyang Wang

Leveraging Explicit Unsupervised Information for Robust Graph
Convolutional Neural Network Learning   102
Chu Zheng, Peiyun Wu, Xiaowang Zhang, and Zhiyong Feng

Content Sharing Prediction for Device-to-Device (D2D)-based Offline
Mobile Social Networks by Network Representation Learning   112
*Qing Zhang, Xiaoxu Ren, Yifan Cao, Hengda Zhang, Xiaofei Wang,
and Victor Leung*

LSimRank: Node Similarity in a Labeled Graph   127
Yang Wu, Ada Wai-Chee Fu, Cheng Long, and Zitong Chen

Fruited-Forest: A Reachability Querying Method Based on Spanning Tree
Modelling of Reduced DAG.   145
*Liu Yang, Tingxuan Chen, Junyu Zhang, Jun Long, Zhigang Hu,
and Victor S. Sheng*

Frequent Semantic Trajectory Sequence Pattern Mining in Location-Based
Social Networks   154
   Zhen Zhang, Jing Zhang, Fuxue Li, Xiangguo Zhao, and Xin Bi

Aligning Users Across Social Networks via Intra and Inter Attentions   162
   Zhichao Huang, Xutao Li, and Yunming Ye

NSTI-IC: An Independent Cascade Model Based on Neighbor Structures
and Topic-Aware Interest   170
   Chuhan Zhang, Yueshuang Yin, and Yong Liu

Knowledge Graph

Knowledge Graph Attention Network Enhanced Sequential
Recommendation   181
   *Xingwei Zhu, Pengpeng Zhao, Jiajie Xu, Junhua Fang, Lei Zhao,
   Xuefeng Xian, Zhiming Cui, and Victor S. Sheng*

TKGFrame: A Two-Phase Framework for Temporal-Aware Knowledge
Graph Completion.   196
   Jiasheng Zhang, Yongpan Sheng, Zheng Wang, and Jie Shao

An Ontology-Aware Unified Storage Scheme for Knowledge Graphs   212
   *Sizhuo Li, Guozheng Rao, Baozhu Liu, Pengkai Liu, Sicong Dong,
   and Zhiyong Feng*

IterG: An Iteratively Learning Graph Convolutional Network
with Ontology Semantics   227
   Xingya Liang, Fuxiang Zhang, Xin Liu, and Yajun Yang

Fine-Grained Evaluation of Knowledge Graph Embedding Models
in Downstream Tasks   242
   Yuxin Zhang, Bohan Li, Han Gao, Ye Ji, Han Yang, and Meng Wang

Learning to Answer Complex Questions with Evidence Graph   257
   Gao Gu, Bohan Li, Han Gao, and Meng Wang

Characterizing Robotic and Organic Query in SPARQL Search Sessions   270
   *Xinyue Zhang, Meng Wang, Bingchen Zhao, Ruyang Liu,
   Jingyuan Zhang, and Han Yang*

Tail Entity Recognition and Linking for Knowledge Graphs.   286
   *Dalei Zhang, Yang Qiang, Zhixu Li, Junhua Fang, Ying He, Xin Zheng,
   and Zhigang Chen*

Natural Answer Generation via Graph Transformer   302
   Xiangyu Li, Sen Hu, and Lei Zou

Diversified Top-k Querying in Knowledge Graphs 319
  Xintong Guo, Hong Gao, Yinan An, and Zhaonian Zou

High Order Semantic Relations-Based Temporal Recommendation Model
by Collaborative Knowledge Graph Learning 337
  Yongwei Qiao, Leilei Sun, and Chunjing Xiao

Temporal Knowledge Graph Incremental Construction Model
for Recommendation 352
  Chunjing Xiao, Leilei Sun, and Wanlin Ji

Recommender Systems

Few-Shot Representation Learning for Cold-Start Users and Items 363
  Bowen Hao, Jing Zhang, Cuiping Li, and Hong Chen

Long Short-Term Memory with Sequence Completion for Cross-Domain
Sequential Recommendation...................................... 378
  Guang Yang, Xiaoguang Hong, Zhaohui Peng, and Yang Xu

IASR: An Item-Level Attentive Social Recommendation Model for
Personalized Ranking 394
  *Tianyi Tao, Yun Xiong, Guosen Wang, Yao Zhang, Peng Tian,
  and Yangyong Zhu*

Spatio-Temporal Self-Attention Network for Next POI Recommendation 409
  *Jiacheng Ni, Pengpeng Zhao, Jiajie Xu, Junhua Fang, Zhixu Li,
  Xuefeng Xian, Zhiming Cui, and Victor S. Sheng*

Joint Cooperative Content Caching and Recommendation
in Mobile Edge-Cloud Networks................................... 424
  Zhihui Ke, Meng Cheng, Xiaobo Zhou, Keqiu Li, and Tie Qiu

Dual Role Neural Graph Auto-encoder for CQA Recommendation 439
  Xing Luo, Yuanyuan Jin, Tao Ji, and Xiaoling Wang

KGWD: Knowledge Graph Based Wide & Deep Framework
for Recommendation 455
  Kemeng Liu, Zhonghong Ou, Yanxin Tan, Kai Zhao, and Meina Song

Seamless Incorporation of Appointment-Based Requests on Taxi-Rider
Match Scheduling 470
  Yongxuan Lai, Shipeng Yang, Anshu Xiong, and Fan Yang

FHAN: Feature-Level Hierarchical Attention Network for Group
Event Recommendation 478
  Guoqiong Liao, Xiaobin Deng, Xiaomei Huang, and Changxuan Wan

KASR: Knowledge-Aware Sequential Recommendation.   493
   Qingqin Wang, Yun Xiong, Yangyong Zhu, and Philip S. Yu

Graph Attentive Network for Region Recommendation
with POI- and ROI-Level Attention.   509
   Hengpeng Xu, Jinmao Wei, Zhenglu Yang, and Jun Wang

Generalized Collaborative Personalized Ranking for Recommendation   517
   Bin Fu, Hongzhi Liu, Yang Song, Tao Zhang, and Zhonghai Wu

Information Extraction and Retrieval

Dynamic Multi-hop Reasoning   535
   Liang Xu, Junjie Yao, and Yingjie Zhang

Multi-hop Reading Comprehension Incorporating
Sentence-Based Reasoning   544
   Lijun Huo, Bin Ge, and Xiang Zhao

Author Contributed Representation for Scholarly Network   558
   Binglei Wang, Tong Xu, Hao Wang, Yanmin Chen, Le Zhang,
   Lintao Fang, Guiquan Liu, and Enhong Chen

Unsupervised Cross-Modal Retrieval by Coupled Dual Generative
Adversarial Networks   574
   Jingzi Gu, Peng Fu, Jinchao Zhang, Lulu Wang, Bo Li,
   and Weiping Wang

GSimRank: A General Similarity Measure on Heterogeneous
Information Network   588
   Chuanyan Zhang, Xiaoguang Hong, and Zhaohui Peng

Multi-task Learning for Low-Resource Second Language
Acquisition Modeling   603
   Yong Hu, Heyan Huang, Tian Lan, Xiaochi Wei, Yuxiang Nie, Jiarui Qi,
   Liner Yang, and Xian-Ling Mao

Multi-view Clustering via Multiple Auto-Encoder   612
   Guowang Du, Lihua Zhou, Yudi Yang, Kevin Lü, and Lizhen Wang

A Method for Place Name Recognition in Tang Poetry Based on Feature
Templates and Conditional Random Field   627
   Yan Zhang, Yukun Li, Jing Zhang, and Yunbo Ye

Machine Learning

MLND: A Weight-Adapting Method for Multi-label Classification Based
on Neighbor Label Distribution.   639
   Lei Yang, Zhan Shi, Dan Feng, Wenxin Yang, Jiaofeng Fang,
   Shuo Chen, and Fang Wang

meanNet: A Multi-layer Label Mean Based Semi-supervised Neural
Network Approach for Credit Prediction   655
   Guowei Wang, Lin Li, and Jianwei Zhang

Multi-task Attributed Graphical Lasso   670
   Yao Zhang, Yun Xiong, Xiangnan Kong, Xinyue Liu, and Yangyong Zhu

Hylo: Hybrid Layer-Based Optimization to Reduce Communication
in Distributed Deep Learning   685
   Wenbin Jiang, Jing Peng, Pai Liu, and Hai Jin

Joint Reasoning of Events, Participants and Locations for Plot
Relation Recognition   700
   Shengguang Qiu, Botao Yu, Lei Qian, Qiang Guo, and Wei Hu

FedSmart: An Auto Updating Federated Learning
Optimization Mechanism   716
   Anxun He, Jianzong Wang, Zhangcheng Huang, and Jing Xiao

Discriminative Multi-label Model Reuse for Multi-label Learning   725
   Yi Zhang, Zhecheng Zhang, Yinlong Zhu, Lei Zhang,
   and Chongjun Wang

Global and Local Attention Embedding Network for Few-Shot
Fine-Grained Image Classification.   740
   Jiayuan Hu, Chung-Ming Own, and Wenyuan Tao

Bayes Classifier Chain Based on SVM for Traditional Chinese Medical
Prescription Generation   748
   Chaohan Pei, Chunyang Ruan, Yanchun Zhang, and Yun Yang

A Spatial and Sequential Combined Method for Web
Service Classification.   764
   Xin Wang, Jin Liu, Xiao Liu, Xiaohui Cui, and Hao Wu

A Pruned DOM-Based Iterative Strategy for Approximate Global
Optimization in Crowdsourcing Microtasks   779
   Lizhen Cui, Jing Chen, Wei He, Hui Li, and Wei Guo

D-GHNAS for Joint Intent Classification and Slot Filling.   794
   Yanxi Tang, Jianzong Wang, Xiaoyang Qu, Nan Zhang, and Jing Xiao

Index-Based Scheduling for Parallel State Machine Replication.   808
    Guodong Zhao, Gang Wu, Yidong Song, Baiyou Qiao,
    and Donghong Han

Author Index   825

Contents – Part II

Blockchain

DHBFT: Dynamic Hierarchical Byzantine Fault-Tolerant Consensus
Mechanism Based on Credit.................................... 3
    Fengqi Li, Kemeng Liu, Jing Liu, Yonggang Fan, and Shengfa Wang

MaSRChain: A Trusted Manuscript Submission and Review System Based
on Blockchain 18
    Fengqi Li, Kemeng Liu, Haoyu Wu, and Xu Zhang

Enabling Efficient Multi-keyword Search Over Fine-Grained Authorized
Healthcare Blockchain System 27
    Yicheng Ding, Wei Song, and Yuan Shen

Data Mining

Debiasing Learning to Rank Models with Generative
Adversarial Networks 45
    Hui Cai, Chengyu Wang, and Xiaofeng He

An Effective Constraint-Based Anomaly Detection Approach
on Multivariate Time Series 61
    Zijue Li, Xiaoou Ding, and Hongzhi Wang

A Method for Decompensation Prediction in Emergency
and Harsh Situations 70
    Guozheng Rao, Shuying Zhao, Li Zhang, Qing Cong, and Zhiyong Feng

Improved Brain Segmentation Using Pixel Separation and Additional
Segmentation Features....................................... 85
    Afifa Khaled, Chung-Ming Own, Wenyuan Tao,
    and Taher Ahmed Ghaleb

Evaluating Fault Tolerance of Distributed Stream Processing Systems 101
    Xiaotong Wang, Cheng Jiang, Junhua Fang, Ke Shu, Rong Zhang,
    Weining Qian, and Aoying Zhou

Predicting Human Mobility with Self-attention and Feature Interaction 117
    Jingang Jiang, Shuo Tao, Defu Lian, Zhenya Huang, and Enhong Chen

Predicting Adverse Drug-Drug Interactions via Semi-supervised
Variational Autoencoders   132
   Meihao Hou, Fan Yang, Lizhen Cui, and Wei Guo

Smarter Smart Contracts: Efficient Consent Management in Health
Data Sharing   141
   Mira Shah, Chao Li, Ming Sheng, Yong Zhang, and Chunxiao Xing

Joint Learning-Based Anomaly Detection on KPI Data   156
   Yongqin Huang, Yijie Wang, and Li Cheng

Parallel Variable-Length Motif Discovery in Time Series Using
Subsequences Correlation.   164
   Chuitian Rong, Lili Chen, Chunbin Lin, and Chao Yuan

Learning Ability Community for Personalized Knowledge Tracing   176
   Juntao Zhang, Biao Li, Wei Song, Nanzhou Lin, Xiandi Yang,
   and Zhiyong Peng

LOCATE: Locally Anomalous Behavior Change Detection in Behavior
Information Sequence   193
   Dingshan Cui, Lei Duan, Xinao Wang, Jyrki Nummenmaa, Ruiqi Qin,
   and Shan Xiao

Hyperthyroidism Progress Prediction with Enhanced LSTM   209
   Haiqin Lu, Mei Wang, Weiliang Zhao, Tingwei Su, and Jian Yang

Text Analysis and Mining

DeepStyle: User Style Embedding for Authorship Attribution
of Short Texts   221
   Zhiqiang Hu, Roy Ka-Wei Lee, Lei Wang, Ee-peng Lim, and Bo Dai

Densely-Connected Transformer with Co-attentive Information
for Matching Text Sequences   230
   Minxu Zhang, Yingxia Shao, Kai Lei, Yuesheng Zhu, and Bin Cui

WEKE: Learning Word Embeddings for Keyphrase Extraction   245
   Yuxiang Zhang, Huan Liu, Bei Shi, Xiaoli Li, and Suge Wang

Contribution of Improved Character Embedding and Latent Posting Styles
to Authorship Attribution of Short Texts   261
   Wenjing Huang, Rui Su, and Mizuho Iwaihara

Utilizing BERT Pretrained Models with Various Fine-Tune Methods
for Subjectivity Detection.   270
   Hairong Huo and Mizuho Iwaihara

A Framework for Learning Cross-Lingual Word Embedding with Topics. . . .   285
  Xiaoya Peng and Dong Zhou

Paperant: Key Elements Generation with New Ideas   294
  Xin He, Jiuyang Tang, Zhen Tan, Zheng Yu, and Xiang Zhao

Turn-Level Recurrence Self-attention for Joint Dialogue Action Prediction
and Response Generation   309
  Yanxin Tan, Zhonghong Ou, Kemeng Liu, Yanan Shi, and Meina Song

Mining Affective Needs from Online Opinions for Design Innovation   317
  Danping Jia and Jian Jin

Spatial, Temporal and Multimedia Databases

Multi-grained Cross-modal Similarity Query with Interpretability   327
  Mingdong Zhu, Derong Shen, Lixin Xu, and Gang Ren

Efficient Semantic Enrichment Process for Spatiotemporal Trajectories
in Geospatial Environment   342
  Jingjing Han, Mingyu Liu, Genlin Ji, Bin Zhao, Richen Liu, and Ying Li

On the Vulnerability and Generality of K–Anonymity Location Privacy
Under Continuous LBS Requests   351
  Hanbo Dai, Hui Li, Xue Meng, and Yingxue Wang

Fine-Grained Urban Flow Prediction via a Spatio-Temporal
Super-Resolution Scheme.   360
  Rujia Shen, Jian Xu, Qing Bao, Wei Li, Hao Yuan, and Ming Xu

Detecting Abnormal Congregation Through the Analysis of Massive
Spatio-Temporal Data   376
  Tianran Chen, Yongzheng Zhang, Yupeng Tuo, and Weiguang Wang

SSMDL: Semi-supervised Multi-task Deep Learning for Transportation
Mode Classification and Path Prediction with GPS Trajectories.   391
  Asif Nawaz, Zhiqiu Huang, and Senzhang Wang

Database Systems

GHSH: Dynamic Hyperspace Hashing on GPU   409
  Zhuo Ren, Yu Gu, Chuanwen Li, FangFang Li, and Ge Yu

A Unified Framework for Processing Exact and Approximate Top-k Set
Similarity Join   425
  Cihai Sun, Hongya Wang, Yingyuan Xiao, and Zhenyu Liu

Quantitative Contention Generation for Performance Evaluation
on OLTP Databases.................................... 441
    Chunxi Zhang, Rong Zhang, Weining Qian, Ke Shu, and Aoying Zhou

Pipelined Query Processing Using Non-volatile Memory SSDs........... 457
    Xinyu Liu, Yu Pan, Wenxiu Fang, Rebecca J. Stones, Gang Wang,
    Yusen Li, and Xiaoguang Liu

Sorting-Based Interactive Regret Minimization 473
    Jiping Zheng and Chen Chen

Tool Data Modeling Method Based on an Object Deputy Model.......... 491
    Qianwen Luo, Chen Chen, Song Wang, Rongrong Li, and Yuwei Peng

Unsupervised Deep Hashing with Structured Similarity Learning 500
    Xuanrong Pang, Xiaojun Chen, Shu Yang, and Feiping Nie

Demo

A New CPU-FPGA Heterogeneous gStore System 517
    Xunbin Su, Yinnian Lin, and Lei Zou

Euge: Effective Utilization of GPU Resources for Serving DNN-Based
Video Analysis...................................... 523
    Qihang Chen, Guangyao Ding, Chen Xu, Weining Qian,
    and Aoying Zhou

Blockchain PG: Enabling Authenticated Query and Trace Query
in Database 529
    Qingxing Guo, Sijia Deng, Lei Cai, Yanchao Zhu, Zhao Zhang,
    and Cheqing Jin

PHR: A Personalized Hidden Route Recommendation System Based
on Hidden Markov Model 535
    Yundan Yang, Xiao Pan, Xin Yao, Shuhai Wang, and Lihua Han

JoyDigit NexIoT: An Open IoT Data Platform for Senior Living 540
    Kai Zhao, Peibiao Yang, Peng Zhang, Sufang Wang, Feng Wang,
    Xu Liu, and Hongyan Deng

Epidemic Guard: A COVID-19 Detection System for Elderly People....... 545
    Wenqi Wei, Jianzong Wang, Ning Cheng, Yuanxu Chen, Bao Zhou,
    and Jing Xiao

Automatic Document Data Storage System Based on Machine Learning 551
    Yu Yan, Hongzhi Wang, Jian Zou, and Yixuan Wang

A Meta-Search Engine Ranking Based on Webpage Information
Quality Evaluation 556
    Yukun Li, Yunbo Ye, and Wenya Xu

Author Index 561

Big Data Analytic

Active Classification of Cold-Start Users in Large Sparse Datasets

Xiang Li[1], Xiao Li[2(✉)], and Tao Wang[2]

[1] Academy of Miltary Science, Beijing, China
lixiang@126.com
[2] National University of Defense Technology, Changsham, China
xiaoli@nudt.edu.cn

Abstract. Many applications need to perform classification on large sparse datasets. Classifying the *cold-start users* who have very few feedbacks is still a challenging task. Previous work has applied active learning to classification with partially observed data. However, for large and sparse data, the number of feedbacks to be queried is huge and many of them are invalid. In this paper, we develop an active classification framework that can address these challenges by leveraging online Matrix Factorization models. We first identify a step-wise data acquisition heuristic which is useful for active classification. We then use the estimations of online Probabilistic Matrix Factorization to compute this heuristic function. In order to reduce the number of invalid queries, we further estimate the probability that a query can be answered by the cold-start user with online Poisson Factorization. During active learning, a query is selected based on the current knowledge learned in these two online factorization models. We demonstrate with real-world movie rating datasets that our framework is highly effective. It not only gains better improvement in classification, but also reduces the number of invalid queries.

1 Introduction

Large sparse data are common in various domains [1,9,10]. For example, the Netflix dataset [1] contains user ratings on more than $17,000$ movies given by $480,000$ users, with a data sparsity of 98.82%. These datasets contain millions of user-item interactions with a large majority of them missing. Many applications need to perform classification on these sparse data. In practice, while it is possible to train a good classifier from the existing users, the classifier can hardly perform well on cold-start users during prediction phase.

Active learning is an effective strategy for the cold-start problems, i.e., the system actively queries for more feedbacks from a user so that classification performance can be improved. In previous work, active learning has been applied to classifying partially observed data [2,3,5,6]. However, none of them are designed for large and sparse datasets. The difficulty is two-fold: the number of potential item queries is huge and most of the queries are invalid since a user only knows a small portion of all the items.

© Springer Nature Switzerland AG 2020
X. Wang et al. (Eds.): APWeb-WAIM 2020, LNCS 12317, pp. 3–10, 2020.
https://doi.org/10.1007/978-3-030-60259-8_1

To address the above challenges, we develop a novel framework to actively classify the cold-start users in a large sparse dataset. We derive a simple yet effective step-wise heuristic function that is useful for active classification. To compute this heuristic function before each query, we use feedback estimations given by an online Probabilistic Matrix Factorization [8] model. To reduce the number of invalid queries, we use online Poisson Factorization model [4] to estimate how likely a user can actually give the feedback. During active learning, our framework iteratively consults and updates these two factorization models for better classification performance and fewer invalid queries. The effectiveness of our framework is evaluated on real-world user-item datasets.

2   Classification for Cold-Start Users

Problem Definition. Consider a large sparse dataset where each instance $\mathbf{x} = \{x_1, \ldots, x_d\}$ corresponds to a user's feedback given to d items, and y is the label of prediction.[1] Suppose the system has a population of active users who have sufficient feedbacks, $S_{train} = \{\mathbf{x}^{(i)}, y^{(i)}\}_{i=1\ldots N_{train}}$. We can learn a good linear classifier $f^* = \mathbf{w}^*\mathbf{x}$ from S_{train} with some convex loss measure $l(y, f)$.

After training, we need to predict the label y_c of a cold-start user $\mathbf{x}_c$ who has no previous feedback. At each round, the system is allowed to actively query one feedback j from the user. $\mathbf{x}_{c,t}$ denotes the temporary state of $\mathbf{x}_c$ at round t, thus $\mathbf{x}_{c,0} = \mathbf{0}$. Each new user $\mathbf{x}_c$ can only provide feedbacks to a subset of items $I_{\mathbf{x}_c}$ and $|I_{\mathbf{x}_c}| \ll d$. The remaining candidate queries for $\mathbf{x}_c$ at each round is $C_{c,t}$, and of which $\mathbf{x}_c$ can only answer queries of $Q_{c,t} := I_{\mathbf{x}_c} \cap C_{c,t}$.

At each round, the system has to choose a query j from $C_{c,t}$. If j belongs to $Q_{c,t}$, the query is valid and the user will answer it so the system observes new feedback $x_{cj} := (\mathbf{x}_c)_j$. After each valid query, we re-evaluate the performance of our classifier on user $\mathbf{x}_c$, and proceed to the next round. Otherwise, the user will keep skipping invalid queries until a valid one appears.

At any round t, we consider two goals: **Goal 1 (Primary).** To maximize the prediction accuracy of the trained classifier on cold-start users $f^*(\mathbf{x}_{t,c})$. **Goal 2 (Secondary).** To minimize the number of queries skipped (invalid queries) by each cold-start user $\mathbf{x}_c$. Our problem prefers a solution that optimizes the primary goal while considers the secondary goal as much as possible.

3   Heuristics for Active Classification

To achieve Goal 1, we need to choose a sequence of queries for $\mathbf{x}_c$ that leads to the best classification accuracy. Here we assume to know $I_{\mathbf{x}_c}$ in advance.

Step-wise Objective. Without loss of generality, we simplify our discussion to binary classification[2], $y \in \{1, -1\}$. At round t, the predicted label of the

---

[1] If a certain feedback is missing, we treat it as 0 by convention.

[2] Our analysis can be extended to other scenarios such as regression and multi-label classification.

cold-start user is given by $\text{sgn}(\mathbf{w}^*\mathbf{x}_{c,t})$, and the probability of it being wrong is $\Pr(y_c\mathbf{w}^*\mathbf{x}_{c,t} \leq 0)$. Our primary goal can be achieved by finding the optimal sequence of queries $s_t^* = (j_1, j_2, \ldots, j_t)$ that minimizes this probability from all feasible query sequences $\mathcal{S}_t = \{s|s \subseteq I_{\mathbf{x}_c}, |s| = t\}$:

$$s_t^* = \min_{s_t \in \mathcal{S}_t} \Pr(y_c\mathbf{w}^*\mathbf{x}_{c,t} \leq 0|s_t) \tag{1}$$

We use a step-wise optimization strategy that can be proved a sufficient condition for the optimality of Eq.(1). Suppose at round t we choose to query feedback j_t, the probability of wrong classification is

$$\Pr(y_c\mathbf{w}^*\mathbf{x}_{c,t} \leq 0|s_t) = \Pr(y_c\mathbf{w}^*\mathbf{x}_{c,t-1} \leq -y_c w_{j_t}^* x_{cj_t}|s_{t-1} \cup \{j_t\}) \tag{2}$$

where $y_c\mathbf{w}^*\mathbf{x}_{c,t-1}$ is a constant and s_{t-1} is already determined. Minimizing the above probability w.r.t. j_t is thus equivalent to

$$j_t = \text{argmax}_{j \in Q_{c,t}}\{y_c w_j^* x_{cj}\} \tag{3}$$

Suppose we indeed found the optimal query sequence s_{t-1}^* for round $t-1$, from Eq.(2) it is obvious that objective (3) will lead to an optimal query sequence for round t, in the sense of classification error minimization. By induction, this proves that *step-wise optimization using Eq. (3) is a sufficient condition for our ultimate goal Eq. (1)*.

Heuristic Function. However, the step-wise objective (3) is not computable: we do not know the value x_j for all candidate $j \in Q_{c,t}$ at round t, and we always cannot know the true label y_c. We use the following heuristic function to approximate Eq.(3):

$$j_t = \text{argmax}_{j \in Q_{c,t}}|w_j^* x_{cj}| \tag{4}$$

In fact, $|w_j^* x_{cj}|$ denotes the amount of *contribution* from feature value x_{cj} to the final prediction output $w^*\mathbf{x}_c$. It can be computed so long as we have a reasonable estimation of x_{cj}.

Skip Reduction. In practice, the system does not know $Q_{c,t}$, but has to choose from $C_{c,t}$ which is set of all candidate queries that are not asked so far. In order to reduce the number of invalid queries (our second goal), it is useful to estimate the probability of a feedback query j being valid, i.e.,

$$o_{cj} := \Pr(x_{cj} > 0) \tag{5}$$

In the next section, we discuss how to estimate x_{cj} and $\Pr(x_{cj} > 0)$ using Probabilistic Matrix Factorization and Poisson Factorization, respectively.

4   Online Feedback Estimation for Cold-Start Users

4.1   Online Probabilistic Matrix Factorization

Given a sparse matrix $X = \{x_{i,j}\}_{[n \times d]}$, the goal of PMF model is to predict the value of entry $x_{i,j}$ by leveraging the low rank property of the sparse matrix with factorized Gaussian priors:

$$U_i \sim \mathcal{N}(0, \sigma_u^2 I_K); \quad V_j \sim \mathcal{N}(0, \sigma_v^2 I_K); \quad x_{ij}|U, V \sim \mathcal{N}(U_i^T V_j, \sigma^2) \qquad (6)$$

where K is the number of latent dimension, σ_u^2, σ_v^2 and σ are prior Gaussian variances.

For our problem, we can train the PMF model using the training set $X_{[N_{train} \times d]}$, where each row of the matrix denotes a training instance $\{\mathbf{x}^{(i)}\}_{i=1...N_{train}}$. When a cold-start user (row) $\mathbf{x}_c$ is added, its latent vector U_c can be computed using closed form solution of the conditional probability of U_c [7,11]. At round t, the conditional probability is given by

$$\Pr(U_{c,t}|V, \mathbf{x}_{c,t}, \sigma^2, \sigma_v^2) = \mathcal{N}(U_{c,t}|\mu_{c,t}^u, \Sigma_{c,t}^u) \qquad (7)$$

where

$$\mu_{c,t}^u = (\sum_{j \in obs(\mathbf{x}_{c,t})} V_j^T V_j + \frac{I_K}{\sigma_u^2})^{-1} \sum_{j \in obs(\mathbf{x}_{c,t})} (x_{cj} V_j)$$

$$\Sigma_{c,t}^u = \sigma^2 \sum_{j \in obs(\mathbf{x}_{c,t})} (V_j^T V_j + \frac{I_K}{\sigma_u^2})^{-1} \qquad (8)$$

$obs(\mathbf{x}_{c,t})$ is the set of already observed feedbacks in $\mathbf{x}_{c,t}$. From Eq.(8), we see that both $\mu_{c,t}^u$ and $\Sigma_{c,t}^u$ can be updated sequentially after receiving each $j \in obs(\mathbf{x}_{c,t})$. Afterwards, we can get the estimation of each unobserved x_{cj} as $\hat{x}_{cj} = V_j^T \mu_{c,t}^u$.

Combining this active process with our query selection heuristic Eq. (4), we can have an active classification framework, whose basic idea is to update a PMF model at each round and use the updated model to compute estimation $\hat{x}_{cj}$. Afterwards, $\hat{x}_{cj}$ is used in the heuristic for selecting a suitable query.

In our experiment, we will show that this strategy is very effective for our primary goal. However, we did not consider the probability of x_{cj} being invalid. As a result, a user may have to skip many invalid queries. Next, we describe an online algorithm that helps to estimate and update o_{cj} during the active classification process.

4.2   Online Poisson Factorization

We use Poisson Factorization [4] to predict o_{cj} at any round t, where a Poisson distribution $Pois(\cdot)$ is used to model each data entry and its conjugate prior Gamma distribution $\Gamma(\cdot, \cdot)$ is used to model the latent user/item vectors:

$$\theta_i \sim \Gamma(a, \xi_i); \quad \beta_j \sim \Gamma(b, \eta_j); \quad o_{ij}|\theta, \beta \sim Pois(\theta_i^T \beta_j) \qquad (9)$$

here $o_{ij} \in \{0, 1\}$ denotes whether each data entry x_{ij} exists or not in a sparse matrix $X_{[n \times d]}$ and θ_i, β_j are $K' \ll \min(n, d)$ dimensional latent user/item vectors. As discussed in [4], compared to Gaussian likelihood, Poisson distribution is more suitable for implicit (0/1) feedbacks, where the amount of 0s and 1s are significantly unbalanced.

To efficiently compute the inference problem involved in Poisson Factorization, [4] introduces latent parameters $z_{ijk} \sim Pois(\theta_{ik} \beta_{jk}), k = 1, \ldots, K'$ that measure the contribution from each latent dimension to o_{ij}. After we have trained a Poisson Factorization model using the training data, we get the MAP solution of β_j. For a cold-start user $\mathbf{x}_c$, its parameters θ_c and z_c have the following conditional distributions:

$$\Pr(\theta_{ck}|\beta, \xi_c, \mathbf{z}_{cj}, \mathbf{o}_c, a) = \Gamma(a + \sum_j z_{cjk}, \xi_c + \sum_j \beta_{jk}) \tag{10}$$

$$\Pr(\mathbf{z}_{cj}|\beta, \theta, o_{cj}) = \text{Mult}(o_{cj}, \frac{\theta_c \beta_j}{\theta_c^{\mathrm{T}} \beta_j}) \tag{11}$$

where $o_{cj} = 1$ if feature x_{cj} exists, and 0 otherwise. After we receive a new observation $o_{cj} = 1$, we can iteratively update z_c and θ_c using Eq. (11) and (10). When updating the conditional distribution of one parameter, we use the MAP solution of the other. Specifically, the MAP of θ_{ck} is $\frac{a + \sum_j \mathbf{z}_{cj} - 1}{\xi + \sum_j \beta_j}$. For the multinational distribution of $\mathbf{z}_{cj}$, we use its mean value $\frac{o_{cj} \theta_c \beta_j}{\theta_c^{\mathrm{T}} \beta_j}$ instead. Similar to the online update of PMF, the item latent vectors β_j are assumed to be fixed during the whole active classification process of $\mathbf{x}_c$.

Algorithm 1. active-dualmf

Require: a cold-start user $\mathbf{x}_c$; Hyper-parameters $\sigma, \sigma_u^2, \sigma_v^2, a, b, \xi, \eta, \psi$;
Require: linear classifier $f^* = \mathbf{w}^* \mathbf{x}$, MAP of item latent feature vectors: V in PMF and β in Poisson Factorsation. all trained from $\mathcal{S}_{train}$;
 Init: $A \leftarrow (\sigma_u^2 I)^{-1}, \mathbf{b} \leftarrow \mathbf{0}, \mathbf{z} \leftarrow \mathbf{0}, \mathbf{x}_{c,0} \leftarrow \mathbf{0}, q \leftarrow 0, \mathcal{C} \leftarrow \{1, 2, \ldots, d\}$
 for $t = 1, 2, \ldots$ **do**
  $\mu_c^u \leftarrow A^{-1} \mathbf{b}$
  $\theta_c \leftarrow \frac{a + \sum_j \mathbf{z}_{cj} - 1}{\xi + \sum_j \beta_j}$ {Eq. (10)}
  repeat
   if $q < \psi$ **then**
    $\forall j \in \mathcal{C} : \hat{x}_{cj} \leftarrow V_j^T \mu_c^u$
    $j_t \leftarrow \max_{j \in \mathcal{C}} |w_j^* \hat{x}_{cj}|$
   else
    $\forall j \in \mathcal{C} : \hat{o}_{cj} \leftarrow \beta_j^T \theta_c$
    $j_t \leftarrow \max_{j \in \mathcal{C}} \hat{o}_{cj}$
   end if
   send query j_t
   $q \leftarrow q + 1$
   $\mathcal{C} \leftarrow \mathcal{C} - \{j_t\}$
  until $x_{cj_t} > 0$ {query j_t is answerable}
  $\mathbf{x}_{c,t} \leftarrow \mathbf{x}_{c,t-1} + x_{cj_t}$
  Classify the user using $f^*(\mathbf{x}_{c,t})$
  Update $A \leftarrow A + V_{j_t} V_{j_t}^T$ {Eq. (8)}
  Update $\mathbf{b} \leftarrow \mathbf{b} + x_{cj_t} V_{j_t}$ {Eq. (8)}
  Update $\mathbf{z}_{cj} \leftarrow \frac{\theta_c \beta_j}{\theta_c^T \beta_j}$ {Eq. (11)}
 end for

Table 1. Experiment Datasets

Datasets	# Users	# Items	Sparsity
Ml-100k	943	1,682	0.937
Ml-1m	6,040	3,952	0.958
Ymovie	7,620	11,914	0.998

4.3   Integrating with Matrix Factorization Models

During active classification, we update both matrix factorization models after receiving each new queried feedback. To compute the heuristic function, we rely more on $\hat{x}_{cj}$ at the earlier rounds. After an enough number of queries, we switch to $\hat{o}_{cj}$. We name this method as *Active classification with dual Matrix Factorization* (active-dualmf), see Algorithm 1. Our algorithm is computationally feasible. At each round, it only needs to perform one update step for each model.

5   Experiments

To evaluate our active classification framework, we use *ml1m*, *ml100k*[3] and *ymovie*[4] datasets. The label of prediction is the gender of each user. These datasets are sparse user-movie rating matrices and are widely used in the collaborative filtering literature. Table 1 shows their meta-information. The label of prediction is the gender of each user. We select 100 users with more than 100 ratings from each gender as the cold-start users, the rest of data are kept as the training set. As described earlier, we first train a linear classifier and all our matrix factorization models using the training set. In prediction, we actively classify each cold-start user starting from no initial feedback. We treat the feedbacks already present in each dataset as the ground truth of valid queries $I_{\mathbf{x}_c}$.

We compare *active-dualmf* to several baseline solutions. **popular**: always selects the most popular item according to the training set. **random**: always randomly selects an item for query. **active-mean**: active classification with mean estimation. Specifically, at round t, select $j_t = \max_j |w_j^* \hat{x}_j^{(m)}|$, where $\hat{x}_j^{(m)}$ is the mean value of the feedback on item j in the training set. **active-poisson**: active classification using only the estimations provided by Poisson Factorization, which is equivalent to using active-dualmf with $\psi = 0$. **active-pmf**: active classification using only the estimations provided by PMF, which is equivalent to using active-dualmf with $\psi = +\infty$.

The hyper-parameters of PMF and Poisson Factorization follow [4,8]. In active-dualmf, we set $\psi = 300$ for all datasets. The experiment results are given in Fig. 1. *Active-dualmf* and *active-pmf* always have highest classification performance. As discussed earlier, both methods estimate the feedback values using

---

[3] http://grouplens.org/datasets/movielens/.
[4] http://webscope.sandbox.yahoo.com/catalog.php?datatype=r.

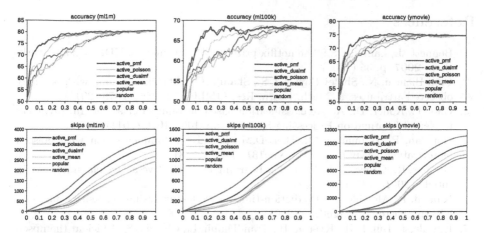

Fig. 1. Experiment results. We measure the classification accuracy and the number of skips at a given t. x-axis measures t divided by the total number of valid feedbacks on average. The last two sub-figures show the impact of parameter ψ in the active-dualmf experiment.

online matrix factorization models and select the query using our heuristic function. The third best method is active-mean, which also has considered the heuristic but cannot accurately estimate the feedback values before each query. The lower three plots of Fig. 1 show the amount of skips a user has performed. We observe that *active-poisson* has the fewest number of skips because each query is selected according to its likelihood of being valid. *Active-dualmf* has almost similar performance as *active-poisson*. The *popular* baseline has the third fewest number of skips. It is understandable that users are more likely to know a popular item. Overall, *active-dualmf* has good performance in both measures. It achieves similar active classification performance as *active-pmf* with much fewer queries skipped.

6   Conclusion

In this paper, we develop an active classification framework for cold-start users. We identify a heuristic function that is effective for query selection. We compute this function with the online feedback estimation given by a probabilistic matrix factorization model. In order to reduce the number of invalid queries, we use online Poisson Factorization to estimate the probability of whether each unobserved query is valid. Our method performs significantly better compared to several baseline solutions.

Acknowledgement. This work is supported by the National Key Research and Development Program of China (2018YFB1004502), the National Natural Science Foundation of China (61702532) and the Key Program of National Natural Science Foundation of China (61532001).

References

1. Bennett, J., Lanning, S.: The netflix prize. In: Proceedings of KDD cup and workshop. **2007**, p. 35 (2007)
2. Cesa-Bianchi, N., Shalev-Shwartz, S., Shamir, O.: Efficient learning with partially observed attributes. J. Mach. Learn. Res. (JMLR) **12**, 2857–2878 (2011)
3. Gao, T., Koller, D.: Active classification based on value of classifier. In: Advances in Neural Information Processing Systems, pp. 1062–1070 (2011)
4. Gopalan, P., Hofman, J.M., Blei, D.M.: Scalable recommendation with poisson factorization. arXiv preprint arXiv:1311.1704 (2013)
5. Greiner, R., Grove, A.J., Roth, D.: Learning cost-sensitive active classifiers. Artif. Intell. **139**(2), 137–174 (2002)
6. Kanani, P., Melville, P.: Prediction-time active feature-value acquisition for cost-effective customer targeting, (2008)
7. Kawale, J., Bui, H.H., Kveton, B., Tran-Thanh, L., Chawla, S.: Efficient thompson sampling for online matrix-factorization recommendation. In: Advances in Neural Information Processing Systems, pp. 1297–1305 (2015)
8. Salakhutdinov, R., Mnih, A.: Bayesian probabilistic matrix factorization using markov chain monte carlo. In: Proceedings of the 25th International Conference on Machine Learning (ICML), pp. 880–887. ACM (2008)
9. Yang, C., et al.: Repolike: amulti-feature-based personalized recommendation approach for open-source repositories. Front. Inf. Technol. Electron. Eng. **20**(2), 222–237 (2019)
10. Zhang, Y., Wu, Y., Wang, T., Wang, H.M.: A novel approach for recommending semantically linkable issues in github projects. Sci. China Inf. Sci. **62**(9), 202–204 (2019)
11. Zhao, X., Zhang, W., Wang, J.: Interactive collaborative filtering. In: Proceedings of the 22nd ACM international conference on Conference on information & knowledge management, pp. 1411–1420. ACM (2013)

Instance-Aware Evaluation of Sensitive Columns in Tabular Dataset

Zheng Gong[1], Kechun Zhao[1], Hui Li[1(✉)] ⓘ, and Yingxue Wang[2]

[1] Xidian University, Xi'an, China
marcogong22@gmail.com, zkc0422@outlook.com, hli@xidian.edu.cn
[2] National Engineering Laboratory for Public Safety Risk Perception
and Control by Big Data, Beijing, China
wangyingxue@csdslab.net

Abstract. Fully discovering knowledge from big data has to publish and share corresponding datasets whenever required. However, the risk for privacy leakage, i.e., record re-identification through some released columns, in the datasets is a fatal problem that prevents these tasks. Therefore, evaluating the sensitivity for different attributes is a prerequisite for dataset desensitization and anonymization, after which datasets can be published and shared in a privacy-preserving way. However, automatically evaluating the sensitivity for attributes is challenging and remains an open problem. In this work, we present a novel-but-simple technique for quantifying the sensitivity in structural database. It automatically evaluates the risks for re-identification for different columns according to *Record-linkage Attack*. Under the support of our scheme, the output sensitivity for the same attribute in different instances of a relational schema varies. Moreover, our scheme can quantify the risks of the columns no matter the semantics of columns are known or not. We also empirically show that the proposed scheme is effective in dataset sensitivity governance comparing with baselines.

Keywords: Data privacy · Record-linkage attack · Sensitivity · Attribute · Relational table

1 Introduction

Exploiting the value behind big data can benefit many applications such as policy-making, interpersonal relationship discovery, etc. However, accomplishing the task will inevitably introduce serious privacy issues. Many attacks that compromise privacy have been proposed over public datasets, which were initially released for research. The majority of these attacks, referred to as *Record-linkage*

Zheng Gong and Kechun Zhao are co-first authors and contribute equally to this work. This work is granted by National Natural Science Foundation of China (No. 61672408, 61972309) and National Engineering Laboratory (China) for Public Safety Risk Perception and Control by Big Data (PSRPC).

X. Wang et al. (Eds.): APWeb-WAIM 2020, LNCS 12317, pp. 11–19, 2020.
https://doi.org/10.1007/978-3-030-60259-8_2

Attack, combine network analysis, data mining and other technologies [2,5] to infer the identities of specific record based on some background knowledge. Specifically, according to *Record-linkage Attack*, for the multivariate structured data, an adversary could link personally identifiable attributes (*e.g.,* social security number), or quasi-identifier (*QI*) attributes (*e.g.,* age, gender), which may not expose the identity of the record independently but can leak the information if combined with other attributes, with his background knowledge to identify a particular or group of individuals in the dataset.

Existing *Record-linkage Attack* resist approach [1] requires user to predefine the sensitive/insensitive attributes. However, this prerequisite can be hardly satisfied, as the data owners could not gain insight into the sensitivity of each attribute. Meanwhile, manually labelling the *QI* or sensitive attributes is inaccurate and subjective. Obviously, it is of great importance if we can *identify and quantify all the "dangerous" attributes according to their risks of unveiling personal information if compromised.* Unfortunately, none of existing technique has explicitly defined such a qualification rule. Existing system[1] can arrange different sensitivity levels to corresponding columns by predefining the formats of some sensitive attributes through regular expressions. However, it is impossible to predefine templates for all attributes we may encounter. Besides, the formats of the entries in the same column may be diverse, even if they exhibit the same semantic meaning. Other techniques adopt some statistical tools to reflect the sensitivity of each column, such as cardinality [3], the proportion of unique values [8] and information entropy [7]. These methods do not take into account the correlation between columns, they consider each column independently. However, *Record-linkage Attack* can be successfully carried out by identifying tuples through *column combinations.*

Therefore, in this work, to address the problem, we present a novel technique for evaluating the sensitivity of each attribute in relational tables. The main contributions of this paper are as follows.

- To the best of our knowledge, we are the first to formally quantify the sensitivity of each column according to their re-identification risks.
- We demonstrate that our technique provides an objective measure for evaluating the sensitivity of each attribute empirically in a series of tables, and can act as a fundamental scheme for further privacy protection and desensitization. This technique is shown to be more realistic and complete than the existing empirical or statistics-driven methods.

The rest of the paper is organized as follows. In Sect. 2, we formally present the adversary model and key definition used in this paper. Our sensitivity evaluation method is proposed in Sect. 3. Empirical studies conducted over a group of datasets are presented in Sect. 4. Section 5 concludes the paper.

---

[1] https://www.dbsec.cn/pro/dms-s.html.

2 Definitions and Adversary Model

Before introducing the details of our framework, we shall first present basic definition and formally define the adversary model.

We adopt the definition of minimal unique column combination in [4], denoted as UCC. In layman's terms, the set of UCC is the set of independent primary keys and composite primary keys in a relational database R. Assume that the adversary has background knowledge κ, with which *Record-linkage Attack* can be performed to infer the real identification of some persons i in R. Obviously, as long as attribute(s) in κ can constitute a UCC of R, the adversary would successfully identify i, which is recognized as a successful attack. On the contrary, if κ doesn't contain any UCC, the adversary can never know if any information he got certainly corresponds to a unique tuple i in R.

Table 1. An Example dataset to be published

MINum	Sex	Age	Zip Code	Birthday	Disease
EN569244	Female	19	721001	1230	Fever
EF863453	Male	23	121000	0422	Pneumonia
EX756421	Female	56	831100	0719	Fever
EA556754	Female	14	201100	0926	Appendicitis
EP974423	Male	23	012000	1111	Leukemia
EN540305	Female	67	831100	1230	Fever
EY775612	Male	19	721001	0717	Leukemia

Table 2. The UCCs of Table 1

UCC
MINum
Age, Disease
Age, Birthday
Birthday, Zip Code
Age, Sex, Zip Code

Table 3. Background knowledge 1

Name	Age	Birthday
Lin	19	1230
Klay	23	0422
Haibara	56	0719
Jessie	14	0926
Charlotte	23	1111
Selena	67	1230
Quinn	19	0717

Table 4. Background knowledge 2

ID Number	MINum
4852	EN569244
8617	EF863453
1713	EX756421
2125	EA556754
3713	EP974423
9905	EN540305
5430	EY775612

For instance, Table 1 (R_e) is an ego dataset containing personal sensitive information, where $MINum$ refers to *Medical Insurance Number*. UCCs of R_e are listed in Table 2. Table 3 (R_1) and 4 (R_2) are the background knowledge κ of an adversary. When an adversary only has Table 3 as his background knowledge (*i.e.*, κ contains only R_1), it is impossible to determine the disease of any person through either *Age* or *Birthday*, but by a combination of both. As the *Age* and *Birthday* can form a *UCC*, the adversary can successfully identify every record in R_e. When κ contains only R_2, since *MINum* is a *UCC* of R_e, the adversary can get the ID number of every patient in Table 1, which may lead to the more disclosure of the private information.

3   The Risk of Re-identification

Given a database instance R with n columns, denoted as $A_1, \ldots, A_n$, for each column combination U over them (it can be viewed as an extensive projection without eliminating duplicate rows), if some rows of U are contained in κ, we denote them by $U \ltimes \kappa$. Suppose the probabilities for $\{A_i\} \ltimes \kappa$ are independent with each other and referred to as $p(A_i)$, respectively, then the success rate for *Record-linkage Attack* with respect to a particular column can be carried out as follows.

Firstly, if a column A_i itself constructs a *UCC* (*i.e.*, a key), the probability of successful attack through A_i should be $p(A_i)$. The reason is that as long as some rows of these columns are contained in κ, the adversary can definitely execute the attack. Secondly, if A_i is an element of some *UCC*s but not a *UCC* itself, the probability of successful attack through it would also depend on other columns that appear in those *UCC*s. Generally, we denote these *UCC*s as $U(A_i) = \{UCC | A_i \in UCC\}$. For each $UCC_j \in U(A_i)$, the adversary needs to cover other columns to successfully implement the attack once A_i is revealed. Suppose the columns that appear along with A_i in UCC_j is $B_1, \ldots, B_k$, let $P(UCC_j \ltimes \kappa)$ be the probability for UCC_j to be revealed (*i.e.*, all the columns of UCC_j for some rows are covered by κ) then its posterior probability, given that A_i is exposed, can be computed as $P(UCC_j \ltimes \kappa | \{A_i\} \ltimes \kappa) = \prod_{r=1}^{k} p(B_r)$. Notably, we also have to take into account the success rate for attacking through other *UCC*s in $U(A_i)$. Given $U(A_i)$, the adversary will successfully complete the attack if $\exists UCC_j \in U(A_i)$ such that $UCC_j \ltimes \kappa$. Therefore, once A_i is exposed, the successful attack probability through any *UCC* that contains A_i would be

$$P(success | \{A_i\} \ltimes \kappa) = 1 - \prod_{UCC_j \in U(A_i)} (1 - P(UCC_j \ltimes \kappa | \{A_i\} \ltimes \kappa)) \qquad (1)$$

Eq. 1 in fact evaluates the posterior probability given that A_i has been exposed. Then the eventual probability for successful attack via A_i should be

$$S(A_i) = p(A_i)P(success | \{A_i\} \ltimes \kappa). \qquad (2)$$

For instance, if we uniformly set the reveal probability of each column in Table 1 as 0.5, respectively, then the sensitivity for the columns can be computed accordingly as follows. $S(MINum) = p(MINum) \times (1 - 0) = 0.5$, as *MINum* itself constructs a *UCC*. $S(Sex) = p(Sex)(1 - (1 - p(Age)p(ZipCode))) = 0.125$. Similarly, the sensitivity for the rest columns are $0.406, 0.313, 0.438, 0.375$, respectively. As discussed above, $S(A_i)$ reflects the probability for successful

Table 5. the UCCs of RPI

UCC	Column combinations	UCC	Column combinations	UCC	Column combinations
UCC_1	Id	UCC_6	Addr.,District3,Hp.,Name	UCC_{11}	Birth.,District4,Hp.
UCC_2	CtfId	UCC_7	Addr.,District4,Hp.,Name	UCC_{12}	Birth.,Hp.,Name
UCC_3	Birth.,Hp.,Zip	UCC_8	Addr.,Fax,Hp.,Name	UCC_{13}	Birth.,CtfTp,Gender,Hp.
UCC_4	Gender,Hp.,Name	UCC_9	Addr.,Hp.,Name,Zip	UCC_{14}	Birth.,Gender,Hp.,Tel
UCC_5	Addr.,Hp.,Name,Tel	UCC_{10}	Birth.,District3,Hp.	UCC_{15}	Addr.,Birth.,Hp.

attack through attribute A_i, according to which we can quantitatively evaluate the attributes based on their risks for *Record-linkage Attack*.

Notably, according to Eq. 2, $S(A_i)$ depends on $p(A_i)$, which refers to the general probability for A_i being revealed to an arbitrary adversary. Obtaining those probabilities seems to be a challenging task. For ease of discussion, we set $p(A_i)$ uniformly as 0.5 in the followings such that we can focus on discussing the intrinsic distribution-driven characteristics of each column, excluding all external scenario-dependent factors.

4   Experiments

To evaluate the performance of our framework, we conduct empirical tests over 2 real-world datasets as follows. The first dataset, denoted as RPI, is a real personal information tabular table containing 14 columns and 6478 tuples. These columns semantically refer to user ID number, birthday (*abbr.,* Birth.), address (*abbr.,* Addr.), mobile number (*abbr.,* Hp.), gender, etc. Another dataset is Pokec[2], the most popular on-line social media in Slovakia. It contains 59 columns including gender, age, hobbies, interest, education, etc. As there are too many null entries, we extract the tuples with relatively less null values. For UCC discovery, we use Metanome Tool [6], an extensible implementation of [4].

4.1   Experimental Results

Sensitivity Justification. In the first group of experiments, given RPI, whose UCCs are listed in Table 5, we *uniformly* set the reveal probabilities for columns as 0.5. Figure 1 shows sensitivity results for each column according to Eq. 2. ID and $CtfID$ exhibit the highest sensitivity. In fact, either ID or $CtfID$ can construct a UCC itself as shown in Table 5. For $Birthday$, an attack is successful only when the adversary gets other columns in UCCs that contain $Birthday$, such as $Mobile$ and Zip of UCC_3 in Table 5. Since the attack on $Birthday$ requires more information, it would be more difficult to succeed when compared with the attacks on ID and $CtfID$. Naturally, its sensitivity should be lower than them, which is justified in Fig. 1.

To further illustrate the effectiveness, we use data masking method to desensitize columns with high sensitivity, and re-compute the sensitivity afterwards.

---
[2] http://snap.stanford.edu/data/soc-Pokec.html.

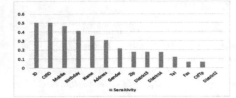

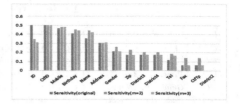

Fig. 1. Sensitivity of RPI ($p = 0.5$)

Fig. 2. Sensitivity of RPI after desensitization

For ID, we separately mask the last m digits of each entry with '$\star$'. Figure 2 shows the sensitivity results before and after the masking. Obviously, a higher level desensitization for ID results in a lower sensitivity, which also justifies the rationality of our evaluation scheme. Notably, the sensitivity of ID (originally 0.5) has dropped significantly to 0.344 and 0.31, respectively; the sensitivity of some other columns increase accordingly. Due to the masking, column ID is no longer a key in the table, and forms new UCCs together with other columns. Consequently, for the columns of newly-formed UCCs with respect to ID, their sensitivity will increase; for the rest columns, their sensitivity will remain unchanged.

Figure 3 shows the results of Pokec. As there are too many columns in Pokec, we limit the number of columns in κ to be no more than 5 in Pokec. The reason for such setting is as follows. There is little chance for an adversary to obtain an extremely strong κ that contains so many columns at the same time, the probability of which obviously decreases exponentially in term of the number of columns. Similar to the phenomenon in the other datasets, the primary key (*user id*) has the greatest sensitivity, and the sensitivity of other columns is affected by the coverage of all UCCs.

Impact of Other Factors. Furthermore, we also adjust the values of some parameters and explore how our model perceives these adjustments. First, we adjust the number of tuples in Pokec, gradually increasing from 10 to 150000, and explore the changes in the sensitivity of each column and the average sensitivity of all columns. According to Fig. 4a, when the number of rows is small, the average sensitivity of all columns (denoted as AS) fluctuates around 0.4. However, when the number of tuples is beyond 35000, the sensitivity of non-key columns decreases significantly. As the number of rows gradually increases, more duplicate values would be produced on a single column or multiple column combinations, which makes it more difficult for an adversary to uniquely re-identify individuals. Meanwhile, the differences on the numbers of tuples lead to different sensitivity for the same columns. It strongly justifies that our model is completely instance-aware.

In order to explore the impact of adversary's κ on sensitivity, we adjust the volume of κ, the maximal number of columns κ contains. Figure 4b shows

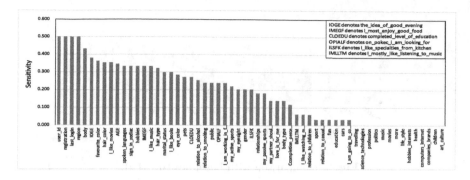

Fig. 3. Sensitivity of Pokec ($p = 0.5$)

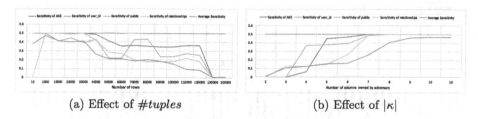

(a) Effect of #tuples

(b) Effect of $|\kappa|$

Fig. 4. Sensitivity changes w.r.t. other factors (in Pokec).

the corresponding results. Apparently, with the enhancement of κ, AS and the sensitivity of other non-primary key columns gradually increase. This is because the more columns an adversary obtains, the easier it is to successfully re-identify individuals. Note that the sensitivity of the primary key of Pokec($user\_id$) always remains stationary during the adjustment above.

These experiments strongly confirm that our model is completely consistent with our subjective perception of sensitivity. That is, as the number of rows of dataset increases and the κ of the adversary enhances, the sensitivity of each column generally decreases and increases, respectively. However, the key of database is not affected by these factors, and its sensitivity remains always the same and the highest.

4.2 Comparison with Other Methods

To the best of our knowledge, we are the first to formally propose the sensitivity of re-identification of a column and quantify it. Traditional techniques adopt some statistical tools to reflect the risks for re-identification, such as cardinality [3] (CDN), the proportion of unique values [8] (POU) and information entropy [7] (IE). We compare with them in following experiments.

Considering that the absolute sensitivity values produced by different methods are incomparable, we only compare the rank of each column accordingly. The more sensitive the column is, the higher it ranks. The comparison results

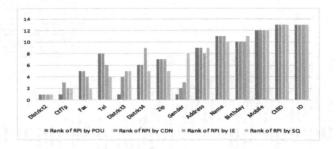

Fig. 5. Comparison with baselines (in RPI).

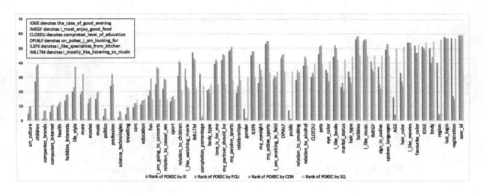

Fig. 6. Comparison with baselines (in Pokec).

for RPI are shown in Fig. 5, where we denote our method as SQ for short. Apparently, CDN, POU and IE produce similar results, which validates that they only consider the distribution of the values in each single column. The ranking results of SQ are consistent with them on some columns (*e.g.*, $CtfID$ and ID), but are quite different on some others (*e.g.*, Tel and $Gender$). Tel ranks higher than $Gender$ in CDN, POU and IE, but it is opposite with respect to SQ. The key reason for this phenomenon is that other methods do not take into account the correlation between columns, they consider each column independently. However, *Record-linkage Attack* can be successfully carried out by identifying tuples through *column combinations*, in which case $Gender$ plays an important role. It is difficult to identify tuples by $Gender$ itself, but its combination with other columns (*e.g.*, UCC_4, UCC_{13} and UCC_{14} in Table 5) can be easily identified. Consequently, it is irrational for CDN, POU and IE to give $Gender$ a relatively low sensitivity level. This justifies our scheme takes into account not only the instance for each column but also the correlation between columns. Similar comparison results for Pokec are shown in Fig. 6, where the differences between SQ and other methods are more observably.

5   Conclusion

In this paper, we present an efficient and pervasive technique for quantifying the sensitivity in structural database. It automatically evaluates the risks for re-identification for different columns according to *Record-linkage Attack*. Under the support of our scheme, the output sensitivity for the same attribute in different instances of a relational schema varies. We have objectively quantified it through a combination of probability model and adversary model. Moreover, the sensitivity quantifying results are basically in line with the common cognition of the public. We also thoroughly show that the proposed scheme is effective in dataset sensitivity governance comparing with baselines.

References

1. Abdelhameed, S.A., Moussa, S.M., Khalifa, M.E.: Privacy-preserving tabular data publishing: a comprehensive evaluation from web to cloud. Comput. Secur. **72**, 74–95 (2018)
2. Backstrom, L., Dwork, C., Kleinberg, J.M.: Wherefore art thou r3579x?: anonymized social networks, hidden patterns, and structural steganography. In: Proceedings of the 16th International Conference on World Wide Web (WWW), pp. 181–190. ACM (2007)
3. Chia, P.H., et al.: Khyperloglog: estimating reidentifiability and joinability of large data at scale. In: Proceedings of the 40th Symposium on Security and Privacy (SP), pp. 350–364. IEEE (2019)
4. Heise, A., Quiané-Ruiz, J., Abedjan, Z.: Scalable discovery of unique column combinations. PVLDB **7**(4), 301–312 (2013)
5. Narayanan, A., Shmatikov, V.: De-anonymizing social networks. In: Proceedings of the 30th Symposium on Security and Privacy (SP), pp. 173–187. IEEE (2009)
6. Papenbrock, T., Bergmann, T., Finke, M., et al.: Data profiling with metanome. PVLDB **8**(12), 1860–1863 (2015)
7. Shlomo, N.: Methods to assess and quantify disclosure risk and information loss under statistical disclosure control. Tech. rep, Government Statistical Service (2018)
8. Skinner, C.J., Elliot, M.: A measure of disclosure risk for microdata. J. Roy. Stat. Soc. B (Stat. Methodol.) **64**(4), 855–867 (2002)

EPUR: An Efficient Parallel Update System over Large-Scale RDF Data

Xiang Kang, Pingpeng Yuan(✉) ⓘ, and Hai Jin ⓘ

National Engineering Research Center for Big Data Technology and System,
Services Computing Technology and System Lab, Cluster and Grid Computing Lab,
School of Computer Science and Technology, Huazhong University of Science
and Technology, Wuhan, China
{xkang,ppyuan,hjin}@hust.edu.cn

Abstract. RDF is a standard model for data interchange on the web
and is widely adopted for graph data management. With the explosive
growth of RDF data, how to process RDF data incrementally and maximize the parallelism of RDF systems has become a challenging problem.
The existing RDF data management researches mainly focus on parallel query, and rarely pay attention to the optimization of data storage
and update. Also, the conventional parallel models for parallel query
optimizations are not suitable for data update. Therefore, we propose a
new design of an efficient parallel update system which is novel in three
aspects. Firstly, the proposed design presents a new storage structure of
RDF data and two kinds of indexes, which facilitates parallel processing. Secondly, the new design provides a general parallel task execution
framework to maximize the parallelism of the system. Last but not least,
parallel update operations are developed to handle incremental RDF
data. Based on the innovations above, we implement an efficient parallel
update system (EPUR). Extensive experiments show that EPUR outperforms RDF-3X, Virtuoso, PostgreSQL and achieves good scalability
on the number of threads.

Keywords: RDF data · Storage · Parallel processing · Batch update

1 Introduction

RDF *(Resource Description Framework)* [10] describes the relationship between
entities in the form of triples, i.e. (subject-predicate-object), also known as (S,
P, O) triples. More and more data providers publish and manage their dataset
with the help of RDF because of its simplicity and flexibility. However, the
rapid growth of RDF data presents new challenges for the storage and update
of traditional RDF system solutions.

One of the challenges in managing the explosive growth of RDF data is
to design an efficient storage structure and a parallel framework to maximize
the parallelism of the RDF system. The storage structure usually needs to be

X. Wang et al. (Eds.): APWeb-WAIM 2020, LNCS 12317, pp. 20–34, 2020.
https://doi.org/10.1007/978-3-030-60259-8_3

specially optimized to facilitate the execution of the parallel framework, such as data partitioning and indexing. The key to improving the performance of RDF systems is to make full use of multi-core resources to accelerate data processing, especially modern computers are equipped with more and more cores. However, most of the existing researches on parallel processing mainly focus on parallel query while parallel data update is often ignored. For example, the parallel query model proposed by RDF-3X [14] does not work well in parallel update, TripleBit [18] with high speed of query processing does not support the update operation. Therefore, a more general parallel framework is urgently needed to improve both query and update performance of RDF systems.

Another challenge is how to update RDF data efficiently and incrementally. Currently, many optimization techniques for data updates of the *Relational Database Management System* (RDBMS) have been developed. However, the optimization techniques for RDBMS are not applicable to RDF systems due to the differences of storage structure. For example, the techniques of PostgreSQL [12] extended from RDBMS has little effect on the processing of RDF data and Virtuoso [4] does not support the incremental data update. Most of conventional RDF systems usually do not support parallel update operations due to the high correlation between RDF data. So, how to efficiently and incrementally update RDF data in parallel still faces many challenges.

To address above challenges and opportunities, we design and implement an efficient parallel update system and refer to it as EPUR. Our main contributions include: (1) We propose a new storage structure that supports multiple data types. Meanwhile, we build statistics and index information to accelerate locating the data. (2) We put forward a general chunk-oriented parallel task execution framework to maximize system parallelism. (3) We implement parallel data update operations based on the proposed new storage structure and chunk-oriented parallel task framework to deal with large-scale RDF data.

The rest of this paper is organized as follows: Sect. 2 describes the new storage structure and indexes. Parallel task processing framework is illustrated in Sect. 3. Section 4 gives introduction to the update operations in detail. We report the experimental results in Sect. 5. Finally, we summary the related work and give conclusion about this paper in Sects. 6 and 7 respectively.

2 Storage Structure and Index Information

2.1 Extended Storage Structure

RDF describes graph data in the form of triples $t = $ *(Subject, Predicate, Object)*, it can also be marked as $S \xrightarrow{P} O$, which means S has property P and the value is O. In the triples, S and P are both strings, but the O in real-world data may have different types. For example, if O represents how much the price of the ticket is, it would be appropriate to use a *float* type, but when the O is used to describe the age, it is better to use *int* type. In view of this, the EPUR uses four tuples (*Subject, Predicate, ObjType, Object*) to optimize the storage format,

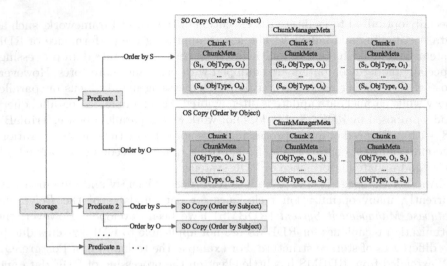

Fig. 1. Chunk-based storage structure

where *ObjType* represents the data type of *Object*. Then, the string is encoded by *String/ID* mapping dictionary while numeric data such as time and age are stored directly according to the literal value.

ChunkManagerMeta		
tripleCount	startPtr	endPtr
8bytes	4bytes	4bytes
pid	soType	length	usedSpace
4bytes	1byte	8bytes	4bytes

ChunkMeta		
ChunkNo	usedSpace	nextChunkNo
8bytes	4bytes	8bytes
lastChunkNo	min	max	updateCount
8bytes	8bytes	8bytes	8bytes

(a) Sturcture of ChunkManagerMeta   (b) Sturcture of ChunkMeta

Fig. 2. Meta data structures

To improve the efficiency of data access, we put the tuples containing the same *Predicate* together, called *Predicate partition*. As shown in Fig. 1, *Chunk Manager* is the operation class of each copy, *Chunk Manager Meta* describes the meta data information of the entire copy, and its structure is shown in Fig. 2a. *Chunk Manager Meta* contains the *ID* of the *Predicate*, *soType* (sorted by *S* or *O*), the number of stored tuples, the beginning and ending memory address of the data. On the basis of *Predicate partition*, we divide each copy into a series of *Chunks* with a unit size of 4KB. The advantage is that the physical storage between different *Chunks* is independent, which is conducive to data parallel operation and can simplify the page operations of the operating system. Similarly, each *Chunk* has its meta data, called *Chunk Meta*, and its structure is shown in Fig. 2b. The *Chunk Meta* records the maximum and minimum *Subject* or *Object* value in the *Chunk*, which can be used to determine the range of values in the current *Chunk*. All *Chunks* are stored continuously. The *next Chunk No* points to the inserted new *Chunk* and is initialized to *NULL*. The *update Count* is used to record the number of updated tuples.

Table 1. Statistical information format

Statistical type	Format
S-P	*Subject, Pre_1, Pre_2*
O-P	*ObjType, Object, Pre_1, Pre_2*
S-P-Count	*Subject, Pre_1, $count_1$, Pr_2, $count_2$*
O-P-Count	*ObjType, Object, Pre_1, $count_1$, Pre_2, $count_2$*

2.2 Statistics and Index Information

Statistics and index information play an important role in locating *Chunk* and are helpful for improving the efficiency of update and query operations. In EPUR, we store four kinds of statistics and two kinds of index information.

Statistical Information. As shown in Table 1, *S-P* and *O-P* list all related *Predicates* of the *Subject* and *Object*. The number of *Subject-Predicate (S-P-Count)* and *Object-Predicate (O-P-Count)* are also recorded, which can be used to estimate the size of the data.

Index Information. EPUR has two kinds of indexes. *Predicate partition index* records the relative position between each *Predicate partition* and starting position of the data according to the *used Space* in *Chunk Manager Meta*. *Predicate partition index* helps EPUR accelerate memory access by directly obtaining the absolute address of each *Predicate partition*. Another index is the *Chunk index*, which is generated from the minimum and maximum value in the *Chunk Meta*. With the help of *Chunk index*, the EPUR can quickly locate the *Chunk* where the data is stored by using binary search.

3 Parallel Task Execution Framework

To maximize the parallelism of RDF system on multi-core processors, it is necessary to provide an effective mechanism to reduce data access conflicts and minimize serial operations when performing data updates. In this section, we first introduce chunk-oriented parallel processing model. Then, we introduce the structure of thread-safe free lock queue model. At last, we describe window based task execution strategy in detail.

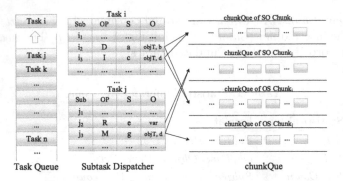

Fig. 3. Chunk-oriented subtask dispatcher

3.1 Chunk-Oriented Parallel Processing Model

In EPUR, *Chunk* is the minimal storage unit of graph data. Therefore, the EPUR decomposes the whole task into a series of chunk level subtasks. These subtasks can be processed at *Chunk* level in parallel, because they can access different *Chunks* independently. As shown in Fig. 3, each *Chunk* has a task queue called *chunkQue*. Illustrated by the example of $Task_i$ and $Task_j$, $Task_i$ and $Task_j$ can be decomposed into i_1, i_2, i_3 and j_1, j_2, j_3, etc. Furthermore, the i_2 and j_2 attempt to delete and read data on different data *Chunks* separately. So, the subtasks are inserted into the *chunkQue* of the corresponding data *Chunk* through subtask dispatcher. Finally, the subtasks in the *chunkQue* are executed in time-stamped order.

3.2 Thread-Safe Free Lock Queue Model

Parallel processing strategies may cause the resource competition unavoidably. The traditional lock mechanism sometimes does not perform well under high concurrency. Therefore, we propose a free lock queue to improve parallel performance. When updating data, the EPUR locates the *Chunks* that need to be updated through the index and allocates *chunkQue* for these *Chunks*. As is shown in Fig. 4, the enqueue and dequeue operations of *chunkQue* are independent of each other. Besides, the model uses atomic variables to count the current number of tasks in the *chunkQue*. The worker thread will bind to a non-empty *chunkQue* and execute the tasks in the enqueue order. When the atomic variable value changes to zero, the worker thread discards the current *chunkQue* and rebinds the new *chunkQue*. In addition, the EPUR adopts fixed size of continuous memory for each *chunkQue* and recycles it through the cursor index of the *chunkQue* to reduce the overhead of allocating and releasing memory.

3.3 Window Based Task Execution

In some cases, the number of subtasks in each *chunkQue* is extremely imbalanced. Massive subtasks in a *chunkQue* will occupy the current worker thread and cause

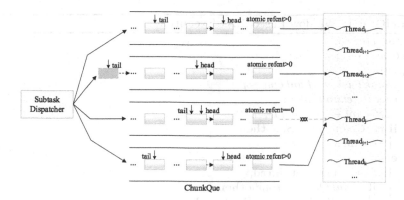

Fig. 4. Thread-safe free lock queue model

the subtasks in other *chunkQue* suffer from waiting for a long time. To minimize the thread blocking during parallel processing, the EPUR sets a window threshold for each *chunkQue* and proposes Algorithm 1. The subtasks in *chunkQue* are processed in three stages. First, if the *chunkQue* is not empty and the number of executed subtasks is less than the window size, subtasks will be executed in order (Line 3–7 in Algorithm 1). Second, when the number of executed subtasks reaches the window size and there are remaining subtasks in the *chunkQue*, the current *chunkQue* will be abandoned and re-registered in the threadpool queue to ensure that all subtasks in *chunkQue* will be executed (Line 9–14). Finally, to reduce the performance loss caused by unnecessary thread switching, the algorithm optimizes the thread switching in second stage. If the idle thread queue in the threadpool is not empty, meaning that no other *chunkQues* are waiting to be executed, so the current *chunkQue* continues to occupy the thread and reset the accumulated count value (Line 15–16).

4 Parallel Update Operation

4.1 Batch Insertion

Batch insert is divided into three phases. The first stage is parallel parsing, followed by parallel data insertion, and finally data sorting and merging.

Parallel Parsing. The data to be inserted is split evenly into slices based on the maximum number of threads that can be executed in parallel. Each thread is responsible for parsing a slice and generating a tuple set. During the parsing period, the system needs to get the corresponding *ID* from the *String/ID* mapping dictionary for string data. If the string cannot be found in the mapping dictionary, the system will add the new string to the mapping dictionary and assign a new *ID* to the string. However, the writing operation on the mapping dictionary is exclusive, and it will prohibit other parsing threads from reading

---

Algorithm 1: Window Based Task Execution

Data: *winSize*

1 *curCount* ← 0;
2 **repeat**
3   *chunkTask* ← *chunkQue.pop()*;
4   execute(*chunkTask*);
5   *curCount* ← *curCount* + 1;
6   **if** *curCount* < *winSize* **then**
7 | continue;
8   **else**
9   suspend current thread;
10   **if** *chunkQue not empty* **then**
11   **if** *idleThreadpool.isEmpty()* **then**
12   re-register the *chunkQue* in *poolQue*;
13   bind current thread to next *chunkQue*;
14   break;
15   *curCount* ← 0;
16   resume current thread;
17   **else**
18 | break;
19 **until** *chunkQue* is empty;

---

and writing to the mapping dictionary to prevent other threads from parsing the data, resulting in a huge overhead. Therefore, the EPUR temporarily stores the tuple containing the new string and continues to parse the next tuple to reduce access conflicts. Compared with building a new data warehouse, there are fewer new strings in the process of inserting data into an existing data warehouse. Therefore, the EPUR performs *ID* mapping and parsing operations on the new strings in the unresolved tuples after all threads have finished parsing, and writes all new *IDs* to the mapping dictionary.

Chunk Level Parallel Insertion. EPUR stores the tuples with same *Predicate* into the same *Predicate partition* and has two copies of data sorted by *S* and *O*. Each *Predicate partition* is continuously stored in units of *Chunks*. After parallel parsing, tuples can be grouped by different *Predicates*. For the tuples containing the new *Predicate*, the EPUR creates a new *Predicate partition* to store the tuples. For tuples that predicates already exist, the EPUR uses the *Predicate partition index* and *Chunk index* to search the *Chunks* in *Predicate partition* where the tuples should be inserted. It should be noted that each *Predicate partition* has two copies of the data, so the same operation should be performed on another copy of the data to achieve data consistency.

Resort and Merge Operations. Before the tuples are inserted, the data in the *Chunks* is already in order. To avoid frequent data movement caused by a large amount of data insertion, the newly inserted tuples are temporarily stored at the end of the *Chunks*. When the *Chunk* space is insufficient, the EPUR will apply for a new *Chunk* to store the tuples and update the *next Chunk No* in *Chunk Meta* to point at the newly applied *Chunk*. Also, the data in the newly applied *Chunk* and source *Chunk* will be merged and resorted after the insertion operation is completed to ensure that the data is still in order.

4.2   Batch Deletion

Batch delete includes two different types: specific tuple deletion and conditional pattern deletion. The parallel method used for deletion is implemented in the same way as insertion based on the chunk-oriented storage. For the specific tuple deletion, the EPUR determines the target *Chunks* in the *SO* and *OS* buffer by index information. To avoid frequent data movement, the EPUR sets the data to zero and marks the data type of the Object temporarily. When the data is persisted to disk, the marked data will be completely deleted and the data in the *Chunks* will be moved to cover the free space. For the conditional pattern deletion, it can be divided into two situations based on whether the predicate is known or not. As with data insertion, data deletion on *Predicate partition* should also consider data consistency.

Predicate Known. The situation of predicate known includes three different modes: $(S, P, ?ObjType, ?O)$, $(?S, P, ObjType, O)$, and $(?S, P, ?ObjType, ?O)$. The last mode is known to delete the data where the *Subject* and *Object* are unknown, which means to delete all the data in the specific partition. If the *Subject* or *Object* is known, which is corresponds to the first two modes. With the help of index information, the EPUR finds the *Chunks* that are involved in the known *Subject* or *Object* in the *Predicate partition*, then deletes those matching tuples.

Predicate Unknown. The situation of predicate unknown includes four different modes: $(S, ?P, ObjType, O)$, $(?S, ?P, ObjType, O)$, $(S, ?P, ?ObjType, ?O)$, and $(?S, ?P, ?ObjType, ?O)$. The last mode means to delete all the data in the database. EPUR searches all *Predicate partitions* according to the *Predicate partition index*, then deletes all the *Predicate partition*. According to the *S-P* or *O-P* of *statistics information* in Table 1, the system can find out which *Predicate partition* the *Subject* or *Object* appears in. So $(S, ?P, ObjType, O)$, $(?S, ?P, ObjType, O)$, and $(S, ?P, ?ObjType, ?O)$ modes can be translated into the predicate known mode to precess. For example, $(s_1, ?P, INT, o_1)$ indicates that all *Predicate partitions* should delete the (s_1, INT, o_1) tuple. The system obtains the *Predicate* through the *statistics information*, suppose the *Predicate* of s_1 includes P_1, P_2, P_3, and the *Predicate* of o_1 includes P_1, P_2, P_5. Then, the system selects the common *Predicate* P_1, P_2 to avoid unnecessary data processing and converts predicate unknown deletion into predicate known conditional pattern deletion. In this example, predicate unknown mode $(s_1, ?P, INT, o_1)$ can be translated into (s_1, P_1, INT, o_1) and (s_1, P_2, INT, o_1).

4.3 Batch Modification

Considering that the memory space occupied by objects of different data types are different and the data in the *Chunks* is in order, directly modifying the data on the original data will cause a large overhead such as *Chunk* compression and segmentation. So, the EPUR breaks down modification operation into two steps, including the deletion of old data and the insertion of new data. The process of batch deletion and insertion have been described in Sect. 4.1 and Sect. 4.2.

5 Evalution

All experiments were run on a dual 14-cores server with 2.40GHz Intel® Xeon® CPU E5–2680, 256GB memory, CentOS 6.5 (2.6.32 kernel), and one 3500GB SAS local disk.

5.1 Datasets

We chose LUBM *(Lehigh University Benchmark)* [6] and BTC 2012 *(Billion Triples Challenge)* [17] to evaluate the update performance of EPUR. LUBM is a program-generated dataset used to describe network of relationships between entities in university. Different from LUBM, BTC is a real-world dataset captured from multiple data sources such as Dbpedia [1] and Freebase [2]. The characteristics of the datasets are shown in Table 2, the most obvious difference between the two data sets is that the number of predicates in BTC is much larger than LUBM.

Table 2. Characteristics of Datasets

Dataset	#Triples	#Subject	#Object	$\#S \cap O$	#Predicate
LUBM	5,000,000	785,288	586,147	180,039	18
BTC	5,000,000	919,129	1,713,351	827,663	57,193

5.2 Performance of Parallel Update Operation

Among the available RDF systems, we selected RDF-3X (latest version GH-RDF-3X), Virtuoso (version 7.2), gStore, and PostgreSQL (Version 10) as comparison systems in the experiment because they represent three different kinds of RDF stores. RDF-3X and gStore are traditional RDF systems that support update operation. Virtuoso is one kind of RDBMS with extensive applicability of RDF. PostgreSQL is a relational RDF store since it has built-in version for RDF and uses snapshot isolation for concurrency control.

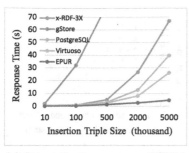

(a) Insert Performance on LUBM

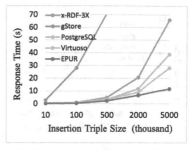

(b) Insert Performance on BTC

Fig. 5. Overall Insert Performance of EPUR

Batch Insertion. The batch insert performance of each system was tested under 5 million records. The experiment results are shown in Fig. 5a and 5b. When the number of data to be inserted is larger than 500,000, EPUR performs far better than RDF-3X and gStore on both LUBM datasets and BTC datasets. The batch insert of gStore does not return results within 20 hours when the data reaches a million so we give up the experiment on gStore. The performance of RDF-3X is good under few data because RDF-3X inserts the data into a temporary in-memory block instead of the source database. RDF-3X will combine the temporary block with original database when the number of data reaches to 500 thousand, which may cause large data consolidation overhead. The snapshot isolation in PostgreSQL for concurrency control works well when the data set is small, but performance degrades as data grows. By comparing the experimental results of LUBM and BTC datasets, it can be seen that the performance of EPUR on LUBM dataset is better than that of BTC. The main reason is that the BTC dataset has more predicates, the amount of data to be inserted into each *Chunk* is small. Each worker thread in EPUR only processes small amount of data, the parallelism of the system is not fully exploited and thread switching also leads to bad locality. Different from RDF-3X, Virtuoso, and EPUR, PostgreSQL has only one copy of data. It is unnecessary for PostgreSQL to consider data consistency. Even through, the performance of EPUR is better than PostgreSQL. In addition, we find that the response time of Virtuoso and PostgreSQL is only about twice as fast as RDF-3X, indicating that multiple threads in Virtuoso and PostgreSQL do not work efficiently.

Batch Deletion. The batch delete performance of each system was tested under 200 thousand records. The virtuoso does not support partial data deletion, so we remove virtuoso in this part of experiment. We can see from Fig. 6a and 6b that EPUR also performs better on LUBM dataset than on BTC dataset. The reason is that the EPUR generates chunk-based subtasks from the same parallel framework as insertion operations when deleting data. Therefore, the deletion operation also faces the overhead problem caused by frequent thread switching.

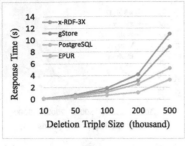
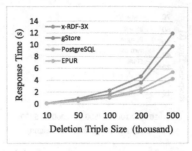

(a) Delete Performance on LUBM   (b) Delete Performance on BTC

Fig. 6. Overall delete performance of EPUR

Instead of removing the target data directly, the EPUR sets the data to be deleted to zero and marks the data type. Since PostgreSQL has only one copy of data and does not need to consider the consistency of the backup data, the deletion performance of PostgreSQL is better than other comparison systems. Also, as the number of deleted data increases, the role of the parallel execution framework in EPUR becomes more apparent, especially on LUBM dataset. When the deleted data reaches 500 thousand, the performance of EPUR is about 2 times higher than other systems.

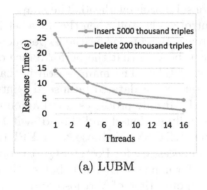
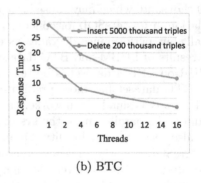

(a) LUBM   (b) BTC

Fig. 7. Scalability with varied threads

5.3   Performance of Parallel Task Execution Framework

Scalability. We evaluated the scalability of EPUR by changing the number of threads in parallel processing. It can be seen from Fig. 7a and 7b that as the number of threads increases from 1 to 8, the performance improvement of insertion and deletion operations on the LUBM dataset is more significant than that on the BTC dataset. The reason is that EPUR deals with subtasks in parallel with *Chunks*, and the number of predicates in the LUBM dataset is less than that in the BTC dataset. Therefore, the data to be inserted or deleted is more centralized in LUBM dataset, resulting in a lower frequency of thread switching, which indicates a higher thread utilization in LUBM. However, when the number of threads increases from 8 to 16, the response time decreases slowly. For LUBM dataset, the data to be inserted or deleted may be concentrated in some of the same *Chunks*. As a result, the number of subtasks in different *chunkQues* varies widely, which may cause some threads in the system to be idle because each *ChunkQue* has only one execution thread at the same time. In contrast to LUBM dataset, the data inserted or deleted is more evenly distributed in the BTC dataset, and the negative impact of thread switching causes the performance improvement of the system to become less apparent.

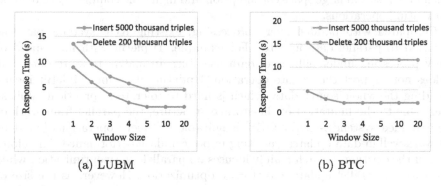

(a) LUBM   (b) BTC

Fig. 8. Update performance with varied window sizes

Window Size. We recorded the response time of insertion and deletion operations under different window sizes to analyze the effect of window size on system performance. It can be seen from Fig. 8a and 8b that the performance of the system does not increase after reaching a certain window size (5 for LUBM and 3 for BTC). Compareing Fig. 8a and 8b, it can be seen that the effect of window size on the LUBM dataset is stronger than that on the BTC dataset. The main reason is that the data to be inserted or deleted in LUBM dataset may be distributed in some of the same *Chunks* due to the small number of predicates, so the expansion of the window size can reduce the overhead caused by unnecessary thread switching. Since the number of predicates in the BTC is much larger than that in the LUBM, the subtasks in each *chunkQue* may be very small or even not up to the window size, resulting in little performance improvement from increasing the window size. Therefore, we can appropriately adjust the window size to obtain better performance according to the characteristics of the data in practical applications.

6 Related Work

6.1 Storage and Parallel Processing

Nowadays, many RDF systems have been developed and can be roughly classified into two types. Their storage structures are quite different. Traditional RDF systems such as RDF-3X [14], TripleBit [18], gStore [20], and Neo4j [11] use graphical structures to describe the relationships between entities. Meanwhile, the systems transform the string into *ID* through *String/ID* mapping dictionary, which also reveals their limitations that they do not support different data types well [7] and cannot perform theta-join [19]. Another type of RDF systems are usually extended from RDBMS, such as Virtuoso [4] and PostgreSQL [12]. For example, PostgreSQL converts RDF data into relational data tables to store, which may result in large space consumption and high time complexity of reading and writing operations.

Compared with parallel query processing, existing RDF systems pay less attention to parallel data updates. For example, TripleBit with high speed of query processing under billions of data uses bitmap matrix to store data, but it does not support the update operation. Updating data for TripleBit means reloading the whole source data, which is hard to tolerate in practical applications. Due to the limitation of the storage structure, the parallel framework of the extended system x-RDF-3X [15] is suitable for query operations but does not work well in data updates, resulting in poor update performance. Therefore, most of the existing research mainly focuses on parallel query optimization while less work on parallel update and storage optimization. However, as the size of data continues to expand, efficient storage structure and online updates methods become more and more important in data management.

6.2 Update

Currently, only a few of RDF systems support online update (incremental) operation, which is unavoidable for the real-world data. When updating the data, database systems typically locks the data and then overwrites the data [9,16] or writes a new copy of the new data [3,5,13]. The former utilizes the lock manager to provide concurrency control, many database systems have shown limited multi-core scalability and even performance degradation because of the bottlenecks latch contention [9]. For example, gStore does not support read-committed isolation and the lock mechanism causes the update performance of the system to degrade. The latter, also known as a multi-version system, allows update transactions to be performed in parallel with read transactions, even if they access the same record. For example, to support update (incremental) operations, x-RDF-3X is extended from RDF-3X, it creates temporary memory block to store the inserted data, and merge with the main database when the temporary memory block is out of space. One drawback of this method is that when the system is unexpectedly powered off, the data in the memory block may lost. Another is that the overhead of maintaining additional storage space can have a negative impact on overall system performance. In addition, some efficient update systems fail to deal with large-scale data. For instance, the update operations of Neo4j are very intuitive but it does not perform well in face of large-scale data. Neo4j is suitable for lightweight data updates without super nodes [8]. Virtuoso has high data loading speed, but does not support partial data update and deletion.

7 Conclusion and Future Work

In this paper, we propose a solution for large-scale RDF data management, including storage and parallel update operations. We design and implement a new storage structure and a general parallel framework to accelerate the update processing of RDF data. The results show that our solution based on chunk-oriented parallel processing makes full use of the potential of multi-cores and achieve better update performance than existing systems. As future work, we will work on extending EPUR for scaling the data and using the distributed computing architecture to optimize the performance, including distributed storage and efficient communication protocols between distributed nodes. Also, we will do further work on parallel queries to play the role of the generic parallel framework.

Acknowledgment. The research is supported by The National Key Research & Development Program of China (No. 2018YFB1402802), NSFC (No. 61672255).

References

1. Bizer, C., et al.: Dbpedia-a crystallization point for the web of data. Web Semant. Sci. Serv. Agents World Wide Web **7**(3), 154–165 (2009)
2. Bollacker, K., Evans, C., Paritosh, P., Sturge, T., Taylor, J.: Freebase: a collaboratively created graph database for structuring human knowledge. In: Proceedings of the 2008 ACM SIGMOD International Conference on Management of Data, pp. 1247–1250. ACM (2008)
3. Dashti, M., Basil John, S., Shaikhha, A., Koch, C.: Transaction repair for multi-version concurrency control. In: Proceedings of the 2017 ACM International Conference on Management of Data, pp. 235–250. ACM (2017)
4. Erling, O.: Virtuoso, a hybrid rdbms/graph column store. IEEE Data Eng. Bull. **35**(1), 3–8 (2012)
5. Faleiro, J.M., Abadi, D.J., Hellerstein, J.M.: High performance transactions via early write visibility. Proc. VLDB Endowment **10**(5), 613–624 (2017)
6. Guo, Y., Pan, Z., Heflin, J.: LUBM: a benchmark for OWL knowledge base systems. Web Semant. Sci. Serv. Agents World Wide Web **3**(2–3), 158–182 (2005)
7. He, L., et al.: Stylus: a strongly-typed store for serving massive RDF data. Proc. VLDB Endowment **11**(2), 203–216 (2017)
8. Holzschuher, F., Peinl, R.: Performance of graph query languages: comparison of cypher, gremlin and native access in neo4j. In: Proceedings of the Joint EDBT/ICDT 2013 Workshops, pp. 195–204. ACM (2013)
9. Jung, H., Han, H., Fekete, A., Heiser, G., Yeom, H.Y.: A scalable lock manager for multicores. ACM Trans. Database Syst. (TODS) **39**(4), 29 (2014)

10. Miller, E.: An introduction to the resource description framework. Bull. Am. Soc. Inf. Sci. Technol. **25**(1), 15–19 (1998)
11. Miller, J.J.: Graph database applications and concepts with neo4j. In: Proceedings of the 2013 Southern Association for Information Systems Conference, **2324** (2013)
12. Momjian, B.: PostgreSQL: introduction and concepts. Addison-Wesley New York, **192** (2001)
13. Neumann, T., Mühlbauer, T., Kemper, A.: Fast serializable multi-version concurrency control for main-memory database systems. In: Proceedings of the 2015 ACM SIGMOD International Conference on Management of Data, pp. 677–689. ACM (2015)
14. Neumann, T., Weikum, G.: The RDF-3x engine for scalable management of RDF data. VLDB J. **19**(1), 91–113 (2010)
15. Neumann, T., Weikum, G.: x-RDF-3x: fast querying, high update rates, and consistency for RDF databases. Proc. VLDB Endowment **3**(1–2), 256–263 (2010)
16. Ren, K., Thomson, A., Abadi, D.J.: Vll: a lock manager redesign for main memory database systems. VLDB J. **24**(5), 681–705 (2015)
17. Semantic Web Challenge: Semantic web challenge 2012, (2012) http://challenge.semanticweb.org/2012/
18. Yuan, P., Liu, P., Wu, B., Jin, H., Zhang, W., Liu, L.: Triplebit: a fast and compact system for large scale rdf data. Proc. VLDB Endowment **6**(7), 517–528 (2013)
19. Zhang, X., Chen, L., Wang, M.: Efficient multi-way theta-join processing using mapreduce. Proc. VLDB Endowment **5**(11), 1184–1195 (2012)
20. Zou, L., Özsu, M.T., Chen, L., Shen, X., Huang, R., Zhao, D.: gStore: a graph-based SPARQL query engine. VLDB J. **23**(4), 565–590 (2013). https://doi.org/10.1007/s00778-013-0337-7

Graph Data and Social Networks

Multiple Local Community Detection via High-Quality Seed Identification

Jiaxu Liu[1], Yingxia Shao[2(✉)], and Sen Su[1]

[1] State Key Laboratory of Networking and Switching Technology,
BUPT, Beijing, China
{jiaxuliu,susen}@bupt.edu.cn

[2] Beijing Key Lab of Intelligent Telecommunications Software and Multimedia,
BUPT, Beijing, China
shaoyx@bupt.edu.cn

Abstract. Local community detection aims to find the communities that a given seed node belongs to. Most existing works on this problem are based on a very strict assumption that the seed node only belongs to a single community, but in real-world networks, nodes are likely to belong to multiple communities. In this paper, we introduce a novel algorithm, HqsMLCD, that can detect multiple communities for a given seed node. HqsMLCD first finds the high-quality seeds which can detect better communities than the given seed node with the help of network representation, then expands the high-quality seeds one-by-one to get multiple communities, probably overlapping. Experimental results on real-world networks demonstrate that our new method HqsMLCD outperforms the state-of-the-art multiple local community detection algorithms.

Keywords: Multiple local community detection · Network embedding · Seed set expansion

1 Introduction

Community structure generally exists in networks [11], where nodes are more densely connected in the same community. Community detection, which aims to discover the community structure of networks, is a fundamental problem in analyzing complex networks and has attracted much attention recently [3, 4, 15]. Most community detection methods detect all communities in the network. However, for a large-scale network, we may not care about all communities in the network, but just a part of it, such as communities that contain a particular node, called seed node. In addition, working on the entire graph is time-consuming, especially on large-scale networks. Sometimes it is also hard or impossible to obtain the complete information of the network, such as the World Wide Web.

Local community detection, which finds the communities of a given seed node, is proposed to handle the above situations, and it has many applications in the real world. For instance, in collaboration networks [14], we may discover

© Springer Nature Switzerland AG 2020
X. Wang et al. (Eds.): APWeb-WAIM 2020, LNCS 12317, pp. 37–52, 2020.
https://doi.org/10.1007/978-3-030-60259-8_4

the working group membership of a particular person through local community detection; and in product networks, the shopping platform may find the products that customers are interested in by detecting the community of purchased products. Most existing algorithms [1,16] for local community detection are based on a strict assumption that the seed node only belongs to a single community, however, in real-world networks, quite a number of nodes appear in multiple communities. It is a more challenging task to detect all local communities related to the seed node, we call this problem *multiple local community detection (MLCD)*. Yang and Leskovec [14] detected multiple hierarchical communities by finding multiple local minima in the local community detection method. He et al. [7] introduced a Local Spectral Subspaces based algorithm (LOSP) to expand different seed sets to communities, which are generated from the ego-network of the given seed node. Kamuhanda and He [9] proposed a Nonnegative Matrix Factorization algorithm to detected multiple communities, and automatically determine the number of detected communities. Hollocou et al. [8] solved the problem by expanding the initial seed to a candidate seed set and applying a local community detection algorithm (e.g., PageRank-Nibble [1]) for seeds in the seed set individually. However, these proposed methods still have the following two problems.

1. Sensitive to the position of the seed node. Existing works select a new community member from nodes around the seed node, for instance, adding surrounding nodes to detected communities one by one until reaching the local optimum of some quality functions (e.g., conductance) [7,14], or applying matrix factorization methods on the subgraph expanded by the seed node [9]. These methods tend to involve correct nodes, if most of the nodes near the seed node belong to the same community as the seed node, and will get high quality (e.g., accuracy) detected communities. Otherwise, they will get low quality communities. Thus, the quality of detected communities is sensitive to the position of the seed node in the community.

2. Insensitive to the local structure of the seed node. Different nodes in a network have different local structures, such as degree centrality, closeness centrality, and betweenness centrality, resulting in different properties of communities. To be concrete, different seed nodes have different numbers of communities that they belong to. However, existing works are insensitive to such characteristics of the seed nodes. The number of detected communities they output is highly related with the input parameters [8,9] or the feature of the entire network [7], and it cannot adaptively change with the number of ground-truth communities of the seed node.

In this paper, we introduce a novel approach HqsMLCD for MLCD to address the above problems. HqsMLCD follows the general framework introduced by MULTICOM [8], and improves the accuracy of detected communities via identifying high-quality seed nodes. HqsMLCD finds high-quality seeds based on network embedding methods, which mitigates the impact of the seed node position. Further, it uses local clustering methods to recognize the local structures of the seed node, and determine the number of high-quality seeds adaptively. Finally,

HqsMLCD expands each high-quality seed to find accurate local communities via existing local community detection methods.

We conducted extensive empirical studies on three real-world networks. The results demonstrate that HqsMLCD achieves the best accuracy of MLCD compared with the state-of-the-art methods, and the trend of the number of detected communities is consistent with the overlapping memberships of the seed node.

The rest of the paper is organized as follows: we present the background and related work in Sect. 2, and we introduce the concept of high-quality seeds in Sect. 3. In Sect. 4, we elaborate on our algorithm HqsMLCD. In Sect. 5, we provide experimental results, and we draw conclusions in Sect. 6.

2 Background and Related Work

Before introducing our algorithm, we present the notations that we use throughout the paper, the problem definition and the general framework of multiple local community detection, and some closely related work.

2.1 Notations

- **Graph.** Let $G = (V, E)$ be an undirected, unweighted graph, where $V = \{v_1, v_2, \cdots, v_n\}$ is the set of n nodes in G, and E is the edge set of G.
- **Communities.** For a seed node v_s, let C_s be the set of ground-truth communities that contain v_s, each community $c_i \in C_s$ is the set of nodes belonging to c_i. Similarly, C_d is the set of communities detected by community detection methods.
- **Network Embedding.** For a graph G, its network embedding $Y_G \in \mathbb{R}^{n \times d}$ is a matrix of vertex latent representation, where d is the dimension of embedding, and $Y_G(v)$ denotes the embedding vector for node v.

2.2 Problem Definition

Multiple Local Community Detection (MLCD). *Given a graph G and a seed node v_s. Multiple local community detection algorithm returns a set of detected communities C_d. For each community $c_i \in C_s$, we consider the most similar community $c_j \in C_d$ as the corresponding detected community of c_i. The algorithm aims to return communities that are as similar as possible to the ground-truth communities, i.e., maximizing*

$$\frac{\sum_{c_i \in C_s} max \{sim \, (c_i, c_j) | c_j \in C_d\}}{|C_s|}, \tag{1}$$

where $sim(c_i, c_j)$ is a metric that measures the similarity between c_i and c_j, generally using F_1 score.

F_1 Score. *Given a ground-truth community c_i and a detected community c_j, F_1 score is defined as*

$$F_1(c_i, c_j) = \frac{2precision(c_i, c_j) \times recall(c_i, c_j)}{precision(c_i, c_j) + recall(c_i, c_j)}, \qquad (2)$$

where $precision(c_i, c_j) = \frac{|c_i \cap c_j|}{|c_j|}$, $recall(c_i, c_j) = \frac{|c_i \cap c_j|}{|c_i|}$.

2.3   General Framework of MLCD

Existing works on multiple local community detection follow a general framework [8,12], which separates into two steps: 1) finding new seeds on the basis of the initial seed node; 2) and then applying local community detection methods to new seeds to obtain multiple detected communities. Figure 1 illustrates the overview of the general framework.

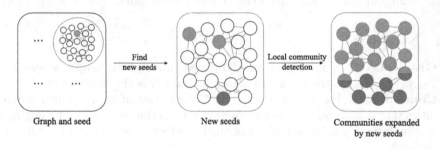

Fig. 1. General framework.

2.4   Related Work

Most of the existing local community detection methods are based on seed set expansion. Specifically, they first take the given seed node as an initial community, then apply a greedy strategy to add nodes to the community until reaching the local or global minimum of some quality functions (e.g., local modularity). Many works improve this method by generating reasonable order of nodes to add to the detected community, such as using random walk [1,2], combining higher-order structure [16], and applying spectral clustering methods [6,7].

The above local community detection methods focus on detecting a single community of the seed node, ignoring the fact that the given seed node may belong to other overlapping communities in the real-word graph. To address this issue, few methods have been introduced. Yang and Leskovec [14] proposed a method which only detects multiple communities by finding multiple local minima of the quality function (e.g., conductance) used in the greedy strategy, which causes that the latter detected community completely contains the former one.

LOSP [7] generates several seed sets from the ego-network of the initial seed node, then expands these seed sets based on their local spectral subspace. Hollocou et al. [8] first found new seeds by clustering the graph which is embedded in a low dimension vector space by a score function of seed set, like Personalized PageRank, then expanded them to multiple communities, however, new seeds are always far away from the initial seed, cause the communities expanded by new seeds including a lot of nodes that beyond the ground-truth communities, and may not contain the initial seed, which is inconsistent with the goal of recovering all the communities of the seed node. Kamuhanda and He [9] applied nonnegative matrix factorization on the subgraph extracted by using Breadth-First Search (BFS) on the initial seed node to solve this problem, it is a novel idea, but the members of detected communities are limited in the range of the subgraph, which ignore the structure of the network, and the number of communities decided by the algorithm is highly related to the size of the subgraph, which is inflexible and illogical. Inspired by MULTICOM [8], Ni et al. [12] proposed a method LOCD following the framework introduced in Sect. 2.3 recently. The difference between LOCD and our work include two main following points. First, we proved the existence of high-quality seeds (Sect. 3.1) and clearly defined quality score and high-quality seeds with graph representation learning. Second, we improved the accuracy of high-quality seeds through clustering methods, and examined the effectiveness through ablation study. Besides, we used more evaluations and baselines in experiments, and tested on more real-world datasets. According to the F_1 score on Amazon in their paper, our work (0.895) outperforms LOCD (0.7863).

3 High-Quality Seeds

According to the general framework of MLCD, we find local communities by expanding seed nodes, different seed nodes result in different detected communities. We call seed nodes that can generate communities close to the ground-truth communities as *high-quality seeds*. In this section, we first empirically verify the existence of high-quality seeds, and then qualitatively analyze how to find them.

3.1 The Existence of High-Quality Seeds

We assume that for all nodes in a ground-truth community, the high-quality ones can generate communities that are more similar to the ground-truth community than other nodes through a certain local community detection method (e.g., PageRank-Nibble [1]). In order to demonstrate the existence of high-quality seeds, we conduct an empirical study.

Three real-world networks Amazon, DBLP and Youtube are used. For each network G, we randomly pick 30 nodes as seed nodes v_s. For a seed node v_s, we choose a ground-truth community c_s that v_s belongs to, then use PageRank-Nibble for v_s and all other nodes belong to c_s to detect their local communities,

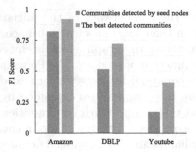
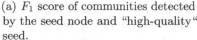
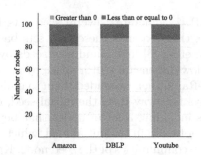

(a) F_1 score of communities detected by the seed node and "high-quality" seed.

(b) Results of difference between average cosine similarity of "same-com-pairs" and "diff-com-pairs".

Fig. 2. Experimental results of high-quality seeds

finally compute the F_1 score. Figure 2(a) illustrates the average F_1 score of communities detected by the 30 seed nodes and the best communities detected by nodes from the ground-truth community that the seed nodes belong to.

We can see that, in the community which the randomly picked seed node belongs to, there exist nodes that can generate a better community than the seed node through a local community detection method, and we call such nodes high-quality seeds.

3.2 High-Quality Seed Identification with Network Representation Learning

Since most existing local community detection methods are based on seed set expansion, which tends to include the neighbors of the seed node into the detected community, high-quality seeds should have high similarity with its neighbors in the same community. Furthermore, the detected community should contain the initial seed node, therefore high-quality seeds are expected to have high similarity with the initial seed node.

In order to find high-quality seeds with the above characteristics, we need a similarity measure that can imply whether nodes belong to the same community. Nowadays, network representation learning (aka., network embedding) is a popular approach to learn low-dimensional representations of nodes and effectively preserve the network structure, like the community structure. Thus intuitively, the similarity between node embeddings could be approximated as the probability of belonging to the same community, so we use node embeddings to select high-quality seeds.

We also conduct an experiment to verify our intuition. First, we randomly pick 100 seed nodes in each of the network Amazon, DBLP, and Youtube, then sample a subgraph around each seed node with BFS, and learn the embeddings of these subgraphs. From each subgraph, we select 50 "same-com-pairs" which refers to node pairs composed of two nodes from the same community, and 50 "diff-com-pairs" which refers to node pairs composed of two nodes from different communities. After that, for each subgraph, we compute the difference between average cosine similarity of "same-com-pairs" and "diff-com-pairs", if the difference is greater than 0, the similarities between node embeddings are considered capable of detecting community relations, and the results as shown in Fig. 2(b).

It shows that most similarities between embeddings of nodes from the same community are greater than those from different communities, which means the similarities could partially reflect the probability of whether belonging to the same community. Thus, network representation learning can be used to find high-quality seeds, the specific quantitive method is introduced in Sect. 4.

4 Multiple Local Community Detection with High-Quality Seeds

In this section, we present our proposed method, Multiple Local Community Detection with High-Quality Seeds (HqsMLCD for short). Our optimizations focus on the selection of new seeds in the general framework described in Sect. 2.3, and we use the new high-quality seeds as the input of local community detection methods to detect multiple communities.

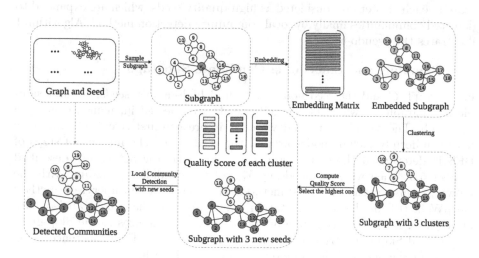

Fig. 3. Framework of HqsMLCD.

Figure 3 shows the overall framework of HqsMLCD. We first use BFS sample a subgraph around the given seed node to find all candidates of high-quality seeds, then apply network representation learning methods on the subgraph to obtain embeddings of candidate nodes. On top of the embeddings, we further cluster the candidate nodes to several clusters. After that, we calculate the *Quality Score* of all candidates in clusters, and nodes with the highest quality

---

Algorithm 1. Multiple Local Community Detection

Input: graph G, initial seed node v_s
1: Initialize:
  $S_h \leftarrow \emptyset$ (high-quality seeds)
  $C_d \leftarrow \emptyset$
2: $G_s \leftarrow$ Sampling(G, v_s)
3: $Y_{G_s} \leftarrow$ Embedding(G_s)
4: $L_{can} \leftarrow$ Clustering(Y_{G_s}) (candidate clusters)
5: **for** l_i in L_{can} **do**
6: **for** v_j in l_i **do**
7:   $q_j \leftarrow$ Compute the quality score of each candidate v_j using Equation 3
8: **end for**
9: $v_h \leftarrow$ node in l_i with the highest quality score q_h
10: $S_h \leftarrow S_h \cup \{v_h\}$
11: **end for**
12: **for** v_i in S_h **do**
13: $c_i \leftarrow$ Local community detection(G, v_i)
14: $C_d \leftarrow C_d \cup \{c_i\}$
15: **end for**
16: **return** C_d

---

score in each cluster are considered as high-quality seeds, which are expanded to detected communities finally by local community detection method. Algorithm 1 illustrates the pseudo-code.

4.1 Sampling and Embedding Candidate Subgraph

For a graph G and the seed node v_s, to find high-quality seeds, we first sample a subgraph G_s where high-quality seeds are selected in, named candidate subgraph. The sampling method we used is breadth-first search (BFS), since it can uniformly include nodes around the seed node. The number of steps of BFS is determined through parameter tuning, and the details are described in Sect. 5.3. Then we get embedding Y_{G_s} of the candidate subgraph with the network representation learning method. We choose the unsupervised method DeepWalk [13] in the implementation, since we don't have any labeled data in advance. DeepWalk feeds random walk paths as sentences to the Skip-gram model, and Skip-gram tries to predict "context" of "word" in "sentence", i.e., predict nearby nodes of the node on a random walk path.

4.2 Clustering Candidate Subgraph

We then cluster the embedded candidate subgraph to several clusters. As illustrated in Fig. 3, candidate nodes in G_s may come from several different ground-truth communities, we want to select one single node as the high-quality seed in each ground-truth community, so that we could recover the correct number of communities, and avoid to miss some ground-truth communities. We choose Density-Based Spatial Clustering of Applications with Noise (DBSCAN)

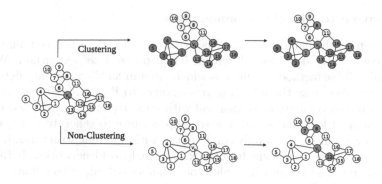

Fig. 4. Example of clustering and non-clustering candidate subgraph.

method [5] in this step, as DBSCAN could automatically decide the number of clusters, i.e., number of detected communities in our algorithm. We use the similarity between node embeddings as the metric of DBSCAN, so we could partition the nodes of different communities flexibly, as we demonstrate in Sect. 3.2.

For instance, given a seed node v_s and its candidate subgraph as in Fig. 4, without clustering, we may generate high-quality seeds that are close to each other, and would lead to the neglect of the nodes in some ground-truth communities as their quality score may less than nodes in other clusters. Besides, without clustering, the number of high-quality seeds should be given as a parameter, which is hard to know in advance in the practice.

4.3 Quality Score and High-Quality Seed Identification

After getting several clusters of candidate nodes, we compute the quality score of every node in all clusters, and select nodes with the highest quality score in each cluster as high-quality seeds. As we mentioned in Sect. 3.2, high-quality seeds have a high possibility of belonging to the same community with their neighbors and the initial seed node v_s. Using cosine similarity between node embeddings approximated as the probability of belonging to the same community, we define the quality score QS of node v as

$$QS(v) = \frac{\sum\limits_{u \in N(v)} Sim\left(Y_{G_s}(u), Y_{G_s}(v)\right)}{|N(v)|} + Sim\left(Y_{G_s}(v), Y_{G_s}(v_s)\right), \qquad (3)$$

where $N(v)$ is the set of neighbors of v. The similarity between the node and its neighbors makes better performance while applying local community detection method on it, and similarity between the node and the seed node v_s ensures v_s be involved in detected communities, which is one of the main goals of MLCD.

4.4 Expand to Detected Communities

In this step, each high-quality seed is expanded to a detected community by a local community detection algorithm based on seed set expansion. We use PageRank-Nibble method [1] which is widely used in local community detection. Further, we also make the following two changes to Pagerank-Nibble: 1) if the current detected community is identical with some community detected before, we find the next local minima of the sweep procedure to generate a larger community, so we could find not only communities with different structures, but also hierarchical communities, which both exist in real-world networks. 2) Inspired by Kamuhanda and He [9] who added the neighbors of initial community members to refine the final community, we also introduce a refinement step which adds the given seed node to the detected community when the detected community doesn't contain it and at least one of its neighbors is involved in the detected community. Finally, we obtain multiple communities as the results. PageRank-Nibble uses conductance as the stop criteria, makes sure the detected communities with low conductance, and combining our selection of seed node, the detected communities can achieve higher similarity with the ground-truth community.

4.5 Time Complexity

Here we analyse the time complexity of each step of HqsMLCD. The time complexity of BFS is $O(n+m)$, where n is the number of nodes, and m is the number of edges in the subgraph. The complexity of both DeepWalk and DBSCAN is $O(nlogn)$. High-quality seeds can be identified with $O(n)$. Pagerank-Nibble costs $O(vol(Supp(p)) + n_p logn_p)$, where p is the PageRank vector, $Supp(p)$ is the support of p, $vol(S)$ denotes the volume of subset S, and $n_p = |Supp(p)|$.

5 Experiments

In this section, we evaluate HqsMLCD on real-world networks. We first introduce the evaluation criteria of our experiments, then we present the basic information of datasets and the state-of-the-art baselines. We present the results on parameter tuning, and the results of comparing HqsMLCD with existing methods.

5.1 Evaluation Criteria

- F_1 **Score.** Defined in Eq. 2
- **Conductance.** The conductance of a set $S \subset V$ is

$$\Phi(S) = \frac{cut(S)}{min(vol(S), vol(V \backslash S))}, \tag{4}$$

where $cut(S)$ is the number of edges with one endpoint in S, and another one not; $vol(S)$ is the sum of the degree of nodes in S.

Table 1. Statistics of read-world datasets

Dataset	Nodes	Edges	Average degree
Amazon	334,863	925,872	5.53
DBLP	317,080	1,049,866	6.62
LiveJournal	3,997,962	34,681,189	17.35

Table 2. Statistics of communities in read-world datasets

Dataset	Number of communities	Average community size	Number of top communities
Amazon	75,149	30.23	1,517
DBLP	13,477	53.41	4,961
LiveJournal	664,414	10.79	4,703

Table 3. The number of nodes with different om

Dataset	$om = 2$	$om = 3$	$om = 4$	$om = 5$
Amazon	3,839	1,652	506	225
DBLP	10,468	2,275	707	221
LiveJournal	19,640	5,819	1,793	926

- **The number of detected communities.** C_d denotes the set of detected communities, and the number of detected communities is $|C_d|$.
- **The seed node coverage.** We expect to find multiple communities that contain the initial seed node v_s, so the coverage of v_s is a key criterion, which is defined as

$$cov(v_s, C_d) = \frac{|\{c_i | v_s \in c_i, c_i \in C_d\}|}{|C_d|}.$$

5.2   Datasets and State-of-the-Art Methods

Datasets. In order to quantify the comparison of algorithm results with the actual situation. We use three real-world networks with ground-truth communities provided by SNAP [10,14]: the product network Amazon, the collaboration network DBLP and the online social network LiveJournal. All three networks are unweighted and undirected, and are widely used in academic literature. Table 1 and Table 2 shows the statistics of them and their ground-truth communities.

We use the top 5,000 communities provided by SNAP as the ground-truth communities in our experiments. The number of ground-truth communities after removing the duplicate shows in Table 2. Then we group the nodes in ground-truth communities according to the number of communities they belong to (i.e., overlapping memberships or om for short [7,9], node with $om = 2$ means it

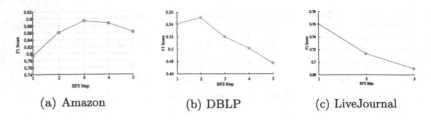

Fig. 5. The average F_1 score of applying different BFS steps in HqsMLCD.

belongs to 2 communities at the same time). The number of nodes with different om of three datasets shows in Table 3. Note that there are too few nodes belonging to more than five communities to achieve meaningful experimental results.

In the following experiments, for each om group, we randomly pick 500 nodes as the initial seed node if there are more than 500 nodes in the group, otherwise, pick all nodes in the group. Besides, we only pick seed nodes whose communities sizes are between 10 and 100 (the range of DBLP is 0 to 200, because of its larger community structure).

Baselines. We compare our algorithm with several state-of-the-art multiple local community detection methods. He et al. [7] generated several seed sets from the ego-network of the initial seed node, then applied LOSP to obtain multiple detected communities. MULTICOM [8] finds new seeds based on the Personalized PageRank score of seed set, then expands new seeds by PageRank-Nibble. MLC [9] uses nonnegative matrix factorization on the subgraph around the initial seed node to get multiple communities. In addition, to verify the effective of clustering proposed in Sect. 4.2, we also consider HqsMLCD-nc as a baseline, which is HqsMLCD without clustering phase.

5.3   Parameter Tuning of the BFS Steps

One of the main parameters of HqsMLCD is the steps of BFS, so we study the effectiveness of it. Figure 5 shows the average F_1 score on Amazon, DBLP and LiveJournal that use different BFS steps in HqsMLCD. We can see that the F_1 score reaches peak value when BFS step equals to a suitable value (e.g., BFS step equals to 3 on Amazon), and the best step of BFS varies on different datasets. The BFS step determines the range of high-quality seeds selection. Too small steps may not contain high-quality seed nodes, but too large steps will contain too much noise. Note that for LiveJournal we only set BFS step to be 1, 2 and 3, because the subgraphs in LiveJournal with steps larger than 3 contain too many noisy nodes, and are too large to be processed efficiently.

5.4   Accuracy Comparison

In this section, we use the F_1 score to measure the accuracy of multiple detected communities. Table 4 lists the average F_1 scores grouped by om of five methods

Table 4. F_1 score results. **Bold** numbers are the best scores, and <u>underlined</u> numbers are the second-best ones.

Dataset	Algorithm	$om = 2$	$om = 3$	$om = 4$	$om = 5$	Mixed om
Amazon	LOSP	0.570	0.562	0.512	0.438	0.546
	MULTICOM	0.809	0.802	0.764	0.872	0.798
	MLC	0.784	0.787	0.774	0.785	0.783
	HqsMLCD-nc	<u>0.843</u>	<u>0.861</u>	<u>0.882</u>	<u>0.884</u>	<u>0.861</u>
	HqsMLCD	**0.882**	**0.901**	**0.907**	**0.890**	**0.895**
DBLP	LOSP	0.528	0.494	0.488	0.443	0.509
	MULTICOM	0.556	0.482	0.497	0.455	0.520
	MLC	0.403	0.361	0.383	0.356	0.384
	HqsMLCD-nc	<u>0.587</u>	<u>0.519</u>	<u>0.537</u>	<u>0.514</u>	<u>0.555</u>
	HqsMLCD	**0.602**	**0.532**	**0.538**	**0.532**	**0.568**
LiveJournal	LOSP	0.601	0.632	0.522	0.598	0.588
	MULTICOM	0.750	0.698	0.698	0.650	0.699
	MLC	0.664	0.710	0.646	<u>0.697</u>	0.679
	HqsMLCD-nc	<u>0.785</u>	<u>0.721</u>	<u>0.712</u>	0.689	<u>0.727</u>
	HqsMLCD	**0.818**	**0.753**	**0.753**	**0.718**	**0.761**

on three datasets, and the last column shows the average F_1 scores of using nodes as seed nodes from all om groups.

We can see that HqsMLCD achieves the best results on three real-world networks, and most results of HqsMLCD-nc outperform the other three base-lines. The advantage of them mainly comes from the high-quality seeds we used to detect local communities. Besides, HqsMLCD is better than HqsMLCD-nc, demonstrating that clustering candidate subgraph is effective.

5.5   Conductance Comparison

We also compare the conductance of the detected communities by different MLCD algorithms. Figure 6 shows the average conductance of communities detected by each algorithm. HqsMLCD and HqsMLCD-nc outperform the other three methods on all three datasets. Note that LOSP, MULTICOM, HqsMLCD-nc, and HqsMLCD all use conductance as the measure to generate detected communities, and our methods still outperform LOSP and MULTICOM, which means the high-quality seeds we select can indeed generate better communities. Comparing with MLC, HqsMLCD also achieves lower conductance. This implies with the help of high-quality seeds, the seed expansion-based method can also surpass the Nonnegative Matrix Factorization-based solution.

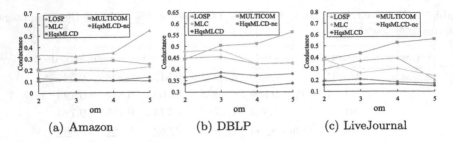

Fig. 6. Conductance results.

5.6   Number of Detected Communities

Here we compare the number of detected communities of different methods to demonstrate the ability to capture the local structures with respect to the given seed node. Figure 7 illustrates the number of detected communities of LOSP, MLC, and HqsMLCD for nodes with different om on Amazon, DBLP, and LiveJournal. Note that MULTICOM and HqsMLCD-nc require the number of detected communities as a input parameter, they have no ability to adaptively determine the number of communities, so we do not visualize them in the figure. The black line represents the number of communities that seed nodes actually belongs to, i.e., om. We can see that the trends of MLC and LOSP remain stable when om increases, but the results of HqsMLCD are consistent with the trend of ground-truth. This phenomenon implies that our algorithm can recognize different local structures and utilize them for community detection.

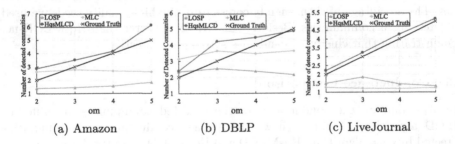

Fig. 7. Number of detected communities.

5.7   Seed Node Coverage

Next we examine the seed node coverage of detected communities. It is an important indicator, as the target of multiple local community detection is to detect multiple communities that the seed node belongs to. We evaluate seed coverage of MULTICOM, MLC, HqsMLCD-nc, and HqsMLCD on Amazon, DBLP and

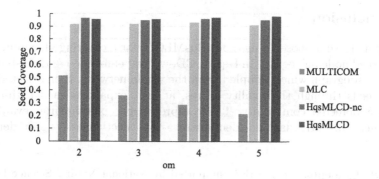

Fig. 8. Seed coverage results.

LiveJournal. Since LOSP includes the seed node in every seed set, we do not compare it here. Figure 8 illustrates the average seed coverage on three datasets grouped by *om*. It is clear to see that HqsMLCD-nc and HqsMLCD outperform MULTICOM and MLC. Note that our method uses the same framework as MULTICOM, but HqsMLCD identifies the high-quality seeds similar to the given seed node via network representation. However, MULTICOM may find new seeds far away from the initial seed node. Therefore, except the community expanded by the initial seed node, the communities generated by new seeds of MULTICOM hardly contain the initial seed node.

5.8   Running Time

At last, we compare the running time of these algorithms on Amazon, DBLP and LiveJournal. For each method, we calculate the average time of detecting all communities of a single seed node on different datasets, Table 5 shows the result. We can see that the running time of LOSP increases rapidly as the size of graph increases, and cost more than 500 s for a single seed node on LiveJournal. Although HqsMLCD doesn't achieve the best time efficiency, HqsMLCD, MLC, and MULTICOM have a similar time cost. Considering the improvement brought by HqsMLCD for the community detection problem, such a little overhead of the time cost is acceptable.

Table 5. Average running time (s) of detecting all communities of a seed node.

Algorithm	Amazon	DBLP	LiveJournal
LOSP	4.24	7.62	538.71
MULTICOM	6.04	9.12	11.37
MLC	1.39	2.82	12.51
HqsMLCD	5.14	6.78	17.19

6   Conclusion

In this paper, we proposed a method, HqsMLCD, for recovering all communities which a seed node belongs to. In HqsMLCD, we first embedded and clustered the candidate subgraph which sampled from the whole network, then selected high-quality seeds through the quality scores, at last, expanded each high-quality seed to a detected community. The comprehensive experimental evaluations on various real-world datasets demonstrate the effectiveness of our detection algorithm.

Acknowledgements. This work is supported by National Natural Science Foundation of China (No. 61702015, U1936104) and The Fundamental Research Funds for the Central Universities 2020RC25.

References

1. Andersen, R., Chung, F., Lang, K.: Local graph partitioning using PageRank vectors. In: FOCS, pp. 475–486 (2006)
2. Bian, Y., Yan, Y., Cheng, W., Wang, W., Luo, D., Zhang, X.: On multi-query local community detection. In: ICDM, pp. 9–18 (2018)
3. Chen, Z., Li, L., Bruna, J.: Supervised community detection with line graph neural networks. In: ICLR (2019)
4. Cui, L., Yue, L., Wen, D., Qin, L.: K-connected cores computation in large dual networks. Data Sci. Eng. **3**(4), 293–306 (2018)
5. Ester, M., Kriegel, H., Sander, J., Xu, X.: A density-based algorithm for discovering clusters in large spatial databases with noise. In: KDD, pp. 226–231 (1996)
6. He, K., Shi, P., Bindel, D., Hopcroft, J.E.: Krylov subspace approximation for local community detection in large networks. TKDD **13**(5), 52 (2019)
7. He, K., Sun, Y., Bindel, D., Hopcroft, J., Li, Y.: Detecting overlapping communities from local spectral subspaces. In: ICDM (2015)
8. Hollocou, A., Bonald, T., Lelarge, M.: Multiple local community detection. SIGMETRICS Perform. Eval. Rev. **45**(3), 76–83 (2017)
9. Kamuhanda, D., He, K.: A nonnegative matrix factorization approach for multiple local community detection. In: ASONAM, pp. 642–649 (2018)
10. Leskovec, J., Krevl, A.: SNAP datasets: stanford large network dataset collection, June 2014. http://snap.stanford.edu/data
11. Newman, M.E.: Modularity and community structure in networks. Proc. Nat. Acad. Sci. **103**(23), 8577–8582 (2006)
12. Ni, L., Luo, W., Zhu, W., Hua, B.: Local overlapping community detection. ACM Trans. Knowl. Discov. Data **14**(1) (2019)
13. Perozzi, B., Al-Rfou, R., Skiena, S.: DeepWalk: online learning of social representations. In: KDD, pp. 701–710 (2014)
14. Yang, J., Leskovec, J.: Defining and evaluating network communities based on ground-truth. Knowl. Inf. Syst. **42**(1), 181–213 (2013). https://doi.org/10.1007/s10115-013-0693-z
15. Ye, Q., Zhu, C., Li, G., Liu, Z., Wang, F.: Using node identifiers and community prior for graph-based classification. Data Sci. Eng. **3**(1), 68–83 (2018)
16. Yin, H., Benson, A.R., Leskovec, J., Gleich, D.F.: Local higher-order graph clustering. In: KDD, pp. 555–564 (2017)

Partition-Oriented Subgraph Matching on GPU

Jing Chen$^{(\boxtimes)}$, Yu Gu, Qiange Wang, Chuanwen Li, and Ge Yu

Northeastern University, Shenyang, China
chenjing@stumail.neu.edu.cn,
{guyu,lichuanwen,yuge}@mail.neu.edu.cn

Abstract. Subgraph isomorphismis a well known NP-hard problem that finds all the matched subgraphs of a query graph in a large data graph. The state-of-the-art GPU-based solution is the vertex-oriented joining strategy, which is proposed by GSI. It effectively solves the problem of parallel write conflicts by taking vertices as processing units. However, this strategy might result in load-imbalance and redundant memory transactions when dealing with dense query graph. In this paper, we design a new storage structure Level-CSR and a new partition-oriented joining strategy. To avoid the influence of vertices with large degrees, we divide the dense vertices in traditional CSR into several GPU-friendly tasks and store them in Level-CSR. Then, an efficient execution strategy is designed based on the partitioned tasks. The partition strategy can improve the load imbalance caused by the irregularity of real-world graphs, and further reduce the redundant global memory access caused by the redundant neighbor set accessing. Besides, to further improve the performance, we propose a well-directed filtering strategy by exploiting a property of real-world graphs. The experiments show that compared with the state-of-the-art GPU based solutions, our approach can effectively reduce the number of unrelated candidates, minimize memory transactions, and achieve load balance between processors.

1 Introduction

Graph analysis has been attracting increasing attention in both industry and research communities. As one of the most fundamental problems in graph analysis, subgraph matching has a wide range of application scenarios, e.g., biomedicine [3], social network [4,8] and knowledge graph [13]. Given a query graph Q and a large data graph G, subgraph matching is to extract all subgraph isomorphic embedding of Q in G. An example of subgraph matching is given in Fig. 1. Figure 1(a) shows a target graph G, Fig. 1(b) shows a query graph Q and Fig. 1(c) shows the matching of Q in G.

Subgraph isomorphism is a well-known NP-hard problem [5]. It has been studied on CPU for decades. Most CPU solutions are based on the backtracking tree search strategy [12] and adopt a heavy pruning techniques to reduce the search space [6,7]. However, the search space is still too large. Therefore, GPU

© Springer Nature Switzerland AG 2020
X. Wang et al. (Eds.): APWeb-WAIM 2020, LNCS 12317, pp. 53–68, 2020.
https://doi.org/10.1007/978-3-030-60259-8_5

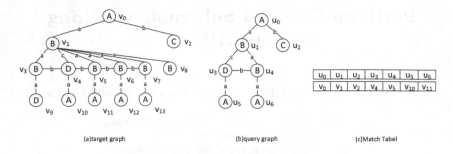

Fig. 1. An example of query and data graph.

acceleration becomes a promising technology to improve efficiency. Since parallel subgraph matching algorithms on GPU will generate intermediate results simultaneously, to avoid the parallel writing conflicts, GpSM [1] and GunrounkSM [9] adopt an edge-oriented [18] join strategy and employ a "2-step output scheme" [1]. In the edge-oriented strategy, each processor takes one edge as a processing unit. The candidate edges are joined through shared vertices. The algorithm performs the same join procedure twice, where the additional joining is to determine the writing address for each processor. Doubling the work makes the edge-oriented strategy inefficient. GSI [2] adopts a vertex-oriented joining strategy and uses a Prealloc-Combine approach to avoid writing conflicts when generating intermediate results in parallel. Different from the edge-oriented approach, the vertex-oriented strategy joins candidate vertices instead of edges through shared edges, and each processor takes one vertex as a processing unit. The vertex-oriented joining strategy avoids work duplication caused by the two-step method. A vertex is joined into intermediate results though multi-edges between itself and the "axis"[1] vertices in the existing result. However, each processor in the vertex-oriented approach has to access the full neighbors of axis vertices. While in the real-world graphs [19], the size of vertices' neighbor sets sharply varies. This strategy might incurs load imbalance and redundant neighbor access.

In this paper, we propose an efficient GPU subgraph isomorphism algorithm based on the partition-oriented joining strategy. Different from the vertex-oriented approach, our approach doesn't take vertices as the minimal processing unit. By carefully partitioning the graph data, we divide all vertices and their neighbors into small fine-grained task partitions and store them in a CSR-based structure for efficient parallel neighbor set accessing. Through the efficient CSR-based index structure, our approach can achieve natural load balance between processors. The redundant global memory access can also be reduced.

Another essential way to improve efficiency and scalability is filtering. We observe that the real-world graph usually follows the power-law distribution. In the subgraph isomorphism problem, that means 1) most edges are connected with a few vertices, and 2) a few vertices might cause most of the invalid intermediate results. Based on these observations, we design a new filtering strategy

---

[1] The vertices that have edges connected with the joined vertex.

Table 1. Notations

Notations	Descriptions
φ	Subgraph isomorphism
g, G and Q	Graph, target graph and guery graph
$Deg(u)$, $C(u)$ and $adj(u)$	Degree, candidate set and neighbors of u
$L_v(u)$, $L(u, u')$	Lable of u and (u, u')
$D(u)$	The joining order of query vertices
M_i	Intermediate results from the ith iteration
$S(u)$, $S(v)$	Encoding of vertex u and v
$V(Q)$	The collection of vertices on the query graph
$P(Q)$	The vertices in $V(Q)$ that have been joined

by considering the different impact of vertices. For vertices with small degrees, lightweight filtering is performed. While for "heavy" vertices, heavy filtering will be carried out by traversing their neighbors. By distinguishing the different types of vertices, we can achieve a better filtering effect with less overhead.

Our contributions are summarized as follows:

- We propose an efficient filtering strategy with only small overhead by exploring the power-law property of real-world graph.
- We propose an efficient partitioned graph data structure Level-CSR, through which we can access the neighbors of vertices in a more efficient and load balanced manner.
- We propose a partition-oriented joining strategy which can reduce both load imbalance and redundant memory access.
- We conduct extensive experimental evaluation on the real data sets, and the result demonstrates that our partition-oriented joining strategy can achieve up to 1.82X speed up over the vertex-oriented strategy and 179X speedup over the edge-oriented joining strategy. And compared with the vertex-orient strategy, our approach can reduce up to 70% memory transactions.

The rest of the paper is organized as follows. Section 2 gives a formal definition of subgraph isomorphism and describes the GPU background. Section 3 provides an overview of the whole process. Section 4 introduces a 2-step filtering strategy. Level-CSR structure and partition-oriented joining strategy are introduced in Sect. 5. Section 6 shows the experimental results. Section 7 concludes the paper.

2   Preliminaries

2.1   Problem Definition

In this paper, we focus on the most general case, where vertices and edges all have labels. We use $g = (V, E, L_v, L)$ to denote the graph, where V is a set of vertices,

E is a set of edges, L_v is a function that associates a vertex u with a label $L_v(u)$, and L is a function that associates a vertex pair (u, u') with a label $L(u, u')$. In the following, we give a formal definition of subgraph iosmorphism and related preliminaries. The frequently used notations are summarized in Table 1.

Definition 1 (Subgraph Isomorphism). Given graphs $Q=(V, E, L_v, L)$ and $G = (V', E', L'_v, L')$, the subgraph isomorphism from Q to G is an injective function $\varphi{:}V \to V'$ that satisfies:
$(1)\forall u \in V, L_v(u) = L'_v(\varphi(u)); (2)\forall(u, u') \in E, (\varphi(u), \varphi(u')) \in E', L(\varphi(u), \varphi(u')) = L'((u, u'))$.

Definition 2 (Subgraph Matching). Given a data graph G and a query graph Q, a subgraph matching finds all subgraphs in G that are isomorphic to Q.

2.2   Related Work

Subgraph Matching on CPU. The research on subgraph matching attracts lasing attention and Ullman algorithm [10] was first proposed to solve this problem. The proposed backtracking method laid the foundation for the subsequent research. VF2 [12] and QuickSI [17] proposed that joining vertices by specific order rather than random selection is an effective way to improve the performance. To reduce cartesian product costs, TurboISO [16] and BoostIso [7] proposed combining similar vertices in query graphs and data graphs. CFL-match [6] proposed a core-forest-leaf based joining method. In CFL-match, the vertices in the query graph are classified into three types: core, forest, and leaf. And the joining order is determined by the types. In recent years, the MapReduce framework has also been introduced to acclearting Subgraph matching [15].

Subgraph Matching on GPU. GpSM [1] and GunrounkSM [9] abandoned the backtracking framework and adopted a breadth-first strategy. The joining order is determined by generating a spanning tree. To write in parallel, both of them choose the "2-step" scheme. For the edge-labeled graph, GSI [2] proposed a new storage structure PCSR, which stores edges separately according to the label. To avoid performing a same join twice as in edge-oriented methods, GSI adopts the pre-allocation strategy to improve performance. There are also parallel subgraph matching algorithms executing based on reducing candidates [14] on GPU. While, in this paper we only focus on the joining based method.

3   Overview

The framework of our algorithm is given in Fig. 2, which consists of three phases: filtering, sorting and joining. In the filtering phase, a set of candidate vertices in data graph G are collected for each query vertex u as $C(u)$. Then, the query vertices' joining order $D(u)$ is determined. And in the joining phase query vertex u joins $C(u)$ by the order determined in the previous phase.

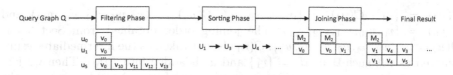

Fig. 2. Framework of algorithm.

3.1 Filtering Phase

Due to the inherent properties of GPU and subgraph isomorphism, a lightweight filtering is prefered. However, the capacity of *global memory* is limited. Besides, we notice that real-world graph data often follow the power-law distribution. It means that the large-degree vertices should be specifically considered. Based on the observation, we design a 2-stage filtering strategy. The details are introduced in Sect. 4.

3.2 Sorting Phase

It has been shown that the matching order of query vertices is a very important factor in reducing the intermediate results. We adopt the methods in CFL-match [6] and GSI as our basis to determine the addition order of query vertices. The sorting runs as follows: we first decompose the query vertices according to the *core-multi-forest* strategy, and then generate two vertex subsets *core* and *forest*. We then iteratively map vertices one by one from query graph to data graph. We first pick the *core* vertex, followed by joining the *forest* layer by layer, until the query graph is finished. In each layer, the joining order is determined by the score of the vertices. The score is determined by $score = \frac{C(u)}{Deg(u)}$ [2]. When u has been determined, the "axis" vertex is determined by the frequency of the edge. The detail process is shown in Fig. 3.

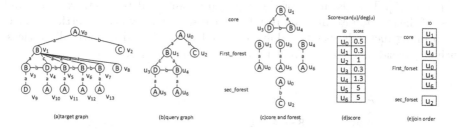

Fig. 3. The process of getting joining order.

3.3 Joining Phase

When the candidate set $C(u)$ of all query vertices are collected and the joining order is obtained, we start the joining phase. Consider the example in Sect. 1. We have $C(u_0) = \{v_0\}$, $C(u_1) = \{v_1\}$, $C(u_2) = \{v_2\}$,

$C(u_3) = \{v_4\}$, $C(u_4) = \{v_3, v_5, v_6, v_7\}$, $C(u_5) = \{v_0, v_{10}, v_{11}, v_{12}, v_{13}\}$ and $C(u_6) = \{v_0, v_{10}, v_{11}, v_{12}, v_{13}\}$. The joining order obtained from Sect. 3.3 is $D(u) = \{u_1, u_3, u_4, u_0, u_5, u_6, u_2\}$. $C(u_1)$ is first taken as the intermediate result, denoted as M_0 such that $M_0 = \{v_1\}$ and u_1 is added into $P(Q)$. Then we join u_3, since u_3 has only one candidate vertex v_4, and $L(v_1, v_4) = L(u_1, u_3) = c$, the intermediate result of the second iteration M_1 is $\{v_1, v_4\}$, and $P(Q)$ is updated to $\{u_1, u_3\}$. In the third iteration, there are two edges connected between $P(Q)$ and u_4, i.e., $L(u_1, u_4) = a$, $L(u_3, u_4) = b$. Therefore the process can be divided into two stages. In the first stage, $C(u_4)$ are joined to the intermediate result through $L(u_1, u_4)$. Then in the second step, $L(u_3, u_4)$ is used to filter out invalid temporary results. Such that only when vertices with both $L(v_1, v) = a$ and $L(v_3, v) = b$ satisfied can produce valid intermediate results Then we continue to iterate until $P(Q) = V(Q)$. The details of the 2-stage joining method are discussed in Sect. 5.

4   Power-Law Distribution Based Flitering Strategy

In the subgraph matching problem, filtering invalid intermediate results is an essential way to improve computing efficiency and reduce space consumption. Since the subgraph matching can produce a large amount of intermediate results and require considerable resources. The CPU-based solutions usually adopt heavyweight filtering methods to reduce the cost from invalid intermediate results. A heavyweight filtering strategy is usually not suitable for GPU architecture since it will incur instruction divergence and random global memory access. However, lightweight filtering methods might result in a large amount of candidates and produce more invalid intermediate results in the joining phase, which limit the processing scale of GPU. Therefore, a more powerful filtering strategy is desired when it comes to large real-world graphs.

We observe that most real-world graphs have the power-law distribution property [19]. That is, most of the edges are connected to a few vertices, and most of the invalid intermediate results are caused by a few heavy vertices. Existing pruning methods usually adopt a unified method to deal with all vertices, without considering the different impacts caused by different vertices.

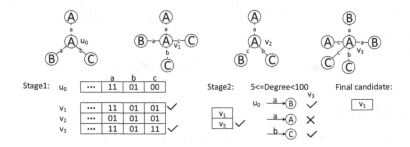

Fig. 4. Filtering phase.

Therefore, in this paper we design and implement a 2-stage filtering strategy for different data vertices. In the lightweight filtering stage, we use the method as proposed in GSI to encode the neighbor information of each vertex as a length-N bit vector signature $S(v)$ for both the data graph and query graph [2]. Then we can obtain the initial candidate set by conducting intersection on the signature between the query graph and data graph. In the second filtering stage, we perform further filtering on vertices whose degrees are between 32 and 512 from candidate sets, by checking whether the first-order neighbors of these vertices can match that of the vertex u in the query graph. The reason for setting the upper bound of vertex degree is that when one's degree is too large, a vertex is much likely to match all the query vertices, so filtering these vertices might consume more resources but with fewer improvements.

An example is illustrated in Fig. 4. The query vertex u_0 has two edges, one with label a and the other with label b. According to the number of different labels of edges, the first stage of filtering is performed. We can see that $S(v_2)$ & $S(u_0) \neq S(u_0)$, then $\{v_1, v_3\}$ is obtained as the initial $C(u_0)$. In the second stage, further filtering is performed. We assume that vertices with the degree $Deg(v) > 5$ are the heavy vertices. Then v_3 will be further pruned, and $C(u_0)$ is updated to $\{v_1\}$.

5   A Partition-Oriented JOIN Execution Strategy

In the subgraph matching problem, the joining process is to add new query vertices into $P(Q)$ and update the intermediate result until $P(Q)$ expands to $V(Q)$. The key to improving performance is to improve the efficiency of the joining process. Extensive researches focus on improving the efficiency of graph-based algorithms on GPU [1,2,9]. However, performing parallel subgraph isomorphic queries efficiently still remains challenging.

5.1   Existing Problems

The vertex-oriented strategy is the state-of-art subgraph matching strategy. This strategy is well designed to increase efficiency and reduce joining overhead. So we use this strategy as our baseline. First of all, we use an simple example to illustrate the joining process. Assume the joining vertex u has 2 edges (u, u_0), (u, u_1) connected with $P(Q)$, and $\sigma_{u_0,u_1}(M)$ is denoted as the result table of u_0 and u_1 in M. For each record (v_i, v_j) in $\sigma_{u_0,u_1}(M)$, we read $adj(v_i)$ and $adj(v_j)$. Then the final result can be expressed as $adj(v_i) \cap adj(v_j) \cap C(u)$. In the first stage, we pre-allocate memory for u through edge (u, u_0) and conduct $adj(v_i) \cap C(u)$. In the second stage, we validate the result generated in the first stage by checking whether $adj(v_i) \cap C(u)$ belongs to $adj(v_j)$. Since different processors have to access different neighbor sets, this strategy might incur the following two problems.

Load Imbalance Between Warps. To coalesce the accessed global memory, the vertex-oriented method assigns one warp to deal with a task. A task is one vertex from intermediate result table M and its neighbor lists. However, the sizes of neighbor lists of real-world graphs vary sharply. Severe load imbalance might occur between warps. In this case, GPU will spend much time on vertices with a large degree. However, for vertices with a small degree, the size of their neighbors is even smaller than the warp size. And hence most threads in this warps are idle. It will result in unnecessary consumption of computing resources.

Redundant Global Memory Access. In the validation stage, to validate the vertex set $adj(v_i) \cap C(u)$ generated in the first stage, the vertex-oriented approach has to access the full neighbors lists of v_j to check whether $adj(v_i) \cap C(u)$ exists. This process in vertex-oriented approach requires a cartesian product and will result in a large amount of memory access. The neighbors set has to be accessed repeatedly. However, only part of the neighbors are required. This stage is time consuming especially when $|adj(v_i) \cap C(u)|$ and $|adj(v_j)|$ are both large. Therefore, reducing redundant memory access in this stage will largely improve the efficiency of the algorithm.

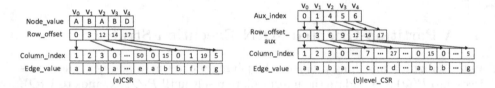

Fig. 5. CSR and Level-CSR.

In order to solve these two problems, we propose 1) a partition-based graph representation named Level-CSR structure, and 2) a partition-based joining strategy, which can reduce both load imbalance and redundant global memory access.

5.2 Level-CSR

The key idea of the load-balancing and memory-efficient joining strategy is to partition the tasks. We first review the traditional storage structure Compressed Sparse Row structure (CSR) as shown in Fig. 5(a). `row_offset` array stores the address of each vertex's neighbors, `column_index` array stores all the neighbors linearly, and `edge_value` stores the corresponding labels. The advantage of traditional CSR is that it allows a vertex to locate its first neighbor in $O(1)$ time, and all neighbors are stored continuously. Therefore the locality can be guaranteed. However, this design has an obvious deficiency. When it requires to visit one of the neighbors of v, the whole $adj(v)$ has to be accessed.

Different from CSR, Level-CSR splits up vertices' neighbors. The `row_offset` array doesn't point to their neighbors in `column_index`. We divide the each

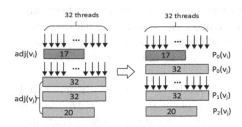 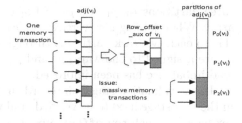

Fig. 6. Reorganize the workload to achieve load balance

Fig. 7. Reducing memory transaction by avoiding invalid data access

neighbor set in `column_index` into multi-partitions with a given partition size N. The sizes of all partitions except the last one are all N. Then we create a secondary index `row_offset_aux` between each vertex and their neighbors, and associate `row_offset` with `column_index`. The `row_offset_aux` array stores the start address of each partition in `column_index`. The `row_offset` array stores the first partition index in the `row_offset_aux` array. Here we give an example in Fig. 5 (b). The `edge_value` array and `node_value` array are the same as those in CSR. As we can see, vertices with degrees less than N are not split, while vertices with degree larger than N are split into several groups. Such that, in the first join stage, the neighbor set of vertices with a large degree can be accessed in parallel. This can reduce the burden of any single processor. In the second stage, this algorithm can quickly determine the neighbor with `row_offset_aux` with fewer memory transactions than accessing all its neighbors.

5.3   Partition-Oriented Joining Strategy

Based on the partitioned graph representation Level-CSR, our partition-oriented joining strategy inherits the same two-stage approach from the vertex-oriented joining. In the first stage, we generate a prefix-sum for each partition instead of each vertex from intermediate results. Then the memory for candidate vertices is pre-allocated based on the prefix-sum. Each partition records its own writing address. When generating intermediate results, we assign a unique warp to deal with one partition. Then the results could be written back in parallel. As in the vertex-oriented strategy, our approach can naturally guarantee inner-warp load balance and memory coalesced accesses. Moreover, our partition-oriented joining strategy can achieve further load balance between warps, which increases the hardware resource utilization.

We give an example in Fig. 6. The vertex-oriented approach assigns one warp to each vertex. Each warp accesses the neighbor set batch by batch in a size of 32. Since the size of $adj(v_i)$ is small, the workload of v_i is light, and some threads are even idle. The size of $adj(v_j)$ is large, so it requires multiple batch operation to complete the whole task. This will result in the load imbalance between warps. In our partition-oriented approach, assume N is set with 32, $adj(v_i)$ will be set as one partition since its size is smaller than N, and $adj(v_j)$ will be divided into three partitions p_0, p_1 and p_2. All of them will be indexed by `row_offset_aux` array. When joining new vertices, we can rearrange the workload with one warp [11] to each two task partitions through `row_offset_aux`, such that $adj(v_i)$ and p_0 are assigned to one warp. p_1 and p_2 are assigned to another warp. Then the load imbalance has been improved.

In the validation stage, all records in (v_i, v_j)'s intermediate results generated in the first stage need to be verified, and we assign one warp to deal with one vertex pair. Through `row_offset_aux`, we can efficiently locate the subset that may contain the vertex v_j to be verified in $adj(v_i)$. As shown in Fig. 7, when testing with traditional CSR structure, the whole neighbor set $adj(v_i)$ has to be accessed, which result in redundant memory transactions. In our partition-oriented strategy, the possible partition can be quickly located through the `row_offset_aux` array. Therefore, the validation of each vertex pair can be finished with fewer memory transactions. The overall joining phase is summarized in Algorithm 1.

Algorithm 1. Joining a new vertex

Input: query graph Q,partial result table M_i corresponding to the query vertices set $P(Q)$, the vertex to be joined and its candidate set $C(u)$,and linking edges E between $P(Q)$ and u.

Output: update intermediate table M_{i+1}

1: select the first edge (u'_0, u), allocate space for write buffer B, offset array $addr$, tasks id T and partition index P.

2: launch a GPU kernel function to generate task for the new vertex;

3: **for** each row m_i (a partial match) in M **do**

4:     Write the match of u'_0 in m_i to T and generate partition index P.

5: **end for**

6: **for** linking edge (u'_i, u) in E **do**

7:     launch a GPU kernel function to join M_i with $C(u)$:

8:     **for** each row task t_i in T **do**

9:         let buf_i be the segment $addr_i$ $addr_{i+1}$ in B

10:        assume that v'_i match u' in t_i

11:        let $N_{p_i}(v'_i, l)$ be the neighbor set partition of v'_i.

12:        **if** (u'_i, u) is the first edge (u'_0, u) **then**

13:            $buf_i = adj_{p_i}(v'_i, l) \setminus m_i \cap C(u)$

14:        **else**

15:            **for** each newly generated result r_j in buf_i **do**

16:                $r_j = r_j \cap adj_{p_j}(v'_i, l)$

17:            **end for**

18:        **end if**

19:     **end for**

20: **end for**

21: allocate memory for intermediate table M'

22: launch a GPU kernel function to link M_i and$B$ to generate M_{i+1}

The core difference between our approach and GSI is the different joining strategies when dealing with vertices that have multiple edges connected to the

Table 2. Dataset description

Dataset[a]	Vertices	Links	$|L_E|$	$|L_V|$	PL-exponent
gowalla	196,591	950,327	10	1	2.65
citeseer	384,413	1,751,463	10	1	2.73
Google	875,713	5,105,039	10	2	2.73
LiveJournal	4,847,571	68,993,773	10	2	2.65
wikipedia-en	4,206,784	101,500,998	10	2	2.21

[a]These datasets are all download from [21]

existing results. When verifying the candidate result through the second and later edges, GSI has to perform a full scan on one's all neighbors to verify whether an edge exists. While in our approach, benefiting from the partition-based level-CSR structure, our strategy only needs to access the necessary neighbors. And the redundant global memory access can be avoided.

5.4   GPU Implementation and Optimizations

Parameter Setting. The setting of parameter N has an important impact on the performance of partition-oriented joining. If N is set to a large value, the system has to access more neighbor subsets in the validation stage. While if N is set to a small value, the storage maintenance cost will increase. On the other hand, each 32 threads are organized and scheduled as a warp. If the partition size is even smaller than the warp size, some threads in a warp may become idle. Therefore, the number of task N assigned to each warp should be divisible by the warp size (32). Since a memory transaction is 128B and each vertex id is stored with 4 Bytes. We set our partition size N to 32, such that each warp can read and process a partition with only one memory transaction.

Shared Memory Optimization. In partition-oriented joining strategy, there are two types of global memory access schemes: 1) reading the neighbor lists from global memory, and 2) writing newly generated results to global memory in the first stage. To further improve the performance, we use shared memory to reduce global memory transactions. Since each warp has M partitions and generates at most $M \times 32$ new results, to reduce the global memory access, we cache all neighbor partitions on shared memory to reduce global memory reading. Then, to avoid global memory writing, we adopt a similar write caching strategy as proposed in GSI. The newly generated intermediate results are cached on shared memory and written back to global memory after all tasks finished. Since each warp handles a limited number of partitions, the system doesn't need to frequently check whether the cache is full and only write back after all partitions are completed.

6   Evaluation

We evaluate our method against the representative edge-oriented method Gunrock [9] and vertex-oriented[2] method GSI [2] separately. All experiments are conducted on a server with ubuntu 16.04. The server is equipped with Intel Silver 4210 2.20GHz CPU, 64G host memory, and a NVIDIA RTX 2080Ti with 34 SMs and 11GB global memory.

Datasets. The experiments are conducted on five real-world datasets, as shown in Table 2. Since the filtering strategy as proposed in this paper targets for power-law distribution. In this paper we choose five datasets that follows the power-law distribution. The power-law exponent metric is also listed in Table 2, which indicates the power-law distribution degree. We randomly assign vertex and edge labels following the power-low distribution. For the query graph, we perform randomly selected data graph until 8 vertices are visited [20]. And then we randomly select two of them and connect them with a randomly chosen edge label, until the average degree reaches 2. For each benchmark, we generate 50 query graphs and report the average query running time.

6.1   Evaluation of Filtering Strategy

To verify the effectiveness of our 2-step filtering strategy, we compare it with the pruning techniques used in GSI that is based on the vertex label and edge label. The metric is the size of the most significant intermediate result, which are the critical bottleneck that limits the scalability of GPU-based subgraph matching. The experiment shows that our 2-step strategy can reduce the intermediate size from 10.1% to 31.6%, as shown in Table 3.

6.2   Comparison with the State-of-the-Art GPU Algorithms and the Evaluation of Scalability

The second set of experiments are to evaluate the performance of our approach to other stare-of-the-art GPU algorithms, the edge-oriented approach in Gunrock and the vertex-oriented approach in GSI [2][3]. As reported in Fig. 8, Our partition-oriented method can achieve up to 179.59X speedup over the edge-oriented method, and 1.06X-1.82X(on average 1.67X) speedup over the vertex-oriented method. In addition, to evaluate the scalability, we generate a series of synthetic graphs datasets using the RMAT[4] graph generator. These graphs are under power-law distribution. Each dataset has n vertices with 3 uniformly assigned vertex labels and $8n$ directed edges with 10 uniformly assigned edge labels. Since the edge-oriented approach runs extremely slow on

---

[2] We use a self-implemented vertex-oriented version since the source code of GSI is not publicly available.

[3] Since our approach only concentrates on the join execution strategy, we don't implement the PCSR structure which is orthogonal to our method for a fair comparison.

[4] https://github.com/farkhor/PaRMAT.

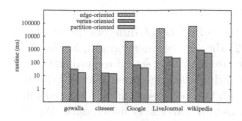
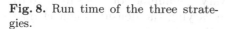

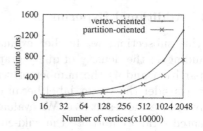

Fig. 8. Run time of the three strategies.

Fig. 9. Scalability test on RMAT benchmark

the largest dataset, we only compare the vertex-oriented and partition-oriented solutions and the results are displayed in Fig. 9. The experiment shows that the partition-oriented approach shows consistently better performance than the vertex-oriented approach, and also shows good scalability.

6.3 The Efficiency of Partition-Oriented Approach

In this subsection, we evaluate the efficiency of our partition-oriented approach. As discussed in Sect. 5, our approach can achieve natural balance since our approach reorganizes the task in a more fine-grained way. Then to verify the effectiveness of our strategy in reducing memory transactions, we calculate the total amount of memory transactions in the verification stage of the algorithm. Table 3 reports the memory transaction amount of vertex-oriented method and partition-oriented method on all five datasets. Our partition-oriented approach can primarily reduce the memory transaction amount from 28% to 70%. In addition, we calculate the additional storage cost caused by the level-CSR structure. As reported in Table 3, the level-CSR structure can bring considerable improvement with little storage overhead. The experiment shows that our approach could effectively improve the performances.

Table 3. Performance of filtering, memory transactions, and storage overhead

Dataset	2-step reduces the candidate set			Global memory transactions			Level-CSR storage overhead		
	1-step	2-step	drop	vertex-oriented	partition-oriented	drop	CSR	level-CSR	overhead
gowalla	577K	465K	19%	991K	316K	68%	15.99M	16.87M	1.05
citeseer	193K	133K	32%	191K	138K	28%	29.56M	31.20M	1.06
Google	1.6M	1.1M	31%	4.9M	1.5M	70%	85.18M	89.07M	1.05
LiveJournal	87.1M	80.1M	8%	83M	38.7M	47%	1427M	1462M	1.02
wikipedia-en	44.4M	37.8M	15%	107M	62.3M	58%	1641M	1676M	1.02

6.4　Additional Experiment

In this subsection, we further evaluate the influence of different parameters including 1) the density of query graph, 2) the size of query graph, 3) the size of partition and 4) the number of vertex label. In this set of experiments, we only consider the vertex label because enlarging the edge label size will drastically reduce the result size. We evaluate both the vertex-oriented and partition-oriented strategy and use the wiki-en dataset in Table 2 as benchmark. We fix the size of query graph with 8 vertices and vary the number of edges from 16 to 32. The result is shown in Fig. 10 (a). Since varying the density might change the joining order and the result size, the runtime doesn't regularly decrease as the number of edges increases. Our partition-oriented strategy shows better performance than vertex-oriented strategy on the dense graph. It is because our partition-oriented strategy performs much better on the validation strategy. To evaluate the influence of the size of query graph. We fix the density of the graph with 3 and vary the number of vertices from 6 to 12. As shown in Fig. 10 (b), although the runtime does not monotically changing because of the randomness of query, our partition-oriented strategy show consistently better performance than the vertex-oriented strategy. An essential parameter in our approach is the partition size N. We evaluate the influence of parameter N by configuring different Ns on two benchmarks, google and wiki-English. We use the same setting with the first experiment, and the graph average degree is 2. As reported in Fig. 10 (c), the algorithm will reach the best performance when N is 32. When N is configured with a small number, some of the threads in each warp will be idle. When set with a large number, the cost of the validation stage will increase,

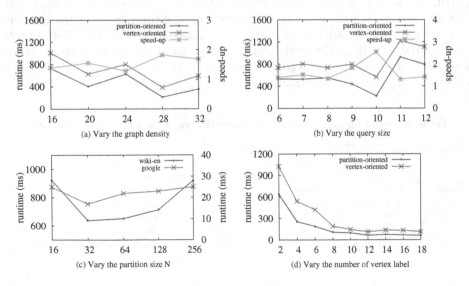

Fig. 10. Experiment of query graph's density, size, partition size and label num of vertices.

since it has to access more invalid neighbor set. The last experiment is to evaluate the influence of vertex labels in the data graph. We use both vertex-oriented and partition-oriented approach. All query graphs have 8 vertices with the average degree 3. We vary the number of vertex labels from 2 to 18. As the number of labels increases, runtime decreases. Both of the two methods demonstrate sharp dropping in runtime because we use dense query graph, and the size of final results drastically decrease. When $|L_v| > 10$, the runtime quickly slows down to zero as candidate sets are already minimal.

7 Conclusion

In this paper, we propose a partition-oriented joining strategy which takes advantage of GPU parallelism to deal with subgraph matching problem. Through carefully partitioning the graph and designing GPU-friendly execution strategy, our approach can reduce both load imbalance and memory transactions in the joining stage. Based on the power-law property of the real-world graph, a well-directed filtering strategy is designed to pruning irrelevant candidate vertices. Experiment results show that our method is efficient and effective.

Acknowledgement. This work is supported by the National Key R&D Program of China (2018YFB10-03400), the National Natural Science Foundation of China (U1811261, 61872070), the Fundamental Research Funds for the Central Universities (N180716010) and Liao Ning Revitalization Talents Program (XLYC1807158).

References

1. Tran, H.-N., Kim, J., He, B.: Fast subgraph matching on large graphs using graphics processors. In: Renz, M., Shahabi, C., Zhou, X., Cheema, M.A. (eds.) DASFAA 2015. LNCS, vol. 9049, pp. 299–315. Springer, Cham (2015). https://doi.org/10.1007/978-3-319-18120-2_18
2. Zeng, L., Zou, L., Özsu, M.T., Hu, L., Zhang, F.: GSI: GPU-friendly subgraph isomorphism. CoRR. abs/1906.03420 (2019)
3. Liu, H., Keselj, V., Blouin, C.: Biological event extraction using subgraph matching. In: ISSMB, pp. 110–115 (2010)
4. Ma, T., Yu, S., Cao, J., Tian, Y., Al-Dhelaan, A., Al-Rodhaan, M.: A comparative study of subgraph matching isomorphic methods in social networks. IEEE Access **6**, 66621–66631 (2018)
5. Garey, M.R., Johnson, D.S.: Computers and Intractability: A Guide to the Theory of NP-Completeness. W. H. Freeman (1979). ISBN 0-7167-1044-7
6. Bi, F., Chang, L., Lin, X., Qin, L., Zhang, W.: Efficient subgraph matching by postponing cartesian products. In: SIGMOD Conference, pp. 1199–1214 (2016)
7. Ren, X., Wang, J.: Exploiting vertex relationships in speeding up subgraph isomorphism over large graphs. PVLDB **8**(5), 617–628 (2015)
8. Liu, G., et al.: Multi-constrained graph pattern matching in large-scale contextual social graphs. In: ICDE, pp. 351–362 (2015)
9. Wang, Y., Davidson, A.A., Pan, Y., Wu, Y., Riffel, A., Owens, J.D.: Gunrock: a high-performance graph processing library on the GPU. In: PPoPP, 11:1–11:12 (2016)

10. Ullmann, J.R.: An algorithm for subgraph isomorphism. J. ACM **23**(1), 31–42 (1976)
11. Hong, S., Kim, S.K., Oguntebi, T., Olukotun, K.: Accelerating CUDA graph algorithms at maximum warp. In: PPOPP, pp. 267–276 (2011)
12. Conte, D., Foggia, P., Sansone, C., Vento, M.: Thirty years of graph matching in pattern recognition. IJPRAI **18**(3), 265–298 (2004)
13. Zou, L., Mo, J., Chen, L., Özsu, M.T., Zhao, D.: gStore: answering SPARQL queries via subgraph matching. PVLDB **4**(8), 482–493 (2011)
14. Son, M.-Y., Kim, Y.-H., Byoung-Woo, O.: An efficient parallel algorithm for graph isomorphism on GPU using CUDA. IJET **7**(5), 1840–1848 (2015)
15. Wang, X., et al.: Efficient subgraph matching on large RDF graphs using MapReduce. Data Sci. Eng. **4**(1), 24–43 (2019)
16. Han, W.-S., Lee, J., Lee, J.-H.: Turbo$_{iso}$: towards ultrafast and robust subgraph isomorphism search in large graph databases. In: SIGMOD, pp. 337–348 (2013)
17. Shang, H., Zhang, Y., Lin, X., Yu, J.X.: Taming verification hardness: an efficient algorithm for testing subgraph isomorphism. PVLDB **1**(1), 364–375 (2008)
18. Kim, S., Song, I., Lee, Y.J.: An edge-based framework for fast subgraph matching in a large graph. In: Yu, J.X., Kim, M.H., Unland, R. (eds.) DASFAA 2011. LNCS, vol. 6587, pp. 404–417. Springer, Heidelberg (2011). https://doi.org/10.1007/978-3-642-20149-3_30
19. Gonzalez, J.E., Low, Y., Gu, H., Bickson, D., Guestrin, C.: PowerGraph: distributed graph-parallel computation on natural graphs. In: OSDI, pp. 17–30 (2012)
20. Yan, X., Yu, P.S., Han, J.: Graph indexing: a frequent structure-based approach. In: SIGMOD, pp. 335–346 (2004)
21. KONECT network dataset - KONECT, April 2017. http://konect.uni-koblenz.de/

An Index Method for the Shortest Path Query on Vertex Subset for the Large Graphs

Zian Pan, Yajun Yang$^{(\boxtimes)}$, and Qinghua Hu

College of Intelligence and Computing, Tianjin University, Tianjin, China
{panzian,yjyang,huqinghua}@tju.edu.cn

Abstract. Shortest path query is an important problem in graphs and has been well-studied. In this paper, we study a special kind of shortest path query on a vertex subset. Most of the existing works propose various index techniques to facilitate shortest path query. However, these indexes are constructed for the entire graphs, and they cannot be used for the shortest path query on a vertex subset. In this paper, we propose a novel index named pb-tree to organize various vertex subsets in a binary tree shape such that the descendant nodes on the same level of pb-tree consist of a partition of their common ancestors. We further introduce how to calculate the shortest path by pb-tree. The experimental results on three real-life datasets validate the efficiency of our method.

Keywords: Shortest path · Vertex subset · Index

1 Introduction

Graph is an important data model to describe the relationships among various entities in the real world. The shortest path query is a fundamental problem on graphs and has been well studied in the past couple of decades. In this paper, we study a special case of the shortest path query problem. Consider the following applications in the real world. In social networks, some users need to investigate the shortest path inside a specified community for two individuals. For example, someone intends to know another by the peoples with the same hobby or occupation. In transportation networks, some vehicles are restricted to a designated area such that they need to know the shortest route inside such area. The query problem in the above applications can be modeled as the shortest path query on a given vertex set for graphs. Given a graph $G(V, E)$ and a vertex subset $V_s \in V$, it is to find the shortest path from the starting vertex v_s to the ending vertex v_e on the induced subgraph of G on V_s.

It is obvious that the shortest path on a vertex subset V_s can be searched by the existing shortest path algorithms, e.g. Dijkstra algorithm. However, these algorithms are not efficient for the shortest path query on the large graphs. Most existing works propose various index techniques to enhance the efficiency of the

© Springer Nature Switzerland AG 2020
X. Wang et al. (Eds.): APWeb-WAIM 2020, LNCS 12317, pp. 69–85, 2020.
https://doi.org/10.1007/978-3-030-60259-8_6

shortest path query on the large graphs. The main idea of these works is that: build an index to maintain the shortest paths for some pairs of vertices in a graph. Given a query, algorithms first retrieve the shortest path to be visited among the vertices in the index and then concatenate them by the shortest paths which are not in the index. Unfortunately, such index techniques cannot be used for the shortest path problem proposed in this paper. It is because the vertex subset V_s is "dynamic". Different users may concern about the shortest path on distinct vertex subset V_s. The indexes for the entire graph G may not be suitable for the induced graph G_s on some given vertex subset V_s. The shortest path searched using the indexes for entire graph G may contain some vertices that are not in V_s. Therefore, the important issue is to develop an index technique such that it can be utilized for answering the shortest path query on various vertex subsets.

In this paper, we propose a novel index, named pb-tree, to make the shortest path query on a vertex subset more efficient for the large graphs. The pb-tree T is a binary tree to organize various vertex subsets of V such that all the vertex subsets in the same level of T form a partition of V. The partition on the lower level is essentially a refinement of that on a higher level. By pb-tree, several vertex subsets with the highest level, which are included in V_s, can be retrieved to answer the shortest path query efficiently on V_s by concatenating the shortest paths maintained in these vertex subsets.

The main contributions of this paper are summarized below. First, we study the problem of the shortest path query on a given vertex subset and develop a novel index pb-tree to solve it. We introduce how to construct pb-tree efficiently. Second, we propose an efficient query algorithm based on pb-tree to answer such shortest path query. Third, we analyze the time and space complexity for pb-tree construction and query algorithm. Forth, we conduct extensive experiments on several real-life datasets to confirm the efficiency of our method.

The rest of this paper is organized as follows. Section 2 gives the problem definition. Section 3 describes what is pb-tree and how to construct it. We introduce how to answer the shortest path query on a vertex subset using pb-tree in Sect. 4 and conduct experiments using three real-life datasets in Sect. 5. Section 6 discusses the related works. Finally, we conclude this paper in Sect. 7.

2   Problem Statement

A weighted graph is a simple directed graph denoted as $G = (V, E, w)$, where V is the set of vertices and E is the set of edges in G, each edge $e \in E$ is represented by $e = (u, v)$, $u, v \in V$, e is called u's outgoing edge or v's incoming edge and v (or u) is called u (or v)'s outgoing(or incoming) neighbor. w is a function assigning a non-negative weight to every edge in G. For simplicity, we use $w(u, v)$ to denote the weight of the directed edge $(u, v) \in E$. A path p in G is a sequence of vertices $(v_1, v_2, \cdots, v_k)$, such that (v_i, v_{i+1}) is a directed edge in G for $1 \leq i \leq k-1$. The weight of path p, denoted as $w(p)$, is defined as the sum of the weight of every edge in p, i.e., $w(p) = \sum_{1 \leq i \leq k-1} w(v_i, v_{i+1})$. Our work can be easily extended to handle the undirected graphs, in which an undirected edge (u, v) is equivalent to two directed edges (u, v) and (v, u).

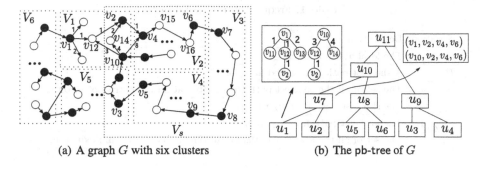

(a) A graph G with six clusters   (b) The pb-tree of G

Fig. 1. A graph G and the pb-tree of it (Color figure online)

In this paper, we study a special kind of shortest path query restricted to a vertex subset. Given a vertex subset $V_s \subseteq V$, an induced subgraph on V_s, denoted as $G_s(V_s, E_s)$, is a subgraph of G satisfying the two following conditions: (1) $E_s \subseteq E$; (2) for any two vertices $v_i, v_j \in V_s$, if $(v_i, v_j) \in E$, then $(v_i, v_j) \in E_s$. We say a path p is in G_s if all the vertices and edges that p passing through are in G_s. Next, we give the definition of the shortest path query on a given vertex subset V_s.

Definition 1 (The shortest path query on a vertex subset). *Given a graph* $G = (V, E, w)$, *a vertex subset* $V_s \in V$, *a source vertex* v_s *and a destination vertex* v_e, *where* $v_s, v_e \in V_s$ *and* G_s *is the induced graph on* V_s, *the short path query on* V_s *is to find a path* p^* *with the minimum weight* $w(p^*)$ *among all the paths in* G_s.

Figure 1(a) illustrates an example graph G and V_s is bounded in red dot line. The shortest path from v_{10} to v_2 on G and V_s are (v_{10}, v_{12}, v_2) and (v_{10}, v_{14}, v_2) respectively because v_{12} is not in V_s.

3   Partition-Based Tree for Shortest Path Query on a Vertex Subset

In this section, we propose a novel index, named **Partition-Based Tree** (or pb-tree for simplicity), to improve the efficiency of the shortest path query on a given vertex subset. A pb-tree, denoted as T, essentially is an index to organize several vertex subsets in a binary tree shape. Specifically, every leaf node in pb-tree T represents a vertex subset, and it can be regarded as a cluster of V. Thus the set of leaf nodes is a partition of V. Every non-leaf node is the super set of its two children. By pb-tree, the nodes in pb-tree which are included in a given V_s can be anchored rapidly and then they can be utilized to answer the shortest path query on V_s. In the following, we first introduce what is pb-tree and then discuss how to construct it. Finally, we explain how to partition a graph into several clusters.

Table 1. Frequently used notations

Notation	Description
$l(u_i)$	The level of the node $u_i \in T$
P_x	A shortest path tree rooted at v_x on G
S_i	The set of all the shortest path trees rooted at all the entries of u_i on G_i
$p^*_{x,y}$	The shortest path from v_x to v_y in G
$a_{x,y}$	The abstract path from v_x to v_y in G
A_i	The set of all the abstract paths for all the pairs of entry and exit in u_i

3.1 What Is Partition-Based Tree?

Definition 2 (Partition). *Given a graph $G(V, E)$, a **partition** $\mathcal{P}$ of G is a collection of k vertex subsets $\{V_1, \cdots, V_k\}$ of V, such that: (1) for $\forall V_i, V_j$ $(i \neq j)$, $V_i \cap V_j = \emptyset$; (2) $V = \bigcup_{1 \leq i \leq k} V_i$. Each $V_i \subseteq V$ is called a cluster in G. A vertex v_x is called an entry of cluster V_i under partition $\mathcal{P}$, if (1) $v_x \in V_i$; and (2) $\exists v_y$, $v_y \notin V_i \wedge v_y \in N^-(v_x)$. Similarly, A vertex v_x is called an exit of cluster V_i, if (1) $v_x \in V_i$; and (2) $\exists v_y$, $v_y \notin V_i \wedge v_y \in N^+(v_x)$. $N^-(v_x)$ and $N^+(v_x)$ are v_x's incoming and outgoing neighbor set, respectively. Entries and exits are also called the border vertices.*

We use $V.entry$ and $V.exit$ to denote the entry set and exit set of G respectively, and use $V_i.entry$ and $V_i.exit$ to denote the entry set and exit set of cluster V_i respectively. Obviously, $V.entry = \bigcup_{1 \leq i \leq k} V_i.entry$ and $V.exit = \bigcup_{1 \leq i \leq k} V_i.exit$.

The pb-tree T is essentially an index to organize various vertex subsets in a similar shape as a binary tree. Given a partition $\mathcal{P}$ of G, a pb-tree can be constructed. Specifically, every leaf node $u_i \in T$ corresponds to a cluster V_i under $\mathcal{P}$ and all leaf nodes consist of the partition $\mathcal{P}$. Every non-leaf node corresponds to the union of the vertex subsets represented by its two children, respectively. Each node in pb-tree has a level to indicate the location of it in the pb-tree. We use $l(u_i)$ to denote the level of the node $u_i \in T$. For every leaf node u_i in T, we set $l(u_i) = 1$. For the root node u_{root} of T, we set $l(u_{\text{root}}) = h$. Note that all the non-leaf nodes on the same level consist of a partition of G and each node can be regarded as a cluster under this partition. The partition comprised of the nodes on the low level is a refinement of the partition on the high level.

There are two kinds of information should be maintained with a pb-tree T. A **shortest path tree set** is maintained for every leaf node and an **abstract path set** is maintained for every non-leaf node. We first introduce the shortest path tree set below.

Given a connected graph $G(V, E)$ and a vertex $v_x \in V$, a shortest path tree rooted at v_x on G, denoted as P_x, is a tree such that the distance from v_x to any other vertex v_y in the tree is exactly the shortest distance from v_x to v_y in G. Every leaf node $u_i \in T$ is essentially a vertex subset of V. Let G_i denote the induced subgraph of G on u_i. The shortest path tree set S_i of u_i is the set of all the shortest path trees rooted at all the entries of u_i on G_i, i.e., $S_i = \{P_x | v_x \in u_i.entry, P_x \subseteq G_i\}$.

We next give the definition of the abstract path for every non-leaf node in pb-tree.

Definition 3 (Abstract Path). *Given a non-leaf node $u_i \in T$, v_x and v_y are the entry and exit of u_i respectively. An abstract path from v_x to v_y, denoted as $a_{x,y}$, is a vertex sub-sequence of the shortest path $p_{x,y}^*$ from v_x to v_y in G such that all the vertices in $a_{x,y}$ are the border vertices of u_i's children.*

Based on above definition, an abstract path $a_{x,y}$ can be considered as an "abstract" of the shortest path $p_{x,y}^*$ by consisting of the border vertices of u_i's children. For every non-leaf node $u_i \in T$, its abstract path set A_i is the set of all the abstract paths for all the pairs of entry and exit in u_i, i.e., $A_i = \{a_{x,y} | v_x \in u_i.entry, v_y \in u_i.exit\}$.

Figure 1(b) shows the pb-tree of graph G in Fig. 1(a). For a leaf node u_1, a shortest path tree set is maintained for it. For a non-leaf node u_7, an abstract path set is maintained for it. For the readers convenience, Table 1 lists some frequently used notations.

3.2 How to Construct Partition-Based Tree?

As shown in Algorithm 1, the pb-tree is constructed in a bottom-up manner. Given a partition $\mathcal{P}$ of G, Algorithm 1 first calls LEAF-NODE (V_i) to construct the leaf node u_i for every cluster $V_i \in \mathcal{P}$ (line 2–4). U is a temporary set to maintain all the nodes on the same level h. In each iteration, Algorithm 1 calls NON-LEAF-NODE (U) to construct the non-leaf nodes on the level $h + 1$ by merging the nodes on the level h (line 5–7). When U is empty, Algorithm 1 terminates and returns the pb-tree T. In the following, we introduce how to construct the leaf nodes and the non-leaf nodes by LEAF-NODE (V_i) and NON-LEAF-NODE (U) respectively.

Algorithm 1: PARTITION-BASED-TREE ($G, \mathcal{P}$)

Input: G, a partition $\mathcal{P}$ of G
Output: the pb-tree T based on $\mathcal{P}$.

1: $T \leftarrow \emptyset, U \leftarrow \emptyset, h \leftarrow 1$;
2: **for** each cluster $V_i \in \mathcal{P}$ **do**
3:     LEAF-NODE (V_i);
4:     $U \leftarrow U \cup \{u_i\}$;
5: **while** $U \neq \emptyset$ **do**
6:     NON-LEAF-NODE (U);
7:     $h \leftarrow h + 1, U \leftarrow U \cup T_h$;
8: **return** T

Algorithm 2: LEAF-NODE (V_i)

1: $u_i \leftarrow V_i$, $S_i \leftarrow \emptyset$;
2: **for** each $v_x \in V_i.entry$ **do**
3:    computes the shortest path tree P_x rooted at v_x on G_i;
4:    $S_i \leftarrow S_i \cup \{P_x\}$
5: interts u_i with S_i into T as a leaf node;

Leaf Node Construction: Given a partition $\mathcal{P}$ of G, all the clusters in $\mathcal{P}$ are the leaf nodes of T. The pseudo-code of LEAF-NODE is shown in Algorithm 2. For each cluster $V_i \in \mathcal{P}$, Algorithm 2 first sets V_i as a leaf node u_i and calculates the shortest path tree set S_i (line 1). There are several methods and we use Dijkstra algorithm to compute the shortest path tree P_x for each entry $v_x \in u_i.entry$ (line 3). Finally, Algorithm 2 inserts u_i with S_i and the crossing paths into pb-tree T as a leaf node (line 5).

Figure 2 depicts a cluster V_1 (Fig. 2(a)) and its shortest path trees rooted at two entries in V_1 (Fig. 2(b)). For example, the shortest path from v_1 to v_2 in G is exactly the simple path from v_1 to v_2 in the shortest path tree P_1.

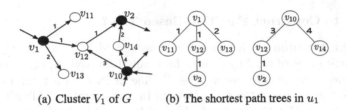

(a) Cluster V_1 of G (b) The shortest path trees in u_1

Fig. 2. Leaf node construction

Non-leaf Node Construction: The non-leaf nodes in pb-tree T are constructed level by level. A temporary set U is utilized to maintain all the nodes on the level h which have been constructed in T and then Algorithm 3 constructs all the non-leaf nodes on the level $h+1$ by merging two nodes with the maximum size of *crossing edge set* in U iteratively. A crossing edge set between node u_i and u_j on the same level of T, denoted as $C_{i,j}$, is the set of all the crossing edges between u_i and u_j, i.e., $C_{i,j} = \{(v_x, v_y) | v_x \in u_i \wedge v_y \in u_j \text{ or } v_x \in u_j \wedge v_y \in u_i\}$. It is worth noting that $C_{i,j} = C_{j,i}$. In each iteration, two nodes u_i and u_j with the maximum $|C_i, j|$ in U are merged into a new node u_k. Note that the $u_k.entry$ and $u_k.exit$ are the subset of $u_i.entry \cup u_j.entry$ and $u_i.exit \cup u_j.exit$ respectively. It is because some of the entries and exits of u_i (or u_j) become the internal vertices of u_k after merging u_i and u_j. Algorithm 3 computes the abstract path set A_k for u_k by Dijkstra algorithm. Finally, u_k is inserted into T with A_k as the parent of u_i and u_j. Note that there may be only one node u_i in U in the final iteration. In this case, u_i will be left in U and be used for constructing the level $h + 2$ of T with all the non-leaf nodes on the level $h + 1$.

Algorithm 3: NON-LEAF-NODE (U)

1: **while** $|U| > 1$ **do**
2:     selects u_i and u_j with the maximum $|C_{i,j}|$ from U;
3:     $u_k \leftarrow u_i \cup u_j$;
4:     computes the abstract path set A_k for u_k;
5:     inserts u_k with A_k into T as the parent node of u_i and u_j;
6:     $U \leftarrow U \setminus \{u_i, u_j\}$

Figure 3 shows the construction of the pb-tree. The leaf nodes are constructed in the same way as Fig. 2. U is $\{u_1, u_2, u_3, u_4, u_5, u_6\}$ in the begining. The algorithm first merges u_1 and u_2 into u_7, because $|C_{1,2}| = 3$ is maximum. The entries of u_7 is v_1 and v_{10}. The algorithm uses the Dijkstra algorithm to compute the shortest paths from v_1 and v_{10}. The shortest path from v_1 to v_6 on V_7 is $(v_1, v_{12}, v_2, v_4, v_{15}, v_{16}, v_6)$, and the abstract path $a_{1,6}$ is (v_1, v_2, v_4, v_6). In the same way, $a_{10,6}$ is maintained as (v_{10}, v_2, v_4, v_6). After that, u_8 is mergred by u_5 and u_6. u_9 is merged by u_3 and u_4. To construct the T_3, U is $\{u_7, u_8, u_9\}$. The algorithm merges u_7 and u_8 into u_{10}, cause $|C_{7,8}| = 2$ is larger than $|C_{8,9}|$ and $|C_{7,9}|$. After that, U is $\{u_9\}$, and u_9 is used to construct the higher level of T. Then U is $\{u_9, u_{10}\}$. u_{11} is constructed by merging u_9 and u_{10}. The abstract paths in those nodes are computed in the same way as computing the abstract paths in u_7.

3.3 How to Partition Graph to Several Clusters

There are several ways to partition a graph to several clusters. For different partitions, the number of entries and exits are different. In our problem, the fewer number of entries and exits makes the smaller size of pb-tree index. Intuitively, the fewer edges among different clusters result in the less number of entries and exits in graphs. Thus it is a problem to find an optimal partition such that the edges among different clusters are sparse and the edges in the same cluster are dense. This problem has been well studied, and there are many effective and efficient algorithms[1,4,17] to solve it. In this paper, We adopt the METIS algorithm[1], which is a classic graph partition algorithm.

3.4 Complexity Analysis

For graph G, let m be the number of edges, k be the number of clusters, α and β be the maximum number of vertices and edges inside the cluster and a be the maximum number of the borders in each cluster.

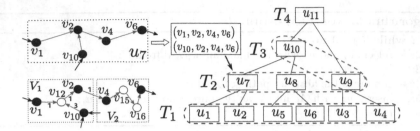

Fig. 3. pb-tree construction

Time Complexity: For each leaf node, the shortest path tree set can be built in $O(a(\alpha \log \alpha + \beta))$ time. All the leaf nodes can be constructed in $O(k\alpha^2 log\alpha + k\alpha\beta)$. As a binary tree, the maximum level of pb-tree is $logk + 1$ and the maximum number of the non-leaf nodes on level h is $\frac{k}{2^{h-1}}$. A non-leaf node on level h is constructed by merging two children. The entry and the exit sets of the two children can be merged in $O(1)$. The time complexity of searching all the neighbors of borders on level h is $O(m)$. The number of borders in a non-leaf node on level h is $O(2^{h-1}a)$, and the number of the vertices in it is $O(2^{h-1}a)$ because abstract paths are computed only by the borders of the children. The Dijkstra algorithm is utilized to compute the abstract paths from each entry. Computing all the abstract paths in a non-leaf node on level h is in $O(2^{h-1}a(2^{h-1}alog(2^{h-1}a) + 2^{2h-2}a^2)) = O(8^{h-1}a^3)$. The time complexity of constructing the non-leaf nodes on level h is $O(4^{h-1}ka^3 + m)$. Because there are $\log k + 1$ levels in pb-tree, then we have

$$\sum_{h=2}^{logk+1} (4^{h-1}ka^3 + m) = mlogk + \frac{4}{3}ka^3(4^{logk} - 1) = mlogk + \frac{4}{3}ka^3(k^2 - 1)$$

Thus the time complexity of constructing all the non-leaf nodes and pb-tree are $O(mlogk + k^3a^3)$ and $O(k\alpha\beta + mlogk + \alpha^3k^3)$ respectively.

Space Complexity: In the worst-case, each shortest path tree in a leaf node contains all the vertices and edges in that node. The number of the shortest path trees in a leaf node is $O(a)$; thus the number of vertices in each leaf node is $O(a\alpha) = O(\alpha^2)$ and the number of edges is $O(a\beta) = O(\alpha\beta)$. The space complexity of leaf nodes is $O(k\alpha^2 + k\alpha\beta)$. For a non-leaf node on level h, the number of the borders is $2^{h-1}a$, and the number of the abstract paths is $O(4^{h-1}a^2)$. In the worst-case, each abstract path contains all the vertices in the node. The space complexity of the non-leaf nodes on level h is $O(a^34^{h-1}k)$. Because there are $\log k + 1$ levels in pb-tree, then we have

$$\sum_{h=2}^{logk+1} (a^34^{h-1}k) = \frac{4}{3}ka^3(4^{logk} - 1) = \frac{4}{3}ka^3(k^2 - 1)$$

Algorithm 4: QUERY-PROCESSING $(q = (V_s, v_s, v_e))$

Input: V_s, v_s, v_e, pb-tree T, G
Output:$p_{s,e}^*$

1: $Q \leftarrow V_s, \tau_s \leftarrow 0$
2: **while** $v_e \in Q$ **do**
3:     gets v_x from Q with minimum τ_x
4:     **if** v_x is expanded by $a_{y,x}$ **then**
5:         PATH-RECOVER $(Q, a_{y,x})$
6:     **if** $v_x \in u_i.entry$ **then**
7:         **if** u_i is a complete node **then**
8:             NODE-IDENTIFY (Q, v_x, u_i)
9:         **else**
10:           PARTIAL-SEARCH (Q, v_x, u_i)
11:     **if** $v_x \notin u_i.entry \vee v_x \in u_i.exit$ **then**
12:        updates the τ of v_x's outgoing neighbors in Q;
13:     dequeues v_x from Q
14: **return** $p_{s,e}^*$

The space complexity of constructing all the non-leaf nodes is $O(k^3 a^3)$, and the space complexity of constructing the pb-tree is $O(k^3 \alpha^3 + k \alpha \beta)$.

4 Query Processing by pb-tree

4.1 Querying Algorithm

In this section, we introduce how to find the shortest path on a given vertex subset by pb-tree. For a vertex subset V_s, all the nodes in pb-tree can be divided into three categories: *Complete node*, *Partial node* and *Irrelevant node*. A node $u \in T$ is a complete node for V_s if all the vertices in u are included in V_s, and it is a partial node if there exists a proper vertex subset of u included in V_s. Correspondingly, u is an irrelevant node if all the vertices in u are outside of V_s. Note that if a node is a complete node, then all its descendant are complete nodes. We propose a Dijkstra-based algorithm on pb-tree to make the query more efficient by expanding the abstract paths in complete non-leaf nodes and the shortest path trees in partial leaf nodes.

The querying algorithm is shown in Algorithm 4. Algorithm 4 utilizes a prior queue Q to iteratively dequeue the vertices in V_s until the ending vertex v_e is dequeued. In each iteration, a vertex v_x is dequeued from Q with the minimum τ_x, where τ_x is the distance from the starting vertex v_s to it. Initially, Q is set as V_s. τ_s is 0 and τ_x is ∞ for other vertices in V_s. If v_x is an exit and it is expanded by an abstract path $a_{y,x}$, Algorithm 4 calls PATH-RECOVER to dequeue all the vertices in the path represented by $a_{y,x}$ from Q (line 4–5) and then updates τ_z for every v_x's outgoing neighbor v_z in Q (line 12). If v_x is an entry of a leaf node u_i, Algorithm 4 calls NODE-IDENTIFY to find the complete node u_j with the highest level such that v_x is still an entry of u_j. NODE-IDENTIFY uses the

---

Algorithm 5: PARTIAL-SEARCH (Q, v_x, u_i)

1: **for** each $v_y \in P_x$ **do**
2:    **if** $v_y \notin V_s$ **then**
3:        deletes the branch below v_y;
4:    **else**
5:        **if** $v_y \in Q$ **then**
6:            updates $p^*_{s,y}$ and τ_y;

Algorithm 6: PATH-RECOVER $(Q, a_{y,x})$

1: **for** each $a_{i,i+1} \subset a_{y,x}$ **do**
2:    **if** $\exists$ a child node u_k of u_j, $a_{i,i+1} \in A_k$ **then**
3:        PATH-RECOVER $(a_{i,i+1})$;
4:    **else**
5:        gets $p^*_{i,i+1}$ by searching P_i
6:        $Q \leftarrow Q \setminus p^*_{i,i+1}$

---

abstract paths to expand the exits of u_j and then updates Q (line 8). Note that u_j may be the leaf node u_i. If such u_j does no exist, the leaf node u_i is a partial node, then Algorithm 4 calls PARTIAL-SEARCH to expand the vertices in u_i and updates Q (line 10). If v_x is not an entry or exit, it must be an internal vertex in a leaf node u_i, then Algorithm 4 updates v_x's outgoing neighbors in Q in the similar way as Dijkstra algorithm (line 12). Algorithm 4 terminates when the ending vertex v_e first dequeued from Q and the τ_e is the shortest distance from v_s to v_e on V_s. Next, we introduce NODE-IDENTIFY, PARTIAL-SEARCH and PATH-RECOVER respectively.

Partial Search: For a partial node u_i and an entry v_x, the shortest path tree P_x of S_i is utilized to expand the shortest paths. Algorithm 5 utilizes BFS to search P_x. For every $v_y \in P_x$, if $v_y \notin V_s$, the branch below v_y can be ignored (line 3). And if $v_y \in Q$, the Algorithm 5 updates the $p^*_{s,y}$ and τ_y (line 6).

Path Recover: For an abstract path $a_{y,x}$ of a complete node u_j, PATH-RECOVER computes $p^*_{y,x}$ in the descendant nodes of u_j. As shown in Algorithm 6, for each sub-abstract path $a_{i,i+1}$ of $a_{y,x}$ which can be found in one of u_j's children, Algorithm 6 calls PATH-RECOVER in that child to compute the $a_{i,i+1}$ (line 3). Otherwise, Algorithm 6 searches the shortest path tree P_i to compute $p^*_{i,i+1}$ (line 5).

Node Identify: Given a leaf node u_i and a vertex $v_x \in u_i.entry$, the pseudo-code of NODE-IDENTIFY is shown in Algorithm 7. It first finds the parent node of u_i. If v_x is an entry of the parent node, and it is a complete node, Algorithm 7 checks the parent node of it in the same way (line 3–4). u_j is the complete node on the highest level and v_x is an entry of it. Then Algorithm 7 searches the shortest path tree P_x to update the exits of u_j in Q, if u_j is a leaf node (line 7). If u_j is a non-leaf node, Algorithm 7 utilizes the abstract paths which start from v_x to update the exits of u_j in Q (line 9).

Algorithm 7: NODE-IDENTIFY (v_x, u_i)

1: finds the parent node u_j of u_i;
2: **while** $v_x \in u_j.entry$ and u_j is a complete node **do**
3:     $u_i \leftarrow u_j$
4:     finds the parent node u_j of u_i;
5: $u_j \leftarrow u_i$
6: **if** u_j is a leaf node **then**
7:     updates the τ of the exits in Q using the shortest path trees in u_j;
8: **else**
9:     updates the τ of the exits in Q using the abstract paths in u_j;

4.2 Example

Figure 4 shows the query process from v_{10} to v_3 on V_s. Initially, Q is set as V_s and τ_{10} is set to 0. In the 1st iteration, v_{10} is dequeued from Q. v_{10} is an entry of a partial node u_1. The algorithm searches the shortest path tree P_{10} in u_1. Because v_{12} is not in V_s, only τ_{14} is updated to 4 and $p^*_{10,14}$ is updated to $(10, 14)$. v_{10} is also an exit of u_1, τ_4 is updated to 8 and $p^*_{10,4}$ is updated to $(10, 4)$. In the 2nd iteration, v_{14} is dequeued from Q. Cause v_{14} is not an entry of u_1, algorithm updates the $p^*_{10,2}$ to $(10, 14, 2)$ by the edge (v_{14}, v_2), and τ_2 is updated to 6. As an exit of u_1, the algorithm searches the outgoing neighbors of v_2 in the 3rd iteration. τ_4 is updated to 7 and $p^*_{10,4}$ is updated to $(10, 14, 2, 4)$. This is the (1) of Fig. 4. In the 4th iteration, because v_4 is an entry of u_2, and it is not an entry of u_7, P_4 in u_2 is searched and τ_6 is updated. In the same way, τ_7 is updated in the next iteration, and $p^*_{10,7}$ is updated to $(10, 14, 2, 4, 15, 16, 6, 7)$. Then v_7 is dequeued from Q. It is an entry of a complete node u_3. The algorithm searches the pb-tree and finds the complete node u_9 with the highest level such that v_7 is an entry of it. That is the (2) of Fig. 4. In u_9, the abstract path $a_{7,5}$ is utilized to update the $p^*_{10,5}$ and τ_5. In the next iteration, v_5 is dequeued from Q and it is expanded by $a_{7,5}$. The algorithm computes $p^*_{7,5}$ by computing $p^*_{7,8}$ in u_3 and $p^*_{9,5}$ in u_4. u_3 and u_4 are the leaf nodes. Therefore, the algorithm searches P_7 in u_3 and P_9 in u_4. All the vertices in $p^*_{7,5}$ are dequeued from Q. After that, τ_3

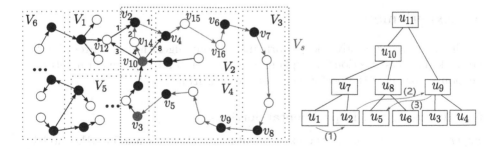

Fig. 4. A shortest path query from v_{10} to v_3 on V_s

and $p_{10,3}^*$ are updated by the edge (v_5, v_3). This is the (3) of Fig. 4. In the next iteration, v_3 is dequeued from Q. The algorithm terminates and returns $p_{10,3}^*$.

4.3   Complexity Analysis

Time Complexity: For a graph G and a vertex subset V_s, let r and q be the number of vertices and edges in G_s, k be the number of clusters, α and a be the maximum number of vertices and borders in each cluster, ψ_c and ψ_p be the number of the complete leaf nodes and the partial leaf nodes. The identification of each node is in $O(1)$, and the number of nodes in pb-tree is $2k - 1$. The time complexity of identifying all the nodes is $O(2k - 1) = O(k)$. For an entry of a complete leaf node, the algorithm finds the complete nodes on a higher level in $O(logk + 1) = O(logk)$, when all the complete nodes are on the highest level. For a complete node on level $logk + 1$, the number of the borders is $O(ka)$. Searching the abstract paths from that vertex is in $O(ka)$. Thus the time complexity of expanding the shortest paths from an entry of a complete leaf node is $O(logk + ka)$. For an entry of a partial leaf node, the algorithm searches the shortest path tree in that node in $O(\alpha)$. For the exits of the complete leaf nodes and the vertices in partial leaf nodes, whose number is $O(\psi_c a + \psi_p \alpha)$, the algorithm searches all the neighbors of it in V_s in $O(\psi_c ar + \psi_p \alpha r)$. For an abstract path, in the worst-case, it is in the node on level $logk + 1$, and all the borders of that node are in the path. The number of the borders is $O(ka)$, and for each pair of the borders, the PATH-RECOVER searches a shortest path tree in a leaf node. The time complexity of computing such an abstract path is $O(ka\alpha)$. The number of the borders in complete nodes is $\psi_c a$. To sum up, because $\psi_c + \psi_p = k, \alpha \geq a$, the time complexity of our method is $O(\psi_c a(logk + ka) + \psi_p a\alpha + \psi_c ar + \psi_p \alpha r + \psi_c a\alpha ka + k) = O(kar + k^2\alpha^3)$. In the worst-case, the number of the complete nodes is zero, and all the shortest path trees can not be utilized. Then time complexity is $O(\psi_p \alpha r) = O(rlogr + q)$, which is the time complexity of the Dijkstra algorithm. In practice, the complexity is much smaller than the worst-case complexity.

Space Complexity: The query algorithm maintains a prior queue Q. In the worst-case, all the vertices in V_s will be dequeued from Q. Therefore, the space complexity is the number of vertices in V_s, i.e. $O(r)$.

5   Experiements

In this section, we study the performance of our algorithm on three real-life network datasets. Section 5.1 explains the datasets and experimental settings. Section 5.2 presents the performance of the algorithms.

5.1   Datasets and Experimental Settings

Experimental Settings. All the experiments were done on a 2.50 GHz Intel(R) Xeon(R) Platinum 8255C CPU with 128G main memory, running on Linux VM-16-3-ubuntu 4.4.0-130-generic. All algorithms are implemented by C++.

Datasets. We use three real road networks from the 9th DIMACS Implementation Challenge (http://users.diag.uniroma1.it/challenge9/download.shtml). All the edges of them are the real roads in the corresponding areas. Table 2 summarizes the properties of the datasets. $|V|$ and $|E|$ are the number of vertices and edges in the road network.

Table 2. Datasets

Dataset	$|V|$	$|E|$	Description
NY	264,346	733,846	New York City Road Network
BAY	327,270	800,172	San Francisco Bay Area Road Network
COL	435,666	1,057,066	Colorado Road Network

Query Set. For each dataset, we use four different kinds of partitions, which partition the graph into 100, 150, 200, and 500 clusters respectively. We construct a pb-tree for each partition. We study the query performance by varying vertex subset V_s. We test 9 kinds of queries, where every query set is a set of queries with a same size of vertex subsets. These vertex subsets contain the 10%, 20%, 30%, 40%, 50%, 60%, 70%, 80% and 90% vertices randomly taken from V. For each query set, we test 100 random queries and report the average querying time as the results for the current query set.

5.2   Experimental Results

Exp-1. Build Time of Index. Figure 5 shows the build time of the pb-tree based on different number of clusters. Observe that, as the number of the clusters increases, the build time of the leaf nodes and the non-leaf nodes are decreased. The main reasons are as follow. As the number of leaf nodes increases, the number of the vertices in a single leaf node decreases. And the time to build the shortest paths tree also decreases. For non-leaf nodes, although the number of all the non-leaf nodes increases, the time to compute the abstract paths based on the Dijkstra algorithm also decreases.

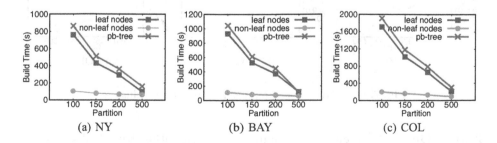

(a) NY   (b) BAY   (c) COL

Fig. 5. Build time of pb-tree

Exp-2. Index Size. Figure 6 shows the size of the pb-tree based on different number of clusters. As the number of the clusters increases, though the size and the number of non-leaf nodes are increased, the size of leaf nodes and the pb-tree are decreased. The main reasons are as follow. On the one hand, as the number of the vertices in a leaf node decreases, the number of the vertices maintained in the shortest path trees also decreases. On the other hand, for more clusters, there will be more non-leaf nodes and more abstract paths in them. Therefore, the size of the non-leaf nodes increases.

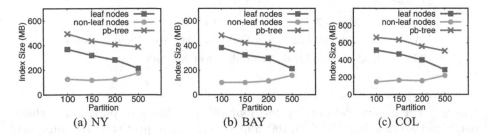

Fig. 6. Index size of pb-tree

Exp-3. Query Time Based on Different Number of Clusters. Figure 7 shows the query time using the four pb-trees based on 100, 150, 200 and 500 clusters on three datasets in four kinds of vertex subsets whose number of the vertices are 90%, 80%, 70% and 60% of the number of the vertices in V. We made two observations. The first one is that for the vertex subsets with the same size, the more clusters the pb-tree is based on, the less time the query processing will take. The reason is that there are more complete nodes and abstract paths can be used. Secondly, as the size of the vertex subsets decreases, the query time also decreases. This is mainly because as the size of the vertex subsets decreases, more vertices are unreachable, and the query results can be returned faster.

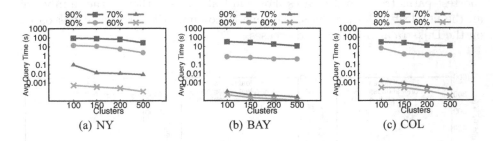

Fig. 7. Query time based on different number of clusters

Exp-4. Query Efficiency. We compared our algorithm with Dijkstra algorithm. Table 3 shows the query times using the pb-tree based on 100 clusters and the Dijkstra algorithm. On each dataset, we find that the Dijkstra algorithm takes more time than our method on each size of vertex subset. We also find that when the size of the vertex subset is 80% of the vertices in V, the time difference between the two methods is minimal. That is because most of the nodes in pb-tree are partial nodes in that case, so most of the abstract paths can not be used. When the size of the vertex subset drops below 50% of the vertices in V, the query times for both methods tend to stabilize. That mainly because most of the vertices are unreachable, and the results can be returned quickly. For our method, the shortest path trees in each leaf node can be used, which makes our method have a better performance than the Dijkstra algorithm.

Table 3. Query times(s)

Dataset	Method	90%	80%	70%	60%	50%	40%	30%	20%	10%
NY	pb-tree	87.0191	13.8673	9.65E-02	5.44E-04	6.48E-05	1.65E-05	2.59E-05	8.78E-05	2.08E-05
	Dijkstra	969.062	102.884	10.26720	4.11E-02	5.74E-04	4.94E-04	2.67E-04	1.60E-04	2.40E-04
BAY	pb-tree	32.8067	0.72000	9.86E-05	4.38E-05	3.22E-05	8.12E-05	3.59E-05	5.77E-05	2.02E-05
	Dijkstra	542.614	10.1591	4.34E-02	9.45E-04	4.52E-04	5.02E-04	1.74E-04	2.91E-04	3.00E-04
COL	pb-tree	30.3478	6.36190	1.48E-03	2.69E-04	6.45E-05	4.98E-05	8.59E-05	5.77E-05	4.85E-05
	Dijkstra	743.509	90.7764	0.494680	8.02E-03	1.15E-03	1.87E-03	1.76E-03	1.21E-03	9.47E-04

6 Related Work

In this section, we will mainly discuss two categories of related work: the first one is the existing algorithms for answering unconstrained shortest path queries; the other one is existing approaches for answering constrained shortest path queries.

In the first category, the traditional shortest path query algorithms, such as the Dijkstra algorithm[5], can be used to solve the problems we supposed in this paper. But it will take a long time to answer the query. The shortest path quad tree is proposed in [13]. Xiao et al. in [16] proposes the concept of the compact BFS-trees. A novel index called TEDI has been proposed by Wei et al. in [15]. It utilizes the tree decomposition theory to build the tree. Ruicheng Zhong et al. propose a G-Tree model in [18]. Goldberg et al. in [6] propose a method which is to choose some vertices as landmark vertices and store the shortest paths between each pair of them. Qiao et al. in [11] propose a query-dependent local landmark scheme. [2] proposes another novel exact method based on distance-aware 2-hop cover for the distance queries. However, those methods can not be used to answer the problem we proposed in this work because the vertices in those pre-computed paths maybe not in the given vertex subset.

In the second category, several works [7,9,10,14] study the constrained shortest path problem on a large graph. A Lagrangian relaxation algorithm for the problem of finding a shortest path between two vertices in a network has been developed in [7]. H. C. Joksch et al. propose a linear programming approach and a dynamic programming approach in [9]. Kurt Mehlhorn et al. present the hull approach, a combinatorial algorithm for solving a linear programming relaxation in [10]. [14] tackles a generalization of the weight constrained shortest path problem in a directed network. Some works aim to answer the query with the constrained edges. Bonchi et al. propose an approximate algorithm for shortest path query with edge constraints in [3]. But the algorithm can not support the exact shortest path query. Michael N. Rice et al. propose a method by precalculating the paths between some of the two vertices with the label of the edge in [12]. Mohamed S. Hassan et al. construct an index called EDP, which is one of the state-of-art methods to answer the query with the constrained edges in [8]. The EDP contains many subgraphs with the same label of edges and stores every shortest path from an inner vertex to a border vertex in each subgraph. Those methods can not be used to solve the problem we proposed in this paper, cause the vertex subset V_s is not constrained by labels or another weight of the edges.

7 Conclusion

In this paper, we study the problem of the shortest path query on a vertex subset. We first give the definition of the shortest path query on a vertex subset. Second, we propose a novel index named pb-tree to facilitate the shortest path query on a vertex subset. We introduce what the pb-tree is and how to construct it. We also introduce how to utilize our index to answer the queries. Finally, we confirm the effectiveness and efficiency of our method through extensive experiments on real-life datasets.

Acknowledgments. This work is supported by the National Key Research and Development Project 2019YFB2101903 and the National Natural Science Foundation of China No. 61402323, 61972275.

References

1. Abou-Rjeili, A., Karypis, G.: Multilevel algorithms for partitioning power-law graphs. In: 20th International Parallel and Distributed Processing Symposium (IPDPS 2006) Proceedings, Rhodes Island, Greece, 25–29 April 2006. IEEE (2006)
2. Akiba, T., Iwata, Y., Yoshida, Y.: Fast exact shortest-path distance queries on large networks by pruned landmark labeling. In: Proceedings of the 2013 ACM SIGMOD International Conference on Management of Data, pp. 349–360 (2013)
3. Bonchi, F., Gionis, A., Gullo, F., Ukkonen, A.: Distance oracles in edge-labeled graphs. In: Proceedings of the 17th International Conference on Extending Database Technology, EDBT 2014, Athens, Greece, 24–28 March 2014, pp. 547–558 (2014)
4. Dhillon, I.S., Guan, Y., Kulis, B.: Weighted graph cuts without eigenvectors a multilevel approach. IEEE Trans. Pattern Anal. Mach. Intell. **29**(11), 1944–1957 (2007)
5. Dijkstra, E.W., et al.: A note on two problems in connexion with graphs. Numer. Math. **1**(1), 269–271 (1959)

6. Goldberg, A.V., Harrelson, C.: Computing the shortest path: a search meets graph theory. In: Proceedings of the Sixteenth Annual ACM-SIAM Symposium on Discrete Algorithms, SODA 2005, Vancouver, British Columbia, Canada, 23–25 January 2005, pp. 156–165 (2005)
7. Handler, G.Y., Zang, I.: A dual algorithm for the constrained shortest path problem. Networks **10**(4), 293–309 (1980)
8. Hassan, M.S., Aref, W.G., Aly, A.M.: Graph indexing for shortest-path finding over dynamic sub-graphs. In: Proceedings of the 2016 International Conference on Management of Data, pp. 1183–1197 (2016)
9. Joksch, H.C.: The shortest route problem with constraints. J. Math. Anal. Appl. **14**(2), 191–197 (1966)
10. Mehlhorn, K., Ziegelmann, M.: Resource constrained shortest paths. In: Paterson, M.S. (ed.) ESA 2000. LNCS, vol. 1879, pp. 326–337. Springer, Heidelberg (2000). https://doi.org/10.1007/3-540-45253-2_30
11. Qiao, M., Cheng, H., Chang, L., Yu, J.X.: Approximate shortest distance computing: a query-dependent local landmark scheme. In: IEEE 28th International Conference on Data Engineering (ICDE 2012), Washington, DC, USA (Arlington, Virginia), 1–5 April 2012, pp. 462–473 (2012)
12. Rice, M.N., Tsotras, V.J.: Graph indexing of road networks for shortest path queries with label restrictions. PVLDB **4**(2), 69–80 (2010)
13. Samet, H., Sankaranarayanan, J., Alborzi, H.: Scalable network distance browsing in spatial databases. In: Proceedings of the ACM SIGMOD International Conference on Management of Data, SIGMOD 2008, Vancouver, BC, Canada, 10–12 June 2008, pp. 43–54 (2008)
14. Smith, O.J., Boland, N., Waterer, H.: Solving shortest path problems with a weight constraint and replenishment arcs. Comput. OR **39**(5), 964–984 (2012)
15. Wei, F.: TEDI: efficient shortest path query answering on graphs. In: Proceedings of the ACM SIGMOD International Conference on Management of Data, SIGMOD 2010, Indianapolis, Indiana, USA, 6–10 June 2010, pp. 99–110 (2010)
16. Xiao, Y., Wu, W., Pei, J., Wang, W., He, Z.: Efficiently indexing shortest paths by exploiting symmetry in graphs. In: 12th International Conference on Extending Database Technology, EDBT 2009, Saint Petersburg, Russia, 24–26 March 2009, Proceedings, pp. 493–504 (2009)
17. Xu, X., Yuruk, N., Feng, Z., Schweiger, T.A.J.: SCAN: a structural clustering algorithm for networks. In: Berkhin, P., Caruana, R., Wu, X. (eds.) Proceedings of the 13th ACM SIGKDD International Conference on Knowledge Discovery and Data Mining, San Jose, California, USA, 12–15 August 2007, pp. 824–833. ACM (2007)
18. Zhong, R., Li, G., Tan, K., Zhou, L.: G-tree: an efficient index for KNN search on road networks. In: CIKM, pp. 39–48 (2013)

Efficient Personalized Influential Community Search in Large Networks

Yanping Wu, Jun Zhao, Renjie Sun, Chen Chen, and Xiaoyang Wang[(✉)]

Zhejiang Gongshang University, Hangzhou, China
yanpingw.zjgsu@gmail.com, junzhao.zjgsu@gmail.com,
renjiesun.zjgsu@gmail.com, {chenc,xiaoyangw}@zjgsu.edu.cn

Abstract. Community search, which aims to retrieve important communities (i.e., subgraphs) for a given query vertex, has been widely studied in the literature. In the recent, plenty of research is conducted to detect influential communities, where each vertex in the network is associated with an influence value. Nevertheless, there is a paucity of work that can support personalized requirement. In this paper, we propose a new problem, i.e., maximal personalized influential community (MPIC) search. Given a graph G, an integer k and a query vertex u, we aim to obtain the most influential community for u by leveraging the k-core concept. To handle larger networks efficiently, two algorithms, i.e., top-down algorithm and bottom-up algorithm, are developed. To further speedup the search, an index-based approach is proposed. We conduct extensive experiments on 6 real-world networks to demonstrate the advantage of proposed techniques.

Keywords: Influential community · Personalized search · k-core

1 Introduction

Retrieving communities and exploring the latent structures in the networks can find many applications in different fields, such as protein complex identification, friend recommendation, event organization, etc. [8,10]. There are two essential problems in community retrieval, that is community detection and community search. Generally, given a graph, community detection problem aims to find all or top-r communities from the graph [12,16], while community search problem is to identify the cohesive communities that contain the given query vertex [6,18]. In this paper, we focus on the category of community search problem, which is very important for personalized applications. For instance, we can conduct better friend recommendation by identifying the important community that contains the query users. Similarly, we can make better event organization by retrieving the community, which contains the user that we want to invite.

In the literature, lots of research tries to find personalized communities by emphasizing the structure cohesiveness. While, in many cases, we also need to

X. Wang et al. (Eds.): APWeb-WAIM 2020, LNCS 12317, pp. 86–101, 2020.
https://doi.org/10.1007/978-3-030-60259-8_7

consider the influence of obtained communities. Recently, there are some research that tries to find communities with large influence, e.g., [1,2,14]. In [14], Li et al. propose a novel community model called k-influential community, where each vertex is associated with a weight (i.e., influence value) in the graph. A community (i.e., subgraph) is essential when it is cohesive and has large influence value. Efficient algorithms are developed to obtain the top-r communities with the largest influence value. Given the importance of the problem, [1,2] try to speedup the search from different aspects. Since influence value is user's natural property, by considering the influence value, it can lead us to identify more significant communities.

Nevertheless, the existing works on influential community detection mainly focus on finding all or top-r influential communities. The personalized situation is not considered. To fill this gap, in this paper, we propose the maximal personalized influential community (MPIC) search problem. Given a graph G, an integer k and a query vertex q, the MPIC is the community with the largest influence value that contains q, and satisfies the k-core (i.e., the degree of each vertex inside is no less than k), connectivity (i.e., the subgraph is connected) and maximal (i.e., no other supergraph satisfies the previous criteria) constraints. As defined in the previous work [14], the influence value of a community is the minimum weight of all the vertices in the community. Given the graph in Fig. 1, if $k = 3$ and the query vertex is v_8, then the vertices in the dotted line is the corresponding MPIC. Note that, the k-core model is also used in the previous works to measure the cohesiveness of the community [1,2,14].

Challenges. The main challenges of the problem lie in the following two aspects. Firstly, the real-world networks, such as social networks, are usually large in size. It is critical for the algorithms to scale for large networks. Secondly, since we investigate the personalized scenario, there may be plenty of queries generated by users in real applications, it is important that the developed algorithms can meet the online requirements.

Contributions. To the best of our knowledge, we are the first to investigate the maximal personalized influential community (MPIC) search problem. The contributions of this paper are summarized as follows.

- We formally define the MPIC search problem.
- To handle large networks, two algorithms, i.e., top-down algorithm and the bottom-up algorithm, are developed based on different searching orders.
- An index-based method is proposed in order to meet the online requirements.
- We conduct extensive experiments on 6 real-world networks to evaluate the performance of proposed techniques. As shown, the developed techniques can significantly speedup the search compared with the baseline.

2 Problem Definition

We consider a network $G = (V, E, \omega)$ as an undirected graph, where V and E denote the vertex set and edge set, respectively. Each vertex $u \in V$ is associated

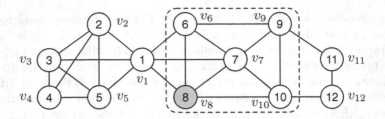

Fig. 1. Running example (The number in the vertex denotes its weight)

Algorithm 1: COMPUTECORE(G, k)
___
    Input   : G : a graph, k : degree constraint
    Output : k-core of G
1 while *exists* $u \in G$ *with* $deg(u, G) < k$ **do**
2 $\lfloor$ $G = G \setminus u$;
3 return G

---

with a weight denoted by $\omega(u)$, representing the influence of vertex u. The vertex weight can be its PageRank score or other user defined value. Without loss of generality, we use the same setting as the previous work for vertex weight, where different vertices have different weights [14]. Note, if that is not the case, we use the vertex id to break the tie. We denote the number of vertices by $n = |V|$ and the number of edges by $m = |E|$. A subgraph $S = (V_S, E_S)$ is an induced subgraph of G, if $V_S \subseteq V$ and $E_S = \{(u,v)|u, v \in V_S, (u,v) \in E\}$. Given a subgraph S, the neighbors of $u \in V_S$ is denoted by $N(u, S) = \{v|v \in V_S, (u,v) \in E_S\}$, and $deg(u, S)$ represents the degree of u in S, i.e., $deg(u, S) = |N(u, S)|$. In this paper, we utilize the k-core model to represent the cohesiveness of a community, which is also widely used in the literature [1,14].

Definition 1 (k-core). *Given a graph G and a positive integer k, a subgraph $S \subseteq G$ is the k-core of G, denoted by $C_k(G)$, if S satisfies the following conditions. (i) $deg(u, S) \geq k$ for each vertex u in S. (ii) S is maximal, i.e., any subgraph $S' \supset S$ is not a k-core.*

To compute the k-core of a graph, we can remove the vertex whose degree is less than k recursively. The time complexity of computing k-core is $O(m)$ [20] and the detailed algorithm is shown in Algorithm 1. To identify important communities, we consider both the cohesiveness and the influence of a community. We employ the widely used influence value to measure the influence of a community [1,14].

Definition 2 (Influence value). *Given an induced subgraph S of G, the influence value of S is the minimum weight of the vertex in V_S, denoted as $f(S)$, i.e., $f(S) = \min_{u \in V_S} \omega(u)$.*

In the previous works, people usually focus on finding all or top-r influential communities [1,2,14]. While, as discussed, in real applications, it is also essential to identify the personalized influential communities for different user queries. Given this requirement, we define the maximal personalized influential community as follows.

Definition 3 (Maximal Personalized Influential Community (MPIC)). *Given a graph G, a positive integer k and a query vertex q, a maximal personalized influential community, short as **MPIC**, is an induced subgraph $\bar{S}$ of G, which meets all the following constraints.*

- *Connectivity: S is connected;*
- *Cohesiveness: each vertex in S has degree at least k;*
- *Personalized: query vertex q is contained in S, i.e., $q \in V_S$;*
- *Maximal: there is no other induced subgraph S' that (i) satisfies the first three constraints (i.e., connectivity, cohesiveness and personalized constraints), (ii) is a supergraph of S, i.e., $S' \supset S$, and (iii) has the same influence value as S, i.e., $f(S) = f(S')$;*
- *Largest: S is the one with the largest influence value and satisfies the previous constraints.*

Problem Definition. Given a graph $G = (V, E, \omega)$, a query vertex q and a positive integer k, we aim to develop efficient algorithm to find the maximal personalized influential community (MPIC) for the query, denoted by **MPIC**(q, k).

Example 1. As shown in Fig. 1, the number in each vertex is the corresponding weight. Suppose $k = 3$ and query vertex is v_8. Then we can see that the subgraph $S_1 = \{v_6, v_7, v_8, v_9, v_{10}\}$ in the dotted line is the corresponding MPIC with influence value of 6. While the subgraph $S_2 = \{v_1, v_2, v_3, v_4, v_5, v_6, v_7, v_8, v_9, v_{10}\}$, which satisfies the first four constraints of MPIC with influence value of 1, is not the MPIC, because it is not the one with the largest influence value.

3 Solutions

In this section, we first introduce some properties about the maximal personalized influential community. Then we develop two approaches, top-down method and bottom-up method by verifying the vertices in different orders. Finally, to support efficient online processing and scale for large networks, an index-based method is proposed based on the bottom-up framework.

3.1 Properties of Maximal Personalized Influential Community

Lemma 1. *Given a graph G, an integer k and a query vertex q, then the influence value of MPIC(q, k) is at most the weight of q, i.e., $f(MPIC(q, k)) \leq \omega(q)$.*

Proof. MPIC(q, k) must contain q. Based on the definition of influence value, we have $f(\text{MPIC}(q, k)) = \min_{u \in \text{MPIC}(q,k)} \omega(u) \leq \omega(q)$. Thus, the lemma holds.

Algorithm 2: TOP-DOWN ALGORITHM

    Input   : G : a graph, k : degree constraint, q : query vertex
    Output : MPIC for the query
1 $C_k(G) \leftarrow$ COMPUTECORE(G, k);
2 **if** $q \notin C_k(G)$ **then**
3 | **return** *error*

4 $C_k(G, q) \leftarrow$ the connected component of $C_k(G)$ that contains q;
5 $S \leftarrow$ sort vertices of $C_k(G, q)$ in descending order based on vertex weights;
6 $Q \leftarrow \emptyset; i \leftarrow 0$;
7 **while** $i < S.size$ **do**
8 | $Q \leftarrow Q \cup \{S[i]\}$;
9 | **If** $S[i] = q$ **then** *break*;
10 | $i \leftarrow i + 1$;

11 **if** $q \in C_k(Q)$ **then**
12 | **return** *the connected component containing* q *in* $C_k(Q)$

13 $i \leftarrow i + 1$;
14 **while** $i < S.size$ **do**
15 | $Q \leftarrow Q \cup \{S[i]\}$;
16 | **if** $q \in C_k(Q)$ **then**
17 | | **return** *the connected component containing* q *in* $C_k(Q)$
18 | $i \leftarrow i + 1$;

Lemma 2. *Given a graph G and two induced subgraphs S_1 and S_2, we have $V_{S_2} \subset V_{S_1}$ and $V_{S_1} = V_{S_2} \cup \{u\}$. If the weight of u is smaller than the influence value of S_2 (i.e., $\omega(u) < f(S_2)$), then the influence value of S_1 is smaller than that of S_2 (i.e., $f(S_1) < f(S_2)$).*

Proof. Based on the definition of influence value, $f(S_1) = \min_{v \in V_{S_1}} \omega(v) \leq \omega(u) < f(S_2)$. Therefore, the lemma holds.

3.2 Top-Down Algorithm

In this section, we present the top-down algorithm which is inspired by the existing influential community detection method [1]. According to Lemma 1, the influence value of the identified MPIC is at most $\omega(q)$. To find the community with the largest influence value, we can first add all the vertices whose weight is no less than $\omega(q)$ and check if we can obtain a community that satisfies the first four constraints of MPIC. If so, we can output the identified community. Otherwise, we can add some vertices with weight smaller than $\omega(q)$ to find the MPIC. The detailed algorithm is shown in Algorithm 2.

In Algorithm 2, we first compute the k-core of G, denoted by $C_k(G)$. Since the MPIC must be inside $C_k(G)$, if q does not belong to the k-core, error code is returned in Line 3, which means we cannot find a MPIC containing q. Otherwise, due to the connectivity constraint, we only need to keep the connected component that contains q. Then we sort the survived vertices in descending order by their weights and store them in S (Lines 4–5). We load the query q and the vertices ranked above q into Q (Lines 7–10). If the k-core $C_k(Q)$ of Q contains q, then we return the connected component containing q, which can be obtained by conducting a BFS from q (Lines 11–12). Otherwise, we add the remaining vertices in S one by one to Q until the k-core of Q contains the query vertex q, and the connected component is returned (Lines 14–18).

Example 2. Consider the graph in Fig. 1. Suppose $k = 3$ and the query vertex is v_8. Following the top-down algorithm, we first compute the k-core of G. Thus, v_{11} and v_{12} are deleted, because they violate the degree constraint. Then we add v_8 and the vertices ranked higher (i.e., $\{v_{10}, v_9\}$) than v_8 into Q. However, they cannot form a 3-core. Then we insert vertex one by one into Q. Until v_6 is added, there is a 3-core containing query v_8, i.e., $\{v_{10}, v_9, v_8, v_7, v_6\}$, which is the MPIC returned.

3.3   Bottom-Up Algorithm

In the top-down algorithm, we first add all the vertices ranked higher than q into Q. After that, by adding each vertex into Q, we need to invoke the k-core computation procedure. Even though the time complexity of k-core computation is $O(m)$, in the worst case, we need to repeat the process n times, which can be time-consuming. Ideally, we can add more vertices into Q for each iteration. However, in order to guarantee the correctness of the algorithm, it is difficult to determine the appropriate number of vertices to be added. If too many vertices are added, we may need a lot of computations to shrink the result. Otherwise, we still need to compute the k-core plenty of times. To reduce the computation cost, in this section, the bottom-up method is proposed, which can avoid computing the k-core repeatedly.

According to Lemma 2, for a given induced subgraph, we can increase its influence value by removing the vertex with the smallest weight. Intuitively, since we aim to find the MPIC, we can iteratively remove the vertices with the smallest weight and keep tracking the other constraints of MPIC, until the MPIC is found. Different from the top-down approach, in the bottom-up method, we visit the vertices in ascending order and remove the unpromising vertices iteratively. The detailed algorithm is shown in Algorithm 3.

For the algorithm, the first three steps are exactly the same as the top-down method (Lines 1–4). Then, we sort the survived vertices in ascending order by the weight of vertex and store them in S (Line 5). Then we try to remove the vertex with the current smallest weight one by one until the query vertex q is met (Lines 6–10). For each vertex u processed, we invoke the DELETE procedure, which details are shown in Lines 11–26. For each processed vertex u, we need to ensure the remained subgraph satisfies the k-core constraint. After deleting a vertex, it may cause its neighbors to have less than k neighbors. Then we remove these vertices as well (Lines 17–20). We put the vertices that violate the degree constraint into R and process them iteratively. When $w = q$ (Line 15), it means

---

Algorithm 3: BOTTOM-UP ALGORITHM

Input   : G : a weighted graph, k : degree constraint, q : query vertex
Output : MPIC for the query

1 $C_k(G) \leftarrow$ COMPUTECORE(G, k);
2 **if** $q \notin C_k(G)$ **then**
3 | **return** *error*

4 $C_k(G, q) \leftarrow$ the connected component of $C_k(G)$ that contains q;
5 $S \leftarrow$ sort vertices of $C_k(G, q)$ in ascending order based on vertex weights;
6 **while** $S \neq \emptyset$ **do**
7 | $D \leftarrow \emptyset$;
8 | $u \leftarrow S.front()$;
9 | **if** DELETE$(u, q, S, D) = 1$ **then**
10 | | **return** $S \cup D$

11 **Procedure** DELETE(u, q, S, D);
12 initialize a queue $R = \{u\}$;
13 **while** $R \neq \emptyset$ **do**
14 | $w \leftarrow R.pop()$;
15 | **if** $w = q$ **then**
16 | | **return** *1*
17 | **for each** $v \in N(w, S)$ **do**
18 | | $deg(v, S) \leftarrow deg(v, S) - 1$;
19 | | **if** $deg(v, S) < k$ **then**
20 | | | $R.push(v)$;
21 | remove w from S;
22 | $D \leftarrow D \cup \{w\}$;

23 **for each** *connected component* S' *in* S **do**
24 | **if** $q \notin S'$ **then**
25 | | remove S' from S;

26 **return** *0*

---

either (i) the input vertex u of DELETE procedure is q, or (ii) $deg(q, S)$ becomes less than k because of the deletion u. In this case, the remained subgraph S and D (i.e, $S \cup D$) form the MPIC. This is because, when we remove the input vertex u, it will cause the remained subgraph does not contain q or q violates the degree constraint. The reason that we keep tracking the deleted vertices D for each DELETE procedure is for case when ii situation happens. Since the identified community should satisfy the connectivity constraint, we can safely remove the connected components in S that do not contain q (Lines 23–25).

Example 3. Consider the graph in Fig. 1. Suppose $k = 3$ and the query vertex is v_8. Following the bottom-up approach, v_{11} and v_{12} are firstly deleted due to the k-core computation. After deleting the vertex v_1 with the smallest weight, the remained graph are separated into two connected components. Therefore,

---

Algorithm 4: INDEX CONSTRUCTION

    Input   : G : a graph
    Output : constructed index

1 **for** k *from* 1 *to* k_{max} **do**
2     $C_k(G) \leftarrow$ COMPUTECORE(G, k);
3     $rn \leftarrow$ empty root node of T_k;
4   **for each** *connected component* S *in* $C_k(G)$ **do**
5   BUILDNODE(k, rn, S);

6 **Procedure** BUILDNODE(k, rn, S);
7 $u \leftarrow$ the vertex with the smallest weight in S;
8 $R \leftarrow \{u\}; D \leftarrow \emptyset$;
9 **while** R *is not empty* **do**
10    $w \leftarrow R.pop()$;
11   **for each** $v \in N(w, S)$ **do**
12       $deg(v, S) \leftarrow deg(v, S) - 1$;
13   **if** $deg(v, S) < k$ **then**
14          $R.push(v)$;
15   remove w from S;
16    $D \leftarrow D \cup \{w\}$;
17 construct an intermediate node crn containing D;
18 append crn to the parent node rn;
19 **for each** *connected component* S' *in* S **do**
20   BUILDNODE(k, crn, S');

---

we can safely remove the connected component $\{v_2, v_3, v_4, v_5\}$ from S since it does not contain the query vertex. Then, we process v_6. As we can see, when processing v_6 in the DELETE procedure, it will result in v_8 violating the degree constraint. Then we can stop and output $\{v_6, v_7, v_8, v_9, v_{10}\}$ as the result.

3.4   Index-Based Algorithm

In the bottom-up approach, we invoke the k-core computation at the beginning of the algorithm and the total cost of checking degree constraint in DELETE only takes $O(m)$ time, which avoids lots of computations compared to the top-down method. However, the bottom-up approach still has some limitations. (i) When deleting the vertices, it still costs a lot for processing very large graphs. (ii) For real applications, different users may have different requirements and there may exist a large amount of queries. Therefore, it is hard for it to meet the online requirement.

Motivated by the requirements, in this section, we propose an index-based algorithm by leveraging the bottom-up framework. In the bottom-up method, for a given k, we try to delete the vertex u with the smallest weight in each iteration by DELETE procedure. Then we can obtain the MPIC for certain vertices, such

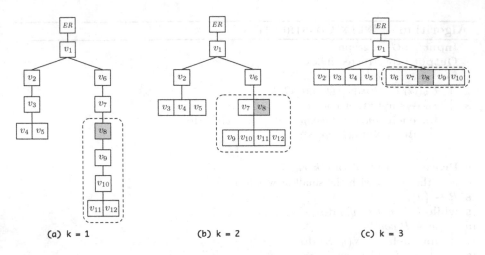

(a) k = 1   (b) k = 2   (c) k = 3

Fig. 2. Example for index construction

as the vertex u and the vertices removed when processing u. If we process the vertices in order, we can obtain the MPICs for all the vertices. Therefore, we can build a tree structure index according to the processing order. Let $k_{\max}$ be the largest core number, i.e., the largest k value for any k-core. If we build a tree index for each k value, then we can answer any given query efficiently. In Algorithm 4, we present the details of how to index the visited vertices effectively. Then we show how to answer a query by utilizing the index.

Index Construction. In Algorithm 4, we build a tree index for each k value from 1 to k_{max} (Lines 1–5). In each iteration, we first compute the corresponding k-core, and for each connected component, we construct the indexed tree nodes by invoking BUILDNODE procedure. The details of BUILDNODE procedure are shown in Lines 6–20. The BUILDNODE procedure is very similar to the DELETE procedure in Algorithm 3. It starts by processing the vertex with the smallest weight (Line 7). When we process a vertex u, it will cause some other vertices violating the degree constraints (Lines 11–14) and we add them and u into D (Line 16). According to the bottom-up method, it means the vertices in D belong to the same MPIC. Then we construct an intermediate node crn that contains the vertices in D, and append it to its parent node rn (Lines 17–18). Then we recursively call the BUILDNODE to process each connected component S' of the remained subgraph S (Lines 19–20). After processing each k, the index is constructed. Based on the construction process, we can see that the MPIC of a vertex consists of its belonged intermediate node and its children nodes in the index.

Example 4. Figure 2 shows the constructed index for the graph in Fig. 1 when $k = 1, 2, 3$. The ER node is the empty root node. It is for the case when the computed k-core in Line 2 of Algorithm 4 is not connected. For $k = 1$, the constructed index is shown in Fig. 2(a). We first process v_1 which will result in 2 connected components. Then we remove v_2 and v_3 and create two intermediate nodes for them, since the removal of them does not make other vertices violate the degree constraint. When deleting v_4, the degree of v_5 becomes less than 1. Then we construct an intermediate node that contains v_4 and v_5. We conduct similar procedure for the other connected component, and the constructed index is shown in the right branch. Similar procedure is conducted for $k = 2, 3$, where the corresponding index are shown in Figs. 2(b) and 2(c).

Query Processing. As we can see, for a given query, the MPIC consists of the intermediate node that contains the query vertex and all its children nodes in the corresponding k index. If we maintain $k_{\max}$ pointers for each vertex to its corresponding intermediate nodes, we can efficiently locate the vertex's intermediate node for a given k and traverse the index to return the result. For a given query, if we cannot find its intermediate node in the index, it means it does not has a MPIC for the query.

Example 5. Consider the graph in Fig. 1. The constructed index is shown in Fig. 2 for $k = 1, 2, 3$. Given the query vertex v_8, the MPIC is the vertices in the dotted line for $k = 1, 2, 3$ respectively.

Discussion. If we do not need to retrieve the specific vertices in MPIC, the index can answer the query in $O(1)$ time by just returning the pointer for the intermediate node. Otherwise, we need to traverse from the intermediate node to obtain all the vertices. In this paper, we use the second case in the experiments, since the first two algorithms will obtain all the vertices in MPIC.

4 Experiments

In this section, we conduct extensive experiments on real-world networks to evaluate the performance of proposed techniques.

4.1 Experiment Setup

Algorithms. Since there is no previous work for the proposed problem, we conduct experiments with the proposed three algorithms, i.e., top-down algorithm, bottom-up algorithm and index-based algorithm. The top-down algorithm serves as the baseline method.

Datasets. We evaluate the algorithms on 6 real-world datasets, i.e., Email, Brightkite, Gowalla, YouTube, Wiki and Livejournal. Table 1 shows the statistic details of the datasets. The datasets are downloaded from the Stanford Network Analysis Platform[1], which are public available. Similar as previous work, we use the PageRank value to serve as the vertex weight [14].

---

[1] http://snap.stanford.edu.

Table 1. Statistics of datasets

Dataset	#Vertices	#Edges	d_{max}	k_{max}
Email	36,692	183,831	1,367	43
Brightkite	58,228	214,078	1,134	52
Gowalla	196,591	950,327	14,730	51
YouTube	1,134,890	2,987,624	28,754	51
Wiki	1,791,488	13,846,826	16,063	72
Livejournal	3,997,962	34,681,189	14,815	360

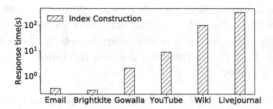

Fig. 3. Index construction time

Parameter and Workload. To evaluate the performance of proposed techniques, we vary the weight of query vertex and k. To generate the query vertices, we sort the vertices according to the weight and divide them into 5 buckets. For each bucket, we randomly select 200 vertices as query vertices. For k, we vary k from 5 to 25 with **10** as the default value. For each setting, we run the algorithms 10 times and report the average response time.

All algorithms are implemented in C++ with GNU GCC 7.4.0. Experiments are conducted on a PC with Intel Xeon 3.2 GHz CPU and 32 GB RAM using Ubuntu 18.04 (64-bit).

4.2   Experiment Result

Results of Index Construction. We first present the index construction time for all datasets, the results are shown in Fig. 3. As we can observe, the index construction phase is very efficient. It only takes 0.290 seconds for Brightkite dataset. For the largest network Livejournal, which has more than 34 million edges, it only takes 325.656 s for constructing the index.

Results of Varying Query Vertex Weight. By varying the query vertex weight, we conduct the experiments on all the datasets. The response time is shown in Fig. 4, where k is set as the default value. As observed, the bottom-up method is much faster than the top-down method, since the top-down method may compute the k-core many times. Among all, the index-based method runs fastest, due to the novel index structure proposed. In the two largest datasets, i.e., Wiki and Livejournal, the index-based method achieves up to 6 orders of

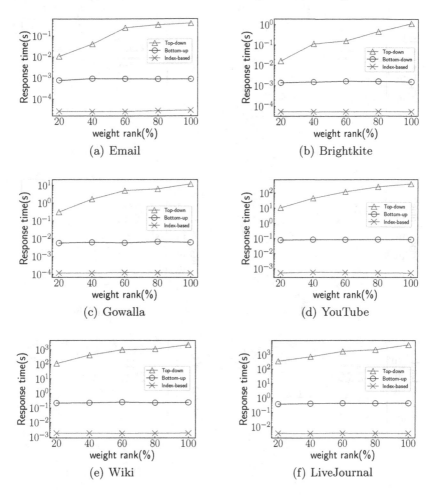

Fig. 4. Experiment results by varying query vertex weight

magnitudes speedup compared with the top-down method. As we can see, the bottom-up and index-based methods are not sensitive to the weight of query vertex. While, for the top-down method, the response time increases when the weight increases. This is because, for query vertex with larger weight, it may compute the k-core more times when adding vertices one by one.

Results of Varying k. We conduct the experiments on all the datasets by varying the query parameter k. The results of response time are shown in Fig. 5, where similar trend can be observed. The bottom-up and index-based methods are significantly faster than the top-down method, and the index-based method is the fastest one for all cases. In the largest dataset, i.e., Livejournal, the index-based method can achieve up to 6 orders of magnitudes speedup compared with the top-down method. With the increase of k, the response time of top-down

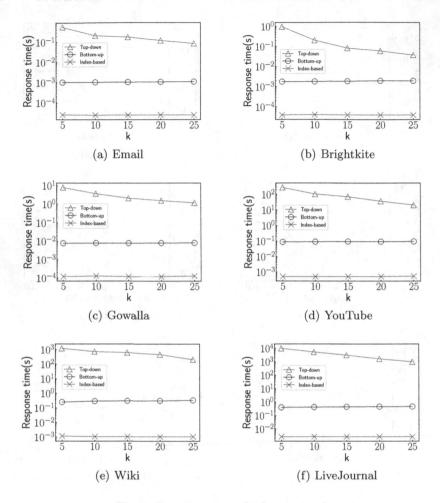

Fig. 5. Experiment results by varying k

method decreases. This is because, for larger k, the identified MPIC tends to be smaller. As shown, the bottom-up and index-based methods can scale well for the parameter k.

Summary. As demonstrated in the experiments, both bottom-up and index-based methods are significantly faster than the top-down method, and they can scale well for different query parameters. Especially for the index-based method, it usually can achieve orders of magnitudes speedup. Given the experiment results, in real applications, users can make a trade-off when selecting algorithms. If index construction is allowed by the applied platform, it would be better to use the index-based method. Otherwise, users can select the bottom-up method, which can also provide competitive performance.

5 Related Work

We present the related work from the following three aspects, i.e., cohesive subgraph mining, community search and influential community detection.

Cohesive Subgraph Mining. Cohesive subgraph mining is a very important tool for graph analysis and can find many applications in different fields [4,17]. In the literature, different models are proposed to measure the cohesiveness of a subgraph, such as k-core [20], k-truss [21], clique [5], etc. There are also some works that try to identify cohesive subgraph on special graphs, such as identifying k-core and k-truss over uncertain graphs [11,19].

Community Search. For cohesive subgraph mining, people usually focus on finding all or high ranked cohesive subgraphs. Given a graph G and query vertices, the community search problem aims to identify a densely connected subgraph that contains the query vertices [8]. To measure the cohesiveness of a community, different models are used. In [6,18], authors use the minimum degree to serve as the metric, which is similar to the k-core constraint. [18] proposes a global search framework to identify the community. Cui et al. [6] develop a local search method to avoid visiting too many vertices. Huang et al. [9] leverage the k-truss model and propose the triangle-connected k-truss community problem. It designs a triangle connectivity-preserving index to efficiently search the k-truss communities. There is lots of research for other kinds of graphs, e.g., attribute graphs and profile graphs [3,7]. [8] presents a comprehensive survey of recent advanced methods for community search problems.

Influential Community Detection. In traditional community detection/ search problems, the influence value of a community has been neglected. In [14], Li et al. present a novel community model called k-influential community. Given a graph G, each vertex is associated with a weight, i.e., influence value. It aims to find the top-r k-influential communities, where the cohesiveness is measured based on the k-core model. In [2], Chen et al. propose the backward searching technique to enable early termination. Recently, Bi et al. [1] develop a local search method, which can overcome the deficiency of accessing the whole graph. Li et al. [15] present an I/O-efficient algorithm to compute the top-r influential communities. In [13], authors further investigate the case when each user is associated with multiple weights. However, as observed, these works aim to identify the influential communities for the whole network, while the personalized case has not been considered.

6 Conclusion

In this paper, we investigate the maximal personalized influential community search problem, which is an important tool for many applications, such as personalized friend recommendation, social network advertisement, etc. In order to scale for large networks, two algorithms, i.e., top-down algorithm and bottom-up algorithm, are developed based on different vertex accessing orders. To fulfill the requirement of online searching, an index based method is proposed. Finally, comprehensive experiments are conducted to verify the advantage of developed techniques on 6 real world datasets.

Acknowledgments. Xiaoyang Wang is supported by NSFC61802345. Chen Chen is supported by ZJNSF LQ20F020007.

References

1. Bi, F., Chang, L., Lin, X., Zhang, W.: An optimal and progressive approach to online search of top-k influential communities. VLDB (2018)
2. Chen, S., Wei, R., Popova, D., Thomo, A.: Efficient computation of importance based communities in web-scale networks using a single machine. In: CIKM (2016)
3. Chen, Y., Fang, Y., Cheng, R., Li, Y., Chen, X., Zhang, J.: Exploring communities in large profiled graphs. TKDE **31**, 1624–1629 (2018)
4. Cheng, J., Ke, Y., Chu, S., Özsu, M.T.: Efficient core decomposition in massive networks. In: ICDE (2011)
5. Cheng, J., Ke, Y., Fu, A.W.C., Yu, J.X., Zhu, L.: Finding maximal cliques in massive networks. TODS **36**, 1–34 (2011)
6. Cui, W., Xiao, Y., Wang, H., Wang, W.: Local search of communities in large graphs. In: SIGMOD (2014)
7. Fang, Y., Cheng, R., Luo, S., Hu, J.: Effective community search for large attributed graphs. VLDB **9**, 1233–1244 (2016)
8. Fang, Y., et al.: A survey of community search over big graphs. VLDB J. 1–40 (2019). https://doi.org/10.1007/s00778-019-00556-x
9. Huang, X., Cheng, H., Qin, L., Tian, W., Yu, J.X.: Querying k-truss community in large and dynamic graphs. In: SIGMOD (2014)
10. Huang, X., Lakshmanan, L.V., Xu, J.: Community search over big graphs: models, algorithms, and opportunities. In: ICDE (2017)
11. Huang, X., Lu, W., Lakshmanan, L.V.: Truss decomposition of probabilistic graphs: semantics and algorithms. In: SIGMOD (2016)
12. Khan, B.S., Niazi, M.A.: Network community detection: a review and visual survey. arXiv (2017)
13. Li, R., et al.: Skyline community search in multi-valued networks. In: SIGMOD (2018)
14. Li, R.H., Qin, L., Yu, J.X., Mao, R.: Influential community search in large networks. VLDB **8**, 509–520 (2015)
15. Li, R.-H., Qin, L., Yu, J.X., Mao, R.: Finding influential communities in massive networks. VLDB J. **26**(6), 751–776 (2017). https://doi.org/10.1007/s00778-017-0467-4
16. Parthasarathy, S., Ruan, Y., Satuluri, V.: Community discovery in social networks: applications, methods and emerging trends. In: Aggarwal, C. (ed.) Social Network Data Analytics, pp. 79–113. Springer, Boston (2011). https://doi.org/10.1007/978-1-4419-8462-3_4
17. Sariyüce, A.E., Pinar, A.: Fast hierarchy construction for dense subgraphs. VLDB (2016)
18. Sozio, M., Gionis, A.: The community-search problem and how to plan a successful cocktail party. In: KDD (2010)

19. Yang, B., Wen, D., Qin, L., Zhang, Y., Chang, L., Li, R.: Index-based optimal algorithm for computing k-cores in large uncertain graphs. In: ICDE (2019)
20. Zhu, W., Chen, C., Wang, X., Lin, X.: K-core minimization: an edge manipulation approach. In: CIKM (2018)
21. Zhu, W., Zhang, M., Chen, C., Wang, X., Zhang, F., Lin, X.: Pivotal relationship identification: the k-truss minimization problem. In: Kraus, S. (ed.) IJCAI (2019)

Leveraging Explicit Unsupervised Information for Robust Graph Convolutional Neural Network Learning

Chu Zheng[1,2], Peiyun Wu[1,2], Xiaowang Zhang[1,2(✉)], and Zhiyong Feng[1,2]

[1] College of Intelligence and Computing, Tianjin University, Tianjin 300350, China
xiaowangzhang@tju.edu.cn
[2] State Key Laboratory of Communication Content Cognition, Beijing, China

Abstract. Most existing graph convolutional networks focus on utilizing supervised information for training semi-supervised graph learning. However, the inherent randomness of supervised information can reduce the robustness of graph convolutional network models in some cases. To cope with this problem, in this paper, we propose a novel semi-supervised graph representation learning method RUGCN by leveraging explicit unsupervised information into training. We first propose a practical training method to ensure unsupervised information measurable by preserving both unsupervised (ranking smoothing) and semi-supervised (Laplacian smoothing) information. And then, we introduce a broadcast cross-entropy function to ensure ranking smoothing run in harmony with Laplacian smoothing. Experiments show that RUGCN achieves competitive results and stronger robustness.

Keywords: Social media · Representation learning · Semi-supervised learning · Graph convolutional network

1 Introduction

Semi-supervised graph embedding methods exploit the graph or structure of data and learning with very few labels [1]. The graph convolutional network (GCN)-based model is an import approach of semi-supervised graph embedding and achieves significant improvement on popular benchmarks. The GCN-based models, including GCN [13], graphSAGE network [4], and so on. However, the GCN-based approaches utilize supervised information with paying little attention to the randomness brought by labeled nodes (an example is shown in Fig. 1), which can weaken the robustness of the model. Firstly, labeled nodes in different position passing different levels of supervised information, in some cases, supervised information can be biased or weak for distant unlabeled nodes. Secondly, the position of labeled nodes as data prior knowledge is independent of models. Thus the randomness is inevitable. Finally, most GCN-based approaches only explicitly take supervised information into consideration, which brings the position randomness into models.

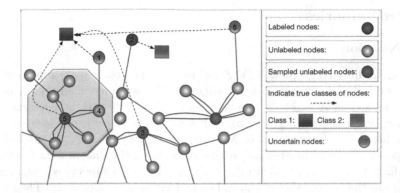

Fig. 1. Suppose nodes in the above graph belong to two classes, and each class has one labeled node in training, i.e., node 2 and one of the uncertain nodes. If we randomly take node 6 as a labeled node, it'll bring the following negative effects. (Color figure online)

To cope with the above limitation in GCN, the key idea of this paper is to explicitly leverage the local semantics of unsupervised information into semi-supervised GCN. This leads us to investigate the connections between semi-supervised and unsupervised graph learning: 1) Most unsupervised graph learning methods are based on consistency prior assumption [2] or label smoothness assumption that adjacent nodes on the graph are more likely to have the same label. The previous proposed semi-supervised graph methods [1] adopt this assumption to regularize models, which is consistent with label smoothness assumption to some extent. 2) A practical strategy proposed by [3], which suggests putting supervised information into a neural network as a plug-in of the unsupervised algorithm, training both unlabeled and labeled data while sharing network parameters. It shows that both semi-supervised and unsupervised information can be trained in a unified framework.

In this paper, based on GCN, we present a novel model *RUGCN*, a robust Graph Convolutional Network for semi-supervised graph embedding. Specifically, in Fig. 1, we sample from the unlabeled nodes to get the blue nodes, and we explicitly maintain each blue node's local semantics(blue line). The contributions of this paper are follows:

- We present a novel practical training method, which makes unsupervised information measurable and simultaneously maintaining both unsupervised and semi-supervised information.
- We introduce a broadcast cross-entropy function to ensure the measured unsupervised information being non-trivial, which first treats the output dimension as a settable parameter and obtains the multi-dimensional node class by utilizing aggregation function.
- Experiments show that RUGCN achieves competitive results, especially in random node classification task.

2   Preliminaries

2.1   Notation

Given an undirected graph $\mathcal{G} = (\mathcal{V}, \mathcal{E})$, where $\mathcal{V} = \{v_1, v_2, \ldots, v_n\}$ represents the vertex set with $|\mathcal{V}| = n$, and $\mathcal{E}$ is the edge set. The symmetric adjacency matrix of $\mathcal{G}$ is defined as $\mathbf{A} \in \mathbb{R}^{n \times n}$ where a_{ij} denotes the edge weight between nodes v_i and v_j, for unweighted graph, $a_{ij} = 1$ if v_i connects to v_j, otherwise $a_{ij} = 0$. We further define feature matrix $\mathbf{X} = \{\mathbf{x}_1, \mathbf{x}_2, \ldots, \mathbf{x}_n\} \in \mathbb{R}^{n \times k}$ where i-th row corresponds to the k-dimensional feature of node v_i, the diagonal degree matrix $\mathbf{D} = \mathrm{diag}\{d_1, d_2, \ldots, d_n\}$ where $d_i = \sum_j a_{ij}$. For simi-supervised learning, $\mathcal{V}_l$ and $\mathcal{V}_u$ are the set of labeled and unlabelled vertices, respectively. The ground truth labels are denoted as $\mathbf{Y}$, and the estimated labels on both labeled and unlabeled vertices are denoted by $\hat{\mathbf{Y}} = \{\hat{\mathbf{Y}}_l, \hat{\mathbf{Y}}_u\} \in \mathbb{R}^{n \times C}$, where C as label class numbers. Our goal is to predict the unknown labels $\mathbf{Y_u}$ in transductive learning.

2.2   Graph Convolutional Network

In our model, we select graph convolution as hidden layer, node feature matrix $\mathbf{X}$ of k-th convolution layer is updated as:

$$\mathbf{X}^{(k)} = \sigma\left(\tilde{\mathbf{D}}^{-\frac{1}{2}}\tilde{\mathbf{A}}\tilde{\mathbf{D}}^{-\frac{1}{2}}\mathbf{X}^{(k-1)}\mathbf{\Theta}\right) \tag{1}$$

where $\tilde{\mathbf{A}} = \mathbf{A} + \mathbf{I}$, $\tilde{\mathbf{D}} = \mathbf{D} + \mathbf{I}$ and $\mathbf{I} = diag\{1\}^n$ is the identity matrix, $\mathbf{\Theta}$ is a trainable parameter matrix and σ represents activation functions. This convolution is essentially a type of Laplacian smoothing [17], thus the main drawback of GCN is over-smoothing, which can lead the features indistinguishable.

3   Methodology

In this section, we explicitly integrate the unsupervised loss into the existing GCNs framework. The overall framework is shown in Fig. 2.

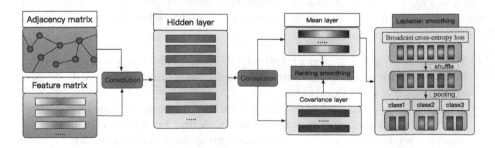

Fig. 2. The network structure of RUGCN.

3.1   Ranking Smoothing

The recently proposed unsupervised Gaussian embedding methods [7,8,11] assume that the target embedding obeys Gaussian distribution. We adopt this idea and calculate the dissimilarity on the top layer of our model, which is similar to graph Laplacian regularization of label propagation algorithms [19]. We denote the top layer output logits as $\mathbf{Z}$, the t-th node output logit $\mathbf{z}_t \sim \mathcal{N}(\mu_t, \Sigma_t)$, where $\mu_t \in \mathbb{R}^D, \Sigma_t \in \mathbb{R}^{D \times D}$ represent the mean vector and covariance matrix, respectively. In other words, $\mathbf{z}_t$ is composed of μ_t and Σ_t.

Dissimilarity. To measure the ranking smoothing between unlabeled node pairs, we choose KL-divergence between two multivariate Gaussian to measure the pair-wise nodes dissimilarities:

$$\mathcal{D}_{KL}(\mathbf{z}_t \| \mathbf{z}_s) = E_{\mathbf{z}_t}\left(\log \frac{\mathbf{z}_t}{\mathbf{z}_s}\right) = \frac{1}{2}\left(\log \frac{\det \Sigma_s}{\det \Sigma_t} - D + tr\left(\Sigma_s^{-1}\Sigma_t\right) + (\mu_s - \mu_t)^T \Sigma_s^{-1}(\mu_s - \mu_t)\right) \tag{2}$$

based on above formula, we define unsupervised loss L_U as follows:

$$L_U = \sum_{(t,s)} \exp\left(\mathcal{D}_{KL}(\mathbf{z}_t \| \mathbf{z}_s)\right), (t, s) \in V_u \tag{3}$$

Sampling. We further parameterize the local ranking scope. We build a subset $\tilde{E}_{uu}$ of E_{uu} to replace the original one:

$$\tilde{E}_{uu}^{(1)} = \{E_{ij}\}, i \in V_u, j \notin V_l, 0 < |N(i)| \leq k \tag{4}$$

where k is a hyperparameter controls the degree of unlabeled nodes.

3.2   Laplacian Smoothing

To avoid the ranking smoothing being trivial, we set up a haperparameter M to keep output dimension D equal to M times the number of label classes C. Thus we have $\mathbf{Z} \in \mathbb{R}^{n \times D}$. Finally, we define the index of each label class based on *shuffle* function and $\hat{\mathbf{Y}}$ formally as follows:

$$\begin{aligned} \text{index}_c &= \textit{Shuffle}(0, 1, ..., |D| - 1), |\text{index}_c| = M, c = 1, 2, ..., C \\ \hat{\mathbf{Y}} &= \text{softmax}(\mathbf{Z}) = \exp(\delta(\mathbf{Z}_{\text{index}_c}))/Z \end{aligned} \tag{5}$$

where δ is a pooling function such as *mean* or *sum* function, Z is a column vector and each element is the corresponding sum of exponential $\mathbf{Z}$. Then we define the final cross-entropy loss over all labeled nodes as:

$$L_X = -\sum_{l \in \hat{\mathbf{Y}}_l} \sum_{c=1}^{C} \hat{\mathbf{Y}}_{lc} \ln \mathbf{Z}_{lc} \tag{6}$$

We treat the output dimensions as a tunable parameter, and we denote above loss function as *broadcast cross-entropy loss*. The overall loss of $RUGCN$ is define as:

$$L = L_X + \alpha * L_U \tag{7}$$

4   Related Works

Unsupervised Learning. DeepWalk [5,6] treats nodes as *words* and random walks as *sentences*, learning embeddings via the prediction of posterior probability between nodes and its neighboring nodes. Yang [18] proves that deepWalk is equivalent to factorize matrix. Some methods are based on ranking, such as LINE [7–9]. Different from the above methods based on local similarity, DGI [12] learns global patch representation via comparing global and local mutual information of embeddings. In summary, these unsupervised learning methods assume local and/or global similarities in data [2].

Semi-supervised Learning. This category includes a majority of GCNs [13, 15]. Most proposed GNNs in existing open-source graph neural network libraries [16] are designed to follow the message-passing architecture, the difference among these GNNs lies in how to design aggregation and update functions, such as spectral graph convolutional neural network [13] and Graph attention neural network [15]. More graph embedding methods can be referred to [10].

5   Experiments

5.1   Experimental Settings

For evaluation, we implement our experiments on three popular citation datasets, namely, CORA [13], Citeseer [1], and Pubmed [13], and an active research fields of authors dataset Coauthor Physics(CPhy) [14]. On each dataset, the research documents are considered as nodes in a graph, their citation relations are considered as edges, and all documents are described by bag-of-words feature vectors. The statistics of all datasets are presented in Table 1. We compare RUGCN performance with four models and two variant models: Label Propagation(LP) [14], a nonparametric model proposed earlier, and we only compare its performance on Planetoid Node Classification. GCN [13], a simple and effective neural network composed of two convolutional layers and has widely used in transductive setting. GAT [15], a multi-head attention-based neural network, which can be applied in both transductive and inductive settings. GraphSAGE [4](GS-mean), an inductive graph learning method which is effective in processing large graphs. GCNNorm, a variant model that denotes the original GCN network structure with the ranking smoothing, we use Euclidean distance as c_2 function to measure the ranking loss. RUGCNOB, a variant model which denotes our proposed RUGCN without broadcast cross-entropy loss, which only uses the traditional cross-entropy.

Table 1. Summary of the datasets.

Dataset	Classes	Features	Nodes	Edges
CORA	7	1,433	2,708	5,278
Citeseer	6	3,703	3,327	4,552
Pubmed	3	500	19,717	44,324
CPhy	5	8,415	34,493	247,962

Table 2. Planetoid split: classification accuracy from 10 random initialization.

Model	CORA	CiteSeer	PubMed
LP	74.4	67.8	70.5
GCN	81.5	70.3	77.8
GAT	81.8	71.4	78.7
GS-mean	76.6	68.6	76.5
GCNNorm	**82.4**	71.9	78.0
RUGCNOB	81.0	70.4	78.5
RUGCN	82.0	**72.1**	**78.8**

Table 3. Random split: classification accuracy from 10 random initialization.

Model	CPhy	Citeseer	Pubmed	CORA
LP	86.6	67.8	70.5	74.4
GCN	92.8	71.9	77.8	81.5
GAT	92.5	71.4	**78.7**	81.8
GS-mean	93.0	71.6	77.4	79.2
GCNNorm	93.2	73.8	78.4	81.8
RUGCNOB	92.5	74.3	78.1	80.5
RUGCN	**93.7**	**75.2**	78.3	**82.4**

5.2   Planetoid Node Classification

In this experiment, we use the fixed data split from Planetoid [7], we adopt the following hyperparameters in this experiment: first hidden layer size is 32 and search trade-off α in $[1, 5, 10]$ for unsupervised information, the learning rate is 0.05, maximal epoch size is 200, weight decay for Adam optimizer is 0.0005, negative slope for Leaky-ReLU is 0.2, we search M in $[2, 5, 10, 15, 20]$, and the degree threshold is $k = 999$. As shown in Table 2, we can see that RUGCN outperforms on Citeseer and PubMed datasets (improve over original GCN by 2.6% and 1.3%), and also perform better than RUGCNOB (improve over CiteSeer by 2.4%), it illustrates the effectiveness of our proposed broadcast cross-entropy loss. GCNNorm achieves the best result on CORA (improve over original GCN by 1.1%). Both GCNNorm and RUGCN achieve better results, while GCNNorm gets the best results on CORA, which shows that the effect of using different methods to measure unsupervised information is various.

5.3   Random Node Classification

To verify the robustness of the model against unbalanced supervised information, we follow the classification method in [14]. In Table 3, GCNNorm also performs better than the original GCN (the highest is 2.6% higher than the original GCN on Citeseer). Compared with the results in Planetoid Node Classification, RUGCNOB and RUGCN both improve better accuracy than original GCN, the main reason being that we use more unlabeled nodes into our ranking smoothing procedure, leading to the better exploitation of unsupervised information and robustness of models in the transductive setting. Although RUGCN has great performance, the GAT is better than RUGCN in PubMed, the main reason may that the attention mechanisms allow the GAT to adjust the message propagation automatically. However, GAT also lacks the interpretation of data.

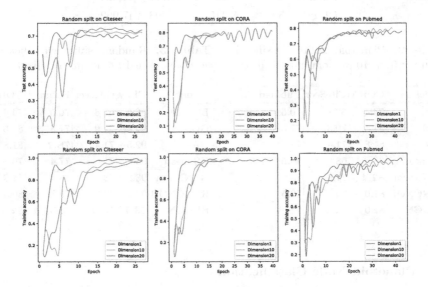

Fig. 3. The training and test accuracy of each epoch in different dimensions.

5.4 Accuracy Analysis of Broadcast Cross-Entropy

To evaluate our broadcast cross-entropy loss function is effective, we select the labeled samples that result in a bad performance in the second classification task. We fix the random seed of this sampling to keep the result of each training is same. We set the number of early-stopping as 10, and only the parameter M can change. Figure 3 shows the accuracy of each epoch with different dimensions M, where $M = 1$ means we use the traditional cross entropy-function, otherwise representing the broadcast cross-entropy function in different parameters. As shown in Fig. 3, the main noticeable fact is that high training accuracy does not mean good generalization. The training accuracy quickly reaches the maximum and becomes flat on dimension 1, which also higher than training accuracy on other dimensions, but the corresponding test accuracy is always not the best result. Besides, when the dimension is 10 or 20, the training accuracy is always under the unsaturated state. In contrast, the test accuracy can reach the highest peak. This also verifies that the proposed broadcast cross-entropy loss can avoid training over-fitting and keep generalization.

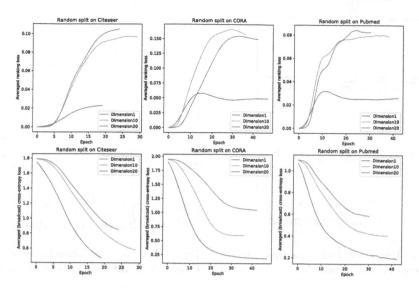

Fig. 4. The supervised loss (broadcast cross-entropy loss) and unsupervised loss (ranking loss) of each epoch in different dimensions.

5.5   Supervised and Unsupervised Loss of RUGCN

We further analyze supervised loss (broadcast cross-entropy loss) and unsupervised loss (ranking loss) of RUGCN in different dimensions, which is shown in Fig. 4, here we set the trade-off parameter as 1 for all datasets. From Fig. 4, we can observe that the curve changes in three data sets tend to be consistent. In the upper three graphs, when we increase the dimension, unsupervised loss increases, and RUGCN needs more epoch for convergence. It illustrates that a higher dimension can enhance the strength of ranking part in RUGCN, and the ranking procedure also extends the time of reaching a steady-state of RUGCN. In the below three graphs, when we increase the dimension, supervised loss is increasing, and became slower gradually. It indicates that supervised and unsupervised loss complement each other in training, resulting in RUGCN not totally rely on supervised loss and alleviate the randomness brought by supervised information.

5.6   Uncertainty and Class-Correlation Visualization

Uncertainty Analysis. In this experiment, we analyze the uncertainty (variance embeddings) of RUGCN, which is shown in Fig. 5. Experimental setting is followed by [8]. Overall, the curves of node variances increase as the log10 degree of nodes (x-axis) increases in CORA and CPhy, this trend of Pubmed is the opposite. Meanwhile, RUGCN's performance increases higher on CORA and CPhy than Pubmed, which indicates the variance embeddings of high degree nodes carry more uncertainties. And the complex connectivity of different datasets shows a different influence on the ranking part of RUGCN.

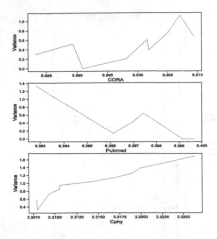

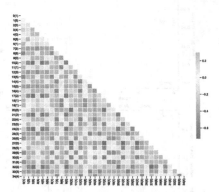

Fig. 5. Uncertainty analysis from randomness classification.

Fig. 6. Pearson correlation heatmap on CORA from randomness classification.

Class-Correlation Analysis. The class-correlation is shown in Fig. 6. We set the $M = 5$, and the CORA have seven classes, resulting in the dimension of node embeddings is 35. The axes represent the predefined class label for each dimension (e.g., 34(9) represents the class 9 of dimension 34). We notice that dimensions that belong to the same class are positively correlated with each other. It illustrates that the class information-passing is reliable, and the RUGCN can well maintain both unsupervised (ranking smoothing) and semi-supervised information (Laplacian smoothing).

6   Conclusions

In this paper, we leverage explicit unsupervised information to improve the robustness of GCN-based semi-supervised learning. Our approach provides a new method of utilizing unsupervised information such as local semantics of unlabelled nodes to optimize semi-supervised learning and a new variant of cross-entropy function. Though RUGCN takes advantage of local semantics of unlabeled nodes, the complex connectivity of unlabeled nodes can still affect the performance of RUGCN. In future work, we will explore the effectiveness of collective semantics of labeled and unlabeled nodes.

Acknowledgments. This work is supported by the National Key Research and Development Program of China (2017YFC0908401) and the National Natural Science Foundation of China (61972455,61672377).

References

1. Sen, P., Namata, G., Bilgic, M., Getoor, L., Gallagher, B., Eliassi-Rad, T.: Collective classification in network data. AI Mag. **29**(3), 93–106 (2008)

2. Zhou, D., Bousquet, O., Lal, T.N., Weston, J., Schölkopf, B.: Learning with local and global consistency. In: NIPS, pp. 321–328 (2003)
3. Weston, J., Ratle, F., Collobert, R.: Deep learning via semi-supervised embedding. In: ICML, pp. 1168–1175 (2008)
4. Hamilton, W.L., Ying, Z., Leskovec, J.: Inductive representation learning on large graphs. In: NIPS, pp. 1024–1034 (2017)
5. Perozzi, B., Al-Rfou, R., Skiena, S.: DeepWalk: online learning of social representations. In: KDD, pp. 701–710 (2014)
6. Grover, A., Leskovec, J.: node2vec: scalable feature learning for networks. In: KDD, pp. 855–864 (2016)
7. Bojchevski, A., Günnemann, S.: Deep gaussian embedding of attributed graphs: unsupervised inductive. CoRR abs/1707.03815 (2017)
8. Zhu, D., Cui, P., Wang, D., Zhu, W.: Deep variational network embedding in Wasserstein space. In: KDD, pp. 2827–2836 (2018)
9. Tang, J., Qu, M., Wang, M., Zhang, M., Yan, J., Mei, Q.: LINE: large-scale information network embedding. In: WWW, pp. 1067–1077 (2015)
10. Cai, H., Zheng, V.M., Chang, K.C.C.: A comprehensive survey of graph embedding: Problems, techniques, and applications. IEEE Trans. Knowl. Data Eng. 30(9), 1616–1637 (2018)
11. He, S., Liu, K., Ji, G., Zhao, J.: Learning to represent knowledge graphs with gaussian embedding. In: CIKM, pp. 623–632 (2015)
12. Veličković, P., Fedus, W., Hamilton, W.L., Liò, P., Bengio, Y., Hjelm, R.D.: Deep graph infomax. CoRR abs/1809.10341 (2018)
13. Kipf, T.N., Welling, M.: Semi-supervised classification with graph convolutional networks. CoRR abs/1609.02907 (2016)
14. Shchur, O., Mumme, M., Bojchevski, A., Günnemann, S.: Pitfalls of graph neural network evaluation. CoRR abs/1811.05868 (2018)
15. Velickovic, P., Cucurull, G., Casanova, A., Romero, A., Liò, P., Bengio, Y.: Graph Attention Networks. CoRR abs/1710.10903 (2017)
16. Fey, M., Lenssen, J.E.: Fast graph representation learning with pyTorch geometric. CoRR abs/1903.02428 (2019)
17. Li, Q., Han, Z., Wu, X.: Deeper insights into graph convolutional networks for semi-supervised learning. In: AAAI, pp. 3538–3545 (2018)
18. Yang, C., Liu, Z., Zhao, D., Sun, M., Chang, E.: Network representation learning with rich text information. In: IJCAI, pp. 2111–2117 (2015)
19. Chapelle, O., Scholkopf, B., Zien, A.: Semi-supervised Learning. MIT Press, Cambridge (2006)

Content Sharing Prediction for Device-to-Device (D2D)-based Offline Mobile Social Networks by Network Representation Learning

Qing Zhang[1], Xiaoxu Ren[1], Yifan Cao[1], Hengda Zhang[1], Xiaofei Wang[1(✉)], and Victor Leung[2]

[1] College of Intelligence and Computing, Tianjin University, Tianjin, China
{qingzhang,xiaoxuren,yifancao,hengdazhang,xiaofeiwang}@tju.edu.cn
[2] The University of British Columbia,
2329 West Mall, Vancouver, B.C. V6T 1Z4, Canada
vleung@ece.ubc.ca

Abstract. With the explosion of cellular data, the content sharing in proximity among offline Mobile Social Networks (MSNs) has received significant attention. It is necessary to understand the face-to-face (e.g. Device-to-Device, D2D) social network structure and to predict content propagation precisely, which can be conducted by learning the low-dimensional embedding of the network nodes, called Network Representation Learning (NRL). However, most existing NRL models consider each edge as a binary or continuous value, neglecting rich information between nodes. Besides, many traditional models are almost based on small-scale datasets or online Internet services, severely confining their applications in D2D scenarios. Therefore, we propose **ResNel**, a RESCAL-based network representation learning model, which aims to regard the multi-dimensional relations as a probability in third-order (3D) tensor space and achieve more accurate predictions for both discovered and undiscovered relations in the D2D social network. Specifically, we consider the Global Positioning System (GPS) information as a critical relation slice to avoid the loss of potential information. Experiments on a realistic large-scale D2D dataset corroborate the advantages of improving forecast accuracy.

Keywords: Content sharing prediction · Network representation learning · Mobile social networks · Device-to-Device (D2D) · Relation network

1 Introduction

Social Network Analysis (SNA) has been pervasive as a means of understanding network structure recently. Network Representation Learning (NRL) can convert

X. Wang et al. (Eds.): APWeb-WAIM 2020, LNCS 12317, pp. 112–126, 2020.
https://doi.org/10.1007/978-3-030-60259-8_9

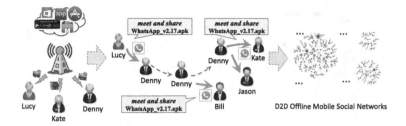

Fig. 1. Content sharing in D2D offline MSNs [23].

social network characteristics into low-dimensional vectors for vertex classification [4], clustering [1] and link prediction [8].

The top 10% videos in YouTube account for around 80% of all the views [3], implying the fact that retransmission of the same files induces network resources wasted. Device-to-Device (D2D) communication is a promising method to cache and share the multimedia contents via short-range communication technologies (e.g. Wi-Fi and Bluetooth) [6,17,19,21], which reduces the repeated downloads and alleviates the backbone traffic pressure [11]. Figure 1 shows representative sharing. Lucy has a WhatsApp installed on her device initially, and then she can share it with her friend Denny via the D2D link. As such, Denny can share with anyone nearby. Hence, D2D Mobile Social Networks (MSNs) come into being. It is noteworthy that each transmission during D2D communication is precious and hard-won because the content is pressing and is shared based on interest and friendship [18]. Thereby, link prediction, also called Content Sharing Prediction (CSP) in realistic offline MSNs is essential and valuable.

Some NRL models explore the link prediction problem from the local network structure. However, the majority of them are conducted on online networks and barely consider various interactions (e.g. content types, sharing time, and geographical information.) or just regard the relation as a binary or continuous value between users (**Challenge 1**). On the other hand, a few studies involving edge relations still exist imprecise separations of correct links and malicious links (**Challenge 2**).

In this paper, We propose ResNel to improve CSP accuracy with the third-order (3D) probability-scored tensor factorization based on social multi-relational embeddings. Due to the location characteristics of D2D communication, we develop a specific relation slice called *Global Positioning System* (GPS). As a result, the sharing-based relation triple can be represented as a 3D tensor, wherein a sender links to a receiver through relations containing App types and GPS, shown in Fig. 2. This paper makes the following contributions:

- To the best of our knowledge, it is a prior work to extend the multi-dimensional relations between users into probability rather than the binary value in a 3D tensor space based on network structures of a real-world large-scale D2D data set.

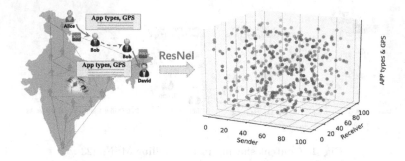

Fig. 2. Illustration of the proposed embedding ResNel from D2D sharing-based MSNs to third-order (3D) tensor space.

- We consider GPS as a critical slice, which can avoid the loss of potential information, separate the true and false triples accurately, as well as detect missing links or forecast the future links in offline MSNs effectively.
- Compared to other state-of-the-art models, experimental results on the real show the better performance of ResNel, with **3–7 times** enhancement in terms of MRR as well as **5.2 times** for mean Hits@k.

2   Related Work

2.1   Network Representation Learning Based on Network Structure

The word vector representation model based on network structure, represented by word2vec model, lately has set off a wave in the area of representation learning, which inspires the research of NRL as well. DeepWalk [10], the first proposed node vectorization model based on the Word2vec, imitates the text generation process via the random walk path. Others, such as node2vec [5] and SDNE [16], tend to learn embeddings of network vertices based on the local network structure. However, they do not adequately consider the rich semantic information over edges but merely regard the single relation as a binary number or a continuous value in the networks, which may lead to the loss of vast potential information. Besides, they conduct their analysis almost on online datasets derived from some popular social networking sites with restricted relations, such as click rate, interest sharing, and retweets. In contrast, some unique edge information, such as GPS or user mobility [12], is seldom considered.

2.2   Link Predictions Based on Relation Extraction

Relation extraction (RE) recent years has been a significant task to enrich Knowledge graph (KG) [7]. Knowledge Representation Learning (KRL), as a crucial method used for RE, maps nodes (entities) or edges (relations) in KG into low-dimensional vector spaces, which is favourable to construction, reasoning and application in Web-scale knowledge bases (KBs). TransE [2], as a widely-used method in KRL, considers the relation in each triple (head, relation, tail) as a translation from the head entity to tail entity. Cunchao Tu et al. [14], considering the text interactions between vertices in social networks, propose a translation-based social relation extraction model (TransNet). TransLink [24] jointly embeds both users and interactive behaviours into a unified low-dimension space. However, both of the transitive models are not fully expressive due to the absolute contradiction imposed on different relation types. Thus, it is necessary to consider the multi-dimensional relations between users.

3 Preliminaries

3.1 Definitions

Definition 1 (Knowledge Network Graph). *Given a directed graph* $\mathcal{G} = \{V_H, E, V_T\}$, *where* $V = V_H \cup V_T$ *is the set of vertices (entities),* V_H *represents the head entity, while* V_T *signifies tail entity. And* $E \subseteq V \times V$ *is the set of edges (relations). We define* $\mathcal{G}$ *be the knowledge network graph (KNG).*

Definition 2 (Social Network Graph). *Given a directed graph* $G = \{V, E\}$, *where* V *is the set of vertices (users) and* $E \subseteq V \times V$ *is the set of edges (various interactions). Besides, the edges in* E *are either labeled as* E_L *(discovered relations) or* E_P *(undiscovered relations), thus existing* $E = E_L + E_P$. *We define* G *be the Social Network Graph (SNG).*

3.2 Multi-relational Prediction Model Based on the Binary Tensor

The Construction of Relational Tensors. The KNG $\mathcal{G}$, with n entities and m relationships, can be represented by a 3D tensor $\mathcal{X} \in \mathbb{R}^{n \times n \times m}$, where the value of a triple represented by the indices (i, j, k) in tensor X is given by the cell x_{ijk}. The scoring scheme is defined as follows:

- The tensor element value is 1 when the relational fact is true, and 0 or -1 otherwise, i.e., $x_{ijk} \in \{0, 1\}$, or $x_{ijk} \in \{-1, 1\}$; $\forall i, j, k$.

Relational Reasoning Based on Knowledge Representation. To perform collective learning on multi-relational data, RESCAL [9] decomposes a tensor into a factor matrix $\mathbf{A} \in \mathbb{R}^{n \times r}$ and a core tensor $\mathcal{W} \in \mathbb{R}^{r \times r \times m}$, where r is the number of latent factors. Note that the k-th slice of the tensor contains k relations among entities, denoted as $\mathbf{X}_k$ and approximately expressed as the following equation by decomposition:

$$\mathbf{X}_k \approx \mathbf{A}\mathbf{W}_k\mathbf{A}^\mathrm{T}, for \ k = 1, \cdots, m. \tag{1}$$

The factor matrices $\mathbf{A}$ and $\mathbf{W}_k$ can be computed by solving the regularized minimization problem,

$$\min_{\mathbf{A},\mathbf{W}_k} \frac{1}{2}\left(\sum_k \parallel \mathbf{X}_k - \mathbf{A}\mathbf{W}_k\mathbf{A}^{\mathrm{T}} \parallel_{\mathrm{F}}^2 + \lambda(\parallel \mathbf{A} \parallel_{\mathrm{F}}^2 + \sum_k \parallel \mathbf{W}_k \parallel_{\mathrm{F}}^2)\right). \tag{2}$$

We use the alternating least-squares (ALS) approach to improve the computational efficiency of (2). Thus the factor matrices $\mathbf{A}$ and $\mathbf{W}_k$ are given by

$$\mathbf{A} \leftarrow [\sum_{k=1}^{m} \mathbf{X}_k\mathbf{A}\mathbf{W}_k^{\mathrm{T}} + \mathbf{X}_k^{\mathrm{T}}\mathbf{A}\mathbf{W}_k][\sum_{k=1}^{m} \mathbf{B}_k + \mathbf{C}_k + \lambda\mathbf{I}]^{-1}, \tag{3}$$

where $\mathbf{B}_k = \mathbf{W}_k\mathbf{A}^{\mathrm{T}}\mathbf{A}\mathbf{W}_k^{\mathrm{T}}, \mathbf{C}_k = \mathbf{W}_k^{\mathrm{T}}\mathbf{A}^{\mathrm{T}}\mathbf{A}\mathbf{W}_k$, and $\mathbf{R}_k \leftarrow ((\mathbf{A} \otimes \mathbf{A})^{\mathrm{T}}(\mathbf{A} \otimes \mathbf{A}) + \lambda\mathbf{I})^{-1}(\mathbf{A} \otimes \mathbf{A})vec(\mathbf{X}_k)$, $\otimes$ is the Kronecker product.

4 Proposed Method

4.1 Multi-relational Prediction Model Based on the Probability-Scored Tensor

The edge in KNG is usually simplified as a binary or a continuous value, which is not enough to present comprehensive edge information. In this work, we use the interactions between vertices to infer richer potential information.

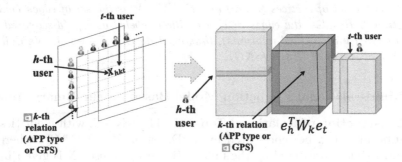

Fig. 3. Tensor decomposition of the relation tensor X.

We redefine SNG by dividing user set V into head user (sender) and tail user (receiver) ($G = \{V_H, E, V_T\}$). The relation measures prediction $r(h,t)$ is generalized by the logistic function:

$$\mathbf{P}_{htk} = \sigma(\varphi(h,t,k)), \tag{4}$$

where $\sigma(x) = \frac{1}{1+e^{-x}}$. $\mathbf{P}_{htk} = x_{ijk}$ corresponds to the valid probability when the relation $r(h,t)$ is true (e.g. $\mathbf{P}_{htk} = P(\mathcal{Y}_{htk} = 1)$). And $\varphi(h,t,k)$ is the scoring function. And we can forecast the probabilities of both discovered and undiscovered triples as follows:

– The tensor element x_{ijk} represents the probability that the fact is 1, i.e., $x_{ijk} \in [0,1]$; $\forall i,j,k$.

4.2   ResNel: RESCAL-based Social NRL Model

Model Foundation. ResNel is proposed based on the probability tensor factorization. According to the observed relation k between entity h and t. We model the scoring function as follows:

$$\varphi(h, t, k) = e_h^T \mathbf{W}_k e_t. \tag{5}$$

Figure 3 models the user multi-dimensional interactions (various APP types and GPS information) in 3D tensor spaces in detail.

Model Solution. Stochastic Gradient Descent (SGD) with mini-batches and AdaGrad are used by minimizing the negative log-likelihood loss function with L_2 regularization on the embeddings of the considered model:

$$\min_{e_h, \mathbf{W}_k, e_t} \sum_{r(h,t) \in \Gamma} f(e_h, \mathbf{W}_k, e_t) + g(e_h, \mathbf{W}_k, e_t), \tag{6}$$

where $f(e_h, \mathbf{W}_k, e_t) = log(1 + exp(-\mathbf{Y}_{htk}\varphi(h, t, k)))$, and $g(e_h, \mathbf{W}_k, e_t) = \lambda(\| e_h \|_2^2 + \| \mathbf{W}_k \|_F^2 + \| e_t \|_2^2)$.

Let λ denote the regularization coefficient and Γ as the training set, rewrite the problem (6) as

$$\Upsilon(\Gamma) = \sum_{r(h,t) \in \Gamma} f(e_h, \mathbf{W}_k, e_t) + g(e_h, \mathbf{W}_k, e_t). \tag{7}$$

We use SGD to solve the problem $f(e_h, \mathbf{W}_k, e_t)$, and the gradients of the scoring function are shown as follows:

$$\begin{aligned}
\nabla_{e_h}\varphi(h, t, k) &= \mathbf{W}_k e_t, \\
\nabla_{\mathbf{W}_k}\varphi(h, t, k) &= e_h e_t^T, \\
\nabla_{e_t}\varphi(h, t, k) &= \mathbf{W}_k^T e_h.
\end{aligned} \tag{8}$$

Therefore, we can finally write the gradient of these parameters for one triple $r(h, t)$. The optimization with respect to embeddings in $\Upsilon(\Gamma)$ can be written as:

$$\begin{aligned}
\nabla_{e_h}\Upsilon(r(h, t)) &= -\mathbf{Y}_{htk}\varphi(h, t, k)\sigma(\mathbf{W}_k e_t) + 2\lambda e_h, \\
\nabla_{\mathbf{W}_k}\Upsilon(r(h, t)) &= -\mathbf{Y}_{htk}\varphi(h, t, k)\sigma(e_h e_t^T) + 2\lambda \mathbf{W}_k, \\
\nabla_{e_t}\Upsilon(r(h, t)) &= -\mathbf{Y}_{htk}\varphi(h, t, k)\sigma(\mathbf{W}_k^T e_h) + 2\lambda e_t.
\end{aligned} \tag{9}$$

Notably, we discuss the SGD for this scoring function in Algorithm 1. If Γ only contains positive triples, we generate η negative triples per positive train triple by corrupting either the head entity or the tail entity of the positive triple, which can be referred to [13], and Λ corresponds to the embeddings $e_h, \mathbf{W}_r, e_t$. Algorithm 1 firstly forms the random entities and relation embeddings of social networks. Then we generate samples, including negative and positive triples. To accurately address the optimal solution, the gradient for parameters Λ is conducted iteratively (lines 3–5). The AdaGrad is used to update the learning

Algorithm 1. SGD for the Social Multi-relational
Prediction Model

Input: Train set Γ, Validation set Γ_v, learning rate α,
embedding dimension k, regularization parameters λ,
negative ratio η, batch size b, max iter m, stopping s.
$\quad e_i \leftarrow randn(k)$, for each $i \in \mathbf{E}$;
$\quad \mathbf{W}_i \leftarrow randn(k, k)$, for each $i \in \mathbf{V}$;
Output: The entities and the relation embeddings e_h,

1.   **for** $i = 1, \cdots, m$ **do**
2. $\quad$ **for** $j = 1, \cdots, |\Gamma|/b$ **do**
3. $\quad\quad$ $\Gamma_b \leftarrow sample(\Gamma, b, \eta)$
4. $\quad\quad$ Update embeddings w.r.t.:
5. $\quad\quad$ $\sum_{r(h,t) \in \Gamma_b} \nabla \Upsilon(r(h,t); \Lambda)$
6. $\quad\quad$ Update learning rate α using AdaGrad
7. $\quad$ **end for**
8. $\quad$ **if** $i \mod s = 0$ **then**
9. $\quad\quad$ **break if MRR** on Γ decreased
10. $\quad$ **end if**
11.   **end for**

---

rate α (line 6). Because the optimization problem is to model the relationship between entities, we can easily quantify the relationship in social networks as a slice and add it to the tensor for the subsequent solution.

A tensor decomposition model is considered to be fully expressed if there exists an embedding of both entities and relationships for any real triples. As a result, we can accurately separate true triples and false triples. Because of the certain contradiction imposed on different relation types, we establish a bound (i.e. the rank of decomposition) with the embedding dimension of entities to ensure that our model is fully expressive by Theorem 1.

Theorem 1. *Given any ground truth over a set of entities* $\mathbf{E}$ *and relations* $\mathbf{V}$, *there exists a ResNel model with n-dimensional head and tail entity embeddings of dimensionality* $n = r$ *and* $r \times r$ *relation embeddings, where n is the number of entities, which accurately represents that ground truth.*

Proof. Let $\mathbf{e_h}$ and $\mathbf{e_t}$ be the n-dimensional one-hot binary vector representations of heal entity e_h and tail entity e_t respectively. For each head entity $e_h^{(i)}$, tail entity $e_t^{(j)}$, as well as relation $r^{(k)}$, we let the i-th and j-th element respectively represent the related vectors e_h and e_t be 1, all other elements 0. Further, if the relation between (e_h, e_t) is true and 0 otherwise, we will set the ij element of the matrix $\mathbf{W} \in \mathbb{R}^{r \times r}$ to 1. Thus the tensor products of these entity embeddings and the relation embedding can accurately represent the original tensor after applying the logistic sigmoid. $\square$

5   Data Preprocessing

We conduct the experiment on the realistic large-scale offline user transmission data set from *Xender*, one of the world's leading mobile APPs for D2D contents sharing [20]. In the dataset, user behaviors contain 9 columns (FileType, MD5, SenderID, ReceiverID, TimeStamp, UserIP, Country, GPS, FilesSize), we select the three most valuable items of which as <APP name, sender, receiver> in 01/08/2016 to conduct our experimental data trace.

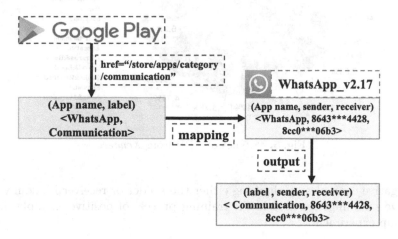

Fig. 4. APP relation tagging from Google Play Store.

5.1   APP Relation Labels and Metadata

In order to accurately predict users' interests sharing and make interest recommendations broadly, we crawl all of the APPs' name and the category in which they fall as their label from Google Play, noting that each different APP corresponds to only one label. Then we match the crawled data table in the form of <APP name, label> properties each row with the experimental data table, converting the APP name to the corrected label. Taking the WhatsApp APP as an example, Fig. 4 shows the process of tagging in detail. The App named WhatsApp is substituted by the Communication relation label after mapping, thus generating the metadata of our experiment, called **Xender-filtered**.

In our experiment, the *Xender*-filtered data set consists of 64,028 transmissions between 72,550 users with 48 relation labels related to APP types. It is worth mentioning that ResNel particularly takes *geographic cosine similarity* [20] into account, which is used as the 49th label in our trail. Specifically, in order to better investigate the labels, we depict the whole 48 types of labels for APP, where the top two are Communication and Tools, shown in Fig. 5.

Considering there are only positive triples in our data set, we generate negative triples based on *local closed-world assumption* [2]. In this way, we can

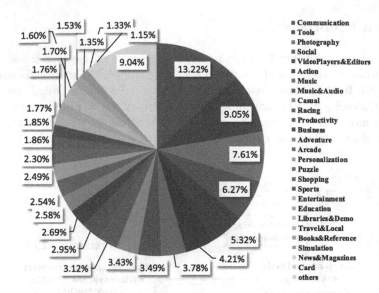

Fig. 5. 48 types of APP from *Xender*.

get negative examples by changing either the sender or receiver randomly. The negative samplings are used in the training process of positive examples in the follow-up experiment.

5.2   DBSCAN Clustering and Geographic Cosine Similarity

Unlike online relations, the content sharing of offline MSNs is limited by geographic positions and always follows the principle of homogeneity. Considering that the actual motion of each user is ranging other than a single point with the diversity of the geographical location in the real world, we use DBSCAN [22] to cluster the users' geographical information. The clusters are then used as feature vectors of the vertices to calculate *geographic cosine similarity* between user pairs. Considering the impact of the latitude, longitude and sample numbers in the cluster, we leverage the scan radius value of 0.05 with the minimum sample number is 1. Thus, we clustered 64,028 transmissions into 5590 clusters. The result of clustering is shown in Fig. 6(a).

Since the geographic similarity of all users is sparse, we select some active user pairs to observe the distribution of geographic similarity. It can be clearly seen from Fig. 6(b) that the geographical locations of active users are always similar, with more than 70% of users having cosine similarities above 0.7, which also manifests that geographical factor has a significant impact on the offline transmission. Therefore, *geographic cosine similarity* is used as the critical relation slice between vertices (users) among the 3D tensor space in ResNel to improve the accuracy of transmission prediction.

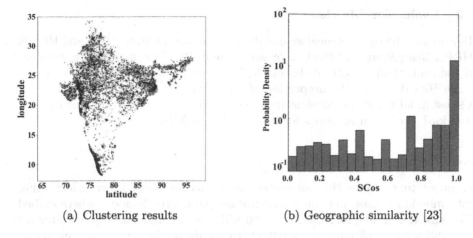

(a) Clustering results   (b) Geographic similarity [23]

Fig. 6. Preprocessing results of location relation.

6 Experiment

We experiment on *Xender*-filtered data set. Compared to a bunch of state-of-the-art models, ResNel not only takes full advantage of the semantic relation between entities but also is fully expressive.

6.1 Baselines

In order to validate the performance of our model, we compare it with some KRL and NRL models:

- **RESCAL** [15] It performs collective learning via the underlying components of the model and provides an efficient algorithm for computing the 3D tensor decomposition.
- **TransNet** [14] It regards the interaction between vertices as a translation operation and formalizes the task of Social Relation Extraction (SRE) to evaluate the capability of NRL method on modelling the relations between vertices.
- **Deepwalk** [10] It receives n-dimensional node embeddings by performing random walks to generate random walk sequences and then employs Skip-Gram to learn node representation.

6.2 Parameter Settings

For ResNel, we use SGD as our optimizer to train embeddings. Concerning hyperparameters, we set the initial learning rate is 0.5, which is tuned at runtime with AdaGrad later. Meanwhile, we try varying the batch size similar to [13], but it makes no difference to the results. Without loss of generality, we deal with 100 batches each epoch, and the ratio of negatives generated every positive training triple is 1.

6.3   Evaluation Metrics

To evaluate the performance, we mainly focus on two metrics: MRR and Hits@k. MRR (*Mean Reciprocal Rank*) represents the mean of the sum of the reciprocal of the rank of all correct labels, and higher value indicates better performance, while Hits@k means the proportion of correct labels ranked in the top k and a substantial value is equivalent to a better effect likewise. All of them are the standard evaluation measures for both KRL and NRL.

6.4   Parameter Sensitivity

In order to evaluate the parameter sensitivity of ResNel, we select different embedding sizes and the regularization parameter lambda, where embedding size ranges in $\{20, 25, 30, 35, 40, 50, 60\}$, and regularization parameter $\lambda \in \{0.1, 0.2, 0.3, 0.4, 0.5, 0.6, 0.7, 0.8, 0.9, 1\}$, to obtain the best hyper-parameters.

Figure 7 shows the evaluation results with the change of regularization parameter lambda and embedding size. As we can see from the left part of Fig. 7, when the regularization parameter lambda changes from 0.1 to 1, the MRR and Hits@k value increase sharply, and then the curve flattens out, which is similar to the trend of the evaluation results with the change of embedding size in the right part of Fig. 7. According to experimental results, we fundamentally conclude that the performance of the ResNel model is best when $\lambda \geq 0.4$, embedding size ≥ 40 meanwhile.

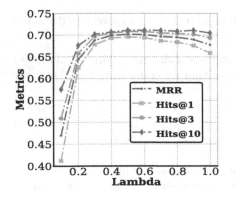 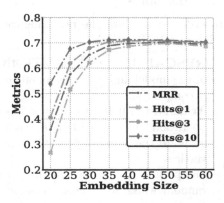

Fig. 7. Parameter sensitivity.

6.5   Experiment Results and Analysis

Figure 8 unfolds a clear comparison between our proposed ResNel and all the baselines in terms of the CSP results with various evaluation metrics. We can see that ResNel achieves remarkable and fantastic improvements than all the baselines.

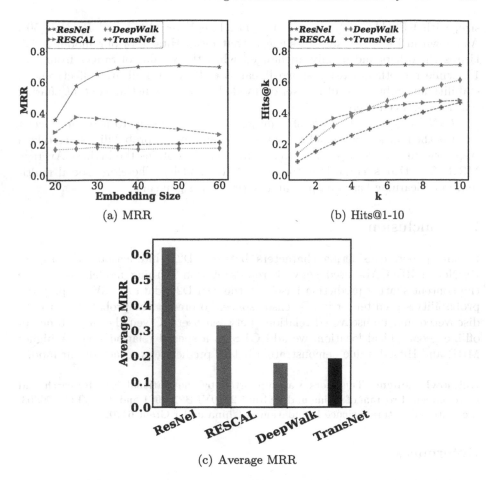

(a) MRR

(b) Hits@1-10

(c) Average MRR

Fig. 8. Evaluation results on *Xender*-filtered data set.

As we can see clearly from Fig. 8(a), MRR of our model keeps linearly growing when embedding size <40 and converges when embedding size ≥40, while baselines have no apparent changes. Furthermore, the best MRR of ResNel attains **0.704** at **50** embedding size, which is a good confirmation of the previous parameter sensitivity settings. Moreover, all NRL models perform poorly on relation prediction task among different indexes on account of ignoring of rich semantic information over edges when representing the structure information of vertexes. Oppositely, ResNel and RESCAL achieve satisfactory results over MRR, which is aligned with a key of taking the details on edges into consideration. In contrast with ResNel, RESCAL also has poor performance on MRR with 12% to 24% categorically lower than ResNel since it only considers a single label on the edge every time, which may be consistent with the situation in KG.

Besides, we make a comparison among Hits@1 to Hits@10 under the condition that all of the contrast models and ResNel keep their best embedding size, with RESCAL (50), TransNet (100), DeepWalk (128), and ResNel (50). As shown in Fig. 8(b), we can suggest that mean Hits@k of our model is **5.2 times** the others and mainly unchanged when the k value of ranges from 1 to 10, while the others exist a sharp linear rise. It richly indicates effectiveness, stability and robustness of ResNel on modelling and predicting content sharing relations between users.

ResNel can avoid the loss of a majority of relations up to a point since it regards the multi-dimensional relations between users as probabilities. To take a step forward, Fig. 8(c) plainly reveals that ResNel obtains the highest Average MRR (**2–6 times** as much as the other NRL models). Therefore, social multi-relational learning based on probability tensor is significant.

7   Conclusion

In this paper, considering characters between D2D interaction, we propose ResNel, a RESCAL-based network representation learning model, to explore the content sharing prediction based on the real D2D data set. We employ the probability-scored tensor in 3D tensor spaces to predict the probability of both discovered and undiscovered relations between users. Given the importance of offline geographical location, we add GPS as a special relation slice. A higher MRR and Hits@k value demonstrate a better predictive accuracy of our model.

Acknowledgment. This work was supported by the National Key Research and Development Program of China under Grant 2019YFB2101901 and 2018YFC0809803, the National Natural Science Foundation of China under Grant 61702364.

References

1. Bedi, P., Sharma, C.: Community detection in social networks. Wiley Interdisc. Rev.: Data Mining Knowl. Disc. **6**(3), 115–135 (2016). https://doi.org/10.1002/widm.1178
2. Bordes, A., Usunier, N., Garcia-Duran, A., Weston, J., Yakhnenko, O.: Translating embeddings for modeling multi-relational data. In: Burges, C.J.C., Bottou, L., Ghahramani, Z., Weinberger, K.Q. (eds.) Advances in Neural Information Processing Systems, pp. 2787–2795 (2013)
3. Cha, M., Kwak, H., Rodriguez, P., Ahn, Y.Y., Moon, S.: I tube, you tube, everybody tubes: analyzing the world's largest user generated content video system. In: Dovrolis, C., Roughan, M. (eds.) Proceedings of the 7th ACM SIGCOMM Conference on Internet Measurement, pp. 1–14. ACM (2007). https://doi.org/10.1145/1298306.1298309
4. Chen, L., Shen, C., Vogelstein, J.T., Priebe, C.E.: Robust vertex classification. IEEE Trans. Pattern Anal. Mach. Intell. **38**(3), 578–590 (2015). https://doi.org/10.1109/TPAMI.2015.2456913
5. Grover, A., Leskovec, J.: node2vec: scalable feature learning for networks. In: Macskassy, S.A., Perlich, C., Leskovec, J., Wang, W., Ghani, R. (eds.) Proceedings of the 22nd ACM SIGKDD International Conference on Knowledge Discovery and Data Mining, pp. 855–864. ACM (2016). https://doi.org/10.1145/2939672.2939754

6. Han, Y., Wang, X., Leung, V., Niyato, D., Yan, X., Chen, X.: Convergence of edge computing and deep learning: A comprehensive survey. arXiv preprint arXiv:1907.08349 abs/1907.08349 (2020). https://doi.org/10.1109/COMST.2020.2970550

7. Lin, Y., Shen, S., Liu, Z., Luan, H., Sun, M.: Neural relation extraction with selective attention over instances. In: Proceedings of the 54th Annual Meeting of the Association for Computational Linguistics. ACL (2016). https://doi.org/10.18653/v1/p16-1200

8. Lu, X., Yu, Z., Guo, B., Zhou, X.: Predicting the content dissemination trends by repost behavior modeling in mobile social networks. J. Netw. Comput. Appl. **42**(3), 197–207 (2014). https://doi.org/10.1016/j.jnca.2014.01.015

9. Nickel, M., Tresp, V., Kriegel, H.P.: A three-way model for collective learning on multi-relational data. In: Getoor, L., Scheffer, T. (eds.) Proceedings of the 28th International Conference on International Conference on Machine Learning, pp. 809–816. Omnipress (2011)

10. Perozzi, B., Al-Rfou, R., Skiena, S.: Deepwalk: Online learning of social representations. In: Macskassy, S.A., Perlich, C., Leskovec, J., Wang, W., Ghani, R. (eds.) Proceedings of the 20th ACM SIGKDD International Conference on Knowledge Discovery and Data Mining, pp. 701–710. ACM (2014). https://doi.org/10.1145/2623330.2623732

11. Shen, S., Han, Y., Wang, X., Wang, Y.: Computation offloading with multiple agents in edge-computing-supported IoT. ACM Trans. Sensor Netw. **16**(1), 1–27 (2019). https://doi.org/10.1145/3372025

12. Sheng, H., et al.: Mining hard samples globally and efficiently for person re-identification. IEEE Internet Things J. (2020). https://doi.org/10.1109/JIOT.2020.2980549

13. Trouillon, T., Welbl, J., Riedel, S., Gaussier, É., Bouchard, G.: Complex embeddings for simple link prediction. In: Balcan, M., Weinberger, K.Q. (eds.) Proceedings of the 33nd International Conference on Machine Learning, pp. 2071–2080. JMLR (2016)

14. Tu, C., Zhang, Z., Liu, Z., Sun, M.: Transnet: translation-based network representation learning for social relation extraction. In: Sierra, C. (ed.) Proceedings of the 26th International Joint Conference on Artificial Intelligence, pp. 2864–2870. IJCAI (2017). https://doi.org/10.24963/ijcai.2017/399

15. Verma, A., Bharadwaj, K.K.: Identifying community structure in a multi-relational network employing non-negative tensor factorization and GA k-means clustering. Wiley Interdisc. Rev.: Data Mining Knowl. Disc. **7**(1), e1196 (2017). https://doi.org/10.1002/widm.1196

16. Wang, D., Cui, P., Zhu, W.: Structural deep network embedding. In: Krishnapuram, B., Shah, M., Smola, A.J., Aggarwal, C.C., Shen, D., Rastogi, R. (eds.) Proceedings of the 22nd ACM SIGKDD International Conference on Knowledge Discovery and Data Mining, pp. 1225–1234. ACM (2016). https://doi.org/10.1145/2939672.2939753

17. Wang, X., Han, Y., Wang, C., Zhao, Q., Chen, X., Chen, M.: In-edge AI: intelligentizing mobile edge computing, caching and communication by federated learning. IEEE Netw. **33**(5), 156–165 (2019)

18. Wang, X., Li, X., Pack, S., Han, Z., Leung, V.C.: STCS: spatial-temporal collaborative sampling in flow-aware software defined networks. IEEE J. Sel. Areas Commun. (2020). https://doi.org/10.1109/JSAC.2020.2986688

19. Wang, X., Wang, C., Li, X., Leung, V.C., Taleb, T.: Federated deep reinforcement learning for Internet of Things with decentralized cooperative edge caching. IEEE Internet Things J. (2020). https://doi.org/10.1109/JIOT.2020.2986803
20. Wang, X., Zhang, Y., Leung, V.C., Guizani, N., Jiang, T.: D2d big data: content deliveries over wireless device-to-device sharing in large-scale mobile networks. IEEE Wireless Commun. **25**(1), 32–38 (2018). https://doi.org/10.1109/MWC.2018.1700215
21. Wang, Y., Wei, L., Vasilakos, A.V., Jin, Q.: Device-to-device based mobile social networking in proximity (MSNP) on smartphones: Framework, challenges and prototype. Future Gener. Comput. Syst. **74**, 241–253 (2017). https://doi.org/10.1016/j.future.2015.10.020
22. Yuan, Z., Jiang, Y., Gidófalvi, G.: Geographical and temporal similarity measurement in location-based social networks. In: Chow, C., Shekhar, S. (eds.) Proceedings of the Second ACM SIGSPATIAL International Workshop on Mobile Geographic Information Systems, pp. 30–34. ACM (2013). https://doi.org/10.1145/2534190.2534192
23. Zhang, Y., Huang, Z., Wang, S., Wang, X., Jiang, T.: Spark-based measurement and analysis on offline mobile application market over device-to-device sharing in mobile social networks. In: 2017 IEEE 23rd International Conference on Parallel and Distributed Systems, pp. 545–552. IEEE (2017). https://doi.org/10.1109/ICPADS.2017.00077
24. Zhou, J., Fan, J.: Translink: user identity linkage across heterogeneous social networks via translating embeddings. In: IEEE INFOCOM 2019-IEEE Conference on Computer Communications, pp. 2116–2124. IEEE (2019). https://doi.org/10.1109/INFOCOM.2019.8737542

LSimRank: Node Similarity in a Labeled Graph

Yang Wu[1(✉)], Ada Wai-Chee Fu[1], Cheng Long[2], and Zitong Chen[1]

[1] The Chinese University of Hong Kong, Hong Kong, China
{yangwu,adafu,ztchen}@cse.cuhk.edu.hk
[2] Nanyang Technological University, Nanyang, Singapore
c.long@ntu.edu.sg

Abstract. The notion of node similarity is useful in many real-world applications. Many existing similarity measurements such as SimRank and its variants have been proposed. Among these measurements, most capture the structural information of a graph only, and thus they are not suitable for graphs with additional label information. We propose a new similarity measurement called LSimRank which measures the similarities among nodes by using both the structural information and the label information of a graph. Extensive experiments on datasets verify that LSimRank is superior over SimRank and other variants on labeled graphs.

Keywords: Node similarity · Labeled graph · Random walk

1 Introduction

The problem of measuring the similarity among nodes is a fundamental one in graph analysis such as collaborative filtering [3], web page ranking [10], link prediction [12], graph clustering [26], spam detection [19], and natural language processing [15]. Among those existing similarity measurements, SimRank is one that is commonly used [8]. It has been shown that SimRank works very well in many applications [3,12,15]. The intuition behind SimRank is that *"two objects are similar if they are referenced by similar objects"*. Based on similar intuitions, quite a few variants of SimRank have also been proposed [3,15].

Many real graphs come with node labels, node similarity for such graphs has been studied in [6,20,23]. However, there are limitations in such work such as giving zero similarity to non-identical labels, assumption of concept taxonomy, and the resulting utility. In this paper, we propose a new similarity measurement among nodes called LSimRank which captures both the node label information and the structural information of the given graph. Our contributions are as follows: (1) Unlike the existing work [6,20], LSimRank can give non-zero similarity among nodes with different yet similar labels. (2) In LSimRank, in order to capture better label information of a node, we consider the label information of its

© Springer Nature Switzerland AG 2020
X. Wang et al. (Eds.): APWeb-WAIM 2020, LNCS 12317, pp. 127–144, 2020.
https://doi.org/10.1007/978-3-030-60259-8_10

neighborhood and compute the label similarity between two nodes using measurements such as total variance distance and Jaccard similarity. (3) Extensive experiments on real datasets verify that LSimRank is superior to SimRank, and superior to SemSim [23] which is the state-of-the-art SimRank measurement for labeled graphs.

This paper is organized as follows. Section 2 reviews the related work. Section 3 provides preliminaries and the problem definition. Section 4 introduces our proposed similarity measurement, LSimRank. Section 5 defines a label similarity measurement between nodes. Section 6 introduces the approximation algorithms for estimating LSimRank values. Section 7 presents the experimental results and Sect. 8 concludes the paper and gives a few directions for future study.

2   Related Work

SimRank, proposed by Jeh and Widom [8], is a widely used similarity measurement in many areas. The idea behind SimRank is that two nodes are similar if their neighbours are similar. They further proposed a Random Surfer-Pairs model to interpret SimRank by random walk pairs, which is very useful in designing approximation algorithms. There are quite many follow-up studies on SimRank, which we review as follows.

Since the computation of the accurate SimRank scores in large graphs is extremely costly, there has been much interest in approximation algorithms for SimRank. The first random walk based approximation algorithm is proposed by Fogaras and Racz [7]. They proposed an index structure called fingerprint trees which to represent reversed random walks in a compact way. Another indexing method called SLING is proposed in [21] which gives near-optimal time complexity and guarantees a small additive error. TSF [16] and READS [9] are dynamic indexing algorithms which will be further described in Sect. 6. Several index-free approximation algorithms are proposed: in [14], the proposed ProbSim estimates SimRank scores with provable approximation guarantees; in [18], a Monte Carlo based algorithm UniWalk can simulate the original BiWalk in computing SimRank scores with a rectified factor.

Variants of Simrank have been proposed to overcome limitations of SimRank and improve the accuracy. SimRank++, proposed by Antonellis et al. [3], adds a new parameter called evidence score to improve the accuracy of SimRank in click graphs. Zhao et al. [25] proposed P-Rank which considers both in-neighbours and out-neighbors in the SimRank computation. In [24], SimRank* is proposed to traverse more incoming paths that are ignored by SimRank, and thus avoids the "zero-SimRank" problem. ASCOS++[5] solves the problem that two nodes can only reach each other through paths of odd lengths and includes the weights of the edges along the paths in the calculation.

Some existing work has studied the node similarity in labeled graphs. [20] proposed a new framework of meta path-based similarity and a new definition of similarity measure, *PathSim*, that captures the subtle similarity semantics among peer objects in networks. [6] introduced a new measurement called NSimGram which uses the label sequences found in paths of bounded length q leading to the nodes. However, these new measurements only apply non-zero similarity to nodes with the same labels. For nodes with different labels, the similarities are always 0. [17,22] focus on the relations between nodes. Such a relation is predefined based on the labels of edges in a path. They measure the similarity between nodes based on paths with particular relations. If two nodes do not follow paths with the given relations which meet at one node, then the similarity is 0.

SemSim [23] boosts the SimRank of labeled graphs with semantics. Our recursive form of LSimRank is similar to SemSim [23]. The advantages of our approach are as follows: 1) SemSim [23] adopts the Lin Score [13] as the label similarity measurement, but it only works in graphs with a taxonomy of the label concepts. We make a in depth study on the label similarity in Sect. 4 and define a new label similarity measurement which does not depend on a concept taxonomy. Experimental studies in Sect. 7 show that our new label similarity measurement is superior to the use of Lin Score. 2). The random surfer-pairs form in SemSim [23] depends on a new graph G^2 which is obtained from the original graph G. If the original graph G is large, the size of G^2 may be very large, as a result, the cost of computing the similarity may be also very high. We introduce the random surfer-pairs form which depends only on the original graph, so the cost of computing the similarity is much lower. We prove that our random surfer-pairs form is equivalent to the recursive form in our technical report [2] concretely. 3). Using our random surfer-pairs form, many sophisticated ideas in existing work can be adopted for approximating the similarity scores as described in Sect. 6.

3   LSimRank

We first define our problem. Given a labeled graph $G = (V, E)$ with the following properties, 1) G can be directed or undirected, 2) each node in G has at least one label and L_G is the set of distinct labels in G, 3) the whole graph G can be easily accessed, where V is the node set and E is the edge set. The problem is to measure the similarity among nodes in G.

In order to measure the similarity between nodes in labeled graphs, we propose LSimRank which captures both the label information and the structural information. The basic intuition of LSimRank can be interpreted as '*two objects are similar if they have similar labels and are referenced by similar objects*'. We measure how similar the labels of two nodes u and v are using a function $L(u, v) \in [0, 1]$. For simplicity, we call $L(u, v)$ the label similarity function. Details of how $L(u, v)$ is defined and computed are given in Sect. 4.

As for SimRank, the process of computing LSimRank can also be recursively propagated beyond the localized neighborhood scope to the entire graph, so that the global structure may be involved. Next, we show the iterative form of LSimRank and then derive the corresponding random surfer-pairs form.

[Recursive Form]. Given a graph G, let $In(u)$ be the in-neighbour set of u and let $LS(u, v)$ denote the LSimRank score between u and v. $C \in (0, 1)$ is a decay factor. The recursive form of LSimRank is defined as follows,

$$LS(u, v) = \begin{cases} \frac{C \cdot L(u,v)}{|In(u)||In(v)|} \sum_{a \in In(u)b \in In(v)} LS(a, b) & \text{if } u \neq v \\ 1 & \text{if } u = v \end{cases} \tag{1}$$

Theorem 1. *The solution to the recursive form of LSimRank in Equation (1) is unique when $C \neq 1$*

Proof. Please see our technical report [2].

[Random Surfer-Pairs Form]. Based on the recursive form in Equation (1), we can obtain the corresponding random surfer-pairs form of LSimRank.

Let $\pi_u = (u_0, u_1, u_2, ..., u_k)$ and $\pi_v = (v_0, v_1, v_2, ..., v_k)$ be two random walks with same length. $u_0 = u$ and $v_0 = v$. Note that k can be any positive number here. Let $I(\pi_u, \pi_v)$ be an indicator function which is 1 if the last node of π_u and π_v is the first meeting point, i.e. $u_k = v_k$ and $u_i \neq v_i$ for $0 \leq i < k$. We denote the length of π_u by $\ell(\pi_u)$.

Define $L'(\pi_u, \pi_v) = \prod_{i=0}^{k} L(u_i, v_i)$ as the label similarity between two random walks π_u, π_v. Then the random surfer-pairs form of LSimRank can be defined as

$$LS'(u, v) = \sum_{\pi_u, \pi_v} I(\pi_u, \pi_v) Pr(\pi_u, \pi_v) L'(\pi_u, \pi_v) C^{\ell(\pi_u)}$$
$$= E[I(\pi_u, \pi_v) L'(\pi_u, \pi_v) C^{\ell(\pi_u)}] \tag{2}$$

where $Pr(\pi_u, \pi_v)$ is the probability of sampling random walks π_u and π_v given starting points u and v. Then we prove that $LS'(u, v)$ in Equation (2) exactly models our original definition of LSimRank by showing that $LS'(u, v)$ equals $LS(u, v)$ in Equation (1). In the proof of the following Lemma, $v \cdot \pi$ stands for a path of node v followed by path π.

Lemma 1. *$LS'(u, v)$ is equivalent to $LS(u, v)$ in Eq. 1.*

Proof. Please see our technical report [2].

Equation (2) considers all the paths up to length ∞, but this can be very expensive. A practical way is to limit the length of paths. Given a positive integer t, only those pathes whose length is no larger than t are considered in Equation (2). The value of t is usually set as 10 in previous works [7, 8, 16].

4   Label Similarity Function

One easy way to define the label similarity is to directly compare the labels of nodes. If u and v have the same label, then $L(u, v) = 1$, otherwise $L(u, v) = 0$. This is in fact the measurement by Lin score [13] given in SemSim [23] when no concept taxonomy is given: suppose two nodes have the same label X, the lowest common ancestor (LCA) of X will be X itself, while for two nodes with different labels there is no LCA for the labels and the conceptual similarity becomes zero. So in graphs without taxonomy, Lin score is too simplistic, since the similarity values can only be 0 or 1. Another weak point of Lin score is that it only considers the labels of u and v, while we have much more information in the graph.

We define a more comprehensive label similarity function based on two intuitions: 1. *"The label information of a node u does not only depends on its own label, but also depends on the labels in its neighborhood"*. 2. *"Closer neighbors of u contribute more to the label information of u than farther neighbors"*. Here, we give one example to show that using the labels of neighbors is very helpful in similarity measurement. Consider a citation network, each node is a conference paper and each edge is a citation relationship. The conference which a paper belongs to is the label of this paper. E.g., paper [8] is from KDD and paper [7] is from WWW. So if we only consider their own labels, then the label similarity is 0 and the LSimRank score is also 0. However, [8] and [7] are closely related, since [8] proposes the definition of SimRank and [7] presents a scalable algorithm to compute approximate SimRank scores. If we consider the labels of of their neighbors, we can find that they are cited by many papers from the same conference, so the label similarity and LSimRank score should not be 0.

Specifically, we propose to define a label vector P_u for each node u in G, which captures the characteristics of the labels in the neighborhood of u within h hops. We use a decay factor of C_l of value in (0,1). For simplicity, each label is represented by an integer. There is one entry $P_u(a)$ for each label a in L_G, initially set to 0. We examine the h-hop neighborhood of u, for each node v in this neighborhood, if v is in i-th hop from u, and the label of v is b, then we add C_l^i to $P_u(b)$. As $C_l \in (0, 1)$, farther neighbors contribute less to the label vector. After processing the h-hop neighborhood, let M be the sum of all entries in P_u, we normalize the values by replacing $P_u(a)$ by $P_u(a)/M$ for each label a in L_G.

The time complexity of computing P_u is $O(d_{max}^h)$, which will increase as h increases, where d_{max} is the maximum degree in G. So a large h will lead to poor time complexity. In our experiment, we only show the results when $h = 1$, since we observe that the results of LSimRank is already acceptable when $h = 1$. We also show the results when $h = 2$ in our technical report [2]. The improvement of the results from $h = 1$ to $h = 2$ is not obvious. So $h = 1$ is often sufficient.

In some graphs, one node may have multiple labels. In order to handle this case, we distribute the contribution of a node to each label equally, which means that if one node has m labels and it is an i-th hop neighbor of node u, then it has $1/m \times C_l^i$ contribution to the count of these m labels in the label vector P_u.

Now, the problem becomes measuring the similarity between two label vectors P_u and P_v. *Total variation distance* and *Kullback-Leibler divergence* are two widely used measurements for computing the distance between probability distributions. However, since Kullback-Leibler divergence is asymmetric, if Kullback-Leibler divergence is used, then LSimRank will also be asymmetric, which means that $L(u, v) \neq L(v, u)$, which is not desirable. So we choose to use total variation distance here. We use D_{TVD} to represent total variation distance.

$$D_{TVD}(P_u, P_v) = \frac{1}{2} \sum_{i=1}^{|L_G|} |P_u(i) - P_v(i)| \tag{3}$$

Since the smaller the distance is, the more similar the two nodes are, we define the label similarity between u and v as

$$L(u, v) = 1 - D_{TVD}(P_u, P_v) \tag{4}$$

Jaccard similarity is another commonly used measurement for the similarity between two vectors.

$$L(u, v) = \frac{\sum_{i=1}^{|L_G|} min(P_u(i), P_v(i))}{\sum_{i=1}^{|L_G|} max(P_u(i), P_v(i))} \tag{5}$$

We call LSimRank with different label similarity functions, *LSimRank-Lin*, *LSimRank-TVD* and *LSimRank-Jaccard*. We will compare these alternatives in the experiments. In the following, we introduce two different strategies for enhancing the computation of label similarity.

4.1   Strategy 1: Pre-computing Label Vectors

In computing LSimRank, we may reuse many label similarity values multiple times. If we compute the label similarity values every time we encounter them in LSimRank computation, it may incur much extra time cost. So if we pre-compute label similarity values, the time cost can be reduced a lot. However, if we pre-compute all label similarity values, the time complexity is $O(|V|^2(d_{max}^h + |L_G|))$ where d_{max} is the maximum degree in the graph and h is the number of hops used in computing the label vectors and we need $O(|V|^2)$ space to store them, which is prohibitive for large graphs. Instead, we can pre-compute the label vector P_u for each node u, then the space cost and time cost of the pre-computation process are reduced to $O(|V||L_G|)$ and $O(|V|d_{max}^h)$, respectively. With the pre-computed label vectors, the time cost of computing one label similarity is $O(|L_G|)$.

It is well known that the degree distribution of nodes in many graphs satisfies power law distribution, which means that only a small portion of nodes have large degrees and most of the nodes have small degrees. Also, in computing the LSimRank scores, those nodes with larger degrees will be used more times than those with small degrees, since more paths go through nodes with large degrees.

Based on this observation, we can design a better method for computing label similarities. We divide all nodes into two sets, large degree set and small degree set, based on their degrees. For example, we put 10% nodes with the largest degrees into the large degree set and put the remaining 90% nodes into the small degree set. For those nodes in the large degree set, we pre-compute the label vectors for them, since these nodes have large degrees and the time cost of computing the label vectors is very expensive. While for those nodes in the small degree set, we do not pre-compute the label vector for them, since their degree is small and the pre-computation of label vectors will not reduce the time cost a lot but incur extra space cost. Let $w = 0.1$. The space cost and time cost of the pre-computation process are $O(w|V||L_G|)$ and $O(w|V|d_{max}^h)$, respectively. In computing the label similarity, the time cost is $O(d_{max}^h + |L_G|)$.

4.2   Strategy 2: Using Similarity Between Labels

With the above optimization algorithm we still have some problems. First, we need $O(|V||L_G|)$ space to store the pre-computed label vectors for each node, which needs large space cost for large graphs. Also, in the querying process, we need to spend extra time $O(|L_G|)$ to compute each label similarity value.

In order to further reduce the cost, we directly use the similarity between labels instead of the label similarity between nodes in computing LSimRank. Suppose we want to compute the similarity between two labels l_1 and l_2, we first randomly select m node pairs $\{(u_1, v_1), (u_2, v_2), ..., (u_m, v_m)\}$ with labels l_1 and l_2. Then we compute the label similarity of these m node pairs and use the average value of these label similarity as the similarity between l_1 and l_2. Let $L^*(l_1, l_2)$ be the similarity between l_1 and l_2, we have $L^*(l_1, l_2) = \sum_{i=1}^{m} L(u_i, v_i)/m$. The computation of $L(u_i, v_i)$ is based on Eq. 4 or 5 Then, for all node pairs (u, v) where u has label l_1 and v has label l_2 or u has label l_2 and v has label l_1, we use the similarity between labels l_1 and l_2 to replace the label similarity between u and v, i.e. $L(u, v) = L^*(l_1, l_2)$.

With this method, the time cost of computing the similarity between labels is $O(m(d_{max}^h + |L_G|)|L_G|^2)$. The space cost of storing the similarity between labels is $O(|L_G|^2)$, which is much smaller than the space cost $O(|V||L_G|)$ for Strategy 1. Note that $|L_G|$ is a small number in most graphs as shown in our experiments. $O(1)$ time is needed for the query process for looking up the label similarity. In our experiments in Sect. 7, using $1\%|V|$ ($m = 1\%|V|$) node pairs is enough for getting accurate results.

We summarize the space and time cost of these two strategies in Table 1.

Table 1. Index space, Indexing time and CPU time for computing one label similarity

	Index space	Indexing time	CPU time
Strategy 1	$O(|V||L_G|)$	$O(|V|d_{max}^h)$	$O(|L_G|)$
Strategy 2	$O(|L_G|^2)$	$O(|V|(d_{max}^h + |L_G|)|L_G|^2)$	$O(1)$

5   Computing LSimRank

In order to solve $LS(u, v)$ in Equation (1), we can rewrite Equation (1) in the following iterative form

$$LS_{k+1}(u, v) = \begin{cases} \frac{C \cdot L(u,v)}{|In(u)||In(v)|} \sum_{a \in In(u) b \in In(v)} LS_k(a, b) & \text{if } u \neq v \\ 1 & \text{if } u = v \end{cases} \quad (6)$$

with the ground state of $LS_0(u, v) = 0$, if $u \neq v$ and $LS_0(u, v) = 1$, if $u = v$. $LS_k(u, v)$ is the LSimRank value between u and v in the k-th iteration. With Equation (6), we can compute $LS_{k+1}(u, v)$ based on $LS_k(u, v)$ recursively.

Theorem 2. *LSimRank scores in Equation (6) has the following properties*

1. *(**Symmetry**)* $LS_k(u,v) = LS_k(v,u)$
2. *(**Monotonicity**)* $0 \leq LS_k(u,v) \leq LS_{k+1}(u,v) \leq 1$
3. *(**Convergence**) The solution to the iterative form of LSimRank always exists and converges to a fixed point $LS^*(u,v)$, which is the theoretical solution to the recursive form of LSimRank in Equation (1).*

Proof. Please see our technical report [2].

Property 3(*Convergence*) guarantees that the unique solution to the recursive LSimRank Equation (1) can be reached by computing $LS_k(u,v)$ iteratively. In [25], it has been shown that such an iterative form converges to the fixed point very quickly, i.e. $k = 5$. The space and time complexity of computing the LSimRank score with Eq. 6 is $O(|V|^2)$ and $O(kd_{max}^2|V|^2)$ respectively.

6 Approximation Algorithms

We have introduced a simple algorithm of computing LSimRank scores in Eq. 6, but the time and space cost of this algorithm is prohibitive on large graphs. So approximation algorithms are necessary for computing LSimRank in real-world applications. All the estimations in the following algorithms is unbiased and the prove is shown in our technical report [2]. The error bounds and the complexities are also shown in our technical report [2].

6.1 Basic Algorithm

Based on the random surfer-pairs form in Eq. 2, we can design a Monte Carlo based approximation algorithm. First, we generate a reverse random walk from each node in the graph. In fact, we do not need to generate totally independent random walks. Instead, we generate a set of coalescing walks: each pair of walks will follow the same path after their first meeting time. More precisely, we start a reversed walk from each node. In each time step, the walks at different nodes independently choose an in-neighbor uniformly. If two walks are at the same node, they follow the same edge. All random walks stop when the length of random walks reaches the maximum length t. If we repeat such simulation process r times, let π_u^i and π_v^i be the truncated random walks in the i-th simulation, which end at the meeting node of the random walks from u and v, then the estimation of $LS(u,v)$ is

$$\widehat{LS(u,v)} = \sum_{i=1}^{r} I(\pi_u^i, \pi_v^i) L'(\pi_u^i, \pi_v^i) C^{\ell(\pi_u^i)} / r \qquad (7)$$

Recently, a few sophisticated approximation algorithms have been proposed to estimate SimRank. However, such algorithms cannot be applied to LSim-Rank directly, since LSimRank considers the labels of nodes. In the following subsections, we propose variants of such algorithms which can be applied for computing LSimRank. In Sect. 6.2, we describe the index-based approximation algorithms and in Sect. 6.3, we describe the index-free approximation algorithms. We compare all these algorithms in Sect. 7.3.

6.2 Index-Based Approximation Algorithms

The existing index-based approximation algorithms for SimRank named SLING [21], FR [7], READS [9] and TSF [16] are frequently cited in SimRank related work. For LSimRank, we propose variants of these algorithms whose names start with 'L-' in the following. We find that for SLING and FR, no simple variants can be applied to handle LSimRank, since we cannot compute the label similarity between random walks based on their indexes, so we focus on READS [9] and TSF [16].

[**L-SAforest**]. In READS [9], the indexing process constructs an SA forest using sampled random walks from each node, then SA sets are formed which contain leaf nodes in the SA forest as the index. If two leaf nodes are in the same SA tree, then they are assigned to the same SA set and the random walks from them have a common meeting point. In the querying process, in order to obtain the SimRank value between nodes, we only need to check if two nodes are in the same SA set or not. However, the index of READS contains no information about the sampled random walks which are necessary for computing the label similarity between random walks in LSimRank. So we need to keep the SA trees as the index. We call the method L-SAforest. The difference between the querying process of L-SAforest and READS is that we should multiply the contribution of each random walk pair with the label similarity between them as the contribution to the LSimRank values. The querying process of L-SAforest is shown in our technical report [2] and the correctness of this method has been proved in [9].

[**L-TSF**]. In TSF [16], R_g one-way graphs are sampled as the index. To sample a one-way graph, each vertex in the reversed graph randomly selects an outgoing edge and $|V|$ such edges compose a one-way graph. In the querying process, the algorithm samples R_q random walks from the query node u with length T on the original graph, then for each sampled random walk, we find the nodes with common meeting points in the sampled random walk in the one-way graph and add the contributions to the corresponding similarity scores.

L-TSF has the same indexing process as TSF, while in the querying process, we multiply the contribution of each random walk pair with the label similarity between the pair as the final contribution to the LSimRank values.

6.3 Index-Free Approximation Algorithms

ProbSim [14] and Uniwalk [18] are two recently proposed index-free algorithms for SimRank. Here we describe variants of these approaches for LSimRank.

[L-ProbSim]. In each simulation, ProbeSim generates a $\sqrt{c}$-walk $W(u) = (u_1, u_2..., u_k)$ from the query node u. Then, on each partial $\sqrt{c}$-walk $W(u, i) = (u_1, ..., u_i)$, $i = 2, ..., k$, we find all the paths in graph G which have meeting points with $W(u, i)$ from each node $v \in |V|$ and the length from u and v to the meeting point should be the same. We compute the contributions to the SimRank score $S(u, v)$ based on these paths from u and v with meeting points. Finally, we sum all contributions in all partial random walks.

In L-ProbeSim, we multiply each contribution with the label similarity between the paths from u and v to the meeting point as the contribution to the LSimRank score. The algorithm of L-ProbeSim shows in our technical report [2]. The difference between this new algorithm and the original one in [14] is that we construct a tree T to store all the paths, which is used to compute the label similarity between paths with meeting points.

[L-UniWalk]. UniWalk extends a path starting from the query node u by 2 steps forwards iteratively. At each iteration, let p be the center point in the path and v be the end point, then we check if p is the first meeting point of two sub-paths, one from u to p and the other from v to p. If yes, then we compute the contribution of these two sub-paths to the SimRank score between u and v. The iteration process stops when the length of the path equals $2l$ where l is a pre-defined maximum length. We sum all contributions in every iteration as the estimation of the SimRank score between u and v.

In L-UniWalk, the difference is that in each iteration, we multiply the contribution to SimRank with the label similarity between two sub-paths as the contribution to LSimRank score between u and v. Note that UniWalk is designed for handling undirected graphs, and the experimental results show that UniWalk performs worse than others in directed graphs.

7   Experimental Results

First, we show the effectiveness of LSimRank in comparison with SimRank. Secondly, we compare the effectiveness all variants of LSimRank mentioned in Sect. 4, i.e. LSimRank-TVD and LSimRank-Jaccard, and related work on labeled graphs, namely SemSim from [23], PathSim from [20], and NSimGram from [6]. Thirdly, we compare the accuracy and cost of different approximation algorithms for LSimRank.

Note that we have also compared the two optimization strategies in Sect. 4 and the details are reported in [2]. We find that LSimRank using optimization Strategy 2 in 4.2 outperforms Strategy 1 in 4.1 in that it is more efficient while producing very similar results. Hence in this section, we only report our results based on Strategy 2.

7.1   Experiment Settings

We run experiments on four real-world datasets which are available in [1,11]. The statistics of these datasets are shown in Table 2. In Wikispeedia, each node

Table 2. Statistics of datasets

Network	$|V|$	$|E|$	$|L|$	
Wikispeedia(WK)	4.6×10^3	1.2×10^5	14	directed
Amazon-meta(AM)	5.5×10^5	1.8×10^6	100	undirected
US-Patents(UP)	3.8×10^6	1.6×10^7	6	directed
Wikipedia Links(WL)	1.2×10^7	3.8×10^8	10	directed

is a Wikipedia article and each edge is a hyperlink between articles. Each node label is the category which the article belongs to. In Amazon-meta, nodes are products (books, music CDs, DVDs and video tapes). If two products are bought together then there is a link between them. The node label is the category which the product belongs to. In Cit-Patents, each node is a patent and each edge represents a citation relationship. The node label is the category which the patent belongs to. Wikipedia Links consists of the wikilinks of the Wikipedia. Nodes are Wikipedia articles, and directed edges are hyperlinks. Wikipedia Links has no node label, so we need to generate the node labels. We use 10 labels and we randomly assign a label to each node with a uniform probability, which follows the generating process in [4]. We use 1-hop neighbors for computing the label similarity between nodes. Our experiments in the technical report [2] show that 1-hop returns similar accuracy compared with 2-hops. All algorithms are implemented in C++, and we conduct experiments on a Linux machine with Intel 3.40GHz CPU, 16GB memory. For fair comparison, we set the decay factors $C = C_l = 0.8$ for all algorithms as in previous work [7–9,21].

7.2   Comparing LSimRank and SimRank

SimRank scores are computed using the brute-force algorithm in [8] and LSim-Rank scores are computed by Eq. 6. We use Strategy 1 in Sect. 4.1 for computing label similarity in LSimRank. Since the computations cost a lot of time on large graphs, we only show the results on WK. In WK, nodes may have multiple labels. In our experiment, we test six query nodes, "Internet", "Computer Science", "Linux", "DNA", "Food" and "Jazz". The query node "Internet" has two labels, "IT"(information technology) and "Citizenship". "Computer Science" and "Linux" have one label, "IT". "DNA" has label "Science". "Food" has label "Everyday Life". "Jazz" has label "Music". Because of the space limit, we only show the results of "Internet". First, we show the top-10 nearest neighbors of the query nodes. Second, we evaluate LSimRank and SimRank based on their performance on the link prediction problem[1].

[**Top-10 Nearest Neighbors**]. Table 3 shows the top-10 nearest neighbors of the query node 'internet' with label 'IT' in *LSimRank-TVD*. Table 3 shows the

---

[1] NDCG and precision are two commonly used metrics in top-k query problems. However, these two metrics cannot be used here, since they need the ground-truth rank of nodes which does not exist in our case.

top-10 nearest neighbors of the query node "internet" with label "Citizenship" in *LSimRank-TVD*. Table 3 shows the top-10 nearest neighbors of the query node "internet" in SimRank. We only show the results of LSimRank-TVD. Other LSimRank algorithms return similar results, so we show them in our technical report [2]. We also show the 10-nearest neighbors of querying "Computer Science(IT)", "Linux(IT)", "DNA(Science)", "Food(Everyday Life)" and "Jazz(Music)" in the technical report [2].

When we use different labels for the query node "Internet", the results of LSimRank are totally different and there is no overlap between them. In addition, if we check the results using label "IT", it is obvious that the results are closely related to "internet" in terms of information technology. And this is also true for label "Citizenship". However, the results of SimRank contain some nodes from both cases using labels "IT" and "citizenship" and also include some unrelated nodes, which means the quality of results is quite poor. This proves that LSimRank can filter many unrelated nodes when we consider node labels. So LSimRank outperforms SimRank in labeled graphs.

Table 3. Top-10 NN for (a) "Internet(IT)" with LSimRank-TVD; (b) "Internet (Citizenship)" with LSimRank-TVD; (c) "Internet" with SimRank

	(a)		(b)		(c)
1	X Window core protocol	1	Local community	1	Japanese grammar
2	HTTP cookie	2	Garden Gnome Liberation Front	2	X Window core protocol
3	Wikisource	3	Creative Commons	3	Local community
4	Napster	4	History of the Internet	4	Telephone exchange
5	Wikispecies	5	Mass media	5	Defaka
6	InterBase	6	Broadcasting	6	Scent of a Woman
7	GNU Project	7	Working poor	7	Weather map
8	GNU Linux naming controversy	8	Publishing	8	Shabo language
9	X Window System	9	Video	9	Garden Gnome Liberation Front
10	World Wide Web	10	FairTax	10	Wikispecies

Table 4. Node ranks: "Internet(IT)"

Adjacent node	LSimRank-TVD	LSimRank-Jaccard	SemSim	PathSim	NSimGram	SimRank
Compact disk	**56**	58	NA	NA	NA	322
World wide web	**5**	13	9	8	15	45
Computer	**54**	59	89	101	138	401
Google	**25**	32	44	39	28	95
Linux	24	28	26	**20**	31	93
Wikipedia	**40**	52	87	78	69	145

Table 5. Node ranks: "Internet(Citizenship)"

Adjacent node	LSimRank-TVD	LSimRank-Jaccard	SemSim	PathSim	NSimGram	SimRank
Mass media	**8**	15	12	13	9	58
Broadcasting	11	**9**	24	14	13	66
Publishing	19	21	35	17	**15**	92
Education	**48**	51	NA	NA	NA	96

Table 6. Node ranks: "Computer Science(IT)"

Adjacent node	LSimRank-TVD	LSimRank-Jaccard	SemSim	PathSim	NSimGram	SimRank
Programming language	11	**9**	13	17	12	42
History of computing hardware	14	15	21	18	**11**	66
Data Encryption Standard	**9**	11	12	21	15	47
Wikisource	**29**	36	NA	NA	NA	49

Table 7. Node ranks: "Linux(IT)"

Adjacent node	LSimRank-TVD	LSimRank-Jaccard	SemSim	PathSim	NSimGram	SimRank
OpenBSD	**9**	7	21	12	10	11
GNU	**4**	6	11	13	5	7
X Window System	12	**11**	19	23	9	15
World Wide Web	**53**	59	NA	NA	NA	109

[**Link Prediction**].Another popular way to evaluate different node similarity measurements is measuring their effectiveness in the link prediction problem [3,5]. The basic idea is to remove some edge from the graph and then check which node similarity measurement can make most useful prediction on the missing edge. First, we remove one edge (u, v) from the graph, then we run the one-to-all query on node u, and we compare the ranks of the similarity scores between (u, v) in different node similarity measurements. The measurement which ranks the similarity score of (u, v) the highest is the best in link prediction.

We experiment on six adjacent edges of the query node "Internet(IT)", four adjacent edges of the query node "Internet (Citizenship)", four adjacent edges of the query node "Computer Science" and four adjacent edges of the query node "Linux". In each experiment, we delete one such edge, then we compute the similarity scores of the node connected with the deleted edge. The results are shown in Tables 4, 5, 6 and 7. The lower the number is, the higher the rank of the node is. "NA" means that the similarity score is 0, which means the measurements does not work here. Here we also include three existing algorithms SemSim [23], PathSim [20] and NSimGram [6] for comparison. In some cases, SemSim, PathSim and NSimGram are "NA", so these algorithms do not work. In most cases, the rank of nodes in LSimRank-TVD and LSimRank-Jaccard are much higher than other algorithms. LSimRank-TVD is slightly better than LSimRank-Jaccard.

In order to see if LSimRank outperform SimRank in more cases and find the best label similarity function, we repeat the link prediction process 1000 times, with randomly chosen query nodes. In Table 8, we show the accuracy of each algorithm in link predictions. The accuracy means the the percentage of link prediction cases in which the corresponding algorithm returns the highest rank. We show the results of WK and AM. There is no taxonomy in WK, so Lin Score [13] in SemSim [23] becomes a simple indicator function as we stated in Sect. 4. As a results, the result of SemSim [23] is very poor. While AM has the taxonomy. We find that in most of the cases, the rank in LSimRank-TVD is the highest among all algorithms mentioned in this section in Table 8. SemSim [23] is used in graphs with taxonomy, but we find that TVD is still slightly better than SemSim [23] in the graph (AM) with taxonomy. In the graph (WK) without taxonomy, TVD is much better than SemSim [23].

Table 8. The accuracy of different algorithms in link predictions

Dataset	LSimRank-TVD	LSimRank-Jaccard	SemSim	PathSim	NSimGram	SimRank
WK	**69.5%**	21.7%	0.9%	3.4%	4.1%	0.4%
AM	**42.5%**	24.3%	29.8%	1.4%	1.7%	0.3%

7.3   Comparing Approximation Algorithms

[**Precision**]. We measure the quality of different approximation algorithms in LSimRank by using precision which is the percentage of top-k nearest neighbors in approximation algorithms among the ground-truth top-k nearest neighbors.

$Precision = |approximated\ top\ k\ nodes\ set \cap exact\ top\ k\ nodes\ set|/k$.

The results of the iterative form of LSimRank in Eq. 6 serves as the ground-truth in our experiments. We only show the precision for the small graph WK, since the computation time cost is prohibitive in large graphs.

In Fig. 1(a), we find that L-SAforest and L-ProbeSim outperform other index and index-free algorithms, respectively. L-TSF performs poorly, since it is based on the assumption that no cycle with length shorter than t exists in the given graph, but this assumption is not true in many graphs. L-UniWalk is designed only for undirect graphs and it performs poorly on directed graphs. In addition, We find that the accuracy is high for nearer neighbors, i.e., when k is small, but the result quality decreases quickly when we estimate more nearest neighbors, i.e., when k is large.

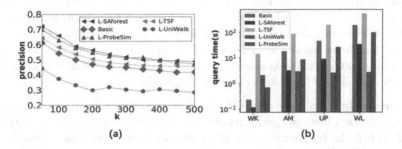

Fig. 1. (a) Top-k query precision, (b) Query time cost

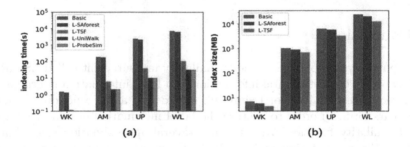

Fig. 2. (a) Indexing time, (b) Index space(a) Indexing time, (b) Index space

[**Querying Efficiency**]. We evaluate the querying efficiency for each approximation algorithm based on the query times. The query times of LSimRank and LSimRank* are shown in Fig. 1(b) and each result is averaged over 100 single source queries. Figure 1(b) shows that L-UniWalk has the lowest querying time cost for large graphs, since the query cost of UniWalk is unrelated to the graph size. But its accuracy is not acceptable as shown in Fig. 1(a). The query time of L-SAforest is slightly higher than L-UniWalk on large graphs. Since L-SAforest improves the accuracy a lot, this is a good trade-off between querying cost and accuracy. While on small graphs, the querying cost of L-SAforest is the lowest. Other algorithms are always worse than L-SAforest.

[**Indexing Cost**]. We compare the time and space cost of the indexing process for all algorithms in Fig. 2(a) and 2(b). The indexing process contains two parts: 1. pre-computing the label similarity, 2. constructing the index for query-ing process. Index-free algorithms (L-ProbeSim and L-Uniwalk) has no cost for constructing the index.

In index-based algorithms, L-TSF has the lowest time and space cost, and the basic algorithm has the highest time and space cost. Although L-TSF has the lowest querying time cost, it has very low precision. So it is an undesirable trade-off. L-SAforest has slightly higher time and space cost than L-TSF, but the cost is still acceptable. So L-SAforest is still the best algorithm in index based algorithms. For index-free algorithms, there is no index cost, but pre-computing the label similarity values takes time. We do not show the index space cost of L-ProbeSim and L-UniWalk, since when the total number of labels $|L|$ is small, the space cost $O(|L|^2)$ is also very small in LSimRank.

[**Recommendations in Practice**]. We have the following recommendations: 1. Total variation distance performs best in computing the label similarity func-tion. 2. When the number of different labels $|L|$ is not very large, LSimRank is superior to LSimRank-Basic in query time and index space cost. 3. We recom-mend to use L-SA Forest or L-ProbeSim for approximation, since they have the highest accuracy with acceptable time and space cost. If we can afford the cost of constructing the index in L-SAforest, then L-SAforest is preferred, otherwise, L-ProbeSim is recommended.

8 Conclusion

In this paper, we propose a new node similarity measurement called LSimRank which captures both structural information and label information in graphs. We give a recursive definition of LSimRank and derive a corresponding random-surfer pairs form. In order to capture the label information of nodes, we define a label similarity function. We introduce several approximation algorithms to speed up the computation of LSimRank. Extensive experiments on datasets verify that LSimRank is superior over SimRank on labeled graphs. There are a few directions for future study. First, it may be helpful to include edge labels in measuring similarity. We can easily extend the label vector to include the edge labels within h-hop neighbors. Second, it may be interesting to design new algorithms to handle dynamic graphs.

References

1. Konect datasets: The koblenz network collection. http://konect.uni-koblenz.de
2. Technical report: LSimRank: Node similarity in a labeled graph. https://www.dropbox.com/sh/19il4hol726ltic/AABsMjX-28wJN4IlYArJS6yYa?dl=0
3. Antonellis, I., Molina, H.G., Chang, C.C.: Simrank++: query rewriting through link analysis of the click graph. Proc. VLDB Endowment **1**(1), 408–421 (2008)
4. Arora, A., Sachan, M., Bhattacharya, A.: Mining statistically significant connected subgraphs in vertex labeled graphs. In: SIGMOD, pp. 1003–1014 (2014)

5. Chen, H.-H., Giles, C.L.: Ascos++: an asymmetric similarity measure for weighted networks to address the problem of simrank. ACM Trans. Knowl. Discov. Data (TKDD) **10**(2), 15 (2015)
6. Conte, A., Ferraro, G., Grossi, R., Marino, A., Sadakane, K., Uno, T.: Node similarity with q-grams for real-world labeled networks. In: Proceedings of the 24th ACM SIGKDD International Conference on Knowledge Discovery & Data Mining, pp. 1282–1291. ACM (2018)
7. Fogaras, D., Rácz, B.: Scaling link-based similarity search. In: Proceedings of the 14th International Conference on World Wide Web, pp. 641–650. ACM (2005)
8. Jeh, G., Widom, J.: Simrank: a measure of structural-context similarity. In: Proceedings of the Eighth ACM SIGKDD International Conference on Knowledge Discovery and Data Mining, pp. 538–543. ACM (2002)
9. Jiang, M., Fu, A.W.-C., Wong, R.C.-W.: Reads: a random walk approach for efficient and accurate dynamic simrank. Proc. VLDB Endowment **10**(9), 937–948 (2017)
10. Jin, R., Lee, V.E., Hong, H.: Axiomatic ranking of network role similarity. In: Proceedings of the 17th ACM SIGKDD International Conference on Knowledge Discovery and Data Mining, pp. 922–930. ACM (2011)
11. Leskovec, J., Krevl, A.: Snap datasets: standford large network dataset collection (2016). http://snap.standford.edu/data
12. Liben-Nowell, D., Kleinberg, J.: The link-prediction problem for social networks. J. Am. Soc. Inf. Sci. Technol. **58**(7), 1019–1031 (2007)
13. Lin, D., et al.: An information-theoretic definition of similarity. In: Icml, vol. 98, pp. 296–304. Citeseer (1998)
14. Liu, Y., Zheng, B., He, X., Wei, Z., Xiao, X., Zheng, K., Lu, J.: Probesim: scalable single-source and top-k simrank computations on dynamic graphs. Proc. VLDB Endowment **11**(1), 14–26 (2017)
15. Rothe, S., Schütze, H.: Cosimrank: a flexible & efficient graph-theoretic similarity measure. In: Proceedings of the 52nd Annual Meeting of the Association for Computational Linguistics (Volume 1: Long Papers), vol. 1, pp. 1392–1402 (2014)
16. Shao, Y., Cui, B., Chen, L., Liu, M., Xie, X.: An efficient similarity search framework for simrank over large dynamic graphs. Proc. VLDB Endowment **8**(8), 838–849 (2015)
17. Shi, C., Kong, X., Huang, Y., Philip, S.Y., Wu, B.: Hetesim: a general framework for relevance measure in heterogeneous networks. IEEE Trans. Knowl. Data Eng. **26**(10), 2479–2492 (2014)
18. Song, J., Luo, X., Gao, J., Zhou, C., Wei, H., Uniwalk, J.X.Y.: Unidirectional random walk based scalable simrank computation over large graph. IEEE Trans. Knowl. Data Eng. **30**(5), 992–1006 (2018)
19. Spirin, N., Han, J.: Survey on web spam detection: principles and algorithms. ACM SIGKDD Explor. Newsletter **13**(2), 50–64 (2012)
20. Sun, Y., Han, J., Yan, X., Yu, P.S., Wu, T.: Pathsim: meta path-based top-k similarity search in heterogeneous information networks. Proc. VLDB Endowment **4**(11), 992–1003 (2011)
21. Tian, B., Xiao, X.: Sling: a near-optimal index structure for simrank. In: Proceedings of the 2016 International Conference on Management of Data, pp. 1859–1874. ACM (2016)
22. Xiong, Y., Zhu, Y., Philip, S.Y.: Top-k similarity join in heterogeneous information networks. IEEE Trans. Knowl. Data Eng. **27**(6), 1710–1723 (2014)
23. Youngmann, B., Milo, T., Somech, A.: Boosting simrank with semantics. In: EDBT, pp. 37–48 (2019)

24. Yu, W., Lin, X., Zhang, W., Chang, L., Pei, J.: More is simpler: effectively and efficiently assessing node-pair similarities based on hyperlinks. Proc. VLDB Endowment **7**(1), 13–24 (2013)
25. Zhao, P., Han, J., Sun, Y.: P-rank: a comprehensive structural similarity measure over information networks. In: Proceedings of the 18th ACM Conference on Information and Knowledge Management, pp. 553–562. ACM (2009)
26. Zhou, Y., Cheng, H., Yu, J.X.: Graph clustering based on structural/attribute similarities. Proc. VLDB Endowment **2**(1), 718–729 (2009)

Fruited-Forest: A Reachability Querying Method Based on Spanning Tree Modelling of Reduced DAG

Liu Yang[1], Tingxuan Chen[1], Junyu Zhang[1], Jun Long[1], Zhigang Hu[1], and Victor S. Sheng[2(✉)]

[1] Central South University, Changsha, China
{yangliu,chentingxuan,zhangjunyu,jlong,zghu}@csu.edu.cn
[2] Texas Tech University, Broadway, Lubbock 2500, USA
victor.sheng@ttu.edu

Abstract. A reachability query is a fundamental graph operation in real graph applications, which answers whether a node can reach another node through a path in a graph. However, the increasingly large amounts of real graph data make it more challenging for query efficiency and scalability. In this paper, we propose a Fruited-Forest (*FF*) approach to accelerate reachability queries in large graphs by constructing four kinds of fruited-forests from a reduced DAG in different traversal orders. We build different binary-label schemes for the four kinds of fruited-forests to cover reachability between nodes as much as possible, and create a corresponding index for the deleted edges which are deleted during the construction of fruited-forests. Our experimental results on 18 large real graph datasets show that our *FF* approach requires less index construct time and a smaller index size, which is more scalable to answer reachability queries compared with other existing works.

Keywords: Reachability query · Fruit-forest · Large graph · DAG reduction · Spanning tree

1 Introduction

Given a directed graph $G = (V, E)$ with n nodes ($n = |V|$), and m edges ($m = |E|$), a reachability query ($u \to v$? $u, v \in V$) is to answer if there exists a path $(u, v) = (v_1, v_2, \cdots, v_p)$ in G where (v_i, v_{i+1}) is an edge in E, for $1 \leq i < p, u = v_1$, and $v = v_p$. If the graphs are in small-scales, a reachability query can be answered by depth-first search (DFS) or reachability transitive closures. However, these methods are not efficient when the graphs grow large, since DFS is inefficient for large-scale datasets and reachability transitive closures occupy a huge storage space.

Inspired by the result of DAG reduction G^ε by [9], we propose a *FF* approach to answer a reachability query, using topological order and topological level to maximize the coverage of unreachable node pairs and reachable node pairs, just

© Springer Nature Switzerland AG 2020
X. Wang et al. (Eds.): APWeb-WAIM 2020, LNCS 12317, pp. 145–153, 2020.
https://doi.org/10.1007/978-3-030-60259-8_11

like the real fruited trees with full of fruits. In addition, we construct the index of transitive closure for each node by a bottom-up method to reduce the index construction time and size.

2 FF Construction from DAG

Given a result of DAG reduction G^ε (Fig. 1), and its topological order, FF can be constructed by four kinds of spanning trees, with different topological orders and constructions, including top-down from left to right, top-down from right to left, bottom-up from left to right, bottom-up from right to left. We use X to represent the topological order of a node from top (node's indegree is 0) to bottom (node's outdegree is 0) and left to right (i.e., left first), $\overline{X}$ from top to bottom and right to left (i.e., right first), $\neg X$ from bottom to up and left to right, and $\neg \overline{X}$ from bottom to up and right to left.

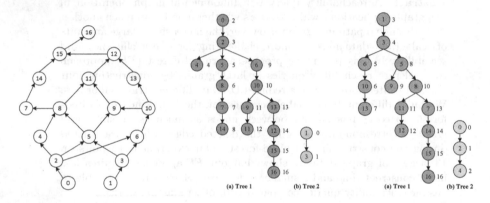

Fig. 1. DAG G^ε **Fig. 2.** ILM-X trees   **Fig. 3.** ILM-$\overline{X}$ trees

Definition 1. ILM-X($\overline{X}$) *Given the topological order* $X(\overline{X})$, *an ILM-X($\overline{X}$) tree* $T_x^\varepsilon(T_{\overline{x}}^\varepsilon)$ *is a* $X(\overline{X})$-*order spanning tree of* G^ε, *where the* __incoming__ *edge to a node* v *in* $T_x^\varepsilon(T_{\overline{x}}^\varepsilon)$ *is from its* __last__ *graph parent node* u, *which has the* __maximum__ *topological order among* v's *parents in* $X(\overline{X})$.

Definition 2. OLM-$\neg X$($\neg \overline{X}$) *Given the topological order* $\neg X(\neg \overline{X})$, *an OLM-$\neg X$($\neg \overline{X}$) tree* $T_{\neg x}^\varepsilon(T_{\neg \overline{x}}^\varepsilon)$ *is a* $\neg X(\neg \overline{X})$-*order spanning tree of* G^ε, *where the* __out__ *edge to a node* v *in* $T_{\neg x}^\varepsilon(T_{\neg \overline{x}}^\varepsilon)$ *is from its* __last__ *graph child* u, *which has the* __maximum__ *topological order among* v's *child in* $\neg X(\neg \overline{X})$.

From the above, the FF constructed from DAG consists of four kinds of forests, i.e., ILM-X, ILM-$\overline{X}$, OLM-$\neg$X and OLM-$\neg\overline{X}$. As shown in Fig. 2, Fig. 3, Fig. 4 and Fig. 5, the number in the circle is the node ID, and the number next to the circle is the topological order of the node.

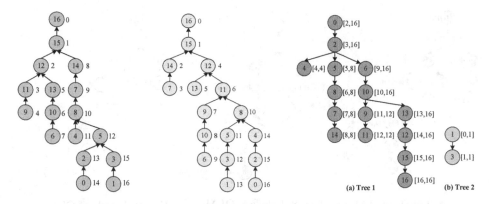

Fig. 4. OLM-¬X tree   **Fig. 5.** OLM-¬X̄ tree   **Fig. 6.** Labels of ILM-X

3 Interval Labeling

We use the constructed trees to create a binary label for each node in this section, so that these trees contain the most information between nodes, including reachability and unreachability information.

Interval Labels for Nodes in FF. We assign a binary label to each node, with the first label representing the topological order of the node, and the second label representing the maximum topological order of the node that can reach in the tree. The following four figures (Fig. 6, Fig. 7, Fig. 8 and Fig. 9) show the interval labels corresponding to ILM-X, ILM-X̄, OLM-¬X and OLM-¬X.

Lemma 1. *Given four different topological orders of X, $\overline{X}$, $\neg X$ and $\neg \overline{X}$, u and v have an ancestor-descendant relationship if and only if the following four conditions meet simultaneously: (1) $X_u < X_v$; (2) $\overline{X_u} < \overline{X_v}$; (3) $\neg X_u > \neg X_v$; (4) $\neg \overline{X_u} > \neg \overline{X_v}$.*

Lemma 2. *Let $I_X(u) = [s, e]$, $I_{\overline{X}}(u) = [s, e]$, $I_{\neg X}(u) = [s, e]$, $I_{\neg \overline{X}}(u) = [s, e]$ be the interval labels assigned to u based on ILM-X, ILM-X̄, OLM-¬X and OLM-¬X̄, respectively. $\forall u, v \in V^\varepsilon$, (1) $I_X(v) \subset I_X(u)$; (2) $I_{\overline{X}}(v) \subset I_{\overline{X}}(u)$; (3) $I_{\neg X}(u) \subset I_{\neg X}(v)$; (4) $I_{\neg \overline{X}}(u) \subset I_{\neg \overline{X}}(v)$. If anyone of the above four conditions is satisfied, u can reach v.*

The Top-Level of Node in FF. The level of the topology is not changed whether the topological order is obtained from left to right or right to left. That is, the depth of the topology remains unchanged, so that we can construct a topological level for each node based on ILM-X trees as shown in Fig. 10.

Lemma 3. *Nodes on the same topological level are mutually unreachable.*

We present our result in Fig. 11 according to above lemmas. The x-axis is the topological order of the nodes, and the y-axis is the topological level of the nodes. Table 1 lists the four different interval labels and the topological level.

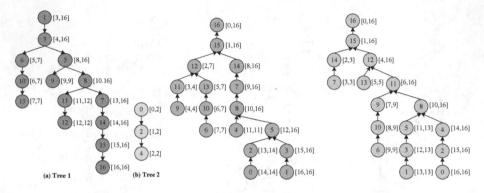

Fig. 7. Labels of ILM-$\overline{X}$ **Fig. 8.** Labels of OLM-$\neg X$ **Fig. 9.** Labels of OLM-$\neg\overline{X}$

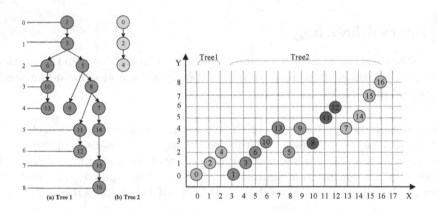

Fig. 10. Topo-level of trees   **Fig. 11.** Bracnches of ILM-X

4   Index of Deleted Edges

Most reachable nodes can be judged quickly from the above constructed FF, since most nodes except the root nodes have only one parent node in the forest. However, one node may have multiple parent nodes in G^ε. That is, because some of the reachability relationships are broken during FF construction. According to the four different kinds of forests we constructed, the original reachability has been retained to the greatest extent, but there is still a part of reachability relationships are broken by deleted edges, so we create an out-index for each node whose original reachability relationships with other nodes are broken.

In order to speed up the index construction and reduce the index size, we propose a bottom-up index construction method by upward step from leaf nodes. Once a node has the deleted reachability, the reachability of the deleted node of the node is added to the index of the node, and as to its parent node, just add the index of the node to the index of its parent node.

Table 1. Labels of nodes in four kinds of trees

ID	Level	ILM(X.Y)	ILM(¬X,Y)	OLM($\overline{\text{X}}$,Y)	OLM(¬$\overline{\text{X}}$,Y)
0	0	(0, 2)	(2, 16)	(16, 16)	(14, 14)
1	0	(3, 16)	(0, 1)	(13, 13)	(16, 16)
2	1	(1, 2)	(3, 16)	(15, 16)	(13, 14)
3	1	(4, 16)	(1, 1)	(12, 13)	(15, 16)
4	2	(2, 2)	(4, 4)	(14, 16)	(11, 11)
5	2	(8, 16)	(5, 8)	(11, 13)	(12, 16)
6	2	(5, 7)	(9, 16)	(9, 9)	(7, 7)
7	4	(13, 16)	(7, 8)	(3, 3)	(9, 16)
8	3	(10, 16)	(6, 8)	(10, 16)	(10, 16)
9	4	(9, 9)	(11, 12)	(7, 9)	(4, 4)
10	3	(6, 7)	(10, 16)	(8, 9)	(6, 7)
11	5	(11, 12)	(12, 12)	(6, 16)	(3, 4)
12	6	(12, 12)	(14, 16)	(4, 16)	(2, 7)
13	4	(7, 7)	(13, 16)	(5, 5)	(5, 7)
14	5	(14, 16)	(8, 8)	(2, 3)	(8, 16)
15	7	(15, 16)	(15, 16)	(1, 16)	(1, 16)
16	8	(16, 16)	(16, 16)	(0, 16)	(0, 16)

5   Answer Reachability Queries

Our *FF* approach presents the following 4-step judgement to answer whether u can reach v:

(1) Are they are on the same topological level based on **Lemma** 3? If they are on the same topological level, u cannot reach v. Otherwise, the second step is performed.

(2) Does an ancestor-descendant relationship exists between u and v based on **Lemma** 1? If it does not exist, u cannot reach v. Otherwise, the third step is performed.

(3) Have they contained relationships between the four different interval labels in the four different forests based on **Lemma** 2? If they do not exist, it means that the reachability of u and v cannot be answered by the constructed *FF*, and then the four step is performed. Otherwise, u can reach v.

(4) Whether v exists in the index of u, if it exists, u can reach v, otherwise, u cannot reach v.

6   Experimental Studies

We conduct a set of experiments in order to compare the performance of our Fruited-Forest (*FF*) algorithm with other reachability approaches. We test the

Table 2. 15 Real Large Graph Datasets

DataSet	$|V|$	$|E|$	$|E|/|V|$
citeseer	693947	312282	0.450
email	231000	223004	0.965
LJ	971232	1024140	1.054
mapped100K	2658702	2660628	1.000
mapped1M	9387448	9440404	1.005
twitter	18121168	18359487	1.013
uniprot22m	1595444	1595442	0.999
uniprot100m	16087295	16087293	0.999
uniprot150m	25037600	25037598	0.999
web	371764	517805	1.392
wiki	2281879	2311570	1.013
citeseerx	6540399	15011259	2.295
dbpedia	3365623	7989191	2.374
go-uniprot	6967956	34770235	4.990
HostLink	12754590	26669293	2.091

efficiency of our algorithm on 15 real large real datasets which are used in [4, 6, 7], as shown in Table 2. As given in [6], we classify the graphs with the average degree smaller than 2 as sparse graphs and the ones with the average degree larger than or equal to 2 as dense graphs.

It is proved that the *BFL* algorithm is more efficient in constructing of index than other algorithms in [4], including *GRAIL* [8], *PWAH8* [3], *TF-Label* [1], *HL* [2], *Feline* [5], *IP+* [7] and *TOL* [10], on 15 real large-scale datasets shown in Table 2. However, *BFL* needs more space to storage index than *TOL* on 15 real large-scale datasets. *BFL* performs best on 13 out of all 15 datasets, except *citeseer* and *email*. Therefore, we only compare experimental results with *BFL*, *TOL*, *GRAIL*. All algorithms, including *FF*, are implemented in C++ and compiled by G++ 6.3.3. All these experiments are performed on the machine with 3.20 GHz Intel Core i5–6500 CPU, 32 GB RAM running on CentOS7/Linux.

We compare *FF* with *BFL*, *GRAIL* and *TOL*, from three aspects, including the index construction time, index size, and query time in 15 real datasets using equal workloads shown in Table 3 and Fig. 12, Fig. 13 and Fig. 14. The query time is the total running time of a total of 1,000,000 reachability queries. The best results are highlighted in **bold** font. For experiments that run longer than 24 h or run more than 32GB of memory, we use "—" instead of the experimental results.

Table 3. Index Construction Time (ms), Index Size (KB) and Query Time (ms) on 15 Real Datasets

DataSet	Index Time				Index Size				Query Time			
	BFL	GRAIL	TOL	FF	BFL	GRAIL	TOL	FF	BFL	GRAIL	TOL	FF
citeseer	86	792.8	250	**83.4**	17132.5	2710.7	10956.8	**1228.8**	39.9	438.3	87.6	**14.2**
email	17	229.4	80	**11.8**	8350.7	**7.5**	3379.2	264.8	50.7	7666.2	75.7	**12.4**
LJ	68	1031.3	75.7	**63.2**	35671	3793.9	15564.8	**844.4**	79.1	3980740.8	90.8	**29.8**
mapped100K	182	2894.2	870	**113.9**	80129	10385.6	45260.8	**460.5**	35.2	365	104.4	21
mapped1M	642	11566.8	3100	**398.7**	275369	36669.7	169267.2	**1614.1**	34.9	429.6	96.632	**23.1**
twitter	1495	—	5880	**666.7**	617821.2	—	333209.6	**2338.9**	31.7	—	97.556	**15.3**
uniprot22m	88	1760.9	580	**79.4**	58683.4	6232.2	25804.8	**613.8**	35.1	478.3	92.3	**10.4**
uniprot100m	1334	25059.3	5200	**1222**	620522.5	62841	292761.6	**22223.3**	36.8	707	95.2	**26.3**
uniprot150m	**692**	34610.1	8090	1004.4	267115.5	97803.1	474828.8	**909.5**	34.2	543.8	97	**6.4**
web	56	368	130	**43.9**	15231	1452.2	5734.4	**885.2**	77.4	439624.2	84	**74.8**
wiki	124	2304.8	750	**73.7**	82699.3	8913.6	38297.6	**251.9**	35.6	734222.5	91.9	**8.2**
citeseerx	**1465**	8264.6	2150	1596.7	292454.5	**25548.4**	116736	236544	**54.5**	31750.9	92.2	131.6
dbpedia	731	16197.3	2240	**667.8**	111779.8	27218.9	58265.6	**13267.4**	58.1	639.3	95	**54.1**
go-uniprot	1812	5425.1	1120	**187.2**	197731.3	13147.1	124620.8	**820.9**	35.5	113331.2	98.2	**9.1**
HostLink	2203	19646	4100	**1547.9**	372529.2	49822.6	231321.6	**32275.4**	71.1	6915906	99.7	**64.8**

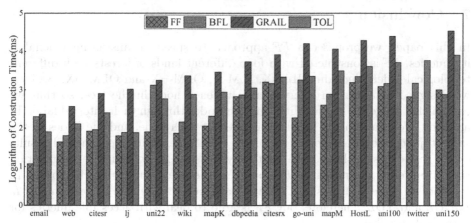

Fig. 12. Index construction time

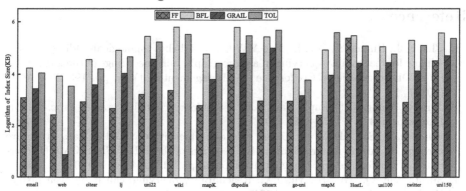

Fig. 13. Index size

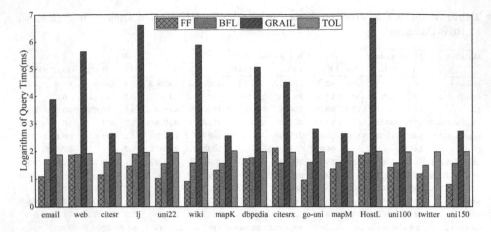

Fig. 14. Query time

7   Conclusion

In this paper, we proposed a *FF* approach to speed up answering reachability queries. *FF* is constructed with four different kinds of forests with different topological orders, including ILM-X, ILM-$\overline{\text{X}}$, OLM-¬X and OLM-¬$\overline{\text{X}}$. Besides, we designed to assign an interval label to each node in the tree, so that we can quickly judge the reachability between nodes through their interval label. In addition, we established a topological level for each node, and the nodes in the same topology level are not reachable to each other. Our experimental results on 15 real datasets showed that not only the index size and the construction time are greatly optimized by *FF*, but also the query time is much shorter. In terms of all three measures, our *FF* approach performed much better than *BFL*, *GRAIL* and *TOL*. Therefore, our *FF* is able to deal with accessible queries for large-scale graphs.

References

1. Cheng, J., Huang, S., Wu, H., Fu, A.W.C.: Tf-label: a topological-folding labeling scheme for reachability querying in a large graph. In: Proceedings of the 2013 ACM SIGMOD International Conference on Management of Data, pp. 193–204. ACM (2013)
2. Jin, R., Wang, G.: Simple, fast, and scalable reachability oracle. Proc. VLDB Endowment **6**(14), 1978–1989 (2013)
3. van Schaik, S.J., de Moor, O.: A memory efficient reachability data structure through bit vector compression. In: Proceedings of the 2011 ACM SIGMOD International Conference on Management of Data, pp. 913–924. ACM (2011)
4. Su, J., Zhu, Q., Wei, H., Yu, J.X.: Reachability querying: can it be even faster? IEEE Trans. Knowl. Data Eng. **29**(3), 683–697 (2016)

5. Veloso, R.R., Cerf, L., Meira Jr, W., Zaki, M.J.: Reachability queries in very large graphs: a fast refined online search approach. In: EDBT, pp. 511–522. Citeseer (2014)
6. Wei, H., Yu, J.X., Lu, C., Jin, R.: Reachability querying: an independent permutation labeling approach. Proc. VLDB Endowment **7**(12), 1191–1202 (2014)
7. Wei, H., Yu, J.X., Lu, C., Jin, R.: Reachability querying: an independent permutation labeling approach. VLDB J. **27**(1), 1–26 (2017). https://doi.org/10.1007/s00778-017-0468-3
8. Yıldırım, H., Chaoji, V., Zaki, M.J.: Grail: a scalable index for reachability queries in very large graphs. VLDB J. Int. J. Very Large Data Bases **21**(4), 509–534 (2012)
9. Zhou, J., Yu, J.X., Li, N., Wei, H., Chen, Z., Tang, X.: Accelerating reachability query processing based on *dag* reduction. VLDB J. Int. J. Very Large Data Bases **27**(2), 271–296 (2018)
10. Zhu, A.D., Lin, W., Wang, S., Xiao, X.: Reachability queries on large dynamic graphs: a total order approach. In: Proceedings of the 2014 ACM SIGMOD International Conference on Management of Data, pp. 1323–1334. ACM (2014)

Frequent Semantic Trajectory Sequence Pattern Mining in Location-Based Social Networks

Zhen Zhang[1(✉)], Jing Zhang[1], Fuxue Li[1], Xiangguo Zhao[2], and Xin Bi[2]

[1] College of Electrical Engineering, Yingkou Institute of Technology,
Yingkou, Liaoning, China
zhangzhenneu@gmail.com,hj2002cn@hotmail.com,lifuxue119@163.com
[2] College of Computer Science and Engineering, Northeastern University,
Shenyang, Liaoning, China
{zhaoxiangguo,bixin}@mail.neu.edu.cn

Abstract. At present, more and more researchers have focused on the study of the frequent trajectory sequence pattern mining in location-based social network (LBSN), in which the trajectories of contributing frequent patterns in users' trajectory database must have same or similar the location coordinates and conform to the semantics and time constraints. In this paper, we focus on the study of users' daily frequent mobile pattern. Excessive limitations on location information may limit the results of mining users' frequent mobile pattern. Therefore, based on the frequent trajectory sequence pattern mining in LBSNs, we first define a new frequent semantic trajectory sequence pattern mining (FSTS-PM) problem that focuses on the study of mining users' frequent mobile pattern. FSTS-PM problem does not consider the location coordinates of the trajectory points, but uses the distance and time constraints among the trajectory points in a trajectory sequence to optimize the user's frequent mobile pattern mining results. Then, we propose the modified PrefixSpan (MP) algorithm which integrates the distance and time filtering mechanism based on the original PrefixSpan to find frequent semantic trajectory sequence pattern. Finally, the extensive experiments verify the performance of MP algorithm.

Keywords: Location-based social networks · Frequent pattern · Trajectory sequence · Mobile pattern

1 Introduction

With the development of GPS technology and the wide application of intelligent terminals, location-based social network (LBSN) services have developed rapidly [1,2], such as Foursquare, Geolife. The most basic trajectory is GPS composed of latitude and longitude coordinates and time. Each trajectory point is usually accompanied by the descriptions of the semantic labels, such as "restaurant" or "hospital". At present, there have been a lot of researches on frequent

© Springer Nature Switzerland AG 2020
X. Wang et al. (Eds.): APWeb-WAIM 2020, LNCS 12317, pp. 154–161, 2020.
https://doi.org/10.1007/978-3-030-60259-8_12

trajectory sequence pattern mining algorithms, so as to find frequent moving sequences of the relationships between users' locations [3–7]. In [5], a spatial-temporal trajectory mining algorithm was proposed. However, mining the lack of semantic trajectory pattern cannot fully convey users' rich movement behaviors. In [6], the semantic dimension was put into the spatial-temporal trajectory sequence pattern. However, a location only corresponded to a semantic label. In fact, a single semantic label sometimes fails to fully describe the spatial location information and limit the mining results. Therefore, in [7], Arya et. al solved the singleness problem of the semantic label.

In this paper, based on the problem of mining users' frequent trajectory sequence pattern, we focus on mining users' daily frequent mobile pattern. Mining users' daily frequent mobile pattern benefits every aspect of people's daily lives. For example, we find that most users will choose to go to the gym for exercise after work, and then go to the restaurant for dinner. Therefore, office→gym→restaurant is the users' daily frequent mobile patten, which is not restricted by spatial conditions. Therefore, users in different cities and even in different countries are likely to contribute to the frequent mobile pattern. However, in the traditional problem of mining users' frequent trajectory sequence pattern, the spatial location information of the frequent elements between the trajectory sequences must be consistent or both within a certain region, which will limit the results of mining users' frequent mobile pattern.

Therefore, in this paper, we define a new frequent semantic trajectory sequence pattern mining (FSTS-PM) problem to mine users' daily frequent mobile pattern. Given a series of users' daily trajectories in LBSN services, an integer threshold, distance and time constraints, FSTS-PM problem is not limited by spatial location information, but needs to satisfy both distance and time constraints between trajectory points. In order to solve FSTS-PM problem, we propose the modified PrefixSpan (MP) algorithm. On the basis of the traditional PrefixSpan [8] sequence pattern mining algorithm, MP algorithm cleverly integrates the distance and time constraints, so as to efficiently filter the nonconforming sequences and speed up the return of algorithm results.

The remainder of this paper is organized as follows: The problem definitions are introduced in Sect. 2. The details of MP algorithm are described in Sect. 3. A series of experimental results are presented in Sect. 4. The paper is concluded in Sect. 5.

2 Problem Definition

In this paper, $P = \{p_1, p_2, \cdots, p_n\}$ represents a series of location, in which each location is composed of two-dimensional latitude and longitude geographic coordinate $p_i = (p_i \cdot longitude, p_i \cdot latitude)$. I represents the set of the semantic label categories. Each location p_i obtains the semantic label set I_i by mining its check-in information (there may be multiple semantic labels on each location).

Definition 1 (Moving Trajectory). A user's moving trajectory is composed of a sequence of locations with the time stamps $< (p_1, t_1),$

Table 1. The semantic trajectory database

No.	Sequence
1	(a,(0,0),0),({abc},(30,40),10),(d,(60,80),30),({ae},(120,160),40),(f,(180,240),50)
2	({ad},(0,0),0),(c,(45,60),20),({df},(90,120),40)
3	({ef},(300,400),0),({df},(450,600),10),(c, (1200,1600),40),({ae},(900,1200),90)
4	({af},(600,800),0),(c,(1200,1600),30),(b, (1800,2400,),60),(c,(450,600),100)

$\cdots, (p_i, t_i), \cdots, (p_n, t_n) >$, in which each element (p_i, t_i) represents the user is on the location p_i at time t_i.

Definition 2 (Semantic Trajectory Database S). A user's semantic trajectory is composed of a semantic sequence with the time stamps and location coordinates $< id, s >=< (I_1, p_1, t_1), \cdots, (I_i, p_i, t_i), \cdots, (I_n, p_n, t_n) >$, in which id is the sequence number, s represents a sequence, and each element (I_i, p_i, t_i) represents the user has check-in at the location p_i at time t_i. The information of check-in contains the semantic label set I_i of the location p_i.

The spatial distance between trajectory points in each trajectory is defined as $Sd(p_i, p_j)$, and the calculation formula is as follows:

$$Sd(p_i, p_j) = \parallel p_i, p_j \parallel \tag{1}$$

where $\parallel p_i, p_j \parallel$ is the Euclidean distance between the trajectory points p_i and p_j.

The evaluation of check-in time interval between each trajectory point in each trajectory is defined as $Td(t_i, t_j)$, and the calculation formula is as follows:

$$Td(t_i, t_j) = t_j - t_i \tag{2}$$

where t_j is the user's check-in time stamp at the trajectory point p_j, and t_i is the user's check-in time stamp at the trajectory point p_i.

Definition 3 (Frequent Semantic Trajectory Sequence Pattern). Let $I = \{i_1, \cdots, i_i, \cdots, i_n\}$ defines a series of semantic items. Any semantic trajectory sequence $< id, s >=< (I_1, p_1, t_1), \cdots, (I_i, p_i, t_i), \cdots, (I_n, p_n, t_n) >$, in which $I_i \in I$ and $p_i \in P$, supports the sub-frequent semantic sequence pattern $\acute{I} = \{\acute{I}_1, \acute{I}_2, \cdots, \acute{I}_m\}$ $(m < n)$ or the trajectory sequence gives the sub-semantic sequence a support, when $1 \le k_1 < k_2 <, \cdots, k_m \le m$, $\{\acute{I}_1 \subseteq I_{k_1}, \acute{I}_2 \subseteq I_{k_2}, \cdots, \acute{I}_m \subseteq I_{k_m}\}$, $Sd(p_{k_i}, p_{k_{i+1}}) \ge \sigma$, $Td(t_{k_i}, t_{k_{i+1}}) \le \gamma$, in which σ and γ are the pre-given distance and time constraints. Similarly, given the semantic trajectory database S, which contains a series of trajectory sequences, an integer threshold δ, and distance and time constraints σ and γ. We can consider the sub-semantic sequence $\acute{I}$ as a frequent semantic trajectory sequence pattern in the semantic trajectory database S when $support(\acute{I}) \ge \delta$.

Example 1 Next, we give an example. Table 1 shows the semantic trajectory database S, which contains the semantic label set $I = \{$Chinese food(a), dessert shop(b), cafe(c), shopping center(d), western restaurant(e), cinema$(f)\}$, minimum support threshold $\delta = 2$, time constraint $\gamma = 50$, distance constraint $\sigma = 500$. In the semantic trajectory database S, the latitude and longitude of each trajectory point is expressed as an integer for the convenience of subsequent calculations. For the number 1 trajectory sequence, the semantic item a appears twice in the number 1 trajectory sequence, so it contributes two sequence lengths. For semantic item a, however, the number 1 trajectory sequence only contributes $support(a) = 1$, and the whole trajectory database S contributes $support(a) = 3$. So the semantic term a is a frequent semantic sequence pattern.

3   MP Algorithm

MP algorithm is based on the most representative frequent sequence pattern mining algorithm prefixSpan.

Definition 4 (Semantic Postfix). Give a user's semantic trajectory sequence $< (I_1, p_1, t_1), \cdots, (I_i, p_i, t_i), \cdots, (I_n, p_n, t_n) >$. For any of the semantic set I_i $(1 \leq i \leq n)$, $< (I_{i+1}, \| p_{i+1}, p_i \|, t_{i+1} - t_i), (I_{i+2}, \| p_{i+2}, p_i \|, t_{i+2} - t_i), \cdots, (I_n, \| p_n, p_i \|, t_n - t_i) >$ defines the semantic postfix.

We demonstrate the steps of mining frequent semantic trajectory sequence pattern by MP algorithm in the semantic trajectory database shown in Table 1. Still assume that the minimum support threshold $\delta = 2$, the time constraint $\gamma = 50$, the distance constraint $\sigma = 500$.

Step 1: Count the number of occurrences of the 1-length frequent semantic sequences. Scan S to find the number of occurrences of all 1-length frequent semantic sequences in the semantic trajectory database: $< a >$: 4; $< b >$: 2; $< c >$: 4; $< d >$: 3; $< e >$: 2; $< f >$: 4 (those exceeding the minimum support threshold 2 can be considered as frequent semantic sequences).

Step 2: Split search space. Based on the step 1, we can divide the search space into six subspaces: (1) the prefix $< a >$; $\cdots$; (6) the prefix $< f >$.

Step 3: Search for the frequent semantic trajectory sequences in subspaces. By creating a postfix database, subsets of semantic sequence patterns can be mined iteratively. Table 2 records the postfix database creation process, which is explained as follows:

First, we need to find a semantic sequence pattern with the prefix $< a >$. According to the definition of semantic postfix, it will form the $< a >$ − postfix database in semantic trajectory database S, which includes four postfix sequence: (1) $(\{abc\}, 50, 10), (d, 100, 30), (\{ae\}, 200, 40), (f, 300, 50) >$; (2) $(\{-d\}, (0, 0, 0), (c, 75, 20), (\{df\}, 150, 40) >$; (3)$< \{-e\}, 0, 0 >$; (4)$< (\{-f\}, 0, 0), (c, 1000, 30), (b, 2500, 60), (c, 250, 100) >$. Then by scanning the $< a >$ − postfix database, the 2-length frequent semantic sequences can be found: $< ac >$: 2; $< ad >$: 2; $< af >$: 2, $< \{ae\} >$: 2.

Table 2. The creation of postfix database

prefix	Postfix database	Frequent pattern
$< a >$	$< (\{abc\}, 50, 10), (d, 100, 30), (\{ae\}, 200, 40), (f, 300, 50) >;$ $< (-d, 0, 0), (c, 75, 20), (\{df\}, 150, 40) >; < \{-e\}, 0, 0 >;$ $< \{-f\}, 0, 0), (c, 1000, 30), (b, 2000, 60), (c, 250, 100) >$	$< a >; < ac >; < ad >;$ $< af >; < \{ae\} >;$ $< acd >; < acf >$
$< b >$	$< (\{-c\}, 0, 0), (d, 50, 20), (\{ae\}, 150, 30), (f, 250, 40) >;$ $< (c, 2250, 40) >$	$< b >$
$< c >$	$< (d, 50, 20), (\{ae\}, 150, 30), (f, 250, 40) >; < (\{df\}, 75, 20) >;$ $< \{ae\}, 500, 50 >; < (b, 1000, 30), (c, 1250, 70) >$	$< c >; < cd >; < cf >;$ $< ca >; < ce >; < cae >$
$< d >$	$< (\{ae\}, 100, 10), (f, 200, 20) >; < (c, 75, 20), (\{df\}, 150, 40) >;$ $< (\{-f\}, 0, 0), (c, 1250, 30), (\{ae\}, 750, 80) >$	$< d >; < df >$
$< e >$	$< (f, 100, 10) >; \{-f\}, 0, 0), (\{df\}, 250, 10), (c, 1500, 40),$ $(\{ae\}, 1000, 90) >$	$< e >; < ef >$
$< f >$	$< (\{df\}, 250, 10), (c, 1500, 40), (\{ae\}, 1000, 90) >; < c, 1000, 30),$ $(b, 2000, 60), (c, 250, 100) >$	$< f >$

Next, we need to loop the above process and divide the semantic sequence containing $< a >$ into 4 subsets: (1) containing the prefix $< ac >$; (2) containing the prefix $< ad >$; (3) contains the prefix $< af >$; (4) containing the prefix $< \{ae\} >$. These subsets create their own postfix databases in the same way that the $< a > -$ postfix database is created:

$< ac > -$ postfix database contains two postfix sequence: (1) $< (d, 50, 20), (\{ae\}, 150, 30), (f, 250, 40) >$; (2) $< (\{df\}, 75, 20)$. Then scan the $< ac > -$ postfix database. And the 3-length frequent semantic sequences can be found: $< acd >$: 2, $< acf >$: 2.

$< ad > -$ postfix database contains two postfix sequences: (1) $< (\{ae\}, 100, 10), (f, 200, 20) >$; (2) $< (\{-f\}, 0, 0) >$. Since it has no hope of having more frequent semantic sequences, the $< ad > -$ postfix database is terminated.

$< af > -$ postfix database has not had any non-empty postfix sequence, so $< af > -$ postfix database is terminated.

$< \{ae\} > -$ postfix database contains a sequence of non-empty postfix: $< (f, 100, 10) >$, which have not had more frequent semantic sequences, so $< ae > -$ postfix database is terminated.

Next we search for the 3-length frequent semantic sequence pattern that contains $< a >$. The semantic sequences containing $< a >$ is divided into two subsets: (1) containing the prefix $< acd >$; (2) containing the prefix $< acf >$. Then create their postfix database: $< acd > -$ postfix database contains two postfix sequences: (1) $< (\{ae\}, 100, 10), (f, 200, 20) >$; (2) $< (-f, 0, 0) >$. The postfix database has not produced more frequent semantic sequence patterns, so terminate the postfix database.

The $< acf > -$ postfix database has not had any non-empty sequences, so the postfix database is terminated.

At this point, all frequent semantic sequence patterns containing $< a >$ prefix finish searching. And the frequent semantic trajectory sequence patterns including $< b >$, $< c >$, $< d >$, $< e >$, and $< f >$ prefixes is similar to the

Table 3. The Description of the experimental datasets

	Foursquare	Brightkite	Geolife
Number of trajectories	30,000	40,000	50,000
Average item	6	7	8
Total number of items	50,000	60,000	70,000

Table 4. The parameter setting

Parameter	Range	Default value
Grid size	2–10 unit	10 unit
Frequent threshold δ	0.1%–0.5%	0.1%
Distance constraint	0.2–1.0 km	1.0 km
Time constraint	60–100 min	100 min

mining of $< a >$ prefix. These postfix databases are created and the final mining results are shown in Table 2.

4 Experiments

4.1 Experiment Setup

We make the experiment on three real LBSN datasets: Foursquare, Geolife, and Brightkite. The basic information for these three datasets is described in Table 3. And the total number of item in the whole trajectory database is 70000. Table 4 shows the changes of experimental parameters. In the experiment, MP algorithm will mainly carry out comparative experiments with NB algorithm. NB algorithm first uses PrefixSpan algorithm to find frequent semantic sequences. Then scan the results of frequent semantic sequence pattern to filter out results that do not meet the distance and time constraints. A series of experiments are conducted on the PC of Microsoft Windows win10, Intel Core i5 CPU, 3.20 GHz, and 16GB memory in java JDK 1.8. Each experiment is taken for 10 times and the average result of 10 experiments will be as the final value.

4.2 Experimental Analysis

The Effect of Grid Sizes on the Efficiency of the Algorithms. The top three figures in Fig. 1 show the running time of MP and NB algorithms with the change of the granularity of grid in Foursquare, Geolife, and Brightkite. We can find that the larger granularity, the longer the running time of the two algorithms. And we can also find that the running time of MP algorithm is less than that NB algorithm.

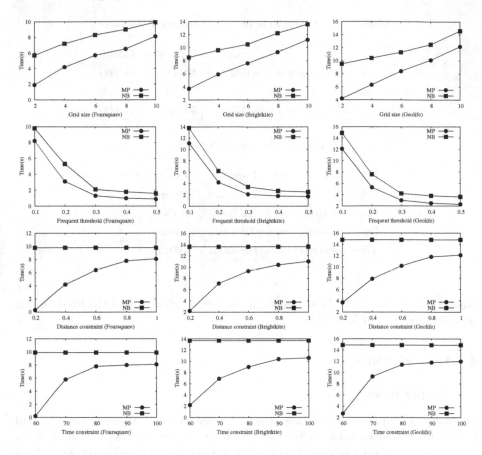

Fig. 1. The effect of four parameters for the algorithms

The Effect of Frequent Threshold on the Efficiency of the Algorithms.
The three figures in the second row of Fig. 1 show the running time of MP and
NB algorithms with the change of frequent threshold in Foursquare, Geolife,
and Brightkite. We can find that the running time of both algorithms decreases
slightly with the increase of frequent threshold. And we can also find that the
running time of MP algorithm is still less than that of NB algorithm.

The Effect of Distance Constraint on the Efficiency of the Algorithms.
The three figures in the third row of Fig. 1 show the running time of MP and
NB algorithms with the change of distance constraint in Foursquare, Geolife, and
Brightkite. First, we can find that the larger the distance constraint, the longer
the running time of MP algorithm will be. However, the running time of NB
algorithm will be basically unchanged. And we can still get the same conclusion
as above: the running time of MP algorithm is less than NB algorithm.

The Effect of Time Constraint on the Efficiency of the Algorithms. The
bottom three figures in Fig. 1 show the running time of MP and NB algorithms

with the change of time constraint in Foursquare, Geolife, and Brightkite. We can find that the longer the time constraint setting, the longer the running time of MP algorithm will be. However, the running time of NB algorithm will be basically unchanged. And we can still get the same conclusion as above: the running time of MP algorithm is less than NB algorithm.

5   Conclusions

In this paper, we focus on mining the users' daily frequent mobile pattern. We first give the definition of FSTS-PM problem. Next, we propose MP algorithm to solve FSTS-PM problem. MP algorithm integrates the distance and time constraint conditions into the process of frequent semantic trajectory sequence mining, and filters out the nonconforming trajectories directly. Finally, the effectiveness of MP algorithm is verified by a large number of experiments.

Acknowledgment. This research is partially supported by the National Natural Science Foundation of China under Grant Nos. 61672145, 61702086, China Postdoctoral Science Foundation under Grant No. 2018M631806, Doctor Startup Foundation of Liaoning Province under Grant No. 2020-BS-288, Natural Science Foundation of Liaoning Province of China under Grant No. 20180550260, Scientific Research Foundation of Liaoning Province under Grant Nos. L2019001, L2019003, Doctoral Business and Innavation Launching Plan of Yingkou City under Grant No. QB-2019-16.

References

1. Hao, F., Zhang, J., Duan, Z., Zhao, L., Guo, L., Park, D.-S.: Urban area function zoning based on user relationships in location-based social networks. IEEE Access **8**, 23487–23495 (2020)
2. Li, Y., Zhao, X., Zhang, Z., Yuan, Y., Wang, G.: Annotating semantic tags of locations in location-based social networks. GeoInformatica **24**(1), 133–152 (2020)
3. Chen, Y., Zhao, X., Lin, X., Wang, Y., Guo, D.: Efficient mining of frequent patterns on uncertain graphs. IEEE Trans. Knowl. Data Eng. **31**(2), 287–300 (2019)
4. Na Deng, X., Chen, D.L., Xiong, C.: Frequent patterns mining in DNA sequence. IEEE Access **7**, 108400–108410 (2019)
5. Lee, A.J.T., Chen, Y.-A., Ip, W.-C.: Mining frequent trajectory patterns in spatial-temporal databases. Inf. Sci. **179**(13), 2218–2231 (2009)
6. Zhang, C., Han, J., Shou, L., Jiajun, L., La Porta, T.F.: Splitter: mining fine-grained sequential patterns in semantic trajectories. PVLDB **7**(9), 769–780 (2014)
7. Arya, K.K., Goyal, V., Navathe, S.B., Prasad, S.: Mining frequent spatial-textual sequence patterns. In: Renz, M., Shahabi, C., Zhou, X., Cheema, M.A. (eds.) DAS-FAA 2015. LNCS, vol. 9050, pp. 123–138. Springer, Cham (2015). https://doi.org/10.1007/978-3-319-18123-3_8
8. Pei, J., Han, J., Mortazavi-Asl, B.: Prefixspan: mining sequential patterns by prefix-projected growth. In: Proceedings of the 17th International Conference on Data Engineering, pp. 215–224 (2001)

Aligning Users Across Social Networks via Intra and Inter Attentions

Zhichao Huang[1,2], Xutao Li[1,2], and Yunming Ye[1,2(✉)]

[1] Harbin Institute of Technology, Shenzhen, Shenzhen 518055, China
yeyunming@hit.edu.cn
[2] Shenzhen Key Laboratory of Internet Information Collaboration,
Shenzhen 518055, China

Abstract. In recent years, aligning users across different social networks receives a significant attention. Previous studies solve the problem based on attributes or topology structure approximation. However, most of them suffer from error propagation or the noise from diverse neighbors. To address the drawback, we design *intra* and *inter* attention mechanisms to model the influence of neighbors in local and across networks. In addition, to effectively incorporate the topology structure information, we leverage neighbors from labeled pairs instead of these in original networks, which are termed as *matched neighbors*. Then we treat the user alignment problem as a classification task and predict it upon a deep neural network. We conduct extensive experiments on six real-world datasets, and the results demonstrate the superiority of the proposed method against state-of-the-art competitors.

Keywords: User alignment · Intra and inter attentions · Matched neighbors

1 Introduction

As the advancement of social networks and Web 2.0, users may have many different social network accounts in diverse social platforms. In particular, these platforms are independent from each other. Thus, an important problem arises, namely how to identify the same user in different platforms, which is well known as *user alignment*. One intuitive solution of user alignment is to compare user profiles such as gender, name, etc [2,6]. However, the user profiles across social networks are often heterogenous or even faked. Consequently, they cannot provide sufficient alignment evidence. Modelling topology structure similarity is also considered in user alignments [3,4]. Specifically, IONE [3] simultaneously learns node context embeddings in local and across networks, while PALE [4] learns local network embeddings independently. In addition, there also exists some attribute based work [1,5], which solves this problem with user attribute similarity comparison. However, most of above methods do not comprehensively exploit the information of both user attributes and topology structures to solve

© Springer Nature Switzerland AG 2020
X. Wang et al. (Eds.): APWeb-WAIM 2020, LNCS 12317, pp. 162–169, 2020.
https://doi.org/10.1007/978-3-030-60259-8_13

the user alignment problem. Recently, method incorporating both user attributes and topology structures is proposed to align users across social networks [7], yet it still remain some drawbacks. For example, the method only consider the local topology structures. Therefore, it cannot propagate node information from neighbors across networks, where it may suffer from error propagation or noise from diverse neighbors.

According to above analysis, there are still two main challenges in user alignment problem: (1)*How to incorporate the topology structures?* For any candidate pair of users, they usually have different topology structures, and incorporating the whole topology structures may introduce some noise. (2)*How to deal with diverse neighbors?* Because of diverse neighbors, it requires taking neighbor influence in local and across networks into consideration. More importantly, the contribution of each neighbor is usually not equal and should be weighted. To address the two challenges, we propose the **INAMA** model in this paper, *i.e.*, using **IN**-tra/-ter **A**ttention **M**echanisms for user **A**lignments. To solve challenge (1), we define **matched neighbors** (See in Sect. 3.1), which preserves the local topology structures by using labeled aligned neighbors instead of the whole neighbors. To address challenge (2), we design **intra** and **inter** attention mechanisms to distinguish the influence of diverse neighbors in local and across networks. Finally, we treat user alignment problem as a supervised classification task and apply a deep neural network to generate the alignment labels. To sum up, the main contributions of the paper are as follows:

- To incorporate topology structure information, we define the matched neighbors, which consists of nodes from labeled aligned neighbors and reduces the error propagation by noisy nodes, to replace the original neighbors.
- To capture effective node information propagation by diverse matched neighbors, two attention mechanisms are designed to distinguish influence of them in local and across networks, respectively.
- Extensive experiments have been conducted on six real-world datasets, and the results demonstrate the superiority of our approach.

2   Related Work

As we know, user profile plays an important role for the same user identification across networks. Many attempts by comparing user names have been extensive studied [2,6]. For example, Zafarani *et al.* [6] aligned users by adding or removing user names' prefix or postfix upon their habits. Yet Kong *et al.* [1] solved the problem according to cosine similarities of TF-IDF textual features. Mu *et al.* [5] proposed latent user space to determine user identities in a metric learning way. Because node attributes are usually diverse and heterogeneous, above methods may be not strong enough to indicate user identities. As aforementioned in the introduction, incorporating topology structures also give the evidence. IONE [3] and PALE [4] are two famous methods to consider topology structures for user alignment, while they ignore the node attributes.

Recently, incorporating both user attributes and topology structures to align users becomes a hot topic. Some matrix decomposing based unsupervised methods are extensive studied [8]. Zhong *et al.* [9] proposed a unsupervised co-training model to integrate both user attributes and relationships with neighbor pairs. MEgo2Vec [7] is a latest model, which designs an ego network for each node pair to learn the structure consistencies and node attribute similarities.

3   Methodology

3.1   Preliminary

In this section, we briefly give necessary definitions and then formally formulate the problem. In order to effectively incorporate the topology structures, we give the definition of *matched neighbors* to instead of using the whole networks as follow:

Definition Matched Neighbors. Let G^s and G^t be the source and target networks, respectively. We use notations N^s and N^t to represent neighbor sets in the two networks, where N^s_v and N^t_u indicate the neighbors of nodes $v \in G^s$ and $u \in G^t$. Existing aligned pairs are denoted as (A^s, A^t), where $A^s_i \in G^s$ and $A^t_i \in G^t$ refer to the corresponding nodes of *i-th* aligned pair. Thus, given two nodes $v \in G^s$ and $u \in G^t$, we construct the *matched neighbors* $M_v \in G^s$ and $M_u \in G^t$ for them by the following steps:

(1) Given two existing aligned pairs (A^s_i, A^t_i) and (A^s_j, A^t_j), if there is a relationship between A^s_i and A^s_j, we add an edge between A^t_i and A^t_j. Similarly, we do the same operation to augment the relationships in source network.

(2) After step (1), we obtain new neighbor sets N^s and N^t for the two augmented networks. Then, we generate matched neighbors for nodes v and u with respect to $M_v = N^s_v \cap A^s$ and $M_u = N^t_u \cap A^t$. Besides, we add each node itself to the matched neighbor set.

When generating matched neighbors done, we can model the local topology similarities between users across networks. Thus, we solve the issue, how to incorporate topology structures, with matched neighbors. In addition, node attributes often plays an important role for aligning users. According to both local topology and node attribute similarities, we can formulate the user alignment problem as follow:

Problem User Alignment Across Social Networks. Let (v, u) be a candidate user pair and M_v and M_u refer to the corresponding matched neighbors, where $v \in G^s$ and $u \in G^t$. Notation X is used to represent the node attributes. Incorporating both user attributes and topology structures, we treat the problem as following classification task:

$$f : (v, u, M_v, M_u, X) \rightarrow \hat{y}, \tag{1}$$

where $\hat{y}$ is a binary value, with 1 indicating the same person, and 0 otherwise.

3.2   The Proposed INAMA Model

According to above analysis, to solve the user alignment problem, we consider both node attributes and topology structures. Specifically, we adopt matched neighbors instead of original topologies. We show the overview framework of our proposed model in Fig. 1.

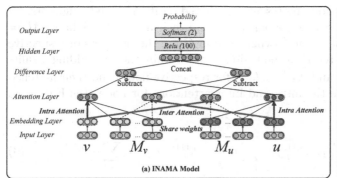 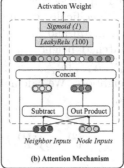

Fig. 1. The illustration of INAMA model. (a) shows the overall architecture, where users v and u are with respect to the nodes from source and target networks, and M_v and M_u represent their matched neighbors. Blue and red lines from *Embedding Layer* to *Attention Layer* are *intra attention* and *inter attention* mechanisms, respectively. (b) introduces the activation unit for *Attention Layer*, which adaptively learns the neighbor influences. (Color figure line)

As shown in Fig. 1(a), our method is composed of three main components: (i) Firstly, we apply an embedding layer to transform raw features into low dimensional dense representations. (ii) Then two attention mechanisms, *i.e.*, intra and inter attentions, are introduced to model the influences of matched neighbors in local and across networks. (iii) Then we concatenate the differences of attention results. Finally, a deep neural network is employed to generate the predictive logits and a binary softmax is used to predict the alignment labels.

Node Embedding. Let the feature size be F and embedding size be d. In embedding layer, a shared feature weight $W^{(0)} \in R^{F \times d}$ and bias $b^{(0)} \in R^{d \times 1}$ are introduced to transform raw features into low dimensional dense representations. Non-linear activation function $tanh$ is adopted in this layer. Therefore, for arbitrary node v, given its node attributes X_v, the node embedding can be formulated as follow:

$$h_v^{(1)} = tanh(W^{(0)^T} h_v^{(0)} + b^{(0)}), \qquad (2)$$

where $h_v^{(0)}$ denotes the raw feature X_v, and $h_v^{(1)}$ represents the embedding result. Through node embedding, we can obtain low dimensional dense representations for all nodes.

Neighbor Attention. After node embedding, we further smooth each node's representation by their matched neighbors' representations. Inspired by [10], we introduce a local activation characteristic of users and adaptively calculate the contribution of each neighbor. In attention layer, we design intra and inter attentions, which model the node information propagation in local and across networks, respectively. According to Fig. 1(b), the novel local activation unit is applied on the matched neighbors, where a weighted sum pooling is performed to adaptively calculate node representation based on its matched neighbors.

Specifically, given a candidate pair (v, u) and their matched neighbors $M_v = [v_1, ..., v_P]$ and $M_u = [u_1, ..., u_Q]$, where P and Q are the numbers of respective matched neighbors. After node embedding, we obtain the embedding results $h_v^{(1)}$, $h_u^{(1)}$, $[h_{v_1}^{(1)}, ..., h_{v_P}^{(1)}]$ and $[h_{u_1}^{(1)}, ..., h_{u_Q}^{(1)}]$ for respective nodes and their matched neighbors. We calculate the intra and inter attentions for node v as Eq. 3 and Eq. 4:

$$h_v^{(2)} = g(h_v^{(1)}; h_{v_1}^{(1)}, ..., h_{v_P}^{(1)}) = \sum_{i=1}^{P} a(h_{v_i}^{(1)}, h_v^{(1)}) \cdot h_{v_i}^{(1)} = \sum_{i=1}^{P} w_i h_{v_i}^{(1)}, \tag{3}$$

$$h_v^{'(2)} = g(h_v^{(1)}; h_{u_1}^{(1)}, ..., h_{u_Q}^{(1)}) = \sum_{i=1}^{Q} a(h_{u_i}^{(1)}, h_v^{(1)}) \cdot h_{u_i}^{(1)} = \sum_{i=1}^{Q} w_i h_{u_i}^{(1)}. \tag{4}$$

Here, $h_v^{(2)}$ and $h_v^{'(2)}$ represent the attentional results of v in local and across networks, $a(\cdot)$ is a feed-forward network with output as the activation weight. Similarly, we calculate intra and inter attention results for node u as $h_u^{(2)}$ and $h_u^{'(2)}$ in the same way. Following the popular setting in attention based methods, we normalize the attention weights within $\sum_i w_i = 1$ in Eq. 3 and Eq. 4.

Objective Function. When neighbor attention process done, we concatenate the differences between the corresponding attention results, $i.e$, $|h_v^{(2)} - h_u^{(2)}|$ and $|h_v^{'(2)} - h_u^{'(2)}|$. Then we apply a function f such as the full connection operation on the concatenation to predict the matching score $\hat{y} = f(|h_v^{(2)} - h_u^{(2)}|; |h_v^{'(2)} - h_u^{'(2)}|)$. Consequently, we can formulate the objective function as the cross entropy loss:

$$\mathcal{L} = \frac{1}{n} \sum_{i=1}^{n} CrossEntropy(\hat{y}_i, y_i), \tag{5}$$

where n is the number of training samples, and $\hat{y}_i$ and y_i refer to the predicted and true labels for i-th candidate pair, respectively.

4   Experiments

4.1   Experimental Setup

Datasets. We collected three pairs of *Social Networking Services* (SNS) datasets (*w.r.t. Douban Online-Offline, Flickr-Lastfm* and *Flickr-Myspace*) from [8]. We also extract three pairs of *academia* datasets. In particular, we employ the co-author network from DBLP[1] and split the whole dataset to three networks in chronological order (*w.r.t.* year 2016, 2017 and 2018). In each network, we select *Yoshua Bengio* as the center node and construct the co-author subnetwork with regard to the nodes, which can be reached from the center node with no more than four-hops. Conference names of conference papers are treated as node attributes. We construct the ground truth in terms of the author identities in DBLP. Because of discrete user attributes, we represent them in one-hot encoding way, with 1 indicating users have the attribute and 0 otherwise. The statistical details are summarized in Table 1.

Table 1. The statistics of datasets.

Dataset	Source network		Target network		#Features	#Matched pairs
	#Nodes	#Edges	#Nodes	#Edges		
Douban Online-Offline	1,118	3,022	3,906	16,328	187	1,118
Flickr-Lastfm	12,974	32,298	15,436	32,638	3	452
Flickr-Myspace	6,714	14,666	10,733	21,767	3	267
DBLP 17-16	9,455	27,721	1,1509	33,858	2,059	1,823
DBLP 18-16	5,562	15,966	1,1509	33,858	1,831	1,028
DBLP 18-17	5,562	15,966	9,455	27,721	1,833	1,156

Baseline Methods. To evaluate the performance of our INAMA method, we compare it with several state-of-the-art methods. Specifically, two conventional supervised methods **KNN** and **SVM** are adopted as baselines. We also consider three recent embedding methods, namely **ULink** [5], **IONE** [3] and **MEgo2Vec** [7], as our baseline methods.

Implementation Details. We employ *Mean Reciprocal Rank* (MRR) to evaluate all methods and the computation can be formulated as follow:

$$MRR = \frac{1}{N} \sum_{i=1}^{N} \frac{1}{hit(x_i)}, \qquad (6)$$

where $hit(x)$ represents the position of the corrected linked user in the returned list of the top-k candidates, and N is the number of test users. For a fair comparison, the embedding size is set as 50 for all embedding methods. We repeat each experiment five times and report the average performance.

---

[1] http://dblp.uni-trier.de/.

4.2   Experimental Results

Main Results. We show the MRR performance in Table 2. According to Table 2, INAMA achieves the best on four datasets (academia datasets and Flickr-Myspace) and the second positions on the remainder two datasets. On academia datasets, INAMA has the average improvements of 18.07%, 34.34% and 13.02% compared to IONE, ULink and MEgo2Vec respectively. The MRR results reveal that our method is much more suitable for the datasets with rich attributes. The reasons are two-folded: (i) INAMA comprehensively exploits both node attributes and topology structures. (ii) Our model simultaneously captures the influence of diverse neighbors in local and across networks.

Table 2. MRR performance on the six datasets (%), where the best and second results are in bold and underline, respectively.

Dataset	KNN	SVM	ULink	IONE	MEgo2Vec	INAMA
Douban Online-Offline	22.48	21.72	27.37	82.94	**89.13**	<u>84.95</u>
Flickr-Lastfm	8.36	7.89	8.40	**16.57**	11.51	<u>14.21</u>
Flickr-Myspace	8.95	9.06	<u>9.20</u>	8.09	9.12	**11.43**
DBLP 17-16	12.65	9.24	18.06	36.22	<u>42.62</u>	**52.07**
DBLP 18-16	12.56	12.61	18.45	32.09	<u>34.33</u>	**55.35**
DBLP 18-17	14.91	11.26	22.03	39.05	<u>46.56</u>	**54.15**

Ablation Studies. In this part, we try four variants of INAMA to figure out the impacts of node features, matched neighbors, intra and inter attentions. We construct one-hot encoding inputs based on node ids to replace the node features and denote it as $\sim id$. We remove the matched neighbors, intra and inter attentions to validate the effectiveness of topology and information propagation influence in local and across networks. The above three variants are denoted as $\sim w/o\,neighbor$, $\sim w/o\,intra$ and $\sim w/o\,inter$. We show the MRR performance of different variants in Table 3. Comparing the results of $\sim id$ with INAMA, node attributes affect our model significantly on datasets with rich attributes. It proves the aforementioned statement that our method is more suitable for datasets with rich inputs. Similarly, the results also validate the effectiveness of matched neighbors. More importantly, by using intra and inter attention manners, our model improves average 2% and 1.9% MRR performance respectively.

Table 3. MRR performance of different variant models.

Dataset	$\sim id$	$\sim w/o\ neighbor$	$\sim w/o\ intra$	$\sim w/o\ inter$	INAMA
Douban Online-Offline	25.53	32.28	81.21	80.86	**84.95**
Flickr-Lastfm	10.13	10.00	11.08	11.94	**14.21**
Flickr-Myspace	9.17	10.93	10.83	10.65	**11.43**
DBLP 17-16	16.34	33.45	50.83	50.55	**52.07**
DBLP 18-16	15.97	28.40	54.44	54.42	**55.35**
DBLP 18-17	16.96	32.61	51.80	52.29	**54.15**

5   Conclusion

In this paper, we propose the INAMA model to solve user alignment problem. To effectively incorporate topology structures, we generate matched neighbors instead of original topology structures. To distinguish information propagation influence in local and across networks, we introduce intra and inter attention mechanisms. Comprehensive experiments on six real-world datasets have been conducted, and the results demonstrate the superiority of the proposed method against state-of-the-art techniques.

Acknowledgments. This research was supported in part by the National Key R&D Program of China, 2018YFB2101100, 2018YFB2101101 and NSFC under Grant Nos. 61972111, U1836107, 61602132 and 61572158.

References

1. Kong, X., Zhang, J., Yu, P.S.: Inferring anchor links across multiple heterogeneous social networks. In: ACM International Conference on Information & Knowledge Management, pp. 179–188 (2013)
2. Liu, J., Zhang, F., Song, X., Song, Y.I., Lin, C.Y., Hon, H.W.: What's in a name?: An unsupervised approach to link users across communities. In: ACM International Conference on Web Search & Data Mining, pp. 495–504 (2013)
3. Liu, L., Cheung, W.K., Li, X., Liao, L.: Aligning users across social networks using network embedding. In: International Joint Conference on Artificial Intelligence, pp. 1774–1780 (2016)
4. Man, T., Shen, H., Liu, S., Jin, X., Cheng, X.: Predict anchor links across social networks via an embedding approach. In: International Joint Conference on Artificial Intelligence, pp. 1823–1829 (2016)
5. Mu, X., Zhu, F., Lim, E.P., Xiao, J., Wang, J., Zhou, Z.H.: User identity linkage by latent user space modelling. In: ACM SIGKDD Conference on Knowledge Discovery & Data Mining, pp. 1775–1784 (2016)
6. Zafarani, R., Liu, H.: Connecting users across social media sites: a behavioral-modeling approach. In: ACM SIGKDD Conference on Knowledge Discovery & Data Mining, pp. 41–49 (2013)
7. Zhang, J., et al.: Mego2vec: embedding matched ego networks for user alignment across social networks. In: ACM International Conference on Information & Knowledge Management, pp. 327–336 (2018)
8. Zhang, S., Tong, H.: Final: fast attributed network alignment. In: ACM SIGKDD Conference on Knowledge Discovery & Data Mining, pp. 1345–1354 (2016)
9. Zhong, Z., Cao, Y., Guo, M., Nie, Z.: Colink: an unsupervised framework for user identity linkage. In: AAAI Conference on Artificial Intelligence, pp. 5714–5721 (2018)
10. Zhou, G., et al.: Deep interest network for click-through rate prediction. In: ACM SIGKDD Conference on Knowledge Discovery & Data Mining, pp. 1059–1068 (2018)

NSTI-IC: An Independent Cascade Model Based on Neighbor Structures and Topic-Aware Interest

Chuhan Zhang, Yueshuang Yin, and Yong Liu[(⊠)]

HeiLongJiang University, Harbin, China
`liuyong123456@hlju.edu.cn`

Abstract. With the rapid development of social networks, discovering the propagation mechanism of information has become one of the key issues in social network analysis, which has attracted great attention. The existing propagation models only take into account individual influence between users and their neighbors, ignoring that different topologies formed by neighbors will have different influence on the target user. In this paper, we combine the influence of neighbor structure on different topics with the distribution of user interest on different topics, propose an propagation model based on structure influence and topic-aware interest, called NSTI-IC. We use an expectation maximization algorithm and a gradient descent algorithm to learn parameters of NSTI-IC. The experimental results on real datasets show that NSTI-IC model is superior to classical IC and structInf-IC models in terms of MSE and accuracy.

Keywords: Social networks · Propagation model · Structure influence · Expectation maximization

1 Introduction

Social network sites such as WeChat, Sina Weibo, Facebook and Twitter make communication among people more closer. These online social networks enable users to retweet, comment, and tag, which make new ideas and products spread quickly. In recent years, it has become one of the hot topics in data mining community to discover the mechanism of information propagation in social networks.

In order to describe the law of information propagation in social networks, various information propagation models have been proposed. Kempe et al. [2] first proposed the Independent Cascade (IC) model and Linear Threshold (LT) model. Liu et al. [3] proposed a TI-IC model by considering the topic distribution of propagation items and the interest distribution of users simultaneously. However, these propagation models mainly consider the interaction between individuals, and do not consider the influence of neighbor structure on individuals. Recent studies have found that the diversity of neighbor structures in social networks is an important factor affecting information propagation, and the probability of propagation is closely related to the number of different structures [5].

© Springer Nature Switzerland AG 2020
X. Wang et al. (Eds.): APWeb-WAIM 2020, LNCS 12317, pp. 170–178, 2020.
https://doi.org/10.1007/978-3-030-60259-8_14

In this paper, we take into consideration the influence of neighbor structure on different topics and the distribution of user interest on different topics, propose a novel information propagation model in social networks – An Independent Cascade Model based on Neighbor Structures and Topic-aware Interest, called NSTI-IC. To learn the parameters of the NSTI-IC model, we first use an expectation maximization algorithm (EM) to obtain the influence probabilities of different structures on different users, and then use a gradient descent algorithm to solve the influence vectors of neighbor structures and the interest vectors of users. Experimental results on two real data sets show that NSTI-IC model is better than classical propagation models in terms of mean square error(MSE), accuracy and other metrics. The source code for this paper can be downloaded from https://github.com/Zhang-chu-han/NSTI-IC.

2   Model Definition

This section begins with some preliminary knowledge, and then introduces the independent cascade model NSTI-IC.

The social network is represented by a directed graph $G = (V, E)$, and the users' historical action log is recorded as L. Each record in L is denoted as a triple $l = (u, i, t)$, which means user u accepted propagation item i at time t. Assume that there is a topic distribution for each propagation item and an interest distribution for each user. For each topic $z \in [1, Z]$, where Z represents the number of topics, we assume that each user has an interest component θ_u^z on topic z. Therefore, each user u has an interest distribution vector $\theta_u = (\theta_u^1, \theta_u^2, \cdots, \theta_u^Z)$ on different topics.

In the propagation process of item i, if user u accepts a propagation item i, we call user u active; otherwise, we call user u inactive. As shown in literature [9], whether or not the current inactive user u becomes active in the propagation of item i depends largely on the possible influence of the active neighbor structures around u on u itself. In this paper, we only consider 20 neighbor structures formed by 2, 3, and 4 active nodes, represented by a set $S = \{s_0, s_1, s_2, \ldots\ldots, s_{19}\}$, as shown in Table 1. White node represents the target user and the red node represents active neighbor nodes before the target user is active.

Because user u has an interest distribution vector $\theta_u = (\theta_u^1, \theta_u^2, \cdots, \theta_u^Z)$ on different topics, we further assume that the influence of structure $s \in S$ on different topics is different, and there is also the influence distribution vector $\theta_s = (\theta_s^1, \theta_s^2, \cdots, \theta_s^Z)$ on different topics for structure s. In the propagation of item i, the probability that user u is activated by active neighbor structure s is defined as $p_{s,u} = \theta_s \bullet \theta_u = \sum\limits_{j=1}^{Z} \theta_s^j \theta_u^j$.

The NSTI-IC model works as follows. At time $t = 0$, only partial nodes $D \subseteq V$ (for example, the initial publisher of weibo) is active nodes on propagation item i; at time $t \geq 1$, if any neighbor node v of u within the period of $(t - \tau, t)$ become active, then structure s consisting of neighbor node v and other active nodes has one chance to activate node u, the activation probability of node u is

$p_{s,u} = \theta_s \bullet \theta_u$. Here τ is defined as the maxmium time interval, which mean that the propagation is valid in this time interval. The effect of this parameter τ will be evaluated in the experiment. If neighbor structure s does not activate node u, neighbor structure s will not attempt to activate node u in the future. When there are multiple active neighbor structures around node u, the probability of node u being activated is $p_u^i = 1 - \prod_{s \in S_i^{(u)}} (1 - \theta_s \bullet \theta_u)^{n_{s,u,i}^+}$, where $S_i^{(u)}$ represents a set of neighbor structures which attempt to activate node u during the propagation of item i, and $n_{s,u,i}^+$ represents the number of instances of neighbor structure s around node u that may influence node u during the propagation of item i. This is because that the same structure can appear multiple times around node u. For example, structure s_4 appear multiple times in Fig. 1. At the same time, we assume that if structure s_i is the substructure of another structure s_k, the function of structure s_i is replaced by structure s_k, and only structure s_k attempts to activate other inactive nodes. As shown in Fig. 1, when an instance of structure s_1 is a substructure of structure s_4, structure s_1 will not attempt to activate node u_0, but structure s_4 will attempt to activate node u_0. When a node is activated, this node and the surrounding active nodes form a new neighbor structure to attempt to other inactive nodes. The propagation process continues until there are no nodes that can be activated.

Table 1. All influence structures consisting of 2, 3 and 4 active neighbor nodes

k	S_k	k	S_k	k	S_k	k	S_k
0		5		10		15	
1		6		11		16	
2		7		12		17	
3		8		13		18	
4		9		14		19	

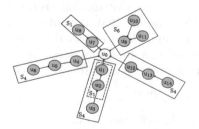

Fig. 1. An example for illustrating the NSTI-IC model

3 Learning Algorithms for NSTI-IC

In this section, we firstly use an EM algorithm to compute the probability $p_{s,u}$ that neighbor structure s activates node u, and then use a gradient descent algorithm to obtain the influence vector $\theta_s = (\theta_s^1, \theta_s^2, \cdots, \theta_s^Z)$ of neighbor structure s and the interest vector $\theta_u = (\theta_u^1, \theta_u^2, \cdots, \theta_u^Z)$ of user u by fixing $p_{s,u}$.

Before using the EM algorithm, the log-likelihood function (Q function) of the complete data needs to be constructed. Let I be the set of all propagation items. A_i^+ represents the set of nodes that are activated during the propagation of item i, and A_i^- represents the set of nodes that are not activated during the propagation of item i. $S_i^{(u)}$ represents the set of neighbor structures that may influence node u during the propagation of item i, and $\bar{S}_i^{(u)}$ represents the set of neighbor structures that have no influence on node u during the propagation of item i. $n_{s,u,i}^+$ represents the number of instances of neighbor structure s that may influence node u during the propagation of item i, and $n_{s,u,i}^-$ represents the number of instances of neighbor structure s that have no influence on node u during the propagation of item i. Referring to the symbol representation of standard EM algorithm, $\widehat{\Theta}$ represents the current estimation of parameters Θ, and the log-likelihood function of complete data is as follows.

$$
Q\left(\Theta, \widehat{\Theta}\right) = \sum_i^{|I|} \{ \sum_{u \in A_i^+} [\sum_{s \in S_i^{(u)}} n_{s,u,i}^+ (\frac{\hat{p}_{s,u}}{\hat{p}_u^i} log p_{s,u} + (1 - \frac{\hat{p}_{s,u}}{\hat{p}_u^i}) log(1 - p_{s,u}))
$$

$$
+ \sum_{s \in \bar{S}_i^{(u)}} n_{s,u,i}^- log(1 - p_{s,u})] + \sum_{u \in A_i^-} \sum_{s \in \bar{S}_i^{(u)}} n_{s,u,i}^- log(1 - p_{s,u}) \}
$$

By calculating the derivative of Q function to $p_{s,u}$, we obtain the following iterative formula.

$$
p_{s,u} = \frac{\sum_{i=1}^{|I|} (n_{s,u,i}^+ \times \frac{\hat{p}_{s,u}}{\hat{p}_u^i})}{\sum_{i=1}^{|I|} (n_{s,u,i}^+ + n_{s,u,i}^-)}
$$

Based on the above formula, we give the pseudo code of EM algorithm, as shown in algorithm 1. In line 1, the algorithm preprocesses the data, calculates all the $S_i^{(u)}, \bar{S}_i^{(u)} (\forall i \in I, \forall u \in V)$, $n_{s,u,i}^+$ and $n_{s,u,i}^- (\forall i \in I, \forall s \in S, \forall u \in V)$ and saves them. In line 2~6, the algorithm randomly initializes the parameter $p_{s,u}$, and then alternately performs E step and M step until convergence.

After obtaining the influence probability $p_{s,u}$ of neighbor structure s on user u, we adjust the structure influence vector $\theta_s = (\theta_s^1, \theta_s^2, \cdots, \theta_s^Z)$ and the user interest vector $\theta_u = (\theta_u^1, \theta_u^2, \cdots, \theta_u^Z)$ to fit the influence probability $p_{s,u}$. Thus, we can construct the following optimization objective. We use a gradient descent algorithm to solve the optimization objective.

$$\underset{s_j \in S, u_k \in V}{\arg\min} \frac{1}{2} \sum_{j=1}^{|S|} \sum_{k=1}^{|V|} (p_{s_j, u_k} - \theta_{s_j} \bullet \theta_{u_k})^2$$

Algorithm 1. An EM algorithm for learning the NSTI-IC model

Input: a social network $G = (V, E)$, an action log L
Output: parameters $p_{s,u}(\forall s \in S, \forall u \in V)$
 1: Scan G and L to obain all $S_i^{(u)}, \bar{S}_i^{(u)}(\forall i \in I, \forall u \in V)$, $n_{s,u,i}^+$ and $n_{s,u,i}^-(\forall i \in I, \forall s \in S, \forall u \in V)$;
 2: **for all** $s \in S$ **do**
 3:     **for all** $u \in V$ **do**
 4:         Init $p_{s,u}$;
 5:     **end for**
 6: **end for**
 7: **repeat**
 8:     **for all** $i \in I$ **do**
 9:         **for all** $u \in V$ **do**
10:             **if** u is active in event i **then**
11:                 $p_u^i = 1 - \prod_{s \in S_i^{(u)}} (1 - p_{s,u})^{n_{s,u,i}^+}$;
12:             **end if**
13:         **end for**
14:     **end for**
15:     **for all** $s \in S$ **do**
16:         **for all** $u \in V$ **do**
17:             $p_{s,u} = \dfrac{\sum\limits_{i=1}^{|I|} \left(n_{s,u,i}^+ \times \frac{\hat{p}_{s,u}}{\hat{p}_u^i} \right)}{\sum\limits_{i=1}^{|I|} \left(n_{s,u,i}^+ + n_{s,u,i}^- \right)}$;
18:         **end for**
19:     **end for**
20: **until** convergence

---

4   Experimental Results and Analysis

4.1   Experimental Setup

We conduct the experiments on a real dataset, Sina Weibo. Sina Weibo is a Chinese social network site similar to Twitter that allows users to comment on Weibo or retweet Weibo to other users, which can be downloaded from http://aminer.org/structinf. The dataset contains a social networks $G(V, E)$ and an action log $L(u, i, t)$. The tuple (u, i, t) contained in L means that user u

affected by i at time t. If user u_j affected by i at time t_j , a friend u_k of user u_j affected by i at time t_k , and t_j is earlier than t_k, then we believe that this affection was propagated from user u_j to user u_k. We use two algorithms StructInf-Basic and StructInf-S2 proposed by [10] to constuct two datasets, Data_Basic and Data_S2, respectively. Data_Basic contains 800 microblogs and 287965 users, and Data_S2 contains 800 microblogs and 419532 users.

4.2   Comparison Models and Metrics

We compare NSTI-IC with the following two models.

1) IC [2]. In this model, each node has two states, active and inactive state. Each active node has only one chance to activate the inactive neighbor node, and this process is irreversible. The stop condition of propagation is that there has no node being activated.
2) StructInf-IC [10]. As shown in [10], different neighbor structures formed by active nodes will have different effects on tatget node. In this paper, we use the StructInf method [10] to compute the influence probability of neighbor structures. These influence probabilities are embedded in the IC model, the propagation mechanism similar to IC model is used to simulate the propagation process of information. We call this model StructInf-IC.

We divide all propagation items into training set and test set in a ratio of 8:2, and ensure that all actions of one propagation item was either in the training set or in the test set. We firstly learn the parameters of the model on the training set, and then predict the propagation result of each new propagation item in the test set according to the learned model. The detailed prediction process is as follows. For each propagation item i, we use the learned model to compute the activated probability for each node, and calculate Mean Square Error (MSE) and accuracy according to the predicted probability and activation threshold. Lastly, we calculate the average value on all propagation items.

4.3   Comparison of Different Models

Comparison on MSE. Table 2 and Table 3 shows MSE of different models on two datasets Data_Basic and Data_S2 respectively. In Data_S2, StructInf-IC is slightly superior to IC in terms of MSE, which indicates that neighbor structure plays an important role in information propagation. NSTI-IC takes into account both the user interests and the influence of neighbor structure, thus NSTI-IC is obviously superior to the existing models.

Table 2. Mean Squared Error of different models in Data_Basic

Model	MSE
IC	0.072
StructInf-IC	0.149
NSTI-IC	0.053

Table 3. Mean Squared Error of different models in Data_S2

Model	MSE
IC	0.153
StructInf-IC	0.144
NSTI-IC	0.109

Comparison on Accuracy. Figure 2 and Fig. 3 show the accuracy of different models with respect to different activation thresholds δ on Data_Basic and Data_S2 respectively. If the activation probability of a node is not less than activation threshold δ, then this node is regarded as an active node.

As can be seen from Fig. 2, the accuracy of StructInf-IC is slightly lower than that of IC, which indicates that on Data_Basic, structure influence have little effect on model accuracy. The accuracy of NSTI-IC is always higher than that of other models on Data_Basic, which shows that the combination of user interest and structure influence can achieve the best prediction effect on Data_Basic. As can be seen from Fig. 3, StructInf-IC is less accurate than NSTI-IC, but is better than IC, which indicates that on Data_S2, neighbor structures play a role in accuracy. NSTI-IC combine the influence of neighbor structures with the user interests on different topics, and it is obviously better than other models in terms of accuracy.

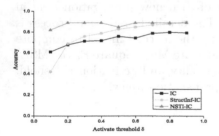

Fig. 2. Accuracy of different models on Data_Basic

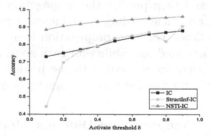

Fig. 3. Accuracy of different models on Data_S2

5   Related Work

In recent years, researchers have paid more and more attention to the influence of neighbor structure on users in social networks. In 2012, Ugander et al. [5] first considered the impact of the diversity structures on users in social networks. They believed that structure was an important factor in individual decision-making, and this idea was later widely applied to different scenarios. In 2017,

Zang et al. [8] quantified the structural mode of information propagation and found new structural mode through the proposed analysis of seven indicators. Later, they found the structural complexity of information propagation was far greater than previously suspected, so they adopted a larger dimensional approach to structural complexity [9]. In 2018, Huang et al. [1] proposed the dynamic prediction problem of ternary relationship. They studied how the third edge affected the strength of existing two edges through time effect and different structural information formed between users. In 2019, Xudong Wu et al. [7] proposed a new measurement method to accurately evaluate the contribution of neighbor structure of each user to information propagation in the social network. Rizi et al. [4] used a graph embedding method to simulate the social influence of activated users on the event. In the same year, Wang et al. [6] used Node2vec to extract the representative characteristics of users, established the multi-label classification model called NNMLInf to predict the social impact.

Although structural influence has been proved to play an important role in information propagation, to the best of our knowledge, no work has considered the joint influence of neighbor structures and topic-aware user interest on information propagation.

6 Conclusion

In this paper, we consider both structure influence and user interest on different topics, and propose an independent cascade model called NSTI-IC based on neighbor structures and topic interest. We use the expectation maximization algorithm and the gradient descent algorithm to learn model parameters. Compared with the existing propagation model, NSTI-IC can predict the propagation results of information more accurately.

Acknowledgment. This work was supported by the National Natural Science Foundation of China (No. 61972135, No. 61602159), the Natural Science Foundation of Heilongjiang Province (No. LH2020F043), and the Innovation Talents Project of Science and Technology Bureau of Harbin (No. 2017RAQXJ094).

References

1. Huang, H., Dong, Y., et al.: Will triadic closure strengthen ties in social networks? ACM Trans. Knowl. Disc. Data (TKDD) **12**(3), 1–25 (2018)
2. Kempe, D., Kleinberg, J., et al.: Maximizing the spread of influence through a social network. In: Proceedings of the 9th ACM SIGKDD International Conference on Knowledge Discovery and Data Mining, pp. 137–146 (2003)
3. Liu, Y., Xie, S., Zhong, Z., Li, J., Ren, Q.: Research on topic-interest based influence maximization algorithm in social networks. J. Comput. Res. Dev. **55**(11), 2406–2418 (2018)
4. Rizi, F.S., Granitzer, M.: Predicting event attendance exploring social influence. In: Proceedings of the 34th ACM/SIGAPP Symposium on Applied Computing, pp. 2131–2134 (2019)

5. Ugander, J., et al.: Structural diversity in social contagion. In: Proceedings of the National Academy of Sciences, pp. 5962–5966 (2012)
6. Wang, X., et al.: NNMLInf: social influence prediction with neural network multi-label classification. In: Proceedings of the ACM Turing Celebration Conference-China, pp. 1–5 (2019)
7. Wu, X., Fu, L., et al.: Collective influence maximization. In: Proceedings of the Twentieth ACM International Symposium on Mobile Ad Hoc Networking and Computing, pp. 385–386 (2019)
8. Zang, C., Cui, P., et al.: Quantifying structural patterns of information cascades. In: Proceedings of the 26th International Conference on World Wide Web Companion, pp. 867–868 (2017)
9. Zang, C., Cui, P., et al.: Structural patterns of information cascades and their implications for dynamics and semantics. arXiv preprint arXiv:1708.02377 (2017)
10. Zhang, J., Tang, J., et al.: Structinf: mining structural influence from social streams. In: Proceedings of the 31th AAAI Conference on Artificial Intelligence (2017)

Knowledge Graph

Knowledge Graph Attention Network Enhanced Sequential Recommendation

Xingwei Zhu[1], Pengpeng Zhao[1(✉)], Jiajie Xu[1], Junhua Fang[1], Lei Zhao[1], Xuefeng Xian[2(✉)], Zhiming Cui[3], and Victor S. Sheng[4]

[1] Institute of AI, Soochow University, Suzhou, China
ppzhao@suda.edu.cn
[2] Suzhou Vocational University, Suzhou, China
xianxuefeng@jssvc.edu.cn
[3] Suzhou University of Science and Technology, Suzhou, China
[4] Texas Tech University, Lubbock, TX, USA

Abstract. Knowledge graph (KG) has recently been proved effective and attracted a lot of attentions in sequential recommender systems. However, the relations between the attributes of different entities in KG, which could be utilized to improve the performance, remain largely unexploited. In this paper, we propose an end-to-end **K**nowledge **G**raph attention network enhanced **S**equential **R**ecommendation (KGSR) framework to capture the context-dependency of sequence items and the semantic information of items in KG by explicitly exploiting high-order relations between entities. Specifically, our method first combines the user-item bipartite graph and the KG into a unified graph and encodes all nodes of the unified graph into vector representations with TransR. Then, a graph attention network recursively propagates the information of neighbor nodes to refine the embedding of nodes and distinguishes the importance of neighbors with an attention mechanism. Finally, we apply recurrent neural network to capture the user's dynamic preferences by encoding user-interactive sequence items that contain rich auxiliary semantic information. Experimental results on two datasets demonstrate that KGSR outperforms the state-of-the-art sequential recommendation methods.

Keywords: Sequential recommendation · Knowledge graph · Graph neural network

1 Introduction

In the age of information explosion, recommender systems are widely used in various fields (e.g., e-commerce, social media, and news portals) to help users discover what they are interested in from mass information. In these scenarios, a user's tastes are usually dynamic and evolving by nature. The key factors of building an effective recommender system are accurately characterizing the user's dynamic preferences and distilling collaborative signal of the items. Sequential

© Springer Nature Switzerland AG 2020
X. Wang et al. (Eds.): APWeb-WAIM 2020, LNCS 12317, pp. 181–195, 2020.
https://doi.org/10.1007/978-3-030-60259-8_15

recommendation, which aims to predict next activity of the user, has attracted many researchers' sights recently.

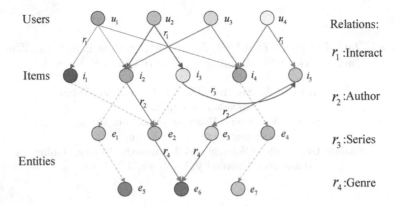

Fig. 1. A book example of knowledge graph. r_2, r_3, and r_4 are from KG.

Various sequential recommendation methods have been proposed and achieved encouraging results. One of the representative work is the classic factorizing personalized markov chain [13] model, which assumes that the previous one action (or previous few) is the foundation of the next activity and successfully characterizes short-range item transitions for the recommendation. However, with the markov assumption, an independent combination of the past interactions may limit the performance of recommendation [18]. Another line of work develops recurrent neural network (RNN) [4,22] methods to encode historical interaction records of each user into a hidden state. The hidden state is further used to predict the next action of the users. RNN methods, which profit in exploring the item-to-item sequential relations with the advanced memory cell structures like long short-term memory (LSTM) [5] and gated recurrent units (GRU) [4], have been successfully equipped for various application scenarios.

More recently, knowledge-enhanced sequential recommender (KSR) [6] applies RNN-based models to capture sequential user preference and further incorporates knowledge graph (KG) to enhance the semantic representation of key-value memory networks. By introducing knowledge-enhanced memory networks to capture attribute-level user preference, KSR has achieved remarkable performance. However, the relations between the attributes of different entities have not been adequately considered. As illustrated in Fig. 1, given a book KG that user u_1 has interacted with books i_1, i_2 and i_4, we predict the next item i_5 interacted by u_1. Between items i_2 and i_5, there are three connections in Fig. 1: the purple, blue, and green solid lines. We believe that these deep-layer connections are helpful in predicting the next item i_5 successfully:

- $i_2 \xrightarrow{-r_1} u_2 \xrightarrow{r_1} i_3 \xrightarrow{r_3} i_5$
- $i_2 \xrightarrow{-r_1} u_3 \xrightarrow{r_1} i_4 \xrightarrow{-r_1} u_4 \xrightarrow{r_1} i_5$
- $i_2 \xrightarrow{r_2} e_2 \xrightarrow{r_4} e_6 \xrightarrow{-r_4} e_3 \xrightarrow{-r_2} i_5$

Taking the last connection as an example, it illustrates that the authors of books i_2 and i_5 are e_2 and e_3 respectively, and the genres of author e_2 and e_3 are both e_6. Considering only the attribute level, items only implicitly capture the collaborative signal of directly connected nodes. And the relationship information that author attributes e_2 and e_3 both connected to the genre attribute e_6 in the third connection could potentially enhance sequential recommendations. However, existing works have not fully exploited the high-order dependency between entities and their local graph contexts in KG.

To this end, in this paper, we put forward a novel **K**nowledge **G**raph attention network enhanced **S**equential **R**ecommendation (KGSR) framework, which introduces a graph attention network into a sequential recommender to explicitly exploit the high-order dependency between different entities in KG. Firstly, we combine user behaviors and item knowledge into a unified relational graph as the KG that we use, and encode all nodes of the KG into vector representations with TransR [10]. Then, the graph attention network module recursively updates each node's embedding according to its embedding and its neighbors' embeddings, where a neural attention mechanism is employed to learn the weight of each neighbor. Finally, the RNN-based network encodes the user's sequential interactions for capturing dynamic user preferences. Therefore, we can fully mine the collaborative signals from the collective user behaviors and knowledge graph, and then predict the user's next interaction.

The contributions of this work are summarized as follows:

- To our best knowledge, we firstly introduce the high-order dependency between entities in KG into sequential recommendation to fully exploit the collaborative signals in interaction and knowledge graph.
- We develop the KGSR for the sequential recommendation in an end-to-end manner, where TransR parameterizes the entities and relations as vector representations, and the graph attention network propagates the information of node's local graph context in the KG, while the RNN-based networks model user's sequential intents.
- We conduct extensive experiments on two benchmark datasets to demonstrate the effectiveness of our proposed method.

2   Related Work

In this section, we review the recent work from three orientations: general recommendation, sequential recommendation, and knowledge-aware recommendation.

2.1   General Recommendation

Traditional recommendation methods, such as k-nearest neighbor [14] and matrix factorization algorithms [8], are often based on the idea of collaborative filtering: matching users based on similar preferences and interests. The datasets used by recommendation systems can generally be classified into explicit feedback datasets and implicit feedback datasets. The recommendation methods using explicit feedback data treat the recommendation as a rating prediction problem. However, most users do not usually rate the items, and the user's implicit feedback (e.g., clicks) is often available. Therefore, most methods focus on processing implicit feedback data to make recommendations. Bayesian personalized ranking (BPR) [12], which optimizes the latent factor model with a pair-wise ranking loss, is a representative method on implicit feedback. General recommendation is good at capturing users' general preferences, but fail to adapt to situations where user interests are often dynamically shifted.

2.2 Sequential Recommendation

The sequential recommendation method is designed to learn the chronological sequence of user interaction and then predict the likely user interaction items for the next step. The classical factorizing personalized markov chain (FPMC) method [13], which is a hybrid model of markov chain and matrix factorization, learns the transformation relationship between item-item to predict the next item based on the last interaction item. Another popular neural network method is recurrent neural networks. LSTM and GRU are two classical methods based on RNN, which have been widely applied in various scenarios such as session-based GRU [4], user-based GRU [2,18,22] and attention-based GRU [9]. Recommender system with external user memory networks [1] is proposed to introduce the memory mechanism to captured item-level and feature-level sequential patterns explicitly.

2.3 Knowledge-Aware Recommendation

Knowledge graph has been widely adopted to address data sparsity and cold start problems and has achieved great success. However, knowledge graph is just widely leveraged in traditional recommendation task scenarios, and remains largely unexploited in the field of sequential recommendation. Collaborative knowledge base embedding (CKE) [20], which is the first work to apply embedding and deep learning methods to extract semantic representations from the knowledge graph automatically, is a representative regularization-based method. One of the representative path-based methods is knowledge-aware path recurrent network (KPRN) [16], which not only encodes both entities and relations in a path into a unified representations, but also performs reasoning based on paths to deduce user preference. Knowledge graph attention network (KGAT) [15] develops an advanced graph attention network method to explicitly perform the propagation of collaborative information between nodes in KG, and it contains both path-based and regularization-based ideas. In addition to non-sequence recommendation methods such as CKE, KPRN and KGAT, KSR has recently successfully introduced KG to enhance sequential recommendation. KSR [6] combines knowledge-enhanced key-value memory networks and GRU to capture attribute-based user preference and sequential user preference, respectively.

Although KSR has made a good improvement on the baseline, it did not fully exploit the multi-layer connection relationship between different entities in KG.

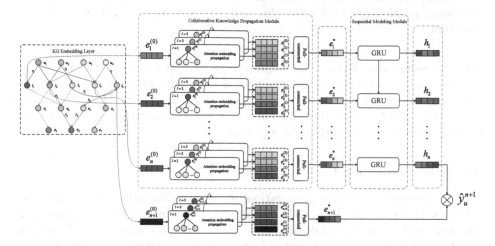

Fig. 2. Illustration of the proposed KGSR model. The left module is the KG embedding layer, the middle is the collaborative knowledge propagation module, and the right is the sequential modeling module.

3 Knowledge Graph Attention Network Enhanced Sequential Recommendation

In this section, we introduce our proposed KGSR model. The overall framework is illustrated in Fig. 2. We first describe the problem statement in our work and then present the architecture of our model in detail.

3.1 Problem Statement

Before introducing our proposed model, we first formally detail some basic concepts and notations involved in our work.

Recommendation System Dataset. We denote a set of users as $\mathcal{U} = \{u_1, u_2, ..., u_{|\mathcal{U}|}\}$ and a set of items as $\mathcal{I} = \{i_1, i_2, ..., i_{|\mathcal{I}|}\}$, where $|\mathcal{U}|$ and $|\mathcal{I}|$ represent the numbers of users and items, respectively. We build the training set's interaction data into a user-item bipartite graph $\mathcal{G}_1 = \{(u, y_{u,i}, i)|u \in \mathcal{U}, i \in \mathcal{I}\}$, where $y_{u,i} = 1$ if user u has already interacted with item i; otherwise, $y_{u,i} = 0$.

Knowledge Graph. All triples in the KG are denoted as $\mathcal{G}_2 = \{(h, r, t)|h, t \in \mathcal{E}, r \in \mathcal{R}\}$, where $\mathcal{E} = \{e_1, e_2, ..., e_{|\mathcal{E}|}\}$ is the set of entities and $\mathcal{R} = \{r_1, r_2, ..., r_{|\mathcal{R}|}\}$ is the set of relations. Each triplet represents that there is a relation r from head entity h to tail entity t.

Hybrid Knowledge Graph. Based on the item-entity alignment set, we combine the user-item bipartite graph $\mathcal{G}_1$ and the KG $\mathcal{G}_2$ into a unified graph $\mathcal{G} = \{(h, r, t)|h, t \in \mathcal{E}', r \in \mathcal{R}'\}$, where $\mathcal{E}' = \mathcal{E} \cup \mathcal{U}$ and $\mathcal{R}' = \mathcal{R} \cup \{Interact\}$. The additional relation $Interact$ is the observed interaction $y_{u,i} = 1$ between user u and item i.

Task Description. We now formulate the sequential recommendation task to be addressed in our work. Taking the hybrid knowledge graph $\mathcal{G}$ and a user u's history interaction sequence $\mathcal{S} = \{s_1^u, ..., s_t^u, ..., s_{|\mathcal{S}|-1}^u\}$, $(s_t^u \in \mathcal{I})$ as the input, where the index t denotes the relative time index, we aim to learn a function to predict the next item $s_{|\mathcal{S}|}^u$ that the user touches.

3.2 KG Embedding Layer

Before executing knowledge propagation, we need to vectorize the entities and relations in the hybrid KG. We first initialize the embedding of entities and relations as $\mathbb{R}_e^d$ and $\mathbb{R}_r^k$ randomly. Then we choose to employ TransR [10], a widely used knowledge graph embedding method, to embed representations of entities. TransR learns the embedding of entities and relations in the graph, requiring entities and relations to satisfy the constraints: $e_h^r + e_r \approx e_t^r$, if the triple (h, r, t) exists in the graph, where $e_h^r = W_r e_h$ and $e_t^r = W_r e_t$, $(e_h, e_t \in \mathbb{R}_e^d$, $e_r \in \mathbb{R}_r^k)$. $W_r \in \mathbb{R}^{k \times d}$ projects the representations of entities into the relation r's space. As described above, given a triplet (h, r, t), we have the energy score as follows:

$$F_{kg}(h, r, t) = \|W_r e_h + e_r - W_r e_t\|_2^2 \qquad (1)$$

The lower score of $F_{kg}(h, r, t)$, the more likely the triplet is true, and vice versa. Similar to BPR, TransR's loss is defined as follows:

$$\mathcal{L}_{kg} = \sum_{(h,r,t,t') \in \Gamma} - \ln \sigma(F_{kg}(h, r, t') - F_{kg}(h, r, t)) \qquad (2)$$

where $\Gamma = \{(h, r, t, t')|(h, r, t) \in \mathcal{G}, (h, r, t') \notin \mathcal{G}\}$. The symbol t' is an entity chosen at random from set $\{e|e \in \mathcal{E}, e \notin t\}$. $\sigma(\cdot)$ represents the logistic sigmoid function.

3.3 Collaborative Knowledge Propagation Module

The KG contains a large amount of entity attribute information. Previously, KSR [6] has been proposed to combine sequential recommender with the attribute information in the existing KG via key-value memory network. However, it ignores the dependency between an entity and its local graph context, which would be insufficient to explore the attributed-based collaborative signal between items. And it is unable to mine global user-item relationships. Our idea is to introduce the graph attention network to capture global user-item and item-item relationships simultaneously. And then, the RNN-based method simulates the sequence, where each item embedding has already contained the global collaborative signal. Next, we present how to propagate node embeddings via graph attention network recursively.

Information Propagation. Given an entity $k \in \mathcal{E}$ and a set of triples $\mathcal{N}_k = \{(h, r, t)|(h, r, t) \in \mathcal{G}, h = k\}$. After a layer of propagation, the node k' ego-network [11], which is merged with the neighbor nodes' embeddings, is represented as follows:

$$e_{\mathcal{N}_k} = \sum_{(h,r,t) \in \mathcal{N}_k} \pi(h, r, t) e_t \tag{3}$$

where $\pi(h, r, t)$ determines how much information is propagated from the neighbor entity t to the entity k. $\pi(h, r, t)$ is formed as follows:

$$\pi'(h, r, t) = (W_r e_t)^\top \tanh (W_r e_h + e_r) \tag{4}$$

$$\pi(h, r, t) = \frac{\exp (\pi'(h, r, t))}{\sum_{(h,r',t') \in \mathcal{N}_h} \exp (\pi'(h, r', t'))} \tag{5}$$

where tanh is the activation function and Eq. 5 is to normalize the relevance scores between entity h and its every neighbor entity. Specifically, when calculating $\pi(h, r, t)$ in Eq. 3, each neighbor of the entity k is the parameter h here.

Information Aggregation. Based on the ego-network obtained above, we merge the entity representation e_k and its ego-network representation $e_{\mathcal{N}_k}$ as the next layer's representation of entity k. The fusion function is formulated as follows:

$$e_k^{(1)} = \text{LeakyReLU}(W^{(1)}(e_k \odot e_{\mathcal{N}_k})) \tag{6}$$

where $W^{(1)} \in \mathbb{R}^{d' \times d}$ is the dimensional transition matrix between two layers, and $\odot$ is the element-wise product. LeakyReLU is the activation function.

Recursive Propagation. In order to explore more information, we stack more propagation layers to gather the multi-layer connection information from the higher-hop neighbors. In the l-th layer, entity k's representation is formulated as follows:

$$e_k^{(l)} = \text{LeakyReLU}(W^{(l)}(e_k^{(l-1)} \odot e_{\mathcal{N}_k}^{(l)})) \tag{7}$$

where the l-th layer's ego-network representation of entity k is defined as follows:

$$e_{\mathcal{N}_k}^{(l)} = \sum_{(h,r,t) \in \mathcal{N}_k} \pi(h, r, t) e_t^{(l-1)} \tag{8}$$

where $e_t^{(l-1)}$ is from the previous information propagation layer, retaining the information of entity t's $(l-1)$-hop neighbors.

Fully-Connected Layer. After the L-layer operation, we learned multiple representations for each entity k, namely $\{e_k^{(1)}, e_k^{(2)}, ..., e_k^{(L)}\}$. We first concatenate them into a single vector as final representation of entity k, as follow:

$$e_k' = e_k^{(0)} \parallel e_k^{(1)} \parallel ... \parallel e_k^{(L)} \tag{9}$$

where $\parallel$ denotes the concatenation operation. We obtain entity embedding set $\mathcal{E}^* = \{e_1', ..., e_k', ..., e_{|\mathcal{E}|}'\}$, where $e_k' \in \mathbb{R}^{d'}$, $d' = d + d^{(1)} + d^{(2)} + ... + d^{(L)}$, and then we project them into a fully-connected layer.

$$e_k^* = e_k' W_s + b_s \tag{10}$$

where $W_s \in \mathbb{R}^{d' \times d}$, $b_s \in \mathbb{R}^d$. We obtain new entity embedding set $\mathcal{E}^* = \{e_1^*, e_2^*, ..., e_{|\mathcal{E}|}^*\}$, and we can form a new item embedding matrix $\mathbf{I}^* \in \mathbb{R}^{|\mathcal{I}| \times d}$ based on item-entity alignment set. Obviously, the user-item and attribute-based item-item collaborative signal is seamlessly injected into the representation learning process via the multi-layer embedding propagation.

3.4   Sequential Modeling Module

Here, we apply a sequential recommendation method to model the user's historical interactions, which usually follow a chronological order. RNN has been proved to be effective in various sequence coding tasks. LSTM and GRU are two typical variants of RNN, which are proposed to solve the deficiency of the RNN method in dealing with long-dependencies. Here we choose GRU as our sequence encoder because GRU has a simpler structure than LSTM and has similar effects in most cases.

Given a user u's interaction sequence $\{s_1^u, ..., s_t^u, ..., s_{|\mathcal{S}|-1}^u\}$, we look up items embedding matrix $\mathbf{I}^* \in \mathbb{R}^{|\mathcal{I}| \times d}$ to obtain the input items' embedding $\{e_1^u, ..., e_t^u, ..., e_{|\mathcal{S}|-1}^u\}$. The current hidden state vertor $h_t^u \in \mathbb{R}^d$ can be computed by GRU-based recommender taking previous hidden state vector h_{t-1}^u and current item's embedding vector e_t^u as input.

$$h_t^u = \mathrm{GRU}(h_{t-1}^u, e_t^u; \Phi) \tag{11}$$

where $\mathrm{GRU}(\cdot)$ is the GRU cell. Φ denotes all relevant parameters of the GRU unit.

3.5   Model Prediction and Learning

Through the calculation of the sequential recommendation method, we obtain the final user preference representation h_t^u. Then, we conduct inner product of user representation h_t^u and item representation e_i^* looked up from matrix $\mathbf{I}^*$, and the score is used for ranking:

$$\hat{y}(u, i) = (h_t^u)^\top e_i^* \tag{12}$$

The higher the score of $\hat{y}(u, i)$, the higher the probability that user u will interact with item i next. Additionally, we optimize the recommendation model with BPR loss [12] as follows:

$$\mathcal{L}_{rec} = \sum_{(u,i,j)\in\mathcal{O}} -\ln\sigma(\hat{y}(u, i) - \hat{y}(u, j)) \tag{13}$$

where $\mathcal{O} = \{(u, i, j)|(u, i) \in \mathcal{Q}^+, (u, j) \in \mathcal{Q}^-\}$ is the training set, and $\mathcal{Q}^+$ denotes the set of observed (positive) interactions between user u and item i while $\mathcal{Q}^-$ indicates the set of unobserved (negative) interaction sampled randomly.

Finally, we minimize the overall objection function, which learns Eq. 2 and Eq. 13 jointly, to train our proposed KGSR model, as follows:

$$\mathcal{L} = \mathcal{L}_{rec} + \mathcal{L}_{kg} + \lambda\|\Theta\|_2^2 \tag{14}$$

where Θ is the set of all trainable parameters, and L_2 regularization is introduced to prevent overfitting.

4 Experiments

In this section, we first present our experimental settings and then compare and analyze our experimental results.

4.1 Dataset Description

To verify the effectiveness of our model KGSR, we conducted a giant amount of comparison experiments on two benchmark datasets: Amazon-book[1] and Yelp2018[2].

- **Amazon-book** is a widely used benchmark dataset in book recommendations, which contains product reviews and metadata from Amazon. To ensure the quality of the datasets, we filter unpopular items and inactive users with fewer than ten records.
- **Yelp2018** comes from the 2018 edition of the Yelp challenge, wherein the local businesses like restaurants and bars are viewed as the items. Similarly, we use the 10-core setting to ensure that each user and item have at least ten interactions.

In addition to the recommendation system datasets, we also need the knowledge graph datasets. The KG used in this paper is released by [15] on GitHub. For Amazon-book, its KG is extracted from Freebase, which provides two-hop neighbor entities of items. In contrast, Yelp2018's KG is extracted from the local business information network (e.g., category, location, and attribute). For clarity, detailed statistics of the two processed datasets are presented in Table 1.

---

[1] http://jmcauley.ucsd.edu/data/amazon.
[2] https://www.yelp.com/dataset/challenge.

Table 1. Statistics of the two datasets.

		Amazon-book	Yelp2018
User-item interaction	Users	70,595	45,805
	Items	24,914	45,043
	Interactions	846,094	1,282,878
Knowledge graph	Entities	88,572	90,961
	Relations	39	42
	Triplets	2,557,656	1,845,261

4.2 Experimental Settings

Evaluation Metrics. To evaluate the performance of each method for the sequential recommendation, we adopt two common Top-N metrics, Hit Rate@10 [19] and NDCG@10 [17,21]. Hit@10 just cares about the probability of the ground-truth and falls into the first ten items predicted, while NDCG@10 is a position-aware metric. In particular, when there is only one test item for each user, Hit@10 is equivalent to Recall@10 and proportional to P@10.

For the test method, we apply the strategy in [3,7]. We take the last one of each user's interaction record as the test set, and then all the remaining interaction records are used as the train set. When testing, the last item in the user interaction sequence is used as the ground-truth, and then it forms final test examples with 100 randomly selected items that are not in the user interaction record. The final result shows the ranking of the ground-truth item among the 101 test examples.

Baselines. We choose the following methods as the baselines to compare with our model:

- **BPR** [12]: Bayesian personalized ranking is a classic method, which uses a pair-wise loss function to model the relative preferences of users.
- **NCF** [3]: Neural collaborative filtering replaces the inner product of traditional MF with a neural architecture, which provides the model with nonlinearity modeling capability.
- **CKE** [20]: Collaborative knowledge base embedding is the first work leveraging structural content from the KG, textual content and visual content for recommender systems. Here, we simply extract knowledge from KG.
- **FPMC** [13]: Factorizing personalized markov chains combines matrix factorization and first-order markov chain for the next-basket recommendation. It could capture both sequential effects and the general interests of users.
- **RUM** [1]: It first utilizes a memory network to improve sequential recommendation, where item-level (RUM^I) and feature-level (RUM^F) are its two variants. We only report the results of RUM^I here.
- **GRU4Rec** [4]: Gated recurrent unit uses an RNN-based method to model user action sequences for the session-based recommendation. It utilizes the

session-parallel mini-batch training process and ranking-based loss functions for improvement.

- **GRU4Rec+**: We use the BPR model to pretrain item embedding and take it as the input of GRU4Rec.
- **KSR** [6]: Knowledge-enhanced sequential recommender is the first time that sequential recommender is integrated with existing KG information by leveraging external memories.

Table 2. Overall performance comparisons on both Amazon-Book and Yelp2018 datasets. Experimental results are reported in terms of Hit@10 and NDCG@10 evaluation methods. Boldface indicates the best results, while the second best is underlined.

	Amazon-Book		Yelp2018	
	Hit@10	NDCG@10	Hit@10	NDCG@10
BPR	0.6511	0.4614	0.8437	0.5768
NCF	0.6890	0.4820	0.8450	0.5790
CKE	0.7515	0.5457	0.8557	0.5918
FPMC	0.6986	0.4835	0.7645	0.5164
RUM	0.7511	0.5412	0.8666	0.5891
GRU4Rec	0.7501	0.5402	0.8553	0.5887
GRU4Rec+	0.7515	0.5398	0.8660	0.5990
KSR	<u>0.7656</u>	<u>0.5550</u>	<u>0.8720</u>	<u>0.6060</u>
KGSR	**0.8056**	**0.5987**	**0.8984**	**0.6432**
Improv.	5.222%	7.865%	3.022%	6.144%

Parameter Settings. The experimental results of the baselines we report are all parameters optimized to the data set. We implement our KGSR model in Tensorflow. We set the depth of graph attention network L as 3 with hidden dimension 64, 32, and 16, respectively. We only use one layer of GRU here. The default Xavier initializer to initialize the model parameters and the embedding size is fixed to 50. We optimize our models with Adam optimizer, where the batch size is fixed at 128. Optimal learning rate $\alpha = 0.0001$ and the coefficient $\lambda = 10^{-5}$ of L2 normalization for our experiments. We apply an embedding dropout technique where the drop ratio $d = 0.1$. We will conduct experiments to analyze the impact of the depth of the graph attention network L and the maximum length of the sequence in the future. We set the depth L of the graph attention neural network to 1, 2, 3, and 4 respectively to analyze the impact of L. To investigate the impact of sparsity, we limit the maximum length of the input sequence to simulate datasets with different degrees of sparsity. The input sequence length is limited to 10, 20, 30, 40, or 50, respectively.

4.3   Performance Comparison

We compare our model with all baselines in terms of Hit@10 and NDCG@10. The results of all models are reported in Table 2. We have the following observations:

- In terms of two evaluation metrics (i.e., Hit Rate and NDCG), our method KGSR consistently performs better than all baseline methods on two benchmark datasets. By using the graph attention network method to propagate signals recursively, KGSR successfully captures the collaborative signals in interactions and the knowledge graph. This indicates importance of the collaborative information in collective user behaviors and knowledge graph to the sequential recommendation method.
- Among all the non-sequential baselines, CKE achieves the most competitive performance on both datasets compared to BPR and NCF. Maybe this is because CKE additionally introduces items' fact information from KG, which can make up for the collaborative information not included in the interaction information between items. BPR achieves comparable performance to NCF on the dense dataset Yelp2018 but performs slightly worse than NCF on the relatively sparse dataset Amazon-book. This proves that the neural network structure introduced by NCF can effectively characterize user-item interactions.
- Among the sequential baselines, FPMC is the only non-neural network method and has the worst performance. RUM uses key-value memory networks to learn the long-term and short-term preferences of users. Compared to GRU4Rec, RUM has obtained advanced sequence recommendation performance. We use BPR pre-trained items embedding as the input to GRU4Rec to optimize GRU4Rec+. With the pre-training, GRU4Rec+ achieves the second-best performance of all baselines, behind KSR. KSR, which uses key-value memory networks to incorporate the user's attribute-level preference and GRU to capture the user's sequence preference, obtains the best performance among all baselines. However, in KSR, entity and relationship representation of KG and the embedding of items require pre-training. The quality of the pre-trained embedding has a great impact on the performance of the KSR, so this may be why although the KSR in terms of our results reported here is better than other baselines, the margin is not very large.
- Finally, we compare our proposed model KGSR with the strongest baseline KSR model. It is clear to see that our model KGSR improves over the KSR w.r.t. NDCG@10 by 7.865% and 6.144% on the Amazon-book and Yelp2018, respectively. By using a graph attention network to simultaneously capture the collaborative signals in interaction and knowledge graph and using GRU to capture user's sequence preference, KGSR naturally combines the side information of the knowledge graph to improve the performance of sequential recommendation. This verifies that our method improves the sequential recommendation performance more effectively compared with KSR.

4.4   Model Analysis and Discussion

The above is an overall comparison of the experimental results. Our model achieved significant improvements across all baselines. In this paragraph, we further experiment and analyze our model to better understand it. We first analyze the effect of the depth L of the graph attention network on the sequential recommendation, and then limit the maximum length of the input sequence interacted by each user to simulate the sparseness of the data. On datasets with different degrees of sparseness, we compare the performance of our model and KSR.

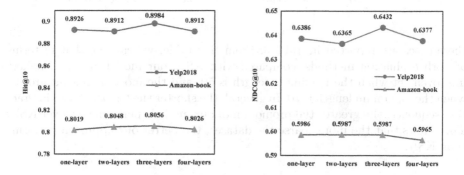

Fig. 3. Influence of depth L of graph attention network.

Influence of Depth L of Graph Attention Network. Previously, we have proved that the introduction of the graph attention network can effectively improve the performance of sequential recommendation. Here we further experimentally analyze the effect of the depth of graph attention network on the final sequential recommendation performance. We set the depth of propagation layers to 1, 2, 3, and 4, respectively. Our experimental results are reported in Fig. 3. From line chart, we can see that the final model performance is optimal when the number of layers is 3. In addition, analyzing Fig. 3 and Table 2, our model with one layer's graph attention network is also better than the best performance baseline KSR, which indicates that the information propagation of graph attention network can effectively capture the collaborative signals in interaction and knowledge graph and improve the sequential recommendation.

Influence of Maximum Length of the Input Sequence. To further study the advantages of our model, we limit the maximum length of input user interaction sequences to 10, 20, 30, 40, and 50, respectively, on the amazon-book dataset. The corresponding average interaction lengths are 6.65, 8.15, 8.86, 9.3, and 9.59, respectively. And the experimental results of our model and KSR under

Table 3. Influence of maximum length of the input sequence on the Amazon-book dataset.

Max len		10	20	30	40	50
Avg len		6.65	8.15	8.86	9.3	9.59
KSR	Hit@10	0.7365	0.7547	0.7588	0.7590	0.7637
	NDCG@10	0.5320	0.5446	0.5446	0.5508	0.5542
KGSR	Hit@10	0.7911	0.7964	0.8019	0.8020	0.8056
	NDCG@10	0.5841	0.5932	0.5953	0.5972	0.5987
Improv.	Hit@10	**7.413%**	5.525%	5.680%	5.665%	5.484%
	NDCG@10	**9.793%**	8.924%	9.310%	8.424%	8.021%

these cases are reported in Table 3. From this table, we can see that in terms of both evaluation methods, compared with KSR, our model has the smallest improvement when the maximum length is 50, and the most significant growth when the maximum length is 10. In general, the shorter the length of user interaction sequence, the greater the promotion of our model's performance over KSR. This shows that the more sparse the dataset, the better our approach performs than KSR.

5 Conclusion

In this paper, we proposed an end-to-end method named **K**nowledge **G**raph attention network enhanced **S**equential **R**ecommendation (KGSR). By exploring multi-layer connectivity in knowledge graph, our method distills the collaborative signals between different entities, which greatly helps sequential methods find relevant items for recommendation accurately. Specifically, our method utilizes TranR to vectorize all entities in knowledge graph. And a graph attention network is introduced to perform information propagation, while the GRU captures the transitions of items in interaction sequences. The graph attention network not only makes up for the insufficiency of the RNN-based method to fully capture the context-dependency of sequence items but also successfully captures the semantic information of items in knowledge graph. Extensive experiments on two benchmarks datasets demonstrate the rationality and effectiveness of our model KGSR.

Acknowledgments. This research was partially supported by NSFC (No. 61876117, 61876217, 61872258, 61728205), Open Program of Key Lab of IIP of CAS (No. IIP2019-1) and PAPD.

References

1. Chen, X., et al.: Sequential recommendation with user memory networks. In: WSDM, pp. 108–116. ACM (2018)

2. Donkers, T., Loepp, B., Ziegler, J.: Sequential user-based recurrent neural network recommendations. In: RecSys, pp. 152–160. ACM (2017)
3. He, X., Liao, L., Zhang, H., Nie, L., Hu, X., Chua, T.S.: Neural collaborative filtering. In: WWW, pp. 173–182. WWW (2017)
4. Hidasi, B., Karatzoglou, A., Baltrunas, L., Tikk, D.: Session-based recommendations with recurrent neural networks. arXiv preprint arXiv:1511.06939 (2015)
5. Hochreiter, S., Schmidhuber, J.: Long short-term memory. Neural computation, pp. 1735–1780 (1997)
6. Huang, J., Zhao, W.X., Dou, H., Wen, J.R., Chang, E.Y.: Improving sequential recommendation with knowledge-enhanced memory networks. In: SIGIR, pp. 505–514. ACM (2018)
7. Kang, W.C., McAuley, J.: Self-attentive sequential recommendation. In: ICDM, pp. 197–206. IEEE (2018)
8. Koren, Y., Bell, R., Volinsky, C.: Matrix factorization techniques for recommender systems. Computer **8**, 30–37 (2009)
9. Li, J., Ren, P., Chen, Z., Ren, Z., Lian, T., Ma, J.: Neural attentive session-based recommendation. In: CIKM, pp. 1419–1428. ACM (2017)
10. Lin, Y., Liu, Z., Sun, M., Liu, Y., Zhu, X.: Learning entity and relation embeddings for knowledge graph completion. In: AAAI (2015)
11. Qiu, J., Tang, J., Ma, H., Dong, Y., Wang, K., Tang, J.: Deepinf: social influence prediction with deep learning. In: SIGKDD, pp. 2110–2119 (2018)
12. Rendle, S., Freudenthaler, C., Gantner, Z., Schmidt-Thieme, L.: BPR: Bayesian personalized ranking from implicit feedback. In: UAI, pp. 452–461. AUAI Press (2009)
13. Rendle, S., Freudenthaler, C., Schmidt-Thieme, L.: Factorizing personalized Markov chains for next-basket recommendation. In: WWW, pp. 811–820. ACM (2010)
14. Sarwar, B.M., Karypis, G., Konstan, J.A., Riedl, J., et al.: Item-based collaborative filtering recommendation algorithms. In: WWW, vol. 1, pp. 285–295 (2001)
15. Wang, X., He, X., Cao, Y., Liu, M., Chua, T.S.: KGAT: knowledge graph attention network for recommendation. arXiv preprint arXiv:1905.07854 (2019)
16. Wang, X., Wang, D., Xu, C., He, X., Cao, Y., Chua, T.S.: Explainable reasoning over knowledge graphs for recommendation. In: AAAI, vol. 33, pp. 5329–5336 (2019)
17. Xu, C., et al.: Graph contextualized self-attention network for session-based recommendation. In: IJCAI, pp. 3940–3946 (2019)
18. Xu, C., et al.: Recurrent convolutional neural network for sequential recommendation. In: WWW, pp. 3398–3404. ACM (2019)
19. Yan, H., Zhao, P., Zhang, F., Wang, D., Liu, Y., Sheng, V.S.: Cross domain recommendation with adversarial examples. In: DASFAA (2020)
20. Zhang, F., Yuan, N.J., Lian, D., Xie, X., Ma, W.Y.: Collaborative knowledge base embedding for recommender systems. In: SIGKDD, pp. 353–362. ACM (2016)
21. Zhang, T., et al.: Feature-level deeper self-attention network for sequential recommendation. In: IJCAI, pp. 4320–4326. AAAI Press (2019)
22. Zhao, P., et al.: Where to go next: a spatio-temporal gated network for next poi recommendation. In: AAAI, vol. 33, pp. 5877–5884 (2019)

TKGFrame: A Two-Phase Framework for Temporal-Aware Knowledge Graph Completion

Jiasheng Zhang[1,2], Yongpan Sheng[3(✉)], Zheng Wang[2,4], and Jie Shao[2,5]

[1] Guizhou Provincial Key Laboratory of Public Big Data, Guizhou University,
Guiyang 550025, China
zjss12358@gmail.com

[2] School of Computer Science and Engineering,
University of Electronic Science and Technology of China, Chengdu 611731, China
shaojie@uestc.edu.cn

[3] School of Big Data & Software Engineering, Chongqing University,
Chongqing 401331, China
shengyp2011@gmail.com

[4] Institute of Electronic and Information Engineering of UESTC,
Dongguan 523808, China
zh_wang@hotmail.com

[5] Sichuan Artificial Intelligence Research Institute, Yibin 644000, China

Abstract. In this paper, we focus on temporal-aware knowledge graph (TKG) completion, which aims to automatically predict missing links in a TKG by making inferences from the existing temporal facts and the temporal information among the facts. Existing methods conducted on this task mainly focus on modeling temporal ordering of relations contained in the temporal facts to learn the low-dimensional vector space of TKG. However, these models either ignore the evolving strength of temporal ordering relations in the structure of relational chain, or discard more consideration to the revision of candidate prediction results produced by the TKG embeddings. To address these two limitations, we propose a novel two-phase framework called TKGFrame to boost the final performance of the task. Specifically, TKGFrame employs two major models. The first one is a relation evolving enhanced model to enhance evolving strength representations of pairwise relations pertaining to the same relational chain, resulting in more accurate TKG embeddings. The second one is a refinement model to revise the candidate predictions from the embeddings and further improve the performance of predicting missing temporal facts via solving a constrained optimization problem. Experiments conducted on three popular datasets for entity prediction and relation prediction demonstrate that TKGFrame achieves more accurate prediction results as compared to several state-of-the-art baselines.

Keywords: Two-phase framework · Temporal evolution · Temporal-aware knowledge graph completion

© Springer Nature Switzerland AG 2020
X. Wang et al. (Eds.): APWeb-WAIM 2020, LNCS 12317, pp. 196–211, 2020.
https://doi.org/10.1007/978-3-030-60259-8_16

1   Introduction

Knowledge graphs (KGs) such as Freebase [2], YAGO [17] and DBpedia [13] have proven to be highly valuable resources for many applications including information extraction [21], semantic search [1] and question answering [6]. However, in fact, KGs with large scales are usually far from complete, because the facts contained in KG are mainly mined from unstructured sources using machine learning and information extraction techniques, and no single source is sufficiently comprehensive as well as technique is sufficiently perfect. Therefore, KG completion[1] is a long-standing but increasingly important task in the research field.

KG embedding, which aims to embed KG elements (i.e., entities and relations) into the latent, low-dimensional, and real-valued vector representations, has been proven to be a powerful technique for KG completion. Over the last few years, several approaches have been developed for this task and two main groups can be distinguished: translational distance-based methods such as TransE [3] and its numerous variants, and semantic matching methods such as RESCAL [16]. Although most of these methods have exhibited both effectiveness and strong generalization capabilities for KG completion, we observed that they only treat KG as a static graph and the assumption in the background is that the facts involved in KG are universally true. Obviously, the assumption is inadequate and inconceivable in many real-world scenarios. In fact, quite of facts in KG are extremely ephemeral or tend to be valid only in a specified time period. An illustration of the comparison between KG and temporal-aware knowledge graph (TKG) based on the topic *"soccer player"* is in Fig. 1. Intuitively, existing approaches may make mistakes without considering the temporal aspects of facts when learning KG embeddings.

In recent years, most of contemporary researchers turn to distributed representations of temporal knowledge graphs (a.k.a TKG embeddings) to deal with the TKG completion problem. It aims to automatically predict missing links in a TKG by making inferences from the existing temporal facts and the temporal information among the facts. A series of representation learning methods for TKG completion, e.g., t-TransE [10], TransE-TAE [9], TTransE [12] and HyTE [5], have been implemented to model the temporal ordering of relations contained in the temporal facts to learn a low-dimensional vector space of TKG. See Sect. 2.2 for more details on TKG embedding methods.

Although existing TKG embedding methods on the above task have achieved preliminary performance improvements, they still suffer from two major limitations: (1) The model ignores the evolving strength of pairwise relations pertaining to the same relational chain, which results in some temporal information loss in the learned embeddings. (2) The model only relies on the learned embeddings to predict the plausibility of missing links in the TKG, and lacks more consideration

---

[1] KG completion, as known as link prediction in KG, aims to automatically predict missing links between entities based on known facts involved in KG.

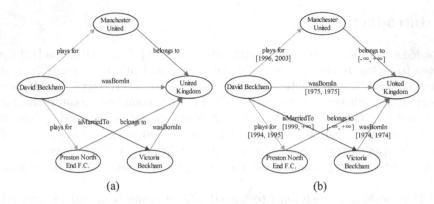

Fig. 1. (a) An example of KG on the topic *"soccer player"*, in which five entities (e.g., *"David Beckham"*, *"United Kingdom"*) are represented as vertices, and four types of relations (e.g., *"plays for"*, *"wasBornIn"*) are represented as directed edges with labels in four different colors between vertices; (b) An example of TKG augmented from (a), in which each directed edge as relation with timestamp represented as $[t_{start}, t_{end}]$ denotes its connected fact that starts in t_{start} and ends in t_{end}, e.g., (*"David Beckham"*, *"plays for"*, *"Manchester United"*) is true only during 1996–2003. Note that, as for some facts with special time intervals, if the facts do not end yet, we represent their timestamps as $[t_{start}, +\bowtie]$, e.g., the fact (*"David Beckham"*, *"isMarriedTo"*, *"Victoria Beckham"*), with the timestamp $[1999, +\bowtie]$; for some facts are factual ones, we represent their timestamps as $[-\bowtie, +\bowtie]$, e.g., the fact (*"Manchester"*, *"belongs to"*, *"United Kingdom"*) with the timestamp $[-\bowtie, +\bowtie]$.

to the further revision of prediction results, leading to a suboptimal performance on TKG completion.

To address the above limitations, we propose a novel two-phase framework called TKGFrame to boost the final performance of TKG completion task. TKGFrame addresses these issues by applying two models, namely relation evolving enhanced model and refinement model. Specifically, in the relation evolving enhanced model, based on the work of Jiang *et al.* [9], a refined temporal evolving matrix is introduced to enhance evolving strength representations of pairwise relations in the same relational chain. For example, for the relation-based chain associated with the same person, the temporal ordering relation *wasBornIn* needs to use greater strength to evolve into *diedIn* than into *graduatedFrom* in the temporal-aware embedding space measured by the refined temporal evolving matrix. This kind of temporal ordering enhanced information can be regarded as a regularization term for a joint optimization problem to learn TKG embeddings. The refinement model formulates the plausibility prediction of missing temporal facts in the TKG from the embeddings as an integer linear programming (ILP) problem, in which two types of additional common-sense constraints for temporality are utilized to effectively filter out those implausible predictions for the purpose of improving the prediction quality. In addition, another advantage of the refinement model is that it would benefit to improve the explainability for the final prediction results by better handling temporal conflicts in relations. By integrating the above two models seamlessly into a complete framework, it can achieve more accurate prediction results. It is worthwhile to highlight our contributions as follows:

- We propose a novel two-phase framework called TKGFrame for TKG completion.
- We present three extensions of TKGFrame based on the idea of incorporating temporal order among relations for learning TKG embeddings [9]: (1) refine a new temporal evolving matrix for better modeling evolving strength representations of pairwise relations pertaining to the same relational chain following the timeline; (2) formulate plausibility measure of the candidate predictions of missing temporal facts as a constrained optimization problem, and propose an ILP approach to solve it as well as avoid implausible predictions from the embedding results; and (3) integrate two models into the proposed TKGFrame seamlessly.
- We conduct extensive experiments on three real-world datasets, newly collected from two popular KG projects, namely YAGO 3 and Wikidata, and compare our results against some state-of-the-art baseline methods on both entity prediction and relation prediction tasks. Experimental results have verified the effectiveness of TKGFrame.
- To illustrate the evaluation of our model and facilitate further research on this topic, we have made the experimental details and source code of the model publicly available[2].

The remainder of this paper is organized as follows. We review related research in this area in Sect. 2. Section 3 provides the details of each model derived from TKGFrame. In Sect. 4, we conduct extensive experimental evaluations and provide an analysis of the effectiveness of our model in terms of entity prediction and relation prediction, respectively. Finally, the conclusions and future work are described in Sect. 5.

2 Related Work

In this section, we provide an overview of the typical methods for KG embedding learning. These approaches have offered state-of-the-art results for KG and TKG completion on several benchmarks. According to whether the temporal-aware information is considered or not in the learned KG embeddings, the methods can be summarized into two major branches, including static KG embedding methods and temporal-aware KG embedding methods.

---

[2] The experimental details and source code of the model are publicly available at https://github.com/zjs123/TKGComplt.

2.1   Static Knowledge Graph Embedding Methods

Static KG embedding methods aim to map each entity and each relation in a KG to a latent, low-dimensional, and real-valued vector representation and compute a score to measure the plausibility for each triple by applying a scoring function to these representations. The well-known TransE model [3] maps entities to vectors and regards r as translations from a head entity h to a tail entity l. Based on TransE, a number of improved models have been proposed, such as TransH [20] and TransR [14]. Specifically, TransE [3] attempts to make $h + r$ and l be as close as possible by adjusting the vectors for the head entity h, relation r, and tail entity l. The TransH model [20] models relations as vectors on a relation-specific hyperplane with an associated translation operation. TransE and TransH both embed the entities and relations into the same space. The TransR model [14] considers separate entity and relation spaces to better capture the differences between entities and relations.

2.2   Temporal-Aware Knowledge Graph Embedding Methods

In recent years, an increasing number of researchers have paid attention to this promising area, and many efforts have been made for learning temporal property among relations and relation embedding simultaneously. Jiang *et al.* [10] took the happen time of facts into account, and proposed a TKG embedding model by simply extending standard TransE model. Jiang *et al.* [9] extended the above work and made an attempt to incorporate temporal order information for TKG completion. Specifically, in this approach, instead of incorporating temporal-aware information in the learned embeddings, it first learns temporal order among relations (e.g., *wasBornIn* → *worksAt* → *diedIn*), and then these relation orders are incorporated as consistency constrains to learn TKG embeddings. However, some explicit temporal relation dependencies in relational chains in the model are not fully considered, which affects the actual quality of the TKG embeddings. In contrast to [9], Dasgupta *et al.* [5] proposed a TKG embedding model called HyTE inspired from the objective of TransH [20], which is able to directly incorporate temporal information in the learned embeddings. Specifically, they firstly divide an input TKG into multiple static subgraphs, each of which is pertinent for a timestamp, and then project all the entities and relations of each subgraph onto the hyperplane specific with a timestamp for joint learning of the hyperplane vectors and the representations of the TKG elements distributed in the subgraphs. TTransE [12] investigated temporal scope prediction over unannotated triples, and extended existing TransE-style scoring functions. TA-TransE [8] utilized digit-level LSTM to learn TKG embeddings combining with existing scoring functions such as TransE and DistMult. For both TTransE and TA-TransE, they verify the effectiveness of the joint learning framework which is based on existing scoring function, with temporal information regularization. In addition, another study in Know-Evolve [19] is mostly focused on factual knowledge evolving. It uses a bilinear model (RESCAL) and employs a deep recurrent neural network in order to learn non-linearly evolving entities.

3   The Proposed Two-Phase Framework

In this section, two models and detailed steps within the proposed TKGFrame are introduced in detail.

3.1   Phase I: Relation Evolving Enhanced Model for TKG Embedding

Our TKG embedding model is expected to better model temporal evolution among facts in the temporal-aware embedding space. For this, Jiang *et al.* [9] firstly propose a key assumption that temporal ordering relations occurring in the facts are associated with each other and evolve in a time dimension. In the guide of this assumption, they attempt to capture the temporal order among relations by using a *temporal evolving matrix* $\mathbf{T} \in \mathbb{R}^{n \times n}$, where n is the dimension of relation embedding, While experimental evidence indicates that $\mathbf{T}$ is indeed helpful for incorporating temporal-aware information to the learned TKG embeddings.

Inspired by the above idea, we refine a new *temporal evolving matrix* $\mathbf{T}_e \in \mathbb{R}^{n \times n}$ for better modeling temporal dependencies in a relational chain. The key distinction between these two forms of *temporal evolving matrices* (i.e., $\mathbf{T}$ and $\mathbf{T}_e$) is that in the former, $\mathbf{T}$ only can separate given prior relation and subsequent relation which share the same head entity in the temporal-aware embedding space, whereas in the latter, $\mathbf{T}_e$ is able to enhance evolving strength representations of pairwise relations pertaining to the same relational. Specifically, for the same person, there exists a temporal dependency, denoted as *wasBornIn* $\rightarrow$ *graduatedFrom* $\rightarrow$ *worksAt* $\rightarrow$ *diedIn*. As a result, for the first case, *wasBornIn* can evolve into *graduatedFrom*, *graduatedFrom* can evolve into *worksAt*, and *worksAt* can evolve into *diedIn* in a time dimension, with the same intensity. For the second case, *wasBornIn* can evolve into *graduatedFrom*, *worksAt* and *diedIn* with the strength as once, twice, and three times, which can be measured by $\mathbf{T}_e$, $\mathbf{T}_e^2$, and $\mathbf{T}_e^3$. Following the similar process introduced above, *graduatedFrom* can also evolve into *worksAt* and *diedIn* in once and twice strength as presented by $\mathbf{T}_e$ and $\mathbf{T}_e^2$, respectively. A simple graphical illustration for this example is shown in Fig. 2. In this way, we enhance the evolvement among temporal ordering relations by exploiting different evolving strength measures. It indicates that the farther distance of the pairwise relations in a relation-based chain, the more evolving strength they need.

As studied in [9], we also formulate TKG embedding as an optimization problem based on a temporal-aware regularization term. Given any two positive training quadruples (e_i, r_i, e_j, t_{r_i}) and (e_i, r_j, e_m, t_{r_j}), they share the same *head entity* and a temporal ordering relation pair $\langle r_i, r_j \rangle$. If $t_{r_i} < t_{r_j}$, we have a pair of positive temporal ordering relations, denoted as $r^+ = \langle r_i, r_j \rangle$, and corresponding negative relation pair $r^- = \langle r_i, r_j \rangle^{-1}$ by inverse. Our optimization requires that positive temporal ordering relation pairs in each relational chain[3] should have lower scores than negative pairs. Therefore, we have a temporal scoring function:

---

[3] The relational chain can be constructed by connecting temporal relations sharing the same head entity ranked by an order of their timestamps.

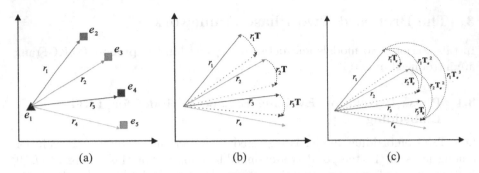

Fig. 2. An illustration of two forms of temporal evolving matrices (i.e., $\mathbf{T}$ and $\mathbf{T}_e$) in the temporal-aware embedding space. For instance, there exist four temporal ordering relations for the same person, denoted as $r_1 = wasBornIn$, $r_2 = graduatedFrom$, $r_3 = worksAt$, $r_4 = diedIn$, ranked in chronological order in a relation-based chain l_r. The relation between entity e_i and entity e_j corresponds to a translation vector r_i by the TransE model, i.e., $\mathbf{e}_i + \mathbf{r}_i \approx \mathbf{e}_j$ when $(\mathbf{e}_i, \mathbf{r}_i, \mathbf{e}_j)$ holds $(j = i + 1, j \leq 5, i = 1)$, as shown in (a). We obtain prior relation's projection $r_i\mathbf{T}$ near subsequent relation $\mathbf{r}_{i+1}$ in the space by projection by $\mathbf{T}$, i.e., $\mathbf{r}_i\mathbf{T} \approx \mathbf{r}_{i+1}$, but $\mathbf{r}_{i+1}\mathbf{T} \neq \mathbf{r}_i$ $(i = 1, 2, 3)$, as shown in (b). Similar to (b), we obtain prior relation's projection $\mathbf{r}_i\mathbf{T}^{j-i}$ near subsequent relation $\mathbf{r}_j$ based on their dependency strength in l_r in the space by projection by $\mathbf{T}_e$, i.e., $\mathbf{r}_i\mathbf{T}_e^{j-i} \approx \mathbf{r}_j$, but $\mathbf{r}_j\mathbf{T}_e^{j-i} \neq \mathbf{r}_i$ $(j = i + 1, j \leq 4, i = 1, 2, 3)$, as shown in (c).

$$g(\langle r_i, r_j \rangle) = \|\mathbf{r}_i\mathbf{T}_e^{j-i} - \mathbf{r}_j\|_{l_1/l_2}, \tag{1}$$

where $\mathbf{T}_e$ is a parameter to be learned by our model from the training data, and $\mathbf{T}_e^n$ is to enhance the evolving strengths of pairwise relations with different dependency distances in the relation-based chain, which has introduced in the earlier parts of this section. We are expected to obtain a low score when the temporal ordering relation pair is in chronological order, and a high score otherwise. Note that $\mathbf{T}_e$ is also an asymmetric matrix, resulting in loss function with asymmetric property, so as to a better modeling of temporal ordering relation pairs.

However, in practice, Eq. 1 cannot ensure that the scores of positive temporal ordering relation pairs are absolutely low to fulfill the projection when the chronological order exists, as pointed by Zhou et al. [22]. Hence, we follow the strategy adopted in modeling previous work [18] and leverage an optimized objective function as the temporal loss function:

$$\mathcal{O}_r = \sum_{r^+ \in \mathcal{D}_r^+} [g(r^+) - \gamma_1]_+ + \mu \sum_{r^- \in \mathcal{D}_r^-} [\gamma_2 - g(r^-)]_+, \tag{2}$$

where $\mathcal{D}_r^+$ and $\mathcal{D}_r^-$ denote the sets of positive temporal ordering relation pairs and negative temporal ordering relation pairs covering all the relation-based chains, respectively. $[\cdot]_+ = max(\cdot, 0)$, $\gamma_1, \gamma_2 > 0$ are two hyperparameters, $\mu > 0$ is used for smoothing as well as to strike a trade-off between the two terms in Eq. 2, and is fixed to 0.5 in our implementation. To summarize, the advantages of Eq. 2 is two-fold: firstly, we are able to directly control the absolute scores of positive and negative temporal ordering relation pairs as needed, with setting $g(r^+) \leq \gamma_1$ and $g(r^-) \geq \gamma_2$ ($\gamma_2 > \gamma_1$ and γ_1 is a relatively small positive value); secondly, we are still expected to preserve the characteristic of the margin-based ranking criterion deriving from TransE model [3], with setting $g(r^-) - g(r^+) \geq \gamma_2 - \gamma_1$.

Moreover, in order to make the temporal-aware embedding space compatible with the observed temporal facts, we make use of the temporal fact set Δ and follow the same scoring function applied in TransE model:

$$f(\mathbf{e}_s, \mathbf{r}, \mathbf{e}_o) = \|\mathbf{e}_s + \mathbf{r} - \mathbf{e}_o\|_{l_1/l_2}. \tag{3}$$

Combining Eq. 2 and Eq. 3, the final optimization problem can be solved by minimizing the joint scoring function as follows:

$$\mathcal{L} = \sum_{t^+ \in \Delta^+} \sum_{t^- \in \Delta^-} [\gamma + f(t^+) - f(t^-)]_+ + \lambda \mathcal{O}_r, \tag{4}$$

where $t^+ \in \Delta^+$ is a positive temporal fact, and $t^- \in \Delta^-$ is a negative temporal fact by randomly replacing head or tail entity of the positive one. In our settings, the constrains are: $\|\mathbf{e}_s\|_2 \leq 1$, $\|\mathbf{r}_i\|_2 \leq 1$, $\|\mathbf{e}_o\|_2 \leq 1$, $\|\mathbf{r}_j\|_2 \leq 1$, $\|\mathbf{r}_i \mathbf{T}_e^n\|_2 \leq 1$, and $\|\mathbf{r}_j \mathbf{T}_e^n\|_2 \leq 1$ for presenting the model from overfitting during training.

The first term in Eq. 4 enforces the resulting temporal-aware embedding space compatible with the whole of observed temporal triples, and the second term further requires the space to be consistent and more accurate. Hyperparameter λ strikes a trade-off between the two terms. We use stochastic gradient descent over shuffled mini-batches to solve this minimization problem.

3.2 Phase II: Refinement Model

After obtaining the TKG embeddings generated from the previous phase, the plausibility prediction of the missing temporal triples from these embeddings inevitably suffers from inferior embedding performance. Hence, in this section, we further model plausibility measure of the candidate predictions as a constrained optimization problem, and propose an integer linear programming (ILP) approach to eliminate implausible predictions from the embedding results. ILP is an optimization model with constraints and the whole of variables are required to be non-negative integers [4].

Objective Function. We first define a decision variable $x_{s,r,o}$ for each candidate quadruple $s_{s,o}^r = (e_s, r, e_o, t_r)$. These variables are binary and indicate whether quadruple s_{so}^r is true or false.

$$x_{s,r,o} = \begin{cases} 1, & \text{if} s_{s,o}^r = (e_s, r, e_o, t_r) \text{ is selected to be retained} \\ 0, & \text{otherwise} \end{cases}.$$

We then define the objective function as follows:

$$min \sum_{x_{s,r,o}} (\min f(s_{s,o}^r) - \theta) \times x_{s,r,o}, \tag{5}$$

where $f(s_{s,o}^r)$ represents the plausibility predicted by the prior embedding model, as computed in Eq. 3. The lower score, the more likely to be valid. θ is the threshold used to select temporal facts with sufficiently high possibility (see implementation details in Sect. 4.2 for its value in our experiments).

Constraints. Inspired in part by the considerations given by [9], we then illustrate two categories of common-sense constraints associated temporality for our ILP model: *temporal disjointness constraint* and *temporal ordering constraint*.

(1) Temporal Disjointness Constraint. It claims that the time intervals of any two temporal facts with a same functional relation (i.e., relation type) and a same head entity, or a same tail entity are non-overlapping. For example, a person can only be spouse of one person during a specified time interval, so $(e_1, wasSpouseOf, e_2, [1994, 1998]) \cap (e_1, wasSpouseOf, e_3, [1992, 2000]) \cap (e_2 \neq e_3) \rightarrow$ false. These constraints can be represented as:

$$x_{s,r,l} + x_{s,r,m} \leq 1, x_{n,r,o} + x_{p,r,o} \leq 1,$$
$$\forall r \in \mathcal{C}_1 \, , \, t_{x_{s,r,l}} \cap t_{x_{s,r,m}} \neq \emptyset, t_{x_{n,r,o}} \cap t_{x_{p,r,o}} \neq \emptyset \qquad (6)$$

where $\mathcal{C}_1$ are functional relations described such as *wasBornIn*, and $t_{x_{s,r,l}}$, $t_{x_{s,r,m}}$ are time intervals for two temporal facts with a common head entity as well as diverse tail entities, respectively. Similarly, $t_{x_{n,r,o}}$, $t_{x_{p,r,o}}$ are also time intervals for two temporal facts with a common tail entity as well as diverse head entities, respectively.

(2) Temporal Ordering Constraint. It claims that some temporal relations occurr in order. Correspondingly, the fact related to the relation always happens before another one. For example, a person must be born before he graduates, so $(e_1, wasBornIn, e_2, t_1) \cap (e_1, graduatedFrom, e_3, t_2) \cap (t_1 > t_2) \rightarrow$ false. These constraints can be represented as:

$$x_{s,r_i,l} + x_{s,r_j,m} \leq 1, \forall (r_i, r_j) \in \mathcal{C}_2, t_{x_{s,r_i,l}} \leq t_{x_{s,r_j,m}} \qquad (7)$$

where $\mathcal{C}_2 = \{(r_i, r_j)\}$ are relation pairs in which each pair has precedent order such as $(wasBornIn, graduatedFrom)$. These relation pairs can be discovered automatically in experimental datasets by statistical strategies and finally manually calibrated.

ILP Model. With the two constraints as described above, we define our final ILP model as follows:

$$\min \quad \sum_{x_{s,r,o}} (\min f(s_{s,o}^r) - \theta) \times x_{s,r,o} \qquad (8)$$

$$\text{s.t.} \quad \forall r \in \mathcal{C}_1 \, , \, t_{x_{s,r,l}} \cap t_{x_{s,r,m}} \neq \emptyset, t_{x_{n,r,o}} \cap t_{x_{p,r,o}} \neq \emptyset$$
$$x_{s,r,l} + x_{s,r,m} \leq 1$$
$$x_{n,r,o} + x_{p,r,o} \leq 1,$$
$$\forall (r_i, r_j) \in \mathcal{C}_2, t_{x_{s,r_i,l}} \leq t_{x_{s,r_j,m}}$$
$$x_{s,r_i,l} + x_{s,r_j,m} \leq 1$$
$$x_{s,r,o} \in \{0, 1\}. \qquad (9)$$

Table 1. Statistics of datasets.

Dataset	#Entity	#Relation	#Triples			Time Interval
			#Train	#Valid	#Test	
YAGO11k	10,623	10	16.4k	2k	2k	[100 - 2017]
Wikidata12k	12,554	24	32.5k	4k	4k	[19 - 2020]
Wikidata11k	11,134	95	112k	14.3k	14.2k	[25 - 2020]

It is obvious that the first constraint restricts the selection of facts with a common head/tail entity and diverse tail/head entity, along with non-overlapping time intervals will be selected. The second constraint restricts that when a pair of facts with precedent ordering relation is selected, but their time intervals do not satisfy this order, they will also be excluded. We minimize this objective function in order to find the best assignment of indicator variables to minimize the overall score of test quadruples while complying with the temporal constraints. We use $PuLP^4$, which is an LP modeler written in python, to solve the problem.

4 Experiments and Analysis

In this section, we first provide an overview of the datasets used in the experiments, and then conduct an extensive experimental evaluation and provide an analysis of the experimental results in terms of entity prediction task and relation prediction task, respectively.

4.1 Datasets

We evaluate our model and baselines on three datasets, which are derived from two popular KG projects, namely YAGO 3 [15] and Wikidata [7]. We distill out all the facts with timestamps and select those ones pertaining to top-N types of frequent time-sensitive relations in each dataset for our experiments. Simple statistics of the datasets are summarized in Table 1. In the following, we detail each dataset.

- **YAGO11k:** This is a subset of YAGO 3 [15] released by HyTE 2018 [5], containing 10,623 distinct entities, 10 types of most frequent time-sensitive relations, and in a total of 20.4k temporal triples. Here the temporal facts in this dataset are in the form of ($\#factID$, $OccurSince$, t_s), ($\#factID$, $OccurUntil$, t_e) indicating the fact is valid during $[t_s : t_e]$, where $\#factID$ denotes a specific fact (e_s, r, e_e).
- **Wikidata12k:** This is a subset of Wikidata released by HyTE 2018 [5], containing 12,554 distinct entities, 24 types of most frequent time-sensitive relations, and in a total of 40.5k temporal triples. This is almost 2 times larger than YAGO11k.

---
[4] https://pypi.python.org/pypi/PuLP.

- **Wikidata11k**: This is a subset of Wikidata released by TA-TransE [8], containing 11,134 distinct entities, 95 types of time-sensitive relations, and in total of 28.5k temporal triples.

For getting the test and validation set for each dataset, we randomly sample roughly 80% of instances as training, 10% as validation and 10% for testing on each dataset.

4.2 Entity Prediction

Compared Baseline Methods. In order to evaluate our model more comprehensively, a suite of state-of-the-art baselines are compared, including the following:

- **TransE** [3][5]. This is a simple but effective traditional distance-based model.
- **TransH** [20] (See footnote 5). This model instead models entities as vectors on a relation-specific hyperplane with an associated translation operation for dealing with the complex relations.
- **TransE-TAE** [9]. This model utilizes a temporal ordering of relations to model the knowledge evolution in the time dimension. Observed relation ordering with respect to the same head entity is modeled as a regularization term in conjunction with TransE scoring function. As no code is available, we implemented it by ourselves.
- **TransH-TAE** [9]. This model performs the operations as same as TransE-TAE for learning temporal ordering among relations, and then incorporates them to TransH scoring function as a regularization term. As no code is available, we implemented it by ourselves.
- **TTransE** [12][6]. This model studies scoring functions that incorporate temporal representation into a TransE-style scoring function, with a focus on the temporal relation prediction task.
- **TA-TransE** [8][7]. This model utilizes digit-level LSTM to learn TKG embeddings combining with existing scoring functions such as TransE and DistMult.
- **HyTE** [5][8]. This model incorporates time associated information in the entity-relation spaces by associating each timestamp with a corresponding hyperplane.
- **TKGFrame**$_{without\_ILP}$. This is the variant of our model. We remove the refinement model in the second phase from TKGFrame, which degenerates to only performed the temporal ordering enhanced model in the first phase for TKG completion. We use the subscript without_ILP to denote this setting.

---

[5] The code for TransE and TransH is from https://github.com/thunlp/OpenKE.
[6] The code for TTransE is from https://github.com/INK-USC/RE-Net/tree/master/baselines.
[7] The code for TA-TransE is from https://github.com/nle-ml/mmkb.
[8] The code for HyTE is from https://github.com/malllabiisc/HyTE.

Evaluation Metrics. The entity prediction task aims to predict missing head or tail entity of a triple as introduced in Definition 3.3. In the testing stage, for each quadruple (e_s, r, e_e, t), we also regard it as a triple without considering its time dimension t, and replace its head/tail entities with all entities in the TKG to construct candidate triples. Then we rank all these entities in descending order of the scores, which are calculated by our scoring function as Eq. 3. Based on the entity ranking list, we adopt two standard metrics from [3]: (1) the mean rank of correct entities (MR), and (2) the proportion of correct entities ranked in top-10 rank entities called Hit@10. As pointed out by Bordes *et al.* [3], the two metrics are desirable but flawed when a corrupted triple exists in the test set. To address this problem, we filter out the whole of corrupted triples that occurred in the test set before ranking. We call the former dataset as *Raw* and the latter one as *Filter* in the evaluation.

Implementation Details. We implement our model and the baselines in PyTorch. All the experiments are performed on an Intel Xeon CPU E5-2640 (v4) with 128 GB main memory, and Nvidia Tesla P100. We initialize all the baselines with the parameter settings in the corresponding papers and then turn them on our datasets for best performance for a fair comparison[9]. For the temporal ordering enhanced model in TKGFrame, we create 100 mini-batches for each epoch during training. The embedding dimension $d \in \{50, 100, 200\}$, margin γ_1 and γ_2 are set in the range of $\{1, 2, 4\}$, learning rate $l \in \{10^{-2}, 10^{-3}, 10^{-4}\}$, negative sampling ratio $n \in \{1, 3, 5\}$, hyperparameter $\lambda \in \{10^{-2}, 10^{-3}, 10^{-4}\}$, and threshold $\theta \in \{10, 11, 12, 13\}$. The best configuration is chosen based on *Raw* MR on the validation dataset. The final parameters are $d = 100$, $\gamma_1 = \gamma_2 = 4$, $l = 10^{-2}$, $n = 3$, $\lambda = 10^{-2}$, $\theta = 11$ and taking l_2-norm for YAGO11k dataset and $d = 100$, $\gamma_1 = \gamma_2 = 4$, $l = 10^{-2}$, $n = 3$, $\lambda = 10^{-2}$, $\theta = 11$ and taking l_1-norm for Wikidata12k dataset. For Wikidata11k, the final configuration are $d = 100$, $\gamma_1 = \gamma_2 = 4$, $l = 10^{-3}$, $n = 3$, $\lambda = 10^{-2}$, $\theta = 11$ and l_1-norm.

Results. Table 2 illustrates the results for entity prediction. We have four major findings. (1) Not surprisingly, temporal-aware embedding models have more obvious advantages than traditional translation-based models such as TransE and TransH on all metrics. This verifies that incorporating temporal information to guide the TKG embedding learning improves the performance of entity predic-

---

[9] We train TransE and TransH on all datasets with embedding dimension $d = 100$, margin $\gamma = 1.0$, learning rate $l = 10^{-3}$ and taking l_1-norm. The configuration of TAE-TransE and TAE-TransH are set as embedding dimension $d = 100$, margin $\gamma_1 = \gamma_2 = 4$, learning rate $l = 10^{-4}$, regularization hyperparameter $t = 10^{-3}$ and taking l_1-norm for YAGO11k and Wikidata12k datasets, and $d = 100$, $\gamma_1 = \gamma_2 = 2$, $l = 10^{-5}$, $t = 10^{-3}$, taking l_1-norm for Wikidata11k. We train TA-TransE and TTransE with the same parameter setting as introduced in [11]. For TA-TransE model, the configuration are embedding dimension $d = 100$, margin $\gamma = 1$, batch size $bs = 512$, learning rate $l = 10^{-4}$ and taking l_1-norm for all the datasets. For HyTE, we initialize the same parameter setting as HyTE, in which embedding dimension $d = 128$, margin $\gamma = 10$, learning rate $l = 10^{-5}$, negative sampling ratio $n = 5$ and using l_1-norm for all the datasets.

Table 2. The experimental results of different methods on three datasets for entity prediction task. The best and second best baseline results in each column are boldfaced and underlined, respectively (the lower are better for MR, and the higher are better for Hit@10).

Dataset	YAGO11k				Wikidata12k				Wikidata11k			
Models	MR		Hit@10(%)		MR		Hit@10(%)		MR		Hit@10(%)	
	Raw	Filter	Raw	Filter	Raw	Filter	Raw	Filter	Raw	Filter	Raw	Filter
TransE	1535.7	1522.2	13.7	15.6	1309.8	1296.1	28.1	37.3	200.5	187.5	47.2	72.3
TransH	1431.9	1419.5	14.1	16.2	1063.6	1050.0	30.2	39.9	193.5	180.9	47.3	73.0
TransE-TAE	1118.1	_1105.1_	16.7	_22.5_	738.0	723.8	33.0	42.6	55.7	42.3	60.4	80.2
TransH-TAE	1124.9	1111.8	17.1	22.4	488.2	_474.1_	36.1	_48.3_	55.1	_42.1_	61.0	_81.8_
TTransE	1172.0	1171.5	12.8	13.3	505.6	503.4	_36.3_	40.4	58.9	56.6	61.5	64.6
TA-TransE	1547.9	1534.9	11.7	13.2	663.0	653.9	34.7	43.7	94.1	85.9	61.2	74.6
HyTE	_590_	–	18.6	–	_237.7_	–	32.6	–	_36.3_	–	**73.8**	–
TKGFrame$_{without\_ILP}$	671.0	662.3	27.5	29.9	439.9	428.1	38.0	50.9	47.1	34.1	64.7	88.0
TKGFrame	**549.6**	**542.1**	**29.0**	**31.3**	**165.5**	**153.8**	**38.1**	**51.7**	**30.9**	**17.6**	_65.4_	**88.6**

tion. (2) Compared with TransE-TAE, TransH-TAE, and TA-TransE, HyTE obtains better performance on *Raw* MR metrics. This demonstrates its superiority to structure the hyperplanes in the entity-relation space compatible with these temporal facts on the datasets. (3) TKGFrame outperforms all the baselines by a significant improvement. The *Raw* MR drops by nearly 6.8%, 30.3% and 14.8%, and *Filter* Hit@10 rises about 39.1%, 7.0% and 8.3% on YAGO11k, Wikidata12k and Wikidata11k dataset, respectively. This demonstrates that the relation evolving enhanced model is beneficial for generating more accurate TKG embeddings, and the refinement model is useful to remove more implausible predictions. In addition, TKGFrame achieves better performance results than TKGFrame$_{without\_ILP}$ on all metrics, illustrating the importance of filtering out implausible predictions from the candidates provided by the relation evolving enhanced model. (4) One interesting observation is that TKGFrame does not outperform HyTE on Wikidata11k with *Raw* Hit@10. One explanation is that because it contains variety of relation types and the distribution of temporal ordering relations especially for the ones in the structure of relational chain is more sparse, this affects the actual quality of the learned TKG embeddings.

4.3   Relation Prediction

Evaluation Metrics. Similar to the entity prediction task, following [3], we adopt two standard metrics for predict missing relation of a quadruple (fact), including MR and Hit@1.

Results. Table 3 shows the results for relation prediction. We have three major findings. (1) TKGFrame outperforms all the baselines by a significant improvement, we verify that the relation evolving enhanced model is valuable to improving the representations of temporal ordered relations in pairwise. (2) The refinement model is indeed able to improve the performance of relation prediction, the

Table 3. The experimental results of different methods on three datasets for relation prediction task. The best and second best baseline results in each column is boldfaced and underlined, respectively (the lower are better for MR, and the higher are better for Hit@1).

Dataset	YAGO11k				Wikidata12k				Wikidata11k			
Models	MR		Hit@1(%)		MR		Hit@1(%)		MR		Hit@1(%)	
	Raw	*Filter*	*Raw*	*Filter*	*Raw*	*Filter*	*Raw*	*Filter*	*Raw*	*Filter*	*Raw*	*Filter*
TransE	1.61	1.60	65.2	66.9	1.26	1.21	85.3	88.2	1.18	1.12	93.6	<u>94.2</u>
TransH	1.57	1.56	67.0	68.1	1.25	1.14	85.5	87.4	1.21	1.15	1.15	92.8
TransE-TAE	1.53	1.51	71.4	72.7	1.23	1.20	85.9	88.9	1.11	<u>1.09</u>	89.6	90.2
TransH-TAE	1.44	<u>1.42</u>	75.5	<u>76.4</u>	1.21	<u>1.11</u>	86.5	<u>89.0</u>	1.23	1.14	84.1	85.4
TTransE	1.47	–	73.8	–	1.22	–	86.0	–	<u>1.08</u>	–	96.3	–
TA-TransE	–	–	–	–	–	–	–	–	–	–	–	–
HyTE	<u>1.38</u>	–	<u>78.4</u>	–	<u>1.12</u>	–	<u>88.8</u>	–	1.10	–	<u>97.2</u>	–
TKGFrame_{without_ILP}	1.29	1.28	77.3	78.2	1.20	1.11	85.0	88.4	1.05	1.03	97.7	98.1
TKGFrame	**1.18**	**1.07**	**86.5**	**86.6**	**1.12**	**1.06**	**92.0**	**92.2**	**1.04**	**1.02**	**97.8**	**98.3**

Raw MR drops by nearly 14.4%, 0% and 3.7%, and the *Filter* Hit@1 rises about 13.3%, 3.5% and 4.3% on YAGO11k, Wikidata12k and Wikidata11k dataset, respectively. This main reason is that two categories of common-sense constraints associated temporality are leveraged to better handle temporal conflicts in relations. Relation prediction can be viewed as a multi-label problem that the same entity pair may have multiple relation labels. For example, (*"Einstein"*, *"ETH Zürich"*) could have two valid relations: *graduatedFrom* and *worksAt*. Though using the temporal constraints, we are aware that the two relations have different valid periods, and therefore we would remove the implausible one to improve Hit@1 accuracy.

5   Conclusion

This paper presents a novel two-phase framework, called TKGFrame, to further improve the performance of the TKG completion task. TKGFrame consists of two major models, namely (1) relation evolving enhanced model and (2) refinement model, corresponding to two phases of TKGFrame. To be specific, the first model attempts to enhance evolving strength representations of pairwise relations in the same relational chain by learning a new temporal evolving matrix, resulting in more accurate TKG embeddings. In the second model, we formulate plausibility measure of candidate predictions of unseen temporal facts in the TKG provided by the embeddings from the first model as a constrained optimization problem, and an ILP model is proposed to solve this problem as well as effectively filter out those implausible prediction results presented conflict strictly in each other. The above two models are seamlessly integrated into TKGFrame, which is beneficial to produce more accurate predictions for TKG completion. Comprehensive experiments on three popular datasets show that the proposed solution outperforms state-of-the-art baselines in terms of entity prediction and relation prediction tasks.

In terms of future work, we attempt to exploit our solution in several kinds of extensions and follow-up studies. One direction is to give greater consideration to enhance the representations of time-sensitive facts by including side information (e.g., type consistency information, accurate textual information) beyond their temporal ordering relations in a relation-based chain that we have considered thus far. A second direction of extension is to a specific consideration regarding the enrichment of temporal ordering relations in pairwise. We will explore using comparing with similar popular facts and timestamp-based label propagation method, to further mine temporal ordering relations, even for some low-resource datasets. A third direction for studying is to further consider using our proposed framework for temporal scope prediction of news facts.

Acknowledgments. This work was supported by Major Scientific and Technological Special Project of Guizhou Province (No. 20183002), Sichuan Science and Technology Program (No. 2020YFS0057, No. 2020YJ0038 and No. 2019YFG0535), Fundamental Research Funds for the Central Universities (No. ZYGX2019Z015) and Dongguan Songshan Lake Introduction Program of Leading Innovative and Entrepreneurial Talents. Yongpan Sheng's research was supported by the National Key Research and Development Project (No. 2018YFB2101200).

References

1. Barbosa, D., Wang, H., Yu, C.: Shallow information extraction for the knowledge web. In: ICDE, pp. 1264–1267 (2013)
2. Bollacker, K., Evans, C., Paritosh, P., Sturge, T., Taylor, J.: Freebase: a collaboratively created graph database for structuring human knowledge. In: SIGMOD, pp. 1247–1250 (2008)
3. Bordes, A., Usunier, N., Garcia-Duran, A., Weston, J., Yakhnenko, O.: Translating embeddings for modeling multi-relational data. In: NIPS, pp. 2787–2795 (2013)
4. Clarke, J., Lapata, M.: Global inference for sentence compression: an integer linear programming approach. J. Artif. Intell. Res. **31**, 399–429 (2008)
5. Dasgupta, S.S., Ray, S.N., Talukdar, P.: Hyte: hyperplane-based temporally aware knowledge graph embedding. In: EMNLP, pp. 2001–2011 (2018)
6. Dong, L., Wei, F., Zhou, M., Xu, K.: Question answering over freebase with multi-column convolutional neural networks. In: ACL-IJCNLP (vol. 1: Long Papers), pp. 260–269 (2015)
7. Erxleben, F., Günther, M., Krötzsch, M., Mendez, J., Vrandečić, D.: Introducing wikidata to the linked data web. In: Mika, P., et al. (eds.) ISWC 2014. LNCS, vol. 8796, pp. 50–65. Springer, Cham (2014). https://doi.org/10.1007/978-3-319-11964-9_4
8. García-Durán, A., Dumančić, S., Niepert, M.: Learning sequence encoders for temporal knowledge graph completion (2018). https://arxiv.org/abs/1809.03202
9. Jiang, T., et al.: Towards time-aware knowledge graph completion. In: COLING, pp. 1715–1724 (2016)
10. Jiang, T., et al.: Encoding temporal information for time-aware link prediction. In: EMNLP, pp. 2350–2354 (2016)
11. Jin, W., et al.: Recurrent event network: global structure inference over temporal knowledge graph (2019). https://arxiv.org/abs/1904.05530

12. Leblay, J., Chekol, M.W.: Deriving validity time in knowledge graph. In: WWW, pp. 1771–1776 (2018)
13. Lehmann, J., et al.: DBpedia-a large-scale, multilingual knowledge base extracted from Wikipedia. Semant. Web **6**(2), 167–195 (2015)
14. Lin, Y., Liu, Z., Sun, M., Liu, Y., Zhu, X.: Learning entity and relation embeddings for knowledge graph completion. In: AAAI, pp. 2081–287 (2015)
15. Mahdisoltani, F., Biega, J., Suchanek, F.M.: Yago3: a knowledge base from multi-lingual wikipedias. In: CIDR (2013)
16. Nickel, M., Tresp, V., Kriegel, H.P.: A three-way model for collective learning on multi-relational data. In: ICML, vol. 11, pp. 809–816 (2011)
17. Suchanek, F.M., Kasneci, G., Weikum, G.: Yago: a core of semantic knowledge. In: WWW, pp. 697–706 (2007)
18. Sun, Z., Hu, W., Zhang, Q., Qu, Y.: Bootstrapping entity alignment with knowledge graph embedding. In: IJCAI, pp. 4396–4402 (2018)
19. Trivedi, R., Dai, H., Wang, Y., Song, L.: Know-evolve: deep temporal reasoning for dynamic knowledge graphs. In: ICML, vol. 70, pp. 3462–3471 (2017)
20. Wang, Z., Zhang, J., Feng, J., Chen, Z.: Knowledge graph embedding by translating on hyperplanes. In: AAAI, pp. 1112–1119 (2014)
21. Xiong, C., Callan, J.: Query expansion with freebase. In: ICTIR, pp. 111–120 (2015)
22. Zhou, X., Zhu, Q., Liu, P., Guo, L.: Learning knowledge embeddings by combining limit-based scoring loss. In: CIKM, pp. 1009–1018 (2017)

An Ontology-Aware Unified Storage Scheme for Knowledge Graphs

Sizhuo Li[1], Guozheng Rao[1,2(✉)], Baozhu Liu[1], Pengkai Liu[1], Sicong Dong[1], and Zhiyong Feng[1,2]

[1] College of Intelligence and Computing, Tianjin University, Tianjin, China
{lszskye,rgz,liubaozhu,liupengkai,sicongdong,zyfeng}@tju.edu.cn
[2] Tianjin Key Laboratory of Cognitive Computing and Application, Tianjin, China

Abstract. With the development of knowledge-based artificial intelligence, the scale of knowledge graphs has been increasing rapidly. The RDF graph and the property graph are two mainstream data models of knowledge graphs. On the one hand, with the development of the Semantic Web, there are a large number of RDF knowledge graphs. On the other hand, property graphs are widely used in the graph database community. However, different families of data management methods of RDF graphs and property graphs have been seperately developed in each community over a decade, which hinder the interoperability in managing large knowledge graph data. To address this problem, we propose a unified storage scheme for knowledge graphs which can seamlessly accommodate both RDF and property graphs. Meanwhile, the concept of ontology is introduced to meet the need for RDF graph data storage and query load. Experimental results on the benchmark datasets show that the proposed ontology-aware unified storage scheme can effectively manage large-scale knowledge graphs and significantly avoid data redundancy.

Keywords: Knowledge graph · Unified storage scheme · Ontology-aware

1 Introduction

Knowledge graphs have become the cornerstone of artificial intelligence. With the applications of artificial intelligence, more and more fields begin to organize and publish their domain knowledge in the form of knowledge graphs. Knowledge graphs can not only describe various entities and concepts which exist in the real world, but also can depict the relationships between these entities and concepts. At present, knowledge graphs have been widely used in the fields of big data analysis [1], knowledge fusion [2], precision marketing [3], and semantic search [4].

As the demand of knowledge-based AI applications, the amount of knowledge graph data has been dramatically increasing. Currently, it is common that knowledge graphs have millions of vertices and billions of edges. Many knowledge graphs in the LOD (Linked Open Data) cloud diagram have more than 1 billion

© Springer Nature Switzerland AG 2020
X. Wang et al. (Eds.): APWeb-WAIM 2020, LNCS 12317, pp. 212–226, 2020.
https://doi.org/10.1007/978-3-030-60259-8_17

triples. For example, the number of triples of the latest version of the DBpedia [5] dataset has reached 13 billion. Meanwhile, a great amount of graph data has been stored as property graphs. Therefore, many systems are developed in graph database industry, including Neo4j [6], TigerGraph [7], and OrientDB [8].

In order to manage large-scale knowledge graph data, two mainstream data models of knowledge graphs have been developed: the RDF (Resource Description Framework) model [9] and the property graph model. RDF is a standard data model developed by the World Wide Web Consortium to represent and manage information on the Semantic Web. In the graph database community, the property graph model is another common data model which has built-in support for vertex and edge properties [10]. At present, these two mainstream data models for knowledge graphs have not been unified in a broader perspective of knowledge graph data management, which hinder the interaction while managing knowledge graphs from different communities. A unified data model helps reduce the cost of development of database management systems and realize the interoperability of different types of knowledge graphs at the same time. It has become an urgent need that RDF and property graphs can be effectively managed in a unified storage scheme.

In this paper, we present a unified storage scheme for both RDF and property graphs. Considering the mature storage management facilities in relational databases, our unified storage scheme for knowledge graphs has been implemented based on an RDBMS, using the relational data model as the physical layer to realize our knowledge graph data model. Since knowledge graphs support querying instance information with rich ontology semantic information, it is necessary to propose an ontology-aware unified storage scheme for knowledge graphs. Ontology is introduced to optimize storage and facilitate query as a heuristic information. Finally, we have designed and realized a prototype system that implements the proposed storage scheme and supports efficient query processing.

Our contributions can be summarized as follows:

1) We propose a novel unified storage scheme for knowledge graphs based on relational data model, which can seamlessly accommodate both RDF and property graphs.
2) We introduce ontology as a rich semantic information to optimize our knowledge graph storage scheme. Additionally, the prefix encoding is adopted to save storage space and reflect the hierarchical information between the ontologies.
3) Extensive experiments on several datasets are conducted to verify the effectiveness and efficiency of our storage scheme. The experimental results show that the triple traversal time of our scheme is less than that of the Neo4j.

The rest of this paper is organized as follows. Section 2 briefly introduces the related work and several formal definitions are given in Sect. 3. The ontology-aware unified storage scheme is described in detail in Sect. 4. Section 5 shows experimental results on benchmark datasets. Finally, we conclude in Sect. 6.

2   Related Work

Relational storage scheme is one of the main methods of storing knowledge graph data. In this section, various relational storage schemes are introduced, including Triple table, Horizontal table, Property table, Vertical partitioning, and Sextuple indexing.

Triple Table. Triple table is a storage scheme with a three-column table in a relational database. The scheme of this table is:

$$triple\_table(subject, predicate, object)$$

Each triple in a knowledge graph is stored as a row in $triple\_table$. The triple table is the simplest way to store knowledge graphs in a relational database. Although the triple table storage scheme is clear, the number of rows in the $triple\_table$ is equal to the number of edges in the corresponding knowledge graph. Therefore, there will be many self-joins after translating a knowledge graph query into an SQL query. The representative system adopting triple table storage scheme is 3store [11].

Horizontal Table. Each row of the horizontal table stores all the predicates and objects of a subject. The number of rows is equal to the number of different subjects in the corresponding knowledge graph. The horizontal table storage scheme, however, is limited by the following disadvantages: (1) the structure of the horizontal table is not stable. The addition, modification or deletion of predicates in knowledge graphs will directly result in the addition, modification or deletion of columns in the horizontal table. The change to the structure of the table often leads to high costs; and (2) the number of columns in the horizontal table is equal to the number of different predicates in the corresponding knowledge graph. In a real-world large-scale knowledge graph, the number of predicates is likely to reach tens of thousands, which is likely to exceed the maximum number of columns in the table allowed by the relational database. The representative system adopting horizontal table storage scheme is DLDB [12].

Property Table. The property table is a refinement of the horizontal table, storing those subjects of the same type in one table, which solves the problem of exceeding the limit of the maximum number of columns in the horizontal table scheme. However, there still exists several drawbacks of the property table storage scheme: (1) the number of predicates is likely to reach tens of thousands in a real-world large-scale knowledge graph and thus a large number of tables need to be created. The number of the tables may exceed the maximum number of tables; and (2) the property table storage scheme can cause the problem of null value. The representative system adopting property table storage scheme is Jena [13].

Vertical Partitioning. The vertical partitioning storage scheme creates a two-column table for each predicate [14]. Subjects and objects of the same predicate will be stored in one table. Compared with the previous storage schemes, the problem of null value is solved. However, the vertical partitioning storage scheme also has its limitation: the number of tables to be created is equal to the number of different predicates in knowledge graphs, and the number of predicates in a real-world large-scale knowledge graph may exceed several thousand, which leads to high cost while maintaining the database. The representative database adopting the vertical partitioning storage scheme is SW-Store [15].

Sextuple Indexing. Six tables are built to store all the six permutations of triples in sextuple indexing storage scheme, namely spo, pos, osp, sop, pso, and ops. The sextuple indexing storage scheme helps alleviate the self-join problem of single table and improve the efficiency of some typical knowledge graph queries. The sextuple indexing storage scheme adopts typical "space-for-time" strategy, therefore, a large amount of storage space is required. Typical systems adopting the sextuple indexing storage scheme are RDF-3X [16] and Hexastore [17].

Inspired by the above relational storage schemes, our unified storage scheme adopts the relational data model as the physical layer to realize our knowledge graph data model. The details of our scheme will be introduced in Sect. 4.

3 Preliminaries

In this section, we introduce several basic background definitions, including RDF graph, property graph, triple partition, and triple classification, which are used in our algorithms.

Definition 1 (RDF Graph). *Let U, B, and L be three infinite disjoint sets of URIs, blank nodes, and literals, respectively. A triple $(s, p, o) \in (U \cup B) \times U \times (U \cup B \cup L)$ is called an RDF triple, where s is the subject, p is the predicate, and o is the object. A finite set of RDF triples is called an RDF graph.*

Definition 2 (Property Graph). *A property graph is a tuple $G = (V, E, \rho, \lambda, \sigma)$ where:*

1) V is a finite set of vertices,
2) E is a finite set of edges and $V \cap E = \emptyset$,
3) $\rho : E \to (V \times V)$ is a mapping that associates an edge with a pair of vertices. For example, $\rho(e) = (v_1, v_2)$ indicates that e is a directed edge from vertex v_1 to v_2,
4) Let Lab be the set of labels. $\lambda : (V \cup E) \to Lab$ is a mapping that associates a vertex or an edge with a label, i.e., $v \in V$ (or $e \in E$) and $\lambda(v) = l$ (or $\lambda(e) = l$), then l is the label for vertex v (or edge e),
5) Let Prop be the set of properties and Val be the set of values. $\sigma : (V \cup E) \times Prop \to Val$ is a mapping that associates a vertex (or edge) with its corresponding properties, i.e., $v \in V$ (or $e \in E$), $p \in Prop$ and $\sigma(v, p) = val$ (or $\sigma(e, p) = val$), then the value of the property p of the vertex v (or edge e) is val.

Definition 3 (Triple Partition). *Let T be a finite set of RDF triples whose values of subjects and objects are not blank nodes. T can be divided into three subsets, including $X(T)$, $Y(T)$, and $Z(T)$.*

$$X(T) = \{(s,p,o) \mid (s,p,o) \in T \wedge p = \mathtt{rdf:type}\} \tag{1}$$

$$Y(T) = \{(s,p,o) \mid (s,p,o) \in T \wedge o \in L\} \tag{2}$$

$$Z(T) = \{(s,p,o) \mid (s,p,o) \in T \wedge p \neq \mathtt{rdf:type} \wedge o \notin L\} \tag{3}$$

The three subsets satisfy the following two conditions: (1) $X(T) \cup Y(T) \cup Z(T) = T$; and (2) $X(T) \cap Y(T) \cap Z(T) = \emptyset$. Since a triple set T is divided into three subsets, the triple classification of T based on triple partition can be defined as Definition 4.

Definition 4 (Triple Classification). *Let C be the set of classes of triples. $C = \{mem, prop, edge\}$. $\varphi : T \rightarrow C$ is a mapping that associates an RDF triple with its corresponding class.*

$$\varphi(t) = \begin{cases} mem & \text{if } t \in X(T) \\ prop & \text{if } t \in Y(T) \\ edge & \text{if } t \in Z(T) \end{cases}$$

The example RDF graph shown in Fig. 1 describes a music knowledge graph where *(LangLang, plays, FateSymphony)* $\in Z(T)$ and $\varphi((LangLang, plays, FateSymphony)) = edge$.

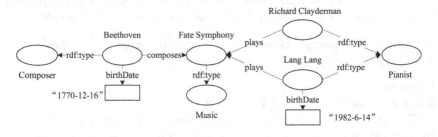

Fig. 1. An example RDF graph.

4   Ontology-Aware Unified Storage Scheme

In this section, we first propose a basic storage scheme for both RDF and property graphs, then we optimize the basic storage scheme by introducing the information of ontology. Finally, we present our data loading algorithm.

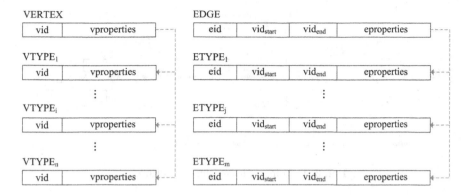

Fig. 2. The basic storage scheme.

4.1   A Basic Storage Scheme

The basic storage scheme is composed of several relations, including VERTEX, EDGE, VTYPE$_1$, VTYPE$_2$,..., VTYPE$_n$ (n is the number of vertex labels), ETYPE$_1$, ETYPE$_2$,..., ETYPE$_m$ (m is the number of edge labels), as shown in Fig. 2. Actually, relation VTYPE$_i$ is a partition of relation VERTEX, while relation ETYPE$_j$ is a partition of relation EDGE.

For property graphs, the first column in VERTEX records the encodings of all the vertices in the property graph, while the properties of those vertices are kept in the second column. Meanwhile, the first column in EDGE holds the encodings of all the edges, while the information of the head vertices, tail vertices, and properties of those edges are kept in the second, third, and forth column, respectively. VTYPE$_i$ ($0 \leqslant i \leqslant n$) records the information of those vertices of the same label, while ETYPE$_j$ ($0 \leqslant j \leqslant m$) records the information of those edges of the same label.

For RDF graphs, the first column of each row in VERTEX records the URI of an instance. The URIs of properties and the corresponding literals of this instance are kept in the second column. Besides, the first column of each row in EDGE holds a predicate p where $\varphi((s, p, o)) = edge$. The subjects and objects of this predicate are stored in the second column and the third column, respectively. VTYPE$_i$ records the information of those vertices of the same type, while ETYPE$_j$ records the information of those edges of the same type.

4.2   The Ontology Information

RDFS (RDF Schema) is an extension of RDF, and it provides the framework to describe application-specific classes and properties. Classes in RDFS are much like classes in object oriented programming languages which allows resources to be defined as instances of classes, and subclasses of classes. More specifically, the class rdfs:Class declares a resource as a class for other resources. The property rdfs:subClassOf is an instance of rdf:property that is used to state that all

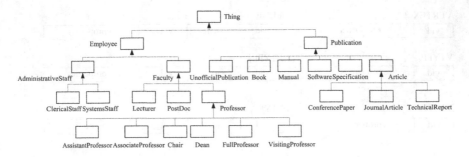

Fig. 3. Ontology hierarchical structure.

the instances of one class are instances of another. Since a class can be further refined into subclasses, an ontology of an RDF graph is actually a hierarchical structure of classes.

Algorithm 1: ONTOLOGYENCODING(T)

Input   : Ontology $T = (V, E, v_0, Label, Id, \mu)$, where $Id = \emptyset$
Output: The encoded ontology T

1 $V_l \leftarrow$ getLeaf($T.V$);   // Get all the leaf node in T
2 **foreach** $v \in V_l$ **do**
3 | **return** $id \leftarrow$ getCode(v);

4 **return** T;
5 **Function** getCode (v)
6 | **if** v isSubclassOf v_j **then**
7 | | $v_j.index \leftarrow |V_l|$;
8 | | $V_l \leftarrow V_l \cup \{v_j\}$;
9 | | **return** getCode(v_j) + $v.index$;
    | | // The plus sign refers to string concatenation
10 | **else**
11 | | **return** $v.index$;

The structure of an ontology can be described in terms of a tree, where the nodes represent classes, and the edges represent the relationships between them. The definition of an ontology can be formally given as:

Definition 5 (Ontology). *An ontology is a 6-tuple $O = (V, E, v_o, Label, Id, \mu)$ where*

1) *V is a finite set of nodes,*
2) *E is a finite set of edges and $V \cap E = \emptyset$,*
3) *v_0 is the root node of the tree structure and $v_0 \in V$,*
4) *Let Label be the set of labels,*

5) Let Id be the set of the encodings of nodes. Each node has a unique encoding, which contains its complete hierarchical information,

6) $\mu : V \rightarrow Id$ is a mapping that associates a node with its corresponding encoding, i.e., $v \in V$ and $\mu(v) = id$, then the encoding of node v is id.

The example ontology hierarchical structure is extracted from Lehigh University Benchmark (LUBM) [18]. The root of the ontology hierarchy is *owl:Thing*, as shown in Fig. 3. Meanwhile, the hierarchical structure is formed by transitivity of the property `rdfs:subClassOf`, e.g., *Publication* has *Article, Book, Manual, Software, Specification,* and *UnofficialPublication* as its direct subclasses.

In order to save storage space and reflect the hierarchical structure of the ontology, we leverage the prefix encoding to encode classes in each ontology. Algorithm 1 shows the recursive procedure of ontology encoding, meaning that it first encodes the leaf node, then upward encodes the nodes until the root *owl:Thing* is encountered.

4.3   An Optimized Storage Scheme

In this section, we modify the basic storage scheme and propose an ontology-aware unified storage scheme for knowledge graphs. The optimized storage scheme is composed of three main relations, including VERTEX, EDGE, and ONTOLOGY, and several auxiliary relations, as shown in Fig. 4. VERTEX and EDGE store the information of all the vertices and edges in a knowledge graph. Meanwhile, the encodings of the ontologies in RDF graphs are kept in relation ONTOLOGY.

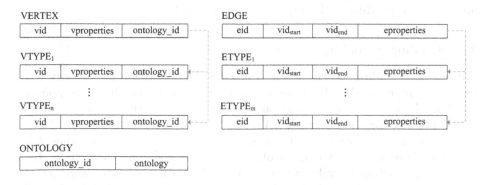

Fig. 4. The ontology-aware unified storage scheme.

The storage scheme of RDF and property graphs in our optimized version is similar to that in the basic version, except for an extra relation ONTOLOGY and an extra field *ontology_id* in relation VERTEX and relation VTYPE$_i$. Since the prefix encoding is adopted to reflect the hierarchical structure between RDF classes, queries assuming the *subClassOf* relationship between an RDF class and its subclasses can be completed by using the keyword "LIKE" in a fuzzy match inquiry process. Therefore, the ontology helps improve the reasoning capability and optimize queries as a heuristic information.

When storing a property graph, the value of *ontology_id* will be left empty. An example scheme for a given property graph is shown in Fig. 5 (a), and the property graph is shown in Fig. 5 (b).

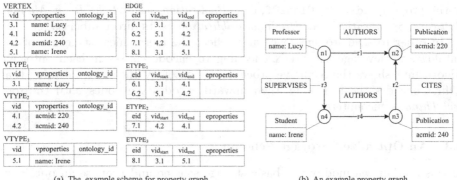

(a). The example scheme for property graph   (b). An example property graph

Fig. 5. Example scheme for a given property graph.

When storing an RDF graph, the first column of each row in **VERTEX** records the URI of an instance, while the third column records the encoding of the corresponding ontology. An example scheme for RDF graph is shown in Fig. 6, and the corresponding RDF graph is shown in Fig. 1.

4.4 Loading Algorithm

We present a loading algorithm which is shown in Algorithm 2 to import RDF data. The input of the algorithm is an RDF graph G and its corresponding ontology T. The processed triples are stored into an auxiliary data structure *VEO*. The auxiliary data structure *VEO* is built on top of our storage scheme.

Algorithm 2 consists of three parts: (1) if $\varphi((s, p, o)) = mem$ (lines 2–5), **getLabel** function is invoked to obtain the corresponding label of o, then **traverse0** function is called to traverse T in depth-first order and get the node v_c with label l, finally function μ gets the ontology encoding of v_c; (2) if $\varphi((s, p, o)) = prop$ (lines 6–9), **getProperty** function is provided to get the property information corresponding to s, then *VEO* is updated with the latest value of properties; and (3) if $\varphi((s, p, o)) = edge$ (lines 10–11), (p, s, o) is inserted into *VEO*.

Theorem 1. *Given an RDF graph G and its corresponding ontology T, we assume that the triples in G are processed and stored into the auxiliary data structure VEO by Algorithm 2. The time complexity of Algorithm 2 is bounded*

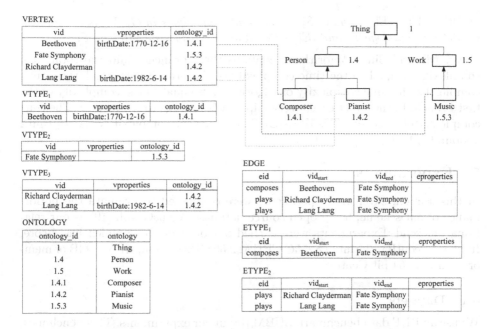

Fig. 6. Example scheme for a given RDF graph.

Algorithm 2: TRIPLELOADING(G, T)

Input : RDF graph G, Ontology $T = (V, E, v_0, Label, Id, \mu)$
Output: The auxiliary data structure VEO

1 **foreach** $(s, p, o) \in G$ **do**
2   **if** $\varphi((s, p, o)) = mem$ **then**
3         $l \leftarrow$ getLabel(o);
4         $v_c \leftarrow$ traverseO(v_0, l);   // Traverse ontology T from v_0
5   insert $(s, \mu(v_c))$ into VEO;   // Get the ontology encoding of v_c

6   **else if** $\varphi((s, p, o)) = prop$ **then**
7         $property \leftarrow$ getProperty(VEO, s);
8         $p \leftarrow property + p + o$;
9   update p in VEO;

10   **else**
11   insert (p, s, o) into VEO;

12 **return** VEO;
13 **Function** traverseO (v, l)
14   **if** $v \neq$ NULL **then**
15   **if** $v.lab = l$ **then**   // Depth-first search
16   **return** v;
17   **else**
18   traverseO($v.firstChild, l$);
19   traverseO($v.nextBrother, l$);

by $O(|S|(|V| + |E|))$, where $|S|$ is the number of triples in G, $|V|$ is the number of nodes in ontology T, and $|E|$ is the number of edges in ontology T.

Proof. (Sketch) Since Algorithm 2 contains three branches and the total time complexity is equal to the time complexity of the branch with the largest time complexity, the time complexity of Algorithm 2 is equal to the complexity of the first branch. In the worst case, every triple in G belongs to class *mem*. The time complexity of traversing T is $|V| + |E|$. Thus, the time complexity of Algorithm 2 is bounded by $O(|S|(|V| + |E|))$ ☐

5 Experiments

In this section, extensive experiments were conducted to evaluate the performance of our scheme, using open source database AgensGraph [19] as our relational backend. Experiments were carried out on a machine which has 4-core, Intel(R) Xeon(R) Platinum 8255C CPU @ 2.50 GHz system, with 16 GB of memory, running 64-bit CentOS 7.

5.1 Datasets

We use an RDF data benchmark LUBM [18] in our experiments. This benchmark is based on an ontology called Univ-Bench for the university domain. Univ-Bench describes universities and departments and the activities that occur at them. The test data of LUBM is synthetically generated instance data over that ontology. Meanwhile, LUBM offers 14 test queries over the data. Table 1 shows the characteristics of the datasets in our experiments.

Table 1. Characteristics of datasets

Dataset	File#	Total size (MB)	V#	E#	Triples#
LUBM1	15	13.6	17,150	23,586	103,397
LUBM2	34	29.3	39,510	54,342	237,210
LUBM3	50	43.5	57,652	79,933	348,105
LUBM4	71	61.1	82,204	113,745	493,844
LUBM5	93	79.6	107,110	148,846	493,844

5.2 Experimental Results

The experimental results show the effectiveness and efficiency of our ontology-aware unified storage scheme. Data insertion and deletion can be completed efficiently. Meanwhile, our scheme is more compact than Neo4j and the traversal time of the triples in our scheme is less than that in Neo4j on all data sets. In our experiments, we provide two versions of the unified storage schemes, one of which is a basic version without the ontology information, while the other is an optimized version with the ontology information.

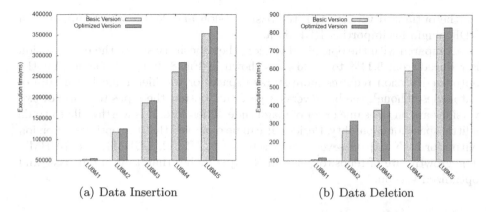

(a) Data Insertion   (b) Data Deletion

Fig. 7. The experimental results of data insertion and deletion on LUBM datasets.

Data Insertion and Deletion. The experimental results show that the average execution speed of the basic version is 4.73% and 9.52% faster than that of the optimized version in data insertion and deletion, respectively, which is not counterintuitive. Though the optimized version is slightly inferior to the basic version, it is complete with the respect to the semantic information. Therefore, it is quite important to measure the tradeoffs between efficiency and reasoning capability.

Actually, the time costs of two versions are on the same order of magnitude, thus are comparative, as shown in Fig. 7. Although the performance of the optimized version is not better than that of the basic version, it is worthwhile to trade the slight overhead for reasoning capability.

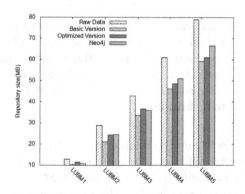

Fig. 8. The experimental results of repository size while inserting data.

Repository Size. We check the change of the file size before and after the data sets being loaded. Experiments were conducted to compare the space required for the optimized version with the basic version and Neo4j, which supports an RDF plugin for importing RDF data.

Compared with the optimized version, the repository size of the basic version is reduced from 5.11% to 13.36%, as shown in Fig. 8. It is reasonable that the optimized version requires more storage space for the hierarchical structure of ontologies. Though the basic version performs better, the repository size of two versions are on the same order of magnitude. Therefore, it is worthwhile to trade a little space for capability. Besides, it can be observed that the optimized version outperforms Neo4j on several data sets, i.e., LUBM2, LUBM4, and LUBM5. The growth rate of repository size in Neo4j is higher than that of our basic and optimized version.

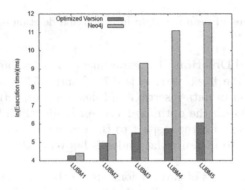

Fig. 9. The experimental results of triple traversal.

Triple Traversal. We also evaluate the time required to traverse all triples in a graph and the experimental results are shown in Fig. 9. The average execution speed in the optimized version is about 99 times faster than that in Neo4j, i.e., our optimization method on average outperforms Neo4j by two orders of magnitude over LUBM data sets. In order to show the results clearly, we change the scale of the Y-axis to logarithmic.

Query Speed. We select four type-related queries from the 14 test queries that LUBM offers: $Q1$ directly refers to the type information of *UndergraduateStudent*, $Q2$ refers to the type information of *GraduateStudent* with some filtering conditions, $Q3$ assumes the *subClassOf* relationship between *Professor* and its subclasses. It is obvious that class *Professor* has a wide hierarchy. $Q4$ assumes the *subClassOf* relationship between *Person* and its subclasses. Similarly, class *Person* features a deep and wide hierarchy.

We compare the basic storage scheme with the optimized storage scheme, and the execution time results of $Q1$, $Q2$, $Q3$, and $Q4$ are shown in Fig. 10. When changing the size of datasets from LUBM1 to LUBM5, query times of these

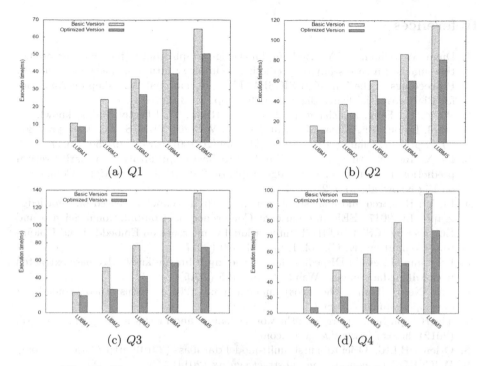

Fig. 10. The experimental results of efficiency on LUBM datasets.

two schemes have increased. Meanwhile, it can be observed that the optimized version has better query efficiency on all 4 queries. Compared with the basic version, the average query time of the optimized version is reduced from 23.24% to 40.33%.

6   Conclusion

This paper proposes a unified storage scheme for both RDF and property graphs and introduces the concept of ontology to reflect the hierarchical relationships between RDF classes. A prototype system of our storage scheme is designed and implemented based on AgensGraph. Extensive experiments on the LUBM benchmark datasets verify the effectiveness and efficiency of our storage scheme.

Acknowledgments. This work is supported by the National Natural Science Foundation of China (61972275), the Natural Science Foundation of Tianjin (17JCY-BJC15400), and CCF-Huawei Database Innovation Research Plan.

References

1. Duan, W., Chiang, Y.Y.: Building knowledge graph from public data for predictive analysis: a case study on predicting technology future in space and time. In: Proceedings of the 5th ACM SIGSPATIAL International Workshop on Analytics for Big Geospatial Data, BigSpatial 2016, pp. 7–13 (2016)
2. Wang, H., Fang, Z., Zhang, L., Pan, J.Z., Ruan, T.: Effective online knowledge graph fusion. In: Arenas, M., et al. (eds.) ISWC 2015. LNCS, vol. 9366, pp. 286–302. Springer, Cham (2015). https://doi.org/10.1007/978-3-319-25007-6_17
3. Fu, X., Ren, X., Mengshoel, O., Wu, X.: Stochastic optimization for market return prediction using financial knowledge graph. In: 2018 IEEE International Conference on Big Knowledge, pp. 25–32 (2018)
4. Li, Y.: Research and analysis of semantic search technology based on knowledge graph. In: 2017 IEEE International Conference on Computational Science and Engineering (CSE) and IEEE International Conference on Embedded and Ubiquitous Computing (EUC), vol. 1, pp. 887–890 (2017)
5. Lehmann, J., et al.: DBpedia-a large-scale, multilingual knowledge base extracted from wikipedia. Semant. Web 6(2), 167–195 (2015)
6. The Neo4j Team: The neo4j manual v3.4 (2018). https://neo4j.com/docs/developermanual/current/
7. TigerGraph Inc.: Tigergraph: the world's fastest and most scalable graph platform (2012). https://www.tigergraph.com/
8. OrientDB Ltd.: Orientdb: first multi-model database (2010). http://orientdb.com/
9. W3C: RDF 1.1 concepts and abstract syntax (2014)
10. Angles, R., Arenas, M., Barceló, P., Hogan, A., Reutter, J., Vrgoč, D.: Foundations of modern query languages for graph databases. ACM Comput. Surv. 50(5), 1–40 (2017)
11. Harris, S., Gibbins, N.: 3store: efficient bulk RDF storage. In: PSSS1 - Practical and Scalable Semantic Systems, Proceedings of the First International Workshop on Practical and Scalable Semantic Systems, vol. 89 (2003)
12. Pan, Z., Heflin, J.: DLDB: extending relational databases to support semantic web queries. In: PSSS1 - Practical and Scalable Semantic Systems, Proceedings of the First International Workshop on Practical and Scalable Semantic Systems, vol. 89 (2003)
13. Wilkinson, K.: Jena property table implementation. In: In SSWS, Athens, Georgia, USA, pp. 35–46 (2006)
14. Abadi, D., Marcus, A., Madden, S., Hollenbach, K.: Scalable semantic web data management using vertical partitioning. In: VLDB, pp. 411–422 (2007)
15. Abadi, D., Marcus, A., Madden, S., Hollenbach, K.: SW-store: a vertically partitioned DBMS for semantic web data management. VLDB J. 18(2), 385–406 (2009). https://doi.org/10.1007/s00778-008-0125-y
16. Neumann, T., Weikum, G.: RDF3X: a RISC-style engine for RDF. Proc. VLDB Endow. - PVLDB 1, 647–659 (2008)
17. Weiss, C., Karras, P., Bernstein, A.: Hexastore: Sextuple indexing for semantic web data management. PVLDB 1, 1008–1019 (2008)
18. Guo, Y., Pan, Z., Heflin, J.: LUBM: a benchmark for owl knowledge base systems. Web Semant. Sci. Serv. Agents World Wide Web 3(2–3), 158–182 (2005)
19. Bitnine-OSS: Agensgraph: a transaction graph database based on PostgreSQL (2017). http://www.agensgraph.org

IterG: An Iteratively Learning Graph Convolutional Network with Ontology Semantics

Xingya Liang[1], Fuxiang Zhang[1], Xin Liu[1], and Yajun Yang[1,2](✉)

[1] College of Intelligence and Computing, Tianjin University, Tianjin, China
{liangxingya,zhangfx,liuxin_tiei,yjyang}@tju.edu.cn
[2] Tianjin Key Laboratory of Cognitive Computing and Application, Tianjin, China

Abstract. Knowledge reasoning aims to infer new triples based on existing triples, which is essential for the development of large knowledge graphs, especially for knowledge graph completion. With the development of neural networks, Graph Convolutional Networks (GCNs) in knowledge reasoning have been paid widespread attention in recent years. However, the GCN model only considers the structural information of knowledge graphs and ignores the ontology semantic information. In this paper, we propose a novel model named IterG, which is able to incorporate ontology semantics seamlessly into the GCN model. More specifically, IterG learns the embeddings of knowledge graphs in an unsupervised manner via GCNs and extracts the semantic ontology information via rule learning. The model is capable of propagating relation layerwisely as well as combining both rich structural information in knowledge graphs and ontological semantics. The experimental results on five real-world datasets demonstrate that our method outperforms the state-of-the-art approaches, and IterG can effectively and efficiently fuse ontology semantics into GCNs.

Keywords: Graph convolutional neural networks · Knowledge reasoning · Knowledge graphs

1 Introduction

With the rapid development of artificial intelligence, Knowledge Graphs (KGs) have become a large-scale semantic network on top of the existing World Wide Web. KGs store facts as triples in the form of (*head entity, relation, tail entity*), abbreviated as (h, r, t). Entities and relations in the real world can be formally described in the form of a KG, where nodes represent entities and edges represent relations. With the development of big data and semantic web technology, a large number of KGs, such as YAGO [15,16], WordNet [9], and Freebase [1], have been developed, which have also supported a wide range of applications, including question answering [22], relation extraction [25], and recommendation systems [5].

© Springer Nature Switzerland AG 2020
X. Wang et al. (Eds.): APWeb-WAIM 2020, LNCS 12317, pp. 227–241, 2020.
https://doi.org/10.1007/978-3-030-60259-8_18

With the emergence of KGs, knowledge reasoning has become a basic service to support upper-level applications and attracted widespread attention. KG-oriented knowledge reasoning is intended to use various learning methods to infer the existing relations between entity pairs, and automatically identify wrong knowledge based on existing data to supplement KGs. For example, if a KG contains facts such as $(HUAWEI, isBasedIn, Shenzhen)$, $(Shenzhen, stateLocatedIn, Guangdong)$, and $(Guangdong, countryLocatedIn, China)$, we can find the missing link $(HUAWEI, headquarterLocatedIn, China)$. The target of knowledge reasoning is not only the attributes and relations between entities, but also the attribute values of entities and the conceptual level of ontologies. For instance, if an entity's ID number is known, the gender, age, and other attributes of this entity can be obtained through inference. Therefore, it is very important to efficiently and accurately realize the knowledge reasoning task on KGS.

To address these knowledge reasoning tasks, one of the solutions is to directly model the triples of KGs through a neural network, and obtain the embeddings of the elements of triples for further reasoning based on a score function. Each entire network forms a scoring function, and the output of the neural network is the scoring value. Socher et al. [14] proposed a neural tensor network named NTN, which replaced the traditional neural network layer with a bilinear tensor layer, and linked the head entity and the tail entity in different dimensions to characterize the entity complex semantic relations between them. Chen et al. [3] introduced a similar neural tensor network model to predict new relations in KGs. By initializing the entity representations learned from text using an unsupervised method, the model can be improved. Recently, Shi and Weninger [13] proposed a shared variable neural network model named ProjE. The main method of ProjE is to treat the entity prediction expectation as a multi-candidate ranking problem, and take the candidate with the highest ranking as the entity prediction result.

With the development of neural networks, GCNs in knowledge reasoning has been paid widespread attention in recent years, and it can perform convolution on arbitrary structural graphs [4,8]. However, GCNs are suitable for processing undirected graphs, and the relations in KGs are directed. Therefore, in order to apply GCNs to knowledge reasoning, Schlichtkrull et al. [12] proposed the Relation Graph Convolutional Networks (R-GCNs) model to solve the problem of knowledge reasoning from a structural perspective. The R-GCN model introduces GCNs into knowledge reasoning for the first time from a graph perspective, and has achieved outstanding results on some datasets on link prediction and entity classification. However, in this method, the evolutionary design based on GCNs is not well described, and for datasets with fewer types of relations, the quality of the processing results will be reduced. Therefore, the R-GCN model is not mature enough compared with other inference models, and there is still abundant room for improvement.

To this end, we propose a novel model named **Iter**atively learning **G**raph convolutional network with ontology semantics (**IterG**) for knowledge reasoning, which learns the embeddings of KGs in an unsupervised manner via GCNs. In particular, the semantic ontology information in KGs is extracted via rule learning. The model is capable of propagating relations layer-wisely as well as combining both rich structural information in KGs and the semantic ontology information. We evaluate our proposed methods with the link prediction task and verify the running performance on public benchmark datasets, i.e., WN18 and FB15K. Experimental results show that our approach achieves better performance compared with the state-of-the-art approaches.

The major contributions of our work are three-fold:

1. We propose an iteratively learning graph convolutional network model **IterG**, which is regarded as a framework to complement the KGs. It can effectively accomplish the knowledge reasoning problem on KGs.
2. To enhance the reasoning ability of the model, we extract the semantic ontology information in KGs via rule learning and integrating semantics into IterG. The model is capable of propagating relations layer-wisely as well as combining both rich structural information in KGs with ontological semantics.
3. The experimental results on five benchmarks demonstrate that our proposed IterG outperforms the current state-of-the-art methods, including both traditional and deep learning based methods. And IterG can effectively and efficiently fuse ontology semantics into GCNs.

The rest of this paper is organized as follows. Section 2 reviews related work. In Sect. 3, the preliminaries of GCNs are introduced. In Sect. 4, we provide the details of the proposed algorithm for learning the embeddings of the entities and relations in KGs. Section 5 shows the experimental results, and we conclude in Sect. 6.

2   Related Work

In this paper, we focus on iteratively learning graph convolutional network and integrating ontology semantics from KGs. Thus the related work includes two parts: knowledge reasoning based on GCNs and rule learning.

2.1   R-GCN Models

The entities in KGs are connected to each other with relations. Each entity and its neighboring entities form a star structure. In a star structure, there is a relation from a central entity to an adjacent entity, and vice versa. In order to be able to learn KGs from the perspective of neighboring entities and apply them to KG completion, Schlichtkrull et al. [12] introduced R-GCNs from the perspective of graphs, which modeled the KGs via encoding the star structure from the micro level. Unlike knowledge reasoning from the perspective of text processing, R-GCN considers the problem of knowledge reasoning from the perspective of structure, which evolved from GCNs. Since GCNs only deal with undirected graphs and KGs are mostly directed graphs, R-GCNs are designed to be adapted to directed relations. The R-GCN model can be viewed as a set of autoencoders, including an encoder and a decoder.

However, the experimental results of the R-GCN model are not stable enough: the improvements obtained on the AIFB and AM standard datasets are significant, whereas the experimental results on the MUTAG and BGS datasets are not good, which is caused by the nature of the datasets. MUTAG, a molecular map data set, is relatively simple from the perspective of both representing atomic bonds and the existence of a certain characteristic. BGS is a rock type data set with hierarchical feature descriptions released by the British Geological Survey, where the relations only indicate the existence of a specific feature or feature hierarchy. To address this issue, an improvement is to introduce the attention mechanism and replace the normalization constants with attention weights [12].

The R-GCN model introduced GCNs to knowledge reasoning for the first time from the perspective of graphs. It has achieved good results on some datasets on link prediction and entity classification. However, in this method, the evolutionary design based on GCNs is not well described, and for datasets with fewer types of relations, the quality of the processing results will be reduced. In addition, the experimental results of R-GCNs lacks comparison with the latest baselines, and the reliability remains to be verified.

2.2   Rule Learning

The rule-based reasoning methods are well-studied in traditional knowledge engineering for decades, which use logical rules for reasoning on KGs. The reasoning component inside the NELL KG uses first-order relational learning algorithms for reasoning [2]. The reasoning component learns the probabilistic rules, and after manual screening and filtering, it brings in specific entities to instantiate the rules and infer new relationship instances from other relationship instances that have been learned. The YAGO KG uses an inference machine named Spass-YAGO to enrich KG content [17]. Spass-YAGO abstracts the triples in YAGO to equivalent rule classes and uses chain superposition to calculate the transitivity of the relationship. The superposition process can be iterated arbitrarily, and the expansion of YAGO is completed by using these rules. Wang et al. [20,21] proposed a first-order probabilistic language model ProPPR (programming with personalized PageRank) for knowledge reasoning on KGs. Paulheim and Bizer [11] proposed two algorithms, SDType and SDValidate which use the statistical distribution of attributes and types to complete triples, and to identify false triples. SDType infers the types of entities by statistically distributing the types of head and tail entities, similar to the weighted voting mechanism, which assigns weight to the voting of each attribute. SDValidate first calculates the frequency of the relation-tail entity, and the low-frequency triples are further calculated by the statistical distribution of attributes and types. The triples with scores less than the threshold are considered to be potentially wrong. Jang et al. [7] proposed a pattern-based method to evaluate the quality of KG triples. This method directly analyzes the data pattern in KGs. According to the assumption that more frequent patterns are more reliable, the patterns with high occurrence rates are selected, including the head entity patterns and the tail entity patterns, etc., and then these patterns are used for triples quality analysis.

Unlike the above previous works, we focus on the GCNs with ontology semantics, and propose an iteratively learning graph convolutional network model called IterG for the knowledge reasoning on large-scale KGs. The model is capable of propagating relations layer-wisely as well as combining both rich structural information in KGs and the ontology semantic information. To the best of our knowledge, the IterG is the first work to integrate ontology semantic information into GCNs for knowledge reasoning.

3 Preliminaries

The notations used throughout this paper are defined first. A KG $G = \{E, R, T\}$ contains a set of entities E, a set of relations R, and a set of triples $T = \{(h, r, t) \mid h, t \in E; r \in R\}$. Given a triple (h, r, t), the symbols h, r, and t denote head entity, relation, and tail entity, respectively. For instance, a triple is $(\texttt{Tianjin}, isLocatedIn, \texttt{China})$, which means that Tianjin is located in China.

3.1 Graph Convolutional Networks

Graph Convolutional Neural Networks (GCNNs) generalize traditional convolutional neural networks to the graph domain. There are mainly two types of GCNNs: spatial GCNNs and spectral GCNNs. Spatial GCNNs view the convolution as "patch operator" which constructs a new feature vector for each node using its neighborhood information. Spectral GCNNs define the convolution by decomposing a graph signal $\mathbf{s} \in R^n$ (a scalar for each vertex) on the spectral domain and then applying a spectral filter g_θ (a function of eigenvalues of L_{sym}) on the spectral components. However, this model requires explicitly computing the Laplacian eigenvectors, which is impractical for real large graphs. A way to avoid this problem is approximating the spectral filter g_θ with Chebyshev polynomials up to k-th order. Defferrard et al. [4] applied this technique to build a k-localized ChebNet, where the convolution is defined as:

$$g_\theta \star \mathbf{s} \approx \sum_{k=0}^{K} \theta'_k T_k(L_{\text{sym}})\mathbf{s}, \tag{1}$$

where $\mathbf{s} \in R^n$ is the signal on the graph, g_θ is the spectral filter, $\star$ denotes the convolution operator, T_k is the Chebyshev polynomials, and $\theta' \in R^K$ is a vector of Chebyshev coefficients. By the approximation, the ChebNet is actually spectrum-free.

However, some disadvantages exist in the first-generation parameter method, for example, the convolution kernel does not have spatial localization. In [8], Kipf and Welling simplified GCNNs by limiting $K = 1$ and approximating the largest eigenvalue λ_{max} of L_{sym} by 2. In this way, the convolution becomes

$$g_\theta \star \mathbf{s} = \theta \left(I + D^{-\frac{1}{2}} A D^{-\frac{1}{2}} \right) \mathbf{s}, \tag{2}$$

where θ denotes the only Chebyshev coefficient left. The advantages of the convolution kernel designed by Eq. (2) are: (1) the convolution kernel has only one parameter, so the complexity of the parameters is greatly reduced; (2) convolution kernel has good spatial localization. We focus on this simplified GCN model in the rest of this paper.

3.2   OWL Web Ontology Language Axioms

In this paper, we mainly study how to integrate ontology semantic information into GCNs. Axioms are the main components of KG ontologies, since they are important to enrich semantics in KGs.

OWL (Web Ontology Language) is a semantic web ontology language with formally defined meaning and is designed to represent rich and complex knowledge about entities and relations. OWL defines multiple types of axioms, which can be used for rule reasoning. Our model is inspired by the IterE [24] model, which proposes seven object attribute expression axioms selected from the OWL ontology language. Essentially, for each type of axioms, we can draw rule conclusions through the embeddings of relations based on the linear mapping hypothesis. For instance, considering axiom SymmetricOP($hasFriend$), if a KG contains the triple ($Alice, hasFriend, Bob$), according to the rule conclusion of symmetric axiom in Table 1, a new triple ($Bob, hasFriend, Alice$) can be inferred. So the axioms that the relations satisfy can be obtained by calculating the similarity between the embeddings of relations and the rule conclusions. In general, the higher the similarity, the more likely the relations is to satisfy the corresponding axioms. The details of the conclusions of each axiom are listed in Table 1, where the rule form $(x, r, x)^1$ of ReflexiveOP(OPE) means reflexive.

Table 1. Seven types of axioms and translated rule formulation.

Object property axiom	Rule form
ReflexiveOP(OPE)	$(x, r, x)^1$
SymmetricOP(OPE)	$(y, r, x) \leftarrow (x, r, y)$
TransitiveOP(OPE)	$(x, r, z) \leftarrow (x, r, y), (y, r, z)$
EquivalentOP(OPE$_1$ ... OPE$_n$)	$(x, r_2, y) \leftarrow (x, r_1, y)$
SubOP(OPE$_1$ OPE$_2$)	$(x, r_2, y) \leftarrow (x, r_1, y)$
InverseOP(OPE$_1$ OPE$_2$)	$(x, r_1, y) \leftarrow (y, r_2, x)$
SubOP(OPChain(OPE$_1$ ... OPE$_n$) OPE)	$(y_0, r, y_2) \leftarrow (y_0, r_1, y_1), (y_1, r_2, y_2)$

4   The IterG Model

In this section, we describe our proposed IterG model in detail. Given a KG $G = \{E, R, T\}$, our objective is to learn structural and ontological information

at the same time and complement each other's advantages, while graph convolutional networks only learn the structural characteristics of nodes without considering the semantic information on the KGs. So we seamlessly integrate ontology semantic information into GCNs via the IterG model.

4.1 Intuition

We first introduce the overall architecture of IterG before reporting the detailed implementation of model's design principle that conforms to the template method design pattern, which is shown in Fig. 1 and includes two main parts: (i) auto-encoder layer and (ii) reasoning layer.

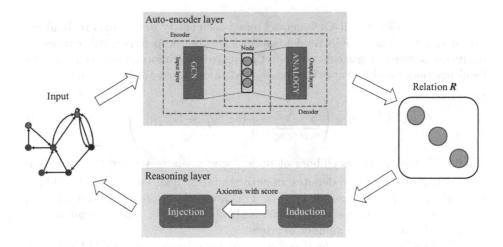

Fig. 1. The IterG architecture.

Auto-encoder layer extracts the structural information from KGs through a two-layer graph convolutional neural network, thereby obtaining the embeddings of nodes and relations.

Reasoning layer uses the embeddings of relations to conduct axiom induction, and then uses the axiom injection to select triples with high confidence and adds them to the original KG for the next iterative learning.

4.2 Graph Auto-Encoder Model

In order to obtain the embeddings of nodes and relations in KGs, we introduce a graph auto-encoder model comprised of an entity encoder and a scoring function (decoder). In this paper, GCNs are used as the encoder and ANALOGY as the decoder. First, we use a two-layer graph convolutional neural network to obtain the embeddings of the nodes in KGs, and then use ANALOGY to get the embeddings of the relations, which is shown in Fig. 2.

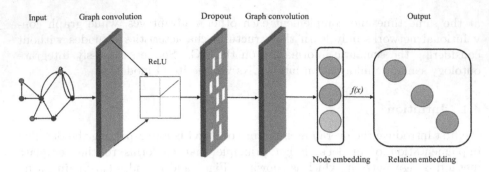

Fig. 2. Graph auto-encoder model.

As the encoder, the R-GCN model maps each entity $v_i \in \mathcal{V}$ to a real-valued vector $e_i \in \mathbb{R}^d$. The R-GCN model use the following propagation rule expressed in the message-passing architecture [6] that aggregates information from a node's local neighbors and forwards the aggregated information to the next layer,

$$h_i^{(l+1)} = \sigma \left(\sum_{r \in R} \sum_{j \in N_i^r} \frac{1}{c_{i,r}} W_r^{(l)} h_j^{(l)} + W_0^{(l)} h_i^{(l)} \right), \tag{3}$$

where N_i^r denotes the neighbors of node i under the relation $r \in R$, $c_{i,r}$ is a normalization constant, δ denotes an activation function, and $h_i^{(l)}$ is the hidden state of i-th node at the relation $r \in R$. This layer-wisely propagation model can be implemented in sparse-dense matrix multiplications and has a computational complexity linear to the number of edges.

ANALOGY is used as the decoder in the experiments and ANALOGY performs well on the standard link prediction task. In ANALOGY, every relation r is associated with a diagonal matrix $M_r \in \mathbb{R}^{d \times d}$ and a triple (h, r, t) is scored as

$$f(h, r, t) = e_h^T R_r e_t. \tag{4}$$

The main innovation of ANALOGY is to apply analogy inference to the KG embedding, which adds constraints to the model's score function to capture the information of the analogy structure in KGs, thereby optimizing the embedding representation of entities and relations in KGs.

4.3   Rule Learning

After graph auto-encoder learning, the learning entity is represented by real-valued vectors and the relation is represented by matrices, which are used for rule learning. In order to learn new rules via relation matrices, we introduce the IterE [24] model, which employs seven object attribute expression axioms selected from the OWL ontology language. IterE is proposed based on the basis of embeddings learned with linear map assumption. Essentially, for each type of axioms, we can draw rule conclusions through the embeddings of relations based on the linear mapping hypothesis. For instance, considering axiom SymmetricOP($hasFriend$), if a KG contains the triple ($Alice, hasFriend, Bob$), according to the rule conclusion of symmetric axiom in Table 1, a new triple ($Bob, hasFriend, Alice$) can be inferred. So the axioms that the relations satisfy can be obtained by calculating the similarity between the relation embeddings and the rule conclusions. In general, the higher the similarity, the more likely the relations is to satisfy the corresponding axioms. The rule conclusions of the OWL axioms are listed in Table 2.

Table 2. OWL axioms and rule conclusion.

Object property axioms	Rule conclusion
ReflexiveOP(r)	$\mathbf{M}_r = \mathbf{I}$
SymmetricOP(r)	$\mathbf{M}_r\mathbf{M}_r = \mathbf{I}$
TransitiveOP(r)	$\mathbf{M}_r\mathbf{M}_r = \mathbf{M}_r$
EquivalentOP(r_1, r_2)	$\mathbf{M}_{r_1} = \mathbf{M}_{r_2}$
subOP($\mathbf{r}_1, \mathbf{r}_2$)	$\mathbf{M}_{r_1} = \mathbf{M}_{r_2}$
inverseOP($\mathbf{r}_1, \mathbf{r}_2$)	$\mathbf{M}_{r_1}\mathbf{M}_{r_2} = \mathbf{I}$
subOP(OPChain(r_1, r_2),r)	$\mathbf{M}_{r_1}\mathbf{M}_{r_2} = \mathbf{M}_r$

Axiom Induction. After we calculated the relation embeddings using the graph auto-encoder model, relation embeddings are used to induce a set of axioms, denoted as A. To this end, IterG employs an effective pruning strategy to generate a possible axiom pool P which contains all possible axioms. Then we calculate the similarity between the relation embeddings and the rule conclusions to predict the score for each axiom $p \in P$.

Before calculating axiom scores with relation embeddings, concrete relations are applied to replace relation variables r, r_1, r_2, and r_3 in Table 2. As long as more than one axioms is satisfied, this axiom will be added to the pool, and a pool of possible axioms P is produced. In general, there are two methods for generating axiom pool. One way is to find possible axioms by traversing all the relations, however, the complexity of this method is too high. Another method is to generate axiom pool using random walks on KGs, but it is cannot be ensured that all possible axioms are covered. Therefore, we adopt a pruning strategy that combines traversal and random selection, which achieves a good balance between complexity and the coverage of possible axioms.

After getting relation embeddings and axiom pool P, a score s_p for each axiom $p \in P$ can be calculated based on the rule conclusions for each type of axioms. $\mathbf{M}_1^p$ and $\mathbf{M}_2^p$ denote the relation embeddings and the rule conclusions, respectively, which may be a single matrix or the dot product of two matrices. Generally, the values of $\mathbf{M}_1^p$ and $\mathbf{M}_2^p$ will be quite similar but not equal during the calculating process. So we calculate the similarity between $\mathbf{M}_1^p$ and $\mathbf{M}_2^p$ and when the higher the similarity, the more confident the axiom p will be.

Axiom Injection. IterG can infer a set of new triplets T_{new} through axiom injection with a KG G and a possible axiom set A, which employs axiom injection to infer new triples. The process of reasoning can be summarized in the following form:

$$(h^p, r^p, t^p) \leftarrow (h_1, r_1, t_1), (h_2, r_2, t_2), ..., (h_n, r_n, t_n) \tag{5}$$

where the right side triples $(h_k, r_k, t_k) \in T$ with $k \in [1, n]$ are generated from the rule conclusions of axioms, and $(h^p, r^p, t^p) \notin T$ is a new inferred triple which will be added into KGs.

A new set of triples $T_{new} = \{(h^p, r^p, t^p) \mid h^p \in E \text{ or } t^p \in E\}$ can be obtained via high-confidence axioms after axiom injection. Thus, the previous KG is updated. Then the process goes back to the graph auto-encoder model to start a new learning iteration.

5 Experimental Evaluation

In this section, our method is evaluated on the link prediction task. Extensive experiments are conducted to verify the validity of our IterG model on both benchmark and real-world KGs.

5.1 Datasets

In this research, we evaluate our models on benchmarks WN18, FB15k, and FB15k-237. Link prediction tasks are usually performed on FB15k and WN18, which are subsets of relational database Freebase and WordNet, respectively. WordNet is a semantic vocabulary KG, which has been widely used in the field of natural language processing. Freebase is a well-known knowledge base containing general facts. We also select FB15k-237 as the experimental data set, which removed all inverse triple pairs, as in [18] Toutanova and Chen found that both FB15k and WN18 have serious flaws. A simple baseline LinkFeat using a linear classifier on the sparse feature vector of the observed training relationship can greatly outperform other methods [18]. Table 3 gives a summary of these datasets.

Table 3. Datasets used in the experiments.

Dataset	WN18	FB15k	FB15k-237
Entities	40,943	14,951	14,541
Relations	18	1,345	237
Train edges	141,442	483,142	272,115
Val. edges	5,000	50,000	17,535
Test edges	5,000	59,071	20,466

In addition to the above three datasets, we also use two sparse datasets WN18-sparse and FB15k-sparse, which contain only sparse entities. It is explored whether IterG really contributes to sparse entity embeddings on sparse datasets. Table 4 gives a summary of these datasets.

Table 4. Sparse datasets used in the experiments.

Dataset	WN18-sparse	FB15k-sparse
Entities	40,943	14,951
Relations	18	1,345
Train edges	141,442	483,142
Val. edges	3,624	18,544
Test edges	3,590	22,013

5.2 Baselines

DisMult [23] is selected as the first baseline, which is a common baseline for link prediction experiment, and it can perform well on standard data sets such as FB15k. However, DisMult cannot model antisymmetric and inverse modes due to the symmetric nature of the model. We add LinkFeat proposed in [18] as a second baseline, which is a simple neighbor-based LinkFeat algorithm.

We further compare IterG to ComplEx [19], HolE [10], and R-GCN [12], which are the state-of-the-art models for link prediction. ComplEx solves the problem of DisMult and can infer symmetric and antisymmetric modes in the complex space. In addition, it can also derive inverse rules because of the existence of conjugate complex numbers. HolE is simlar to ComplE, however, HolE replaces the vector-matrix product with circular correlation. Finally, we also compare with IterE on sparse datasets.

5.3 Experimental Settings

The experimental settings are mainly divided into two parts, including graph auto-encoder model and rule learning. We first introduce the experiment settings of the graph auto-encoder model. For FB15k and WN18, a basic decomposition, with a single encoding layer and two basic functions, is employed to obtain the results. For FB15k-237, when the block dimension is 5×5 and embedding dimensional equals 500, the block decomposition performs the best. Before normalization, encoder is regularized via edge dropout. The dropout rate of the self-loops is equal to 0.2, and the dropout rate of the other edges is equal to 0.4. And $l2$ regularization is applied to the decoder with a parameter of 0.01. Adam optimizer is used in the graph auto-encoder model with a learning rate of 0.01. Finally, our model and baselines are trained with full-batch optimization.

Then we introduce the experimental settings of the rule learning part. In the part of axiom induction, the minimum axiom probability p is set to 0.5 and the inclusion probability t is set to 0.95. For axiom injection, in order to choose axioms with high confidence as much as possible and introduce as little noise as possible, a threshold θ is set for each dataset and axioms with scores $s_{axiom} > \theta$ are regarded as high quality axioms.

5.4   Results

Two commonly evaluation metrics are employed to provide results: Mean Reciprocal Rank (MRR) and Hits@n, which can be calculated in the raw and the filtered setting [12]. The experimental results show both filtered and raw MRR, and filtered Hits@1, Hits@3, and Hits@10.

Table 5. Results on the Freebase and WordNet datasets.

Model	FB15k					WN18				
	MRR		Hits @			MRR		Hits @		
	Raw	Filtered	1	3	10	Raw	Filtered	1	3	10
LinkFeat		0.779			0.804		0.938			0.939
DistMult	0.248	0.634	0.522	0.718	0.814	0.526	0.813	0.701	0.921	0.943
R-GCN	**0.251**	0.651	0.541	0.736	0.825	0.553	0.814	0.686	0.928	**0.955**
HolE	0.232	0.524	0.402	0.613	0.739	**0.616**	0.938	0.930	0.945	0.949
ComplEx	0.242	**0.692**	0.599	0.759	0.840	0.587	0.941	**0.936**	0.945	0.947
IterG	0.245	0.684	**0.603**	**0.765**	**0.853**	0.592	**0.943**	0.933	**0.947**	0.951

Table 6. Results on FB15k-237.

Model	MRR		Hits @		
	Raw	Filtered	1	3	10
LinkFeat		0.063			0.079
DistMult	0.100	0.191	0.106	0.207	0.376
R-GCN	**0.158**	0.248	**0.153**	0.258	0.414
IterG	0.153	**0.253**	0.148	**0.267**	**0.421**
CP	0.080	0.182	0.101	0.197	0.357
TransE	0.144	0.233	0.147	0.263	0.398
HolE	0.124	0.222	0.133	0.253	0.391
ComplEx	0.109	0.201	0.112	0.213	0.388

Table 5 demonstrates the experimental results of the IterG model and other models on FB15k and WN18. On the FB15k and WN18 datasets, IterG outperforms the DistMult, but is not as good as LinkFeat like all other systems on these two dataset. Compared with R-GCNs, the experimental results of IterG are also improved, which exactly demonstrates that the semantic information in KGs is effective for knowledge reasoning, and the ontology semantic information can improve the performance of GCNs.

Table 7. Results on the sparse datasets.

Model	FB15k-sparse					WN18-sparse				
	MRR		Hits @			MRR		Hits @		
	Raw	Filtered	1	3	10	Raw	Filtered	1	3	10
TransE	0.335	0.418	0.102	0.711	0.847	0.255	0.398	0.258	0.486	0.645
DistMult	0.558	0.738	0.593	0.875	0.931	0.324	0.600	**0.618**	0.651	0.759
ComplEx	0.677	0.911	0.890	0.933	0.944	0.327	0.616	0.540	0.657	0.761
ANALOGY	0.675	**0.913**	0.890	**0.934**	**0.944**	0.331	0.620	0.543	0.661	0.763
R-GCN	0.673	0.907	**0.894**	0.933	**0.944**	0.328	0.613	0.537	0.659	0.763
ITerE	0.675	0.901	0.870	0.931	**0.948**	0.359	0.613	0.529	0.662	0.767
IterG	**0.682**	0.908	0.885	0.923	0.945	**0.365**	**0.617**	0.548	**0.667**	**0.768**

The results of the IterG model and other models on FB15k-237 are demonstrated in Table 6. It can be inferred from the results that our IterG model is much better than DistMult, highlighting the importance of a separate encoder model. And in FB15k-237, the performance of the LinkFeat is worse than other models since inverse relations have been deleted. As aforementioned, the performance of IterG and R-GCN on FB15k-237 is similar. The IterG model is further compared with other models and it also exhibits superior performance. The above results indicate that the ontology semantic information can effectively enhance the reasoning ability of IterG.

In Table 7, we evaluate the IterG model and other models on sparse datasets. First, the link prediction results of IterG perform better than ANALOGY, which means most of the triplets injected into GCNs learning are useful. And the link prediction results also show that learning axioms from graph auto-encoder model works well. Second, IterG outperforms IterE on WN18-sparse and FB15k-sparse, which shows that GCNs can better extract the structural information in KGs, thereby generating more accurate relation embeddings. The results show that, even in the sparse datasets, our IterG model demonstrates its superiority over other models.

Based on the experimental results, we can conclude that: (1) the results in link prediction demonstrate that IterG outperforms all baselines, which indicates that IterG is capable of fusing ontology semantic information into GCNs, and (2) ontology semantic information in the IterG model can significantly improve the knowledge reasoning ability of GCNs.

6 Conclusion

In this paper, we propose an novel GCN framework, named IterG, for knowledge reasoning. In IterG, the structural and ontology semantic information on KGs are extracted at the same time, and the rule learning and GCNs are seamlessly fused to better accomplish the knowledge reasoning task. In particular, to enhance the reasoning ability of the model, we extract the ontology semantic information in KGs via rule learning. The model is capable of propagating relations layer-wisely as well as combining both rich structural information in KGs with the ontology semantic information. The evaluation on five real-world datasets demonstrates that our method outperforms the state-of-the-art approaches, and IterG can effectively and efficiently fuse ontology semantics into GCNs.

Acknowledgements. This work is supported by the National Natural Science Foundation of China (61972275).

References

1. Bollacker, K., Evans, C., Paritosh, P., Sturge, T., Taylor, J.: Freebase: a collaboratively created graph database for structuring human knowledge. In: Proceedings of the 2008 ACM SIGMOD international conference on Management of data, pp. 1247–1250 (2008)
2. Carlson, A., Betteridge, J., Kisiel, B., Settles, B., Mitchell, T.M.: Toward an architecture for never-ending language learning. In: Proceedings of the Twenty-Fourth AAAI Conference on Artificial Intelligence, AAAI 2010, Atlanta, Georgia, USA, 11–15 July 2010 (2010)
3. Chen, D., Socher, R., Manning, C.D., Ng, A.Y.: Learning new facts from knowledge bases with neural tensor networks and semantic word vectors. arXiv preprint arXiv:1301.3618 (2013)
4. Defferrard, M., Bresson, X., Vandergheynst, P.: Convolutional neural networks on graphs with fast localized spectral filtering. In: Advances in Neural Information Processing Systems, pp. 3844–3852 (2016)
5. Felfernig, A., et al.: Persuasive recommendation: serial position effects in knowledge-based recommender systems. In: de Kort, Y., IJsselsteijn, W., Midden, C., Eggen, B., Fogg, B.J. (eds.) PERSUASIVE 2007. LNCS, vol. 4744, pp. 283–294. Springer, Heidelberg (2007). https://doi.org/10.1007/978-3-540-77006-0_34
6. Gilmer, J., Schoenholz, S.S., Riley, P.F., Vinyals, O., Dahl, G.E.: Neural message passing for quantum chemistry. In: Proceedings of the 34th International Conference on Machine Learning, vol. 70, pp. 1263–1272. JMLR. org (2017)
7. Jang, S., Choi, J., Yi, M.: Semi-automatic quality assessment of linked data without requiring ontology (2015)
8. Kipf, T.N., Welling, M.: Semi-supervised classification with graph convolutional networks. arXiv preprint arXiv:1609.02907 (2016)
9. Miller, G.A.: Wordnet: a lexical database for English. Commun. ACM **38**(11), 39–41 (1995)
10. Nickel, M., Rosasco, L., Poggio, T.: Holographic embeddings of knowledge graphs (2015)

11. Paulheim, H., Bizer, C.: Improving the quality of linked data using statistical distributions. Int. J. Semant. Web Inf. Syst. **10**(2), 63–86 (2014)
12. Schlichtkrull, M., Kipf, T.N., Bloem, P., van den Berg, R., Titov, I., Welling, M.: Modeling relational data with graph convolutional networks. In: Gangemi, A., et al. (eds.) ESWC 2018. LNCS, vol. 10843, pp. 593–607. Springer, Cham (2018). https://doi.org/10.1007/978-3-319-93417-4_38
13. Shi, B., Weninger, T.: ProjE: embedding projection for knowledge graph completion. In: Thirty-First AAAI Conference on Artificial Intelligence (2017)
14. Socher, R., Chen, D., Manning, C.D., Ng, A.: Reasoning with neural tensor networks for knowledge base completion. In: Advances in Neural Information Processing Systems, pp. 926–934 (2013)
15. Suchanek, F.M., Kasneci, G., Weikum, G.: Yago: a core of semantic knowledge. In: Proceedings of the 16th International Conference on World Wide Web, pp. 697–706 (2007)
16. Suchanek, F.M., Kasneci, G., Weikum, G.: Yago: a large ontology from wikipedia and wordnet. J. Web Semant. **6**(3), 203–217 (2008)
17. Suda, M., Weidenbach, C., Wischnewski, P.: On the saturation of YAGO. In: Giesl, J., Hähnle, R. (eds.) IJCAR 2010. LNCS (LNAI), vol. 6173, pp. 441–456. Springer, Heidelberg (2010). https://doi.org/10.1007/978-3-642-14203-1_38
18. Toutanova, K., Chen, D.: Observed versus latent features for knowledge base and text inference. In: The 3rd Workshop on Continuous Vector Space Models and their Compositionality (2015)
19. Trouillon, T., Welbl, J., Riedel, S., Gaussier, É., Bouchard, G.: Complex embeddings for simple link prediction. International Conference on Machine Learning (ICML) (2016)
20. Wang, W.Y., Mazaitis, K., Cohen, W.W.: Programming with personalized pagerank: a locally groundable first-order probabilistic logic (2013)
21. Wang, W.Y., Mazaitis, K., Lao, N., Mitchell, T., Cohen, W.W.: Efficient inference and learning in a large knowledge base: Reasoning with extracted information using a locally groundable first-order probabilistic logic. Comput. Sci. (2014)
22. Weston, J., et al.: Towards AI-complete question answering: a set of prerequisite toy tasks. Comput. Sci. (2015)
23. Yang, B., Yih, W.t., He, X., Gao, J., Deng, L.: Embedding entities and relations for learning and inference in knowledge bases. arXiv preprint arXiv:1412.6575 (2014)
24. Zhang, W., et al.: Iteratively learning embeddings and rules for knowledge graph reasoning. In: The World Wide Web Conference, pp. 2366–2377 (2019)
25. Zhou, G., Su, J., Zhang, J., Zhang, M.: Exploring various knowledge in relation extraction. In: ACL, Meeting of the Association for Computational Linguistics, Conference, June, University of Michigan, USA (2005)

Fine-Grained Evaluation of Knowledge Graph Embedding Models in Downstream Tasks

Yuxin Zhang[1], Bohan Li[1,2,3], Han Gao[1], Ye Ji[1], Han Yang[4], and Meng Wang[5(✉)]

[1] Nanjing University of Aeronautics and Astronautics, Nanjing 211100, China
[2] Key Laboratory of Safety-Critical Software, Ministry of Industry and Information Technology, Nanjing 211100, China
[3] Collaborative Innovation Center of Novel Software Technology and Industrialization, Nanjing 210000, Jiangsu, China
[4] Peking University, Beijing 100000, China
[5] Southeast University, Nanjing 211100, China
meng.wang@seu.edu.cn

Abstract. Knowledge graph (KG) embedding models are proposed to encode entities and relations into a low-dimensional vector space, in turn, can support various machine learning models on KG completion with good performance and robustness. However, the current entity ranking protocol about KG completion cannot adequately evaluate the impacts of KG embedding models in real-world applications. However, KG embeddings is not widely used as word embeddings. An asserted powerful KG embedding model may not be effective in downstream tasks. So in this paper, we commit to finding the answers by using downstream tasks instead of entity ranking protocol to evaluate the effectiveness of KG embeddings. Specifically, we conduct comprehensive experiments on different KG embedding models in KG based recommendation and question answering tasks. Our findings indicate that: 1) Modifying embeddings by considering more complex KG structural information may not achieve improvements in practical applications, such as updating TransE to TransR. 2) Modeling KG embeddings in non-euclidean space can effectively improve the performance of downstream tasks.

Keywords: Knowledge graph · Embedding model · Evaluation

1 Introduction

Knowledge graph is a collection of fact triples in form of <subject, predicate, object>. Many downstream tasks have achieved better performance by using facts in the KG, such as question answering system [1], recommendation system [17,22], and natural language processing tasks [15]. Recently, the knowledge graph embedding (KGE) models aim to formalize the latent semantics implied

© Springer Nature Switzerland AG 2020
X. Wang et al. (Eds.): APWeb-WAIM 2020, LNCS 12317, pp. 242–256, 2020.
https://doi.org/10.1007/978-3-030-60259-8_19

in the facts into low-dimensional continuous vector space. The generated embeddings in turn can support various machine learning models on KG completion with good performance and robustness. It is intuitive that the KG embeddings should also improve the performance of machine learning based downstream applications seamlessly.

Since first work [3] proposed the TransE model based on semantic translation theory for KGE, more researchers dedicated their focus to improving the models on KG completion. One direction to modify KGE models is to consider more complex KG structural information, such as TransH [20], TransR [8], and HolE [11]. Xiao et al. [21] deem that the original KGE models could not well depict the characteristics of KG due to the ill-posed algebraic system and over strict geometric forms, and proposed the ManifoldE based on the manifold principle. Afterward, another direction of improving KGE models is to encode KG into non-Euclidean presentation spaces. For instance, Sun et al. [14] proposed a novel method of embedding multi-relational graphs with non-Euclidean manifolds, which embeds KG into complex vector spaces. Kolyvakis et al. [7] proposed a HyperKG model using hyperbolic space to reflect the topological characteristics of KG better. The detailed review on KGE can be found in [18].

The traditional evaluation method of the KGE model is the entity ranking (ER) protocol. ER protocol first removes the head entities in the test triples in order and replaces them with other entities in the dictionary. Then it calculates the energy of the test triples with these corrupt triples and orders them in ascending order. At last, we use the rank of the correct triples in test as the KGE evaluation indicator. The whole process is repeated while removing the tail entity instead of the head entity. Although the ER protocol can reflect the performance of the KGE model to some extent on KG completion, there is no systematic analysis of the KGE improvements in downstream tasks. Recent advances in KGE model have reached around 90% accuracy on traditional benchmark. Why are KG embeddings not widely used as word embeddings in downstream tasks? Is an asserted improved KG embedding model really also effective in downstream tasks? In this paper, we commit to finding the answers.

Specifically, we conduct comprehensive experiments on different KG embedding models in KG based recommendation and question answering tasks. In the same representation space, the embedding of different KGE modeling methods is used as a pre-training result, which is measured by downstream task experiments. Meanwhile, we experiment with KGE models which in different representation spaces. In addition, we perform multiple sets of experiments on the KGE dimension in the downstream task to try to find the impact of the embedded dimension on the downstream tasks.

The consistent experimental results indicate that: 1) The traditional evaluation protocol has limitations, and the existing KGE model's ability to capture knowledge is overestimated. 2) Modifying embeddings by considering complex KG structural information may not achieve improvements in practical applications. For instance, in KGE downstream tasks, the recommendation task model only depends on the entity embedding. Therefore, the TransR model with improved relational embedding does not improve performance in recommendation tasks. 3) Encoding KG in non-euclidean space can effectively improve the performance of KG embeddings in downstream tasks. For example, the embedding result of HyperKG based on hyperbolic space has a certain hierarchical structure, while the model based on Euclidean space does not have. Hence, HyperKG has better performance in the question answering tasks which need to predict the answer entities accurately.

2   Preliminaries

Knowledge graph consists of the entity set $\mathcal{E}$, the relation set $\mathcal{R}$ and the set $\mathcal{K} \subset \mathcal{E} \times \mathcal{R} \times \mathcal{E}$ of fact triples (h, r, t), where $h, t \in \mathcal{E}$ and $r \in \mathcal{R}$. We refer to h, r and t as the head entity, relation, and tail entity to the triple, respectively [18]. KGE models translate entity h, t and relation r into low-dimensional dense continuous vectors $\mathbf{h}, \mathbf{t} \in \mathbb{R}^{d_e}$ and $\mathbf{r} \in \mathbb{R}^{d_r}$, where d_e and d_r is the dimension of the embedding. In this work, we mainly consider the currently prevalent translation distance KGE models, which guarantee the effectiveness of the embedding models by minimizing the semantic deviation distance of fact triples. The semantic translational distance induces a ranking: triples with short distance are considered more likely to be true than triples with long distance. Traditional translation distance KGE models are based on Euclidean space, but in recent years, more models based on non-euclidean space have proposed. We find that these new models have more characteristics derived from their respective spaces compared to the traditional KGE model based on Euclidean space. However, the differences of final performance and characteristics of these KGE models are unclear. Therefore, we select the most classic KGE models as the evaluation object according to the following two criterias:

- Choose KGE models based on different embedding spaces to analyze their characteristics and the final embedding performance;
- Choose KGE models based on the same embedding space to measure the impact of modeling methods on model of performance.

TransE [3]. TransE is the most representative translational distance model. In 2013, Mikolov et al. [9] found translation invariance in word vector space such as *"China - Beijing ≈ America - Washington"*. In the same year, Bordes et al. [3] proposed the TransE model by treating relations as translation vectors between entities. The TransE model represents entities and relationships in the same space, the relationship vector $\mathbf{r}$ is the translation between the head entity vector $\mathbf{h}$ and the tail entity vector $\mathbf{t}$, that is, $\mathbf{h} + \mathbf{r} \approx \mathbf{t}$. TransE's semantic translation distance is calculated in Euclidean space. The scoring function is defined as the distance between $\mathbf{h} + \mathbf{r}$ and $\mathbf{t}$, i.e.,

$$s(\mathbf{h}, \mathbf{r}, \mathbf{t}) = -\|\mathbf{h} + \mathbf{r} - \mathbf{t}\|_{1/2}. \tag{1}$$

The score is expected to be small if (h, r, t) holds.

TransH [20]. In order to overcome the limitations of the TransE model in dealing with 1-to-n, n-to-1 and n-to-n relationships, the TransH model transforms the fact tuples onto the hyperplane of the relationship. For each fact triple (h, r, t), TransH first projects the head entity $\mathbf{h}$ and tail entity $\mathbf{t}$ onto the relational hyperplane along the normal vector $\mathbf{w}_r$ of the relation $\mathbf{r}$. The head entity projection vector $\mathbf{h}_\perp$ and tail entity projection vector $\mathbf{t}_\perp$ are represented as follows:

$$\mathbf{h}_\perp = \mathbf{h} - \mathbf{w}_r^\top \mathbf{h} \mathbf{w}_r, \quad \mathbf{t}_\perp = \mathbf{t} - \mathbf{w}_r^\top \mathbf{t} \mathbf{w}_T. \tag{2}$$

The translation distance of the TransH model is also calculated in Euclidean space. For a given fact triple (h, r, t), there is $\mathbf{h}_\perp + \mathbf{r} \approx \mathbf{t}_\perp$. The scoring function is defined as follows:

$$s(\mathbf{h}, \mathbf{r}, \mathbf{t}) = -\|\mathbf{h}_\perp + \mathbf{r} - \mathbf{t}_\perp\|_2^2. \tag{3}$$

TransR [8]. The TransH model still embeds entities and relationships in a same semantic space, which limits the model's expressiveness. TransR embeds entities and relationships into different semantic spaces, which strengthens the model's modeling ability. For each fact triple (h, r, t), TransR first projects the entity vector from the entity space to the relationship space through the projection matrix $\mathbf{M}_r$ of the relationship $\mathbf{r}$, which is represented by $\mathbf{h}_\perp$ and $\mathbf{t}_\perp$ as follows:

$$\mathbf{h}_\perp = \mathbf{M}_r \mathbf{h}, \quad \mathbf{t}_\perp = \mathbf{M}_r \mathbf{t}. \tag{4}$$

The projections are then assumed to be connected by $\mathbf{r}$ on the relation space with a low error if (h, r, t) holds, i.e., $\mathbf{h}_\perp + \mathbf{r} \approx \mathbf{t}_\perp$. The scoring function is accordingly defined as:

$$s(\mathbf{h}, \mathbf{r}, \mathbf{t}) = -\|\mathbf{h}_\perp + \mathbf{r} - \mathbf{t}_\perp\|_2^2. \tag{5}$$

HolE [11]. Different from the above-mentioned semantic translation models, HolE is a classic semantic matching model. The model calculates the credibility of facts by measuring the similarity of latent semantics of entities and relations embodied in their vector space representations. For a given fact triple (h, r, t), the HolE model first uses a loop operation to form the head and tail entities of the fact into the form $\mathbf{h} \star \mathbf{t} \in R$. Then, the credibility of the combined vector and relationship representation are calculated. The scoring function of HolE is as follows:

$$s(\mathbf{h}, \mathbf{r}, \mathbf{t}) = \mathbf{r}^\top (\mathbf{h} \star \mathbf{t}) = \sum_{i=0}^{d-1} [\mathbf{r}]_i \sum_{k=0}^{d-1} [\mathbf{h}]_k \cdot [\mathbf{t}]_{(k+i) \mod d}, \tag{6}$$

where $d = d_e = d_r$.

ManifoldE [21]. Although the embedding ability of the above models is improving, they still calculate the translational distance in the Euclidean space. The geometric form of semantic translation model based on Euclidean space is over strict. The ManifoldE model loosens the previously over strict geometric form, placing the tail entity $\mathbf{t}$ in the fact triplet approximately on the manifold (sphere space, hyperplane space, etc.), extending from a point to a manifold that resembles a high-dimensional spherical. The intuitive geometric form is a hyperspherical surface with $\mathbf{h} + \mathbf{r}$ as the center of the sphere and the relation radius D_r. The scoring function is defined as:

$$\mathcal{M}(\mathbf{h}, \mathbf{r}, \mathbf{t}) = \|\mathbf{h} + \mathbf{r} - \mathbf{t}\|_2^2, \tag{7}$$

$$s(\mathbf{h}, \mathbf{r}, \mathbf{t}) = \left\|\mathcal{M}(\mathbf{h}, \mathbf{r}, \mathbf{t}) - D_r^2\right\|^2. \tag{8}$$

HyperKG [7]. The HyperKG model learns the hyperbolic embedding of entities and relationships, which can reflect the topological characteristics of the knowledge graph better. Kolyvakis et al. [7] defined the term embedding as $\mathbf{h} + \Pi_\beta \mathbf{t}$, where Π is a hyperparameter controlling the number of successive circular shifts. The scoring function is accordingly defined as:

$$s(\mathbf{h}, \mathbf{r}, \mathbf{t}) = d_p \left(\mathbf{h} + \Pi_\beta \mathbf{t}, \mathbf{r}\right). \tag{9}$$

RotatE [14]. To improve the inference ability of the translation model, the RotatE model defines each relationship as the rotation from the head entity h to the tail entity t in the complex vector space. For a given fact triple (h, r, t), we expect that:

$$\mathbf{t} = \mathbf{h} \circ \mathbf{r}, \quad \text{where } |r_i| = 1, \tag{10}$$

and $\circ$ is the Hadmard (or element-wise) product. The scoring function of RotatE is as follows:

$$s(\mathbf{h}, \mathbf{r}, \mathbf{t}) = \|\mathbf{h} \circ \mathbf{r} - \mathbf{t}\|. \tag{11}$$

3   Tasks and Evaluation Protocols

The Entity ranking (ER) protocol is the most widely used protocol for evaluating the performance of a KGE models. However, for a given relationship, it can only focus on a small part of all possible facts due to the limitations of its measurement methods. For this reason, the ER protocol overestimates the performance of the KGE models and cannot perform fine-grained evaluation of the models. We attempt to use specific KGE downstream tasks to measure embedding models in different spaces in order to dig more characteristics of models, as well as conduct comprehensive evaluation and analysis on model performance. We adopt question answering and recommendation system, which are the two kinds of the most common downstream tasks of KGE, as the performance metrics. In this section, we introduce each KGE downstream task models and discuss the relationship between the KGE models and the downstream task models.

3.1   Question Answering

Compared with other question answering systems, the KEQA models [6] only rely on the upper-level embedding of entities and relationships, which not require additional information. The KEQA models aim at common simple questions, and the main idea is to ensure that the models can accurately identify entity and predicate (relation) in the question to improve the accuracy of the answer. Instead of directly inferring entities and predicates, the KEQA models combine the representations of entities and predicates in the KG embedding space, and design a joint distance metric, which returns the three learning vectors closest to the facts in KG as candidate answers. The KEQA models are mainly divided into the following three parts.

Predicate and Head Entity Learning Model. Take a question as input, and return a vector, as far as possible to ensure that the vector is close to the embedding obtained by the KGE model. This module mainly contains a simple neural network composed of the bidirectional recursive neural network layer and injection layer. Its core idea is to assign different weights according to the order of words in the question. The purpose is to find a spot in the predicate space as news headlines predicate representation and a spot in the entity embedding space as its entity representation.

Head Entity Detection Model. In this module, the model selects one or more consecutive words from the problem as the name of the header entity, so that the scope of entity search can be reduced from all entities in KG to part of entities with the same or similar names. Same as the previous module, this process also uses a bidirectional recursive neural network (such as LSTM) model for implementing the head entity tag detection task.

Joint Search on Embedding Spaces. If the head entity in a fact triple belongs to candidate head entities, then this fact is included in the candidate facts of the question. The model designs a joint distance measure of the structure and relationship information retained in KGE. The proposed joint distance metric is defined as:

$$\underset{(h,\ell,t)\in\mathcal{K}}{\text{minimize}} \|\mathrm{p}_\ell - \hat{\mathrm{p}}_\ell\|_2 + \beta_1 \|e_h - \hat{e}_h\|_2 + \beta_2 \|f(e_h, \mathrm{p}_\ell) - \hat{e}_t\|_2 \\ - \beta_3 \sin [n(h), \text{HED}_{\text{entity}}] - \beta_4 \sin [n(\ell), \text{HED}_{\text{non}}]. \tag{12}$$

Function $n(.)$ returns the name of the entity or predicate. HEDentity and HEDnon denote the tokens that are classified as entity name and non-entity name by the HED model. Function $sim[\cdot, \cdot]$ measures the similarity of two strings. Function $f(.)$ define as the KG embedding algorithm. β_1, β_2, β_3, and β_4 are predefined weights to balance the contribution of each term. Finally, according to the ranking results, the most appropriate facts are selected from the candidate set, and the tail entity of the fact triple is used as the final answer.

3.2   Recommendation Systems

DKN. The DKN model [16] is an online news recommendation system that provides customers with personalized news recommendations. Unlike other recommendation systems, news recommendation systems are full of knowledge entities and common sense because of the high concentration of news language. DKN is a content-based deep recommendation framework for click prediction. It takes candidate news and a set of user click news history as input and calculates the prediction probability of a user clicking candidate news. The key component of DKN is a multi-channel and word-entity-aligned knowledge-aware convolutional neural network (KCNN) that fuses semantic-level and knowledge-level representations of news. KCNN is an extension of the traditional CNN model, which allows the flexible integration of knowledge in knowledge graphs into sentence representation learning. After extracting knowledge from candidate news, the KCNN module stacks the word embedding, entity embedding, and context embedding of the candidate news as the initialization input of the module. The three embedded matrices are aligned and stacked as follows:

$$\bar{e} = \frac{1}{|\text{context}(e)|} \sum_{e_i \in \text{context}(e)} \mathbf{e}_i, \tag{13}$$

$$W = [[\mathbf{w}_1 g(\mathbf{e}_1) g(\bar{\mathbf{e}}_1)] [\mathbf{w}_2 g(\mathbf{e}_2) g(\bar{\mathbf{e}}_2)] \ldots [\mathbf{w}_n g(\mathbf{e}_n) g(\bar{\mathbf{e}}_n)]] \in \mathbb{R}^{d \times n \times 3}, \tag{14}$$

where $\mathbf{w}_{1:n}$ represents the word embedding, $g(e_{1:n})$ represents the transformed entity embeddings, and $g(\bar{e}_{1:n})$ represents the transformed context embeddings.

Through the KCNN module, the embedding of candidate news and user click news can be obtained. Then the attention module can be used to convert user clicks into user embeddings. Finally, DNN is used to calculate the probability of the user clicking on the news. We use the AUC score of DKN as an indicator of recommendation performance.

Translational Models for Item Recommendation. The above two downstream task models both use KGE as auxiliary information to help downstream models better complete their tasks, while this model uses the semantic translation model to recommend products directly. It does not belong to the downstream application task of KGE, but we still take it as the evaluation index of KGE model in different spaces. The reason is that we analyze the process of the model and find that the final evaluation index of the model is the performance of completing missing facts. Wang et al. [19] proposed that the traditional ER is not suitable for the task of knowledge base completion (KBC) performance evaluation due to its limitations, but the PR protocol they proposed is not suitable for application model datasets because of high computational cost. The task of this model is to recommend products (tail entities) to users (head entities). In short, it is to complete the original KG triples (users, recommendations, products). Different from ER protocol and PR protocol, this model can not only effectively measure the performance of model KBC but also test large-scale datasets. We use P@5 as an indicator of model recommendation performance [13].

4   Experimental Study

We use KGE downstream task models introduced in Sect. 3 to conduct experimental studies to evaluate the performance of various KGE models in different spaces. All datasets, experimental results, and source code in the experimental research are public, and for the convenience of other research works, we also provide data and log information generated during the experimental intermediate process. For all embedding models in different spaces, we evaluate the performance of different dimensions and different downstream tasks of KGE, so as to explore the characteristics of embedding models in different spaces and provide suggestions and help for future research on KGE and downstream task models. Experimental results show that the existing KGE model's ability to acquire knowledge is overestimated, and the traditional measurement protocol may even lead to misleading conclusions. We find that the HyperKG and RotatE models based on non-Euclidean space can provide excellent performance for KGE downstream tasks. As for models in Euclidean space, the performance of TransE, TransH, and TransR lags behind, especially the TransR model with a more complex structure performs the worst on most downstream tasks. The experimental results show that KGE models based on non-Euclidean space generalizing points to relaxed geometric forms can effectively improve the ability of KGE model entity embedding and relation embedding. KGE models based on Euclidean space limit their performance because of extremely strict geometrical forms. Modifying embeddings by considering more complex KG structural information may not achieve improvements in practical applications. When the embedding models rely too much on additional information, the performance of embedding the entity and relationship will decrease.

4.1   Hyperparameter Settings of KGE

To keep effort tractable, we verify the MRR (for ER) of the data according to the datasets to select the best hyperparameters. For the embedding models in different presentation spaces, we performed an exhaustive grid search on the following hyperparameter settings: learning rate $\eta \in \{0.0001, 0.001, 0.01, 0.05, 0.1\}$, margin hyperparameter $\gamma \in \{0.5, 1, 2, 3, 4\}$. In order to analyze the relationship between the dimensions of the embedding models and the downstream tasks of KGE, we select the best hyperparameters in different dimensions of $de \in \{50, 100, 150, 200, 250, 300\}$ to obtain the final model. We trained each model for up to 1000 epochs during the grid search. Therefore, the expression ability of the embedding models is maximized.

4.2   Experiments on KEQA

Datasets. Instead of the typical evaluation of embedding models, we use the real dataset corresponding to the specific downstream application model. The subsets of traditional knowledge graphs (such as FB15K, WN18, FB-237, etc.) are not suitable for downstream models, and the scale of these datasets is too

Table 1. The statistics of the question answering datasets.

	FB2M	FB5M	SimpleQuestions
# Relations	4,641	5,279	1,837
# Entities	647,657	751,227	131,681
# Training	1,604,874	1,780,111	75,910
# Validation	N.A	N.A	10,845
# Test	N.A	N.A	21,687

Table 2. The performance of KEQA with different objective functions on FB2M.

	$\|\mathbf{p}_\ell - \hat{\mathbf{p}}_\ell\|_2$	$\|\mathbf{e}_h - \hat{\mathbf{e}}_h\|_2$	$\|f(\mathbf{e}_h, \mathbf{p}_\ell) - \hat{\mathbf{e}}_t\|_2$
TransE	0.701	0.173	0.703
TransH	0.711	0.185	0.727
TransR	0.714	0.171	0.734
ManifoldE sphere	N.A	N.A	N.A
RotatE	0.716	0.188	**0.738**
HyperKG	**0.723**	**0.196**	0.727

small to be necessary for research in this experiment. We first introduce the knowledge graph subset and question answering dataset used in KEQA model experiments.

FB2M and FB5M: Freebase is a real and credible KG dataset. The commonly used data sets for evaluating KGE models, such as FB15K and FB237, are all subsets of Freebase. The KEQA model uses two large subsets of Freebase: FB2M and FB5M. Their corresponding statistics are shown in Table 1, and the repeated facts have been deleted.

SimpleQuestions: It contains more than ten thousand simple questions associated with corresponding facts. All these facts belong to FB2M. It has been used as the benchmark for the recent QA-KG methods [2,4,10].

Performance Results. In order to evaluate the effect of KGE on the performance of KEQA model under different embedding spaces, the embedding algorithm mentioned in Sect. 2 is applied to the dataset FB2M or FB5M to learn P and E. Note that P and E are not the additional sources of information. Then, the KEQA model is applied to predict the header entities and predicates of each question in the test set. The performance of the model is measured by the accuracy of predicting header entities and predicates, and the evaluation criteria are defined as accurate predictions of new questions. The performance of KEQA that based on different KGE models on SimpleQuestions about FB2M and FB5M are listed in Fig. 1(a) and Fig. 1(b), respectively.

From graph (a) and (b) in Fig. 1, we can clearly find that the performance of the embedding models in different spaces in the KEQA task is divided into three parts. It is worth noting that Manifold Sphere model is precarious, and its embedding performance is random. This is related to the algebraic form and embedding space of the Manifold Sphere model. The embedding of spherical space depends too much on the initialization of the sphere radius, which directly determines the upper limit of embedding performance of the model. Therefore, unlike other models, the Manifold Sphere model in spherical embedding space has poor robustness and poor embedding performance overall. Besides, the performance of KEQA based on semantic translation models is significantly better than that based on semantic matching models, and as the dimensions increase, the performance of KEQA based on semantic translation models continues to improve. In contrast, the performance of KEQA based on semantic matching continues to decline. For semantic translation-based models, the performance of the embedding models in non-Euclidean space is more satisfactory than that of the Euclidean space, especially when embedding at a low dimension. This means that HyperKG in hyperbolic embedding space and RotatE in complex vector space can successfully and efficiently capture the structural and semantic features of entities and relationships. For the embedding models such as TransE, TransH, and TransR in the traditional Euclidean space, there is no significant difference in performance when the embedding dimension is less than 200. But as the dimensions increase, the TransH and TransR models with stronger generalization capabilities achieve better results. The performance of each model declines on the larger data scale FB5M dataset but remained consistent on the whole.

To better understand the performance changes of different KGE models, we study three terms dependent on KGE model in the KEQA objective function (Eq. 12) and analyze the influence of embedding models on related terms in the KEQA objective function under different spaces. We choose the embedding dimension with the best performance and perform three sets of experiments, respectively. Each set of experiments only retains one of the terms as the new objective function. The performance of KEQA with different objective functions on FB2M is summarized in Table 2.

From the results in Table 2, we draw three main observations. First, HyperKG and RotatE can provide better embedding and improve prediction accuracy in the module of predicate representation prediction and the module of head entity representation prediction. Second, among the embedding methods based on Euclidean space, although TransR can provide better relational embedding, its entity embedding performance is inferior. In addition, we find that TransH's entity embedding performs significantly better than TransE and TransR, which is different from our normal cognition.

4.3   Experiments on DKN

Datasets. The news data for the DKN experiments came from Bing News' server logs. Each log mainly includes the user id, news title, news url, timestamp, and click identifier (0 means no click, 1 means click). The news dataset is divided into two parts, which are randomly sampled from October 16, 2016, to June 11, 2017, as a training set, and randomly selected from June 12, 2017, to August 11, 2017, as a test set. Besides, the original author of the model retrieves all entities that appear in the dataset and entities within their one hop in Microsoft Satori knowledge graph, and extract all edges (triples) with confidence greater than 0.8 among them. Table 3 shows the basic statistics of the news dataset and the extracted knowledge graph. After a simple analysis of the dataset distribution, we find that the average word count of each news headline is 7.9 words and the entity word count is 3.7 words, which indicates that entities occupy almost half of news headlines. The high frequency of the entity in the news headline indicates the importance of the entity, hence, the embedding effect of the entity will have a significant impact on the performance of the model.

Table 3. The statistics of the extracted knowledge graph.

	The extracted knowledge graph
# Relations	1,166
# Entities	36,350
# Triples	772,258
avg.# entities per title	3.7

Performance Results. The comparison results of different KGE models are shown in Fig. 1(c). The critical components of DKN model and KCNN mainly make use of entity embedding and context embedding, so the final performance of DKN model depends on the entity embedding of KGE models. There are several main conclusions to be drawn from this observation. First, the performance of DKN models based on different KGE models shows a clear hierarchical structure, and there is a vast difference in performance between different KGE models. HyperKG based on hyperbolic space has the best performance, while RotatE based on complex vector space is slightly inferior, but both are better than the Trans series based on Euclidean space. Second, we find that the dimensions of entity embedding have little effect on the final performance of the DKN model. The reason is that in KCNN, the word embedding, entity embedding, and context embedding need to be uniformly mapped to the same dimension (50 dimensions), so the difference brought by the entity embedding dimension is eliminated during the compression process. Third, TransH performance based on Euclidean space is significantly better than TransR. Although TransR is an optimization model for TransH, the entity embedding ability is worse than TransH. It is worth noting that TransR improves the generalization ability of the model by embedding entities and relationships in different spaces, and can effectively deal with multi-relationship problems. However, a part of the semantic information is embedded in the transformation matrix at the same time, which may be the cause of the poor embedding performance of TransR.

4.4 Experiments on Item Recommendation

Datasets. The dataset is MoviesLens 1M [5]. MoviesLens 1M is a classic dataset for evaluating recommendation systems, and it contains 1,000,209 anonymous ratings of approximately 3,900 movies made by 6,040 MovieLens users. Enrico Palumbo et al. [12] construct corresponding knowledge graphs using mapped DBpedia data. Furthermore, We purify the knowledge graph to get a refined dataset. The basic statistics of the knowledge graph constructed are shown in Table 4.

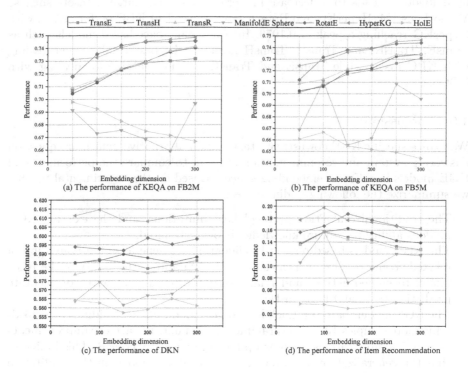

Fig. 1. Results of downstream tasks using different KGE.

Table 4. The statistics of MovieLens 1M datasets.

	MovieLens 1M
# Relations	19
# Entities	29,166
# Triples	3,974,676

Performance Results. Unlike the other two KGE downstream application models, the item recommendation task is to use the translation model to recommend products for users. Instead of measuring the ability of the KGE model to embed entities or relationships, it measures the KBC performance of the entire KGE model, that is, the ability to complete triples of facts that did not exist currently. The comparison of the results of different KGE models is shown in Fig. 1(d). We find that the KBC performance of most embedding models is related to dimensions, and KBC performance is maximized at 100–150 dimensions. After that, as the dimension increases, the more noise introduced by embedding leads to a decrease in performance. For large datasets such as MoviesLens 1M, HyperKG and RotatE have a excellent KBC performance, with HyperKG reaching a peak of 0.1976. In Euclidean space-based models such as TransE, TransH, and TransR, TransH achieves the best results when dealing with KBC tasks, while TransE and TransR are not suitable for dealing with KBC tasks.

4.5   Discussion

We utilize specific KGE downstream tasks as an alternative, which are question answering system and recommendation system, to compare the performance of KGE models in different embedding spaces. Based on the experimental results, we summarize the following findings:

- The traditional evaluation protocol has limitations, and the existing KGE model's ability to capture knowledge is overestimated.
- The KGE models based on non-Euclidean space generalize the points into a relaxed geometric form, which can effectively improve the ability of the KGE model to embed entities and relationships, especially in terms of accurate prediction tasks and KBC tasks;
- The KGE models based on Euclidean space, modifying embeddings by considering more complex KG structural information may not achieve improvements in practical applications, such as updating TransE to TransR. This indicates that the generalization improvement of embedded models in the traditional Euclidean space cannot improve their performance, especially when the models rely on the transformation matrix excessively.

5   Conclusion

We investigate whether the current KGE models based on different embedding spaces can provide good support for KGE downstream application tasks, as well as the differences between the models. We believe that the commonly used KGE evaluation protocol is inappropriate for answering these two questions, and take the downstream task as an alternative. The experimental results prove this hypothesis, traditional evaluation protocols overestimate the ability of the KGE model to capture knowledge, and many KGE models perform poorly in downstream tasks. Besides, we found that using Non-Euclidean space as embedding space is an effective generalization method, which can improve the ability of model knowledge acquisition and enrich knowledge characteristics.

Acknowledgements. We are very grateful to Professor Li Xue of the Neusoft for his help in this article. This work is supported in part by the National Natural Science Foundation of China (grants No. 61772268 and 61906037); State Key Laboratory for smart grid protection and operation control Foundation; Association of Chinese Graduate Education (ACGE); the Fundamental Research Funds for the Central Universities (NS2018057, NJ2018014).

References

1. Abujabal, A., Yahya, M., Riedewald, M., Weikum, G.: Automated template generation for question answering over knowledge graphs. In: Proceedings of the 26th international Conference on World Wide Web, pp. 1191–1200. International World Wide Web Conferences Steering Committee (2017)
2. Bordes, A., Usunier, N., Chopra, S., Weston, J.: Large-scale simple question answering with memory networks. arXiv preprint arXiv:1506.02075 (2015)
3. Bordes, A., Usunier, N., Garcia-Duran, A., Weston, J., Yakhnenko, O.: Translating embeddings for modeling multi-relational data. In: Advances in Neural Information Processing Systems, pp. 2787–2795 (2013)
4. Golub, D., He, X.: Character-level question answering with attention. arXiv preprint arXiv:1604.00727 (2016)
5. Harper, F.M., Konstan, J.A.: The movielens datasets: history and context. ACM Trans. Interact. Intell. Syst. (TIIS) 5(4), 1–19 (2015)
6. Huang, X., Zhang, J., Li, D., Li, P.: Knowledge graph embedding based question answering. In: Proceedings of the Twelfth ACM International Conference on Web Search and Data Mining, pp. 105–113. ACM (2019)
7. Kolyvakis, P., Kalousis, A., Kiritsis, D.: HyperKG: hyperbolic knowledge graph embeddings for knowledge base completion. arXiv preprint arXiv:1908.04895 (2019)
8. Lin, Y., Liu, Z., Sun, M., Liu, Y., Zhu, X.: Learning entity and relation embeddings for knowledge graph completion. In: Twenty-Ninth AAAI Conference on Artificial Intelligence (2015)
9. Mikolov, T., Yih, W.T., Zweig, G.: Linguistic regularities in continuous space word representations. In: Proceedings of the 2013 Conference of the North American Chapter of the Association for Computational Linguistics: Human Language Technologies, pp. 746–751 (2013)
10. Mohammed, S., Shi, P., Lin, J.: Strong baselines for simple question answering over knowledge graphs with and without neural networks. In: Proceedings of NAACL-HLT, pp. 291–296 (2018)
11. Nickel, M., Rosasco, L., Poggio, T.: Holographic embeddings of knowledge graphs. In: Thirtieth AAAI Conference on Artificial Intelligence (2016)
12. Palumbo, E., Rizzo, G., Troncy, R., Baralis, E., Osella, M., Ferro, E.: Translational models for item recommendation. In: Gangemi, A., et al. (eds.) ESWC 2018. LNCS, vol. 11155, pp. 478–490. Springer, Cham (2018). https://doi.org/10.1007/978-3-319-98192-5_61
13. Steck, H.: Evaluation of recommendations: rating-prediction and ranking. In: Proceedings of the 7th ACM Conference on Recommender Systems, pp. 213–220. ACM (2013)

14. Sun, Z., Deng, Z.H., Nie, J.Y., Tang, J.: Rotate: knowledge graph embedding by relational rotation in complex space. arXiv preprint arXiv:1902.10197 (2019)
15. Wang, G., et al.: Label-free distant supervision for relation extraction via knowledge graph embedding. In: Proceedings of the 2018 Conference on Empirical Methods in Natural Language Processing, pp. 2246–2255 (2018)
16. Wang, H., Zhang, F., Xie, X., Guo, M.: DKN: deep knowledge-aware network for news recommendation. In: Proceedings of the 2018 World Wide Web Conference, pp. 1835–1844. International World Wide Web Conferences Steering Committee (2018)
17. Wang, M., Liu, M., Liu, J., Wang, S., Long, G., Qian, B.: Safe medicine recommendation via medical knowledge graph embedding. arXiv preprint arXiv:1710.05980 (2017)
18. Wang, Q., Mao, Z., Wang, B., Guo, L.: Knowledge graph embedding: a survey of approaches and applications. IEEE Trans. Knowl. Data Eng. **29**(12), 2724–2743 (2017)
19. Wang, Y., Ruffinelli, D., Gemulla, R., Broscheit, S., Meilicke, C.: On evaluating embedding models for knowledge base completion. arXiv preprint arXiv:1810.07180 (2018)
20. Wang, Z., Zhang, J., Feng, J., Chen, Z.: Knowledge graph embedding by translating on hyperplanes. In: Twenty-Eighth AAAI Conference on Artificial Intelligence (2014)
21. Xiao, H., Huang, M., Zhu, X.: From one point to a manifold: knowledge graph embedding for precise link prediction. arXiv preprint arXiv:1512.04792 (2015)
22. Zhang, F., Yuan, N.J., Lian, D., Xie, X., Ma, W.Y.: Collaborative knowledge base embedding for recommender systems. In: Proceedings of the 22nd ACM SIGKDD International Conference on Knowledge Discovery and Data Mining, pp. 353–362. ACM (2016)

Learning to Answer Complex Questions with Evidence Graph

Gao Gu[1], Bohan Li[1,2,3], Han Gao[1], and Meng Wang[4(✉)]

[1] Nanjing University of Aeronautics and Astronautics, Nanjing 211100, China
[2] Key Laboratory of Safety-Critical Software, Ministry of Industry and Information Technology, Nanjing 211100, China
[3] Collaborative Innovation Center of Novel Software Technology and Industrialization, Nanjing 210000, Jiangsu, China
[4] Southeast University, Nanjing 211100, China
meng.wang@seu.edu.cn

Abstract. Text-based end-to-end question answering (QA) systems have attracted more attention for their good robustness and excellent performance in dealing with complex questions. However, this kind of method lacks certain interpretability, which is essential for the QA system. For instance, the interpretability of answers is particularly significant in the medical field, in that interpretable answers are more credible and apt to acception. The methods based on knowledge graph (KG) can improve the interpretability, but suffer from the problems of incompleteness and sparseness of KG. In this paper, we propose a novel method (EGQA) to solve complex question answering via combining text and KG. We use Wikipedia as a text source to extract documents related to the question and extract triples from the documents to construct a raw graph (i.e., a small-scale KG). Then, we extract the evidence graphs from the raw graph and adopt Attention-based Graph Neural Network (AGNN) to embed them to find the answer. Our experiments conduct on a real medical dataset Head-QA, which shows that our approach can effectively improve the interpretability and performance of complex question answering.

Keywords: Question answering · Evidence graph · Neural network

1 Introduction

QA systems provide people with needed information and are widely used in many fields, such as medical, financial, and e-commerce [3]. Most approaches are focused on answering simple questions, while complex questions have always been one of the challenges in QA. Great use of data is available with the widespread usage of the internet, which provides one of the best sources to obtain information and accelerate the development of the text-based QA system [8]. With the rapid development of deep learning, text-based end-to-end QA systems emerge in recent years, which has achieved better performance in answering complex

© Springer Nature Switzerland AG 2020
X. Wang et al. (Eds.): APWeb-WAIM 2020, LNCS 12317, pp. 257–269, 2020.
https://doi.org/10.1007/978-3-030-60259-8_20

questions with good robustness. However, this kind of approach also has an apparent weakness, which is the lack of interpretability. Interpretability is essential and necessary in many domains, especially in the medical field, where the uninterpretable answer is often not trusted enough to be adopted by medical staff when it comes to the vital health of patients. As shown in Fig. 1, the text-based end-to-end QA system outputs the answer without interpretability.

Recently, with the emergence of KG, numerous KG-based QA methods have been proposed [5]. For a given natural language problem, the KG-based QA system mainly solves it by semantically parsing, and then make use of the KG to query and deduce to obtain the answer. On account of the characteristics of KG's structure, this kind of method can provide the interpretability of answers by outputting the subgraph related to the questions and answers. However, the existing KG is suffering from the problems of incomplete and sparse, which limits the performance of KG-based QA approaches. As shown in Fig. 1, the KG-based QA system cannot find the answer to this question due to the incompleteness of KG.

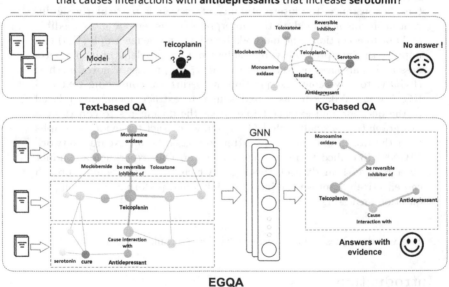

Fig. 1. A text-based QA system can find the answer but cannot provide nterpretability, while the KG-based QA system cannot find the answer because the missing node in the KG. Our approach EGQA can find the answer with interpretability.

For this reason, we propose a method (EGQA) to answer complex questions by combining text and KG, which can make up for the weakness of the two kinds of methods and provide interpretability while improving the performance. Our method includes three parts. Firstly, we use Wikipedia as the source of the text, extract the five most relevant documents according to the question. Then, we extract the triples from documents to construct a raw graph (i.e., a small-scale knowledge graph), and the raw graph is denoised and optimized to obtain several candidate evidence graphs, and AGNN is used to embed them to obtain the feature of question. At last, we adopt the TextCNN to embed the question and compare it with the candidate evidence graphs to find the most relevant evidence graph to obtain the candidate nodes of answer and rank the candidate nodes to find the final answer. As shown in Fig. 1, through our method, an interpretable answer is found.

The main contributions of this paper are as follows:

- We propose a novel model combining text and KG to answer complex questions, which makes up for the deficiency of previous works;
- We provide interpretability of the answer with guaranteed accuracy, making the answer more credible;
- We verify our model on a real-world medical dataset, and the results demonstrate that the model can effectively improve the performance of complex questions with interpretability.

2   Related Work

2.1   Text-Based End-to-end QA Systems

Text-based end-to-end QA system commonly can be divided into three subtasks: question analysis, document retrieval, and answer generation, the different processing of the three subtasks result in different approaches. With the development of machine learning, the performance of text-based end-to-end systems has improved in recent years.

Hermann et al. [9] defined an approach to solving machine reading tasks and provides large-scale supervised reading comprehension data, which can learn to read real documents and answer complex questions with little prior knowledge of language structure. Hewlett et al. [10] presented WIKIREADING, a large-scale natural language understanding task, and publicly-available dataset. Its task is to predict the value of text from Wikipedia's structured knowledge base by reading the text of the corresponding article in Wikipedia. Wang et al. [18] presented the gated self-matching networks for reading comprehension style QA, which is designed to answer questions in a given document. Yu et al. [22] proposed a novel QA architecture called QANet. Instead of recurrent networks, its encoder only contains convolution and self-attention, where convolution models local interactions and self-attention models global interactions. Xiao et al. [20] proposed a multi-hop QA model, which can find the answers from multiple related documents. Lu et al. [14] proposed a new unsupervised method that combines evidence from multiple documents retrieved dynamically to answer complex questions. Although text-based end-to-end QA systems use powerful machine learning models to improve performance and increase the accuracy of answers effectively, such methods lack interpretability and lead to reduced reliability of the answers.

2.2 Knowledge Graph-Based QA Systems

The traditional knowledge graph-based question answering system can be divided into three types. The first one is based on semantic parsing [1]. The main idea is to convert natural language into a series of logical forms, which can express the entire question to semantics, and then query in the knowledge graph through a query language to find the answer. These approaches rely on the first step of semantic parsing from natural language to logical forms, which has the problem of the error transmission, resulting in poor performance of the models and low recall rate. The second is based on information extraction [12]. This type of method extracts the entities in the question and queries the knowledge graph to obtain the subgraph centered on the entity. Each node or edge in the subgraph can be used as a candidate answer. Although this kind of method can improve the recall rate, it is still limited by the incompleteness of the KG because it depends on the mapping from natural language to the KG. The third is based on vector modeling [2]. The questions and candidate answers are embedded in distributed representation. The distributed representations are trained by training data to make the score of the vector representation of the questions and correct answers as high as possible. This type of method effectively avoids errors in semantic parsing and improves the performance of models. However, these methods are also limited by the incompleteness of KG. In recent years, with the rapid development of deep learning, the mainstream knowledge graph-based QA systems mainly utilize deep learning to improve traditional methods and have achieved excellent performance. However, all of these models focus on improving the performance of QA systems but make the interpretability worse and worse.

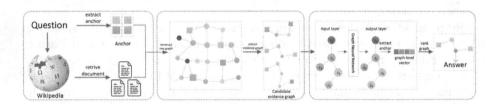

Fig. 2. Overview of EGQA

3 Our Methods

As shown in Fig. 2, we mainly introduce our model from four parts: (1) find documents from Wikipedia according to the given question, (2) build the raw graph based on the SPO (Subject-Predication-Object) triples extracted from the documents, (3) extract the candidate evidence graphs from the raw graph, and (4) use the AGNN to find the most relevant evidence graph to find the final answer. We elaborate on each part in the following subsections.

3.1   Document Retrieval

To reduce the search cost, we adopt a classic document retrieval system proposed by [4]. This system converts all articles into TF-IDF (Term Frequency - Inverse Document Frequency) weighted bag-of-word vectors. Assume that m documents form a collection of documents: $D = \{N_1, N_2, \ldots, N_m\}$, and the number of occurrences of the phrase j in the document N_j is denoted as C_{ij}, the TF and IDF of the phrase j are:

$$\text{TF} = \frac{C_{ij}}{\sum_{j=1}^{n} C_{ij}}, \tag{1}$$

$$\text{IDF} = \log \frac{m}{h+1}, \tag{2}$$

where n is the number of phrase j in document N_i, and h is the total number of documents containing phrase j. Thus, the comprehensive frequency of phrase j in the document N_j can be calculated as $\text{TF} * \text{IDF}$. We utilize bigram counts as the participle model, and then map each phrase to a hash value using the feature hash table [19], and we can encode each documents into a dictionary containing the frequencies of each phrase.

After extracting the most related documents, we define each set of information in the document as a triple of two entities and a relationship which is represented as (S, P, O). We adopt Open IE [15] to extract the required information and use the NLTK package to perform POS tagging and NER on the extracted documents in the preprocessing. As for the processing of SPO triples, we use named entities and the extracted tokens as the processing objects respectively. Regarding triples, we mainly extract them based on the dependency syntax. After eliminating irrelevant words without dependent structure, the results of dependency syntactic analysis are analyzed together with specific statements to generate triples.

Since the SPO triples depend on different text during extraction, the quality of the triples varies. We use the same procedure as [14] to take the paired distance between the parts of the triples as the confidence index of each triple relationship. Suppose that in a SPO triple, the distance of S and P, P and O are d_1 and d_2, the confidence indices of $S - P$ and $P - O$ are:

$$b_{S-P} = \frac{1}{d_1 + 1}, \tag{3}$$

$$b_{P-O} = \frac{1}{d_2 + 1}. \tag{4}$$

When the same SPO pair appears in different documents $\{S_i\}$, their common score is:

$$b = \sum_{s_i} \frac{1}{d_i + 1}. \tag{5}$$

3.2 Raw Graph Construction

We use graphs to represent the knowledge involved in the documents. We form the raw graph based on the SPO triples extracted from the related documents, and then extract the candidate evidence graphs. The raw graph is represented as $G = (V, E)$ where V is the set of nodes and E is the set of edges.

A complex question often requires information from multiple documents and we use triples from multiple documents to build the raw graph. In contrast to the other models, this may generate a lot of noise and synonym entities which can be resolved in the subsequent extraction process. In order to determine the importance of different nodes, we assign different weights to nodes and edges during the construction process. The allocation of weights is mainly based on the premise that the more an item is relevant to the token mentioned in the question, the more important it is to solve the problem.

We refer to the method proposed by [14], which does not take the predicate in the triple as an edge but as a single node, i.e., each SPO triple can form two entity nodes and one predicate nodes in the graph. If the node S or node O already exist in the graph, an edge will be extended from the existing node to connect the new node. Due to the same entity node may appear in different forms in multiple triples, we use entity-mention dictionary [11], a dictionary (shown as Table 1) compiled from a large knowledge base, including the probability that the same text form points to different standard entities.

Table 1. Mention dictionary

Mention	Entity	Probability
007	007_(Shanty_Town)	0.1000
007	5th_Ward_Boyz	0.0182
007	James_Bond	0.1318
007	James_Bond_(literary_character)	0.3045

We can calculate the similarity of two nodes via this dictionary, i.e., when two nodes have the same standard form of entity e, the similarity is the difference of probabilities, otherwise the similarity is zero. The similarity of two word phrases i, j can be calculated as:

$$\text{sim}_{i,j} = \begin{cases} |\text{dic}\,[i, e] - \text{dic}\,[j, e]|, & i \rightarrow e \text{ and } j \rightarrow e \\ 0, & \not\exists\ e \end{cases}, \quad (6)$$

where dic denotes mention dictionary. When there are two nodes whose similarity exceeds the threshold, we connect them by a bidirectional edge, whether the node is an entity or a predicate. When setting the weight of each node, we first observe whether there is a standard entity e pointed by both a token of the question and the node. If there is and the similarity is higher than the threshold, it is used as the weight; otherwise, the similarity is set as zero. The weight of node v is calculated as:

$$W_v = \begin{cases} \text{sim}_{v,q}, & \text{sim}_{v,q} > S \\ 0, & \text{sim}_{v,q} < S \end{cases}, \tag{7}$$

where q is the token of the question which is close to the node v, and S is the threshold. With regard to the edges in the triples, we use the confidence index obtained in the previous extraction as the weight:

$$W_e = b_{v1-v2}, \tag{8}$$

where v_1 and v_2 are the two nodes connected by the edge e. The articles in Wikipedia often contain descriptions of the entity, and the characteristics of its syntactic patterns are very easy to profile. For example, we can extract the attribute relation like *(xenobiotic, chemical substance)* and establish the corresponding attribute node from the statement *"A xenobiotic is a chemical substance found within an organism that is not naturally produced or expected to be present within the organism"*, the attribute node can perform filtering function when ranking the answer node later.

3.3 Evidence Graph Construction

After constructing the raw graph, we need to find the relevant nodes with the question in the raw graph. Here we use the previous entity-mention dictionary to find the nodes that have a certain degree of similarity to the token in the question and regard them as anchors to extract key information.

Definition 1 (Anchor). *Suppose there is a token set $\{q_1, q_2, q_3, ..., q_n\}$ in the question, when there is node v in the raw graph, it meets the condition $\text{sim}_{v,q_i} > S$ with any question token q_i, where S is the similarity threshold, then we called node v as an anchor.*

After getting the anchors, our goal is to construct the evidence graphs containing the answer node from the raw graph.

Definition 2 (Evidence Graph). *Suppose there is token set $\{q_1, q_2, q_3, ..., q_n\}$ in the question, and each token q_i corresponds to a collection of corresponding anchors set as $\{V_1^i, V_2^i ... V_n^i\}$, and if there is a subgraph (V, E), where V contains at least one node in each anchor set, then we call it as an evidence graph.*

In the process of evidence graph construction, in order to improve the efficiency and accuracy, it is necessary to ensure that the number of edges is as small as possible and the sum of weights is as large as possible. Regarding the construction of evidence graphs, we refer to the classic algorithm as [6]. we use each anchor node as the initial state of a tree and make them grow synchronously. We select the edges and nodes with larger weights at each step. When two trees meet, we merge them; when any tree covers at least one node in each anchor node set, the tree stops growing and exists as a candidate evidence graph. We set a maximum value to limit the number of candidate evidence graphs, and select graphs with larger comprehensive weight when there are candidate results more than the limited number.

3.4 Answer Generation

After obtaining the candidate evidence graphs of the question, we need to choose the graph which can obtain the correct answer. The previous method [21] compares graphs by analyzing the differences between nodes, which only mechanically calculates the features at the node level of the graph, lacking the analysis of the overall structure. Hence, we utilize AGNN [16] to analyze the features of candidate evidence graphs.

When training the model of the evidence graph, we need a standard value to form the loss with the output of evidence graph. We use TextCNN [13] to obtain a vector representation of a question, which first encodes the question as a collection of tokens, and then converts each token into a word2vec vector that we have pre-trained according to Wikipedia. After extracting features from the one-dimensional convolutional layer, the set consisting of these word vectors enter a MaxPooling layer to make the length of the sentence vectors uniform, and the final output vector V_q can be used as a question representation when constructing candidate graphs later.

AGNN [16] is a model based on GNN to process graphs with state of the art performance. It replaces the original fully-connected layers with the attention mechanism, which can make each node in the graph learn the characteristics of neighboring nodes dynamically and adaptively during the propagate process, and reduce parameters to improve efficiency at the same time. The AGNN estimates which neighbor is more relevant to the node during each iteration of the graph node and measures its contribution accordingly.

For an evidence graph G, we extract all the nodes and edges from it, where the edges are encoded in COO format, i.e., set up two lists, and the first list contains the index of the source node, while the index of the target node is specified in the second list. Regarding the nodes, we use the vector of word2vec obtained from Wikipedia to go through a linear layer as the initialization state of each node:

$$H_i^{(1)} = W^T X_i + b, \tag{9}$$

We applied AGGN's attention-based propagation layer to realize information intersection between nodes. Different from the previous GNN, AGNN uses scalars to transfer information between a node and its neighbors in each propagation layer:

$$H^{(t+1)} = P^{(t)} H^{(t)}, \tag{10}$$

where $P^{(t)}$ is a matrix of $n * n$, n represents the number of nodes, each element in the matrix represents the delivery parameters of two nodes, the parameters of non-adjacent nodes are represented by zero. The propagation mode of the nodes is as follows:

$$H^{(t+1)} = \sum_{j \in N(i) \cup \{i\}} P_{ij}^{(t)} H_j^{(t)}, \tag{11}$$

$$P_i^{(t)} = \mathrm{softmax}\left(\left[\beta^{(t)} \cos\left(H_i^{(t)}, H_j^{(t)}\right)\right]_{j \in N(i) \cup \{i\}}\right), \tag{12}$$

where *cos* represents the cosine similarity of two vectors, and $N(i)$ represents the neighbors of node i in the graph.

In terms of output, we take the output vector with anchor in the model to pass through the previous TextCNN, and take its representation in the hidden layer as the final graph-level output vector. After obtaining the target evidence graph, we select the entity nodes other than the anchors as the candidate answers, and then rank the candidate answers by comparing the type node of the answer with the predict type of the answer to find the final answer.

4 Experiments

4.1 Dataset

In our experiment, we use Wikipedia as the source of information. We apply wikiextractor[1], a python package that decoded all information on Wikipedia into text, with each keyword corresponding to a document, excluding the content other than text. Data in Wikipedia performs well in multiple areas of testing, indicating its wide coverage. Considering the application scenario of interpretable QA, we choose an area with high interpretable requirement which is medical, and chose a latest dataset containing complex questions. We extracted data from HEAD-QA [17], which consists a set of questions from exams to obtain a professional position in the Spanish health system that are challenging even for highly professional people. This dataset contains six specific subdivisions, and we selecte a total of 2288 questions in the two parts of Pharmacology and Medicine as our experimental dataset.

4.2 Baselines

To measure the effectiveness of our model, we choose two Text-based QA methods and two KG-based QA methods as baselines.

DrQA [4]: DrQA is an open domain question answering system based on RNN and multi-task learning, which is trained on a large-scale corpus.

QUEST [14]: QUEST is a question answering system based on document information extraction. It extracts the documents related to the question from the open corpus, then builds the documents into graphs, extracts the graphs through Steiner Tree, and finally outputs the answer nodes from the Steiner Tree.

STAGG [21]: STAGG is a KG-based QA system that turns questions into semantic graphs of a certain length and then turns the semantic graphs into SPARQL to query the answers in the knowledge graphs.

OQA [7]: OQA extracts information from different knowledge bases at same time. It analyzes the problem structure, and finally translates the question into a structured query statement to get an answer.

---

[1] https://github.com/attardi/wikiextractor.

Table 2. Statistics of the questions in HEAD-QA

Category	Question	Train	Graph	Positive	Negative
Pharmacology	1139	457	55721	523	55198
Medicine	1149	455	57723	567	57156

Table 3. Evaluation results on the HEAD-QA test set

	MRR	Hits@5	Precision@1
DrQA	0.327	0.341	0.312
QUEST	0.329	0.346	0.314
STAGG	0.286	0.324	0.278
OQA	0.276	0.312	0.269
EGQA	**0.354**	**0.361**	**0.335**

4.3 Training and Evaluation

During the training of AGNN, we use part of the data as the train set and validation set, the rest of the data as the test set. We need both positive and negative evidence graph of the question for training. So when we extract a candidate evidence graph from the documents for each question, we examine the non-anchor nodes for each candidate evidence graph, which is positive when a node is very close to the real answer, otherwise it is negative. The information about all the evidence graphs is shown in Table 2.

In each round of training, we calculate the features of the graph by taking the cosine similarity of the output vector of each evidence graph and the question vector as the reward function:

$$f(g) = \cos(v_g, v_q), \tag{13}$$

where v_g is the output vector of the graph g through AGNN, and v_q is the output vector of the question through TextCNN. Its loss function is set as:

$$\text{loss}(\mathbf{x}, \mathbf{y}) = \frac{\sum_i \max(0, (1 - x[y] + x[i]))}{x.\,\text{size}}, \tag{14}$$

where x is the set composed of the value of the evidence graph after the reward function, y is the distribution of the positive graph in x while i is the distribution of the remaining negative graph, and $x.$ size is the length of x. By calculating for the loss function, we can implement parameter updates for both TextCNN and AGNN. We use Adam optimizer to train the model with a learning rate as 0.01. In order to prevent overfitting of the model, we use a layer of Dropout in the model to actively forget some dimensions of the vector, and the forgetting rate is set at 30%. Since the word2vec vector dimension of the node is 300, we also added two linear layers to compress the vector.

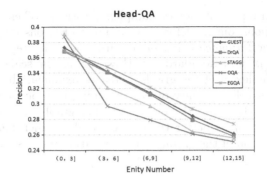

Fig. 3. Evaluation results by entity number

Since the evidence graph outputs a non-standard form of the answer extracted from the text, in order to adapt it to the multi-option characteristics of the dataset, we compare the output answer with all the options and select the one with the maximum percentage of the shared token as the selection object. Because there may be multiple answer nodes with different priorities in one evidence graph, we use the following evaluation metrics: the main metric is Mean Reciprocal Rank (MRR), we also adopt Precision@1 (P@1) the probability that the most likely answer node predicts accurately directly and Hits@k, the probability that the top-k answers contain the correct answer.

4.4 Results

As shown in Table 3, EGQA performed better than all the baselines in the test set. It can be proved that the system which extract documents from Wikipedia in real time and construct evidence graphs for complex question is proved to be more advantageous than the previous system. As can be seen from the Table 3, end-to-end methods such as DrQA perform significantly better than those purely KG-based QA methods such as OQA, and their performance is very close our method EGQA. This means that the end-to-end approaches can often extract more information from the text than the KG-based methods, and can achieve good results on complex questions on the basis of not pursuing interpretability.

Since our primary goal is to ensure efficiency while dealing with complex questions, we test performance for all models based on the complexity of questions. As shown in Fig. 3, when the number of the entities in the question is small, i.e., only a few entities are involved, the methods based on knowledge graph perform very well. This approach can guarantee the accuracy close to that of text-based QA, and can also provide the interpretability of the answer through the output of subgraph of KG. However, as the entities and relationships involved in the question increase, the accuracy of the KG-based QA methods decreases dramatically, largely due to the limitation that KG-based QA methods rely too much on the mapping from natural language to logical language or semantic graph, which often leads to poor representation on complex questions. When dealing with simple one-hop questions, our model is very similar to KG-based QA methods, but KG-based QA's performance is better because the entity representation of the knowledge graph is more standardized. However, as the scale of the questions increases, the complexity of the graph increases exponentially, so we can take advantage of the excellent ability of deep learning to process large-scale graph data to extract the characteristics of the evidence graphs. Our model in dealing with complex questions is better than other models which benefits from both information extraction of the graph and information process by deep learning.

5   Conclusion

In this paper, we propose a method to combine text and KG to solve complex questions. The method works by extracting knowledge graphs from wikipedia and using a trained graph neural network to get the answers. Experiments on the real dataset HEAD-QA show that our method can better deal with complex questions and provide interpretability compared with the baselines. In the future work, we intend to consider more methods in text information extraction to eliminate excessive noise in the raw graph and improve the accuracy of triples. At the same time, we also consider applying the idea of the current model to more tasks such as text reading comprehension. By extracting the text content in real time, we can analyze the importance of different sub-graphs of the raw graph, so as to extract the main body of the article and make an overview.

Acknowledgements. This work is supported in part by National Natural Science Foundation of China (grants No. 61772268 and 61906037); State Key Laboratory for smart grid protection and operation control Foundation; Association of Chinese Graduate Education (ACGE); the Fundamental Research Funds for the Central Universities (NS2018057, NJ2018014).

References

1. Bao, J., Duan, N., Yan, Z., Zhou, M., Zhao, T.: Constraint-based question answering with knowledge graph. In: Proceedings of COLING 2016, the 26th International Conference on Computational Linguistics: Technical Papers, pp. 2503–2514 (2016)
2. Bordes, A., Chopra, S., Weston, J.: Question answering with subgraph embeddings. arXiv preprint arXiv:1406.3676 (2014)
3. Bouziane, A., Bouchiha, D., Doumi, N., Malki, M.: Question answering systems: survey and trends. Procedia Comput. Sci. **73**, 366–375 (2015)
4. Chen, D., Fisch, A., Weston, J., Bordes, A.: Reading wikipedia to answer open-domain questions. arXiv preprint arXiv:1704.00051 (2017)
5. Diefenbach, D., Lopez, V., Singh, K., Maret, P.: Core techniques of question answering systems over knowledge bases: a survey. Knowl. Inf. Syst. **55**(3), 529–569 (2017). https://doi.org/10.1007/s10115-017-1100-y
6. Ding, B., Yu, J.X., Wang, S., Qin, L., Zhang, X., Lin, X.: Finding top-k min-cost connected trees in databases. In: 2007 IEEE 23rd International Conference on Data Engineering, pp. 836–845. IEEE (2007)

7. Fader, A., Zettlemoyer, L., Etzioni, O.: Open question answering over curated and extracted knowledge bases. In: Proceedings of the 20th ACM SIGKDD International Conference on Knowledge Discovery and Data Mining, pp. 1156–1165. ACM (2014)
8. Gupta, P., Gupta, V.: A survey of text question answering techniques. Int. J. Comput. Appl. **53**(4), 975–8887 (2012)
9. Hermann, K.M., et al.: Teaching machines to read and comprehend. In: Advances in neural information processing systems, pp. 1693–1701 (2015)
10. Hewlett, D., et al.: Wikireading: A novel large-scale language understanding task over wikipedia. arXiv preprint arXiv:1608.03542 (2016)
11. Hoffart, J., et al.: Robust disambiguation of named entities in text. In: Proceedings of the Conference on Empirical Methods in Natural Language Processing, pp. 782–792. Association for Computational Linguistics (2011)
12. Hu, S., Zou, L., Yu, J.X., Wang, H., Zhao, D.: Answering natural language questions by subgraph matching over knowledge graphs. IEEE Trans. Knowl. Data Eng. **30**(5), 824–837 (2017)
13. Kim, Y.: Convolutional neural networks for sentence classification. arXiv preprint arXiv:1408.5882 (2014)
14. Lu, X., Pramanik, S., Saha Roy, R., Abujabal, A., Wang, Y., Weikum, G.: Answering complex questions by joining multi-document evidence with quasi knowledge graphs. In: Proceedings of the 42nd International ACM SIGIR Conference on Research and Development in Information Retrieval, pp. 105–114. ACM (2019)
15. Mausam, M.: Open information extraction systems and downstream applications. In: Proceedings of the Twenty-Fifth International Joint Conference on Artificial Intelligence, pp. 4074–4077. AAAI Press (2016)
16. Thekumparampil, K.K., Wang, C., Oh, S., Li, L.J.: Attention-based graph neural network for semi-supervised learning. arXiv preprint arXiv:1803.03735 (2018)
17. Vilares, D., Gómez-Rodríguez, C.: Head-qa: A healthcare dataset for complex reasoning. arXiv preprint arXiv:1906.04701 (2019)
18. Wang, W., Yang, N., Wei, F., Chang, B., Zhou, M.: Gated self-matching networks for reading comprehension and question answering. In: Proceedings of the 55th Annual Meeting of the Association for Computational Linguistics (Volume 1: Long Papers), pp. 189–198 (2017)
19. Weinberger, K., Dasgupta, A., Attenberg, J., Langford, J., Smola, A.: Feature hashing for large scale multitask learning. arXiv preprint arXiv:0902.2206 (2009)
20. Xiao, Y., et al.: Dynamically fused graph network for multi-hop reasoning. arXiv preprint arXiv:1905.06933 (2019)
21. Yih, S.W.T., Chang, M.W., He, X., Gao, J.: Semantic parsing via staged query graph generation: question answering with knowledge base (2015)
22. Yu, A.W., et al.: Qanet: Combining local convolution with global self-attention for reading comprehension. arXiv preprint arXiv:1804.09541 (2018)

Characterizing Robotic and Organic Query in SPARQL Search Sessions

Xinyue Zhang[1], Meng Wang[1,2(✉)], Bingchen Zhao[3], Ruyang Liu[1],
Jingyuan Zhang[1], and Han Yang[4]

[1] Southeast University, Nanjing, China
{zangxy216,meng.wang}@seu.edu.cn
[2] Key Laboratory of Computer Network and Information Integration
(Southeast University), Ministry of Education, Nanjing, China
[3] Tongji University, Shanghai, China
[4] Peking University, Beijing, China

Abstract. SPARQL, as one of the most powerful query languages over knowledge graphs, has gained significant popularity in recent years. A large amount of SPARQL query logs have become available and provided new research opportunities to discover user interests, understand query intentions, and model search behaviors. However, a significant portion of the queries to SPARQL endpoints on the Web are robotic queries that are generated by automated scripts. Detecting and separating these robotic queries from those organic ones issued by human users is crucial to deep usage analysis of knowledge graphs. In light of this, in this paper, we propose a novel method to identify SPARQL queries based on session-level query features. Specifically, we define and partition SPARQL queries into different sessions. Then, we design an algorithm to detect loop patterns, which is an important characteristic of robotic queries, in a given query session. Finally, we employ a pipeline method that leverages loop pattern features and query request frequency to distinguish the robotic and organic SPARQL queries. Differing from other machine learning based methods, the proposed method can identify the query types accurately without labelled data. We conduct extensive experiments on six real-world SPARQL query log datasets. The results demonstrate that our approach can distinguish robotic and organic queries effectively and only need 7.63×10^{-4} s on average to process a query.

Keywords: SPARQL · Session search · Query classification

1 Introduction

With the rapid development of Semantic Web technologies, more and more data are published as knowledge graphs in Resource Description Framework (RDF) [11] triple form (*subject, predicate, object*). SPARQL [9], as one of the most widely used query languages for accessing knowledge graphs, has become the de-facto standard in this context. Currently, there are approximately

X. Wang et al. (Eds.): APWeb-WAIM 2020, LNCS 12317, pp. 270–285, 2020.
https://doi.org/10.1007/978-3-030-60259-8_21

1.5×10^{11} RDF triples from different domains[1] that can be explored by 557 SPARQL endpoints on the Web[2]. As a result, numerous SPARQL query logs are generated every day and have recently become available for researchers to discover user interests, understand query intentions, and model search behaviors [15,17].

Motivations: Conducting extensive analysis of massive SPARQL logs is challenging. One of the main problems is that there is a significant portion of queries to SPARQL endpoints that are robotic queries. Robotic queries are usually generated and issued by automated scripts or programs for index size inferring, data crawling, or malicious attacking, while organic queries imply the real information need of human users. Raghuveer [15] pointed out that 90% of queries in USEWOD dataset [3] are requested by less than 2% no-human users. Similarly, in DBpedia[3] SPARQL query log dataset, 90% queries are provided by only 0.4% automated software programs. It indicates that robotic queries dominate organic ones in terms of volume and query load. Therefore, it is crucial to pre-process query logs by detecting and separating robotic queries from organic queries before diving into deep analysis works.

Most of existing methods [4,15] on distinguishing between robotic and organic query are mainly based on agent names recorded in SPARQL logs [4,15] and query request frequency [15]. However, each of them has disadvantages. For agent names, it is simple and effective to select organic queries from trusted agents, but the trusted agent list needs to be manually specified and is not always available. Following the specification of Apache's log format[4], agent names will be recorded on 400 error and 501 error only. Besides, smart crawlers can fake agent names by adding them to the request header. For query request frequency, how to determine an appropriate threshold is annoying. Therefore, recognizing the different types of queries only by the agent name or frequency is not enough. Moreover, several machine learning based methods [10,19] have been proposed to detect robotic queries in conventional search engines. However, they rely on user demography features and sufficient labelled training data, which are usually missing in SPARQL search scenarios.

Solutions: Given the above observations, in this paper, we propose a framework to classify robotic and organic queries by detecting features of robotic queries in SPARQL session-level. Specifically, we organize sequences of queries as sessions which are defined considering the time and semantic constraints. Then, according to three types of loop patterns that distribute in robotics queries, *i.e.*, single intra loop pattern, the sequence of intra loop pattern, and inter loop pattern, we design algorithms to detect each pattern. Our loop detection algorithm is a training-free process which focuses on detecting characteristic of robotic queries and has high efficiency with a complexity of $O(nlogn)$ where n presents the session length.

---

[1] http://linkeddata.org/.

[2] https://sparqles.ai.wu.ac.at/availability.

[3] https://wiki.dbpedia.org/.

[4] http://httpd.apache.org/docs/current/mod/mod_log_config.html.

Finally, we implement a pipeline method that takes query request frequency and loop pattern features into consideration to distinguish robotic and organic queries. To guarantee the high precision for organic queries, a rule has been specially set to relax the constraint of robotic queries, *i.e.*, if one session that comes from one user is detected with loop patterns, then all the sessions of the same user will be classified into robotic queries. Moreover, our method can provide the explanation for each identified query (*i.e.*, filtered by frequency, or the specific loop pattern).

Contributions: The contributions of this paper are summarized as follows:

- We propose an efficient and simple pipeline method in SPARQL session-level to distinguish between organic and robotic queries.
- We design a new training-free algorithm that can accurately detect loop patterns that is an important characteristic for robotic queries, with a complexity of $O(nlogn)$ where n is the session length.
- We conduct extensive experiments on six real-world SPARQL query log datasets. The results indicate that our approach is effective and efficient.

Organization: The remainder of this paper is organized as follows. Sect. 2 presents basic SPARQL query log analysis. The details of our method (including preliminary, loop pattern detection algorithm, and query classifying method) are described in Sect. 3. In Sect. 4, we show experiments on real-world SPARQL queries to demonstrate the effectiveness and efficiency of our method. Sect. 5 discusses related work. Finally, conclusions are presented in Sect. 6.

2   SPARQL Query Log Analysis

Before we design our query detection algorithm, we first collect real-world SPARQL query logs and present basic analysis.

2.1   Datasets

We use data collected from six different SPARQL endpoints: affymetrix[5], dbsnp[6], gendr[7], goa[8], linkedspl[9], and linkedgeodata[10]. The first five datasets are a part of Bio2Rdf [2] which is a bioinformatic RDF cloud. The linkedgeodata [20] makes the information collected by the OpenStreetMap project [7] available as an RDF knowledge graph. All these SPARQL logs have been modified into RDF format like LSQ [18], which makes them easy to analyze.

---

[5] http://affymetrix.bio2rdf.org/sparql.
[6] http://dbsnp.bio2rdf.org/sparql.
[7] http://gendr.bio2rdf.org/sparql.
[8] http://goa.bio2rdf.org/sparql.
[9] http://linkedspl.bio2rdf.org/sparql.
[10] http://linkedgeodata.org/sparql.

Table 1. Statistics of SPARQL query logs.

Dataset	Queries	Executions	Users	Begin time	End time
affymetrix	618,796/630,499	1,782,776/1,818,020	1,159	2013-05-05	2015-09-18
dbsnp	545,184/555,971	1,522,035/1,554,162	274	2014-05-23	2015-09-18
gendr	564,158/565,133	1,369,325/1,377,113	520	2014-01-16	2015-09-18
goa	630,934/638,570	2,345,460/2,377,718	1,190	2013-05-05	2015-09-18
linkedgeodata	651,251/667,856	1,586,660/1,607,821	26,211	2015-11-22	2016-11-20
linkedspl	436,292/436,394	756,806/757,010	107	2014-07-24	2015-09-18

In our collected data, every SPARQL query and execution is identified by a unique id. One query can have multiple executions. We recognize different users by their encrypted IP address. The basic information about the datasets in this paper can be found in Tabble 1. The *queries* column indicates the number of queries without parse error and the number of all the queries. The *executions* column presents executions without parse error and the number of all the executions. We also list the number of users and the time interval of the data.

2.2 Preliminary Analysis

We perform preliminary analysis about query distributions over users and time span, as well as query template repetitions.

Distribution of Queries Executed by Users: As mentioned above, many prior works [15, 18] have noticed that most SPARQL queries are provided by few no-human users, and we also find the similar phenomenon in our data. We first group queries by users and then sort users by the number of queries they execute. Then we calculate how many users contribute to 95% executions at least. Results can be found in Table 2. In terms of the number of executions, 95% executions are contributed by very few users (less than 7%) in all the datasets, and less than 0.5% in the sum of all datasets.

Table 2. 95% executions are contributed by α% users.

Dataset	affymetrix	dbsnp	gendr	goa	linkedspl	linkedgeodata	all
α	1.47	3.65	1.54	1.60	1.87	6.80	0.40

Table 3. The percentage (β%) of unique templates

Dataset	affymetrix	dbsnp	gendr	goa	linkedspl	linkedgeodata	all
β	0.25	0.28	0.16	0.20	0.67	0.19	0.28

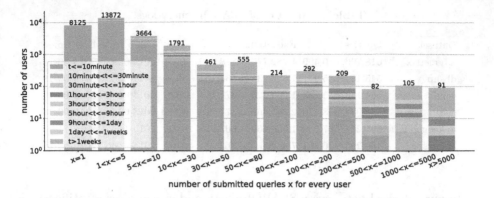

Fig. 1. Distributions of the number of submitted queries x and time span t of the submitted queries for every user. The X-axis indicates different intervals about the number of submitted queries, Y-axis means how many users are in this interval. Different colors in the bar mean different time spans of these users.

Distributions of Queries, Users, and Time Span Together: We associate users with the number of queries they submit and the time span of these submitted queries for each user, as illustrated in Fig. 1. In terms of the number of users, most users execute 1–80 queries within 1 h.

Query Template Repetition: As mentioned by Raghuveer [15], robotic queries tend to use fixed query templates. We extract the query template for every query in our data. We match the extracted query templates to calculate the percentage of unique templates over all queries, which means that the lower the number is, the more repetitions of templates are in queries. The query templates are extracted by replacing IRI, variable and literal with _IRI_, _VAR_, _LIT_ respectively like [15]. We calculate the similarity between two templates based on string edit distance by fuzzywuzzy[11]. The query template repetition results of six datasets are reported in Table 3. We find that the percentage of unique templates behind queries is less than 0.7%. For all the data sets except linkedgeodata, the number of unique templates is about 0.3% of the number of all queries. The results indicate that the large repetitive query templates exist in real-world queries.

3   Our Method

In this section, we present the definition of SPARQL query session based on time and semantic constraints, as well as descriptions of three loop patterns, which are important features of robotic queries and characterized by the distribution of query templates in a given SPARQL query session. Then, we design a loop pattern detection algorithm to capture the loop features of robotic queries. Finally, we implement a pipeline method that leverages query request frequency and loop pattern features to solve the organic and robotic query identifying problem.

---

[11] https://pypi.org/project/fuzzywuzzy/.

3.1   Preliminaries

Definition 1. *Term(q): term set of one query.* All variables and specific terms (i.e. RDF IRIs) used in the query are included in the term set.

Definition 2. *Session.* Considering a sequence of queries $q_1, q_2, q_3 \cdots q_n$[12], which is ordered by time and executed by one user. We define a SPARQL query sequence as a **session** if it satisfies the following two constraints:

– If we use $time(q)$ to represent the time when query q is executed, this sequence of queries satisfies $time(q_n) - time(q_1) < time\_threshold$.
– For any continuous query pair (q_i, q_{i+1}) in this sequence, it satisfies $term(q_i) \cap term(q_{i+1}) \neq \emptyset$.

In this paper, we set *time_threshold* to 1 h. The reason why we include variables in the term set is that users usually do not change variable names they use in a query. If two continuous queries executed by one user share one variable, we can infer that two queries have some potential correlations and should be included in the same session. Next, we introduce three types of loop patterns in the SPARQL session-level.

Single Intra Loop Pattern: Robotic queries often come from a loop in automated scripts or programs trying to collect enough information to satisfy their uses. In these sessions, the structure of queries remains the same, but variables, literals, or IRIs are changing. (1) In some cases, machines want to collect all the information about one specified *subject*, then in queries, only *predicates* are changing as shown in below Example 1. (2) For cases in which machines want to find out the same information shared by some *subjects*, the *subjects* are changing, as shown in Example 2. (3) If a machine wants to collect the *subjects* with certain types or values, then only *objects* are changing (see Example 3). (4) There are also cases in which the numeric values in SPARQL constraint operators *FILTER*, *OFFSET* and *LIMIT* and the string values in *REGEX* functions are changing.

```
Example1: predicate change
{ ?s  <http://bio2rdf.org/affymetrix_vocabulary:x-flybase>   ?o}
{ ?s  <http://bio2rdf.org/affymetrix_vocabulary:x-omim>   ?o }
```

```
Example2: subject change
{<http://linkedgeodata.org/triplify/node2957398896> rdfs:label ?label}
{<http://linkedgeodata.org/triplify/node1885439658> rdfs:label ?label}
```

```
Example3: object changing
{?item rdf:type <http://www.openlinksw.com/schemas/rdfs/TechArticle#this>}
{?item rdf:type <http://wordnet.okfn.gr/resource/synset-noun-2> }
```

---

[12] We only consider queries without parse errors and merge the same queries in adjacent positions. For instance, a sequence $[0, 1, 1, 1, 2]$ (in which $0, 1, 2$ means the query id) can be processed to $[0, 1, 2]$.

All the cases described above remain the structure of the original SPARQL query and change one or more variables, IRIs, and literal values. This is to say, the query templates behind queries in this kind of loop are the same. This is the so-called *single intra loop pattern*. If we use 0 to represent the template index, '+' means appearing one or more times, then the single intra loop pattern can be expressed by $[0+]$.

Sequence of Intra Loop: In our dataset, excepting the single intra loop introduced above, we also notice there are *sequences of intra loops*. This type of loop pattern shows up when, for example, the machine gets one target attribute for all the *subjects*, then queries for another attribute. If we use numbers to represent template index, '+' means appearing one or more times, then this loop pattern can be expressed by $[0 + 1 + \cdots]$.

Inter Loop Pattern: Another type of loop pattern is *inter loop pattern*, which is used, for instance, to query all the features for one *subject*, then change to another *subject*. Using the same method as above, inter loop pattern can be expressed by $[(01 \cdots)+]$. Notice 0,1 here can be a single query or a intra loop.

3.2   Loop Pattern Detection Algorithm

In this section, we introduce our loop pattern detection algorithm, as shown in Fig. 2. In a nutshell, the algorithm we implement contains the following steps:

- **Step1:** *Generate templates*, we organize the queries as sessions (Such as *QuerySeq* in Fig. 2) defined in Sect. 3.1, and replace each query in the original session with its corresponding template index to generate a sequence of template index.
- **Step2:** *Merge the same items in adjacent positions*, we merge the continuous same items and generate a sequence of template index without repetitions in adjacent positions (*i.e. TmpltSeqWoRep*). An example of this step is shown in Fig. 2.
- **Step3:** *Is it a single intra loop?*, we detect a single intra loop pattern which can be expressed as $[0+]$. Therefore, if *TmpltSeqWoRep* only contains one template index, then this session has intra loop pattern.
- **Step4:** *Is it a sequence of intra loop?*, we detect the *sequences of intra loop* which have the order like $[0 + 1 + \cdots]$. We recognize such pattern by calculating the percentage of *len(TmpltSeqWoRep)* and *len(QuerySeq)* and regard sessions with this value lower than *thre*1 as sessions with *sequence of intra loop patterns*. We design this step because if merging the same items in adjacent positions can let the length of the session shrink to lower than a threshold, there must be so many repetitions in adjacent positions. The set of *thre*1 is provided in Sect. 3.2.
- **Step5:** *Is it a inter loop*, we detect *inter loops* which has the pattern like $[(01)+]$. Details about this function can be found in *Inter Loop Detection* section below.

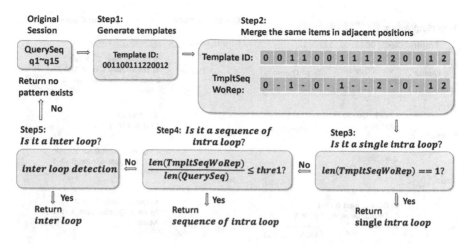

Fig. 2. Overview of loop pattern detection algorithm.

If a session contains one of the patterns described above, then we think queries of this session can be classified into robotic queries. All the thresholds mentioned in Algorithms are determined by experiments in *Thresholds Setting* section below.

Inter Loop Detection: As described in Sect. 3.1, the inter loop pattern can be expressed by $[(01...)+]$. We detect this pattern by calculating the maximum subsequence which loops over the entire session. We use a *Queue* to store this subsequence. A detailed example is provided by Fig. 3. Scanning the input ($TmpltSeqWoRep$) from left to right, add the item that do not exist in *Queue* into *Queue* (step1–2 in Fig. 3). For items that are already in *Queue*, the subsequence beginning from a specific item in $TmpltSeqWoRep$ should be matched against subsequence in *Queue*. The subsequence can match over the sequence in *Queue* from the beginning (step3–4 and step6–8) or the middle. Also, *Queue* can be extended like step5. Notice that Fig. 3 is only the first step of *Detect inter loop* function. The percentage of $len(Queue)$ and $len(QuerySeq)$, presents in what extent intra loop pattern exists. Therefore, if this value is lower than $thre2$, then we think a inter loop pattern exists in this session.

Thresholds Setting: In order to find 2 thresholds mentioned in Sect. 3.2, we extract $3,000$ sessions in all the data randomly to find different features in sessions with different lengths. We use len_ori, $len1$, $len2$ to indicate $len(QuerySeq)$, $len(TmpltSeqWoRep)$, $len(Queue)$ in the following sections. len_ori, is just the length of original session; $len1$ means the length of session after removing the continuous same template index; $len2$ is the length of maximum subsequence which appears in a session, corresponding to the length of *Queue* in Fig. 3. We consider three kinds of features:

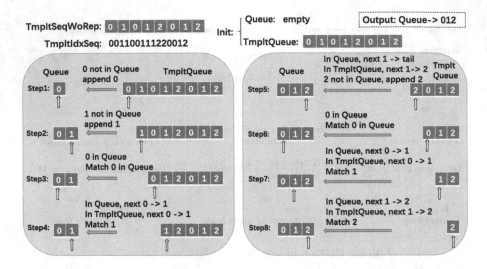

Fig. 3. An example of *inter loop detection*

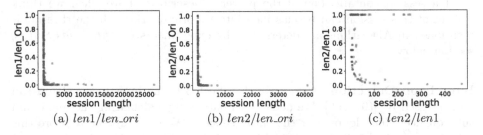

(a) *len1/len_ori*   (b) *len2/len_ori*   (c) *len2/len1*

Fig. 4. Distribution of *len1/len_ori*, *len2/len_ori* and *len2/len1*.

- Distribution of *len1/len_ori* in sessions with different lengths, which can present the distribution of intra loop, both *single intra loop* and *sequence intra loop pattern*.
- Distribution of *len2/len_ori* in sessions with different lengths, which can present the distribution of *intra loop* and *inter loop pattern*.
- Distribution of *len2/len1* in sessions with different lengths, which can present the distribution of *inter loop*, because *len2* is computed based on *TmpltIdxWoRep*.

The Distribution of three features can be seen in Fig. 4. In terms of *len1/len_ori*, sessions with lengths more than 100 are almost 0, which indicates there are lots of *intra loops*. On the contrary, in shorter sessions with lengths less than 100, distribution of *len1/len_ori* is different. The turning point of *len1/len_ori* in Fig. 4a is about 0.1, therefore, we set *thre1* to 0.1. Using the same method, according to Fig. 4b, we set *thre2* to 0.1.

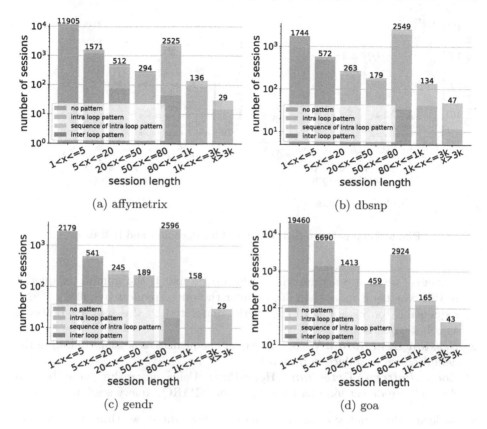

(a) affymetrix

(b) dbsnp

(c) gendr

(d) goa

Fig. 5. Loop pattern distribution in affymertrix, dbsnp, gendr and goa.

Comparing three figures in Fig. 4, we can conclude that most of the sessions with lengths longer than 100 contain *intra loop patterns*. In sessions with lengths of 100–500, there are a few *inter loop patterns* existing.

Complexity: Considering the process in Fig. 2, assuming that the length of the original session is n, step3 and step4 have the complexity of constant. The complexity of step2 is linear, and the complexity for step1 and step5 which contains the operation of finding an item in an ordered list is $O(nlogn)$. Therefore, the complexity of our loop pattern detection algorithm is $O(nlogn)$.

3.3 Robotic and Organic Query Classification Pipeline Method

We design a pipeline method to classify robotic and organic queries by leveraging query request frequency and loop patterns, which contains the following steps:

1) *Frequency Test:* For a query sequence ordered by time and generated by one user, we check the query request frequency first. For every query in this

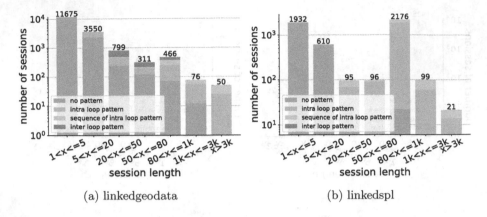

(a) linkedgeodata   (b) linkedspl

Fig. 6. Loop pattern distribution in linkedgeodata and linkedspl.

sequence, we create a time window in 30 min and if the number of queries in this window is more than 30, we infer the query request frequency of this sequence is too high and all the queries generated by this user are detected as robotic queries.

2) **Session Generation:** We organize query sequences as sessions following the definition we introduce in Sect. 3.1.

3) **Loop Pattern Detection Algorithm:** Using algorithm described in Sect. 3.2, we detect loop patterns based on SPARQL query sessions.

Considering the number of organic queries is very small, we think the recall of robotic query classification is more important. Therefore, we set a rule: if one of the sessions of one user can be detected as a loop pattern, all the queries of the same user will be classified into robotic queries. Note that, the agent name constraint can also be added into this pipeline before the *Frequency Test*. Usually, some browser-related agent names are selected as a sign of organic queries.

4   Experiments

To scrutinize the effectiveness and efficiency of the proposed method, We conduct experiments on six real-world datasets. We first evaluate the loop pattern detection algorithm and its average runtime. Then, we validate the effectiveness of our pipeline method to classify robotic and organic queries, as well as the efficiency for a query and a session.

4.1   Loop Pattern Detection

We detect three loop patterns mentioned in Sect. 3.1 using our loop pattern detection algorithm. Results shown in Fig. 5 and Fig. 6 indicate our algorithm can recognize all the sessions with lengths more than 1,000 in 5/6 datasets and

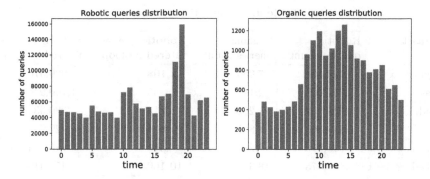

Fig. 7. Query Request Time (UTC) distribution of the linkedgeodata.

most sessions with lengths of 80–1,000. For dbsnp, gendr, and linkedspl, there are loop patterns distributed in sessions with lengths of 50–80.

Also, in different datasets, the distribution of different patterns is a little different. The most common loop pattern in all the datasets is the *single intra loop pattern*. The second common loop pattern is the *sequence of intra loop pattern*, which appears in dbsnp in particular. Besides, in linkedgeodata, there is a considerable number of *inter loop patterns*. Most sessions with lengths of more than 80 can be detected, which illustrates our algorithm can capture features of robotic queries. For the efficiency, experiments on linkedspl dataset show our algorithm can process a query in 2.37×10^{-4} s, and a session in 0.001 s on average.

4.2 Robotic and Organic Query Classification

Our pipeline method utilizes the query request frequency and loop patterns to identify robotic and organic queries. The classification results are reported in Table 4. We also list the number of robotic queries filtered by different constraints. Query request frequency can filter out the most robotic queries and our Loop Pattern Detection Algorithm can filter out a considerable number of robotic queries. Even though the number of queries filtered by loop pattern detection is smaller than the number of queries filtered by frequency, it is still a fairly big number considering the number of organic queries. Taking gendr as an example, the overall number of organic queries is 1262, but the number of queries filter by loop pattern is 1214, which will disturb analysis work if they are mixed up.

Table 4. Classification results.

Dataset	Robotic queries count	Organic queries count	Robotic queries filtered by loop	Robotic queries filtered by freq
affymetrix	990,684	7,659	1,108	989,576
dbsnp	1,191,001	2,146	55	1,190,946
gendr	981,549	1,262	1,214	980,335
goa	1,430,506	1,827	624	1,429,882
linkedspl	745,810	1,230	376	745,434
linkedgeodata	1,480,573	18,380	10,160	1,470,413

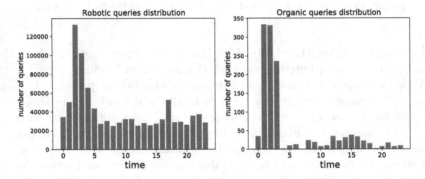

Fig. 8. Query Request Time (UTC) distribution of gendr.

Furthermore, considering there is no ground truth in robotic and organic query classification tasks, we visualize the distribution of queries requested to endpoints at different times within one day and use the difference of distributions in robotic and organic queries to evaluate the effectiveness of our methods. Results can be seen in Fig. 7 and Fig. 8. We only show two canonical distributions here. The rest datasets are similar to these two distributions. The distributions in both linkedgeodata and gendr for organic queries follow a strong daily rhythm. Like [4], with most activities happening during the European and American day and evening. This indicates a direct human involvement. For robotic queries, most of them are uniformly distributed. An interesting thing here is that, in 1:00–3:00 in gendr, we check queries in this time interval and find most of the queries are very likely to come from an automated script that examines the availability of endpoint every day. These kinds of queries are hard to remove for two reasons: 1) They do not have a high request frequency. 2) They do have diversity in the session-level. But we can notice their existence by the visualization we present here, and we can remove such queries manually. Besides, the experiment shows that our pipeline method can process a query in 7.63×10^{-4} s and a query sequence from one user in 5.33 s on average.

5 Related Work

SPARQL Log Analysis: SPARQL log analysis can provide rich information in many aspects. Many prior works [1,8,13,14,21] have focused on the analysis of SPARQL query logs. They analyze SPARQL queries from statistical features (*i.e.* occurrences of triple patterns), shape related features (*i.e.* occurrences of SPARQL queries with a shape of tree), etc. However, these works mainly analyze SPARQL queries in isolation. Features between queries have not been fully analyzed. Currently, similarity between queries in a query sequence which is from the same user and ordered by time (in [15], this sequence is called as *session*) has been noticed by [5,14,15]. The similarity feature has been utilized in query augmentation based on the analysis of previous (historic) queries [12,16,23]. In [16], authors define *session* based on the definition of [15] but add a 1-h time window constraint. Our work moves onward by adding a semantic constraint on the definition of *session*. Raghuveer [15] introduce *intra* and *inter loop patterns* which are characteristics of robotic queries from the session viewpoint. Then, they evaluate the prevalence of these patterns in USEWOD dataset [3] by loop detection technique they design. However, the method they introduce is quite simple and can not satisfy the need to distinguish between robotic and organic queries. In light of this, we classify loop patterns more carefully and give a specific definition of these patterns. Furthermore, according to the features of each pattern, we design an algorithm to detect loop patterns, which can be used in the robotic and organic query classification scenario.

Robotic and Organic Query Classification: The need to distinguish between machines and humans in SPARQL search is recognized by [4,15,17]. Rietveld *et al.* [17] find organic queries and robotic queries have very different features. In [15], robotic queries are recognized by query request frequency and the agent names. Bielefeldt *et al.* [4] are the first to introduce an idealised view of organic and robotic queries. They separate wikidata [22] SPARQL query logs into organic queries and robotic queries mainly by manually specified agent lists. They have published this classified dataset. Based on this dataset, Bonifati *et al.* [6] analyze different features of both queries. However, as we mentioned above, distinguishing robotic and organic queries by agent names and query request frequency has drawbacks. In this paper, we consider an important characteristic, *i.e.*, loop pattern, and design a pipeline method for robotic and organic queries classification problem leveraging query request frequency and loop pattern detection algorithm. Experiments on six real-world SPARQL query logs indicate that our method is more effective and efficient.

6 Conclusion

In this paper, we propose a novel method to distinguish robotic and organic queries based on SPARQL session-level query features. We first organize queries as sessions. Then, we design an algorithm to detect loop patterns, which is an important characteristic of robotic queries. Furthermore, we implement a pipeline method to separate robotic queries from organic queries by leveraging query request frequency and loop patterns. Our method does not require user demography features and sufficient labelled training data. The effectiveness and efficiency of our method has been validated by experiments on six real-world SPARQL query log datasets.

Acknowledgement. This work was supported by National Science Foundation of China with Grant Nos. 61906037 and U1736204; National Key Research and Development Program of China with Grant Nos. 2018YFC0830201 and 2017YFB1002801; the Fundamental Research Funds for the Central Universities.

References

1. Arias, M., Fernández, J.D., Martínez-Prieto, M.A., de la Fuente, P.: An empirical study of real-world sparql queries. arXiv preprint arXiv:1103.5043 (2011)
2. Belleau, F., Nolin, M.A., Tourigny, N., Rigault, P., Morissette, J.: Bio2RDF: towards a mashup to build bioinformatics knowledge systems. J. Biomed. Inform. **41**(5), 706–716 (2008)
3. Berendt, B., Hollink, L., Hollink, V., Luczak-Rösch, M., Möller, K., Vallet, D.: USEWOD 2011: 1st international workshop on usage analysis and the web of data. In: The 20th International Conference on World Wide Web, pp. 305–306 (2011)
4. Bielefeldt, A., Gonsior, J., Krötzsch, M.: Practical linked data access via SPARQL: the case of wikidata. In: The 11th Workshop on Linked Data on the Web, pp. 1–10 (2018)
5. Bonifati, A., Martens, W., Timm, T.: An analytical study of large SPARQL query logs. VLDB J. 1–25 (2017)
6. Bonifati, A., Martens, W., Timm, T.: Navigating the maze of wikidata query logs. In: The World Wide Web Conference, pp. 127–138 (2019)
7. Haklay, M., Weber, P.: OpenStreetMap: user-generated street maps. IEEE Pervasive Comput. **7**(4), 12–18 (2008)
8. Han, X., Feng, Z., Zhang, X., Wang, X., Rao, G., Jiang, S.: On the statistical analysis of practical SPARQL queries. In: The 19th International Workshop on Web and Databases, pp. 1–6 (2016)
9. Harris, S., Seaborne, A., Prud'hommeaux, E.: SPARQL 1.1 query language. W3C Recommendation **21**(10), 778 (2013)
10. Kang, H., Wang, K., Soukal, D., Behr, F., Zheng, Z.: Large-scale bot detection for search engines. In: The 19th International Conference on World Wide Web, pp. 501–510 (2010)
11. Klyne, G., Carroll, J.J., McBride, B.: Resource description framework (RDF): concepts and abstract syntax. W3C Recommendation (2004)
12. Lorey, J., Naumann, F.: Detecting SPARQL query templates for data prefetching. In: Cimiano, P., Corcho, O., Presutti, V., Hollink, L., Rudolph, S. (eds.) ESWC 2013. LNCS, vol. 7882, pp. 124–139. Springer, Heidelberg (2013). https://doi.org/10.1007/978-3-642-38288-8_9
13. Möller, K., Hausenblas, M., Cyganiak, R., Grimnes, G.A., Handschuh, S.: Learning from linked open data usage: patterns & metrics. In: The WebSci10: Extending the Frontiers of Society On-Line, pp. 1–8 (2010)

14. Picalausa, F., Vansummeren, S.: What are real SPARQL queries like? In: The International Workshop on Semantic Web Information Management, pp. 1–6 (2011)
15. Raghuveer, A.: Characterizing machine agent behavior through SPARQL query mining. In: The International Workshop on Usage Analysis and the Web of Data, pp. 1–8 (2012)
16. Rico, M., Touma, R., Queralt Calafat, A., Pérez, M.S.: Machine learning-based query augmentation for SPARQL endpoints. In: The 14th International Conference on Web Information Systems and Technologies, pp. 57–67 (2018)
17. Rietveld, L., Hoekstra, R., et al.: Man vs. machine: Differences in SPARQL queries. In: The 4th USEWOD Workshop on Usage Analysis and the Web of of Data, pp. 1–7 (2014)
18. Saleem, M., Ali, M.I., Hogan, A., Mehmood, Q., Ngomo, A.-C.N.: LSQ: the linked SPARQL queries dataset. In: Arenas, M., et al. (eds.) ISWC 2015. LNCS, vol. 9367, pp. 261–269. Springer, Cham (2015). https://doi.org/10.1007/978-3-319-25010-6_15
19. Shakiba, T., Zarifzadeh, S., Derhami, V.: Spam query detection using stream clustering. World Wide Web 21(2), 557–572 (2017). https://doi.org/10.1007/s11280-017-0471-z
20. Stadler, C., Lehmann, J., Höffner, K., Auer, S.: LinkedGeoData: a core for a web of spatial open data. Semant. Web 3(4), 333–354 (2012)
21. Stegemann, T., Ziegler, J.: Pattern-based analysis of SPARQL queries from the LSQ dataset. In: International Semantic Web Conference (Posters, Demos & Industry Tracks), pp. 1–4 (2017)
22. Vrandečić, D., Krötzsch, M.: Wikidata: a free collaborative knowledgebase. Commun. ACM 57(10), 78–85 (2014)
23. Zhang, W.E., Sheng, Q.Z., Qin, Y., Yao, L., Shemshadi, A., Taylor, K.: SECF: improving SPARQL querying performance with proactive fetching and caching. In: The 31st Annual ACM Symposium on Applied Computing, pp. 362–367 (2016)

Tail Entity Recognition and Linking
for Knowledge Graphs

Dalei Zhang[1], Yang Qiang[2], Zhixu Li[1,3($\boxtimes$)], Junhua Fang[1], Ying He[3],
Xin Zheng[3], and Zhigang Chen[4]

[1] School of Computer Science and Technology, Soochow University, Hefei, China
{dlzhang,zhixuli,jhfang}@suda.edu.cn
[2] King Abdullah University of Science and Technology, Jeddah, Saudi Arabia
[3] IFLYTEK Research, Suzhou, China
qiangyanghm@hotmail.com
[4] State Key Laboratory of Cognitive Intelligence, iFLYTEK,
Hefei, People's Republic of China
{yinghe,xinzheng3,zgchen}@iflytek.com

Abstract. This paper works on a new task - Tail Entity Recognition and
Linking (TERL) for Knowledge Graphs (KG), i.e., recognizing ambiguous entity mentions from the tails of some relational triples, and linking these mentions to their corresponding KG entities. Although plenty
of work has been done on both entity recognition and entity linking,
the TERL problem in this specific scenario is untouched. In this paper,
we work towards the TERL problem by fully leveraging KG information with two neural models for solving the two sub-problems, i.e., tail
entity recognition and tail entity linking respectively. We finally solve the
TERL problem end-to-end by proposing a joint learning mechanism with
the two proposed neural models, which could further improve both tail
entity recognition and linking results. To the best of our knowledge, this
is the first effort working towards TERL for KG. Our empirical study
conducted on real-world datasets shows that our models can effectively
expand KG and improve the quality of KG.

Keywords: Tail Entity Recognition and Linking · Infobox Linking ·
Knowledge Graph

1 Introduction

Nowadays, Knowledge Graphs (KG) has become the most popular way to store
factual knowledge in the form of triples *(head, predicate, tail)*. While in a relational triple *head* and *tail* denote two entities in a relation *predicate*, in an
attribute triple *tail* is the value of an attribute *predicate* for an entity *head*.
In recent years, KG have been successfully applied to a wide variety of applications including semantic search [4], question answering [22], and recommendation
systems [28] etc.

© Springer Nature Switzerland AG 2020
X. Wang et al. (Eds.): APWeb-WAIM 2020, LNCS 12317, pp. 286–301, 2020.
https://doi.org/10.1007/978-3-030-60259-8_22

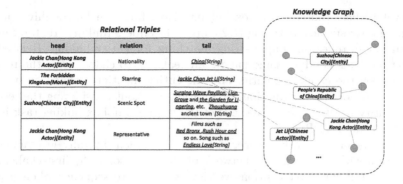

Fig. 1. Example triples requiring tail entity recognition and linking

Despite their usefulness and popularity, KG are often incomplete and noisy due to the unclean and incomplete data sources employed at the KG construction stage. While most existing efforts are focused on relation prediction [25] and entity typing [15] for KG, this paper solely pays attention to recognizing entity mentions from the *tail* of some triples and linking them to their corresponding KG entities. As the examples shown in Fig. 1, in these triples, the *predicate* is a relation, but the *tail* appears just as a plain string, where one or more entity mentions are unrecognized and unlinked to their corresponding KG entities. For example, the *"Starring"* of *"The Forbidden"* is *"Jackie Chan Jet Li"*, but *"Jackie Chan Jet Li"* is a plain string. The two entity mentions *"Jackie Chan"* and *"Jet Li"* are not detected and linked to their corresponding entities in KG. This kind of phenomenon widely exists in manually-constructed KG and KG that are generated from encyclopedia's infobox [18] such as DBPedia [1] and Yago [2]. According to our sampling statistics on BaiduBaike [21], among 20 millions relational triples extracted from 16 millions entities' infobox, more than 12 millions triples have their tail entity mentions unrecognized and unlinked to the corresponding KG entities. Therefore, it is crucial to perform **Tail Entity Recognition and Linking (TERL)** for these triples.

Generally, two nontrivial challenging sub-problems in TERL should be tackled: one is to identify all the hidden entity mentions that might be mixed with each other from the tails of triples, the other is to link these entity mentions to their corresponding KG entities. Although plenty of work has been done on both Named Entity Recognition (NER) [6,19] and Entity Linking (EL) [5,11,26], the two problems are mainly studied on document-level or sentence-level. But the texts in TERL are even shorter, i.e., phrase-level, which means the entity mentions has much less textual context to be leveraged in TERL. Thus, traditional NER and EL approaches could hardly be applied successfully on TERL.

Fortunately, we have plenty of KG information about the triple and the candidate entities of the mentions that could be leveraged. There is also some pioneer work conducted on the second challenge by addressing a similar problem called infobox linking [18], which aims at linking entity mentions in the infobox of encyclopedias. Existing infobox linking algorithms can be roughly put into two categories: surface matching [7,23] and relatedness ranking [10,18]. Surface matching only relies on simple string matching for entity linking. Relatedness ranking methods conduct some hand-craft features to characterize the relatedness between the candidate entity and the entity mentions, which do not take full advantage of KG information. In addition, without considering the recognition of entity mentions from the tails of the triples, infobox linking task is just a sub-problem of TERL.

In this paper, we work towards the TERL problem by fully leveraging KG information with a deep neural network method. To solve the first challenge of TERL, i.e., tail entity recognition, we view it as a word sequence labeling problem. The tail entity recognition result is not only decided by the textual context within the tail element, but also the *relation* in the triple. An entity mention may have multiple aspects, and different relations focus on different aspects of entity mentions. Therefore, we innovatively propose a Relation Projection layer on top of BiLSTM layer [13] to extract some relation features, and the conditional random fields (CRFs) [16] are used as the last layer, to predict the label of each word and model sequence label dependencies. For the second challenge, different from the existing approaches on infobox linking above, we propose to learn embedding vectors for entity mentions and KG entities based on the *tags* in KG. Particularly, we propose a concept of relation tags and considering each tags has different importance to entity mention and candidate entities, we introduce attention mechanism here to obtain mention and entities representations. Then, we calculate the similarity scores between an entity mention representation and each of its candidate KG entity representation. Finally, we choose the most similar mention-entity pair as the linking result.

However, if we tackle the two sub-tasks separately, the relatedness between the two sub-tasks is not employed, and the errors generated in the tail entity recognition stage would propagate to tail entity linking. Therefore, we propose to solve the TERL problem in an end-to-end manner by jointly learning the above two models for tail entity recognition and tail entity linking. To achieve this, we apply a sharing mechanism for multi-task training using BiLstm-Projection layers as a shared feature extractor. In this way, we could leverage their relatedness and increase the correlation of the tail entity recognition module and the tail entity linking module.

We summarize our contributions as follows:

- To the best of our knowledge, this is the first effort working towards Tail Entity Recognition and Linking (TERL) for KG.
- We propose neural models for the two sub-problems of TERL, i.e., entity mentions recognition and entity linking for the tails of triples respectively.
- We finally solve the TERL problem end-to-end by proposing a joint learning mechanism for the two proposed neural models, which could further improve both entity mentions recognition and entity linking results.
- Our empirical study conducted on real-world datasets demonstrates that our model outperforms state-of-the-art approaches on the two sub-problems of

TERL, i.e. entity mentions recognition and entity linking for the tails of triples respectively.

Roadmap: The rest of the paper is organized as follows. We cover the related work in Sect. 2 and then formally define the problem in Sect. 3. After introducing our models in Sect. 4, we present our empirical study in Sect. 5. We conclude the paper in Sect. 6.

2   Related Work

In this section, we firstly present the existing work on Named Entity Recognition (NER) and Entity Linking (EL) respectively, and then introduce some recent work on Infobox Linking.

2.1   Named Entity Recognition (NER)

NER is a task that seeks to locate and classify named entities in unstructured texts. The majority of the existing NER systems treat the task as a word sequence labeling problem and model it using conditional random fields (CRFs) [16] on top of hand-engineered features or, more recently, using BiLstm [17,20] capable of learning hidden lexical and syntactic features. In addition, NER systems have been achieving state-of-the-art results by using word contextual embeddings, obtained with language models [9].

One sub-problem in TERL can also be taken as a special kind of NER problem. Compared to the existing NER problems which are mainly studied on document-level or sentence-level, the NER problem in TERL is more challenging given that the texts in TERL are even shorter, which means the entity mentions lack enough textual context information in TERL.

2.2   Entity Linking (EL)

EL is the task of associating a specific textual mention of an entity in a given document with a large target catalog of entities in KG. Current approaches to EL make extensive use of deep neural networks and distributed representations [12, 24, 26], which have achieved state-of-art results where context-aware word, span and entity embeddings, together with neural similarity functions, are essential in these frameworks. These methods assume that the entity mentions have been given, which ignore the important dependency between NER and EL.

2.3   Infobox Linking

Infobox linking is similar to TERL which considers the tail entity mention has been detected. Infobox Linking aims at linking entity mentions to their corresponding KG entities. To address this problem, some existing methods have been proposed, including surface name matching [7] and relatedness ranking [10,18].

Surface Matching. This kind of methods [7] are simply based on string matching without using KG information and entity linking techniques. They extract values from infobox directly and use string matching to find the entities which should be linked. In specific, if there exists an entity name exactly matched with the infobox value, then the value will be replaced by the link to the matched entity. However, the ambiguity of entity name and the inconsistency of surface name make this method inaccurate.

Relatedness Ranking. In order to take advantage of KG information, some approaches based on machine learning models have been proposed. [29] propose an infobox linking method by designing seven features for candidate entities and then exploit a logistic regression model to determine the relevance of infobox's value and candidate entity. [18] extend the features set used in the above method and propose a boosting-based approach using GBDT and logistic regression to increase the reliability of the proposed model.

3 Problem Definition

A typical KG consists of a number of *facts*, usually in the form of triples denoted as *(head, predicate, tail)*, where *head* is an entity, *tail* can be either another entity or an attribute, and *head* entity links to *tail* by *predicate*. If the *tail* of the triple is an entity, we call this triple as a *Relation Triple*, otherwise we call it an *Attribute Triple*.

A widely existing problem to KG constructed manually and KG generated from encyclopedia's infobox is that many relation triples have their *tails* appear just as plain strings, where one or more entity mentions are unrecognized and unlinked to their corresponding KG entities. To solve this problem, we propose a new task - Tail Entity Recognition and Linking (TERL) for Knowledge Graphs (KG), aiming at recognizing ambiguous entity mentions contained in the tail of some relation triples, and linking these mentions to their corresponding entities in KG. More formally, we define the TERL task as follows:

Definition 1. Tail Entity Recognition and Linking (TERL). *For a relation triple (head,relation,tail_string) in KG, where tail_string is a plain string without links, the task of TERL recognizes all the entity mentions $M = \{m_1, m_2, ...\}$ from the tail_string. And then, for each $m_i \in M$, TERL identifies its corresponding candidate entity set $C(m_i) = \{e_{i,1}, e_{i,2}, ...\}$ from the KG, and finally links m_i to its corresponding entity $e_{i,j} \in C(m_i)$.*

4 Our Approach

Given a relation triple *(head, relation, tail_string)*, our model firstly uses Relation-aware Tail Entity Recognition Module to detect entity mentions in *tail_string*. This part will be introduced in Sect. 4.1. Then the Tail Entity Linking module links these mentions to their corresponding entities in KG, as will be covered in Sect. 4.2. We further design a sharing mechanism to jointly learn the two modules, which will be presented in Sect. 4.3.

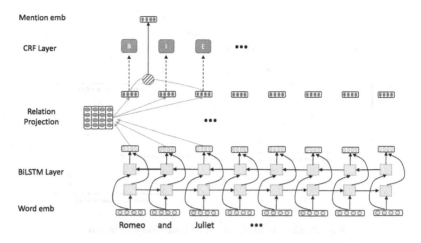

Fig. 2. The architecture of Our Tail Entity Recognition model

4.1 Relation-Aware Tail Entity Recognition

Given a relation triple *(head, relation, tail_string)*, this module aims at recognizing all entity mentions from *tail_string*, which can be modeled as a sequential text labeling problem. Particularly, for an input *tail_string* M with s character $\{w_1, w_2, ..., w_s\}$, where w_i denotes the *i-th* character in M, our task is to assign a label l_i to each character w_i, where $l_i \in \{B, I, O, E\}$, where the labels B, I, E represent the *begin, middle, end* words of an entity and the label O represents the other words.

Figure 2 describes the architecture of our model for tail entity recognition. Briefly, for each token in *tail_string*, we use the pre-trained word embeddings [8] to represent them, and then apply a Bi-LSTM layer to learn the semantics among them. Apart from that, we design a Relation Projection layer to learn token representations, which is followed by a CRF layer. Finally, we employ the outputs of CRF layer to detect entity and the outputs of Relation Projection to learn the shared mention embeddings for linking. More details are shown as follows.

Relation-Aware Tokens Representation Learning. In this section, we briefly introduce how to get the relation-aware representation of each token in the input *tail_string*. We feed the pre-trained word embedding of each token into a bi-directional LSTM layer to learn hidden states. The forward and backward outputs are concatenated to construct token representation:

$$h_{w_i} = [\overrightarrow{h_{w_i}}; \overleftarrow{h_{w_i}}] \qquad (1)$$

where $\overrightarrow{h_{w_i}}$ and $\overleftarrow{h_{w_i}}$ denote the forward and backward hidden state of BiLSTM layer.

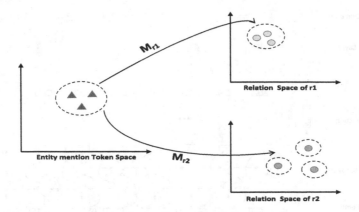

Fig. 3. Simple illustration of Relation Projection

The entity recognition results are decided not only by the textual context within the *tail_string*, but also the *relation* in the triples. For instance, given two relation triples *(William Shakespeare, Work, Romeo and Juliet)* and *(Romeo and Juliet, Characters , Romeo and Juliet)*, the two *tail_string* are same and an existing NER model may output one same results. However, considering the *relation* in triples, the NER results should be different. If the *relation* is *"Work"*, the whole string *"Romeo and Juliet"* is an entity mention. For the relation *"Characters"*, two entity mentions *"Romeo"* and *"Juliet"* should be detected. Thus, we take the *relation* of triples into account. To achieve this, we innovatively propose a Relation Projection layer to capture the hidden relation information. Particularly, we design a Relation Projection (RP) Layer on top of the BiLSTM layer to extract the hidden relation features. For each relation r, we set a projection matrix $\boldsymbol{W_r}$, which may project entity mentions from token space to relation space. Figure 3 describes a simple illustration of Relation Projection. With the mapping matrix, we define the projected of token as:

$$\boldsymbol{w}_i^r = \boldsymbol{h}_i \boldsymbol{W}_r \qquad (2)$$

where $\boldsymbol{W}_r$ is the projection matrix for relation r.

Entity Detection. Different common NER problem, TERL task only need predict entity boundaries. Formally, given the *tail_string* M with s words $M = \{w_1, w_2, ..., w_s\}$, and one entity $E_{i,j}$ where it is composed by a continuous word sequence $(w_i, w_{i+1}, ..., w_j)$. Specially, we tag the boundary word w_i as *"B"* and w_j as *"E"*. The word inside entities assigned with label *"I"* and non-entity word are assigned with *"O"* labels.

We recognize entity as shown in Fig. 2. For each token in *tail_string*, we predict a boundary label by feeding its relation-aware representation $\boldsymbol{w}_i^r$ into a ReLU activation function. Considering conditional Random Fields (CRFs) [16] always perform well in modeling sequence label dependencies (e.g., label "I" must be after "B"), we use a CRF layer as the last layer.

Given a training set $\{(M_i, y_i)\}$, the loss function in Tail Entity Recognition is shown as follows:

$$L_{ER} = - \sum_i \log(p(\boldsymbol{y}|\boldsymbol{M})) \tag{3}$$

where $p(\boldsymbol{y}|\boldsymbol{M})$ is a family of conditional probability over all possible label sequence $\boldsymbol{y}$ given M.

Apart from that, we also learn the shared entity mention representation in this stage. We average the representation for each token within $E_{i,j}$ to represent the shared entity mention. The shared representation of entity mention $E_{i,j}$ is obtained as follows:

$$E_{i,j} = \frac{1}{j-i+1} \sum_{k=i}^{j} \boldsymbol{w}_k^r \tag{4}$$

where $\boldsymbol{w}_k^r$ is the relation-aware representation for the k-th token in sequence M. If necessary, the shared mention representation will be sent into the Tail Entity Linking module.

4.2 Relation Tags-Aided Mention and Entity Representation Learning for Tail Entity Linking

Given a relation triple *(head,relation,tail_string)*, m is an entity mention contained in *tail_string*. This module links the entity mention m to its corresponding entity in KG. The key of this task is getting appropriate representations of entity mention and candidate entities.

Traditional entity linking makes mention representations aware of their local context. In our task, however, contexts are not available to mentions, which hinders us to gain more useful information from local contexts. Fortunately, there exists a large number of tags in KG. To represent mention and candidate entities well, our method fully leverages tag information. Briefly, we collect relevant tag information from KG and use attention mechanism to get mention representations and candidate entity representations. Then we select the candidate entity as the corresponding one, which has the most similar representation to the mention representation (Fig. 4).

Mention Representation Using Attentive Relation Tags. In this part, we propose a concept of Relation tags and explain how to get mention representations. For a relation r, we construct a triple set $triple_r = \{(S, r, O)\}$ from KG, where S is an entity set and O is another entity set. We do statistics to each entity's tags in the set O, and take the top k tags with the highest frequency as the Relation tags of r, denoted as $Tag_r = \{tag_1^r, tag_2^r, ..., tag_k^r\}$. m is an entity mention contained in *tail_string*. We organize m and Tag_r as a new sequence $m\_Tag_r = \{m, tag_1^r, ..., tag_k^r\}$. Considering tags in the Relation tags should be paid different attentions by assigning different weights for

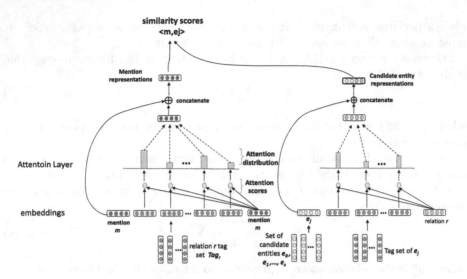

Fig. 4. Our Tail Entity Linking Module Architecture shown for the triple *(head,r,m)* and candidate entity e_j .

contributing mention representation learning. For example, in a triple *("Rush Hour(1998 film)", "Starring", "Jackie Chan")*, the Relation tags of relation *"Starring"* is { *"Actor"*, *"Singer"*, ...}. In common sense, the tag *"Actor"* has greater effect on mention *"Jackie Chan"* than tag *"Singer"*. Based on this observation, the mention-aware tag representation tag_m can be built using attention mechanism [27]:

$$z_{sm} = (W_Q E_m)(W_K tag_s^r)^\top \tag{5}$$

$$\alpha_s^r = \frac{\exp(z_{sm})}{\sum_{s=1}^k \exp(z_{sm})} \tag{6}$$

$$tag_m = \sum_{s=1}^k \alpha_s^r (W_V tag_s^r) \tag{7}$$

where matrix W_Q, W_K and W_V are trainable parameters, tag_s^r is the word embedding of the s-th tag in the set Tag_r. E_m is the shared entity mention embedding mentioned in Eq. 4. The final mention representation is generated by concatenating the representation of m and tag_m:

$$x_m = [E_m ; tag_m] \tag{8}$$

Attention-Based Candidate Entity Representation. The candidate entities generation is mainly based on the string comparison of mentions and names of entities in KG. To generate candidate entity set which contains possible entities, it is necessary to build a mention-entity dictionary D that contains a vast amount of information on the surface forms of entities, such as name variations, abbreviations, aliases, etc.

Given a triple $(head, r, m)$, the candidate entity set of m is denoted as $C(m) = \{e_0, e_1, ..., e_n\}$, what we need to do is to learn the representations for each entity in $C(m)$. The method of achieving candidate entity representations is similar to the way of learning mention representations. Considering that each tag of a candidate entity e_j contributes differently to the relation r. For instance, the tag "Actor" is more important than the tag "Singer" to the relation "Starring". We introduce attention mechanism to tackle this problem. In details, we firstly get the tags of entity e_j from KG denoted as $Tag^{e_j} = \{tag_1, tag_2..., tag_n\}$, then we use attention mechanism on Tag^{e_j} and relation r, to get the relation-aware representation e_j^r:

$$z_q = (\boldsymbol{W_1}r)(\boldsymbol{W_2}\boldsymbol{tag_q^{e_j}})^\top \tag{9}$$

$$\alpha_q^r = \frac{\exp(z_q)}{\sum_{q=1}^n \exp(z_q)} \tag{10}$$

$$e_j^r = \sum_{q=1}^n \alpha_q^r(\boldsymbol{W_3}\boldsymbol{tag_q^r}) \tag{11}$$

where matrix $\boldsymbol{W_1}, \boldsymbol{W_2}$ and $\boldsymbol{W_3}$ are trainable parameters. r is the word embedding of relation r. $\boldsymbol{tag_q^{e_j}}$ means the q-th tag embedding of candidate entity e_j and α_q^r is the weight of $\boldsymbol{tag_q^{e_j}}$.

To merge some semantic information, we concatenate e_j and e_j^r. The final representation of candidate entity e_j is x_j:

$$\boldsymbol{x_{e_j}} = [e_j; e_j^r] \tag{12}$$

where e_j is word embedding of entity e_j.

Entity Linking Score. We use cosine similarity to compute the final score between mention representation $\boldsymbol{x_m}$ and each candidate entity representation $\boldsymbol{x_{e_i}}$. Then we select the candidate entity $\hat{e}$ with the highest score as the corresponding entity in KG:

$$\boldsymbol{score_m} = Cosine(\boldsymbol{x_m}, \boldsymbol{C_m}) \tag{13}$$

where $\boldsymbol{x_m}$ is the mention representation of m and matrix $\boldsymbol{C_m}$ contains all the candidate entity representations. The linking loss function is the cross entropy:

$$L_{EL} = -\sum_{i=1}^T \sum_{m=1}^{M(i)} y_m^\top log(softmax(\boldsymbol{score_m})) \tag{14}$$

where T is the total number of relational triple *(head,relation,tail_string)* in training data, and $M(i)$ denotes the number of mention in i-th *tail_string*. The golden entity for mention m is represented by the one-hot vector $y_m^\top$.

4.3 Joint Learning

It's not a good choice to train Entity Recognition (ER) and Entity Linking (EL) independently since the errors generated from ER can propagate to EL. That is, the wrong ER decision will decrease the performance of the linking module. Luckily, this problem can be avoided by proper context understanding (i.e. EL).

Therefore, we apply a joint learning strategy to learn these two parts jointly. In details, we apply a parameter sharing mechanism for multi-task training using BiLSTM and Relational Projection layers as shared feature extractor. Firstly we get the shared mention representation (Eq. 4) from the extractor. Then the shared mention representations will be propagated into EL module. Parameter sharing greatly reduces the risk of overfitting and increases the correlation of ER module and tail EL module. During the training phase, we feed the ground-truth labels into ER module so that the EL module will be trained without affection from incorrect entity recognition. The joint learning loss is then obtained by summing the individual loss:

$$L = L_{ER} + L_{EL} \tag{15}$$

where L_{ER} and L_{EL} denote the loss function for ER module and EL module, respectively.

In addition, due to the fact ER module may detect some incorrect mentions that should not be linked. For instance, the incorrect mention *"Romeo and Juliet"* has corresponding entity in KG but it should not be linked to KG. This fact influences both ER and EL modules. In this case, we design another loss function to improve the performance of joint learning model. The NNEL (No-Need Entity Linking) loss is shown as follows:

$$L_{NNEL} = \sum_{i=1}^{T} \sum_{m=1}^{\widehat{M}(i)} max(score(m)) \tag{16}$$

where the T is the total number of *Relational Triple* in training data, $\widehat{M}(i)$ denotes the number of entity mentions in i-th *tail_string* which do not need to be linked. The $score(m)$ represents the cosine similarity scores between m and candidate entity set $C(m)$. So the final joint learning loss function is shown as follows:

$$L = L_{ER} + L_{EL} + L_{NNEL} \tag{17}$$

5 Experiments

5.1 Datasets and Metrics

We crawl entity articles from BaiduBaike [21] and HudongBaike [3] which contain information including infoboxes, descriptions and tags. In order to obtain amount of data without tremendous manual annotation efforts, we collect anchor texts that contain hyperlink to the reference entity from infoboxes. Suppose that for

Table 1. Comparison of ER results in the test set.

Methods	Baidupedia			Hudongpedia		
	Recall	Precision	F1	Recall	Precsion	F1
BiLstm-CRF (Huang et al.)	73.84%	84.56%	78.83%	72.63%	85.32%	78.46%
Bert case (Devlin et al.)	75.94%	89.19%	82.03%	75.71%	89.12%	81.86%
BiLstm-RT-CRF (Only NER)	86.93%	91.12%	88.97%	86.52%	90.68%	88.54%
Joint Learning model	**89.48%**	**91.20%**	**90.34%**	**89.51%**	**91.08%**	**90.28%**
Joint Learning model (+NNEL Loss)	89.38%	91.05%	90.20%	88.32%	90.79%	89.53%

an entity article e, its infobox has several relations, one relation value m is an anchor text which is linked to an entity e_m. These elements construct a relation triples denoted as $(e, relation, m)$, and the corresponding entity of m in KG is e_m. The rest candidate entities for m to construct negative examples in the way we introduce in Sect. 4.2. To reduce manual cost, we simulate real KG data in which one or more entity mentions included in tail element and create two datasets using these relation triples from BaiduBaike and HudongBaike respectively. The dataset1 (denoted as Baidupedia) includes 54000 triples and dataset2 (denoted as Hudongpedia) includes 50000 triples.

As for the evaluation metrics, we use *Recall*, *Precision* and *F*1 to evaluate the performance of the Tail Entity Recognition and like the existing state-of-the-art infobox linking model [18], we use *Precision* to assess the performance of the Tail Entity Linking task.

5.2 Baseline Methods

We compare our joint learning model with NER and infobox linking models separately on BaiduPedia and HudongPedia. We choose two state-of-the-art NER models including BiLstm-CRF [14] and Bert-base [9], and some state-of-the-art infobox linking models as baselines. The details of baseline infobox linking models are as follows. BoW Model [7] proposes a straightforward method which is to compare the context of the mention and the description of candidate entities. LR Ranking Model [29] convertes the ranking problem into a classification problem and solves it using logistic regression. SVM Ranking Model [10] designs a svm model which uses a max-margin loss to train the model. GBDT+LR Model [18] extends the feature set used in LR Ranking Model and proposes a boosting-based approach.

5.3 Results

Comparison with Individual Modules. TERL task considers one or more entity mentions existing in *tail_string*, which can be solved by joint learning model in this paper. In order to prove the effectiveness of our joint learning model on both tasks, we compare the joint learning model with popular NER and Infobox Linking models separately. And to understand whether the joint learning approach is advantageous for NER and EL, we also compare the results obtained by the same models when training with separate objectives.

1. **Comparison with NER models.** The comparison results for NER can be found in Table 1. Our single BiLSTM-RT-CRF method surpasses all competitors on NER by a large margin, at least 10% on *Recall* in both datasets. This means our method can detect different entity mentions in a same *tail_string* depending the different *relation* in triple. It can be attributed to the Relation Projection Layer which can capture the relation information well. Our joint learning model achieves best performance on all metrics in that entity recognition can benefit from tail entity linking and each wrong entity detection can be avoided by proper context understanding. The results explains the *relation* in triple and joint learning can influence entity detection in our scenario. The performance on two datasets have no significant difference, which shows that our model can achieve good results in different KG. The NNEL Loss does not improve the performance in NER stage, because incorrect span may have been captured in common joint learning model.

2. **Comparison with EL models.** In the EL case, in order to perform a fair comparison, the mentions that are linked by the Tail Entity Linking system correspond to the ones detected by the joint learning approach. We compare our joint learning model with several state-of-the-art infobox linking models. And to evaluate our joint learning model, we compare joint learning model with individual linking module. The results can be observed in Table 2. The joint learning model obviously increases the linking precision. In addition, the *Precision* of **Joint Learning model (+NNEL Loss)** can reach 93.69% in BaiduPedia and can reach 89.87% in Hudongpedia, which is much higher than other models. The results show the NNEL loss has great influence on tail entity linking task, and as expected, the NNEL Loss can reduce the number of incorrect mentions that should not be linked. It is noticeable that the results of these models on the two datasets perform a little difference on *Precision*, which results from the following reasons. (1) Entities in the Baidupedia have an average of 6 tags while entities in the Hudongpedia have 4 tags averagely. Therefore, our model which based on entity tag information, performed better on Baidupedia. (2) As mentioned in Sect. 2, these baselines extract features from entity description that provides a concise summary of salient information of entity with hyperlink. The entity description information are less in Hudongpedia than in the Baidupedia. So, the final result of Hudongpedia is not so good as that in the Baidupedia.

The results in Table 1 and Table 2 show that, as expected, Entity Recognition could benefit from Infobox Linking and vice versa. This indicates that by leveraging the relatedness of the tasks, we can achieve better results. In addition, the results prove the NNEL loss has significant influence on TERL task, especially in the EL stage.

Table 2. Comparison of EL results in the test set.

Methods	BaiduPedia	HudongPedia
	Precision	Precision
BoW Model (Chen et al.)	59.31%	61.28%
LR Ranking Model (Xu et al.)	82.12%	78.63%
SVM Ranking Model (Dredze et al.)	85.21%	80.72%
GBDT+LR Model (Li et al.)	88.39%	82.21%
Only Linking	89.96%	85.21%
Joint Learning model	90.99%	86.46%
Joint Learning model (+NNEL Loss)	**93.69%**	**89.87%**

6 Conclusions

In this paper, we work towards the TERL problem by fully leveraging KG information with two neural models for solving the two sub-problems, i.e., tail entity recognition and tail entity linking respectively. We propose an end-to-end framework to solve the TERL problem by proposing a joint learning mechanism for the two proposed neural models, which could further improve both entity recognition and entity linking results. Our experiments on real-world datasets demonstrate that our model performs much better than baseline models and can solve TERL task which are not taken into account by other methods.

Acknowledgments. This research is partially supported by National Key R&D Program of China (No. 2018AAA0101900), Natural Science Foundation of Jiangsu Province (No. BK2019 1420), National Natural Science Foundation of China (Grant No. 61632016), Natural Science Research Project of Jiangsu Higher Education Institution (No. 17KJA5 20003), the Suda-Toycloud Data Intelligence Joint Laboratory and a project funded by the Priority Academic Program Development of Jiangsu Higher Education Institutions.

References

1. https://wiki.dbpedia.org/
2. http://www.yago.com/
3. https://baike.com/
4. Berant, J., Chou, A., Frostig, R., Liang, P.: Semantic parsing on freebase from question-answer pairs. In: Proceedings of the 2013 Conference on Empirical Methods in Natural Language Processing, pp. 1533–1544 (2013)
5. Bunescu, R., Paşca, M.: Using encyclopedic knowledge for named entity disambiguation. In: 11th Conference of the European Chapter of the Association for Computational Linguistics (2006)
6. Cao, P., Chen, Y., Liu, K., Zhao, J., Liu, S.: Adversarial transfer learning for Chinese named entity recognition with self-attention mechanism. In: Proceedings of the 2018 Conference on Empirical Methods in Natural Language Processing (2018)

7. Chen, Z., et al.: Cuny-blender tac-kbp2010 entity linking and slot filling system description. In: TAC (2010)
8. Cui, Y., et al.: Pre-training with whole word masking for chinese bert. arXiv preprint arXiv:1906.08101 (2019)
9. Devlin, J., Chang, M.W., Lee, K., Toutanova, K.: Bert: Pre-training of deep bidirectional transformers for language understanding. arXiv preprint arXiv:1810.04805 (2018)
10. Dredze, M., McNamee, P., Rao, D., Gerber, A., Finin, T.: Entity disambiguation for knowledge base population. In: Proceedings of the 23rd International Conference on Computational Linguistics, pp. 277–285. Association for Computational Linguistics (2010)
11. Globerson, A., Lazic, N., Chakrabarti, S., Subramanya, A., Ringaard, M., Pereira, F.: Collective entity resolution with multi-focal attention. In: Proceedings of the 54th Annual Meeting of the Association for Computational Linguistics (Volume 1: Long Papers), pp. 621–631 (2016)
12. He, Z., Liu, S., Li, M., Zhou, M., Zhang, L., Wang, H.: Learning entity representation for entity disambiguation. In: Proceedings of the 51st Annual Meeting of the Association for Computational Linguistics (Volume 2: Short Papers), pp. 30–34 (2013)
13. Hochreiter, S., Schmidhuber, J.: Long short-term memory. Neural Comput. $9(8)$, 1735–1780 (1997)
14. Huang, Z., Xu, W., Yu, K.: Bidirectional lstm-crf models for sequence tagging. arXiv preprint arXiv:1508.01991 (2015)
15. Jin, H., Hou, L., Li, J., Dong, T.: Attributed and predictive entity embedding for fine-grained entity typing in knowledge bases. In: Proceedings of the 27th International Conference on Computational Linguistics, COLING (2018)
16. Lafferty, J., McCallum, A., Pereira, F.C.: Conditional random fields: probabilistic models for segmenting and labeling sequence data (2001)
17. Lample, G., Ballesteros, M., Subramanian, S., Kawakami, K., Dyer, C.: Neural architectures for named entity recognition. arXiv preprint arXiv:1603.01360 (2016)
18. Li, X., Yang, J., Zhang, R., Ma, H.: A novel approach on entity linking for encyclopedia infoboxes. In: Zhao, J., Harmelen, F., Tang, J., Han, X., Wang, Q., Li, X. (eds.) CCKS 2018. CCIS, vol. 957, pp. 103–115. Springer, Singapore (2019). https://doi.org/10.1007/978-981-13-3146-6_9
19. Lin, B.Y., Lu, W.: Neural adaptation layers for cross-domain named entity recognition. arXiv preprint arXiv:1810.06368 (2018)
20. Liu, L., et al.: Empower sequence labeling with task-aware neural language model. In: Thirty-Second AAAI Conference on Artificial Intelligence (2018)
21. Murphy, T.I.: Line spacing in latex documents. https://baike.baidu.com/. Accessed 4 Apr 2010
22. Nathani, D., Chauhan, J., Sharma, C., Kaul, M.: Learning attention-based embeddings for relation prediction in knowledge graphs. arXiv preprint arXiv:1906.01195 (2019)
23. Niu, X., Sun, X., Wang, H., Rong, S., Qi, G., Yu, Y.: Zhishi.me - weaving Chinese linking open data. In: Aroyo, L., et al. (eds.) ISWC 2011. LNCS, vol. 7032, pp. 205–220. Springer, Heidelberg (2011). https://doi.org/10.1007/978-3-642-25093-4_14
24. Radhakrishnan, P., Talukdar, P., Varma, V.: Elden: improved entity linking using densified knowledge graphs. In: Proceedings of the 2018 Conference of the North American Chapter of the Association for Computational Linguistics: Human Language Technologies, Volume 1 (Long Papers), pp. 1844–1853 (2018)

25. Shi, B., Weninger, T.: Open-world knowledge graph completion. In: Thirty-Second AAAI Conference on Artificial Intelligence (2018)
26. Sun, Y., Lin, L., Tang, D., Yang, N., Ji, Z., Wang, X.: Modeling mention, context and entity with neural networks for entity disambiguation. In: Twenty-Fourth International Joint Conference on Artificial Intelligence (2015)
27. Vaswani, A., et al.: Attention is all you need. In: Advances in neural information processing systems, pp. 5998–6008 (2017)
28. Wang, H., Zhang, F., Zhao, M., Li, W., Xie, X., Guo, M.: Multi-task feature learning for knowledge graph enhanced recommendation. In: The World Wide Web Conference, WWW (2019)
29. Xu, M., et al.: Discovering missing semantic relations between entities in Wikipedia. In: Alani, H., et al. (eds.) ISWC 2013. LNCS, vol. 8218, pp. 673–686. Springer, Heidelberg (2013). https://doi.org/10.1007/978-3-642-41335-3_42

Natural Answer Generation
via Graph Transformer

Xiangyu Li, Sen Hu, and Lei Zou[✉]

Peking University, Beijing, China
{xiangyu_li,husen,zoulei}@pku.edu.cn

Abstract. Natural Answer Generation (NAG), which generates natural answer sentences for the given question, has received much attention in recent years. Compared with traditional QA systems, NAG could offer specific entities fluently and naturally, which is more user-friendly in the real world. However, existing NAG systems usually utilize simple retrieval and embedding mechanism, which is hard to tackle complex questions. They suffer issues containing knowledge insufficiency, entity ambiguity, and especially poor expressiveness during generation. To address these challenges, we propose an improved knowledge extractor to retrieve supporting graphs from the knowledge base, and an extending graph transformer to encode the supporting graph, which considers global and variable information as well as the communication path between entities. In this paper, we propose a framework called G-NAG, including a knowledge extractor, an incorporating encoder, and an LSTM generator. Experimental results on two complex QA datasets demonstrate the efficiency of G-NAG compared with state-of-the-art NAG systems and transformer baselines.

Keywords: Question answering · Natural Answer Generation · Graph transformer

1 Introduction

Natural Answer Generation (NAG), which devotes to providing fluent answers in the form of natural language sentences, has received much attention in recent years. Compared with traditional question answering (QA) systems that merely offer accurate Answer Semantic Units (*ASU*) [10], NAG could satisfy users in real-world scenarios where fluency is of strong demand.

Generally, the popular NAG framework consists of three modules, as shown in Fig. 1-a. Knowledge extractor recognizes the topic entity and retrieves its related triples from the underlying Knowledge Base (KB). After Knowledge encoder representing these candidate triples and the question as two sequences, Generator could generate the natural answer with an attention mechanism. Existing NAG systems have achieved some success focused on simple problems (one topic entity), such as [6,10,27].

© Springer Nature Switzerland AG 2020
X. Wang et al. (Eds.): APWeb-WAIM 2020, LNCS 12317, pp. 302–318, 2020.
https://doi.org/10.1007/978-3-030-60259-8_23

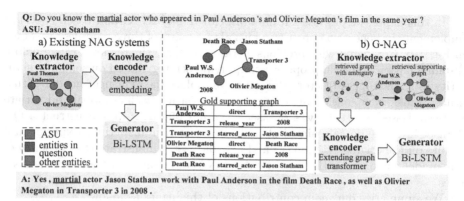

Fig. 1. Natural Answer Generation process of an example question.

However, there are still many non-trivial issues due to linguistic complexity that the above systems do not perform well. (1) In Knowledge extractor. On the one hand, existing NAG systems recognize one topic entity and retrieve its one-hop neighbors related to the question. When a question contains more entities and multi-hop relations, they may leave out some critical entities. Take Q in Fig. 1 as an example, the *ASU* Jason Statham should be retrieved through 2-hops from the mentioned entities in question so that it may be left by previous knowledge extractor with one-hop retrieval mechanism. On the other hand, without considering the global structure in KB, the above systems do disambiguation before retrieving triples. Thus, they may choose irrelevant entities far apart from others, such as Paul Thomas Anderson which may be confused with the correct entity Paul W.S. Anderson but unrelated to the question in Fig. 1-a. (2) In Knowledge encoder. Previous NAG systems encode triples as a sequence, such as a list by LSTM [10,27] or key-value structure by Memory Network [6], which is too simple to express complicated semantic information. For the same example, triple-list or key-value could not represent the topological structure of the supporting graph clearly, which is the key to generate answers logically.

We focus on these challenges above and propose some novel solutions. (1) In Knowledge extractor, we consider to retrieve multi-hop triples around mentioned entities, such as 2-hops, as some may not appear in questions but useful for answer generating. Since multi-hop retrieval may return a supporting graph with much redundancy, we propose a simplifying method based on semantic similarity, as shown in Fig. 1-b. Meanwhile, we solve entity ambiguity after retrieving triples based on the global structure in KB to choose correct entities. (2) In Knowledge encoder. Since graph transformer [13] is proposed to generate summarization and achieve excellent performance, we employ an extending graph transformer as encoder, which has more capacity to encode complicated pairwise relationships than the sequence structure. To fit the NAG problem, we introduce the communication path and two extra vertices to capture global or variable information, respectively (to be discussed in Sect. 2.3).

In this paper, we propose a framework called G-NAG (Graph-based NAG) to implement the generation process, which also consists of three modules, as shown in Fig. 1-b. Compared with previous work, we enlarge the retrieval range before disambiguation and then propose a simplifying strategy based on semantic similarity in Knowledge extractor. Moreover, we replace the sequence encoder with a graph transformer considering communication path as well as global and variate vertices. Based on `Wikimovie` dataset [16] and `DBpedia`, we reconstruct a QA dataset in movie domain aimed at multi-hop question answering. Experimental results on the original `Wikimovie` and new dataset demonstrate the efficiency of our model compared with state-of-the-art NAG systems and transformer baselines.

We summarize our main contributions of this paper as follow:

- We design a generation framework G-NAG, which generates natural and logical answer based on KB. To our knowledge, it is the first framework that aims at addressing complex NAG problem.
- We present a novel knowledge extractor which enlarges retrieval range before disambiguation and simplifies triples based on semantic similarity to gain the supporting graph.
- We propose an extending graph transformer to represent the supporting graph, which considers the communication path and captures global or variable information by extra vertices.
- We implement experiments on two datasets in the movie domain. The results demonstrate that G-NAG performs better compared with existing NAG approaches and transformer baselines, especially in complex natural answer generation problems.

2   Methodology

In this section, we introduce the notations employed in this paper.

Basic Definition: We denote a given question as Q, and its accurate Answer Semantic Units as ASU. There is only one type of ASU for each question, i.e., the ASU maybe two actors but not an actor and a writer. The generated natural answer is denoted as A, and knowledge triples in KB are in the form $\langle s, p, o \rangle$, where s, o are entity vertices (ent) and p is relation edge (rel).

Graph Definition: We define the initial graph by multi-hop retrieval as a inter-connected graph set $\mathbb{G} = [G_i = (V_q, V_o, E_i)]$, where vertex $v \in V_q$ is mentioned in question, $v \in V_o$ denotes other retrieved vertex, and E_i is a set of relation edges that link vertices. After disambiguation and graph simplifying, the final supporting graph is denoted as G. In encoding section, we convert G to an unlabeled graph $G' = (V', P')$, where V' is a set of all vertices and P' is a matrix describing communication path among vertices.

2.1   Framework Overview

Our G-NAG framework consists of three modules: Knowledge Extractor, Incorporating Encoder, and Generator. We depict an overview with a concrete example in Fig. 2.

In Knowledge Extractor: Given the question Q, G-NAG maps each entity phrase to its candidate linking vertices $v \in V_q$ in underlying KB. Allowing for the ambiguity of phrase linking, k-hop neighbors of these $v \in V_q$ are retrieved from KB. These triples construct a large graph, which could be divided into an inter-connected graph set $\mathbb{G}$, as illustrated in Fig. 2 a-I. Then for disambiguation, we employ a cost-distance strategy as a-II. Further, G-NAG removes redundant vertices and edges by semantic similarity to acquire a simplified supporting graph G as shown in Fig. 2 a-III. In Incorporating Encoder: G-NAG obtains the embedding of supporting graph and question through concatenating a novel graph transformer (to be discussed in Sect. 2.3) and bi-LSTM, as shown in Fig. 2-b. Specially, we consider the communication path between vertices-pair in graph attention calculation. Before encoding, we convert the supporting graph G to an unlabeled bipartite graph G', which contains global and variate vertices (to be discussed in Sect. 2.2).

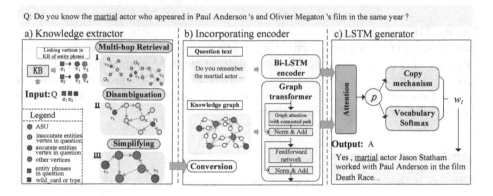

Fig. 2. Natural Answer Generation process of an example question.

In Generator: G-NAG predicts output word w_t at each time step t by generating from vocabulary or copying from supporting graph G and question Q via a soft switch p. As illustrated in Fig. 2-c, token with underline is copied from question text, and the colored token is from the graph, while other ordinary words are generated from the vocabulary.

2.2   Knowledge Extractor

We propose an improved knowledge extractor in this section to provide a more accurate supporting graph. Specifically, we enlarge the extraction range by multi-hop retrieval before entity disambiguation, then solve the ambiguity based on the global graph structure, and simplify the graph by semantic similarity eventually.

In the offline phase, following a similar procedure to [25], G-NAG encodes the underlying KB into a common low-dimensional vector space. We employ TransE, which refers to that p of each triple is represented as translation operation from head vertex s to tail vertex o. Take triple $\langle s, p, o \rangle$ as an example, o should be the closest vertex of $s + p$, while semantically similar vertices should be closed as well.

Multi-hop Retrieval

Given Q, we map each entity phrase $enti$ to its candidate linking vertices $v \in V_q$ in KB, while a entity phrase $ent1$ may be matched more than one vertex as a set, such as $v_{ent1} = [v_i^1] \subseteq V_q$. Allowing for the ambiguity of phrase linking temporarily, we retrieve k-hop neighbors of each linking vertex to construct a large graph. As some linking vertices are far apart in KB, the large graph could be divided into a graph set $\mathbb{G} = [G_i = (V_q, V_o, E_i)]$ where G_i are unconnected to each other, V_q denotes linking vertices for entity phrase in question and V_o denotes the other vertices retrieved. Factual questions usually have only a group of core multi-hop relationships, that is, the distances between exact entities are all within a fixed number of hops, so target entities are rarely distributed on two completely different graphs G_i.

Entity Disambiguation

In this stage, G-NAG deals with the ambiguous vertices in V_q. To ensure the integrity of the supporting graph, we remain at most M graphs in $\mathbb{G}$ with more linking entity phrases (Assume n graphs cover all entity phrases and denote m as a parameter). Then considering one of the remaining graphs G_i, we compute its cost motivated by [25] formulated as follow:

$$M = max(m, n), \quad Cost_{G_i} = \sum_{(s,p,o) \in G_i} \|s + p - o\|_2^2 \tag{1}$$

Because of the cumulative effect of error, the candidate G with the minimum cost could be selected with the strongest internal relevance.

Moreover, we propose a minimum-distance method to delete redundant linking vertices in G for each entity phrase. Take $v_{ent1} = [v_1, v_2]$ in Fig. 3-a as an example, we define the shortest path (number of edges) between v_1 and each vertex of v_{ent2} as the minimum-distance between v_1 and v_{ent2}. Then we rank vertices v in the same v_{entj} according to the minimum-distance sum of v and other v_{entj}. Further, we only keep the vertex with the minimum sum in each v.

Graph Simplifying

In this stage, G-NAG deletes redundant vertices in V_o. For each vertex $v \in V_o$ in graph, we keep it if there exists a communication path between two linking vertices $v_i, v_j \in V_q$ containing it. In other words, we remove $v \in V_o$ only related to one entity phrase, which means a weak correlation with Q. Here, we regard two vertices as isomorphic if they share the same neighborhood and connect every common neighbor vertex with edges of the same relation. Then we merge isomorphic vertices and concatenate their text attributions as one vertex.

G-NAG further deletes redundant vertices in V_o using aggregated semantic similarities based on word embedding [9]. For this step, we only consider the alternative vertex $v \in V_o$ that could be removed without affecting the connectivity of the graph. Specifically, for each vertex, we concatenate triples containing it as a word sequence T, then use Word2Vec [15] to compute string similarities between T and question Q following [20]. Where, w represents a word of the string, and the average is used as the aggregation functions. Finally, we keep the top-k alternative vertices in V_o with a higher score.

$$Similarity(Q, T) = Agg \ cos(w_Q, w_T) \tag{2}$$

Different from existing NAG systems, which match triples with the question directly, G-NAG performs multi-hop retrieval in entity-level without considering relation phrases, then simplifies the graph based on semantic similarity. This strategy allows G-NAG to handle implicit relations, where predicates are missed in question, more effectively.

In addition, we identify the wild-card, i.e., *who*, *when* or main type phrase, i.e., *actress* in Fig. 1, in question text, which will be the text attribution of variate vertex described in next section.

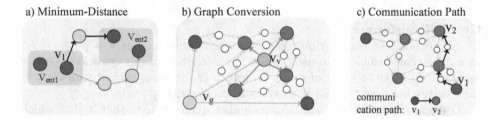

Fig. 3. Example of minimum distance, graph conversion and communication path

2.3   Incorporating Encoder

The encoder receives discrete inputs (question text and supporting graph defined before) and encodes them into numerical representations jointly [3], to accomplish neural network feeding.

Graph Conversion

Inspired by [2,13], we convert the extracted graph to an unlabeled bipartite graph. Specifically, we replace each relation edge with two vertices, where one represents the forward direction of the relation and the other represents the reverse. The key difference with the above work is G-NAG introduces two extra vertices v_v, v_g to capture effective information.

Specifically, global vertex connects to vertices $v \in V_q$ mentioned in the question to update the global state following the reasoning perspective as humans. Besides, variate vertex connects to other retrieved vertices $v \in V_o$ and global vertex, where its text attribution is a wild-card, i.e., who, or ASU type recognized by knowledge extractor, i.e., actor. Therefore, the variate vertex v_v concerns the other retrieved vertices $v \in V_o$ except for these mentioned in question, while global vertex v_g mainly grasps the whole graph via mentioned vertices $v \in V_q$ and variate vertex v_v.

As shown in Fig. 3-b, global vertex v_g, which concentrates information via two mentioned vertices and the variate vertex, could reach all vertices in G'. Therefore, we initialize the decoder state using global vertex representation after self-attention following [13, 26]. Moreover, since the variate vertex has specific text attribution, it focuses more on other involved vertices $v \in V_o$ especially ASU, which is of vital importance for the generation. The conversion result is $G' = (V', P')$, where V' is a vertex set and P' is a matrix storing communication path between every vertices-pair. Take vertices pair v_1, v_2 as an example in Fig. 3-c, a sequence of vertex text attribution along the path from v_1 to v_2 expresses the communication path. Note we choose the shortest path between vertices-pair (numbers of edges) and adopt embedding average when two or more equal length paths exist.

Graph Transformer

In this section, the text attribution of vertices is embedded as $V = [v_i], v_i \in R^d$ in a dense continuous space using bi-LSTM described in the Question encoder section, which is the input of graph transformer. Same as typical transformer, each vertex has 3 vector representations $\mathbf{q}(query)$, $\mathbf{k}(key)$, $\mathbf{v}(value)$.

Our graph transformer maintains a similar architecture as that in [13], which is proposed to generate summarization in the scientific domain. Compared with summarization generation, there are two differences in our task that is also challenges for encoding.

- Entities in supporting graph could be divided into mentioned vertices $v \in V_q$ and other retrieved vertices $v \in V_o$, while the former linked by entity phrases are related to answers but the latter may be ASU or supplementary information that could be omitted.
- There are closer relationships between entities than that of a summarization since the supporting graph is for a specific question in NAG, not for a scientific topic.

Therefore, we improve the graph transformer as following.

For each original vertex, G-NAG employs self-attention over the whole converted graph while [13] only calculates on local neighborhoods. This design allows vertex to capture more information except for neighborhoods since the supporting graph in the NAG task is smaller and more logically connected than that in the long-text summarization generation task.

Besides, we extend the conventional self-attention architecture by explicitly encoding the communication path between vertices-pair v_i, v_j in the alignment model motivated by [22]. Specifically, we encode the communication path described following into d-size dimension space and add it to vertex v_j's $\mathbf{k}(key)$ vector for calculation. Thus, we represent v_i as the weighted sum of all vertices' $\mathbf{v}(value)$ vectors with the consideration of communication path, formulated as follow:

$$\hat{v}_i = \underset{n=1}{\overset{N}{\|}} \sum_{j \in V} \alpha_{ij}^n W_V^n v_j, \ where \ a_{ij}^n = \frac{exp((\mathbf{W_k k_j} + \mathbf{W_R r_{ij}})^\top W_Q q_i)}{\sum_{z \in V} exp((\mathbf{W_k k_z} + \mathbf{W_R r_{iz}})^\top W_Q q_i)} \quad (3)$$

where $\|$ represents concatenation, α_{ij}^n is normalized attention coefficient computed by self-attention mechanism per head, and W_V^n is transformation's weight matrix of $\mathbf{v}(value)$. For each attention function α, W_K, W_Q are transformation's weight matrix of $\mathbf{k}$ (key) and $\mathbf{q}$ $(query)$, where r_{ij} denotes the embedded communication path between v_i, v_j and $W_R \in R^{d*d}$ is a parameter matrix of $\mathbf{r}$.

For global and variate vertex, we compute their representation over neighbor vertices without path encoding respectively. As discussed before, we capture retrieved information by variate vertex and obtain global state by global vertex, which allows graph transformer to better articulate global patterns and *ASU* location. Since the edges around each extra vertex do not represent real relation in KB, we only contextualize global and variate vertices' representation by attending over their neighborhoods. As a result, these two vertices' representations are calculated attending over their neighborhoods in G' formulated as follows. Here, $\mathcal{N}_g$ denotes the neighborhoods of v_g and the representation calculation of v_v is the same as v_g.

$$\hat{v}_g = \underset{n=1}{\overset{N}{\|}} \sum_{j \in \mathcal{N}_g} \alpha_j^n W_V^n v_j, \quad where \ a_j^n = \frac{exp((\mathbf{W_k k_g})^\top W_Q q_i)}{\sum_{z \in \mathcal{N}_g} exp((\mathbf{W_k k_z})^\top W_Q q_g)} \quad (4)$$

Finally, we adopt the conventional transform architecture, which is composed of a stack of D = 6 identical layers. As illustrated in Fig. 2 b, each layer consists of a self-attention mechanism and feed-forward network, both around by a residual connection. The final representation of vertices is denoted as $V^D = [v^D]$.

In the following, we describe the representation of the communication path between vertices-pair. Given a vertex sequence along the communication path between two vertices, we concatenate the text attribution p_i of each vertex as sequence $p = [p_i]$. Then, we acquire d-sized corresponding embedding sequence $s = [s_i]$ inspired by the label sequence embedding procedure in [28]. Considering continuous or discrete representations separately, we employ the average method and self-attention method to calculate representation vector r_{ij}.

Average Method: Calculate the averaged embedding as the representation vector of the communication path.

Self-attention Method: Use attention function as presented in Eq. 4 to acquire the representation of s as $h^s = [h_i^s]$, then define a weight γ to calculate weighted sum of h^s as r:

$$\gamma_i = \frac{exp(e_i)}{\sum_{k=0}^{L} exp(e_k)}, e_i = v^\top tanh(W_{h^s} h_i^s + b) \tag{5}$$

where L denotes the length of communication path.

Question Encoder

The question encoder transforms the question text into a vector representation by Recurrent Neural Network (RNN). The tokens of the question q_i are fed into a single-layer bidirectional LSTM [11] one by one, producing a sequence of concatenated encoder hidden states hq_i. While hq_i is expressed by $[\overrightarrow{hq_i}, \overleftarrow{hq_{L-i+1}}]$, which are encoded by a forward and a backward RNN independently. We use encoder state $hq_L = [\overrightarrow{hq_L}, \overleftarrow{hq_1}]$ to represent the whole question, while encoder output list hq_i is stored for attention distribution calculation.

2.4   Generator

To predict answer words y_t in each time step, we use LSTM decoder. During training, decoder accepts the embedding of previous output words $y_{<t} = y_1, y_2, ..., y_{t-1}$, a context vector c_t with attention on inputs, and decoder hidden state of previous step s_{t-1} to update hidden state: $s_t = f(y_{t-1}, s_{t-1}, c_t)$. Inspired by Copynet [7], we apply the copy mechanism to deal with the unknown or special words expected to appear in the answer sentence. In the following, we describe the generation process in decoder at each time step.

Firstly, we initialize the decoder state using global vertex representation as s_0. Then we compute the graph context vector c_g using N-headed attention as follows, which is a weighted sum of vertex representations.

$$c_g = s_t + \overset{N}{\underset{n=1}{\|}} \sum_{i \in V} \alpha_i^n W_G^n v_i^D, \qquad where \; \alpha_i = \frac{exp((\mathbf{W_k k_i})^\top W_Q s_t)}{\sum_{z \in V} exp((\mathbf{W_k k_z})^\top W_Q s_t)} \tag{6}$$

Similarly, the question context vector c_q is computed attending over the question text as in [1]. Then we concatenate c_g and c_q as final context vector c_t. Below, parameters W_h, W_s, b^* are learned during training, and L indicates the length of question sequence.

$$c_q = \sum_{j=1}^{L} \beta_j^n h_j, \; where \; \beta_j = \frac{exp(e_j)}{\sum_{k=0}^{L} exp(e_k)}, e_j = v^\top tanh(W_h h_j + W_s s_t + b^*) \tag{7}$$

G-NAG model generates answer words both from vocabulary based on attention and copying words via pointing. Therefore, we define a soft switch g within

0 to 1, which chooses between predicting a vocabulary word by distribution P_v or copying a word via attention distribution $[\alpha_i, \beta_j]$. Eventually, we acquire a final probability distribution over the extend vocabulary as follows.

$$P(w) = gP_{copy}(w) + (1-g)P_v(w), \; where \; g = sigmoid(W_h^\top h_t + W_s^\top s_t + b_g) \quad (8)$$

$$P_{copy} = \sum\nolimits_{j:w_j=w}(\alpha_j + \beta_j) \qquad P_v = softmax(W_{v1}(W_{v2}[s_t, c_t] + b_1) + b_2) \quad (9)$$

Besides, we minimize negative log-likelihood of the target word w_t^* for each time step, and the overall loss is defined as their sum.

$$\mathcal{L} = \frac{1}{T}\sum\nolimits_{t=0}^{T}(-logP(w_t^*)) \quad (10)$$

3   Experiment

3.1   Datasets

Our model attempts to generate natural answers, especially for complex questions that contain logical relations between entities. To our knowledge, there is not an existing dataset naturally fitted to this problem. Thus, we tailor the Wikimovie[1] dataset [16] according to our requirements as wikimovie*. Moreover, we reconstruct a multi-hop dataset wikimovie-multihop from the Wikimovie and DBpedia by manual annotation. The original Wikimovie dataset consists of simple question-ASU pairs, external KB and natural sentences from Wikipedia about the movie, which covers 10 topics. To expand knowledge, we search cast members' related triples in DBpedia by DBpedia Lookup Service. Statistics of the two datasets are available in Table 1.

Table 1. Data statistics of dataset

Dataset	Total movie num	QA-pairs	Avg length of question	Avg length of answer	Avg triples per QA-pair
wikimovie*	6429	12037	17	14	4.7
multihop	13066	34472	15	15	5.5

wikimovie*: Take each natural sentence in Wikimovie as an ideal answer, we search the related triples in underlying KB and choose one o (*object*) among the triples as *ASU*. Then let annotators generate the corresponding question, which contains the triple information mentioned in the answer without variate and movie name as Example 1. We remove the QA-pair if its *ASU* is not unique. Since each natural sentence in Wikimovie is around one movie, the related graph is star-like and within 2-hops.

---

[1] http://fb.ai/babi.

Example 1. Given the natural answer "*Resident Evil is a 2013 English movie directed by Paul Anderson and starring Li_Bingbing*". One possible question is "*What is the language of the 2013 film by Paul Anderson and Li_Bingbing*".

`wikimovie-multihop`: We extract sub-graph randomly in underlying KB with limited size, while the sub-graph should contain more than 2-hop relations between entities, but no more than 4-hop for the longest path. Then for each sub-graph, we mask one vertex to be *ASU* that is not in the border. Based on the sub-graph, let annotators generate QA pairs in natural language sentences, while the question must be answerable and the answer should contain all information without missing. Note that entities not essential for reasoning *ASU* could be omitted or replaced, i.e., in 2008 replaced by in the same year in Sect. 1. After annotators providing 460 QA pairs, we extend the dataset by replacing the sub-graph in underlying KB with the same graph structure.

3.2   Evaluation Metrics

Automatic Evaluation: Similar to existing NAG systems [10,27], we compute ASU-acc to evaluate the correctness of *ASU*. Following [5], we adopt some word-overlap based metrics (WBMs)[2] including BLEU-4 [19], and METEOR [4] to measure the co-occurrences of references and generated answers.

Manual Evaluation: Further, it is hard to automatically evaluate the naturalness and correctness of generated answers. Following [17], we employ a manual evaluation to measure the Naturalness and Correctness respectively by a score among 0–5, where the higher the score, the better the evaluation. The Kappa coefficient for inter-annotator is 0.744, and the p-value for scores is less than 0.01.

3.3   Comparison Models

Throughout existing researches on the natural language answer generation problem, we compare our model (G-NAG) with state-of-the-art NAG models from different perspectives.

- GenQA [27], a standard seq2seq model with attention using encoder-decoder structure. It retrieves the best-matched triple by MLP and encodes it with the question encoded by LSTM to generate a natural answer.
- COREQA [10], a similar structure to GenQA. Moreover, it retrieves more one-hop triples and introduces the copy mechanism.
- HM-NAG [6], an improvement of COREQA. It encodes all related triples in key-value structure without matching with the question and selects proper triples completely by attention during generation.

---

[2] WBMs are implemented in https://github.com/Maluuba/nlgeval.

Except for existing NAG systems, we compare several baselines containing graph attention or transformer. Since these models have no knowledge extractor module, we feed the same simplified graph after converting as input.

- GraphWriter [13], a graph2seq model for summarization containing graph transformer without variate vertex and communication path during the self-attention calculation.
- Transformer [23], a sequence transformer proposed originally without graph structure.

3.4 Implementation Details

In knowledge extractor, we recognize entity phrases by StanfordCoreNLP tools and use Word2Vec [15] with 300 dimension vectors trained on the EN-wiki dataset to compute string similarities. Besides, we keep the top-2 alternative vertices in V_o with a higher score, and set $k = 2$, $m = 3$ in extractor module.

In experiments, G-NAG and baseline models are trained for about 40 epochs with the learning rate as 0.03, where gradients are updated by Adam [12] learning rule. In both datasets, we add word occurring more than 5 times into vocabulary and the state size of word embedding and batch size are both set to 256. For the transformer, we set layer D as 6, attention heads as 4, following the setting in [13], and use a self-attention based method to encode the communication path described in Sect. 2.3.

3.5 Result

Table 2 shows the answer generation performance on the `wikimovie*` dataset. From the result, we can see that G-NAG performs better than NAG baselines[3] both in the automatic or manual evaluation due to the improved knowledge extractor. Meanwhile, G-NAG outperforms GraphWriter and Transformer in ASU-acc, BLEU-4, and METEOR with stronger information express-ability of graph embedding method.

Table 2. Performances on dataset *Wikimovie**

Model	GenQA	COREQA	HM-NAG	GraphWriter	Transformer	G-NAG
ASU-acc	0.6506	0.6680	0.6818	0.8171	0.7913	**0.8310**
BLEU-4	0.3421	0.3792	0.3879	0.4282	0.4014	**0.4419**
METEOR	0.3722	0.3990	0.4113	0.4527	0.4371	**0.4809**
Natural	2.5	2.7	2.7	**3.4**	3.1	**3.4**
Correctness	2.0	2.5	2.7	3.4	3.1	**3.6**

---

[3] Since different tailoring for the dataset, the result of HM-NAG is not the same as it reported.

Considering manual evaluation, both G-NAG and GraphWriter, employing graph transformer, could generate fluent natural answers with the same score in Naturalness. Moreover, our G-NAG obtains a higher score in Correctness as it introduces two extra vertices and communication path embedding into the self-attention calculation.

Next, we prove the effectiveness of our model in `wikimovie-multihop` dataset in Table 3. Compared with G-NAG, ASU-acc metrics of NAG baselines are unsatisfactory as they use one-hop triple retrieval, which solves complex relations hardly in a multi-hop situation. Meanwhile, we see that G-NAG achieves higher ASU-acc than GraphWriter and Transformer which are fed with the same supporting graph since G-NAG has more ability to capture the *ASU* by variate vertex representation.

Table 3. Performances on dataset *Wikimovie-multihop*

Model	GenQA	COREQA	HM-NAG	GraphWriter	Transformer	G-NAG
ASU-acc	0.3071	0.4129	0.4513	0.7544	0.7403	**0.7816**
BLEU-4	0.1608	0.2011	0.2106	0.3322	0.3078	**0.3471**
METEOR	0.2034	0.2351	0.2509	0.3777	0.3541	**0.3912**
Natural	2.1	2.3	2.4	3.1	3.0	**3.2**
Correctness	1.7	2.1	2.2	3.2	2.9	**3.3**

A comparison in manual evaluation between sequence-based knowledge representation, such as NAG baselines or Transformer, and graph transformer-based framework proves the express-ability of graph transformer. We analyze that sequence-based systems may miss information during retrieving or generating stage, therefore the generated answers get a low score. Further, as for graph transformer, G-NAG could generate more logical and perfect answers than GraphWriter, which is reflected in BLEU-4 and Correctness metrics.

Table 4. Performances on implicit relation dataset *Wikimovie**

Model	GenQA	COREQA	HM-NAG	GraphWriter	Transformer	G-NAG
ASU-acc	0.5217 (−0.129)	0.5513 (−0.117)	0.5904 (−0.091)	0.7744 (−0.0430)	0.7502 (−0.041)	**0.7909** (**−0.040**)
BLEU-4	0.2904 (−0.052)	0.3122 (−0.067)	0.3212 (−0.067)	0.3884 (−0.040)	0.3571 (−0.044)	**0.4037** (**−0.038**)
METEOR	0.3317	0.3520	0.3688	0.4243	0.3914	**0.4427**
Natural	2.3	2.6	2.6	**3.4**	3.0	**3.4**
Correctness	1.8	2.2	2.3	3.2	2.7	**3.5**

As mentioned in Sect. 2.2, G-NAG can handle implicit relations in questions, which is a challenge to NAG but the common situation in daily life, i.e., Q in Fig. 2. Thus, we select the QA pairs in `Wikimovie`* where the questions have no obvious attribute or relational predicates. As shown in Table 4, G-NAG performs better than NAG baselines as it extracts triples depending more on the entity, not the relation, which is reflected in the decline value of ASU-acc and BLEU-4 compared with Table 3. Moreover, G-NAG keeps retrieved vertices as well as relation edges with higher scores in graph simplifying so as to identify these implicit relations. Furthermore, we can see that although the automatic metrics have fallen, the Naturalness and Correctness of G-NAG stay essentially flat because of the ability of generator module. However, G-NAG may generate redundant information in this situation, which will be discussed in the case study.

Table 5. Example outputs of various systems versus Gold.

Question*	Do you remember the *César-winner* actress who appeared in director Rupert Sanders' and Drew Goddard's film in the same year?
Knowledge	(movie-1, release_year, 2012), (movie-1, directed_by, Rupert Sanders), (movie-1, starred_actor, ASU), (movie-2, release_year, 2012), (movie-2, directed_by, Drew Goddard), (movie-2, starred_actor, ASU)
HM-NAG	*César-winner* Rupert Sanders worked with Rupert Sanders in the film Snow White and the Huntsman, and Drew Goddard in the film Bad Times at the El Royale in the same year
GraphWriter	*César-winner* **Kristen Stewart** worked with Rupert Sanders in the film Snow White and the Huntsman in 2012, and Drew Goddard in the film The Cabin in the Woods
G-NAG	*César-winner* **Kristen Stewart** worked with Rupert Sanders in the film Snow White and the Huntsman, and Drew Goddard in the film The Cabin in the Woods in 2012
Gold	Yes, *César-winner* **Kristen Stewart** worked with Rupert Sanders in the film Snow White and the Huntsman, as well as Drew Goddard in The Cabin in the Woods in 2012
Question*multi*	What is the release date of the *animated* movie by Kurt Frey and Ben Stassen?
Knowledge	(movie-1,directed_by,Ben Stassen), (movie-1,written_by,Ben Stassen), (movie-1, written_by, Kurt Frey), (movie-1, release_year, ASU)
HM-NAG	Haunted Castle is a *animated* film written by writer Kurt Frey and Ben Stassen
GraphWriter	Haunted Castle is a **2001** *animated* horror film written by writer Kurt Frey and directed by Ben Stassen
G-NAG	Haunted Castle is a **2001** *animated* horror film written by writer Kurt Frey and directed by co-writer Ben Stassen
Gold	Written by Kurt Frey and directed by co-writer Ben Stassen, Haunted Castle is a **2001** *animated* film

3.6 Case Study

Table 5 gives some outputs from our model, GraphWriter, and HM-NAG which performs better than the other two NAG baselines. *ASU* and other entities in this table are marked as **bold** and *italics* separately, while copy words marked as <u>underline</u> and superscript denotes the dataset QA pairs from. Besides, we use (movie-1,movie-2) to denote mentioned movies in the order that they appear in gold answers.

In Case 1, though HM-NAG recognizes entities correctly, it fails to generate *ASU* and accurate movie names because of triple missing. Meanwhile, because GraphWriter does not consider path information in the attention calculation, it has not a comprehensive grasp of graph structure to generate *year* in the right position. In Case 2, when the given question contains implicit relations, it is hard for HM-NAG to recognize all accurate relations and *ASU*. Moreover, even fed with a more accurate graph, GraphWriter misses the relation reflected in gold answer by *co-writer*. As implicit relation affects the simplifying stage, G-NAG obtains a supporting graph with more redundant entities while it generates extra information as *horror*.

4 Related Work

Our work belongs to the NAG task and draws inspiration from the research fields of graph-to-sequence, and copying mechanism.

NAG: [10,27] propose an end-to-end model to encode question and related knowledge as a sequence. Further, [6] put these triples into Key-Value memory proved effective by [16]. The above work provides a feasible framework consists of retrieving and generating that is followed by G-NAG. However, limited by the simple retrieval and sequence representation structure, these systems do not perform well in complex questions, which stimulates us to make improvements.

Graph-to-Sequence: To find alternative representation structure for NAG, we notice that converting graph to sequence is wildly studied from different aspects. The above work proves that the graph is an effective structure to encode complex information [14], which fits our requirements. As for graph representation, the key idea is to learn a mapping to embed nodes as points in a low-dimensional vector space. Motivated by [13,24,28], we employ graph transformer considering communication path to encode the supporting graph.

Attention and Copy Mechanism: Since unknown or special words in source text may impede predicting, Copying based on Attention has been proven extremely useful for a broad range of text generation tasks. To judge where to copy from, Copynet [7] utilizes the soft attention distribution to produce an output sequence containing elements from the input. This solution is applied to dialogue system [7], NMT [8], summarization [18,21], QA system [10], etc.

5   Conclusion and Future Work

In this paper, we propose a novel generating framework based on graph transformer to address the natural answer generation problem (NAG). The model we put forward, named G-NAG, improves knowledge extraction by multi-hop retrieval before disambiguation and simplifying strategy. Besides, it mainly increases express-ability by an extending graph transformer to encode the supporting graph for generating. Experimental results on two closed-domain datasets demonstrate that our model significantly outperforms existing NAG models, and prove the effectiveness of graph attention and transformer meanwhile. In the future, we expect G-NAG to find the balance between enlarging retrieval range and controlling graph size. Moreover, we try to solve the repetition problems by coverage model or other approaches.

Acknowledgement. This work was supported by NSFC under grant 61932001 and 61961130390.

References

1. Bahdanau, D., Cho, K., Bengio, Y.: Neural machine translation by jointly learning to align and translate. arXiv preprint arXiv:1409.0473 (2014)
2. Beck, D., Haffari, G., Cohn, T.: Graph-to-sequence learning using gated graph neural networks, pp. 273–283. Association for Computational Linguistics, Melbourne. https://www.aclweb.org/anthology/P18-1026
3. Cho, K., et al.: Learning phrase representations using RNN encoder-decoder for statistical machine translation. arXiv preprint arXiv:1406.1078 (2014)
4. Denkowski, M., Lavie, A.: Meteor universal: language specific translation evaluation for any target language, pp. 376–380. ACL (2014)
5. Elsahar, H., Gravier, C., Laforest, F.: Zero-shot question generation from knowledge graphs for unseen predicates and entity types. ACL (2018)
6. Fu, Y., Feng, Y.: Natural answer generation with heterogeneous memory. In: Proceedings of the 2018 Conference of the North American Chapter of the Association for Computational Linguistics: Human Language Technologies (2018)
7. Gu, J., Lu, Z., Li, H., Li, V.O.: Incorporating copying mechanism in sequence-to-sequence learning. arXiv preprint arXiv:1603.06393 (2016)
8. Gulcehre, C., Ahn, S., Nallapati, R., Zhou, B., Bengio, Y.: Pointing the unknown words. arXiv preprint arXiv:1603.08148 (2016)
9. Hasibi, F., Balog, K., Bratsberg, S.E.: Dynamic factual summaries for entity cards. In: Proceedings of the 40th International ACM SIGIR Conference on Research and Development in Information Retrieval, pp. 773–782. ACM (2017)
10. He, S., Liu, C., Liu, K., Zhao, J.: Generating natural answers by incorporating copying and retrieving mechanisms in sequence-to-sequence learning. In: Proceedings of the 55th Annual Meeting of the Association for Computational Linguistics (2017)
11. Hochreiter, S., Schmidhuber, J.: Long short-term memory. Neural Comput. **9**(8), 1735–1780 (1997)
12. Kingma, D.P., Ba, J.: Adam: a method for stochastic optimization. arXiv preprint arXiv:1412.6980 (2014)

13. Koncel-Kedziorski, R., Bekal, D., Luan, Y., Lapata, M., Hajishirzi, H.: Text generation from knowledge graphs with graph transformers. arXiv preprint arXiv:1904.02342 (2019)

14. Lin, P., Song, Q., Wu, Y.: Fact checking in knowledge graphs with ontological subgraph patterns. Data Sci. Eng. **3**(4), 341–358 (2018)

15. Mikolov, T., Sutskever, I., Chen, K., Corrado, G.S., Dean, J.: Distributed representations of words and phrases and their compositionality. In: Advances in Neural Information Processing Systems, pp. 3111–3119 (2013)

16. Miller, A., Fisch, A., Dodge, J., Karimi, A.H., Bordes, A., Weston, J.: Key-value memory networks for directly reading documents. arXiv preprint arXiv:1606.03126

17. Mohammed, S., Shi, P., Lin, J.: Strong baselines for simple question answering over knowledge graphs with and without neural networks. In: ACL, pp. 291–296 (2018)

18. Nallapati, R., Zhou, B., Gulcehre, C., Xiang, B., et al.: Abstractive text summarization using sequence-to-sequence RNNS and beyond. arXiv preprint arXiv:1602.06023

19. Papineni, K., Roukos, S., Ward, T., Zhu, W.J.: BLEU: a method for automatic evaluation of machine translation. Association for Computational Linguistics (2002)

20. Reinanda, R., Meij, E., de Rijke, M.: Mining, ranking and recommending entity aspects. In: Proceedings of the 38th International ACM SIGIR Conference on Research and Development in Information Retrieval, pp. 263–272. ACM (2015)

21. See, A., Liu, P.J., Manning, C.D.: Get to the point: summarization with pointer-generator networks. arXiv preprint arXiv:1704.04368 (2017)

22. Shaw, P., Uszkoreit, J., Vaswani, A.: Self-attention with relative position representations. arXiv preprint arXiv:1803.02155 (2018)

23. Vaswani, A., et al.: Attention is all you need. In: Advances in Neural Information Processing Systems, pp. 5998–6008 (2017)

24. Veličković, P., Cucurull, G., Casanova, A., Romero, A., Lio, P., Bengio, Y.: Graph attention networks. arXiv preprint arXiv:1710.10903 (2017)

25. Wang, R., Wang, M., Liu, J., Chen, W., Cochez, M., Decker, S.: Leveraging knowledge graph embeddings for natural language question answering. In: Li, G., Yang, J., Gama, J., Natwichai, J., Tong, Y. (eds.) DASFAA 2019. LNCS, vol. 11446, pp. 659–675. Springer, Cham (2019). https://doi.org/10.1007/978-3-030-18576-3_39

26. Xu, K., Wu, L., Wang, Z., Feng, Y., Witbrock, M., Sheinin, V.: Graph2seq: gEraph to sequence learning with attention-based neural networks. arXiv preprint arXiv:1804.00823 (2018)

27. Yin, J., Jiang, X., Lu, Z., Shang, L., Li, H., Li, X.: Neural generative question answering. arXiv preprint arXiv:1512.01337 (2015)

28. Zhu, J., Li, J., Zhu, M., Qian, L., Zhang, M., Zhou, G.: Modeling graph structure in transformer for better AMR-to-text generation (2019)

Diversified Top-k Querying in Knowledge Graphs

Xintong Guo[✉], Hong Gao, Yinan An, and Zhaonian Zou

Harbin Institute of Technology, Harbin, China
{xintong.guo,honggao,znzou}@hit.edu.cn
1170300428@stu.hit.edu.cn

Abstract. The existing literatures of the query processing on knowledge graphs focus on an exhaustive enumeration of all matches, which is time-consuming. Users are often interested in diversified top-k matches, rather than the entire match set. Motivated by these, this paper formalizes the diversified top-k querying (DTQ) problem in the context of RDF/SPARQL and proposes a diversification function to balance importance and diversity. We first prove that the decision problem of DTQ is NP-complete, and give a baseline algorithm with an approximation ratio of 2. Secondly, an index-based algorithm with the early termination property is proposed. The index is adept in parallel diversified top-k selection in multicore architectures. Using real-world and synthetic data, we experimentally verify that our algorithms are efficient and effective in computing meaningful diversified top-k matches.

Keywords: Diversified top-k query · RDF/SPARQL · Parallel graph processing

1 Introduction

Query processing on the RDF graph has been well studied. Some systems [15] rely on relational join to get the results, and some [18] rely on subgraph isomorphism algorithm. The query response time is reasonable since the query graph is quite small in most applications. As knowledge graphs are growing in size, the number of isomorphic subgraphs in such RDF graphs can be excessively large. Users usually prefer seeing a ranked result list rather than a list of unranked matches. The top-k graph pattern matching problem is introduced under the circumstances. A score function is used to measure the quality of subgraphs based on the weight on nodes/edges. Only the k best subgraphs are returned. Unfortunately, the resulting subgraphs are often highly overlapped and dominated by some very high weight nodes/edges, while more representative subgraphs may be missed. Finally, diversity is introduced into search results to remedy the situation.

Example 1 *A fraction of an RDF graph is shown in Fig. 1(a). The graph has weights on nodes such that a higher weight implies higher importance. A user wants to find*

© Springer Nature Switzerland AG 2020
X. Wang et al. (Eds.): APWeb-WAIM 2020, LNCS 12317, pp. 319–336, 2020.
https://doi.org/10.1007/978-3-030-60259-8_24

a director of the romance film and the birthplace of this director. The corresponding SPARQL query is "?movie directedBy ?director; ?movie rdf:type Romance;?director birthPlace ?country", as shown in Fig. 1(b). There are many matching subgraphs in G_D. We limit the number of matches to a small k. In this example, let us set $k = 2$. The question is which set of two matches is better. If we return (mo_1, d_1, c_1) and (mo_1, d_2, c_2) as matches for $(?movie, ?director, ?country)$, we have the max total weight in all answers. But mo_1 appears in both answers. The results seem redundant to the user. Instead, the disjoint matches (mo_1, d_1, c_1) and (mo_2, d_2, c_2) form a better solution set, as balancing both diversity and importance. Hence, in selecting the top-k matches, we aim to reduce the overlapping information among the matches and improve the importance.

To achieve the trade-off between importance and diversity, we study the Diversified Top-k Querying (DTQ) problem. The importance of a result set is measured by the sum of its nodes' weight. The diversity is measured by a distance function. To the best of our knowledge, this is the first study to consider both the importance score and diversity of a result on the knowledge graph.

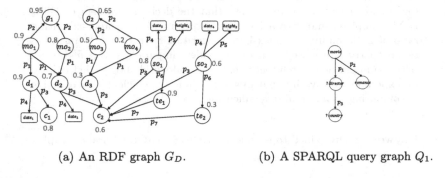

(a) An RDF graph G_D.   (b) A SPARQL query graph Q_1.

Fig. 1. An example; the meanings of the vertex labels are: mo-movie; d-director; g_1-romance; g_2-comedy; c - country; so-soccer player; te-soccer team; p_1-directedBy; p_2-rdf:type; p_3-birthPlace; p_4-birthDate; p_5-hasHeight; p_6-team; p_7-isLocatedIn.

There are two major challenges of solving DTQ: (1) Assume that we can generate and store all matches for a query, the remaining problem becomes how to select a set with both high importance and high diversity. Though the state-of-the-art [11] provides an approximation ratio of 2, it requires $O(\frac{1}{2}kn^2)$ time, where n is the number of matches. When n is large, the runtime is unacceptable. (2) Generating all matches may be prohibitively costly. So a ranking-while-matching mechanism is preferable to return k matches without an exhaustive search, while still having a good result.

We propose two algorithms for DTQ targeting on the above challenges. Our contributions are summarized as follows.

- We formalize the *Diversified Top-k Querying problem* in the knowledge graph and prove the decision version of this problem is NP-complete.

– We develop an approximation algorithm DTQ-Base with a guarantee of 2 in $O(kn)$ time, where n indicates the total number of matches.
– To solve the DTQ problem more efficiently, we propose a heuristic algorithm DTQ-Index based on the Backbone index. We generate diversified top-k matches using the runtime version of the Backbone index, which leverages multicore processing to maximize throughput and reduce latency.
– Using both real-world and synthetic datasets, we empirically verify the efficiency and effectiveness of our algorithms. The studies show that DTQ-Base is much faster than state-of-the-art algorithms, and DTQ-Index achieves competitive results with DTQ-Base while taking much less time.

The rest of this paper is organized as follows. Section 2 reviews the related work. Section 3 introduces some notions and defines the problem. The proposed approach consists of two phases: offline index construction and online query processing, which are elaborated in Sects. 4 and 5, respectively. We present experimental results with detailed insights in Sect. 6. Conclusions are made in Sect. 7.

2   Related Work

The proposed problem falls into the category of the top-k graph pattern matching problem. Top-k graph pattern matching is to retrieve k best matches from the match set. Many different forms of top-k queries have been studied in the literature [10,12]. Gupta et al. [12] rank the results based on edge weight, and rely on exhaustive indexes on every node. To provide more flexibility of top-k pattern matching, Cheng et al. [10] extend matching semantics by allowing the edge to path mapping, and propose to rank matches based on their compactness. Unfortunately, the resulting subgraphs from the above methods are often highly overlapped and not very representative.

Under the circumstances, diversity is introduced to graph pattern matching in [7,11,16,17]. Result diversification is a bi-criteria optimization problem for balancing relevance and diversity. Arnaout et al. [7] follow a rank-after-matching paradigm, which is not efficient especially for large graphs for which the number of matches could be enormous and hence computing all the matches could be very time-consuming. Fan et al. [11] designate an output node in the query graph, then the result only includes a set of nodes that are matches of the output node. Yang et al. [17] consider diversity solely and measure diversity by the number of nodes covered by all the matches. Wang et al. [16] also extend edge to path mapping and use the diversification strategy in [17].

Our work differs from prior work in the following aspects: (1) Diversified top-k graph pattern matching is typically a bi-criteria optimization problem of relevance and diversity. As SPARQL is our query language, our work seeks an exact match without relevance problem. Importance and diversity are two significant concerns in our setting. (2) Most work [10,12] in top-k graph pattern matching suppose weight on edges to reflect the strength of connection between nodes, while we suppose weight on nodes to reflect the importance. (3) Existing solutions utilize subgraph matching algorithms to find top-k results, which are difficult to be parallelized intrinsically. Our work, however, uses a novel index to support parallel execution.

3   Problem Definition

The Resource Description Framework (RDF) [1] is a data model developed by the World Wide Web Consortium (W3C) to represent billions of facts in the knowledge graphs. The SPARQL query language [2] correspondingly provides a triple-pattern-based format to query over RDF stores. Their formal definitions are presented as follows.

Definition 1. *An **RDF data graph** $G_D(V_D, E_D, L_D, \psi_D, W_D)$ is a directed, labeled multi-graph, where V_D is a set of data nodes, $E_D \subseteq V_D \times V_D$ is the set of directed edges, $|E_D|$ denotes the number of triples in G_D. L_D is the set of edge labels, and ψ_D is a labeling function with $\psi_D : E_D \rightarrow L_D$. W_D is an importance mapping function defined on the node set as $W_D : V_D \rightarrow R \in [0,1]$.*

Definition 2. *A **SPARQL query graph** $G_Q(V_Q, E_Q, L_Q, Vars, \phi_Q)$ is a directed, labeled multi-graph, where V_Q is the set of query nodes, $E_Q \subseteq V_Q \times V_Q$ is the set of directed edges, L_Q is the set of edge and node labels, $Vars$ are the variables to be answered, and ϕ_Q is a labeling function with $\phi_Q : V_Q \cup E_Q \rightarrow Vars \cup L_D$.*

For example, Fig. 1(a) shows an example RDF graph with $|V_D| = 21$ nodes and $|E_D| = 24$ edges. Figure 1(b) shows a query Q_1 with four nodes. $V_Q = \{?movie, ?director, romance, ?country\}$, and $Vars = \{?movie, ?director, ?country\}$.

Processing a SPARQL query graph G_Q against an RDF graph G_D is analogous to finding all subgraph isomorphisms of G_Q in G_D. The group of all matches is denoted as $\mathbb{M}(G_D, Q_D)$. For the sake of brevity, we will use the node set (tuple notation) to refer to the match induced by the node set. For example, the subgraph (mo_1, d_1, c_1) is a match of Q_1 in G_D.

Definition 3. *Given a match $m_i = (m_i^V, m_i^E)$ of a SPARQL query G_Q in an RDF graph G_D, where m_i^V and m_i^E are the node set and edge set in this match respectively, the **Importance Score** of m_i is defined as*

$$\delta_I(m_i) = \frac{1}{|Vars|} \sum_{v_j \in m_i^V} W_D(v_j) \tag{1}$$

$|Vars|$ is used to normalize δ_I to $[0,1]$. For example, the importance score for the match (mo_1, d_1, c_1) is 0.87.

Definition 4. *Given two matches $m_i = (m_i^V, m_i^E)$ and $m_j = (m_j^V, m_j^E)$, their* ***Distance*** *is defined as*

$$\delta_D(m_i, m_j) = 1 - \frac{|m_i^V \cap m_j^V|}{|m_i^V \cup m_j^V|} \tag{2}$$

The distance function measures the "dissimilarity" of two matches. For example, the distance of match (mo_1, d_1, c_1) and (mo_1, d_2, c_2) is $1 - \frac{|(mo_1, d_1, c_1) \cap (mo_1, d_2, c_2)|}{|(mo_1, d_1, c_1) \cup (mo_1, d_2, c_2)|} = 1 - \frac{1}{5} = 0.8$.

Based on $\delta_I()$ and $\delta_D()$, we give the formal definition of our DTQ problem.

Definition 5. *Given an RDF graph G_D, a SPARQL query G_Q, a positive integer k and a parameter $\lambda \in [0,1]$, the* ***Diversified Top-k Querying Problem*** *is to find a set of k matches M such that*

$$F(M) = \underset{M \subseteq \mathbb{M}(G_D, Q_D)}{\arg\max} \left[(k-1)(1-\lambda) \cdot \sum_{m_i \in M} \delta_I(m_i) + 2\lambda \cdot \sum_{m_i, m_j \in M,\ i<j} \delta_D(m_i, m_j) \right]$$

$$\tag{3}$$

λ is a predefined parameter to strike a balance between the two factors. The diversity metric is scaled down with 2λ, since there are $\frac{k(k-1)}{2}$ factors for the difference sum, while only k factors for the important sum. DTQ is to find a set of k matches from $\mathbb{M}(G_D, Q_D)$ such that the bi-criteria objective function is maximized.

Theorem 1. *The decision problem of DTQ is NP-complete.*

Proof. The decision problem of DTQ is in NP since one can guess a k-element set M and then check whether $M \subseteq \mathbb{M}(G_D, Q_D)$ and $F(M) \geq LB$ in PTIME. To show the lower bound LB, observe that by setting $\lambda = 1$, DTQ is reduced to the k-diverse set problem [14] as its special case, which is known to be NP-hard [14]; hence DTQ is NP-hard. Thus, DTQ is NP-complete. $\qquad\square$

3.1 DTopk-Base Algorithm

DTQ is nontrivial to approximate, which is suggested by results for the max-sum diversification [9]. Despite the hardness, we provide a simple greedy algorithm with an approximation guarantee of 2. Suppose we have computed and stored $\mathbb{M}(G_D, Q_D)$, $\delta_I(m_i)$ and $\delta_D(m_i, m_j)$ for all matches $m_i, m_j \in \mathbb{M}(G_D, Q_D)$. DTopk-Base first initializes an empty set S for top-k matches. Next, it iteratively selects a match u that maximize $F_u'(S) = \frac{1}{2}(k-1)(1-\lambda)\delta_I(u) + 2\lambda d(u, S)$, where $d(u, S) = \sum_{v \in S} \delta_D(u, v)$. Then add it to S. This process repeats k times and outputs S. We denote it as DTopk-Base shown in Algorithm 1.

DTopk-Base runs in time proportional to k times the cost of computing $F_u'(S)$ for all u. Suppose $n = |\mathbb{M}(G_D, Q_D)|$. As $\delta_I(\cdot)$ is modular, the value of

$\frac{1}{2}(k-1)(1-\lambda)\delta_I(u)$ will not change in each iteration. $d(u, S)$ for all u can be updated in $O(n)$, so each $F'_u(S)$ is amortized only $O(1)$. Hence, the total time complexity of DTopk-Base is $O(kn)$. DTopk-Base achieves a 2-approximation ratio, and we prove it in the Appendix.

Algorithm 1. DTopk-Base Algorithm

Input: $\mathbb{M}(G_D, Q_D)$: all matches; $\delta_I(\cdot)$: importance function; $\delta_D(\cdot, \cdot)$: distance function; k: a cardinality constraint
Output: S: a diversified result set, where $|S| = k$ and $S \subseteq \mathbb{M}(G_D, Q_D)$
1: $S = \emptyset$
2: **while** $|S| < k$ **do**
3:    find $u \in \mathbb{M}(G_D, Q_D) \backslash S$, maximizing $F'_u(S) = \frac{1}{2}(k-1)(1-\lambda)\delta_I(u) + 2\lambda d(u, S)$
4:        $S = S \cup u$
5: **return** S

3.2   DTopk-Index Overview

Algorithm 1 requires $\mathbb{M}(G_D, Q_D)$ to be computed firstly. Thus, it is not efficient especially for large knowledge graphs. To rectify this, we present a heuristic algorithm for DTQ, denoted as DTopk-Index. DTopk-Index selectively generates matches with high important score and high diversity gain. DTopk-Index consists of two phases: offline index construction and online query processing. In the offline phase, given a knowledge graph G_D, we extract its Backbone index. In the online phase, given a SPARQL query G_Q, we first process it against the Backbone index to prune unnecessary part. The remaining part, called the runtime Backbone index, generates partial results in parallel. Then, we enumerate diversified top-k matches from the partial results in a level-wise manner to get a high-quality set. We will discuss the details in the next two sections.

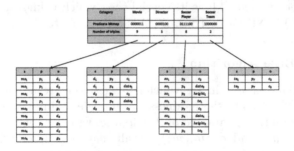

Fig. 2. Backbone index of G_D in Fig. 1(a)

Algorithm 2. Backbone Index Construction

Input: G_D: RDF graph, $C = \{c_1, c_2, \cdots, c_l\}$: categories
Output: Backbone index BI-top, BI-bottom
1: **for** every triple t in G_D **do**
2:     sid, pid, oid = encode(t)
3:     insert (sid, pid, oid) to encode_table ET
4:     **if** pid not in Sub_preds[sid] **then**
5:         Sub_preds[sid].append(pid)
6:         Sub_bitmap[sid] = makeBitmap(Sub_preds[sid])
7: **for** each c_i in C **do**
8:     initialize $BI - top[c_i]$ and $BI - bottom[c_i]$
9: **for** every triple t in ET **do**
10:     send (sid, pid, oid) to corresponding category BI-bottom[c_j]
11:     BI-top[c_j].cnt++
12:     BI-top[c_j].bitmap=BI-top[c_j].bitmap$\wedge$ Sub_bitmap[sid]
13: **return** BI-top, BI-bottom

4   Offline Index Construction

4.1   Backbone Index

Entities in the RDF graph could be classified into different categories. For example, in DBPedia 2015-10 dump, there are 453 entity categories, like Person, Place, Work and so on. We can get the categories from the ontology of knowledge graph and rdf:type value. Entities of the same category are likely to share the same set of predicates. For example, in the DBPedia dataset, for entities in the Movie category, they always contain predicates like director, producer, starring and so forth.

Based on this observation, this paper proposes a novel Backbone index based on the entities' category and predicates set. The Backbone index (BI) consists of two-level structures. The top-level structure is indexed according to the category; each index instance is composed of the $\langle entity\ category, predicate\ bitmap, the\ number\ of\ triples \rangle$. The bottom-level structure contains all the triples belonging to this category; each instance is composed of $\langle subject, predicate, object \rangle$.

As most knowledge graphs are auto-constructed by crawling from webpages, the incompleteness is unavoidable. For example, in Fig. 1(a), the birthDate value of director d_3 is missing. So the predicate bitmap of category Director will be the conjunction of each entity's predicate bitmap. Predicate bitmap is in the form of $p_7 p_6 \cdots p_1$, where p_i has the same definition in Fig. 1. Predicate bitmap of d_1 and d_2 is 0001100, and predicate bitmap of d_3 is 0000100, so the predicate bitmap of Director will be 0000100.

Taking the example in Fig. 1(a), G_D contains four categories, namely Movie, Director, Soccer player, and Soccer team. And its Backbone index is shown in Fig. 2.

4.2   Implementation

The Backbone index can be easily extracted by two linear scans on the knowledge graph. The algorithm is presented in Algorithm 2. On the first scan, we encode

RDF strings into numerical IDs to avoid the storage overheads (Line 2–3). Besides, we store every new predicate for each subject in Sub_preds. Multi-value is common in the RDF graph. We only store per *predicate* once in each bitmap. A new predicate bitmap is iteratively constructed for a distinct subject (Line 4–6). On the second scan, we send (sid, pid, oid) to the corresponding category, then update BI-top (Line 9–12).

The time complexity of BI construction is linear to the triple count in the knowledge graph, which is $O(2|E_D|)$. The space complexity of BI-top is too small to be omitted. We compactly store each triple in BI-bottom using three integers of 4 bytes, one for each triple component, namely sid, pid, and oid. The space complexity of the Backbone index is $O(12|E_D|)$ bytes.

5   Diversified Top-k Querying Processing

In this section, we present a novel algorithm DTopk-Index for generating diversified top-k matches. Briefly, it works as follows: (1) Given a SPARQL query G_Q, we first decompose it into a sequence of star subqueries. Then, multithreading is leveraged to match these subqueries to the Backbone index to get partial results. These results are called the runtime Backbone index. (2) We generate diversified top-k matches in a level-wise manner using the runtime Backbone index.

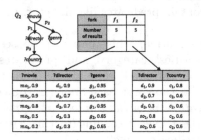

Fig. 3. Q_2 and its runtime Backbone index

5.1   Runtime Backbone Index

Incoming SPARQL query is first decomposed into a sequence of disjoint forks. A fork is a star-shaped subquery. The triple patterns in a fork share identical subject join variable. For example, Q_2 in Fig. 3 is decomposed into two forks, $f_1 = \{?movie\ p_1\ ?director,\ ?movie\ p_2\ ?genre\}$ and $f_2 = \{?director\ p_3\ ?country\}$. Then, each fork matches to zero or more categories. According to BI-top in Fig. 2, f_1 is mapped to $\{c_1(Movie)\}$ and f_2 is mapped to $\{c_2(Director), c_3(Soccer\ player)\}$. This mapping uses query structure information to eliminate the non-promising part in BI, e.g., $\{c_4(Soccer\ Team)\}$.

Instead of the whole Backbone index, we only need a fraction of it, called the runtime Backbone index BI_R regarding the SPARQL query. BI_R also consists of two-level structures. The top-level structure $BI_R - top$ is indexed according to the forks in query; each index instance is composed of the $\langle fork, the\ number\ of\ partial\ results \rangle$. The bottom-level structure $BI_R - bottom$ contains all the partial results belonging to this fork. We also store the node weight with partial results together.

The implementation is straightforward. Relevant triples can be immediately identified at query time and loaded into main memory in linear I/O time regarding the size, by reading the BI corresponding to categories in the fork. Then, triples within the fork are joined on the subject. Loading triples and joining them on subject are carried out separately on each fork since there is no dependence among forks. That offers us a great opportunity to improve efficiency by multithreading. We assign the individual fork for evaluation to a distinct thread.

Algorithm 3 summarizes BI_R construction steps. First, we decomposed G_Q into a group of forks (Line 1). Each fork is evaluated on a distinct thread (Line 2). Each fork matches to a set of categories according to the bitmap in $BI - top$. We load triples in them to a cached table CT. Note that only triples with corresponding predicates in f will be loaded (Line 3–5). Finally, triples in CT with the identical subject are joined to produce partial results for this fork (Line 6–7). After all forks finish, we do a synchronization (Line 8).

Clearly, finding the diversified top-k matches in G_D (or BI) is equivalent to finding them in BI_R. The size of BI_R is much smaller than that of BI most of the time. Besides, the time complexity of this algorithm is dominated by the slowest fork. If a fork has plenty of triples to deal with, we can further divide categories into multiple threads. All we need is merging partial results that belong to the same fork in the end. The selection of parallel granularity is quite flexible.

The reason why we use fork as the basic join unit lies in the high coverage of almost-star-shaped graph patterns in real-world query logs [8]. Users tend to build their queries gradually by a sequence of star queries. Generating partial results of forks in parallel is of paramount importance to improve efficiency.

In Fig. 3 we show the BI_R for Q_2. For fork f_1, we load all triples which contains predicate p_1 and p_2 from BI-bottom[c_1]. For fork f_2, we load all triples which contains predicate p_3 from BI-bottom[c_2] and BI-bottom[c_3]. Each fork has 5 partial results after self-join.

Algorithm 3. DTopk-Index Phase 1: runtime Backbone index construction

---

Input: BI: Backbone index; G_Q: a SPARQL query
Output: BI_R: runtime Backbone index
1: forks=Decompose(G_Q)
2: **for** each f in forks *in parallel* **do**
3:    C=MatchCategory(BI-top,f)
4:    **for** each c_j in C **do**
5:        CT=Load(BI-bottom[c_j],f)
6:    $BI_R - bottom[f] = Join(CT, f)$
7:    $BI_R - top[f].cnt = |BI_R - bottom[f]|$
8: *synchronization*
9: **return** BI_R

5.2 Diversified Top-k Match Computation

In this subsection, we assemble the partial results in the runtime Backbone index to perform ranking and matching simultaneously. We carry on the assembling process in two stages.

The first stage of our solution aims to maximize diversity. We adopt a level-wise generation paradigm which eases diversity constraint gradually. We start by selecting a fork f_h from BI_R and call it *head fork*. Usually, the fork with the minimum instance count is selected for better selectivity. The instances in $BI_R - bottom[f_h]$ are sorted by the variables' total weight in descending order. These instances are the start points to expand partial results into full ones. Now, we initialize the solution set $S = \emptyset$ and start the level-wise generation progress. At Level 0, we scan the sorted $BI_R - bottom[f_h]$ in a top-down manner to collect a maximal set of disjoint matches in S and move on to Level 1. Let S_i be the set of matches generated at Level i, each $m \in S_i$ contains at most i identical nodes in each m_j, where $\forall m_j \in S_0 \cup S_1 \cup \cdots \cup S_{i-1}$. There are $|Vars|$ variable in G_Q, so there are $|Vars| - 1$ levels at most. The search terminates whenever k matches are collected in S.

Algorithm 4 shows the pseudo code for Stage 1. S is initially empty and $level = 0$ (Line 1–2). We choose a fork from runtime Backbone index BI_R and sort instances by weight in descending order (Line 3–4). At Level 0, we start from each instance in $BI_R - bottom[f_h]$ to generate all disjoint matches (Line 5–8). If $|S| < k$, we ease the diversity constraint level by level, where $level \in \{1, 2, \cdots, |Vars| - 1\}$. At Level i, the newly generated match should overlap with $m_j \in S$ at most i nodes (Line 9–13). Once k matches are obtained, Stage 1 terminates and records S, tr pointer and $level$.

Since BI_R is stored in tabular format, we use relational join to present our subfunction $FindDisjointMatch(tr, G_Q, BI_R)$ and $FindMatch(tr, level, G_Q, BI_R, S)$. The join operator conforms with three major principles: (1) We create a linear order of the forks $f_1, f_2, \cdots, f_k$, where f_1 is the head fork. The matching will be conducted in this order.. (2) The partial match is greedily joined with the candidate with the highest weight. This makes matches with higher importance scores be generated prioritized. (3) At Level i, the new match should have at most i overlapped nodes with any match in S. We use an extra counter to record the number of overlapped nodes in a partial match.

Algorithm 4. DTopk-Index Phase 2 Stage 1
___
Input: BI_R: runtime Backbone index; G_Q: a SPARQL query; k: a cardinality constraint; f_h: head fork
Output: S: a result set; tr: stopping instance; $level$: stopping level
1: $S = \emptyset$
2: $level = 0$
3: $f_h \leftarrow HeadFork(BI_R)$
4: Sort($BI_R - bottom[f_h]$)
5: **for** each tr in $BI_R - bottom[f_h]$ **do**
6:    $S = S \cup FindDisjointMatch(tr, G_Q, BI_R, S)$
7:    **if** $|S| == k$ **then**
8:       **return** $S, tr, 0$
9: **for** $level \in \{1, 2, \cdots, |Vars| - 1\}$ **do**
10:    **for** each tr in $BI_R - bottom[f_h]$ **do**
11:       $S = S \cup FindMatch(tr, level, G_Q, BI_R, S)$
12:       **if** $|S| == k$ **then**
13:          **return** $S, tr, level$
___

Stage 1 makes sure S as diversified as possible. At Stage 2, we continue with a mechanism SWAP, which keeps loosening the grip on diversity in exchange for high importance score. SWAP resumes the level-wise match generation, continuing at the level and instance of $BI_R - bottom$ where Stage 1 ends. The new match may swap with a match in S. Our SWAP mechanism allows us to set up an early termination criterion for this stage, which can significantly improve efficiency.

We sort matches in S based on the importance score in descending order. Suppose the sorted list is $S = \{m_1, m_2, \cdots, m_k\}$ and m_k has minimum importance score. We only replace m_k with the new match. For the swapping condition, recall Eq. 3, we have

$$F(S) = (k-1)(1-\lambda)\sum_{i=1}^{k}\delta_I(m_i) + 2\lambda\sum_{i<j}\delta_D(m_i, m_j), \; where \; m_i, m_j \in S$$

$$= F(S \setminus m_k) + [(k-1)(1-\lambda)\delta_I(m_k) + 2\lambda\sum_{i=1}^{k-1}\delta_D(m_k, m_i)] \qquad (4)$$

We use $F(m_k)$ to denote the contribution of m_k, then $F(m_k) = (k-1)(1-\lambda)\delta_I(m_k) + 2\lambda\sum_{i=1}^{k-1}\delta_D(m_k, m_i)$. The contribution of a new generated match m_{k+1} is $F(m_{k+1}) = (k-1)(1-\lambda)\delta_I(m_{k+1}) + 2\lambda\sum_{i=1}^{k-1}\delta_D(m_{k+1}, m_i)$. If $F(m_{k+1}) > F(m_k)$, we swap m_{k+1} with m_k to get a better S. We rearrange the inequality and formalize the swapping condition.

Swapping Condition. We swap the next candidate m_{k+1} with m_k, if:

$$(k-1)(1-\lambda)(\delta_I(m_{k+1}) - \delta_I(m_k)) > 2\lambda(\delta_D(m_k, S \setminus m_k) - \delta_D(m_{k+1}, S \setminus m_k)) \quad (5)$$

We keep generating new match and see whether swapping condition is satisfied. If it is satisfied, we swap and reorder the S based on importance score.

Stopping Condition. Stage 2 can terminate if the following inequality is satisfied:

$$\delta_I(m_k) > \delta_I(m_{k+1}) \qquad (6)$$

We stop once the important score of the new match is lower than m_k. As we generate match from $BI_R - bottom[f_h]$, there is an assumption that instance with a high score in $BI_R - bottom[f_h]$ is more likely to produce high-quality match. It is realistic in many domains. For example, an influential researcher is more likely to produce high-quality papers published in top conferences.

Stage 2 is described in Algorithm 5. First, we sort each match in S by importance score (Line 1). Then, we resume match generation at which Stage 1 stops (Line 2–8). For every new match, we check whether TerminationCondition is satisfied. If not, go on. Swap m_k and m_{k+1} if SwappingCondition is satisfied. When all matches at Level i have been generated, and if $i < |Vars| - 1$, we continue with the next level. This recursive process continues until either we can terminate early or $j > |Vars| - 1$ (Line 9–16).

Algorithm 5. DTopk-Index Phase 2 Stage 2

Input: S: a temporal result set; BI_R: runtime Backbone index; G_Q: a SPARQL query; tr:start instance; $level$: start level; k: a cardinality constraint; f_h: head fork.
Output: S: a diversified top-k result set
1: Sort(S)
2: **for** instance in $\{BI_R - bottom[f_h][tr + 1], \cdots, BI_R - bottom[f_h][end]\}$ **do**
3:     $m_{k+1} = FindMatch(instance, level, G_Q, BI_R, S)$
4:     **if** TerminationCondition(m_{k+1}, m_k) **then**
5:         **return** S
6:     **else if** SwappingCondition(m_{k+1}, m_k) **then**
7:         $S = (S \setminus m_k) \cup m_{k+1}$
8:         Sort(S)
9: **for** $j \in \{level + 1, level + 2, \cdots, |Vars| - 1\}$ **do**
10:     **for** each instance in $BI_R - bottom[f_h]$ **do**
11:         $m_{k+1} = FindMatch(instance, j, G_Q, BI_R, S)$
12:         **if** TerminationCondition(m_{k+1}, m_k) **then**
13:             **return** S
14:         **else if** SwappingCondition(m_{k+1}, m_k) **then**
15:             $S = (S \setminus m_k) \cup m_{k+1}$
16:             Sort(S)

Example 2. *Consider Q_2 in Fig. 3. Let $k = 3$ and $\lambda = 0.5$, we rank forks in BI_R by the number of instances. We randomly select f_1 as the head fork. We sort instances in BI-bottom[f_1] in descending order of weight. First, linear scan BI-bottom[f_1] from top to bottom to generate a set of disjoint matches, which are (mo_1, d_1, g_1, c_1) and (mo_3, d_3, g_2, c_2). Since $k = 3$, and $|S| = 2 < k$, we continue to search for matches having overlapping nodes with S. We move on to Level 1, the overlap size is set to 1. Still, we linear scan BI-bottom[f_1] from top to bottom to generate new matches. We get match (mo_2, d_2, g_1, c_2). Now $|S| = k$, so Stage 1 terminates. We sort S in descending order as $(mo_1, d_1, g_1, c_1, 0.89)$, $(mo_2, d_2, g_1, c_2, 0.76)$ and $(mo_3, d_3, g_2, c_2, 0.51)$ (normalized by $|Vars|$). We begin Stage 2. We resume from Level 1 and instance (mo_3, d_3, g_2), and there is no other match. There is no match in Level 2, either. We move to Level 3. Now, $(mo_1, d_2, g_1, c_2, 0.79)$ is obtained and its weight is larger than $(mo_3, d_3, g_2, c_2, 0.51)$. We examine whether the Swapping Condition is satisfied. The answer is no. Finally, $(mo_4, d_3, g_2, c_2, 0.44)$ is generated, and its score is lower than $(mo_3, d_3, g_2, c_2, 0.51)$. Stage 2 terminates and return $S = \{(mo_1, d_1, g_1, c_1), (mo_2, d_2, g_1, c_2), (mo_3, d_3, g_2, c_2)\}$.*

Table 1. Data Statistics

Dataset	Triples (M)	$S \cup O$ (M)	P	C	Raw size (GB)	Index time (sec)	Index size (MB)
LUBM100	13.88	3.30	17	12	2.46	75	167
WatDiv10m	10.91	1.05	86	24	1.54	46.3	131
DBPedia	31.38	13.55	670	453	3.52	117.9	376.6
DBLP	176.63	45.17	27	4	30.64	752	2120

6 Experiments

In this section, we conduct several experiments to verify the effectiveness and efficiency of our diversified top-k querying algorithms.

Datasets: Table 1 describes the datasets, where S, P, O, and C denote the unique subjects, predicates, objects and categories. We use two synthetic datasets LUBM100 [3] and WatDiv10m [4]. Each node in LUBM100 and WatDiv10m is assigned a weight chosen randomly between 0 and 1. We also use two real datasets DBLP [5] and DBPedia 2015-10 core [6]. The importance of a node v in DBLP and DBPedia is defined as $\frac{log(v_{out\_degree})}{log(max\_out\_degree)}$. This setting follows an intrinsic nature: as an author in DBLP, the more papers he writes, the more likely he is an influential researcher.

Queries: We use the benchmark queries in LUBM and WatDiv. For DBLP and DBPedia, we manually choose some meaningful queries from their query logs. Size of a SPARQL query is defined as $|Q| = |V_q| + |E_q|$. To fully test our methods, we make sure the number of matches for each query is larger than 10k.

Algorithms: There is no ground-truth algorithm of the DTQ problem. Because it is impracticable to enumerate all k-subsets of results when their counts are over 10k. We implemented our algorithms DTopk-Base and DTopk-Index. The problem of finding the diversified top-k matches in a heterogeneous network has been studied earlier [11], so we adapt its method in our DTQ problem setting. We denote it as DTopk-Fan, which is also a 2-approximation method.

Hardware: We implement three algorithms in C++, having the O3 optimization flag enabled and the OpenMP framework to enable multithreaded execution. We set them up on a machine with 128 GB RAM, 480GB SSD, and two Intel Xeon CPUs (6 cores each), running 64-bit CentOS 7.

We run all the experiments 5 times and report their mean. We use the single-thread version of DTopk-Index without a special statement.

6.1 Results

Exp1-Backbone Index. The last two columns in Table 1 show the Backbone index size and construction time. Generating the Backbone index is very fast. Even for the largest graph DBLP, the index creation takes up to 13 min. The index size is ten times smaller than the raw size.

Exp2-Effectiveness Study. We evaluate the effectiveness the three methods, DTopk-Base, DTopk-Index vs. DTopk-Fan. We measure effectiveness by computing $F(\cdot)$ and the ratio $IR = \frac{|M(G_D, Q_D)|}{|\mathbb{M}(G_D, Q_D)|}$, where $M(G_D, Q_D)$ indicates the number of matches identified by the algorithms when they terminate. Apparently, $IR = 1$ for DTopk-Base and DTopk-Fan as they examine all the matches (results are not shown in figures). Figure 4 illustrates the results.

Effect of Varying the k: Fixing Q and $\lambda = 0.5$, we vary k from 5 to 25. As shown in Fig. 4(b), the ratio IR of DTopk-Index increases from 0.09 to 0.23 when k increases from 5 to 25. The reason is that, for a larger k, more matches have to be identified and examined by the algorithms. Other datasets show the same trend in Fig. 4(f), 4(j), and 4(l). Comparing DTopk-Base and DTopk-Fan, the $F(\cdot)$ has distinguishable differences in DBLP, while LUBM, WatDiv, and DBPedia do not. This phenomenon stems mainly from many nodes have a really high weight (high out-degree) in DBLP. The node weight follows uniform distribution in LUBM, WatDiv, and DBPedia. The selection strategy in DTopk-Base can pick up nodes with high weight quickly than DTopk-Fan.

Effect of Varying the $|Q|$: Fixing $k = 5$ and $\lambda = 0.5$, we vary $|Q|$ from 3 to 11. The results shown in Fig. 4 tell us that DTopk-Index effectively reduces excessive matches and achieve competitive result comparing to DTopk-Base and DTopk-Fan. Taking LUBM as an example, DTopk-Index produces no more than 25% matches in Fig. 4(d), but the $F(\cdot)$ is very close to that of DTopk-Base and DTopk-Fan in Fig. 4(c).

Exp3-Efficiency Study We next evaluate the efficiency of the three algorithms. For DTopk-Base and DTopk-Fan, the runtime includes time to generate all matches.

Effect of Varying the k: Fixing Q and $\lambda = 0.5$, we vary k from 5 to 25. The results are shown in Figs. 5(a)–5(d). DTopk-Fan and DTopk-Index are more sensitive to the increase of k than DTopk-Base. A possible explanation is the select function of DTopk-Base can be updated incrementally. Recall function $F_u'(S) = \frac{1}{2}(k-1)(1-\lambda)f_u(S) + 2\lambda d(u, S)$ in DTopk-Base, for a match u, $f_u(S)$ actually equals to $\delta_I(u)$, and $d(u, S)$ denotes the distance between u and every element in the existing solution set S. Suppose at iteration i, match v is added to S. At iteration $i + 1$, we could update $F_u'(S + v) = \frac{1}{2}(k-1)(1-\lambda)f_u(S) + 2\lambda[d(u, S) + d(u, v)] = F_u'(S) + 2\lambda d(u, v)$. This update costs just a little time. The time complexity of DTopk-Fan is $O(\frac{1}{2}kn^2)$, as it iteratively selects two matches m_1, m_2 that maximize $F'(m_1, m_2) = (1-\lambda)(\delta_I(m_1) + \delta_I(m_2)) + 2\lambda\delta_D(m_1, m_2)$. So DTopk-Fan is always slower than DTopk-Base and DTopk-Index.

Effect of Varying the $|Q|$: Fixing $k = 5$ and $\lambda = 0.5$, we vary $|Q|$ from 3 to 11. In Figs. 5(e)–5(f), as $|Q|$ grows, it takes more time to produce all matches, so runtime also grows in DTopk-Base and DTopk-Fan. For some very complicated queries, like $|Q| = 11$ in WatDiv, both DTopk-Base and DTopk-Fan take more than 1000 s to finish, which is unacceptable in real-world applications. In contrast, DTopk-Index always finishes within a reasonable time as it produces much fewer matches.

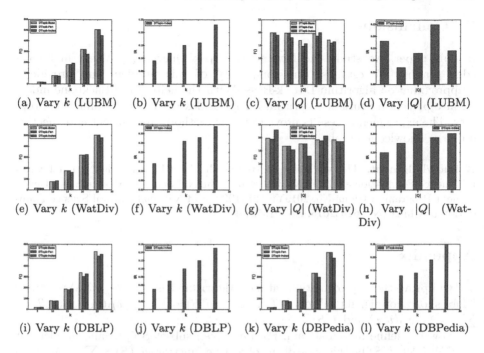

Fig. 4. Effectiveness evaluation, fixing $\lambda = 0.5$

Effect of Multi-Threads: In Fig. 5(g)–5(h), we compare the workload latency using multi-threaded implementations. We combine 5 queries in LUBM and Wat-Div, and vary thread from 1 to 10. The response time decreases by 69% and 65% on LUBM and WatDiv, respectively. The primary trend of DTopk-Index is almost linearly downward with an increasing number of threads. This efficiency improvement lies in the parallelization of forks in the runtime Backbone index, which encourages us to seek parallelization when assembling forks in the future work.

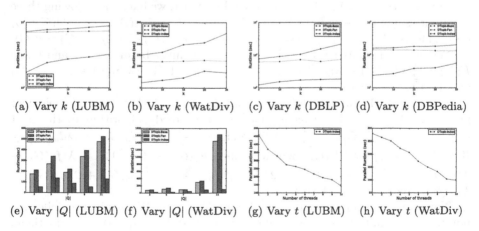

Fig. 5. Efficiency evaluation, fixing $\lambda = 0.5$, and t represents thread

7   Conclusions

In this paper, we study the Diversified Top-k Querying problem in knowledge graphs. We establish the complexity of this problem and provide a 2-approximation algorithm DTopk-Base. With the help of the Backbone index, we also present a heuristic algorithm DTopk-Index with early-termination property. The experimental results prove that our methods are efficient and effective on large knowledge graphs.

Acknowledgment. This work is supported by the Joint Funds of the National Natural Science Foundation of China No. U19A2059, the National Key Research and Development Program of China No. 2019YFB2101902, and National Natural Science Foundation of China (No. 61532015, No. 61672189).

Appendix

We will prove the approximation ratio of Algorithm 1 is 2. $\mathbb{M}(G_D, Q_D)$ is named $\mathbb{M}$ for short. For disjoint subsets $S, T \subseteq \mathbb{M}$, let $d(S) = \sum_{u,v \in S} \delta_D(u, v)$, $d(S, T) = \sum_{u \in S, v \in T} \delta_D(u, v)$ and $f(S) = \sum_{u \in S} \delta_I(u)$.

Now we define marginal gain. For any given subset $S \subseteq \mathbb{M}$ and an element $u \in \mathbb{M} \backslash S$, let $F(S)$ be the value of the objective function, $d_u(S) = \sum_{v \in S} \delta_D(u, v)$ be the marginal gain on the diversity, $f_u(S) = f(S+u) - f(S) = f(u) = \delta_I(u)$ be the marginal gain on the importance, and $F_u(S) = (1-k)(1-\lambda)f_u(S) + 2\lambda d_u(S)$ be the total marginal gain on the objective function. Let $f'_u(S) = \frac{1}{2}(k-1)(1-\lambda)f_u(S)$ and $F'_u(S) = f'_u(S) + 2\lambda d_u(S)$.

We utilize the a theorom in [13]: Given a metric distance function $d(\cdot, \cdot)$, and two disjoint sets X and Y, the following inequality holds: $(|X| - 1)d(X, Y) \geq |Y|d(X)$.

Let O be the optimal solution and G be the greedy one at the end of the Algorithm 1. Let G_i be the greedy solution at the end of step i, $i < k$; let $A = O \cap G_i$, $B = G_i \backslash A$ and $C = O \backslash A$. By Lemma 1, we have the following three inequalities: (1) $(|C| - 1)d(B, C) \geq |B|d(C)$; (2) $(|C| - 1)d(A, C) \geq |A|d(C)$; (3) $(|A| - 1)d(A, C) \geq |C|d(A)$. Besides, we have (4) $d(A, C) + d(A) + d(C) = d(O)$.

When $k = 1$, match u with the largest $\delta_I(u)$ must be in both G and O, so $F(G) = \frac{1}{2}(k-1)(1-\lambda)f_u(S) + 2\lambda d_u(S) = \frac{1}{2}(k-1)(1-\lambda)\delta_I(u) + 0 = \frac{1}{2}F(O)$ apparently.

When $k > 1$, suppose $|C| = 1$ and $i = k - 1$. Let v be the element in C, and let u be the element taken by the greedy algorithm in the next step, and then $F'_u(G_i) \geq F'_v(G_i)$. Therefore, $\frac{(k-1)(1-\lambda)}{2}f_u(G_i) + 2\lambda d_u(G_i) \geq \frac{(k-1)(1-\lambda)}{2}f_v(G_i) + 2\lambda d_v(G_i)$, which implies $F_u(G_i) = (k-1)(1-\lambda)f_u(G_i) + 2\lambda d_u(G_i) \geq \frac{(k-1)(1-\lambda)}{2}f_u(G_i) + 2\lambda d_u(G_i) \geq \frac{(k-1)(1-\lambda)}{2}f_v(G_i) + 2\lambda d_v(G_i) \geq \frac{1}{2}F_v(G_i)$, hence $F(G) \geq \frac{1}{2}F(O)$.

Now we can suppose that $k > 1$ and $|C| > 1$. We apply the following non-negative multipliers to Inequality. (1) (2) (3) and Eq. (4) and add them:

$(1) \times \frac{1}{|C|-1} + (2) \times \frac{|C|-|B|}{k(|C|-1)} + (3) \times \frac{i}{k(k-1)} + (4) \times \frac{i|C|}{k(k-1)}$; then we have $d(A, C) + d(B, C) - \frac{i|C|(k-|C|)}{k(k-1)(|C|-1)}d(C) \geq \frac{i|C|}{k(k-1)}d(O)$.

Since $k > |C|$, we have $d(C, G_i) = d(C, A + B) = d(C, A) + d(C, B) \geq \frac{i|C|}{k(k-1)}d(O)$. Suppose P is a set, we define function $f'(P) = \sum_{x \in P} f'_x(P)$. Then, $\sum_{v \in C} f'_v(G_i) = f'(C \cup G_i) - f'(G_i) = f'(O) - f'(G)$. Therefore,

$$\sum_{v \in C} F'_v(G_i) = \sum_{v \in C}[f'_v(G_i) + 2\lambda d(\{v\}, G_i)]$$

$$= \sum_{v \in C} f'_v(G_i) + 2\lambda d(C, G_i) \geq (f'(O) - f'(G)) + 2\lambda \times \frac{i|C|}{k(k-1)}d(O)$$

Let u_{i+1} be the element taken at step $(i+1)$, and then we have $F'_{u_{i+1}}(G_i) \geq \frac{1}{k}(f'(O) - f'(G)) + \frac{2\lambda i}{k(k-1)}d(O)$. Summing over all i from 0 to $k-1$, we have $F'(G) = \sum_{i=0}^{i=k-1} F'_{u_{i+1}}(G_i) \geq (f'(O) - f'(G)) + \lambda d(O)$. Hence, $F'(G) = f'(G) + 2\lambda d(G) \geq f'(O) - f'(G) + \lambda d(O)$, and $F(G) = (k-1)(1-\lambda)f(G) + 2\lambda d(G) = 2f'(G) + 2\lambda d(G) \geq f'(O) + \lambda d(O) = \frac{1}{2}[(k-1)(1-\lambda)f(O) + 2\lambda d(O)] = \frac{1}{2}F(O)$.

So the approximation ratio of Algorithm 1 is 2. This completes the proof.   □

References

1. http://www.w3.org/TR/rdf-concepts/
2. http://www.w3.org/TR/rdf-sparql-query/
3. http://swat.cse.lehigh.edu/projects/lubm/
4. http://dsg.uwaterloo.ca/watdiv/
5. https://dblp.uni-trier.de/xml/
6. http://downloads.dbpedia.org/2015-10/core-i18n/
7. Arnaout, H., Elbassuoni, S.: Result diversity for RDF search. In: KDIR (2016)
8. Bonifati, A., Martens, W., Timm, T.: An analytical study of large SPARQL query logs. VLDB J. 1–25 (2019)
9. Borodin, A., Lee, H.C., Ye, Y.: Max-sum diversification, monotone submodular functions and dynamic updates. In: PODS (2012)
10. Cheng, J., Zeng, X., Yu, J.X.: Top-k graph pattern matching over large graphs. In: 2013 IEEE 29th International Conference on Data Engineering (ICDE), pp. 1033–1044 (2013)
11. Fan, W., Wang, X., Wu, Y.: Diversified top-k graph pattern matching. PVLDB **6**, 1510–1521 (2013)
12. Gupta, M., Gao, J., Yan, X., Çam, H., Han, J.: Top-k interesting subgraph discovery in information networks. In: 2014 IEEE 30th International Conference on Data Engineering, pp. 820–831 (2014)
13. Ravi, S.S., Rosenkrantz, D.J., Tayi, G.K.: Heuristic and special case algorithms for dispersion problems. Oper. Res. **42**, 299–310 (1994)
14. Vieira, M.R., et al.: On query result diversification. In: 2011 IEEE 27th International Conference on Data Engineering, pp. 1163–1174 (2011)

15. Wang, X., Chai, L., Xu, Q., Yang, Y., Li, J., Wang, J., Chai, Y.: Efficient subgraph matching on large RDF graphs using mapreduce. Data Sci. Eng. **4**, 24–43 (2019). https://doi.org/10.1007/s41019-019-0090-z

16. Wang, X., Zhan, H.: Approximating diversified top-k graph pattern matching. In: Hartmann, S., Ma, H., Hameurlain, A., Pernul, G., Wagner, R.R. (eds.) DEXA 2018. LNCS, vol. 11029, pp. 407–423. Springer, Cham (2018). https://doi.org/10. 1007/978-3-319-98809-2_25

17. Yang, Z., Fu, A.W.C., Liu, R.: Diversified top-k subgraph querying in a large graph. In: SIGMOD Conference (2016)

18. Zou, L., Özsu, M.T.: Graph-based RDF data management. Data Sci. Eng. **2**, 56–70 (2016). https://doi.org/10.1007/s41019-016-0029-6

High Order Semantic Relations-Based Temporal Recommendation Model by Collaborative Knowledge Graph Learning

Yongwei Qiao[1](✉), Leilei Sun[2], and Chunjing Xiao[2]

[1] Engineering Technology Training Center, Civil Aviation University of China, Tianjin, China
qiaoyongwei76@126.com
[2] School of Computer Science and Technology, Civil Aviation University of China, Tianjin, China

Abstract. Knowledge graph (KG) as the source of side information has been proven to be useful to alleviate the data sparsity and cold start. Existing methods usually exploit the semantic relations between entities by learning structural or semantic paths information. However, they ignore the difficulty of information fusion and network alignment when constructing knowledge graph from different domains, and do not take temporal context into account. To address the limitations of existing methods, we propose a novel High-order semantic Relations-based Temporal Recommendation (HRTR), which captures the joint effects of high-order semantic relations in Collaborative Knowledge Graph (CKG) and temporal context. Firstly, it automatically extracts different order connectivities to represent semantic relations between entities from CKG. Then, we define a joint learning model to capture high-quality representations of users, items, and their attributes by employing TransE and recurrent neural network, which captures not only structural information, but also sequence information by encoding semantic paths, and to take their representations as the users'/items' long-term static features. Next, we respectively employ LSTM and attention machine to capture the users' and items' short-term dynamic preferences. At last, the long-short term features are seamlessly fused into recommender system. We conduct extensive experiments on real-world datasets and the evaluation results show that HRTR achieves significant superiority over several state-of-the-art baselines.

Keywords: Collaborative knowledge graph · High-order semantic relation · Structural information · Temporal recommendation

1 Introduction

Collaborative Filtering (CF) is the most popular recommendation strategy, which exploits users' historical interactions to infer their preferences. However,

X. Wang et al. (Eds.): APWeb-WAIM 2020, LNCS 12317, pp. 337–351, 2020.
https://doi.org/10.1007/978-3-030-60259-8_25

they usually suffer from the data sparsity and cold start problem. Various types of side information have been incorporated to address it, such as social networks [7], temporal context [11] and user/item attributes [14]. Knowledge graph (KG) as the source of auxiliary data has been widely adopted to enhance recommendation. It connects various entities and links from different topic domains as nodes and edges to develop insights on recommendation.

Some state-of-art methods utilizing KG are proposed to boost recommendation quality. Meta-path based methods extract paths between two entities to represent different semantic relations, which leverages the relations of item-item [19], user-user [1,10,21], and user-item [6,9]. They can generate effective recommendation by modeling the user preference based on the semantic relations. Because the extracted meta-paths rely on manually designed features based on domain knowledge, they are always incomplete to represent all semantic relations. KG embedding based methods [14,16,20] automatically learn the embeddings of entities to capture entity semantics and incorporate them to recommendation framework. But A major limitation of these KG embedding methods is less intuitive and effective to represent the connection semantic relations of entities. For example, Zhang et al. [20] extracted items' semantic representations from structural content, textual content and visual content by capturing entity semantics via TransR, but ignored the high-order semantic relations between paired entities for recommendation. Then, some methods try to seek a way which not only can capture the semantic relations of entities and paths, but also not rely on handcrafted features and domain knowledge. Sun et al. [12] employed recurrent neural network (RNN) to learn semantic representations of both entities and high order paths to improve recommendation.

Almost all above methods rely on knowledge graph which includes various information from different domains. However, information fusion and network alignment are also very difficult. To address the limitations of constructing knowledge graph, a solution is to design a lightweight Collaborative Knowledge Graph (CKG) by only utilizing the facts in one domain as knowledge. CKG that often includes the interaction behaviors of users on items and side information for items (e.g., item attributes and external knowledge) and users (e.g., age, zip code, and occupation). Wang et al. [17] proposed Knowledge Graph Attention Network (KGAT), which explicitly models high-order connectivities in CKG and recursively propagates the embedding from a node's neighbors to refine its representation. But it only considered the high-order relations between users and items. Wang Hongwei et al. [15] proposed RippleNet which extends a user's potential preference along links in the CKG. These methods model user's preference by utilizing the high-order semantic representations and relations into recommender system, while they don't consider temporal influence. Xiao et al. [18] proposed KGTR which captures the joint effects of interactions by defining three categories relationships in CKG and considers the effect of temporal context. It can obtain the first and second order semantic relations by TransE and the embeddings of user's and item's various attributes, however, can not learn the high-order semantic relations.

Considering the limitations of existing solutions, we believe it is critical to develop a model that can effectively exploit high-order connections in CKG and take temporal information into account. To this end, we propose a novel High-order semantic Relations-based Temporal Recommendation (HRTR), which captures the joint effects of high-order semantic relations in CKG for recommendation. HRTR firstly mines semantic relations about some entities from different order connectivities. Then, it jointly learns high-quality representations of users, items, and their attributes to capture structural knowledge by employing TransE [2] and to explore sequence information by using recurrent neural network to encode semantic paths, which are regard as the users'/items' long-term static features. Next, by splitting the users' interactions with a time window, the users' short-term dynamic preferences are learned by LSTM [5]. The set of users who have recently interacted with an item is used to explore the items' short-term features by attention mechanism [13]. At last, the long-term and short-term preferences of users and items are integrated to recommend an item list to a user.

We summarize our main contributions as follows:

- We propose a joint learning model to capture high-quality representations of entities in a lightweight Collaborative Knowledge Graph, which not only can capture structural information, but also can explore sequence information by automatically encoding extracted semantic paths.
- We seamlessly fuse high-quality representations of entities and temporal context for recommendation, which effectively captures the users' and items' stable long-term and short-term dynamic preferences.
- We conduct experiments on real-world datasets, and the results show the significant superiority of HRTR over several state-of-the-art baselines.

2   Related Work

In this section, we review existing works on meta path based methods, KG embedding based methods, and semantic relation based methods, which are most related to our work.

2.1   Meta Path Based Methods

Meta path based methods capture the relations between two entities in KG by defining meta-paths, which are predefined by using handcrafted features based on domain knowledge. They generally infer a user preference by leveraging the different entity similarity of item-item [19], user-item [6,9], and user-user [1,10, 21]. HeteRec [19] learned the user preference on an item connected with his/her rated item via different meta paths. SemRec [10] captured semantic similarity among users by introducing the weighted meta path. Wang et al. [1] and Zheng et al. [21] respectively proposed matrix factorization model to regularize user similarity derived from meta path. SimMF [9] extended matrix factorization based model by adding meta path based user-item similarity. They successfully model the user preference based on the semantic relations, but they heavily rely on manually designed features based on domain knowledge and can not completely represent all semantic relations between two entities.

2.2 KG Embedding Based Methods

KG embedding based methods first capture the entity embedding by exploiting the structural information of KG and incorporate the learned entity embeddings into a recommendation framework. CKE proposed by Zhang et al. [20] combined CF with item embeddings obtained via TransR [8]. DKN [16] combined the treated entity embeddings with CNN for news recommendation. SHINE [14] embed three types of networks by designing deep autoencoders for celebrity recommendations. But a major limitation of these KG embedding methods is less intuitive and effective to represent the semantic relations of entities.

2.3 Semantic Relation Based Methods

Another kind of methods effectively improves the performance of recommendation by mining the high-order semantic relations or integrating various other information and strategies to capture better representations for recommendation. Sun et al. [12] employed RNN to model different order semantics of paths to characterize user preferences. Wang et al. [17] proposed knowledge graph attention network (KGAT), which recursively propagates the embedding from a node's neighbors to refine its representation and discriminates the importance of neighbors by using an attention mechanism. Wang Hongwei et al. [15] proposed RippleNet which extends a user's potential preference along links in CKG. These methods model users' preferences by utilizing the high-order semantic representations and relations, while they do not consider temporal influence. Xiao et al. [18] proposed KGTR which captures the joint effects of interactions by defining three categories relationships and temporal context.

Different from these works, our proposed method not only can effectively exploit semantics of entities and high-order connectivities, but also take the long-short term preferences of users and items into account.

3   Our Proposed Model

Let $U = \{u_1, u_2, \cdots\}$ and $V = \{v_1, v_2, \cdots\}$ denote the sets of users and items, respectively. $M = \{M_{uv} | u \in U, v \in V\}$ is a sparse user-item interaction matrix that consists of users, items, and the interactions which include rating, browsing, clicking and so on. Meanwhile, there are various attributes of users and items, such as gender, age, occupation, which are significant auxiliary information for recommendation result. We aim to build temporal personalized recommendation model for a user based on the semantic embeddings of users, items and their attributes, and then recommend items to users.

The overview of our proposed HRTR is shown as Fig. 1, which consists of three parts: (1) learning high quality semantic representations of users, items and their attributes by TransE and RNN; (2) training long-short term preferences of users and items, in which the learned semantic representations are considered as the long-term features, the short-term features of users and items are captured by LSTM and attention machine based on the learned semantic embeddings and interactions, repectively; (3) predicting how likely a user interacts an item by integrating these learned long-short term preferences into a sigmoid based prediction model.

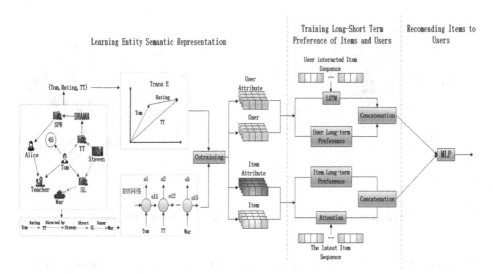

Fig. 1. The framework of high order semantic relations temporal recommendation

3.1   Different Order Semantic Relations Mining

Designing Collaborative Knowledge Graph. Given U, V, M as well as users'/items' attributes, user-item interaction graph and user/item attribute graph are defined, which is regarded as the formal construction of Collaborative Knowledge Graph (CKG).

As illustrated in Fig. 2, taking movie data as an example, the users and items are treated as entities. When there is an observed interaction between user u and item i (e.g., purchases, clicks, ratings), a link will be constructed between them. Here, user-item interaction graph G_1 is denoted as $G_1 = \{(u, m_{uv}, i) | u \in U, i \in V, m_{uv} \in R'\}$, and R' is the interaction sets. In addition to the interactions, users/items have different types of side information to profile them. The user/item attribute graph G_2 is defined to organize the side information in the form of directed graph. Formally, it is presented as $G_2 = \{(h', r', t') | h' \in$

$U \cup V, t' \in \Psi, r' \in \Omega\}$, where Ψ is the attribute values set, Ω is the attribute set and contain canonical relations and their inverse direction. (h', r', t') describes that there is a semantic relationship r' from h' to t'. For example, $(Tom, age, 45)$ states the fact that Toms age is 45. Then, Collaborative Knowledge Graph which encodes user interactions and the side information of users and items is defined as a unified graph $G = \{(h, r, t), h, t \in \varepsilon, r \in R\}$, where $\varepsilon = U \cup V \cup \Psi$, $R = R' \cup \Omega$.

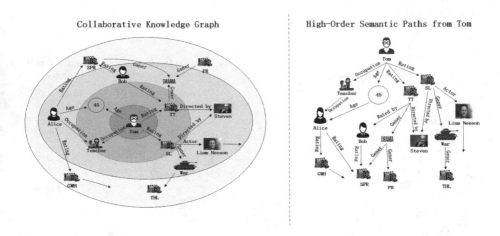

Fig. 2. Different order semantic relations mining on CKG

Different Order Semantic Relations Mining. The key to successful recommendation is to fully exploit the high-order relations in CKG, which represents the way to learn the embedding of entities by using the first-order, second-order or even higher-order semantic relations, respectively. Formally, we define the L-order relations between nodes as a multi-hop relation path: $e_0 \xrightarrow{r_1} e_1 \xrightarrow{r_2} \cdots \xrightarrow{r_L} e_L$, where $e_l \in \varepsilon$ and $r_l \in R$, (e_{l-1}, r_l, e_l) is the $l - th$ triplet, and L is the length of relation path. Then we can denote the semantic relation paths that reach any node from e_0 with different length l. As shown in Fig. 2, for an entity "Tom", we can exploit the first-order semantic relations, $Tom \xrightarrow{age} 45$, $Tom \xrightarrow{occupation} teacher$, $Tom \xrightarrow{rating} TheTerminal(TT)$ and $Tom \xrightarrow{rating} Schindler'sList(SL)$, which represents the attributes of Tom, and his rating activities, respectively. They can be easily extended to the second-order semantic relations, which contains more richer semantics. For example, $Tom \xrightarrow{age} 45 \xrightarrow{-age} Alice$, $Tom \xrightarrow{occupation} teacher \xrightarrow{-occupation} Alice$, $Tom \xrightarrow{rating} TT \xrightarrow{-rating} Bob$, $Tom \xrightarrow{rating} SL \xrightarrow{directedby} Steven$, which indicates semantic relations between Tom and Alice, Bob, Steven relying on common attributes, rating on one item TT, or the relationship on SL. However, to exploit such high-order relations, there are challenges: 1) the number of semantic paths increases dramatically with the order size, which will lead to more computation in training it, and 2) the different order relations are of different importance to recommendation, which requires the model to carefully define them.

Generally, shorter semantic paths indicate stronger relations, while longer ones may represent more semantic relations. To increase model efficiency, We only consider the semantic paths with the length less than a threshold and take the semantic relations started from an entity of user or item into account.

3.2 Semantic Relation Learning

We aim to parameterize entities and relations as vector representations to improve recommendation, which not only learns the structural information, but also the sequence information of semantic relations. Here we employ TransE [2], a widely used method, on CKG to capture this structural knowledge. Sequence information of semantic paths is exploited by adopting RNN.

Structural Embedding. To capture this structural information, TransE is used to learn it by optimizing the probability $P(h, r, t)$ of the relational triples (h, r, t), which exists in the graph. So the probability $P(h, r, t)$ is formalized as follows:

$$L_{SE} = P(h, r, t) = \sum_{(h,r,t^+)\in CKG} \sum_{(h,r,t^-)\in CKG^-} \sigma(g(h, r, t^+) - g(h, r, t^-)) \quad (1)$$

where $\sigma(x) = 1/(1 + exp(x))$ is sigmoid function. The CKG and the CKG^- are the positive and negative instances set, respectively. $g(\cdot)$ is the energy function which represents the correlation from h to t in the relation r. The score of $g(\cdot)$ is lower if the triplet is more likely to be true. Here, we define $g(h, r, t)$ as follow:

$$g(h, r, t) = ||e_h + e_r - e_t||_{L_1/L_2} + b_1 \quad (2)$$

where e_h, e_r, e_t are the embedding of h,r and t; b_1 is a bias constant. The relations of entities are modeled through the triples, which can inject the direct connections into embedding to increase the model representation ability.

Sequence Embedding. Structural embedding can capture entity semantics and semantic relations between entities, however, can not study the semantic relations of high-order paths. By regarding the entities in different high-order semantic paths as a sequence, we naturally think that recurrent neural networks are suitable for modeling different order semantic paths. This is mainly because that it has capability in modeling sequences with various lengths. To this end, we adopt RNN to learn the semantics of entities by encoding the semantic paths with different lengths, and then a pooling operation is used to get the final semantic representation.

Assume n paths of different lengths from an user u_i to any another entity e_j, i.e., $p_l = e_0 \xrightarrow{r_1} e_1 \xrightarrow{r_2} \cdots\cdots \xrightarrow{r_T} e_T$ with $e_0 = u_i$, the RNN learns a representation

h_{lt} for each entity e_t in p_l, which considers both the embeddings of entities in the path and the order of these entities. It encodes the sequence from the beginning entity of the path e_0 to the subsequent entity e_t. For entity e_t

$$O_{lt} = \delta(W \cdot O_{l(t-1)} + H \cdot h_{lt} + b_2) \tag{3}$$

where W is the linear transformation parameters for the previous step, H is for current step; b_2 is the bias term; δ is the sigmoid function. $O_{l(t-1)}$ is a learned hide state by encoding the subsequence from e_0 to e_{t-1}, O_{lt} is a learned hide state after learning the embedding of h_{lt} at step t. For n paths from a user entity u_i, their last representations are $O_{1T_1}, O_{2T_2} \cdots O_{nT_n}$, where T_n is the length of p_n. Based on this, we get the entity representation $O[u_i]$ by adding a max pooling or an average pooling operation towards all the n paths. Similarly, we can get the representation $O[v_j]$ of item v_j. So the objective function can be defined as:

$$L_{SP} = \sum_{(u_i, v_j) \in CKG^+} -\ln \delta(\hat{y}(u_i, v_j) - y(u_i, v_j)) \tag{4}$$

where the probability $\hat{y}(u_i, v_j) = \delta(O[u_i]^T O[v_j])$ is predicted by conducting inner product of user and item representations, CKG^+ is positive instances set, $\sigma(\cdot)$ is the sigmoid function.

Finally, we have the objective function to jointly learn Eqs. (1) and (4), as follows:

$$L = L_{SE} + L_{SP} \tag{5}$$

We optimize L_{SE} and L_{SP} alternatively. Specifically, all representations for nodes are updated by randomly sampling a batch of instances h, r, t, t'; hereafter, we randomly sample some users or items and mine semantic paths starting from them, and update the representation for all nodes. Then we can get the embeddings of users, items and their attributes U_L, V_L, U_a, V_a, which are regard as the long term preferences of users and items for temporal recommendation.

3.3   Training Long-Short Term Preference of Users and Items

Users Long-Short Preference. A user preference is compose of the long-term and short-term preference. The long-term preference indicates the stable interest, which is represented by semantic presentations of the user's interacted items and their attributes. The short-term preference indicates a user's dynamic interest, which are learned by LSTM here. The size of time window t is the key issue when modeling the user dynamic preference. The more fine-grained interest changes can be captured by using smaller time window, but the training data is very sparse and the learning process is difficult. On the contrary, the larger time window will has sufficient training data, while the model is less adaptive for capturing dynamics changes of a user preference. To this end, we adopt the latest n items to model the user short term preference, which ensures the enough training data to train the user preference. Instead of inputting the user interacted history in form of items sequence into LSTM, the learned semantic representations of the interacted items and their attributes are regarded as pre-train input of LSTM. This makes the training faster and more effective. Finally, the output of LSTM U_S is taken as the user short-term preference.

Items Long-Term Preference. Similar to the user preference, the item preferences are also made up of two parts. The learned semantic representations of items and their attributes are regarded as their long-term preferences. Their short-term features are determined by the popularity of them changing over time. We think that the most fashionable items currently have a greater contribution to user preference. Here, we adopt attention machine to capture the short-term characteristics of items because of its capability of keeping the contextual sequential information and exploiting the relationships between items. At last, the items recently viewed by all users are used as attention input. Similar to [13], the attention vector for items $(1, 2, \cdots I)$ are calculated by using Eq. (6) at each output time t.

$$V'_s = \sum (\delta(z^T tanh(W_c c_t + W_y y_i))y_i) \tag{6}$$

where z , W_c, W_y are learnable parameters, c_t is the training item at time t and y_i is i-th item in input sequence. $\delta(\cdot)$ is a sigmoid function. Lastly, c_t and V'_s are concatenated as the next input c_{t+1}. The final output V_s can be regarded as items' dynamic preferences.

3.4   Recommending Items to Users

Our task is to predict items which the user likely to prefer to when giving the long-short term preferences of users, items and their attributes. They can be concatenated into a single vector as the input of a standard multi-layer perceptron (MLP), as follow:

$$U_P = U_L \| U_a \| U_S$$
$$V_P = V_L \| V_a \| V_S \tag{7}$$

where $\|$ is the concatenation operation. $\hat{y}_{uv}$ is used to represent the probability of the user u interact with the item v. It is represented by Eq. (8)

$$\hat{y}_{uv} = \sigma(h^T O_L) \tag{8}$$

where O_L is output of MLP. For any $l - th$ layer, O_l is defined as Eq. (9)

$$\varnothing_l = \phi_l(\lambda_l O_{l-1} + \vartheta_l) \tag{9}$$

where $\phi_l, \lambda_l, \vartheta_l$ are the ReLU activation function, weight matrix and bias vector for the l-th layer's perceptron, respectively. O_{l-1} is the $l - 1$-th layer's output of MLP. U_P and V_P are the input of input layer.

We treat y_{uv} as label, which represents the actual interaction. 1 means user u has interacted with item v, and 0 otherwise. Therefore, the likelihood function is defined as Eq. (10):

$$p(y, y^- | \Theta_f) = \prod_{(u,v) \in y} \hat{y}_{uv} \prod_{(u,v) \in y^-} (1 - \hat{y}_{uv}) \tag{10}$$

Taking the negative logarithm of the likelihood, we gain the objective function as Eq. (11):

$$
\begin{aligned}
L &= - \sum_{(u,v) \in y} \log \hat{y}_{uv} - \sum_{(u,v) \in y^-} \log(1 - \hat{y}_{uv}) \\
&= - \sum_{(u,v) \in y \cup y^-} y_{uv} \log \hat{y}_{uv} + (1 - y_{uv}) \log(1 - \hat{y}_{uv})
\end{aligned}
\tag{11}
$$

where y^- is the negative instances set, which is uniformly sampled from unobserved interactions with the sampling ratio related to the number of observed interactions. The output of each neuron is controlled in [0,1] by using sigmoid function. The learning will stop when their output is near to either 0 or 1.

We adopt adaptive gradient algorithm to optimize our model, which automatically adapts the step size to reduce the efforts in learning rate tuning. In the recommendation stage, candidate items are ranked in ascending order according to the prediction result, and we recommend the top ranked items to users.

4 Experiments

In this section, we perform experiments to evaluate HRTR. We first introduce experimental setup, including the datasets, baselines, evaluation metrics and parameter settings, and then present the experiment results against the related baselines.

4.1 Experimental Setup

Dataset Description. To demonstrate the effectiveness of HRTR, We conduct experiments on two public datasets. The one is MovieLens-1M[1] which consists of 6,040 users, 3,952 items and approximately 1M explicit ratings. Besides the user-item ratings, it also includes some auxiliary information about users and items, such as age, occupation, zip code, genre, title, director, etc. Ratings ranging from 1 to 5 are transformed into either 1 or 0, where 1 indicates a user have rated an item, otherwise 0. Another one is Yelp[2], which contains 4700000 review information, 156000 businesses and 110000 users. Here we consider businesses, for example movie theaters, as items. We set the threshold to 10, which represents that a user has at least 10 interactions.

For each user, his/her interactions are first sorted based on interactive time, and the latest one is regarded as the test positive instance and others are utilized as positive instances for training. Finally we randomly sample four negative instances for per positive one, and randomly sample 99 unrated items as the test negative instances.

---

[1] https://grouplens.org/datasets/movielens/.
[2] https://www.yelp.com/dataset/challenge.

Evaluation Metrics. Hit Ratio (HR) and Normalized Discounted Cumulative Gain (NDCG) are used to evaluate the performance of a ranked list [4]. The HR intuitively measures whether the recommendation list includes the test item. The NDCG measures the ranking of the test item in top-K list. We calculate HR and NDCG for each test user and take the average score as the final results.

Baselines. To validate the effectiveness of our proposed HRTR, we compare it with the following state-of-the-art baselines

- NCF [3]: It uses a multi-layer perceptron replacing the inner product to learn the user-item interactions.
- MCR [6]: It is a meta path based model, which extracts qualified meta paths as similarity between a user and an item.
- CKE [20]: It is a collaborative KG embedding based method, which learns item latent representations by combining structural, textual and visual information in a unified framework.
- KGTR [18]: It is a semantic relation plus temporal method, which defines three relationships in CKG to express interactions for recommendation.

Parameter Settings. For structural embedding training, the embedding size is fixed to 100, hyper parameter b_1 is set to 7, and L_1 is taken as distance metric. For sequence embedding training, the threshold of the longest semantic path length is set to 6. A longer path hardly improves performance but brings heavier computational overhead. We implement HRTR in Python based on the Keras framework and employ mini-batch Adam to optimize it. For MovieLens dataset, 16 items are selected as the input of LSTM for one user to learn his/her short term preference. For Yelp, 8 items are selected to mine users' preference. We select items which interacted by all users in the latest hour as input of attention to learn the items' short term features.

We find out other optimal parameters for HRTR by experiment and take HR and NDCG as metrics to evaluate them. We apply a grid search to find out the best values for hyperparameters: the dimension of representation vector d is tuned in $\{50, 100, 150, 200\}$, the batch size s is searched in $\{128, 256, 512, 1024, 2048\}$. Due to space limitation and the same trend, only the results on MovieLens are shown in Fig. 3. From Fig. 3 we can see that HR@10 and NDCG@10 firstly increase and then decrease with the increase of d. The performance of HRTR is best when $d = 100$. As s increases, its performance increases rapidly and tends to be stable with different batch size and the best performance is obtained when bach size is set to 2048. So we set $s = 2048$ and $d = 100$ as the optimal parameters for MovieLens, while for Yelp $s = 2048$ and $d = 150$. The optimal parameters of baselines are set to their recommended values.

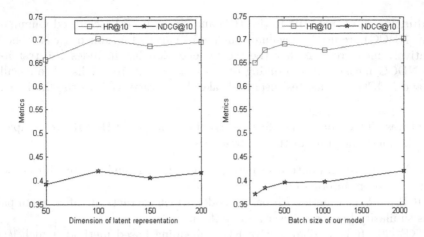

Fig. 3. The performance of our HRTR with different dimensions and batch sizes

4.2   Results and Analysis

Results Analysis of HRTR. Here, we report the performance of our HRTR for top@k recommendation on MovieLens, where k is tuned in {5, 10, 15, 20, 25, 30}. Firstly, the batch size is set to 2048 and the dimension is tuned in {50, 100, 150, 200}, the results are shown in Fig. 4. Some interesting observations can be noted from Fig. 4. With increasing of k, HR@k and NDCG@k are improved rapidly and tend to be stable. In general, HR@k and NDCG@k get better results when $d = 100$, while the difference is very slight. The result is consistent with the analysis in parameter settings. That shows it is not sensitive to vector dimension.

As shown in Fig. 5, we also tested the top@k item recommendations, when vector dimension is fixed to 100 while batch size is searched in {512, 1024, 2048}. We can observe that HR@k and NDCG@k increase when k varies from 5 to 30. HR@k and NDCG@k all get the better performance when batch size becomes larger and it is obvious for NDCG@k. Due to the same trends, the results on Yelp are not described in detail.

Comparing HRTR with Baselines. Table 1 summarizes the performance of all methods on two datasets and the best performance is boldfaced. MCR without considering temporal information and CKE without employing semantic paths achieve poor performance compared with other methods. This confirm that semantic path and temporal context are useful to provide better recommendation. MCR highly outperforms all models if the ranking list is short. That is mainly because MCR exploits the entity relation in the KG by introducing meta paths relying on domain knowledge, which has its superiority when requiring shorter recommendation list. The performance of KGTR is closest to HRTR.

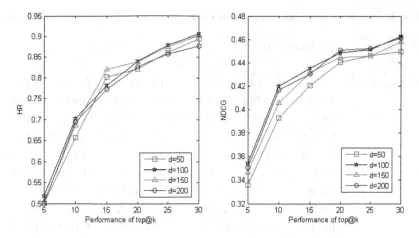

Fig. 4. HR@K and NDCG@K results with different dimensions

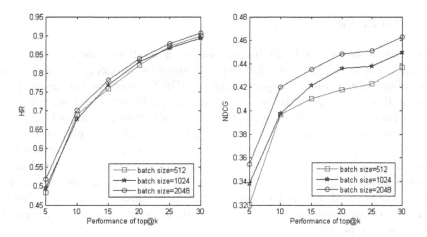

Fig. 5. HR@K and NDCG@K results with different batch size

The reason is that they all consider semantic relation with temporal context. While HRTR is still superior to KGTR. The mainly reason is that HRTR can capture high order semantic relation, KGTR can not do it. For sparser Yelp dataset, HRTR achieves significantly better performance than other methods, that shows that HRTR is more suitable for sparser data.

Table 1. Performance of all comparison methods across all the evaluation metrics.

Datesets	Methods	HR@k			NDCG@k		
		5	10	20	5	10	20
MovieLens-1M	NCF	0.5339	0.6812	0.8204	0.3501	0.4102	0.4403
	MCR	**0.5764**	0.5873	0.6079	**0.4354**	0.4001	0.3809
	CKE	0.4251	0.5736	0.7345	0.1585	0.1698	0.1999
	KGTR	0.5402	0.6978	0.8303	0.3603	**0.4232**	0.4501
	HRTR	0.5102	**0.6989**	**0.8312**	0.3412	0.4120	**0.4508**
Yelp	NCF	0.1123	0.1360	0.2011	0.1650	0.1123	0.0543
	MCR	**0.1202**	0.1143	0.1156	**0.1815**	0.1828	0.1798
	CKE	0.0931	0.1098	0.1172	0.1212	0.1131	0.0821
	KGTR	0.1102	0.1179	0.1206	0.1528	0.1698	0.1658
	HRTR	0.1090	**0.1379**	**0.2152**	0.1811	**0.1903**	**0.1822**

5 Conclusions

In this paper, we proposed a High-order semantic Relations-based Temporal Recommendation model (HRTR) that explores the joint effects of different semantic relations in CKG and temporal context. HRTR overcame the limitations of
existing KG-aware methods by jointly learning different order semantic relations between entities, which not only captures structural information, but also
explores sequence information in CKG. HRTR respectively exploited the users'
and items' long and short term features, which could capture their stable and
temporal dynamic preferences. Extensive experiments were conducted on real
datasets and the experimental results demonstrated the significant superiority of
HRTR over state-of-the-art baselines. In future, we plan to design an effectively
unified model to simultaneously explore the structural and sequence information
to improve the performance.

Acknowledgement. This work was partially supported by grants from the National
Natural Science Foundation of China (No. U1533104; U1933114), the Fundamental
Research Funds for the Central Universities (No. ZXH2012P009) and Civil Aviation
Science and Technology Project (No. MHRD20130220)

References

1. Wang, Y., Xia, Y., Tang, S., Wu, F., Zhuang, Y.: Flickr group recommendation with
   auxiliary information in heterogeneous information networks. Multimedia Syst.
   23(6), 703–712 (2016). https://doi.org/10.1007/s00530-015-0502-5
2. Bordes, A., Usunier, N., Garcia-Duran, A., Weston, J., Yakhnenko, O.: Translating
   embeddings for modeling multi-relational data. In: Advances in neural information
   processing systems, pp. 2787–2795 (2013)
3. He, X., Liao, L., Zhang, H., Nie, L., Hu, X., Chua, T.S.: Neural collaborative
   filtering. In: Proceedings of WWW, pp. 173–182. WWW (2017)

4. He, X., Tao, C., Kan, M.Y., Xiao, C.: Trirank: review-aware explainable recommendation by modeling aspects (2015)
5. Hochreiter, S., Schmidhuber, J.: Long short-term memory. Neural Comput. **9**(8), 1735–1780 (1997)
6. Hu, B., Shi, C., Zhao, W.X., Yu, P.S.: Leveraging meta-path based context for top-N recommendation with a neural co-attention model. In: Proceedings of the 24th ACM SIGKDD International Conference on Knowledge Discovery & Data Mining, pp. 1531–1540 (2018)
7. Jamali, M., Ester, M.: A matrix factorization technique with trust propagation for recommendation in social networks. In: Proceedings of the 2010 ACM Conference on Recommender Systems RecSys 2010, Barcelona, Spain, 26–30 September 2010 (2010)
8. Lin, Y., Liu, Z., Sun, M., Liu, Y., Zhu, X.: Learning entity and relation embeddings for knowledge graph completion. In: Proceedings of AAAI (2015)
9. Shi, C., Liu, J., Zhuang, F., Yu, P.S., Wu, B.: Integrating heterogeneous information via flexible regularization framework for recommendation. Knowl. Inf. Syst. **49**(3), 835–859 (2016). https://doi.org/10.1007/s10115-016-0925-0
10. Shi, C., Zhang, Z., Luo, P., Yu, P.S., Yue, Y., Wu, B.: Semantic path based personalized recommendation on weighted heterogeneous information networks. In: Proceedings of the 24th ACM International on Conference on Information and Knowledge Management (2015)
11. Sun, Y., Yuan, N.J., Xie, X., Mcdonald, K., Zhang, R.: Collaborative intent prediction with real-time contextual data. **35**(4), 30 (2017)
12. Sun, Z., Yang, J., Zhang, J., Bozzon, A., Huang, L.K., Xu, C.: Recurrent knowledge graph embedding for effective recommendation. In: Proceedings of the 12th ACM Conference on Recommender Systems, pp. 297–305. ACM (2018)
13. Vinyals, O., Kaiser, L., Koo, T., Petrov, S., Sutskever, I., Hinton, G.: Grammar as a foreign language. Eprint Arxiv, pp. 2773–2781 (2015)
14. Wang, H., Zhang, F., Hou, M., Xie, X., Guo, M., Liu, Q.: Shine: signed heterogeneous information network embedding for sentiment link prediction (2018)
15. Wang, H., et al.: Ripplenet: propagating user preferences on the knowledge graph for recommender systems. In: Proceedings of the 27th ACM International Conference on Information and Knowledge Management, pp. 417–426 (2018)
16. Wang, H., Zhang, F., Xie, X., Guo, M.: DKN: deep knowledge-aware network for news recommendation (2018)
17. Wang, X., He, X., Cao, Y., Liu, M., Chua, T.S.: KGAT: knowledge graph attention network for recommendation. In: Proceedings of the 25th ACM SIGKDD International Conference on Knowledge Discovery & Data Mining, pp. 950–958 (2019)
18. Xiao, C., Xie, C., Cao, S., Zhang, Y., Fan, W., Heng, H.: A better understanding of the interaction between users and items by knowledge graph learning for temporal recommendation. In: Nayak, A.C., Sharma, A. (eds.) PRICAI 2019. LNCS (LNAI), vol. 11670, pp. 135–147. Springer, Cham (2019). https://doi.org/10.1007/978-3-030-29908-8_11
19. Xiao, Y., Xiang, R., Sun, Y., Sturt, B., Han, J.: Recommendation in heterogeneous information networks with implicit user feedback. In: Proceedings of the 7th ACM Conference on Recommender Systems (2013)
20. Zhang, F., Yuan, N.J., Lian, D., Xie, X., Ma, W.Y.: Collaborative knowledge base embedding for recommender systems. In: Proceedings of the 22nd ACM SIGKDD, pp. 353–362. ACM (2016)
21. Zheng, J., Liu, J., Shi, C., Zhuang, F., Li, J., Wu, B.: Recommendation in heterogeneous information network via dual similarity regularization. Int. J. Data Sci. Analytics **3**(1), 35–48 (2016). https://doi.org/10.1007/s41060-016-0031-0

Temporal Knowledge Graph Incremental Construction Model for Recommendation

Chunjing Xiao(✉), Leilei Sun, and Wanlin Ji

School of Computer Science and Technology, Civil Aviation University of China,
Tianjin, China
chunjingxiao@163.com

Abstract. Knowledge graph (KG) has been proven to be effective to improve the performance of recommendation because of exploiting structural and semantic paths information in a static knowledge base. However, the KG is an incremental construction process with interactions occurring in succession. Although some works have been proposed to explore the evolution of knowledge graph, which updates the entity representations by considering the previous interactions of related entities. However, we believe that the semantic path information between the involved entities and the occurring interaction itself also can refine their representations. To this end, we propose a temporal knowledge graph incremental construction model, which updates the entity representations by considering interaction itself and high-order semantic paths information. Specifically, different length semantic paths between user and item are automatically extracted when an interaction occurs. Then we respectively employ recurrent neural network and standard multilayer perceptron (MLP) to capture different length path semantic information and interaction itself information for updating the entity representations. Finally, we use MLP to predict the probability that a user likes an item after seamlessly integrating these variations into a unified representation. We conduct experiments on real-world datasets to demonstrate the superiority of our proposed model over all state-of-the-art baselines.

Keywords: Knowledge graph · Semantic path · User interaction · Recurrent neural network

1 Introduction

Recommender system (RS) recently has been active in various fields. Similar to the event detection method [13], the goal of RS is to find items that the user are more interested by using user's historical behaviors. Matrix Factorization (MF)-based methods [2,8] have achieved great success, however, their performances will be significantly reduced when the data is sparse and they lack the further exploration of hidden relationship encoded in datasets (e.g., user-item pair).

X. Wang et al. (Eds.): APWeb-WAIM 2020, LNCS 12317, pp. 352–359, 2020.
https://doi.org/10.1007/978-3-030-60259-8_26

To address theses limitations, researchers try to utilize knowledge graph (KG) to help us discover potential interrelationships between users, items and user-item pairs. Meta path-based methods [3,4,11] mainly add entity similarity (user-user, item-item and user-item) derived from meta paths in KG into collaborative filtering (e.g., the latent factor model [5] (LFM)). However, they heavily rely on handcrafted features and domain knowledge, and are not enough to fully capture the critical paths of the entity relationship. KG embedding based methods [9–12] automatically learn the embeddings of entities in KGs by using structural information and entity properties, but ignore the path semantic information. Recurrent Knowledge Graph Embedding (RKGE) [6] not only learned the entity representations, but also the semantic paths. However, all KG-aware methods mentioned above can get better performance by assuming that KG has been fully constructed and is static. In fact, the knowledge graph construction is a temporal and incremental process. When an interaction occurs, entities and edges are added to KG. Knowledge graph evolutionary methods [1,7,14] learned better entity representations by introducing the temporal order of interactions. However, they did not consider the impact of high-order semantic path in KG when updating the entity representations.

Considering the limitations of existing methods, we propose a temporal knowledge graph incremental construction model for recommendation (KGCR), which not only considers interaction itself, but also high-order semantic paths information when updating their representations. Specifically, it automatically extracts different length paths between user-item pairs when an interaction occurs. Then the entity representations are updated by exploring the impact of interact itself and semantic paths learning by recurrent neural network (RNN) and MLP, respectively. Finally, we use MLP to predict the recommendation results after seamlessly integrating these variations into a unified representation. The experimental results show its superiority over other state-of-the art baselines.

2 Methodology

Given user-item interaction data and auxiliary information about users and items, our goal is to incrementally construct knowledge graph based on the order of interaction occurring, which not only considers the previous representations of the two involved entities, but also the impact of interaction itself and high-order semantic paths. The overall framework of KGCR is shown in Fig. 1, which consists of three parts: 1) extracting different length semantic paths between user and item when a user interact with an item at t time; 2) employing RNN and MLP to respectively mine the impact of semantic representations in different length paths and interaction itself of the user and item; 3) Training and recommendation after fusing these impacts into a unified MLP model.

2.1 Incremental Temporal Knowledge Graph

We regard the interactions between users and items as temporal sequence, and then traditional static KG need to be augmented into incremental temporal KG.

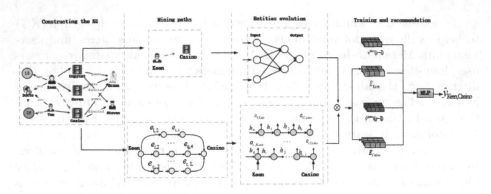

Fig. 1. The overall framework of KGCR.

When a user interacts with an item at time t, an edge will be added between them, as shown in Fig. 1. Here, we extend triplet representation for static KG to introduce time dimension and incremental temporal knowledge graph G_T is denoted as $G_T = \{(u, y_{ui}, i, t) | u \in U, i \in I, y_{ui} \in R'\}$, where R' is the interaction sets (e.g.,purchases, clicks, ratings), $y_{ui} = 1$ if a user interacts with an item, otherwise 0, $t \in R^+$ is the occurring time of this interaction. So an incremental temporal KG containing M edges corresponding M observed interactions can be regarded as the globally ordered set $D = \{(u, y_{ui}, i, t_m)\}_{m=1}^M$, where $0 \leq t_1 \leq t_2 \leq \cdots t_m \leq \cdots t_M$. In addition to the interactions, users/items are profiled by their different types of side information, which is organized in the form of directed graph G_a. Formally, it is denoted as $G_a = \{(h, r, t) | h \in U \cup I, r \in \Psi, t \in \Lambda\}$, where Ψ is the attribute set and consists of their canonical and inverse relations, Λ is the attribute value set. When users/items are firstly joined to G_T, their attributes are also added. Then G_T and G_a can be denoted as a unified graph $G = G_T \cup G_a$.

2.2   Semantic Paths Mining

Having an observed interaction at time t, KGCR regards it as an incoming event that will alter the semantic representations of entities. As shown in Fig. 1, for entity pair $(Keen, Casino)$, we can exploit different order semantic paths to mining their different semantic relations. For example, Keen likes Casino can be inferred by: 1) $Keen \xrightarrow{interact} Seven \xrightarrow{genre} Drama \xrightarrow{-genre} Casino$, 2) $Keen \xrightarrow{interact} Seven \xrightarrow{genre} Drama \xrightarrow{-genre} Copycat \xrightarrow{directedby} Steven \xrightarrow{direct} Casino$, 3) $Keen \xrightarrow{occupation} Doctor \xrightarrow{-occupation} Tom \xrightarrow{interact} Casino$. These paths capture semantic relations of 1) belonging to the same genre, 2) belonging to the same genre and being directed by the same director, or 3) being watched by users with same occupation. Thus, we exploit entity relations to update involved entity representations when an interaction occurs. So the semantic relations between entity pair (u, i) is denote as a multi-hop relation path:

$e_0 \xrightarrow{r_1} e_1 \xrightarrow{r_2} \cdots \xrightarrow{r_L} e_L$, where $e_l \in U \cup I \cup \Lambda$ and $r_l \in R' \cup \Psi$, (e_{l-1}, r_l, e_l) is the $l-th$ triplet, and L is the length of relation path.

2.3   Evolution of Semantic Presentations for Entities

Given an interaction $m = (u_k, y_{ui}, i_n, t_m) \in D$, and assume that m is user u_k's s-th interaction while it is i_n's q-th interaction. Then we update the their representations with the following function, respectively:

$$\boldsymbol{\nu}^{u_k}(t_s) = \delta_1(\boldsymbol{w}_t^u \boldsymbol{\nu}^{u_k}(t_{s-1}) + \boldsymbol{w}^z \boldsymbol{\lambda}^{u_k}(t_s-)) \tag{1}$$

$$\boldsymbol{\nu}^{i_n}(t_q) = \delta_1(\boldsymbol{w}_t^i \boldsymbol{\nu}^{i_n}(t_{q-1}) + \boldsymbol{w}^z \boldsymbol{\lambda}^{i_n}(t_q-)) \tag{2}$$

where $\boldsymbol{w}_t^u, \boldsymbol{w}_t^i, \boldsymbol{w}^z$ are training parameters, $t_s = t_q = t_m$ is the time of observed interaction, t_{s-1} is the time of the latest interaction in which u_k was involved, t_s- represents the time that m is just to happen. $\boldsymbol{\nu}^{u_k}(t_{s-1})$ and $\boldsymbol{\nu}^{u_k}(t_s)$ respectively indicates latest vector representation of u_k before and after considering the impact of an interaction m. Vectors in Eq. 2 are similar to Eq. 1, so they will not be described in detail. Here $\boldsymbol{\lambda}^{u_k}(t_s-)$ is equal to $\boldsymbol{\lambda}^{i_n}(t_q-)$, which represents the influence due to this interaction and is expressed in a unified form $\boldsymbol{\lambda}(t_m)$. It consists of two part: 1) $g_1(\boldsymbol{\nu}^{u_k}(t_{s-1}), \boldsymbol{\nu}^{i_n}(t_{q-1}))$ represents the interplay of two involved entities; 2) $g_2(\boldsymbol{h}^{u_k}, \boldsymbol{h}^{i_n})$ indicates the impact of different length semantic paths. Thus, it is defined as follow:

$$\boldsymbol{\lambda}(t_m) = \delta_2(g_1(\boldsymbol{\nu}^{u_k}(t_{s-1}), \boldsymbol{\nu}^{i_n}(t_{q-1})) + g_2(\boldsymbol{h}^{u_k}, \boldsymbol{h}^{i_n})) \tag{3}$$

where $\delta_1(\cdot)$ and $\delta_2(\cdot)$ are nonlinear functions, which can be equal (softmax in our case). $g_1(\boldsymbol{\nu}^{u_k}(t_{s-1}), \boldsymbol{\nu}^{i_n}(t_{q-1}))$ is computed as:

$$g_1(\boldsymbol{\nu}^{u_k}(t_{s-1}), \boldsymbol{\nu}^{i_n}(t_{q-1})) = \phi_l(\boldsymbol{\nu}^{u_k}(t_{s-1})^T, \boldsymbol{\nu}^{i_n}(t_{q-1})) \tag{4}$$

where ϕ_l is the l layer ReLU operation. $g_2(\boldsymbol{h}^{u_k}, \boldsymbol{h}^{i_n}))$ is learned by RNN.

Assume that the threshold of semantic path length is set to L and there are j_l paths with l lengths between entity pair (u_k, i_n), p_l^γ is the γ-th semantic paths having l length, which is represented as $p_l^\gamma = e_l^{\gamma_0} \xrightarrow{r_1} e_l^{\gamma_1} \xrightarrow{r_2} \cdots \cdots \xrightarrow{r_l} e_l^{\gamma_l}$ with $e_l^{\gamma_0} = u_k, e_l^{\gamma_l} = i_n$. For entity $e_l^{\gamma_l}$

$$\boldsymbol{h}_l^{\gamma_t} = \delta(\boldsymbol{W} \cdot \boldsymbol{h}_l^{\gamma_{(t-1)}} + \boldsymbol{H} \cdot \boldsymbol{\nu}_l^{\gamma_t} + b_2) \tag{5}$$

where $\boldsymbol{W}, \boldsymbol{H}$ are parameter matrix; b_2 is the bias term; δ is activation function (sigmoid function in our case); $\boldsymbol{\nu}_l^{\gamma_t}$ is a vector representation of entity $e_l^{\gamma_t}$. $\boldsymbol{h}_l^{\gamma_{(t-1)}}$ is a learned hide state by encoding the subsequence from $e_l^{\gamma_0}$ to $e_l^{\gamma_{(t-1)}}$, $\boldsymbol{h}_l^{\gamma_t}$ is a learned hide state after learning the embedding of $\boldsymbol{\nu}_l^{\gamma_t}$ at step t.

So $\boldsymbol{h}_l^{\gamma_0}$ and $\boldsymbol{h}_l^{\gamma_l}$ can be regarded as the updated user and item latent representations after learning the semantic information of paths p_l^γ. Then we can explore $\boldsymbol{h}_l^{u_k}$ and $\boldsymbol{h}_l^{i_n}$ after learning all the paths with l length. They can be further considered as the input of training all semantic paths with $l+1$ length. $\boldsymbol{h}^{u_k}$ and $\boldsymbol{h}^{i_n}$ can be obtained through pooling all different length semantic paths.

2.4   Efficient Training for Recommendation

We treat the representations $\boldsymbol{\nu}^{u_k}(t_s)$ and $\boldsymbol{\nu}^{i_n}(t_q)$ as the input of MLP to train this model. Its output $\hat{y}_{ui}$ indicates the probability of the user u_k interacts with the item i_n, which is shown as Eq. 6

$$\hat{y}_{ui} = \phi_l(\boldsymbol{\nu}^{u_k}(t_s), \boldsymbol{\nu}^{i_n}(t_q)) \tag{6}$$

where ϕ_l is the l layer ReLU activation operation. By applying negative sampling, we gain the objective function as Eq. 7:

$$
\begin{aligned}
L &= - \sum_{(u,i)\in D} \log \hat{y}_{ui} - \sum_{(u,i)\in D^-} \log(1 - \hat{y}_{ui}) \\
&= - \sum_{(u,i)\in D\cup D^-} y_{ui} \log \hat{y}_{ui} + (1 - y_{ui}) \log(1 - \hat{y}_{ui})
\end{aligned}
\tag{7}
$$

where D^- is the negative instances set. Our model is optimized using adaptive gradient algorithm, and in the recommendation stage, the top ranked items are recommended after we rank candidate items in ascending order.

3   Experimental Results

3.1   Experimental Setting

Dataset Description and Evaluation Metrics. To demonstrate the effectiveness of our KGCR, we adopt two real-world public datasets from different domains for empirical study. The first one is Movielens_100k dataset and is combined with IMDB. The second one is Yelp, which is much sparser than Movielens_100k. If a user interacts with an item (e.g. rating or writing a review), the feedback is set to 1, otherwise 0. Hit Ratio (HR@K) and Normalized Discounted Cumulative Gain (NDCG@k) are adopted to evaluate the effectiveness of KGCR, and the recommendation list is tuned in {5, 10, 15}.

Baselines. To validate the superiority of KGCR, we compare it with several baselines: (1) NCF [2]: It is a deep neural networks framework to model interactions, which replaces inner product with MLP. (2) MCRec [3]: It is a path-based model, which extracts qualified meta-paths as connectivity between a user and an item. (3) RKGE [6]: It is a KG embedding approach, which learns semantic representations of entities and entity paths. (4) CKE [12]: It is a representative regularization-based method, which exploits semantic embeddings derived from TransR to enhance matrix factorization. (5) KGAT [9]: It explicitly models the high-order relationship in KG and recursively propagates the entity representation to its neighbors.

Parameter Settings. We randomly initialize parameters with Gaussian distribution, and optimize it by SGD. For hyper parameters, the batch size is searched in {512, 1024, 2048}, the learning rate is tuned in {0.0001, 0.0005, 0.001, 0.005}. The vector dimension varies among {10, 20, 50, 100 }. The layers of MLP is set in {32, 16, 1}. For baselines, we employ the suggested values in the original papers for most parameters.

3.2 Experiment Results and Analysis

Impacts of Semantic Path Lengths. As proposed by Sun et al. [6], shorter paths are more useful to exploit the entity relations because of more clearer semantic meanings. Here, we tune the length of semantic paths in {2, 4, 6, 8, 10,12} and input to KGCR. Figure 2 depicts the results on the two datasets. From the results, we observe that the performance of KGCR firstly increase and then decrease with the path length increasing. It shows that proper path length has a critical impact on performance.

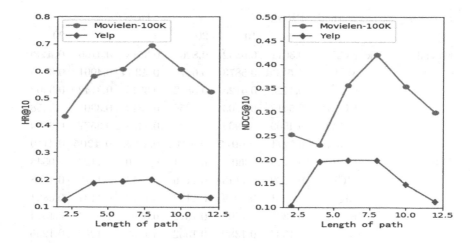

Fig. 2. HR@10 and NDCG@10 of different length of paths on two Datasets

Impact of Interaction Itself and Semantic Paths. To better assess the impact of interaction itself and semantic paths, we firstly compare KGCR with its variation KGCR_N without considering the influence of them. From the results, as shown in Table 1, we can see that KGCR is superior to KGCR_N, which shows it is necessary to consider both interaction itself and semantic paths.

Comparing KGCR with Baselines. We compare the proposed KGCR with baselines, the results are summarized in Table 2. We can observe that KGCR consistently achieves the best performance. That mainly because that KGCR incrementally updates entity representations by considering the influence of interaction itself and semantic paths, while MCRec, CKE and RKGE are always

Table 1. Comparison KGCR with KGCR_N.

Datesets	Methods	HR@k			NDCG@k		
		5	10	20	5	10	20
MovieLens_100k	KGCR	0.5271	0.6942	0.8212	0.3505	0.420	0.4110
	KGCR_N	0.4877	0.5448	0.7031	0.3078	0.2033	0.2988
Yelp	KGCR	0.1398	0.1402	0.2167	0.1832	0.1983	0.1804
	KGCR_N	0.1102	0.1254	0.1723	0.1098	0.1035	0.0964

based on the assumption that the knowledge graph is already constructed and is static, KGAT ignores topological information and NCF does not take auxiliary information in KG. The performance of KGCR on Yelp is better than all other methods, that implies that KGCR is more suitable for sparser data.

Table 2. Comparison of KGCR and baselines.

Datesets	Methods	HR@k			NDCG@k		
		5	10	20	5	10	20
MovieLens_100k	NCF	0.5011	0.6832	0.8204	0.3513	0.4166	**0.4280**
	MCRec	**0.5764**	0.5873	0.6079	**0.4354**	0.4001	0.3809
	CKE	0.4723	0.5125	0.6812	0.3013	0.3142	0.3902
	RKGE	0.5412	0.6703	0.7256	0.3312	0.3301	0.3458
	KGAT	0.4509	0.5902	0.6902	0.3468	0.3577	0.3529
	KGCR	0.5271	**0.6942**	**0.8212**	0.3505	**0.4205**	0.4110
Yelp	NCF	0.1123	1360	0.2011	0.1650	0.1123	0.0543
	MCRec	0.1202	0.1143	0.1156	0.1815	0.1828	0.1798
	CKE	0.0931	0.1098	0.1172	0.1212	0.1131	0.0821
	RKGE	0.1325	0.1401	0.1312	0.0894	0.1254	0.1024
	KGAT	0.1334	0.1382	0.1552	0.1758	0.1268	0.1256
	KGCR	**0.1398**	**0.1402**	**0.2167**	**0.1832**	**0.1983**	**0.1804**

4   Conclusion

In this paper, we proposed KGCR, which updates the entity representations when an interaction occurs. it overcame the limitations of existing KG-aware methods by combining interplay of two involved entities with the variations brought from high-order semantic paths. That were respectively employed by applying RNN and MLP. Through extensive experiments on real-world datasets, we demonstrated the superiority of our proposed model over all state-of-the-art baselines. For future works, we plan to extend the variations to other entities by recursively propagating the entity embeddings in knowledge graph.

Acknowledgement. This work was partially supported by grants from the National Natural Science Foundation of China (No. U1933114), the Fundamental Research Funds for the Central Universities (No. ZXH2012P009) and Civil Aviation Science and Technology Project (No. MHRD20130220).

References

1. Goyal, P., Kamra, N., He, X., Liu, Y.: DynGEM: deep embedding method for dynamic graphs. arXiv preprint arXiv:1805.11273 (2018)
2. He, X., Liao, L., Zhang, H., Nie, L., Hu, X., Chua, T.S.: Neural collaborative filtering. In: Proceedings of the 26th International Conference on World Wide Web, pp. 173–182 (2017)
3. Hu, B., Shi, C., Zhao, W.X., Yu, P.S.: Leveraging meta-path based context for top-N recommendation with a neural co-attention model. In: Proceedings of the 24th ACM SIGKDD International Conference on Knowledge Discovery and Data Mining, pp. 1531–1540 (2018)
4. Luo, C., Pang, W., Wang, Z., Lin, C.: Hete-CF: social-based collaborative filtering recommendation using heterogeneous relations. In: 2014 IEEE International Conference on Data Mining, pp. 917–922. IEEE (2014)
5. Shi, Y., Larson, M., Hanjalic, A.: Collaborative filtering beyond the user-item matrix: a survey of the state of the art and future challenges. ACM Comput. Surv. (CSUR) **47**(1), 1–45 (2014)
6. Sun, Z., Yang, J., Zhang, J., Bozzon, A., Huang, L.K., Xu, C.: Recurrent knowledge graph embedding for effective recommendation. In: Proceedings of the 12th ACM Conference on Recommender Systems, pp. 297–305 (2018)
7. Trivedi, R., Farajtabar, M., Biswal, P., Zha, H.: DyRep: learning representations over dynamic graphs (2018)
8. Wang, H., Wang, N., Yeung, D.Y.: Collaborative deep learning for recommender systems. In: Proceedings of the 21th ACM SIGKDD International Conference on knowledge Discovery and Data Mining, pp. 1235–1244 (2015)
9. Wang, X., He, X., Cao, Y., Liu, M., Chua, T.S.: KGAT: knowledge graph attention network for recommendation. In: Proceedings of the 25th ACM SIGKDD International Conference on Knowledge Discovery and Data Mining, pp. 950–958 (2019)
10. Wang, X., He, X., Wang, M., Feng, F., Chua, T.S.: Neural graph collaborative filtering. In: Proceedings of the 42nd International ACM SIGIR Conference on Research and Development in Information Retrieval, pp. 165–174 (2019)
11. Wang, X., Wang, D., Xu, C., He, X., Cao, Y., Chua, T.S.: Explainable reasoning over knowledge graphs for recommendation. In: Proceedings of the AAAI Conference on Artificial Intelligence, vol. 33, pp. 5329–5336 (2019)
12. Zhang, F., Yuan, N.J., Lian, D., Xie, X., Ma, W.Y.: Collaborative knowledge base embedding for recommender systems. In: Proceedings of the 22nd ACM SIGKDD International Conference on Knowledge Discovery and Data Mining, pp. 353–362 (2016)
13. Zhang, X., Chen, X., Yan, C., Wang, S., Li, Z., Xia, J.: Event detection and popularity prediction in microblogging. Neurocomputing **149**(pt.c), 1469–1480 (2015)
14. Zhou, L., Yang, Y., Ren, X., Wu, F., Zhuang, Y.: Dynamic network embedding by modeling triadic closure process. In: Thirty-Second AAAI Conference on Artificial Intelligence (2018)

Recommender Systems

Few-Shot Representation Learning for Cold-Start Users and Items

Bowen Hao[1,2], Jing Zhang[1,2(✉)], Cuiping Li[1,2], and Hong Chen[1,2]

[1] Key Laboratory of Data Engineering and Knowledge Engineering
of Ministry of Education, Renmin University of China, Beijing, China
{jeremyhao,zhang-jing,licuiping,chong}@ruc.edu.cn
[2] School of Information, Renmin University of China, Beijing, China

Abstract. Existing recommendation algorithms suffer from cold-start issues as it is challenging to learn accurate representations of cold-start users and items. In this paper, we formulate learning the representations of cold-start users and items as a few-shot learning task, and address it by training a representation function to predict the target user (item) embeddings based on limited training instances. Specifically, we propose a novel attention-based encoder serving as the neural function, with which the K training instances of a user (item) are viewed as the interactive context information to be further encoded and aggregated. Experiments show that our proposed method significantly outperforms existing baselines in predicting the representations of the cold-start users and items, and improves several downstream tasks where the embeddings of users and items are used.

Keywords: Cold-start representation learning · Few-shot learning · Attention-based encoder

1 Introduction

Existing recommendation systems (RS) such as Matrix Factorization [14] and Neural Collaborative Filtering [11] are facing serious challenges when making cold-start recommendations, i.e., when dealing with a new user or item with few interactions for which the representation of the user or the item can not be learned well.

To deal with such cold-start challenges, some researches are conducted which can be roughly classified into two categories. The first category incorporates side information such as knowledge graph (KG) to alleviate the cold-start issues [3,25,26,28]. Specifically, these methods first pre-process a KG by some knowledge graph embedding methods such as TransE [1], TransH [27] and so on, and then use the entities' embeddings from KG to enhance the corresponding items' representations. For instance, Zhang et al. [28] learn item representations by combining their embeddings in the user-item graph and the KG. Cao et al. [3] and Wang et al. [25] jointly optimize the recommendation and KG embedding

© Springer Nature Switzerland AG 2020
X. Wang et al. (Eds.): APWeb-WAIM 2020, LNCS 12317, pp. 363–377, 2020.
https://doi.org/10.1007/978-3-030-60259-8_27

tasks in a multi-task learning setting via sharing item representations. However, existing KGs are far from complete and it is not easy to link some items to the existing entities in KG due to the missing entities in KG or the ambiguous issues.

The second category uses meta learning [2] to solve the cold-start issues. The goal of meta learning is to design a meta-learner that can efficiently learn the meta information and can rapidly adapt to new instances. For example, Vartak et al. [21] propose to learn a neural network to solve the user cold-start problem in the Tweet recommendation. Specifically, the neural network takes items from user's history and outputs a score function to apply to new items. Du et al. [4] propose a scenario-specific meta learner framework, which first trains a basic recommender, and then tunes the recommendation system according to different scenarios. Pan et al. [16] propose to learn an embedding generator for new ads by making use of previously learned ads' features (e.g., the attributes of ads, the user profiles and the contextual information) through gradient-based meta-learning.

All these KG-based and meta learning based methods aim to directly learn a powerful recommendation model. Different from these methods, in this paper, we focus on how to learn the representations of the cold-start users and items. We argue that the high-quality representations can not only improve the recommendation task, but also benefit several classification tasks such as user profiling classification, item classification and so on (which is justified in our experiments). Motivated by the recently proposed inductive learning technique [7,23], which learns node representations by performing an aggregator function over each node and its fixed-size neighbours, in this paper, we aim to learn the high-quality representations of the cold-start users and items in an inductive manner. Specifically, we view the items that a target user interacts with as his/her contextual information and view the users that a target item interacts with as its contextual information. We then propose an attention-based context encoder (AE), which adopts either soft-attention or multi-head self-attention to integrate the contextual information to estimate the target user (item) embeddings.

In order to obtain a AE model to effectively predict the cold-start user and item embeddings from just a few interactions, we formulate the cold-start representation learning as a few-shot learning task. In each episode, we suppose a user (item) which has enough interactions with items (users) as the target object to predict. Then AE is asked to predict this target object using only K contextual information, i.e., for each target user, AE is asked to use K interacted items to predict his/her representation, while for each target item, AE is asked to use K interacted users to predict the representation of the target item. This training scheme can simulate the real scenarios where there are cold-start users or cold-start items which only have a few interactions.

We conduct several experiments based on both intrinsic and extrinsic embedding evaluation. The intrinsic experiment is to evaluate the quality of the learned embeddings of the cold-start users and items, while the extrinsic experiments are three downstream tasks that the learned embeddings are used as inputs. Experiments results show that our proposed AE can not only outperform the baselines in the intrinsic evaluation task, but also benefit several extrinsic evaluation tasks such as personalized recommendation, user classification and item classification.

Our contributions can be summarized as: (1) we formulate the cold-start representation learning task as a K-shot learning problem and propose a simulated episode-based training schema to predict the target user or item embeddings. (2) We propose an attention-based context encoder which can encode the contextual information of each user or each item. (3) Experiments on both intrinsic and extrinsic embedding evaluation tasks demonstrate that our proposed method is capable of learning the representations of cold-start users and items, and can benefit the downstream tasks compared with the state-of-the-art baselines.

2 Approach

In this section, we first formalize learning the representations of cold-start users and cold-start items as two separated few-shot learning tasks. We then present our proposed attention-based encoder (AE) in solving both these two tasks.

2.1 Few-Shot Learning Framework

Problem Formulation. Let $U = \{u_1, \cdots, u_{|U|}\}$ be a set of users and $I = \{i_1, \cdots, i_{|I|}\}$ be a set of items. I_u denotes the item set that the user u has selected. U_i denotes the user set in which each user $u \in U_i$ selects the item i. Let M be the whole dataset that consists of all the (u, i) pairs.

Problem 1: Cold-Start User Embedding Inference. Let $D_T^{(u)} = \{(u_k, i_k)_{k=1}^{|T^u|}\}$ be a meta-training set, where $i_k \in I_{u_k}$, $|T^u|$ denotes the number of users in $D_T^{(u)}$. Given $D_T^{(u)}$ and a recommendation algorithm[1] (e.g., Matrix factorization) that yields a pre-trained embedding for each user and item, denoted as $e_u \in \mathbf{R}^d$ and $e_i \in \mathbf{R}^d$. Our goal is to infer embeddings for cold-start users that are not observed in the meta-training set $D_T^{(u)}$ based on a new meta-test set $D_N^{(u)} = \{(u_k', i_k')_{k=1}^{|N^u|}\}$, where $i_k' \in I_{u_k'}$, $|N^u|$ denotes the number of users in the meta-test set $D_N^{(u)}$.

Problem 2: Cold-Start Item Embedding Inference. Let $D_T^{(i)} = \{(i_k, u_k)_{k=1}^{|T^i|}\}$ be a meta-training set, where $u_k \in U_{i_k}$, $|T^i|$ denotes the number of items in $D_T^{(i)}$. Given $D_T^{(i)}$ and a recommendation algorithm that yields a pre-trained embedding for each user and item, denoted as $e_u \in \mathbf{R}^d$ and $e_i \in \mathbf{R}^d$. Our goal is to infer embeddings for cold-start items that are not observed in the meta-training set $D_T^{(i)}$ based on a new meta-test set $D_N^{(i)} = \{(i_k', u_k')_{k=1}^{|N^i|}\}$, where $u_k' \in U_{i_k'}$, $|N^i|$ denotes the number of items in $D_N^{(i)}$.

---

[1] We also select some node embedding methods (e.g., DeepWalk [17], LINE [20]) which accept user-item bipartite graph as input and output a pre-trained embedding for each user and item.

Note that these two tasks are symmetrical and the difference between these two tasks is that the roles of users and items are swapped. For simplicity, we present the cold-start user embedding inference scenario, and the cold-start item embedding inference scenario is similar to the cold-start user embedding inference scenario if we simply change the role of the users and items. In the following parts, we omit the subscript and simply use D_T and D_N to denote the meta-training set and meta-test set in both two tasks.

For the cold-start user embedding inference task, D_N is usually much smaller than D_T, and the cold-start users in D_N only have selected a few items, i.e., there are few (u'_k, i'_k) pairs in D_N. Thus it is difficult to directly learn the user embedding from D_N. Our solution is to learn a neural model f_θ parameterized with θ on D_T. The function f_θ takes the item set I_u of user u as input, and outputs the predictive user embedding $\hat{e}_u$. The predictive user embedding is expected to be close to its target embedding. Note that the user in D_T has enough interactions, thus the pre-trained embedding e_u is convincing and we view it as the target embedding.

In order to mimic the real scenarios that the cold-start users only have interacted with few items, we formalize the training of the neural model as a few-shot learning framework, where the model is asked to predict cold-start user embedding with just a few interacted items. To train the neural function f_θ, inspired by [24], we form episodes of few-shot learning tasks. In the cold-start user inference task, in each episode, for each user u_j, we randomly sample K items from I_{u_j} and construct a positive support set $\mathbf{S}_{u_j^+}^K = \{i_{u_j^+, k}\}_{k=1}^K$, where $i_{u_j^+, k}$ is sampled from I_{u_j} and denotes the k-th sampled item for the target user u_j. We also randomly sample K negative items and construct a negative support set $\mathbf{S}_{u_j^-}^K = \{i_{u_j^-, k}\}_{k=1}^K$, where each item $i_{u_j^-, k}$ is not in I_{u_j}. Based on the sampled items, the model f_θ is expected to predict more similar embedding to the target user embedding when given $\mathbf{S}_{u_j^+}^K$ and more dissimilar embedding when given $\mathbf{S}_{u_j^-}^K$. We use cosine similarity to indicate whether the predicted embedding is similar to the target embedding. To further optimize the neural model f_θ, we minimize the regularized log loss defined as follows [10]:

$$L = -\frac{1}{|T_u|} \sum_{j=1}^{|T_u|} (\log(\sigma(\hat{y}_{u_j^+})) + \log(1 - \sigma(\hat{y}_{u_j^-}))) + \lambda ||\theta||^2, \tag{1}$$

where $\hat{y}_{u_j^+} = \cos(f_\theta(\mathbf{S}_{u_j^+}^K), u_j)$, $\hat{y}_{u_j^-} = \cos(f_\theta(\mathbf{S}_{u_j^-}^K), u_j)$, θ denotes the parameters of the proposed model f_θ, σ is a sigmoid function, the hyper-parameter λ controls the strength of L_2 regularization to prevent overfitting. Once the model f_θ is trained based on D_T, it can be used to predict the embedding of each cold-start user u' in D_N by taking the item set I'_u as input. Similarly, we can also design another neural model g_ϕ to learn the representations of cold-start items. Specifically, g_ϕ can be trained on D_T, and can be used to predict the embedding of each cold-start item i' in D_N by taking the user set U'_i as input.

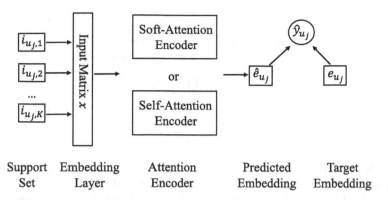

Fig. 1. The proposed attention-based encoder f_θ framework. g_ϕ is similar to f_θ if we simply swap the role of the users and items.

2.2 Attention-Based Representation Encoder

In this section, we detail the architecture of the proposed neural model f_θ (g_ϕ is similar if we simply swap the role of the users and items). For the cold-start user embedding inference task, the key idea is to view the items that a user has selected as his/her contextual information, and we expect f_θ to be able to analyze the semantics of the contextual information, to aggregate these items for predicting the target user embedding. Using AE as f_θ, a more sophisticated model to process and aggregate contextual information can be learned to infer target user embedding.

Embedding Layer. As mentioned before, we first train a recommendation (node embedding) algorithm on the whole dataset M to obtain the pre-trained embeddings e_u and e_i. Note that we view e_i as contextual information, and e_u in D_T as target user embedding. Both e_u and e_i are fixed. Given each target user u_j and the support set $\mathbf{S}_{u_j}^K = \{\mathbf{S}_{u_j^+}^K \cup \mathbf{S}_{u_j^-}^K\}$, we map the support set $\mathbf{S}_{u_j}^K$ to the input matrix $x^{K \times d} = [e_{i_1}, \cdots, e_{i_K}]$ using the pre-trained embeddings, where K is the number of interacted items, d is the dimension of pre-trained embeddings. The input matrix is further fed into the aggregation encoder.

Aggregation Encoder. We present two types of aggregation encoder, namely soft-attention encoder and self-attention encoder.

(1) Soft-attention Encoder. Inspired by [10] that uses soft-attention mechanism to distinguish which historical items in a user profile are more important to a target user, in this paper, we first calculate the attention score between the target user embedding e_{u_j} and each item embedding e_{i_k} that he/she has selected, then we use weighted average items' embeddings to represent the predicted user embedding $\hat{e}_{u_j}$:

$$a_{u_j i_k} = \frac{\exp(r(e_{u_j}, e_{i_k}))}{\sum_{k'=1}^{K} \exp(r(e_{u_j}, e_{i_{k'}}))}, \tag{2}$$

$$r(e_{u_j}, e_{i_k}) = W_1^T \text{RELU}(W_2(e_{u_j} \odot e_{i_k})), \tag{3}$$

$$\hat{e}_{u_j} = \frac{1}{K} \sum_{k=1}^{K} a_{u_j i_k} e_{i_k}, \tag{4}$$

where r is soft-attention neural function that has the element-wise operation $\odot$ between the two vectors e_{u_j} and e_{i_k}, $W_1 \in \mathbf{R}^{d \times 1}$, $W_2 \in \mathbf{R}^{d \times d}$ are two weight matrices, RELU is an activate function, K is the number of interacted items.

(2) Self-attention Encoder. Same as [22], our self-attention encoder consists of several encoding blocks. Each encoding block consists of a self-attention layer and a fully connected layer. Using such encoding blocks can enrich the interactions of the input items to better predict the target user embedding.

Self-attention layer consists of several multi-head attention units. For each head unit h, we view the input matrix x into query, key and value matrices. Then linear projections are performed to map the query, key, value matrices to a common space by three parameters matrices W_h^Q, W_h^K, W_h^V. Next we calculate the matrix product $xW_h^Q(xW_h^K)^T$ and scale it by the square root of the dimension of the input matrix $\frac{1}{\sqrt{d_x}}$ to get mutual attention matrix. We further multiply the attention matrix by the value matrix xW_h^V to get the self attention vector $a_{self,h}$ for head h:

$$a_{self,h} = \text{softmax}(\frac{xW_h^Q(xW_h^K)^T}{\frac{1}{\sqrt{d_x}}})xW_h^V. \tag{5}$$

We concatenate all the self attention vectors $\{a_{self,h}\}_{h=1}^{H}$ and use a linear projection W^O to get the self-attention output vector $SA(x)$, where H is the number of heads. Note that $SA(x)$ can represent fruitful relationships of the input matrix x, which has more powerful representations:

$$SA(x) = \text{Concat}(a_{self,1}, \cdots, a_{self,H})W^O. \tag{6}$$

A fully connected feed-forward network (FFN) is performed to accept $SA(x)$ as input and applies a non-linear transformation to each position of the input matrix x. In order to get higher convergence and better generalization, we apply residual connection [9] and layer normalization [13] in both self-attention layer and fully connected layer. Besides, we do not incorporate any position information as the items in the support set $\mathbf{S}_{u_j}^K$ have no sequential dependency. After averaging the encoded embeddings in the final FFN layer, we can obtain the predicted user embedding $\hat{e}_{u_j}$.

Given the target user embedding e_{u_j} and the predicted user embedding $\hat{e}_{u_j}$, the regularized log loss are performed to train AE (Eq. 1). For the self-attention model, the parameters $\theta = [\{(W_h^Q, W_h^K, W_h^V)\}_{h=1}^H, \{(w_l, b_l)\}_{l=1}^H, W^O]$, where w_l, b_l are the weights matrix and bias in the l-th FFN layer, for the soft-attention model, the parameters $\theta = [W_1, W_2]$. Figure 1 illustrates the proposed model f_θ.

3 Experiment

In this section, we present two types of experiments to evaluate the quality of embeddings resulted by the proposed AE model. One is an intrinsic evaluation which involves two tasks: cold-start user inference task and cold-start item inference task. The other one is an extrinsic evaluation on three downstream tasks: (1) Personalized recommendation, (2) Item classification and (3) User classification.

Table 1. Statistics of the datasets.

Dataset	#Users	#Items	#Interactions	#Sparse Ratio
MovieLens-1M	6,040	3,706	1,000,209	4.47%
Pinterest	55,187	9,916	1,500,809	0.27%

3.1 Settings

We select two public datasets, namely MovieLens-1M[2] [8] and Pinterest[3] [6]. Table 1 illustrates the statistics of the two datasets. For simplicity, we detail the settings of training f_θ (the settings of training g_ϕ is similar if we simply swap the roles of users and items). For each dataset, we first train the baseline on the whole dataset M to get the pre-trained user embedding e_u and item embedding e_i. We then split the dataset into meta-training set D_T and meta-test set D_N according to the number of interactions for each user. In MovieLens-1M, the users in D_T interact with more than 40 items, and this splitting setting results 4689 users in D_T and 1351 users in D_N. In Pinterest, the users in D_T interact with more than 30 items, and this results 13397 users in D_T and 41790 users in D_N[4]. We use D_T to train f_θ, and use D_N to do downstream tasks. The pre-trained e_u in D_T is viewed as target user embedding and e_i is viewed as contextual information.

---

[2] https://grouplens.org/datasets/movielens/.

[3] https://www.pinterest.com/.

[4] When training g_ϕ, in MovieLens-1M, the items in D_T interact with more than 30 users, and this results 2819 items in D_T and 887 items in D_N. In Pinterest, the items in D_T interact with more than 30 users, and this results 8544 items in D_T and 1372 items in D_N.

Table 2. Performance on cold-start user and item embedding evaluation. We use averaged cosine similarity as the evaluation metric.

Methods	MovieLens (user)		Pinterest (user)		MovieLens (item)		Pinterest (item)	
	3-shot	8-shot	3-shot	8-shot	3-shot	8-shot	3-shot	8-shot
LINE	0.623	0.709	0.499	0.599	0.423	0.593	0.516	0.578
AEw-LINE	0.680	0.749	0.502	0.644	0.460	0.602	0.534	0.585
AEo-LINE	**0.926**	**0.962**	**0.926**	**0.928**	**0.726**	**0.802**	**0.726**	**0.804**
AEe-LINE	**0.964**	**0.990**	**0.984**	**0.987**	**0.797**	**0.849**	**0.783**	**0.845**
DW	0.413	0.535	0.504	0.596	0.489	0.528	0.526	0.563
AEw-DW	0.445	0.568	0.518	0.630	0.496	0.521	0.564	0.596
AEo-DW	**0.828**	**0.835**	**0.847**	**0.892**	**0.603**	**0.784**	**0.664**	**0.736**
AEe-DW	**0.866**	**0.887**	**0.950**	**0.988**	**0.767**	**0.834**	**0.739**	**0.820**
MF	0.399	0.503	0.444	0.524	0.579	0.729	0.503	0.569
AEw-MF	0.424	0.512	0.492	0.556	0.592	0.743	0.524	0.589
AEo-MF	**0.836**	**0.945**	**0.646**	**0.813**	**0.713**	**0.809**	**0.698**	**0.823**
AEe-MF	**0.949**	**0.971**	**0.799**	**0.857**	**0.849**	**0.932**	**0.837**	**0.908**
FM	0.542	0.528	0.539	0.564	0.535	0.543	0.474	0.495
AEw-FM	0.568	0.559	0.583	0.584	0.553	0.573	0.495	0.513
AEo-FM	**0.702**	**0.803**	**0.809**	**0.826**	**0.723**	**0.809**	**0.694**	**0.804**
AEe-FM	**0.810**	**0.866**	**0.948**	**0.968**	**0.817**	**0.870**	**0.794**	**0.867**
GS	0.693	0.735	0.584	0.664	0.593	0.678	0.642	0.682
AEw-GS	0.704	0.744	0.624	0.642	0.624	0.686	0.654	0.694
AEo-GS	**0.806**	**0.896**	**0.825**	**0.906**	**0.747**	**0.828**	**0.712**	**0.812**
AEe-GS	**0.951**	**0.972**	**0.912**	**0.984**	**0.869**	**0.942**	**0.816**	**0.903**
GAT	0.723	0.769	0.604	0.684	0.613	0.698	0.684	0.702
AEw-GAT	0.724	0.784	0.664	0.682	0.664	0.726	0.694	0.712
AEo-GAT	**0.846**	**0.935**	**0.886**	**0.916**	**0.757**	**0.868**	**0.725**	**0.821**
AEe-GAT	**0.969**	**0.981**	**0.952**	**0.991**	**0.869**	**0.950**	**0.846**	**0.912**

3.2   Baseline Methods

We select the following baseline models for learning the user and item embeddings, and compare our method with the corresponding baseline methods.

Matrix Factorization (MF) [12]: Learns user and item representations by decomposing the rating matrix.

Factorization Machine (FM) [18]: Learns user and item representations through considering the first-order and high-order interactions between features. For fair comparison, we only use the users and items as features.

LINE [20]: Learns node embeddings through maximizing the first-order proximity and the second-order proximity between a user and an item in the user-item bipartite graph.

DeepWalk (DW) [17]: Learns node embeddings through first performing random walk to sample sequences of nodes from the user-item bipartite graph, and then using Skip-Gram algorithm to learn user and item embeddings.

GraphSAGE (GS) [7]: Learns node embeddings through aggregating node information from a node's local neighbors. We first formalize the user-item interaction ratings as a user-item bipartite graph, and then aggregate at most third-order neighbours of each user (item) to update the user (item) representation. We find using second-order neighbours can lead to the best performance.

GAT [23]: Learns node embeddings through adding attention mechanism upon the GraphSAGE method. We also find using second-order neighbours can lead to the best performance.

AE-Baseline: Is our proposed method which accepts the pre-trained embeddings of items (users), and predicts the final embeddings of the corresponding users (items) by the trained f_θ or g_ϕ. We use the name AE-baseline to denote the pre-trained embeddings are produced by the corresponding baseline method. We compare our model AE with these baselines one by one. To verify the effectiveness of the attention part, we have three variant models: **(1) AEo-baseline** which uses soft-attention as attention encoder. **(2) AEe-baseline** which uses self-attention as attention encoder. **(3) AEw-baseline** which discards the attention part and use multilayer perceptron (MLP) to replace it.

3.3   Intrinsic Evaluation: Evaluate Cold-Start Embeddings

Here we illustrate the settings in the cold-start user inference task. We select both MovieLens-1M and Pinterest datasets to do evaluation. As mentioned before, we train our model f_θ on D_T. However, in order to make effective evaluation of the predicted user embeddings, the target users should be obtained from the users with sufficient interactions. Thus in this task, we drop out D_N and split the meta-training set D_T into training set T_r and test set T_e with ratio 7:3. We first use each baseline method to train the meta-training set D_T to get the target user embedding. Then for each user in T_e, we randomly drop out other items and only maintain K items to predict the user embedding. This simulates the scenario that the users in the test set T_e are cold-start users. We train f_θ on T_r and do the evaluation on T_e. After trained on T_r, f_θ outputs the predicted user embeddings in T_e based on the K interacted items. For each user, we calculate the cosine similarity between the predicted user embedding and the target user embedding, and average them to get the final cosine similarity to denote the quality of the predicted embeddings. For all the baseline methods, we use T_r and the T_e (each user in T_e only has K items) to obtain the predicted user embeddings and calculate the average cosine similarity. In our experiments, K is set as 3 and 8, the number of encoding blocks is 4, the number of heads H is 2, the parameter λ is 1e-6, the batch size is 256, the embedding dimension d is 16 and the learning rate is 0.01.

Experimental Results. Table 2 lists the performance of the proposed model AEo-baseline, AEe-baseline and other baselines under K-shot training settings. The results show that our proposed AEo-baseline and AEe-baseline significantly improve the quality of the learned embeddings comparing with each baseline. Besides, we have four findings: (1) Compared with AEw-baseline, both AEo-baseline and AEe-baseline have better performance, which demonstrates adding attention mechanism is useful. (2) The performance of AEe-baseline is better than AEo-baseline, which implies that using self-attention is better than using soft-attention. The reason is that multi-head self-attention has a more powerful representation ability than soft-attention. (3) When K is relative small (i.e., $K = 3$), the performance of all the baselines gets lower, while the proposed method AEo-baseline and AEe-baseline still have a good performance. (4) Some competitive baselines such as GraphSAGE and GAT can alleviate the cold-start problem by aggregating user's (item's) information from user's (item's) first-order or high-order neighbours, however, their performance is lower than our proposed method. The reason is that for the cold-start users and the cold-start items, there are still few high-order neighbours. Both (3) and (4) demonstrates all the baselines are difficult to deal with the cold-start issues, while our model is capable of generating good representations for cold-start users and items.

3.4 Extrinsic Evaluation: Evaluate Cold-Start Embeddings on Downstream Tasks

To illustrate the effectiveness of our proposed method in dealing with learning the representations of the cold-start users and items, we evaluate the resulted embeddings on three downstream tasks: (1) Personalized recommendation (2) User classification and (3) Item classification. For each task, for the proposed method, we use f_θ and g_ϕ to generate the user and item embeddings in D_N to do evaluation; for the baseline methods, we directly train the baseline on M and use the resulted user and item embeddings to do evaluation.

Personalized Recommendation Task. Personalized recommendation task aims at recommending proper items to users. Recent approaches for recommendation tasks use randomly initialized user and item embeddings as their inputs, which often get suboptimal recommendation performance. We claim that a high-quality pre-trained embeddings can benefit the recommendation task.

We use MovieLens-1M and Pinterest datasets and select Neural Collaborative Filtering (NCF) [11] as the recommender. We first randomly split D_N into training set and test set with ratio 7:3, and then feed the user and item embeddings generated by our model or the baselines into the GMF and MLP unit in NCF as pre-trained embeddings, which are further fine-tuned during training process. During the training process, for each positive pairs (u, i), we randomly sample one negative pairs. During the test process, for each positive instance, we randomly sample 99 negative instance [11]. We use Hit Ratio of top m items (HR@m), Normalized Discounted Cumulative Gain of top m items (NDCG@m) and Mean Reciprocal Rank (MRR) as the evaluation indicator.

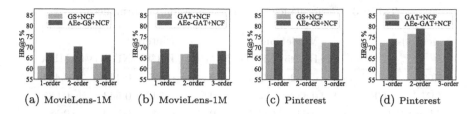

(a) MovieLens-1M   (b) MovieLens-1M   (c) Pinterest   (d) Pinterest

Fig. 2. Recommendation performance of GraphSAGE, GAT and our proposed method when using first-order and high-order neighbours.

The hyperparameters we used are the same as [11]. Table 3 illustrates the recommendation performance. Note that the method NCF represents using the randomly initialized embeddings. The results show that: (1) Using pre-trained embeddings can improve the recommendation performance. (2) Our model beats all the baselines. (3) Compared with AEw-baseline+NCF method which uses MLP layer to replace the attention encoder, using soft-attention and self-attention can improve the performance. (4) Due to the strong representation ability of multi-layer self-attention mechanism, the performance of using self-attention encoder is better than using soft-attention encoder. All the above analysis shows that our proposed method has the ability of learning high-quality representations of cold-start users and items. We further show the recommendation performance of GraphSAGE (GS), GAT and our proposed method AEe-GS, AEe-GAT when using first-order, second-order and third-order neighbours of target users and target items. Figure 2 illustrates the recommendation performance. The results show that all the methods have better performance when using second-order neighbours. Besides, our proposed method significantly beats GS and GAT due to the strong representation ability.

Item Classification Task. We evaluate the encoded item embeddings in AE through a multi-label classification task. The goal is to predict multi-labels of items given the user-item interactive ratings. Intuitively, similar items have a higher probability belonging to the same genre, thus this task needs high-quality item embeddings as input features. We select MovieLens-1M dataset, in which the movies are divided into 18 categories (e.g., Comedy, Action, War). Note that each movie belongs to multi genres, for example, the movie 'Toy Story (1995)' belongs to there genres, namely animation, children's, and comedy. We use logistic regression classifier which accepts the item embeddings as input features to do evaluation. Specifically, we first randomly split D_N into training set and test set with ratio 7:3, and then use item embeddings generated by our model or the baselines as input features. Next we train the logistic regression classifier in the training set and finally evaluate the performance in the test set. Micro-averaged F1-score is used as an evaluation metric. Table 4 illustrates the item classification performance. The result shows that our proposed model beats all the baselines, which verifies our model can produce high-quality item representations. Besides, the performance of AEw-baseline is lower than AEo-baseline and AEe-baseline;

Table 3. Performance on recommendation performances.

Methods	MovieLens			Pinterest		
	HR@5	NDCG@5	MRR	HR@5	NDCG@5	MRR
NCF	0.392	0.263	0.260	0.627	0.441	0.414
LINE + NCF	0.633	0.631	0.648	0.642	0.543	0.587
AEw-LINE + NCF	0.641	0.637	0.652	0.644	0.549	0.582
AEo-LINE + NCF	**0.659**	**0.640**	**0.664**	**0.651**	**0.568**	**0.590**
AEe-LINE + NCF	**0.666**	**0.646**	**0.679**	**0.659**	**0.585**	**0.593**
DW+NCF	0.621	0.620	0.634	0.587	0.392	0.367
AEw-DW + NCF	0.628	0.624	0.643	0.593	0.403	0.369
AEo-DW + NCF	**0.646**	**0.640**	**0.663**	**0.624**	**0.483**	**0.402**
AEe-DW+NCF	**0.673**	**0.643**	**0.684**	**0.652**	**0.462**	**0.433**
MF + NCF	0.558	0.577	0.579	0.711	0.660	0.666
AEw-MF + NCF	0.562	0.564	0.581	0.718	0.672	0.678
AEo-MF + NCF	**0.573**	**0.583**	**0.589**	**0.726**	**0.702**	**0.693**
AEe-MF + NCF	**0.597**	**0.591**	**0.595**	**0.748**	**0.725**	**0.736**
FM + NCF	0.448	0.286	0.265	0.641	0.453	0.424
AEw-FM + NCF	0.451	0.291	0.271	0.652	0.482	0.482
AEo-FM + NCF	**0.482**	**0.334**	**0.326**	**0.723**	**0.702**	**0.672**
AEe-FM + NCF	**0.495**	**0.357**	**0.346**	**0.756**	**0.721**	**0.729**
GS + NCF	0.657	0.664	0.657	0.743	0.642	0.681
AEw-GS + NCF	0.668	0.672	0.675	0.753	0.652	0.693
AEo-GS + NCF	**0.683**	**0.693**	**0.684**	**0.778**	**0.683**	**0.723**
AEe-GS + NCF	**0.703**	**0.724**	**0.704**	**0.782**	**0.693**	**0.735**
GAT + NCF	0.667	0.672	0.664	0.765	0.664	0.702
AEw-GAT + NCF	0.684	0.681	0.682	0.771	0.674	0.719
AEo-GAT + NCF	**0.694**	**0.702**	**0.704**	**0.782**	**0.693**	**0.723**
AEe-GAT + NCF	**0.713**	**0.724**	**0.735**	**0.793**	**0.713**	**0.746**

AEe-baseline has the best performance, which verifies adding attention encoder can improve the performance; due to the strong representation ability, using self-attention is a better choice than using soft-attention.

User Classification Task. We further evaluate the encoded user embeddings in AE through a classification task. The goal is to predict the age bracket of users given the user-item interactions. Intuitively, similar users have same tastes, thus they have a higher probability belonging to the same age bracket. We select MovieLens-1M dataset, and the users are divided into 7 age brackets, (i.e., Under 18, 18–24, 25–34, 35–44, 44–49, 50–55, 56+). We use logistic regression classifier which accepts user embeddings as input features to do evaluation. Specifically, we first randomly split D_N into training set and test set with ratio 7:3, and

Table 4. Performance on item classification and user classification task.

Methods	Movielens-1M	
	Items classification (micro-averaged F1 score)	Users classification (averaged F1 score)
LINE	0.6052	0.3031
AEw-LINE + NCF	0.6111	0.3067
AEo-LINE + NCF	**0.6478**	**0.3294**
AEe-LINE	**0.6620**	**0.3309**
DW	0.5335	0.2605
AEw-DW+ NCF	0.5435	0.2685
AEo-DW + NCF	**0.5687**	**0.2799**
AEe-DW	**0.5707**	**0.2894**
MF	0.4791	0.2273
AEw-MF + NCF	0.4852	0.2291
AEo-MF + NCF	**0.5364**	**0.2368**
AEe-MF	**0.5496**	**0.2477**
FM	0.4809	0.2803
AEw-FM + NCF	0.4883	0.2894
AEo-FM + NCF	**0.4912**	**0.3194**
AEe-FM	**0.5062**	**0.3286**
GS	0.5931	0.2941
AEw-GS + NCF	0.6012	0.3011
AEo-GS + NCF	**0.6342**	**0.3134**
AEe-GS	**0.6546**	**0.3295**
GAT	0.6135	0.3147
AEw-GAT + NCF	0.6243	0.3256
AEo-GAT + NCF	**0.6464**	**0.3456**
AEe-GAT	**0.6646**	**0.3673**

then use user embeddings generated by our model or the baselines as input features. Next we train the logistic regression classifier in the training set and finally evaluate the performance in the test set. Averaged F1-score is used as an evaluation metric. Table 4 shows the user classification performance. The result shows that our method beats all baselines, which further demonstrates our model is capable of learning the high-quality representations.

4   Related Work

Our work is highly related to the meta learning method, which aims to design a meta-learner that can efficiently learn the meta information and can rapidly adapt to new instances. It has been successfully applied in Computer Vision (CV) area and can be classified into two groups. One is the metric-based method which learns a similarity metric between new instances and instances in the training set. Examples include Matching Network [24] and Prototypical Network [19]. The other one is model-based method which designs a meta learning model to directly predict or update the parameters of the classifier according to the training data. Examples include MAML [5] and Meta Network [15]. Recently, some works attempt to use meta learning to solve the cold-start issue in the recommendation systems. Pan et al. [16] propose to learn a embedding generator for new ads by making use of previously learned ads' features through gradient-based meta-learning. Vartak et al. [21] propose to learn a neural network which takes items from user's history and outputs a score function to apply to new items. Du et al. [4] propose a scenario-specific meta learner, which adjust the parameters of the recommendation system when a new scenario comes. Different from these methods that aim to directly learn a powerful recommendation model, we focus on how to learn the representations of the cold-start users and items, and we design a novel attention-based encoder that encode the contextual information to predict the target embeddings.

5   Conclusion

We present the first attempt to solve the problem of learning accurate representations of cold-start users and cold-start items. We formulate the problem as a few-shot learning task and propose a novel attention-based encoder AE which learns to predict the target users (items) embeddings by aggregating only K instances corresponding to the users (items). Different from recent state-of-the-art meta learning methods which aim to directly learn a powerful recommendation model, we focus on how to learn the representations of cold-start users and items. Experiments on both intrinsic evaluation task and three extrinsic evaluation tasks demonstrate the effectiveness of our proposed model.

Acknowledgments. This work is supported by National Key R&D Program of China (No. 2018YFB1004401) and NSFC (No. 61532021, 61772537, 61772536, 61702522).

References

1. Bordes, A., Usunier, N., Garcia-Duran, A., Weston, J., Yakhnenko, O.: Translating embeddings for modeling multi-relational data. In: NeurIPS 2013 (2013)
2. Brazdil, P., Giraud-Carrier, C.G., Soares, C., Vilalta, R.: Metalearning - Applications to Data Mining. Cognitive Technologies. Springer, Heidelberg (2009). https://doi.org/10.1007/978-3-540-73263-1
3. Cao, Y., Wang, X., He, X., Hu, Z., Chua, T.S.: Unifying knowledge graph learning and recommendation: towards a better understanding of user preferences. In: WWW 2019. ACM (2019)
4. Du, Z., Wang, X., Yang, H., Zhou, J., Tang, J.: Sequential scenario-specific meta learner for online recommendation. In: SIGKDD 2019 (2019)

5. Finn, C., Abbeel, P., Levine, S.: Model-agnostic meta-learning for fast adaptation of deep networks. In: ICML 2017, pp. 1126–1135. JMLR.org (2017)
6. Geng, X., Zhang, H., Bian, J., Chua, T.S.: Learning image and user features for recommendation in social networks. In: ICCV 2015, pp. 4274–4282 (2015)
7. Hamilton, W., Ying, Z., Leskovec, J.: Inductive representation learning on large graphs. In: NeurlPS 2017, pp. 1024–1034 (2017)
8. Harper, F.M., Konstan, J.A.: The movielens datasets: history and context. TIIS **5**(4), 1–9 (2016)
9. He, K., Zhang, X., Ren, S., Sun, J.: Deep residual learning for image recognition. In: CVPR 2016, pp. 770–778 (2016)
10. He, X., He, Z., Song, J., Liu, Z., Jiang, Y.G., Chua, T.S.: NAIS: neural attentive item similarity model for recommendation. IEEE Trans. Knowl. Data Eng. **30**(12), 2354–2366 (2018)
11. He, X., Liao, L., Zhang, H., Nie, L., Hu, X., Chua, T.S.: Neural collaborative filtering. In: WWW 2017, pp. 173–182 (2017)
12. Koren, Y., Bell, R., Volinsky, C.: Matrix factorization techniques for recommender systems. Computer **42**(8), 30–37 (2009)
13. Lei Ba, J., Kiros, J.R., Hinton, G.E.: Layer normalization. arXiv preprint arXiv:1607.06450 (2016)
14. Linden, G., Smith, B., York, J.: Amazon.com recommendations: item-to-item collaborative filtering. IEEE Internet Comput. **7**(1), 76–80 (2003)
15. Munkhdalai, T., Yu, H.: Meta networks. In: ICML 2017, pp. 2554–2563. JMLR.org (2017)
16. Pan, F., Li, S., Ao, X., Tang, P., He, Q.: Warm up cold-start advertisements: improving CTR predictions via learning to learn id embeddings. In: SIGIR 2019 (2019)
17. Perozzi, B., Al-Rfou, R., Skiena, S.: DeepWalk: online learning of social representations. In: SIGKDD 2014, pp. 701–710. ACM (2014)
18. Rendle, S.: Factorization machines with libFM. TIST **3**(3), 57 (2012)
19. Snell, J., Swersky, K., Zemel, R.: Prototypical networks for few-shot learning. In: NeurlPS 2017, pp. 4077–4087 (2017)
20. Tang, J., Qu, M., Wang, M., Zhang, M., Yan, J., Mei, Q.: Line: large-scale information network embedding. In: WWW 2015, pp. 1067–1077 (2015)
21. Vartak, M., Thiagarajan, A., Miranda, C., Bratman, J., Larochelle, H.: A meta-learning perspective on cold-start recommendations for items. In: NeurlPS 2017, pp. 6904–6914 (2017)
22. Vaswani, A., et al.: Attention is all you need. In: NeurlPS 2017, pp. 5998–6008 (2017)
23. Velickovic, P., Cucurull, G., Casanova, A., Romero, A., Liò, P., Bengio, Y.: Graph attention networks. In: ICLR 2018 (2018)
24. Vinyals, O., Blundell, C., Lillicrap, T., Wierstra, D., et al.: Matching networks for one shot learning. In: NeurlPS 2016, pp. 3630–3638 (2016)
25. Wang, H., Zhang, F., Zhao, M., Li, W., Xie, X., Guo, M.: Multi-task feature learning for knowledge graph enhanced recommendation. In: WWW 2019 (2019)
26. Wang, X., He, X., Cao, Y., Liu, M., Chua, T.: KGAT: knowledge graph attention network for recommendation. In: SIGKDD 2019, pp. 950–958 (2019)
27. Wang, Z., Zhang, J., Feng, J., Chen, Z.: Knowledge graph embedding by translating on hyperplanes. In: AAAI 2014 (2014)
28. Zhang, F., Yuan, N.J., Lian, D., Xie, X., Ma, W.Y.: Collaborative knowledge base embedding for recommender systems. In: SIGKDD 2016. ACM (2016)

Long Short-Term Memory with Sequence Completion for Cross-Domain Sequential Recommendation

Guang Yang[1](✉) ⓘ, Xiaoguang Hong[1](✉), Zhaohui Peng[1](✉), and Yang Xu[2](✉)

[1] School of Computer Science and Technology, Shandong University, Jinan, China
loggyt@yeah.net, {hxg,pzh}@sdu.edu.cn
[2] Shandong Normal University, Jinan, China
zzmylq@gmail.com

Abstract. As the emerging topic to solve the loss of time dimension information, sequential recommender systems (SRSs) has attracted increasing attention in recent years. Although SRSs can model the sequential user behaviors, the interactions between users and items, and the evolution of users' preferences and item popularity over time, the challenging issues of data sparsity and cold start are beyond our control. The conventional solutions based on cross-domain recommendation aims to matrix completion by means of transferring explicit or implicit feedback from the auxiliary domain to the target domain. But most existing transfer methods can't deal with temporal information. In this paper, we propose a Long Short-Term Memory with Sequence Completion (SCLSTM) model for cross-domain sequential recommendation. We first construct the sequence and supplement it in which two methods are proposed. The first method is to use the intrinsic features of users and items and the temporal features of user behaviors to establish similarity measure for sequence completion. Another method is to improve LSTM by building the connection between the output layer and the input layer of the next time step. Then we use LSTM to complete sequential recommendation. Experimental results on two real datasets extracted from Amazon transaction data demonstrate the superiority of our proposed models against other state-of-the-art methods.

Keywords: Cross-domain sequential recommendation · Long short-term memory · Sequence completion

1 Introduction

With the explosively growing amount of online information, recommender system (RS) is playing an indispensable role in our daily lives as well as in the Internet industry for the problem of information overload. The traditional RSs [1], including the content-based, collaborative filtering and hybrid collaborative filtering RSs, model the user-item interactions in a static way and lost the time dimension.

In the real world, users' shopping behaviors usually happen successively in a sequence, rather than in an isolated manner. Taking the real events of someone U_1

© Springer Nature Switzerland AG 2020
X. Wang et al. (Eds.): APWeb-WAIM 2020, LNCS 12317, pp. 378–393, 2020.
https://doi.org/10.1007/978-3-030-60259-8_28

depicted in Fig. 1 as an example, U_1 bought a bag of infant formula milk, a baby stroller and diapers successively. So we can all guess about the likelihood of buying baby bottles. Likewise, the sequential dependencies can be seen in next case. Before U_2 started a vacation, he booked a flight, several tickets for some tourist attractions and rented a car successively, and his next action may be booking a local hotel. In such a case, based on the location of each attraction and car rental company, we can guess the location of the hotel. In the above scenario, each of U_2's next actions depends on the prior ones and therefore all the four consumer behaviors are sequentially dependent. Such kind of sequential dependencies commonly exist in actual data but cannot be well captured by the conventional collaborative filtering RSs or content-based RSs [2], which essentially motivates the development of sequential RSs.

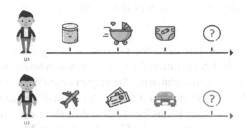

Fig. 1. Two examples of sequential RSs

Furthermore, user interest is dynamic rather than static over time [30]. How to capture user interest accurately to enhance the accuracy of recommendation results is an enormous practical challenge in RSs. For example, many people want to watch horror movies when Halloween comes and love movies are always popular on Valentine's Day. Such dynamics are of great significance for precisely profiling a user or an item for more accurate recommendations. The traditional RSs can't capture the dynamic change of interest or behavior well when sequential recommender systems (SRSs) are competent for the task.

In conclusion, sequential recommender systems meet our requirements for these objective situations, so they can greatly improve recommendation performance [3].

Unfortunately, recommender systems are generally faced with data sparsity and cold start problems in that users interact with only an extremely tiny part of the commodities on a website or a directory and sequential recommender systems are no exception. As a promising solution to address these issues, cross-domain recommender systems [4, 5] have gained increasing attention in recent years. This kind of algorithm tries to utilize explicit or implicit feedbacks from multiple auxiliary domains to improve the recommendation performance in the target domain. As shown in Fig. 2, commodities are divided into different domains according to their attributes or categories. Users who have active data in both domains are called linked users and we mark them with dashed red box. Users who only have active data in the target domain are called cold start users. Our goal is to make recommendations for cold start users by linked users. Linked users serve as a bridge for our model to transfer knowledge across domains. Existing studies [4, 5, 6, and 7] can't process sequence data. The sequence is split into separate data to fill in the user/item matrix and all temporal information is discarded. Therefore, how to deal with sequence data for cross-domain recommender systems remain an open problem.

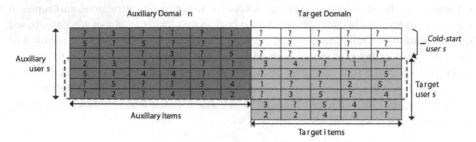

Fig. 2. Illustration of the cross-domain recommendation for cold-start users

To address the above challenges, we propose a Long Short-Term Memory with Sequence Completion (SCLSTM) model for cross-domain sequential recommendation in this paper. Specifically, we first construct the sequence and supplement it in which two methods are proposed. The first method is to use the intrinsic features of users and items and the temporal features of user behaviors to establish similarity measure for sequence completion. Another method is to improve Long Short-Term Memory network (LSTM) by building the connection between the output layer and the input layer of the next time step. Complete the sequence by adding this input logic unit. Then we use LSTM to complete sequential recommendation. Our major contributions are summarized as follows:

- We define the concept of sequence completion and propose two methods of sequence completion. One uses similarity measure, the other uses improved LSTM.

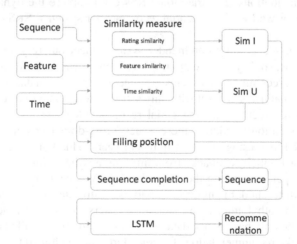

Fig. 3. SCLSTM with similarity measure recommendation framework

- We propose a Long Short-Term Memory with Sequence Completion (SCLSTM) model for cross-domain sequential recommendation, which can solve data sparsity and cold start problems of sequential recommender systems.
- We systematically evaluate our proposal through comparing it with the state-of-the-art algorithms on the dataset of Amazon[1]. The results confirm that our new method substantially improves the recommendation performance.

2 Sequence Completion

In real life, there are many sequences, such as a piece of text, a pulse signal and a melody. When we read a damaged book, it is difficult for us to understand it accurately. We must fill these sequences with external knowledge to solve these problems. For example, look at a fragmentary passage, "The Spider-Man series broke ground by featuring, a from behind Spider-Man's secret identity." Almost all superhero fans understand what it means. "The Spider-Man series broke ground by featuring Peter Parker, a high school student from Queens behind Spider-Man's secret identity." Why has this happened? These superhero fans use their animation knowledge to picture the sentence. We formally define the sequence completion as follows.

Definition 1. (Sequence Completion) For a sequence S_m of missing elements, the missing elements are recovered by analyzing the effective elements and context knowledge. Make the sequence S_m close to the complete sequence S. ($\min\{|S - S_m|\}$).

Take a word recognition as an example, given a word "spi_er" with a missing letter, we guess that the word is "spinner", "spider" or others according to dictionary information. Then, according to the context information, the word "spider" is determined. But when the word with a missing letter becomes "s_er", it's very difficult to determine what it really means. Common algorithms, especially RNN (Recurrent Neural Network)-based algorithms, can use sequence data to classify and are actually sequence completion algorithms. But these algorithms face two difficult problems. First of all, the sparser the data, the worse the algorithm performance. Especially the cold start problem is a fatal blow to these supervised algorithms. Secondly, the sequence of recommender system is quite different from the common sequence. Limited by the sampling method and platform, we cannot capture all the sequence data. Take book purchase record of Amazon as an example, the channels for users to obtain books include hypostatic stores, websites and libraries, even could borrow them from friends. But we can only collect part of the data through Amazon, so we can't get the real complete sequence on reading records.

For these reasons and more, we propose two novel algorithms of sequence completion.

3 SCLSTM with Similarity Measure

We propose a recommendation framework called SCLSTM based on similarity measure model and the framework is as shown in Fig. 3. First, we extract three kinds of data from

---

[1] https://www.amazon.com.

the logs, which they are users-items interaction sequences, users/items feature graph and users action time list. Then, we use these three groups of data to build three similarity measure models for users and items. The rating similarity, feature similarity and time similarity are calculated respectively, and combining three models to get user similarity SimU and item similarity SimI. Next, the user similarity is used to determine the location and length of sequence completion and item similarity is used to determine the content of sequence completion. Based on the previous step, we complete sequence completion and get relatively complete sequence data. Finally, we use the sequence we just obtained as input and use the LSTM model to recommend.

3.1 User and Item Similarity Measures

Rating Similarity Measure
We decide to use the classic cosine similarity algorithm to calculate rating similarity. We can compute the first similarity measure between user a and b as follows:

$$PR_{ab} = \frac{\sum_{e \in I(a,b)} (r_{ae} - \overline{r_a})(r_{be} - \overline{r_b})}{\sqrt{\sum_{e \in I(a,b)} (r_{ae} - \overline{r_a})^2} \sqrt{\sum_{e \in I(a,b)} (r_{be} - \overline{r_b})^2}} \tag{1}$$

$$Sim_{ab}^R = e^{-\omega PR_{ab}} (\omega > 0) \tag{2}$$

Where ω is a predefined parameter. Given two users a and b, r_{ae} represents the user's rating of the item e and $\overline{r_a}$ represents the average score of user a. If they have commonly rated items, $I(a, b)$ represents the set of common items. $|I(a, b)|$ represents the size of the set. Here, we adopt an exponential function to transform users' rating difference into a similarity value. The greater the value of *Sim*, the greater the similarity.

For items, our formula has the same principle and form. Given two items c and d, we can compute the similarity measure between item c and d as follows:

$$PR_{cd} = \frac{\sum_{e \in I(c,d)} (r_{ec} - \overline{r_c})(r_{ed} - \overline{r_d})}{\sqrt{\sum_{e \in I(c,d)} (r_{ec} - \overline{r_c})^2} \sqrt{\sum_{e \in I(c,d)} (r_{ed} - \overline{r_d})^2}} \tag{3}$$

$$Sim_{cd}^R = e^{-\omega PR_{cd}} (\omega > 0) \tag{4}$$

Feature Similarity Measure
In e-commerce websites, users and merchandise have many characteristics besides the shopping records. For example, mobile phones have many features such as brand, price, color and screen size, etc. These features are just as important as the rating matrix but often ignored by similarity measure. We decided to use similarity search on graph to deal with these similarity measure [26]. First of all, we use user features and commodity features to create two graphs. Users, items and their features are the nodes on the graph. An edge indicates that the user/item owns the feature. If two nodes have similar neighbors

in the network, we think they are similar. We can compute the second similarity measure between node a and b as follows:

$$Sim_{ab}^F = \frac{\sum_{i=1}^{|I(a)|} \sum_{j=1}^{|I(b)|} Sim^F\left(I_i(a), I_j(b)\right)}{|I(a)||I(b)|} \tag{5}$$

$$Sim_{ab}^F = 0, \; if I(a) = \emptyset \; or \; I(b) = \emptyset \tag{6}$$

$$Sim_{aa}^F = 1 \tag{7}$$

$$Sim_{ab}^F = Sim_{ba}^F, \text{symmetric} \tag{8}$$

Where $I(a)$ represents the entry neighborhood of node a, $|I(a)|$ represents the size of the neighborhood. This recursive algorithm is the same on two graphs, so we can express it uniformly.

Time Similarity Measure

With the advent of the era of mass information that consists of great time span data, the importance of temporal information is highlighted. Intuitively, the older the data is, the less time weight will be in similarity calculation, so the conventional research always use the forgetting curve to model the time factor. However, the time difference between different events or behaviors also contains important information. Sequence can represent relative time difference, but absolute time difference is often ignored. In the case of movies, we can measure the similarity of two movies by the number of people watching them together. But there are two difficult problems in the actual calculation. First of all, for many similar films, we can no longer distinguish the similarity differences in detail by traditional algorithms. Secondly, most of the time, what we are looking for is the next movie that we will see immediately after this movie, rather than the movie that will be seen eventually. So we created a model using time difference to compute similarity. The basic idea is that the closer the two movies are viewed, the more relevant they are. Take another example of a computer journal, the time interval between the author's papers published on TOC and TPDS is very short. Therefore, we can think that TOC and TPDS themes are very similar, and the level is very close. In order to solve the above problems, we created a time similarity measure model as follows:

$$\Delta T_{c,d|u_i} = \frac{\sum_{j=1}^{k_{cd}} g\left(t_{c|u_i} - t_{d|u_i}\right)}{k_{cd} t_m} \tag{9}$$

$$\Delta T_{c,d} = \frac{|I(c)||I(d)|}{|I(c,d)|} \cdot \frac{\sum_{i=1}^{|I(c,d)|} \Delta T_{c,d|u_i}}{|I(c,d)|} \tag{10}$$

$$Sim_{cd}^T = e^{-\mu \Delta T_{c,d}} \; (\mu > 0) \tag{11}$$

Where μ is a predefined parameter. Take shopping behavior as an example, $\Delta T_{c,d|u_i}$ represents the average time interval between the purchase of items c and d by user u_i. $t_{c|u_i}$ represents the time when user u_i purchases commodity c at one time. t_m represents the average time interval of user u_i's shopping behavior. Because users may buy the same product multiple times, k_{cd} represents the number of times user u_i purchases commodity c. $g\left(t_{c|u_i} - t_{d|u_i}\right)$ indicates that for each $t_{c|u_i}$, we select the closest $t_{d|u_i}$ to calculate the time difference. When there are two closest times, select the one that can get a positive value. $I(c, d)$ represents a set of users who jointly purchase two items.$|I(c, d)|$ represents the size of the set. $I(c)$ represents a set of users who purchased item c. $\Delta T_{c,d}$ represents the average time interval between the purchase of items c and d by all common users. The first half of the formula ensures that hot users/items do not affect the accuracy of the formula in Eq. 10. Here, we adopt an exponential function to transform users' rating difference into a similarity value.

In the later experiments, we verified the superiority of our innovative similarity algorithm. Finally, we combine the three categories of similarity:

$$Sim = \alpha\, Sim^R + \beta Sim^F + \gamma Sim^T \tag{12}$$

Where α, β and γ are the weights to control the importance of the three parts and Sim is the similarity we finally get.

3.2 Sequence Completion with Similarity Measure

First of all, given a cold start user a, we design a formula to calculate the heterogeneous similarity between user a and item c, so as to get the most similar top-N items with user a, and restrict these items from the target domain.

$$Sim_{ac} = \frac{\sum_{i \in I_c} Sim_{ai}}{|I(c)|} \tag{13}$$

Then, we change the Sim^T model slightly, and change the absolute time to the relative time, we can get a similarity model Sim^{RT} and ΔT^{RT} about the relative time.

Given a rating sequence of user a, j is an element in the sequence and i is an element in the set of top-N. The filling fraction formula is as follows:

$$f_{ij} = \frac{1}{n_i} Sim_{ai} Sim_{ji}^{RT} \tag{14}$$

Find the largest f_{ij}, fill its corresponding element i into the sequence, and fill in the front or back of position j. The front and back are determined by the positive and negative of ΔT^{RT}. n_i indicates the number of times the element i has been filled in the sequence.

Finally, the sequence is updated and the filling fraction is calculated repeatedly. The algorithm is repeated l times and $l < N$. The rating scores are calculated together as follows:

$$r_{ai} = \overline{r_a} + \tau \sum_{k=1}^{m} Sim_{ak}^R (r_{ki} - \overline{r_k}) \tag{15}$$

Where τ is a predefined parameter, and $\tau > 0$. Finally, the filling sequence S' is obtained. The pseudocode of the proposed sequence completion algorithm is shown in Algorithm 1.

Algorithm 1 sequence completion

Input : $S_{av} = (s_{av_t})$: user a rating sequence for items.

        $I(a)$: the set of most similar top-N items with user a.

        l: the sequence length that we set, $l < N$.

Output: S'_{av}: the filling sequence we obtained.

  1:    **while** $k \leq l$ **do**

  2:      **for** each item j in S_{av} **do**

  3:        **for** each item i in $I(a)$ **do**

  4:          $f_{ij} = \frac{1}{n_i} Sim_{ai} Sim_{ji}^{RT}$;

  5:        $f_{cd} = max(f_{ij})$;

  6:        **if** $\Delta T_{cd}^{RT} > 0$ **then**

  7:         Fill element c into the sequence, immediately after d;

  8:        **else** Fill element c into the sequence, ahead of d;

  9:        $k++$;

 10:   **return** S'_{av};

3.3 Sequential Recommendation

Through Long Short-Term Memory network (LSTM) [28], we finally get the recommended results for cold start users. We choose Cross Entropy Loss to find the error.

4 SCLSTM with Improved LSTM

Another model is to improve LSTM by building the connection between the output layer and the input layer of the next time step. Complete the sequence by adding this input logic unit. We can see the architecture of the model in Fig. 4.

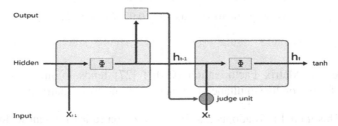

Fig. 4. Improved LSTM framework

By adding a judgment unit, we decide whether to take the output of this step as the input of the next step, so as to move the whole sequence backward. The algorithm uses the filling fraction formula in the previous chapter. The formula of judgment unit is as follows:

$$Ip_t = \begin{cases} Op_{t-1}, & \text{if } W_i f_{Op_{t-1} x_{t-1}} + b_i \geq W_j f_{x_t x_{t-1}}, \text{ then } t++; \\ x_t, & \text{if } W_i f_{Op_{t-1} x_{t-1}} + b_i < W_j f_{x_t x_{t-1}} \end{cases} \tag{16}$$

Where Ip_t represents the input of time step t, Op_{t-1} represents the output of time step $t-1$ and x_t represents the sequence element of time step t. f_{ij} is the filling fraction formula in

Eq. 14. $t++$ means to insert Op_{t-1} into the sequence, then the remaining elements move backward in turn. W_i and W_j is the weight parameter and b_i is the deviation parameter. They were trained together with other parameters of LSTM. In the process of propagation of neural networks, when $Ip_t = Op_{t-1}$, the propagation actually stops. Therefore, the number of iterations must be greater than the length of the maximum sequence.

5 Experiments

5.1 Experiments Settings

We use the Amazon dataset [29] to evaluate the performance of our model and baselines. There are ratings, simple attribute and reviews in total spanning from May 1996 to July 2014. It has 21 categories of items and we choose the three most widely used categories in cross-domain recommendation to perform the experiment. In order to gain better experiment performance, we filter the content in the dataset. We grab data from IMDb[2] and Google[3] to supplement features of users and items. The statistics of the two datasets are given in Table 1. We compare our model with the following baselines:

Table 1. The statistics of the two datasets

	Dataset 1		Dataset 2	
Domain	Movies	Books	Movies	CDs
Users	3479		4237	
Items	3983	2473	4302	5766
Ratings	19011	13002	43658	30263
Density	0.00193	0.00132	0.00176	0.00122

CMF: Collective Matrix Factorization (CMF) [27] tends to incorporate different sources of information by simultaneously factorizing multiple matrices.

EMCDR: This model [25] adopts matrix factorization to learn latent factors first and then utilize an MLP network to map the user latent factors.

Markov-RS: Markov chain-based sequential recommender systems [10] adopt Markov chain models to model the transitions over user-item interactions in a sequence, for the prediction of the next interaction.

LSTM: Given a sequence of historical user-item interactions, an RNN-based sequential recommender system [28] tries to predict the next possible interaction by modelling the sequential dependencies over the given interactions.

---

[2] https://www.imdb.com/.
[3] https://www.google.com/.

5.2 Evaluation Metric

In both data sets, we choose the domain with sparse data as the target domain. We select some users randomly in the target domain and hide their information as cold start users. In our experiments, we set the proportions of cold start users as 70%, 50% and 30% of the initial users respectively. The proportion is denoted as ϕ. We adopt Root Mean Square Error (RMSE) and Hit Ratio defined as follows as the evaluation metrics.

$$\text{RMSE} = \sqrt{\sum_{r_{ac} \in I_{test}} \frac{\left(r_{ac} - \widehat{r_{ac}}\right)^2}{|I_{test}|}} \tag{17}$$

Where I_{test} is the set of test ratings. r_{ac} denotes an observed rating in I_{test}. $\widehat{r_{ac}}$ represents the predictive value of r_{ac}. $|I_{test}|$ is the number of test ratings.

$$\text{Hit Ratio} = \frac{\sum_u G(T_u \in R(u, t))}{|U|} \tag{18}$$

Where $G(\cdot)$ is an indicator function, $R(u, t)$ is a set of items recommended to user u at a specified time period t, T_u is the test item that user u accessed at a specified time period t and $|U|$ is size of all test sets. If the test item appears in the recommendation set, we call it a hit.

5.3 Experimental Results

The experimental results of RMSE on "Movies & Books" are shown in Table 2, and the results on "Movies & CDs" are presented in Table 3. The best performance of these models is shown in boldface. Because the data in the movie domain is relatively dense, we regard the movie domain as an auxiliary domain in both datasets. Our approaches are SCLSTM with similarity measure (SCLSTM1) and SCLSTM with improved LSTM (SCLSTM2). The parameters α, β and γ were finally determined to be 0.3, 0.1 and 0.6 in Eq. 14.

Table 2. Recommendation performance on "Movies & Books"

	RMSE		
ϕ	70%	50%	30%
CMF	1.4621	1.3305	1.2648
EMCDR	1.3583	1.0048	0.9496
Markov-RS	1.4365	1.4008	1.3701
LSTM	1.2543	1.1568	0.9970
SCLSTM1	**0.9477**	**0.9432**	0.9376
SCLSTM2	0.9951	0.9765	**0.9320**

Table 3. Recommendation performance on "Movies & CDs"

	RMSE		
φ	70%	50%	30%
CMF	1.6255	1.6118	1.6032
EMCDR	1.6753	1.1238	1.1494
Markov-RS	1.4213	1.4077	1.3653
LSTM	1.2775	1.2203	1.0988
SCLSTM1	**1.1380**	1.0776	1.0152
SCLSTM2	1.2203	**1.0377**	**0.9961**

We evaluate the performance of different models under different values of φ by RMSE model. From Tables 2 and 3, one can draw the conclusion that SCLSTM1 and SCLSTM2 are superior to all the state-of-the-art methods in cross-domain recommendation for cold start users. LSTM, SCLSTM1 and SCLSTM2 all perform better than CMF and EMCDR which proves the effectiveness of deep learning methods in cross-domain recommendation, even though the algorithm is not specially designed for cross-domain recommendation. With the increasing sparsity of data, the efficiency of all algorithms has declined. But we can see that the efficiency of SCLSTM1 fall less than those of other algorithms. Its performance is the most stable of all algorithms. When the data is denser, SCLSTM2 performs better than SCLSTM1. When the data becomes sparse, the performance of SCLSTM1 begins to exceed that of SCLSTM2. This is closely related to the advantage of SCLSTM1 as an algorithm based on similarity measure.

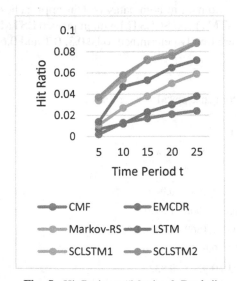

Fig. 5. Hit Ratio on "Movies & Books"

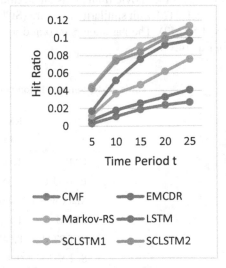

Fig. 6. Hit Ratio on "Movies & CDs"

Distinguished from other recommender systems, the most important feature of sequence recommendation is that its input and output are sequences. With this, we can not only recommend, but also recommend the right products at the right time. RMSE can't express this feature, but Hit Ratio can. Specified time period t represents the continuous t-times shopping behavior. We predict the t-times shopping information, and then compare it with the real t-length sequence. If there is one data coincidence, it means one hit. For the non-sequence recommendation algorithms CMF and EMCDR and the sequence recommendation algorithm Markov-RS which cannot output sequence data, we use Top-t data instead of prediction data. Figure 5 and 6 show that the results of Hit Ratio vary with t while $\phi = 30\%$. As you can see from the graph, the smaller the t, the greater the ratio of our two algorithms over other algorithms. With the increase of ϕ, t is fixed to 5 because of the sparse data in Fig. 7 and 8. Combining these four graphs, we can see that our two algorithms show great superiority in Hit Ratio.

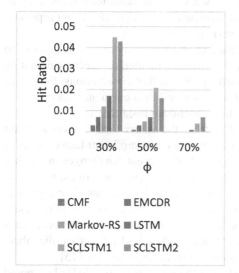 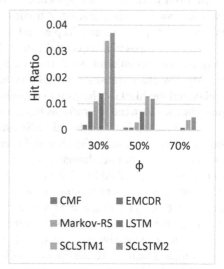

Fig. 7. Hit ratio on "Movies & Books" with t = 5

Fig. 8. Hit ratio on "Movies & CDs" with t = 5

Finally, we use collaborative filtering with different similarity algorithms to predict movie ratings in the Amazon movie dataset and utilize RMSE to evaluate the performance of all similarity algorithms. The similar algorithms we compare are Euclidean Distance (ED), Chebyshev Distance (CD), Cosine Similarity (CS), Personalized PageRank (PPR), SimRank (SR) [26], Jaccard Coefficient (JC) and our Time Similarity Measure (TS). The experimental results are shown in Fig. 9 and our algorithm shows great superiority.

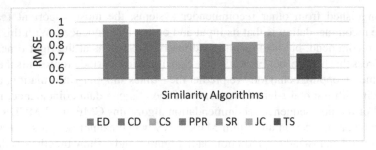

Fig. 9. Similarity algorithm performance

6 Related Work

Sequential Recommender Systems. Existing works about sequential recommender systems (SRSs) mostly consist of traditional sequence models [8–10], latent representation models [11–15], and deep neural network models [16–21].

Yap [8] proposed a sequential pattern-based recommender system which can mine frequent patterns on sequence data. Garcin [9] proposed a method of directly calculating the Markov chain transition probability based on the explicit observations. Feng [10] embedded the Markov chains into a Euclidean space and then calculates the transition probabilities between interactions based on their Euclidean distance.

Factorization machine-based SRSs usually utilize the matrix factorization or tensor factorization to factorize the observed user-item interactions into latent factors of users and items for recommendations [11, 12]. Such methods presents challenges in the face of data sparsity. Embedding-based SRSs learn a latent representations for each user and item for the subsequent recommendations by encoding all the user-item interactions in a sequence into a latent space. Specifically, some works take the learned latent representations as the input of a network to further calculate an interaction score between users and items, or successive users' actions [13, 14], while other works directly utilize them to calculate a metric like the Euclidean distance as the interaction score [15].

Deep neural networks nearly dominate SRSs in the past few years. Wu [16] proposed a method of capturing the long-term dependencies in a sequence with long short-term memory (LSTM) model while Hidasi [17] utilized gated recurrent unit (GRU) model and Quadrana [18] utilized hierarchical RNN. Both models are based on the improvement of recurrent neural network (RNN). A few works [19, 20] developed convolutional neural networks (CNN)-based SRSs. They first put all sequence data into a matrix, and then treat such a matrix as an image in the time and latent spaces. However, due to the limited sizes of matrix dimension CNN-based SRSs cannot effectively capture long-term dependencies. This is an obvious defect for sequence recommendation. Wu [21] transformed sequence data into directed graphs by mapping each sequence to a path and taking each interaction as a node in the graph, and then utilized graph neural network (GNN)-based SRSs to commendation.

Cross-Domain Recommender Systems. Cross-domain recommender systems have gained increasing attention in recent years. Existing studies [4–7] including the knowledge aggregation-based cross-domain recommender systems and the knowledge transfer-based cross-domain recommender systems and the latter methods is the focus of current research. Pan [22] proposed an adaptive models sharing potential features between two domains. Unlike adaptive algorithms, Pan [23] proposed a cooperative algorithms by learning potential features simultaneously between two domains, and optimizing a common objective function. Li [24] proposed a model based on rating patterns transfer.

7   Conclusion and Future Work

In this paper, we propose a Long Short-Term Memory with Sequence Completion model for cross-domain sequential recommendation. We first construct the sequence and supplement it in which two methods are proposed. Then we use LSTM to complete sequential recommendation. Experimental results on two real datasets extracted from Amazon transaction data demonstrate the superiority of our proposed models against other state-of-the-art methods. The current context of a user or commodity may greatly affect the user's choice of goods. When making recommendations, this should be taken into account. Therefore context-aware cross-domain sequential recommendations would be an important direction in our future works.

Acknowledgments. This work was supported by Shandong Provincial Key Research and Development Program (Major Scientific and Technological Innovation Project) (No. 2019JZZY010105), and NSF of Shandong, China (No. ZR2017MF065).

References

1. Dong, X., Yu, L., Wu, Z., Sun, Y., Yuan, L., Zhang, F.: A hybrid collaborative filtering model with deep structure for recommender systems. In: AAAI 2017, pp. 1309–1315 (2017)
2. Kang, W.-C., Wan, M., McAuley, J.J.: Recommendation through mixtures of heterogeneous item relationships. In: CIKM 2018, pp. 1143–1152 (2018)
3. Wang, S., Hu, L., Wang, Y., Cao, L., Sheng, Q.Z., Orgun, M.A.: Sequential recommender systems: challenges, progress and prospects. In: IJCAI 2019, pp. 6332–6338 (2019)
4. Song, T., Peng, Z., Wang, S., Fu, W., Hong, X., Yu, P.S.: Review-based cross-domain recommendation through joint tensor factorization. In: Candan, S., Chen, L., Pedersen, T.B., Chang, L., Hua, W. (eds.) DASFAA 2017. LNCS, vol. 10177, pp. 525–540. Springer, Cham (2017). https://doi.org/10.1007/978-3-319-55753-3_33
5. Wang, X., Peng, Z., Wang, S., Yu, Philip S., Fu, W., Hong, X.: Cross-domain recommendation for cold-start users via neighborhood based feature mapping. In: Pei, J., Manolopoulos, Y., Sadiq, S., Li, J. (eds.) DASFAA 2018. LNCS, vol. 10827, pp. 158–165. Springer, Cham (2018). https://doi.org/10.1007/978-3-319-91452-7_11
6. Cantador, I., Fernández-Tobías, I., Berkovsky, S., Cremonesi, P.: Cross-domain recommender systems. In: Ricci, F., Rokach, L., Shapira, B. (eds.) Recommender Systems Handbook, pp. 919–959. Springer, Boston, MA (2015). https://doi.org/10.1007/978-1-4899-7637-6_27

7. Ignacio, F.-T., Cantador, I., Kaminskas, M., Ricci, F.: Cross-domain recommender systems: a survey of the state of the art. In: Spanish Conference on Information Retrieval, vol. 24 (2012)
8. Yap, G.-E., Li, X.-L., Yu, P.S.: Effective next-items recommendation via personalized sequential pattern mining. In: Lee, S.-G., Peng, Z., Zhou, X., Moon, Y.-S., Unland, R., Yoo, J. (eds.) DASFAA 2012. LNCS, vol. 7239, pp. 48–64. Springer, Heidelberg (2012). https://doi.org/10.1007/978-3-642-29035-0_4
9. Garcin, F., Dimitrakakis, C., Faltings, B.: Personalized news recommendation with context trees. In: RecSys 2013, pp. 105–112 (2013)
10. Feng, S., Li, X., Zeng, Y., Cong, G., Chee, Y.M., Yuan, Q.: Personalized ranking metric embedding for next new POI recommendation. In: IJCAI 2015, pp. 2069–2075 (2015)
11. Rendle, S., Freudenthaler, C., Schmidt-Thieme, L.: Factorizing personalized Markov chains for next-basket recommendation. In: WWW 2010, pp. 811–820 (2010)
12. Hidasi, B., Tikk, D.: General factorization framework for context-aware recommendations. Data Min. Knowl. Discov. 30(2), 342–371 (2015). https://doi.org/10.1007/s10618-015-0417-y
13. Wang, P., Guo, J., Lan, Y., Xu, J., Wan, S., Cheng, X.: Learning hierarchical representation model for nextbasket recommendation. In: Proceedings of the 38th International ACM SIGIR Conference on Research and Development in Information Retrieval, pp. 403–412 (2015)
14. Wang, S., Hu, L., Cao, L., Huang, X., Lian, D., Liu, W.: Attention-based transactional context embedding for next-item recommendation. In: AAAI 2018, pp. 2532–2539 (2018)
15. He, R., Kang, W.-C., McAuley, J.J.: Translation-based recommendation: a scalable method for modeling sequential behavior. In: IJCAI 2018, pp. 5264–5268 (2018)
16. Wu, C.-Y., Ahmed, A., Beutel, A., Smola, A.J.: How Jing: recurrent recommender networks. In: WSDM 2017, pp. 495–503 (2017)
17. Hidasi, B., Karatzoglou, A., Baltrunas, L., Tikk, D.: Session-based recommendations with recurrent neural networks. In: ICLR (Poster) (2016)
18. Quadrana, M., Karatzoglou, A., Hidasi, B., Cremonesi, P.: Personalizing session-based recommendations with hierarchical recurrent neural networks. In: RecSys 2017, pp. 130–137 (2017)
19. Tang, J., Wang, K.: Personalized top-N sequential recommendation via convolutional sequence embedding. In: WSDM 2018, pp. 565–573 (2018)
20. Yuan, F., Karatzoglou, A., Arapakis, I., Jose, J.M., He, X.: A simple convolutional generative network for next item recommendation. In: WSDM 2019, pp. 582–590 (2019)
21. Wu, S., Tang, Y., Zhu, Y., Wang, L., Xie, X., Tan, T.: Session-based recommendation with graph neural networks. In: Proceedings of the AAAI Conference on Artificial Intelligence, vol. 33, pp. 346–353 (2019)
22. Pan, W., Xiang, E.W., Liu, N.N., Yang, Q.: Transfer learning in collaborative filtering for sparsity reduction. In: AAAI 2010 (2010)
23. Pan, W., Liu, N.N., Xiang, E.W., Yang, Q.: Transfer learning to predict missing ratings via heterogeneous user feedbacks. In: IJCAI 2011, pp. 2318–2323 (2011)
24. Li, B., Yang, Q., Xue, X.: Can movies and books collaborate? cross-domain collaborative filtering for sparsity reduction. In: IJCAI 2009, pp. 2052–2057 (2009)
25. Man, T., Shen, H., Jin, X., Cheng, X.: Cross-domain recommendation: an embedding and mapping approach. In: IJCAI 2017, pp. 2464–2470 (2017)
26. Jeh, G., Widom, J.: SimRank: a measure of structural-context similarity. In: KDD 2002, pp. 538–543 (2002)
27. Singh, A.P., Gordon, G.J.: Relational learning via collective matrix factorization. In: KDD 2008, pp. 650–658 (2008)
28. Hochreiter, S., Schmidhuber, J.: Long short-term memory. Neural Comput. 9(8), 1735–1780 (1997)

29. McAuley, J.J., Pandey, R., Leskovec, J.: Inferring networks of substitutable and complementary products. In: KDD 2015, pp. 785–794 (2015)
30. Wang, S., Hu, X., Yu, P.S., Li, Z.: MMRate: inferring multi-aspect diffusion networks with multi-pattern cascades. In: KDD 2014, pp. 1246–1255 (2014)

IASR: An Item-Level Attentive Social Recommendation Model for Personalized Ranking

Tianyi Tao[1], Yun Xiong[1,2]([✉]), Guosen Wang[1], Yao Zhang[1], Peng Tian[1], and Yangyong Zhu[1,2]

[1] Shanghai Key Laboratory of Data Science, School of Computer Science, Fudan University, Shanghai, China
{tytao17,yunx,gswang17,yaozhang18,tianpeng,yyzhu}@fudan.edu.cn
[2] Shanghai Institute for Advanced Communication and Data Science, Fudan University, Shanghai, China

Abstract. Most recommender systems provide recommendations by listing the most relevant items to a user. Such recommendation task can be viewed as a personalized ranking problem. Previous works have found it advantageous to improve recommendation performance by incorporating social information. However, most of them have two primary defects. First, in order to model interaction between users and items, existing works still resort to biased inner production, which has proved less expressive than neural architectures. Second, they do not delicately allocate weights of social neighbor influence based on the user feature or the item feature in a recommendation task. To address the issues, we propose an **I**tem-level **A**ttentive **S**ocial **R**ecommendation model, IASR for short, in this paper. It employs an item-level attention mechanism to adaptively allocate social influences among trustees in the social network and gives more accurate predictions with a neural collaborative filtering framework. Extensive experiments on three real-world datasets are conducted to show our proposed IASR method out-performs the state-of-the-art baselines. Additionally, our method shows effectiveness in the cold-start scenario.

Keywords: Social recommendation · Personalized ranking · Attention mechanism

1 Introduction

In recent years, recommender systems are gaining growing popularity due to the rapid growth of the Internet, which also brings the issues of information explosion and information overload. Many large companies, e.g., e-commerce companies like Amazon and eBay, video companies like Netflix and Hulu and social networking companies like Facebook have all built successful recommender systems to improve their services and make more profits. One of the most commonly

© Springer Nature Switzerland AG 2020
X. Wang et al. (Eds.): APWeb-WAIM 2020, LNCS 12317, pp. 394–408, 2020.
https://doi.org/10.1007/978-3-030-60259-8_29

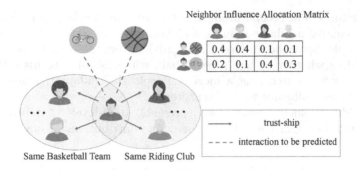

Fig. 1. A real-world example of item-aware neighbor influence allocation.

used approaches for building recommender systems is collaborative filtering, in which past interactions between users and items are utilized for modeling the latent features of users and items. Among a vast majority of existing collaborative filtering models, matrix factorization (MF) [15,23] is known as the most popular one. The basic idea is to represent users and items in a low-dimensional latent space by decomposing the interaction matrix into two low-dimension ones. Therefore, a user's interaction with an item can be modeled by the inner product of the corresponding latent features.

Traditional recommender systems suffer from cold-start problems. In most real-world scenarios, many cold users exist in recommendation problem. Cold users are users have few or even no consumption histories. To alleviate cold-start problems, researchers proposed many social recommendation methods [17, 29,32]. By integrating social information, users' features can be modeled not only from historical interactions' perspective but also from the social connections' perspective.

Roughly speaking there are mainly two types of recommender systems. The first type uses social connections to guide the sampling process of training pairs. Representative works are [20,26,29,32]. The basic idea of this type of approaches is to categorize items into detailed sets for each user with the help of social connections. For example, in [32], items are categorized into three classes for user u—items consumed by u, items not consumed by u but consumed by u's friends/trustees, items neither consumed by u nor u's friends/trustees. With detailed categorization, such models apply different assumptions to give the sets an ordered rank, which can be used for guiding the sampling process. The second type, however, directly utilizes social connections to build latent features for MF. Representative methods are [7,25]. Taking [7] as an example, the TrustSVD model is built on top of the famous SVD++ [14] model. [7] redesigns the predict function by adding a new term which reflects the neighbors' influences.

Although both types of methods mentioned above can improve the ranking performance to some extent, there still exist two unresolved problems. The first problem is that they employ biased inner products of items' and users' latent features, which is reported in [9] to be less expressive than deep neural network based structures. The second problem is that existing works pay little attention to how to control neighbor influences elaborately. We present Fig. 1 as a real-world example. Someone may take more advice from his basketball teammates when deciding whether to buy a basketball, while listening to his riding club-mates more when purchasing a bicycle. People shall adapt the proportion of social neighbors' influence for different items.

To address such issues, we present Item-level Attentive Social Recommendation, IASR for short. The main contributions of our work are as follows:

1. We substitute the traditional inner product module to a multi-layer percep-tron structure to capture high-level and non-linear interaction information.
2. We present a neural network based attention module to elaborately model trustee influences with respect to not only user features but also item features.
3. Extensive experiments on three real-world datasets show better performance of our IASR model against existing state-of-the-art approaches. Moreover, our proposed IASR model alleviates the cold-start problems as proved by the experimental results.

2   Related Work

In this section, we will review the most related works from two perspectives. The first is social recommendation for personalized ranking, which is the gen-eral target of our work. The second is applications of attention mechanism in recommender systems.

2.1   Social Recommendation for Personalized Ranking

In [11], Hu et al. raise their opinion that implicit data are of great importance in recommender systems. Following in [22], Rendle et al. present a bayesian per-sonalized ranking. Rendle et al. pioneeringly point out that the main task of recommender systems should not be the regression of explicit ratings. However, researcher should focus on a classification problem more, which is to decide the preference order when given one user with two items. Since then, many approaches about personalized ranking have been proposed. In [26], Wang et al. follow the work in [32] by defining strong and weak ties in a social network, which can help categorize the while item set even more delicately. In [31], an embedding based social recommender is proposed by identifying semantic friends. Later in [29], Yu et al. extend the work in [31] to heterogeneous networks, and propose a model to identify implicit friendships, with whose help the item set is catego-rized into five ordered sets just like [26,32], generating more fine-grained train-ing samples for BPR loss function. Apart from BPR-based ranking approaches, there also exist other approaches [5,25]. [5,25] study users' exposure in implicit data, and try to model them accurately by studying social influences, and finally enhance ranking results.

2.2   Attention Mechanism in Recommender Systems

Attention mechanism is first introduced for machine translation problems in [1] and gets popular in many research areas [4], e.g. QA [10, 16, 24] and document classification [12, 28]. Attention mechanisms draw researchers' attention for mainly three reasons. First, such models achieve great improvements in related areas. Second, they handle a critical problem in recurrent neural networks (RNN) that is the performance degradation when input size is very large. Last, they are able to provide extra interpretability. Many recommender systems employ attention mechanism as well. He et al. propose a neural network model in [8] which uses an attention network to distinguish which historical items in a user profile is of greater importance. In [3], Cao et al. use attention mechanism to help aggregate members' embeddings to form a group embedding in terms of each item. This is a similar work to ours. However, our work do not need explicit group information, allowing it to be more widely applicable. In [30], Yu et al. develop a neural attentive interpretable recommendation system that can assign attentive weights to interacted items of a user, which will later contribute to modeling user's profile.

3   Method

In this section, we present our IASR model. First of all, we briefly overview our model. We then describe our model in detail. Lastly, we discuss the optimization method for our model.

Before discussing the model, we need to formulate the task. In our work, we focus on giving personalized ranking under implicit data settings, with the help of social network data. Here we define $\mathcal{U} = \{u_1, \ldots, u_n\}$ as the user set of n users, as well as $\mathcal{I} = \{i_1, \ldots, i_m\}$ as the item set of m items. The implicit feedback is defined as a matrix $\boldsymbol{R} \in \{0, 1\}^{n \times m}$ with $r_{u,i}$ denoting the value in the u-th row and i-th column of $\boldsymbol{R}$. $r_{u,i} = 1$ when the interaction between user u and item i is observed, and $r_{u,i} = 0$ otherwise. Additionally, we define $\boldsymbol{T} \in \{0, 1\}^{n \times n}$, whose u-th row, v-th column's value $t_{u,v}$ denotes the observation of trust-ship from user u to user v. Similarly, $t_{u,v} = 1$ if such trust-ship is observed, and $t_{u,v} = 0$ vice versa. With all these data given, our model should be able to give the order of all items for each user, according to his or her personal preferences.

3.1   Model Overview

Figure 2 shows the overview of our IASR model. Formally, we use $\boldsymbol{p}_u \in \mathbb{R}^{d_u \times 1}$ to denote user u's embedding and $\boldsymbol{q}_i \in \mathbb{R}^{d_i \times 1}$ to denote item i's embedding. Here d_u and d_i means the dimension for users' and items' embedding vectors respectively, and they do not have to be the same thanks to the neural network design which will be discussed later. However, for the convenience of model presentation, we assume they have the same size, and use d to denote the dimension. IASR accepts user u and item i as inputs, and through $\boldsymbol{T}$, all the trustees of user u can be

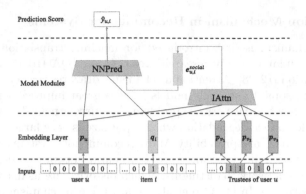

Fig. 2. The overview of our IASR model.

looked up. Trustees of user u can be denoted as a set $\mathcal{N}_u = \{v | t_{u,v} = 1\}$. The general steps of our model are as follows:

$$e_{u,i}^{social} = IAttn(\boldsymbol{p}_u, \boldsymbol{q}_i, \mathcal{N}_u), \tag{1}$$

$$\hat{y}_{u,i} = NNPred(\boldsymbol{p}_u, \boldsymbol{q}_i, e_{u,i}^{social}), \tag{2}$$

where $IAttn$ denotes the Item-level Attention module and $NNPred$ denotes the Neural Network Prediction module. $IAttn$ accepts $\boldsymbol{p}_u$, $\boldsymbol{q}_i$ and $\mathcal{N}_u$, adaptively allocates trustee weights, and then generates the aggregated social representation $e_{u,i}^{social}$. $NNPred$ accepts the social representation along with embeddings of the user and the item, and then gives the final prediction. Both modules will be discussed in the following parts. In advance of introducing these two modules, a brief introduction of the K-way Vector Aggregator will be given, which is a component both utilized in the Item-level Attention module and the Neural Network Prediction module.

3.2 Model Details

K-Way Vector Aggregator Following the ideas in [21], which proposes a factorization machine model to capture all the single variables and pairwise interactions in a single vector, we extend the factorization machine model to a higher perspective, i.e., from single vector to multiple vectors.

Figure 3 illustrates our design of k-way vector aggregator. A k-way vector aggregator accepts k vectors of the same size $d^{in} \in \mathbb{N}$ and extracts their first-order and second-order information into a new vector of size $d^{out} \in \mathbb{N}$:

$$\boldsymbol{v}^{pooling1} = \left\| \begin{matrix} k \\ \\ i=1 \end{matrix} \right. (\boldsymbol{v}_i^{in}), \tag{3}$$

$$\boldsymbol{v}^{pooling2} = \left\| \begin{matrix} k \\ \\ i=1, j=1, i<j \end{matrix} \right. (\boldsymbol{v}_i^{in} \odot \boldsymbol{v}_j^{in}), \tag{4}$$

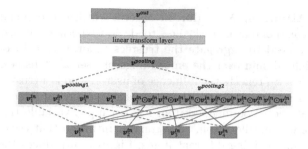

Fig. 3. Illustration of a 4-way vector aggregator.

$$v^{pooling} = (v^{pooling1} \| v^{pooling2}), \tag{5}$$

$$v^{out} = VA(v_1^{in}, \dots, v_k^{in}) \tag{6}$$

$$= W_{kwa} v^{pooling} + b_{kwa}, \tag{7}$$

where $\|$ represents the concatenation operation among vectors, $v_i^{in} \in \mathbb{R}^{d^{in}}$ means the i-th input vector and $v^{pooling} \in \mathbb{R}^{d^{pooling}}$ denotes a hidden pooling layer which is the concatenation of $v^{pooling1} \in \mathbb{R}^{d^{pooling1}}$ and $v^{pooling2} \in \mathbb{R}^{d^{pooling2}}$.

Here $v^{pooling1}$ contains the first-order information of the input vectors by simply joining them up into a large vector. Hence the size of $v^{pooling1}$, i.e., $d^{pooling1}$, is $k \times d^{in}$. Similarly, $v^{pooling2}$ is the concatenation of second-order informative vectors. Each second-order informative vector (e.g. $v_1^{in} \odot v_2^{in}$) is the hadamard product of two different input vectors and thus its size $d^{pooling2}$ is $\frac{k \times (k-1)}{2} d^{in}$. We put $v^{pooling1}$ and $v^{pooling2}$ together to form $v^{pooling}$, and then feed it into a linear transformation, notated by a weight matrix $W_{kwa} \in \mathbb{R}^{d^{out} \times d^{pooling}}$ and a bias vector $b_{kwa} \in \mathbb{R}^{d^{out}}$, projecting all the first-order information and second-order information into a new latent space of dimension $v^{out} \in \mathbb{R}^{d^{out}}$.

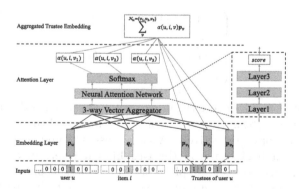

Fig. 4. Illustration of item-level attentive social representation aggregation.

Item-Level Attention Module. In order to utilize the social information in a single recommendation task, i.e., to decide whether to recommend item i to user u, we need to aggregate the trustees' information. In our model, we perform a weighted sum over the embeddings of user u's trustees. The weight, denoted by $\alpha(u, i, v)$, reflects the influence of user v, who is a trustee of user u, on deciding whether to recommend item i to user u. Different from most previous works, we treat the recommended item i as an input variable that contributes in learning the weight allocation, based on our intuition that trustees' influence varies when recommending different items. Figure 4 introduces the structure of this component. More precisely, we have the following definitions:

$$o(u, i, v) = MLP^{social}(VA^{social}(\boldsymbol{p}_u, \boldsymbol{q}_i, \mathcal{N}_u)), \tag{8}$$

$$\alpha(u, i, v) = softmax(o(u, i, v)) = \frac{\exp(o(u, i, v))}{\sum_{v'}^{\mathcal{N}_u} \exp(o(u, i, v'))}, \tag{9}$$

$$e_{u,i}^{social} = IAttn(\boldsymbol{p}_u, \boldsymbol{q}_i, \mathcal{N}_u) \tag{10}$$

$$= \sum_v^{\mathcal{N}_u} \alpha(u, i, v)\boldsymbol{p}_v, \tag{11}$$

where $e_{u,i}^{social}$ denotes the output of this component, VA^{social} a 3-way vector aggregator accepting the embeddings of user u, item i and a trustee v, MLP^{social} a neural attention network which is capable of expressing non-linear information.

In (8), for each trustee of user i's, we project recommendee embedding, item embedding and trustee embedding to a score denoted by $o(u, i, v)$ via VA^{social}, MLP^{social} step by step. Nextly in (9), we normalize the scores using a softmax function, ensuring their summation to be 1. Lastly, we treat the normalized scores, denoted by $\alpha(u, i, v)$, as weights, and calculate the weighted sum of the embeddings of trustees as the aggregated trustee embedding, which is exactly the output of this component. We further detail the structure of the neural attention network, i.e., MLP^{social}, as follows:

$$\begin{cases} \boldsymbol{e}_1 = \sigma(\boldsymbol{W}_1 \boldsymbol{e}^{in} + \boldsymbol{b}_1) \\ \quad \cdots\cdots \\ \boldsymbol{e}_h = \sigma(\boldsymbol{W}_h \boldsymbol{e}_{h-1} + \boldsymbol{b}_h) \\ \boldsymbol{e}^{out} = \boldsymbol{w}^T \boldsymbol{e}_h \end{cases}, \tag{12}$$

where $\boldsymbol{e}^{in}$, $\boldsymbol{e}_i$, $\boldsymbol{e}^{out}$ and h denote the input vector of the network, the i-th hidden layer of the network, the output vector of the network and the number of hidden layers in this network, respectively. Also, we use $\boldsymbol{W}_i$ and $\boldsymbol{b}_i$ to represent the weight matrix and bias vector in the i-th hidden layer. In order to capture the non-linear information, we apply a non-linear activation function $\sigma(\cdot)$, e.g. sigmoid, tanh or ReLU, to each hidden layer. In the end, the last layer's output $\boldsymbol{e}_h$ will be transformed to a score value with vector $\boldsymbol{w}$.

In order to avoid too expensive computation cost on those users who have a large number of friends, we use a hyper-parameter N_n to control the number of trustees participating in the aggregation. That is if a user u has a neighbor size larger than N_n, we will randomly select N_n neighbors to complete the aggregation.

Neural Network Prediction Module. With trustees' embeddings aggregated, we are now able to give the prediction of a recommendation task. Figure 5 shows the structure of this part.

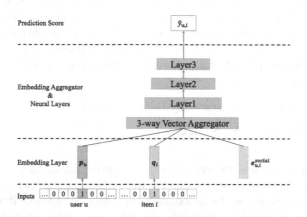

Fig. 5. Illustration of the neural network prediction module.

Similar to the designs of neural attention network in Sect. 3.2, we use a neural network to predict the score of recommendation. We have the following definitions:

$$e_{u,i}^{agg} = VA^{pred}(\boldsymbol{p}_u, \boldsymbol{q}_v, e_{u,i}^{social}), \tag{13}$$

$$score_{u,i} = MLP^{pred}(e_{u,i}^{agg}), \tag{14}$$

$$\hat{y}_{u,i} = NNPred(\boldsymbol{p}_u, \boldsymbol{q}_i, e_{u,i}^{social}) \tag{15}$$

$$= \sigma(score_{u,i}), \tag{16}$$

where $e_{i,j}^{social}$ represent the aggregated trustee embedding for recommendation task over the user-item pair $< i, j >$. VA^{pred} is a 3-way vector aggregator accepting the embeddings of user u, item i and user u's aggregated trustee embedding in respect to item i. MLP^{pred} means a neural network for prediction which will be discussed shortly after. $\hat{y}_{u,i}$ is the prediction score. Since we are looking into recommendations over implicit data in our work, $\hat{y}_{u,i}$ should be a real number in the range of $[0, 1]$. We use a sigmoid function $\sigma(\cdot)$ to normalize the prediction score.

MLP^{pred} shares the same structure as (12). However, they do not share the same settings for network depth and layer widths. Thus their parameters are learned unrelatedly. We adopt the fashion that not sharing the same network among social part and prediction part in our model because their outputs do not share a same semantic space.

3.3   Model Optimization Method

Unlike rating prediction under explicit interaction settings, our task is more like a classification problem rather than a regression problem that is to classify an input triplet $<u, i, j>$ where u denotes the user and i, j the two items into two categories: u prefer i over j and u prefer j over i. In order to solve this classification problem, most existing works apply a pairwise optimization method [22,26,32]. However, in our work, we use noise contrastive estimation loss like [27] in optimization instead of a pair-wise fashion. For an observed interaction $<u, i>$, we have:

$$l(u, i, \theta) = \log \sigma(score_{u,i}) + E_{j \sim p(j)}[\log \sigma(-score_{u,j})], \tag{17}$$

$$\mathcal{L}(U, I, \theta) = \sum_u \sum_i l(u, i, \theta) \tag{18}$$

where $l(u, i, \theta)$ is the loss in terms of one observed interaction, $p(j)$ denotes a noise distribution where an item j can be drawn from, $\mathcal{L}(U, I, \theta)$ means the complete form of loss function. In practical, $p(j)$ which is the distribution of noisy samples can be replaced by uniform sampling from all observed interactions. Also, since the accurate expectation of the distribution is expensive to calculate, we directly draw N_s samples from observed interactions to substitute the latter term $E_{j \sim p(j)}[\log \sigma(-score_{u,j})]$ in (17) where N_s is another hyper-parameter denoting the number of samples drawn for computing the NCE loss. We adopt such sampling approach for the reason that the training data distribution is a natural option for noise distribution $p(j)$. Since our model is designed in an end-to-end fashion, loss can be easily back-propagated to update user and item embeddings, model parameters as well.

4   Experiments

4.1   Experimental Settings

Datasets. We conduct experiments on following 3 real-world datasets:

CiaoDVD. Ciao is an European online-shopping website[1]. **CiaoDVD** is a dataset crawled from the entire category of DVDs from website in December, 2013. This dataset contains user ratings and trust relationships. This dataset is first introduced in [6].

Delicious. Delicious is originally founded in 2003 as a social bookmarking service[2]. This dataset contains social information and bookmarking information, and is introduced in [2].

---

[1] https://www.ciao.co.uk/.

[2] https://del.icio.us/(not available when paper is written).

Epinions. This dataset is collected from Epinions.com web site, which is also a European online-shopping website, with a crawler introduced in [18,19]. This dataset is publicly accessible[3].

Since interactions in **CiaoDVD** and **Epinions** are explicit ratings, we treat them as implicit interactions in our experiments by simply view a rating as an observed consumption interaction.

Baseline Methods. To show the better performance of personalized ranking provided by our IASR model, we compare it with the following baselines:

Random. This method gives an random order for each item list.

MostPopular. This method ranks items in the query according to their popularity which is defined by their occurrences in the training set. This is a non-personalized baseline.

MF-BPR. This method is proposed in [22] by Rendle et al. By replacing the point-wise optimizing approach with the bayesian pair-wise optimizing way, traditional MF method can achieve better performance in the task of personalized recommendation in implicit datasets.

NeuMF. Proposed by He et al. [9], this model replaces the inner product with a neural architecture. It has the capability to learn the non-linearity information form user-item interactions.

TBPR. Proposed in [26], this is an extensive work of **MF-BPR**. It divide the item set into 5 non-overlapping and ordered sets by bringing in the idea of strong and weak ties.

SERec. Proposed in [25], this work looks into user exposures by utilizing social network information. It integrates social exposure into collaborative filtering to improve recommendation under implicit data settings.

Parameter Settings. We implement our model based on Pytorch[4]. The code can be found here[5]. We make the validation set the same way as the test set. User and item embeddings are trained from scratch. All hidden layers are randomly initialized with a Gaussian distribution of mean 0 and standard deviation 0.1. We use the Adam optimizer [13] to optimize the loss function and apply mini-batch gradient descent to better utilize GPU. Mini-batch size is searched in {128, 256, 512}. Weight decay is searched in {0.000001, 0.00001, 0.0001, 0.001}. Learning rate is searched in {0.001, 0.005, 0.01, 0.05, 0.1}. Embedding sizes d is set to 64. We empirically employ a 3-layer tower structure in the neural networks following [9], that is the size of every hidden layer is half of the last hidden layer. ReLU activation is used as the non-linear function in our neural networks.

---

[3] http://www.trustlet.org/downloaded_epinions.html.
[4] https://pytorch.org/.
[5] https://github.com/tytao17/IASR.

Table 1. Performance of baseline methods and our method

Dataset	Metrics	Rand	MP	MF-BPR [22]	NeuMF [9]	TBPR [26]	SERec [25]	IASR
CiaoDVD	HR@5	0.0316	0.0789	<u>0.1368</u>	0.1158	0.1263	0.0842	**0.1579**
	HR@10	0.0842	0.1579	<u>0.2211</u>	0.1789	0.2158	0.1368	**0.2474**
	NDCG@5	0.0191	0.0469	0.0765	0.0663	<u>0.0827</u>	0.0546	**0.1098**
	NDCG@10	0.0360	0.0714	0.1036	0.0861	<u>0.1125</u>	0.0719	**0.1383**
	MRR	0.0456	0.0694	0.0926	0.0792	<u>0.1036</u>	0.0724	**0.1262**
Delicious	HR@5	0.0581	0.1002	<u>0.3030</u>	0.2138	0.1936	0.0623	**0.3914**
	HR@10	0.1086	0.1507	<u>0.3838</u>	0.2955	0.2727	0.1170	**0.4731**
	NDCG@5	0.0345	0.0659	<u>0.2498</u>	0.1532	0.1411	0.0374	**0.3241**
	NDCG@10	0.0506	0.0821	<u>0.2757</u>	0.1794	0.1668	0.0547	**0.3504**
	MRR	0.0555	0.0821	<u>0.2610</u>	0.1645	0.1570	0.0586	**0.3292**
Epinions	HR@5	0.0508	0.3039	0.4620	<u>0.4478</u>	0.4010	0.0489	**0.4665**
	HR@10	0.0995	0.4213	**0.5929**	0.5796	0.5216	0.0926	<u>0.5919</u>
	NDCG@5	0.0299	0.2134	<u>0.3384</u>	0.3263	0.2919	0.0282	**0.3465**
	NDCG@10	0.0454	0.2513	<u>0.3809</u>	0.3692	0.3310	0.0422	**0.3869**
	MRR	0.0520	0.2188	<u>0.3315</u>	0.3210	0.2896	0.0498	**0.3404**

Table 2. Performance of baseline methods and our method over cold users

Dataset	Metrics	Rand	MP	MF-BPR [22]	NeuMF [9]	TBPR [26]	SERec [25]	IASR
CiaoDVD	HR@5	0.0476	0.0794	0.1111	**0.1587**	0.0952	0.0794	**0.1587**
	HR@10	0.1111	0.1587	0.1587	<u>0.2063</u>	0.1905	0.1746	**0.2698**
	NDCG@5	0.0269	0.0489	0.0568	**0.0875**	0.0676	0.0468	<u>0.0835</u>
	NDCG@10	0.0477	0.0739	0.0725	<u>0.1029</u>	0.0976	0.0778	**0.1176**
	MRR	0.0531	0.0723	0.0727	0.0889	**0.0924**	0.0695	<u>0.0913</u>
Delicious	HR@5	0.0543	0.0886	<u>0.1257</u>	0.1000	0.0971	0.0600	**0.2457**
	HR@10	0.0914	0.1486	<u>0.2114</u>	0.1629	0.2000	0.1257	**0.3314**
	NDCG@5	0.0320	0.0631	<u>0.0852</u>	0.0611	0.0635	0.0375	**0.1880**
	NDCG@10	0.0440	0.0821	<u>0.1123</u>	0.0812	0.0969	0.0583	**0.2156**
	MRR	0.0512	0.0828	<u>0.1048</u>	0.0797	0.0900	0.0620	**0.1996**
Epinions	HR@5	0.0558	0.3176	<u>0.3863</u>	0.3691	0.3090	0.0258	**0.4335**
	HR@10	0.0944	0.3863	<u>0.5107</u>	0.4979	0.3648	0.0644	**0.5365**
	NDCG@5	0.0340	0.2157	<u>0.2804</u>	0.2609	0.2318	0.0169	**0.3350**
	NDCG@10	0.0461	0.2381	<u>0.3204</u>	0.3024	0.2505	0.0291	**0.3684**
	MRR	0.0551	0.2102	<u>0.2796</u>	0.2600	0.2341	0.0405	**0.3350**

4.2   Performance Comparison

Table 1 and Table 2 detail the performance of different models. In Table 2, cold users are defined as users with fewer than 5 interactions in the training set. **SERec** reports bad results because of hardship in tuning parameters, so we skip it in this section. In each row, the best result is in boldface while the second best result is underlined. From the presented results, we can see that:

1. **Random** shows the worst performance while **MostPopular** shows the second worst performance in most cases, since they have no personalized knowledge about the datasets.
2. **MF-BPR** shows surprisingly good results than other state-of-the-art methods, for its great simplicity and generality.
3. In some cases, **NeuMF** shows the second best performance, because it can capture non-linear information as our model.
4. Also in some cases, **TBPR** shows the second best performance for its utilization of social information.
5. In most cases, our proposed **IASR** model outperform all the compared baseline methods. We believe it is for the combination of two advantages.
6. Out proposed **IASR** model shows little performance degradation in cold-user settings, which certifies its ability to solve cold-start problems in recommendation systems.

Table 3. Results of random user-item pairs selected from test set of **Delicious**

User	Item	Trustees and weights									
#870	#127	#29	#60	#61	#269	#484	#538	#802	#881	-	-
		0.211	0.094	0.130	0.091	0.089	0.092	0.089	**0.205**	-	-
#961	#786	#172	#240	#378	#380	#573	#590	#657	#723	#1043	#1185
		0.077	0.097	0.089	0.081	**0.112**	0.105	0.110	0.105	0.108	**0.117**
#1111	#813	#122	#153	#356	#578	#735	#1140	#1166	-	-	-
		0.121	0.136	0.147	**0.147**	0.147	**0.153**	0.150	-	-	-
#1185	#785	#172	#240	#355	#536	#567	#573	#590	#657	#797	#961
		0.075	0.085	**0.105**	0.097	**0.105**	0.107	0.100	0.105	**0.102**	**0.111**

4.3 Attention Mechanism Analysis

To evaluate the effectiveness of item-level attention mechanism, we conduct some case studies. Presented in Table 3, we randomly draw 4 users from test set of **Delicious** whose positive test items are ranked top-5. For each user, we give his or her id and positive test item id, as well as his or her trustees' ids with allocated weights below them. Weights in **bold** font denote the interaction between this trustee and the positive item can be observed in the training set. We can see in these nicely ranked cases, our model tends to allocate greater weights to those who have interacted with the item, thus helps rank this item in a higher position. It proves the effectiveness of the attention mechanism in our IASR model.

4.4 Hyper-parameter Analysis

Our IASR model is mainly related to two hyper-parameters, N_n for controlling the maximum neighbor size and N_s for controlling the NCE sampling size. We study these two parameters on **Delicious** and **CiaoDVD**. On both datasets, we set the embedding size to 16, N_s to 255 when studying N_n and N_n to 10 when studying N_s.

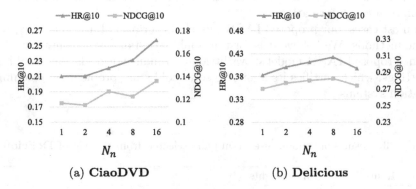

(a) **CiaoDVD**   (b) **Delicious**

Fig. 6. Performance of IASR using different neighbor size N_n on **CiaoDVD** and **Delicious**.

From Fig. 6, we can find on **CiaoDVD**, larger neighbor size N_n brings better performance while on **Delicious** the performance starts to decrease when N_n is set too large. We believe drawing too many neighbors in aggregation phase may bring some unnecessary noise thus finding a optimal neighbor size for a specific dataset is important.

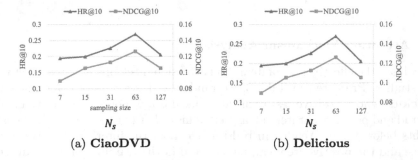

(a) **CiaoDVD**   (b) **Delicious**

Fig. 7. Performance of IASR using different sampling size N_s on **CiaoDVD** and **Delicious**.

From Fig. 7, we can find on both datasets, the metrics HR@10 and NDCG@10 improve while the sampling size grows from a small value, and start to drop when the sampling size becomes too large. This indicates larger sampling size helps the learning process of IASR in general, however too aggressive sampling size settings will hurt the learning process.

5   Conclusion and Future Work

In this work, we devise a neural network based model which utilizes item-level attention for social recommendation. With neural networks, our model is endowed with the ability to explore the non-linearity in user item interactions. With attention mechanism, our model can adaptively allocate trustees' influences in recommendation tasks. We compare our model with other state-of-the-art models on three real-world datasets to show the effectiveness of our model in not only common recommendation tasks but also those for cold users.

In the future, our work can be extended to two major directions. First, we can bring in more external information rather than social networks, which can be used to train the users' and items' latent features more accurately. Second, we will study how the adaptively learned trustees' weights change over time by utilizing some session based datasets.

Acknowledgements. This work is supported in part by the National Natural Science Foundation of China Projects No. U1936213, No. U1636207, and the Shanghai Science and Technology Development Fund No. 19511121204, No. 19DZ1200802.

References

1. Bahdanau, D., Cho, K., Bengio, Y.: Neural machine translation by jointly learning to align and translate. arXiv preprint arXiv:1409.0473 (2014)
2. Cantador, I., Brusilovsky, P.L., Kuflik, T.: Second workshop on information heterogeneity and fusion in recommender systems (HetRec2011) (2011)
3. Cao, D., He, X., Miao, L., An, Y., Yang, C., Hong, R.: Attentive group recommendation. In: SIGIR, pp. 645–654 (2018)
4. Chaudhari, S., Polatkan, G., Ramanath, R., Mithal, V.: An attentive survey of attention models. arXiv preprint arXiv:1904.02874 (2019)
5. Chen, J., Feng, Y., Ester, M., Zhou, S., Chen, C., Wang, C.: Modeling users' exposure with social knowledge influence and consumption influence for recommendation. In: CIKM, pp. 953–962 (2018)
6. Guo, G., Zhang, J., Thalmann, D., Yorke-Smith, N.: ETAF: an extended trust antecedents framework for trust prediction. In: ASONAM, pp. 540–547 (2014)
7. Guo, G., Zhang, J., Yorke-Smith, N.: TrustSVD: collaborative filtering with both the explicit and implicit influence of user trust and of item ratings. In: AAAI (2015)
8. He, X., He, Z., Song, J., Liu, Z., Jiang, Y.G., Chua, T.S.: Nais: neural attentive item similarity model for recommendation. TKDE **30**(12), 2354–2366 (2018)
9. He, X., Liao, L., Zhang, H., Nie, L., Hu, X., Chua, T.S.: Neural collaborative filtering. In: WWW, pp. 173–182 (2017)
10. Hermann, K.M., et al.: Teaching machines to read and comprehend. In: Advances in Neural Information Processing Systems, pp. 1693–1701 (2015)

11. Hu, Y., Koren, Y., Volinsky, C.: Collaborative filtering for implicit feedback datasets. In: ICDM, pp. 263–272 (2008)
12. Kiela, D., Wang, C., Cho, K.: Dynamic meta-embeddings for improved sentence representations. In: EMNLP, pp. 1466–1477 (2018)
13. Kingma, D.P., Ba, J.: Adam: A method for stochastic optimization. arXiv preprint arXiv:1412.6980 (2014)
14. Koren, Y.: Factorization meets the neighborhood: a multifaceted collaborative filtering model. In: SIGKDD, pp. 426–434 (2008)
15. Koren, Y., Bell, R., Volinsky, C.: Matrix factorization techniques for recommender systems. Computer **8**, 30–37 (2009)
16. Lu, J., Yang, J., Batra, D., Parikh, D.: Hierarchical question-image co-attention for visual question answering. In: NeurIPS, pp. 289–297 (2016)
17. Ma, H., Yang, H., Lyu, M.R., King, I.: SoRec: social recommendation using probabilistic matrix factorization. In: CIKM, pp. 931–940 (2008)
18. Massa, P., Avesani, P.: Trust-aware recommender systems. In: RecSys, pp. 17–24 (2007)
19. Massa, P., Souren, K., Salvetti, M., Tomasoni, D.: Trustlet, open research on trust metrics. SCPE **9**(4) (2008)
20. Pan, W., Chen, L.: GBPR: group preference based Bayesian personalized ranking for one-class collaborative filtering. In: IJCAI (2013)
21. Rendle, S.: Factorization machines. In: ICDM, pp. 995–1000 (2010)
22. Rendle, S., Freudenthaler, C., Gantner, Z., Schmidt-Thieme, L.: BPR: Bayesian personalized ranking from implicit feedback. In: UAI, pp. 452–461 (2009)
23. Sarwar, B.M., Karypis, G., Konstan, J.A., Riedl, J., et al.: Item-based collaborative filtering recommendation algorithms. WWW **1**, 285–295 (2001)
24. Sukhbaatar, S., Weston, J., Fergus, R., et al.: End-to-end memory networks. In: NeurIPS, pp. 2440–2448 (2015)
25. Wang, M., Zheng, X., Yang, Y., Zhang, K.: Collaborative filtering with social exposure: a modular approach to social recommendation. In: AAAI (2018)
26. Wang, X., Lu, W., Ester, M., Wang, C., Chen, C.: Social recommendation with strong and weak ties. In: CIKM, pp. 5–14 (2016)
27. Wu, G., Volkovs, M., Soon, C.L., Sanner, S., Rai, H.: Noise contrastive estimation for scalable linear models for one-class collaborative filtering. arXiv preprint arXiv:1811.00697 (2018)
28. Yang, Z., Yang, D., Dyer, C., He, X., Smola, A., Hovy, E.: Hierarchical attention networks for document classification. In: NAACL-HLT, pp. 1480–1489 (2016)
29. Yu, J., Gao, M., Li, J., Yin, H., Liu, H.: Adaptive implicit friends identification over heterogeneous network for social recommendation. In: CIKM, pp. 357–366 (2018)
30. Yu, S., Wang, Y., Yang, M., Li, B., Qu, Q., Shen, J.: NAIRS: a neural attentive interpretable recommendation system. In: WSDM, pp. 790–793 (2019)
31. Zhang, C., Yu, L., Wang, Y., Shah, C., Zhang, X.: Collaborative user network embedding for social recommender systems, pp. 381–389 (2017)
32. Zhao, T., McAuley, J., King, I.: Leveraging social connections to improve personalized ranking for collaborative filtering. In: CIKM, pp. 261–270 (2014)

Spatio-Temporal Self-Attention Network for Next POI Recommendation

Jiacheng Ni[1], Pengpeng Zhao[1]($\boxtimes$), Jiajie Xu[1], Junhua Fang[1], Zhixu Li[1], Xuefeng Xian[2]($\boxtimes$), Zhiming Cui[3], and Victor S. Sheng[4]

[1] Institute of AI, Soochow University, Suzhou, China
ppzhao@suda.edu.cn
[2] Suzhou Vocational University, Suzhou, China
xianxuefeng@jssvc.edu.cn
[3] Suzhou University of Science and Technology, Suzhou, China
[4] Texas Tech University, Lubbock, TX, USA

Abstract. Next Point-of-Interest (POI) recommendation, which aims to recommend next POIs that the user will likely visit in the near future, has become essential in Location-based Social Networks (LBSNs). Various Recurrent Neural Network (RNN) based sequential models have been proposed for next POI recommendation and achieved state-of-the-art performance, however RNN is difficult to parallelize which limits its efficiency. Recently, Self-Attention Network (SAN), which is purely based on the self-attention mechanism instead of recurrent modules, improves both performance and efficiency in various sequential tasks. However, none of the existing self-attention networks consider the spatio-temporal intervals between neighbor check-ins, which are essential for modeling user check-in behaviors in next POI recommendation. To this end, in this paper, we propose a new Spatio-Temporal Self-Attention Network (STSAN), which combines self-attention mechanisms with spatio-temporal patterns of users' check-in history. Specifically, time-specific weight matrices and distance-specific weight matrices through a decay function are used to model the spatio-temporal influence of POI pairs. Moreover, we introduce a simple but effective way to dynamically measure the importances of spatial and temporal weights to capture users' spatio-temporal preferences. Finally, we evaluate the proposed model using two real-world LBSN datasets, and the experimental results show that our model significantly outperforms the state-of-the-art approaches for next POI recommendation.

Keywords: Self-Attention Network · Point-of-Interest · Recommender system

1 Introduction

Nowadays, due to the popularity of Location-based Social Networks (LBSN), such as Foursquare and Yelp, users can share their locations and experiences

© Springer Nature Switzerland AG 2020
X. Wang et al. (Eds.): APWeb-WAIM 2020, LNCS 12317, pp. 409–423, 2020.
https://doi.org/10.1007/978-3-030-60259-8_30

with friends. As a result, huge amounts of check-in data have been accumulated with an increasing need of Point-of-Interest (POI) recommendation, which also gains great research interest in recent years. Different from traditional recommendation, spatio-temporal information (i.e., time intervals and geographical distances) of users' check-ins is critical in POI recommendation. However, integrating spatio-temporal transitions into recommendation is a long-term challenge.

To model users' sequential patterns, the Markov Chain based model is an early approach for sequential recommendation. Factorizing Personalized Markov Chain (FPMC) models users' sequential information through factorizing user-item matrix and utilizing item-item transitions for next basket recommendation [14]. However, the Markov assumption is difficult to establish a more effective relationship among factors. With the development of deep learning, Recurrent Neural Network (RNN) has been successfully applied to capture the sequential user behavior patterns, some examples are Long Short-Term Memory (LSTM) [8] and Gated Recurrent Units (GRU) [4].

Some recent works have extended RNN to model the spatio-temporal information, which capture the transition patterns of user check-ins, for POI recommendation and demonstrate the effectiveness. Time-LSTM equips LSTM with time gates, which are specially designed, to model time intervals [26]. ST-RNN models local temporal and spatial contexts with time-specific transition matrices for different time intervals and distance-specific transition matrices for different geographical distances [13]. HST-LSTM combines spatio-temporal influences into LSTM model naturally to mitigate the data sparsity in location prediction problem [10]. Also by enhancing LSTM network, STGN introduced spatio-temporal gates to capture spatio-temporal information between check-ins [24]. However, RNN-based models are difficult to preserve long-range dependencies. Moreover, these methods need to compute step by step (i.e., computation of the current time step should wait for the results of the last time step), which leads to these models hard to parallelize.

Recently, a new sequential model Self-Attention Network (SAN) was proposed, which is easy to parallelize and purely based on a self-attention mechanism instead of recurrent modules [16]. It achieves state-of-the-art performance and efficiency in various sequential tasks [17,22]. The essence of the self-attention network is to capture long-term dependencies by calculating the weight of attention between each pair of items in a sequence. Actually, a pure self-attention network treats a sequence as a set, essentially without considering the order of the items in a sequence. The order of the items in a sequence is extremely important for sequential modeling tasks. To model the order information of the sequence, Tan et al. [15] applied the positional embedding to encode the sequential position information for semantic role labeling. Moreover, SASRec [9] applied position embedding into the self-attention mechanism to consider the order of the items. ATRank [25] divided items' time into intervals whose length increases exponentially, where each interval represents a time granularity. However, none of the above self-attention networks take the spatio-temporal information into consideration. It is dramatically important to consider time intervals and geographical distances between neighbor items for next POI recommendation. Hence, how to integrate time intervals and geographical distances into the self-attention network is a big challenge.

To this end, in this paper, we propose a new Spatio-Temporal Self-Attention Network (STSAN) by incorporating spatio-temporal information between check-ins into a self-attention block for next POI recommendation. Specifically, we map the time and distance intervals between two check-ins to a weight between two POIs by a decay function. In this way, POI i will get a high attention score on POI j if their spatio-temporal intervals are relatively short, and vice versa. Furthermore, in order to capture the dynamic spatio-temporal preferences of different users, we combine the spatial and temporal weights adaptively and incorporate them into the self-attention block. Experimental results show that incorporating spatio-temporal information into the self-attention block can significantly improve the performance of next POI recommendation.

To summarize, our contributions are listed as follows.

- We propose a novel framework, Spatio-Temporal Self-Attention Network (STSAN), to model time and distance intervals through a decay function and incorporate the weight values into a self-attention block for next POI recommendation.
- We introduce a simple but effective way to adaptively measure the importance of spatial and temporal weight, which can capture the spatio-temporal preferences of different users.
- We conduct extensive experiments on two representative real-world datasets, i.e., Gowalla and Foursquare, to demonstrate the effectiveness of our proposed model. The experimental results show that our proposed STSAN outperforms state-of-the-art methods, especially RNN-based models.

2   Related Work

In this section, we give a brief review of POI recommendation and discuss related work from two aspects, which are traditional POI recommendation and leveraging neural networks for POI recommendation.

2.1   Traditional POI Recommendation

Matrix Factorization (MF) is a traditional method to learn users' general taste, which factorizes a user-item rating matrix into two lower dimensionality matrices, each of which represents the latent factors of users or items [11]. Cheng et al. [1] firstly fused MF with geographical and social influence by modeling the probability of a user's check-in as a Multi-center Gaussian Model for POI recommendation. Yao et al. [20] extended the traditional MF-based approach by exploiting a high-order tensor instead of a traditional user-item matrix to model multi-dimensional contextual information. Another line of work focuses on Markov Chain based methods, which estimate an item-item transition matrix and use it for predicting next item. For instance, FPMC fuses matrix factorization and first-order Markov Chains to capture the long-term preference and short term transitions respectively [14]. FPMC-LR employs FPMC to model the personalized POI transitions and aims to recommend POIs for next hours by merging consecutive check-ins in previous hours [2]. PRME, proposed by [5], uses a metric embedding method to model the sequential patterns of POIs. He et al. [6] further proposed a tensor-based latent model, which fuses the observed successive check-in behavior with the latent behavior preference of each user to address a personalized next POI recommendation problem.

2.2 Neural Networks for POI Recommendation

With the impressive achievement of deep learning methods in different domains such as computer vision and natural language processing, there exist various methods employing and extending deep neural networks for POI recommendation. Yang et al. [18] proposed a deep neural architecture named PACE, which jointly learns the embeddings of users and POIs to predict both user preferences and various context associated with users and POIs. Zhang et al. [23] presented a unified framework named NEXT to learn user's next movement intention and incorporate meta-data information and temporal contexts for next POI recommendation. Recurrent Neural Network (RNN) has been successfully employed to capture users' dynamic preferences from the sequence of check-ins. ST-RNN [13], which employs time-specific and distance-specific transition matrices to characterize dynamic time intervals and geographical distances respectively, was first proposed to model the spatial and temporal contexts for the next location prediction. Recently, HST-LSTM was proposed to mitigate the data sparsity in the location prediction problem by combining the spatio-temporal influences into the LSTM model [10]. A more recent work STGN equipped LSTM with the new time and distance gates to model time and distance intervals between neighbor check-ins and extract users' long-term and short-term interests [24]. Though RNN-based methods are efficient in modeling sequential patterns, they still suffer from several weaknesses, such as large time consuming, being hard to parallelize and preserve long-range dependencies.

3 Our Approach

In this section, we first formalize the problem statement of next POI recommendation and then present the architecture of our Spatio-Temporal Self-Attention Network (STSAN) for next POI recommendation.

3.1 Problem Statement

In the setting of next POI recommendation, we denote a set of users as $U = \{u_1, u_2, ..., u_{|U|}\}$ and a set of POIs as $V = \{v_1, v_2, ..., v_{|V|}\}$, where $|U|$ and $|V|$

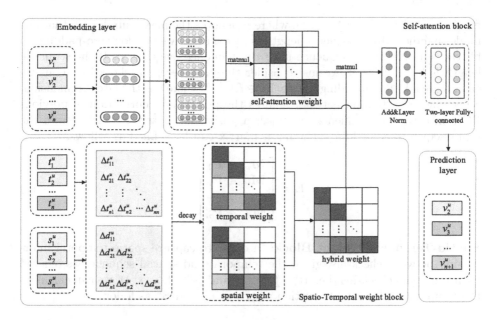

Fig. 1. The architecture of our proposed STSAN.

are the number of users and POIs respectively. For a user $u \in U$, we use $L^u = (v_1^u, v_2^u, ..., v_{|L|}^u)$ to denote a sequence of check-ins in chronological order. And each check-in record v_i^u is associated with its timestamp t_i^u and its geographic coordinates s_i^u of a POI. The goal of next POI recommendation is to predict possible top-k POIs that a user may visit at next time step, given the user historical check-ins.

3.2 Spatio-Temporal Self-Attention Network

As we mentioned above, spatial and temporal information is essential in POI recommendation. Thus, we propose a spatio-temporal self-attention network (STSAN) to integrate time and distance intervals into a self-attention block through a decay function. As shown in Fig. 1, STSAN consists of four components, i.e., Embedding layer, Spatio-Temporal weight block, Self-attention block and Prediction layer. Specifically, we first transform the sparse representation of POIs (i.e., one-hot representation) into a unique latent vector. This latent vector has a lower dimension and can capture precise semantic relationships between POIs. For spatial and temporal context, we utilize a decay function to measure the importance of time and distance intervals, forming a hybrid weight matrix. Then a user's sequential patterns are learned by a self-attention network, where the hybrid weight matrix is integrated into. Finally, we predict the next POI with a higher probability score.

Embedding Layer: As the length of user's check-in sequence is not fixed, we transform the training sequence $L^u = (v_1^u, v_2^u, ..., v_{|L|}^u)$ into a sequence with a fixed length $\hat{L}^u = (v_1^u, v_2^u, ..., v_n^u)$, where n denotes the maximum length that our model handles. If the sequence length is less than n, we employ zero-padding to fill the left side of the sequence until the sequence length is n. If the sequence length is larger than n, we just consider the most recent n check-ins. Thus we can create a POI embedding matrix $\mathbf{M} \in \mathbb{R}^{|V| \times d}$ where d is the latent dimension. Since the self-attention network ignores the positional information of previous POIs in a check-in sequence, we inject a positional matrix $\mathbf{P} \in \mathbb{R}^{n \times d}$ into the input sequence embedding. The input matrix can be defined as follows:

$$
\mathbf{E} = \begin{bmatrix} \mathbf{M}_{v_1} + \mathbf{P}_1 \\ \mathbf{M}_{v_2} + \mathbf{P}_2 \\ ... \\ \mathbf{M}_{v_n} + \mathbf{P}_n \end{bmatrix} \tag{1}
$$

Spatio-Temporal Weight Block: In order to capture spatio-temporal information between check-ins, given the temporal and spatial sequence associated with the user's check-ins (i.e., $(t_1^u, t_2^u, ..., t_n^u)$ and $(s_1^u, s_2^u, ..., s_n^u)$), we can calculate the temporal and spatial transition matrices $\mathbf{T}^u$ and $\mathbf{S}^u$ as follows:

$$
\mathbf{T}_{ij}^u = \begin{cases} \Delta t_{ij}^u, & i \geqslant j \\ 0, & i < j \end{cases} \tag{2}
$$

$$
\mathbf{S}_{ij}^u = \begin{cases} \Delta d_{ij}^u, & i \geqslant j \\ 0, & i < j \end{cases} \tag{3}
$$

where Δt_{ij}^u and Δd_{ij}^u are the time intervals and distance intervals between check-in v_i^u and check-in v_j^u respectively. Since the smaller the spatio-temporal intervals between two POIs, the more related the two POIs are. We use an interval-aware decay function to convert the time and distance intervals into an appropriate weight. Hence the temporal weight matrix $\hat{\mathbf{T}}^u$ and the spatial weight matrix $\hat{\mathbf{S}}^u$ can be calculated as follows:

$$
\hat{\mathbf{T}}_{ij}^u = \begin{cases} g(\Delta t_{ij}^u), & i \geqslant j \\ 0, & i < j \end{cases} \tag{4}
$$

$$
\hat{\mathbf{S}}_{ij}^u = \begin{cases} g(\Delta d_{ij}^u), & i \geqslant j \\ 0, & i < j \end{cases} \tag{5}
$$

where g is the decay function, which is defined as $g(x) = 1/log(e + x)$. Due to the nature of sequences, the model should consider only the previous POIs when predicting the current POI. Thus we employ the future blinding that ignores the influence of future POIs. That is to say, if POI v_j is behind POI v_i in a sequence, the attention score of v_i on v_j will be 0. What's more, spatial and temporal contexts are not always the same important for capturing the patterns of check-in sequence. For instance, a user may decide to visit a museum near the restaurant where he or she had dinner on the previous day. Although the time intervals of two check-ins are long (i.e., more than 24 h), the restaurant and the museum are close geographically. Thus we utilize a learnable weight factor α that the model can adjust adaptively while training to balance the influence of the spatial and temporal contexts. The hybrid weight is the adaptive combination of the temporal weight and the spatial weight, which is defined as follows:

$$\mathbf{H} = \alpha \cdot \hat{\mathbf{T}} + (1 - \alpha) \cdot \hat{\mathbf{S}}, \tag{6}$$

where $0 < \alpha < 1$. Finally we convert it through a linear projection:

$$\hat{\mathbf{H}} = \mathbf{W}\mathbf{H} + \mathbf{b}, \tag{7}$$

where $\mathbf{W} \in \mathbb{R}^{n \times n}$ is a global learnable projection matrix, and $\mathbf{b} \in \mathbb{R}^{n \times n}$ is the bias, which can capture the high-order spatio-temporal transition patterns of all check-in sequences and make the model more flexible.

Self-Attention Block: We can obtain the embedding matrix $\mathbf{E}$ from the above embedding layer as the input of self-attention block, given a check-in sequence $(v_1, v_2, ..., v_n)$. In order to model the transition patterns of the sequence, we use the self-attention network proposed by [16], which can capture the relationships between POIs in the sequence. Firstly, the scaled dot-product attention is defined as follows:

$$Attention(\mathbf{Q}, \mathbf{K}, \mathbf{V}) = softmax(\frac{\mathbf{Q}\mathbf{K}^T}{\sqrt{d}})\mathbf{V}, \tag{8}$$

where $\mathbf{Q}, \mathbf{K}, \mathbf{V}$ represent query, key, and value respectively, d denotes the latent dimension of each POI. In the self-attention block, the query, the key and the value are equal to $\mathbf{E}$. We also convert them to three matrices through a linear projection and feed them into an attention layer:

$$\mathbf{W}_{SA} = softmax(\frac{\mathbf{E}\mathbf{W}^Q(\mathbf{E}\mathbf{W}^K)^T}{\sqrt{d}}), \tag{9}$$

$$\mathbf{F} = STSA(\mathbf{E}) = \hat{\mathbf{H}}\mathbf{W}_{SA}(\mathbf{E}\mathbf{W}^V), \tag{10}$$

where $\mathbf{W}^Q, \mathbf{W}^K, \mathbf{W}^V \in \mathbb{R}^{d \times d}$ are the projection matrices and $\hat{\mathbf{H}}$ is the hybrid weight matrix obtained from the spatio-temporal weight block. We argue that layer normalization is beneficial for stabilizing and accelerating at the training process [12], which is defined as follows:

$$LayerNorm(\mathbf{x}) = \tilde{\alpha} \odot \frac{\mathbf{x} - \mu}{\sqrt{\sigma^2 + \epsilon}} + \tilde{\beta}, \tag{11}$$

where $\mathbf{x}$ is an input vector with all features of a sample, $\odot$ is an element-wise product (i.e., the Hadamard product), σ and μ are the variance and the mean of $\mathbf{x}$ respectively, $\tilde{\alpha}$ and $\tilde{\beta}$ are learned scaling factors and bias terms. Since existing methods have demonstrated that the last visited POI plays an important role on predicting next POI [7,14], we also utilize a residual connection to propagate the last POI's embedding to the final layer.

$$\hat{\mathbf{F}} = \mathbf{E} + LayerNorm(\mathbf{F}), \tag{12}$$

In order to learn more complex transitions between POIs, we apply a two-layer fully-connected layer with the ReLU activation function.

$$\mathbf{O} = ReLU(\hat{\mathbf{F}}\mathbf{W}_1 + \mathbf{b}_1)\mathbf{W}_2 + \mathbf{b}_2, \tag{13}$$

where $\mathbf{W}_1, \mathbf{b}_1, \mathbf{W}_2, \mathbf{b}_2$ are model parameters.

Prediction Layer: After the self-attention block, we predict the next POI based on $\mathbf{O}_t$, given the first t POIs. We calculate the user's preference for POIs through a dot product operation as follows:

$$r_{v_i,t} = \mathbf{O}_t \mathbf{M}_{v_i}^T, \tag{14}$$

where $r_{v_i,t}$ is the relevance of POI v_i being the next POI given the first t POIs. A high score r_{v_i} means a high relevance. $\mathbf{O}_t$ denotes the t-th line of $\mathbf{O}$, and $\mathbf{M} \in \mathbb{R}^{|V| \times d}$ is a POI embedding matrix. Note that the model inputs a sequence $(v_1, v_2, ..., v_n)$ and its excepted output is a 'shifted' version of the same sequence $(v_2, v_3, ..., v_{n+1})$. After training process, we can generate next POI recommendations by the last row of matrix $\mathbf{O}$.

3.3   Network Training

During the training process, we apply the binary cross-entropy loss as the optimization objective function of our model as follows:

$$-\sum_{v_i \in L^u} \sum_{t \in [1,2,...,n]} [log(\sigma(r_{v_i,t})) + \sum_{v_j \notin L^u} log(1 - \sigma(r_{v_j,t}))], \tag{15}$$

In each training epoch, for each target POI v_i in each sequence, we randomly sample a negative POI v_j. And we use Adam to optimize the parameters in our model, which is a variant of gradient descent and can adapt the learning rate for each parameter by performing a little update for frequent parameters and heavily update for infrequent parameters.

3.4   Complexity Analysis

Space Complexity: Compared with SASRec [9], whose total number of parameters is $O(|V|d + nd + d^2)$ from the embedding layer, self-attention layers, feed-forward networks and layer normalization, our proposed model needs to consider the time and the distance intervals of all POI pairs in a user's check-in sequence. Thus the space complexity of our model inevitably grows but is acceptable, which is $O(|U|n + |V|d + nd + d^2)$.

Time Complexity: The time complexity of our model consists mostly of the spatio-temporal weight block and the self-attention block. Hence it is $O(|U|n^2 + n_{epoch}n^2d)$, where n_{epoch} is the number of epochs at the training process. If the total number of users $|U|$ is equal to $n_{epoch}d$, our model will be about twice slower than the original self-attention network. Although the time

Table 1. Statistics of the datasets after preprocessing

Dataset	#User	#POI	#Check-in	Density
Gowalla	51089	106735	3136810	0.058%
Foursquare	3376	11860	584028	1.459%

complexity of our model increases to some extent for the computation of spatial and temporal transition matrices, the parallelism nature of the self-attention network has not been destroyed. Thus our model is also much faster than those RNN-based methods, whose computation on time step t should wait for the results of time step $t - 1$.

4 Experiments

In this section, we first describe datasets, evaluation metrics and baseline methods used in our experiments. Then we evaluate the performance of STSAN compared with the state-of-the-art baseline methods and analyze our experimental results.

4.1 Datasets

We conducted experiments on two public available LBSNs datasets (i.e., *Gowalla*[1] and *Foursquare*[2]), which have user-POI interactions, timestamps of check-ins and locations of POIs. *Gowalla* is a location-based social networking website where users share their locations by checking-in and the dataset was generated worldwide from February 2009 to October 2010 [3]. *Foursquare* contains check-ins in New York and Tokyo collected from April 2012 to February 2013 [19]. Each check-in of the two datasets is associated with its timestamp and geographic coordinates. For both datasets, we remove users with fewer than 10 check-ins and POIs visited by fewer than 10 users. The statistics of the two datasets are summarized in Table 1. We sort each user's check-ins according to the chronological order and take the early 70% of users' check-ins as the training data, the last 30% as the testing data.

4.2 Evaluation Metrics and Implementation Details

To evaluate the recommendation performance of STSAN and the baseline methods, we adopt two widely used evaluation metrics, i.e., Recall and Normalized Discounted Cumulative Gain (NDCG). Recall measures the accuracy of the recommendation. For an instance in the testing set, Recall@K is 1 if the visited POI appears in the set of top-K recommended POIs, and 0 otherwise. NDCG

---

[1] http://snap.stanford.edu/data/loc-gowalla.html.
[2] https://sites.google.com/site/yangdingqi/home/foursquare-dataset.

is a position-aware metric, which assigns larger weights on higher positions. In this paper, we choose $K = \{5, 10\}$ to illustrate different results of Recall@K and NDCG@K. In the default version of STSAN, we set the embedding size d to 100 on *Gowalla* and 50 on *Foursquare*. The maximum sequence length n is set to 50 on both datasets. Following [9], we implement our experiments in *Tensorflow* and apply the mini-batch Adam optimizer to optimize the parameters in our model. We set the learning rate to 0.001 initially. The number of epochs is set to 200, the batch size is 128 and we apply only one self-attention block.

4.3 Baselines

We compare our proposed model STSAN with the following representative methods, which are briefly described as follows.

- **RNN:** This is a traditional recurrent architecture, which only considers the sequence of POIs in its hidden unit while ignoring additional contextual information [21].
- **ST-RNN:** It replaces the single transition matrix in RNN to model spatio-temporal contexts by including time-specific and distance-specific transition matrices during model learning [13].
- **HST-LSTM:** It combines spatio-temporal influences into a LSTM model naturally to mitigate the data sparsity in the location prediction problem [10].
- **STGN:** Enhancing LSTM network, STGN introduces the spatio-temporal gates to capture the spatio-temporal relationships between successive check-ins [24]. We use its variation named STGCN, which uses couple input and forget gates.
- **SASRec:** This is a strong sequential model, which applies self-attention mechanisms to capture long-term sequential semantics [9].
- **T-SAN:** This is a variant of our proposed model with only temporal context.
- **S-SAN:** This is a variant of our proposed model with only spatial context.
- **STSAN:** This is our proposed model.

4.4 Performance Comparison

In this subsection, we analyze the performance of the proposed STSAN, comparing with eight baselines on two datasets. Our experimental results in terms of Recall@K and NDCG@K are shown in Table 2. From the table we can see the following observations: Compared with the standard RNN, ST-RNN, HST-LSTM, and STGN perform better on the two datasets. This confirms that incorporating time and distance information into the standard RNN architecture is critical for improving the POI recommendation performance. SASRec achieves a better performance, comparing with RNN-based methods. This confirms the advantages of self-attention mechanisms to model sequential patterns. Although ST-RNN, HST-LSTM and STGN take the spatio-temporal information into consideration,

Table 2. Experimental results of STSAN and baselines. The best performing method in each row is boldfaced.

Dataset	Method	Topk = 5		Topk = 10	
		Recall	NDCG	Recall	NDCG
Gowalla	RNN	0.0893	0.0674	0.1136	0.0756
	ST-RNN	0.0967	0.0706	0.1229	0.0792
	HST-LSTM	0.1128	0.0816	0.1433	0.0905
	STGN	0.1348	0.1020	0.1714	0.1139
	SAN	0.2093	0.1440	0.2812	0.1672
	T-SAN	0.2660	0.1896	0.3418	0.2140
	S-SAN	0.2369	0.1699	0.3092	0.1934
	STSAN	**0.3113**	**0.2287**	**0.3699**	**0.2478**
Foursquare	RNN	0.1206	0.0809	0.1799	0.0999
	ST-RNN	0.1306	0.1087	0.1867	0.1197
	HST-LSTM	0.2067	0.1546	0.2662	0.1738
	STGN	0.2366	0.1736	0.3018	0.1920
	SAN	0.3966	0.2746	0.5140	0.3126
	T-SAN	0.4177	0.2922	**0.5286**	0.3282
	S-SAN	0.4046	0.2871	0.5149	0.3229
	STSAN	**0.4243**	**0.3033**	0.5221	**0.3350**

they perform worse than SASRec, which may be due to the weakness of RNN architectures. Finally, our proposed model STSAN achieves the best recommendation performance regardless of the datasets and the evaluation metrics. This proves that STSAN can better capture long-term and short-term preferences like SASRec. Although SASRec has also achieved a better result than RNN-based methods, it cannot incorporate the time and the distance intervals, which are essential for POI recommendation. Our proposed STSAN outperforms SASRec as the time and the distance intervals can be correctly combined into the self-attention block.

4.5 Discussions

In this subsection, we explore the effectiveness of spatio-temporal components in our architecture via an ablation study and investigate the influence of hyperparameters.

Effectiveness of Spatio-Temporal Context: In order to explore the effectiveness of spatial and temporal context, we illustrate the performance of SASRec, T-SAN, S-SAN and STSAN in Table 2. SASRec applies the original self-attention block following [9]. Both T-SAN and S-SAN are variants of our proposed model with only temporal context or spatial context respectively. For T-SAN, we replace the hybrid weight matrix **H** as the temporal transition matrix

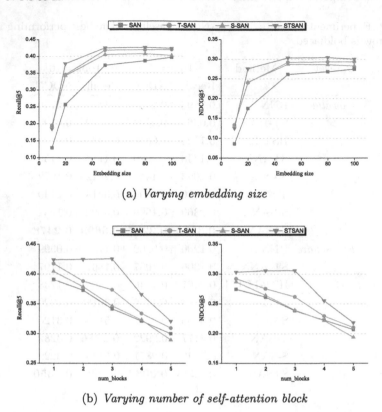

(a) *Varying embedding size*

(b) *Varying number of self-attention block*

Fig. 2. Performance with different embedding sizes and number of self-attention block.

$\hat{\mathbf{T}}$ calculated by Eq. (2). For S-SAN, the hybrid weight matrix $\mathbf{H}$ is replaced by the spatial transition matrix $\hat{\mathbf{S}}$ calculated by Eq. (3). As we can see from the experimental results, both T-SAN and S-SAN outperform SASRec. This suggests that incorporating the temporal weight and the spatial weight into self-attention block yields a significant improvement in POI recommendation. Moreover, STSAN combines spatial and temporal context through dynamically learning to give the proper weight to spatial and temporal transition matrices. Thus, it achieves the best performance among these methods. This means that time and distance intervals are both critical for improving the recommendation performances.

Influence of Hyper-parameters: Figure 2(a) shows the performance of four self-attention based models with different embedding sizes on *Foursquare*. As we can see from our experimental results, high dimensions can capture more characteristic information of POIs. On the other hand, the performance of four models is almost unchanged when the embedding size exceeds 50. This demonstrates that the model with a larger dimension cannot capture more useful patterns of POIs. The original self-attention mechanism (Transformer) proposed by [16]

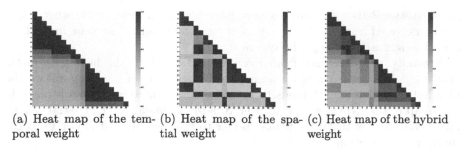

(a) Heat map of the temporal weight

(b) Heat map of the spatial weight

(c) Heat map of the hybrid weight

Fig. 3. Visualization of the spatio-temporal weight at random sampled sequences of user A on *Foursquare*.

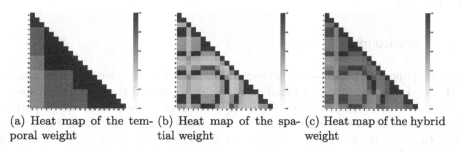

(a) Heat map of the temporal weight

(b) Heat map of the spatial weight

(c) Heat map of the hybrid weight

Fig. 4. Visualization of the spatio-temporal weight at random sampled sequences of user B on *Foursquare*.

stacks several self-attention blocks to capture complicated sequential patterns. We conduct the experiments of our model with varying the number of self-attention blocks on *Foursquare*. Figure 2(b) shows that a larger number of self-attention blocks cannot significantly improve the recommendation performance. This may be because the hierarchical self-attention structure may increase the number of model parameters and the model may suffer over-fitting.

4.6   Visualization of Attention Weight

As we mentioned above, different users may have different spatio-temporal interests. In this subsection, we seek to reveal the different influence of time and distance intervals on the check-in sequences of different users through the visualization of three weight matrices (i.e., the temporal weight matrix $\hat{\mathbf{T}}$, the spatial weight matrix $\hat{\mathbf{S}}$ and the hybrid weight matrix $\mathbf{H}$). We randomly choose two check-in sequences among all users and convert these three weight matrices of each sequence into heat maps as shown in Fig. 3 and 4, which only shows the last 20 positions of each sequence. From the visualizations, we can conclude as follows.

Firstly, the heat map of the temporal weight indicates that more recent POIs will obtain more attention (a higher weight) due to the decay function. In reality, two POIs that a user visited in a short time tend to have similar characteristics.

Similarly, two POIs with short distance intervals are related to each other, which can be depicted from the heat map of the spatial weight. The heat map of the hybrid weight is a fusion of the two heat maps above.

Secondly, as we can see from Fig. 3(c) and Fig. 4(c), the heat map of the hybrid weight of user A is more similar to the heat map of the temporal weight. This indicates that user A tends to be more time focused. On the contrary, the heat map of the hybrid weight of user B is more similar to the spatial weight. This demonstrates that user B may prefer to walk out so that closer POIs can obtain more attention.

Overall, the visualizations of the spatio-temporal weight show the effectiveness of our proposed model in dynamically capturing users' spatial and temporal preferences.

5   Conclusion

In this paper, we proposed a spatio-temporal self-attention based model named STSAN for next POI recommendation. We incorporated the time and distance intervals between check-ins in a sequence to enhance the recommendation performance of standard self-attention networks. Specifically, we designed a decay function to obtain the weight of spatio-temporal intervals. Furthermore, we combined the spatial and the temporal weight dynamically to capture the spatio-temporal interests of the user through an adaptive factor. Extensive experimental results on two real-world datasets showed that STSAN outperforms the state-of-the-art methods. This demonstrates the effectiveness of our STSAN in modeling the spatio-temporal information into the self-attention network. In the future, we will consider richer context information, such as social relationships and textual contents to further improve the performance for next POI recommendation.

Acknowledgements. This research was partially supported by NSFC (No. 61876117, 61876217, 61872258, 61728205), Open Program of Key Lab of IIP of CAS (No. IIP 2019-1) and PAPD.

References

1. Cheng, C., Yang, H., King, I., Lyu, M.R.: Fused matrix factorization with geographical and social influence in location-based social networks. In: AAAI (2012)
2. Cheng, C., Yang, H., Lyu, M.R., King, I.: Where you like to go next: successive point-of-interest recommendation. In: IJCAI, pp. 2605–2611 (2013)
3. Cho, E., Myers, S.A., Leskovec, J.: Friendship and mobility: user movement in location-based social networks. In: SIGKDD, pp. 1082–1090. ACM (2011)
4. Chung, J., Gulcehre, C., Cho, K., Bengio, Y.: Empirical evaluation of gated recurrent neural networks on sequence modeling. arXiv preprint arXiv:1412.3555 (2014)
5. Feng, S., Li, X., Zeng, Y., Cong, G., Chee, Y.M., Yuan, Q.: Personalized ranking metric embedding for next new POI recommendation. In: IJCAI, pp. 2069–2075 (2015)

6. He, J., Li, X., Liao, L., Song, D., Cheung, W.K.: Inferring a personalized next point-of-interest recommendation model with latent behavior patterns. In: AAAI, pp. 137–143 (2016)
7. He, R., McAuley, J.: Fusing similarity models with Markov chains for sparse sequential recommendation. In: ICDM, pp. 191–200. IEEE (2016)
8. Hochreiter, S., Schmidhuber, J.: Long short-term memory. Neural Comput. 9(8), 1735–1780 (1997)
9. Kang, W.C., McAuley, J.: Self-attentive sequential recommendation. In: ICDM, pp. 197–206. IEEE (2018)
10. Kong, D., Wu, F.: HST-LSTM: a hierarchical spatial-temporal long-short term memory network for location prediction. In: IJCAI, pp. 2341–2347 (2018)
11. Koren, Y., Bell, R.M., Volinsky, C.: Matrix factorization techniques for recommender systems. IEEE Comput. 42(8), 30–37 (2009)
12. Lei Ba, J., Kiros, J.R., Hinton, G.E.: Layer normalization. arXiv preprint arXiv:1607.06450 (2016)
13. Liu, Q., Wu, S., Wang, L., Tan, T.: Predicting the next location: a recurrent model with spatial and temporal contexts. In: AAAI, pp. 194–200 (2016)
14. Rendle, S., Freudenthaler, C., Schmidt-Thieme, L.: Factorizing personalized Markov chains for next-basket recommendation. In: WWW, pp. 811–820. ACM (2010)
15. Tan, Z., Wang, M., Xie, J., Chen, Y., Shi, X.: Deep semantic role labeling with self-attention. In: AAAI, pp. 4929–4936 (2018)
16. Vaswani, A., et al.: Attention is all you need. In: NIPS, pp. 5998–6008 (2017)
17. Xu, C., et al.: Graph contextualized self-attention network for session-based recommendation. In: Kraus, S. (ed.) IJCAI, pp. 3940–3946 (2019)
18. Yang, C., Bai, L., Zhang, C., Yuan, Q., Han, J.: Bridging collaborative filtering and semi-supervised learning: a neural approach for poi recommendation. In: SIGKDD, pp. 1245–1254. ACM (2017)
19. Yang, D., Zhang, D., Zheng, V.W., Yu, Z.: Modeling user activity preference by leveraging user spatial temporal characteristics in LBSNs. IEEE Trans. 45(1), 129–142 (2015)
20. Yao, L., Sheng, Q.Z., Qin, Y., Wang, X., Shemshadi, A., He, Q.: Context-aware point-of-interest recommendation using tensor factorization with social regularization. In: SIGIR, pp. 1007–1010. ACM (2015)
21. Yu, F., Liu, Q., Wu, S., Wang, L., Tan, T.: A dynamic recurrent model for next basket recommendation. In: SIGIR, pp. 729–732. ACM (2016)
22. Zhang, T., et al.: Feature-level deeper self-attention network for sequential recommendation. In: Kraus, S. (ed.) IJCAI, pp. 4320–4326 (2019)
23. Zhang, Z., Li, C., Wu, Z., Sun, A., Ye, D., Luo, X.: Next: a neural network framework for next POI recommendation. arXiv preprint arXiv:1704.04576 (2017)
24. Zhao, P., et al.: Where to go next: a spatio-temporal gated network for next POI recommendation. In: AAAI, pp. 5877–5884 (2019)
25. Zhou, C., et al.: Atrank: an attention-based user behavior modeling framework for recommendation. In: AAAI, pp. 4564–4571 (2018)
26. Zhu, Y., et al.: What to do next: modeling user behaviors by time-LSTM. In: IJCAI, pp. 3602–3608 (2017)

Joint Cooperative Content Caching and Recommendation in Mobile Edge-Cloud Networks

Zhihui Ke[1,2], Meng Cheng[3], Xiaobo Zhou[1,2(✉)], Keqiu Li[1,2], and Tie Qiu[1,2]

[1] College of Intelligence and Computing, Tianjin University, Tianjin 300350, China
{ke_zhihui,xiaobo.zhou,keqiu,qiutie}@tju.edu.cn
[2] Tianjin Key Laboratory of Advanced Networking (TANK), Tianjin, China
[3] School of Information Science, Japan Advanced Institute of Science and Technology
(JAIST), Nomi, Ishikawa 923-1292, Japan
m-cheng@jaist.ac.jp

Abstract. In mobile edge-cloud networks, multiple edge nodes form a mesh network to cooperate with each other. To maximize the benefit of resource-limited edge nodes, the content providers jointly optimize the content caching and recommendation decisions. However, the cooperation between edge nodes complicates both the content caching and recommendation decisions. To solve this problem, in this paper, we propose an efficient joint cooperative content caching and recommendation scheme in edge-cloud networks. Specifically, we formulate the joint cooperative content caching and recommendation problem as an integer-linear programming problem to minimize the average download delay, with controllable user preference distortion tolerance. We propose an efficient heuristic algorithm to solve the formulated problem due to its NP-hardness. We evaluate the performance of the proposed scheme with the MovieLens dataset. The simulation results demonstrate that the proposed scheme can decrease the average download latency by up to 37% and improve average cache hit rate by up to 24%, as compared with state-of-the-art solutions.

Keywords: Edge-cloud networks · Content caching ·
Recommendation system · Edge computing

1 Introduction

With the paradigm shift from mobile cloud computing to mobile edge computing, mobile edge-cloud (MEC) network has emerged as a promising solution to address the conflict between explosively increasing mobile traffic data caused by 5G, Internet of Things (IoT) [3,15] or Intelligent Connected Vehicle (ICV) [16] and the scarce backhaul network bandwidth. In mobile edge-cloud networks, the content providers (CPs) can cache some of its content items in edge nodes that is in the close proximity of mobile users. Since the requests of these content

© Springer Nature Switzerland AG 2020
X. Wang et al. (Eds.): APWeb-WAIM 2020, LNCS 12317, pp. 424–438, 2020.
https://doi.org/10.1007/978-3-030-60259-8_31

items can be served at the edge node, benefits are obtained such as redundant data transmission reduction, backhaul network bandwidth saving, user quality of experience (QoE) improvement, etc [19]. As the storage space of edge nodes are limited to cache all the content items, the content caching policy have to be properly designed to maximize the benefits of MEC network [10].

Various content caching polices have been proposed during the past decade, of which the average download delay and cache hit rate are two important performance metrics. To maximize the cache hit rate, a natural design is to rank the content items according to its popularity which usually follows Zipf distribution, and cache the top K content items in the edge node [14]. Note that in MEC networks, all edge nodes forms a mesh network and can cooperate with each other [12]. More specifically, a user request that can not only be served by the local edge node but also by its neighboring nodes which have the item. In the worst case, this request will be directed to the cloud platform. Obviously, the cooperation between edge nodes further improve the cache hit rate and reduce the average download delay. Taking the cooperation between edge nodes into consideration, several cooperative content caching policies were proposed recently to maximize the cache hit rate and minimize the download delay, which utilize the convex optimization method [8,18] or deep reinforcement learning method [9,20]. Nevertheless, these popularity based content caching policies assume that the popularity of content items is pre-known, or at least can be accurately predicted, which is difficult in practical scenarios where the preferences of users change dynamically.

Recently, more and more CPs use recommendation systems to generate personalized recommendation lists of short videos, songs, movies or other content items to cater the preference of individual users. Recommendation system not only improves the satisfaction of users but also boosts the number of content requests. For example, more than 80% video traffic are driven by recommendation system at Netflix [5]. In MEC networks, the content caching and recommendation policies of the CP are mutually dependent and interacting. On the one hand, the recommendation lists will change the user request statistics, which further affect the content caching policy. On the other hand, the recommendation system are prone to recommend the content items that cached in the edge node to maximize the cache hit rate. In view of this, some researchers propose to jointly design and optimize the content caching and recommendation policies in small cell networks where a single edge node is deployed [1,2,11] or multiple edge nodes without cooperation [6]. However, due to the fact that the cooperation between edge nodes complicates both the content caching and recommendation policies, an efficient joint cooperative content caching and recommendation scheme is still missing in MEC networks.

In this paper, inspired by [1,2,11], we propose an efficient joint cooperative content caching and recommendation scheme in MEC networks. The main contributions of this paper are summarized as follows.

1. We formulate the joint content caching and recommendation problem as integer-linear programming (ILP) to minimize the average download latency, where the cooperation between edge nodes is taken into account.
2. We propose an approximate but practical heuristic algorithm to solve the ILP problem formulated due to its NP-hardness. First, the original problem is decoupled into two subproblems, recommendation-aware cooperative content caching problem and caching-aware recommendation problem. Lagrangian relaxation and dual decomposition methods were used to further decompose the recommendation-aware cooperative content caching problem into two subproblems and subgradient method is employed to solve it. We also propose an efficient algorithm to deal with the caching-aware recommendation problem.
3. We evaluate the performance of the proposed algorithm using real world dataset. Experiment results demonstrate that the proposed algorithm can efficiently improve caches performance and decrease the average download latency in comparison with existing caching strategies.

The reminder of this paper is organized as follows. In Sect. 2, we introduce the system model. In Sect. 3, we formulate the joint cooperative content caching and recommendation problem as an ILP problem to minimize the average download delay. The heuristic algorithm to solve the ILP problem formulated is detailed in Sect. 4. In Sect. 5 we present simulation results to evaluate the performance of the proposed algorithm. Finally, we conclude the paper in Sect. 6.

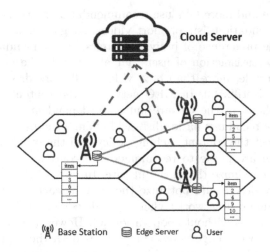

Fig. 1. A MEC based cooperative caching region.

2   System Model

2.1   Network Model

We consider a MEC network which consists of a cloud server and N base stations (BSs), as shown in Fig. 1. Each BS has equipped with an edge server E_n, $n = 1, 2, \cdots, N$ with storage capacity S_n. E_n is connected to the cloud server via the backhaul link with a data transmission rate $d_{n,0}$. Besides, all the edge servers are connected with each other to form a mesh network, where $d_{n,m}$ denotes the data transmission rate between E_n and E_m, $m = 1, 2, \cdots, N$, $m \neq n$.

Assume there is a CP deploy its network service in this MEC network to serve U users that randomly scattered over the coverage areas of all the BSs. Let U_n denote the number of users within the coverage area of BS n, we have $U = \sum_{n=1}^{N} U_n$. The CP has in total I content items, where s_i denotes the size of item i, $i = 1, 2, \cdots, I$. The CP deploys its content items at the cloud server, and also caches a part of the items at the edge servers. When a user in the coverage area of BS n requests item i, it will be delivered in three ways. (1) Local delivery: if E_n has cached item i, then it will deliver item i to the user directly. (2) Inter-edge delivery: if E_n has not cached item i but another edge servers has, E_n will fetch item i from the other edge server and then deliver it to the user. (3) Cloud delivery: if none of the edge servers has cached item i, E_n will fetch it from the cloud server and then deliver it to the user.

Let $\mathbf{y} = \{y_{n,i}, n \in [1, N], i \in [1, I]\}$ denote the caching decision, where $y_{n,i} = 1$ indicates item i is cached at E_n, and $y_{n,i} = 0$ otherwise. Let $\mathbf{z} = \{z_{n,i,m}, n, m \in [1, N], i \in [1, I]\}$ denote the content delivery decision, where $z_{n,i,m} = 1$ indicates an inter-edge delivery of item i from E_m to E_n, and $z_{n,i,m} = 0$ otherwise. Obviously, we have $z_{n,i,n} = y_{n,i}, \forall n \in [1, N], \forall i \in [1, I]$. We denote the download delay of cloud delivery as $L_{n,i,0}$, so we have $L_{n,i,0} = s_i/d_{n,0}$. Similarly, we denote the download delay of local delivery and inter-edge delivery as $L_{n,i,m}$, where

$$L_{n,i,m} = \begin{cases} 0, & \text{if } m = n, \\ s_i/d_{n,m}, & \text{if } m \neq n. \end{cases} \tag{1}$$

2.2   Recommendation Model

Apparently, different users have different preference on the content items, which can be obtained via conventional recommendation algorithms (e.g., collaborative filtering) based on the comments or visiting history of the users. Denote the preference of users as $\mathbf{q} = \{q_{u,i}, u \in [1, U], i \in [1, I]\}$, where $0 \leq q_{u,i} \leq 1$ is the preference of user u on item i. After obtaining $\mathbf{q}$, the recommendation system selects the top R items and recommend them to user u.

To allow some flexibility to adapt to the cache decisions, we introduce a recommendation window for user u that contains the top K_u items according to the preference, where $R \leq K_u \leq I$. Let $\mathcal{W}_u$ denote the set of candidate items inside the recommendation window. Then the CP will select R items from $\mathcal{W}_u$ according to some selection criteria and recommended them to user u.

In the best case, the CP recommends the top R items from the recommendation window to the user, which are exactly the top R items according the preference of the user. On the contrary, in the worst case, the CP recommend the bottom R items from the recommendation window to the user. Obviously, the quality of recommendation is deteriorated in the worst case. Here we introduce User Preference Distortion (UPD) to quantitatively measure the gap between the best and worst cases, which is expressed as [2]

$$T_u(K_u, R) = 1 - \frac{\sum_{i=K_u-R+1}^{K_u} q_{u,i}}{\sum_{i=1}^{R} q_{u,i}} \tag{2}$$

It can be seen from (2) that the window size K_u plays an important role in determining the caching efficiency and quality of recommendation. More specifically, with smaller K_u, the UPD is smaller, leading to better quality of recommendation. However, the cached content items may have less chance of being recommended. On the other hand, with larger K_u, more cached content items can be recommended to the user, however the UPD is also larger. The CP has to make a tradeoff between the caching efficiency and quality of recommendation. Let $t_u \in [0,1)$ denote the UPD tolerance, i.e., as long as $T_u(K_u, R) \leq t_u$, the user is satisfied with the recommendation result. Therefore, the maximum window size can be obtained as

$$K_u^* = \max\{K_u | T_u(K_u, R) \leq t_u\}. \tag{3}$$

2.3   User Request Model

Let $\mathbf{x} = \{x_{u,i}, u \in [1,U], i \in [1,I]\}$ denote the recommendation result, where $x_{u,i} = 1$ indicates item i is recommended to user u, and $x_{u,i} = 0$ otherwise. When R items are recommended to user u, these items will be requested with higher possibility. In other words, the recommendation result has an impact on the user request. To capture the impact of recommendation on user u, we introduce a vector $\mathbf{r}_u = [r_{u,1}, r_{u,2}, \cdots, r_{u,I}]$, where

$$r_{u,i} = x_{u,i} \cdot \frac{1}{R}. \tag{4}$$

The probability of user u requests item i can be obtained as

$$p_{u,i} = a_u \cdot r_{u,i} + (1 - a_u) \cdot q_{u,i}, \tag{5}$$

where a_u denotes the sensitivity of user u to the recommendation result.

Given the definitions above, the local content popularity $q_{n,i}$, i.e., the probability that item i requested by the users in the coverage of BS n, can be obtained as

$$q_{n,i} = \sum_{u=1}^{U_n} p_{u,i}. \tag{6}$$

3   Problem Formulation

The problem of joint cooperative caching and recommendation (JCCR) in mobile edge-cloud networks can be described as follows: for a given network topology, the storage capacity of each edge server and the preference of users, how should the CP place the content items on each edge server and which items should be recommended to users such that the average download latency is minimized? This is also equivalent to maximizing the cache hit rate. Therefore, the JCCR problem can be formulated as

$$\mathbf{P_1}: \quad \max_{\mathbf{x,y,z}} \sum_{n=1}^{N} \sum_{i=1}^{I} \sum_{m=1}^{N} q_{n,i} \cdot z_{n,i,m} \cdot (L_{n,i,0} - L_{n,i,m}) \tag{7}$$

$$\text{s.t.} \quad \sum_{i=1}^{I} s_i \cdot y_{n,i} \leq S_n, \quad \forall n \in [1,N] \tag{8}$$

$$z_{n,i,m} \leq y_{m,i}, \quad \forall n \in [1,N], i \in [1,I], m \in [1,N] \tag{9}$$

$$\sum_{m=1}^{N} z_{n,i,m} \leq 1, \quad \forall n \in [1,N], i \in [1,I] \tag{10}$$

$$\sum_{i \in \mathcal{W}_u} x_{u,i} = R, \quad \forall u \in [1,U] \tag{11}$$

$$x_{u,i} \in \{0,1\}, \quad \forall u \in [1,U], \forall i \in \mathcal{W}_u \tag{12}$$

$$y_{n,i} \in \{0,1\}, \quad \forall n \in [1,N], \forall i \in [1,I] \tag{13}$$

$$z_{n,i,m} \in \{0,1\}, \quad \forall n \in [1,N], \forall i \in [1,I], \forall m \in [1,N] \tag{14}$$

Constraint (8) ensures that the total size of the items cached on an edge server does not exceeds its storage capacity. Inequality (9) indicates that an item can be fetched from the edge server m only if it caches that item. Inequality (10) reflects the cooperation among the edge servers. Specifically, the users within the coverage of BS n will fetch item i from E_n if item i is cached on E_n. Otherwise, the users will fetch item i from another edge server that has this item. Constraint (11) guarantees R items within recommendation window are recommended to each user. Since $\mathbf{P_1}$ is an ILP problem which is NP-hard, in the next section, we propose a heuristic algorithm to solve this problem.

4   Algorithm Design

In this section, we present the heuristic algorithm designed to solve $\mathbf{P_1}$. As the content caching and recommendation are mutually dependent, solving $\mathbf{P_1}$ is intractable. Instead, we use a two stage approach, namely recommendation-aware cooperative content caching and caching-aware recommendation, to address the problem of cooperative content caching and recommendation respectively.

4.1   Recommendation-Aware Cooperative Content Caching

In the recommendation-aware cooperative content caching stage, first we set $K_u = R$ to obtain a tentative recommendation result as

$$x'_{u,i} = \begin{cases} 1, & \text{if item } i \in \mathcal{W}_u, \\ 0, & \text{otherwise.} \end{cases} \tag{15}$$

With $\mathbf{x}'$, $\mathbf{P}_1$ can be simplified as

$$\mathbf{P}_2: \quad \max_{\mathbf{y},\mathbf{z}} \sum_{n=1}^{N} \sum_{i=1}^{I} \sum_{m=1}^{N} q_{n,i} \cdot z_{n,i,m} \cdot (L_{n,i,0} - L_{n,i,m}) \tag{16}$$

$$\text{s.t.} \quad (8),(9),(10),(13),(14).$$

The cooperative caching problem $\mathbf{P}_2$ is still an ILP problem, but is a generalized assignment problem. We leverage Lagrangian relaxation and dual decomposition method [13] to solve the problem, as this problem is convex. By combining the objective function (16) and constraint (9) by Lagrangian multiplier $\boldsymbol{\eta} = \{\eta_{n,i,m}, \ n,m \in [1,N], \ i \in [1,I]\}$, the Lagrangian dual problem of $\mathbf{P}_2$ can be expressed as

$$\min_{\boldsymbol{\eta}} \quad L(\boldsymbol{\eta}) \tag{17}$$

$$\text{s.t.} \quad \eta_{n,i,m} \geq 0, \forall n \in [1,N], \forall i \in [1,I], \forall m \in [1,N],$$

where the Lagrangian function $L(\boldsymbol{\eta})$ is expressed as

$$L(\boldsymbol{\eta}) = \max_{\mathbf{y},\mathbf{z}} \left\{ \sum_{n=1}^{N} \sum_{i=1}^{I} \sum_{m=1}^{N} q_{n,i} \cdot z_{n,i,m} \cdot (L_{n,i,0} - L_{n,i,m}) \right.$$

$$\left. + \sum_{n=1}^{N} \sum_{i=1}^{I} \sum_{m=1}^{N} q_{n,i} \cdot \eta_{n,i,m} \cdot (y_{m,i} - z_{n,i,m}) \right\} \tag{18}$$

$$\text{s.t.} \quad (8),(10),(13),(14).$$

By separating $\mathbf{y}$ and $\mathbf{z}$, the Lagrangian function $L(\boldsymbol{\eta})$ can be further decomposed into two subproblems $\mathbf{P}_3$ and $\mathbf{P}_4$ as

$$\mathbf{P}_3: \quad \max_{y} \sum_{n=1}^{N} \sum_{i=1}^{I} \sum_{m=1}^{N} q_{n,i} \cdot \eta_{n,i,m} \cdot y_{m,i} \tag{19}$$

$$\text{s.t.} \quad (8),(13).$$

and

$$\mathbf{P}_4: \quad \max_{z} \sum_{n=1}^{N} \sum_{i=1}^{I} \sum_{m=1}^{N} q_{n,i} \cdot (L_{n,i,0} - L_{n,i,m} - \eta_{n,i,m}) \cdot z_{n,i,m} \tag{20}$$

$$\text{s.t.} \quad (10),(14).$$

respectively.

Algorithm 1. Recommendation-aware Cooperative Content Caching

Input: N, I, U, U_n, $q_{u,i}$, $L_{n,i,0}$, $L_{n,i,m}$, s_i, S_n
Output: y, z
1: Initialize $l = 0$, $\theta_1 = +\infty$, $\theta_2 = -\infty$, d=2, and assign η with random positive values;
2: Calculate $x'_{u,i}$, $\mathbf{r}_u$, $p_{u,i}$ and $q_{n,i}$ according to (15) (4), (5) and (6), respectively;
3: **while** termination criterion not satisfied **do**
4:    Calculate $\alpha_{m,i}$ according to (21);
5:    Obtain y by solving $\mathbf{P}_3$ with the DP algorithm;
6:    Update θ_2 according to (22);
7:    Obtain z according to (23);
8:    Update θ_1 according to (24);
9:    **if** θ_1 has not decreased for the last 10 consecutive iterations **then**
10:      d = d/2;
11:   **end if**
12:   Update η according to (25);
13:    $l = l + 1$;
14: **end while**
15: **return** y, z

After the decomposition, $\mathbf{P}_2$ can be solved in an iterative way, which is summarized in Algorithm 1. The key steps are as follow, where l denotes the index of iteration.

1. First, we fix η and solve P_1 to obtain the caching decision y (Lines 4–6). Apparently, $\mathbf{P}_3$ can be further decomposed into N independent one-dimensional knapsack problems if we regard

$$\alpha_{m,i} = \sum_i^N q_{n,i} \cdot \eta_{n,i,m} \tag{21}$$

as the profit of assigning item i to edge server E_m. Dynamic Programming(DP) algorithm can be then utilized to solve these independent knapsack problems [17]. Note that with y, we can solve P_2 using a greedy algorithm to obtain a lower bound θ_2. Denote the value of the objective function of (16) with y and the greedy algorithm as $v(O)$, we have

$$\theta_2 = \max\{\theta_2, v(O)\}. \tag{22}$$

2. Next, with the given η and y, we solve P_4 to obtain the content delivery decision z (Lines 7–8). Similarly, we further decompose P_4 into $N \times I$ one-dimensional knapsack problems, where the optimal solutions are given by

$$z_{n,i,m} = \begin{cases} 1, & \text{if } \beta_{n,i,m} = \max\{\beta_{n,i,m}|y_{m,i} = 1, m \in [1,N], m \neq n\}, \\ 0, & \text{otherwise.} \end{cases} \tag{23}$$

Here $\beta_{n,i,m} = q_{n,i} \cdot (L_{n,i,0} - L_{n,i,m} - \eta_{n,i,m})$. Note that after solving P_3 and P_4, we obtain a upper bound θ_1. Denote the value of $L(\eta)$ with $\mathbf{y}$ and $\mathbf{z}$ as $v(L)$, we have

$$\theta_1 = \min\{\theta_1, v(L)\}. \tag{24}$$

3. Finally, after obtaining $\mathbf{y}$ and $\mathbf{z}$, we update $\boldsymbol{\eta}$ by

$$\eta_{n,i,m} = [\eta_{n,i,m} - \lambda \cdot g_{n,i,m}]^+, \tag{25}$$

where $g_{n,i,m} = (y_{m,i} - z_{n,i,m}) \cdot q_{n,i}$ is the subgradient direction, $\lambda = d \cdot (\theta_1 - \theta_2)/\|\mathbf{g}\|^2$ is the step size (Lines 9–12). Parameter d is initially set as $d = 2$, and it will reduce to half of its current value if θ_1 does not decrease after 10 iterations.

The whole process is repeated until either one of the following conditions is met: (1) $l > 600$, (2) $d \leq 0.005$, (3) $(\theta_1 - \theta_2)/\theta_1 < 0.01$ and (4) θ_1 remains unchanged after 20 consecutive iterations.

In Algorithm 1, the time complexity of solving P_3 is $O(N \cdot I \cdot \max(S_n))$, moreover, the complexity of solving P_4 is $O(N \cdot I \cdot N) = O(I \cdot N^2)$. Therefore, the total computational complexity of Algorithm 1 is given by $O(U \cdot I + (N \cdot I \cdot \max(S_n) + I \cdot N^2) \cdot l) = O(N \cdot I \cdot \max(S_n, N) \cdot l)$.

4.2   Caching-Aware Recommendation

As stated above, the recommendation decisions of the CP is affected not only by the preference of the users, but also by the caching decision $\mathbf{y}$ and content delivery decision $\mathbf{z}$ obtained from Algorithm 1. Next, we show how to make the recommendation decision for user u in the coverage of BS n.

1. First, given the UPD tolerance t_u, we obtain the maximum window size K_u^* according to (3). Given the preference of users $\mathbf{q}$, the set of candidate items inside the recommendation window, $\mathcal{W}_u$, can also be obtained. We sort $\mathcal{W}_u$ in decreasing order according to the user preference, and obtain a new set $\mathcal{V}_u = \{v_u(k) \mid k \in [1, K_u^*], \ v_u(k) \in [1, I]\}$.
2. Reorder $\mathcal{V}_u$ as follows: for $v_u(k)$, $k = 1, 2, \cdots, K_u^*$, if $z_{n,v_u(k),n} = 0$, move $v_u(k)$ to the last position of $\mathcal{V}_u$.
3. Reorder $\mathcal{V}_u$ again as follows: for $v_u(k)$, $k = 1, 2, \cdots, K_u^*$, if $\sum_{m=1}^{N} z_{n,v_u(k),m} = 0$, move $v_u(k)$ to the last position of $\mathcal{V}_u$.
4. Finally, recommend the top R items of $\mathcal{V}_u$ to user u.

The procedures of caching-aware recommendation are summarized in Algorithm 2. The computational complexity is $O(U \cdot \max(K_u^*) + U \cdot \max(K_u^*) + U \cdot \max(K_u) \cdot I) = O(U \cdot \max(K_u^*) \cdot I)$.

5   Performance Evaluation

In this section, we evaluate the performance of the proposed scheme with the popular *MovieLens Dataset* [7]. We randomly select 600 users and 2000 movies,

Algorithm 2. Caching-aware Recommendation

Input: y, z, q, t_u;
Output: the recommendation list $\widetilde{R} = \{\widetilde{R}_u, u \in [1, U]\}$;
1: **for** $u \in [1, U]$ **do**
2:     Calculate K_u^* according to (3);
3:     Obtain $\mathcal{V}_u$ by reordering $\mathcal{W}_u$;
4:     **for** $k \in [1, K_u^*]$ **do**
5:       **if** $z_{n,v_u(k),n} = 0$ **then**
6:         Move $v_u(k)$ to the last position of $\mathcal{V}_u$;
7:       **end if**
8:     **end for**
9:     **for** $k \in [1, K_u^*]$ **do**
10:      **if** $\sum_{m=1}^{N} z_{n,v_u(k),m} = 0$ **then**
11:        Move $v_u(k)$ to the last position of $\mathcal{V}_u$;
12:      **end if**
13:     **end for**
14:     Add top R items of $\mathcal{V}_u$ to $\widetilde{R}_u$;
15: **end for**
16: **return** $\widetilde{R}$

---

where the data includes user ratings of movies in a 0–5 rating scale. Let $c_{u,i}$ denotes the ratings of user u on movie i. Then, the user preference can be obtained as

$$q_{u,i} = \frac{\sum_{v=1}^{U} \max\{0, sim(u,v)\} \cdot c_{v,i}}{\sum_{i=1}^{I} \sum_{v=1}^{U} \max\{0, sim(u,v)\} \cdot c_{v,i}}, \tag{26}$$

where $sim(u,v), u, v \in [1, U]$ is the similarity between user u and v which is obtained using collaborative filtering algorithm [4]. For simplicity, we assume the storage capacity of all the edge servers are the same. The other parameters for simulations are listed in Table 1.

Table 1. Simulation parameters

Parameter	Value
N	7
U	600
I	2000
s_i	$[1, 4]$
$d_{n,0}$	1
$d_{n,m}$	10
a_u	$(0.5, 0.7]$
t_u	$[0, 1]$

We compare the performance of the proposed scheme with other three schemes listed as follows.

1. Local Popularity Caching (**LPC**): This is a local content popularity based caching policy that is widely adopted, where each edge server caches the most popular items. Note that in LPC, the caching decisions are made purely based on content popularity without taking the recommendation decisions into account. The local content popularity can be obtained from (6) by setting $\mathbf{x} = \mathbf{0}$ and $a_u = 0$.
2. **CawR**: This is a joint caching and recommendation scheme proposed in [2], where the caching and recommendation decisions are made jointly for each edge server. However, in CawR, the edge servers can not communicate with each other.
3. **CawR-2**: This is an improved version of CawR. In CawR-2, the caching decisions are made in the same way as CawR. However, the recommendation decisions are made according to Algorithm 2.

The average download latency of the four schemes are shown in Fig. 2. As can be seen from the figure, the average download latency of all the four schemes decrease as the storage capacity increases from 20 to 100. However, the average download latency of CawR, CawR-2 and the proposed scheme decrease at a faster speed. Moreover, the average download latency of LPC is the highest. Compared with CawR, the average download latency of CawR-2 is reduced by 24% when the storage capacity is 100, which indicates the effectiveness of caching-aware recommendation algorithm proposed in this paper. Compared with CawR-2, there is around 13% performance gain with the proposed scheme when the storage size is 100. This shows the proposed recommendation-aware cooperative edge caching can further decrease the download latency. In other words, the proposed scheme achieves 37% performance gain compared with the original CawR scheme when the storage size is 100. It is also shown from the figure that the UPD tolerance has an impact on the average download latency. As compared with the case with $t_u = 0$, if the users can accept a small distortion (i.e., $t_u = 0.05$), the average download latency with CawR, CawR-2 and the proposed scheme can be further reduced by around 10%. It is also found from the figure that, the performance of CawR and CawR-2 decrease as the number of recommended items increase. However, the proposed scheme is more robust.

In Fig. 3, we show the average cache hit rate of the four schemes. The average cache hit rate of LPC is the lowest in all the cases. As the storage capacity of the edge servers increases from 20 to 100, the average cache hit rate also increases. This is because with larger storage capacity, more items can be cached at the edge servers. The average cache hit rate of the proposed scheme has around 13% and 24% gain over that of CawR-2 and CawR, respectively, which is consistent with the results shown in Fig. 2. It is also found that with t_u increases from 0 to 0.05, the average hit rate of CawR, CawR-2 and the proposed scheme also increases. This is because the recommendation window size is larger with $t_u = 0.05$, therefore the cached items are more likely to be recommended to the users. However, there is a tradeoff between the cache hit rate and the satisfaction

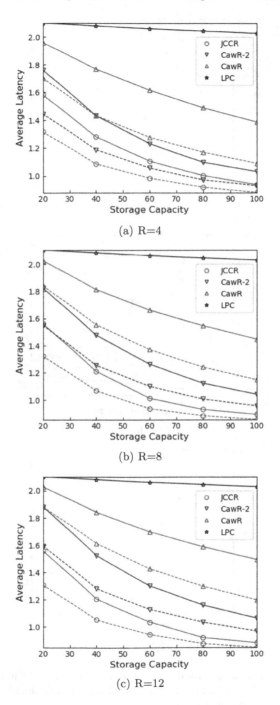

(a) R=4

(b) R=8

(c) R=12

Fig. 2. The average download latency of LPC, CawR, CawR-2 and the proposed scheme, where (a) $R = 4$, (b) $R = 8$ and (c) $R = 12$. Solid lines and dashed lines correspond to $t_u = 0$ and $t_u = 0.05$, respectively.

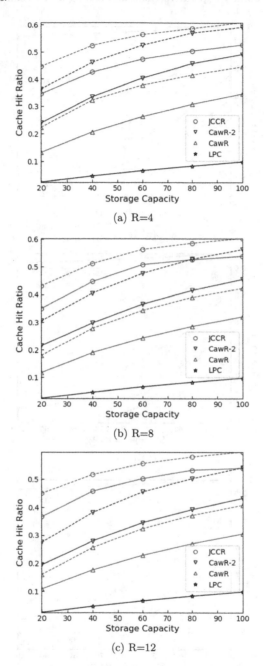

Fig. 3. The average cache hit rate of LPC, CawR, CawR-2 and the proposed scheme, where (a) $R = 4$, (b) $R = 8$ and (c) $R = 12$. Solid lines and dashed lines correspond to $t_u = 0$ and $t_u = 0.05$, respectively.

of users on the recommended items. If t_u is too large, the satisfaction of users might be hurt, resulting in the users turn to other competitive CPs.

6 Conclusion

In this paper, we propose an efficient joint cooperative content caching and recommendation scheme for edge-cloud networks where multiple edge nodes form a mesh network to cooperate with each other. First, we formulate the joint cooperative content caching and recommendation problem as an ILP problem. Then, we propose an efficient two-stage heuristic algorithm to solve the ILP problem since it is NP-hard. The first stage is recommendation-aware cooperative content caching, and the second stage is caching-aware recommendation. We validate the effectiveness of the proposed scheme with the MovieLens dataset. Experiment results demonstrated that the proposed scheme achieves superior performance as compared with the state-of-the-art solutions in terms of average download latency and average cache hit rate. A tradeoff between cache hit rate and the satisfaction of the users on the recommendation results is left as a future study.

Acknowledgments. This work is supported in part by National Key R&D Program of China under Grant 2018YFB1004700, in part by the National Natural Science Foundation of China under Grant No. 61702365, and also in part by the Natural Science Foundation of Tianjin under Grant No. 18ZXZNGX00040 and 18ZXJMTG00290.

References

1. Chatzieleftheriou, L.E., Karaliopoulos, M., Koutsopoulos, I.: Caching-aware recommendations: nudging user preferences towards better caching performance. In: IEEE INFOCOM 2017-IEEE Conference on Computer Communications, pp. 1–9. IEEE (2017)
2. Chatzieleftheriou, L.E., Karaliopoulos, M., Koutsopoulos, I.: Jointly optimizing content caching and recommendations in small cell networks. IEEE Trans. Mob. Comput. **18**(1), 125–138 (2018)
3. Chen, N., Qiu, T., Zhou, X., Li, K., Atiquzzaman, M.: An intelligent robust networking mechanism for the internet of things. IEEE Commun. Mag. **57**(11), 91–95 (2019)
4. Ekstrand, M.D., Riedl, J.T., Konstan, J.A., et al.: Collaborative filtering recommender systems. Found. Trends® Hum.-Comput. Interact. **4**(2), 81–173 (2011)
5. Gomez-Uribe, C.A., Hunt, N.: The netflix recommender system: algorithms, business value, and innovation. ACM Trans. Manag. Inf. Syst. (TMIS) **6**(4), 1–19 (2015)
6. Guo, K., Yang, C.: Temporal-spatial recommendation for caching at base stations via deep reinforcement learning. IEEE Access **7**, 58519–58532 (2019)
7. Harper, F.M., Konstan, J.A.: The movielens datasets: history and context. ACM Trans. Interact. Intell. Syst. (TiiS) **5**(4), 19 (2016)
8. Jiang, W., Feng, G., Qin, S.: Optimal cooperative content caching and delivery policy for heterogeneous cellular networks. IEEE Trans. Mob. Comput. **16**(5), 1382–1393 (2016)

9. Jiang, W., Feng, G., Qin, S., Liang, Y.C.: Learning-based cooperative content caching policy for mobile edge computing. In: ICC 2019–2019 IEEE International Conference on Communications (ICC), pp. 1–6. IEEE (2019)

10. Li, L., Zhao, G., Blum, R.S.: A survey of caching techniques in cellular networks: research issues and challenges in content placement and delivery strategies. IEEE Commun. Surv. Tutorials **20**(3), 1710–1732 (2018)

11. Liu, D., Yang, C.: A learning-based approach to joint content caching and recommendation at base stations. In: 2018 IEEE Global Communications Conference (GLOBECOM), pp. 1–7. IEEE (2018)

12. Mao, Y., You, C., Zhang, J., Huang, K., Letaief, K.B.: A survey on mobile edge computing: the communication perspective. IEEE Commun. Surv. Tutorials **19**(4), 2322–2358 (2017)

13. Palomar, D.P., Chiang, M.: A tutorial on decomposition methods for network utility maximization. IEEE J. Sel. Areas Commun. **24**(8), 1439–1451 (2006)

14. Qiu, L., Cao, G.: Popularity-aware caching increases the capacity of wireless networks. IEEE Trans. Mob. Comput. (2019)

15. Qiu, T., Li, B., Zhou, X., Song, H., Lee, I., Lloret, J.: A novel shortcut addition algorithm with particle swarm for multi-sink internet of things. IEEE Trans. Ind. Inform. (2019)

16. Siegel, J.E., Erb, D.C., Sarma, S.E.: A survey of the connected vehicle landscape–architectures, enabling technologies, applications, and development areas. IEEE Trans. Intell. Transp. Syst. **19**(8), 2391–2406 (2017)

17. Vazirani, V.V.: Approximation Algorithms. Springer, Heidelberg (2013)

18. Yang, L., Chen, Y., Li, L., Jiang, H.: Cooperative caching and delivery algorithm based on content access patterns at network edge. In: Leung, V.C.M., Zhang, H., Hu, X., Liu, Q., Liu, Z. (eds.) 5GWN 2019. LNICST, vol. 278, pp. 99–123. Springer, Cham (2019). https://doi.org/10.1007/978-3-030-17513-9_8

19. Yao, J., Han, T., Ansari, N.: On mobile edge caching. IEEE Commun. Surv. Tutorials **21**(3), 2525–2553 (2019)

20. Zhong, C., Gursoy, M.C., Velipasalar, S.: Deep multi-agent reinforcement learning based cooperative edge caching in wireless networks. In: ICC 2019–2019 IEEE International Conference on Communications (ICC), pp. 1–6. IEEE (2019)

Dual Role Neural Graph Auto-encoder for CQA Recommendation

Xing Luo, Yuanyuan Jin, Tao Ji, and Xiaoling Wang[✉]

Shanghai Key Laboratory of Trustworthy Computing, East China Normal University,
3663 North Zhongshan Road, Shanghai, China
xluo@stu.ecnu.edu.cn, seijyy@qq.com, taoji.cs@gmail.com,
xlwang@sei.ecnu.edu.cn

Abstract. Matching between questions and suitable users is an appealing and challenging problem in the research area of community question answering (CQA). Usually, different from the traditional recommendation systems where a user has only a single role, each user in CQA can play two different roles (dual roles) simultaneously: as a requester and as an answerer. For different roles, users usually have varying interests and expertise in different topics and knowledge domains, which is rarely addressed in the previous methods. Besides, based on an explicit single link between two users, existing methods cannot capture implicit associations between their possibly similar roles. Therefore, in this paper, we propose the structure of a dual role graph and employ the link prediction approach to make CQA recommendation on the graph. Moreover, we develop a *Dual Role Neural Graph auto-encoder* (DRNGae) framework, which can: 1) encode the dual role graph structure to capture the implicit dual role correlation by propagating high-order information embeddings of graph neural network; 2) learn variable weights with the dual role feature preferences from dual role content information by self-attention mechanism; 3) reconstruct the graph structure to predict the possible interaction links. Experimental studies on real-world datasets verify our design and prove that our model achieves significantly better performance than baselines in link prediction (95.3% AUC, 96.2% AP on Citeseer dataset) and CQA recommendation (79.5% recall@25, 76.7% ndcg@25 on Yahoo! answer dataset).

Keywords: CQA recommendation · Dual role graph · Graph neural network · Self-attention

1 Introduction

With the explosive growth of e-commerce and social media platforms, community question answering (CQA) has become more and more popular as a web service. People are sharing their knowledge (answering questions) and seeking information (requesting questions and getting answers). Typical Q&A websites

© Springer Nature Switzerland AG 2020
X. Wang et al. (Eds.): APWeb-WAIM 2020, LNCS 12317, pp. 439–454, 2020.
https://doi.org/10.1007/978-3-030-60259-8_32

like Yahoo! Answers[1] and Zhihu[2], where users can collide with the sparks of collective wisdom, make it more easily and accurately to find information what their needs.

Though CQA website advantages over traditional information retrieval, it has thousands of questions posted daily, which make it also faces several unique challenges. First, The large number of questions makes it difficult for a general user to find a suitable question to answer in a short time [5]. Second, [11] show that many questions cannot be resolved immediately, which means that requesters may have to wait a long time to get a satisfactory answer. So, if the site can automatically recommend new questions or suitable answerers, It can help questions to be answered as soon as possible, which will increase user engagement and benefit the development of CQA websites. Judging by this, providing recommendation service is an essential part of the CQA social network.

Since the explicit link between users' interaction, the recommendation is actually to predict the non-obvious association links between users and items in the network. Therefore, more and more researchers regard the recommendation task as a link prediction task, and the core problem is how to embed the bipartite graph of users and items. A user-item association graph-based algorithm is proposed for making collaborative filtering recommendations [2]. [3] proposes a ranking factor graph (RFG) model to capture the general social patterns of link formation in heterogeneous social networks. However, these approaches fail to capture high-order information about user-item interactions and ignores the different importance of node-independent content information. To solve it, We catch the high-order relations and content information by using graph neural network [9] and self-attention network [19] respectively.

As the particularity of CQA recommendation, each user in the CQA website can play two different roles (dual role) simultaneously: the requester and the answerer. We take an illustrative example to show the distinction and connection between the two roles of users. Fig. 1 lists some questions requested and answered by two users in CQA. As we can see, user A (a computer scientist) who as a requester only wants to learn cooking is more likely to request questions about cooking while as an answerer to answer many computer-related questions based on his specialty, the request and answer of user B (a chef) are the opposite of user A. Obviously, there is an implicit connection between the two roles: the preferences of a user in the two roles are different, and users may have similar relationships in some role. Hence, it is necessary to take into account both requester and answerer preferences of users simultaneously in CQA. [22] proposes a topic probabilistic framework, and modeling the two roles to analyze the latent topic information for users, but are not suitable for discovering and modeling the varies personality preferences on the same topic. To overcome this limitation, in this work, we naturally view CQA recommendation as a link prediction problem on a dual role graph, which can enhance answerer-question-requester interaction to embed different preferences of two roles.

---

[1] http://answers.yahoo.com/.
[2] http://www.zhihu.com/.

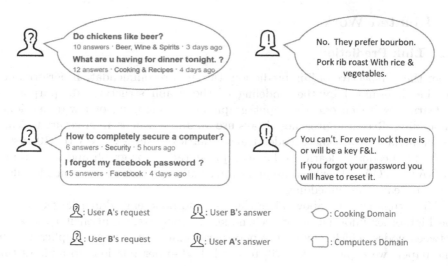

Fig. 1. An example of the user in CQA.

This paper proposes a Dual Role Neural Graph auto-encoder (DRNGae) framework to model the dual role preferences for CQA recommendation. Varying preferences of the two roles are learned by modeling explicit content features (e.g., answer text and question text) and implicit correlation. Specifically, we first construct an input graph with dual role that contains the interaction information, where the content features of the node can be embedded as optional components. Then, the graph neural network is used to capture the hidden dual role correlation by propagating high-order information embedding in the graph, and the self-attention network is used to calculate different weights for the two roles' different feature preferences from the content information. Finally, the graph structure is reconstructed to predict the possible interaction between the users and the questions through the auto-encoder structure.

To summarize, our major contributions include:

1. We propose a novel dual role neural graph-based auto-encoder framework for CQA recommendation, which explicitly models the different preferences of the users' two roles with implicit correlation.
2. We introduce the graph neural network to capture the implicit dual role correlation and self-attention mechanism focus on modeling different feature preferences for the dual role.
3. We achieve state-of-the art performance in link prediction (95.3% AUC, 96.2% AP on Citeseer dataset) and CQA recommendation (79.5% recall@25, 76.7% ndcg@25 on Yahoo! answer dataset).

2 Related Work

2.1 Link Prediction

From the perspective of link prediction, the final recommendation performance can be determined by the modeling of the graph structure. Its purpose is to learn how to encode the input graph into a mapping of low-dimensional embedding. Recent approaches always use an auto-encoder architecture to learn the embedding via some encoder transformation, like GAE/VGAE [10] use a GCN [9] encoder to learn the latent representation for graph and its variants ARGA/ARVGA [14], which use an adversarially regularized auto-encoder algorithm to learn the embedding.

Unfortunately, the above algorithms of the node embedding largely ignore the high-order information of each node. It can't extract implicit association between nodes, which may lead to poor performance in practical application. In this paper, we explore GNN [20] to catch high-order relations to address this issue.

2.2 Ranking Recommendation

Another related research is to learn a ranking model to generate the recommended list of recommendations. In recent years, more and more researches use the graph-based method, which exploits the interactions graph to catch user preference. For example, GC-MC [1] adopts GCN encoding the first-order neighbors to represent the users and items. HOP-Rec [23] enhances the user's representation through random walks in which the user interacts with multi-hop items to build the recommender model.

The most related work considering the dual roles in CQA is DRM [22], which maps the two roles of users into two asker and answerer space with a probabilistic framework. it proposes a dual role model (DRM) to modeling the latent topic information for users' embedding. However, the latent topics they get can not highlight the importance of different topics, which masks the individual differences between users on the same topic.

Despite their success, these approaches are not sufficient to detect implicit interactions between the dual roles of users for CQA recommendation since the dual roles hide the implicit interaction of users. In this work, we catch high-order relations to capture the implicit dual role interaction on a dual role graph by graph neural network, And utilize the self-attention network to represent the user's preferences of two roles.

3 DRNGae: Dual Role Neural Graph Auto-encoder

In this section, we first characterize our proposed Dual Role Neural Graph auto-encoder (DRNGae) framework, schematically depicted in Fig. 2, and formalize the notation used in it. And then introduce how to use the graph topology and node features to reconstruct the graph structure for predict the unobserved links.

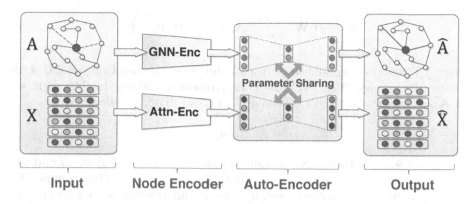

Fig. 2. Schematic depiction of the Dual Role Neural Graph auto-encoder (DRNGae) framework, which the Node Encoder learn the node representation and the Auto-Encoder is trained to reconstruct the graph structure to predict the hidden links (the red dashed linkes at Input denotes the unobserved possible links, then we predict them in the Output the red solid line). (Color figure online)

3.1 Problem Definition and Framework

As show in Fig. 2, the input is a undirected graph $G = \{A, X\}$. where $A \in \mathbb{R}^{N \times N}$ (N is the number of nodes), is an adjacency matrix representing the topological structure of the graph G, of which $A \in \{A_{ij} = 1, A_{ij} = 0\}^{N \times N}$, where 1 represents the currently known positive edge with node i and j, 0 represents the non-existent negative edge with node i and j, and $X \in \mathbb{R}^{N \times F}$ (F is the dimension of feature matrix embedding) is an optional feature matrix of available explicit features associated with each node, i.e. content information.

Give a graph G, our purpose is to map the topology of nodes a_i and the node features x_i to low-dimensional vectors $a_i^{gnn} \in \mathbb{R}^N$ and $x_i^{attn} \in \mathbb{R}^F$ by GNN network and Self-Attention network respectively in the node encoder part. And then, the auto-encoder architecture is to learn a set of low-dimensional latent variables $z_i \in \mathbb{R}^D$ (D is the dimension of embedding) with the formal format $\text{Enc}(a_i^{gnn}, x_i^{attn})$ that can generate approximate reconstruction vector $\hat{a}_i$ (at link prediction stage, we disregard the output $\hat{x}_i$), which minimizes the error between a_i and $\hat{a}_i$, thereby maintaining the global graph structure of A for predict the possible interaction links.

3.2 Node Encoder

GNN Encoder. In a (undirected) graph G, GNN is a multi-layer network. In each layer, the multi-hop neighbor informations can be aggregated to maintain a set of node representations.

As follows the graph neural network [9,20], let $\mathcal{N}(i)$ be neighbours of node i in G. We denotes a_i^l to be the node vector representation of i at the l-th GNN layer. a_i^l is obtained by:

$$a_i^l = g\left(\mathbf{W}^G \sum_{j \in \mathcal{N}(i)} \mathbf{A}_{ij}^l a_j^{l-1} + \mathbf{B}^G a_i^{l-1}\right) \tag{1}$$

where $g()$ denotes a non-linear activation function (we use Leaky-ReLU with negative input slope 0.1), $\{\mathbf{W}^G, \mathbf{B}^G\}$ are parameter matries. In this work, we set $\mathbf{A}_{ij}^1 = \mathbf{A}_{ij}, a_i^0 = a_i$, and $l = 3$, so a_i^{gnn} is equal to a_i^3, as follows:

$$a_i^{gnn} = a_i^3$$

We can see that the GNN naturally catches high-order relations to find the implicit correlation between nodes. Taking the first two layers for example [8]: for every node i at the second layer, a_i^2 contains information of its 1-hop neighbours a_j^1. Since a_j^1 has already encoded its own 1-hop neighbours at the first layer, a_i^2 actually encodes information of its 2-hop neighbours. In short, the new node representation a_i^l contains both the previous layer vector a_i^{l-1} and a weighted aggregation of neighbour vectors a_j^{l-1}. This is, $a_i^{gnn} = a_i^3$ is the new node representation of a_i which be an adjacency vector of the i-th node in $\mathbf{A}$.

Attn Encoder. Self attention is a special case of attention mechanism, which has been successfully applied to many research topics including NLP [19] and QA [12]. So in this paper, self-attention is applied to capture feature-ferture transitions of each node feature sequence itself without regard to their distances. We have the feature sequence embedding of each node feature $(\mathbf{x}_i)$, i.e., $\mathbf{x}_i = [x_i^1, x_i^2, ..., x_i^n]$. Then, we feed them into the self-attention layer to better capture the global feature preference. Lastly, each node feature (x_i^{attn}) after the attention layer can be formulated as:

$$x_i^{attn} = \text{mean-pooling}\left(\text{softmax}\left(\frac{(\mathbf{x}_i\mathbf{W}^Q)(\mathbf{x}_i(\mathbf{W}^K)^\top)}{\sqrt{d_k}}\right)(\mathbf{x}_i\mathbf{W}^V)\right) \tag{2}$$

where the projection matrices $\{\mathbf{W}^Q, \mathbf{W}^K, \mathbf{W}^V\}$ and d_k is the dimension of sequence embedding.

3.3 Auto-encoder

Encoder Model. We first get the new node representation vector a_i^{gnn} with high-order information by GNN Encoder module. And the aim of the encoder model $\text{Enc}(a_i^{gnn}, z_i)$ is : $\mathbb{R}^N \to \mathbb{R}^D$. We take a simple inference model parameterized by stacking two layers $(t = [0, 1])$:

$$z_i^{t+1} = \text{Enc}(a_i^{gnn}, z_i^t; \mathbf{W}^t, \mathbf{B}^t) \tag{3}$$

each layer of the network can be expressed with the function $\text{Enc}(a_i^{gnn}, z_i^t; \mathbf{W}^t, \mathbf{B}^t)$ as follows:

$$\text{Enc}(z_i^t, a_i^{gnn}; \mathbf{W}^t, \mathbf{B}^t) = \sigma(a_i^{gnn} \oplus z_i^t; \theta) \tag{4}$$

Here, z_i^t is the input for layer, and z_i^{t+1} is the output after layer. For simplicity, we set θ contains all the weight units parameters $\mathbf{W}^t$ and bias units parameter $\mathbf{B}^t$ which need to learn in the encoder model and $\sigma(\cdot)$ denotes a non-linear activation function (we use ReLU$(\cdot) = max(0, \cdot)$). $\oplus$ is the concat function. In this paper, if the feature matrix $\mathbf{X}$ is available, we set $z_i^0 = x_i^{attn} \in \mathbb{R}^F$, which can get by training with Attn encoder. So the set of low-dimensional latent variables $z_i \in \mathbb{R}^D$ is constructed as follows:

$$z_i^1 = \text{MLP}(a_i^{gnn} \oplus x_i^{attn}; \theta^0) \tag{5}$$

$$z_i^2 = \text{MLP}(a_i^{gnn} \oplus z_i^1; \theta^1) \tag{6}$$

this encoder model $\text{Enc}(z_i, a_i^{gnn}) = q(z_i|a_i^{gnn}, x_i^{attn})$ encodes both graph structure and node features into a representation $z_i = q(z_i|a_i^{gnn}, x_i^{attn}) = z_i^2$. Similarly, if the feature matrix $\mathbf{X}$ doesn't exist, encoder model $\text{Enc}(z_i, a_i^{gnn}) = q(z_i|a_i^{gnn})$ which only consider the graph structure $\mathbf{A}$. The next chapters are introduced by assuming $\mathbf{X}$ is available.

Decoder Model. Our decoder model aims to reconstruct the node vector a_i of the graph structure $\mathbf{A}$ to predict the unobserved links on it. For reconstructing it, we consider to stack two layers of the decoder part to obtain an approximate vector $(\hat{a_i}^{gnn} \oplus \hat{x_i}^{attn})$ of the graph node's high-order embedding and node feature's attention embedding as follows:

$$\hat{a_i}^{gnn} \oplus \hat{x_i}^{attn} = \text{Dec}(\hat{a_i}^{gnn}, \hat{x_i}^{attn}|z_i) \tag{7}$$

$$\text{Dec}(\hat{a_i}^{gnn}, \hat{x_i}^{attn}|z_i) = \text{MLP}\left(\text{MLP}(z_i; (\theta^1)^\top); (\theta^0)^\top\right) \tag{8}$$

and then training a link prediction layer to predicts the node vector $\hat{a_i}$ for link prediction:

$$\hat{a_i} = \text{MLP}(\hat{a_i}^{gnn}; (\mathbf{W}^G)^\top) \tag{9}$$

Inference and Learning. Many studies [1,21] have shown that parameter sharing is a very effective form of regularization, which helps to improve the learning and generalization ability of the model. So, we constrain our framework by sharing the weight units parameters $\mathbf{W}^t$ that can reduce parameters nearly twice as much as unconstrained architecture, but notice that the bias units parameters $\mathbf{B}^t$ do not share. The parameters θ are learned via backpropagation and optimized by minimizing the Masked Balanced Cross-Entropy (MBCE) [16] loss, which only allows the contribution of parameters related to the observation edge. However, the number of observed (positive) edges is usually significantly less than the number of un-observed (negative) edges, resulting in extreme class imbalance [13]. In this work, we define a weight factor ζ as the multiplier of positive class in the cross-entropy loss formula to deal with class imbalance. So, in the end, we can compute the MBCE loss of each node vector a_i as follows:

$$\mathcal{L}_{a_i} = -a_i log(\varphi(\hat{a_i})) \cdot \zeta - (1 - a_i)log(1 - \varphi(\hat{a_i})) \tag{10}$$

$$\mathcal{L}_{\text{MBCE}} = \frac{m_i \odot \mathcal{L}_{a_i}}{\sum m_i}. \tag{11}$$

Here, $\zeta = 1 - \frac{\# \text{ positive links}}{\# \text{ negative links}}$, $\varphi(\cdot)$ is the sigmoid function, $\odot$ is the Hadamard product, and m_i is the boolean function: $m_i = 0$, if $a_i = \mathbf{0}$, else $m_i = 1$.

Loss with Node Feature. Node feature, also called side information, can encode information complementary to the topological structure of the input graph, which has been proved to improve the prediction performance of the model [10, 21] significantly. If the explicit node features matrix $\mathbf{X} \in \mathbb{R}^{N \times F}$ is available, we can compute the augmented $\mathcal{L}$ loss which contains both graph structure and node feature informations to simply improve performance, and as follows:

$$\mathcal{L} = \mathcal{L}_{\text{MBCE}} + \mathcal{L}_{x_i} \tag{12}$$

$$\mathcal{L}_{x_i} = -x_i^{attn} log(\varphi(\hat{x}_i^{attn})) - (1 - x_i^{attn})log(1 - \varphi(\hat{x}_i^{attn})) \tag{13}$$

where x_i^{att} and $\hat{x}_i^{att}$ can be obtained through the Attn encoder module and Decoder Model calculation respectively.

4 Node Encoder: Dual Role GNN and Feature Self-attention

In this section, we first introduce how to use GNN to represent the higher-order information of nodes (a_i^{gnn}) to capture the implicit dual role correlation in dual role graph. Then we propose an attention-based model to modeling dual role feature preferences (x_i^{attn}) of a user with two roles.

4.1 Dual Role GNN

In a CQA website, each user always plays two different roles (dual role) simultaneously: the answerer and the requester. In light of this situation, we consider the decomposition of a tripartite graph into two role's bipartite graphs and represent the node information of the two roles, respectively. For the convenience of distinction, we use superscript $(\cdot)^a$ to indicate the answerer role and $(\cdot)^r$ to indicate the requester role.

As illustrated in Fig. 3 (left), $\mathbf{A}$ is the adjacency matrix of the topological structure of input graph $\mathbf{G}$, which can be divided into two-subgraph (Answerer-Question Graph and Requester-Question Graph) adjacency matrices ($\mathbf{A}^a$ and $\mathbf{A}^r$), then we can represent the nodes of these two subgraphs with GNN layers respectively, so as to extract the higher-order information under dual role graphs, finally, a new node representation (a_i^{gnn}) of the user is computed by synthesizing the node vectors (answerer role vector $(a_i^{a\text{-}gnn})$ and requester role vector $(a_i^{r\text{-}gnn})$) of dual roles that contain two roles' higher-order information as follows:

$$a_i^{gnn} = \text{mean-pooling}\left(a_i^{a\text{-}gnn}, a_i^{r\text{-}gnn}\right)$$

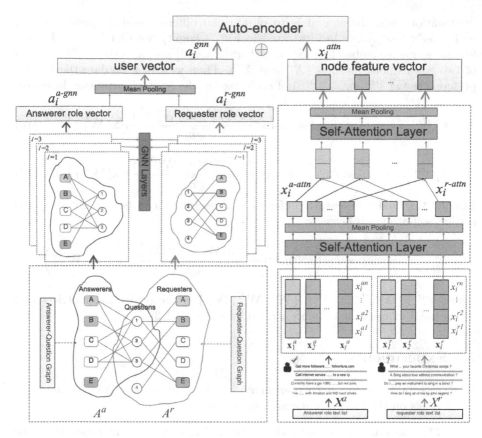

Fig. 3. The architecture of Dual Role GNN (left) and Dual Role Feature Self-Attention (right)

Similar to Eq. (1), the hidden representation for the answerer role vector and requester role vector are computed as follows:

$$(a_i^{a\text{-}gnn})^l = g\left(\mathbf{W}^G \sum_{j\in\mathcal{N}(i)} (a^a)_{ij}^l (a^a)_j^{l-1} + \mathbf{B}_1^G (a^a)_i^{l-1}\right) \tag{14}$$

$$(a_i^{r\text{-}gnn})^l = g\left(\mathbf{W}^G \sum_{j\in\mathcal{N}(i)} (a^r)_{ij}^l (a^r)_j^{l-1} + \mathbf{B}_2^G (a^r)_i^{l-1}\right) \tag{15}$$

where the $\mathbf{W}^G$ shares between the dual role graph and also shared in Eq. (9).

4.2 Dual Role Feature Self-attention

For dual role, we use two attention layers to capture the different preferences of the dual role. The first is to obtain the different weight of each role's feature information, and the second is to obtain the different feature preferences of each user's dual roles. As illustrated in Fig. 3 (right), we first have each node feature sequence embedding ($\mathbf{x}_i^a = [x_i^{a1}, x_i^{a2}, ..., x_i^{an}]$ and $\mathbf{x}_i^r = [x_i^{r1}, x_i^{r2}, ..., x_i^{rn}]$) of two roles's node features ($\boldsymbol{X}^a$ and $\boldsymbol{X}^r$). Then we can formulate the feature preferences ($x_i^{a\text{-}attn}$ and $x_i^{r\text{-}attn}$) of each role by the first self-attention layer as:

$$x_i^{a\text{-}attn} = \text{mean-pooling}\left(\text{softmax}(\frac{(\mathbf{x}_i^a \mathbf{W}_1^Q)(\mathbf{x}_i^a (\mathbf{W}_1^K)^\top)}{\sqrt{d_{k1}}})(\mathbf{x}_i^a \mathbf{W}_1^V)\right) \qquad (16)$$

$$x_i^{r\text{-}attn} = \text{mean-pooling}\left(\text{softmax}(\frac{(\mathbf{x}_i^r \mathbf{W}_2^Q)(\mathbf{x}_i^r (\mathbf{W}_2^K)^\top)}{\sqrt{d_{k2}}})(\mathbf{x}_i^r \mathbf{W}_2^V)\right) \qquad (17)$$

Finally, the dual role feature preferences of each user can be computed by the second self-attention layer as:

$$x_i^{attn} = \text{mean-pooling}\left(\text{softmax}(\frac{(\mathbf{x}_i^{ar}\mathbf{b}fW_3^Q)(\mathbf{x}_i^{ar} (\mathbf{W}_3^K)^\top)}{\sqrt{d_{k3}}})(\mathbf{x}_i^{ar} \mathbf{W}_3^V)\right)$$

where $\mathbf{x}_i^{ar} = [x_i^{a\text{-}attn}, x_i^{r\text{-}attn}]$, $\{\mathbf{W}_i^Q, \mathbf{W}_i^K, \mathbf{W}_i^V\}$ is the projection matrices and d_{ki} is the dimension of sequence embedding ($i = [1, 2, 3]$).

5   Experiments

In this section, we conduct experiments for demonstrating the effectiveness of our models on the following research questions:

1. **RQ1**: Can our models outperform other link prediction methods from the perspective of link prediction?
2. **RQ2**: How does DRNGae perform as compared with state-of-the-art recommendation methods?
3. **RQ3**: Does dual roles help the DRNGae?

5.1   Link Prediction (RQ1)

Datasets. To verify the effectiveness of solving the recommendation problem from the perspective of link prediction, we conduct experiments on three benchmark graph datasets: $Cora, Citeseer, PubMed$ for the link prediction task, and the results are shown in Table 1. Each dataset takes scientific publications as nodes and citation relationships as edges. The feature in each document is a unique word. See [17] for the details.

Baselines. To demonstrate the effectiveness, we compared our algorithms against the following link prediction task methods:

- **DeepWalk (DW)** [15]: is a new representation method for learning the latent space representation of nodes in a social network.

Table 1. Statistics of the datasets for link prediction task.

Dataset	Nodes	Links	Node features	Density
Cora	2708	5429	1433	0.00144
Citeseer	3327	4732	3703	0.00083
PubMed	19717	44338	500	0.00023

Table 2. Statistics of Yahoo! Answers dataset.

Dataset	User number	Question number	Answer number
User-10	1643	1160	33195
User-15	810	648	23567
User-25	342	261	14988

- **Spectral Clustering (SC)** [18]: is an effective clustering method for learning social embedding based on graph theory.
- **VGAE** [10]: utilize a variational graph auto-encoder to embed the graph structure and content information.
- **ARVGA** [14]: considers a adversarially regularization approach into a variational graph auto-encoder for learning graph embedding.

Metrics. We adopt two widely used metrics to evaluate the performance: AUC score (the area under a receiver operating characteristic curve) and AP score (average precision). We divided the $\{Cora, Citeseer, PubMed\}$ dataset into train/validation/test sets same as [10,14], and show the mean AUC and AP score after 10 standard error iterations, on which initializing the random weights of the fixed data segments.

Implementation Details. First, we randomly set a group of elements in the adjacency matrix as the missing state, and collect their indexes as the validation set. Then, training the auto-encoder to generate a set of predictions (a list of 1 and 0) for those missing indexes to evaluate the final results. In all experiments, We train 100 epochs with a mini-batch size of 64 samples and set the dimension of the hidden layer fixed in [512, 256, 128]. We use Adam algorithm for gradient descent optimization in the learning rate at [0.0001, 0.001, 0.01] and employ a regularization form of early stopping to prevent overfitting on the validation set. For other baselines, we keep the same settings as the corresponding papers.

Experimental Results. The details of the experimental results are shown in Table 3. As we can see, our model achieves outstanding performance for link prediction with and without node features, and adding node features improves predictive performance across datasets significantly. The margin in the results between DRNGae and other methods has further proved that it is feasible for CQA recommendation from the perspective of link prediction.

5.2   CQA Recommendation (RQ2)

Datasets. We download the Yahoo! Answer datasets from the Yahoo! Answer Datasets API[3] for experiments. Then the whole dataset (U, Q, A) is divided

---

[3]   https://webscope.sandbox.yahoo.com/

Table 3. Results for Link Prediction. * denote experiments do not support node features.

Method	Cora		Citeseer		PubMed	
	AUC	AP	AUC	AP	AUC	AP
SC* [18]:	0.846	0.885	0.805	0.850	0.842	0.878
DW* [15]	0.831	0.850	0.805	0.836	0.844	0.841
DRNGae*	**0.893**	**0.914**	**0.857**	**0.889**	**0.925**	**0.928**
VGAE [10]:	0.914	0.926	0.908	0.920	0.944	0.947
ARVGE [14]	0.924	0.926	0.924	0.930	**0.965**	**0.968**
DRNGae	**0.940**	**0.949**	**0.953**	**0.962**	0.963	0.964

into three subsets according to the number of questions answered by users. We divide 80% of each subset into training sets and 20% into test sets, in which the training set is only used for parameter estimation and the test set is used for evaluation. The statistical details of all subsets are shown in Table 2. It can be seen that each data set contains a user set, a question set and an answer set. For example, the user set, question set and answer set of User-10 are defined as U-10, Q-10 and A-10 respectively. We take the users who answered more than 10 questions as the user set U-10, and then take the number of questions (answers) that be requested (answered) by these users as question set Q-10 (answer set A-10). And so on for the other subsets.

Baselines. We compared our proposed DRNGae against state-of-the-art methods:

- **DRM** [22]: propose a dual role model to extract latent topic information through PLSA [7] to analyze the effect of different roles in CQA.
- **GC-MC** [1]: encode the user and item representation only with the first-order neighborhood in graph by adopting an auto-encoder structure.
- **HOP-Rec** [23]: is a state-of-the-art graph-based model, which uses random walk with the high-order neighborhood information to enhance the representation of users and items.

Metrics. We make a top-N recommendation from the perspective of link prediction. For each node (user node or question node), we predict the links between a user node and each question nodes and recommending the appropriate questions to the user. Similarly, for a question node, recommending the question to top-N users who are the most qualified to answer it. Following [23], we employ two metrics to evaluate the effectiveness of top-N recommendation: recall@K and ndcg@K. We report the mean metrics for all users/questions in the test set.

Experimental Results. Figure 4 shows the performance comparison results of the top-N recommendation. As can be seen, DRNGae consistently yields the

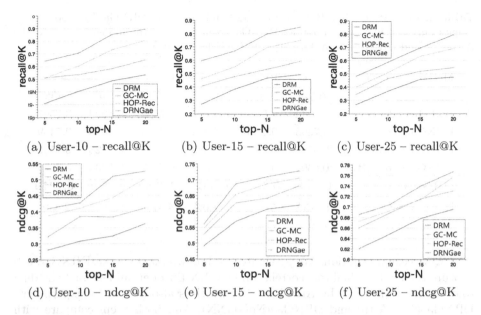

(a) User-10 – recall@K   (b) User-15 – recall@K   (c) User-25 – recall@K

(d) User-10 – ndcg@K   (e) User-15 – ndcg@K   (f) User-25 – ndcg@K

Fig. 4. Performance of top-N recommendation where N in $[5, 10, 15, 20]$ on the three datasets.

best performance on all the datasets. It validates the superiority of the model that we proposed. In particular, in all datasets, the recall and ndcg scores of DRNGae increased by about 10% and 2% compared with the strongest baseline, respectively, i.e., HOP-Rec. DRNGae outperforms GC-MC, which means the implicit user correlation from the higher-order information of the user plays an active role. The GNN can naturally catch high-order relations, which makes the results more efficient than other topic model-based methods. DRNGae outperforms HOP-Rec, which means the implicit correlation and different weights of dual role has positive effects on CQA recommendation.

5.3   Is Dual Role Helpful? (RQ3)

As there is little work on CQA recommendation with the dual role, it is curious to see whether using the dual role of users is beneficial to the recommendation task. Towards this end, we further investigated the contribution of the dual role for the DRNGae and the influence of components. The results are summarized in Table 4. The DRNGae^a indicates that the method only uses a single role (answerer role) of a user to experiment. As we can see, compared with DRNGae^a, two metrics are improved on three datasets, which improves 13.75%, 17.0%, 19.43% at recall@20 and 5.31%, 4.37%, 2.83% at ndcg@20. And we can see that as N becomes larger (User-N), the interaction data of dual role users decreases sharply, resulting in the positive influence of Dual Role undermined. This result is highly encouraging, indicating the effectiveness of using a dual role

Table 4. Influence of Dual Role at recall@20 and ndcg@20. DRNGae^a denote experiments only consider answerer role, DRNGae(Non-GNN) is the model only used the Attn-Enc and DRNGae(Non-Attn) is only GNN-Enc used in.

Method	User-10		User-15		User-25	
	recall	ndcg	recall	ndcg	recall	ndcg
HOP-Rec [23]:	0.8044	0.5028	0.7501	0.7064	0.6899	0.7567
DRNGae^a	0.7863	0.4986	0.7274	0.6984	0.6653	0.7459
DRNGae(Non-GNN)	0.8515	0.5099	0.7983	0.7129	0.7328	0.7592
DRNGae(Non-Attn)	0.8809	0.5181	0.8334	0.7199	0.7738	0.7635
DRNGae	**0.8944**	**0.5251**	**0.8510**	**0.7289**	**0.7946**	**0.7670**
%Improv.	13.75%	5.31%	17.0%	4.37%	19.43%	2.83%

for CQA recommendation. We attribute the improvement to the DRNGae can capture the implicit dual role correlation by GNN-Encoder, and extract the dual role feature preferences by Attn-Encoder, which is also proved by experiments DRNGae(Non-Attn) and DRNGae(Non-GNN). And both them compare with DRNGae^a and find that the influence of GNN-Encoder is more powerful which mean that the implicit dual role correlation is more important.

6   Conclusion and Future Work

In this paper, we explicitly incorporated the dual role of user into the reconstruction function of auto-encoder architecture for CQA recommendation. We devised a new model DRNGae, which captures the implicit dual role correlation by extracting high-order information on the dual role graph. And learn variable weights for dual role feature preferences to help improve the model performance. Experiments on a great quantity of real-world datasets show that the proposed model is rational and effective.

In the future, we will further improve DRNGae by taking the temporal dynamic information into account the preferences of dual roles since the behavior of users will change with time [4]. In addition, we are interested in exploring the method of adversarial learning [6] between the two roles, which may improve the performance of DRNGae.

References

1. van den Berg, R., Kipf, T.N., Welling, M.: Graph convolutional matrix completion. arXiv preprint arXiv:1706.02263 (2017)
2. Chen, H., Li, X., Huang, Z.: Link prediction approach to collaborative filtering. In: Proceedings of the 5th ACM/IEEE-CS Joint Conference on Digital Libraries (JCDL 2005), pp. 141–142. IEEE (2005)

3. Dong, Y., et al.: Link prediction and recommendation across heterogeneous social networks. In: 2012 IEEE 12th International Conference on Data Mining, pp. 181–190. IEEE (2012)
4. Du, N., Wang, Y., He, N., Sun, J., Song, L.: Time-sensitive recommendation from recurrent user activities. In: Advances in Neural Information Processing Systems, pp. 3492–3500 (2015)
5. Guo, J., Xu, S., Bao, S., Yu, Y.: Tapping on the potential of Q&A community by recommending answer providers. In: Proceedings of the 17th ACM Conference on Information and Knowledge Management, pp. 921–930. ACM (2008)
6. He, X., He, Z., Du, X., Chua, T.S.: Adversarial personalized ranking for recommendation. In: The 41st International ACM SIGIR Conference on Research & Development in Information Retrieval, pp. 355–364. ACM (2018)
7. Hofmann, T.: Unsupervised learning by probabilistic latent semantic analysis. Mach. Learn. 42(1–2), 177–196 (2001)
8. Ji, T., Wu, Y., Lan, M.: Graph-based dependency parsing with graph neural networks. In: Proceedings of the 57th Annual Meeting of the Association for Computational Linguistics, pp. 2475–2485 (2019)
9. Kipf, T.N., Welling, M.: Semi-supervised classification with graph convolutional networks. arXiv preprint arXiv:1609.02907 (2016)
10. Kipf, T.N., Welling, M.: Variational graph auto-encoders. arXiv preprint arXiv:1611.07308 (2016)
11. Li, B., King, I.: Routing questions to appropriate answerers in community question answering services. In: Proceedings of the 19th ACM International Conference on Information and Knowledge Management, pp. 1585–1588. ACM (2010)
12. Li, X., et al.: Beyond RNNs: positional self-attention with co-attention for video question answering. In: The 33rd AAAI Conference on Artificial Intelligence, vol. 8 (2019)
13. Menon, A.K., Elkan, C.: Link prediction via matrix factorization. In: Gunopulos, D., Hofmann, T., Malerba, D., Vazirgiannis, M. (eds.) ECML PKDD 2011. LNCS (LNAI), vol. 6912, pp. 437–452. Springer, Heidelberg (2011). https://doi.org/10.1007/978-3-642-23783-6_28
14. Pan, S., Hu, R., Long, G., Jiang, J., Yao, L., Zhang, C.: Adversarially regularized graph autoencoder for graph embedding. arXiv preprint arXiv:1802.04407 (2018)
15. Perozzi, B., Al-Rfou, R., Skiena, S.: Deepwalk: online learning of social representations. In: Proceedings of the 20th ACM SIGKDD International Conference on Knowledge Discovery and Data Mining, pp. 701–710. ACM (2014)
16. Sedhain, S., Menon, A.K., Sanner, S., Xie, L.: Autorec: autoencoders meet collaborative filtering. In: Proceedings of the 24th International Conference on World Wide Web, pp. 111–112. ACM (2015)
17. Sen, P., Namata, G., Bilgic, M., Getoor, L., Galligher, B., Eliassi-Rad, T.: Collective classification in network data. AI Mag. 29(3), 93–93 (2008)
18. Tang, L., Liu, H.: Leveraging social media networks for classification. Data Mining Knowl. Discov. 23(3), 447–478 (2011)
19. Vaswani, A., et al.: Attention is all you need. In: Advances in Neural Information Processing Systems, pp. 5998–6008 (2017)
20. Veličković, P., Cucurull, G., Casanova, A., Romero, A., Lio, P., Bengio, Y.: Graph attention networks. arXiv preprint arXiv:1710.10903 (2017)
21. Vukotić, V., Raymond, C., Gravier, G.: Bidirectional joint representation learning with symmetrical deep neural networks for multimodal and crossmodal applications. In: Proceedings of the 2016 ACM on International Conference on Multimedia Retrieval, pp. 343–346. ACM (2016)

22. Xu, F., Ji, Z., Wang, B.: Dual role model for question recommendation in community question answering. In: Proceedings of the 35th International ACM SIGIR Conference on Research and Development in Information Retrieval, pp. 771–780. ACM (2012)
23. Yang, J.H., Chen, C.M., Wang, C.J., Tsai, M.F.: HOP-rec: high-order proximity for implicit recommendation. In: Proceedings of the 12th ACM Conference on Recommender Systems, pp. 140–144. ACM (2018)

KGWD: Knowledge Graph Based Wide & Deep Framework for Recommendation

Kemeng Liu, Zhonghong Ou$^{(\boxtimes)}$, Yanxin Tan, Kai Zhao, and Meina Song

Beijing University of Posts and Telecommunications, Beijing, China
{liukemeng,zhonghong.ou,kaizhao,mnsong}@bupt.edu.cn, tobytyx@gmail.com

Abstract. Knowledge Graph (KG) contains rich real-world auxiliary information, which can be leveraged to improve the performance of recommender systems. Nevertheless, existing recommender systems usually sample and aggregate neighbor entities and relations that link to target items to enrich the representations of items or users, whereas ignoring combinatorial features among different neighbor entities and relations. To resolve the problem mentioned above, we propose an end-to-end Knowledge Graph based Wide & Deep (KGWD) framework to leverage combinatorial features effectively. At the wide level, KGWD introduces a novel Triplet Compressed Interaction Network (TriCIN) to generate high-order combinatorial features among different triplets associated with the target item automatically. At the deep level, KGWD discovers users' potential long-distance preferences by mining multi-hop neighbor information over the KG. We conduct experiments on three real-world datasets, i.e., Yelp2018, Last-FM, and Amazon-book, to evaluate the performance of KGWD. Experimental results demonstrate that KGWD outperforms state-of-the-art schemes significantly. Specifically, in all three datasets, KGWD improves the F1-score by more than 5% over the state-of-the-art.

Keywords: Recommender systems · Knowledge graph · Wide & Deep

1 Introduction

General recommender systems usually perform recommendations through user-item interactions, e.g., Collaborative Filtering (CF) [1–3], whereas the accuracy and diversity are limited. Due to problems of data sparsity and cold start of CF-based schemes, researchers started to take auxiliary information into recommender systems to enrich representations of items and users. Prior studies [4–9] demonstrate that combining auxiliary information improves performance of recommender systems effectively.

In recent years, Knowledge Graph (KG) has been proposed to describe relations between entities. It provides useful information implying users' potential preferences, which can be leveraged to improve the performance of recommendations. Existing KG-based recommendation schemes can be roughly divided

© Springer Nature Switzerland AG 2020
X. Wang et al. (Eds.): APWeb-WAIM 2020, LNCS 12317, pp. 455–469, 2020.
https://doi.org/10.1007/978-3-030-60259-8_33

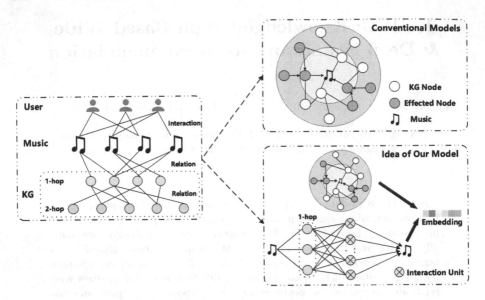

Fig. 1. The comparison between the ideas of conventional KG-based models and our model.

into two categories, i.e., path-based schemes and embedding-based schemes. **Path-based schemes** select different patterns of paths among entities in the KG by path selection algorithms [5,11] or defining meta-path patterns [10,12]. This type of schemes rely on the selection or definition of meta-paths heavily. Moreover, defining meta-path requires domain knowledge and consumes a large amount of labor. **Embedding-based schemes** employ Knowledge Graph Embedding (KGE) [13] algorithms to represent the information of the KG, and integrate them with the items or users in recommender systems. This type of schemes gradually become the mainstream direction of KG-based recommender systems, including CKE [4], KGCN [7], and KGAT [8]. Although embedding-based schemes can effectively integrate information of the KG into recommender systems, they take into consideration the internal relationship along KG paths only, and ignore combinatorial features among different triplets from different paths. This leaves a large space for improvement.

Combinatorial features are generated by transformation of raw features. They can be leveraged to infer a user's more precise preferences for personalized recommendations. A number of schemes have been proposed for combinatorial feature selection and generation, e.g., [14–16]. Conventional combinatorial feature generation methods not only rely on domain knowledge heavily, but also are time-consuming and laborious. Thus, new schemes have been proposed to generate combinatorial features automatically, including FM [17], NFM [3], and xDeepFM [18], which improves the performance of recommender systems. Nevertheless, these schemes are all KG-free, making them incapable of leveraging the strengths of KG.

Figure 1 shows the comparison of the ideas of conventional KG-based models and ours. It shows that the existing approaches enrich the representations of the items by integrating the internal relationship along KG paths only, ignoring the combinatorial features among the KG triplets. In face of limitations of existing approaches, we propose an end-to-end Knowledge Graph based Wide & Deep (KGWD) framework in this paper. KGWD consists of a wide part and a deep part. The **wide** part generates bounded degree high-order combinatorial features automatically at triplet-wise level; the **deep** part propagates information of multi-hop neighbors to the target item. Compared with the state-of-the-art schemes, KGWD can leverage explicit information between neighbors and implicit combinatorial features in the KG, leading to performance improvement.

The contributions of this paper are summarized as follows:

- We introduce a novel Triplet Compressed Interaction Network (TriCIN) to model users' implicit preferences by generating high-order combinatorial features at triplet-wise level automatically.
- We propose a KGWD framework to leverage both wide and deep information simultaneously. KGWD models users' long distance preferences along KG paths, and takes into consideration the triplet-wise combinatorial features to discover users' personalized preferences.
- We conduct extensive experiments on three real-world datasets, which demonstrate the effectiveness of KGWD. Specifically, KGWD improves the F1-score by more than 5% over the state-of-the-art in all three datasets.

2   Related Work

There are two categories of studies relevant to our work, corresponding to the wide and deep part of KGWD, respectively. The wide part is corresponding to combinatorial feature generation, whilst the deep part is relevant to neighbor information propagation.

2.1   Combinatorial Feature Generation

Combinatorial features can be considered as the combinations of rules that indicate users' potential preferences. For example, FM [17] models second-order cross features as pairwise dot product of raw feature vectors, including both useful and useless combinations. NFM [3] is a variant of FM, which combines deep neural network with FM. Wide & Deep [19] and DeepFM [20] introduce a hybrid framework that takes into consideration both low-order and high-order feature interactions. Based on Wide & Deep, DCN [21] introduces a Cross Net to generate bounded degree high-order features at bit-wise level automatically, while xDeepFM [18] proposes a Compress Interaction Network (CIN) to generate bounded degree combinatorial features at vector-wise level. Nevertheless, these studies do not leverage KG to generate features. To make full use of KG, we introduce a TriCIN, which can model the users' implicit preferences by generating combinatorial features at triplet-wise level over the KG.

2.2 Neighbor Information Propagation

The neighbors of a target item in KG usually contain a lot of attribute information, which implies users' potential preferences. How to model neighbor information of the target item is a critical procedure for KG-based recommender systems. Zhang et al. [4] proposed CKE, which combines CF with structural, textual, and visual content in a unified framework. Wang et al. [6] proposed RippleNet, which learns users' embeddings by simulating the propagation of user preferences over the links in the KG. Inspired by Graph Convolution Network (GCN) [22], KGCN [7] and KGAT [8] were proposed to model neighbor information and propagate them from neighbors to center recursively. We propose to propagate neighbor information to enrich the item representations and discover the users' long distance preferences. With the integration of both implicit combinatorial features and explicit information between neighbors in the KG, KGWD can acquire a more comprehensive profile of the user's preferences.

3   The KGWD Framework

In this section, we introduce the KGWD framework. We first formulate the KG-based recommendation problem, then present the architecture of KGWD from whole to part.

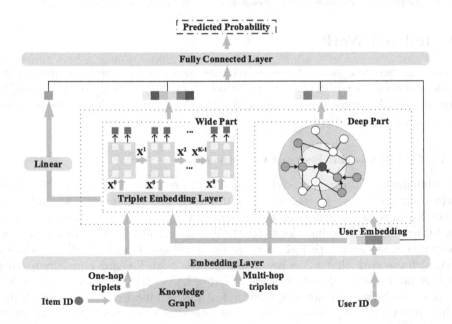

Fig. 2. The overall architecture of KGWD.

3.1   Problem Formulation

In a general recommendation scenario, there is a set of M users $U = \{u_1, u_2\, u_3, ..., u_m\}$, and a set of N items $I = \{i_1, i_2, i_3, ..., i_n\}$. There are also historical interactions between users and items, which can be represented by a user-item interaction matrix. The user-item matrix $Y \in R^{M \times N}$ is defined according to users' explicit and implicit feedback, e.g., clicking, browsing, or purchasing. In user-item matrix Y, $y_{ui} = 1$ indicates that user u interacts with item i, while $y_{ui} = 0$ indicates the opposite.

In KG-based recommender systems, in addition to the user-item matrix, there is a KG G, which contains auxiliary information related to items. The KG is a directed graph that is composed of triplets (h, r, t), where $h, t \in E$ is the head and tail entity, respectively, and $r \in R$ is the relation between h and t. Moreover, there exists an item-entity alignment set that is used to map the items to the entities of KG.

The objective of KGWD is to learn a predicted function $\hat{y}_{ui} = F(u, i | \Theta, Y, G)$ according to the given user-item interaction matrix Y and the KG G. $\hat{y}_{ui}$ denotes the probability of user u interacting with item i, and Θ denotes the model parameters of function F.

3.2   The Architecture of KGWD

The overall architecture of KGWD is illustrated in Fig. 2. KGWD takes a user u and an item i as input, and outputs the predicted probability that user u interacts with item i. The item i is also a seed that is used to find the multi-hop neighbors in the KG. We use the first-hop neighbors to generate combinatorial features in the wide part, and use the multi-hop neighbor information to model users' long distance preferences in the deep part. The embeddings of entities and relations of the KG will be learned automatically through this end-to-end framework.

The Wide Part. The wide part of KGWD framework is inspired by the idea of high-order combinatorial feature generation. The combinations of different neighbors of the target item imply the users' potential preferences. Thus, we propose a Triplet Compressed Interaction Network (TriCIN) to generate high-order combinatorial features at triplet-wise level for each pair (u, i). The term **wide** refers to the wide range of features that can be selected.

TriCIN consists of a Triplet Embedding Layer (TEL) and a CIN [18]. The architecture of TEL is illustrated in Fig. 3. For each pair (u, i) to be predicted, we first find the first-hop neighbors of item i in the KG. Herein, we define $S^i_{neighbor}$ as the set of first-hop neighbors of the target item i in the KG, which consists of relations and tail entities. For each triplet (h, r, t) in $S^i_{neighbor}$, TEL projects h and t into the vector space of r through a transformation matrix:

$$e^r_h = W_r e_h, \; e^r_t = W_r e_t. \tag{1}$$

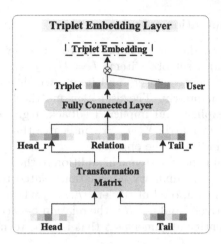

Fig. 3. The architecture of Triplet Embedding Layer (TEL).

Wherein $e_h, e_t \in \mathbb{R}^k$ and $e_r \in \mathbb{R}^d$ are the embeddings for h, t, and r, respectively; k and d are the dimensions of embeddings. $W_r \in \mathbb{R}^{d \times k}$ is the transformation matrix, which projects the entities from the k-dimension entity space into the d-dimension relation space.

In recommender systems, triplets can be considered as the meta paths that contain users' preferences. In order to retain the information of a triplet, we concatenate e_h^r, e_r, and e_t^r, and feed the concatenated embedding into a fully connected layer for aggregation:

$$e_{triplet_j} = \sigma(W Concat(e_h^r, e_r, e_t^r)). \tag{2}$$

Wherein $e_{triplet_j}$ is the embedding for triplet j; $\sigma(\cdot)$ is an activation function, e.g., ReLU or LeakyReLU; W is the parameter vector of the fully connected layer.

Moreover, user information is introduced to distinguish the influence of different triplets. The final representation of triplet j is formulated as follows:

$$e_{triplet_j}^u = e_u \circ e_{triplet_j}. \tag{3}$$

Wherein $e_{triplet_j}^u$ is the embedding for triplet j associated with user u; e_u is the embedding for user u; $\circ$ denotes the Hadamard product ($<a_1, a_2, a_3> \circ <b_1, b_2, b_3> = <a_1 b_1, a_2 b_2, a_3 b_3>$). The triplet j here is one of the neighbors of item i in the KG.

CIN is a scheme proposed by Lian et al. [18] to generate high-order combinatorial features at vector-wise level automatically. The order of feature interactions grows with the network depth. Here, we define the low-order feature matrix as follows:

$$X^0 = [e_{triplet_1}^u, e_{triplet_2}^u, ..., e_{triplet_m}^u]. \tag{4}$$

Herein, $\boldsymbol{X}^0 \in \mathbb{R}^{m \times d}$ is the low-order feature matrix that is composed of the raw embedding for $triplet_j$ associated with user u; m is the number of the first-hop neighbor set $S^i_{neighbor}$.

Then, we take $\boldsymbol{X}^0$ as input, and the k-order feature embeddings are formulated as follows:

$$\boldsymbol{X}^k_{h,*} = \sum_{i=1}^{H_{k-1}} \sum_{j=1}^{m} \boldsymbol{W}^{k,h}_{ij} (\boldsymbol{X}^{k-1}_{i,*} \circ \boldsymbol{X}^0_{j,*}), 1 \le h \le H_k. \tag{5}$$

Wherein $\boldsymbol{X}^0_{j,*} = \boldsymbol{e}^u_{triplet_j}$ is the j-th triplet embedding associated with user u, H_{k-1} denotes the number of feature embeddings in the $(k-1)$-th layer, $\boldsymbol{W}^{k,h} \in \mathbb{R}^{H_{k-1} \times m}$ is the parameter matrix for the h-th feature embeddings.

After calculating the high-order feature embeddings, sum pooling is applied on each feature map of the hidden layer:

$$p^k_i = \sum_{j=1}^{D} \boldsymbol{X}^k_{i,j}, k \in [1,T], i \in [1, H_k]. \tag{6}$$

Wherein D denotes the dimension of embedding, T denotes the depth of the network. Then TriCIN concatenates all pooling embeddings $\boldsymbol{p}^k = Concat(p^k_1, p^k_2, ..., p^k_{H_k})$ with length H_k to form the final triplet-wise representation:

$$\boldsymbol{e}_{wide} = Concat(\boldsymbol{p}^1, \boldsymbol{p}^2, ..., \boldsymbol{p}^T) \in \mathbb{R}^{\sum_{i=1}^{T} H_i}. \tag{7}$$

The Deep Part. The other part of KGWD is the deep part. The term **deep** refers to the depth of neighbors used to enrich representations of items in the KG. The deep part of KGWD leverages the information of multi-hop neighbors along the KG to discover users' long distance preferences. It also integrates the influence of users into the neighbor weights. Namely, the influence of different neighbors are closely related to users, head entities, and relations.

To predict a (u, i) and its neighbor triplet set $N_h = \{(h, r, t) | (h, r, t) \in G\}$, we represent the embeddings for neighbors as the linear combination of tail entities, where the weights are computed according to the user u and the triplet (h, r, t):

$$\boldsymbol{e}^u_{N_h} = \sum_{(h,r,t) \in N_h} \pi(u, h, r, t) \boldsymbol{e}_t. \tag{8}$$

Wherein $\boldsymbol{e}^u_{N_h}$ is the embedding of the neighbor information corresponding to user u; $\pi(u, h, r, t)$ denotes the weights, which influence the information propagation from t to h on each triplet (h, r, t). $\pi(u, h, r, t)$ is formulated as follows:

$$\pi(u, h, r, t) = Mean(\boldsymbol{e}_u \circ \sigma(\boldsymbol{e}_h + \boldsymbol{e}_r)). \tag{9}$$

Wherein $\boldsymbol{e}_u \in \mathbb{R}^d, \boldsymbol{e}_h \in \mathbb{R}^k, \boldsymbol{e}_r \in \mathbb{R}^d$ are embeddings of the user, the head entity, and the relation, respectively. We set d equal to k for the sake of simplicity.

$Mean(\cdot)$ is the mean function; $\sigma(\cdot)$ is an activation function. Hereafter, we apply softmax function to normalize the influence coefficients:

$$\pi(u,h,r,t) = \frac{exp(\pi(u,h,r,t))}{\sum_{(u,h,r',t')\in N_h} exp(\pi(u,h,r',t'))}. \tag{10}$$

Note that the influence coefficients take into consideration both users and triplets, which effectively discover different users' preferences.

The final step is the aggregation of head entity and the neighbor information $e_{N_h}^u$. Based on KGAT [8], we apply bi-interaction aggregator to acquire the aggregation:

$$\begin{aligned} e_{deep} &= LeakyReLU(\boldsymbol{W}_1(e_h + e_{N_h})) \\ &+ LeakyReLU(\boldsymbol{W}_2(e_h \circ e_{N_h})). \end{aligned} \tag{11}$$

Wherein $\boldsymbol{W}_1, \boldsymbol{W}_2 \in \mathbb{R}^{d' \times d}$ are the trainable weight matrices. By analogy, the multi-hop neighbor information propagation can be realized.

3.3   Model Prediction

Besides the triplet-wise combinatorial features from the wide part and neighbor information from the deep part, there is a linear part in Fig. 2 (the leftmost path), which models the low-order embeddings of triplets associated with user u:

$$e_{triplet}^u = Concat(e_{triplet_1}^u, e_{triplet_2}^u, \cdots, e_{triplet_m}^u). \tag{12}$$

$$e_{linear} = \boldsymbol{W}_{linear} e_{triplet}^u. \tag{13}$$

Wherein $\boldsymbol{W}_{linear}$ are the parameters of the linear part.

Then we concatenate all embeddings together, and feed them into a fully connected layer for the predictions:

$$e_{input} = Concat(e_{linear}, e_{wide}, e_{deep}, e_u). \tag{14}$$

$$\hat{y} = sigmoid(\boldsymbol{W}_{output} e_{input}). \tag{15}$$

Wherein $\boldsymbol{W}_{output}$ are the parameters of the fully connected layer; e_{wide} and e_{deep} are the output of the wide part and the deep part, respectively; e_u denotes the embedding for user u.

3.4   Parameter Learning

To optimize parameters of our framework, we choose the Binary Cross Entropy Loss (BCELoss):

$$\mathcal{L} = -\frac{1}{N} \sum_{i=1}^N y_i log \hat{y}_i + (1 - y_i) log(1 - \hat{y}_i) \tag{16}$$

Wherein N denotes the number of training instances; y_i and $\hat{y}_i$ are the ground truth and the predicted probability of the user u interacting with the item i, respectively.

After adding the L2-regularization, the complete loss function is defined as follows:

$$\mathcal{J} = \mathcal{L} + \lambda||\Theta||_2^2. \tag{17}$$

Wherein λ is the hyper-parameter of L2-regularization; Θ denotes all parameters of KGWD.

4   Experiments

4.1   Datasets

We utilize the datasets released by KGAT [8] to evaluate the effectiveness of KGWD, which include three public datasets: Yelp2018, Last-FM, and Amazon-book. Freebase[1] is the KG used for Amazon-book and Last-FM, while the item knowledge extracted from the local business information network is used as KG data for Yelp2018.

- **Yelp2018**[2]: A dataset released from Yelp challenge 2018. Only businesses, e.g., restaurants and bars, are seen as items interacted with users for recommendations in this paper.
- **Last-FM**[3]: A widely used music recommendation dataset, which contains users' historical music listening records from Last.FM online music system. Only a subset of records are used.
- **Amazon-book**[4]: A subset of Amazon-review, which is a dataset used for product recommendation. Only the records of book products are used.

Statistics of the three datasets are summarized in Table 1. All history interactions are treated as positive instances. 80% of interactions of each user are randomly selected as the training set, while the remaining are used as the test set. Moreover, we randomly select 10% of interactions from the training set as the validation set. For the training set and validation set, a negative sampling approach is used to generate a negative instance for each positive instance, which the user does not interact with. In order to reduce the test time, we generate negative samples with the positive/negative ratio of 1/5 for the test set.

4.2   Baselines

We compare the proposed KGWD framework with the following six baselines.

---

[1] https://developers.google.com/freebase/data.
[2] https://www.yelp.com/dataset/challenge.
[3] https://grouplens.org/datasets/hetrec-2011/.
[4] http://jmcauley.ucsd.edu/data/amazon/.

Table 1. Statistics of the three datasets used.

	Yelp2018	Last-FM	Amazon-book
#Users	45,919	23,566	70,679
#Items	45,538	48,123	24,915
#Interactions	1,185,068	3,034,796	847,733
#Entities	90,961	58,266	88,572
#Relations	42	9	39
#Triplets	1,853,704	464,567	2,557,746

- **FM** [17]: generates second-order features by dot product between inputs. We take users, items, and the first-hop neighbors as the raw features and feed them into FM.
- **NFM** [3]: combines the linear characteristic of FM and the nonlinear characteristic of deep neural networks by concatenating the FM under the deep neural networks.
- **xDeepFM** [18]: a CTR prediction model based on FM, where CIN is proposed to generate vector-wise combinatorial features.
- **xDeepFM+TEL:** extends xDeepFM with our proposed Triplet Embedding Layer, and generates combinatorial features at triplet-wise level for recommendations. It is equivalent to the KGWD without the deep part.
- **KGCN** [7]: an end-to-end model inspired by GCN [22]. It enriches the item's representations by integrating their associated attributes in the KG. It can be considered as the KGWD without the wide part to compare with the whole KGWD.
- **KGAT** [8]: another GCN based model. It proposes a collaborative KG and a bi-interaction aggregator, which enriches the item's representations.

Herein, FM and NFM both generate second-order features among input attributes, while xDeepFM and xDeepFM+TEL generate high-order combinatorial features at vector-wise level and triplet-wise level. KGCN and KGAT are both embedding-based methods, which enrich representations of items by neighbor information propagation in the KG.

4.3   Experiment Setup

Evaluation Metrics. In recommendation scenarios, both CTR prediction and top-K recommendation prediction need to be evaluated. We adopt F1 score to evaluate the performance of CTR prediction, and NDCG@K to evaluate the performance of top-K recommendation prediction. Herein, K is set to 20 by default. All experimental results are reported as average for all users in the test set.

Parameters Setting. We optimize the KGWD framework with Adam optimizer, where the batch size is set to 1024. We use Xavier initializer [23] to initialize the trainable parameters. The embedding size is fixed to 32 for Yelp2018 and Last-FM, 8 for Amazon-book. In the wide part, the number of first-hop triplets is set to 30 for Yelp2018, 35 for Last-FM and Amazon-book. In the deep part, the number of neighbor hops is fixed to 3 and the number of neighbors per hop is fixed to 6 for all datasets. We set the learning rate and L2 regularization coefficient to $1e-3$ and $1e-5$, respectively.

For baselines, we fix the dimension of embeddings the same as KGWD corresponding to different datasets for a fair comparison. For FM-based baselines, the number of feature fields is set the same as the number of first-hop triplets in the wide part of KGWD. For KGCN, the number of neighbor hops and the neighbor nodes of each hop are also set the same as that in the deep part of KGWD. The learning rate is set to $1e-3$ for all baselines except KGAT, and the learning rate of KGAT is set by default. The L2 regularization coefficient is set to $1e-8$ for KGCN, while the others are set as $1e-5$. The other hyper-parameters of baselines are set as default.

Table 2. The performance of KGDW compared with other baselines.

Category	Model	Yelp2018		Last-FM		Amazon-book	
		F1	NDCG@20	F1	NDCG@20	F1	NDCG@20
Wide	FM	0.6363	0.8497	0.5649	0.8430	0.4801	0.7750
	NFM	0.6204	0.8686	0.5792	0.8939	0.4831	0.7621
	xDeepFM	0.5531	0.8335	0.4650	0.7596	0.5070	0.8010
	xDeepFM+TEL	0.5609	0.8470	0.4653	0.7631	0.5233	0.7983
Deep	KGCN	0.6203	0.8433	0.6230	0.8418	0.4704	0.7504
	KGAT	0.6201	0.9083	0.4890	0.8881	0.5659	**0.8764**
Wide & Deep	KGWD	**0.7277**	**0.9121**	**0.7178**	**0.9323**	**0.6145**	0.8580

4.4 Results and Discussion

Overall Comparison. The overall results are presented in Table 2. From the table, we make the following major observations:

- In general, KGWD outperforms the state-of-the-art baselines in most cases, which demonstrates the effectiveness of our framework. Note that the improvement of F1-score is larger than NDCG@20, which demonstrates that KGWD performs better on CTR predictions than on Top-K predictions.
- The performance of KGCN and KGAT are better than the baselines in the wide category, which demonstrates that neighbor information along paths in the KG can discover users' preferences. Nevertheless, the results of KGWD demonstrate that combinatorial features of triplets play an important role for performance improvement.

- xDeepFM+TEL performs better than xDeepFM in most cases, which demonstrates that generating combinatorial features at triplet-wise level is helpful for discovering users' potential preferences. It also demonstrates that the TEL we propose can effectively model the triplet information in the KG.

KGWD performs better on more dense datasets, i.e., Yelp2018 and Last-FM. Instead, Amazon-book is a sparser datasets with lots of triplets in the KG, KGWD may introduce noises from the KG and performs worse than KGAT on the metric NDCG@20. It demonstrates that KGWD can discover more information from the KG, and the triplet-wise combinatorial features and neighbor information along paths in the KG are useful supplementary for recommendations.

Model Analysis. The main idea of KGWD is the combination of combinatorial features at triplet-wise level and neighbor information along paths over the KG, which are corresponding to the wide part and the deep part, respectively. Since these two parts are partially based on xDeepFM and KGCN, we compare the results of KGWD, xDeepFM+TEL, and KGCN. As shown in Table 2, for three different datasets, KGWD increases by 16.68%, 25.25%, and 9.12% on F1 score, and 6.51%, 16.92%, and 5.97% on NDCG@20 over xDeepFM+TEL. Meanwhile, KGWD increases by 10.74%, 9.48%, and 14.41% on F1 score, and 6.88%, 9.05%, and 10.76% on NDCG@20 over KGCN. The results demonstrate that performance improvement of using combinatorial features at triplet-wise or neighbor information along paths alone is limited. Nevertheless, when KGWD combines these two aspects together, the performance improvement is significant, which demonstrates the effectiveness of our framework.

Table 3. The Performance of KGWD with different dimension of embedding.

D	Yelp2018		Last-FM		Amazon-book	
	F1	NDCG@20	F1	NDCG@20	F1	NDCG@20
8	0.7233	0.9110	0.6512	0.8922	**0.6116**	**0.8547**
16	0.7260	0.9113	0.6921	0.9159	0.6044	0.8484
32	**0.7261**	**0.9122**	**0.7174**	**0.9316**	0.6041	0.8486

4.5   Parameters Analysis

The Performance of Dimension of Embedding. In this experiment, we vary the dimension of embedding D to investigate its influence on recommendations on different datasets. The results are shown in Table 3. From the table, we can see that increasing D can help improve performance on Yelp2018 and Last-FM, which indicates that a larger D is likely to encode more information of users and items. Note that the performance on Amazon-book decreases along with an increasing D. This is likely because the Amazon-book dataset is sparse, and a larger D may introduce noise rather than useful information.

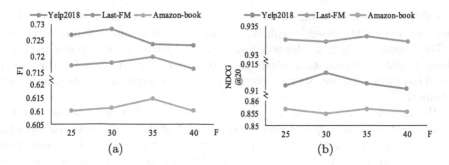

Fig. 4. The Performance of KGWD with different number of neighbors selected in the wide part.

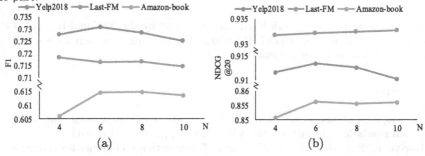

Fig. 5. The Performance of KGWD with different numbers of neighbors selected in the deep part.

The Performance of Different Numbers of Neighbors Selected in the Wide Part. The first-hop neighbors in the wide part are the raw features used in combinatorial feature generation. Thus, we vary the number of neighbors F in the wide part to investigate its influence on recommendations on different datasets. From Fig. 4, we observe that increasing F initially improves performance, whereas a too large F adversely harms performance. This is likely because a large F causes overfitting.

The Performance of Different Numbers of Neighbors Selected in the Deep Part. The number of neighbors of each hop N is an important hyperparameter in the deep part. To explore the impact of N, we conduct experiments with different N on KGWD. The results are shown in Fig. 5. From the figure, we find that increasing N improves the performance of KGWD, because more neighbors per hop can capture more users' long distance preferences. Nevertheless, a too large N may introduce noises and cause overfitting. Moreover, a larger N also takes more memory and increases the computational burden.

5   Conclusions

In this paper, we proposed an end-to-end Knowledge Graph based Wide & Deep (KGWD) framework for recommender systems. KGWD introduces a novel

TriCIN to generate combinatorial features from the KG at triplet-wise. Moreover, to model the users' explicit and implicit preferences more effectively, KGWD combines both triplet-wise combinatorial features (wide part) and path-along neighbor information (deep part) together. Experiments on three real-world datasets demonstrate that our framework outperforms the state-of-the-art schemes.

We plan to carry out future work from the two directions below. (1) The influence of different triplet-wise combinatorial features is different. Introducing attention mechanism to the wide part is an important future work direction. (2) Considering the relations between triplet-wise combinatorial features and neighbor information can better combine the advantages of these two aspects, which is also a future direction worth working on.

Acknowledgement. This work is supported in part by the National Key R&D Program of China (Grant No. 2017YFB1401500). Engineering Research Center of Information Networks, Ministry of Education.

References

1. Sarwar, B.M., Karypis, G., Konstan, J.A., et al.: Item-based collaborative filtering recommendation algorithms. In: WWW 2001, pp. 285–295 (2001)
2. Koren, Y., Bell, R., Volinsky, C.: Matrix factorization techniques for recommender systems. Computer **8**, 30–37 (2009)
3. He, X., Chua, T.S.: Neural factorization machines for sparse predictive analytics. In: Proceedings of the 40th International ACM SIGIR Conference on Research and Development in Information Retrieval, pp. 355–364. ACM (2017)
4. Zhang, F., Yuan, N.J., Lian, D., et al.: Collaborative knowledge base embedding for recommender systems. In: Proceedings of the 22nd ACM SIGKDD International Conference on Knowledge Discovery and Data Mining, pp. 353–362. ACM (2016)
5. Wang, X., Wang, D., Xu, C., et al.: Explainable reasoning over knowledge graphs for recommendation. In: Proceedings of the AAAI Conference on Artificial Intelligence, vol. 33, pp. 5329–5336 (2019)
6. Wang, H., Zhang, F., Wang, J., et al.: RippleNet: propagating user preferences on the knowledge graph for recommender systems. In: Proceedings of the 27th ACM International Conference on Information and Knowledge Management, pp. 417–426. ACM (2018)
7. Wang, H., Zhao, M., Xie, X., et al.: Knowledge graph convolutional networks for recommender systems. In: The World Wide Web Conference, pp. 3307–3313. ACM (2019)
8. Wang, X., He, X., Cao, Y., et al.: KGAT: knowledge graph attention network for recommendation. arXiv preprint arXiv:1905.07854 (2019)
9. Wang, H., Zhang, F., Hou, M., et al.: SHINE: signed heterogeneous information network embedding for sentiment link prediction. In: Proceedings of the Eleventh ACM International Conference on Web Search and Data Mining, pp. 592–600. ACM (2018)
10. Zhao, H., Yao, Q., Li, J., et al.: Meta-graph based recommendation fusion over heterogeneous information networks. In: Proceedings of the 23rd ACM SIGKDD International Conference on Knowledge Discovery and Data Mining, pp. 635–644. ACM (2017)

11. Sun, Z., Yang, J., Zhang, J., et al.: Recurrent knowledge graph embedding for effective recommendation. In: Proceedings of the 12th ACM Conference on Recommender Systems, pp. 297–305. ACM (2018)
12. Hu, B., Shi, C., Zhao, W.X., et al.: Leveraging meta-path based context for top-n recommendation with a neural co-attention model. In: Proceedings of the 24th ACM SIGKDD International Conference on Knowledge Discovery & Data Mining, pp. 1531–1540. ACM (2018)
13. Wang, Q., Mao, Z., Wang, B., et al.: Knowledge graph embedding: a survey of approaches and applications. IEEE Trans. Knowl. Data Eng. **29**(12), 2724–2743 (2017)
14. He, X., Pan, J., Jin, O., et al.: Practical lessons from predicting clicks on ads at Facebook. In: Proceedings of the Eighth International Workshop on Data Mining for Online Advertising, pp. 1–9. ACM (2014)
15. Lian, J., Zhang, F., Xie, X., et al.: Restaurant survival analysis with heterogeneous information. In: Proceedings of the 26th International Conference on World Wide Web Companion. International World Wide Web Conferences Steering Committee, pp. 993–1002 (2017)
16. Lian, J., Xie, X.: Cross-device user matching based on massive browse logs: the runner-up solution for the 2016 CIKM cup. arXiv preprint arXiv:1610.03928 (2016)
17. Steffen, R.: Factorization machines. In: IEEE 10th International Conference on Data Mining (ICDM), pp. 995–1000 (2010)
18. Lian, J., Zhou, X., Zhang, F., et al.: xDeepFM: combining explicit and implicit feature interactions for recommender systems. In: Proceedings of the 24th ACM SIGKDD International Conference on Knowledge Discovery & Data Mining, pp. 1754–1763. ACM (2018)
19. Cheng, H.T., Koc, L., Harmsen, J., et al.: Wide & deep learning for recommender systems. In: Proceedings of the 1st Workshop on Deep Learning for Recommender Systems, pp. 7–10. ACM (2016)
20. Guo, H., Tang, R., Ye, Y., et al.: DeepFM: a factorization-machine based neural network for CTR prediction. arXiv preprint arXiv:1703.04247 (2017)
21. Wang, R., Fu, B., Fu, G., et al.: Deep & cross network for ad click predictions. In: Proceedings of the ADKDD 2017. ACM (2017). Article no. 12
22. Kipf, T.N., Welling, M.: Semi-supervised classification with graph convolutional networks. arXiv preprint arXiv:1609.02907 (2016)
23. Glorot, X., Bengio, Y.: Understanding the difficulty of training deep feedforward neural networks. In: Proceedings of the Thirteenth International Conference on Artificial Intelligence and Statistics, pp. 249–256 (2010)

Seamless Incorporation
of Appointment-Based Requests
on Taxi-Rider Match Scheduling

Yongxuan Lai[1,2]($\boxtimes$), Shipeng Yang[1,2], Anshu Xiong[1,2], and Fan Yang[1,3]

[1] Shenzhen Research Institute, Xiamen University, Shenzhen 518057, China
laiyx@xmu.edu.cn, wydn12345@qq.com, 837412842@qq.com
[2] School of Informatics, Xiamen University, Xiamen 361005, China
[3] School of Aerospace Engineering, Xiamen University, Xiamen 361005, China
yang@xmu.edu.cn

Abstract. Rider demand responsive systems (RDRS) makes a match between numerous requests and vehicles, it is a challenging problem to make the maximal match as soon as the real-time requests pop up in the RDRS. Much research has been addressed on this issue. However, there is still not much work on handling the appointment-based requests. In this paper, we propose an algorithm called BMF (Bipartite Minimal-cost Flow) to solve the taxi-rider match scheduling problem with appointment-based rider requests on a time-dependent road network. Riders and vehicles are modeled as vertices in a bipartite graph, and the maximal utility calculation is transformed to the *minimal cost flow problem* that could be solved efficiently. Experimental results show that the proposed scheme can effectively decrease the average waiting time of riders (>44% reduction) at the cost of acceptable increase on the running time.

Keywords: Appointment-based request · Taxi-rider match · Rider demand responsive system

1 Introduction

In recent years, there has been increasing concern about the Rider Demand Responsive Systems (RDRS) [2, 7]. The taxi-rider matching is usually viewed as a kind of spatial matching problem that aims to match two sets of objects with optimization goals based on their spatial locations [9,12,13]. Appointment-based taxi service has been a kind of business of taxi companies for long. However, the appointment-based requests are not well studied and integrated into the existing RDRS platform. The appointment-based requests usually processed separately in a semi-manual approach; and in some taxi-hailing platforms the service is simply not provided. Riders' user experience would degrade sharply with the growth of the waiting time when the scheduled pickup is late. As the road networks are affected by various factors [1], it is still hard to incorporate the changing

© Springer Nature Switzerland AG 2020
X. Wang et al. (Eds.): APWeb-WAIM 2020, LNCS 12317, pp. 470–477, 2020.
https://doi.org/10.1007/978-3-030-60259-8_34

traveling time information for the match of appointment-based requests. The system should be flexible enough to dynamically adjust the matching pairs when better matching opportunities emerge in realtime. In this paper, we propose an efficient utility-based algorithm that integrates the real-time and appointment-based requests for RDRS. The major contributions of this paper are as follows:

- We propose an algorithm assigns both the real-time and appointment-based requests within the same framework.
- We propose an algorithm called BMF (Bipartite Minimal-cost Flow) to solve the taxi-rider match scheduling problem.
- We conduct experiments on real-world historical origin-destination datasets to verify the effectiveness of the proposed methods.

To the best of our knowledge, the proposed scheme is the first to efficiently integrate and process both the real-time and appointment-based requests within the same framework.

2 Related Work

According to whether requests are predefined or dynamically added, the problem could be classified into the *static* and the *dynamic* RDRS. The static RDRS problem could be viewed as a special member of the general class of the Dial-a-Ride Problem (DARP) [2,3]. The static version of RDRS corresponds to the static DARP where all customer/rider queries are known in priori, on which existing works on the DARP have primarily focused. Also, as the general DARP is NP-hard, only small instances that involve a few cars and dozens of requests can be solved optimally, usually by resorting to integer linear programming techniques. In dynamic RDRS problem, requests are popped up in real-time. Tong et al. [9,10] viewed the RDRS as the online minimum bipartite matching problem in real-time spatial data. The authors evaluated four representative online algorithms, and argued that Greedy significantly outperforms the other algorithms in almost all practical cases. Tong et al. [11] developed a two-step framework that integrates offline prediction for the flexible two-sided online task assignment. The problem of task assignment in spatial data is also called spatial matching problem [12,13], which aims to match two sets of objects with optimization goals based on their spatial locations. Yiu et al. [13] proposed an algorithm of edge-pruning strategies based on the spatial properties of the problem for optimal assignment. Hassan et al. [5] proposed a framework that formulates the online spatial task assignment as the multi-armed bandit problem. Recent works have used reinforcement learning to provide optimization algorithms for matching problem. Tang et al. model the ride dispatching problem as a Semi Markov Decision Process to account for the temporal aspect of the dispatching actions [8]. [6] proposed a multi-agent reinforcement learning solution to the ride dispatching problem. Most of the existing approaches for the dynamic RDRS problem only handle the real-time tasks/requests, and the pair of assignments could not be revoked once they are matched. In this paper we consider both the real-time and appointment-based requests within the same framework, and the vehicles and requests are set in a flexible way to be revokable to maximize the overall utility.

3   Preliminaries and Problem Definition

3.1   Road Network

The road network is represented by a directed graph $G_r = (V_r, E_r)$, where V_r is a set of vertices and $E_r \subseteq V_r \times V_r$ is a set of ordered pairs of vertices, with a weight function $w : (E_r, t) \rightarrow \mathbb{R}$ mapping edges to time-dependent real-valued weights. For simplicity, we denote $w(u, v, t)$ as the weight of an edge $e(u, v) \in E_r$ at time t, and it represents the amount of time required to reach v starting from u at time t. Given two vertices x_1, x_k, we also denote $w(x_1, x_k, t)$ as the minimal accumulated weight from node x_1 to x_k if there is a path $\{x_1 \rightarrow x_2 ... \rightarrow x_k\}$.

3.2   Query Set

Each request, e.g. q, is associated with a submission timestamp t_0, an origin location o, a destination location d, and a preferred time window $[t_1, t_2]$. The requests could be categorised into two types: the real-time requests, and the appointment-based requests, which are denoted as Q_1, Q_2 respectively:

$$\begin{cases} q \in Q_1, & if \ q.t_1 \in [t_0, now + T_1] \\ q \in Q_2, & if \ q.t_1 \in (now + T_1, \infty) \end{cases} \tag{1}$$

where now is the current time, T_1 is the minimal time gap for making appointments. The appointment set Q_2 could further be divided into two parts by another time factor $T_2 > T_1$:

$$\begin{cases} q \in Q_2^1, & if \ q \in Q_2, \ q.t_1 \in (now + T_1, now + T_2] \\ q \in Q_2^2, & if \ q \in Q_2, \ q.t_1 \in (now + T_2, \infty) \end{cases} \tag{2}$$

Then the *ready set* of requests are denoted as Q and defined as follows:

$$Q = Q_1 \cup Q_2^1 \tag{3}$$

3.3   Utility of Assignment

We denote $u(c, q, t)$ as the utility of a real-time request based assignment, and it consists of a trajectory-related utility $trac(c, q, t)$ and a service-related utility $serv(c, q, t)$. The utilities are defined as follows:

$$u(c, q, t) = \alpha * trac(c, q, t) + (1 - \alpha) * serv(c, q, t), \alpha \in [0, 1] \tag{4}$$

$$trac(c, q, t) = \frac{U}{w(c, q, t)}, \quad w(c, q, t) = w(l_c, q.o, t) \tag{5}$$

$$serv(c, q, t) = \begin{cases} (1 + \Delta(c, q, t))^{-1}, & pt(c, q, t) < q.t_1 \\ 1 + e^{-\Delta(c, q, t)}, & q.t_1 \leq pt(c, q, t) \leq q.t_2 \\ 0, & pt(c, q, t) > q.t_2 \end{cases} \tag{6}$$

where U is a predefined factor to normalize the cost for vehicle c traveling to pick up q, l_c is the location of vehicle c, $pt(c, q, t)$ is the expected time point of picking up q by vehicle c and $\Delta(c, q, t)$ is the length of time when the pickup is ahead or behind the time point $pt(c, q, t)$.

For an appointment-based request $q \in Q_2$, the utility is defined similar to the real-time request except an amplifying factor in service-related utility:

$$serv(c, q, t) = \begin{cases} (1 + \Delta(c, q, t))^{-1}, & pt(c, q, t) < q.t_1 \\ K * (1 + e^{-\Delta(c, q, t)}), & q.t_1 \leq pt(c, q, t) \leq q.t_2 \\ 0, & pt(c, q, t) > q.t_2 \end{cases} \tag{7}$$

where $K \geq 1$ is a parameter that amplifies the utility of serving appointment requests compared to real-time requests. For the sake of concise, the utilities are also denoted as $u(c, q)$, $serv(c, q)$, $trac(c, q)$ respectively if time t is known in the context.

3.4 Utility of Match

From the view of the whole road network G_r, given a set of requests Q, a set of vehicles C, and current time t, the overall utility of a match $\mathcal{M}$ between Q and C is:

$$util(G_r, Q, C, \mathcal{M})_t = \sum_{(c, q, t) \in \mathcal{M}} u(c, q, t) \tag{8}$$

where with assignment (c, q, t) vehicle c could only serve request q during the trip. Suppose $\mathbb{M}$ is the set of matches, the goal of the RDRS system is to find a match that maximises $util(G_r, Q, C, \mathcal{M})_t$:

$$\mathcal{M}^*_t = \underset{\mathcal{M}}{\operatorname{argmax}} \{util(G_r, Q, C, \mathcal{M})_t : \mathcal{M} \in \mathbb{M}\} \tag{9}$$

4 Matching Riders and Vehicles

4.1 Building Bipartite Graph

The proposed scheme first builds a bipartite graph $G_b(V_b, E_b)$ based on sets of vehicles and requests. As illustrated in Fig. 1, the set of vehicles is positioned on the left (C), and the set of requests is positioned on the right (Q). Each pair of vehicle and request is connected by an edge if the vehicle is able to pick up the rider before the end of the desired time window, i.e. $pt(c, q, t) \leq q.t_2$ for vehicle c and request q. Two special nodes denoted by $Source$ and $Sink$ are also added, where $Source$ connects to each of the vehicles and $Sink$ connects to each of the requests. Every edge (v_i, v_j) has a $capacity$ and a $cost$ $weight$ attached to it, which are defined as follows:

$$cap(v_i, v_j) = 1, \quad (v_i, v_j) \in E_b \tag{10}$$

$$cw(v_i, v_j) = \begin{cases} -u(v_i, v_j), & v_i \in C, \ v_j \in Q \\ 0, & v_i = Source \ || \ v_j = Sink \end{cases} \tag{11}$$

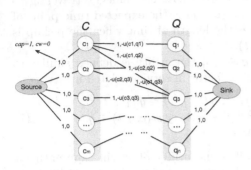

Fig. 1. An example of graph G_b that illustrates the possible match between vehicles and requests. Each edge in the graph is attached with a capacity *cap* and cost weight *cw*.

Fig. 2. Distributions of origin-destination pairs on the Xiamen Island, Fujian Province, China. The red/blue point indicates the origin/destination of a trip. (color figure online)

Algorithm 1: Bipartite Match Algorithm

---
1 $d = min(|C|, |Q|)$;
2 **while** $d > 0$ **do**
3 $\quad$ $\mathcal{M} \leftarrow MCFP(G_b, Source, Sink)$;
4 $\quad$ **if** $\mathcal{M}$ *is a feasible match* **then** break;
5 $\quad$ **else** $d = d - 1$;

6 **return** $\mathcal{M}$;

4.2 Solving the Minimum-Cost Flow Problem

Having the graph G_b built, we transform the static maximal match utility problem defined at Eq. 9 to the following *minimum-cost flow problem* (MCFP) [4]:

$$\text{minimize} : \sum_{(u,v) \in E_b} cw(u,v) * f(u,v) \tag{12}$$

where $f(u,v)$ is the flow through edge (u,v), $f(u,v) = 1$ means there is an assignment (u,v) in the match. When Eq. 12 has the minimal-cost maximum flow, $\mathcal{M}^*$ has the largest overall utility defined at Eq. 9 because the cost weight is set $-u(v_i, v_j)$ in G_b in Eq. 11. Algorithm 1 is the pseudocode of the procedures searching the maximal flow and maximal match utility.

5 Experimental Study

5.1 Experimental Settings

We conduct the experiments with real-world road network of Xiamen island and Xiamen Taxi Trip Datasets. The schemes are implemented in Java 1.8 and

Table 1. Overall performance of the schemes.

Schemes/metrics	Average waiting time (s)	Average matching time (s)	Success ratio of real-time requests	Success ratio of appointment requests	Overall satisfaction ratio	Average income (RMB)
DFM	182.59	0.057	0.5509	0.9147	0.5975	65.26
MFM	193.55	0.073	0.9207	0.9535	0.9242	78.44
MUM	114.46	0.081	0.9347	0.9535	0.9375	79.26
BMF	**107.21**	**0.130**	**0.9375**	**0.9535**	**0.9400**	**79.50**

experiments are run on a desktop server with Intel Core i5 (4 cores), 8 G DDR3 RAM. The origin-destination pairs (Fig. 2) of trips are extracted from taxi operating table of the Xiamen Trip Dataset. The interval between two sequential requests is 3 s and the total simulation time is 1 h.

To study the performances, we also conduct other three algorithms besides the proposed BMF scheme: (1) Distance First Match(DFM): matches a request to the nearest taxi and the matched pairs is irrevocable; (2) Maximum Flow Match (MFM): is adopted based on [9], which uses bipartite graph to match taxis and requests as more as possible; (3) Maximum Utility Match (MUM): uses bipartite graph to match taxis and requests based on the utility calculation similar to BMF, but the requests are not revokable.

5.2   Result Analysis

Overall Performance. By default, the number of vehicles is 300, the length of the pickup window is 5 min, the percentage of appointment-based requests is 10%, the amplifying factor K is 1.5, and the balance factor α is 0.5. The time gap T_1 and T_2 are set 5 and 30 min respectively.

Table 1 presents the overall performance of the schemes. The proposed BMF scheme has the shortest waiting time at 107.21 s. Compared to other schemes, it gains more than 44% of reduction of the average waiting time of riders. Also, BMF has the highest overall request satisfaction ratio at 0.94. The performance of MUM is similar to BMF and has better performance than other schemes. Yet because the assignment is not revokable, taxis might have to fulfill requests even when better matches appear. Compare to other schemes, BMF scheme has larger matching time per epoch. This is because of the extra complexity solving the MCFP problem. The overall income of drivers are also showed in the table. As depicted in Table 1, the proposed BMF scheme has the highest average income. We follow the pricing strategies in Xiamen City and charge 20 RMB additional service fee for the appointment-based requests.

Impact Factors. We also vary other parameters, i.e., the number of taxis, the width of preferred pickup window to study their impact on the schemes. Figure 3 depicts the impact of the number of taxis. From the figure, we could see that the average waiting time of riders for the successful requests decreases as the number of taxis grows for all the schemes. Yet the waiting time of BMF and MUM changes more sharply, which decreases from above 150 s to about 66 s. Figure 4 illustrates the impact of the preferred pickup window of requests, which is set to 1, 3, 5 and 7 min. From Fig. 4 we could see that the satisfaction ratio and income increase as the preferred pickup window grows for all the schemes, but the performance on the average waiting time degrades. This is understandable as larger pickup window means more flexibility on the time, and hence more chance for taxis being able to pickup the riders. So the income of drivers also increases from about 40 RMB to near 80 RMB for most of the schemes except DFM. As the DFM scheme adopts a distance-first approach for the matching, the increased pickup window has less impact on the average waiting time, and its average income is about 13 RMB less than other schemes.

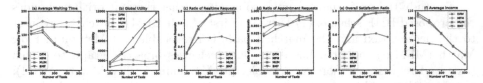

Fig. 3. Impact of number of taxis on (a) the average waiting time, (b) global utility, (c) ratio of real-time requests, (d) ratio of appointment, (e) overall success ratio, and (f) average income.

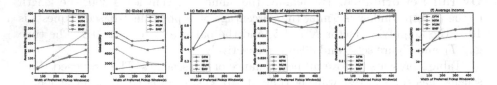

Fig. 4. Impact of the interval of preferred pickup window on (a) the average waiting time, (b) global utility, (c) ratio of real-time requests, (d) ratio of appointment, (e) overall success ratio, and (f) average income.

6   Conclusions

We have proposed an algorithm called BMF to solve the taxi-rider match scheduling problem on the time-dependent road network. The trajectory and service related utilities are defined, based on which the maximal utility calculation is transformed to the minimal cost flow problem that could be solved efficiently. The scheme integrates and processes both the real-time and appointment-based requests, and requests could be revoked to maximize the overall utility. Experimental results show that the proposed scheme can effectively decrease the waiting time of riders.

Acknowledgements. This research is in part supported by the Natural Science Foundation of China (61672441, 61872154, 61862051), the Shenzhen Basic Research Program (JCYJ20170818141325209, JCYJ20190809161603551), Natural Science Foundation of Fujian(2018J01097), Special Fund for Basic Scientific Research Operation Fees of Central Universities (20720200031).

References

1. Abadi, A., Rajabioun, T., Ioannou, P.A.: Traffic flow prediction for road transportation networks with limited traffic data. IEEE Trans. Intell. Transp. Syst. **16**(2), 653–662 (2015)
2. Attanasio, A., Cordeau, J.F., Ghiani, G., Laporte, G.: Parallel tabu search heuristics for the dynamic multi-vehicle dial-a-ride problem. Parallel Comput. **30**(3), 377–387 (2004)
3. Cordeau, J.F., Laporte, G.: The dial-a-ride problem: models and algorithms. Ann. Oper. Res. **153**(1), 29–46 (2007). https://doi.org/10.1007/s10479-007-0170-8
4. Goldberg, A.V., Tarjan, R.E.: Finding minimum-cost circulations by canceling negative cycles. J. ACM (JACM) **36**(4), 873–886 (1989)
5. Hassan, U.U., Curry, E.: A multi-armed bandit approach to online spatial task assignment. In: Ubiquitous Intelligence and Computing, pp. 212–219. IEEE (2014)
6. Li, M., et al.: Efficient ridesharing order dispatching with mean field multi-agent reinforcement learning, pp. 983–994 (2019)
7. Ma, S., Zheng, Y., Wolfson, O.: T-share: a large-scale dynamic taxi ridesharing service. In: 2013 IEEE 29th International Conference on Data Engineering (ICDE), pp. 410–421. IEEE (2013)
8. Tang, X., Qin, Z.T., Zhang, F., Wang, Z., Ye, J.: A deep value-network based approach for multi-driver order dispatching. In: The 25th ACM SIGKDD International Conference (2019)
9. Tong, Y., She, J., Ding, B., Chen, L., Wo, T., Xu, K.: Online minimum matching in real-time spatial data: experiments and analysis. Proc. VLDB Endow. **9**(12), 1053–1064 (2016)
10. Tong, Y., She, J., Ding, B., Wang, L., Chen, L.: Online mobile micro-task allocation in spatial crowdsourcing. In: 2016 IEEE 32nd International Conference on Data Engineering (ICDE), pp. 49–60. IEEE (2016)
11. Tong, Y., et al.: Flexible online task assignment in real-time spatial data. Proc. VLDB Endow. **10**(11), 1334–1345 (2017)
12. Wong, R.C.W., Tao, Y., Fu, A.W.C., Xiao, X.: On efficient spatial matching. In: Proceedings of the 33rd International Conference on Very Large Data Bases, pp. 579–590 (2007). VLDB Endow
13. Yiu, M.L., Mouratidis, K., Mamoulis, N., et al.: Capacity constrained assignment in spatial databases. In: Proceedings of the 2008 ACM SIGMOD International Conference on Management of Data, pp. 15–28. ACM (2008)

FHAN: Feature-Level Hierarchical Attention Network for Group Event Recommendation

Guoqiong Liao[1], Xiaobin Deng[1,2(✉)], Xiaomei Huang[1], and Changxuan Wan[1]

[1] School of Information Management, Jiangxi University of Finance and Economics, Nanchang, China
liaoguoqiong@163.com, dengxiaobin83@163.com, huangxm501@126.com, wanchangxuan@263.net
[2] Jiangxi Water Resources Institute, Nanchang, China

Abstract. Recommending events to groups is different from to single-user in event-based social networks (EBSN), which involves various complex factors. Generally, group recommendation methods are either based on recommendation fusion or model fusion. However, most existing methods neglect the fact that user preferences change over time. Moreover, they believe that the weights of different factors that affect group decision-making are fixed in different periods. Recently, there are a few works using the attention mechanism for group recommendation. Although they take into account the dynamic variability of user preferences and the dynamic adjustment of user features weights, they haven't discussed more features of groups and events affecting group decision-making. To this end, we propose a novel Feature-level Hierarchical Attention Network (FHAN) for group event recommendation for EBSN. Specifically, group decision-making factors are divided into group-feature factors and event-feature factors, which are integrated into a two-layer attention network. The first attention layer is constructed to learn the influence weights of words of group topics and event topics, which generates better thematic features. The second attention layer is built to learn the weights of group-feature factors and event-feature factors affecting group decision-making, which results in better comprehensive representation of groups and events. All influence weights of different features in the model can be dynamically adjusted over time. Finally, we evaluate the suggested model on three real-world datasets. Extensive experimental results show that FHAN outperforms the state-of-the-art approaches.

Keywords: Event-based social network · Hierarchical attention network · Group recommendation · CNN

1 Introduction

With the rapid development of social network services, Event-Based Social Networks (EBSN) have emerged and become more and more popular, such as Meetup, Plancast, Douban, etc. Through the platforms, it is easier for people to organize and participate in events or activities such as going to concerts with friends, watching movies with

© Springer Nature Switzerland AG 2020
X. Wang et al. (Eds.): APWeb-WAIM 2020, LNCS 12317, pp. 478–492, 2020.
https://doi.org/10.1007/978-3-030-60259-8_35

family and attending academic meetings with colleagues, Differing from ordinary social networks, EBSN generally don't serve for a single user, but rather for groups attending activities together. Therefore, recommending events to groups has become an important task for EBSN.

The group recommendation systems usually fuse the preferences of each user in a group when recommending [1], which may occur at different stages of recommendation process. In generally, preference fusion methods can be divided into two categories [6, 8, 23]: recommendation fusion and model fusion. Among them, the recommendation fusion is to first generate a recommendation or calculate a prediction score for each group member, and then generate a group recommendation or a group prediction score [2, 5]; the model fusion is to first fuse member preference models for generating a group preference model, and then make recommendations [3, 7–9]. Whether using the methods based on recommendation fusion or model fusion, the user preferences in the group are usually considered in a static form, which is inconsistent with the real situation that user preferences may change over time. Moreover, these methods believe that the weights of factors that affect group decision-making are fixed in different periods. [26, 27] proposed the group recommendation methods based on attention mechanism, which take into account the dynamic variability of user preferences and the dynamic adjustment of the weights of user feature factors. However they haven't considered more features of groups and events such as the categories of groups, the locations of events, the cost of events, the topics of groups and events, etc.

The motivation of the solution in this paper is: group participation in an event activity is affected by a variety of factors, and different factors have different influence weights on the group's decision whether to participate in an event activity and the influence weights are not fixed, but change over time. For example, multiple members of a family form a group and decide whether to go to cinema together. There are some factors that affect them to go to cinema together: (1) Whether the content of the movie meets their interests; (2) The price of movie ticket; (3) The movie broadcast time; (4) The distance which is from the cinema to home and so on. If the movie theater is far away from their home, "distance" may be an important factor for them to consider when the family decides whether to go to cinema. If the family buys a private car over time, traveling becomes very convenient. So when the family considers whether to watch a movie next time, "distance" may be not an important factor for them to consider. Therefore, the influence weight of "distance" has changed when they decide whether to watch a movie.

To this end, we propose a novel method called Feature-level Hierarchical Attention Network (FHAN) for recommending events to groups in EBSN. In order to capture the dynamic attributes of influencing factors, we use the attention networks that can automatically assign the weight of each factor and adjust it dynamically. The hierarchical structure can better generate different levels of group features and event features. Specifically, we first embed the original features both of groups and events into a low-dimensional dense vector space. Then we use a convolutional neural network and an attention mechanism to learn the topical characteristics of groups and events. The influence weights of group theme features, event theme features, and other features are learned through another attention mechanism. Weights and feature vectors are weighted and summed, and then be sent to a fully connected neural network. Thus, a high-level group representation and event representation are obtained. The contributions of the paper can be summarized as follows:

- For recommending events to groups, we build a feature-level hierarchical attention network framework with good scalability. To best of our knowledge, it is the first work to generalize a framework using feature-level attention for group event recommendation in EBSN.
- Through the feature-level hierarchical attention network, not only can we learn the influence weights of different words on the group topics and event topics, resulting in better theme characteristics, but also learn the influence weights of the group-feature factors and event-feature factors. The influence weights can be dynamically adjusted over time. Finally, a high-level comprehensive feature representation of group and event are generated for group event recommendation.
- We have performed experiments on three real datasets, to verify that the suggested model have better performance than the state-of-art models.

The remaining of the paper is organized as follows: Sect. 2 introduces the related works; the problem statement is discussed in Sect. 3; Sect. 4 describes the details of FHAN; Comparative experiments on real datasets are conducted in Sect. 5, and we summarize the work in the end.

2   Related Work

Group recommendation is different from traditional recommendation, and mainly uses preference fusion methods for recommendation, which can be divided into model-based fusion methods and recommendation-based fusion methods [24].

The model fusion method fuses user preferences of group to generate a group preference model, and then group recommendation is produced based on the group preference model. Yu et al. [8] proposed a model fusion method based on item feature scores. The process of model fusion is to find the preference model with the smallest global distance of user preference models in the group as the group preference model. Yuan et al. [4] proposed a probabilistic model called COM to simulate the generation of group preferences for events. COM aggregates the preferences of group members with different weights to estimate the group's preferences for events, thereby performing group recommendation. Kagita et al. [10] proposed a fusion method based on priority sequence mining and virtual user model. The user preference model is composed of a series of item sequences. It constructs a virtual user preference model through priority sequence mining to achieve preference fusion.

The recommendation fusion method fuses users' prediction score or a list of recommended items to obtain a group prediction score or a group recommendation list. O'Connor et al. [23] combined the user recommendation list with the least pain strategy to get the group recommendation list. Chen et al. [11] used genetic algorithm to optimize the weights of group members, and proposed a group recommendation method combining collaborative filtering and genetic algorithm. The research results of Naamani-Dery et al. [12] show that a balance can be found between the size of the recommendation list and the cost of group preference extraction, and the scale of the group recommendation list can be reduced by iterative preference extraction.

Whether it is a method based on traditional recommendation fusion or model fusion, they did not consider that the preferences of users in the group change dynamically over time, and they did not even consider the influence weights of group feature and event feature on the decision-making problem.

Recently, attention mechanism has become a research hotspot. There are a large number of applications in the fields of natural language processing, statistical learning, image video and recommendation systems [13–17].

Researchers engaged in the research of recommendation systems have introduced the attention mechanism to improve the recommendation performance. Chen et al. [18] proposed Attention Collaborative Filtering (ACF) model and introduced a novel attention mechanism in collaborative filtering to solve challenging of item and component-level implicit feedback in multimedia recommendation. He et al. [15] proposed a neural network model called NAIS to solve the problem of collaborative filtering of projects. The key of NAIS is the attention network and it can distinguish which historical item in the users' portrait is more important for prediction. Ying et al. [19] proposed a novel two-layer hierarchical attention network that expresses users' long-term and short-term preferences through different layers of attention, forming final preferences, and recommending the next item that users may be interested in. Zhou et al. [20] proposed a modeling framework called ATRank for user heterogeneous behavior sequences based on attention mechanism, and applied it to recommendation scenarios. Chen et al. [21] proposed a probabilistic model HTPF, which takes into account both user attention and preferences in social recommendation.

The above studies are applied to the traditional recommendation system. It provides a good research idea for the combination of attention mechanism and group recommendation. Cao et al. [27] proposed the AGREE model. For the first time, the attention mechanism in neural networks is used for group recommendation. However, this method doesn't consider the influence weights of the item features. Vinh Tran et al. [26] proposed the MoSAN model, which introduces attention mechanism to group recommendation. This method can model complex group decision-making processes. But it lacks in-depth mining features of the topics both of groups and events. Moreover, it doesn't consider the comprehensive impact of both group features and event features on group decisions.

3 Problem Statement

Let $G = \{g_1, g_2, \dots g_L\}$ denote a set of groups; $U = \{u_1, u_2, \dots u_N\}$ denote a set of users; $E = \{e_1, e_2, \dots e_M\}$ denote a set of events; where L, N and M are the total numbers of groups, users and events, respectively. Each group consists of several users.

The decision whether a group participate an event is influenced by group-feature factors and event-feature factors. In this paper, we just list some important factors for discussion. The group-feature factors mainly include topic users and category of a group, and the event-feature factors include topic time, distance and cost of an event. Whether it is a group feature or an event feature, the degree of influence on the decision is different. Moreover, the influence weights are not fixed, but change with time.

Our goal is to predict the group's preference for the event, given group g and event activity e.

Input: group original features, event original features, target group g, target event e.

Output: group $g's$ preference score for event e.

4   FHAN Model

This section introduces suggested feature-level hierarchical attention group event recommendation (FHAN) model. We show the general framework first, and then describe the specific situations at each layer.

4.1   Model Framework

Our FHAN model architecture is shown in Fig. 1, which is a feature-level hierarchical attention network. The bottom layer is the decision factors that influence the group participation event. The left side is the group-feature factors and the right side is the event-feature factors. We first embed all factors into the low-dimensional dense vector space through embedding. For factors other than group topics and event topics, we directly use their low-dimensional dense vectors as their feature vectors. The topics of group and event are generally the main factors affecting group decision-making, and are generally described in text. Therefore, we construct the first-level attention network to learn about this part of the elements, which uses the attention mechanism to capture the weights of the words' impact on text sentences. The convolution and pooling operation of the convolutional neural network are used to obtain the final semantics of the text. Finally, the topic features of group and event are obtained through the fully connected layer learning.

After obtaining the feature vectors of group-feature factors and event-feature factors, in order to capture how various factors influence the decision of group participation event, we build the second-level attention network. It can automatically learn the impact weight of each factor through the attention mechanism. The weights and feature vectors are weighted and summed, and then we send it to the fully connected network. After that, we obtain high-level representation of group and event. Finally, the representation of group and event is multiplied to obtain the group's prediction score for event.

This paper provides a general model framework. The influencing factors are not limited to those listed in the model framework. Users can compress or expand according to their own conditions. At the same time, the attention mechanism can also be appropriately adjusted. For example, if the different influence weights of users in the group on event preferences are to be considered, the attention mechanism can be added before "group users" mapping feature vectors.

4.2   Embedding Layer

One-Hot encoding is usually used as an embedding vector of attributes, but it is too sparse and the relationship between the data is lost. Therefore, this paper does not use One-Hot coding. Instead, we encode a digital dictionary containing raw data such as

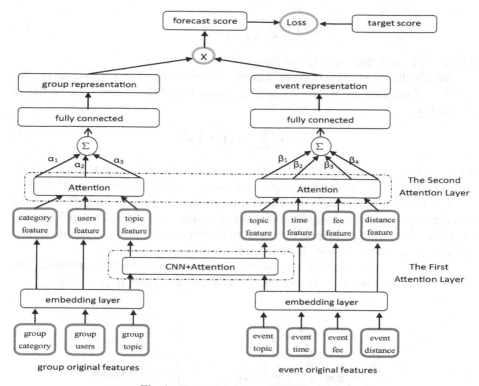

Fig. 1. The architecture of FHAN model

group category, group users, group topic, event topic, event time, event cost, and event distance. Then a dictionary embedding matrix will be constructed and the embedding vector of each factor will be obtained through look-up table. The category embedding vector $g_{category}$ of group, user embedding vector g_{users} of group, event time embedding vector e_{time}, event cost embedding vector e_{fee}, and event distance embedding vector $e_{distance}$ are directly used as their respective feature vectors.

4.3 First Attention Layer

Figure 2 is the expanded form of the first attention layer. First, the topics of group and event are mapped to a low-dimensional vector space through embedding. The dimension set in this paper is 30, which is enough to express text semantics. Let $K = \{1,2,3, ..., 30\}$. The input vectors of this layer are $X_1, X_2, X_3....X_{30}$. The topics are text composed of words. There is a contextual relationship between words. The context at different positions has different weights on the semantic impact of words. We can learn the influence weights of words through the attention mechanism. Take the vector X_3 as an example and directly use the similarity to calculate the weights. Formula 1 is to calculate the influence weights. Formula 2 is to calculate the weighted sum of the weights and the vectors.

$$\gamma_{3,i} = \frac{X_i X_3}{\sum_{i \in K \cap i \neq 3} X_i X_3}, \tag{1}$$

$$\mathbf{Y}_3 = \sum_{i \in K \cap i \neq 3} \gamma_{3,i} \mathbf{X}_i, \tag{2}$$

where $\gamma_{3,i}$ is the influence weight of the i-th input vector on $\mathbf{X}_3$.

We get the weighted sum of each input vector through the attention layer: $\mathbf{Y}_1$, $\mathbf{Y}_2$, $\mathbf{Y}_3 \ldots \mathbf{Y}_{30}$. Then use the convolution operation to get the feature map, as shown in formula 3.

$$\mathbf{A} = f\left(\sum \mathbf{W}_0 \mathbf{Y} + \mathbf{b}_0\right), \tag{3}$$

where $\mathbf{A}$ is the feature map output by the convolution layer, f is the ReLu activation function, $\mathbf{W}_0$ and $\mathbf{b}_0$ are filtering weights and filtering offset parameters, respectively.

The main function of the Pooling layer is down-sampling, which further reduces the number of parameters by removing unimportant features in the feature map. There are many Pooling methods. This paper uses Max Pooling, which is to take the maximum value in the feature as the sample value after sampling.

After the convolution and pooling layers, the input vector is finally transformed into low-dimensional dense topic feature vectors for group and event: $\mathbf{g}_{topic}$ and $\mathbf{e}_{topic}$.

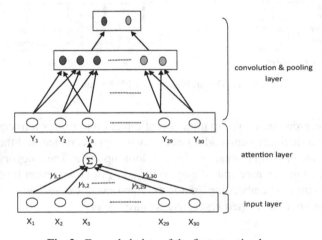

Fig. 2. Expanded view of the first attention layer

4.4 Second Attention Layer

The influence weights of group-feature factors and event-feature factors are calculated through neural network learning. Equations 4 and 5 show the calculation of group-feature factors' affecting weights. For the calculation of event-feature factors' affecting weights, see Eq. 6 and 7.

$$\mathbf{h}_i = \varnothing(\mathbf{W}_i \mathbf{g}_i + \mathbf{b}_i), \tag{4}$$

$$\alpha_i = \frac{exp\left(\mathbf{u}_i^T \mathbf{h}_i\right)}{\sum_{i \in \{\text{categry}:1,\text{users}:2,\text{topic}:3\}} exp\left(\mathbf{u}_i^T \mathbf{h}_i\right)}, \tag{5}$$

$$\mathbf{h}_j = \varnothing\left(\mathbf{W}_j \mathbf{e}_j + \mathbf{b}_j\right) \tag{6}$$

$$\beta_j = \frac{exp\left(\mathbf{u}_j^T \mathbf{h}_j\right)}{\sum_{j \in \{\text{topic}:1,\text{time}:2,\text{fee}:3,\text{distance}:4\}} exp\left(\mathbf{u}_j^T \mathbf{h}_j\right)}, \tag{7}$$

where $\mathbf{W}_i$, $\mathbf{b}_i$ and $\mathbf{u}_i$ denote model parameters of group-feature factors, $\mathbf{W}_j$, $\mathbf{b}_j$ and $\mathbf{u}_j$ denote model parameters of event-feature factors, $\mathbf{h}_i$ and $\mathbf{h}_j$ represent implicit representations of group-feature factors and event-feature factors, $\mathbf{g}_i$ and $\mathbf{e}_j$ are feature vector of the factors generated by the embedding layer and the first attention layer, respectively. $\varnothing$ is the activation function and we use *tanh* as the activation function. α_i and β_j are the influence weights of group-feature factors and event-feature factors, respectively. Finally, we calculate the attention-weighted summation of group features and event features to obtain the group feature vector $\mathbf{g}_{\text{group}}$ and event feature vector $\mathbf{e}_{\text{event}}$ at this stage.

$$\mathbf{g}_{\text{group}} = \sum_{i \in \{\text{categry}:1,\text{users}:2,\text{topic}:3\}} \alpha_i \mathbf{g}_i, \tag{8}$$

$$\mathbf{e}_{\text{event}} = \sum_{j \in \{\text{topic}:1,\text{time}:2,\text{fee}:3,\text{distance}:4\}} \beta_j \mathbf{e}_j. \tag{9}$$

4.5 Fully Connected Layer and Output Layer

We send the group feature vector $\mathbf{g}_{\text{group}}$ and the event feature vector $\mathbf{e}_{\text{event}}$ to the fully connected layer to further learn the features. Then map them to vector space of the same dimension at the same time. Finally, the final representation vector of the group $\mathbf{g}$ is multiplied with the final representation vector of the event $\mathbf{e}$ to obtain a prediction score.

$$\mathbf{g} = tanh\left(\mathbf{W}_{\text{group}} \mathbf{g}_{\text{group}} + \mathbf{b}_{\text{group}}\right), \tag{10}$$

$$\mathbf{e} = tanh(\mathbf{W}_{\text{event}} \mathbf{e}_{\text{event}} + \mathbf{b}_{\text{event}}), \tag{11}$$

$$\hat{y}_{ge} = \mathbf{g} \cdot \mathbf{e}^T. \tag{12}$$

4.6 Model Training

We take the group's rating for event as a regression task. We use supervised method to train the model and take the mean square error as the loss function. AdamOptimizer as the optimizer is used to optimize the mean square error function.

$$\mathcal{L} = \frac{1}{N} \sum (\hat{y} - y)^2, \tag{13}$$

where N represents the number of samples in the training dataset, y and $\hat{y}$ denote the real target score and prediction score in the training dataset.

5 Experiment

In this section, we compare the experimental results of FHAN with other five baseline methods and three variant methods on three real datasets. Generally speaking, our experimental goal is to answer the following research questions (RQ):

- RQ1: How does FHAN perform as compared to existing advanced methods?
- RQ2: How does attention affect FHAN model?
- RQ3: How does FHAN model perform with different hyper-parameters values?

5.1 Experiment Setup

Datasets. We performed experiments on three real datasets. The first two datasets are from two different cities on the Meetup[1] website: Philadelphia and Montgomery. There are 239 groups and 22358 events in the Philadelphia dataset, and 1347 groups and 25408 events in the Montgomery dataset. The actual score data of the two datasets is a floating point number between 0–5. We discarded the data with zero score. The zero score is most likely that the user did not participate in scoring and does not represent the true score. Both datasets include various group-feature factors and event-feature factors, such as group category, group users, group topic, group latitude and longitude, event topic, event time, event cost, and event latitude and longitude. This paper calculates the distance which is from the group location to the event location according to the latitude and longitude of the group and the event. The distance is considered as an event-feature factor. So the group-feature factors and event-feature factors contained in Philadelphia and Montgomery datasets are: group topic, group category, group users, event topic, event time, event fee, event distance.

The third dataset comes from MovieLens 1M. This dataset contains more than 100 million comments from more than 6,000 users on nearly 4,000 movies. Since MovieLens 1M contains only users and no groups. This paper first divides users who have rated the same movie into a group, so that we have nearly 4,000 groups. Then take the user-rated movies as events that the group has participated in. If there are multiple users rating a movie at the same time, we take their average score as the score for a group participating movie event. Therefore, the group's score for movie ratings ranges from 1 to 5. Each group is equivalent to participating in multiple movie events. Finally, we generate a new dataset MovieLens New. The new dataset includes one group-feature factor and two event-feature factors: group users, event topic and event time.

Table 1 is the statistical information of the three datasets. We divide the three datasets into training dataset and testing dataset.

Evaluation Metrics. We use two indicators to evaluate model performance: Root Mean Square Error (RMSE) and Mean Absolute Error (MAE). For the two metrics, a smaller metric value indicates better recommendations.

---

[1] http://www.meetup.com/.

Table 1. Statistics of datasets.

Datasets	Philadelphia	Montgomery	MovieLens New
Group	239	1347	3952
Event	22358	25408	3952
Score	(0, 5]	(0, 5]	[1, 5]

$$RMSE = \sqrt{\frac{1}{|T|} \sum_{(g,e) \in T} (\hat{y}_{ge} - y_{ge})^2}, \tag{14}$$

$$MAE = \frac{1}{|T|} \sum_{(g,e) \in T} |\hat{y}_{ge} - y_{ge}|, \tag{15}$$

where g and e represent groups and events, and T is the number of samples in the test set, $\hat{y}_{ge}$ and y_{ge} denote the prediction score and real target score in the test set.

Baselines. We compared our model FHAN with baseline methods as follows.

- **Random:** An algorithm that predicts a random score based on the distribution of the training set, assuming the distribution is normal.
- **CF** [25]: The similarity between users or projects is combined with the user's historical scoring data to calculate the user's preference for the project. This method has the problems of sparse data and cold start.
- **NMF** [22]: The generalized structure of matrix factorization and the structure of multi-layer perceptron are combined, and the linear features of matrix factorization and the non-offline features of neural networks are combined in the modeling user-item interaction.
- **AGREE** [27]: It is the first to use the attention mechanism in neural networks for group recommendation. This model considers that the members of the group have different weights for different items. The user-item interaction information is used to improve the effect of group recommendation. AGREE is similar to the variant method in our model framework that puts an attention mechanism before the "group user" embedding vector instead of the "group topic" and lacks another attention mechanism.
- **MoSAN** [26]: It uses an attention mechanism to obtain the influence of each user in the group. The model can learn the influence weights of users in the group, and it recommends items to the group based on the weights and preferences of its members. The method can model complex group decision-making processes. This method considers different contexts when calculating the influence weights of users in a group, which is similar to the structure of our model removing "CNN + Attention" and only considering the issue of user-user interactions attention weights.
- **FHAN0:** A variant of the model in this paper, which removes the attention mechanism based on the model FHAN.

Table 2. Performance comparison of different methods

Training	Metrics	Algorithms								
		Random	CF	NMF	AGREE	MoSAN	FHAN 0	FHAN 1-1	FHAN 1-2	FHAN
Philadelphia (50%)	RMSE	0.744	0.611	0.573	0.501	0.498	0.527	0.488	0.485	**0.421**
	MAE	0.492	0.384	0.384	0.363	0.369	0.379	0.375	0.369	**0.338**
Philadelphia (70%)	RMSE	0.712	0.558	0.561	0.493	0.489	0.515	0.472	0.471	**0.402**
	MAE	0.483	0.371	0.373	0.358	0.365	0.372	0.369	0.363	**0.311**
Philadelphia (90%)	RMSE	0.699	0.55	0.551	0.482	0.48	0.505	0.465	0.461	**0.385**
	MAE	0.471	0.363	0.363	0.349	0.354	0.365	0.359	0.356	**0.292**
Montgomery (50%)	RMSE	0.751	0.622	0.575	0.506	0.499	0.526	0.485	0.483	**0.425**
	MAE	0.493	0.383	0.384	0.364	0.369	0.381	0.377	0.371	**0.339**
Montgomery (70%)	RMSE	0.711	0.556	0.561	0.491	0.487	0.513	0.477	0.476	**0.412**
	MAE	0.484	0.375	0.375	0.359	0.366	0.374	0.368	0.364	**0.313**
Montgomery (90%)	RMSE	0.697	0.552	0.549	0.483	0.482	0.508	0.464	0.463	**0.382**
	MAE	0.473	0.361	0.362	0.348	0.353	0.368	0.355	0.359	**0.288**
MovieLens New (50%)	RMSE	1.592	0.985	0.981	0.891	0.881	0.922	0.882	0.883	**0.834**
	MAE	1.226	0.751	0.743	0.693	0.699	0.723	0.699	0.698	**0.645**
MovieLens New (70%)	RMSE	1.573	0.976	0.967	0.883	0.874	0.913	0.871	0.872	**0.825**
	MAE	1.218	0.743	0.737	0.685	0.691	0.712	0.695	0.691	**0.634**
MovieLens New (90%)	RMSE	1.505	0.923	0.916	0.862	0.862	0.892	0.863	0.86	**0.816**
	MAE	1.207	0.728	0.724	0.679	0.68	0.703	0.689	0.682	**0.625**

- **FHAN1-1:** A variant of the model in this paper. It is equivalent to the model that the second-level attention mechanism is removed and the first-level attention mechanism is retained in FHAN.
- **FHAN1-2:** A variant of the model in this paper. It is equivalent to the model that the first-level attention mechanism is removed and the second-level attention mechanism is retained in FHAN.

Parameter Settings. The dimensions of the embedding matrix are 32 dimensions for the two datasets on Meetup and the MovieLens New dataset is 256 dimensions. The learning rate is set to 0.0001. We take AdamOptimize as optimizer. The dropout is set to 0.2 and the batch_size is set to 256. The convolution sliding window window_sizes = {2, 3, 4, 5}. The number of convolution kernels is 8. The attention_size is set to 8. Epoch = 20.

5.2 Overall Performance Comparison (RQ1)

On three datasets, we compared the FHAN model with other baseline methods, as shown in Table 2. We have the following observations: (1) Our FHAN model achieves the best on all three datasets, which is better than the current advanced methods. On both indicators, it is less than 0.05 compared to each baseline method, which shows that our model has clearly improved in terms of performance; (2) The models that use attention (including the baseline method and our model method) perform better than models that do not use attention, indicating that the attention mechanism has played a role in improving model performance; (3) The AGREE and MoSAN models are inferior to our FHAN model, because they only consider the impact weight of "group users" factor and the MoSAN model does not fully mine the topic semantics of groups and events; (4) The higher the proportion of the training dataset, the better the performance of each model, which shows that training with a large amount of data can better fit the model and can learn better features. Training with a small amount of data will cause the model to be under-fitting.

5.3   The Role of Attention on the Model (RQ2)

From the experimental results of the model FHAN and the variant models FHAN0, FHAN1-1, FHAN1-2, the hierarchical attention model is better than the model without attention or with the single-layer attention. It indicates that two attention mechanisms layers have a positive effect on the model. The first attention layer promotes the model to capture the influence weights of words in text semantics, resulting in better topic feature vectors for group and event. The second attention layer enables the model to automatically calculate the influence weights of group-feature factors and event-feature factors, resulting in more excellent comprehensive feature vectors of group and event.

In order to better understand the dynamic changes of the weights generated by the attention mechanism in the model, we take the Philadelphia city dataset as an example, and sort the training data set by the time of the event. We take out 50%, 70%, and 90% of the data volume, respectively. We examine the change in the output values of the second-level attention weights. As shown in Fig. 3, Fig. 3(a) is the changes in the attention weights of group-feature factors at three different moments, reflecting that the influence weight of the group topic is decreasing, and the influence weights of the user and category of the group are increasing. The reason may be that more consideration is given to: how the opinions of the users in the group are unified and whether the type of event activity is consistent with the type of group attention. Figure 3(b) shows the changes in attention weights of event-feature factors at three different moments, reflecting that the topic impact weight of the event is first rise and then fall, the cost and distance impact weights of the event are decreasing, and the time impact weight of the event is increasing. The reason may be that the group's interest in the event's topical declines after rising, and group does not care much about the cost of participating in the event and the location of the event. They are more concerned about whether they have time to participate in the event.

5.4   Effect of Hyper-parameters on Model Performance (RQ3)

There are mainly two hyper-parameters in the FHAN model: Attention Size and Group Size. Since the two urban datasets on Meetup are basically the same in terms of the impact of hyper-parameters on model performance, this paper selects the Philadelphia city data representative Meetup dataset.

Attention Size. The attention size may affect the model's ability to evaluate source information and choose an appropriate recommendation strategy. In order to study the effect of attention size, we tested the model performance when the attention size was 8, 16, 32 and 64, as shown in Fig. 4. The results show that FHAN is robust to changes in attention size. For the Meetup dataset, we set the attention size to 8, and it is possible to calculate the feature vectors with a small attention size. However, excessive attention size may cause over-fitting and degrade model performance. For the MovieLens New dataset, because it is not sensitive to the choice of attention size, we also set the attention size to 8.

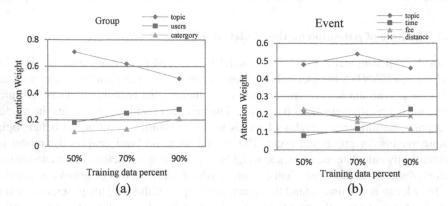

Fig. 3. The changes of attention weight

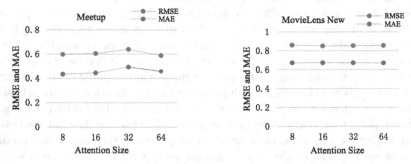

Fig. 4. Impact of attention size: RMSE and MAE of FHAN model on two datasets.

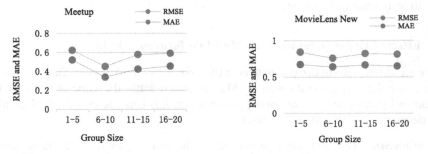

Fig. 5. Impact of group size: RMSE and MAE of FHAN model on two datasets.

Group Size. To study the performance of FHAN model on different group sizes, we run the experiments when the group size was {1–5, 6–10, 11–15, 16–20} members. As shown in Fig. 5, the results show that the FHAN model performs best at a group size of 6–10 members.

6 Conclusions

In this paper, we propose a model called FHAN to solve the problem of recommending events to groups. The FHAN model not only captures the influence weights of words when learning the topic feature of group and event, but also captures the influence decision weights of group-feature factors and event-feature factors when learning the comprehensive features of group and event. These impact weights are not fixed but dynamically adjusted. Finally, we generate a high-level comprehensive feature representation of group and event, which makes the prediction score of the group participation event more accurate. Experimenting on three real datasets, our FHAN model performs best. In future research work, we intend to further optimize the model and improve the model recommendation performance.

Acknowledgement. This research was supported in part by the National Natural Science Foundation of China (No. 61772245), the Jiangxi Provincial Graduate Innovation Fund (No. YC2019-B093) and the Science and Technology Project of Jiangxi Provincial Department of Education (No. GJJ181349).

References

1. Garcia, I., Pajares, S., Sebastia, L., et al.: Preference elicitation techniques for group recommender systems. Inf. Sci. **189**, 155–175 (2012)
2. Baltrunas, L., Makcinskas, T., Ricci, F.: Group recommendations with rank aggregation and collaborative filtering. In: RecSys, pp. 119–126 (2010)
3. Berkovsky, S., Freyne, J.: Group-based recipe recommendations: analysis of data aggregation strategies. In: RecSys, pp. 111–118 (2010)
4. Yuan, Q., Cong, G., Lin, C.Y.: COM: a generative model for group recommendation. In: SIGKDD, pp. 163–172 (2014)
5. De Campos, L.M., Fernández-Luna, J.M., Huete, J.F., et al.: Managing uncertainty in group recommending processes. User Model. User-Adap. Interact. **19**(3), 207–242 (2009). https://doi.org/10.1007/s11257-008-9061-1
6. Jameson, A., Smyth, B.: Recommendation to groups. In: Brusilovsky, P., Kobsa, A., Nejdl, W. (eds.) The Adaptive Web. LNCS, vol. 4321, pp. 596–627. Springer, Heidelberg (2007). https://doi.org/10.1007/978-3-540-72079-9_20
7. Masthoff, J.: Group recommender systems: combining individual models. In: Ricci, F., Rokach, L., Shapira, B., Kantor, P.B. (eds.) Recommender Systems Handbook, pp. 677–702. Springer, Boston, MA (2011). https://doi.org/10.1007/978-0-387-85820-3_21
8. Yu, Z., Zhou, X., Hao, Y., et al.: TV program recommendation for multiple viewers based on user profile merging. User Model. User-Adap. Interact. **16**(1), 63–82 (2006). https://doi.org/10.1007/s11257-006-9005-6

9. Seko, S., Yagi, T., Motegi, M., et al.: Group recommendation using feature space representing behavioral tendency and power balance among members. In: RecSys, pp. 101–108 (2011)

10. Kagita, V.R., Pujari, A.K., Padmanabhan, V.: Virtual user approach for group recommender systems using precedence relations. Inf. Sci. **294**(3), 15–30 (2015)

11. Chen, Y.L., Cheng, L.C., Chuang, C.N.: A group recommendation system with consideration of interactions among group members. Expert Syst. Appl. **34**(3), 2082–2090 (2008)

12. Naamani-Dery, L., Kalech, M., Rokach, L., et al.: Preference elicitation for narrowing the recommended list for groups. In: RecSys, pp. 333–336 (2014)

13. Cho, K., Courville, A., Bengio, Y.: Describing multimedia content using attention-based encoder-decoder networks. IEEE Trans. Multimedia **17**(11), 1875–1886 (2015)

14. Lee, J., Shin, J.H., Kim, J.S.: Interactive visualization and manipulation of attention-based neural machine translation. In: EMNLP, pp. 121–126. ACL (2017)

15. He, X., He, Z., Song, J., et al.: NAIS: neural attentive item similarity model for recommendation. IEEE TKDE **30**(12), 2354–2366 (2018)

16. Kiela, D., Wang, C., Cho, K.: Dynamic meta-embeddings for improved sentence representations. In: EMNLP, pp. 1466–1477 (2018)

17. Li, X., Zhao, B., Lu, X.: MAM-RNN: multi-level attention model based RNN for video captioning. In: IJCAI, pp. 2208–2214 (2017)

18. Chen, J., Zhang, H., He, X., et al.: Attentive collaborative filtering: multimedia recommendation with item- and component-level attention. In: SIGIR, pp. 335–344 (2017)

19. Ying, H., Zhuang, F., Zhang, F., et al.: Sequential recommender system based on hierarchical attention networks. In: The 27th International Joint Conference on Artificial Intelligence (2018)

20. Zhou, C., Bai, J., Song, J., et al.: ATRank: an attention-based user behavior modeling framework for recommendation. In: AAAI (2018)

21. Chen, J., Wang, C., Shi, Q., et al.: Social recommendation based on users' attention and prefence. Neurocomputing **341**, 1–9 (2019)

22. He, X., Liao, L., Zhang, H., et al.: Neural collaborative filtering. In: WWW, pp. 173–182 (2017)

23. O'connor, M., Cosley, D., Konstan, J.A., Riedl, J.: PolyLens: a recommender system for groups of users. In: Prinz, W., Jarke, M., Rogers, Y., Schmidt, K., Wulf, V. (eds.) ECSCW, pp. 199–218. Springer, Dordrecht (2001). https://doi.org/10.1007/0-306-48019-0_11

24. Yujie, Z., Yulu, D., Xiangwu, M.: Research on group recommender systems and their applications. Chin. J. Comput. **4**, 745–764 (2016)

25. Breese, J.S., Heckerman, D., Kadie, C.: Empirical analysis of predictive algorithms for collaborative filtering. In: Proceedings of the 14th Conference on Uncertainty in Artificial Intelligence, Madison, USA, pp. 43–52 (1998)

26. Vinh Tran, L., Nguyen Pham, T.A., Tay, Y., et al.: Interact and decide: medley of sub-attention networks for effective group recommendation. In: SIGIR, pp. 255–264 (2019)

27. Cao, D., He, X., Miao, L., et al.: Attentive group recommendation. In: SIGIR, pp. 645–654 (2018)

KASR: Knowledge-Aware Sequential Recommendation

Qingqin Wang[1], Yun Xiong[1,2(✉)], Yangyong Zhu[1,2], and Philip S. Yu[3]

[1] Shanghai Key Laboratory of Data Science, School of Computer Science,
Fudan University, Shanghai, China
{qqwang18,yunx,yyzhu}@fudan.edu.cn
[2] Shanghai Institute for Advanced Communication and Data Science,
Fudan University, Shanghai, China
[3] Computer Science Department, University of Illinois at Chicago,
Chicago, IL 60607, USA
psyu@uic.edu

Abstract. The goal of sequential recommendations is to capture the transitions of users' interests. Most existing methods utilize sequential neural networks to model interaction records, mapping items into latent vectors. Although such methods do explore the transitions of items in interaction sequences, they only capture the sequence dependencies of items, neglecting the deep semantic relevance between items. Such limited information contributes less to catching the complicated sequential behaviors of users accurately. In this paper, we propose a novel model Knowledge-Aware Sequential Recommendation (KASR), which captures sequence dependencies and semantic relevance of items simultaneously in an end-to-end manner. Specifically, we first convert the interaction records into a knowledge-transfer interaction sequence, which reflects the fine-grained transitions of users' interests. Next, we further recursively aggregate information in the knowledge graph based on a specific relation attention network, to explicitly capture the high-order relevance between items. A knowledge-aware GRU is later introduced to explore the sequential and semantic relevance between items automatically. We have conducted extensive experiments on three real datasets, and the results demonstrate that our method outperforms the state-of-the-art models.

Keywords: Recommendation systems · Recurrent neural networks · Sequential prediction · Knowledge graph

1 Introduction

Recommendation systems are ubiquitous, extracting useful information from online resources to help us locate data sources quickly. As the interests of users always change dynamically, to simulate dynamic and evolving preferences for

X. Wang et al. (Eds.): APWeb-WAIM 2020, LNCS 12317, pp. 493–508, 2020.
https://doi.org/10.1007/978-3-030-60259-8_36

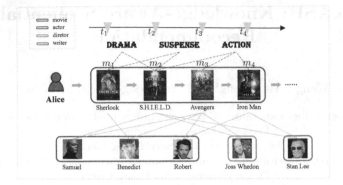

Fig. 1. Example of relevant attributes of movies.

better user experience, Sarver et al. [15] proposed the sequential recommendation, which aims to predict the next item following a specific interaction sequence.

Sequential recommendations have great value in web applications, such as product prediction in online e-commerce, news exposure on the website, page push in a click session. For capturing sequential users' behaviors, some work [12,16] is proposed to predict the next item based on Markov Chains. Recently, the majority of studies have introduced powerful deep learning algorithms into sequential recommendations. Some research [4,5] proposes recurrent neural networks to capture the contextual relevance of items in interaction sequences. In addition, other existing work [8,24] designs networks to capture users' long-term preferences and local interests simultaneously. By encoding interaction sequences into hidden vectors, the above methods do capture users' dynamic preferences, but they also have some limitations. Since the hidden vectors only contain the associated information in each dependent sequence, it is insufficient to capture the complicated preferences of users accurately. Furthermore, previous methods only consider the transitions of items in sequences but neglect the fact that the attributes of items are often related to each other. As a real example shown in Fig. 1, Alice has watched four movies recently that are regarded as her interaction sequence $[m_1, m_2, m_3, m_4]$. It is observed that m_1 and m_2 belong to the same subjects, while both m_2 and m_3 are directed by *Joss Whedon*. The attribute association between movies reflects the fine-grained sequential preferences of users. By mining rich semantic information in KG, we may infer that Alice will watch an action movie next time directed by *Joss Whedon* or written by *Stan Lee*.

The attributes of items are not isolated but linked up with each other, forming a knowledge graph (KG) [23]. To capture fine-grained users' preferences, many non-sequential methods [20,21,26] introduce KG to enhance the modeling of knowledge-aware recommendations. Still, these non-sequential methods model each static user-item interaction independently, failing to capture the contextual relevance of items and cannot be applied to sequential prediction. For sequential recommendations, Huang et al. [6] utilize TransE [1] to get pre-trained entity embedding to incorporate external KG into sequential recommendations. However, KSR [6] regards KG embedding and recommendation as two independent tasks with shared item embedding. Such separate modeling cannot fuse sequence dependencies and semantic relevance accurately. Since instead of directly plugging high-order relations into the model optimized for the recommendation, such a method only explores users' preferences in an implicit way, which may ignore long dependency in sequences and affect the final performance [21]. Therefore, it is urgent and intuitive but challenging to design a unified model to capture both the sequence of interactive records and the semantic information in KG simultaneously.

Considering the above issues, we propose a novel model KASR, to capture the sequence dependency and semantic relevance of items simultaneously. Different from the existing knowledge-aware recommendation models, our method judiciously integrates KG embedding into sequential recommendations in an end-to-end manner. In detail, we first introduce a knowledge-transfer interaction sequence based on relevant attributes between items, which incorporates the semantics of KG and reflects the fine-grained transitions of users' potential interests. To fully capture the high-order semantic relevance of items, a specific relation attention network is proposed to recursively aggregate information in KG. Furthermore, we present the knowledge-aware GRU that unifies the knowledge-transfer interaction sequence and high-order information aggregation in KG, automatically exploring the sequential and semantic relevance to capture the implicit preferences of users. To our best knowledge, this is the first effort to integrate KG embedding into sequential recommendations in an end-to-end manner. Our contributions are summarized as follows:

1. We propose an end-to-end model that captures both sequential dependency and semantic relevance of items, exploring the intrinsic correlation between KG embedding and sequential recommendations.
2. We introduce the relation attention network to explicitly aggregates the high-order relevance in KG, and a unified knowledge-aware GRU directly plugs the relevance into the modeling of interaction sequences.
3. Extensive experiments are conducted on three real-world datasets, and the results show that our model outperforms the state-of-the-art baselines.

2   Problem Definition

In this section, we formally define the basic notations used in this paper. Supposing that we have n items represented as $\mathcal{V} = \{v_1, v_2, ..., v_n\}$. Our task focuses on the recommendation with implicit feedback, where we sort the interaction items generated by a user at time t according to relative time to form the interaction sequence, denoted as $S_t = [v_1, v_2, ..., v_t]$.

A knowledge graph can be considered as $\mathcal{G} = (\mathcal{E}, \mathcal{R})$, which includes a large number of entity-relation-entity triples that represent the facts in the real world.

$\mathcal{E}$ and $\mathcal{R}$ are the set of entities and relations, and each triple is represented as $\{(e_i, r_{ij}, e_j)|e_i, e_j \in \mathcal{E}; r_{ij} \in \mathcal{R}\}$, where r_{ij} denotes the relation between the entity e_i and e_j. In knowledge-aware sequential recommendations, each item v_i corresponds to an entity e_i in KG, so that the interaction sequence $S_t = [v_1, v_2, ..., v_t]$ can be equivalently denoted as $S_t = [e_1, e_2, ..., e_t]$. As mentioned earlier, attributes between items are always linked with each other. We denote the relevant attributes between entity e_i and e_j as the set $\mathcal{A}^{(e_i, e_j)}$. What's more, given an origin sequence S_t, we formally define the corresponding knowledge-transfer interaction sequence as $S_t^a = [e_1, \mathcal{A}^{(e_1, e_2)}, e_2, ..., e_{t-1}, \mathcal{A}^{(e_{t-1}, e_t)}, e_t]$, where $\mathcal{A}^{(e_{t-1}, e_t)}$ denotes the relevant attributes between any two adjacent entities.

Based on the preliminaries above, given an interaction sequence S_t as well as knowledge graph $\mathcal{G}$, our task is to infer the next item following the sequence at time $t + 1$. Specifically, our model outputs a probability vector $\hat{\mathbf{y}} \in \mathbb{R}^n$, where n denotes the number of candidate items and $\hat{\mathbf{y}}_i$ indicates the probability of the i-th candidate item being selected next time.

3   The Proposed Method

In this section, we introduce the Knowledge-Aware Sequential Recommendation model (Fig. 2). Given an interaction sequence, KASR outputs the probability of all the corresponding candidate items being selected next time.

3.1   Knowledge-Transfer Interaction Sequence

Users' interests always change dynamically, and the characteristics of interacted items will affect the change. To capture the fine-grained preferences of users at the attribute level, we explore the transitions of users' interests by mining the relevance between items. In reality, there is usually more than one related attribute between any item-pair, which has different priorities to describe their relevance. Inspired by [9], the degree of nodes reflects the structure and semantic in a graph, and nodes with a larger degree always represent stronger characteristics. For an interaction sequence S_t, we extract T relevant attribute nodes between two items and keep the degree of nodes as large as possible, as the connections to construct a knowledge-transfer sequence S_t^a. The validity of sampling based on degrees will be demonstrated in the experimental part.

The formal description of constructing a knowledge-transfer interaction sequence is shown in Algorithm 1. We first sort the neighbor nodes of all entities in the descending order of degrees (Line 2–4). Then, loop through any adjacent item-pair in S_t and extract their relevant attributes in $\mathcal{G}$. For adjacent items v_i and v_j, we map them to the corresponding entity and obtain the intersection of neighbor nodes $\mathcal{L}_I$, which contains all the relevant attributes between e_i and e_j (Line 6–9). Then, we extract T connection attributes from $\mathcal{L}_I$ while keeping the degree of nodes as large as possible (Line 10–12). Note, for the last entity e_t, we use the padding node as its relevant attributes at the current time.

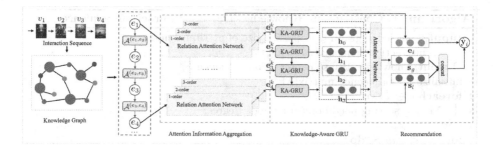

Fig. 2. The workflow of KASR model. Given an interaction sequence, the original interaction sequence is converted into a knowledge-transfer sequence first. Then, we aggregate the high-order semantic information of entities in KG. A knowledge-aware GRU explores sequential relevance and high-order connectivities between items simultaneously. Finally, we calculate the probability that candidate items may be selected based on hidden vectors.

Finally, all entities are spliced one after another by connection attributes to form the knowledge-transfer interaction sequence S_t^a (Line 13), which implicitly reflects the fine-grained transitions of users' interests. It is worth mentioning that the knowledge-transfer sequence we introduced can be easily extended to items in multiple contexts. For simplicity, we only consider the relevant attributes between adjacent items.

3.2 Attention Information Aggregation

Relation Attention Network. Knowledge graph is a natural graph structure, where each node is cooperatively characterized by its neighbor nodes. Each entity e_i is denoted as an entity embedding $\mathbf{e}_i \in \mathbb{R}^d$ and each relation r_{ij} is denoted as a relation embedding $\mathbf{r}_{ij} \in \mathbb{R}^d$. Here, d is the dimension size. $\mathcal{N}_{(e_i)} = \{(e_i, r_{ij}, e_j) | (e_i, r_{ij}, e_j) \in \mathcal{G}\}$ denotes the set of neighbor nodes to e_i. To capture the different contributions of each neighbor to e_i, we integrate the relation features to improve self-attention [19] to compute the attention score:

$$g(e_i, r_{ij}, e_j) = \mathbf{W}_r \cdot (\mathbf{e}_i \odot \mathbf{r}_{ij} \odot \mathbf{e}_j) + \mathbf{b}_r, \tag{1}$$

$$\alpha_{(e_i, e_j)} = \frac{\exp(g(e_i, r_{ij}, e_j))}{\sum_{(\hat{e}_i, \hat{r}_{ij}, \hat{e}_j) \in \mathcal{N}_{(e_i)}} \exp(g(\hat{e}_i, \hat{r}_{ij}, \hat{e}_j))}, \tag{2}$$

where $\mathbf{W}_r \in \mathbb{R}^{d \times d}$ and $\mathbf{b}_r \in \mathbb{R}^d$ are weight matrices applied to every triple. $\odot$ denotes the dot product operation. The output normalized coefficient $\alpha_{(e_i, e_j)}$ represents the contribution of neighbor e_j to e_i.

High-Order Information Aggregation. Relation attention calculates the different contributions of neighbor nodes, which makes it possible for us to aggregate features of neighbors to capture the semantic relevance of items. Formally, the neighborhood aggregation information of entity e_i is defined as:

Algorithm 1: Constructing Knowledge-Transfer Interaction Sequence

---

Input: knowledge graph $\mathcal{G} = (\mathcal{E}, \mathcal{R})$, size of attribute nodes T;
　　　　interaction sequence $S_t = [v_1, v_2, \cdots, v_t]$

Output: knowledge-transfer interaction sequence S_t^a

1　initialize S_t^a, adjacency matrix $\mathbf{M}$;
2　**foreach** $e \in \mathcal{E}$ **do**
3　$\quad$ $\mathbf{M}[e] = $ sorting neighbors(e) by node degree;
4　**end**
5　**for** $[v_i, v_j]$ *in* S_t **do**
6　$\quad$ mapping $[v_i, v_j]$ to entities $[e_i, e_j]$;
7　$\quad$ $\mathcal{L}_{e_i} \leftarrow \mathbf{M}[e_i]$;
8　$\quad$ $\mathcal{L}_{e_j} \leftarrow \mathbf{M}[e_j]$;
9　$\quad$ $\mathcal{L}_I \leftarrow Interaction(\mathcal{L}_{e_i}, \mathcal{L}_{e_j})$;
10　$\quad$ **foreach** e *in* $\mathcal{L}_I$ **do**
11　$\quad$ $\quad$ add e to $\mathcal{A}^{(e_i, e_j)}$ util T nodes in $\mathcal{A}^{(e_i, e_j)}$;
12　$\quad$ **end**
13　$\quad$ $S_t^a \leftarrow concat(S_t^a, [e_i : \mathcal{A}^{(e_i, e_j)}])$;
14　**end**
15　**return** S_t^a;

$$\mathbf{e}_{\mathcal{N}_{(e_i)}} = \sum_{(e_i, r_{ij}, e_j) \in \mathcal{N}_{(e_i)}} \alpha_{(e_i, e_j)} \cdot \mathbf{e}_j, \tag{3}$$

where $\alpha_{(e_i, e_j)}$ controls how much information entity e_i aggregates from neighbor node e_j. The output vector $\mathbf{e}_{\mathcal{N}_{(e_i)}} \in \mathbb{R}^d$ indicates the aggregated neighbor information of node e_i. Finally, we combine the features of the central node e_i itself and neighbor nodes to update $\mathbf{e}_i$ as:

$$f_{agg}(\mathbf{e}_i, \mathbf{e}_{\mathcal{N}(e_i)}) = \sigma\left(\mathbf{W}_f \cdot [\mathbf{e}_i \,\|\, \mathbf{e}_{\mathcal{N}(e_i)}] + \mathbf{b}_f\right), \tag{4}$$

where $\mathbf{W}_f \in \mathbb{R}^{d \times 2d}$ and $\mathbf{b}_f \in \mathbb{R}^d$ are weight matrices, and $\|$ is the concatenation operation. σ is the sigmoid function. Information in KG propagates layer by layer along with relations. Inspired by previous methods [20,21], we can stack multi-layer information aggregation to explore the high-order semantic relevance between entities. Formally, we iteratively define k-order information aggregation of e_i as:

$$\mathbf{e}_i^k = f_{agg}(\mathbf{e}_i^{k-1}, \mathbf{e}_{\mathcal{N}(e_i)}^{k-1}), \tag{5}$$

where $\mathbf{e}_i^{k-1}$ and $\mathbf{e}_{\mathcal{N}(e_i)}^{k-1}$ are the node's feature itself and aggregation information at the previous layer, respectively. We use $\mathbf{e}_i$ as the initial feature. After k-layer attention information aggregation, the updated embedding $\mathbf{e}_i^k$ contains the high-order semantic information that transfers and accumulates multi-layer.

3.3   Knowledge-Aware GRU

The knowledge-transfer interaction sequence S_t^a implicitly reflects the fine-grained transitions of users' interests. For an entity pair $[e_t \rightarrow \mathcal{A}^{(e_t,e_{t+1})} \rightarrow e_{t+1}]$ in S_t^a, the connection attributes $\mathcal{A}^{(e_t,e_{t+1})}$ express how the user's interests transfers from e_t to e_{t+1}, which is taken as the transferred embedding of user at time t:

$$\mathbf{e}_t^a = \sum_{e_i \in \mathcal{A}^{(e_t,e_{t+1})}} \mathrm{softmax}\left(D(e_i)\right) \cdot \mathbf{e}_i, \tag{6}$$

where $D(e_i)$ calculates the degree of attribute node e_i in KG, and $\mathbf{e}_i$ represents its embedding. Then, the improved knowledge-aware GRU (KA-GRU) computes the current hidden state vector $\mathbf{h}_t$ conditioned on the hidden state $\mathbf{h}_{t-1}$, transferred embedding $\mathbf{e}_t^a$ and the aggregated information $\mathbf{e}_t^k$:

$$\hat{\mathbf{e}}_t = \mathbf{W}_d \cdot \left([\mathbf{e}_t^a \parallel \mathbf{e}_t^k]\right), \tag{7}$$

$$\mathbf{h}_t = \mathrm{KA\text{-}GRU}(\mathbf{h}_{t-1}, \hat{\mathbf{e}}_t; \varPhi), \tag{8}$$

where $\mathbf{W}_d \in \mathbb{R}^{d \times 2d}$ controls the contribution of the item's high-order information and transfer knowledge to users' preferences. $\varPhi$ includes all the parameters of KA-GRU networks to be learned.

3.4   Recommendation and Training

After feeding S_t^a into KA-GRU, we obtain t hidden vectors, which encode the sequential and semantic relevance between interactive items. The hidden state $\mathbf{h}_t$ indicates the user's current interest at time t, and we regard it as the sequence's local representation $\mathbf{s}_l$. And all the t hidden states imply the user's long-term preferences, which are considered as global representation $\mathbf{s}_g$:

$$\mathbf{s}_g = \sum_{i=1}^{t} \alpha_i \cdot \mathbf{h}_i, \tag{9}$$

$$\alpha_i = \mathbf{W}_s \cdot \sigma(\mathbf{W}_l \mathbf{h}_t + \mathbf{W}_g \mathbf{h}_i), \tag{10}$$

where α_i guides the different priorities of each item in S_t. $\mathbf{W}. \in \mathbb{R}^{d \times d}$ are weight matrices. $\mathbf{s}_l \in \mathbb{R}^d$ is combined with $\mathbf{s}_g \in \mathbb{R}^d$ as the representation of sequence to compute the score of candidate item e_i:

$$\mathbf{y}_i = \left(\mathbf{W}_p \cdot (\mathbf{s}_l \parallel \mathbf{s}_g)^{\mathrm{T}}\right) \cdot \mathbf{e}_i. \tag{11}$$

Here, $\cdot^T$ represents transpose and $\mathbf{W}_p \in \mathbb{R}^{d \times d}$ is the weight matrix. After that, we can get the output score $\mathbf{y} \in \mathbb{R}^n$ for all candidate items, which is fed into a softmax function:

$$\hat{\mathbf{y}} = \mathrm{softmax}(\mathbf{y}), \tag{12}$$

where the normalized scores $\hat{\mathbf{y}} \in \mathbb{R}^n$, and each element indicates the probability that corresponding candidate item that will be selected next time.

Table 1. Statistics of three datasets.

Datasets	# Users	# Items	# Interactions	# KG Triples
MovieLens-1M	5,216	2,344	644,952	20,195
Amazon-Book	7,521	2,467	357,562	681,101
Last-FM	14,143	47,890	2,385,889	2,228,651

To optimize the proposed model, we opt for the cross-entropy loss function. For each sequence S_t, the loss is defined as the cross-entropy between the predicted probability and the ground truth. We formally define the optimization function as:

$$\mathcal{L}(\Theta) = -\sum_{i=1}^{n} \mathbf{y}_i \log(\hat{\mathbf{y}}_i) + (1 - \mathbf{y}_i)\log(1 - \hat{\mathbf{y}}_i) + \lambda \|\Theta\|_2^2, \qquad (13)$$

where $\mathbf{y}$ is the one-hot vector of the ground truth item, and Θ is parameters of our model, including all the weights of networks and the embedding table of entities and relations. The last term is L_2 regularization to prevent overfitting. Finally, we apply Back-Propagation Through Time (BPTT) to optimize parameters of the objective function.

4 Experiments

In this section, we conduct experiments with related baselines on three real-world datasets and report the comparison results.

4.1 Datasets

To evaluate the proposed model, we conduct experiments on three real-world datasets, which vary in terms of application scenario, size, and sparsity. For the knowledge graph, we extract triples subsets from the open Knowledge Base [27] in recommendation systems.

MovieLens-1M[1] is a widely used personalized movie rating dataset, which consists of a large number of 1 to 5 explicit ratings on the Movie-Lens website.

Amazon-Book[2] is selected from the widely used dataset Amazon-review in production recommendation where data is collected from the world-leading e-commerce platform.

Last-FM[3] is a music dataset from Last.fm online system, and we view the tracks as items. Since the Last-FM music dataset is very large, we take the subset where the timestamp is from Jan 2010 to May 2010.

---

[1] https://grouplens.org/datasets/movielens/.
[2] https://jmcauley.ucsd.edu/data/amazon/.
[3] https://grouplens.org/datasets/hetrec-2011/.

Following previous methods [20, 21], we have filtered out items without corresponding entities in KG for all datasets. To ensure the quality of the datasets, we only keep users with at least 20 interactions and items with at least 5 interactions, while explicit interaction is converted into implicit feedback. Then, we group interaction records by users and sort them in ascending order of timestamps to build interaction sequences. The basic statistics of three datasets are summarized in Table 1, and the code is available at https://github.com/qqingwang/KASR.

4.2   Experimental Setup

Baselines. To prove the effectiveness of our model, we compare it with the three lines of related methods that will be mentioned in the related work section, baselines as following:

- **BPR** [11] is one of the most common comparison models which utilizes Bayesian Personalized Ranking to sort items in pairs.
- **NCF** [3] is a state-of-the-art recommendation model that replaces the inner product with a neural architecture to implement Matrix Factorization.
- **CKE** [26] first proposes to incorporate structural, textual, and visual knowledge to improve recommendation performance. For fairness, we implement a simplified CKE by only using KG in this paper.
- **FPMC** [12] is a classic hybrid model that combines Matrix Factorization and Markov Chain to explores sequential features and users' interests for the next prediction.
- **GRU4REC** [4] proposes an RNNs-based deep learning model for sequential recommendation firstly. It utilizes session-parallel mini-batch training process and employs a ranking-based loss function.
- **STAMP** [8] is a hybrid model that constructs two network structures to capture the users' general preferences and current interests of the last click in an interaction sequence.
- **KSR** [6] incorporates KG into sequential recommendations based on Memory Networks. Different from our models, KSR models interaction sequences and KG as two independent tasks and ignores their intrinsic relevance.
- **SRGNN** [24] constructs sequences as graph structure data and utilizes graph neural networks to model complex transitions of items, thus obtaining accurate item embedding.

Implementation Details. In sequential recommendation, our task is to predict the next item after a specific sequence. For simplicity, we segment the ordered interaction records into short item sequences by a sliding window of length 10 to 20. For each user, we hold the latest two sequences as valid data and test data, respectively, and the remaining are for training. We adopt the widely used leave-one-out method [3,25] to evaluate performance. Considering the massive scale of data and the time-consuming calculation, we randomly sampled 500 items (including the target item) that are not in the interaction sequence as candidate items. We predict the probability of 500 items being selected and rank items

Table 2. Performance comparison of different methods.

Model	MovieLens-1M			Amazon-Book			Last-FM		
	HR	NDCG	MRR	HR	NDCG	MRR	HR	NDCG	MRR
BPR	0.272	0.136	0.105	0.306	0.183	0.123	0.359	0.169	0.135
NCF	0.389	0.188	0.139	0.388	0.236	0.172	0.599	0.320	0.241
CKE	0.423	0.206	0.143	0.430	0.206	0.154	0.621	0.303	0.223
FPMC	0.432	0.192	0.140	0.515	0.257	0.178	0.598	0.299	0.212
GRU4REC	0.584	0.297	0.215	0.562	0.312	0.240	0.620	0.443	0.371
STAMP	0.594	0.308	0.221	0.583	0.322	0.252	0.639	0.450	0.372
KSR	0.621	0.315	0.228	0.628	0.370	0.292	0.675	0.502	0.449
SRGNN	0.602	0.306	0.223	0.613	0.359	0.283	0.681	0.517	0.457
KASR	**0.638**	**0.332**	**0.243**	**0.654**	**0.402**	**0.321**	**0.707**	**0.529**	**0.468**

according to it. Following previous methods [6,25], we use metric Hit Ratio (HR), Normalized Discounted Cumulative Gain (NDCG), and Mean Reciprocal Rank (MRR) to evaluate the ranking performance. HR measures whether the target item is presented on the top list, NDCG and MRR measure the ranking quality. Due to space limitations, we only report the above metrics of the top-20 recommendation list, the metrics of top-5 and top-10 follow the same result.

For all baselines above, we either apply a grid search for hyper-parameters based on validation or follow the original parameter settings. In our model KASR, we adopt a 2-layer GRU network, where the hidden size and embedding size are fixed to 100, and batch size is fixed to 128. During training, the learning rate $\alpha = 0.0005$ and the coefficient $\lambda = 10^{-7}$ of L_2 normalization. We adopt an embedding dropout technique where the drop ratio is set to 0.2. Besides, we search the number T of relevant attributes between two items and layers K of information aggregation from 1 to 4. We uniformly sample N neighbors of each entity as its neighbors set, and the size of N is tested in $\{2, 4, 8, 16\}$. We will discuss how the key hyperparameters affect the performance in Sect. 4.5.

4.3   Performance Comparison

Comparative results of KASR with the other eight baseline methods are presented in Table 2. Among all baselines, the proposed model KASR outperforms other methods in terms of all metrics on all three datasets. In conventional methods, NCF obtains better results than BPR in all cases, and CKE incorporates KG in collaborative filtering and improves performance. In general, the performance of conventional recommendations is worse than that of sequential recommendations, which shows that non-sequential models are not suitable for recommending the next item. Our method explores the dependency of items in interaction sequences and achieves better results than all conventional models.

The basic sequential model FPMC performs poorly than other sequential methods, which indicates that it is insufficient to model sequential features

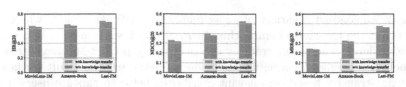

Fig. 3. Performance comparison of knowledge-transfer in interaction sequence.

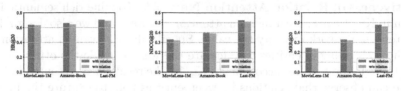

Fig. 4. Performance comparison of relation aggregation attention.

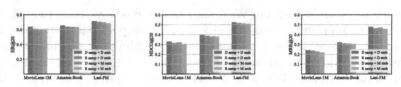

Fig. 5. The influence of the degree of nodes on results.

by only considering the transitions between successive items. Both GRU4REC and STAMP explicitly capture users' long-term preferences and current interests, which outperform conventional methods and FPMC. None of the above vanilla methods consider side-information or explore the semantic relevance between items. KSR introduces Memory Networks to capture users' preferences at the attribute level, and its performance exceeds the simple sequential models above. However, as mentioned earlier, KSR ignores the intrinsic correlation between recommendation and KG embedding. Instead, our method introduces the knowledge-transfer interaction sequence to capture the fine-grained transitions of users' interests and explore the high-order relevance between items simultaneously, which considers the intrinsic correlation and achieves better results. Besides, SRGNN utilizes graph neural networks to model more complex transitions between items. It gets the second-best results on the Last-FM dataset, only inferior to KASR. Different from SRGNN, our model applies graph neural networks to the knowledge graph. By aggregating the high-order information, KASR captures the inherent semantic relevance of items in KG while modeling the interactive sequences and achieves the best results. Experimental results show that our method greatly improves performance.

4.4 Study of Different Variants

Effectiveness of Transfer Knowledge. We introduce the knowledge-transfer sequence to capture the fine-grained transitions of users' preferences. As shown in Fig. 3, we conduct a variety of experiments to verify its benefit, where 'w/o' means that the transferred embedding in Eq. 7 has been removed. It is obvious that considering knowledge-transfer can accurately predict the next item with a higher score, achieving a better result on all datasets. The result verifies that knowledge-transfer based on relevant attributes helps to capture users' preferences more accurately.

Effectiveness of Relation Attention Network. To mine rich semantic information in KG, we propose a relation attention network, and we also design different attention network to verify the value. Specifically, one vanilla attention only uses the embedding of entities to calculate the weight, while the other one considers the relation features according to Eq. 1. The results are presented in Fig. 4, and we can observe that relations between entities help to capture the inherent semantic association between items genuinely and achieves better results.

Influence of Node's Degree. We design several model variants to explore the influence of nodes degree. As shown in Fig. 5, 'D samp' extracts attribute nodes based on degree and 'R samp' extracts randomly. Similarly, 'D emb' represents transferred embedding based on the degree of nodes, while 'M emb' indicates the average of all attributes. It can be observed that "D samp + D emb" achieves the best results on the three datasets, while "R samp + M emb" gets the worst results. Therefore, it is necessary to consider the degree of nodes.

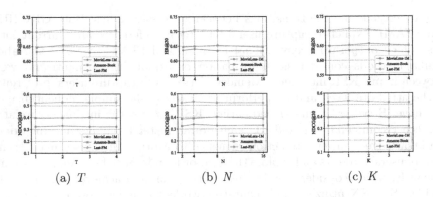

Fig. 6. Hyperparameter analysis on three datasets.

4.5   HyperParameter Analysis

In this section, we examine the influence of three key parameters in our method: the number T of connection attributes in knowledge-transfer sequences, size N of sampling neighbor nodes, and layers K in information aggregation.

As in Fig. 6 (a), the model achieves the best results when $T = 2$ or $T = 3$. It verifies that considering more relevant knowledge between items helps better capture transitions of users' interests. Moreover, T with a too large value may bring some noise and reduce the performance. Next, we conduct extensive

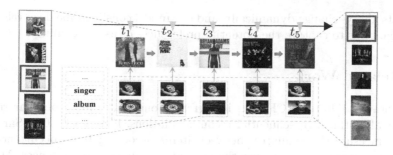

Fig. 7. A real case of interaction sequence from the Last-FM dataset, where the green box represents the prediction ranked list for music at a specific time t, and the red box is the music of ground truth selected by the user. (Color figure online)

experiments to evaluate the model with different size N of neighbor nodes when aggregating information. Figure 6 (b) shows the experimental results, where the Amazon-Book dataset gets the best performance when $N = 8$, and the other two datasets achieve the best results when $N = 4$. Since the KG of Amazon-Book is sparse, aggregating more neighbor nodes may get richer relevant information. It is necessary to choose an appropriate value of N. Besides, we vary the different K-order aggregation to study the impact of high-order relevance between items, where $K = 0$ means no information is aggregated. Figure 6 (c) indicates that high-order information aggregation can improve performance, and the model achieves the best performance when the value of K is in [1,2]. However, with an increase of K value, aggregation may capture more irrelevant information and decrease performance. In general, although the above parameters have a slice of influence on results, they are still robust.

4.6 Case Study

Experimental results have shown that our method can predict the next item accurately. The primary benefit of KASR is that it fully explores the sequential dependency of items and mines the semantic association between items at the same time, capturing the potential interests of users more deeply. We act as a real example from the Last-FM dataset in Fig. 7, where the record is music. In this example, we present two types of attributes of items, including "singer" and "album". We can observe that the user listens to a lot of music from different albums of the same singer. At the time t_3, as the user has already listened to two music from the same album, KASR captures more users' preferences at attributes "album" and tends to recommend the next music from the same album. However, the user selects music from the singer's other two albums at t_3 and t_4, which shows his interest point in the singer's various albums. KASR is capable of capturing the fine-grained transitions of the user's interest point from "album" to "singer", and it is more likely to expose the singer's other new albums that have never appeared before at time t_5. The real example shows that users' interests always change dynamically, and our model considers the deep relevance between items to capture the potential preferences of users genuinely.

5 Related Work

Collaborative Filtering (CF) [11] is currently one of the most popular recommender algorithms. In sequential recommendations, inspired by CF, Sarver et al. [14] measure the similarity between items according to co-occurrence frequency in sequences. To capture the context information in sequences, Markov Decision Process [16] is proposed to model sequential interactions. FPMC [12] is a hybrid model of Matrix Factorization (MF) [7] and Markov Chain (MC), which explores the sequential feature between two clicks. Chen et al. [2] propose a logistic Markov embedding method to predict the next playlist. However, MC-based methods assume that past items are independent of each other, which is actually inappropriate for sequential recommendations.

Some existing research applies deep learning in recommendation systems, e.g., CF-based on Restricted Boltzmann Machines [13] and hierarchical representation encoder-decoder model [22]. NCF [3] replaces the inner product in MF with a neural architecture. Inspired by natural language processing, RNNs are introduced into sequential recommendations. Hidasi et al. [4] first propose RNNs to model session recommendations and introduce a training strategy [5] for p-RNN. Xu et al. [18] apply data augmentation and method shifts to improve the performance. STAMP [8] considers the current interest and long-term preferences of users simultaneously. Recently, a new study [24] utilizes graph neural networks to model sequences and explore relevance between items.

To solve the problem of sparse data and cold start, many studies have introduced side-information into recommendations, including social networks [17], knowledge graphs [26], and text descriptions [10]. KG contains rich semantic information between the items, and many efforts utilize deep learning to enhance the performance of knowledge-aware recommendations. Especially, CKE [26] introduces the knowledge graph into deep CF. RippleNet [20] explores users' hierarchical preferences based on Memory Network. KGCN [21] applies graph neural networks to capture the higher-order feature between items. However, these methods are for non-sequential recommendation task. KSR [6] first integrates external KG into the sequential recommendations. Different from our model, KSR ignores the intrinsic relevance between KG and interaction sequences.

6 Conclusion

In this paper, we propose a novel model KASR, which integrates the knowledge graph into sequential recommendations in an end-to-end manner. Our method mainly has three benefits. First, we deeply explore the fine-grained transitions of users' interests based on the relevant attributes in the knowledge-transfer interaction sequence. Second, the attention information aggregation explicitly explores the high-order semantic relevance between items, which implies users' preferences. Finally, a knowledge-aware GRU is introduced to automatically capture the sequential relevance and high-order connectivities between items for predicting the next item. Experiments have been conducted on real datasets to evaluate our model, and the results show KASR achieves better performance than other start-of-the-art methods.

Acknowledgement. This work is supported in part by the National Natural Science Foundation of China Projects No. U1936213, No. U1636207, the Shanghai Science and Technology Development Fund No. 19511121204, No. 19DZ1200802, NSF under grants III-1526499, III-1763325, III-1909323, and CNS-1930941.

References

1. Bordes, A., Usunier, N., Garcia-Duran, A., Weston, J., Yakhnenko, O.: Translating embeddings for modeling multi-relational data. In: NIPS, pp. 2787–2795 (2013)
2. Chen, S., Moore, J.L., Turnbull, D., Joachims, T.: Playlist prediction via metric embedding. In: ICDM, pp. 714–722. ACM (2012)
3. He, X., Liao, L., Zhang, H., Nie, L., Hu, X., Chua, T.S.: Neural collaborative filtering. In: WWW, pp. 173–182. ACM (2017)
4. Hidasi, B., Karatzoglou, A., Baltrunas, L., Tikk, D.: Session-based recommendations with recurrent neural networks. In: ICLR (2015)
5. Hidasi, B., Quadrana, M., Karatzoglou, A., Tikk, D.: Parallel recurrent neural network architectures for feature-rich session-based recommendations. In: RecSys, pp. 241–248. ACM (2016)
6. Huang, J., Zhao, W.X., Dou, H., Wen, J.R., Chang, E.Y.: Improving sequential recommendation with knowledge-enhanced memory networks. In: SIGIR, pp. 505–514. ACM (2018)
7. Koren, Y., Bell, R., Volinsky, C.: Matrix factorization techniques for recommender systems. IEEE Comput. **8**, 30–37 (2009)
8. Liu, Q., Zeng, Y., Mokhosi, R., Zhang, H.: STAMP: short-term attention/memory priority model for session-based recommendation. In: KDD, pp. 1831–1839. ACM (2018)
9. Lu, Y., Shi, C., Hu, L., Liu, Z.: Relation structure-aware heterogeneous information network embedding. In: AAAI, pp. 4456–4463 (2019)
10. Rendle, S.: Factorization machines with libFM. TIST **3**(3), 57 (2012)
11. Rendle, S., Freudenthaler, C., Gantner, Z., Schmidt-Thieme, L.: BPR: Bayesian personalized ranking from implicit feedback. In: UAI. AUAI Press (2009)
12. Rendle, S., Freudenthaler, C., Schmidt-Thieme, L.: Factorizing personalized Markov chains for next-basket recommendation. In: WWW. ACM (2010)
13. Salakhutdinov, R., Mnih, A., Hinton, G.: Restricted Boltzmann machines for collaborative filtering. In: ICML, pp. 791–798. ACM (2007)
14. Sarwar, B.M., Karypis, G., Konstan, J.A., Riedl, J., et al.: Item-based collaborative filtering recommendation algorithms. In: WWW, pp. 285–295. ACM (2001)
15. Schafer, J.B., Konstan, J., Riedl, J.: Recommender systems in e-commerce. In: ICEC, pp. 158–166. ACM (1999)
16. Shani, G., Heckerman, D., Brafman, R.I.: An MDP-based recommender system. J. Mach. Learn. Res. **6**(Sep), 1265–1295 (2005)

17. Song, W., Xiao, Z., Wang, Y., Charlin, L., Zhang, M., Tang, J.: Session-based social recommendation via dynamic graph attention networks. In: WSDM, pp. 555–563. ACM (2019)
18. Tan, Y.K., Xu, X., Liu, Y.: Improved recurrent neural networks for session-based recommendations. In: DLRS, pp. 17–22. ACM (2016)
19. Vaswani, A., et al.: Attention is all you need. In: NIPS, pp. 5998–6008 (2017)
20. Wang, H., et al.: RippleNet: propagating user preferences on the knowledge graph for recommender systems. In: CIKM, pp. 417–426. ACM (2018)
21. Wang, H., Zhao, M., Xie, X., Li, W., Guo, M.: Knowledge graph convolutional networks for recommender systems. In: WWW, pp. 3307–3313. ACM (2019)
22. Wang, P., Guo, J., Lan, Y., Xu, J., Wan, S., Cheng, X.: Learning hierarchical representation model for nextbasket recommendation. In: SIGIR. ACM (2015)
23. Wang, Q., Mao, Z., Wang, B., Guo, L.: Knowledge graph embedding: a survey of approaches and applications. TKDE **29**(12), 2724–2743 (2017)
24. Wu, S., Tang, Y., Zhu, Y., Wang, L., Xie, X., Tan, T.: Session-based recommendation with graph neural networks. In: AAAI, vol. 33, pp. 346–353 (2019)
25. Xue, H.J., Dai, X., Zhang, J., Huang, S., Chen, J.: Deep matrix factorization models for recommender systems. In: AAAI, pp. 3203–3209 (2017)
26. Zhang, F., Yuan, N.J., Lian, D., Xie, X., Ma, W.Y.: Collaborative knowledge base embedding for recommender systems. In: KDD, pp. 353–362. ACM (2016)
27. Zhao, W.X., et al.: KB4Rec: a data set for linking knowledge bases with recommender systems. Data Intell. **1**(2), 121–136 (2019)

Graph Attentive Network for Region Recommendation with POI- and ROI-Level Attention

Hengpeng Xu[1], Jinmao Wei[1(✉)], Zhenglu Yang[1(✉)], and Jun Wang[2]

[1] College of Computer Science, Nankai University, Tianjin, China
xuhengpeng@mail.nankai.edu.cn, {weijm,yangzl}@nankai.edu.cn
[2] College of Mathematics and Statistics Science, Ludong University, Shandong, China
junwang@mail.nankai.edu.cn

Abstract. Due to the prevalence of human activity in urban space, recommending ROIs (region-of-interest) to users becomes an important task in social networks. The fundamental problem is how to aggregate users' preferences over POIs (point-of-interest) to infer the users' region-level mobility patterns. We emphasize two facts in this paper: *(1)* there simultaneously exists ROI-level and POI-level implicitness that blurs the users' underlying preferences; and *(2)* individual POIs should have non-uniform weights and more importantly, the weights should vary across different users. To address these issues, we contribute a novel solution, namely GANR[2] (Graph Attentive Neural Network for Region Recommendation), based on the recent development of attention network and Neural Graph Collaborative Filtering (NGCF). Specifically, to learn the user preferences over ROIs, we provide a principled neural network model equipped with two attention modules: the POI-level attention module, to select informative POIs of one ROI, and the ROI-level attention module, to learn the ROI preferences. Moreover, we learn the interactions between users and ROIs under the NGCF framework. Extensive experiments on two real-world datasets demonstrate the effectiveness of the proposed framework.

Keywords: Region recommendation · Graph neural network · Location-based social networks · Attention mechanism · Multi-context

1 Introduction

The rapid urbanization process has been nurturing big and complex urban space and changing our lifestyles on an unprecedented scale and speed. Urban region-level activities modeling is widely recognized as a fundamental task. Researchers [1–3] have found that a large proportion of visitors visited multiple POIs resided in small regions. Different from POI, ROI refers to the integrated urban areas with specific functionalities that attract users' attentions and activities. Character users' preferences among these regions is benefit us to develop

© Springer Nature Switzerland AG 2020
X. Wang et al. (Eds.): APWeb-WAIM 2020, LNCS 12317, pp. 509–516, 2020.
https://doi.org/10.1007/978-3-030-60259-8_37

a better region recommendation for users. In this paper, we endeavor to recommend a set of nearby locations rather than an individual location, i.e., region recommendation. Such recommendation satisfies the requirements of urbanization and modern civilization, while filtering the latent information of a particular urban region from user-generated spatio-temporal data.

Most of the existing location recommendation solutions are designed to recommend POIs [4,5]. However, if we direct applied these location methods to region recommendation, it means that we treat the user ROI preferences as the average POI preferences located in one ROI. Recently, a few ROI recommendation related studies have appeared [2,6]. Pham et al. [7] utilized the interactions between POIs to improve recommendation performances and reduce the region recommendation problem to the geometric intersection problem. Xu et al. [2] utilized the ConvLSTM network to learn the global and personal preferences of users over regions, while it still ignored the correlation between users' preferences over POI-level and ROI-level. As such, these solutions are insufficient to capture the complicated dynamic process of making check-in decisions by users, resulting in the suboptimal performance of region recommendation.

Recommending an ROI is more complicated than recommending a POI since different POIs differentially contribute to users' attentions and activities in a region. In this work, we approach the fundamental problem in region recommendation, i.e., how to aggregate the preference of POIs located in the same region to decide users' check-in activities on regions. The key challenges here are how to design an expressive model to appropriately learn the user preferences in one region and how to adapt his/her preferences when this user interacts with other regions. Based on the above analysis, when designing graph neural network architecture with attention mechanism for ROI recommendation, we need to address the following new issues:

(1) **ROI-level attention**, which models users' preferences on different regions. Each user is associated with a set of regions via tracking their check-in history data. However, a set of check-in regions feedback does not necessarily indicate equal region preferences. To better characterize users' preferences, the implicit feedback in the region-level requires different attentions on the set of regions.

(2) **POI-level attention**, which learns the importance of neighbors in the same region. For each POI in one region, POI-level attention aims to learn the importance of neighbors in the same region and assign different attention values to them. Therefore, how to design a model that can discover the subtle differences of POIs in the same region and learn their weights properly is desired.

In this paper, we propose a novel graph neural network architecture, dubbed Graph Attentive Neural Network for region recommendation (GANR^2), which is equipped with both ROI- and POI- level attentions. The ROI-level attention is able to learn the importance of each ROI and assign proper weights to them, which can represent users' preferences over ROIs. Meanwhile, POI-level attention is able to learn the importance of POIs located in the same ROI, and assign

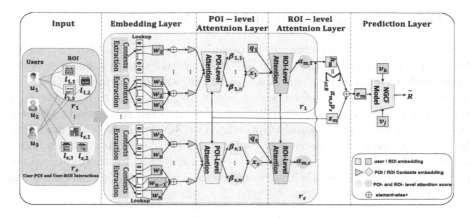

Fig. 1. Illustration of GANR²: the left part depicts the user-POI and user-ROI interactions, and the right part is the representation of GANR².

different attention values to these POIs, which can represent inside each ROI users' preferences on different POIs. Specifically, we employ the state-of-the-art NGCF framework to learn the user-region interactions. Extensive evaluations demonstrate that GANR² achieves superior recommendation performance on real-world datasets.

2 Preliminaries

2.1 Problem Definition

Suppose we have M users $\mathcal{U} = \{u_1, u_2, ...u_M\}$, N POIs $\mathcal{P} = \{p_1, p_2, ..., p_N\}$, and S regions $\mathcal{R} = \{r_1, r_2, ..., r_S\}$. The s-th region $r_s \in \mathcal{R}$ consists of a set of POIs, i.e., region components with POI index $\mathcal{B}_s = \{B_{s,1}, B_{s,2}, ..., B_{s,\lfloor B_s \rfloor}\}$, where $B_{s,\lfloor * \rfloor} \in \mathcal{P}$, and $|B_s|$ is the size of the region r_s. There are two kinds of observed interaction data among $\mathcal{U}$, $\mathcal{P}$, and $\mathcal{R}$, namely, user-ROI interactions and user-POI interactions. We use $Y = [y_{i,j}]_{M \times S}$ to denote the user-ROI interactions and $X = [x_{i,j}]_{M \times N}$ to denote the user-POI interactions. In our work, we also leverage heterogeneous contexts associated with each POI, such as temporal features, category feature. Specially, we use C_n to denote the properties of POI p_n, including temporal popularity features, category features, etc.

Inspired by the works [8,9], we utilize density-based cluster method to detect regions. Specially, we first use the grid-based methods to split the urban area into small regions, and then calculate the popularity of each region grid. Finally, we merge them with density-based algorithms into ROIs.

Given a target user u_m, our task is defined as recommending a list of ROIs that user u_m may interacted in, which is formally defined as follows:

Input: Users $\mathcal{U}$, POIs $\mathcal{P}$, ROIs $\mathcal{R}$, User-ROI interactions , User-POI interactions X, and POI contexts C.

Output: A personalized ranking function that map an ROI to a real value for each user $\tilde{y} : \mathcal{R} \rightarrow \mathbb{R}$.

3 Graph Attentive Neural Network

Figure 1 depicts the architecture of our neural network model GANR[2]. At a high level, our model employs the embedding-based graph attentive neural network framework. Given a user u_m, an ROI r_s, and the n-th POI p_n in the ROI r_s, we use α_{ms} to denote u_m's preference degree w.r.t. r_s and β_{msn} to represent u_m's preference degree w.r.t. p_n in r_s. We use two attention subnetworks to learn the two preference scores jointly. Specially, the ROI-level attention module is to learn the users' preferences over regions and POI-level attention module is to learn users' preferences over POIs in the same region. Furthermore, we use an embedding layer to deal with heterogeneous contexts in a unified manner to generate POI's feature content.

3.1 Model

In addition to explicitly parameterizing each user u_m with z_m, GANR[2] also models users based on the set of ROIs that they check-in. Therefore, each ROI r_s is associated with two factor vectors. One is denoted as v_s, which is the basic ROI vector in the latent factor model. The other one, denoted as q_s, is the auxiliary region latent vector which is used to characterize the users based on the set of ROIs they interact with. The overall preference degree of a user is obtained through the sum: $e_m = z_m + \sum_{s \in Y_m} \alpha_{ms} q_s$.

Next we elaborate the three components.

Embedding Layer. Given the users' check-in history data, we supply all pieces of information except the POI p to represent the POI's content. However, the factors in the context set C is heterogeneous in terms of data type. Here, we introduce two types of features that we have extracted from POIs.

Category Features. Given a POI p_n, we first extract the textual content feature $f_n c$ from POIs' categories by using one-hot representation, and then transform it to latent vector through the embedding layer.

Popular Temporal Features. Intuitively, a popular POI will have a higher visiting probability (a.k.a. its popularity). In this paper, we exploit two kinds of popularity features, that is, overall popularity and temporal popularity.

ROI-Level Attention. The purpose of ROI-level attention is to learn a user's latent factors by considering the ROIs that a user u_m has interacted with.

To alleviate the limitation of the mean-based aggregator, an intuitive solution is to tweak α_{ms} to be aware of the target user u_m, i,e., assigning an individualized weight for each (u_m, r_s) pair as follows:

$$h_m = \delta\left(W \cdot \left\{ \sum_{s \in C_m} \alpha_{ms} q_s \right\} + b\right), \tag{1}$$

where α_{ms} denotes the attention weight of the interactions with r_s in contributing to the user u_m's latent factor when characterizing u_m's preference from the interaction history Y_m. Specially, we parameterize the ROI-level attention score α_{ms} with a two-layer neural network, which we call the ROI-level attention network. The input to the attention network is the context-aware ROI representation x_s, the neighborhood ROI latent and auxiliary vector v_s and q_s, and the user latent vector z_m. Formally, the attention network is defined as

$$\alpha_{ms}^* = w_1^T . \delta(W_{1u}z_m + W_{1v}v_s + W_{1p}q_s + W_{1x}x_s + b_1) + c_1, \qquad (2)$$

where $W(1*)$ and bias b_1 are the first layer parameters, the vector w_1 and bias c_1 are the second layer parameters, and $\delta(x)$ is the ReLU function.

The final attention weights are obtained by normalizing the above attentive scores with the softmax function, which can be interpreted as the contribution of the interaction to the user u_m's latent presentation as

$$\alpha_{ms} = \frac{\exp(\alpha_{ms}^*)}{\sum_{s \in Y_m} \exp(\alpha_{ms}^*)}. \qquad (3)$$

POI-Level Attention. The goal of POI-level attention is to assign POIs in the same ROI attentive weights that are consistent with user preference, and then apply the weighted sum to construct the ROI content representation. We use $|s*|$ to denote the size of the set and x_{sn} to denote the context embedding of POI p_n. Each ROI r_s may be encoded into a variable-sized set of POI component features x_{s*}. We perform an attention mechanism with a two-layer neural network to extract these POIs that are critical to generate the ROI representation, and model a user's preference degree in each POI in the same ROI by relating POI-level attention β_{msn} with user's latent vector z_m. The POI context embedding x_{sn} is represented as follows:

$$x_s = \delta(W . \left\{ \sum_{n \in B_s} \beta_{msn} x_{sn} \right\} + b), \qquad (4)$$

$$\beta_{msn}^* = w_2^T . \delta(W_{2u}z_m + W_{2x}x_{ms} + b_2) + c_2, \qquad (5)$$

$$\beta_{msn} = \frac{\exp(\beta_{msn}^*)}{\sum_{n \in B_s} \exp(\beta_{msn}^*)}, \qquad (6)$$

where the matrices W_{2*} and bias b_2 are the first layer parameters, the vector w_2 and bias c_2 are the second layer parameters, and $\delta(x)$ is the ReLU function.

3.2   Interaction Learning with NGCF

NGCF is a graph neural network based framework for item recommendation [10]. In our model, after we have obtained the ROI-level latent vectors h_m for the user u_m, u_m's final representation is represented as $h_m + z_m$. Following the mainstream recommender models [10], we first build a parameter matrix as an embedding look-up table as follows:

$$E = [h_1 + z_1, ..., h_M + z_M, v_1, ..., v_S]. \qquad (7)$$

Table 1. Comparisons on two datasets evaluated by Recall and NDCG.

Method	NYC		TKY	
	Recall	NDCG	Recall	NDCG
USG	0.1462	0.1633	0.1031	0.1762
PACE	0.2187	0.2078	0.1615	0.2425
GeoDCF	0.2864	0.3108	0.2146	0.3563
NGCF	0.2541	0.28152	0.1973	0.3242
GANR^2	**0.316**	**0.3599**	**0.2265**	**0.3845**

Then, we construct the Laplacian matrix $\mathcal{L}$ as [10]. By implementing the matrix-form propagation rule, we can simultaneously update representations for all users and ROIs in a rather efficient way. After propagating with L layers, we obtain multiple representations for the user u_m, namely $\{e^1_{um}, ..., e^L_{um}\}$, where $e^l_{um} = h^l_{um} + z^l_{um}$ and $e^l_{rs} = v^l_s$. Here, we also concatenate them to construct the final embedding for a user. We do the same operation on ROIs by concatenating the item representations $\{e^1_{rs}, ..., e^L_{rs}\}$ learned by different layers to the final ROI embedding as

$$e^*_{um} = e^1_{um}||...||e^L_{um}, \, e^*_{rs} = e^1_{rs}||...||e^L_{rs}, \tag{8}$$

where $||$ is the concatenation operation. Finally, we conduct the inner product to estimate the user's preference towards the target ROI as

$$\widetilde{y}(u_m, r_s) = {e^*_{um}}^T e^*_{rs}. \tag{9}$$

4   Experiments

4.1   Experimental Setup

Datasets. We evaluate our model on public Foursquare check-in datasets collected from two big cities, namely, New York (NYC) and Tokyo (TKY) [11]. To evaluate the effectiveness of top-K recommendation and preference ranking, we adopt two widely-used evaluation protocols: recall@K and ndcg@K. By default, we set $K = 20$. We report the average metrics for all users in the test set

Baselines. We compare GANR^2 with several representation methods: USG [4], PACE [5], GeoDCF [1], NGCF [12].

4.2   Performance Comparison

We first compare the recommendation performance of all methods. Table 1 shows the overall rating prediction error w.r.t. Recall and NDCG on NYC and TKY datasets. Our proposed GANR2 achieves the best performance on both datasets, significantly outperforming the state-of-the-art MF and Hybrid methods (the average improvement over the second best baseline GeoDCF is 9.25%).

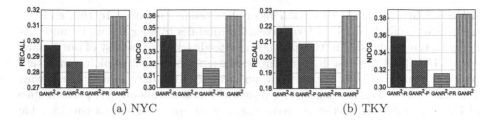

(a) NYC

(b) TKY

Fig. 2. Effect of attention mechanisms on NYC and TKY.

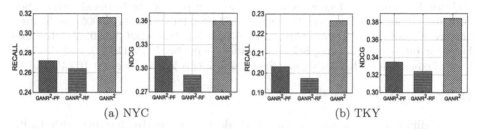

(a) NYC

(b) TKY

Fig. 3. Effect of POI and ROI context information on NYC and TKY.

4.3 Model Analysis

Effects of Attention Mechanisms at ROI- and POI- Level. To get a better understanding of GANR^2, we evaluate the key components of GANR^2, that is, ROI- and POI-level attentions. We compare GANR^2 with its three variants:(1) GANR^2-P: the POI-level attention of GANR^2 is eliminated; (2) GANR^2-R: the ROI-level attention score α of GANR^2 is eliminated during aggregating ROIs; (3) GANR^2-PR: two attention mechanisms (ROI-level attention α and POI-level attention β) are both eliminated. As suggested in Fig. 2, GANR^2-P and GANR^2-R yields worse performance than GANR^2, which validates the benefits of the ROI-level and POI-level attentions in aggregation.

Effects of Context Information of POI, ROI. GANR^2 provides embedding layer to integrate the context of information to model users' preferences GANR^2. In this subsection, we compare GANR^2 with its two variants: (1) GANR^2-PF: the user-POI interactions is removed; (2) GANR^2-RF: both the user-POI interactions and the context information about POIs are removed. As shown in Fig. 3, in terms of analyzing POI context information, GANR^2-PF performs worse than GANR^2, indicating that POI context information is important to learn user latent vector and boost the recommending ROI performance.

5   Conclusions

In this paper, we have proposed a graph attentive neural network for region recommendation (GANR^2) to address the implicit feedback in ROI- and POI-level. We observe that the user preferences over ROI- and POI-level are usually neglected in conventional location recommendation methods. To this end, we introduce the ROI- and POI-level attention modules to infer the users' underlying preferences encoded in the implicit user feedback. To the best of our knowledge, GANR^2 is the first ROI recommendation model that exploits an attention mechanism to learn the aggregation strategy from data in a dynamic way. The extensive experiments on two real-world datasets validate the performance of GANR^2 over state-of-the-art recommendation approaches by a considerable margin.

Acknowledgements. This work was supported in part by the National Natural Science Foundation of China under Grant No. 61772288, U1636116, 11431006, the Natural Science Foundation of Tianjin City under Grant No. 18JCZDJC30900, the Research Fund for International Young Scientists under Grant No. 61750110530, and the Ministry of education of Humanities and Social Science project under grant 16YJC790123.

References

1. Rafailidis, D., Crestani, F.: GeoDCF: deep collaborative filtering with multi-faceted contextual information in location-based social networks. In: Berlingerio, M., Bonchi, F., Gärtner, T., Hurley, N., Ifrim, G. (eds.) ECML PKDD 2018. LNCS (LNAI), vol. 11052, pp. 709–724. Springer, Cham (2019). https://doi.org/10.1007/978-3-030-10928-8_42
2. Xu, H., Zhang, Y., Wei, J., Yang, Z., Wang, J.: Spatiotemporal-aware region recommendation with deep metric learning. In: Li, G., Yang, J., Gama, J., Natwichai, J., Tong, Y. (eds.) DASFAA 2019. LNCS, vol. 11448, pp. 491–494. Springer, Cham (2019). https://doi.org/10.1007/978-3-030-18590-9_73
3. Yuan, J., Zheng, Y., Xie, X.: Discovering regions of different functions in a city using human mobility and POIs. In: SIGKDD, pp. 186–194. ACM (2012)
4. Ye, M., Yin, P., Lee, W.C., Lee, D.L.: Exploiting geographical influence for collaborative point-of-interest recommendation. In: SIGIR, pp. 325–334 (2011)
5. Yang, C., Bai, L., Zhang, C., Yuan, Q., Han, J.: Bridging collaborative filtering and semi-supervised learning: a neural approach for POI recommendation. In: SIGKDD, pp. 1245–1254 (2017)
6. Yuan, Q., Zhang, W., Zhang, C., Geng, X., Cong, G., Han, J.: PRED: periodic region detection for mobility modeling of social media users. In: SDM, pp. 263–272 (2017)
7. Pham, T.A.N., Cong, G.: A general model for out-of-town region recommendation. In: International World Wide Web Conference (WWW), pp. 401–410 (2017)
8. Ester, M., Kriegel, H.P., et al.: A density-based algorithm for discovering clusters in large spatial databases with noise. In: KDD, pp. 226–231 (1996)
9. Zhang, B., Zhang, L., Guo, T., Wang, Y., Chen, F.: Simultaneous urban region function discovery and popularity estimation via an infinite urbanization process model. In: SIGKDD, pp. 2692–2700 (2018)
10. Fan, W., et al.: Graph neural networks for social recommendation. In: The World Wide Web Conference (WWW), pp. 417–426 (2019)
11. Yang, D., Zhang, D., Zheng, V.W., Yu, Z.: Modeling user activity preference by leveraging user spatial temporal characteristics in LBSNs. IEEE Trans. Syst. Man Cybern. 45(1), 129–142 (2015)
12. Wang, X., He, X., Wang, M., Feng, F., Chua, T.S.: Neural graph collaborative filtering. arXiv preprint arXiv:1905.08108 (2019)

Generalized Collaborative Personalized Ranking for Recommendation

Bin Fu[1], Hongzhi Liu[1(✉)], Yang Song[2], Tao Zhang[3], and Zhonghai Wu[1(✉)]

[1] Peking University, Beijing, China
{binfu,liuhz,wuzh}@pku.edu.cn
[2] BOSS Zhipin NLP Center, Beijing, China
songyang@kanzhun.com
[3] BOSS Zhipin, Beijing, China
kylen.zhang@kanzhun.com

Abstract. Data sparsity is a common problem in collaborative ranking for personalized recommendation with implicit feedback. Several previous work tried to 'borrow' feedback information from users' neighborhood as their prior preferences to alleviate this problem. However, they emphasize the overlapping interests of users and their neighborhood while de-emphasize the importance of users' own specific taste, which leads to under-personalization. In addition, they ignore the collaborative influence among items which is also important for preference learning.

To solve these problems, we propose an effective collaborative ranking method *G*eneralized *C*ollaborative *P*ersonalized *R*anking (**GCPR**), which utilizes the collaborative influence among users and items in a unified framework. It strengthens the specific taste of users by using inner-basket influence of items to enhance the personalization. In addition, it utilizes cross-basket influence of items to dig more collaborative items to further alleviate the sparsity problem. Then, we utilize generalized AUC to learn a confidence-based listwise preference, and propose a post-training based on self-paced learning to solve the top-biased problem of the generalized AUC. Experimental results on four public real-world datasets show that GCPR achieves better performance than traditional collaborative filtering (CF) methods and state-of-the-art collaborative ranking methods.

Keywords: Collaborative ranking · Implicit feedback · Personalization · Sparsity

1 Introduction

Recommender systems have been studied to resolve the issue of information overload in various fields during the past decades, like products-to-customer recommendation in e-commerce platforms and people-to-people recommendation in social networks, etc. The key of personalized recommendation with implicit

© Springer Nature Switzerland AG 2020
X. Wang et al. (Eds.): APWeb-WAIM 2020, LNCS 12317, pp. 517–532, 2020.
https://doi.org/10.1007/978-3-030-60259-8_38

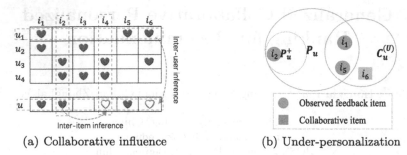

(a) Collaborative influence   (b) Under-personalization

Fig. 1. A simple example illustrates: (a) collaborative influence includes inter-user (blue dashed) and inter-item (green dashed) influence. ♥ denotes the observed 'like', and ♡ is the 'like' inferred from collaborative influence. Previous CR work only consider the inter-user influence (blue dashed arrow), which is exemplified as user u 'borrows' i_6 from his/her neighbor u_1 to alleviate his/her preference sparsity (i.e. $u_1 \overset{i_6}{\dashrightarrow} u$). (b) the non-overlapping observed items between u and his/her neighborhood (i.e. P_u^+ where $P_u^+ \subseteq P_u$) is assigned with a lower confidence (i.e. 0) than $P_u \backslash P_u^+$. (Color figure online)

feedback is to learn preference from users' past behaviors [3–5], i.e. learning the relative preference of each user on items. However, users often gave feedbacks on a small proportion of items, which let this preference learning suffer from the sparsity problem.

Bayesian Personalized Ranking (BPR) [13] is a well-known pairwise preference learning method. It assumes users prefer the items given positive feedback than the others. However, these partial orders are coarse-grained (caused by sparsity), and its assumption of independence between users does not always hold [11]. To solve these problems, several collaborative ranking (CR) methods [9,11,12] have been proposed to utilize the inter-user influence to refine the preference relations. Figure 1 is a simple example which illustrates how this inter-user influence work (blue dashed line in Fig. 1(a)). Besides the preference relations $\{i_1,i_2,i_5\} \succ_u \{i_3,i_4,i_6\}$ (BPR), they acquire preference relations $\{i_6\} \succ_u \{i_3,i_4\}$ via the inter-user influence, which alleviates the sparsity problem to some extent.

However, those CR methods above have two drawbacks: (1) non-overlapping observed items between u and his/her neighborhood (P_u^+ in Fig. 1(b)) are always weighted lower than overlapping observed items (e.g. i_1 and i_5 in Fig. 1(b)), which means they relatively overemphasize those observed items shared with user neighbors, while de-emphasizing the importance of non-shared personalized interests. This will lead to under-personalization. (2) They ignore the inter-item influence which is also important for preference learning. In Fig. 1(a), there exists inter-item influence between observed item i_2 and unobserved item i_4, which are always appeared together. Through i_2, we have a high level of confidence that u may also like i_4, which can alleviate the sparsity problem from a different aspect.

To solve these problems, we design a new CR method called GCPR (Generalized Collaborative Personalized Ranking) based on implicit feedbacks. The main contributions of this paper include: (1) we consider two types of inter-item influences: inner-basket influence is to enhance the personalized specific preferences and cross-basket influence to alleviate the sparsity problem. (2) We utilize generalized AUC to learn a confidence-based listwise preference, and propose a post-training based on self-paced learning to solve its top-biased problem. (3) Extensive experiments are conducted, and the results show that GCPR outperforms traditional CF methods and state-of-the-art CR methods.

2 Background

2.1 Bayesian Personalized Ranking

Preference is the ordering relation between items according to user's taste [1], and preference learning (PL) deals with the learning of these preferences from the feedbacks [4]. Pairwise PL [3] is one of the most widely-used PL. In PL, utility function and preference relation (PR) [4] are used to denote the prediction function and pairwise preference ($\succ$), respectively. To keep consistent with the given preferences, utility function $f(\cdot)$ for item-pair (i, j) of user u, should satisfy

$$i \succ_u j \Leftrightarrow f(u; i) > f(u; j) \tag{1}$$

where $i \succ_u j$ means user u prefers item i to item j.

Rendle [13] proposed a well-known PL method BPR for personalized ranking based on Bayesian inference, which assumes a user prefers the items given positive feedbacks P_u to other items $I \backslash P_u$, $i \succ_u j$ where $i \in P_u$ and $j \in I \backslash P_u$. BPR tries to maximize the posterior probability, i.e.

$$p(\Theta | \succ_u) \propto p(\succ_u | \Theta) p(\Theta)$$

where Θ is the model parameters. BPR is a basic and effective PL method with theoretical basis.

2.2 Collaborative Personalized Ranking

While PRs in BPR are coarse with only comparing items with positive feedback and those without, which let BPR suffer from sparsity.

To solve this problem, some BPR extensions have been proposed with considering inter-user influence. GBPR [11] proposes *group preference* $i_{G_u} \succ_u j$, derived from the global group of the user, and then enhance individual preference. PRIGP [12] splits the observed items from user's neighborhood into *item groups* according to their cumulative number of occurrences for both sparsity and personalization. However, PRIGP treats all the neighbors equally and ignores the degree of inter-user influence. In a different way, CML [6] uses metric learning to learn latent factors of users and items in the same compact space to reduce the impact of sparsity to some extent. CPLR [9] considers the degree of inter-user influence on the preferences of both observed and unobserved items, and acquires more explicit (i.e. $\succ_u$) and implicit (i.e. confidence) PRs.

Table 1. Notations and denotations.

Notation	Description	Notation	Description
U	User set	I	Item set
u	A user	i	An item
R	Feedback matrix	r_{ui}	Feedback of u on i
P_u	Observed items of u	P_u^+	Non-overlapping items of u
N_u	Nearest neighbors of u	N_i	Nearest neighbors of i
E_u	Collaborative itemset of u	c_{ui}	The confidence that u likes i
τ	Inter-user influence degree	ψ	Inter-item influence degree
$\mathcal{L}$	Loss	Θ	Model parameter(s)
θ	Coupling coefficient	$\gamma(\cdot)$	Relativeness function

However, only the potential preferences influenced by the user neighborhood are included by the inter-user influence of GBPR, PRIGP and CPLR, but those collaborative items which are related (e.g., similar and complementary) to the observed items are ignored. For example, people who has bought a computer would like to buy computer accessories or just replace it with a new one. These potential interests can be transductive inferred by the internal properties of items. This negligence make GBPR, PRIGP and CPLR still suffer from sparsity. Another problem is that they only assign confidences (aka. weights) to the overlapping observed items between user and neighborhood (Fig. 1(b)), which means the confidence of personal interests (P_u^+) is lower than the sharing interests ($P_u \backslash P_u^+$). However, the personal interests reflects the specific taste of user, which is crucial for personalized recommendation, and this leads to under-personalization.

3   Our Approach

3.1   Problem Definition

Let u denote a user and i denote an item. The implicit feedback[1] matrix R is defined as:

$$r_{ui} = \begin{cases} 1, \text{ if } (u,i) \text{ interaction is observed.} \\ 0, \text{ otherwise.} \end{cases}$$

Let P_u represent the items with observed feedbacks of u, i.e., $P_u = \{i|i \in I, r_{ui} = 1\}$, and $I \backslash P_u$ denote the items without observed feedbacks. Table 1 shows the notations and corresponding descriptions used in this paper.

Our goal is to generate a personalized ranking list of items from $I \backslash P_u$ for each user u using the implicit feedbacks.

---

[1] We consider the implicit feedback since it is more common than explicit feedback.

3.2 Generalized Collaborative Personalized Ranking (GCPR)

We firstly give the objective function, and detail how to obtain collaborative preference and calculate confidence. Then, the optimization and a post-training process based on self-paced learning to solve the top-biased problem in listwise ranking are presented. Finally, the algorithm is shown and analyzed.

Objective Function. For user u, we denote the collaborative itemset from collaborative influences as E_u. Then, I is divided into three non-overlapping subsets: the observed itemset P_u, the collaborative (unobserved) itemset E_u and the left unobserved itemset L_u, where $L_u = I - P_u - E_u$.

We assume there exists a listwise preference relation: user prefers the observed items from P_u over E_u and L_u, and prefer E_u over L_u, i.e. $P_u \succ_u E_u \succ_u L_u$, and can be simplified:

$$P_u \succ_u E_u, \quad E_u \succ_u L_u \tag{2}$$

which is equivalent to $i \succ_u k$, $k \succ_u j$ where $\forall i \in P_u$, $\forall k \in E_u$ and $\forall j \in L_u$.

To learn the listwise preference above, we try to maximize the generalized AUC [17,18], i.e. $GAUC_f = \frac{1}{|U|} \sum_{u \in U} GAUC_f(u)$, to find a utility function $f(\cdot)$,

$$GAUC_f(u) = \frac{\sum_{i \in P_u, k \in E_u} \mathbb{1}(f(u;i) > f(u;k)) + \sum_{k \in E_u, j \in L_u} \mathbb{1}(f(u;k) > f(u;j))}{|P_u||E_u| + |E_u||L_u|}$$

where $f(u;i)$ is the predicted feedback and $\mathbb{1}(\cdot)$ is binary indicator function.

Further, we simplify $GAUC$ by removing constants and replace $\mathbb{1}(\cdot)$ with the sigmoid function $\sigma(\cdot)$ like BPR [13], and define min_ΘGCPR-OPT $(\mathcal{L})$ as follows,

$$
\begin{aligned}
\mathcal{L} &= -ln(\prod_{u \in U} \prod_{i \in P_u, k \in E_u, j \in L_u} p(i >_u k >_u j)) + Reg(\Theta) \\
&\approx \sum_{u \in U} \left[\sum_{i \in P_u} \sum_{k \in E_u} \mathcal{L}_{uik} + \sum_{k \in E_u} \sum_{j \in L_u} \mathcal{L}_{ukj} \right] + \lambda_\Theta ||\Theta||_2^2 \\
&= -\sum_{u \in U} \left[\sum_{i \in P_u} \sum_{k \in E_u} c_{uik} ln(\sigma(\hat{r}_{uik})) + \sum_{k \in E_u} \sum_{j \in L_u} c_{ukj} ln(\sigma(\hat{r}_{ukj})) \right] + \lambda_\Theta ||\Theta||_2^2
\end{aligned}
\tag{3}
$$

where $\hat{r}_{uik} = \hat{r}_{ui} - \hat{r}_{uk}$, $\hat{r}_{ui} = f(u;i) = W_u V_i^T$ and $\Theta = \{W, V\}$. W and V denote the latent factor matrices of U and I, respectively. $W \in \mathbb{R}^{|U| \times d}$ and $V \in \mathbb{R}^{|I| \times d}$. λ_Θ is the regularization coefficient. c_{uik} and c_{ukj} are the pairwise confidence coefficients, which describe how much confidence that we have with the preference relations $i \succ_u k$ and $k \succ_u j$, respectively.

Collaborative Preference. The foundation of personalized ranking recommendation is that *a portion of unobserved items would be preferred by user, and they should be ranked ahead of other unobserved items.* To find those items, for user u, we collect the unobserved items as E_u by transductive inferring from the collaboration of users and items in a heuristic way. Collaborative preferences are those ordering relations between E_u and L_u (i.e., $E_u \succ L_u$).

E_u contains items from inter-user influence ($C_u^{(U)}$) and items from inter-item influence ($C_u^{(I)}$). $C_u^{(U)}$ is based on the assumption that *the items liked by similar users would be also preferred by user u*, and $C_u^{(I)}$ is based on the assumption that *items similar to those items liked by user u would also be preferred by u*.

$$E_u = C_u^{(U)} \cup C_u^{(I)} \tag{4}$$

$C_u^{(U)}$ is transductive inferred from u's neighborhood with similar taste,

$$C_u^{(U)} = \{t \mid \exists\, u' \in N_u, t \in P_{u'},\, t \notin P_u\} \tag{5}$$

where N_u is the nearest neighbors of user u.

$C_u^{(I)}$ is transductive inferred based on the relatedness (e.g., similarity and complementarity) between P_u (as a basket) and $I \backslash P_u$, i.e. observed items have influence on some of unobserved items (***cross-basket influence***),

$$C_u^{(I)} = \{t \mid \exists\, i \in P_u, t \in N_i,\, t \notin P_u\} \tag{6}$$

where N_i is the nearest neighbors of item i.

In Fig. 1(a), $C_u^{(I)} = \{i_4\}$ since i_4 is one of the nearest neighbors of i_2 where $i_2 \in P_u$, and this cross-basket influence can be exemplified as $i_2 \xrightarrow{i_4} u$. Then, a new listwise PR $\{i_1, i_2, i_5\} \succ_u \{i_4, i_6\} \succ_u \{i_3\}$ can alleviate the sparsity problem.

Confidence of Preference. The information granularity of implicit feedbacks is coarse, e.g. buy or not buy, which does not reflect the preference intensity. To solve this problem, we calculate the confidence of preference based on the inner-basket influence and cross-basket influence between items.

We assume item i' has influence on another item i because item i' appears in the nearest neighbors N_i,

$$\psi(i' \dashrightarrow i) = \gamma(i', i) \cdot \mathbb{1}(i' \in N_i) \tag{7}$$

where $\gamma(\cdot)$ is a non-negative relativeness function and $\psi(\cdot)$ is asymmetric.

Based on the assumption above, inter-item influence also exists in P_u (***inner-basket influence***). Items in P_u may receive influences from others in P_u,

$$c_{ui}^{(IB)} = \sum_{i' \in P_u, i' \neq i} \psi(i' \dashrightarrow i) \tag{8}$$

where $i \in P_u$. For an observed item i, if it is more related to other observed items, i would be more preferred by the user and get a larger confidence.

Similarly, the degree of ***cross-basket influence*** of observed items on $C_u^{(I)}$,

$$c_{uk}^{(CB)} = \sum_{i' \in P_u} \psi(i' \dashrightarrow k) \tag{9}$$

where $k \in C_u^{(I)}$. Then, a unified formula of confidence is as following,

$$c_{ui}^{(I)} = \sum_{i' \in P_u, i' \neq i} \psi(i' \dashrightarrow i) \tag{10}$$

where $i \in P_u \cup C_u^{(I)}$. Similarly, we get the confidence from inter-user influence,

$$c_{ui}^{(U)} = \sum_{u' \in N_u} \tau(u' \dashrightarrow u) \cdot \mathbb{1}(i \in P_{u'}) \tag{11}$$

$$\tau(u' \dashrightarrow u) = \gamma(u', u) \cdot \mathbb{1}(u' \in N_u) \tag{12}$$

where $i \in P_u \cup C_u^{(U)}$. $\tau(u' \dashrightarrow u)$ is the inter-user influence degree from u' to u.

As in Sect. 1 and Sect. 2.2, $c_{ui}^{(U)}=0$ and $\forall i \in P_u^+$, which results in under-personalization. This can be alleviated by fusing the inter-user and inter-item influence. We use the simple weighted average to combine $c_{ui}^{(U)}$ and $c_{ui}^{(I)}$ after their normalizations,

$$c_{ui} = \theta \, \bar{c}_{ui}^{(U)} + (1 - \theta) \, \bar{c}_{ui}^{(I)} \tag{13}$$

where $\bar{c}_{ui}^{(U)} = |E_u \cup P_u| * c_{ui}^{(U)} / \sum_{k \in E_u \cup P_u} c_{uk}^{(U)}$. θ is a coupling coefficient, $\theta \in [0, 1]$.

The confidence can be used to finely tune the intensity of preference relations in preference learning. To control its variance, p-norm is used, i.e., $(c_{ui})^p$. We set $p < 1$ to shrink the confidences close to 1. For an item triple (i, k, j) from (P_u, E_u, L_u), the pairwise confidence is calculated,

$$c_{uik} = \frac{(c_{ui})^p + \mu}{(c_{uk})^p + \mu}, \quad c_{ukj} = (c_{uk})^p + \mu \tag{14}$$

where μ is a smooth constant. p and μ are set 0.9 and 1, respectively.

$\gamma(\cdot)$ in Eq. (7) and Eq. (11) is a relativeness measure function defined on pairs of users/items based on R. For simplicity, Jaccard similarity is used in this paper.

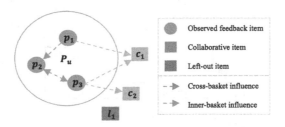

Fig. 2. A simple example illustrates inner-basket and cross-basket influence.

Example. A simple example in Fig. 2 shows how the *inner-basket* and *cross-basket influence* alleviate sparsity and enhance personalization. Dotted arrow denotes source item has influence on end item ($\psi(\cdot)$ in Eq. (7)). And dotted arrows in P_u are *inner-basket influence*, and dotted arrows out from P_u reflect *cross-basket influence*. Through *cross-basket influence*, $C_u^{(I)} = \{c_1, c_2\}$ can be found and assigned with confidence according to Eq. (6) and Eq. (9) to alleviate the sparsity. Through *inner-basket influence*, $\{p_2, p_3\}$ are weighted with different confidences according to Eq. (8), to enhance the personalization. Note that, actually, left-out items are more than observed items and collaborative items.

Optimization. $\mathcal{L}$ can be optimized by stochastic gradient descent (SGD), and updating rules are given in Eq. (15). Uniformly sampling strategy is used: randomly pick a user u from U, then an item triad (i, k, j) is randomly picked from (P_u, E_u, L_u).

$$\Theta \leftarrow \Theta - \eta \cdot \frac{\partial \text{GCPR-OPT}}{\partial \Theta} \tag{15}$$

where η is the learning rate. The gradients of the parameters in Θ are calculated,

$$\frac{\partial \text{GCPR-OPT}}{\partial W_u} = -c_{uik}\sigma(-\hat{r}_{uik})(V_i - V_k) - c_{ukj}\sigma(-\hat{r}_{ukj})(V_k - V_j) + 2\lambda_\Theta W_u$$

$$\frac{\partial \text{GCPR-OPT}}{\partial V_i} = -c_{uik}\sigma(-\hat{r}_{uik})W_u + 2\lambda_\Theta V_i$$

$$\frac{\partial \text{GCPR-OPT}}{\partial V_k} = c_{uik}\sigma(-\hat{r}_{uik})W_u - c_{ukj}\sigma(-\hat{r}_{ukj})W_u + 2\lambda_\Theta V_k$$

$$\frac{\partial \text{GCPR-OPT}}{\partial V_j} = c_{ukj}\sigma(-\hat{r}_{ukj})W_u + 2\lambda_\Theta V_j$$

Post-training. In personalized ranking, top-biased problem is that top positions are not treated more important than lower positions. min_ΘGCPR-OPT in Eq. (3) is optimized based on generalized AUC in which top-biased problem exists.

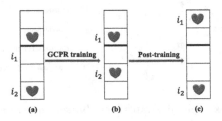

Fig. 3. A simple example shows the transformation of the item-list of user u for top-2 recommendation (a) before training, (b) after traning and (c) after post-training.

A simple example in Fig. 3 illustrates a case of top-2 recommendation, and the transformation of the ranking item-list of u: (a) before training, (b) after training and (c) after post-training. After GCPR training, GCPR put items i_1 and i_2 to proper positions to minimize the ranking loss $\mathcal{L}$, where $\mathcal{L} = \mathcal{L}(i_1) + \mathcal{L}(i_2)$, which reaches the stable trade-off of these two ranking losses. $\mathcal{L}(i_1) = \sum_{i_1 >_u j} \mathcal{L}_{ui_1j}$ and $\mathcal{L}(i_2) = \sum_{i_2 >_u j} \mathcal{L}_{ui_2j}$. $\mathcal{L}(i_1) < \mathcal{L}(i_2)$ due to i_1 ranks more close to the top than i_2. While, a better result is shown in Fig. 3(c) for top-2 recommendation, which can be realized by putting more attention on the ranking of i_1.

To solve this problem, we adopt self-paced learning (SPL) [8,19]. The idea of SPL is to learn 'easy' samples first and then gradually learn 'complex' samples, which simulates the process of human learning. The solution strategy of SPL is to assign different weights to these samples: larger weights on 'easy' samples and smaller weights on 'complex' samples. We assume that, after the convergence of GCPR training, the larger the ranking loss ($\mathcal{L}(i)$) of the item is, the more complex it is. We adjust $\mathcal{L}$ to $\mathcal{L} = \omega_{i_1}\mathcal{L}(i_1) + \omega_{i_2}\mathcal{L}(i_2)$ where $\omega_{i_1} > \omega_{i_2} > 0$. Due to $\mathcal{L}(i_1) < \mathcal{L}(i_2)$, and we simply let $\omega_i = \frac{1}{\sigma(\mathcal{L}(i))+1}$.

Since $\mathcal{L}(i)$ can be decomposed into pairs of items, i.e. $\mathcal{L}(i) = \sum_{i >_u j} \mathcal{L}_{uij} = -\sum_{i >_u j} ln\sigma(\hat{r}_{uij})$, we realize SPL in a smooth way by auto-tuning the weight of pairwise ranking loss as follows,

$$\omega_{uik} = \frac{1}{\sigma(\mathcal{L}_{uik}) + 1} \tag{16}$$

ω_{ukj} is calculated similar with ω_{uik}. The whole loss function is redefined as:

$$\mathcal{L} = \sum_{u \in U} \left[\sum_{i \in P_u} \sum_{k \in E_u} \omega_{uik} c_{uik} \mathcal{L}_{uik} + \sum_{k \in E_u} \sum_{j \in L_u} \omega_{ukj} c_{ukj} \mathcal{L}_{ukj} \right] + \lambda_\Theta \|\Theta\|_2^2 \tag{17}$$

Algorithm. The pseudo-code of GCPR is shown in Algorithm 1, which consists of three stages: setup, training and post-training. In setup stage, $|N_u|$ ($|N_i|$) nearest neighbors are found for each user u (item i) based on $\gamma(\cdot)$, and then the whole items are split into three overlapping itemsets: P_u, E_u and L_u. In training stage, for each time, we randomly sample a user u and an item triad (i, k, j), then calculate the gradients and update Θ. The post-training stage adjusts the weights of different item-pair losses according to Eq. (16) and Eq. (17).

In setup stage, we adopt inverted index [2] to speed up the nearest neighbors retrieval since R is sparse. Assuming that, user (item) and its $|U_{co-like}|$ ($|I_{co-liked}|$) neighbors co-like (be co-liked by) at least one item (user), the complexity is $O(|U||U_{co-like}| + |I||I_{co-liked}|)$. Since $|N_u| \leq |U_{co-like}|$ and $|N_i| \leq |I_{co-liked}|$, the lower bound is $O(|U||N_u| + |I||N_i|)$, and further simplified as $O(|U| + |I|)$ since $|N_u|$ and $|N_i|$ are usually preset small. The complexity of training stage and post-training stage are $O(Td)$ and $O(T'd)$. The whole complexity is $O(|U||U_{co-like}| + |I||I_{co-liked}| + Td + T'd)$.

Algorithm 1. Generalized Collaborative Personalized Ranking (GCPR)

Input: Implicit feedback matrix R; user set U; item set I; the size of nearest neighbors $|N_u|$ and $|N_i|$; dimension of latent factor d; regulization coefficient λ_Θ, and learning rate of GCPR training η and post-training η'; number of iteration in GCPR training T and post-training T'.

Output: The latent factors W and V.

1: **Setup:**
2: **for** each item $i \in I$ **do**
3:     Select $|N_i|$ nearest neighbors and form N_i based on $\gamma(\cdot)$.
4: **for** each user $u \in U$ **do**
5:     Select $|N_u|$ nearest neighbors and form N_u based on $\gamma(\cdot)$.
6:     Split the itemset I into three parts: P_u, E_u and L_u, and calculate the confidences of items in $P_u \cup E_u$ according to Eq.(13).
7: **Training:**
8: Randomly initialize the parameters W and V.
9: **for** $i = 1$ to T **do**
10:     Randomly select a user u from U.
11:     Randomly select an item triad (i, k, j) from (P_u, E_u, L_u), and get c_{ui} and c_{uk}.
12:     Calculate the gradients and update W and V, according to Eq.(15).
13: **Post-training:**
14: **for** $i = 1$ to T' **do**
15:     Randomly select a user u from U.
16:     Randomly select an item triad (i, k, j) from (P_u, E_u, L_u), and get c_{ui} and c_{uk}.
17:     Calculate the item-pair loss $\mathcal{L}_{uik}$ and $\mathcal{L}_{ukj}$, and their weights ω_{uik} and ω_{ukj}.
18:     Calculate the gradients and update W and V, according to Eq.(16) and Eq.(17).

4   Experiments

4.1   Datasets

Four public real-world datasets for recommendation task are adopted: Netflix5K5K[2], Amazon[3], ML-100K[4] and Delicious2K[5]. Netflix5K5K contains 282,474 ratings with 5000 users on 5000 movies. Amazon describes 195,791 buying records with 6170 users on 2753 items from Amazon website. ML-100K includes 1,000,209 ratings given by 6040 users on 3,952 movies. Delicious2K describes the tag information from user on online bookmarks, which collects 230,942 user-tag records with 1,867 users and 40,897 tags. The same as [9,11,13], we consider ratings higher than 3 as positive feedbacks. Table 2 shows these datasets.

---

[2] https://www.netflix.com/, please refer to [9].
[3] http://jmcauley.ucsd.edu/data/amazon/.
[4] https://grouplens.org/datasets/movielens/.
[5] https://grouplens.org/datasets/hetrec-2011/.

Table 2. Statistic of datasets.

Dataset	User	Item	Size	Density(%)
Netflix5K5K	5000	5000	151,256	0.61
Amazon	6170	2753	195,791	1.15
ML-100K	943	1682	100,000	6.30
Delicious2K	1867	40,897	230,942	0.30

4.2 Evaluation Metrics

Some common evaluation metrics for top-N recommendation are used, including Precision (Pre@N), Recall (Recall@N), Mean Average Precision (MAP@N [15]), Mean Reciprocal Rank (MRR@N [16]), Normalized Discounted Cumulative Gain (NDCG@N [7]). All the experiments are under the same five-fold cross-validation.

4.3 Baselines

Nine representative recommendation algorithms are used as baselines, including traditional CF methods: POP, UCF, ICF [14], WRMF [10], and several CR methods: BPR [13], GBPR [11], PRIGP [12], CML [6], CPLR [9].

- **POP.** The items are ranked by the popularity for all users.
- **UCF.** User-based Collaborative Filtering collects the items from the nearest neighbors of the user and ranks them by the aggregation.
- **ICF** [14]. Item-based Collaborative Filtering recommends the items which are most similar to the observed itemset.
- **WRMF** [10]. Weighted Regularized Matrix Factorization considers different weights for user's preferences in matrix factorization.
- **BPR** [13]. Bayesian Personalized Ranking is a basic pairwise learning method.
- **GBPR** [11]. Group Bayesian Personalized Ranking relaxes the inter-user independence assumption of BPR by introducing the group preference.
- **PRIGP** [12]. Personalized Ranking with Item Group considers those items with observed feedbacks from user's nearest neighbors and splits them into *item groups* with ranking relations.
- **CML** [6]. Collaborative Metric Learning uses metric learning, i.e. replaces dot-product in BPR with hinge loss of Euclidean distance, to consider the triangle inequality between user-item, user-user and item-item relationships.
- **CPLR** [9]. Collaborative Pairwise Learning to Rank considers the inter-user influence on both items with observed feedbacks and those without.

4.4 Implementation and Parameter Setting

We implemented our model using TensorFlow[6]. Let $topN = 10$, $d = 100$, $\eta = 0.1$, and $T = 10000*|U|$. For post-training, let $T' = 1000*|U|$ and $\eta' = 0.001$. We

---

[6] https://www.tensorflow.org.

Table 3. Prediction performance (ave. of five-fold cross-validation) of nine baselines and GCPR. The best results of all are in **bold**, and the best among nine baselines are underlined. *, ** indicate $p \leq 0.01$, and $p \leq 0.001$ based on the Wilcoxon signed rank test.

Dataset	Metric	Model										Improve
		POP	UCF	ICF	WRMF	BPR	GBPR	PRIGP	CML	CPLR	GCPR	
Netflix5K5K	Prec@10	8.2	12.8	12.1	12.0	13.3	13.2	13.3	<u>13.3</u>	12.8	**13.8**	3.8%*
	Recall@10	11.5	<u>20.5</u>	18.2	20.4	20.2	20.3	19.8	20.3	18.6	**22.3**	8.8%**
	MAP@10	4.6	<u>9.7</u>	8.7	9.1	9.6	9.6	9.3	9.2	8.6	**11.0**	13.4%**
	MRR@10	20.7	32.9	31.1	29.6	<u>33.0</u>	32.8	32.4	31.5	31.4	**35.1**	6.4%*
	NDCG@10	25.9	38.3	36.3	36.3	<u>38.5</u>	38.4	37.8	37.5	36.8	**40.6**	5.5%*
ML-100K	Prec@10	11.8	20.7	18.4	20.7	22.2	21.2	20.5	<u>22.2</u>	22.0	**22.7**	2.3%
	Recall@10	10.9	22.7	19.4	22.9	23.8	23.1	21.9	<u>24.3</u>	23.4	**25.2**	3.7%*
	MAP@10	5.2	12.1	10.5	11.8	12.7	11.7	11.1	<u>12.7</u>	12.4	**13.9**	9.4%**
	MRR@10	31.5	49.3	46.0	46.3	50.5	47.9	46.3	<u>50.5</u>	50.3	**53.2**	5.3%*
	NDCG@10	36.8	54.7	51.1	52.9	56.0	53.7	52.4	<u>56.0</u>	55.6	**58.3**	4.1%*
Amazon	Prec@10	1.3	4.4	4.5	4.5	4.6	4.8	4.4	<u>5.0</u>	4.3	**5.2**	4%*
	Recall@10	2.7	9.8	10.1	10.7	10.2	10.8	9.8	<u>11.2</u>	9.6	**11.8**	5.4%**
	MAP@10	1.0	4.6	4.9	4.5	4.3	4.6	4.4	<u>5.0</u>	4.1	**5.5**	10%**
	MRR@10	4.3	14.2	15.1	13.9	13.8	14.4	13.9	<u>15.6</u>	13.1	**16.5**	5.7%**
	NDCG@10	5.8	17.7	18.3	17.9	17.7	18.3	17.4	<u>19.5</u>	16.9	**20.4**	4.6%*
Delicious2K	Prec@10	6.8	16.6	17.1	15.7	18.2	17.2	16.0	17.4	<u>18.7</u>	**20.2**	8%**
	Recall@10	7.0	16.9	17.5	16.0	18.5	17.5	16.3	17.9	<u>19.1</u>	**20.9**	9.4%**
	MAP@10	3.4	10.1	10.9	8.4	11.1	10.4	9.8	10.4	<u>11.7</u>	**14.1**	20.5%**
	MRR@10	19.5	45.1	49.0	40.8	49.0	46.4	44.8	46.1	<u>50.4</u>	**53.9**	6.9%**
	NDCG@10	23.1	50.0	52.7	47.5	53.6	51.3	49.5	51.0	<u>54.8</u>	**58.0**	5.8%*

explore regularization coefficient λ_Θ in $\{100, 10, \dots 0.0001\}$ for WRMF, BPR, GBPR, PRIGP, CML and GCPR. $|N_u|$ and $|N_i|$ are explored in $\{5, 10, 20, 50, 100, 200\}$ same in UCF, ICF, PRIGP, CPLR and GCPR. For WRMF, the confidence weight coefficient α is chosen from $\{1, 2, 3, 4, 5\}$. For GBPR, the size of group $|G|$ and ρ are chosen from $\{1, 2, 3, 4, 5\}$ and $\{0.2, 0.4, 0.6, 0.8, 1.0\}$, respectively. For PRIGP, α is chosen from $\{0.001, 0.01, \dots 10\}$. We use the CML implementation[7] and tune the margin m in $\{0.01, 0.05, \dots 5, 10\}$. α, β and γ of CPLR are chose in $\{0, 1\}$ [9]. The coupling coefficient θ of GCPR is explored in $\{0, 0.2, 0.4, 0.6, 0.8, 1\}$. Grid search is used to find the best parameter(s) for all the methods.

4.5 Results and Analysis

Prediction Performance. Table 3 lists the results of nine baselines and GCPR with five metrics (@top-10) on datasets, and we can get following conclusions: (1) GCPR consistently outperforms the baselines on all datasets across various metrics. GCPR not only performs much better than traditional CF methods, but also beats PL methods. (2) Among nine baselines, CML and CPLR are two state-of-the-art CR methods. CML performs better on ML-100K and Amazon while CPLR performs better on the sparsest dataset Delicious2K. (3) GBPR and

---

[7] https://github.com/changun/CollMetric.

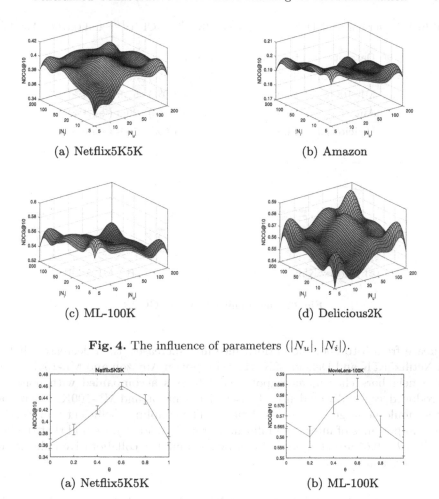

Fig. 4. The influence of parameters ($|N_u|$, $|N_i|$).

(a) Netflix5K5K

(b) ML-100K

Fig. 5. The influence of parameter θ.

PRIGP perform unstable, even worse than BPR on ML-100K and Delicious2K, due to that they ignore the influence degree. (4) Since POP, UCF, ICF and WRMF are not ranking-oriented, their performances are not as good as CR methods in most cases. Interestingly, among four datasets, the improvement of GCPR over others is relevant with the sparsity. GCPR improves most on the sparsest dataset Delicious2K and least on the densest dataset ML-100K. BPR, GBPR, PRIGP, CML and CPLR suffer from the sparsity, and GBPR, PRIGP and CPLR suffer from the under-personalization. The results confirm that GCPR effectively deal with the problems of under-personalization and sparsity.

Effects of Parameters. Figure 4(a–d) examines the effect of varying the neighborhood size ($|N_u|$ and $|N_i|$) on the performance of GCPR. When $|N_u|$ and $|N_i|$

Table 4. Performance (NDCG@10,%) of GCPR$^{(CB)}$, GCPR$^{(IB)}$ and the best baseline.

Dataset	Best Baseline	GCPR$^{(CB)}$	GCPR$^{(IB)}$
Netflix5K5K	38.5	39.8 (+3.4%)	39.1 (+1.6%)
ML-100K	56.0	57.7 (+3.0%)	57.9 (+3.4%)
Amazon	19.5	20.5 (+5.1%)	20.3 (+4.1%)
Delicious2K	54.8	55.7 (+1.6%)	56.8 (+3.6%)

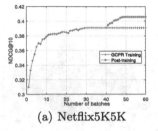   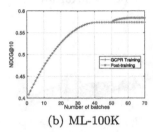

(a) Netflix5K5K   (b) ML-100K

Fig. 6. The training curves of GCPR.

increase from 5 to 200, the performance first increases, then decreases slightly on Netflix5K5K and Delicious2K while sharply on Amazon and ML-100K. With more neighbors chosen, more potential interests accompanied with noise are introduced, especially on denser datasets like Amazon and ML-100K. The proper sizes should be larger on sparser data set. The coupling coefficient θ in Eq. (13) is the importance of inter-item influence. From Fig. 5(a–b), we find that the best results ($\theta = 0.6$) are always produced by combing the collaborative influence on both users and items.

Effectiveness of Cross-Basket and Inner-Basket Influence. *Cross-basket influence* can help alleviate the sparsity and *inner-basket influence* can enhance personalization. GCPR$^{(CB)}$, GCPR$^{(IB)}$ are GCPR variants only including *cross-basket influence* and *inner-basket influence*, respectively. Table 4 shows they perform better than other baselines, and by combining *cross-basket* and *inner-basket influence*, GCPR always performs best.

Impact of Post-training. Figure 6 shows the performance of GCPR without and with post-training, after the convergence of GCPR training, further training GCPR with self-paced learning leads to a significant improvement, about 1.8% and 1.6% absolute improvement on NDCG@10. Self-paced learning can put more effort on learning the observed items and collaborative items at the top positions, which can alleviate the top-biased problem of GAUC.

5   Conclusion

To solve the under-personalization and sparsity problems in previous CR methods, we propose utilizing inner-basket influence and cross-basket influence of items, and then we design a generalized collaborative ranking method (GCPR). To learn the listwise preference of users, we design an objective function based on generalized AUC with preference confidence. Further, self-paced learning is used to solve the top-biased problem in generalized AUC. Experimental results show that GCPR is an effective CR method for personalized recommendation. For future work, we will try to improve GCPR in the setting of explicit feedback.

Acknowledgements. This work was partially sponsored by National 863 Program of China (Grant No. 2015AA016009).

References

1. Brafman, R.I., Domshlak, C.: Preference handling - an introductory tutorial. AI Mag. **30**(1), 58–86 (2009)
2. Cohen, W.W.: Integration of heterogeneous databases without common domains using queries based on textual similarity. In: SIGMOD Conference, pp. 201–212. ACM Press (1998)
3. Fürnkranz, J., Hüllermeier, E.: Pairwise preference learning and ranking. In: Lavrač, N., Gamberger, D., Blockeel, H., Todorovski, L. (eds.) ECML 2003. LNCS (LNAI), vol. 2837, pp. 145–156. Springer, Heidelberg (2003). https://doi.org/10.1007/978-3-540-39857-8_15
4. Fürnkranz, J., Hüllermeier, E.: Preference learning: an introduction. In: Fürnkranz, J., Hüllermeier, E. (eds.) Preference Learning, pp. 1–17. Springer, Heidelberg (2010). https://doi.org/10.1007/978-3-642-14125-6_1
5. de Gemmis, M., Iaquinta, L., Lops, P., Musto, C., Narducci, F., Semeraro, G.: Learning preference models in recommender systems. In: Fürnkranz, J., Hüllermeier, E. (eds.) Preference Learning, pp. 387–407. Springer, Heidelberg (2010). https://doi.org/10.1007/978-3-642-14125-6_18
6. Hsieh, C., Yang, L., Cui, Y., Lin, T., Belongie, S.J., Estrin, D.: Collaborative metric learning. In: WWW, pp. 193–201. ACM (2017)
7. Järvelin, K., Kekäläinen, J.: Cumulated gain-based evaluation of IR techniques. ACM Trans. Inf. Syst. **20**(4), 422–446 (2002)
8. Jiang, L., Meng, D., Mitamura, T., Hauptmann, A.G.: Easy samples first: self-paced reranking for zero-example multimedia search. In: ACM Multimedia, pp. 547–556. ACM (2014)
9. Liu, H., Wu, Z., Zhang, X.: CPLR: collaborative pairwise learning to rank for personalized recommendation. Knowl.-Based Syst. **148**, 31–40 (2018)
10. Pan, R., et al.: One-class collaborative filtering. In: ICDM, pp. 502–511. IEEE Computer Society (2008)
11. Pan, W., Chen, L.: GBPR: group preference based Bayesian personalized ranking for one-class collaborative filtering. In: IJCAI, pp. 2691–2697. IJCAI/AAAI (2013)
12. Qiu, S., Cheng, J., Yuan, T., Leng, C., Lu, H.: Item group based pairwise preference learning for personalized ranking. In: SIGIR, pp. 1219–1222. ACM (2014)

13. Rendle, S., Freudenthaler, C., Gantner, Z., Schmidt-Thieme, L.: BPR: Bayesian personalized ranking from implicit feedback. In: UAI, pp. 452–461. AUAI Press (2009)
14. Sarwar, B.M., Karypis, G., Konstan, J.A., Riedl, J.: Item-based collaborative filtering recommendation algorithms. In: WWW, pp. 285–295. ACM (2001)
15. Shi, Y., Karatzoglou, A., Baltrunas, L., Larson, M., Hanjalic, A., Oliver, N.: TFMAP: optimizing MAP for top-n context-aware recommendation. In: SIGIR, pp. 155–164. ACM (2012)
16. Shi, Y., Karatzoglou, A., Baltrunas, L., Larson, M., Oliver, N., Hanjalic, A.: CLiMF: learning to maximize reciprocal rank with collaborative less-is-more filtering. In: RecSys, pp. 139–146. ACM (2012)
17. Song, D., Meyer, D.A.: Recommending positive links in signed social networks by optimizing a generalized AUC. In: AAAI, pp. 290–296. AAAI Press (2015)
18. Waegeman, W., Baets, B.D.: A survey on roc-based ordinal regression. In: Fürnkranz, J., Hüllermeier, E. (eds.) Preference Learning, pp. 127–154. Springer, Heidelberg (2010). https://doi.org/10.1007/978-3-642-14125-6_7
19. Zhao, Q., Meng, D., Jiang, L., Xie, Q., Xu, Z., Hauptmann, A.G.: Self-paced learning for matrix factorization. In: AAAI, pp. 3196–3202. AAAI Press (2015)

Information Extraction and Retrieval

Dynamic Multi-hop Reasoning

Liang Xu[1], Junjie Yao[1(✉)], and Yingjie Zhang[2]

[1] East China Normal University, Shanghai, China
xulyeng@gmail.com, junjie.yao@cs.ecnu.edu.cn
[2] Shanghai Electric Vehicle Public Data Collecting, Monitoring and Research Center,
Carlsbad, USA
zhangyingjie@shevdc.org

Abstract. Multi-hop reasoning is an essential part of the current reading comprehension and question answering areas. The reasoning methods have been extensively studied, and most of them are generally focused on the pre-retrieval based inference, with the help of a few paragraphs. These methods are fixed and unable to cope with dynamic and complex questions. Here, we propose to utilize the dynamic graph reasoning network for multi-hop reading comprehension question answering.

Specifically, the new approach continuously infers the clue entities and candidate answers based on the question and clue paragraphs. The clue entities and candidate answers extracted at each hop are used as new nodes to expand the dynamic graph. Then we iteratively update the semantic representation of the questions via dynamic question memory, and apply the graph attention network to encode the information of inference paths. Extensive experiments on two datasets verify the advantage and improvements of the proposed approach.

Keywords: Multi-hop reasoning · Graph attention network · Commonsense

1 Introduction

Question answering (QA) has been a popular topic in recent years. In particular, machine reasoning methods have been studied extensively to support QA services. Prominent ones include reading comprehension CommonsenseQA [12] and multi-hop HotpotQA [16]. However, machine reasoning, especially multi-hop reasoning is still a challenging problem [5]. Most of the work [2] are established in two parts: retrieving paragraphs and reasoning. Retrieving paragraphs and reasoning are separated. The retriever is consequently unable to cover all the necessary informative paragraphs, and the ability of reasoning depends largely on the results of the earlier retriever.

Current models for single document QA tend to seek answers in sentences matched by the question, which does not involve complex reasoning. Complex

This work was supported by NSFC grant 61972151, the Open Research Fund of KLATASDS-MOE.

logical reasoning can better verify the model's reasoning ability. Earlier work [11] used Bi-attention flow between questions and context, and pre-trained model such as Bert [4] to capture the implied relationship between questions and context. With the development of graph neural networks, more and more work [5,15] completes the inference of complex logic by constructing inference graphs.

Figure 1 presents an example of multi-hop reading comprehension. We complete the document retrieval based on the raw question text in the first stage, which retrieves the information of the beginning and end hop. The information required by the middle hop may not be related to the initial input.

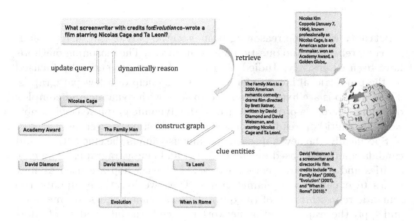

Fig. 1. Stages of Multi-hop reasoning: retrieving documents, constructing dynamic graph, and updating query.

In this paper, we propose a novel framework for question-answer based on dynamic graph processing. The retrieved information, and the question representation will change iteratively. In the current hop, we use the key entities called *clue entities* in the question and context to retrieve information called *clue paragraphs*. Based on the previous hop *clue paragraphs*, we then reasoned to obtain the next hop *clue entities* and *candidate answers* until we find the correct answer. This kind of dynamic iteration process of retrieval-reasoning can provide an explicit inference paths.

Complex multi-hop reading comprehension QA requires explicit inference paths to illustrate the rigor of its reasoning logic. Previous deep learning based models cannot provide a sufficient explanation of the reasoning process. We use *clue entities* and *candidate answers* to dynamically construct graph, then utilize the graph attention network [13] to aggregate the information of the inference paths. With the deepening of reasoning, the expression of the question has different from the original question. We use a dynamic memory network to update iteratively the semantic information of the question at each hop.

The contribution of this work can be summarized as follows: 1). We propose a novel framework of dynamical graph reasoning for multi-hop reading comprehension open-domain questioning answer; 2). Experiments on two datasets verify the improvements, compared with the baselines; 3). The new approach reveals novel explainability.

2   Related Works

Machine Reading Comprehension: Compared with traditional rule-based machine reading comprehension methods, models based on deep learning are better at mining semantic information of context, resulting in a significant performance improvement. R-NET [14] is an end-to-end neural networks model for reading comprehension QA. It matches the question and passage with gated attention-based recurrent networks to obtain the question-aware passage representation. BIDAF [11] network, a multi-stage hierarchical process that represents the context at different levels of granularity and uses bidirectional attention flow mechanism to obtain a query-aware context representation without early summarization.

Open-Domain QA: However, open-Domain QA is not limited to reasoning on certain documents, but to find supporting evidence to answer questions based on prior knowledge or large-scale document sets. Recently, DrQA [2] leverages a neural model to extract the accurate answer from retrieved paragraphs, usually called retrieval-extraction framework. Rajarshi et al. [3]uses gated recurrent unit to update the query at each step conditioned on the state of the reader and the reformulated query is used to re-rank the paragraphs by the retriever. Kenton et al. [8]treats evidence retrieved from open corpus as a latent variable, and jointly learns the retriever and reader from question-answer string pairs and without any IR system.

Graph Neural Network: Graph modeling is incresingly used in reasoning. Entity-GCN [1] considers three different types of edges that connect different entities in the entity graph. DFGN [15] constructs a dynamic entity graph, wherein each reasoning step irrelevant entities are softly masked out, and a fusion module is designed to improve the interaction between the entity graph and the documents. Cognitive Graph QA [5] employs an machine reading comprehension model to predict answer spans and possible next-hop spans, and then organizesthem into a cognitive graph. Compared with previous work, our architecture extends the query memory mechanism and the underlying graph reasoning model.

3   Dynamic Graph Reasoning

3.1   Proposed Framework

The proposed framework in Fig. 2. It consists of three core modules: Multi-level Features Extraction, Dynamic Question Memory, Dynamic Graph Attention Reasoning. The multi-level features extraction module iteratively extracts

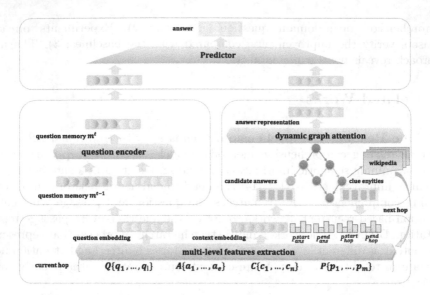

Fig. 2. Dynamic graph reasoning framework.

the *clue entities* and *candidate answers*, the dynamic graph reasoning module encodes the information of the inference paths, and the dynamic question memory is updated accordingly at each hop.

Our approach encodes the question memory dynamically. We first take the raw question text as the initialization of clue paragraphs, and extract the key information in the clue paragraphs as the clue entities, then retrieve paragraphs related to clue entities as the next hop clue paragraphs. The clue entity and candidate answers are used as nodes, and an dynamic graph is established according to the progressive relationship in the reasoning process.

Each node has two vector embeddings representation, one is the question memory and the other is the context semantic embedding. The context semantic embedding requires the graph attention neural network model GAT [13] aggerate neighbor information of the inference paths, and the question memory update is based on the memory of the previous hop and the question semantic embedding of the current hop via dynamic memory network [7].

3.2 Multi-level Features Extration

We take questions and choices, and related documents as input to the module to obtain multi-level features that include question embedding, context semantic embedding, and clue entities and candidate answers.

We use clue entities x to retrieve related document $para[x]$ from Wikipedia. Then we transform these document mentioned clue entities x in previous hop as $clue[x]$ in current hop to extract candidate answers a and useful next-hop clue entities y from the $para[x]$. Utilizing "pointer vectors" $S_{hop}, E_{hop}, S_{ans}, E_{ans}$

as additional learnable parameters to predict targeted spans. The probability $P_{ans}^{start}[i]$ and $P_{ans}^{end}[i]$ of the ith input token to be the start and end position of an candidate answer span respectively. The process extract the candidate answers based on the start and end position of the span. The same process is followed by clue entities span. We use the next hop clue entities y to extract relevant documents $para[y]$ from Wikipedia, and use the predecessor documents $para[x]$ which extracted clue entities y as current hop clue paragraphs $clue[y]$. Both are put into the model to extract the further hop candidate answers and clue entities.

3.3   Dynamic Question Memory

For multi-hop reasoning QA, the characterization of the question should be updated progressively. For the different candidate answers obtained by reasoning, the question representation also changes accordingly. The question representation for the final correct answer has changed significantly from the original question. In its general form, the question memory module is comprised of an attention mechanism as well as a recurrent network with which it updates its memory [7]. During each iteration, the attention mechanism attends over the question vector representations E and the previous memory m^{i-1}. The scoring function S takes as input the feature set $z(E, m)$ and produces a scalar score. We use a gating function as our attention mechanism. For each iteration i, the mechanism takes the vector representation E of current question and a previous memory m^{i-1} as inputs to compute gating.

$$g^i = S(E, M^{i-1}) = \sigma\Big(W_2tanh\big(W_1z(E, m^{i-1}) + b_1\big) + b_2\Big) \qquad (1)$$

Based on the previous memory m^{i-1}, we update the question memory for each time of the multi-level features extraction. The initial state of this GRU is initialized to the question vector itself: $m^0 = E^0$.

$$h_t^i = g^iGRU(E, h_{t-1}^i) + (1 - g^i)h_{t-1}^i \qquad (2)$$

$$m^i = GRU(h_t^i, m^{i-1}) \qquad (3)$$

3.4   Dynamic Graph Attention Reasoning

The nodes of a dynamic graph are dynamically added based on the reasoning of each hop. At each reasoning hop, we will obtain new candidate answers and clue entities as new nodes to expand the dynamic graph. At the same time, we use the context semantic vector outputed by the feature extraction module as the initialization vector representation of the dynamic graph nodes and the current hop question memory vector as the question memory of the candidate answers nodes. The dynamic graph can effectively aggregate the information of the inference paths through the encoding of multiple neural attention layers. There may be multiple paths passing through the same node. Therefore, Using the attention mechanism for different paths of this node will capture the information differences of different inference paths more finely.

We use graph attention networks (GAT) [13] to encode the information of different inference paths. Specifically, GAT takes all the nodes as input, and updates node feature through its neighbors in the graph. The input to our layer is a set of node features h; module produces a new set of node features h' as its output. Then performing a shared attentional mechanism a to computes attention coefficients, and applying the LeakyReLU nonlinearity:

$$a_{ij} = \frac{exp\Big(LeakyRelu\Big(W_{e_{ij}}[h_i||h_j] \Big) \Big)}{\sum_{j \in \mathcal{N}_i} exp\Big(LeakyRelu\Big(W_{e_{ik}}[h_i||h_k] \Big) \Big)} \tag{4}$$

Where $W_{e_{ij}}$ is the weight matrix corresponding to the edge type e_{ij} between the i-th and j-th nodes. Where $W \in R^{d \times d}$ is a weight matrix to be learned, $\sigma(\cdot)$ denotes an activation function, and a_{ij} is the attention coefficients, which can be calculated by:

$$h'_i = \sigma\Big(\sum_{j \in \mathcal{N}_i} a_{ij} W h_j \Big) \tag{5}$$

4   Experiments

4.1   Experiments Setup

Datasets: We use CommonSenseQA[1] and HotpotQA[2] for the evaluation. CommonSenseQA is a dataset for multi-choices commonsense question answering which inferences correct answer with prior knowledge. It collected 12,247 commonsense questions which each question has only one correct answers and four distractors. The full-wiki dump of HotpotQA contains training set (90,564 questions), a development set (7,405 questions). We have selected several powerful basic models, including MUPPET [6], CogQA [5], ESIM+ELMO [16], CoS-E [10], KagNet [9].

4.2   Quantitative Study of Commonsense Reason

In CommonSenseQA, multiple options are given along with the question, and the model needs to pick the one option as correct answer. The accuracy of the answer is the main indicator of the evaluation model. The results on the CommonSenseQA dataset showing in Fig. 3 illustrates that our model outperform all comparison models.

---

[1] https://www.tau-nlp.org/commonsenseqa.
[2] https://hotpotqa.github.io.

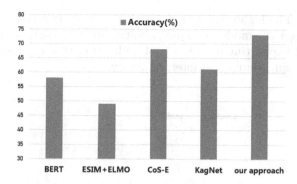

Fig. 3. Comparisons with different models on commonsenseQA.

From the comparison chart of accuracy, our approach makes the accuracy higher. Compared to other models that only use the raw question text as context material, we use external knowledge sources like Wikipedia as supporting facts for inference, and make full use of the semantic information of the relevant documents retrieved. Although there is often a complex reasoning relationship between external knowledge and question, our model can handle them well and thus exhibit higher accuracy. In addition, since we iteratively use external sources as supporting facts, the path of inference is explicit and interpretable.

4.3 Quantitative Study on Question Answering

For the evaluation of HotpotQA, Exact Match (EM), precision, recall and F1 score of not only answers but also sentence-level supporting facts to verify the model's reasoning ability and explainability.

Accuracy Results: The results on HotpotQA dataset are listed in Table 1. Not only Exact Match (EM), precision, recall and F1 score of our proposed approach performs much better than the baseline model and MUPPET, but also strong competition with the latest models CogQA.

Table 1. Answer results of HotpotQA.

Methods	Answer			
	EM	F1	Pre	Recall
Baseline	17.70	26.40	27.56	27.71
MUPPET	31.09	39.22	41.20	42.76
CogQA	36.56	48.49	51.29	49.06
Our Approach	34.03	45.73	48.60	46.05

Explainability Study: For multi-hop reading comprehension QA, not only need to gain the final answer, often the internal process of multi-hop reasoning is very critical. The higher the comprehensive evaluation metrics of supporting facts, the stronger the model reasoning ability. Our proposed model achives the highest value of supporting facts in Fig. 4, indicating that our model has strong multi-hop reasoning ability and interpretability.

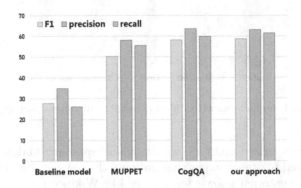

Fig. 4. Supporting facts and joint metric on HotpotQA

Query memory mechanism provides iterative memory for our reasoning at each hop, and updates simultaneously clue entities and documents, which make it more accurate to get support facts. The dynamic graph attention neural network has greater advantages in aggregating inference paths information, and obtaining accurate reasoning answers.

5   Conclusion

We design a novel cyclic iterative reasoning framework to tackle complex inference tasks. We continually looking for clue entities and candidate answers to construct dynamic and explicit inference graph, using an attention mechanism to capture information about the different inference paths, and cyclically updating context information. Compared to other models, the proposed approach shows advantages and improvements, not only in accuracy but also in qualitative studies. In future work, we will continue to expand the existing progress.

References

1. Cao, N.D., Aziz, W., Titov, I.: Question answering by reasoning across documents with graph convolutional networks. In: NAACL, pp. 2306–2317 (2019)
2. Chen, D., Fisch, A., Weston, J., Bordes, A.: Reading Wikipedia to answer open-domain questions. In: ACL, pp. 1870–1879 (2017)
3. Das, R., Dhuliawala, S., Zaheer, M., McCallum, A.: Multi-step retriever-reader interaction for scalable open-domain question answering. In: ICLR (2019)

4. Devlin, J., Chang, M., Lee, K., Toutanova, K.: BERT: pre-training of deep bidirectional transformers for language understanding. In: NAACL-HLT, pp. 4171–4186 (2019)
5. Ding, M., Zhou, C., Chen, Q., Yang, H., Tang, J.: Cognitive graph for multi-hop reading comprehension at scale. ACL **2019**, 2694–2703 (2019)
6. Feldman, Y., El-Yaniv, R.: Multi-hop paragraph retrieval for open-domain question answering. In: ACL, pp. 2296–2309, July 2019
7. Kumar, A., et al.: Ask me anything: dynamic memory networks for natural language processing. In: ICML, pp. 1378–1387 (2016)
8. Lee, K., Chang, M., Toutanova, K.: Latent retrieval for weakly supervised open domain question answering. In: ACL, pp. 6086–6096 (2019)
9. Lin, B.Y., Chen, X., Chen, J., Ren, X.: KagNet: knowledge-aware graph networks for commonsense reasoning. In: Proceedigs of EMNLP-IJCNLP (2019)
10. Rajani, N.F., McCann, B., Xiong, C., Socher, R.: Explain yourself! Leveraging language models for commonsense reasoning. In: ACL (2019)
11. Seo, M.J., Kembhavi, A., Farhadi, A., Hajishirzi, H.: Bidirectional attention flow for machine comprehension. In: ICLR (2017)
12. Talmor, A., Herzig, J., Lourie, N., Berant, J.: CommonsenseQA: a question answering challenge targeting commonsense knowledge. In: NAACL (2019)
13. Veličković, P., Cucurull, G., Casanova, A., Romero, A., Liò, P., Bengio, Y.: Graph attention networks. In: ICLR, pp. 1–12 (2018)
14. Wang, W., Yang, N., Wei, F., Chang, B., Zhou, M.: Gated self-matching networks for reading comprehension and question answering. In: ACL, pp. 189–198 (2017)
15. Xiao, Y., et al.: Dynamically fused graph network for multi-hop reasoning (2019). arxiv:1905.06933Comment. Accepted by ACL 19
16. Yang, Z., et al.: HotpotQA: a dataset for diverse, explainable multi-hop question answering. In: EMNLP, pp. 2369–2380 (2018)

Multi-hop Reading Comprehension Incorporating Sentence-Based Reasoning

Lijun Huo[1], Bin Ge[1], and Xiang Zhao[1,2(✉)]

[1] Science and Technology on Information Systems Engineering Laboratory, National University of Defense Technology, Changsha, China
xiangzhao@nudt.edu.cn
[2] Collaborative Innovation Center of Geospatial Technology, Wuhan, China

Abstract. Multi-hop machine reading comprehension (MRC) requires models to mine and utilize relevant information from multiple documents to predict the answer to a semantically related question. Existing work resorts to either document-level or entity-level inference among relevant information, which can be too coarse or too subtle, resulting less accurate understanding of the texts. To mitigate the issue, this research proposes a sentence-based multi-hop reasoning approach named SMR. SMR starts with sentences of documents, and unites the question to establish several reasoning chains based on sentence-level representations. In addition, to resolve the complication of pronouns on sentence semantics, we concatenate two sentences, if necessary, to assist in constructing reasoning chains. The model then synthesizes the information existed in all the reasoning chains, and predicts a probability distribution for selecting the correct answer. In experiments, we evaluate SMR on two popular multi-hop MRC benchmark datasets - WikiHop and MedHop. The model achieves 68.3 and 62.9 in terms of accuracy, respectively, exhibiting a remarkable improvement over state-of-the-art option. Additionally, qualitative analysis also demonstrates the validity and interpretability of SMR.

Keywords: Reading comprehension · Multi-hop question answering · Sentence representation · Text understanding

1 Introduction

Machine reading comprehension (MRC) is an important and desired aspect in natural language understanding. Its purpose is to use machines to extract desired information and knowledge automatically, based on a given question and some documents. Compared to the basic tasks in natural language processing, such as named entity recognition and relation extraction, MRC is a more complicated and higher-level task, which requires deeper understanding of semantics.

In recent years, to verify the effect of MRC models, many data sets have been developed, represented by SQuAD [10]. Most of the existing datasets are aimed at single-hop MRC task such that each question corresponds to a document, and the information for solving the question is restricted to that document. In other words, there is not a reasoning process among several documents, which nevertheless does not reflect real-life scenarios.

To better evaluate MRC models in a more realistic setting, the task of multi-hop MRC is delivered, where to answer a given question, multiple supporting documents are necessary. In other words, the multi-hop MRC task requires models to make reasoning hops among documents based on the information of the question, in order to find enough useful knowledge for predicting the answer. We focus on multi-hop MRC in this paper.

The multi-hop MRC task is notoriously challenging from at least the following three aspects. First, for each question, there are many supporting documents, but only a small portion of them contain information to resolve the question, and the rest are interference. Most existing MRC models find it difficult to handle documents of large scale, and have little anti-interference capability. Second, the information to resolve the question is distributed among multiple documents, which requires effective reasoning to form a reliable chain of information clue. However, current models are weak at performing effective reasoning over multiple documents. Third, there may be multiple possible chains of information clue formed by reasoning, which need to be screened and evaluated by quadratic sorting. The quality of this operation brings great uncertainty to MRC models in unveil the correct reasoning chain.

In view of these difficulties, in contrast to existing work resorting to either document-level or entity-level reasoning, which can be too coarse or too subtle, we propose SMR, a progressive model based on sentence-level reasoning. It is naturally inspired by the reading comprehension strategy of human. When human deal reading comprehension, one usually finds the keywords from the question firstly, and then searches for a sentence semantically related to the keywords in the supporting documents. Next, based on the knowledge of the current sentence, she reasons for the subsequent logical sentence to locate it, which is considered to be a hop. Finally, all the sentences extracted from the supporting documents make up a reasoning chain of information clue, and the answer can be finally derived.

To imitate the aforementioned process, SMR finds a sentence existing in the supporting documents according to the main entity in the question, to start the reasoning. Then, it employs a Sentence Selector, which iteratively selects a relevant sentence as an intermediate reasoning node, resulting in a complete chain. In this way, SMR will construct multiple reasoning chains, and in the end, it leverages an Answer Predictor to infer the answer, which integrates the information of the reasoning chains, as well as the question to derive a probability distribution of answers.

Further, sentences in human language often contain pronouns, and accurate resolution of pronouns and the nouns they refer to are essential for guiding reasoning, e.g., to link the pronoun 'it' in $sent_2$ of Fig. 1 with the noun 'the Johannesburg Zoo' in $sent_1$. Although existing co-reference resolution methods may help, it is practically non-trivial to conduct it without mistakes, in which case mistakes will be propagated to MRC. To alleviate the issue, we propose to concatenate two sentences (e.g., $sent_1$ and $sent_2$) into one concatenation sentence (e.g., $sent_3$). Hence, when the model needs to reason from $sent_1$ to $sent_2$, it will choose $sent_3$ as a node instead to avoid extra hopping, which substantially reduces the difficulty in overly long reasoning.

Fig. 1. Representation enrichment via concatenation of adjacent sentences.

Contributions. In summary, the proposed model SMR consists of three modules: Sentence Represent, Sentence Selector and Answer Predictor. And we make the following contributions in this paper:

- We proposed to leverage sentence-based reasoning for MRC, which constructs multiple chains that connect sentences relevant to the question;
- We introduce sentence concatenation to handle the potential issue of co-reference in context for effective sentence-based reasoning;
- We achieve competitive accuracy results on popular multi-hop datasets, and SMR is demonstrated to be able to explain the reasoning process.

Organization. We discuss related work in Sect. 2. Section 3 introduces the model SMR in details, including sentence representation, sentence selector and answer predictor. Then, we report the experimental study with in-depth analysis in Sect. 4, and conclude the paper in Sect. 5.

Note that existing multi-document MRC datasets have different formats, corresponding to various types of multi-document MRC. This research mainly focuses on the popular multi-hop datasets WikiHop and MedHop [8], where one needs to choose the correct answer from the given candidate set to the given question, based on a collection of documents.

2 Related Work

In recent years, various multi-hop MRC datasets have been developed, and these datasets all demand models to understand the semantics of texts and find the internal relationship between texts. However, their questions have different forms. For example, HotpotQA [9] and TriviaQA [17] contain {question, document set, answer}, where the answer must be generated, and the question is a natural language text. On the other hand, QAngaroo WikiHop and MedHop [8] contain {question, document set, answer, candidates}, where the answer is an entity presented in the given candidate set, and the question consists of an entity and a relationship. Some others such as Who Did What [18] and Children's Book Test [19] provide cloze-style MRC datasets, on which the models need to predict the missing word/entity in questions.

According to the characteristics of these data sets, researchers have developed various models to handle the tasks. For example, [8] fuses multiple documents into a long one, and then uses the single-hop MRC model with bidirectional attention mechanism to deduce the answer. However, because the documents after fusion are too long and the model has no information skipping capability, the performance of the model is far less accurate than that in the single-hop task.

With the assistance of knowledge guidance, [2] enables the model to integrate the semantics of documents, but the approach is difficult to apply due to the fact that external knowledge tends to be limited to a specific field.

Focus on reasoning, [4] gathers all possible reasoning paths according to the entities contained in the documents, and then scores each path to select the correct reasoning path. However, the method extracts many invalid paths that are apt to bring in interference and waste computing resources.

[5, 6] uses graph neural networks [20] to obtain the relationship between entities, and adds self-attention mechanism [7] into the model, which obtains a gain in the result. However, the model has poor interpretability owing to lack explicit reasoning, and meanwhile it is of high complexity and low efficiency.

The research in this paper was inspired by the research by EPAr [3], which creates a document explorer to select documents to build an inference tree. We follow the same framework to establish SMR, but substantially differ by incorporating sentence-based reasoning, explicit paths and sentence concatenation (to be introduced in Sect. 3). The innovative design implements a MRC model with higher accuracy and better interpretability (to be detailed in Sect. 4) (Fig. 2).

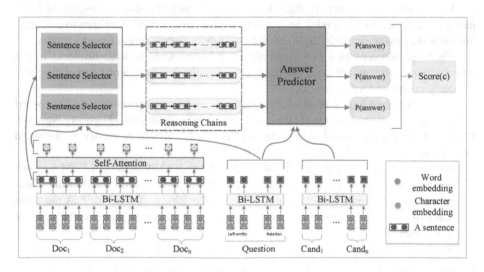

Fig. 2. Framework of sentence-based MRC.

3   Model

In the section, we introduce our proposed model for multi-hop MRC, which comprises three modules.

Before delving into the details, we first formally define the task that is investigated in this paper.

Task Definition. In the task of multi-hop MRC [8], there is a question q and a set of supporting documents T'. In particular, the question q is provided in the form of a tuple $(l_e, r, ?)$, where l_e is the left entity, and r represents the relation between l_e and the unknown right entity, which is the answer. In addition, there is also a candidate set $C' = \{c'_\eta\}_{\eta=1}^H$ containing the correct answer. The purpose is to predict the unknown right entity from C'.

In the sequel, we explain our proposed model, which first performs sentence segmentation and semantic encoding (Sect. 3.1), then inferences to build the multi-hop chains based on the encoded semantics (Sect. 3.2), and finally mines the evidence of the multi-hop chains to rank the candidates for finding the answer (Sect. 3.3).

3.1 Sentence Representation

We first conduct text preprocessing and word encoding methods. Then, we divide the supporting documents into single sentences and concatenation sentences. Subsequently, we explain the encoding methods of these steps.

Word Encoding. The goal of word encoding is to characterize the question and supporting documents as vectors for inputting into neural networks.

We first filter documents to reduce the number of interfering documents and the GPU memory occupied by the model. In practice, we use the TF-IDF algorithm to calculate and rank the cosine similarity between the question and each supporting document.

Then, we intercept the top-N supporting documents with the least similarity as the new supporting document set $T = \{t_n\}_{n=1}^N$. We apply the same word embedding and semantic encoding for l_e, r and T.

For word embedding, we combine character embedding and pre-trained Glove word embedding [12] as the initial word embedding and input them into a Highway Network [21] to obtain the final word representation. We use $\mathbf{L}'$, $\mathbf{R}'$ and $\mathbf{X}'$ to denote the word embedding of l_e, r and T respectively.

For semantic encoding, we pass $\mathbf{L}'$, $\mathbf{R}'$, and $\mathbf{X}'$ through a bidirectional LSTM network [22] with v hidden units and concatenate the bidirectional output of LSTM as the word-level semantic representation. We use $\mathbf{L} \in \mathbb{R}^{Q_l \times v}$, $\mathbf{R} \in \mathbb{R}^{Q_r \times v}$, $\mathbf{X} \in \mathbb{R}^{N \times J \times v}$ as the word encoding of l_e, r and T, respectively, where Q_l, Q_r, J are the word-level lengths of l_e, r and T respectively.

Since each candidate c'_η can be found in the supporting document set T, we take out the word encoding corresponding to c'_η in $\mathbf{X}$, average it at the word-level and then get $\mathbf{c}_\eta \in \mathbb{R}^v$ as the semantic encoding of c'_η.

Sentence Encoding. The Sentence Encoding mainly divides each document into several sentences and converts each sentence to a vector.

We first cut a documents t into multiple sentences to obtain the single sentence set $\mathbf{D}^o = \{\mathbf{d}_i^o\}_{i=i}^I$ s.t. $\mathbf{d}_i^o \in \mathbb{R}^{K \times v}$ where I is the number of single sentences contained in t, K is the number of words that make up a single sentence and $\mathbf{d}_{ik}^o$ is the corresponding word encoding in X. We then connect all two adjacent single sentences in the document to obtain the concatenation sentence set $\mathbf{D}^b = \{\mathbf{d}_i^b\}_{i=1}^{I-1}$, $\mathbf{d}_i^b$ can be given as

$$\mathbf{d}_i^b = \mathbf{d}_i^o \| \mathbf{d}_i^o \; and \; 1 \leq i < I, \tag{1}$$

where $\|$ is used to indicate concatenation. Next, we joint $\mathbf{D}^o$ and $\mathbf{D}^b$ to complete the sentence division of t and get the sentence set $\mathbf{D}$; that is,

$$\mathbf{D} = \mathbf{D}^o \cup \mathbf{D}^b, \tag{2}$$

where $\cup$ refers to union.

We adopt the same operation for all supporting documents and get the word-level sentence encoding $\mathbf{S}$ of T; that is,

$$\mathbf{S} = \mathbf{D}_1 \cup \mathbf{D}_2 \cup \ldots \cup \mathbf{D}_N = \{s_1, \ldots, s_{I'}\}, \tag{3}$$

where I' is the number of total sentences including single sentence and concatenation sentence of T. We apply a self-attention mechanism [7] to implement vector representation of sentences and get the sentence-level sentence encoding set $\mathbf{E}$ of T. Specifically, the formula we use to transform a sentence s_i into a vector representation $\mathbf{e}_i \in \mathbb{R}^v$ is as follows (K is considered as the length of all sentences for simplicity); that is,

$$\begin{aligned} a_{ik} &= \tanh(\mathbf{W}_2 \tanh(\mathbf{W}_1 s_{ik} + \mathbf{b}_1) + \mathbf{b}_2), \\ \hat{a}_i &= \text{softmax}(a_i), \\ \mathbf{e}_i &= \sum_{k=1}^{K} \hat{a}_{ik} s_{ik} \end{aligned} \tag{4}$$

3.2 Sentence Selector

In the section, we utilize a hierarchical memory network [23] to construct sentence-based reasoning chains.

We define two phases for Sentence Selector: selecting a node and establishing a hop edge. In the selecting phase, the model extracts a sentence that is most relevant to the network memory state $\mathbf{m}$ as the starting node of the current hop. During the establishing phase, the model updates $\mathbf{m}$ to prepare for jumping the next node, which can be compared to generating the current jump edge.

We choose to use the left entity as the starting node of the inference chain, so the model initializes $\mathbf{m}$ with the last state of $\mathbf{L}$ and updates it with a Gated Recurrent Unit (GRU) [14].

Selecting a Node. At each hop h, the model calculates the correlation between each sentence encoding $\mathbf{e}_i$ in $\mathbf{E}$ and current memory state $\mathbf{m}^h$ based on the bilinear-similarity and obtains a node selection distribution P_{sent}, which can be described as

$$p_i = e_i^{\mathrm{T}} \mathbf{W}_P \mathbf{m}^h,$$

$$P_{sent} = \text{softmax}(p). \tag{5}$$

Then, we choose the sentence $s_i \in S$ as the starting node of the current hop, where i satisfies

$$P_{sent}(i) = \max(P_{sent}). \tag{6}$$

Establishing a Hopping Edge. After selecting the starting node of h hop, the model calculates the bilinear-similarity of $\mathbf{m}^h$ and each word s_{ik} in s_i and normalizes it to obtain a weight μ; that is,

$$v_k = \mathbf{s}_{ik}^T \mathbf{W}_m \mathbf{m}^h,$$
$$\mu = \text{softmax}(v). \tag{7}$$

Now, we use μ to calculate the weighted average $\bar{s}_i$ of all the words in s_i and then input it into a GRU cell to update $\mathbf{m}^h$, which can be described as

$$\bar{s}_i = \sum_{k=1}^K s_{ik} \mu_k,$$
$$\mathbf{m}^{h+1} = \mathbf{GRU}(\bar{s}_i, \mathbf{m}^h). \tag{8}$$

Afterwards, we can combine the two sections together as a recurrent unit U,

$$\left(s_{h+1}, \mathbf{m}^{h+1} \right) = U(\mathbf{m}^h). \tag{9}$$

U can continuously select nodes by updating m. Looping for U H times, we can get a H-hop reasoning chain $S_{chain} = \{s_1, s_2, \ldots, s_H\}$ where each sentence s_h is selected iteratively as a node by U in S. To reduce the fortuity of reasoning chain generation, we repeat Sentence Selector M times to generate M possible H-hop reasoning chains for the model.

3.3 Answer Predictor

In the section, the model mainly predicts the probability of each candidate as the answer based on the H-hop reasoning chains obtained in Sentence Selector. Each chain may be a logical reasoning path from one entity to another.

Therefore, the model also introduces the question as auxiliary evidence to select the answer that meets the requirements of the question. Answer Predictor consists of two parts: reasoning chain information integration and calculating the probability distribution of answers.

Information Integration. Since the predicted answer exists in the last hop s_H of a reasoning chain, we calculate the attention σ between the first $H - 1$ hop of chain and the question for each word in s_H. Then, σ is used to compute the weighted average $\mathbf{x} \in \mathbb{R}^v$ of s_H. The formulas can be expressed as

$$\mathbf{x} = \sum_{k=1}^{K} \mathbf{s}_{Hk}\sigma_k. \tag{10}$$

For calculating σ, we first horizontally stitch the top $H - 1$ hop of $\mathbf{S}_{chain}$ to obtain s_{fore}; that is,

$$s_{fore} = \mathbf{s}_1 \| \mathbf{s}_2 \| \ldots \| \mathbf{s}_{H-1}. \tag{11}$$

Then we calculate an information victor δ^k though adopting a LSTM with an attention mechanism [24] to encode s_{fore} and the top $k - 1$ words of s_H. In the meanwhile, considering the impact of the question on σ, we calculate the α-correlation [3] ε^k of δ^k with the left entity and relationship, mathematically,

$$\begin{aligned}
a_i^k &= \omega^{\mathrm{T}}\tanh\left(\mathbf{W}_a s_{fore}^i + \mathbf{W}_b \mathbf{v}^k + \mathbf{b}\right), \\
c^k &= \mathrm{softmax}(a^k), \\
\mathbf{g}^k &= \sum_i c_i^k s_{fore}^i, \\
\delta^k &= \mathbf{LSTM}(\mathbf{s}_H^{k-1}, \mathbf{v}^{k-1}, \mathbf{g}^{k-1}), \\
\varepsilon^k &= \alpha\left(\delta^k, \mathbf{l}\right) + \alpha\left(\delta^k, \mathbf{r}\right)
\end{aligned} \tag{12}$$

where $\mathbf{v}^k$ is the hidden states of LSTM at the kth step, $\mathbf{l}$ and $\mathbf{r}$ are the final state of $\mathbf{L}$ and $\mathbf{R}$ respectively. In addition, α can be defined as

$$\alpha(x, y) = \mathbf{W}_{\alpha 1}^{\mathrm{T}}((\mathbf{W}_{\alpha 2} x + \mathbf{b}) \circ y), \tag{13}$$

where $\circ$ represents element-wise multiplication.

Finally, ε integrating the information of $\mathbf{S}_{chain}$ and the question can be used to calculate attention σ,

$$\sigma = \mathrm{softmax}(\varepsilon). \tag{14}$$

Probability Distribution Evaluation. After the above, we get a vector $\mathbf{x}$ of highly integrated reasoning chains and problem information. Thus, we can use $\mathbf{x}$ to calculate a probability distribution P_{answer} of candidate $\mathbf{c}_i$ as the answer; that is,

$$\begin{aligned}
\theta_i &= \mathbf{W}_{\theta 1}\mathrm{Relu}(\mathbf{W}_{\theta 2}[\mathbf{c}_i; \mathbf{x}; \mathbf{c}_i \circ \mathbf{x}] + \mathbf{b}_{\theta 2}) + \mathbf{b}_{\theta 1}), \\
P_{answer} &= \mathrm{softmax}(\theta),
\end{aligned} \tag{15}$$

where Relu is the activation.

We calculate P_{answer} for all reasoning chains and get the answer probability distribution set $\tilde{P}_{answer} = \{P_{answer}^i\}_{i=1}^{M}$. Aggregating the results of all reasoning chains, the score of the candidate $\mathbf{c}_\eta$ as the answer can be given as

$$score(\mathbf{c}_\eta) = \sum_{i=1}^{M} P_{answer}^i(\mathbf{c}_\eta). \tag{16}$$

4   Experiments

In the section, we describe the data sets used to evaluate the model, parameter settings, and experimental configurations firstly; additionally, we demonstrate the results and ablation studies of the proposed model.

4.1   Datasets

We use WikiHop and MedHop [8] data sets to evaluate our proposed model; in particular, we exploit the unmasked version of them.

WikiHop is a massive multi-hop MRC data set which provides about 43.8k samples for training set and 5.1k samples for development set. Each sample contains an average of 13.7 supporting documents, which can be divided into about 50 sentences and documents are collected from Wikipedia. The question of each sample contains an entity and a relationship. They form a triple of the WikiData knowledge base with the unknown answer that is contained in the provided candidate set.

MedHop is smaller dataset which consists of 1.6K samples for training set and 342 samples for development set. It mainly focuses on the domain of molecular biology and its each sample including a question, a document set and a candidate set has the same structure as the samples of WikiHop. And the difference is that each document set includes an average of 9.6 supporting documents, and can be divided into about 40 sentences.

In experiments, we use all samples in the training set to train our proposed model and all samples in the development set to adjust the hyper-parameters of the model.

4.2   Experimental Settings

We use NLTK [15] to divide the supporting document set into word tokens and sentence tokens in different granularity and the candidate set and the question into word tokens.

We use the 300-dimensional Glove pre-trained word embedding (with 840B tokens and 2.2 M vocabulary size) [12] to represent initial word tokens. The number of hidden units of all LSTM-RNN [22] is 100. We use dropout [25] with probability 0.5 for every trainable layer. We select top-10 documents which contains an average of 30 single sentences and 20 concatenation sentences after filtering by using the TF-IDF algorithm in each sample.

We use cross entropy loss to measure the level of model training, and use the Adam optimizer to train our model and set the learning rate at 0.001. We train 20k steps using four Nvidia 1080Ti GPUs. On each GPU, the batch size is fixed at 4, and the total batch size is 20. We use accuracy as an indicator for the multi-hop MRC task.

4.3   Result and Analysis

Table 1 presents the results of our proposed multi-hop MRC model on development set and test set[1] of WikiHop, and we compare it with the results that were reported in their original papers.

---

[1] We are in the process of obtaining the results on the hidden test set.

Table 1. Accuracy on the WikiHop development set and test set, where "-" denotes that the values are unavailable currently.

Model	Accuracy (%)	
	Dev	Test
BiDAF [26]	–	42.9
Entity-GCN [13]	64.8	67.6
CFC [7]	66.4	70.6
BAG [27]	66.5	69.0
EEPath [4]	67.1	–
EPAr [3]	67.2	69.1
SMR (ours)	**68.3**	–

We can observe that our proposed model achieves the highest accuracy of 68.3 on the development set for all the models in the table. Compared to the best previous result whose accuracy is 67.2, it is a 1.1 improvement on development set. It's worth noting that our model no use pre-trained language models such as ELMO [16] and Bert [11] which has been shown to give MRC models a significant gain. Therefore, to be fair, the result of the proposed model doesn't compare with those of the pre-trained language model.

We also show the results on MedHop in Table 2. We have a noticeable improvement on MedHop test set. In addition, our proposed model is more interpretable because the sentence-level reasoning chain it generates can be regarded as an explicit path for human reasoning.

Table 2. Accuracy on the MedHop test set, where the results marked "*" were originally reported by [8].

Model	Accuracy (%)
Max -mention*	9.5
Document -cue*	44.9
BiDAF [26]	47.8
Majority -candidate -per -query -type*	58.4
EPAr [3]	60.3
SMR (ours)	**62.9**

In order to reveal how SMR model based on sentence reasoning can realize reasoning and find the answer, we illustrate an example in Fig. 3 to visualize this process. In SMR, relevant supporting documents are screened out, and the sentence sets containing single and concatenation sentences are obtained by sentence division. Relying on the sentences set, SMR constructs two different reasoning chains: $chain_1$ and $chain_2$. Through the SR, SS and AP modules, our model predicts the answer: 'loon op zand'. It can be seen from Fig. 3 that the process of SMR predicting the answer constructs a reasoning path consistent with human cognition.

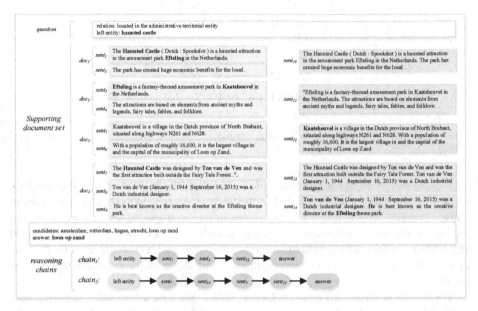

Fig. 3. Sample case of SMR reasoning process.

In the process of constructing the reasoning chains, our model uses self-attention [7] to integrate all the words in a sentence into a vector which represents the semantics of the sentence. EPAr [3] does the same at the document level as well. Because sentences have fewer words, less information is lost in the process than documents, which is the advantage of SMR compared to EPAr. EEPath [4] takes out all possible paths as the basis for predicting the answer. Our model builds valid reasoning path by integrating sentence information and the obtained path has some logic, so our model has more accurate path and higher efficiency compared with EEPath.

SMR use sentence sets which contain single and concatenation sentences to generate T-hop inference chains, which can deal with the pronouns among the sentences well. As $chain_1$ and $chain_2$ in Fig. 3, $sent_5$ and $sent_6$ are two single sentences from the same document, and $sent_{12}$ is the concatenation of the two sentences. In the reasoning process, $sent_3$ chooses $sent_{12}$ as the node of one hop instead of $sent_5$ or $sent_6$. Although containing the key word: 'Kaatsheuvel', $sent_5$ is difficult to reason to $sent_6$ because $sent_6$ used a pronoun 'it' to express the keyword but the model does not understand the meaning of the pronoun. And $sent_6$ contains important intermediate information for predicting the answer and must be a node in the chain of reasoning. Jumping from the $sent_3$ to $sent_{12}$

can not only capture the key word information contained in $sent_5$, but also match the pronoun in $sent_6$ with the key word.

Therefore, the existence of concatenation sentence can make the model more suitable for the situation where there are and there are no pronouns in the inference chain. If the concatenation sentence is too long, the process of integrating it into a vector will lose too much semantic information. Therefore, the model combines two adjacent single sentences into a concatenation sentence, which can satisfy most cases. Meanwhile, the existence of a single sentence avoids the model choosing unnecessary concatenation sentences as nodes such as the second node of $chain_1$ choosing $sent_3$ instead of $sent_{11}$.

4.4 Ablation Study

In order to better understand the contributions of different modules to the performance of our proposed model, we designed several ablation studies (Table 2) on the WikiHop development set.

If removing the sentence-based reasoning from the model, we will encode the documents directly using the self-attention mechanism [7] and replace sentence encoding **S, E** with the resulting document vectors. Then we carry out multi-hop reasoning at the document level and the accuracy of SMR will reduce by 1.1 absolutely. This proves the validity of our proposed reasoning at the sentence level for the multi-hop MRC task.

If we only use one reasoning chain in the model, that is, we don't repeat SC module, the accuracy of SMR will decrease by 2.2%. This demonstrates that constructing multiple inference chains can reduce the randomness of reasoning path generation indeed. If the TF-IDF algorithm isn't used to filter the documents, the accuracy of the model we obtained will be reduced by 1.9%. This proves that removing some irrelevant articles can help to get more accurate reasoning chains, while the model will occupy fewer computing resources and achieve higher training efficiency due to the reduction of supporting documents (Table 3).

Table 3. Ablation results on the WikiHop development set.

Model	Accuracy (%)	
	Dev	Δ
Full model	68.3	–
- document-based reasoning	67.2	1.1
- one reasoning chain	66.1	2.2
- TF-IDF algorithm	66.4	1.9
- single sentence	65.6	2.7
- concatenation sentence	65.1	3.2

We also investigate the effect of single sentences and concatenation sentences on the model effect. Specifically, we use single-sentence set $\mathbf{D}^o$ instead of all sentence set $\mathbf{D}$ for T-hop reasoning and the accuracy is reduced by 2.7%. At the same time, we also replace $\mathbf{D}$ with the concatenation sentence set $\mathbf{D}^b$ and the accuracy is reduced by 3.2%. According to the ablation, we can infer that using only the single sentence set may prevent the model from understanding the meaning of pronouns that may exist. However, the merely using concatenation sentence set can lead to excessive interference between sentences in the reasoning process. Therefore, the combined using of single sentences and concatenation sentences can better cope with the presence of pronouns in adjacent sentences and reduce the negative influence between sentences to improve the performance of the model.

5 Conclusion

In this paper, we have proposed a multi-hop MRC model sentence-based reasoning named SMR, where sentences play a pivotal role in constructing reasoning chains. Besides, we innovatively use concatenation sentence to deal with the semantic encoding of pronouns in a single sentence, which has been proved by experiments to improve the model effect significantly. We also presented that SMR can illustrate its reasoning through hopping across multiple sentences. The superior performance on WikiHop and MedHop data sets verifies the effectiveness of SMR.

In the future, we will verify the effect of SMR after adding the pre-trained language model, although it has achieved excellent performance. We also plan to focus on generative models incorporating sentence-based reasoning like Masque [1]. Moreover, it is of interest to investigate other types of multi-hop MRC datasets, e.g., the newly proposed benchmark HotpotQA [9].

Acknowledgement. This work was partially supported by NSFC under grants Nos. 61872446, 61902417 and 71971212, and PNSF of Hunan under grant No. 2019JJ20024.

References

1. Nishida, K., et al.: Multi-style generative reading comprehension. ACL (1), 2273–2284 (2019)
2. Wang, C., Jiang, H.: Explicit utilization of general knowledge in machine reading comprehension. ACL (1), 2263–2272 (2019)
3. Jiang, Y., Joshi, N., Chen, Y.-C., Bansal, M.: Explore, propose, and assemble: an interpretable model for multi-hop reading comprehension. ACL (1), 2714–2725 (2019)
4. Kundu, S., Khot, T., Sabharwal, A., Clark, P.: Exploiting explicit paths for multi-hop reading comprehension. ACL (1), 2737–2747 (2019)
5. Tu, M., Wang, G., Huang, J., Tang, Y., He, X., Zhou, B.: Multi-hop reading comprehension across multiple documents by reasoning over heterogeneous graphs. ACL (1), 2704–2713 (2019)
6. Ding, M., Zhou, C., Chen, Q., Yang, H., Tang, J.: Cognitive graph for multi-hop reading comprehension at scale. ACL (1), 2694–2703 (2019)
7. Zhong, V., Xiong, C., Keskar, N.S., Socher, R.: Coarse-grain fine-grain coattention network for multi-evidence question answering. ICLR (Poster) (2019)

8. Welbl, J., Stenetorp, P., Riedel, S.: Constructing datasets for multi-hop reading comprehension across documents. TACL **6**, 287–302 (2018)
9. Yang, Z., et al.: HotpotQA: a dataset for diverse, explainable multi-hop question answering. EMNLP, pp. 2369–2380 (2018)
10. Rajpurkar, P., Zhang, J., Lopyrev, K., Liang, P.: SQuAD: 100, 000+ questions for machine comprehension of text. EMNLP, pp. 2383–2392 (2016)
11. Devlin, J., Chang, M.-W., Lee, K., Toutanova, K.: BERT: Pre-training of deep bidirectional transformers for language understanding. NAACL-HLT (1), 4171–4186 (2019)
12. Pennington, J., Socher, R., Manning, C.D.: Glove: global vectors for word representation. EMNLP, 1532–1543 (2014)
13. De Cao, N., Aziz, W., Titov, I.: Question answering by reasoning across documents with graph convolutional networks. NAACL-HLT (1), 2306–2317 (2019)
14. Cho, K., et al.: Learning phrase representations using RNN encoder-decoder for statistical machine translation. EMNLP, pp. 1724–1734 (2014)
15. Bird, S., Loper, E.: NLTK: the natural language toolkit. ACL (Poster and Demonstration) (2004)
16. Peters, M.E., et al.: Deep contextualized word representations. NAACL-HLT, pp. 2227–2237 (2018)
17. Joshi, M., Choi, E., Weld, D.S., Zettlemoyer, L.: TriviaQA: a large scale distantly supervised challenge dataset for reading comprehension. ACL (1), pp. 1601–1611 (2017)
18. Onishi, T., Wang, H., Bansal, M., Gimpel, K., McAllester, D.A.: Who did what: a large-scale person-centered cloze dataset. EMNLP, pp. 2230–2235 (2016)
19. Hill, F., Bordes, A., Chopra, S., Weston, J.: The goldilocks principle: reading children's books with explicit memory representations. ICLR (2016)
20. Battaglia, P.W., et al.: Relational inductive biases, deep learning, and graph networks. CoRR abs/1806.01261 (2018)
21. Srivastava, R.K., Greff, K., Schmidhuber, J.: Highway Networks. CoRR abs/1505.00387 (2015)
22. Hochreiter, S., Schmidhuber, J.: Long short-term memory. Neural Comput. **9**(8), 1735–1780 (1997)
23. Chandar, S., Ahn, S., Larochelle, H., Vincent, P., Tesauro, G., Bengio, Y.: Hierarchical Memory Networks. CoRR abs/1605.07427 (2016)
24. Bahdanau, D., Cho, K., Bengio, Y.: Neural machine translation by jointly learning to align and translate. ICLR (2015)
25. Srivastava, N., Hinton, G.E., Krizhevsky, A., Sutskever, I., Salakhutdinov, R.: Dropout: a simple way to prevent neural networks from overfitting. J. Mach. Learn. Res. **15**(1), 1929–1958 (2014)
26. Seo, M., Kembhavi, A., Farhadi, A., Hajishirzi, H.: Bidirectional attention flow for machine comprehension. ICLR (2017)
27. Cao, Y., Fang, M., Tao, D.: BAG: bi-directional attention entity graph convolutional network for multi-hop reasoning question answering. NAACL-HLT (1), 357–362 (2019)

Author Contributed Representation
for Scholarly Network

Binglei Wang, Tong Xu$^{(\boxtimes)}$, Hao Wang, Yanmin Chen, Le Zhang, Lintao Fang,
Guiquan Liu, and Enhong Chen

School of Computer Science and Technology, University of Science and Technology
of China, Hefei, China
blwang59@gmail.com, tongxu@ustc.edu.cn,
{wanghao3, ymchen16}@mail.ustc.edu.cn, zhangle0202@gmail.com,
flt@mail.ustc.edu.cn, {gqliu,chenen}@ustc.edu.cn

Abstract. Scholarly network analysis is a fundamental topic in academia domain, which is beneficial for estimating the contribution of researchers and the quality of academic outputs. Recently, a popular fashion takes advantage of network embedding techniques, which aims to learn the scholarly information into vectorial representations for the task. Though great progress has been made, existing studies only consider the text information of papers for scholarly network representation, while ignoring the effects of many intrinsic and informative features, especially the different influences and contribution of authors and cooperations. In order to alleviate this problem, in this paper, we propose a novel Author Contributed Representation for Scholarly Network (ACR-SN) framework to learn the unique representation for scholarly networks, which characterizes the different authors' contribution. Specifically, we first adopt a graph convolutional network (GCN) to capture the structure information in the citation network. Then, we calculate the correlations between authors and each paper, and aggregate each embedding of authors according to their contribution by using the attention mechanism. Extensive experiments on two real world datasets demonstrate the effectiveness of ACR-SN and reveal that authors' contribution to the paper varies with the corresponding authorities and interested fields.

Keywords: Scholarly network embedding · Scholar cooperation · Graph convolutional network

1 Introduction

Recent years have witnessed the rapid accumulation of scholarly data, containing rich information of research publishing records with citation networks, which provides unprecedented opportunities for scholarly network analysis [25]. Indeed, with the help of scholarly network analysis, on one hand, we could uncover the trend of research. On the other hand, it is convenient for researchers to choose an appropriate partner and evaluate the influence of work from the micro view.

© Springer Nature Switzerland AG 2020
X. Wang et al. (Eds.): APWeb-WAIM 2020, LNCS 12317, pp. 558–573, 2020.
https://doi.org/10.1007/978-3-030-60259-8_41

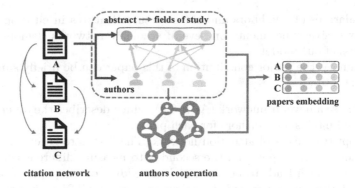

Fig. 1. The overview of scholarly network embedding.

Towards scholarly network analysis, there are many kinds of studies, such as predicting the authorities of authors [12], predicting the influence of paper [4] and paper recommendation [24]. Though large efforts have been made, the researchers usually consider the paper textual information, while the great benefits of academic cooperation are largely under-explored. In fact, cooperation is of great importance for scholars, especially for young researchers. Therefore, in this paper, we aim to study a more comprehensive scholarly network analysis by considering cooperation effects.

In academic networks, dissertations are often considered as research units that can be clustered to higher levels by domains or authors [26]. As shown in Fig. 1, three papers (i.e., A, B, C) can form a citation network, e.g., paper A cites paper B and C. We can make deep analysis about their abstract contents and authors. Specifically, the abstracts generally reflect their study fields and the authors can constitute a co-author relationship which demonstrates the authority of each researcher in different fields. Moreover, different authors may make different contribution to a paper, due to their various authorities and areas of interest. Collaboration in each paper can be obtained by summarizing the embedded vector of each author. By combining these aspects, the preliminary performance of the dissertations is fully formed. In addition, the cited neighbours of the paper are often in closer research fields in the citation network. Therefore, this constraint on similarity should be retained when learning the scholarly network.

Along this line, we propose a novel scholarly network embedding framework called Author Contributed Representation for Scholarly Network (ACR-SN). We first extract the study fields from paper abstract and embed authors of the papers. Then we combine authors embedding and study fields in the paper through the novel author-paper attention mechanism, which could capture the authors' influences and interests. Considering the different contribution of authors to a certain paper, the contribution attention layer is introduced to form the initial representation of papers from the aggregation of authors embedding. Next, we utilize graph convolutional network (GCN) to preserve the citation based similarities of neighbors and the structural features in citation network. Finally, extensive experiments on several scholarly networks demonstrate the effectiveness of our model.

In summary, the major contribution of this paper can be briefly summarized as follows:

- We propose a novel framework (ACR-SN), which describes the different influences and interests of authors for each paper.
- We adopt two layers of attention network. The first is to catch the influence of authors in the paper, and the second is to measure different contribution of authors which leads to better initial embedding of the paper. Considering the similarities in paper and its references, we use GCN to incorporate the paper attributes in information diffusion of the network.
- We conduct extensive experiments on two real world datasets, which demonstrate our ACR-SN framework shows significant performance in many downstream tasks including paper classification and citation prediction.

2   Related Work

In this section, we will summarize the related works in scholarly data analysis and network embedding techniques.

Scholarly Data Analysis. Scholarly data contains multiple scholarly entities, e.g., papers and authors, as well as multiple scholarly relations, e.g., citations among papers, co-authors relationship among authors [25]. Among different scholarly networks, there are various analysis and applications. As for the citation network, research [4] predicts the influence of paper, and research [24] recommends paper based on citation and hierarchical structure of scientific knowledge. For a more comprehensible way of research articles organization, some researchers form a study map [20]. As for the co-author network, some researchers predict the influence and authority of authors using cooperation information [12]. Some studies also analyze authors' contribution with different relations among them [17]. Among these various analysis in scholarly network, the embedding of scholarly entities, authors and papers both are the fundamental issues to solve. This paper focuses on citation networks, and the research object is paper.

Network Embedding. Network embedding is intensively studied these years. The aim of network embedding is to get a low dimensional representation which can model the structure and some other properties of network. There are mainly three kinds of methods:

The first kind of methods are based on matrix-factorization, for example, the well-known Laplacian eigenmaps (LE) [3] and graph factorization (GF) [1]. These methods utilize the eigenvectors as the network representation.

The second kind is based on random walk. These methods use truncated random walk to get the neighbors representation of nodes to decrease the complexity. DeepWalk [16] and node2vec [7], as two typical methods, are also based on inner product of node pairs. However, unlike the matrix-factorization methods, these methods learn nodes embedding to maximize the probability of visiting two nodes on one truncated random walk, rather than using a deterministic node similarity measure.

The third kind of embedding methods combine node attributes and network structure. The previous two methods learn the node represetation from the structure of network, while node attributes are ignored. Unlike them, TADW [27] is based on deepwalk while incorporateing node information. In scholarly network embedding field, Paper2vec [6] combines graph and text information of paper to form the representation. Except for the supervised representations, there are some unsupervised methods, such as UPPSNE [28], and SANE [22], which use pairwise node embedding to represent node; MCNE [23], which learns multiple preference of users in the social network. Also there are some task specific methods, for example, LSNE [5] is a link-oriented signed network embedding method, and DLPQV [11] uses network embedding method to evaluate the quality of patents. Furthermore, some researchers use deep learning methods, which expand the convolution from Euclidean domain to non-Euclidean domain, and these methods are called graph convolutional networks. Among these methods, GCN [9] uses the first-order neighbors to simplify the filter in convolutional network. To get representation inductively, GraphSAGE [8] learns the aggregation of a node's neighbor, instead of learning a deterministic node embedding. GAT combines attention mechanism into graph convolutional network, considering different influence of nodes' neighbours. Additionally, there is some improvement methods like Geom-GCN [15], which proposes geometric aggregation scheme for graph neural networks to overcome the weakness of message-passing neural networks used in GCN. The deep learning based embedding methods inspire us to use GCN to represent articles in citation network.

3   Preliminary and Problem Definition

In this section, we give the definition to the scholarly network embedding problem. To get a better embedding of paper, here we use both author cooperation and text information of paper to represent it. Let p denote a paper from the corpus P. For the information in paper, we use $x_p \in 1 \times d$ to denote the abstract text of p, which consists of the averaged d-dimensional words embeddings of words in the abstract. As for the citations among papers, this relationship can be represented by an adjacency matrix $C \in \mathbb{R}^{|P| \times |P|}$, where $c_{ij} \in \{0, 1\}$ denotes if there is citation relationship between paper p_i and paper p_j. There is also a set of authors Au of the research papers, and each paper p corresponds to an author group au_p, which is a subset of Au.

Given the preliminaries above, we define the problem to solve in this paper:

Table 1. Summary of notations.

Notation	Definition
G	Graph
P	Set of papers in scholarly network
C	Adjacency matrix of paper citations in scholarly network
Au	Set of paper authors
au_i	Authors group of paper i
X	Text embedding of paper
x_i	Text embedding of paper $i, l \times d$
d	Dimension of embeddings
V	Embedding of the papers in the network, $|P| \times d$
v_i	Embedding of the paper $i, 1 \times d$
$\Theta^{(i)}$	Parameters in layer i of GCN
k	Number of paper classes
Z	Paper classification prediction, $|P| \times k$
l	Number of words in paper p
$author_j$	Embedding of author $j, 1 \times d$
ac_{ij}	Importance of author j to the paper $i, 1 \times d$
$nhid$	Number of hidden layers in GCN
$\odot$	Element-wise multiplication

Definition 1. *Scholarly Network: A scholarly network would be denoted as $G = (P, C, Au, X)$, where P is a set of paper, C is a set of citations and references among these papers. X is the text information in paper, here is the average word embeddings of each paper's abstract.*

Definition 2. *Scholarly Network Embedding: Given a scholarly network $G = (P, C, Au, X)$, the aim of scholarly network representation is to get a representation v_i of each paper p_i in a low-dimension space, combining the information of paper and the corresponding authors. The target is to lessen the classification loss between the categories predicted using representation v_i and true labels.*

4   Author Contributed Representation for Scholarly Network Framework

In this section, we propose a model ACR-SN to represent paper in scholarly network, the framework of which is shown in Fig. 2. The whole structure of our model consists of three parts: 1) Paper information input; 2) Author-abstract pairwise attention and author contribution attention layer, which is to fully capture the influence of the authors and learn the attribute of paper from its

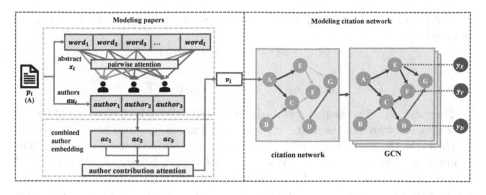

Fig. 2. Framework of Author Contributed Representation for Scholarly Network (ACR-SN). The left part is papers modeling and right is citation network modeling.

abstract; 3) graph convolutional network which is utilized to preserve the structure and transmit the node embeddings in the citation network. The notations are shown in Table 1.

4.1 Network Input

The input of ACR-SN is a citation network, in which each node is a paper, containing authors and abstracts. Take paper i as an example, author j in author group au_i author is mapped to an embedding vector $author_j$ using one hot embedding, word k in the abstracts also reflect to a same dimensional vector $word_k$ by word2vec embedding method. To construct embedding for each paper with the author and abstract information, our model is introduced as below.

4.2 Modeling Papers

Paper modeling is the core part of our method, which aims to capture author and abstract information. It consists of two layers of mechanism. The first layer is a pairwise attention between authors and study areas of the paper, which captures the author's expertise and interest in the areas covered by the paper to generate the embeddings of authors in each paper. The second layer is used to captures the different contribution of authors to the same paper.

Paper-Author Pairwise Attention. The abstract of paper i could be split into several topics through the words embeddings $word_k$. Meanwhile, the authors in au_i also appear in multiple papers, indicating that they have different research interests. To emphasize differences in authors' interests and papers' topics, here we utilize a pairwise method to model the interaction between papers and authors. The details of this attention layer are shown below.

For paper i and author j in au_i, the representation of paper i is calculated as follows:

$$ac_{ij} = Mean(x_i \odot author_j), \tag{1}$$

$$ac_i = \left[ac_{i1}, \ldots, ac_{ij}, \ldots, ac_{|au_i|}\right]. \tag{2}$$

Here $x_i \in \mathbb{R}^{l \times d}$ is the paper embedding matrix, which is the average of lookup vectors of the words in the abstract of paper i, and l is the total number of words. $author_j$ is the embedding of author j in au_i. $\odot$ represents the elementwise product between these vectors. Notice that $author_j \in \mathbb{R}^d$ would be filled to $\mathbb{R}^{l \times d}$ automatically, and $ac_{ij} \in \mathbb{R}^{1 \times d}$ is column average of the elementwise product, representing the embedding of author j in paper i. After column concatenation, the aggregated paper representation vector is $ac_i \in \mathbb{R}^{|au_i| \times d}$.

After generating the authors embeddings, we use another attention layer to aggregate them to form the embedding of paper. The second attention layer is the author attention, which is discussed in the next subsection.

Author Attention. To get the paper representation, an intuitive idea is to stack the representation of authors together and use the average pooling to get paper representation vector. However, this idea ignores the fact that each author may contributes to the paper differently. So we introduce the attention mechanism to apply different importance to each author. The attention layer is a linear layer to learn each author's contribution a_i to the paper i. The detailed attention weight learning progress is shown below:

$$a'_i = W \cdot ac_i + b, \tag{3}$$

where $ac_i \in \mathbb{R}^{|au_i| \times d}$ is the vectors of the authors' representations of paper i. $A_i \in \mathbb{R}^{1 \times d}$ is the attention weight of the authors to the paper i, and b is the bias vector. The output $a'_i \in \mathbb{R}^{|au_i|}$ is the attention weights of authors of paper i. The attention weight a_i is normalized by the softmax function:

$$a_i = \frac{exp(a'_{ij})}{\sum_{j=1}^{|au_i|} exp(a'_{ij})}. \tag{4}$$

Here a'_{ij} is the j-th component of a'_i. The normalization makes sure each author's attention weight is in $[0, 1]$, and the sum of authors contribution is 1.

The paper representation v_i is calculated in the following form:

$$v_i = ac_i \cdot a_i. \tag{5}$$

In this equation, ac_i and a_i are calculated in Eq. (2) and Eq. (4), and the output $v_i \in \mathbb{R}^d$ is the representation vector of paper i. After the calculation in this subsection, the initial embedding of articles is formed. By using two layers of attention in authors and abstracts, we incorporate different kinds of information in scholarly data. To combine the citation structure and learn an accurate representation, we will introduce the GCN framework in the next section.

4.3 Modeling Citation Network

In this part we will show how to use GCN to form the final representation of paper i under the constraint of similarities in its citations.

Here all papers in the dataset P compose a feature matrix $V \in |P| \times d$, where $|P|$ is the number of papers in the citation network, d is dimension of feature vectors. The citation network can be presented in adjacency matrix C, which is generated from paper set P and citations in this network; the degree matrix is denoted as D. Following the spectral approaches in graph neural network, GCN limits the convolution operation to one-localized to avoid overfitting, and uses renormalization trick to refrain from numerical instabilities and exploding or vanishing gradients. So the aggregator in GCN is $\hat{C}X$, where $\hat{C} = \tilde{D}^{-\frac{1}{2}}\tilde{C}\tilde{D}^{-\frac{1}{2}}$ which is a normalization trick in GCN [9], in which $\tilde{C} = C + I_N, \tilde{D}_{ij} = \sum_j \tilde{A}_{ij}$. The forward process is described in the following part.

The input of this part is the representation matrix of paper V, consists of vectors calculated by Eq. (5). The weight in the first layer is denoted as $\Theta^{(0)}$, and the calculation in first layer is shown as below:

$$F = \hat{C}V\Theta^{(0)}, \tag{6}$$

where $\Theta^{(0)} \in \mathbb{R}^{|P| \times nhid}$ is the weight of first layer. $nhid$ is the number of hidden layers in GCN. The output $F \in \mathbb{R}^{|P| \times nhid}$ is the input of next graph convolution layers. The structure of the next layer is similar to the first layer, except the ReLU unit and softmax layer.

$$Z = softmax(\hat{C}ReLU(F)\Theta^{(1)}), \tag{7}$$

where $Z \in \mathbb{R}^{|P| \times k}$ is the convolved signal matrix, and k is the final number of classification of papers. The softmax layer is applied row-wise. The weight in this layer is $\Theta^{(1)} \in \mathbb{R}^{nhid \times k}$. The output of the model is the probability of each type which the paper is divided into. And the next subsection will show the learning process.

4.4 Model Learning

Objective Function. For the proposed ACR-SN model, we use cross entropy shown in Eq. 8 to promise that papers are divided into correct area as much as possible. As mentioned in GCN [9], the loss function is defined in cross-entropy form to maximize the similarity of node representation to the node label:

$$L = -\sum_{l \in Y_L} \sum_{f=1}^{k} Y_{lf} ln Z_{lf}. \tag{8}$$

Here Y_L is the labeled set. k is the number of node classes. Y_{lf} is the vector of true labels, and Z_{lf} is the predicted possibilities of each paper in each class. To optimize our model, we use Adam optimizer to learn the parameters.

Parameter Initialization. In the cooperation attention part, we initialize the authors initial weight to all 1 vectors, assuming all the authors contributes equally to the paper features. For the initial author embedding, we use word embedding to get low dimension one hot embedding of authors and words. As for words in the abstract, we use word2vec to generate their initial embeddings. For all the words in the abstract in the dataset, we select the top 3000 frequent words for a brief embedding. The author and word embedding are randomly initialized and can be learned during training.

In the GCN part, we initialize the weight with a Gaussian distribution, with a mean of 0 and deviation of $1/\sqrt{out_{dimension}}$.

5   Experiments

5.1   Experimental Settings

Datasets. For the purpose of learning the embedding of papers in the scholarly network, here we conduct the experiments on two scholarly networks to demonstrate the effectiveness of our proposed model ACR-SN:

- Semantic Scholar [2]. This is an open scholarly database. Here we downloaded the 2017-10-30 version from the Semantic Scholar website. In [14], they constructed DBLP dataset by extracting four study fields, namely Database, Data Mining, Artificial Intelligence and Computer Vision. In this paper, we also used these four areas, and filtered the data in Semantic Scholar dataset to extract the paper in these fields. After the preprocessing step, there are 48,878 papers. The max connected subgraph contains 46,637 papers and 174,185 citation links.
- DBLP [18]. This is a famous paper dataset in computer science. After filtering out the papers in the four areas mentioned before, there are 78,939 papers in the dataset.

The detailed statistics of datasets is shown in Table 2. These two datasets are both popular in scholarly data mining. The number of four kinds of papers is

Table 2. The statistics of datasets.

Datasets		Semantic scholar	DBLP
#Nodes		48,878	62,137
#Links		174,622	319,222
#Authors		47,343	77,260
Study fields	DB	4,579	6,340
	DM	23,851	10,956
	AI	7,754	20,915
	CV	12,694	23,962

basically balanced, except for the relatively small ones in Database field. The quantity of authors and papers are similar in both datasets. And DBLP is slightly larger compared with Semantic Scholar dataset.

Baselines. As mentioned in the Sect. 2, we selected several state-of-the-art methods to demonstrate the effectiveness of our learned scholarly network embedding by ACR-SN:

Structure-based Methods:

- **Node2vec** [7], different from DeepWalk [16], it designs a biased truncated random walks to efficiently explore diverse neighborhood and utilizes the skip-gram model to learn the node embedding.
- **LINE** [19] is a method that defines the first-order and second-order proximity of network structure to obtain the node representation, respectively.

Combined Methods:

- **Node2vec+attr** is a method using combined features of Node2vec and paper attributes to classify the paper.
- **LINE+attr** also combines the representation of LINE with paper features.
- **UPP-SNE** [28], which is the abbreviation of user profile preserving social network embedding, learns the node embedding by preserving the structure of network and node attributes simultaneously.
- **Paper2vec** [6] solves the problem similar to our method. This method learns the embedding of paper from text information, and uses the citation network structure to jointly refine the learned embedding.

Deep Learning based Methods:

- **GraphSAGE** [8] is a general inductive network embedding framework which generates embedding by aggregating features from a node's neighbors.
- **GCN** [9] optimizes the node embedding in a semi-supervised framework, which has the similar objective function with our method.
- **GAT** [21] considers different weights of neighbors to a node in a network, using attention mechanism in graph neural network.
- **ACR-SN-avg** is the reduced version of our proposed model ACR-SN without containing the attention part.

Evaluation. In the classification experiments, the evaluation metric we used is Accuracy, which is defined by the portion between nodes classified correctly and the total number of nodes:

$$accuracy = \frac{\#nodes\ classified\ correctly}{\#nodes}. \tag{9}$$

As for the link prediction task, we used average precision(AP) and area under curve(AUC) to evaluate the effectiveness of experiments. For each experiment, we randomly selected 10% to 90% from the dataset as training set, and split the remaining part to validation set and test set.

Table 3. The experimental results of node classification on semantic scholar.

Methods	Training ratio								
	0.1	0.2	0.3	0.4	0.5	0.6	0.7	0.8	0.9
Node2vec	0.7002	0.7035	0.7040	0.7063	0.7076	0.7069	0.7082	0.7068	0.7144
LINE	0.6368	0.6421	0.6436	0.6457	0.6445	0.6460	0.6461	0.6464	0.6571
Node2vec+attr	0.7344	0.7442	0.7481	0.7505	0.7513	0.7525	0.7544	0.7565	0.7627
LINE+attr	0.6883	0.7046	0.7138	0.7167	0.7115	0.7192	0.7177	0.7117	0.7308
UPP-SNE	0.6113	0.6160	0.6187	0.6192	0.6196	0.6205	0.6210	0.6267	0.6230
Paper2vec	0.6869	0.6915	0.6933	0.6969	0.6972	0.6967	0.6993	0.7003	0.7122
GraphSAGE	0.4748	0.4748	0.4877	0.4884	0.4886	0.4903	0.4885	0.4898	0.5018
GCN	0.7141	0.7193	0.7162	0.7334	0.7332	0.7387	0.7429	0.7427	0.7480
GAT	**0.7958**	**0.7982**	**0.7968**	**0.8013**	0.7997	0.7998	0.8050	0.8080	0.8130
ACR-SN-avg	0.7683	0.781	0.7926	0.8012	**0.8052**	**0.8096**	**0.8155**	0.8205	0.8287
ACR-SN	0.7770	0.7888	0.7953	0.8000	0.8044	0.8079	0.8144	**0.8212**	**0.8295**

Table 4. The experimental results of node classification on DBLP.

Methods	Training Ratio								
	0.1	0.2	0.3	0.4	0.5	0.6	0.7	0.8	0.9
Node2vec	0.7199	0.7272	0.7295	0.7322	0.7344	0.7367	0.7347	0.7281	0.7269
LINE	0.6862	0.6894	0.6929	0.6951	0.6988	0.6999	0.7015	0.7034	0.7049
Node2vec+attr	0.7078	0.7204	0.7249	0.7298	0.7322	0.7345	0.7320	0.7256	0.7258
LINE+attr	0.6897	0.7024	0.7119	0.7136	0.7148	0.7104	0.7171	0.7118	0.7235
UPP-SNE	0.3747	0.3778	0.3793	0.3786	0.3794	0.3802	0.3798	0.3750	0.3791
Paper2vec	0.3700	0.3731	0.3772	0.3785	0.3799	0.3805	0.3791	0.3756	0.3777
GraphSAGE	0.3653	0.3680	0.3722	0.3746	0.3752	0.3780	0.3761	0.3750	0.3767
GCN	0.3957	0.3945	0.3995	0.4049	0.4172	0.4142	0.4046	0.4038	0.4056
GAT	0.5436	0.5439	0.5321	0.5374	0.5353	0.5384	0.5424	0.5449	0.5460
ACR-SN -avg	0.7292	0.7541	0.7634	0.7703	0.7732	0.7739	0.7779	**0.7829**	**0.7808**
ACR-SN	**0.7300**	**0.7553**	**0.7623**	**0.7739**	**0.7770**	**0.7748**	**0.7792**	0.7778	0.7777

Implementation Details. We implemented our method ACR-SN based on Pytorch framework. We used Adam optimizer and set the learning rate to 0.005. The epoch is set to 300 to reach a stable accuracy performance. The embedding dimension d here is set to 128, and the output layer size(number of paper areas) is 4. Similar to [9], we used a two layer GCN, the hidden layer dimension is 16. In each iteration, we used a full dataset and perform batch gradient descent. The memory usage is $\mathcal{O}(|E|)$ for the usage of sparse storage method. For the Node2vec, we set the walk length to 5, and the window size to 3. For LINE, we used both the first and second neighbors and set the negative samples to 5.

For the link prediction task, we split the 80% of total edges as train-set,10% as validation-set and the rest as test-set. For each set of edges we randomly generated the same size of negative edges that did not appear in the original graph, that is 50% true edges versus 50% false edges.

5.2   Results and Analysis

Here we utilize two tasks to validate the effectiveness of the method. 1). Node Classification: this task is to conduct the classification of papers. 2). Link Prediction: this task is to determine whether there is a citation link between two arbitrary papers. These two tasks are widely used in network embedding field. Next, we will introduce the details of these experimental results:

Node Classification. Table 3 and Table 4 illustrate the detailed results on Semantic Scholar and DBLP datasets. On Semantic Scholar dataset, the proposed ACR-SN outperforms structure-based method (Node2vec, LINE) and the combined methods (Node2vec+attr, LINE+attr, UPP-SNE, Paper2vec), which demonstrates the efficiency of our proposed method. The comparison results between these two kinds of methods demonstrate that structure feature is necessary, and attributes of nodes also play an important role in learning the node representation. The results of Node2vec+attr and LINE+attr reveal that the intuitive combination of structure feature and attributes improve the representation ability compared with structure-based methods, while pairwise attention and author attention in ACR-SN catch the features of paper more effectively. Furthermore, Our method performs better on the unique scholarly datasets compared with UPP-SNE. Also, the utilization of graph convolutional network learn the network structure information better than the CBOW model used in Paper2vec. Finally, ACR-SN achieves higher accuracy than GCN and GraphSAGE, which indicates that our model is more suitable on the scholarly datasets. But on lower training ratio, GAT gains slightly higher accuracy than ACR-SN.

As for DBLP dataset, ACR-SN gain higher accuracy than most baselines. Surprisingly, the structure-based methods (Node2vec, LINE) achieve higher accuracy than the combined methods. The addition of node attributes reduces the experimental performance, which illustrates that content and combined methods are sensitive to the scholarly datasets. The decrease in accuracy indicates that some of the baselines are also sensitive to data imbalance.

In order to demonstrate the effectiveness of attention mechanism, we compare ACR-SN with its variant ACR-SN-avg on the task of node classification, and show the experimental results on Table 3 and Table 4. ACR-SN-avg is the variant of ACR-SN without considering the second attention layer, which uses the average of author embeddings instead of the attention network. The results show that our method gains higher accuracy than the average method under the small training ratio. It demonstrates that the author's contribution attention layer can distinguish the different importance of authors, and achieve a better paper classification result.

Link Prediction. The link prediction task is to determine if there exits the citation relationship in a pair of papers based on their learned node embeddings. Figure 3 shows the link prediction results on semantic scholar dataset. As shown in Fig. 3, we observe that ACR-SN gains the highest AUC among these compared

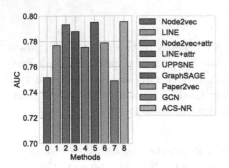
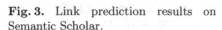
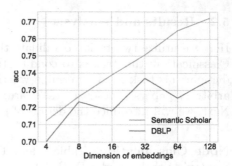

Fig. 3. Link prediction results on Semantic Scholar.

Fig. 4. Parameter Sensibility of the Embedding Dimensions.

methods. Specifically, our method ACR-SN is trained on node classification task, and we use these learned embedding on the link prediction task, which is a cross-task experiment. Comparing to the unsupervised methods like Node2vec, LINE and GraphSAGE, ACR-SN achieves the highest average precision on Semantic Scholar dataset. This result demonstrates that our method can learn the paper embedding effectively.

Table 5. The Distribution of Author Attention Weights in the paper.

Papers	Authors	Weights
Mixture Representations for Inference and Learning in Boltzmann Machines	Neil D. Lawrence	0.0932
	Christopher M. Bishop	0.8024
	Michael I. Jordan	**0.1044**
Loopy Belief Propagation for Approximate Inference: An Empirical Study	Kevin P. Murphy	0.4036
	Yair Weiss	0.2436
	Michael I. Jordan	**0.3528**

Parameter Sensibility Analysis. In our model, embedding dimension is an important parameter. So in Fig. 4, we can observe that with the embedding dimension of paper increasing, the accuracy in node classification is in a rising trend. In DBLP dataset, the accuracy shows the fluctuation. While in Semantic Scholar dataset, the performance of higher embedding dimension is better. As a result, we use the same 128 dimension of paper embedding in all experiments.

5.3   Case Study

From the scholarly dataset, we choose two papers of Michael I. Jordan, professor of UCB, to demonstrate the different contribution of authors in a paper. We select two papers [10] and [13] in his different developing phase, published in 1999 and 2013 respectively. The authors' attentions in these two papers are shown in Table 5. Michael I. Jordan plays different roles in these papers. In both papers, he is the last author. In the first paper, according to our attention calculation, he contributes about ten percent to the paper fewer than the second author, while in the second paper the attention value suggests that the authors contribute nearly averaged to this work. It suggests that the author contributes to paper in different stages differently, and the various contribution could help us to better comprehend the relationship between the authors and papers.

6   Conclusion

In this paper, we proposed a novel scholarly network embedding framework called ACR-SN, for scholarly network analysis. Specifically, we proposed two attention networks for capturing the authors' influences and contribution, respectively. Then we utilized a GCN method to model the diffusion of papers' attributes influences. Extensive experiments show the effectiveness of ACR-SN in many applications including paper classification and citation prediction.

There are still some further directions in the future. First, we would combine the citation network with co-author network. Second, we would deepen the study of co-author relationship for the scholarly network analysis.

Acknowledgements. This work was supported in part by National Natural Science Foundation of China (Grant No. 61703386), the Anhui Sun Create Electronics Company Ltd., under Grant KD1809300321, in part by the National Key R&D Program of China under Grant 2018YFC0832101, and in part by the National Key New Product Plan of China under Grant 2014GRC30006.

References

1. Ahmed, A., Shervashidze, N., Narayanamurthy, S., Josifovski, V., Smola, A.J.: Distributed large-scale natural graph factorization. In: Proceedings of the 22nd International Conference on World Wide Web, pp. 37–48. ACM (2013)
2. Ammar, W., et al.: Construction of the literature graph in semantic scholar. arXiv preprint arXiv:1805.02262 (2018)
3. Belkin, M., Niyogi, P.: Laplacian eigenmaps and spectral techniques for embedding and clustering. In: Advances in Neural Information Processing Systems, pp. 585–591 (2002)
4. Dong, Y., Johnson, R.A., Chawla, N.V.: Will this paper increase your h-index? Scientific impact prediction. In: Proceedings of the Eighth ACM International Conference on Web Search and Data Mining, pp. 149–158 (2015)
5. Du, D., et al.: Solving link-oriented tasks in signed network via an embedding approach. In: 2017 IEEE International Conference on Systems, Man, and Cybernetics (SMC), pp. 75–80. IEEE (2017)
6. Ganguly, S., Pudi, V.: Paper2vec: combining graph and text information for scientific paper representation. In: Jose, J.M., Hauff, C., Altıngovde, I.S., Song, D., Albakour, D., Watt, S., Tait, J. (eds.) ECIR 2017. LNCS, vol. 10193, pp. 383–395. Springer, Cham (2017). https://doi.org/10.1007/978-3-319-56608-5_30

7. Grover, A., Leskovec, J.: node2vec: scalable feature learning for networks. In: Proceedings of the 22nd ACM SIGKDD International Conference on Knowledge Discovery and Data Mining, pp. 855–864. ACM (2016)
8. Hamilton, W., Ying, Z., Leskovec, J.: Inductive representation learning on large graphs. In: Advances in Neural Information Processing Systems, pp. 1024–1034 (2017)
9. Kipf, T.N., Welling, M.: Semi-supervised classification with graph convolutional networks. arXiv preprint arXiv:1609.02907 (2016)
10. Lawrence, N.D., Bishop, C.M., Jordan, M.I.: Mixture representations for inference and learning in Boltzmann machines. arXiv preprint arXiv:1301.7393 (2013)
11. Lin, H., Wang, H., Du, D., Wu, H., Chang, B., Chen, E.: Patent quality valuation with deep learning models. In: Pei, J., Manolopoulos, Y., Sadiq, S., Li, J. (eds.) DASFAA 2018. LNCS, vol. 10828, pp. 474–490. Springer, Cham (2018). https://doi.org/10.1007/978-3-319-91458-9_29
12. Ma, Y., Uzzi, B.: Scientific prize network predicts who pushes the boundaries of science. Proc. Natl. Acad. Sci. **115**(50), 12608–12615 (2018)
13. Murphy, K., Weiss, Y., Jordan, M.I.: Loopy belief propagation for approximate inference: an empirical study. arXiv preprint arXiv:1301.6725 (2013)
14. Pan, S., Wu, J., Zhu, X., Zhang, C., Wang, Y.: Tri-party deep network representation. Network **11**(9), 12 (2016)
15. Pei, H., Wei, B., Chang, K.C.C., Lei, Y., Yang, B.: Geom-GCN: geometric graph convolutional networks. In: International Conference on Learning Representations (ICLR) (2020)
16. Perozzi, B., Al-Rfou, R., Skiena, S.: DeepWalk: online learning of social representations. In: Proceedings of the 20th ACM SIGKDD International Conference on Knowledge Discovery and Data Mining, pp. 701–710. ACM (2014)
17. Petersen, A.M.: Quantifying the impact of weak, strong, and super ties in scientific careers. Proc. Natl. Acad. Sci. **112**(34), E4671–E4680 (2015)
18. Sinha, A., et al.: An overview of Microsoft Academic Service (MAS) and applications. In: Proceedings of the 24th International Conference on World Wide Web, pp. 243–246. ACM (2015)
19. Tang, J., Qu, M., Wang, M., Zhang, M., Yan, J., Mei, Q.: Line: large-scale information network embedding. In: Proceedings of the 24th International Conference on World Wide Web, pp. 1067–1077. International World Wide Web Conferences Steering Committee (2015)
20. Tao, S., Wang, X., Huang, W., Chen, W., Wang, T., Lei, K.: From citation network to study map: a novel model to reorganize academic literatures. In: Proceedings of the 26th International Conference on World Wide Web Companion, pp. 1225–1232 (2017)
21. Veličković, P., Cucurull, G., Casanova, A., Romero, A., Lio, P., Bengio, Y.: Graph attention networks. arXiv preprint arXiv:1710.10903 (2017)
22. Wang, H., et al.: A united approach to learning sparse attributed network embedding. In: 2018 IEEE International Conference on Data Mining (ICDM), pp. 557–566. IEEE (2018)
23. Wang, H., et al.: MCNE: an end-to-end framework for learning multiple conditional network representations of social network. In: Proceedings of the 25th ACM SIGKDD International Conference on Knowledge Discovery & Data Mining, pp. 1064–1072 (2019)
24. West, J.D., Wesley-Smith, I., Bergstrom, C.T.: A recommendation system based on hierarchical clustering of an article-level citation network. IEEE Trans. Big Data **2**(2), 113–123 (2016)

25. Xia, F., Wang, W., Bekele, T.M., Liu, H.: Big scholarly data: a survey. IEEE Trans. Big Data **3**(1), 18–35 (2017)
26. Yan, E., Ding, Y.: Scholarly networks analysis. In: Alhajj, R., Rokne, J. (eds.) Encyclopedia of Social Network Analysis and Mining, pp. 1643–1651. Springer, New York (2014). https://doi.org/10.1007/978-1-4614-6170-8_249
27. Yang, C., Liu, Z., Zhao, D., Sun, M., Chang, E.: Network representation learning with rich text information. In: Twenty-Fourth International Joint Conference on Artificial Intelligence (2015)
28. Zhang, D., Yin, J., Zhu, X., Zhang, C.: User profile preserving social network embedding. In: IJCAI International Joint Conference on Artificial Intelligence (2017)

Unsupervised Cross-Modal Retrieval by Coupled Dual Generative Adversarial Networks

Jingzi Gu[1,2], Peng Fu[1], Jinchao Zhang[1(✉)], Lulu Wang[1], Bo Li[1,2], and Weiping Wang[1,2]

[1] Institute of Information Engineering, Chinese Academy of Sciences, Beijing, China
{gujingzi,fupeng,zhangjinchao,wanglulu,libo,wangweiping}@iie.ac.cn
[2] School of Cyber Security, University of Chinese Academy of Sciences, Beijing, China

Abstract. Textual-visual cross-modal retrieval has become a hot research topic in both computer vision and natural language processing communities. However, existing deep cross-modal hashing methods either rely on amounts of labeled information or have no ability to learn an accuracy correlation between different modalities. In this paper, we address the unsupervised cross-modal retrieval problem using a novel framework called coupled dual generative adversarial networks (CDGAN). This framework consists of two cycle networks: a text-to-image-to-text(t2t) network and an image-to-text-to-image(i2i) network. The t2t network is used to learn the relation among an original text, the generated image and the generated text using the similarity of original and generated image-text, and the i2i network is used to learn the relation among an original image, the generated text and the generated image. Therefore, two groups of mixed hash codes of image-text are learned in this framework. Furthermore, our proposed CDGAN seamlessly couples these two cycle networks with generative adversarial mechanism so that the hash codes can be optimized simultaneously. Extensive experiments show that our framework can well match images and sentences with complex content, and it can achieve the state-of-the-art cross-modal retrieval results on two popular benchmark datasets.

Keywords: CDGAN · Cross-modal · Retrieval

1 Introduction

With the rapid growth of data, how to efficiently and accurately retrieve the required information from massive data of heterogeneous modalities becomes a hot research topic. Thus, cross-modal retrieval [1,20–23,25] which aims to enable flexible retrieval across different modalities (e.g., texts vs. images), plays a key role in information retrieval. Specifically, retrieved images (resp. texts) are highly relevant to a given textual (resp. image) query. However, the challenge

© Springer Nature Switzerland AG 2020
X. Wang et al. (Eds.): APWeb-WAIM 2020, LNCS 12317, pp. 574–587, 2020.
https://doi.org/10.1007/978-3-030-60259-8_42

of cross-modal retrieval is to measure the similarity between different types of data, which is referred to as the heterogeneity gap.

In order to bridge the heterogeneity gap, most existing methods are proposed to learn a common space for different modalities. By projecting cross-modal data into the latent space, the correlations across different modalities can be effectively and efficiently measured by their hamming distance. These cross-modal methods can be generally categorized into two groups: supervised methods and unsupervised methods.

Recently, supervised hashing methods [13,20,24] are used to capture the correlation between different modalities, and this kind of method can further exploit the semantic labels to learn more consistent hash codes for the semantic-relevant cross-modal data. However, label data collection is infeasible, as it is time-consuming and labor-intensive. Different from supervised methods, unsupervised cross-modal hashing methods can leverage unlabeled data to realize efficient cross-modal retrieval. Therefore, this kind of method is more flexible and applicable in real world applications. Among unsupervised deep hashing methods, Unsupervised Generative Adversarial Cross-modal Hashing (UGACH) [27] captures the underlying manifold structure by a graph-based unsupervised correlation. Unsupervised coupled Cycle generative adversarial Hashing networks (UCH) [9] can be optimized to learn common representation and hash codes simultaneously. However, most unsupervised methods learn a single group of hash codes for each modal by preserving semantic correlation between different modalities, and ignore the underlying manifold structure in a certain elevated status.

In this paper, we propose a novel unsupervised cross-modal retrieval using generative adversarial network called CDGAN. Coupled dual generative adversarial networks are designed to build two cycle networks in a unified framework, where two groups of mixed original and generated data hash codes are learned in the network. In each modal, a group hash codes consist of the original data hash codes and the generated data hash codes, and we call it mixed hash codes. Thus, the hash codes can provide more feature information. Specifically, hash codes of the original and pseudo data are similar and can be optimized simultaneously. The main contributions of our paper are outlined as follows:

(1) We design an unsupervised cross-modal retrieval framework by coupled dual generative adversarial networks. Mixed hash codes can be obtained in each modal, which can capture more underlying manifold structure across different modalities.
(2) In the proposed networks, mixed hash codes of multi-modal learning can interact with each other and achieve optimal performance when network is convergence in a unified framework.
(3) Experiments on two real-world datasets with image-text modalities show that CDGAN can outperform other baselines and achieve the state-of-the-art performance in cross-modal retrieval applications.

2   Related Work

In this section, we introduce some representative supervised and unsupervised cross-modal hashing methods. Specifically, the most related work on topic of unsupervised cross-modal hashing methods are reviewed, which can be roughly categorized into the shallow and the deep schemes, according to whether they use the deep networks.

In supervised methods, Deep Visual semantic Hashing (DSVH) [24], Cross-modal Correlation Learning With Multigrained Fusion by Hierarchical Network (CCL) [26], Deep Cross-Modal Hashing (DCMH) [13], Scalable Deep Multimodal Learning for Cross-Modal Retrieval (SDML) [12], Self-Supervised Adversarial Hashing (SSAH) [1], and Cross-Modal Adaptive Message Passing for Text-Image Retrieval (CAMP) [28] encode individual modalities into their corresponding features by constructing two different pathways in deep networks, and this method significantly mitigate the modality gap and achieve superior retrieval performance. SSAH learns hash codes by preserving semantic correlation with label information networks between different modalities. CAMP takes comprehensive and fine-grained cross-modal interactions into account. However, supervised methods use labeled semantic information that requires massive labor cost, making it infeasible in real-world applications. Our paper focuses on unsupervised field that is lacks sufficient explorations.

In unsupervised methods, for shallow structure Canonical Correlation Analysis (CCA) [3] projects data from different modalities into a common hamming space to maximize their correlations. CVH [14] is proposed to consider both intra-view and inter-view similarities to keep the cross-modal relationship. Hashing (CMFH) [5] learns unified hash codes by collective matrix factorization. Latent Semantic Sparse Hashing (LSSH) [7] is proposed to utilize the sparse coding and the matrix factorization to extract the latent features for images and texts. Fusion Similarity Hashing (FSH) [6], explicitly embeds the graph-based fusion similarity across modalities into a common Hamming space. However, it is illustrated that deep cross-modal hashing methods are usually more effective than shallow structure.

Recently, deep learning with neural networks based unsupervised cross-modal hashing methods [15] have been widely used to learn hash codes. Unsupervised Generative Adversarial Cross-modal Hashing (UGACH) [27] captures the underlying manifold structure across different modalities by a graph-based unsupervised correlation. Unsupervised coupled Cycle generative adversarial Hashing networks (UCH) [9] can optimize simultaneously to learn common representation and hash codes. However, only one group of hash codes can be learned in these deep methods, the lack of the hash codes expression leads to be insufficient in cross-modal retrieval. In contrast, our CDGAN can effectively build the modality correlation by a framework that can directly learning coupled dual cycle framework. Besides, the hash codes are updated iteratively to preserve various data information.

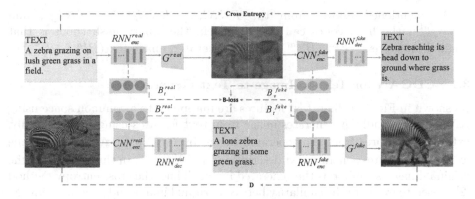

Fig. 1. The proposed unsupervised generative cross-modal learning framework. The entire framework consists of two training paths: text-to-image-to-text, and image-to-text-to-image. It includes nine networks: two sentence encoders RNN_{enc}^{real} and RNN_{enc}^{fake}, two image encoders CNN_{enc}^{real} and CNN_{enc}^{fake}, two sentence decoders RNN_{dec}^{real} and RNN_{dec}^{fake}, two image generators G^{fake} and G^{real}, one image discriminator D. Furthermore, it also has four networks for generating binary codes B_v^{real}, B_v^{fake}, B_t^{real}, and B_t^{fake}.

3   CDGAN Cross-Modal Network

As demonstrated in [9], learning binary codes that preserve the neighborhood structure of the original data is an effective improvement for the unsupervised training of deep hashing network. Specifically, we learn the mixed hash codes, which can preserve more information. Figure 1 shows the overall architecture for the proposed cross-modal retrieval learning framework, named CDGAN. The entire system consists of three training parts: text-to-image-to-text generative feature learning, image-to-text-to-image generative adversarial feature learning, and the hash codes learning part. The first part is t2t. At first, a pseudo image is generated from the input text. Then, a pseudo text is generated from the pseudo image. Finally, we make the original text be similar to the pseudo text. At the same time, the second part i2i is from image generates a text, and then from text generate image, at last, the original image is similar with pseudo image. In the third part, our method generates two group mixed hash codes of each modal, and the binary codes of original image-text and the generated image-text are similar. The input data is image-text data pair.

The t2t part: the t2t networks integrate by text-to-image(t2i), image-to-text(i2i), and binary hash code learning. It generates an image from the textual feature, and then generate a sentence from the embedded pseudo image.

The i2i part: t2t is a dual structure by integrating both image-to-text(i2t) and text-to-image(t2i). It generates an sentence from the embedded generative image, and then generate a image from the textual feature.

As mentioned above, from the RNN_{enc}^{real}, RNN_{enc}^{fake}, CNN_{enc}^{real}, and CNN_{enc}^{fake}, the hash codes can be got. Then, the binary hash codes is that original image-text(B_v^{real}, B_t^{real}) and the generated image-text(B_v^{fake}, B_t^{fake}).

3.1 CDGAN for Text-to-Image-to-Text Generation

As shown in Fig. 1, at first, text features are mapped into a common space using RNN_{enc}^{real}. Secondly, it generates image from text features using G^{real}. Thirdly, extracting features from the generated image by CNN_{Enc}^{fake}. At last, from the extracting features generate text description by RNN_{dec}^{fake}. In this procedure, the original image is similar as the generated image. Thus, the cross entropy method [2] is used to evaluate the similarity between original image and generated image. Then, binary codes of original and generated text are generated.

3.2 CDGAN for Image-to-Text-to-Image Generation

As shown in Fig. 1, at first, image features are extracted into a common space using CNN_{enc}^{real}. Secondly, it generates text from image features using RNN_{dec}^{fake} generator. Thirdly, extracting features from the generated text by RNN_{enc}^{fake}. At last, from the extracting features generate image using G^{fake}. In this procedure, the original image is similar as the generated image. Thus, the discriminator D is used to judge the similarity between original text and generated text. Then, binary codes of original and generated images are generated.

3.3 Text-to-Image Generation

For the text-to-image training part (t2i), our goal is to encourage the text feature t to be able to generate an image that is similar to the text. We adopt an attentional generative adversarial network [16], which has an significantly outperformance for generating realistic image.

At first, the text encoder is a recurrent neural network (RNN)[8] that extracts semantic vectors from the text description, which includes word and sentence embedding pair (w, em).

$$(w, em) = RNN_{enc}(\theta_t) \tag{1}$$

Then, for the image generating procedure, we adept attentional generative network [16]. In our network, it has m generators ($G_0, G_1, ..., G_{m-1}$), which take the hidden states ($F_0, F_1, ..., F_{m-1}$) as input. Specifically, we use h to represent the sentence vector, and V_i is the generated image. Here, $z \sim N(0, 1)$ is a noise vector usually sampled from a standard normal distribution. And F_i^{attn} is the proposed attention model at the $i - th$ stage image generation. The adversarial loss for G_i is defined as:

$$h_0 = F_0(z, em) \tag{2}$$
$$h_i = F_i(h_{i-1}, F_i^{attn}(h_{i-1}, (w, em))) \tag{3}$$
$$V_i = G_i(h_i)i \in 1, 2, 3, ..., m - 1 \tag{4}$$

A natural way to model such a conditional distribution is to use a GAN [17,18], which consists of a discriminator and a generator. The discriminator is trained to distinguish the real samples from the generated samples. And the generator is used to generate image. In each training stage, the generator G and discriminator D are trained alternately. At the $i-th$ stage, the generator G_i has a corresponding discriminator D_i. The adversarial loss for G_i is defined as:

$$L_{G_i} = -\tfrac{1}{2}E_{V_i \sim p_{V_i}}[log(D_i(V_i))]$$
$$-\tfrac{1}{2}E_{V_i \sim p_{V_i}}[log(D_i(V_i, em))] \tag{5}$$

where V_i is a generated image sampled from the distribution p_{V_i} in the $i-th$ stage. The first part is the visual realism unconditional loss to distinguish whether the image is real or fake. While the second part is the conditional loss determines whether the image matches the sentence or not.

After a training step of G_i, each D_i is trained to discriminate the input is real or fake by minimizing the loss defined as follows:

$$L_{D_i} = -\tfrac{1}{2}E_{V_i^G \sim p_{V_i^G}}[log(D_i(V_i^G))]$$
$$-\tfrac{1}{2}E_{V_i \sim p_{V_i}}[log(1 - D_i(V_i))]$$
$$-\tfrac{1}{2}E_{V_i^G \sim p_{V_i^G}}[log(D_i(V_i^G, em))]$$
$$-\tfrac{1}{2}E_{V_i \sim p_{V_i}}[log(1 - D_i(V_i, em))] \tag{6}$$

where V_i^G is from the real image distribution $p_{V_i^G}$ in the $i-th$ stage.

The final objective function of the generator G is as follows:

$$L_G = \sum_{i=0}^{m-1} L_{G_i} \tag{7}$$

Then, the final objective function of the discriminator D is as follows:

$$L_D = \sum_{i=0}^{m-1} L_{D_i} \tag{8}$$

3.4   Image-to-Text Generation

For the image-to-text part, our goal is to encourage the image visual feature to be able to generate sentences that are similar to the image caption. As for image encoding, it is a Convolutional Neural Network (CNN) that maps images to semantic vectors and is pre-trained on ImageNet. Where θ_v and θ_t are the parameters of the image and text decoders, CNN_{enc} and RNN_{dec} transform the encoded vectors into a common embedding space, and x_v and y_t are the resulting mapped vectors for the image and the text. We formulate the image encoders and text decoders as:

$$x_v = CNN_{enc}(\theta_v) \tag{9}$$
$$y_t = RNN_{dec}(\theta_t) \tag{10}$$

Algorithm 1. The learning algorithm for CDGAN

Input: Q $= (v, t)$.
Output: binary hash codes for database points $\mathbf{B}_v$, $\mathbf{B}_t$.
Initialization: initialize θ_v, θ_t mini-batch size
M and iteration number n.
repeat
    Function:text-to-image-to-text
    Draw text-to-image .
    1: Text encoding $\rightarrow t^{real}$ by RNN_{enc}^{real}
    2: Update t^{real} by (1)
    3: Update image generator G_i using (5).
    4: Update image discriminator D_i using (6).
    Draw image-to-text .
    5: Image encoding$\rightarrow v^{fake}$ by CNN_{enc}^{fake}
    6: Update v^{fake} by (9)
    7: Update text generator RNN_{dec}^{fake} using (10).
    Function:image-to-text-to-image
    Draw image-to-text .
    1: Image encoding$\rightarrow v^{real}$ by CNN_{enc}^{real}
    2: Update v^{real} by (9)
    3: Update text generator RNN_{Dec}^{real} using (10).
    Draw text-to-image .
    4: Text encoding $\rightarrow t^{fake}$ by RNN_{enc}^{fake}
    5: Update t^{fake} by (1)
    6: Update image generator G_i using (5).
    7: Update image discriminator D_i using (6).
    Update hash codes B
until a fixed number of iterations

The whole alternating learning algorithm for the proposed CDGAN is briefly outlined in Algorithm 1.

3.5   Hash Codes Learning

$\mathbf{B}_v$ and $\mathbf{B}_t$ are the binary codes of image and text. In this paper, T_v and T_t are the transformation functions which map the encoded vectors into hash codes. $\mathbf{B}_v^{real}$ is the binary codes of real image, $\mathbf{B}_v^{fake}$ is the binary codes of generating image, $\mathbf{B}_t^{real}$ is the binary codes of real text, and $\mathbf{B}_t^{fake}$ is the binary codes of generating text. The binary hash codes of image $\mathbf{B}_v$ consist of $\mathbf{B}_v^{real}$ and $\mathbf{B}_v^{fake}$. And the binary hash codes of text $\mathbf{B}_t$ consist of $\mathbf{B}_t^{real}$ and $\mathbf{B}_t^{fake}$. Then, we can get the binary hash codes by the following formulation:

$$\mathbf{B}_v^{real} = T_v(CNN_{enc}^{real}(\theta_v)) \tag{11}$$

$$\mathbf{B}_v^{fake} = T_v(CNN_{enc}^{fake}(\theta_v)) \tag{12}$$

$$\mathbf{B}_t^{real} = T_t(RNN_{enc}^{real}(\theta_t)) \tag{13}$$

$$\mathbf{B}_t^{fake} = T_t(RNN_{enc}^{fake}(\theta_t)) \tag{14}$$

At last, the binary codes of image and text are similar. Thus, the binary codes loss is calculated using the following formulation (15):

$$\min_{\theta_v, \theta_t} J(\mathbf{B}) = \| \mathbf{B}_v^{real} - \mathbf{B}_t^{real} \|_F^2 + \| \mathbf{B}_v^{fake} - \mathbf{B}_t^{real} \|_F^2$$

$$+ \| \mathbf{B}_v^{real} - \mathbf{B}_t^{fake} \|_F^2 + \| \mathbf{B}_v^{fake} - \mathbf{B}_t^{fake} \|_F^2 \tag{15}$$

3.6   Optimization

The discrete constraint is the major difficulty to optimize the objective function (15). In deep hashing network, we can generate the strict binary hash codes $\mathbf{B}_v$ and $\mathbf{B}_t$ by (16) and (17). $sgn(\cdot)$ is the sign function that outputs $+1$ for positive input and -1 otherwise on each element. Then, we can generate the strict binary hash codes by:

$$\mathbf{B}_v = sgn_v(\lambda CNN_{enc}^{real}(\theta_v) + (1 - \lambda)CNN_{enc}^{fake}(\theta_v)) \tag{16}$$

$$\mathbf{B}_t = sgn_t(\lambda RNN_{enc}^{real}(\theta_t) + (1 - \lambda)RNN_{enc}^{fake}(\theta_t)) \tag{17}$$

However in the backward propagation, the gradient of the sign function is zero for all nonzero input. To handle this vanishing gradients problem, we follow [4,11] to adopt tanh function in function (18) and (19):

$$\mathbf{B}_v = tanh_v(\lambda CNN_{enc}^{real}(\theta_v) + (1 - \lambda)CNN_{enc}^{fake}(\theta_v)) \tag{18}$$

$$\mathbf{B}_t = tanh_t(\lambda RNN_{enc}^{real}(\theta_t) + (1 - \lambda)RNN_{enc}^{fake}(\theta_t)) \tag{19}$$

4   Experiments

4.1   Datasets

Two popular benchmark datasets in cross-modal retrieval: MIRFlickr-25K [10] and Microsoft COCO [19] are used for evaluation.

The original MIRFLICKR-25K dataset [10] consists of 25,000 images collected from Flickr website. And each image is associated with several textual tags, in witch the image-text pair is annotated with at least one of the 24 unique labels. 20,015 image-text pairs are used in our experiment, because the unlabeled data is removed. We take 2,000 image-text pairs as the query set and the remaining as the retrieval database. The text for each point is represented as a 1386-dimensional bag-of-words vector. For supervised baselines, we select 5,000 image-text from retrieval set to construct training set.

We also evaluate our approach on the MSCOCO dataset [19]. It contains 82,783 training images and 40,504 validation images. Each image has five different sentences and is labeled with at least one of 80 unique labels. In our experiment, 122,218 image-text pairs are used to formulate the dataset where 2,000 image-text pairs are randomly selected as a query set and the remaining 120,218 pairs are regarded as a retrieval set. For supervised methods 6,000 image-text pairs are randomly selected to construct training set from retrieval set.

4.2 Baselines and Evaluation

We compare our method with six methods, including several unsupervised shallow-structure-based methods (CVH [14], CMFH [5], STMH [4], LSSH [7] and FSH [6]), and deep-structure-based methods (CMSSH [11] and UCH [9]). CMSSH is supervised method and UCH is unsupervised method. For fair comparison, deep network CNN-F is used to extract deep features for all shallow structure based methods.

To evaluate CDGAN, we choose three metric methods. Firstly, the mean average precision (MAP) is a widely used metric to measure the accuracy of the hamming ranking protocol. Secondly, the precision and recall for the returned points given any hamming radius are adopted to evaluate the retrieval performance. Finally, in this paper, visual results of text-to-image retrieval can demonstrate the quality of the retrieved image generated by our conditional GAN and image-to-text retrieval prove the quality of the generated text.

4.3 Implementation Details

We experiment with image encoder ResNet152. For ResNet152, we obtain the global image feature by taking a mean-pooling over the last spatial image features. The dimensions of the image feature vectors is 2048 for ResNet152 and then reduce the dimension to 16, 32, and 64. As for text preprocessing, we convert all sentences to lower case, resulting in a vocabulary words.

We set the word embedding size to 300 and the dimensionality of the joint embedding space to 1024 and then reduce the dimension to 16, 32, and 64. For the sentence encoder, we use a GRU-based encoder to get the abstract feature representation. The number of hidden units of both GRUs is set to 1024. For the sentence decoder, we adopt a one-layer GRU-based decoder which has the same hidden dimensions as the GRU-based encoder.

In each t2i part, there are three generators for images in total, where dimensions are 64×64, 128×128, 256×256. Followed [16], a pre-trained bi-directional GRU was used to calculate the semantic embedding from text descriptions. The sentence length is 24.

4.4 Experiment Results

The Mean Average Precision (MAP). The MAP results are presented in Table 1. We group these compared methods into two categories: supervised and

Table 1. The MAP results of baselines and CDGAN on MIRFLICKE-25K and COCO datasets.

Task	Method	MIRFLICKE-25K			COCO		
		16 bits	32 bits	64 bits	16 bits	32 bits	64 bits
I → T	CVH	0.5869	0.5753	0.5722	0.4744	0.4755	0.4590
	STMH	0.5742	0.5821	0.6023	0.4054	0.4149	0.4065
	LCMH	0.5592	0.5691	0.5852	0.4212	0.4515	0.4411
	LSSH	0.5891	0.6041	**0.6243**	0.4689	0.4735	0.4853
	FSH	0.5802	0.5839	0.5914	0.4530	0.4894	0.4942
	CMSSH	0.5981	0.5935	0.6007	0.5034	0.5161	0.5172
	OURS	**0.6102**	**0.6120**	0.6141	**0.5297**	**0.5242**	**0.5256**
T → I	CVH	0.5985	0.5954	0.5892	0.4702	0.4745	0.4589
	STMH	0.5855	0.584	0.6222	0.3911	0.4220	0.4491
	LCMH	0.5614	0.5693	0.5821	0.4510	0.4714	0.4712
	LSSH	0.5830	0.5882	0.6014	0.4565	0.4606	0.4653
	FSH	0.5757	0.5764	0.5832	0.4711	0.5092	0.5149
	CMSSH	0.5984	0.5932	0.6007	0.5036	0.5164	0.5178
	OURS	**0.6113**	**0.6122**	**0.6141**	**0.5291**	**0.5249**	**0.5251**

Table 2. Comparison results between the proposed CDGAN and UCH. The results are evaluated on COCO according to the MAP score.

Task	Method	COCO		
		16 bits	32 bits	64 bits
I → T	UCH	0.5014	0.5147	**0.5371**
	OURS	**0.5297**	**0.5242**	0.5256
T → I	UCH	0.4861	0.4992	0.5212
	OURS	**0.5291**	**0.5249**	**0.5251**

unsupervised. CMSSH is traditional supervised methods information, achieve relatively good performance on retrieval tasks. And LCMH, FSH, and LSSH is unsupervised methods, which can achieve comparable performance in general. In Table 1, we compare our CDGAN with five cross-modal methods with the output dimensions of 16 bits, 32 bits and 64 bits. Then the results show that CDGAN significantly outperforms all the other baselines. From the experimental results, our proposed CDGAN outperforms other competitors by comparing all these methods. In detail, the MAP of our method is higher than that of the baseline methods in MIRFLICKR-25K and MSCOCO. $I \rightarrow T$ denotes that the query is image and the database is text, and $T \rightarrow I$ denotes that the query is text and the database is image. The best results for MAP are shown in bold.

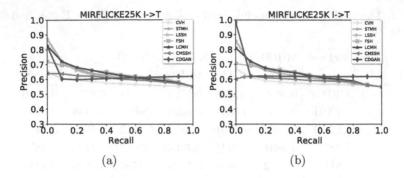

Fig. 2. The Precision-Recall curves on MIRFLICKR-25K.

Fig. 3. Visual results of text-to-image generation.

Comparison CDGAN with UCH. We additionally compare our proposed CDGAN with UCH, which is a representative unsupervised deep learning based method proposed recently in MSCOCO dataset. Table 2 shows the results of comparison between UCH and CDGAN in term of MAP values on MSCOCO datasets. It is obvious that our proposed CDGAN outperforms UCH with different code lengths.

The main reason may be that UCH just calculates single hash codes, which causes that the hash codes is lack of accuracy and thus the retrieval performance is constrained. With no need to build similarity matrix, our CDGAN exploiting modality correlation by generating modality data with couple-dual-GAN. In each modal it can learn more powerful representations. Therefore, more reliable various group hash codes can be achieved with the proposed CDGAN method.

Precision-Recall Curves. The Precision-Recall curves was used to evaluate the visual-semantic similarity between the images and their text descriptions. Additionally, the Precision-Recall curves is obtained by varying the hamming radius from 0 to 64 with a step size 1. Figure 2 shows Precision-Recall curves of all methods with 64-bit hash codes on MIRFLICKR-25K datasets. If one method's Precision-Recall is not completely wrapped by another method's P-R Precision-Recall. Usually equilibrium point is used to measure which one is better. The equilibrium point is the value when $P = R$. if this value is large, the performance of the learner is better. In the Fig. 2, the equilibrium point of CDGAN is about 0.65. Thus, the Precision-Recall curves of CDGAN can get a good performance than other methods.

Results of Text-to-Image Generation. Figure 3 shows some examples of text-to-image. There are three groups data in Fig. 3, at first, the original text is as input, and then the generated images is behind the text. Although the quality of the generated images is not the same as the original images, they still contain the shapes, colors, and backgrounds of the object. These experiment results show that our model can generate certainly good images from the text in the same data pair. Thus, our model can preserves the complex underlying image-text relations.

5   Conclusions

In this paper, we proposed a novel unsupervised coupled dual generative adversarial hashing network in cross-modal retrieval for large-scale datasets. The uniqueness of our method is that mixed hash codes can be learned in an unified framework without using any label information. Moreover, in a training procedure hash codes learn alternately, and achieve optimal performance at the same time. Experiments on two widely-used datasets show that our proposed model can significantly outperform other baselines and can achieve the state-of-the-art performance in real applications.

Acknowledgments. This work was supported by the Strategic Priority Research Program of the Chinese Academy of Sciences (XDC02050200).

References

1. Chao, L., Cheng, D., Ning, L., Wei, L., Xinbo, G., Dacheng, T.: Self-supervised adversarial hashing networks for cross-modal retrieval. In: Proceedings of the IEEE Conference on Computer Vision and Pattern Recognition (CVPR), June 2018
2. ChunHung, L., Lee, C.K.: Minimum cross entropy thresholding. Pattern Recognit. **26**(4), 617–625 (1993)
3. Hardoon, D.R., Szedmak, S., Shawe-Taylor, J.: Canonical correlation analysis: an overview with application to learning methods. Neural Comput. **16**(12), 2639–2664 (2004)

4. Di, W., Xinbo, G., Xiumei, W., Lihuo, H.: Semantic topic multimodal hashing for cross-media retrieval. In: Proceedings of the Twenty-Fourth International Joint Conference on Artificial Intelligence, Argentina, pp. 3890–3896 (2015)
5. Guiguang, D., Yuchen, G., Jile, Z.: Collective matrix factorization hashing for multimodal data. In: IEEE Conference on Computer Vision and Pattern Recognition, USA, pp. 2083–2090 (2014)
6. Hong, L., Rongrong, J., Yongjian, W., Feiyue, H., Baochang, Z.: Cross-modality binary code learning via fusion similarity hashing. In: IEEE Conference on Computer Vision and Pattern Recognition, USA, pp. 6345–6353 (2017)
7. Jile, Z., Guiguang, D., Yuchen, G.: Latent semantic sparse hashing for cross-modal similarity search. In: The 37th International ACM SIGIR Conference on Research and Development in Information Retrieval, Australia, pp. 415–424 (2014)
8. Kyunghyun, C., et al.: Learning phrase representations using RNN encoder-decoder for statistical machine translation. In: Proceedings of the 2014 Conference on Empirical Methods in Natural Language Processing, pp. 1724–1734 (2014)
9. Li, C., Deng, C., Wang, L., Xie, D., Xianglong, L.: Coupled cyclegan: unsupervised hashing network for cross-modal retrieval. In: The Thirty-Third AAAI Conference on Artificial Intelligence, USA, pp. 176–183 (2019)
10. Huiskes, M.J., Lew, M.S.: The MIR flickr retrieval evaluation. In: Proceedings of the 1st ACM SIGMM International Conference on Multimedia Information Retrieval, Canada, pp. 39–43 (2008)
11. Bronstein, M.M., Bronstein, A.M., Michel, F., Paragios, N.: Data fusion through cross-modality metric learning using similarity-sensitive hashing. In: The Twenty-Third IEEE Conference on Computer Vision and Pattern Recognition, USA, pp. 3594–3601 (2010)
12. Peng, H., Liangli, Z., Dezhong, P., Pei, L.: Scalable deep multimodal learning for cross-modal retrieval. In: Proceedings of the 42nd International ACM SIGIR Conference on Research and Development in Information Retrieval, France, USA, pp. 635–644 (2019)
13. Qing-Yuan, J., Wu-Jun, L.: Deep cross-modal hashing. In: IEEE Conference on Computer Vision and Pattern Recognition, CVPR, USA, pp. 3270–3278 (2017)
14. Shaishav, K., Raghavendra, U.: Learning hash functions for cross-view similarity search. In: Proceedings of the 22nd International Joint Conference on Artificial Intelligence, Spain, pp. 1360–1365 (2011)
15. Shupeng, S., Zhisheng, Z., Chao, Z.: Deep joint-semantics reconstructing hashing for large-scale unsupervised cross-modal retrieval. In: International Conference on Computer Vision, Korea (South), pp. 3027–3035 (2019)
16. Tao, X., et al.: AttnGAN: fine-grained text to image generation with attentional generative adversarial networks. In: IEEE Conference on Computer Vision and Pattern Recognition, USA, pp. 1316–1324 (2018)
17. Tingting, Q., Jing, Z., Duanqing, X., Dacheng, T.: MirrorGAN: learning text-to-image generation by redescription. In: IEEE Conference on Computer Vision and Pattern Recognition, USA, pp. 1505–1514 (2019)
18. Tingting, Q., Weijing, Z., Miao, Z., Zixuan, M., Duanqing, X.: Ancient painting to natural image: a new solution for painting processing. In: IEEE Winter Conference on Applications of Computer Vision, USA, pp. 521–530 (2019)
19. Lin, T.-Y., et al.: Microsoft COCO: common objects in context. In: Fleet, D., Pajdla, T., Schiele, B., Tuytelaars, T. (eds.) ECCV 2014. LNCS, vol. 8693, pp. 740–755. Springer, Cham (2014). https://doi.org/10.1007/978-3-319-10602-1_48

20. Venice Erin, L., Jiwen, L., Yap-Peng, T., Jie, Z.: Cross-modal deep variational hashing. In: IEEE International Conference on Computer Vision, pp. 4097–4105. IEEE Computer Society, Italy (2017)
21. Zhang, X., Lai, H., Feng, J.: Attention-aware deep adversarial hashing for cross-modal retrieval. In: Ferrari, V., Hebert, M., Sminchisescu, C., Weiss, Y. (eds.) ECCV 2018. LNCS, vol. 11219, pp. 614–629. Springer, Cham (2018). https://doi.org/10.1007/978-3-030-01267-0_36
22. Yiling, W., Shuhui, W., Qingming, H.: Online asymmetric similarity learning for cross-modal retrieval. In: Proceedings of the IEEE Conference on Computer Vision and Pattern Recognition (CVPR), July 2017
23. Cao, Y., Liu, B., Long, M., Wang, J.: Cross-modal hamming hashing. In: Ferrari, V., Hebert, M., Sminchisescu, C., Weiss, Y. (eds.) ECCV 2018. LNCS, vol. 11205, pp. 207–223. Springer, Cham (2018). https://doi.org/10.1007/978-3-030-01246-5_13
24. Cao, Y., Long, M., Wang, J., Yang, Q., Yu, P.S.: Deep visual-semantic hashing for cross-modal retrieval. In: Proceedings of the 22nd ACM SIGKDD International Conference on Knowledge Discovery and Data Mining, USA, pp. 1445–1454 (2016)
25. Yuming, S., Li, L., Ling, S., Jingkuan, S.: Deep binaries: encoding semantic-rich cues for efficient textual-visual cross retrieval. In: Proceedings of the IEEE International Conference on Computer Vision, October 2017
26. Yuxin, P., Jinwei, Q., Xin, H., Yuxin, Y.: CCL: cross-modal correlation learning with multigrained fusion by hierarchical network. IEEE Trans. Multimed. 20(2), 405–420 (2018)
27. Zhang, J., Peng, Y., Yuan, M.: Unsupervised generative adversarial cross-modal hashing. In: Proceedings of the Thirty-Second AAAI Conference on Artificial Intelligence, USA, pp. 539–546 (2018)
28. Zihao, W., et al.: CAMP: cross-modal adaptive message passing for text-image retrieval. In: International Conference on Computer Vision, Korea (South), pp. 5763–5772 (2019)

GSimRank: A General Similarity Measure on Heterogeneous Information Network

Chuanyan Zhang[1](✉) ⓘ, Xiaoguang Hong[1], and Zhaohui Peng[2]

[1] Shandong University, Jinan 250101, China
chuanyan_zhang@sina.cn, hxg@sdu.edu.cn
[2] Shandong University, Qingdao 266237, China
pzh@sdu.edu.cn

Abstract. Measuring similarity of objects in information network is a primitive problem and has attracted many studies for widely applications, such as recommendation and information retrieval. With the advent of large-scale heterogeneous information network that consist of multi-type relationships, it is important to research similarity measure in such networks. However, most existing similarity measures are defined for homogeneous network and cannot be directly applied to HINs since different semantic meanings behind edges should be considered. This paper proposes GSimRank that is the extended form of the famous SimRank to compute similarity on HINs. Rather than summing all meeting paths for two nodes in SimRank, GSimRank selects linked nodes of the same semantic category as the next step in the pairwise random walk, which ensure the two meeting paths share the same semantic. Further, in order to weight the semantic edges, we propose a domain-independent edge weight evaluation method based on entropy theory. Finally, we proof that GSimRank is still based on the expected meeting distance model and provide experiments on two real world datasets showing the performance of GSimRank.

Keywords: Similarity measure · Heterogeneous information network · Semantic relation · Entropy

1 Introduction

Heterogeneous information networks (HINs), the logical graphs involving multiple typed objects and multiple typed links, have been used to represent the underlaying data in many applications, such as the bibliographic networks, social networks and knowledge network encoded in Wikipedia. In recent years, HIN analysis has attracted a lot of attention since its superior ability of complicate data model. Unlike traditional homogeneous information networks which only carry inter-node *structural* information, HINs further encompass *semantic* information that explain the nodes and their interactions. Such semantic information present new opportunities to many data-driven problems. In particular, we are interested in the similarity measure between objects in HINs. Typically, the objects can be organized into a graph $G = (V, E)$, where the nodes V model the

© Springer Nature Switzerland AG 2020
X. Wang et al. (Eds.): APWeb-WAIM 2020, LNCS 12317, pp. 588–602, 2020.
https://doi.org/10.1007/978-3-030-60259-8_43

objects and the edges E model their interactions. Given a node $u \in V$, how do we measure the similarity of other nodes to u?

Similarity measure plays a fundamental role in network analysis. For example, similarity measure provides object distances in HINs for classification and clustering and it is also helpful to identify similarity objects in recommender systems and information retrieval systems. Similarity computation has been extensively studied for traditional categorical and numerical data types in relational data. Generally, these researches fall into one of the following 2 categories: (1) content-based similarity measures, treating each object as a bag of attributes or as a vector of feature weights, likely Similarity Join [2]; (2) link-based similarity measures, focusing on the linkages between objects, such as personalized PageRank [4], SCAN [5] and SimRank [8]. Based on the evaluation of [10], link-based similarity measures produce better correlation with human judgments compared with content-based measures. For most studies leveraging link information in networks, they are focused on homogeneous networks or bipartite networks, disregarding the subtlety of difference types among nodes and edges which carry different semantic meanings. If we adopt these link-based similarity measures to HINs, it does not make sense to mix them without distinguishing their semantics. Specifically, with various types of interconnected objects, different *semantic edges of similarity* arise from different underlying reasons. As shown in Fig. 1, for the same object (e.g., paper p_1), there could be multiple classes of similarity with different result objects (e.g., paper p_2 for the same mentioned term "*HIN*", and paper p_4 for the same author a_3).

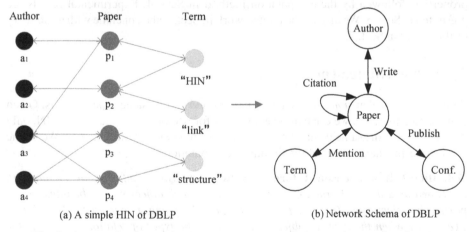

(a) A simple HIN of DBLP   (b) Network Schema of DBLP

Fig. 1. A network schema of DBLP and a simple HIN about author, conf. and paper.

To distinguish the different semantics behind edges of HINs, Sun Y. et al. defines meta paths on network schema and proposes PathSim to measure the similarity by symmetric path instances [11]. Although PathSim could achieve peer similarity, it does not count the asymmetric valuable paths. That is to say, PathSim is a kind of local similarity measure. Besides, even meta path can distinguish the different semantics, PathSim does not weight their contributions. When PathSim is computed on HINs, meta path should be designed and selected by experts firstly. These limitations also exist in other meta path-based distance measures, such as PCRW [12] and HeteSim [13]. Recently, Yuan F. et al. propose a family of Metagraph-based similarity (MGS) that utilize a learning-to-rank technique to automatically learns the right parameters for desired semantic similarity measure [1]. However, its performance is limited by the training datasets.

In this paper, we study the similarity problem between same typed objects on HINs. To produce a global and semantic-aware similarity measure, we propose *GSimRank*, a general form of the famous *SimRank* on HINs. GSimRank ensures that similar objects are more likely to be related to some other *similar objects of the same type*. Concretely, GSimRank is still based on the pairwise random walk model which promises a global score. To distinguish different semantic edges on the meeting paths, we constrain the random walk under the same semantic edge selection. Suppose (u, v) is a node pair in pairwise random walk, then (a, b) is the next step node pair if and only if same-typed a, b link to u, v respectively. Further, we propose a domain-independent unsupervised weighting method based on *entropy theory* to weight the contributions of different semantic edges of G. The intuition is that given a specific semantic relation, the edge distribution determines its capacity of object property representation. If a semantic relation has higher capacity, i.e., its edge instance could be more valuable to identify the linked objects, it is more important for similarity computation. Extensive experimental studies on synthetic and real datasets demonstrates the effectiveness of GSimRank on HINs.

The rest of the paper is organized as follows. Section 2 defines the problem of similarity computation on HINs. Section 3 describes our proposed GSimRank and its properties, followed by the computation method in Sect. 4. Experimental results are presented in Sect. 5. We discuss the related work in Sect. 6 and conclude with a summary of this paper in Sect. 7.

2   Problem Statement

First, we declare that *similarity* is a measure defined on two same-typed objects. Given a link-based measure, we can compute a value s for two objects u and v on a HIN, only if u and v are of the same type; otherwise, u and v are *relevant* with a score s. We define some concepts that are crucial for similarity computation.

Definition 1. Heterogeneous Information Network. *An   information   network is defined as a directed graph $G = (V, E)$ where each object $v \in V$ belongs to one particular object type $\phi(v) \in A$, and each link $e \in E$ belongs to one particular relation $\varphi(e) \in E$. When the types of objects $|A| > 1$ or the types of relations $|E| > 1$, the network is called **heterogeneous information network**; otherwise, it's **homogeneous information network**.*

To study the semantic relationships of HINs, network schema is an efficient technique as shown in Fig. 1 and the definition is as follow.

Definition 2. Network Schema. *A meta template for G with the object mapping $\phi :$ $V \rightarrow A$ and edge mapping $\varphi : E \rightarrow R$, is a directed graph defined over object types A and semantic relations R, denoted as $T_G = (A, R)$. A sematic edge of R is defined as a tuple $R(X, Y)$ where X and Y are node type, and $X, Y \in A$.*

Definition 3. Meta Path. *Meta path is a type of path defined on the network schema* $T_G = (A, R)$ *of* G, *denoted as* $T = (A_1 \ldots A_{l+1})$, *describing a composite relation* $R = R_1 \circ R_2 \circ \ldots \circ R_l$ *between object type* A_1 *and* A_{l+1} *where* $\circ$ *denotes the composition operator on the semantic edges, and for* $1 \leq i \leq l$, $R(A_i, A_{i+1})$.

We use t to denote a path of G. Suppose $t = (v_1 \ldots v_l)$ and $T = (A_1 \ldots A_l)$. If $\phi(v_i) = A_i$ for $1 \leq i \leq l$, we say t is a **path instance** of T, $t \in T$. GSimRank is a general form of SimRank, in which G^2 and *node pair* are two important concepts. In this paper, we give the extended definitions on HINs. Given a HIN G, node pair are two ordered nodes of the same type, e.g., if $(u, v) \in A_i$, (u, v) is a node pair. G^2 is a HIN based on G, where each node represents an ordered node pair of G, and (a, b) points to (c, d) in G^2 if a points to c and b points to d in G.

Due to the various semantic edges (a.k.a. semantic classes) on HINs, it is difficult to distinguish and mix them in a unified link-based distance measure. First, we give an **axiom**: *if two same-typed nodes u and v of G both link to a node x, we can say u and v are similar since $e(u, x)$ and $e(v, x)$ belong to a same semantic relation*. For example, in Fig. 1, p_1 and p_2 are similar for their common mentioned term "*HIN*". Then, we can extend this axiom to measure the similarity through longer paths. As shown in Fig. 1, the author a_1 and a_2 have no common neighbor. But we know that a_1 writes p_1; a_2 writes p_2; p_1 and p_2 are similar. Hence, we can infer that a_1 and a_2 have a certain similarity score since they *write* the similar papers. In conclusion, we can get an **inference**: *given a node pair (u, v) of G, we can compute the similarity score, denoted as $s(u, v)$, through counting the similarity scores of its neighbor node pairs in G^2*. Finally, the problem statement of this paper is defined as follow.

Definition 4. Semantic-aware Similarity. *Given any node pair (u, v) of a HIN G, the semantic-aware similarity of (u, v), denoted as $s(u, v)$, is a weighted sum of its neighbor node pairs according to their semantic relations between them so that each rise of $s(u, v)$ stems from same semantic aspects.*

3 GSimRank

3.1 Motivation

To measure similarity of objects based on their relationships, SimRank first formally introduced the famous intuition that "two objects are similar if they are related to similar objects." SimRank has successfully applied this idea on homogeneous information networks and bipartite networks. Detailly, SimRank score of node pair (u, v), denoted as $s'(u, v)$, specifies how soon two random surfers are expected to meet at same node. If $u = v$, $s'(u, v) = 1$, otherwise,

$$s'(u, v) = \frac{c}{|\Gamma(u)||\Gamma(v)|} \sum_{i=1}^{|\Gamma(u)|} \sum_{j=1}^{|\Gamma(v)|} s'(\Gamma_i(v), \Gamma_j(v)) \tag{1}$$

where c is the decay factor ($0 < c < 1$), $\Gamma(*)$ is the neighbor set of node $*$ (in *or* out, but not in *and* out), and $|\Gamma(*)|$ is the set size. SimRank is based on "random surfer-pairs model" on graph, and its equivalent form is

$$s'(u, v) = \sum_{t:(u,v) \rightsquigarrow (x,x)} P[t]c^{l(t)} \qquad (2)$$

Specially, Eq. (2) is defined on G^2, and the summation is taken over all tours t of G^2, which is composed by 2 *same-length* paths of G: $t(u \ldots x)$ and $t(v \ldots x)$. $P[t]$ is the traveling probability on graph and $l(t)$ is the length of a tour t. These two equations make SimRank be a state-of-art measure for similarity. However, SimRank cannot be directly applied on HINs without the ability of semantic distinguishing. Taking Fig. 1 as an example, if we compute $s'(p_1, p_3)$ based on Eq. (1), a meeting path may be t : $(p_1, p_3) \rightarrow (a_3, a_3)$ which expresses that 2 papers p_1 and p_3 are both written by a same author a_3 so that it's reasonable for similarity computation. At the same time, there are some unreasonable meeting paths arising the final similarity score, likely t : $(p_1, p_3) \rightarrow (a_3, "structure") \rightarrow (p_4, p_4)$ which can be considered as the combination of two random walking paths: $t(p_1 a_3 p_4)$ and $t(p_3 "structure" p_4)$. The sematic logic of t for $s'(p_1, p_3)$ can be translated as follows: (1) p_1 and p_4 are similar since their common author a_3; (2) p_3 and p_4 are similar for the same term "*structure*"; (3) p_1 and p_3 have a certain similarity. Obviously, this logic is not reasonable without semantic consistency, and this tour t should not be counted into $s'(p_1, p_3)$.

3.2 Basic GSimRank Equation

To distinguish the semantics of HINs for similarity computation, we design GSimRank based on the intuition that "two same-typed objects are similar if they are related to similar same-typed objects." Effectively, it inherits the iterative definition form of SimRank and rises the score through same semantic relation every time. Given a HIN $G = (V, E)$ with the network schema $T_G = (A, R)$, and two object $u, v \in A_i$, the GSimRank score between them are denoted as $s(u, v)$. If $u = v$, $s(u, v) = 1$; otherwise,

$$s(u, v) = \frac{c}{|\Gamma(u)||\Gamma(v)|} \sum_{k=1}^{|A(u,p)|} \sum_{i=1}^{|A_k(u)|} \sum_{j=1}^{|A_k(v)|} s\big(A_{k,i}(u), A_{k,j}(v)\big) \qquad (3)$$

where $A(u, v)$ is the object type set about the in/out-neighbors of u and v, $A_k(*)$ is the in/out-neighbors of the given node $*$ of the type A_k and $A_{k,i}(*)$ is the ith element of $A_k(*)$.

In detail, the similarity score $s(u, v)$ depends on the similarities of their neighbor nodes. Comparing with the classic SimRank of Eq. (1) that sums the similarities of all possible neighbor pairs, i.e., $s'\big(\Gamma_i(u), \Gamma_j(v)\big)$, GSimRank only exploits neighbor node pairs, i.e., $s\big(A_{k,i}(u), A_{k,j}(v)\big)$. It ensures the semantic consistency for similarity computation. Practically, only the similarities between linked objects of same type should be considered, which make the semantic of two links consistent. In the perspective of object and attribute, it is more easily to explain. Suppose the neighbors of a given object u in G are its attribute values. That's to say if $\exists A_{k,i}(u) \in \Gamma(u), A_{k,i}(u)$, is the value of u in attribute A_k. Thus, the score $s(u, v)$ in Eq. (3) is computed based on the values of their corresponding attributes. For example, if we compute $s(p_1, p_2)$ in Fig. 1, $\Gamma(p_1) = \{a_1, a_3, "HIN"\}$ and $\Gamma(p_2) = \{a_2, "HIN", "link"\}$. GSimRank only sums the similarities of same attributes: $s("HIN", "HIN")$, $s(a_1, a_2)$, $s(a_3, a_2)$ and $s("HIN", "link")$. While SimRank counts all the similarities, likely $s'(a_1, "link")$, $s'(a_3, "HIN")$ and so on. These different attribute similarities make the semantic relations confused on HINs.

3.3 Weighting Semantic Relations

Different semantic relations have different contribution for the similarity of object on HINs. Practically, many studies have confirmed this opinion [9]. However, few works straightforward study this problem for similarity. In this paper, we propose a sematic relation weighting approach based on entropy theory.

Definition 5. Semantic Relations. *Given a network schema* $T_G = (A, R)$, *semantic relation describes the symmetric relationship between two object types* $A_i, A_j \subseteq A$, *denoted as* $SR(A_i, A_j, \kappa)$, *with a semantic* κ, *and* $SR(A_i, A_j, \kappa) = SR(A_j, A_i, \kappa)$.

For example, $SR(paper, term, mention)$ is a semantic relation that describes the *mention* relationship between *paper* and *term* in Fig. 1. Since the semantic between two object types is usually unique in T_G, we use $SR(paper, term)$ for short. Specially, distinct from the *ordered* semantic edge, semantic relation is symmetric. Based on Definition 5, **semantic weighting problem** in this paper is to weight the contribution w_k for each semantic relation $SR_k(*, *)$ so that if the κ of SR_k is more important for the link-based similarity measure, w_k should be higher.

We propose an entropy-based approach to the semantic weight problem for similarity. Generally, given a semantic relation $SR(A_i, A_j)$, $e(u, v)$ is an edge instance of $R(A_i, A_j)$ if $e(u, v) \in E, u \in A_i, v \in A_j$. The intuition of our method is that "the edge distribution of a semantic relation SR is more chaotic, the edge instance of SR represent more properties of its linked objects." For example, in Fig. 1, the similarities between papers can be computed via $R(paper, paper)$ or $R(paper, conf.)$. Generally, the edge distribution of semantic relation "*citation*" is more disorder than "*publish*" since the paper number is far more than conf. and a paper citing another paper is more stochastic than published in a conference. Thus, $SR(paper, paper)$ is more credible than $SR(paper, conf.)$ for similarity search. In special case, if all papers of a DBLP HIN are published in one conf., the semantic relation $SR(paper, conf.)$ is useless for similarity computation since we cannot distinguish papers according to their *conf.* attribute. We can use entropy to measure the disorder or chaos of a given semantic relation [14]. To computer the entropy of $SR(A_i, A_j)$, we first study the corresponding semantic edge $R(A_i, A_j)$, and propose the following assumption:

Assumption 1. *Given a semantic edge* $R(A_i, A_j)$, *selecting one node from* A_i *and* A_j *respectively to create an edge instance of* R *is a random variable, denoted as* R_{ij}.

Based on the assumption, creating an edge $e(v_{ix}, v_{jy})$ of G, $v_{ix} \in A_i, v_{jy} \in A_j$, is a random event as shown in Fig. 2. Detailly, the random variable R_{ij} depends on two random variables A_i and A_j, and selecting v_{ix} and v_{jy} are two random events for A_i and A_j

respectively. Therefore, the probability of edge $e(v_{ix}, v_{jy})$, denoted as p_{xy}, is computed by

$$p_{xy} = p(A_i = v_{ix})p(A_j = v_{jy}) = \frac{d_j(v_{ix})}{\sum_m d_j(v_{im})} \frac{d_i(v_{jy})}{\sum_n d_i(v_{jn})} \quad (4)$$

where $d_i(*)$ is the degree of node $*$ pointing to nodes of A_i.

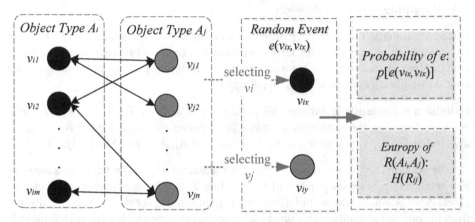

Creating edges of $R(A_i, A_j)$ as a Random Variable R_{ij}

Fig. 2. An illustration of entropy computation for a given semantic edge R.

Further, the entropy of $R(A_i, A_j)$, denoted as $H(R_{ij})$, is

$$H(R_{ij}) = -\sum_{x=1}^{|A_i|} \sum_{y=1}^{|A_j|} p_{xy} \log p_{xy} \quad (5)$$

Obviously, we have $H(R_{ij}) = H(R_{ji})$ base on Eq. (5). Finally, the weight of $SR(A_i, A_j)$, denoted as w_{ij}, is computed by

$$w_{ij} = \frac{2H(R_{ij})}{\sum_{A_k \in A} \sum_{A_l \in A} H(R_{kl})} \quad (6)$$

All the edge instances of $SR(A_i, A_j)$ have the same weight w_{ij}. considering the weights of semantic relations for similarity, Eq. (3) of GSimRank can be rewritten as

$$s(u, v) = \frac{c}{|\Gamma(u)||\Gamma(v)|} \sum_{k=1}^{|A(u,p)|} w_{xk} \left\{ \sum_{i=1}^{|A_t(v)|} \sum_{j=1}^{|A_k(v)|} s(A_{k,i}(u), A_{kj}(v)) \right\} \quad (7)$$

where $\phi(u) = A_x$, and w_{xk} is the weight of $SR(A_x, A_k)$. Specially, in homogeneous information network or bipartite network, Eq. (7) is equivalent to Eq. (1) of SimRank since $w_{xk} \equiv 1$ and $|A(u, v)| = 1$.

3.4 Properties of GSimRank

Some good properties of GSimRank are shown in Theorem 1.

Theorem 1. *Basic Properties of GSimRank:*

1. *Symmetric:* $s(u, v) = s(v, u)$;
2. *Self-maximum:* $s(u, v) \in [0, 1]$. *If* $u = v$, $s(u, v) = 1$.

Proof. Since $\phi(u) = \phi(v)$, given A_k, w_{xk} is same for both $s(u, v)$ and $s(v, u)$. If $A_{k,i}(u) = A_{k,j}(v)$, it's symmetric for $s\big(A_{k,i}(u), A_{k,j}(v)\big) = s\big(A_{k,j}(v), A_{k,i}(u)\big) = 1$; otherwise, Eq. (7) of GSimRank will continue the counting until a node pair (a, b) makes $A_{k,i}(a) = A_{k,j}(b)$ in $(k)^{th}$ iteration and we can infer that the similarity score s is symmetric in $(k - 1)^{th}$ iteration. Therefore, $s(u, v) = s(v, u)$ based on back forward propagation. $\square$

In general, given u and v of a HINs G, let $s'(u, v)$ be the result of SimRank via Eq. (1). Since the constraint of node pairs in Eq. (3), and the weight w in Eq. (7) are all less than 1, we can get $s(u,v) \leqslant s'(u,v)$. Because $s'(u,v) \in [0, 1]$, $s(u,v) \leqslant 1$ and $s(u, u) = 1$. In each iteration of Eq. (7), $s\big(A_{k,j}(v), A_{k,i}(u)\big)$ are nonnegative. Thus, $s(u,v) \geqslant 0$. $\square$

SimRank has an important intuitive model based on "random surfers", i.e., random surfer-pairs model. GSimRank, an extended form of SimRank on HINs, are still based on "random surfers". We will show that GSimRank score $s(u, v)$ measures how soon two random surfer paths are expected as the same node if they started at the same-typed nodes and randomly walked the graph subject to *a same meta path*. Distinct from PathSim, GSimRank counts all possible path instances, i.e., both symmetric and asymmetric meta paths could be utilized for similarity computation.

First, we extend the concept of expected meeting distance (EMD) in classical Sim-Rank to *constrained expected meeting distance* (CEMD). Given any strong connected HIN G, let u, v be any two nodes in G. The EMD $m'(u, v)$ is formally defined as

$$m'(u, v) = \sum_{t:(u,v) \rightsquigarrow (x,x)} P[t]l(t) \tag{8}$$

Due to the "infinite EMD" problem of tours, SimRank designs the *expected-f meeting distance*, which computes the expected $f(l(t))$, where $f(z) = c^z$, instead of computing expected length $l(t)$ in Eq. (8). And the formula of *expected-f meeting distance* is shown in Eq. (2). Based on Eq. (2), we define $m(u, v)$, the similarity between u and v of same type in G based on CEMD, as

$$m(u, v) = \sum_{\substack{T:A_i \rightsquigarrow A_j \\ A \subseteq T_G}} \sum_{\substack{t:(u,v) \rightsquigarrow (x,x) \\ t \in T}} P[t]c^{l(t)} \tag{9}$$

where T is the meta path of T_G, $\phi(u) = A_i$, and t is a path instance of T. We will show that $m(u, v)$ exactly models our original definition of GSimRank by showing that $m(u, v)$ satisfies the GSimRank Eq. (3).

First, if $u = v$, $m(u, v) = s(u, v) = 1$ since $l(t) = 0$. If there is no path t from (u, v) to any singleton nodes, in which case $m(u, v) = 0$, it's easy to see that $s(u, v) = 0$

from Eq. (3) since no similarity would flow to (u, v). Otherwise, consider the tours t from (u, v) to a singleton node x in which the first step is to their out-neighbors $O_k((u, v))$ of A_k, i.e., $t_a : u \to A_{k,i}(u) \rightsquigarrow x$ and $t_b : v \to A_{k,j}(v) \rightsquigarrow x$. Here we use two paths in step on G to instead t on G^2, formally written as $t = t_a \| t_b$. Then, the tours from $(A_{k,i}(u), A_{k,j}(v))$ to x is denoted as t'. For each t we can derive a corresponding t' by splitting the edges $e((u, v), (A_{k,i}(u), A_{k,j}(v)))$ of G^2 at the beginning. And corresponding to the path instance t and t', we derive meta path T' from T where $T' : A_k \rightsquigarrow A(x)$ by splitting the meta edge $(A(u), A_k)$. We use $A(u, v)$ to denote the bijection that takes each T' from T via A_k. Moreover, the probability of traveling t is

$$p[t] = \frac{1}{|O(u)||O(v)|} p[t']$$ (10)

Now, we can rewrite the sum of Eq. (9) in the first step by splitting meta path T and its corresponding path instance t at the same time:

$$
\begin{aligned}
m(u, v) &= \sum_{\substack{T:A_i \rightsquigarrow A_j \\ A \subseteq T_G}} \sum_{\substack{t = t_a \| t_b \\ t_a, t_b \in T}} P[t] c^{l(t)} \\
&= \sum_{A_k}^{|A(u,v)|} \sum_{\substack{A_{k,i}(u) \\ A_{k,j}(v)}}^{|O_k(u,v)|} \sum_{\substack{T':A_k \rightsquigarrow \phi(x) \\ A \subseteq T_G}} \sum_{\substack{t' = t_a' \| t_b' \\ t_a', t_b' \in T'}} \frac{1}{|O(u)||O(v)|} P[t'] c^{l(t)+1} \\
&= \frac{c}{|O(u)||O(v)|} \sum_{A_k}^{|A(u,v)|} \sum_{\substack{A_{k,i}(u) \\ A_{k,j}(v)}}^{|O_k(u,v)|} \sum_{\substack{T':A_k \rightsquigarrow \phi(x) \\ A \subseteq T_G}} \sum_{\substack{t' = t_a' \| t_b' \\ t_a', t_b' \in T'}} P[t'] c^{l(t)} \\
&= \frac{c}{|O(u)||O(v)|} \sum_{k=1}^{|A(u,v)|} \sum_{i=1}^{|A_k(u)|} \sum_{j=1}^{|A_k(v)|} m(A_{k,i}(u), A_{k,j}(v))
\end{aligned}
$$ (11)

Obviously, out-edges in Eq. (11) can be swapped for in-edges. Therefore, Eq. (11) is identical to Eq. (3) of GSimRank. Since the solution of Eq. (3) is unique (proof in Sect. 5), $s(u, v) = m(u, v)$ for any node pair $(u, v), u, v \in V$. We have the following theorem.

Theorem 2. *The GSimRank score, defined in Eq. (3), between two nodes is their constrained expected meeting distance traveling back-edges, for $f(z) = c^z$.*

In the same way, the weigh parameters w can also be integrated into Eq. (11). Based on Theorem 1, we have the following inferences:

Corollary 1. *The GSimRank score $s(u, v)$, defined in Eq. (7), between two nodes is their constrained expected meeting distance $m(u, v)$, defined in Eq. (9) and weigh parameters w of semantic relations computed by Eqs. (4)–(6).*

Corollary 2. *The GSimRank score between two nodes is semantic aware, i.e., each meeting path that rises the final score is semantic constancy. Formally, for each meeting path $t = t_a \| t_b, t_a(a_1, \ldots, a_m), t_b(b_1, \ldots, b_m)$, we can get that $\phi(a_i) = \phi(b_i)$ and $R(\phi(a_{i-1}), \phi(a_i)) = R(\phi(b_{i-1}), \phi(b_i)), 1 < i \leq m$.*

4 Computing GSimRank

A basic solution to the GSimRank equations can be reached by iteration to a fixed-point. For each node type A_i of G, let n_i be the node number of type A_i. Since the definition of GSimRank that similarity only exists between same-typed nodes, we keep n_i^2 entries $s^k(*, *)$, where $s^k(u, v)$ gives the score between a and b on iteration k, and $u, v \in A_i$. For G, we will have entries $s^k(*, *)$ of length $\sum_{i=1}^{|A|} n_i^2$. We can successively compute $s^{k+1}(*, *)$ based on $s^k(*, *)$. First, we initialize $s^0(*, *)$:

$$s^0(u, v) = \begin{cases} 1 \ (\text{if } u = v) \\ 0 \ (\text{if } u \neq v) \end{cases} \tag{12}$$

To compute $s^{k+1}(u, v)$ based on $s^k(*, *)$, we use the GSimRank Eq. (3) or Eq. (7) to get (taking Eq. (3) for example):

$$s^{k+1}(u, v) = \frac{c}{|I(u)||I(v)|} \sum_{k=1}^{|A(u,v)|} \sum_{i=1}^{|A_k(\omega)|} \sum_{j=1}^{|A_k(0)|} s^k\big(A_{k,i}(u), A_{k,j}(v)\big) \tag{13}$$

for $u \neq v$, and $s^{k+1}(u, v) = 1$ for $u = v$. We update the similarity of (u, v) using the similarity scores of its neighbor node pairs from the previous iteration k.

Theorem 3. *Given a HIN $G = (V, E)$, there exists a unique solution of GSimRank, and $\lim_{k \to \infty} s^k(u, v) = s(u, v)$ for any node pair (u, v) of G.*

Proof. First, we will prove the existence of a solution based on our basic algorithm for GSimRank. Based on the initialization, we get $s^1(u, v) \geqslant s^0(u, v)$. Since there are no non-negative functions or parameters in GSimRank equation, we can infer the fact based on iteration:

$$0 \leqslant s^k(u, v) \leqslant s^{k+1}(u, v) \leqslant 1 \textit{ for any } (u, v).$$

By the Completeness Axiom of calculus, we can get $\lim_{k \to \infty} s^k(u, v) = s(u, v)$, i.e., each sequence $\{s^k(u, v)\}$ converges to a limit $s(u, v)$. If we plug all the limit into Eq. (13), we can get the GSimRank equation form. Therefore, the limits satisfy the GSimRank equation. Now, we have proved the uniqueness.

Suppose $s_1(u, v)$ and $s_2(u, v)$ are two solutions for (u, v), and $s_1(u, v) > s_2(u, v)$. Based on Eq. (7), there must exist: $s_1^{m-1}\big(A_{k,i}(u), A_{k,j}(v)\big) > s_2^{m-1}\big(A_{k,i}(u), A_{k,j}(v)\big)$.

If $m \leqslant n$, based on the iteration of Eq. (7), there must exist (a, b), $a \neq b$, and $s_1^0(a, b) > s_2^k(a, b)$, $k \geqslant 0$. This contradicts the monotonicity fact above.

If $m > n$, we have:

$$s_1^{n-1}\big(A_{k,i}(u), A_{k,j}(v)\big) \neq s_2^{n-1}\big(A_{k,i}(u), A_{k,j}(v)\big) \textit{ or}$$
$$s_1^{n+1}\big(A_{k,i}(u), A_{k,j}(v)\big) > s_2^{n+1}\big(A_{k,i}(u), A_{k,j}(v)\big).$$

Both these two situations derive that $s_1^0(a, b) \neq s_2^0(a, b)$ and $a \neq b$. This also contradicts our initial conditions.

Therefore, the solution of GSimRank is unique and $\lim_{k \to \infty} s^k(u, v) = s(u, v)$. $\square$

Let us analyze the time and space requirements of GSimRank. Let $\bar{n}$ be the average of $|A_i|$ and $|A| = m$, the final space complexity is $O(m\bar{n}^2)$. Let $\bar{d}$ be the average of in-neighbor pairs and K is the number of iterations until convergence. The time required is $O(Km\bar{n}^2\bar{d})$ since in each iteration, all node pairs in Eq. (3) are updated with values from their in-neighbor pairs. Obviously, the space requirement of GSimRank is far less than SimRank, which needs $O(|V|^2)$.

5 Experiments

5.1 Experiment Setting

In this section, we report on some preliminary experiments to show that GSimRank scores do in fact extend SimRank similarity into HINs derived from practical data sets. We ran experiments on two data sets.

DBLP Dataset. The first is a subset of DBLP, which contains 128,651 papers and 31,264 authors from 160 famous conferences and journals about *machine learning*, *database*, *data mining* and *information retrieval* in last 10 years. Then, we extract 4256 terms from paper titles and create a DBLP HIN based on the network schema in Fig. 1 with an added $R(paper, year)$.

IMDB Datasets. The second data set is about movies from IMDb which includes movies, genres, directors, actors, years, gross (integer, in millions), rating, reviewer number (integer, in thousands) and length (integer, in minutes). The Movie HIN is designed based on movie centric network schema (i.e., other type nodes only link to movie node). Detailly, the IMDb network includes 1482 movies, 112 genres, 529 directors and 4795 actors (Table 1).

Table 1. Summary of datasets.

Datasets	#node	#edge	#node type	#semantic relations
DBLP	164,341	963,258	5	4
IMDb	8,547	16,651	9	8

A good evaluation for measuring similarity is difficult to design without extensive standard datasets. Thus, we first create two datasets based on some heuristic rules and adopt NDCG and MAP to evaluate the similarity measures [1]. Although admittedly not definitive or exhaustive, this method does illustrate empirically important aspects of GSimRank. In our experiments, we only focus on the similarities between *papers* in DBLP HIN and *movies* in Movie HIN. We create the similar set for each object u based on *co-reference* rules as follow:

- *Paper similar set*: If paper v has *a* "*coauthor*", "*co-conf.*" or "*co-term*" node with u, we set $v \in S_C(u)$. Further, for each condition, add one point for similarity rank (e.g., if v satisfies all the 3 conditions, it has the top score 3).
- *Movie similar set*: If movie v has *a* "*co-actor*", "*co-director*" or "*co-genre*" node with u, we set $v \in S_C(u)$, and rank them as paper similar set.

5.2 Baselines

We evaluate our proposed method against baseline methods, as follows.

- GSR: The proposed GSimRank measure.
- RWR: Random walk with restart [15], a widely used relevance measure on graphs. We set the restart probability $c = 0.15$.
- SR: The SimRank measure. We run SimRank on HINs only considering the structure information, with decay factor $c = 0.85$.
- GSR-W: GSimRank measure with uniform weights. That is, we do not differentiate the importance of semantic relations, i.e., $w_{xk} = 1$ in Eq. (7).
- PS: The PathSim measure, designed for peer similarity search on HINs based on meta path. We adopt the meta path (*PTPAP*) for DBLP HIN and (*MGMDM*) for Movie HIN respectively (short for first letter).
- HS: The HeteSim relevance measure, is designed for relevance search in HINs based on SimRank. We use the same meta paths as PathSim.
- MGP: The Metagraph based proximity measure. MGP is a supervised learning method for semantic proximity search on HINs. We choose "*mention*" for DBLP; "*direct*" for IMDb. The size of Metagraph is limited in 2 to 5 and 20% are reserved for training as advised.

5.3 Performance and Analysis

Comparison to Baselines. We report the NDCG and MAP of the rankings produced by these similarity measure in Table 2.

Table 2. Performance of baselines

Datasets	Metrics	RWR	SR	PS	HS	MGP	GSR-W	GSR
DBLP	NDCG	0.2418	0.3562	0.6049	0.6275	0.7841	0.7663	**0.8015**
	MAP	0.2864	0.3751	0.5814	0.5649	0.7561	0.7218	**0.7824**
IMDb	NDCG	0.2159	0.3472	0.5994	0.5827	0.7625	0.7124	**0.7926**
	MAP	0.2315	0.3505	0.5418	0.5569	0.7052	0.6703	**0.7686**

The key findings are summarized as follow. (1) GSR performs consistently better than all other algorithms in any case. Detailly, these methods can be divided into 3 levels based on their performances. Without semantic distinguishing capability, RWR and SimRank cannot work well in HINs. Many objects that don't belong to the same class with the query node are returned. PathSim and HeteSim returned the same-typed objects based on specific meta paths and they perform better than RWR and SimRank, and their evaluations are close. The same meta paths designed for them may be an important reason. MGP algorithm performs most closely to our proposed method. (2) GSR performs better than GSR-W, by more than 8%, which demonstrates the various semantic relations of HINs do have different contributions for similarity search and our proposed weighting method is effective. (3) The performances on DBLP are better than on IMDb, especially for PS and HS. Since IMDb has richer semantics than DBLP, limited meta paths cannot fully exploit them. MGP has the same problem due to the given semantic class. Meanwhile, GSR performs stable.

Extensive Studies on Top-k Similarity Search. First, we select the most top-k similar nodes as test datasets. As Fig. 3 shown, $k = \{10, 20, 50\}$. GSR still perform better than other measures. Further, GSR is sensitive to top-k similar objects. When $k = 10$, the score raises by more than 10% than its global value. With k increasing, the performance of GSR drops sharply.

Convergence. In this paper, we define the convergence of GSimRank is that for any given node, the rank of its similar objects does not change, and the error of similarity score is less than 10^{-4}. Generally, GSimRank can converge in 7 iterations as shown in Fig. 4. First, semantic weights do not affect the convergence speed visibly. Second, considering the differences between DBLP and IMDb, data scale and semantic amount

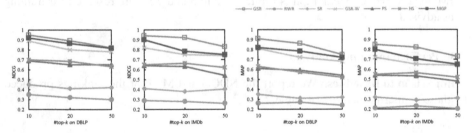

Fig. 3. Top-k similarity search test.

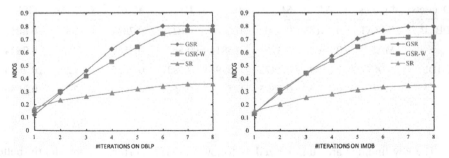

Fig. 4. Convergence speeds of various baselines.

have no influence on convergence speed (i.e., iterations). Another key finding is that the speed in first 4 iterations is much faster than the following iterations.

6   Related Work

This paper focus on link-based similarity measure on information networks. Personalized PageRank [17] computers the probability starting from a source node to a target node in a given network based on random walk with restart. The following works extend it for online queries [15] and the top-k search [18]. However, it is an asymmetrical similarity measure. SimRank [4] computes the similarity of two objects by their neighbors' similarities. Since its briefly intuition and solid mathematical theory, many extended variants of SimRank are proposed [16, 19]. Because of its computational complexity, many following works focus on its fast computation [3], [7]. However, these measures are designed for homogeneous networks or bipartite networks.

PathSim [11], first defining *Network Schema* and *Meta Path* on HINs to distinguish the different semantics behind edges, measures the similarity of same-typed objects based on symmetric path instances of specific meta path. Now meta path-based distances are widely used for HIN analysis [6, 9]. Although PathSim can product peer similarity, it is still a local measure for HINs without considering the asymmetric meta paths. PCRW [12] measures the entity proximity in a labeled directed graph constructed by rich metadata of scientific literature. But PCRW is restricted by its asymmetric property. HeteSim extends SimRank for HINs based on meta path [13]. However, it aims to measure the relevance of different-typed objects, but not the similarity of the same-typed objects. To exploit the semantic relations of HINs, some learning methods are proposed based on meta paths [9]. Recently, Yuan F. et al. propose a family of MGS that utilize a learning-to-rank technique to automatically learns the right parameters for desired semantic similarity measure [1]. However, the performance of supervised methods relies on the quality of training datasets.

7   Conclusion

In this paper, we study the similarity measure problem in HINs and propose GSimRank, which selects linked nodes of the same semantic category as the next step in the pairwise random walk, which promises the semantic consistency of two meeting paths. Further, entropy theory is firstly utilized to weight the semantic edges for similarity computation. Finally, GSimRank is still based on the expected meeting distance model. In the further, we will study the fast computation of GSimRank, and research its applications on graph embedding, context-aware recommendation and other problems of graph data analysis.

Acknowledgement. This research is supported by Shandong Provincial Key Research and Development Program no. 2019JZZY010105, NSF of Shandong, China no. ZR2017MF065.

References

1. Fang, Y., Lin, W., et al.: Metagraph-based learning on heterogeneous graphs. IEEE Trans. Knowl. Data Eng. 1–15 (2019)
2. Xiao, C., Wang, W., Lin, X., et al.: Top-k set similarity joins. In: Proceedings of the 25th International Conference on Data Engineering, pp. 916–927 (2009)
3. Wei, Z., He, X., et al.: PRSim: sublinear time SimRank computation on large power-law graphs. In: Proceedings of the ACM SIGMOD, pp. 1042–1059 (2019)
4. Jeh, G., Widom, J.: Scaling personalized web search. In: Proceedings of the 12th International Conference on World Wide Web, pp. 271–279 (2003)
5. Xu, X., Yuruk, N., Feng, Z., Schweiger, T.A.J.: SCAN: a structural clustering algorithm for networks. In: Proceedings of the 13th ACM SIGKDD, pp. 824–833 (2007)
6. Li, Y., Li, W.: Meta-path augmented response generation. In: The Proceedings of the AAAI Conference on Artificial Intelligence, vol. 33, pp. 9971–9972 (2019)
7. Wang, Y., Chen, L., Che, Y., Luo, Q.: Accelerating pairwise SimRank estimation over static and dynamic graphs. VLDB J. **28**(1), 99–122 (2018). https://doi.org/10.1007/s00778-018-0521-x
8. Jeh, G., Widom, J.: SimRank: a measure of structural-context similarity. In: Proceedings of the Eighth ACM SIGKDD, pp. 538–543 (2002)
9. Fang, Y., Lin, W., Zheng, V.W., Wu, M., Chang, K.C., Li, X.: Semantic proximity search on graphs with metagraph-based learning. In: ICDE, pp. 277–288 (2016)
10. Maguitman, A.G., et al.: Algorithmic computation and approximation of semantic similarity. In: Proceedings of World Wide Web, pp. 431–456 (2006)
11. Sun, Y., Han, J.H., et al.: PathSim: meta path-based top-k similarity search in heterogeneous information networks. Very Large Data Bases **4**(11), 992–1003 (2011)
12. Lao, N., et al.: Relational retrieval using a combination of path-constrained random walks. In: Proceedings of the European Conference on Machine Learning, pp. 53–67 (2010)
13. Shi, C., Kong, X., Huang, Y., Yu, P.S., Wu, B.: HeteSim: a general framework for relevance measure in heterogeneous networks. IEEE Trans. Knowl. Data Eng. **26**(10), 2479–2492 (2014)
14. Zhang, X., Mei, C., Chen, D., Li, J.: Feature selection in mixed data. Pattern Recogn. **56**, 1–15 (2016)
15. Tong, H., Faloutsos, C., Pan, J.Y.: Fast random walk with restart and its applications. In: Proceedings of the Sixth International Conference on Data Mining, pp. 613–622 (2006)
16. Jin, R., Lee, V.E., Hong, H.: Axiomatic ranking of network role similarity. In: Proceedings of the 17th ACM SIGKDD International Conference on Knowledge Discovery and Data Mining, pp. 922–930 (2011)
17. Daniel, F., Balazs, R.: Towards scaling fully personalized PageRank. In: Proceedings of the Algorithms and Models for the Web-Graph: Third International Workshop (2004)
18. Gupta, M., Pathak, A., Chakrabarti, S.: Fast algorithms for top-k personalized PageRank queries. In: Proceedings of the World Wide Web Conference (2008)
19. Cai, Y., Li, P., Liu, H., He, J., Du, X.: S-SimRank: combining content and link information to cluster papers effectively and efficiently. In: Tang, C., Ling, C.X., Zhou, X., Cercone, N.J., Li, X. (eds.) ADMA 2008. LNCS (LNAI), vol. 5139, pp. 317–329. Springer, Heidelberg (2008). https://doi.org/10.1007/978-3-540-88192-6_30

Multi-task Learning for Low-Resource Second Language Acquisition Modeling

Yong Hu[1,2], Heyan Huang[1(✉)], Tian Lan[1], Xiaochi Wei[3], Yuxiang Nie[1], Jiarui Qi[1], Liner Yang[4], and Xian-Ling Mao[1]

[1] School of Computer Science and Technology,
Beijing Institute of Technology, Beijing, China
{huyong,hhy63,maoxl}@bit.edu.cn, lantiangmftby@gmail.com,
jerrrynie@gmail.com, Rita2663269@gmail.com
[2] CETC Big DataResearch Institute Co., Ltd., Guiyang, China
[3] Baidu Inc., Beijing, China
weixiaochi@baidu.com
[4] Beijing Language and Culture University, Beijing, China
lineryang@gmail.com

Abstract. Second language acquisition (SLA) modeling is to predict whether second language learners could correctly answer the questions according to what they have learned, which is a fundamental building block of the personalized learning system. However, as far as we know, almost all existing methods cannot work well in low-resource scenarios due to lacking of training data. Fortunately, there are some latent common patterns among different language-learning tasks, which gives us an opportunity to solve the low-resource SLA modeling problem. Inspired by this idea, we propose a novel SLA modeling method, which learns the latent common patterns among different language-learning datasets by multi-task learning and are further applied to improving the prediction performance in low-resource scenarios. Extensive experiments show that the proposed method performs much better than the state-of-the-art baselines in the low-resource scenario. Meanwhile, it also obtains improvement slightly in the non-low-resource scenario.

Keywords: Second language acquisition modeling · Multi-task learning

1 Introduction

Knowledge tracing (KT) is a task of modeling how much knowledge students have obtained over time so that we can accurately predict how students will perform on future exercises and arrange study plans dynamically according to their real-time situations [1, 7]. Particularly, second language acquisition (SLA) modeling is a kind of KT in the filed of language learning. With the increasing importance of language-learning activity in people's daily life [4], SLA modeling attracts much more attention and we focus on SLA modeling in this paper.

© Springer Nature Switzerland AG 2020
X. Wang et al. (Eds.): APWeb-WAIM 2020, LNCS 12317, pp. 603–611, 2020.
https://doi.org/10.1007/978-3-030-60259-8_44

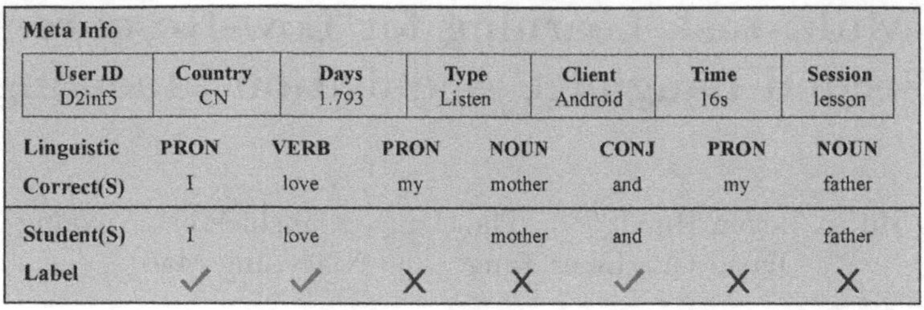

Meta Info						
User ID D2inf5	**Country** CN	**Days** 1.793	**Type** Listen	**Client** Android	**Time** 16s	**Session** lesson
Linguistic	PRON	VERB	PRON	NOUN	CONJ	PRON	NOUN
Correct(S)	I	love	my	mother	and	my	father
Student(S)	I	love		mother	and		father
Label	✓	✓	✗	✗	✓	✗	✗

Fig. 1. Illustration of an example of SLA modeling task

SLA modeling is the learning process of a specific language, thus each SLA modeling task has a corresponding language, e.g., English, Spanish, and French. Meanwhile, each language is composed of many exercises, and an exercise is the smallest data unit. For an exercise, there are three possible types, i.e., *listen*, *Translation*, and *Reverse Tap*, and the answers to the exercises are all sentences regardless of the type of the exercise. In an exercise, the student will be asked to write the answer sentence, and the student-provided sentence and the correct sentence will be compared word by word to evaluate the ability of the student. As an English exercise shown in Fig. 1, there are three words correctly answered, i.e., "*I*", "*love*" and "*and*". Therefore, SLA modeling task is to predict whether students can answer each word correctly according to the exercise information (meta-information, correct sentence with corresponding linguistic information). Thus, it can be simply token into a word-level binary classification task.

In SLA modeling task, low-resource is a common phenomenon which affects the training process significantly. Specifically, this phenomena is mainly caused by two reasons: (1) For some specific language-learning datasets, e.g. Czech, the size of dataset may be very small because we cannot collect enough language-learning exercises; (2) For a user, he/she will encounter cold start scenario when starting to learn a new language. However, almost all existing methods for SLA modeling task train a model separately for each language-learning dataset and thus their performance largely depends on the size of training data. Thus, they can hardly work well in low-resource scenarios.

Intuitively, there are lots of common patterns among different language-learning tasks, such as the learning habits of users and grammar learning skills. If the latent common patterns across these language-learning tasks can be well learned, they can be used to solve the low-resource SLA modeling problem. Inspired by this idea, we propose a novel multi-task learning method for SLA modeling, which is a unified model to process several language-learning datasets simultaneously. Specifically, the proposed model learns shared features across all language-learning datasets jointly, which is the inner nature of the language-learning activity, and can be taken as important prior-knowledge to deal with small language-learning datasets. Moreover, the embedding information of a user is shared, so the learning habits and language talents of the user could be shared

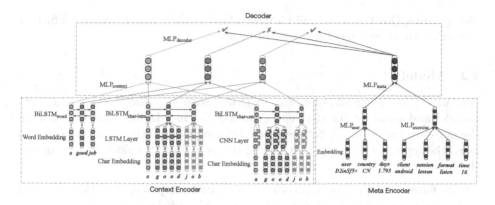

Fig. 2. Illustration of our encoder-decoder structure

in the unified model. Therefore, when a user begins to learn a new language, the unified model can work well even though there is no exercise data for this user.

Extensive experiments show that our method performs much better than the state-of-the-art baselines in low-resource scenarios, and it also obtains improvement slightly in the non-low-resource scenario. Additionally, we have publicly released our codes to facilitate follow-on researchers.[1] (Fig. 2)

2 Methods

2.1 Problem Definition

Suppose there are N second language-learning datasets $\{D^1, D^2, .., D^N\}$, and the kth dataset D^k is composed of M^k exercises $\{e_1^k, e_2^k, ..., e_{M^k}^k\}$, where e_j^k is the jth exercise in the kth dataset.

There are two kinds of information in an exercise e_j^k, i.e., the meta information and the language related context information. The meta information contains two user-related information: (1) user: the unique identifier for each student, e.g., *D2inf5*, (2) country: student's country, e.g., *CN*, and the following five exercise-related information: (1) days: the number of days since the student started learning this language, e.g., 1.793, (2) client: the student's device platform, e.g., *android*, (3) session: the session type, e.g., *lesson*, (4) format (or type): exercise type, e.g., *Listen*, (5) time: the amount of time in seconds that the student answer, e.g., 16 s. This is shared among all language datasets. The information of the context in the exercise e_j^k includes the word sequence, that is $\{w_{e_j^k}^1, w_{e_j^k}^2, ..., w_{e_j^k}^l\}$, and word's linguistic sequences, such as $\{p_{e_j^k}^1, p_{e_j^k}^2, ..., p_{e_j^k}^l\}$, which is the POS-tagging of each word. This is unique to each language-learning dataset. At last, e_j^k has a word level label sequence $\{y_{e_j^k}^1, y_{e_j^k}^2, ..., y_{e_j^k}^l\}$, where $y_{e_j^k} \in \{0, 1\}$. $y_{e_j^k} = 0$ means this word is answered correctly, and $y_{e_j^k} = 1$ means

---

[1] https://github.com/nghuyong/MTL-SLAM.

the opposite. Our task is to build a model based on users' exercises, and further to predict word-level label sequence of future exercises.

2.2 Model

Our model is an encoder-decoder structure with two encoders, i.e., a meta encoder and a context encoder, and a decoder. We use the meta encoder to learn the non-linear relationship between meta information, use the context encoder to learn the representation of a sequence of words and use the decoder to generate the final prediction of each word.

Meta Encoder: The meta encoder is a multi-layer perceptron (MLP) based neural network. It takes the metadata as inputs, and these inputs are first converted into high-dimensional representations by the embedding layers. Then, we separately concatenate the user-related embeddings and the exercise-related embeddings, and send them into MLP_{user} and $MLP_{exercise}$ to get the representation of r^{user} and $r^{exercise}$, respectively. Finally, we concatenate these two features and obtain the final representation of whole meta information r^{meta} by MLP_{meta}. The meta encoder can be formulated as

$$r^{user} = MLP_{user}([x^{user}, x^{countries}, x^{days}])$$
$$t = MLP_{exercise}([x^{format}, x^{session}, x^{client}, x^{time}]) \tag{1}$$
$$r^{meta} = MLP_{meta}([r^{user}, r^{exercise}])$$

where for the sake of simplicity, the variables are omitted from the subscript e_j^k.

Context Encoder: The context encoder consists of three sub-encoders, i.e., a word level context encoder and two character level context encoders. The word level encoder can capture better semantics and longer dependency than the character level encoders [10]. By modeling the character sequence, we can partially avoid the out-of-vocabulary (OOV) problem [5]. Furthermore, we only use the word sequence in the datasets without using provided linguistic information here. The previous work [8] has pointed out that the linguistic information given by the datasets has mistakes. We can learn certain word information and linguistic rules through two character level encoders.

Given the word sequence $\{w_{e_j^k}^1, w_{e_j^k}^2, ..., w_{e_j^k}^l\}$, we first obtain the word representation through $Embedding^{word}$, and then obtain the sentence representation g_t through $BiLSTM_{word}$. Define that each word consists of a sequence of characters $w_t = \{c_1, c_2, ..., c_M\}$. For character-level modeling, we first obtain the character representation through $Embedding^{char}$, and then calculate the word representation through CNN or LSTM, and get the whole sentence representation $\hat{g}_t$ and $\tilde{g}_t$ through BiLSTM. At last, we concatenate g_t, $\hat{g}_t$ and $\tilde{g}_t$, and send the result to a MLP, and get the final output of the context encoder $r_t^{context}$.

The process is formulated as

$$
\begin{aligned}
x_t &= Embedding^{word}(w_t) \qquad m_i = Embedding^{char}(c_i) \\
(g_1, g_2.., g_l) &= BiLSTM_{word}(x_1, x_2, .., x_l) \\
\hat{h}_{w_t} &= LSTM(m_1, m_2, .., m_l) \qquad \tilde{h}_{w_t} = CNN(m_1, m_2, .., m_l) \\
(\hat{g}_1, .., \hat{g}_l) &= BiLSTM_{char-lstm}(\hat{h}_{w_1}, .., \hat{h}_{w_l}) \\
(\tilde{g}_1, ..., \tilde{g}_l) &= BiLSTM_{char-cnn}(\tilde{h}_{w_1}, ..., \tilde{h}_{w_l}) \\
r_t^{context} &= MLP_{context}([g_t, \hat{g}_t, \tilde{g}_t])
\end{aligned}
\tag{2}
$$

Decoder: The decoder takes the output of meta encoder r^{meta} and the output of context encoder $r_t^{context}$ as inputs, the prediction of word w_t is computed with a MLP. It is formulated as

$$
p_t = MLP_{decoder}([r_t^{context}, r^{meta}])
\tag{3}
$$

where the activation function of $MLP_{decoder}$ is sigmoid function.

Table 1. The statistics of Duolingo SLA modeling dataset

	en_es	es_en	fr_en
#Exercises (Train)	824,012	731,896	326,792
#Exercises (Dev)	115,770	96,003	43,610
#Exercises (Test)	114,586	93,145	41,753
#Unique words	2,226	2,915	2,178
#Unique users	2,593	2,643	1,213

2.3 Multi-task Learning

Suppose there are N languages, and each has a corresponding dataset. Since our task is to predict the exercise accuracy of language learners on each language, we can regard these predictions as different tasks. Therefore, there are N tasks. We use cross-entropy loss for each task, which encourages the correct predictions and punishes the incorrect ones. Specifically, we have

$$
Loss_{D_k} = -\frac{1}{N} \sum_{t=1}^{N} (\alpha y_t \cdot log(p_t) + (1 - \alpha)(1 - y_t) \cdot log(1 - p_t))
$$

$$
Loss_{final} = \sum_{k=1}^{N} Loss_{D_k}
\tag{4}
$$

where α is the hyper parameter to balance the negative and positive samples.

In multi-task learning, parameters in meta encoder and decoder are shared, and each task only has its own parameters of the context encoder part. In this way, the common patterns extracted from all language datasets can be utilized simultaneously by the shared meta encoder and decoder.

3   Experients

3.1   Datasets and Settings

We conduct experiments on Duolingo SLA modeling shared datasets, which have three datasets and are collected from English students who can speak Spanish (en_es), Spanish students who can speak English (es_en), and French students who can speak English (fr_en) [9]. Table 1 shows basic statistics of each dataset.

We compare our method with the following state-of-the-art baselines:

- <u>LR</u> Here, we use the official baseline provided by Duolingo [9]. It is a simple logistic regression using all the meta information and context information.
- <u>GBDT</u> Here, we use NYU's method [8], which is the best method among all tree ensemble methods. It uses an ensemble of GBDTs with existing features and manually constructed features based on psychological theories.
- <u>RNN</u> Here, we use singsound's method [6], which is the best method among all sequence modeling methods. It uses an RNN architecture and encoder four features: exercise, context, linguistic and user features.
- <u>ours-MTL</u> It is our encoder-decoder model **without** multi-task learning. Thus, we will separately train a model for each language-learning dataset.

SLA modeling is actually the word level binary classification task, so we use area under the ROC curve (AUC) [3] and F_1 score [2] as evaluation metric.

3.2   Experiment on Small-Scale Datasets

We first verify the advantages of our method in cases where the training data of a language dataset is insufficient. Specifically, we gradually decrease the size of training data from 400K (300K for fr_en) 1K and keep the development set and test set. For our multi-task learning method, we reduce the training data of one language dataset and keep the remaining other two datasets unchanged.

As shown in Fig. 3, our method obtain a huge improvement compared with all baselines when the training data of a language dataset is insufficient. For example, as shown in AUC/en_es in Fig. 3, using 1K training data, our multi-task learning method still could get the AUC score of 0.738, while the AUC score of <u>ours-MTL</u> is only 0.640, and existing <u>RNN</u>, <u>GBDT</u> and <u>LR</u> methods are 0.659, 0.658 and 0.650 respectively. Therefore, the performance of introducing the multi-task learning **increases by nearly ten percent**. Moreover, to achieve the same performance as our multi-task learning 1K training data, the methods without multi-task learning require more 10K training data, which is **ten times more than ours**. Thus, multi-task learning utilizes data from all language-learning datasets simultaneously and effectively alleviate the problem of lacking data in a single language-learning dataset.

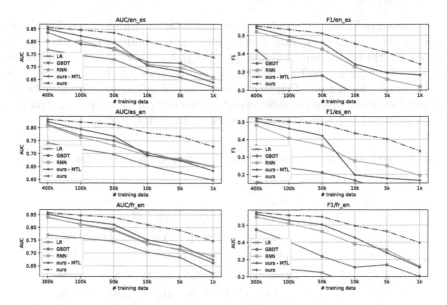

Fig. 3. Comparison of our method and baselines on training data of different sizes

Table 2. The statistics of two users (the following number is the number of words in exercises)

User	Dataset	Train	Dev	Test
RWDt7srk	*es_en*	361	68	19
	fr_en	519	80	51
t6nj6nr/	*es_en*	562	245	274
	fr_en	998	0	0

Table 3. Comparison of our method and baselines in the cold start scenario

Methods	AUC	F_1
LR [9]	0.765	0.083
GBDT [8]	0.751	0.187
RNN [6]	0.771	0.276
Ours-MTL	0.770	0.210
Ours	**0.881**	**0.411**

3.3 Experiment in the Cold Start Scenario

Further, we can directly predict a user's answer on a language without any training exercises of this user on this language at all. This is cold start scenario and also the situation that the language-learning platforms must consider.

Specifically, it can be found that user *RWDt7srk* and *t6nj6nr/* are all English speakers and learn both Spanish and French, so they have exercise data both in *es_en* and *fr_en*. The statistics are shown in Table 2. For baseline methods, we remove the data of these two users on the training set as well as development set of *es_en*, and then train a model. At last, we use the trained model to directly predict the data of these two users on the *es_en* test set. For our multi-task method, the training data of these two users is also removed from the *es_en*, but *fr_en* and *en_es* are unchanged.

As shown in Table 3, if we do not use multi-task learning to predict the new users directly, the performance will be very poor. Compared with the method without multi-task learning, such as ours-MTL, our multi-task learning method increases by **11%** on ACU and **20%** on F_1. Because of the multi-task learning, the user information of these two users has been learned through the *fr_en* dataset. Therefore, although there is no training data of these two users on *es_en*, we can still obtain good performance with multi-task learning.

Table 4. Comparison of our method with existing methods among different languages

Methods	*en_es*		*es_en*		*fr_en*	
	AUC	F_1	AUC	F_1	AUC	F_1
LR [9]	0.774	0.190	0.746	0.175	0.771	0.281
GBDT [8]	0.859	0.468	0.835	0.420	0.854	0.493
RNN [10]	0.861	0.559	0.835	0.524	0.854	0.569
GBDT+RNN [6]	0.861	0.561	0.838	**0.530**	0.857	0.573
Ours-MTL	0.863	**0.564**	0.837	0.527	0.857	0.575
Ours	**0.864**	**0.564**	**0.839**	**0.530**	**0.860**	**0.579**

3.4   Experiment in the Non-low-Resource Scenario

In this section, we will observe the performance of our method in the non-low-resource scenario. Specifically, we use all the data on the three language datasets and this is exactly 2018 public SLA modeling challenge held by Duolingo.[2] Here, we add a new baseline GBDT+RNN. This is SanaLabs's method [6] which combines the prediction of a GBDT and an RNN, and it's also the current best method on the 2018 public SLA modeling challenge.

As shown in Table 4, although the improvement is not very big, our method surpasses all existing methods on all three datasets and refreshes the best scores on all three datasets. Therefore, our method also gains improvement slightly in the non-low-resource scenario.

4   Conclusion

In this paper, we propose a novel multi-task learning method for SLA modeling. As far as we know, this is the first work applying multi-task neural network to SLA modeling. Extensive experiments show that our method performs much better than state-of-the-art baselines in low-resource scenarios, and it also obtains improvement slightly in the non-low-resource scenario. The long version of this work is at https://arxiv.org/abs/1908.09283.

---

[2] http://sharedtask.duolingo.com/2018.html.

Acknowledgments. The work was supported by National Key R&D Plan (No. 2018YFB1005100), NSFC (No. 61772076, 61751201 and 61602197), NSFB (No. Z181100008918002), Major Project of Zhijiang Lab (No. 2019DH0ZX01), Open fund of BDAlGGCNEL, CETC Big Data Research Institute Co., Ltd (No. w-2018018) and Funds of Beijing Advanced Innovation Center for Language Resources (No. TYZ19005).

References

1. Bauman, K., Tuzhilin, A.: Recommending learning materials to students by identifying their knowledge gaps. In: RecSys Posters (2014)
2. Goutte, C., Gaussier, E.: A probabilistic interpretation of precision, recall and F-score, with implication for evaluation. In: Losada, D.E., Fernández-Luna, J.M. (eds.) ECIR 2005. LNCS, vol. 3408, pp. 345–359. Springer, Heidelberg (2005). https://doi.org/10.1007/978-3-540-31865-1_25
3. Hanley, J.A., McNeil, B.J.: The meaning and use of the area under a receiver operating characteristic (ROC) curve. Radiology **143**(1), 29–36 (1982)
4. Larsen-Freeman, D., Long, M.H.: An Introduction to Second Language Acquisition Research. Routledge, Abingdon (2014)
5. Luong, M.T., Sutskever, I., Le, Q.V., Vinyals, O., Zaremba, W.: Addressing the rare word problem in neural machine translation. arXiv preprint arXiv:1410.8206 (2014)
6. Osika, A., Nilsson, S., Sydorchuk, A., Sahin, F., Huss, A.: Second language acquisition modeling: an ensemble approach. arXiv preprint arXiv:1806.04525 (2018)
7. Pelánek, R.: Bayesian knowledge tracing, logistic models, and beyond: an overview of learner modeling techniques. User Model. User-Adapted Interact., 313–350 (2017). https://doi.org/10.1007/s11257-017-9193-2
8. Rich, A., Popp, P.O., Halpern, D., Rothe, A., Gureckis, T.: Modeling second-language learning from a psychological perspective. In: Proceedings of the Thirteenth Workshop on Innovative Use of NLP for Building Educational Applications, pp. 223–230 (2018)
9. Settles, B., Brust, C., Gustafson, E., Hagiwara, M., Madnani, N.: Second language acquisition modeling. In: Proceedings of the Thirteenth Workshop on Innovative Use of NLP for Building Educational Applications, pp. 56–65 (2018)
10. Xu, S., Chen, J., Qin, L.: CLUF: a neural model for second language acquisition modeling. In: Proceedings of the Thirteenth Workshop on Innovative Use of NLP for Building Educational Applications, pp. 374–380 (2018)

Multi-view Clustering via Multiple Auto-Encoder

Guowang Du[1], Lihua Zhou[1(✉)], Yudi Yang[1], Kevin Lü[2], and Lizhen Wang[1]

[1] School of Information, Yunnan University, Kunming 650500, China
{dugking,yudiyang}@mail.ynu.edu.cn, {lhzhou,lzhwang}@ynu.edu.cn
[2] Brunel University, Uxbridge UB8 3PH, UK
Kevin.lu@brunel.ac.uk

Abstract. Multi-view clustering (MVC), which aims to explore the underlying structure of data by leveraging heterogeneous information of different views, has brought along a growth of attention. Multi-view clustering algorithms based on different theories have been proposed and extended in various applications. However, existing of most MVC algorithms are shallow models. They learn structure information of multi-view data by mapping multi-view data to low-dimensional representation space directly, which ignore the Non-linear structure information hidden in each view. This weakens the performance of multi-view clustering to a certain extent. In this paper, we propose a multi-view clustering algorithm based on multiple Auto-Encoder, named MVC-MAE, to cluster multi-view data. MVC-MAE algorithm adopts Auto-Encoder to capture the non-linear structure information of each view in a layer-wise manner. To exploit the consistent and complementary information contained in different views, we also incorporate the local invariance within each view and consistent and complementary information between any two views. Besides, we integrate the representation learning and clustering into a unified step, which jointly optimizes these two steps. Extensive experiments on three real-world datasets demonstrate a superior performance of our algorithm compared with 13 baseline algorithms in terms of two evaluation metrics.

Keywords: Multi-view clustering · Auto-Encoder · Complementary information · Consistent information · Local geometrical information

1 Introduction

Multi-view data is ubiquitous in many real-world applications, where data are collected from different information sources or distinct feature extraction approaches. For instance, an image can be described by color, texture, edges and so on. A piece of news may be simultaneously reported by languages of different countries. Since different views may describe distinct perspectives of data, only using the information of a single view is usually not sufficient for multi-view learning tasks. Therefore, it reasonable and critical to explore the actual clustering structure by synthesizing heterogeneous information from multiple views.

© Springer Nature Switzerland AG 2020
X. Wang et al. (Eds.): APWeb-WAIM 2020, LNCS 12317, pp. 612–626, 2020.
https://doi.org/10.1007/978-3-030-60259-8_45

As there are a lot of unlabeled multi-view data in real life, unsupervised learning, especially multi-view clustering, has attracted widespread interests from researchers. To exploit the heterogeneous information contained in different views, various MVC algorithms have been investigated from different theory aspects, such as graph-based clustering algorithms [1], spectral clustering-based algorithms [2], subspace clustering based algorithms [3], non-negative matrix factorization based algorithm [4, 5], and canonical correlation analysis based algorithms [6, 7]. Although existing multi-view clustering algorithms have achieved reasonable performance, most of them use shallow and linear embedding models to reveal the underlying clustering structure in multi-view data, which are not capable of modeling the non-linear nature of complex data.

To overcome this drawback, one effective way is integrating deep learning into clustering algorithms to utilize the feature learning ability of neural networks. For the single-view clustering tasks, DEC [8] designed a clustering embedding layer by minimizing the KL(Kullback Leibler)-divergence between the predicted cluster label distribution with the predefined one. On the other hand, several works have devoted to developing deep multi-view clustering algorithms, e.g., deep canonical correlation analysis (DCCA) [6] and multi-view deep matrix factorization (DMF-MVC) [9]. DCCA is a deep multi-view clustering algorithm that learns the data of each view and finally fuses information of different views into a common consensus representation, and then conducts some clustering approaches such as k-means on the learned representation. DMF-MVC used a deep Semi-NMF structure to capture the non-linear structure and generate a valid consensus at the last level. However, these two algorithms cannot simultaneously model consistent and complementary information among multiple views. Exploring consistent or complementary information among multiple views is also an important research direction [10]. Some algorithms [4, 5] focus on exploring consistent information with different formulations, while other algorithms [3, 11] concentrate on exploring complementary information. While effectual, most existing algorithms only use one kind of information and cannot simultaneously model consistent and complementary information among multiple views. Recently, [12, 13] have also shown that simultaneously discerning these two kinds of information can achieve better representation learning, but they belong to semi-supervised learning-based methods by exploiting the partial label information of multi-view data. Therefore, learning a low-dimensional representation across multiple views via neural networks is still worth exploring.

In this paper, we propose a Multi-view Clustering algorithm based on Multiple Auto-Encoder, named MVC-MAE (see Fig. 1). Specially, MVC-MAE first employs multiple Auto-Encoders to capture the Non-linear structure information in multi-view data to derive the low-dimensional representation of different views. Then, MVC-MAE designs a novel regularization inspired Cross-Entropy, which guarantees the obtained low-dimensional representation more consistent and complementary between any two views. Also, to protect the local invariance within each view, we also incorporate the local regularization. In addition, some MVC algorithms need to perform a post-processing step (e.g., k-means) after obtaining the low-dimensional representation. However, the learned representation may not be best suited for clustering. Based on DEC, we incorporate the clustering embedding layer into our algorithm, which can achieve mutual benefit for the clustering step and representation learning. We summarize the following contributions of this paper:

- We propose a novel deep multi-view clustering algorithm (MVC-MAE), which can joint capture the hierarchical information, preserve the local geometrical information within each view, model explicitly consistent and complementary information, and obtain the clustering assignments.
- A novel regularization strategy based on the objection function of Cross-Entropy is proposed. This strategy can force the low-dimensional representation of the same sample in different views to be as consistent and complementary as possible.
- Extensive experiments on three datasets show that our proposed algorithm outperforms 13 baseline algorithms in terms of two evaluation metrics.

The rest of this paper is arranged as follows. Section 2 describes some related work. Section 3 introduces a novel MVC algorithm and gives a detailed interpret. Extensive experiments are conducted in Sect. 4. Finally, we give some conclusions in Sect. 5.

2   Related Work

For existing multi-view clustering algorithms, we can group these algorithms into six categories from different theoretical aspects. First, some algorithms adopt NMF techniques to cluster multi-view data, which aims to obtain a consensus indicator factorization among multi-view data. Liu et al. [4] developed an MVC algorithm from the perspective of NMF (MultiNMF), which seeks a latent consensus factor through NMF among various views. To capture the local geometric information, Wang et al. [5] incorporated the graph regularization and MultiNMF. The second category of algorithms is to use a Subspace Clustering algorithm to solve this problem. DiMSC [3] extended subspace clustering into the multi-view domain, and utilize the Hilbert Schmidt Independence Criterion (HSIC) as a diversity term to explore the complementarity of multi-view representations. Thirdly, some spectral clustering algorithms have also been proposed to cluster multi-view data. CoregSC [14] developed a typical multi-view clustering method based on spectral clustering and kernel learning in a co-training style. The fourth category of algorithms is canonical correlation analysis (CCA) for multi-view clustering, which uses CCA to project the multi-view high dimensional data into a low-dimensional subspace. Kamalika et al. [15] proposed an MVC algorithm based on CCA, which projects the data in each view to a lower-dimensional subspace. Fifth, most of the people explore multi-view features with graph-based models. This category of algorithms seeks to find a fusion graph across all views and then uses graph-cut algorithms or other technologies (e.g., spectral clustering) on the fusion graph to produce the clustering results. Nie et al. [16] proposed a novel Auto-weighted Multiple Graph Learning (AMGL) framework to learn a set of weights automatically for all the graphs, and this process does not need any parameter. All of the above five kinds of algorithms belong to the shallow model, but they are not able to fully capture the non-linear and hierarchical structure information within each view.

The last category of algorithms is a multi-view clustering algorithm based on deep learning theory, and these algorithms may intersect with algorithms of the first five categories. Inspired by deep learning, some deep multi-view clustering algorithms have been proposed recently. There are two kinds of algorithms. One is deep multi-view clustering based on matrix factorization, and the other is deep multi-view clustering based on Canonical Correlation Analysis (CCA). DMF-MVC [9] extends deep matrix clustering to multi-view clustering cases. Another algorithm is deep multi-view clustering based on Association analysis, such as DCCA. In DCCA [6], two networks are used to extract the non-linear features of each view, and CCA maximizes the correlation between the extracted features at the top layer.

Our MVC-MAE is a deep multi-view clustering algorithm based on Auto-Encoder, too. It is different from the existing multi-view cluster algorithms in that it not only captures the consistent and complementary information across different views as well as the local geometrical information but also incorporates a clustering embedding layer to train the clustering step together with representation learning.

3 The Proposed Algorithm

In this section, we present MVC-MAE to cluster multi-view data in detail.

3.1 Notations

For multi-view data, let $X = \{X^{(s)} \in \Re^{m \times n^s}\}_{s=1}^{S}$ represent the original data of all views, where S denotes the number of views, n^s is the feature dimension of s-th view, m is the number of samples, $X^{(s)}$ represents the s-th view multi-view data and $X_i^{(s)}$ represents the i-th sample of s-th view. $C_{Cluster}$ represents the number of clusters.

3.2 MVC-MAE Algorithm

The critical point of synthesizing multi-view information to cluster multi-view data is to reasonably fuse within-view information and between-views information to derive more high-quality results. It is obviously that only using the shallow models cannot capture the complex information within each view and considering only one of complementary or consistent information among multiple views is insufficient to cluster multi-view data. MVC-MAE captures the hierarchical information by Auto-Encoder and respects the local geometrical information by constructing an affinity graph within each view, preserves the consistent and complementary information among different views by a regularization strategy between any two views. In addition, we also incorporate the clustering embedding layer into our algorithm, which aims to integrate representation learning and clustering into a step. The architecture of MVC-MAE is shown in Fig. 1.

Non-linear Structure Information. In unsupervised learning, Auto-Encoder [17] has been popularly practiced in various areas, mainly due to its unique feature learning ability. Deep Auto-Encoder is an excellent framework to capture non-linear structure information between the low-dimensional representation and the input data. Deep Auto-Encoder is composed of two components, i.e., the encoder component and encoder

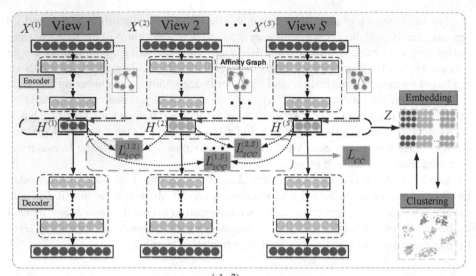

Fig. 1. The architecture of MVC-MAE. $L_{2CC}^{(s1,s2)}$ denotes the regularization loss of consistent and complementary information between two views $X^{(s1)}$ and $X^{(s2)}$, L_{CC} denotes the sum of losses between any two views, and Z denotes the concatenation of learned low-dimensional representations (i.e., $\{H^{(s)}\}_{s=1}^{S}$) from different views. At the clustering step, the clustering embedding layer performs clustering based on Z, and in return, adjusting Z according to the current clustering result.

component, where the encoder component consists of multiple non-linear functions that map the input data to the representation space and the decoder component consists of multiple non-linear functions mapping the representations in representation space to reconstruction space.

In our algorithm, MVC-MAE contains multiple encoder components $\{E^{(s)}\}_{s-1}^{S}$ and multiple decoder components $\{D^{(s)}\}_{s=1}^{S}$, where they are composed of K layers non-linear functions. For the s-th view, we denote the encoder component $E^{(s)}$ and the decoder component $D^{(s)}$, respectively, and denote the learned representation $H^{(s)}$. Here, to better optimize Deep Auto-Encoder, we adopt a modified loss function [18], as follows:

$$L_{AE} = \sum_{s=1}^{S} \sum_{i=1}^{m} \left\| \left(\tilde{X}_i^{(s)} - X_i^{(s)} \right) \right\| \odot B_i^{(s)} \right\| = \sum_{s=1}^{S} \left\| \left(X^{\tilde{(s)}} - X^{(s)} \right) \odot B^{(s)} \right\| \quad (1)$$

where $X^{(s)}$ and $\tilde{X}^{(s)}$ denote the real samples and the reconstructed samples of s-th view, respectively, $\odot$ means the Hadamard product and $B_i^{(s)} = \{B_{i,j}^{(s)}\}_{j=1}^{n}$. If $X_{i,j} = 0$, $B_{i,j}^{(s)} = 1$, else $B_{i,j}^{(s)} = \beta > 1$. By minimizing the loss function of Eq. (1), the revised Auto-Encoder not only smoothly captures the data manifolds as well as preserves the similarity among samples [19], but also imposes more penalty on the reconstruction error of the non-zero elements than that of zero elements [18].

Local Geometrical Information. To respect the local geometrical structure, we construct the affinity graphs $\{W^{(s)}\}_{i=1}^{S}$ for each view by adopting Euclidean distance in which $W_{i,j}^{(s)} = 1$ if one of $X_i^{(s)}$ and $X_j^{(s)}$ is among k nearest neighbors of the other [20]. As a result, we maximize the following likelihood estimation:

$$L_{Local} = \sum_{s=1}^{S} \prod_{W_{i,j}^{(s)}} (P_{i,j}^{(s)}) \tag{2}$$

Where $P_{i,j}^{(s)} = P_{i,j}^{(s,s)}$ is the joint probability between the i-th sample and the j-th sample in the $X^{(s)}$ view, which is defined as follow:

$$P_{i,j}^{(s,s)} = \frac{1}{1 + \exp(-H_i^{(s)}(H_j^{(s)})^T)} \tag{3}$$

Therefore, we can respect the local geometrical structure within each view by minimizing the negative log-likelihood as follows:

$$L_{Local} = \sum_{s=1}^{S} (-\sum_{W_{i,j}^{(s)}>0} \log P_{i,j}^{(s)}) \tag{4}$$

Consistent and Complementary Information. The complementary principle of multi-view data refers to some unique knowledge contained in each view, which is not available in other views. On the other hand, the consistent of multi-view data means that there is some common knowledge in each view. Since different views can describe the same sample from different perspectives, the proposed algorithm should preserve consistent and complementary information contained in multi-view data as much as possible. In other words, the key of MVC is how to capture consistent and complementary low-dimensional representation across different views. A straightforward method is to concatenate these representations directly as the final representation result. It cannot guarantee consistent information between multi-view data. Another widely used method is to enforce multi-view data to share the same representation layer. However, it will lose too much complementary information from multi-view data due to the same representation layer.

To preserve consistent and complementary information, we design a novel regularization strategy inspired by the cross-entropy loss function of binary classification. First, we review the loss function of the cross-entropy of the binary classification:

$$L_B(Y^t|Y^p) = -\sum_{i=1}^{m} (Y_i^t \log(Y_i^p) + (1 - Y_i^t) \log(1 - Y_i^p))$$

$$= -\sum_{i=1}^{m} (\log(Y_i^p)^{Y_i^t} + \log(1 - Y_i^p)^{(1-Y_i^t)})$$

$$= -\sum_{i=1}^{m} \log\left((Y_i^p)^{Y_i^t} \cdot (1 - Y_i^p)^{(1-Y_i^t)}\right)$$

$$= -\prod_{i}^{m}\left((Y_i^p)^{Y_i^t} \cdot (1 - Y_i^p)^{(1-Y_i^t)}\right) \tag{5}$$

where Y_i^t denotes the label of i-th sample and Y_i^p denotes the prediction probability of i-th sample. In the binary classification problem, the set of true labels maybe 0 or 1. When the true label is 1, only the first term is calculated: $L_B(Y^t|Y^p) = -\sum_{i=1}^{m} \log\left((Y_i^p)^{Y_i^t} \cdot 1\right)$; otherwise, only the second term is calculated: $L_B(Y^t|Y^p) = -\log\left(1 \cdot (1 - Y_i^p)^{(1-Y_i^t)}\right)$.

Take multi-view clustering as with two views an example. For the low-dimensional representations of two views from the same sample, we hope them to be as consistent as possible; for low-dimensional representations of different samples from different views, we want their differences to be as large as possible. As a result, we propose to maximize the following loss function:

$$
\begin{aligned}
L_{2CC}^{(s1,s2)} \\
&= \prod_{i,j}^{m}\left((P_{i,j}^{(s1,s2)})^{C_{i,j}^{(s1,s2)}} (1 - P_{i,j}^{(s1,s2)})^{1-C_{i,j}^{(s1,s2)}}\right) \\
&= \sum_{i,j=1}^{m} \log\left((P_{i,j}^{(s1,s2)})^{C_{i,j}^{(s1,s2)}} (1 - P_{i,j}^{(s1,s2)})^{1-C_{i,j}^{(s1,s2)}}\right) \\
&= \sum_{i,j=1}^{m} \log\left((P_{i,j}^{(s1,s2)})^{C_{i,j}^{(s1,s2)}} (1 - P_{i,j}^{(s1,s2)})^{1-C_{i,j}^{(s1,s2)}}\right) \\
&= \sum_{i,j=1}^{m} \left(C_{i,j}^{(s1,s2)} \log(P_{i,j}^{(s1,s2)}) + (1 - C_{i,j}^{(s1,s2)}) \log(1 - P_{i,j}^{(s1,s2)})\right)
\end{aligned} \tag{6}
$$

where $s1 = 1$, $s2 = 2$, and $P_{i,j}^{(s1,s2)}$ is the joint distribution between $X^{(s1)}$ and $X^{(s2)}$ views, which is defined as follows:

$$P_{i,j}^{(s1,s2)} = \frac{1}{1 + \exp(-H_i^{(s1)}(H_j^{(s2)})^T)} \tag{7}$$

For $C_{i,j}^{(s1,s2)}$ in Eq. (6), we interpret it as whether two representations $H_i^{(s1)}$ and $H_j^{(s2)}$ from two views describe the same sample: if they are from the same sample, $C_{i,j}^{(s1,s2)}$ is 1, otherwise $C_{i,j}^{(s1,s2)}$ is 0. Formally, $C_{i,j}^{(s1,s2)} \in \{0, 1\}$ denotes whether $H_i^{(s1)}$ and $H_j^{(s2)}$ are from the same sample. In detail, $C_{i,j}^{(s1,s2)} = 1$ if $i = j$. Otherwise, $C_{i,j}^{(s1,s2)} = 0$. So when $C_{i,j}^{(s1,s2)} = 1$, we maximize the first term of the loss function so that the two representations may be consistent while pushing away them when $C_{i,j}^{(s1,s2)} = 0$. Of course, the two samples are not entirely same, so complementary information is retained between two views. Furthermore, if two samples $X_i^{(s)}$ and $X_j^{(s)}$ are similar according to the local geometrical information, the representation $H_i^{(s)}$ and $H_j^{(s)}$ should also be similar, although they are from different samples. They should not be pushed away. Equation (6) is relaxed as follows:

$$L_{2CC}^{(s1,s2)} = \sum_{i,j=1}^{m} \left(C_{i,j}^{(s1,s2)} \log(P_{i,j}^{(s1,s2)}) \right) + \sum_{i,j=1, W_{i,j}^{s1}=0, W_{i,j}^{s2}=0}^{m} \left((1 - C_{i,j}^{(s1,s2)}) \log(1 - P_{i,j}^{(s1,s2)}) \right)$$

(8)

However, the number of views of most real-world multi-view data may be greater than two, so we first construct Eq. (6) to save the loss function between pairs of views, and then maximize them uniformly. The final optimized loss function is shown in formula (9):

$$L_{CC} = \sum_{s1=1}^{S} \sum_{s2=s1+1}^{S} L_{2CC}^{(s1,s2)}$$

(9)

We concatenate the representations of different views as input for the next step. Meanwhile, the concatenation approach can also preserve the complementary information in each view to some extent.

Clustering Loss. To preserve the clustering structure of low-dimensional representation, a clustering embedding loss (CEL [8]) is adopted, which is measured by KL-divergence in MVC-MAE. Specifically, based on the learned representation of different views, we concatenate them as $Z = \overset{S}{\underset{s=1}{||}} H^{(s)}$, where $||$ represents concatenation operation. Given the initial cluster centroids $\{\mu_j\}_{j=1}^{C_{Cluster}}$, according to [8], we use the Student's t-distribution as a kernel to measure the similarity between the representation Z_i and centroid μ_j:

$$Q_{i,j} = \frac{(1 + \|Z_i - \mu_j\|^2)^{-1}}{\sum_{j'} (1 + \|Z_i - \mu_{j'}\|^2)^{-1}}$$

(10)

where $Q_{i,j}$ is interpreted as the probability of assigning the sample i to cluster j. To this end, we define our objective as a KL divergence loss between the soft assignment $Q_{i,j}$ and the auxiliary distribution $E_{i,j}$ as follows:

$$L_{CLU} = \sum_i \sum_j E_{i,j} \log \frac{E_{i,j}}{Q_{i,j}}$$

(11)

where $E_{i,j}$ is computed by raising $Q_{i,j}$ to its second power and normalizing it with the frequency per cluster as follow:

$$E_{i,j} = \frac{Q_{i,j}^2 / f_i}{\sum_{j'} Q_{i,j'}^2 / f_{j'}}$$

(12)

where $f_j = \sum_i Q_{i,j}$ are soft cluster frequencies.

During the training procedure, we optimize the clustering loss according to Eq. (11) to help Auto-Encoder adjust the representation Z and obtain the final clustering results.

Total Loss. By integrating the above loss functions, we jointly optimize the following loss function:

$$L = L_{AE} + \alpha L_{Local} + \gamma L_{CC} + \theta L_{CLU} \tag{13}$$

Where α, γ and $\theta > 0$ are hyper-parameters. By minimizing the loss function, we obtain the final clustering results directly from the last optimized Q, and the cluster of Z_i is obtained as $\arg\max(Q_i)$, which is the most likely assignment.

3.3 Model Optimization

To optimize the proposed algorithm, we apply the optimizer Adam to minimize the objective in Eq. (13). Besides, in order to avoid falling into a local optimal solution, we first use a big learning rate (e.g., 1e−3) for layer-wise pre-training, and then use a smaller learning rate (e.g., 1e−5) for fine-tuning. After pre-training, we initialize cluster centers $\{\mu_j\}_{j=1}^{C_{Cluster}}$ by employing k-means on Z and calculate the soft clustering assignments distributions of all samples through Eq. (12). Then in the following training, the cluster centers $\{\mu_j\}_{j=1}^{C_{Cluster}}$ are updated together with the embedding Z using the optimizer Adam based on the gradients of L_{CLU} with respect to $\{\mu_j\}_{j=1}^{C_{Cluster}}$ and Z. We calculate target distribution E with Q by Eq. (12), calculate clustering loss L_{CLU} according to Eq. (11) and update our proposed algorithm by minimizing Eq. (13). Finally, we obtain the clustering labels with final Q by Eq. (10).

4   Experiments

4.1   Experiments Setting

Datasets. The experiment results are measured on three real-world datasets, including one text dataset, two image datasets. The statistics of the three datasets including HW2source[1], 100leaves[2] and BBCSport[3] are shown in Table 1.

Table 1. Statistics of three benchmark datasets

Dataset	#instance	#view	#cluster	#d$_1$	#d$_2$	#d$_3$
BBCSport	544	2	5	3183	3203	–
HW2sources	2000	2	10	76	240	–
100leaves	1600	3	100	64	64	64

---

[1] https://archive.ics.uci.edu/ml/datasets/One-hundred+plant+species+leaves+data+set.
[2] https://cs.nyu.edu/roweis/data.html.
[3] http://mldlxg.ucd.ie/datasets/segment.html.

Table 2. The configurations of MVC-MAE on different datasets. We only show the architecture of the encoder (the third column). The decoder reverses the encoder. The number of clustering embedding layer is set to the number of clusters in the corresponding dataset (the fourth column).

Dataset	#View	#neurons in each layer of encoder	#neurons in clustering embedding layer
BBCSport	View 1	3183-256-64-16	5
	View 2	3203-256-64-16	
HW2sources	View 1	76-512-128-32	10
	View 2	240-512-128-32	
100leaves	View 1	64-500-100	100
	View 2	64-500-100	
	View 3	64-500-100	

Compared Algorithms. We compare the proposed MVC-MAE with the following clustering algorithms: NMF [21] (Single View), AE [22] (Single View), CoregSC, Multi-NMF, MultiGNMF, DiMSC, RMSC [23], MVCF [24], MVGL [25], SWML [26], AMGL [16], DCCA, DMF-MVC. Meanwhile, for enhancing the comparison experiments. AE-Concat (AE-C) and AE-ConcatShallow (AE-CS) are also developed to test evaluation. The number of each layer of AE-C is the same as that of MVC-MAE and AE-CS's Encoder and Decoder Component only contain one layer non-linear function. AE-C is a single view clustering algorithm which concatenates the features of each view as its input. AE-CS is the shallow version of AE-C. Among those MVC algorithms, which require an additional clustering step, we use k-means or spectral clustering to cluster the learned representation according to the original paper. We implement our proposed algorithm, AE, AE-C and AE-CS by using TensorFlow framework and adopt LeakRelu [27] as the activation function of all internal layers except for the input, output and clustering embedding layer. For our algorithm, the layer configurations for different datasets are shown at Table 2. α, γ and θ are set to 10, 0.1 and 0.1, respectively.

Evaluation Metrics. In order to measure the clustering performance of different algorithms, two standard clustering evaluation metrics are adopted, i.e., Clustering Accuracy (ACC) and Normalized Mutual Information (NMI) [6]. These measures range in [0, 1], and the larger the value, the better the clustering performance.

4.2 Clustering Performance

For each experiment, we run each algorithm 20 times on each dataset and then record the average results as well as the standard deviations. Note that 0.00 means that the value is close to zero, and 0 denotes zero. The results performance on three real-world datasets is shown in Tables 3 where the best results are highlighted in bold. Note That since DCCA can only deal with two views, it can't give clustering results for 100leaves with three views.

Table 3. Cluster performance on three datasets

Type	Algorithm	Accuracy (%)			Normalized mutual information (%)		
		Digits	BBCSport	100leaves	Digits	BBCSport	100leaves
Single view	NMF-1 View	70.15(0)	37.86(0.00)	35.62(0.00)	63.00(0)	24.60(0.00)	66.17(0)
	NMF-2 View	71.00(0)	44.60(0)	20.87(0.00)	68.74(0)	51.90(0)	52.49(0)
	NMF-3 View	–	–	37.75(0.00)	–	–	66.40(0.00)
	AE-1 View	69.45(2.40)	48.49(7.39)	60.28(1.31)	63.85(1.89)	30.75(7.43)	80.90(0.51)
	AE-2 View	71.97(6.17)	44.98(1.26)	20.61(1.32)	70.13(3.72)	53.88(2.41)	54.53(1.62)
	AE-3 View	–	–	47.66(1.84)	–	–	73.18(0.6)
	AE-CS	84.45(1.88)	46.54(6.49)	62.88(1.62)	79.58(0.99)	21.02(9.73)	83.25(0.51)
	AE-C	87.39(1.26)	51.61(3.1)	66.4(1.16)	80.03(1.52)	49.89(2.7)	85.35(0.4)
Multi-view	Multi-NMF	88.28(1.2)	86.01(3.17)	67.15(2.4)	80.58(1.5)	74.25(2.16)	86.35(0.8)
	Multi-GNMF	92.05(0)	44.57(0)	69.31(0)	86.0(0)	12.74(0)	86.88(0)
	CoregSC	79.35(6.05)	43.31(2.11)	65.19(2.30)	76.43(0.01)	22.55(0.59)	84.57(0.00)
	DMF-MVC	73.88(0.17)	68.38(0)	23.66(0.57)	78.69(0.32)	51.04(0)	53.95(0.31)
	DiMSC	38.28(1.8)	85.91(0.1)	51.84(1.4)	35.64(0.9)	70.75(0.2)	74.48(0.7)
	RMSC	77.52(0.9)	87.78(1.4)	74.09(0.4)	74.49(1.9)	**81.51(2.5)**	89.83(0.6)
	MVCF	82.53(3.7)	66.49(1.1)	79.06(1.1)	76.13(2.1)	46.08(1.4)	90.09(0.9)
	MVGL	72.04(6.7)	35.35(4.3)	81.06(1.5)	79.35(2.21)	15.04(5.3)	91.30(0.8)
	SwML	73.65(0)	36.21(0)	80.94(0)	80.38(0)	1.55(0)	92.07(0)
	AMGL	72.15(0.02)	35.99(0.00)	87.99(1.6)	76.69(0.02)	1.45(0.00)	76.32(0.02)
	DCCA	74.5(4.8)	77.21(3.5)	–	70.5(3.6)	61.92(3.2)	–
	MVC-MAE	**94.64(0.16)**	**93.15(0.20)**	**90.56(0.81)**	**88.46(0.25)**	80.68(0.49)	**96.54(0.22)**

Although NMF and AE are the single-view clustering algorithms, the clustering results of AE are better than those of NMF in all datasets. This is because AE algorithm belongs to the deep learning algorithm, which can capture the complex hierarchical information in data. The clustering results of AE-C are better than those of AE algorithm in most datasets. This demonstrates that integrating information from multiple views can improve the performance of MVC. The clustering results of AE-C are higher than those of AE-CS. This indicates that deep AE can better capture hierarchical information hidden in multi-view data. MVC algorithms usually can achieve better clustering performance than single-view clustering algorithms on most datasets. On the other hand, the clustering performance of some MVC algorithms is lower than that of the single-view clustering algorithm, which indicates that the MVC algorithm needs further exploration.

MVC-MAE is superior to all the compared algorithms in two evaluation metrics on most datasets. These results clearly show that the proposed algorithm is a promising MVC algorithm. Although both DCCA and DMF-MVC are deep MVC algorithms, they cannot achieve the desired performance. For DCCA, it cannot capture complementary information. For DMF-MVC, although it is a deep non-negative matrix factorization structure, the non-linear activation function is not added between layers, so it is not able to fully capture hierarchical information in each view. And it also cannot capture the complementary information. DiMSC can capture complementary information in the dataset, but it does not achieve a good result on all datasets because it is just a shallow model and requires an extra clustering step. Multi-NMF and Multi-GNMF are proposed based on NMF, and they show good results, but both are poor with MVC-MAE.

In all methods, RMSC can suppress a certain degree of noise, so it also obtains good experimental results. The three methods of MVCF, MVGL, and SwML can learn the weight of consistent information of different views. Although these algorithms have achieved excellent results, they are all inferior to MVC-MAE. This shows MVC-MAE's superiority and proves the importance of complementary information in multi-view data.

4.3 Ablation Study of the Proposed Algorithm

In this section, we present some ablation study of MVC-MAE. Effectiveness of capturing consistent and complementary information among views: we present Eq. (13) without parameter γ as MVC-MAE-No-CC. From the clustering results in Tables 4, MVC-MAE achieves better performance than MVC-MAE-No-CC, which demonstrates that capturing consistent and complementary information among different views can improve the clustering results.

Effectiveness of capturing the local geometric information within each view on clustering performance: we present Eq. (13) without parameters α as MVC-MAE-No-Local. From the clustering results in Table 4, MVC-MAE achieves better performance than MVC-MAE-No-Local, which demonstrates that capturing the local geometrical information in each view is an important factor.

Effectiveness of the fusion ways of the low-dimensional information on clustering performance: After obtaining low-dimensional representations, different from the fusion ways of the low-dimensional information of MVC-MAE, we sum all the representations and average them to get the representations Z as to the input of CEL. We represent this algorithm as MVC-MAE-Mean. From the clustering results in Table 4, MVC-MAE distinctly achieves better performance than MVC-MAE-Mean, which shows that the way of concatenating low-dimensional representations can retain more information.

Table 4. Cluster performance on Ablation study

Algorithm	Accuracy (%)			Normalized Mutual Information (%)		
	Digits	BBCSport	100leaves	Digits	BBCSport	100leaves
MVC-MAE$_{No-CC}$	92.20(0.14)	90.43(0.62)	89.69(1.45)	86.01(0.23)	75.57(0.68)	96.33(0.36)
MVC-MAE$_{No-Local}$	92.23(0.19)	87.76(0.51)	89.92(1.22)	86.07(0.32)	69.34(0.99)	96.37(0.35)
MVC-MAE$_{Mean}$	87.45(0.89)	84.56(0.62)	85.62(0.85)	77.08(0.46)	64.67(0.36)	93.63(0.42)
MVC-MAE	**94.64(0.16)**	**93.15(0.20)**	**90.56(0.81)**	**88.46(0.25)**	**80.68(0.49)**	**96.54(0.22)**

4.4 Parameter Sensitivity

In the proposed algorithm, we will evaluate the effect of the hyper-parameters, including three parameters: α, γ, and θ. To study the influence of each parameter change, we vary one parameter each time and fix the others. The performance variation of these parameters is shown in Fig. 2. We can see that the performance is relatively stable without clear trends. This shows that our algorithm has better robustness and does not need to adjust complex parameters.

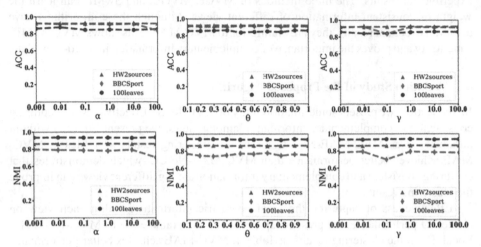

Fig. 2. ACC and NMI of MVC-MAE on three datasets with various α, γ, θ.

5   Conclusion

In this paper, we proposed a deep multi-view clustering algorithm. Unlike many existing MVC algorithms, which usually work in a single layer formulation, we adopt Auto-Encoder to capture the Non-linear structure information within each view. Consistent and complementary information among multiple views is considered in our algorithm. Meanwhile, to maintain the local geometrical information within each view, our algorithm encodes the affinity graph to preserve them. The clustering embedding layer is also incorporated to jointly optimize the representation learning and clustering. Experiments on three datasets verified the effectiveness of MVC-MAE compared with 13 algorithms.

Acknowledgments. This work was supported by the National Natural Science Foundation of China (61762090, 61262069, 61966036, and 61662086), The Natural Science Foundation of Yunnan Province (2016FA026), the Project of Innovative Research Team of Yunnan Province (2018HC019), and Program for Innovation Research Team (in Science and Technology) in University of Yunnan Province (IRTSTYN), the Education Department Foundation of Yunnan Province (2019J0005, 2019Y0006), Yunnan University's Research Innovation Fund for Graduate Students, and the National Social Science Foundation of China (18XZZ005).

References

1. Wang, H., Yang, Y., Liu, B., Fujita, H.: A study of graph-based system for multi-view clustering. Knowl.-Based Syst. **163**, 1009–1019 (2019)

2. Huang, S., Kang, Z., Tsang, I.W., Xu, Z.: Auto-weighted multi-view clustering via kernelized graph learning. Pattern Recogn. **88**, 174–184 (2019)
3. Cao, X., Zhang, C., Fu, H., Liu, S., Zhang, H.: Diversity-induced multi-view subspace clustering. In: Proceedings of the IEEE Conference on Computer Vision and Pattern Recognition, pp. 586–594. IEEE-CS (2015)
4. Liu, J., Wang, C., Gao, J., Han, J.: Multi-view clustering via joint nonnegative matrix factorization. In: Proceedings of the 13th SIAM International Conference on Data Mining, pp. 252–260. SIAM (2013)
5. Wang, Z., Kong, X., Fu, H., Li, M., Zhang, Y.: Feature extraction via multi-view non-negative matrix factorization with local graph regularization. In: 2015 IEEE International Conference on Image Processing, pp. 3500–3504. IEEE (2015)
6. Andrew, G., Arora, R., Bilmes, J., Livescu, K.: Deep canonical correlation analysis. In: Proceedings of the 30th International Conference on Machine Learning, pp. 1247–1255. MIT Press (2013)
7. Chaudhuri, K., Kakade, S.M., Livescu, K., Sridharan, K.: Multi-view clustering via canonical correlation analysis. In: Proceedings of the 26th Annual International Conference on Machine Learning, pp. 129–136. ACM (2009)
8. Xie, J., Girshick, R., Farhadi, A.: Unsupervised deep embedding for clustering analysis. In: Proceedings of the 33nd International Conference on Machine Learning, pp. 478–487. MIT Press (2016)
9. Zhao, H., Ding, Z., Fu, Y.: Multi-view clustering via deep matrix factorization. In: Proceedings of the 31th AAAI Conference on Artificial Intelligence, pp. 2921–2927. AAAI Press (2017)
10. Yang, Y., Wang, H.: Multi-view clustering: a survey. Big Data Min. Anal. **1**(2), 83–107 (2018)
11. Luo, S., Zhang, C., Zhang, W., Cao, X.: Consistent and specific multi-view subspace clustering. In: Proceedings of the 32th AAAI Conference on Artificial Intelligence, pp. 3730–3737. AAAI Press (2018)
12. Xu, C., Guan, Z., Zhao, W., Niu, Y., Wang, Q., Wang, Z.: Deep multi-view concept learning. In: Proceedings of the 27th International Joint Conference on Artificial Intelligence, pp. 2898–2904. AAAI Press (2018)
13. Guan, Z., Zhang, L., Peng, J., Fan, J.: Multi-view concept learning for data representation. IEEE Trans. Knowl. Data Eng. **27**(11), 3016–3028 (2015)
14. Kumar, A., Rai, P., Daume, H.: Co-regularized multi-view spectral clustering. In: Advances in Neural Information Processing Systems, pp. 1413–1421. AAAI Press (2011)
15. Houthuys, L., Langone, R., Suykens, J.A.: Multi-view kernel spectral clustering. Inf. Fusion **44**, 46–56 (2018)
16. Nie, F., Li, J., Li, X., et al.: Parameter-free auto-weighted multiple graph learning: a framework for multiview clustering and semi-supervised classification. In: Proceedings of the 25th International Joint Conference on Artificial Intelligence, pp. 1881–1887. AAAI Press (2016)
17. Hinton, G.E., Salakhutdinov, R.R.: Reducing the dimensionality of data with neural networks. Science **313**(5786), 504–507 (2006)
18. Wang, D., Cui, P., Zhu, W.: Structural deep network embedding. In: Proceedings of the 22nd ACM SIGKDD International Conference on Knowledge Discovery and Data Mining, pp. 1225–1234. MIT Press (2016)
19. Salakhutdinov, R., Hinton, G.: Semantic hashing. Int. J. Approximate Reasoning **50**(7), 969–978 (2009)
20. Cai, D., He, X., Han, J., Huang, T.S.: Graph regularized nonnegative matrix factorization for data representation. IEEE Transa. Pattern Anal. Mach. Intell. **33**(8), 1548–1560 (2010)
21. Lee, D.D., Seung, H.S.: Learning the parts of objects by non-negative matrix fac-torization. Nature **401**(6755), 788–791 (1999)
22. Hinton, G.E., Osindero, S., Teh, Y.W.: A fast learning algorithm for deep belief nets. Neural Comput. **18**(7), 1527–1554 (2006)

23. Xia, R., Pan, Y., Du, L., Yin, J.: Robust multi-view spectral clustering via low-rank and sparse decomposition. In: Proceedings of the 28th AAAI Conference on Artificial Intelligence, pp. 2149–2155. AAAI Press (2014)
24. Zhan, K., Shi, J., Wang, J., Wang, H., Xie, Y.: Adaptive structure concept factor ization for multiview clustering. Neural Comput. **30**(4), 1080–1103 (2018)
25. Zhan, K., Zhang, C., Guan, J., Wang, J.: Graph learning for multiview clustering. IEEE Trans. Cybern. **48**(10), 2887–2895 (2017)
26. Nie, F., Li, J., Li, X., et al.: Self-weighted multiview clustering with multiple graphs. In: Proceedings of the 26th International Joint Conference on Artificial Intelligence, pp. 2564–2570. AAAI Press (2017)
27. Maas, A.L., Hannun, A.Y., Ng, A.Y.: Rectifier nonlinearities improve neural net-work acoustic models. In: Proceedings of the 30th International Conference on Machine Learning, vol. 30, p. 3. MIT Press (2013)

A Method for Place Name Recognition in Tang Poetry Based on Feature Templates and Conditional Random Field

Yan Zhang[1], Yukun Li[1,2(✉)], Jing Zhang[1], and Yunbo Ye[1]

[1] Tianjin University of Technology, Tianjin 300384, China
liyukun_tjut@163.com
[2] Tianjin Key Laboratory of Intelligence Computing and Novel Software
Technology, Tianjin, China

Abstract. Tang poetry is an important aspect of ancient Chinese culture. Given that Tang poetry has unique features in text structure, how to use entity recognition, knowledge graph and other information processing technologies to research poetry is of great importance. However, the existing artificial neural network methods for named entity recognition require a large number of labeled training sets, while Chinese Tang poetry has not been labeled with a good training set. Besides, the grammatical structure of Tang poetry is far from modern Chinese. Therefore, for place name recognition in poetry, the existing neural network methods do not perform well. This article studies and analyzes the metrical form of Tang poetry, finds the metrical rules of place names, and summarizes the feature templates based on the metrical rules. According to the feature templates of Tang poetry, a method of combining feature templates with conditional random field is proposed. Experimental results prove the effectiveness of the proposed method.

Keywords: Tang poetry · Place name recognition · Feature templates · Conditional random field

1 Introduction

The named entity recognition is an important research direction in the natural language processing (NLP) project. It detects and labels the corpus in the text and divides it into predetermined categories, such as time, place names, person names, institutions, etc. As a sub-task of named entity recognition, place name recognition has become more mature in English, but Chinese grammar is well different from that of English. Inverted sentences are more commonly used in English, while subject-predicate-object structures are more common in Chinese, which makes the task of identifying place names in Chinese more challenging than in English [1].

In recent years, China has attached great importance to the study of traditional culture, and Tang poetry is a representative of Tang Dynasty culture and an important part of the study of Chinese culture. Recognizing the place names of Tang poetry helps us to know where the literati in Tang Dynasty tend to go, so that we can dig deeper

X. Wang et al. (Eds.): APWeb-WAIM 2020, LNCS 12317, pp. 627–635, 2020.
https://doi.org/10.1007/978-3-030-60259-8_46

into the cultural heritage of the region [1]. The grammatical structure of Tang poetry is very different from that of modern Chinese. Tang poetry text is concise, the meaning of words is diversified, and the requirements for structure and rhythm are extremely high, while the structure of modern Chinese is much freer than that of Tang poetry, and the meaning of words is relatively low. At present, there is no labeled corpus of the Tang poetry dataset, which is not conducive to learning without human intervention.

Based on the problems above, this article performs entity recognition on place names in Tang poetry. We chose to use conditional random field because it supports custom feature templates and can better learn features in the absence of relevant training sets. According to its grammatical structure and rhythm, a general feature template for Tang poetry is proposed and combined with the conditional random field method to improve the precision of Tang poetry place name recognition.

2 Related Work

In early period, place name recognition was a method based on rule and dictionary. After that, with the emergence of statistical machine learning, method based on Hidden Markov Model (HMM) and conditional random field (CRF) is applied in entity recognition tasks. In recent years, the method of deep learning has broken a new path for the problem of natural language processing and drawn wide attention from the academic community. Getting rid of the shackles of feature engineering, deep neural network can automatically learn word relationships through corpora and extract contextual features to achieve the purpose of entity recognition. Wang et al. proposed a Chinese-oriented deep learning model Char2Vec-Bilstm. Based on the long-short-term memory model (LSTM), a bidirectional long-short-term memory model (BILSTM) was used to learn the complex dependencies in Chinese [2]. In the same way, Bill et al. combined the bidirectional long-short-term memory model with conditional random field (BILSTM-CRF), and obtained a mature named entity recognition model, which has outstanding performance [3]. The attention mechanism can learn long-term dependencies by establishing a direct connection between each character, and can better understand the semantic information in sentences. Wu et al. combined the attention mechanism with the BILSTM-CRF model to realize the improvement of BILSTM-CRF in Chinese named entity recognition [4].

Since the Qin period, the ancient Chinese style structure has become more unified. The language structure of each dynasty after the Qin Dynasty was developed on the basis of the Qin Dynasty language structure. Given that related work about Tang poetry place name recognition has not been found yet, we focus on understanding the related work on place name recognition in the ancient language and hope to find inspiration. On the basis of the pre-Qin corpus, Huang et al. used conditional random field to identify the place names of Qin Kingdom, and achieved good results [5]. Based on the marked corpus of ancient books, Li et al. conducted place name recognition based on conditional random field, and verified the performance of the model through cross-validation [6].

3 Method

3.1 Preliminary Knowledge

Conditional random field (CRF) is a probability distribution model P (Y|X) given X, which is used to solve the problem of sequence labeling. The recognition of place names in Tang poetry is to label each word in the sequence. In the final analysis, it is the labeling problem. CRF is an undirected graph of probability [7], the dots represent labels, the edges between each two dots represents the weight of the path. The input of the conditional random field is the word sequence index after the word segmentation X $(x_1, x_2, x_3 \ldots x_n)$, Y $(y_1, y_2, y_3, \ldots y_n)$ is used as the output label sequence. For example, the sentence "'故人西辞黄鹤楼'", the meaning is "The old man said goodbye to the Yellow Crane Tower in the West", the result after word segmentation is represented by key-value pair word_alphabet: {0: '故', 1: '人', 2: '西', 3: '辞', 4: '黄', 5: '鹤', 6: '楼'}, the BIO tags form used in this article is represented by key-value pairs as label_alphabet: {0: 'B-LOC', 1: 'I-LOC', 2: 'O'}. Based on the method above, the specific form of the observation sequence input into the conditional random field is {0, 1, 2, 3, 4, 5, 6}, corresponding to the index in word_alphabet. The output is {2, 2, 2, 2, 0, 1, 1}, corresponding to the index in label_alphabet.

Modern Chinese has four tones, the first, the second, the third and the fourth. In Tang poetry, in order to simplify the rhythmic style, the ancient literati used level and oblique tones, "平仄通"(Ping Ze Tong) instead of four tones. "平"(Ping) represents the first and second tones, and "仄"(Ze) represents the third and fourth tones, "通"(Tong) represents any of the four tones, and the same set of tones is also called the rhyme [8]. This article uses the BIO tags for the labeling of sequences, where B-LOC represents the first word of the place name, I-LOC means the part after the first word of place name, O means non-place name.

3.2 Feature Templates Selecting

Tang poetry can be divided into five character quatrains, seven character quatrains, five character rhythms, seven character rhythms, whose rhythm is represented by "平仄通" [8], as shown in Table 1:

Through understanding the metrical pattern form of Tang poetry, it is known that the word can only be quoted from one rhyme sections, that is, a complete word is likely to appear in the same rhyme sections [9], and the word for place name will not exceed four words. With this rule, this article uses the unigram form to represent the feature template: U: %x[row, col], where U represents the template form describing unigram feature, row represents the row in the corpus, and col represents the column in the corpus. This representation refers to the current offset row, the value of column col. For example, "故人西辞黄鹤楼", assuming the current word is "辞", the templates we set and the meaning of each template are shown in Table 3, and the training set using BIO tags, and keep the part of speech, as shown in Table 2:

In Table 2, the second column in the table uses POS tags, f represents a position word, v represents a verb, and ns represents a place noun (ns0 represents the first word of a place noun). From the Table 3, assuming the current position is "黄", feature function

Table 1. This table introduces the labeled form of the training set of this article.

Form	Sentence	Metric
five character quatrains	至今思项羽(Missing XiangYu up to now.)	仄平通仄仄
five character rhythms	白日依山尽(Mountains cover the white sun.)	仄仄平平仄
seven character quatrains	夜发清溪向三峡(Leaving the Clear Stream for Three Gorges.)	仄通平平仄平平
seven character rhythms	潭州官舍暮楼空(In the evening, I saw that there were no people in the Tanzhou government building.)	平平仄仄仄平通

Table 2. This table introduces the labeled form of the training set of this article.

Character	Part of Speech	Label
故	n0	O
人	n1	O
西	f	O
辞	v	O
黄	ns0	B-LOC
鹤	ns1	I-LOC
楼	ns2	I-LOC

"func = if(output = B-LOC and feature = "U14: 辞/黄/鹤/楼") return 1 else return 0" produced by the template "U14: %x[−1,0]/%x[0,0]/%x[1,0]/%x[2,0]". That is, if the current position is labeled as "B-LOC", the current position is "黄", the previous position is "辞", the next position is "鹤", and the last two positions are "楼", then the output is 1, otherwise 0. The feature function output obtained at each training position from these templates is entered into a conditional random field to adjust feature weights (feature weights are described below), and then the purpose of improving the precision of place name recognition during testing is achieved.

3.3 Model Generation

The previous section introduced the selection of templates based on the rhythm of Tang poetry, and showed the conditional random field model. In summary, the training process of the model can be obtained, as shown in Algorithm 1:

Table 3. This table indicates the template and the meaning of the template representation.

Template	Expressed Meaning
U00:%x[-3,0]	故
U01:%x[-2,0]	人
U02:%x[-1,0]	西
U03:%x[0,0]	辞
U04:%x[1,0]	黄
U05:%x[2,0]	鹤
U06:%x[3,0]	楼
U07:%x[-1,0]/%x[0,0]	西/辞
U08:%x[0,0]/%x[1,0]	辞/黄
U09:%x[-2,0]/%x[-1,0]/%x[0,0]	人/西/辞
U10:%x[-1,0]/%x[0,0]/%x[1,0]	西/辞/黄
U11:%x[0,0]/%x[1,0]/%x[2,0]	辞/黄/鹤
U12: %x[-3,0]/%x[-2,0]/%x[-1,0]/%x[0,0]	故/人/西/辞
U13: %x[-2,0]/%x[-1,0]/%x[0,0]/%x[1,0]	人/西/辞/黄
U14: %x[-1,0]/%x[0,0]/%x[1,0]/%x[2,0]	西/辞/黄/鹤
U15: %x[0,0]/%x[1,0]/%x[2,0]/%x[3,0]	辞/黄/鹤/楼
U16:%x[-1,1]/[0,1]	f/v
U17:%x[0,1]/[1,1]	v/ns0

Algorithm 1. Save model

```
Input: N
Output: model
1.   RebuildFeatures(FeatureIndex)
2.   for t = 1,2,…,N do
3.       cost = Calcost(t)
4.       cost = ForwardBackward(cost)
5.       FeatureIndex = FeatureIndex + cost
6.   End for
7.   model = Save(FeatureIndex)
8.   return model
```

In Algorithm 1, the weight set *FeatureIndex* is initialized by using the *RebuildFeatures* function, and then the training set *N* is looped. At the beginning of, the path weight is calculated for the first time according to the labeled training set. Then, based on the feature template, a forward-backward algorithm is used to adjust the obtained path weights. Finally, the adjusted weight cost is added to the weight sct *FeatureIndex*. The undirected graph obtained by labels (dots) and weights (edges) is the conditional random field model we finally trained.

3.4 Feature Calculation and Sequence Labeling

What affects the final path probability and result are the two features in the above probability undirected graph, the state feature and the transition feature. The state feature is defined on nodes and indicate that a node has a certain attribute. The transition feature is defined on the edge, indicating whether two states will transit due to a certain feature [10]. The state feature refers to attributes such as {"place", "noun", "time", "institution name"}, and transfer characteristics refer to {"preposition before place name", "preposition before person name"} [10], etc.

By defining observation sequence X (x_1, x_2, x_3 ... x_n) and the state sequence is Y (y_1, y_2, y_3, ... y_n), transition features k_1 {t_1, t_2, t_3, ... t_{k_1}}and state feature k_2 {s_1, s_2, s_3, ... s_{k_2}}, when node i has feature s_j, $s_j = 1$ of x_i. Otherwise, $s_j = 0$. For example: "黄鹤楼" has state feature: {"place", "noun"}, which can be expressed as "$s_l = s_j(y_i, x, i) \in \{0,1\}, l = 1, 2, .. k_1, i = 1, 2, ... n$". Similarly, considering the transition feature of the preceding conjunction, this can be expressed as "$t_k = t_k(y_{i-1}, y_i, x, i) \in \{0, 1\}$, $k = 1, 2, .. k_2, i = 2, 3, ... n$". Then we can get feature functions, the number is $k = k_1 + k_2$ [11]. For each feature function, it has a corresponding weight. The weight here is obtained through the function training parameter adjustment generated by the feature template above. If we define the weight of the transition feature as λ_k, the weight of the state feature is μ_l. Then when the result is the observation sequence X (x_1, x_2, x_3 ... x_n) and the state sequence is Y (y_1, y_2, y_3, ... y_n), the sum of the features of all nodes is:

$$score = \sum\nolimits_{i,k} \lambda_k t_k (y_{i-1}, y_i, X, i) + \sum\nolimits_{i,l} \mu_l s_l(y_i, X, i) \tag{1}$$

For example, it can be learned from the above that the input sequence of "故人西辞黄鹤楼". The first half of the formula represents the transition feature score, and the second half of the formula represents the state feature score. Define the transition feature score as $T[y_{i-1}][y_i]$ and the state score as $E[x_i][y_i]$, then the score of this output sequence is "$score = \sum_{i=1}^6 T[y_{i-1}][y_i] + \sum_{i=1}^6 E[x_i][y_i]$". Using this feature sum to calculate the probability of the state sequence, the higher probability becomes the optimal state sequence [11]. The probability summation is performed on all possible output sequences, and the optimal label sequence is finally output according to the probability size (P (Y|X) takes the maximum value) as the output of the conditional random field [11]. The overall flowchart can be shown in Fig. 1:

So far, the method in this paper is summarized as follows: firstly input the observation sequence X, and use the conditional random field model trained by the feature template to get the highest probability sequence labeling, which achieves the purpose of Tang poetry place name recognition in this paper.

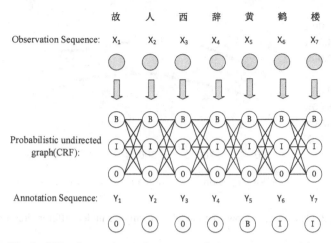

Fig. 1. This picture shows the process of place name recognition.

4 Experiment

4.1 Data Preprocessing and Training

The data set used in this experiment is the People's Daily Corpus. We get 58433 place names. Based on this data set, this paper annotates 100 Tang poetry with place names by experts, among which, five character quatrains, seven character quatrains, five character rhythms, seven character rhythms account for 23%, 26%, 26% and 25%, a total of 2608 labeled characters, including 231 place names. Then, this paper selects 48 Tang poetry with place names as the final test set of this experiment, among them, four types of Tang poetry each account for 25%, a total of 1152 label characters, of which place name labels account for 102.

For the method proposed in this paper, the feature threshold for participating in the training was set as 3 times to avoid the influence of individual features on the training results; the number of training iterations is set to 100, 200, 300, 400 and 500, and the optimal model is obtained by comparing the results. The evaluation criteria for the final experiment were evaluated using precision (P), recall (R), and F value.

4.2 Experiments and Results

We train the model by setting different number of iterations, and get the optimal model from it. The comparison results are shown in Fig. 2:

It can be seen from the Fig. 2 that before the number of iterations is 300, because the obtained features are gradually increasing, all three indicators show an upward trend. When the number of iterations is 300, the performance of the model is optimal. After more than 300 times, the performance of the model decreases due to overfitting.

Compare the results with the previous experiments, as shown in Table 4, it can be seen that the method proposed in this paper is higher than the existing methods in terms of precision, recall rate and F value. This means that our method can better learn the

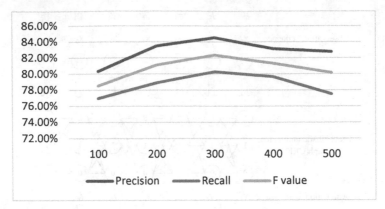

Fig. 2. This picture shows the model performance under different iterations.

metrical features of Tang poems, so as to better recognize place names. Therefore, the method proposed in the text is of certain feasibility and significance for further research.

Table 4. This table shows the comparison results of the methods.

Method	Precision	Recall	F value
LSTM-CRF	77.56%	71.35%	74.33%
BILSTM-CRF	78.92%	72.41%	75.52%
Attention-BILSTM-CRF	80.64%	74.72%	77.57%
Feature template combine CRF	84.51%	80.26%	82.33%

5 Conclusion

This paper uses a method based on the combination of feature templates and conditional random field. We summarize feature templates through the metrical structure and grammatical structure of Tang poetry and use the feature functions generated by conditional random field to label sequences. The method obtained an F value of 82.33% on the Tang poetry testing set we constructed. Compared with other existing neural network methods, the effect is better, but the overall precision and recall rate are still lower than the named entity recognition tasks in other fields. We still need to find more features to improve the performance of the model in the future.

References

1. Nadeau, D., Sekine, S.: A survey of named entity recognition and classification. LingvisticÆę Investigationes **30**(1), 3–26 (2007)

2. Wang, Y., Xia, B., Liu, Z., Li, Y., Li, T.: Named entity recognition for Chinese telecommunications field based on Char2Vec and Bi-LSTMs. In: ISKE, pp. 1–7 (2017)
3. Lin, B.Y., Xu, F.F., Luo, Z., Zhu, K.Q.: Multi-channel BiLSTM-CRF model for emerging named entity recognition in social media. In: NUT@EMNLP, pp. 160–165 (2017)
4. Guohua, W., Tang, G., Wang, Z.: An attention-based BiLSTM-CRF model for Chinese clinic named entity recognition. IEEE Access 7, 113942–113949 (2019)
5. Huang, S., Wang, D., He, L.: Research on the construction of automatic recognition model of ancient Chinese place names based on pre-qin corpus. Library Inf. Serv. **59**(12), 135–140 (2015)
6. Li, N.: Construction of automatic recognition model for place names of local records and ancient books in the library based on digital culture. Library **2018**(05), 67–73 (2018)
7. Poostchi, H., Borzeshi, E.Z.: BiLSTM-CRF for Persian named-entity recognition ArmanPersoNERCorpus: the first entity-annotated Persian dataset. In: LREC (2018)
8. Wei, J.,: Symbiosis and reorganization of Yu Wensuo's translation of tang poetry. Foreign Lang. Foreign Lang. Teach. **2019**(05), 126–134 + 151 (2019)
9. Chen, G.: The monument of Tang poetry: "Nine families annotate Du's Poetry". In: Learning Times, 13 Sept 2019. (006)
10. Yang, F., Zhao, J., Zou, B.: CRFs-based named entity recognition incorporated with heuristic entity list searching. In: IJCNLP 2008, pp. 171–174 (2008)
11. Das, A., Garain, U.: CRF-based named entity recognition @ICON 2013. CoRR abs/1409.8008 (2014)

Machine Learning

MLND: A Weight-Adapting Method for Multi-label Classification Based on Neighbor Label Distribution

Lei Yang, Zhan Shi[✉], Dan Feng, Wenxin Yang, Jiaofeng Fang, Shuo Chen,
and Fang Wang

Wuhan National Laboratory for Optoelectronics,
Huazhong University of Science and Technology, Wuhan, China
{leiyang,zshi,dfeng,ywx,shuochen,wangfang}@hust.edu.cn, fjf1227@qq.com

Abstract. In multi-label classification, each training sample is associated with a set of labels and the task is to predict the correct set of labels for the unseen instance. Learning from the multi-label samples is very challenging due to the tremendous number of possible label sets. Therefore, the key to successful multi-label learning is exploiting the label correlations effectively to facilitate the learning process. In this paper, we analyze the limitations of existing methods that add label correlations and propose MLND, a new method which extracts the label correlations from neighbors. Specifically, we take neighbor's label distribution as new features of an instance and obtain the label's confidence according to the new features. Nevertheless, the neighbor information is unreliable when the intersection of nearest neighbor samples is small, so we use information entropy to measure the uncertainty of the neighbor information and combine the original instance features with the new features to perform multi-label classification. Experiments on three different real-world multi-label datasets validate the effectiveness of our method against other state-of-the-art methods.

Keywords: Multi-label learning · Label correlations · Neighbor label correlation features · Label distribution

1 Introduction

With the advent of the big data era, a large amount of data has been generated from different domains. Manual analysis, classification, and summarization will consume a lot of manpower, which is increasingly difficult to complete. In order to mine the potential information in the data, data mining and machine learning have developed rapidly. Classification has become an important research focus in the field of machine learning.

In many real-world applications, objects often have multiple semantic meanings and each of them is associated with a set of labels simultaneously. For example, in text categorization [7,15], a document may be related to many topics,

© Springer Nature Switzerland AG 2020
X. Wang et al. (Eds.): APWeb-WAIM 2020, LNCS 12317, pp. 639–654, 2020.
https://doi.org/10.1007/978-3-030-60259-8_47

such as history, culture and even dynasty; in bioinformatics, each gene may be associated with a number of functional classes, such as metabolism, transcription and protein synthesis [5]; resulting in the traditional single-label classification is insufficient while dealing with semantic diversity thus the multi-label classification has become an important research focus [2,3]. In multi-label learning, explicitly assigning a set of category labels to each object can intuitively reflect the multiple semantic information possessed by the ambiguous object. Formally, the goal of learning is to find a mapping function $f : x \rightarrow 2^y$ from the feature space to the space of label sets, i.e. the power set of all labels. Therefore, the key challenge of learning from multi-label data relies on the enormous number of output space, i.e. the number of possible label sets grows exponentially as the number of class labels increases. For example, for a label space with 30 labels ($q = 30$), the number of possible label sets would exceed one billion (i.e. 2^{30}).

In order to cope with the challenge of exponential-sized output space, it is essential to facilitate the multi-label classification learning process by leveraging the correlations among different labels. For example, the probability of an article being annotated with label sports would be high if we know it has been labeled stadium and soccer; an image is unlikely to be labeled as river if it is related to desert. The existence of some labels will affect the existence of other labels to some extent. Therefore, capturing the dependency of labels in the classification process is deemed to be crucial for the achievement of multi-label learning techniques. However, the model complexities are usually high when the label correlations are considered.

In this paper, we present an effective yet computational efficient way to address the label correlations. We consider the local label dependency and extract the label correlations from the neighboring instances. Then, we take the label distribution extracting from the nearest neighbor instances label set as new features and use the low-complexity and parallel single-label BR (Binary Relevance) method to calculate the probability of the label appearance. However, when the intersection of similar samples is small, the similarity is unreliable, so we propose a method to measure the reliability of the neighbor information to revise the error in neighbor-based classification result adaptively to improve the accuracy of multi-label learning.

2   Related Work

2.1   Problem Transformation Methods

This category of algorithms tackles multi-label learning problem by transforming it into several single-label problems or multi-class problems. The basic idea of BR method [12] is decomposing the multi-label learning problem into several independent binary classification problems. The computational complexity of BR is low because each of the binary classifier can be trained in parallel while this method ignores the relationship among labels which affect the accuracy of multi-label classification. Read et al. proposes the CC (Classifier Chains) algorithm and ECC (Ensembles of Classifier Chains) algorithm [9] which are high-order approaches with considering the correlations among labels in a random manner. However, these methods lose the opportunity of parallel implementation due to its chaining property. LP (Label-Powerset) [13] proposed by Tsoumakas et al. transforms the multi-label learning problem into several multi-class classification problems which considering a set of labels as an entirety, the label correlations among labels is included in the classification, but the cost of the LP method is to increase the number of entire labels, resulting in only a small number of instances per label, while generating high computational complexity. RAKEL (Random K-labelsets) [14] combines the LP method and integrated learning to compensate for the shortcomings of the LP method. The RAKEL algorithm reduces the computational complexity, resulting in a more uniform distribution of multiple classes, avoiding the problem of too few training samples of LP, but the classification accuracy is very random.

2.2   Algorithm Adaptation Methods

The main idea of the algorithm adaptation methods adapt the existing machine learning techniques to deal with multi-label data directly. Cheng and Hüllermeier proposed a novel multi-label learning algorithm IBLR (Instance-Based Learning by Logistic Regression) [4], which combines K-nearest neighbor learning and logistic regression to compensate for the K-nearest neighbor learning does not take correlations between labels into account. However, the relationship between labels is considered fixed in IBLR, and the real samples differ in the importance of different labels and do not have a fixed impact. The Rank-SVM (Ranking Support Vector Machine) [8] uses the relationship between two labels, which belongs to the second-order strategy. Since the Rank-SVM only defines the margin over hyperplanes for relevant-irrelevant label pairs, it is difficult to add the association of multiple labels to the model, thus limit its performance.

2.3   Mining Label Feature

This category of algorithms improve multi-label learning by mining label features from the known information. In 2015, Zhan and Zhang proposed a multi-label learning method based on specific-label features [16]. In detail, the LIF-TACE (multi-label learning with Label-specIfic FeaTures viA Clustering Ensemble) method generates the label-specific features by clustering the multi-label training samples in a label-wise style, which ignores the utilization of label correlations to improve classification performance. In 2018, Zhang et al. believes that multi-label learning performance can be improved by enriching the labelling information. Therefore, an algorithm called MLFE (Multi-label Learning with Feature-induced labeling information Enrichment) [18] is proposed to enrich the labelling information of the training set by leveraging the structural information in feature space through sparse reconstruction of the training set.

3   Proposed Method

In the formal definition of multi-label classification, $x \in R^d$ is the input space of the d-dimensional feature vector, $Y = \{1, 0\}^m$ is the value of the output space, and the output space is the label set $L = \{l_1, l_2, l_3, \cdots, l_m\}$ and the set consists of $m = |L|$ possible labels. For a given training set $D = \{(x_i, y_i)|1 \leq i \leq n\}$, training the d-dimensional train instances $x_i = \{x_{i1}, x_{i2}, \cdots, x_{id}\}$, the corresponding category label is $y_i = \{y_{i1}, y_{i2}, \cdots, y_{im}\}$, if the instance x_i has the label l_m in the label set, y_{im} takes the value 1, otherwise is 0. The task of the multi-label classification algorithm is to learn a hypothesis $f : x \rightarrow 2^y$ from D which can assign a set of proper labels for the test instance x.

As reviewed in Sect. 2, previous approaches tackle the problem of multi-label learning in various ways, these methods show that exploiting label correlations in the process of multi-label learning can improve the accuracy of multi-label classifier. However, the more relations among labels are considered, the higher computational complexity of the model is needed. If only a part of the label correlations is considered, the high-order dependencies will not be captured. If all the dependencies are considered, the complex relationship of the labels is difficult to handle. Our goal is to find a simple and efficient way to improve the accuracy of multi-label learning by exploiting the neighbor label correlations. Therefore, we propose a method to consider high-order label correlations with low computational complexity. In this section, we detail the algorithm based on neighbor label distribution, named MLND, i.e. Multi-label Learning based on Neighbor label Distribution. The MLND algorithm design consists of two parts. The first part presents the method for extracting label correlations from neighboring instances as new features, and the second part presents the design methods for combine new features and original sample features.

3.1   Algorithm of Extracting Neighbor Label Correlations

BRKNN [11] is an adaptation of the KNN (K Nearest Neighbors) algorithm that is conceptually equivalent to using BR in conjunction with the KNN algorithm. It considers the percentage of the k nearest neighbors that include the current label to obtain the confidence c_λ for a label. Let $Y_j (j = 1 \cdots k)$ be the label sets of the k nearest neighbors of an instance x, the calculation equation of the label λ confidence is:

$$c_\lambda = \frac{1}{k} \sum_{j=1}^{k} I_{(Y_j)}(\lambda) \tag{1}$$

Where $k = N(x)$, $N(x)$ denote the set of KNNs of x identified in the training set, $I_{(Y_j)} : L \rightarrow \{0, 1\}$ is a function that outputs 1 if its input label λ belongs to set Y_j and 0 otherwise. The classification method is that if half or more of the k nearest neighbors have the label λ or c_λ is the largest, the instance x also has the label λ. This method is simple and has a good classification effect. However, the label with the largest proportion of k nearest neighbors is directly assigned to the instance, which is too simple and easy to generate errors.

In this paper, we consider the high-order relationship between all labels to improve classification accuracy. For an instance x, we consider that it possesses the same label with most of its nearest neighbors. That is, the labels of local similar samples have correlations, wherein labels that exist simultaneously at high frequencies are correlated. If the features of two samples are close, they tend to be more similar, and the similar samples have a high probability of belonging to the same type. First, we use the Euclidean metric to measure distances between instances and get a set of similar samples. That is, the neighboring instances with similar features to instance x can be regarded as instance clusters with similar features. The label distribution in the cluster label set is related to the sample label, wherein a plurality of labels that exist simultaneously in a high proportion have the correlations. For example, pictures with similar features should have similar content labels. Then we obtain the distributions of the related labels according to the label distribution percentage in the cluster label set and regard them as new features. Establishing classifier that are characterized by the new feature vector and the objective function is whether instance x has the label l_k.

Algorithm 1. calculating the new features

1: Identify the K-nearest neighbor $N(x_i)$ of x_i
2: **for** $l \in L$ **do**
3:     sum=0
4:     **for** $j \in N(x_i), j \in \{0, 1, \cdots, k\}$ **do**
5:         **if** $l \in Y_j$ **then**
6:             $I_{(Y_j)}(l) = 1$
7:         **else**
8:             $I_{(Y_j)}(l) = 0$
9:         **end if**
10:         sum$+=I_{(Y_j)}(l)$
11:     **end for**
12:     $c_l = \frac{1}{k} \times sum$
13: **end for**
14: $C = \{c_{l_1}, c_{l_2}, c_{l_3}, \ldots, c_{l_m}\}$
15: **for** $l \in L$ **do**
16:     **if** $l \in y_i$ **then**
17:         $t_l = 1$
18:     **else**
19:         $t_l = 0$
20:     **end if**
21: **end for**
22: $T = \{t_{l_1}, t_{l_2}, t_{l_3}, \ldots, t_{l_m}\}$
23: Decision tree training set is$\{[c_{l_1}, c_{l_2}, c_{l_3}, \ldots, c_{l_m}], T\}$

The decision tree is used to classify the new features, because the decision tree can preferentially select features according to the degree of influence of each label. Measure the splitting criteria of the features and construct a topology map of the importance of the label, forming a decision tree from top to bottom. Let the label set $L = \{l_1, l_2, l_3, \ldots, l_m\}$, and the set consists of $m = |L|$ labels. For a given training sample set $D = \{(x_i, y_i)|1 \leq i \leq n\}$, the decision tree is used to predict the label correlations. The training set is $\{[c_{l_1}, c_{l_2}, c_{l_3}, \cdots, c_{l_m}], T\}$, where c_{l_m} is the percentage of the label obtained from the label set of the neighboring instances. Calculate according to Eq. (1) to get the percentage of the label to form the new feature vector. The corresponding output space is $t_i = \{1, 0\}$. If the sample x_i has a label in the label set, the value of t_i is 1, otherwise is 0. Train the classifier to get an objective function, and then use the trained function to make the decision. The existence probability of the label l_k is obtained from the label percentage.

3.2   Combining New Features and Sample Original Features

In this paper, the BR method is used to transform multi-labels into multiple binary problems. Since the binary classification algorithms can solve problems in parallel when adding high-order label correlations, which is beneficial to improve computational efficiency. Moreover, the BR method can select different algorithms, such as decision trees, random forests, SVMs, neural networks, etc.

This paper proposes a MLND multi-label classification algorithm, we combine the new features and the original features to improve the classification accuracy. The overall design of the algorithm is shown in Fig. 1. The BR method is used to classify the feature dataset. First, predict the existence probability p_r of the label l based on the new features. Since the reliability of the neighbor prediction results is different, the classification result based on the neighbor label distribution is dynamically adjusted, and then the result based on the original feature vector is added to the result of the new features to correct the classification result.

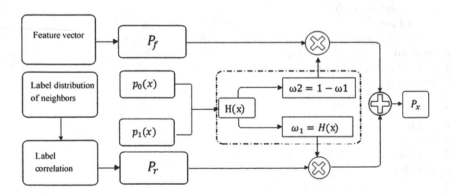

Fig. 1. MLND algorithm

When the classification based on the new features is unreliable, we use information entropy to measure the reliability of neighbor information. The entropy value is used to set a suitable weight for the neighbor-based classifier, and the classification result based on the neighbor label distribution is corrected. If the reliability based on the new features classification is high, the larger weight of neighbor-based classification part which is ω_1 can help to reserve the good result of neighbor label relationship p_r. At the same time, adjust the result p_f based on the original features. However, if the reliability based on the new features classification is low, the larger weight of original features part ω_2 can improve the power of original features and help to correct more errors made by the BR based Decision Tree classifier. Therefore, the new features and the original features classification result can be integrated to improve the classification accuracy.

$$P = \omega_1 \cdot p_r + \omega_2 \cdot p_f$$
$$\omega_1 + \omega_2 = 1 \qquad (2)$$

For each sample x, each label l, the reliability of the nearest neighbor information is calculated according to the probability that the neighbor prediction label l occurs or not occur. According to the principle of maximum entropy [6], the generalization performance of the classifier is proportional to the entropy value [1]. Therefore, the information entropy is used to measure the amount of information gathered from neighbors. The greater entropy means the neighbors are more informative and leads to better performance of the classifier. Conversely, the smaller entropy means the neighbors contain less informative and leads to worse performance of the classifier. The calculation equation of information entropy is shown in (3):

$$H(x) = -\sum_{x \in X} p(x) \log p(x) \qquad (3)$$

For instance, predicting the label l of the unseen instance based on neighbor information, and calculate the neighbor-based information entropy according to the probability of the existence and non-existence probability. For each sample, the neighbor information can be counted according to the MAP (maximum a posteriori probability) principle, and the occurrence probability of the label l can be obtained. The calculation equation for calculating the occurrence and non-occurrence probability of the label l is as shown in (4):

$$p_1(x) = P(H_1^l)P(E_{\vec{c}_t(l)}^l | H_1^l)$$
$$p_0(x) = P(H_0^l)P(E_{\vec{c}_t(l)}^l | H_0^l) \qquad (4)$$

Zhang and Zhou proposed the MLKNN [17] algorithm which combines the traditional KNN method and the Bayesian method to tackle the multi-label classification problem. In this paper, we use the conclusions of the MLKNN [17] algorithm to calculate the existence and non-existence probability of a label. The process of modelling MLKNN is as follows: Given an instance x and its associated label set $Y_x \in Y$, Y is the set of all labels, the total number of labels is defined as m, if there is a label l in Y_x, then $Y_x(l) = 1$, otherwise $Y_x(l) = 0$. $N(x)$ denote the KNNs of x identified in the training set. For instance x, $\vec{C}_x(l)$ counts the number of neighbors of x belonging to the l_{th} class, and the membership counting vector can be defined as:

$$\vec{C}_x(l) = \sum_{a \in N(x)} \vec{y}_a(l) \quad (l \in Y) \tag{5}$$

For each test instance t, the K-nearest neighbor set $N(t)$ is first identified. For the label l, let H_1^l be the event that the instance t has label l, while H_0^l be the event that the instance t has not label l. Furthermore let $E_j^l (j \in \{0, 1, \cdots, k\})$ denote the event that, among the K-nearest neighbors of t, there are exactly j instances which have label l. Therefore, based on the membership counting vector $\vec{C}_t$, the Eq. (6) for whether the instance t has the label l is determined using the MAP principle and the Bayesian principle:

$$
\begin{aligned}
\vec{y}_t(l) &= \arg\max_{b \in \{0,1\}} P(H_b^l | E_{\vec{c}_t(l)}^l) \\
&= \arg\max_{b \in \{0,1\}} \frac{P(H_b^l) P(E_{\vec{c}_t(l)}^l | H_b^l)}{P(E_{\vec{c}_t(l)}^l)} \\
&= \arg\max_{b \in \{0,1\}} P(H_b^l) P(E_{\vec{c}_t(l)}^l | H_b^l) \quad (l \in Y)
\end{aligned}
\tag{6}
$$

Where $P(H_b^l)$ represents a prior probability whether the instance t has the label l, when $b = 1$, $P(H_1^l)$ is equal to the number of samples possessing the label l divided by the total number of samples n. When $b = 0$, $P(H_0^l)$ is equal to the number of samples without the label l divided by the total number of samples.

$$
\begin{aligned}
P(H_1^l) &= \frac{\sum_{i=1}^n \vec{y}_t(l)}{n} \\
P(H_0^l) &= 1 - P(H_1^l)
\end{aligned}
\tag{7}
$$

Thus the calculation of the posterior probability is obtained:

$$
\begin{aligned}
P(E_{\vec{c}_t(l)}^l | H_1^l) &= \frac{c[j]}{\sum_{p=0}^k c[p]} \\
P(E_{\vec{c}_t(l)}^l | H_0^l) &= \frac{c'[j]}{\sum_{p=0}^k c'[p]}
\end{aligned}
\tag{8}
$$

First, for each label l, calculating $c[j](j = 1, 2, 3 \cdots)$, which represents the number of training instances with label l whose KNNs contain exactly j instances with label l. Correspondingly, calculating $c'[j](j = 1, 2, 3 \cdots)$, which represents the number of training instances without label l whose KNNs contain exactly j instances with label l. Moreover, the input argument s is a smoothing parameter controlling the strength of uniform prior.

Then, we use the prior and posterior probability obtained from MLKNN algorithm to calculate the occurrence and non-occurrence probability of the label

---

Algorithm 2. Calculating the reliability of neighbor features

---

1: **for** $l \in L$ **do**
2:   $P(H_1^l) = (s + \sum_{i=1}^{n} \vec{y}_{x_i}(l))/(s \times 2 + n))$
3:   $P(H_0^l) = 1 - P(H_1^l)$
4: **end for**
5: Identify $N(x_i)$ of x_i, $i \in \{1, 2, \cdots, n\}$
6: **for** $l \in L$ **do**
7:   **for** $j \in \{0, 1, \cdots, k\}$ **do**
8:     $c[j] = 0; c'[j] = 0$
9:   **end for**
10:   **for** $i \in \{0, 1, \cdots, n\}$ **do**
11:     $\delta = \vec{C}_x(l) = \sum_{a \in N(x)} \vec{y}_a(l) \quad (l \in Y)$
12:     **if** $(\vec{y}_{x_i}(l) == 1)$ **then**
13:       $c[\delta] = c[\delta] + 1$
14:     **else**
15:       $c'[\delta] = c'[\delta] + 1$
16:     **end if**
17:   **end for**
18:   **for** $j \in \{0, 1, \cdots, k\}$ **do**
19:     $P(E_j^l | H_1^l) = (s + c[j])/(s \times (k+1) + \sum_{p=0}^{k} c[p])$
20:     $P(E_j^l | H_0^l) = (s + c'[j])/(s \times (k+1) + \sum_{p=0}^{k} c'[p])$
21:   **end for**
22: **end for**
23: For instance t, calculate the K nearest neighbor sample $N(t)$
24: **for** $l \in L$ **do**
25:   $\vec{C}_t(l) = \sum_{a \in N(t)} \vec{y}_a(l)$
26:   $p_1(x) = P(H_1^l) P(E_{\vec{c}_t(l)}^l | H_1^l)$
27:   $p_0(x) = P(H_0^l) P(E_{\vec{c}_t(l)}^l | H_0^l)$
28:   $\omega_1 = H(x) = -(p_1(x) \log p_1(x) + p_0(x) \log p_0(x))$
29: **end for**

---

l, and information entropy is used to calculate ω_1 which represents the weight of the neighbor-based classification.

$$\omega_1 = -(p_1(x) \log p_1(x) + p_0(x) \log p_0(x))$$
$$\omega_2 = 1 - \omega_1 \tag{9}$$

Where $p_1(x)$ and $p_0(x)$ are described in Eq. (3). As the new features and ordinary sample features need to be combined to obtain the overall decision, the classifier output is converted into probability, and different confidence can be synthesized according to the weight. Combining the new features with the original features, and get the final result:

$$P_x = \omega_1 \cdot p_r + \omega_2 \cdot p_f \tag{10}$$

Determine whether the label l exists based on the final confidence:

$$y_l = \begin{cases} +1, & if \quad P_x \geq \frac{1}{2} \\ \\ -1, & if \quad P_x < \frac{1}{2} \end{cases} \tag{11}$$

3.3 Algorithm Analysis

MLND algorithm reduces feature dimension in exchange for shorter execution time and adopts the first-order strategy to tackle the label correlation features, which can reduce execution time by using multi-core parallelism. The complexity and time overhead of the MLND algorithm is analyzed in detail below.

In this paper, the K-D tree structure is used to solve the problem of brute force calculating in low efficiency of K nearest neighbors. The computational complexity is $O(D \times N \times \log N)$ when establishing the K-D tree on the N samples whose feature vector is D-dimensional. When calculating the new features of the neighboring instances, first calculate the complexity of the neighbor label set is $O(N)$. Then, the percentage of each label in the neighbor label set is counted, the time complexity is $O(N \times K \times |L|)$. The maximum a posteriori probability of the neighbor label is calculated when calculating the reliability of the neighbor, including two steps of statistical prior probability and posterior probability, the total time complexity of them is $2 \times O(N \times K \times |L|)$. Since the percentage of the neighbor label set can be counted together with the prior probability, the total time complexity of processing the new features and the reliability is $O(N) + 2 \times O(N \times K \times |L|)$. The new features of the N instances after processing is $|L|$ dimensional. It can be classified into single-label classification by exploiting pruning decision tree, and it has computational complexity of $O(|L| \times N \times \log N)$. Therefore, when adding new features, the total computational complexity that needs to be increased is $O(D \times N \times \log N)$, $O(N) + 2 \times O(N \times K \times |L|)$, $O(|L| \times N \times \log N)$ the sum of these three parts, each of which can be multi-core multi-threaded calculation. The time complexity scales linearly with the number of labels $|L|$, the number of neighbors K, the feature dimension D. And the time complexity scales in $O(n \log n)$ relationship with the number of samples N. Therefore, the time complexity of the algorithm is low.

4   Evaluation

4.1 Experiment Environment and Datasets

The hardware platform used in our experiments is a single machine containing 6-core 2.00 GHz Intel(R) Xeon(R) CPU E5-2620 with 4 GB memory. The experiment program is developed in Python on the Linux platform.

In our experiment, we use three real-world datasets in the audio (Emotions), image (Scene), and biological (Yeast) [17] domains. An overview is given in Table 1. Emotions is a multi-label dataset for music emotional classification. The Scene is a natural scene dataset for semantic indexing. Yeast is a gene functional analysis dataset, each gene in the Yeast dataset is associated with a set of functions.

Table 1. Datasets

Dataset	Samples	Features	Total labels	Average labels	Distinct subsets	Domain
Emotions	593	72	6	1.868	27	Audio
Scene	2407	294	6	1.074	15	Image
Yeast	2417	103	14	4.237	198	Biological

4.2 Evaluation Metrics

We used four sample-based evaluation metrics and two label based evaluation metrics to evaluate the multi-label learning performance in the experiments [10].

Sample-Based. For the first three metrics, the smaller the value the better the performance of the classification method. For average precision, on the other hand, the larger the value the better the performance.

- *Hamming loss* is used to measure the proportion of labels whose relevance is predicted inaccurately.

$$HammingLoss = \frac{1}{p} \sum_{i=1}^{p} \frac{XOR(Y_{ij}, P_{ij})}{|L|} \tag{12}$$

- The *Coverage* evaluation is used to examine the search depth required to cover all the relevant labels in the label ordering of instance predictions.

$$coverage = \frac{1}{p} \sum_{i=1}^{p} \max rank f(x_i, y) - 1 \tag{13}$$

- *Ranking Loss* computes the case where the unrelated labels are located before the relevant labels in the label ordering of the sample predictions.

$$rloss = \frac{1}{p} \sum_{i=1}^{p} \frac{1}{|Y_i| \, |\overline{Y_i}|} \times |R_i| \, , where$$

$$R_i = \left\{ (y', y'') | f(x_i, y') \leq f(x_i, y''), (y', y'') \in Y_i \times \overline{Y_i} \right\} \tag{14}$$

- *Average precision* (Ap) is used to evaluate the average fraction of relevant labels ranked higher than a particular label.

$$AvePre = \frac{1}{p} \sum_{i=1}^{p} \frac{1}{|Y_i|} \sum_{y \in Y_i} \frac{|P_i|}{rank f(x_i, y)}, where$$

$$P_i = \left\{ y' | rank f(x_i, y') \leq rank f(x_i, y), y' \in Y_i \right\} \tag{15}$$

Label-Based. Based on the label evaluation [14], there are four performance evaluation metrics for the binary classification: accuracy, precision, recall, and harmonic mean F1-score. The category-based multi-label evaluation metrics use the combined results of the above four metrics. The calculation of these measures for all labels can be achieved using two averaging operations, called F1-Macro and F1-Micro.

4.3   Result and Analysis

Results on Decision Tree. We adopts the decision tree binary classification, and compare the accuracy of the three datasets of Scene, Yeast and Emotions in the pruning decision tree. The number of nearest neighbors considered is set to 30 in the Scene dataset and Yeast dataset, and the number of nearest neighbors in the Emotions is set to 10, and each evaluation metric reaches the optimal value. The experimental results illustrate in Table 2 that after adding neighbor label distribution features to the decision tree, there is no obvious change in Hamming Loss. However, Ranking Loss is decreased by 29%–32% and Average Precision is improved by 15%–22%, Coverage is declined by 30%–60%, and F1-macro and F1-micro are increased by 1%–5%.

Table 2. Experiment results on the decision tree, random forest and neural network

Data	Algorithm	Ranking loss	Coverage	Average percision	F1-macro	F1-micro	Hamming loss
Sence	DT	0.449	2.374	0.555	0.585	0.58	–
	MLND-DT	0.151	0.862	0.775	0.589	0.583	–
Yeast	DT	0.557	11.549	0.49	0.391	0.536	–
	MLND-DT	0.234	7.699	0.683	0.408	0.577	–
Emotions	DT	0.602	4.074	0.526	0.515	0.525	–
	MLND-DT	0.308	2.639	0.68	0.539	0.564	–
Sence	RF	0.134	0.78	0.804	0.606	0.609	–
	MLND-RF	0.094	0.575	0.849	0.711	0.696	–
Yeast	RF	0.227	7.582	0.714	0.342	0.594	–
	MLND-RF	0.186	6.872	0.743	0.451	0.61	–
Emotions	RF	0.219	2.173	0.762	0.573	0.602	–
	MLND-RF	0.198	2.124	0.771	0.602	0.626	–
Sence	MLP	0.08	0.498	0.855	0.728	0.718	0.099
	MLND-MLP	0.076	0.478	0.863	0.751	0.744	0.088
Yeast	MLP	0.201	6.875	0.735	0.427	0.611	0.223
	MLND-MLP	0.183	6.668	0.743	0.424	0.641	0.206
Emotions	MLP	0.424	3.366	0.556	0.088	0.243	0.375
	MLND-MLP	0.386	2.946	0.582	0.185	0.259	0.369

Results on Random Forest. The binary classification uses a random forest to compare the accuracy of the three datasets of Scene, Yeast, and Emotions with and without the neighbor label distribution features. When the number of Scene nearest neighbors, the number of Yeast nearest neighbors, and the number of Emotions nearest neighbors are 30, each evaluation metric preforms the best value. The experimental results show in Table 2 that after adding the new features in the random forest, the three datasets have no change in the Hamming Loss. Nevertheless, the Ranking loss is dropped by 2%–5% and Average Precision is improved by 1%–4.5%, the Coverage is increased by 2%–30%, and the F1-macro and F1-micro are increased by 1%–11%.

Results on Neural Network. The binary classification uses a neural network to compare the accuracy of the three data sets of Scene, Yeast, and Emotions to join neighbor features and not join neighbor features. When setting the number of Scene neighbors, the number of Yeast neighbors, and the number of Emotions neighbors are 10, each evaluation metric preforms the optimal value, and the number of iterations set here is 1000. The experimental results show in Table 2 that after adding the neighbor label distribution features in the neural network, Hamming Loss is declined by 1%–2%, Ranking Loss is decreased by 0.4%–3.8% and Average Precision is improved by 0.8%–2.6%, Coverage is increased by 3%–13%, F1-macro and F1-micro have increased by 2%–10%.

These results show that the new features improve the accuracy of decision tree, random forest and neural network.

Table 3. Experiment results on different algorithms

Dataset	Algorithm	Hamming loss	Coverage	Ranking loss	Average percision	F1-Macro	F1-Micro
Scene	MLND	**0.088**	**0.478**	**0.076**	**0.863**	**0.751**	**0.744**
	BR	0.1368	1.3345	0.2465	0.7109	0.6285	0.6194
	CC	0.1444	1.3504	0.2489	0.7176	0.6126	0.6001
	RAKEL	0.1368	1.0994	0.2010	0.7280	0.6285	0.6194
Yeast	MLND	**0.206**	**6.668**	**0.183**	**0.743**	**0.427**	**0.641**
	BR	0.2454	9.2398	0.3097	0.6216	0.3920	0.5857
	CC	0.2682	8.8423	0.3238	0.6295	0.3966	0.5499
	RAKEL	0.2449	9.5088	0.3300	0.6431	0.3911	0.5861
Emotions	MLND	**0.242**	**2.124**	**0.198**	**0.771**	**0.602**	**0.626**
	BR	0.2474	2.5507	0.2915	0.7014	0.5868	0.6020
	CC	0.2550	2.5351	0.3066	0.6827	0.5760	0.5878
	RAKEL	0.2474	2.5522	0.2931	0.7035	0.5868	0.6020

Comparison of MLND Algorithm and Advanced Algorithm. In this paper, we compare MLND with several state-of-the-art multi-label learning methods, including BR [12] algorithm, CC [9] and RAKEL [14] algorithm. The results are reported in Table 3, numbers in bold represent the highest accuracy in each column. On the natural scene dataset Scene and gene function classification dataset Yeast, the MLND algorithm in the neural network has the highest accuracy and outperforms all other methods such as BR, CC and RAKEL. On the music emotion classification dataset Emotions, the MLND in the random forest is compared with the multi-label algorithm BR, CC, RAKEL. Hamming loss, coverage, Ranking loss, Average precision, F1-Macro, F1-Micro and other metrics are better than BR, CC and RAKEL algorithms. Besides, the efficiency of MLND algorithm with other algorithms on the neural network are compared in Fig. 2. The result indicates that MLND algorithm can improve the accuracy with low computational complexity.

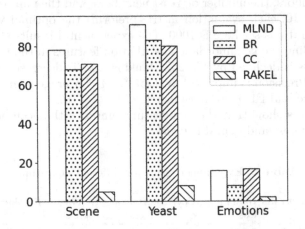

Fig. 2. Training time

5   Conclusion

In this paper, we propose a new algorithm MLND that extracts label correlations from neighboring instances. It considers high-order label correlations in the case of low computational complexity. The probability of label occurrence is calculated by a single-label classification method with low complexity and parallelism, and the same method is used to classify the ordinary features. Then the neighbor feature prediction results are corrected according to the reliability of the neighbor information, combining the new features with the ordinary features to perform multi-label learning. The experimental results indicate that the proposed MLND method which considers the neighbor label ditribution can improve the accuracy of different algorithms. Furthermore, we compare MLND with several advanced multi-label learning methods. The results show that MLND is significantly superior to the compared algorithms BR, CC and RAKEL.

Acknowledgment. This work is supported by NSFC No. 61772216, 61821003, U1705261.

References

1. Berger, A.L.: A maximum entropy approach to natural language processing. Comput. Linguist. **22**(1), 39–71 (1996)
2. Bucak, S.S., Jin, R., Jain, A.K.: Multi-label learning with incomplete class assignments. In: CVPR 2011, pp. 2801–2808 (2011)
3. Burkhardt, S., Kramer, S.: Multi-label classification using stacked hierarchical Dirichlet processes with reduced sampling complexity. Knowl. Inf. Syst. **59**(1), 93–115 (2019). https://doi.org/10.1007/s10115-018-1204-z
4. Cheng, W., Hüllermeier, E.: Combining instance-based learning and logistic regression for multilabel classification. Mach. Learn. **76**(2–3), 211–225 (2009). https://doi.org/10.1007/s10994-009-5127-5
5. Elisseeff, A., Weston, J.: A kernel method for multi-labelled classification. In: Proceedings of the 14th International Conference on Neural Information Processing Systems: Natural and Synthetic, NIPS 2001, pp. 681–687. MIT Press, Cambridge (2001). http://dl.acm.org/citation.cfm?id=2980539.2980628
6. Jaynes, E.: Information theory and statistical mechanics, **106**(4), 620–630 (1957)
7. Katakis, I., Tsoumakas, G., Vlahavas, I.: Multilabel text classification for automated tag suggestion. In: Proceedings of the ECML/PKDD 2008 Discovery Challenge (2008)
8. Lee, C.P., Lin, C.J.: Large-scale linear rankSVM. Neural Comput. **26**(4), 781–817 (2014)
9. Read, J., Pfahringer, B., Holmes, G., Frank, E.: Classifier chains for multi-label classification. Mach. Learn. **85**(3), 333 (2011). https://doi.org/10.1007/s10994-011-5256-5
10. Schapire, R.E., Singer, Y.: Boostexter: a boosting-based system for text categorization. Mach. Learn. **39**(2–3), 135–168 (2000). https://doi.org/10.1023/A:1007649029923
11. Spyromitros, E., Tsoumakas, G., Vlahavas, I.: An empirical study of lazy multilabel classification algorithms. In: Darzentas, J., Vouros, G.A., Vosinakis, S., Arnellos, A. (eds.) SETN 2008. LNCS (LNAI), vol. 5138, pp. 401–406. Springer, Heidelberg (2008). https://doi.org/10.1007/978-3-540-87881-0_40
12. Trohidis, K., Tsoumakas, G., Kalliris, G., Vlahavas, I.: Multi-label classification of music by emotion. EURASIP J. Audio Speech Music Process. **2011**(1), 4 (2011). https://doi.org/10.1186/1687-4722-2011-426793
13. Tsoumakas, G., Katakis, I., Vlahavas, I.: Mining multi-label data. In: Maimon, O., Rokach, L. (eds.) Data Mining and Knowledge Discovery Handbook, pp. 667–685. Springer, Boston (2010). https://doi.org/10.1007/978-0-387-09823-4_34
14. Tsoumakas, G., Vlahavas, I.: Random k-Labelsets: an ensemble method for multilabel classification. In: Kok, J.N., Koronacki, J., Mantaras, R.L., Matwin, S., Mladenič, D., Skowron, A. (eds.) ECML 2007. LNCS (LNAI), vol. 4701, pp. 406–417. Springer, Heidelberg (2007). https://doi.org/10.1007/978-3-540-74958-5_38

15. Van Linh, N., Anh, N.K., Than, K., Dang, C.N.: An effective and interpretable method for document classification. Knowl. Inf. Syst. **50**(3), 763–793 (2016). https://doi.org/10.1007/s10115-016-0956-6
16. Zhan, W., Zhang, M.L.: Multi-label learning with label-specific features via clustering ensemble, pp. 129–136 (2017)
17. Zhang, M.L., Zhou, Z.H.: ML-KNN: a lazy learning approach to multi-label learning. Pattern Recognit. **40**, 2038–2048 (2007)
18. Zhang, Q.W., Zhong, Y., Zhang, M.L.: Feature-induced labeling information enrichment for multi-label learning. In: AAAI (2018)

meanNet: A Multi-layer Label Mean Based Semi-supervised Neural Network Approach for Credit Prediction

Guowei Wang[1], Lin Li[1(✉)], and Jianwei Zhang[2]

[1] School of Computer Science and Technology, Wuhan University of Technology, Wuhan 430070, China
{wangguowei,cathylilin}@whut.edu.cn
[2] Faculty of Science and Engineering, Iwate University, Morioka 0208551, Japan
zhang@iwate-u.ac.jp

Abstract. Currently, semi-supervised deep learning usually combines supervised and unsupervised way to train its model, which intends to make good use of the information of unlabeled data. When applying semi-supervised learning in credit prediction, the distribution of credit data has its own characteristics. It is observed that there are multiple data-dense divisions even for one class because credit prediction needs to be considered from multiple perspectives. We argue that utilizing this information can improve the performance of semi-supervised learning. In this paper, we propose a novel multi-layer label mean based semi-supervised deep learning for credit prediction which is called meanNet. Our multi-layer structure approach takes into consideration class center points in different layers. We estimate the class center points of each class and the goal of multi-layer label mean is to maximize the distance of class center points at each layer. In addition, we add the cost-sensitive loss function to meanNet for the inconsistent misclassification cost between classes of credit datasets. Experiments are conducted on two public financial datasets and the results show that our approach can improve the credit prediction performance compared with popular baselines.

Keywords: Credit prediction · Label mean · Cost sensitive function · Semi-supervised deep learning

1 Introdction

With the rapid development of the internet industry, the number of small business has increased as well. In the face of banks' complicated lending process, it is difficult for small business to get loans in time, which is not conducive to the development of small business [1,2]. Credit evaluation is the content of long-term research in financial field [3]. Plenty of machine learning methods are applied to credit evaluation, such as logistic regression, neural networks, support vector machines (SVMs) and decision trees [4]. In general, an effective credit

© Springer Nature Switzerland AG 2020
X. Wang et al. (Eds.): APWeb-WAIM 2020, LNCS 12317, pp. 655–669, 2020.
https://doi.org/10.1007/978-3-030-60259-8_48

risk assessment model can help banks and financial institutions to reduce losses caused by credit misjudgment.

In face of the expertise involved, collecting large amounts of labeled data is expensive. However, it is relatively easy and cheap to get unlabeled data. Credit prediction is also a classification problem with insufficient supervised information [20]. Due to lack of sufficient labeled data for credit data (discussed further in Sect. 2.1), semi-supervised methods attract researchers' interest. Traditional machine learning based semi-supervised methods consider estimating the labels of unlabeled data to train their models [20–23]. Currently, semi-supervised deep learning methods try to study more information from unlabeled data. Mainly in the field of image [8–12], medical [25,26] and review aspect identification [27], semi-supervised deep learning methods are better than traditional ones.

In credit prediction, there are two major problems. Firstly, corporate and personal credit is affected by many factors, such as income, possession of assets, etc. We have observed that credit datasets have multiple data-dense divisions (discussed further in Sect. 3.2). The main problem is that current semi-supervised deep learning methods do not fully utilize such information when learning from unlabeled data. This multi-center distribution can be used to improve the performance of prediction. In addition, it is worse to wrongly predict class "bad" as class "good" (Money may be loaned to people with bad credit) than reverse case. Thus, the other problem is to solve the inconsistent cost of positive and negative misclassification.

In this paper, we propose a novel multi-layer label mean based semi-supervised deep learning to effectively deal with the above problems. To best of our knowledge, our approach is the first work which uses label mean for credit prediction. We estimate the center points of positive and negative samples and work by maximizing the margin between the class center points to improve accuracy for semi-supervised neural network. The goal of multi-layer label mean is to maximize the difference for each class center point at each hidden layer. In addition, we add cost-sensitive loss function in the supervised part to solve the problem that the negative misclassification causes greater losses.

The main contributions of this paper are as follows:

(1) We investigate the predictive effectiveness of semi-supervised neural networks in credit prediction and consider using multi-layer label mean for multiple data-dense divisions.
(2) We propose meanNet and combine our meanNet with cost-sensitive function for credit prediction.
(3) We evaluate popular semi-supervised methods on real credit datasets under different labeled rates. Compare with several popular baselines under different evaluation indicators. The experimental results show that meanNet can significantly improve the performance for credit prediction.

This paper is organized as follows. Section 2 introduces the related work on semi-supervised deep learning and the applications of semi-supervised learning in credit prediction. Section 3 discusses the main problems in credit prediction,

Sect. 4 describes the over-all framework of our approach. Section 5 provides the experimental setup and analyzes the results. Section 6 concludes this paper.

2 Related Work

2.1 Characteristics of Credit Data

Credit prediction is a typical classification problem. However, a significant proportion of unlabeled data and the high-cost of manual labeling data in real world lead to a serious shortage of training samples. The imbalance between positive and negative samples is also a problem to be faced in credit prediction [5,20,23]. The misclassification cost of default is more than the cost of non-default [6].

2.2 Semi-supervised Deep Learning

Facing the lack of labeled data, an effective solution is to use semi-supervised learning (SSL). Chapelle et al. [7] summarized the research progress of machine learning in the field of SSL. In recent years, various SSL methods have also been proposed, among which semi-supervised neural networks perform well. Previous methods tried to combine supervised and unsupervised loss to get more information from unlabeled data. An example of a typical semi-supervised deep learning method is Ladder Network [8]. Ladder Network integrated unsupervised loss into supervised loss. Using a small amount of labeled data got accuracy close to supervised neural networks on the Mnist dataset. Pezeski et al. [9] verified the effectiveness of Ladder Network through a large number of comparative experiments. Temporal Ensembling performed well on several semi-supervised image classification datasets [10]. Mean Teacher is a model that averages model weights rather than prediction of labels [11]. It used fewer labeled data than Temporal Ensembling to improve the accuracy on the test datasets. MixMatch is a new algorithm that unifies the advantages of the current semi-supervised deep learning methods proposed by Google [12].

The existing semi-supervised deep learning methods combine the supervised prediction loss with the unsupervised loss, but those methods do not consider the distribution of samples. In a specific field, the data distribution has multiple dense divisions. The distance of class center points also has a crucial impact on the results of classification.

2.3 Semi-supervised Learning for Credit Prediction

In the field of traditional machine learning, Li et al. [20] used a semi-supervised SVM [21] to solve credit scoring with reject inference. Zhang et al. [22] used semi-supervised SVM to predict the credit of small business and compared with several machine learning methods. Kennedy et al. [23] compared semi-supervised one-class classification (OCC) algorithms with supervised two-class classification algorithms on low-default portfolio (LDP). The experimental results showed that OCC algorithms can alleviate LDP problem.

Except for meanS3VM [13], the above traditional SSL methods do not consider class center issues. meanS3VM tried to transform data features to a kernel space for estimating the class center points. However, it only used a single high dimensional space to estimate the points.

Semi-supervised deep learning is less researched in credit prediction. We make use of the structure of semi-supervised deep learning to fully utilize unlabeled data by considering the multi-layer class center points.

3   Problem Formulation

In Sect. 3, we first give notations. Then, we discuss the problem of multiple class center points in samples and how the previous approach "meanS3VM" implements label mean in a single high-dimensional space. Based on the credit data distribution we observed, our meanNet tries to introduce label mean [13] into a semi-supervised neural network.

3.1   Notations

A credit dataset contains N labeled samples $\{(x_1, y_1), (x_2, y_2), \ldots, (x_N, y_N)\}$ and M unlabeled samples $\{(x_{N+1}), (x_{N+2}), \ldots, (x_{N+M})\}$. $x_i \in \mathbb{R}^d$ denotes that feature matrix of a sample is d-dimension, and $y_i \in \{0, 1\}$ is the collection of values for data labels. When $y_i = 0$, it means this sample is positive. and the value of 1 means it is negative. We assume $N \ll M$ in the credit dataset.

3.2   Credit Data Distribution

Traditionally, the credit of individuals or companies will be evaluated in several viewpoints, such as assets, past credit and income, etc. Therefore, credit datasets distribution will show multiple data-dense divisions. We normalize the data features from 0 to 1 and use t-SNE [14] to visualize the dataset distribution on 2-D space. The visualized result is shown in the Fig. 1. In this 2-D space, we can observe that the two classes overlap in feature space. We will discuss the influence of this situation on our experiments in Sect. 5.4.

3.3   Label Mean

Traditional semi-supervised SVMs [15] need to predict the labels on unlabeled data and then retrain models. meanS3VM estimates the label means of unlabeled data. Its classification performance is close to that of supervised SVM. meanS3VM maps unlabeled samples separately to two points in reproducing kernel Hilbert space (RKHS) [16]. The brief process is shown in Fig. 2. We assume that M^+ and M^- denote the number of positive and negative samples in unlabeled data, respectively. $\hat{m}^+$ and $\hat{m}^-$ denote the estimated center points of samples for the true center points of samples m^+ and m^- on unlabeled data, respectively.

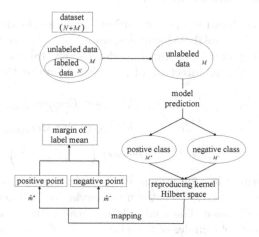

Fig. 1. An example of credit dataset visualization. Normalize the digitized data features to [0,1] and use t-SNE to visualize the data. Data is reduced to 2-D space. The dataset has two classes (1 and 2) and multiple data-dense divisions of each class.

Fig. 2. meanS3VM uses RKHS to get the estimate class center points for label mean.

Although meanS3VM tried to use multiple kernel learning (MKL) [24] for labeled data. It does not consider the case that the structure of a single high-dimensional space does not satisfy the distribution of samples when estimating the class center points of unlabeled data. Another problem is that using MKL for labeled data will take up extra main memory. It causes meanS3VM to be not suitable for big data applications.

Intuitively, the greater interval between two classes, the greater difference in the distribution of two classes. In this situation, classification problems are easier to solve. Considering that there are multiple dense divisions in data distribution, mapping the features of data into a single high-dimensional space does not effectively utilize unlabeled data. Therefore, we combine the multi-layer structure of a neural network and label mean as meanNet to maximize the distance between center points of samples of each class.

4 Our meanNet

In this section, we first introduce the structure of meanNet. The semi-supervised deep learning methods mentioned [10–12] followed Ladder Network [8] idea. Their research is from the point of the prediction of unlabeled data to improve the quality of semi-supervised learning and is orthogonal to us. Thus, we use Ladder Network as the basic framework. Then we explain how to introduce multi-layer label mean to each hidden layer of the semi-supervised deep learning method. In addition, we add cost-sensitive loss function for the inconsistent misclassification cost of credit datasets.

4.1 The Architecture of meanNet

We briefly introduce the structure of meanNet. Consider the credit dataset has N labeled samples and M unlabeled samples, and $N \ll M$. The main architecture of meanNet is a deep denoising AutoEncoder (dAE) [18] and adding noise into each hidden layer. The architecture of meanNet contains three parts (see the Fig. 3):

$$\tilde{x}, \tilde{z}^{(1)}, \ldots, \tilde{z}^{(L)}, \tilde{h}^{(1)}, \ldots, \tilde{h}^{(L)}, \tilde{y} \in Encoder_{noise}(x) \tag{1}$$

$$x, z^{(1)}, \ldots, z^{(L)}, h^{(1)}, \ldots, h^{(L)}, y \in Encoder_{clean}(x) \tag{2}$$

$$\hat{x}, \hat{z}^{(1)}, \ldots, \hat{z}^{(L)} \in Decoder\left(\tilde{z}^{(1)}, \ldots, \tilde{z}^{(L)}\right) \tag{3}$$

meanNet has three loss functions. cSC is the cost-sensitive cross entropy function for supervised part, UC is the unsupervised cost function and the third part is label mean distance. The goal of label mean is to maximize the distance between center points of samples of two classes. In order to convert problem into a convex optimization problem, we have modified label mean distance that will be discussed in Eq. (11). We call the transformation form of label mean distance as LMD. The goal of the final optimization is to minimize the weighted sum of the three loss functions by means of gradient descent.

4.2 The Details of meanNet

Our meanNet fully utilizes of unlabeled data by mapping the feature matrix of class center points of samples to multiple high dimensional spaces and maximizing the distance between the class center points. We combine the cost-sensitive function with meanNet for credit datasets.

As shown in Fig. 3, $x, \tilde{y}$ and y are the original feature matrix of input, the output of the layer L in the noise path and the output of the layer L in the clean path, respectively. $\tilde{z}^{(l)}$ is the variable after linear transformation, Normalization and adding noise of the layer l. $z^{(l)}$ defined same as $\tilde{z}^{(l)}$ but does not add noise. $\hat{z}^{(l)}$ is the output of Decoder layer l. $\tilde{h}^{(l)}$ and $h^{(l)}$ are variables after activation function. The layers corresponding to Corrupted Encoder and Decoder are connected by the variable $\tilde{z}$ and $\hat{z}$. The loss function of meanNet consists of three parts.

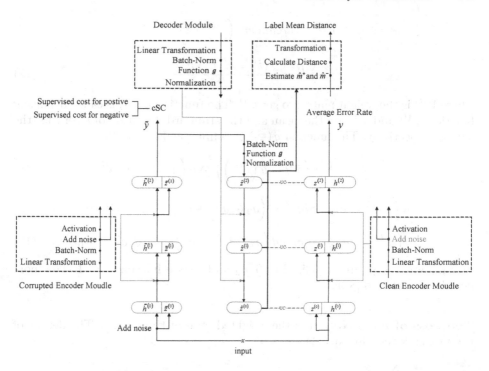

Fig. 3. The architecture of meanNet with two layers. meanNet contains three loss functions. cSC is the supervised cost using cross entropy and cost-sensitive function. UC is the unsupervised cost using MSE (Mean-Square Error). Label Mean Distance is the distance between estimated class center points which is called LMD.

The Architecture of Corrupted Encoder. In this part, the input $\tilde{x}$ is the original feature matrix which adds the Gaussian noise. Each layer of the Encoder is converted by linear transformation. Then, the followed step is batch normalization. Finally, after the activation function, the output of each hidden layer is obtained. The definitions are in Eq. (4) and (5),

$$\tilde{z}^{(l)} = batchnorm\left(W^{(l)} \cdot \tilde{h}^{(l-1)}\right) + Noise \tag{4}$$

$$\tilde{h}^{(l)} = activation\left(\gamma^{(l)}\tilde{z}^{(l)} + \beta^{(l)}\right) \tag{5}$$

where $W^{(l)}$ is the weight matrix to get $\tilde{z}^{(l)}$. $Noise$ is the Gaussian noise in which the mean is 0 and the variance is σ $\left(\mathcal{N}\left(0,\sigma^2\right)\right)$. $\odot$ means element-wise multiplication between two matrices. $\gamma^{(l)}$ and $\beta^{(l)}$ [19] are the scale and shift before using activation function. If the noise $\left(\mathcal{N}\left(0,\sigma^2\right)\right)$ is removed from Eq. (4), the structure will be clean Encoder.

The Architecture of Decoder. Each layer of the Decoder combines the variable $\tilde{z}^{(l)}$ from the Corrupted Encoder and the variable $\hat{z}^{(l+1)}$ from the Decoder to get $\hat{z}^{(l)}$. Detailed description refers to the following Eq. (6) and (7),

$$u^{(l)} = batchnorm\left(V^{(l)} \cdot \hat{z}^{(l+1)}\right) \tag{6}$$

$$\hat{z}^{(l)} = \frac{g\left(\tilde{z}^{(l)}, u^{(l)}\right) - \mu^{(l)}}{\sigma^{(l)}} \tag{7}$$

where $V^{(l)}$ is the weight matrix to get $u^{(l)}$. The function $g\left(\cdot, \cdot\right)$ is called denoising function. $\mu^{(l)}$ and $\sigma^{(l)}$ are the mean and the standard deviation of layer l for the batch, respectively. The function $g\left(\cdot, \cdot\right)$ is defined as Eq. (8),

$$g\left(\tilde{z}^{(l)}, u^{(l)}\right) = \left(\tilde{z}^{(l)} - \mu\left(u^{(l)}\right)\right) \odot v\left(u^{(l)}\right) + \mu\left(u^{(l)}\right) \tag{8}$$

$$\mu\left(u^{(l)}\right) = a_1 \odot Sigmoid\left(a_2 \odot u^{(l)} + a_3\right) + a_4 \odot u^{(l)} + a_5 \tag{9}$$

$$v\left(u^{(l)}\right) = a_6 \odot Sigmoid\left(a_7 \odot u^{(l)} + a_8\right) + a_9 \odot u^{(l)} + a_{10} \tag{10}$$

a_1, a_{3-6} and a_{8-10} are initialized to 0. a_2 and a_7 are initialized to 1. The more details can refer to [8,9].

The Loss of meanNet. It is the weighted sum of three parts. The details of the loss is defined in Eq. (11),

$$Loss = -\sum_{i=1}^{N}(\log\left(P\left(\tilde{y}_i = y_i^*|x_i, y_i^* = 0\right)\right) + c\log\left(P\left(\tilde{y}_i = y_i^*|x_i, y_i^* = 1\right)\right))$$
$$+ \sum_{i=1}^{M}\sum_{l=0}^{L}\lambda_l \left\|z_i^{(l)} - \hat{z}_i^{(l)}\right\|^2 + \sum_{l=0}^{L}\theta_l \frac{1 - cos\_dis\left(\hat{m}_l^+, \hat{m}_l^-\right)}{2} \tag{11}$$

where $\tilde{y}$ and y^* are the prediction of labeled data and the true label of labeled data, respectively. The first part is the cost-sensitive cross entropy function. c is the sensitive coefficient ($c \geqslant 1.0$). cSC is the total cost for the supervised part. λ_l and θ_l are the weight coefficient for UC and LMD at layer l, respectively. LMD is the variant of cosine distance function. The function turns the maximization problem to a minimization problem. The function cos_dis is used to calculate the cosine distance between two estimated class center points. $\hat{m}_l^+$ and $\hat{m}_l^-$ are the feature matrix of estimated positive and negative center points at layer l, respectively.

5 Experiments

5.1 Datasets and Evaluation Measures

We collect two credit datasets (Ping-An[1] and LC07-15[2]) to demonstrate the effectiveness of our meanNet. Table 1 is a brief introduction for the two credit datasets, where #Number, #Ratio and #Feature are the number of samples, the proportion of negative(default) samples in the datasets and the feature dimension, respectively.

Table 1. Description of two datasets.

Dataset	#Number	#Ratio(%)	#Feature
Ping-An	40000	14.73	490
LC07-15	887438	17.53	150

Due to the difference in magnitude between features, we normalize the features of the credit datasets. Finally, we retain the 46-dimensional features of Ping-An and 38-dimensional features of LC07-15. In preliminary experiments, we found that class imbalance impedes the performance of prediction. In particular, the models in the comparative experiments may overemphasize the majority (non-default) class while paying insufficient attention to the minority (default) group. In order to solve the imbalance of credit datasets, we use SMOTE [17] to balance data.

Each experiment randomly divides train set and test set, and randomly selects labeled data. We select 20% from datasets as test sets and assume that the labeled data for the credit datasets is 5%, 10% and 20%. Each set of mean-Net runs 10 times for each dataset. In our experiments, in order to ensure the objectivity of experiments, we take the average result as the final result through the experiments. We use the convolutional neural network as the basis network for our approach and implement meanNet using TensorFlow. To evaluate our approach, we compare meanNet with Ladder Network [8], Π-Model [10], Mean Teacher [11], MixMatch [12] and meanS3VM [13].

To ensure the comparability of the methods in the comparison experiments, we tune the mentioned semi-supervised neural networks as much as possible to obtain better performance for each method. More importantly, for the hyperparameters of meanNet, we first try to tune the hyperparameters on Ladder Network and then lock these on Ladder Network and meanNet except θ. In other words, we only try to find θ on meanNet.

In general, most of the classification problems use accuracy [8] to evaluate the prediction effect. Due to the characteristics of credit prediction, false positive rate (FPR) and F1 [22] should be comprehensively considered.

---

[1] https://www.kesci.com.

[2] https://www.kaggle.com.

5.2   Experimental Results on Ping-An Dataset

In addition to the hyperparameters that we need to tune, we use random initialization for other parameters. The learning rate is initialized to 0.002 and start decay to zero after 60% iteration process. The mini-batch size is set to 100. meanNet with the sensitive coefficient c has a large space for exploration, and we search it from 1.0 to 10.0. Finally, we get that the negative samples misclassification sensitivity coefficient c is 1.3. We rummaged the Gaussian noise with a search grid from 0.001 to 0.5. The Gaussian noise $\mathcal{N}(0, \sigma^2)$ is initialized to $\mathcal{N}(0, 0.01)$. The filter of each layer is 3-by-3 and channel sizes are $[1, 2, 12, 12, 20]$. λ is $[0.1, 0.01, 0.01, 0.01, 0.001]$ for UC. θ is $[0.1, 0.01, 0.01, 0.01, 0.001]$ for LMD. The average results of 10 times run are shown in Table 2.

Table 2. Test results on Ping-An dataset (Ladder Network [8], Π-Model [10], Mean Teacher [11], MixMatch [12] and meanS3VM [13]).

Labeled	Model set	FPR(%)	Accuracy(%)	F1
5%	meanS3VM	38.31(±5.74)	64.28(±2.76)	67.19(±4.15)
	Π-Model	50.31(±3.71)	68.28(±3.52)	73.27(±3.16)
	Mean teacher	36.39(±2.64)	68.67(±1.74)	70.22(±2.18)
	MixMatch	35.39(±1.80)	69.57(±1.55)	71.03±1.94)
	Supervised only (Ladder)	38.92(±4.37)	64.57(±2.38)	67.56(±2.31)
	Ladder ($c = 1.0$)	27.61(±3.52)	76.70(±0.82)	80.26(±1.25)
	Ladder ($c = 1.3$)	26.03(±2.96)	76.87(±1.02)	80.12(±1.52)
	meanNet ($c = 1.0$)	25.49(±3.83)	78.19(±0.62)	**80.89(±0.97)**
	meanNet ($c = 1.3$)	**23.14(±2.09)**	**78.31(±0.36)**	80.62(±1.04)
10%	meanS3VM	35.61(±3.63)	67.50(±2.93)	70.58(±3.41)
	Π-Model	47.41(±4.21)	70.45(±2.41)	74.95(±3.27)
	Mean teacher	33.08(±3.62)	71.08(±1.67)	72.27(±2.71)
	MixMatch	34.53(±2.31)	70.72(±1.97)	72.21(±2.26)
	Supervised only (Ladder)	36.94(±2.93)	66.21(±1.31)	68.82(±1.75)
	Ladder ($c = 1.0$)	25.63(±4.61)	79.29(±0.38)	82.69(±0.91)
	Ladder ($c = 1.3$)	23.91(±2.58)	79.36(±0.27)	82.57(±0.52)
	meanNet ($c = 1.0$)	24.23(±2.98)	80.71(±0.28)	83.45(±0.67)
	meanNet ($c = 1.3$)	**21.82(±2.37)**	**81.32(±0.66)**	**83.75(±1.10)**
20%	meanS3VM	32.63(±3.89)	70.69(±2.31)	73.21(±2.39)
	Π-Model	46.39(±3.49)	71.17(±2.03)	75.50(±2.44)
	Mean teacher	32.57(±2.48)	72.49(±1.77)	73.36(±1.09)
	MixMatch	31.82(±1.73)	73.23(±1.16)	74.79(±1.39)
	Supervised only (Ladder)	35.26(±3.48)	67.37(±1.75)	70.13(±2.46)
	Ladder ($c = 1.0$)	22.91(±1.12)	80.18(±0.45)	84.62(±0.47)
	Ladder ($c = 1.3$)	20.17(±1.72)	80.25(±0.38)	83.40(±0.55)
	meanNet ($c = 1.0$)	22.48(±1.42)	82.97(±0.48)	85.34(±0.70)
	meanNet ($c = 1.3$)	**20.05(±1.24)**	**83.34(±0.55)**	**85.60(±0.61)**

Applying multi-layer label mean to semi-supervised deep learning, and combine cost-sensitive function for the characteristic of credit prediction can improve the performance of prediction. Obviously, meanNet has the best performance compared to meanS3VM and other semi-supervised neural networks.

Default is more costly than non-default in the domain of credit prediction. Therefore, FPR is a significant evaluation index for credit prediction and is lower the better. Compared to Ladder Network, after the cost-sensitive loss function is added to meanNet, FPR is reduced by up to 4.47%. Moreover, meanNet makes better use of unlabeled data and the accuracy is improved by 2.79% than Ladder Network. Overall, our approach is up to 3.16% more accurate than Ladder Network, with a maximum reduction of 4.47% on FPR.

As the proportion of labeled data increases, we can find that the gap between Ladder Network and meanNet is decreasing for FPR. Especially when labeled data is 20%, there is almost no difference between Ladder Network and meanNet on FPR. Our meanNet uses multi-layer label mean, which performs well when labeled data is fewer.

5.3 Experimental Results on LC07-15 Dataset

Similar Ping-An dataset, the feature matrix is retained 38-dimension. The learning rate is initialized to 0.004. c is found as 1.2 after searching. Channel sizes of each layer are $[1, 2, 8, 12, 16]$ and the Gaussian noise $\mathcal{N}(0, 0.001)$. Other hyperparameters are same as Sect. 5.2. The average results of 10 times run are shown in Table 3.

In the results of LC07-15 dataset, meanNet is also better in terms of accuracy than the other networks and meanS3VM. After combining meanNet with the cost-sensitive loss function in the supervised part, FPR is reduced by up to 4.45% than Ladder Network. In terms of FPR and F1, the cost-sensitive loss function can effectively reduce FPR.

It can be seen from Table 3 that the cost-sensitive loss function will reduce the accuracy for meanNet. The cost-sensitive loss function has a penalty effect on the misclassification of default samples. Therefore, our meanNet with the cost-sensitive loss function has an outstanding effect on FPR, which affects the accuracy. Whether using cost sensitive function should highly depend on specific actual applied circumstances.

666   G. Wang et al.

Table 3. Test results on LC07-15 dataset (Ladder Network [8], Π-Model [10], Mean Teacher [11], MixMatch [12] and meanS3VM [13]).

Labeled	Model set	FPR (%)	Accuracy (%)	F1
5%	meanS3VM	38.53(±3.28)	63.01(±1.14)	65.88(±2.28)
	Π-Model	56.98(±3.07)	63.56(±1.92)	70.26(±2.76)
	Mean teacher	39.70(±1.54)	63.25(±2.75)	65.25(±2.81)
	MixMatch	40.44(±2.84)	62.18(±2.16)	64.11(±2.39)
	Supervised only (Ladder)	41.54(±3.79)	61.35(±2.36)	63.82(±2.58)
	Ladder ($c = 1.0$)	32.43(±1.10)	77.60(±0.15)	80.76(±0.29)
	Ladder ($c = 1.2$)	31.11(±1.73)	77.45(±0.20)	80.60(±0.22)
	meanNet ($c = 1.0$)	32.44(±1.26)	**78.31**(±0.18)	**81.27**(±0.25)
	meanNet ($c = 1.2$)	**30.06**(±2.56)	78.27(±0.27)	81.01(±0.43)
10%	meanS3VM	36.47(±2.89)	64.14(±0.89)	66.62(±1.42)
	Π-Model	54.74(±3.27)	66.06(±1.35)	72.38(±2.61)
	Mean teacher	38.20(±1.73)	64.68(±2.14)	66.59(±1.79)
	MixMatch	359.5(±2.61)	68.25(±1.63)	70.38(±1.94)
	Supervised only (Ladder)	39.21(±3.04)	63.83(±2.71)	65.17(±2.54)
	Ladder ($c = 1.0$)	31.93(±0.91)	78.03(±0.15)	81.10(±0.28)
	Ladder ($c = 1.2$)	31.23(±1.75)	77.96(±0.16)	80.90(±0.45)
	meanNet ($c = 1.0$)	30.34(±1.69)	**78.79**(±0.16)	**81.60**(±0.47)
	meanNet ($c = 1.2$)	**29.25**(±1.64)	78.73(±0.13)	81.43(±0.28)
20%	meanS3VM	33.94(±3.41)	64.48(±1.35)	67.56(±2.18)
	Π-Model	53.24(±4.53)	68.20(±3.42)	74.28(±2.85)
	Mean teacher	34.46(±3.08)	67.90(±2.11)	69.53(±2.38)
	MixMatch	32.21(±1.29)	70.40(±2.12)	72.01(±1.83)
	Supervised only (Ladder)	37.29(±2.09)	65.77(±1.74)	68.25(±2.67)
	Ladder ($c = 1.0$)	31.45(±1.43)	78.36(±0.21)	81.20(±0.26)
	Ladder ($c = 1.2$)	28.99(±1.27)	78.23(±0.18)	80.83(±0.31)
	meanNet ($c = 1.0$)	30.60(±0.59)	**79.52**(±0.15)	**82.17**(±0.28)
	meanNet ($c = 1.2$)	**27.00**(±1.02)	79.40(±0.17)	81.82(±0.30)

5.4   Discussion

We showed how meanNet used multi-layer label mean to improve the performance of semi-supervised learning. The proposed approach is simple and easy to implement with semi-supervised neural networks. Meanwhile, we verified the performance of several popular methods on credit datasets. There are still some issues to discuss:

(1) Currently, popular semi-supervised neural networks provide an idea of introducing unlabeled data into neural networks for learning. Although this can

increase the diversity of training samples, models [8,10–12] in the experiments have less consideration for data distribution.

(2) As said in Sect. 3.2, credit datasets have some hard samples. This means that some positive and negative samples are similar in feature space. Models [8,10–12] in the experiments were validated on image datasets and did not consider the situation. Therefore, we consider using multi-layer label mean to solve hard samples in credit prediction. For UC, meanNet and Ladder Network are reconstructed from the feature perspective, that is to say, keep the output of each layer between clean Encoder and Decoder consistent. This sub-task does not disturb supervised learning [8,9]. Π-Model, Mean Teacher and MixMatch define the unsupervised part from another perspective. The unsupervised loss function is to reduce the differences between the prediction of sub-networks for unlabeled data.

(3) Not surprisingly, the thought of multi-layer label mean may be applied to other domains. Since the idea of meanNet is based on real data distribution, any data with a distribution similar to credit data can try to use multi-layer label mean to improve the performance of prediction.

(4) meanNet with a weighted loss function on each layer has a much larger search space for exploration. And we follow Ladder Network [8] to search hyperparameters. Meanwhile, when exploring the effect of different Gaussian noise settings on the experiments, we found an interesting phenomenon that Gaussian noise cannot be set as large as the other networks [8,10–12] for credit data (Therefore we set it to $\mathcal{N}(0, 0.01)$ or $\mathcal{N}(0, 0.001)$).

6   Conclusions and Future Work

In this paper, we propose an approach by enhancing Ladder Network for credit prediction. Specifically, the loss function of multi-layer label mean is to maximize the difference between positive and negative center points of samples. Meanwhile, we use the cost-sensitive loss function to solve the inconsistent misclassification cost between positive and negative samples in credit prediction. Experimental results on two credit datasets show that meanNet is performing well. The proposed multi-layer label mean loss effectively improves the prediction accuracy and the cost-sensitive loss effectively reduces the FPR for credit prediction. Considering more practical situations, an obvious future line of research will therefore be to extend our work to multi-classification problems.

Acknowledgment. This work was partly supported by JSPS KAKENHI Grant Number 19K12230.

References

1. Berger, A.N., Frame, W.S.: Small business credit scoring and credit availability. J. Small Bus. Manag. **45**(1), 5–22 (2007)

2. Rostamkalaei, A., Freel, M.: The cost of growth: small firms and the pricing of bank loans. Small Bus. Econ. **46**(2), 1–18 (2015). https://doi.org/10.1007/s11187-015-9681-x

3. He, H., Zhang, W., Zhang, S.: A novel ensemble method for credit scoring: adaption of different imbalance ratios. Expert Syst. Appl. **98**, 105–117 (2018)

4. Lessmann, S., Baesens, B., Seow, H.V., Thomas, L.C.: Benchmarking state-of-the-art classification algorithms for credit scoring: an update of research. Eur. J. Oper. Res. **247**(1), 124–136 (2015)

5. Fiore, U., Santis, A.D., Perla, F., Zanetti, P., Palmieri, F.: Using generative adversarial networks for improving classification effectiveness in credit card fraud detection. Inf. Sci. **479**(Apr), 448–455 (2019)

6. Garca, V., Marqus, A.I., Snchez, J.S.: Exploring the synergetic effects of sample types on the performance of ensembles for credit risk and corporate bankruptcy prediction. Inf. Fus. **47**, 88–101 (2019)

7. Chapelle, O., Schölkopf, B., Zien, A.: Semi-Supervised Learning. MIT Press, Cambridge (2006)

8. Rasmus, A., Valpola, H., Honkala, M., Valpola, H., Raiko, T.: Semi-Supervised Learning with Ladder Network. In: Advances in Neural Information Processing Systems (NIPS), pp. 3546–3554 (2015)

9. Pezeshki, M., Fan, L., Brakel, P., Courville, A., Bengio, Y.: Deconstructing the ladder network architecture. In: International Conference on Machine Learning (ICML), pp. 2368–2376 (2016)

10. Laine, S., Aila, T.: Temporal ensembling for semi-supervised learning. In: International Conference on Learning Representations (ICLR) (2017)

11. Tarvainen, A., Valpola, H.: Mean teachers are better role models: weight-averaged consistency targets improve semi-supervised deep learning results. In: Advances in Neural Information Processing Systems (NIPS), pp. 1195–1204 (2017)

12. Berthelot, D., Carlini, N., Goodfellow, I., Papernot, N., Oliver, A., Raffel, C.A.: Mixmatch: a holistic approach to semi-supervised learning. In: Advances in Neural Information Processing Systems (NIPS), pp. 5050–5060 (2019)

13. Li, Y., Kwok, J.T., Zhou, Z.: Semi-supervised learning using label mean. In: International Conference on Machine Learning (ICML), pp. 663–640 (2009)

14. van der Maaten, L., Hinton, G.: Visualizing data using t-SNE. J. Mach. Learn. Res. **9**(Nov), 2579–2605 (2008)

15. Joachims, T.: Transductive inference for text classification using support vector machines. In: International Conference on Machine Learning (ICML), pp. 200–209 (1999)

16. Gretton, A., Borgwardt, K.M., Rasch, M., Schölkopf, B., Smola, A.J.: A kernel method for the two-sample-problem. In: Advances in Neural Information Processing Systems (NIPS), pp. 513–520 (2006)

17. Kovács, G.: An empirical comparison and evaluation of minority oversampling techniques on a large number of imbalanced datasets. Appl. Soft Comput. **83**, 105662 (2019)

18. Valpola, H.: From neural PCA to deep unsupervised learning. In: Advances in Independent Component Analysis and Learning Machines, pp. 143–171 (2015)

19. Ioffe, S., Szegedy, C.: Batch normalization: accelerating deep network training by reducing internal covariate shift. In: International Conference on Machine Learning (ICML), pp. 448–456 (2015)

20. Li, Z., Tian, Y., Li, K., Zhou, F., Yang, W.: Reject inference in credit scoring using semi-supervised support vector machines. Expert Syst. Appl. **74**, 105–114 (2017)

21. Tian, Y., Luo, J.: A new branch-and-bound approach to semi-supervised support vector machine. Soft Comput. **21**, 245–254 (2017). https://doi.org/10.1007/s00500-016-2089-y

22. Zhang, J., Li, L., Zhu, G., Meng, X., Xie, Q.: A comparison study of semi-supervised SVM algorithms for small business credit prediction. In: International Conference on Behavioral, Economic and Socio-cultural Computing (BESC), pp. 1–6 (2016)

23. Kennedy, K., Namee, B.M., Delany, S.J.: Using semi-supervised classifiers for credit scoring. J. Oper. Res. Soc. **64**(4), 513–529 (2013)

24. Bach, R.R., Lanckriet, G.R.G., Jordan, M.I.: Multiple kernel learning, conic duality, and the SMO algorithm. In: International Conference on Machine Learning (ICML), pp. 41–48 (2004)

25. Abdelhameed, A., Bayoumi, M.: Semi-supervised deep learning system for epileptic seizures onset prediction. In: International Conference on Machine Learning and Applications (ICMLA), pp. 1186–1191 (2018)

26. Perone, C.S., Cohen-Adad, J.: Deep semi-supervised segmentation with weight-averaged consistency targets. arXiv preprint arXiv:1807.04657 (2018)

27. Ding, Y., Yu, C., Jiang, J.: A neural network model for semi-supervised review aspect identification. In: Kim, J., Shim, K., Cao, L., Lee, J.-G., Lin, X., Moon, Y.-S. (eds.) PAKDD 2017. LNCS (LNAI), vol. 10235, pp. 668–680. Springer, Cham (2017). https://doi.org/10.1007/978-3-319-57529-2_52

Multi-task Attributed Graphical Lasso

Yao Zhang[1], Yun Xiong[1,2(✉)], Xiangnan Kong[3], Xinyue Liu[3],
and Yangyong Zhu[1,2]

[1] School of Computer Science, Shanghai Key Laboratory of Data Science,
Fudan University, Shanghai, China
{yaozhang18,yunx,yyzhu}@fudan.edu.cn
[2] Shanghai Institute for Advanced Communication and Data Science,
Fudan University, Shanghai, China
[3] Worcester Polytechnic Institute, Worcester, MA, USA
{xkong,xliu4}@wpi.edu

Abstract. Sparse inverse covariance estimation, *i.e.*, Graphical Lasso,
can estimate the connections among a set of random variables basing
on their observations. Recent research on Graphical Lasso has been
extended to multi-task settings, where multiple graphs sharing the same
set of variables are estimated collectively to reduce variances. However,
different tasks usually involve different variables. For example, when we
want to estimate gene networks w.r.t different diseases simultaneously,
the related gene sets vary. In this paper, we study the problem of multi-
task Graphical Lasso where the tasks may involve different variable sets.
To share information across tasks, we consider the attributes of variables and assume that the structures of graphs are not only determined
by observations, but influenced by attributes. We formulate the problem
of learning multiple graphs jointly with observations and attributes, *i.e.*,
Multi-task Attributed Graphical Lasso (MAGL), and propose an effective algorithm to solve it. We rely on the LogDet divergence to explore
latent relations between attributes of the variables and linkage structures
among the variables. Multiple precision matrices and a projection matrix
are optimized such that the ℓ_1-penalized negative log-likelihood and the
divergence are minimized.

Keywords: Graphical lasso · Multi-task learning · LogDet divergence

1 Introduction

Gaussian Graphical Models (GGMs) [25] provide a powerful framework for
describing the dependencies among a set of variables and have been attracting much attention in the fields of finance, social networks and bio-informatics,
etc.[16,28]. In these applications, some of the edges between the nodes are usually unknown and must be inferred from observations of the node activities.
It has been shown that the non-zero elements of the precision matrix, *i.e.*, the
inverse of the covariance matrix, correspond to the edges in the underlying graph

© Springer Nature Switzerland AG 2020
X. Wang et al. (Eds.): APWeb-WAIM 2020, LNCS 12317, pp. 670–684, 2020.
https://doi.org/10.1007/978-3-030-60259-8_49

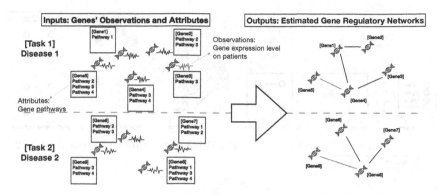

Fig. 1. An illustration of multi-task attributed Graphical Lasso. The tasks are to estimate gene regulatory networks for two diseases collectively to reduce the variance of the estimates. Each gene is accompanied by its expression level on different patients as observations, and pathways it belongs to as attributes. Similar attributes drive certain pairs of variables to be connected (shown in red). (Color figure online)

[25]. Thus structure learning of a GGM is equivalent to estimating its precision matrix, which can be solved via Graphical Lasso (GLasso) [7].

In some cases, multiple GLasso tasks are involved and each contains several observations. Observations in different tasks may come from different distributions, but they are all on the same set of variables. For example, researchers may want to estimate gene regulatory networks for cancer patients and healthy subjects separately using their gene expression levels. Since the gene networks in multiple tasks are highly related, we often estimate multiple precision matrices collectively. The multi-task Graphical Lasso could borrow strength across tasks and reduce the variance of the estimates [19]. There have been some recent work on the multi-task Graphical Lasso [3,12,24,27], but they assume that the sets of variables across tasks are identical and the nonzero patterns in precision matrices are similar across multiple graphs. This is not always the case in the real world where each task could have its own associated variable set. For instance, our tasks are to estimate gene regulatory networks for multiple diseases collectively, but sets of genes involved may not be identical across these diseases. We try to consider multiple sets of variables in multiple tasks.

It is not clear how to jointly solve tasks with different variable sets, but there is a key observation that variables are often accompanied by attributes that might help. For example, each gene is associated with attributes, such as gene families, pathways and related-diseases. In this paper, we study the problem of multi-task attributed Graphical Lasso, where the goal is to simultaneously estimate multiple graphs by exploiting the relationship between attributes and graph structures as illustrated in Fig. 1.

Despite the significance, the multi-task attributed Graphical Lasso is highly challenging due to:

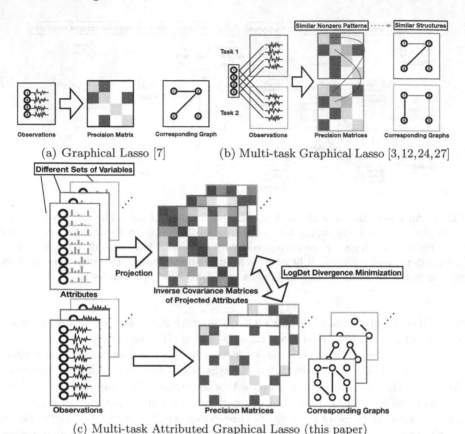

(a) Graphical Lasso [7]   (b) Multi-task Graphical Lasso [3,12,24,27]

(c) Multi-task Attributed Graphical Lasso (this paper)

Fig. 2. (a) Graphical Lasso estimates a single precision matrix and the corresponding graph from observations of variables. (b) Multi-task Graphical Lasso estimates graphs jointly from multiple sets of observations under assumption that the nonzero patterns in precision matrices should be similar. (c) Multi-task attributed Graphical Lasso accepts attributes as side information and supports different sets of variables across tasks. It assumes that the structures of graphs are related to the attributes of variables.

- **Heterogeneity of Variables**: Since the sets of variables are not necessarily identical across tasks, the existing methods based on the assumption that the similar nonzero patterns in precision matrices are no longer applicable. It is challenging to share information across tasks with heterogeneous sets of variables to improve the quality of estimates.
- **Relations between Attributes and Graphs**: Previous methods do not utilize the attributes and infer the graphs by only using observations of variables. But in attributed graphs, connectivities between variables are also influenced by their attributes. It is challenging to define the relationship between attributes and graphs. Besides, how to inject attributes into the multi-task framework is unclear.

To address these issues, we present a novel method called MAGL (Multi-task Attributed Graphical Lasso), which uses the LogDet divergence [18] to build a connection between structures and attributes. Multiple precision matrices and a projection matrix are simultaneously optimized so that the ℓ_1-penalized negative log-likelihood is minimized, meanwhile the LogDet divergence between the precision matrix of graphs and the inverse covariance matrix of projected attributes in each task is also minimized. Since the information is shared indirectly through the projection matrix, our formulation supports heterogeneous sets of variables.

We illustrate the differences between our proposal and existing related problem settings in Fig. 2. The main contributions of our paper are as follows: (1) We study the problem of multi-task attributed Graphical Lasso, and incorporate attributes into the framework of multi-task Graphical Lasso by using the LogDet divergence. (2) We propose an efficient algorithm to solve MAGL using block coordinate descent and augmented Lagrangian method. (3) The conducted experiments illustrate the effectiveness of the proposal.

2 Problem Formulation

In this section, we briefly review some related concepts and notions. We then formulate the problem of multi-task attributes Graphical Lasso.

• **Notations:** In this paper, $\Re$ stands for the set of all real numbers. The space of symmetric matrices is denoted by $\mathcal{S}^n$. The cone of positive semi-definite matrices is denoted by $\mathcal{S}^n_+$, and its interior is $\mathcal{S}^n_{++}$. $\|X\|_1 = \sum_{i,j} |X_{ij}|$ is the element-wise ℓ_1 norm. $\|X\|_F^2 = \sum_{i,j} X_{ij}^2$ is the squared Frobenius norm. $\mathrm{Tr}(\cdot)$ and $\det(\cdot)$ denote the trace and the determinant of a matrix respectively. $\sigma(X)$ returns all singular values of X. $\mathbb{1}\{\text{condition}\}$ is the indicator function.

2.1 Preliminaries

Graphical Lasso: Assume we have a set of samples $X \in \Re^{p \times n}$ drawn i.i.d. from a p-variate Gaussian distribution: $x_j \sim \mathcal{N}_p(\mathbf{0}, \Sigma)$, $j = 1, \ldots, n$, where $\Sigma \in \mathcal{S}^p_{++}$, and x_j is the j-th column of X. A natural way to estimate the precision matrix $\Theta = \Sigma^{-1}$ is via maximum log-likelihood estimation (MLE). The log-likelihood function takes the form (up to a constant) $l(S, \Theta) = \log \det \Theta - \mathrm{Tr}(S\Theta)$, where $S = \frac{1}{n} X X^T \in \mathcal{S}^p_+$ is the sample covariance matrix. However, the MLE fails when $p > n$ because S becomes singular. Even if $p \leqslant n$ and S is not singular, S^{-1} is usually dense. To obtain a meaningful estimate, the ℓ_1 regularization has been employed to induce sparsity. This leads to the sparse inverse covariance matrix estimation problem, also known as Graphical Lasso (GLasso) [7]: $\min_\Theta -l(S, \Theta) + \lambda\|\Theta\|_1$, where $\lambda > 0$ is an ℓ_1 regularization parameter.

LogDet Divergence: The LogDet divergence [18] is proposed to measure the "closeness" between two matrices $X, Y \in \mathcal{S}^p_{++}$. It is defined as

$$D_{ld}(X, Y) = \mathrm{Tr}(XY^{-1}) - \log \det(XY^{-1}) - p.$$

The LogDet divergence is non-negative, and $D_{ld}(X, Y) = 0$ if and only if $X = Y$. It is convex in the first argument. It has been shown [4] that the KL divergence between two multivariate Gaussian distributions with the same mean vector, $\mathcal{N}(\mu, \Theta^{-1})$ and $\mathcal{N}(\mu, \Omega^{-1})$, is proportional to the LogDet divergence between the corresponding precision matrices:

$$KL\left(\mathcal{N}(\mu, \Theta^{-1}), \mathcal{N}(\mu, \Omega^{-1})\right) = \frac{1}{2} D_{ld}(\Theta, \Omega).$$

2.2 Multi-task Attributed Graphical Lasso

Consider that we are given $K \geqslant 2$ tasks, each consisting of not only variables' activities $X^k \in \mathbb{R}^{p_k \times n_k}$, but also attributes $A^k \in \mathbb{R}^{p_k \times m}$, where the i-th row of A^k is the i-th variable's attributes in the k-th task. The samples within each task X^k are identically distributed with a p_k-variate Gaussian distribution with zero mean and covariance matrix $\left(\Theta^k\right)^{-1} \in \mathcal{S}_{++}^{p_k}$. Further we assume that the structures of graphs are influenced by the variables' attributes. We wish to borrow information across the K tasks to estimate the K precision matrices jointly.

For notational simplicity, we assume that $p_i = p$ and $n_i = n$ $\forall i$, but our formulation and algorithm can be easily adapted to the general setting. We formulate the problem of multi-task attributed Graphical Lasso (MAGL) as

$$\min_{\substack{\Theta^k, U \\ 1 \leqslant k \leqslant K}} \sum_{k=1}^{K} \left[-l\left(S^k, \Theta^k\right) + \lambda_1 \|\Theta^k\|_1\right] + \lambda_2 \sum_{k=1}^{K} D_{ld}\left(\Theta^k, \Omega^k\right) + \frac{\lambda_3}{2} \|U\|_F^2, \quad (2.1)$$

where $\Omega^k = \left(\epsilon I + A^k U U^T (A^k)^T\right)^{-1}$, and $U \in \mathbb{R}^{m \times d}$ is a projection matrix from a m-dimensional input space to a d-dimensional output space. $\lambda_1, \lambda_2, \lambda_3, \epsilon > 0$ are the model parameters. The first part in the objective function is the sum of K GLasso problems. We view the projected attributes $A^k U \in \mathbb{R}^{p \times d}$ as d samples drawn from the Gaussian distribution $\mathcal{N}_p\left(0, (\Omega^k)^{-1}\right)$. $\Omega^k = \left(\epsilon I + A^k U U^T (A^k)^T\right)^{-1}$ is the estimate of the inverse of the precision matrix, where ϵ is used to make it non-singular. Now, $D_{ld}(\Theta^k, \Omega^k)$ is the KL divergence between the two Gaussian distributions. By this means, we build a connection between the structures of graphs and the variables' attributes. We also use the squared Frobenius norm of U to prevent overfitting. As illustrated in Fig. 2(c), the Problem 2.1 finds K precision matrices and a projection matrix that minimize the negative log-likelihood of data, and meanwhile minimize the divergence between the precision matrices of data and projected attributes in each task.

3 Methodology

We propose an algorithm based on block coordinate descent to alternatively update $\{\Theta^k\}_{k=1}^K$ and U until convergence. Subproblems then are solved by the Augmented Lagrangian Method (ALM).

Algorithm 1. Multi-task Attributed Graphical Lasso (Problem 2.1)

Require: $\{(S^k, A^k)\}_{k=1}^K, d, \lambda_1, \lambda_2, \lambda_3 > 0, \epsilon = 0.01, \rho_0 = 2, \gamma = 1.05$
 1: Randomly initialize U
 2: **repeat**
 3:     Solve Problem 3.1 for $\{\Theta^k\}_{k=1}^K$
 4:     Initialize $Y^k = \mathbf{0}, \rho = \rho_0$
 5:     **repeat**
 6:         Solve Problems 3.3 and 3.4 for $\{Z^k\}_{k=1}^K$
 7:         Solve the linear system 3.5 for U
 8:         Update $Y^k := Y^k + \rho(Z^k - \tilde{A}^k U)$
 9:         Update $\rho := \gamma \cdot \rho$
10:     **until convergence**
11: **until convergence**
12: **return** $\{\Theta^k\}_{k=1}^K, U$

Update Θ^k: To update $\{\Theta^k\}_{k=1}^K$, with U fixed, we can decompose the Problem 2.1 into K independent parts (suppressing superscript k for simplicity):

$$\text{argmin}_\Theta -l(S, \Theta) + \lambda_1 \|\Theta\|_1 + \lambda_2 D_{ld}(\Theta, \Omega) = \text{argmin}_\Theta -l(\tilde{S}, \Theta) + \frac{\lambda_1}{1 + \lambda_2}\|\Theta\|_1, \tag{3.1}$$

which is a Graphical Lasso problem with a scaled and shifted covariance matrix

$$\tilde{S} = \frac{1}{1 + \lambda_2}\left[S + \lambda_2 \left(\epsilon I + AUU^T A\right)\right].$$

This problem can be seen as a "supervised" Graphical Lasso since the LogDet term hopes two distributions to be similar. Since $\tilde{S}$ is positive semi-definite, Problem 3.1 can be solved by most classical Graphical Lasso solvers efficiently [2,15,21,29].

Update U: The Problem 2.1 with $\{\Theta^k\}_{k=1}^K$ fixed can be re-organized into

$$\min_U \quad \sum_{k=1}^K [-\log\det(I + \frac{A^k}{\sqrt{\epsilon}}UU^T \left(\frac{A^k}{\sqrt{\epsilon}}\right)^T) + \text{Tr}\left((A^k)^T \Theta^k A^k UU^T\right)] \\ + \frac{\lambda_3}{2\lambda_2}\|U\|_F^2. \tag{3.2}$$

Though Problem 3.2 is not convex, we could use the Augmented Lagrangian Method (ALM) to solve it effectively. It can then be rewritten as

$$\min_{\substack{Z^k, U \\ 1 \leqslant k \leqslant K}} \quad \sum_{k=1}^K \left[-\log\det\left(I + Z^k(Z^k)^T\right) + \text{Tr}\left(H^k UU^T\right)\right] + \frac{\lambda_3}{2\lambda_2}\|U\|_F^2,$$

$$\text{s.t.} \quad Z^k = \tilde{A}^k U,$$

where $Z^k \in \Re^{p \times d}$ are auxiliary variables, and $H^k = (A^k)^T \Theta^k A^k$, $\tilde{A}^k = \frac{A^k}{\sqrt{\epsilon}}$. The augmented Lagrangian function is given by

$$\mathcal{L}_\rho \left(U, \{Z^k\}, \{Y^k\} \right)$$
$$= \sum_{k=1}^{K} \left[-\log \det \left(I + Z^k (Z^k)^T \right) + \text{Tr} \left(H^k U U^T \right) \right.$$
$$\left. + \text{Tr} \left((Y^k)^T (Z^k - \tilde{A}^k U) \right) + \frac{\rho}{2} \|Z^k - \tilde{A}^k U\|_F^2 \right] + \frac{\lambda_3}{2\lambda_2} \|U\|_F^2,$$

where $\rho > 0$ is a penalty parameter and $Y^k \in \Re^{p \times d}$ are dual variables. Solving Problem 3.2 is equivalent to minimizing $\mathcal{L}_\rho \left(U, \{Z^k\}, \{Y^k\} \right)$ with a sufficiently large ρ. In practice, we minimize $\{\mathcal{L}_{\rho_t}\}_{t=0}^\infty$ iteratively with a monotonic increasing sequence $\{\rho_t\}_{t=0}^\infty$ satisfying $\lim_{t \to \infty} \rho_t \to \infty$.

Given the initial $U_0, Z_0^k, Y_0^k, \rho_0$, we do the following block coordinate updates:
Step 1: Compute optimal $\{Z_{t+1}^k\}$ with U_t and $\{Y_t^k\}$ fixed. The $\mathcal{L}_{\rho_t}$ is separable w.r.t Z^k, so minimizing $\mathcal{L}_{\rho_t}$ over Z^k takes the form (suppressing k) of

$$\underset{Z}{\text{argmin}} - \log \det(I + ZZ^T) + \frac{\rho_t}{2} \|Z - (\tilde{A}U_t - \frac{1}{\rho_t} Y_t)\|_F^2. \quad (3.3)$$

The above problem can be converted to a set of scalar minimization problems using the following theorem [17]:

Theorem 1. *For unitarily invariant function $F(Z) = f \circ \sigma(Z)$, assuming the singular value decomposition of $R \in \Re^{p \times d}$ is $R = U \Sigma_R V^T$, $\Sigma_R = diag(\{\sigma_{R,i}\}_{i=1}^{\min(p,d)})$, the optimal solution to the problem*

$$\min_Z \ F(Z) + \frac{\rho}{2} \|Z - R\|_F^2$$

is $Z^\star = U \Sigma_Z^\star V^T$, with $\Sigma_Z^\star = diag(\{\sigma_i^\star\}_{i=1}^{\min(p,d)})$ obtained by solving scalar minimization problems

$$\sigma_i^\star = \underset{x}{\text{argmin}} \, f(x) + \frac{\rho}{2} (x - \sigma_{R,i})^2, \ i = 1, \ldots, \min(p, d). \quad (3.4)$$

Since $F(Z) = -\log \det(I + ZZ^T) = -\sum_{i=1}^{\min(p,d)} \log(1 + \sigma_{Z,i}^2)$, $F(Z)$ is a unitarily invariant function with $f(\sigma_{Z,i}) = -\log(1 + \sigma_{Z,i}^2)$, where $\sigma_{Z,i}$ is the i-th singular value of Z. By checking the gradient equation of Problem 3.4, we can find that the optimal $\sigma_i^\star$ is the non-negative root of the cubic equation:

$$g(x) = x^3 - \sigma_i x^2 + (1 - \frac{2}{\rho_t}) x - \sigma_i = 0,$$

where $\sigma_i \geq 0$ is the i-th singular value of $\tilde{A}U_t - \frac{1}{\rho_t} Y_t$. Observe that there exists at least one non-negative root. Besides, by checking the discriminant of the cubic

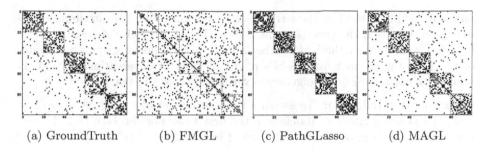

(a) GroundTruth   (b) FMGL   (c) PathGLasso   (d) MAGL

Fig. 3. The precision matrices learned by three comparing methods.

equation, we can find that the equation $g(x) = 0$ only has one real root if $\rho_t \geq 2$ or a triple root 0 if $\rho_t = 2$ and $\sigma_i = 0$. Therefore, Problem 3.4 has a unique optimum if $\rho_t \geq 2$, so does Problem 3.3.

Step 2: Compute optimal U_{t+1} with $\{Z_{t+1}^k\}$, $\{Y_t^k\}$ fixed. The gradient equation is

$$\left[\sum_k \left(2H^k + \rho_t (\tilde{A}^k)^T \tilde{A}^k \right) + \frac{\lambda_3}{\lambda_2} I \right] U_{t+1} = \sum_k \left[(\tilde{A}^k)^T (Y_t^k + \rho_t Z_{t+1}^k) \right]. \quad (3.5)$$

Thus the optimal U_{t+1} can be solved from this linear system.

Step 3: Update the dual variables:

$$Y_{t+1}^k := Y_t^k + \rho_t (Z_{t+1}^k - \tilde{A}^k U_{t+1}), \ \forall k.$$

Step 4: Update the penalty parameter $\rho_{t+1} = \gamma \cdot \rho_t$, where $\gamma > 1$.

The algorithm for MAGL is summarized in Algorithm 1.

4   Experiments

4.1   Data Collection

We evaluate the proposed method on real-world datasets and synthetic datasets:

• **DBLP** is a subset of a bibliographical network. Following settings in [23], we extracted 20 conferences and top-5000 authors among 4 areas from 2006 to 2015. After removing stop words in paper titles, we get 679 frequent terms as the vocabulary to generate bag-of-words representations as authors' activities. Here we assume the life cycle of each author is 5 years, *i.e.*, the length of the PhD program. Given a year, each author is accompanied by a one-hot attribute vector of length 5, which indicates the stage he was in. The tasks are to estimate connections among authors in each year.

• **AML** contains two groups of gene expression levels of AML (acute myeloid leukemia) studies [8,11] used in [9]. Each gene is categorized into at least one pathway, which is used as its attributes. Specifically, the j-th attribute of the i-th gene $A_{ij} = 1$ if the gene is in the j-th pathway, otherwise $A_{ij} = 0$.

The generative method of synthetic data is as follows: given the number of tasks K, the number of variables p, the number of observations n, and the number of classes m, first we generate variables' classes in two ways:

- **Dataset-1 (Ordered):** We assign a random integer $c_i^1 \in \{c \in \mathbb{N} \mid -\lfloor m/2 \rfloor \leqslant c \leqslant m\}$ to each variable as its class in the first task. For the k-th ($k > 1$) task, the i-th variable's class is randomly picked in the set $c_i^k \in \{c_i^{k-1}, c_i^{k-1} + 1\}$.

- **Dataset-2 (Unordered):** $c_i^k \in \{c \in \mathbb{N} \mid 1 \leqslant c \leqslant m\}$ is always randomly picked for all tasks. The i-th variable's attribute vector in the k-th task a_i^k is a vector of all zeros, except that the c_i^k-th element is 1 if $1 \leqslant c_i^k \leqslant m$. The element of a precision matrix $(\Sigma^k)^{-1}_{ij}$ is nonzero with the probability $\frac{(4-t)p}{\sum_{u,v} \mathbb{1}\{\delta_{uv}^k = t\}}$ if $\delta_{ij}^k = t \in \{0, 1, 2\}$, otherwise $\frac{p}{\sum_{u,v} \mathbb{1}\{\delta_{uv}^k \geqslant 3\}}$, where $\delta_{ij}^k = |c_i^k - c_j^k|$. By this means, the number of nonzero off-diagonal elements in each precision matrix is about $10p$. We calculate the sample covariance matrix S^k using n samples.

Dataset-1 simulates the case that there is a natural order among multiple tasks, and tasks share a common set of variables, while Dataset-2 does not assume the identical variable sets nor orderliness among tasks.

4.2   Compared Methods

To validate the effectiveness of our proposal, we test the following methods: (1) **GLasso** [7] is the vanilla Graphical Lasso. We fit a GLasso model for each task separately. (2) **PathGLasso** [9] takes a sample covariance matrix and a set of pathways as input. It assumes that a pair of variables will not be connected if they do not participate together in any pathways. We fit a PathGLasso model independently for each task. (3) **FMGL** [27] jointly estimates multiple tasks of Graphical Lasso using a sequential fused ℓ_1 penalty for adjacent precision matrices. It requires that the tasks have a natural order. (4) **JGL** [3] jointly estimates multiple tasks of Graphical Lasso under the assumption that all graphs have similar non-zero patterns by using fused penalty or group lasso penalty. (5) **MAGL** is our proposal, which makes use of attributes and jointly estimates multiple tasks. All comparing methods have a parameter λ_1 for the ℓ_1 penalty. FMGL and JGL have an extra parameter λ_2 to weight the penalty terms. MAGL uses λ_2 to weight the LogDet divergence term and λ_3 for regularization.

4.3   Experiment Settings

To test whether these methods can correctly recover the nonzero patterns and fit the data distributions, we use F1 score and Relative Log-likelihood as the evaluation metrics. The larger the value, the better the performance.

To ensure a fair comparison, the parameter λ_1 is searched using the bisection technique to make the number of edges in the estimated graphs approximately equal to the number of edges in the true graphs. The λ_2 for FMGL, JGL and

MAGL is determined by cross validation. Besides, for MAGL, we simply let the dimension of the output space of projection $d = 100$, and the regularization parameter $\lambda_3 = 1$ throughout the experiments. Other default values for algorithm parameters are: $\epsilon = 0.01, \rho_0 = 2, \gamma = 1.05$.

Table 1. Results on Dataset-1.

K	m	p	F1↑					Log-likelihood (%)↑				
			GLasso	PathGLasso	FMGL	JGL	MAGL	GLasso	PathGLasso	FMGL	JGL	MAGL
5	3	500	0.3375	0.3375	0.3408	0.3419	**0.3423**	1.2412	1.2412	1.2502	1.2426	**1.2546**
		1000	0.4256	0.4321	0.4302	0.4297	**0.4372**	1.1843	1.2264	1.1977	1.1913	**1.2268**
	5	500	0.3325	0.3477	0.3365	0.3321	**0.3524**	1.2116	1.2234	1.2222	1.2086	**1.2416**
		1000	0.4222	0.4396	0.4286	0.4286	**0.4410**	1.1848	1.2020	1.1977	1.2004	**1.2235**
	10	500	0.3248	**0.3375**	0.3280	0.3273	0.3345	1.2421	1.2647	1.2554	1.2517	**1.2863**
		1000	0.4124	0.4301	0.4167	0.4138	**0.4352**	1.2243	1.2783	1.2348	1.2274	**1.2875**
10	3	500	0.3434	0.3435	0.3499	0.3499	**0.3543**	1.1182	1.1181	1.1430	1.1427	**1.1441**
		1000	0.4192	0.4282	0.4264	0.4236	**0.4425**	1.1201	1.1465	1.1442	1.1305	**1.1523**
	5	500	0.3381	**0.3526**	0.3447	0.3426	0.3521	1.1191	1.1450	1.1401	1.1330	**1.1487**
		1000	0.4012	0.4105	0.4100	0.4081	**0.4237**	1.1457	1.1683	1.1732	1.1611	**1.1795**
	10	500	0.3401	0.3532	0.3448	0.3430	**0.3629**	1.2343	1.2394	**1.2481**	1.2398	1.2450
		1000	0.3877	0.3970	0.3923	0.3891	**0.4075**	1.2342	1.2653	1.2514	1.2410	**1.2828**

4.4 Experiment Results

Following the settings in literatures [3,27,28], we only show numerical results on synthetic datasets, since ground truth in real datasets is hard to obtain. For example, the network structure in DBLP does not correspond to its Gaussian graphical model. Case studies on real-world datasets are conducted instead.

We first summarize our findings on synthetic data. We show the averaged result of 5 runs with different random seeds for each experiment.

Before we show the quantitative results, we manually generate a toy example and show the learned Θ^1 in Fig. 3. Because FMGL, GLasso and JGL show the similar patterns, we only show the result of FMGL. We can see that in the ground truth, most non-zero elements appear on the diagonal blocks. FMGL cannot capture the block structures, and thus performs poorly. For PathGLasso, pathway constraints are employed so that non-zeros elements on off-diagonal blocks are not allowed. Our proposal, MAGL, learns a precision matrix that is closest to the ground truth because block structures are revealed by finding a projection matrix across tasks. Since MAGL does not constrain non-zero patterns, elements on off-diagonal blocks are also successfully recovered.

Our first set of experiments are conducted on the synthetic Dataset-1. The results are shown in Table 1. As we can see, MAGL performs well in most cases. This is because our proposal considers the relations between attributes of variables and linkage structures among variables, and shares information across tasks

Table 2. Results on Dataset-2.

K	m	p	F1↑			Log-likelihood (%)↑		
			GLasso	PathGLasso	MAGL	GLasso	PathGLasso	MAGL
5	3	500	0.3318	0.3318	**0.3576**	1.2449	1.3013	**1.3143**
		1000	0.4170	0.4341	**0.4346**	1.1842	1.2182	**1.2216**
	5	500	0.3300	0.3378	**0.3401**	1.2247	1.2348	**1.2553**
		1000	0.4136	0.4372	**0.4448**	1.1704	1.2361	**1.2642**
	10	500	0.3237	**0.3306**	0.3294	1.2334	1.2456	**1.2877**
		1000	0.4073	0.4249	**0.4293**	1.2260	1.2774	**1.2831**
10	3	500	0.3404	0.3404	**0.3541**	1.1304	1.1414	**1.1568**
		1000	0.4117	0.4188	**0.4332**	1.1217	1.1451	**1.1532**
	5	500	0.3321	0.3391	**0.3448**	1.1079	1.1101	**1.1200**
		1000	0.3986	0.4027	**0.4163**	1.1478	1.1698	**1.1741**
	10	500	0.3350	0.3516	**0.3606**	1.2275	1.2797	**1.2859**
		1000	0.3785	0.3999	**0.4003**	1.2280	1.2331	**1.2453**

to improve the quality of estimates. FMGL does not perform well due to the fact that the sequential fused ℓ_1 penalty only considers the values in the adjacent precision matrices and may hardly capture the global property. Another multi-task method, JGL, performs worse than GLasso in some cases, due to the inappropriate assumption, $i.e.$, similar non-zeros patterns across tasks. We can notice that due to the generative methods of datasets and pathways, by excluding a large number of impossible edges, PathGLasso gains a huge advantage when m is large w.r.t F1. Nevertheless, as illustrated in Fig. 3, missing elements on off-diagonal blocks lower the log-likelihood scores.

The experimental results on Dataset-2 are shown in Table 2, which reveals the similar patterns. FMGL and JGL are not tested here because the sets of variables are not the same in different tasks and there is no oder among them.

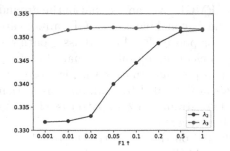 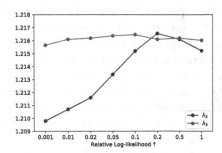

Fig. 4. The influence of $\lambda_{2,3}$.

• **Parameter Study:** In this subsection, we test the performance of MAGL under different λ_2 and λ_3. The results are shown in Fig. 4. We can see that MAGL is robust w.r.t. λ_3. The performance is also stable w.r.t. λ_2 in a wide range. Specifically, as λ_2 grows, the F1 score increases as well but after some point, the log-likelihood decreases slightly. Recall that Problem 3.1 uses a scaled and shifted covariance matrix, and hence a large λ_2 may skew the data distribution and harm the likelihood.

4.5   Case Study

We also apply MAGL to the DBLP and AML datasets. Because of lack of the ground truth, we only show the results qualitatively.

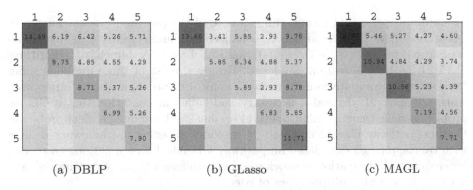

(a) DBLP   (b) GLasso   (c) MAGL

Fig. 5. Co-author patterns on DBLP. The number in cell (i, j) indicates how often co-author activities happened between authors in stage-i and stage-j.

For DBLP dataset, we count the number of co-author activities happened in different stages and show them in Fig. 5(a). For example, about 14.49% co-authors activities are between authors who are both in the Stage-1, *i.e.*, the 1st year of PhD. We apply MAGL and GLasso on the dataset and count the number of edges in the learned graphs. From Figs. 5(b) and 5(c) we can see that, with the help of authors' attributes (*i.e.*, life stages), MAGL reveals co-author patterns better.

In AML dataset, since the attributes of variables (genes) are pathways, the i-th row of U can be viewed as the latent features of the i-th pathway. We map U into a 2-dimensional plane using t-SNE [20] and show it in Fig. 6. As we can see, points are clustered. Take a closer look and we find that the points in bottom-left corner correspond to pathways in which genes are involved in Signaling, and top-left points are pathways involved in Regulation, which means MAGL could make use of attributes properly to help it improve the performance.

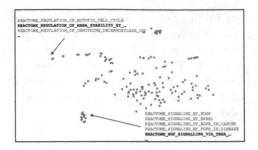

Fig. 6. Visualization of projection matrix on AML dataset.

5 Related Work

To obtain a sparse and meaningful estimate of the precision matrix, numerous researchers have considered the ℓ_1 penalized minimum negative log-likelihood estimation problem [1, 5–7], *i.e.*, Graphical Lasso. A bunch of algorithms [2, 15, 21, 29] have also been developed. However, most of these methods suffer from intensive computation. To make Graphical Lasso applicable in large problems, [26] and [21] derived a necessary and sufficient condition that a GLasso problem can be decomposed into several smaller sized and independent problems. Further, pathway Graphical Lasso [9] provides an efficient framework dealing with overlapping blocks. Based on pathway Graphical Lasso, [30] uses a related heterogeneous information network to provide different types of "pathways" and learn a graph with multiple types of edges.

Recently, there are some prior works on multi-task Graphical Lasso that learn multiple precision matrices simultaneously for related tasks. These methods differ in the choice of penalty functions: [14] suggested to estimate multiple Graphical Lasso by replacing the ℓ_1 norm with an $\ell_{1,\infty}$ norm. [10] proposed a non-convex hierarchical penalty. [12,13,19] assumed that there are common (sub)structures among multiple graphs. [3] estimated multiple precision matrices jointly using a pairwise fused penalty or grouping penalty. [27] considered the case that multiple tasks have a natural order and proposed a sequential fused penalty. A necessary and sufficient condition for the graphs to be decomposable is also given. [22] proposed a method on the assumption that the network differences are introduced from node perturbations. Different from the aforementioned methods that inspected the values in precision matrices, [24] utilized the structure information directly. However, these methods all require that the sets of variables are the same among tasks. Besides, they only focus on the variables' observations and cannot deal with attributed graphs.

6 Conclusion

In this paper, we incorporate variables' attributes into the framework of multi-task Graphical Lasso, and propose Multi-task Attributed Graphical Lasso

(MAGL). We introduce the LogDet divergence to bridge graphs structures and attributes so that information could be shared across multiple tasks. The experiments on synthetic datasets show the effectiveness of MAGL, and the case studies demonstrated that our method can produce a meaningful result. As for future work, we could try other ways to connect variables' observations and attributes. Besides, we will consider applying our proposal to more real world applications.

Acknowledgement. This work is supported in part by the Shanghai Science and Technology Development Fund No. 19511121204, No. 19DZ1200802, and the National Natural Science Foundation of China Projects No. U1636207, No. U1936213.

References

1. Banerjee, O., Ghaoui, L.E., d'Aspremont, A.: Model selection through sparse maximum likelihood estimation for multivariate gaussian or binary data. JMLR **9**(Mar), 485–516 (2008)
2. Cai, T., Liu, W., Luo, X.: A constrained l1 minimization approach to sparse precision matrix estimation. JASA **106**(494), 594–607 (2011)
3. Danaher, P., Wang, P., Witten, D.M.: The joint graphical lasso for inverse covariance estimation across multiple classes. J. R. Stat. Soc. Ser. B Stat. Methodol. **76**(2), 373–397 (2014)
4. Davis, J.V., Dhillon, I.S.: Differential entropic clustering of multivariate gaussians. In: NeurIPS, pp. 337–344 (2007)
5. Duchi, J.C., Gould, S., Koller, D.: Projected subgradient methods for learning sparse Gaussians. In: UAI (2008)
6. Fan, J., Liao, Y., Liu, H.: An overview of the estimation of large covariance and precision matrices. ECONOMET J. **19**(1), C1–C32 (2016)
7. Friedman, J., Hastie, T., Tibshirani, R.: Sparse inverse covariance estimation with the graphical lasso. Biostatistics **9**(3), 432–441 (2008)
8. Gentles, A.J., Plevritis, S.K., Majeti, R., Alizadeh, A.A.: Association of a leukemic stem cell gene expression signature with clinical outcomes in acute myeloid leukemia. JAMA **304**(24), 2706–2715 (2010)
9. Grechkin, M., Fazel, M., Witten, D., Lee, S.: Pathway graphical lasso. In: AAAI, pp. 2617–2623 (2015)
10. Guo, J., Levina, E., Michailidis, G., Zhu, J.: Joint estimation of multiple graphical models. Biometrika **98**(1), 1–15 (2011)
11. Haferlach, T., et al.: Clinical utility of microarray-based gene expression profiling in the diagnosis and subclassification of leukemia: report from the international microarray innovations in leukemia study group. Int. J. Clin. Oncol. **28**(15), 2529–2537 (2010)
12. Hara, S., Washio, T.: Common substructure learning of multiple graphical Gaussian models. In: Gunopulos, D., Hofmann, T., Malerba, D., Vazirgiannis, M. (eds.) ECML PKDD 2011. LNCS (LNAI), vol. 6912, pp. 1–16. Springer, Heidelberg (2011). https://doi.org/10.1007/978-3-642-23783-6_1
13. Hara, S., Washio, T.: Learning a common substructure of multiple graphical Gaussian models. Neural Netw. **38**, 23–38 (2013)
14. Honorio, J., Samaras, D.: Multi-task learning of Gaussian graphical models. In: ICML, pp. 447–454 (2010)

15. Hsieh, C., Sustik, M.A., Dhillon, I.S., Ravikumar, P.D.: QUIC: quadratic approximation for sparse inverse covariance estimation. JMLR **15**(1), 2911–2947 (2014)
16. Huang, S., et al.: Learning brain connectivity of Alzheimer's disease by sparse inverse covariance estimation. NeuroImage **50**(3), 935–949 (2010)
17. Kang, Z., Peng, C., Cheng, J., Cheng, Q.: Logdet rank minimization with application to subspace clustering. Comput. Intell. Neurosci. **2015**, 68 (2015)
18. Kulis, B., Sustik, M., Dhillon, I.: Learning low-rank kernel matrices. In: ICML, pp. 505–512 (2006)
19. Lee, W., Liu, Y.: Joint estimation of multiple precision matrices with common structures. JMLR **16**(1), 1035–1062 (2015)
20. Maaten, L.V.D., Hinton, G.: Visualizing data using T-SNE. JMLR **9**(Nov), 2579–2605 (2008)
21. Mazumder, R., Hastie, T.: The graphical lasso: new insights and alternatives. EJS **6**, 2125 (2012)
22. Mohan, K., London, P., Fazel, M., Witten, D., Lee, S.: Node-based learning of multiple Gaussian graphical models. JMLR **15**(1), 445–488 (2014)
23. Sun, Y., Han, J., Gao, J., Yu, Y.: itopicmodel: information network-integrated topic modeling. In: ICDM, pp. 493–502 (2009)
24. Tao, Q., Huang, X., Wang, S., Xi, X., Li, L.: Multiple Gaussian graphical estimation with jointly sparse penalty. Sig. Process. **128**, 88–97 (2016)
25. Whittaker, J.: Graphical Models in Applied Multivariate Statistics. Wiley, Hoboken (2009)
26. Witten, D.M., Friedman, J.H., Simon, N.: New insights and faster computations for the graphical lasso. J. Comput. Graph Stat. **20**(4), 892–900 (2011)
27. Yang, S., Lu, Z., Shen, X., Wonka, P., Ye, J.: Fused multiple graphical lasso. SIOPT **25**(2), 916–943 (2015)
28. Yin, H., Liu, X., Kong, X.: Coherent graphical lasso for brain network discovery. In: ICDM (2018)
29. Yuan, X.: Alternating direction methods for sparse covariance selection. Optimization Online (2009)
30. Zhang, Y., Xiong, Y., Liu, X., Kong, X., Zhu, Y.: Meta-path graphical lasso for learning heterogeneous connectivities. In: SDM, pp. 642–650 (2017)

Hylo: Hybrid Layer-Based Optimization to Reduce Communication in Distributed Deep Learning

Wenbin Jiang[✉], Jing Peng, Pai Liu, and Hai Jin

National Engineering Research Center for Big Data Technology and System,
Services Computing Technology and System Lab, Cluster and Grid Computing Lab,
School of Computer Science and Technology,
Huazhong University of Science and Technology, Wuhan 430074, China
{wenbinjiang,crystalpeng,liunxpaisley,hjin}@hust.edu.cn

Abstract. In distributed deep learning training, the synchronization of gradients usually brings huge network communication overhead. Although many methods have been proposed to solve the problem, limited effectiveness has been obtained, since these methods do not fully consider the differences of diverse layers. We propose a novel hybrid layer-based optimization approach named Hylo to reduce the communication overhead. Two different strategies are designed for gradient compression of two types of layers (convolution layer and fully-connected layer). For convolution layers, only some important convolution kernels are chosen for gradient transmission. For fully-connected layers, all gradients are quantized to 2 bits with an adaptive gradient threshold. The experimental results show that Hylo brings obvious accelerations for distributed deep learning systems, while with little accuracy loss. It achieves training speedups up to 1.31× compared to state-of-the-art works.

Keywords: Distributed deep learning · Communication optimization · Gradient · Convolution layer · Fully-connected layer

1 Introduction

With the advent of the big data era, *deep learning* (DL) has become a research hotspot in academia and industry. With the continuous increase of the scale of *convolutional neural networks* (CNNs) and data in DL systems, the traditional mode of single-machine training cannot meet the requirements any more, which results in distributed DL systems arising. Data parallelism is a major scheme for distributed DL [1], where multiple machine nodes are used to train a network model concurrently and each node is in charge of a part of the data-set.

There are several *parameter servers* (PSs) and workers [2]. Workers calculate the gradient matrices locally and upload them to servers. Servers update parameters with the aggregated gradients after collecting all the gradient matrices from all workers. Data parallelism significantly improves the effectiveness of

© Springer Nature Switzerland AG 2020
X. Wang et al. (Eds.): APWeb-WAIM 2020, LNCS 12317, pp. 685–699, 2020.
https://doi.org/10.1007/978-3-030-60259-8_50

DL on deeper and larger models [3]. However, with the increase of the number of nodes, gradient exchange and parameter update make network bandwidth a serious bottleneck of the distributed training, and even offset the earning of training time savings from distributed computing.

Some efforts have been made to alleviate the communication bottleneck. MXNET-MPI [4] proposes a generic framework supporting both PS and MPI programming paradigms which can alleviate the communication pressure on the server side. Poseidon [5] combines the advantages of PS and *sufficient factor broadcasting* (SFB). These methods alleviate communication pressure to some extent, but the effect is limited.

In recent years, to deploy CNNs on mobile devices, a lot of works try to reduce the CNN model size by pruning or compressing the weights of various layers without weakening original accuracies obviously, such as [6,7]. Similar to this idea, some methods have been proposed to reduce traffic volume in distributed DL through quantization or sparsification, such as [8–11]. However, these works do not fully consider the diversification of the gradient matrices of different types of layers and various networks.

Our proposed Hylo is a novel layer-based optimization, which takes the gradient matrix characteristics of various types of layers and various networks into account, and adopts different compression algorithms for them to reduce the amount of gradient transmission. Hylo adaptively sparsifies and quantizes the gradients of the *convolution* (CONV) layers and the *fully-connected* (FC) layers with different strategies according to their different characteristics, respectively, which can significantly reduce the DL training time with little loss of accuracy.

2   Related Work

In order to solve the communication bottleneck problem of distributed DL training, many schemes have been proposed, including various hybrid communication strategies and methods to reduce communication traffic. The communication traffic can be reduced by gradient sparsification and gradient quantization.

Hybrid Communication. MXNET-MPI [4] optimizes communication by exchanging gradients with both MPI and PS. MXNET-MPI groups nodes and synchronizes them with MPI within a group. A master is specified for each group to communicate with the servers to update parameters, which can alleviate the communication pressure on the server side to some extent. However, when there is a particularly large number of training nodes, the amount of gradients needed to be transmitted is still large.

Poseidon [5] introduces a hybrid communication strategy that combines the advantages of PS and SFB by being aware of both the mathematical property of DL models and the structures of computing clusters. SFB decomposes a gradient matrix into two vectors called *sufficient factors* (SFs). SFs are broadcasted to servers, which then reconstruct the gradient matrix locally. The matrix property of CONV layer does not allow the matrix to be decomposed into two vectors, so the gradient matrix of CONV layer can only be transmitted with PS.

However, the gradient matrix of FC layer can be decomposed, so Poseidon chooses the way with less communication overhead in PS and SFB to transmit the gradients of FC layers.

Gradient Sparsification. Gradient sparsification reduces communication overhead by selecting partial gradients in the gradient matrix for transmission.

Strom [10] proposes a gradient sparsification method for FC layers. Only gradients larger than a constant threshold are transmitted to servers. However, it is difficult for users to choose a suitable threshold, while it is not appropriate to maintain the same threshold throughout the training. To solve this problem, Dryden et al. [12] propose a sparsification approach by setting a suitable threshold to keep a fixed proportion of gradients to be transmitted. This technique requires to sort the entire gradient matrix for gradient selection, which is a computationally expensive task. Only the top $k\%$ gradients are transmitted to servers. Aji and Heafield [8] also transmit a proportion of gradients, but sample only 0.1% to 1% of the gradients and perform top-k selection on these samples to estimate the threshold. Positive gradients and negative gradients are treated separately. Similarly, DGC [13] uses proportion-based sampling and achieves higher sparsification ratio. Only 0.1% of original gradients are transmitted. However, it requires additional approaches to compensate for the loss of accuracy due to high sparsification ratio.

Gradient Quantization. In general, the parameters of a neural network model are represented by 32-bit floating-point numbers. Gradient quantization reduces the space required for each gradient by sacrificing precision.

Seide et al. [9] propose a quantization scheme for gradients, which quantizes each gradient to $\{0, 1\}$. However, it quantizes gradients column-wise over the gradient matrix, so a floating-point scaler is needed for each column which increases communication overhead. DoReFaNet [11] reduces the bit widths of gradients and weights to 2 and 1, respectively. DoReFaNet reduces both the overhead of gradient communication and weight communication, but it has obvious accuracy loss. Huilgol [14] proposes a quantization method named 2Bit, which has been accepted by MXNet officially and integrated into the main project. 2Bit quantizes gradients to $\{-1, 0, 1\}$ through a constant threshold. However, it is not easy to select a suitable threshold and it is inappropriate to use a fixed threshold throughout the training process. Also using 2-bit gradients, TernGrad [15] quantizes gradients to $\{-1, 0, 1\}$ by making sure that the mean of the gradients before and after quantization is unchanged. However, it takes more time to quantize the gradients than 2Bit.

3   Hybrid Communication Optimization Based on Layer Characteristics

Different from the previous works, our proposed Hylo takes advantage of the characteristics of different layers and different networks to optimize gradient sparsification and quantization.

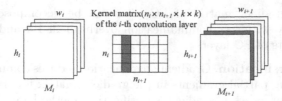

Fig. 1. The process of transforming the input feature maps into the output feature maps

It pays main attention to build a new kernel-level sparsification approach for CONV layers and an adaptive quantization method for FC layers according to their characteristics, respectively. Namely, the selection of the two approaches is decided by the type of the specified layer. For CONV layers, just some important kernels are selected, of which the gradients are transmitted. This strategy greatly reduces the computation time compared to sorting the whole gradient matrix. For FC layers, all gradients are quantized to 2 bits with an automatically adjustable threshold according to the values of gradients. Hylo has less side-effect on training accuracy and no additional approaches are required to compensate for the degradation. Benefiting from above hybrid layer-based optimization, obvious better performance can be obtained.

We will discuss them in detail in the following subsections.

3.1   Kernels Selection for Convolution Layers

We sort the kernels in each CONV layer according to the means of the corresponding absolute values of gradients in these kernels, which can indicate the degrees of the importance of the kernels for the current round of update. Then the gradients of some important kernels are transmitted.

A CONV layer consists of multiple filters, each with the same number of CONV kernels. Through CONV operations, input feature maps are transformed into output feature maps. As shown in Fig. 1, h_i/w_i is the height/width of the input feature maps M_i. n_i denotes the number of input channels for the i-th CONV layer. The i-th CONV layer $\in \mathbb{R}^{n_i \times n_{i+1} \times k \times k}$ consists of n_{i+1} 3D filters $\in \mathbb{R}^{n_i \times k \times k}$, each of which is composed of n_i 2D CONV kernels $\in \mathbb{R}^{k \times k}$. Each filter generates one feature map. The i-th CONV layer transforms the input feature maps $M_i \in \mathbb{R}^{h_i \times w_i \times n_i}$ into the output feature maps $M_{i+1} \in \mathbb{R}^{h_{i+1} \times w_{i+1} \times n_{i+1}}$ [7].

Figure 2 shows the absolute values of gradients of two CONV kernels in the first CONV layer of Inception-BN trained on CIFAR10. K_1 and K_2 denote the two CONV kernels $\in \mathbb{R}^{3 \times 3}$, respectively. It is observed that the absolute values of gradients in the same CONV kernel are close to each other and of the same order of magnitude, while the absolute values of gradients in different CONV kernels may be significantly different. The similar rule also exists in other CONV layers. Based on this observation, the importance of a CONV kernel can be represented by the mean of all absolute values of gradients in the CONV kernel. The gradients can then be filtered in units of CONV kernel.

The absolute values of gradients
of K_1 in the 4-th iteration

2. 60E-01	2. 64E-01	1. 30E-01
2. 02E-01	2. 17E-01	2. 20E-01
5. 85E-01	4. 96E-01	4. 12E-01

The absolute values of gradients
of K_1 in the 8-th iteration

2. 78E-02	5. 21E-02	1. 21E-02
5. 58E-02	3. 47E-02	2. 94E-02
1. 25E-02	6. 48E-02	5. 47E-02

The absolute values of gradients
of K_2 in the 4-th iteration

8. 97E-03	8. 65E-03	2. 70E-03
1. 56E-03	3. 65E-03	3. 34E-03
6. 11E-04	1. 87E-03	1. 75E-03

The absolute values of gradients
of K_2 in the 8-th iteration

8. 94E-03	1. 22E-01	3. 51E-01
3. 92E-01	4. 42E-01	6. 10E-01
7. 99E-01	8. 05E-01	7. 73E-01

Fig. 2. The absolute values of gradients of two CONV kernels in the first CONV layer of Inception-BN trained on CIFAR10 in the first epoch

For a CONV layer, we evaluate the importance of the gradients of each CONV kernel by the mean of the absolute values of gradients in this CONV kernel. The higher the mean, the greater the influence of the gradients of the CONV kernel is. According to the importance, we sort all CONV kernels, and only transmit gradients of the top $k\%$ CONV kernels. The rest gradients are cached and accumulated for the next iteration to maintain the training accuracy in high level. As for the choice of k, it will be discussed in detail later.

Figure 3 shows a concrete illustration. The white squares represent the CONV kernels with gradients of zeros, the dark blue squares represent the most important $k\%$ CONV kernels, and the light blue squares represent the least important $1 - k\%$ CONV kernels. The latest gradients of each kernel are accumulated into the corresponding kernel in the residual accumulation matrices and used to evaluate the importance of the kernels in this iteration. The gradients of the top $k\%$ kernels are transmitted to the servers and used to update the weights of the corresponding kernels. The gradients of the remaining kernels are cached in the residual accumulation matrices for the next iteration.

3.2   Layer-Adaptive Transmission Rate for Convolution Layers

Blindly pursuing a large compression ratio is not a good idea for DL training acceleration. When compression ratio reaches a certain degree, as the number of gradients to be transmitted is already small, which produces little communication traffic, further increasing compression ratio can not benefit the acceleration ratio much any more, but would lead to more accuracy loss.

In a CNN, the scales of the parameter matrices of different CONV layers vary largely. Generally, there is an increase trend along with the serial number of the corresponding layer increasing, as shown in Fig. 4. Moreover, the scales of both CONV layers and FC layers of networks trained on different data-sets also vary a lot. The Inception-BN trained on ImageNet has 33 layers, of which each has more than one hundred thousand parameters, while Inception-BN trained on CIFAR10 has only 5 such layers.

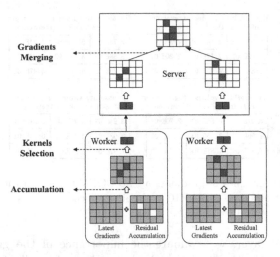

Fig. 3. Kernels selection for CONV layers (Color figure online)

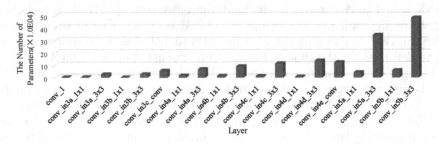

Fig. 4. The scales of the parameter matrices of CONV layers of Inception-BN trained on CIFAR10

For the layers with a small parameter matrix, generally, communication optimization would not bring obvious speedup. The communication cost of these layers is considerable low and therefore the reduced communication time by the communication optimization can be ignored. If considering the extra calculation cost generated by the optimization, the benefit from the optimization becomes more unattractive, especially when training a network with a large number of layers and a small number of parameters in each layer. For example, when training ResNet-164 on CIFAR10, there are about 500 layers requiring gradient exchange, but only 3.8% of these layers have more than thirty thousand parameters.

Therefore, we set a threshold $CommLT$ to filter the layers for communication optimization. Only the layers of which the number of parameters are larger than $CommLT$ are optimized. In other words, the transmission rates of the other CONV layers are 100%.

Generally, gradients are transmitted layer by layer. When selecting CONV kernels for gradient transmission, it is unreasonable to use the same top $k\%$ for different layers in a network or layers in different networks. Therefore, we build a layer-adaptive k for each layer according to the number of parameters. Our goal is to select an appropriate k to make the number of gradients transmitted reduced to a sufficiently small value $GradTN$ after the CONV kernels being selected. A further smaller k would not lead to greater acceleration. Generally, the larger the number of parameters in the layer, the smaller k is. Suppose p_i is the number of parameters in the i-th layer. The value of k_i of the i-th layer is decided by

$$k_i = 100GradTN/p_i \qquad (1)$$

The values of $CommLT$ and $GradTN$ for different networks are decided according to experience. These values also potentially depend on network bandwidths. In the future, we will exploit an adaptive approach to determine the values of $CommLT$ and $GradTN$.

3.3   Quantization for Fully-Connected Layers

For networks trained on small data-set, such as CIFAR10 and CIFAR100, each usually has only one FC layer. Since the parameter scale of this FC layer is not large, we do not optimize communication for this FC layer.

Networks trained on ImageNet often have FC layers with large parameter scales. Therefore, we quantize these layers. Due to the large number of parameters in these FC layers, it is computationally expensive for sorting the corresponding gradients and setting a threshold for choosing some important gradients for transmission, as we do for CONV layers by applying sparsification. Quantization becomes a better choice. We quantize each gradient of the FC layers to three numerical $\{-1, 0, 1\}$ by a specified threshold, and use two bits to encode it. The gradients of which the absolute values are smaller than the threshold are accumulated to a residual accumulation matrix. The residual accumulation matrix is used for new gradients in the next iteration. A similar idea has been implemented in MXNet. Different from it, our proposed approach applies an automatically adjustable threshold instead of a fixed one.

For the threshold, we adjust it according to the variation of gradients as the training goes on. Let g denote the gradient matrix. $abs(\cdot)$ returns the absolute value of the included element. Figure 5 shows the variation trends of the means of $abs(g)$ of the FC layers from Inception-BN and ResNet-164 trained on CIFAR10, respectively. Both the means of $abs(g)$ excessively decrease as the epoch goes up. Trainings on ImageNet follow the same rule. Therefore, changing the threshold for quantization to meet the variation of the gradients is necessary.

Concretely, we obtain a 2-bit compressed gradient g_{ci} by

$$g_{ci} = \begin{cases} 00 & abs(g_{ri}) < mean(abs(g_r)) \\ 01 & g_{ri} \geq mean(abs(g_r)) \\ 11 & g_{ri} \leq -mean(abs(g_r)) \end{cases} \qquad (2)$$

where g_r denotes the new residual accumulation matrix of the FC layer which is accumulated by the latest gradients and the gradients in the residual accumulation matrix of the last iteration, and g_{ri} is an element of g_r; g_c denotes the

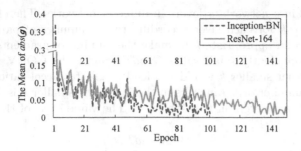

Fig. 5. The means of $abs(g)$ for the FC layers of Inception-BN and ResNet-164 trained on CIFAR10

compressed matrix, and g_{ci} is an element of g_c. Here, $mean(\cdot)$ returns the mean of all elements, and the threshold is set to the mean of $abs(g_r)$.

When receiving the compressed matrix g_c, a server decompresses it by

$$g_{di} = \begin{cases} 0 & g_{ci} = 00 \\ mean(abs(g_r)) & g_{ci} = 01 \\ -mean(abs(g_r)) & g_{ci} = 11 \end{cases} \qquad (3)$$

where g_{di} is an element of g_d that is the decompressed matrix.

Figure 6 shows an example of the process flow of gradient quantization for a FC layer. For convenience, only a 4×4 gradient matrix is considered. After quantization, a quantized gradient matrix g_q is obtained. Each gradient in g_q can be represented by 2 bits. After compression, the resulting 32-bit floating-point number g_c stores all the 2-bit represented gradients. The server decompresses each element of g_c to $\{-threshold, 0, threshold\}$. Obviously, there is a deviation between the decompressed gradients and the original gradients, which will be stored in the residual accumulation matrix for the next iteration.

4   Evaluation

The work of this paper is implemented on MXNet, and the evaluation experiments are performed on a GPU cluster. First, we investigate the convergence of Hylo in Sect. 4.1. Second, the speedup ratios are explored in Sect. 4.2. Finally, we explore the compression ratios of data communicated at different networks and layers in Sect. 4.3. In all experiments, *Stochastic Gradient Descent* (SGD) with momentum is adopted and the momentum is set at 0.9.

The GPU cluster for our distributed DL training tasks comprises six physical machines. The hardware configurations are shown in Table 1. All machines are connected with an Intel Corporation I350(1GbE) switch. We compare the convergences and speedup ratios with the baseline (MXNet without any communication optimization), 2Bit [14], and TernGrad [15] on some typical models.

Three typical data-sets, CIFAR10, CIFAR100, and ImageNet, are used for our experiments. Two networks with different characteristics are trained on each

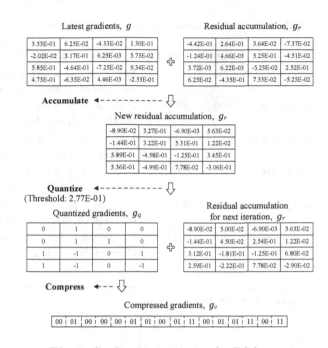

Fig. 6. Gradient quantization for FC layers

Table 1. Hardware configurations of machines

GPU	CPU	Memory	Network adapter
NVIDIA Tesla P100	Intel Xeon CPU E5-2680 v4 @ 2.40 GHz	256 GB	Intel Corporation I350(1GbE)

data-set. Inception-BN trained on CIFAR10 and CIFAR100 has a small number of layers but some layers have a relatively large number of parameters. ResNet-164 and DFN-MR have more layers but fewer parameters per layer. ResNet-50 and Inception-BN trained on ImageNet also have a large number of layers, while most of which have a very large number of parameters. Table 2 lists details of some training hyperparameters.

4.1 Convergence Experiments

For CIFAR10 and CIFAR100, the aforementioned four methods are applied on each network. Table 3 lists the Top-1 validation accuracies. It shows that Hylo converges to the similar accuracy as the baseline does, sometimes even a little better. 2Bit and TernGrad converge to lower accuracies. Figure 7 shows the accuracy curves with epoch as the abscissa. The accuracy curve of Hylo basically matches the one of the baseline, while 2Bit and TernGrad have poorer accuracies.

Table 2. Configurations of some hyperparameters

Data-set	Network	Epoch	Base LR	Adjustment of LR
CIFAR10	Inception-BN	60	0.1	Decreased by a factor of 0.94 at each epoch until it reaches 10^{-8}
	ResNet-164	150	0.1	Decreased by a factor of 0.1 at 100th, 130th epoches
CIFAR100	Inception-BN	60	0.05	Decreased by a factor of 0.94 at each epoch until it reaches 10^{-8}
	DFN-MR	100	0.05	Decreased by a factor of 0.94 at each epoch until it reaches 10^{-8}
ImageNet	Inception-BN	110	0.2	Decreased by a factor of 0.94 at each epoch until it reaches 10^{-8}
	ResNet-50	90	0.2	Decreased by a factor of 0.1 at 30th, 60th epoches

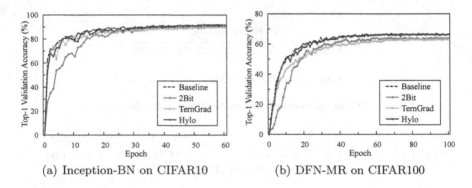

(a) Inception-BN on CIFAR10   (b) DFN-MR on CIFAR100

Fig. 7. Training results with 6 workers (validation accuracy vs. epoch)

For ImageNet, we make accuracy comparisons among Hylo, the baseline, and 2Bit. Table 4 lists the Top-1 validation accuracies. Hylo converges to the similar accuracy as the baseline does, while 2Bit converges to lower accuracy for ResNet-50. The experimental results show that a large number of parameters in DL networks are redundant indeed. Ignoring the gradients with small absolute values temporarily and delaying the transmission of them until they are accumulated to large enough values will not have obvious side-effect on accuracy. In addition, since large transmission rates are used for layers with small parameter scales, the training accuracies are guaranteed.

Table 3. Comparison of Top-1 validation accuracies on CIFAR10 and CIFAR100

Data-set	Network	Workers	Mini-batch size	Training method	Top-1 validation accuracy
CIFAR10	Inception-BN	2	64	Baseline	91.78%
				2Bit	91.35%
				TernGrad	90.85%
				Hylo	**91.98% (+0.20%)**
		6	192	Baseline	91.92%
				2Bit	90.74%
				TernGrad	90.32%
				Hylo	**91.99% (+0.07%)**
	ResNet-164	2	64	Baseline	94.50%
				2Bit	94.13%
				TernGrad	90.77%
				Hylo	94.44%
		6	192	Baseline	94.35%
				2Bit	93.85%
				TernGrad	90.39%
				Hylo	94.03%
CIFAR100	Inception-BN	2	64	Baseline	71.23%
				2Bit	70.88%
				TernGrad	67.69%
				Hylo	**71.55% (+0.32%)**
		6	192	Baseline	70.43%
				2Bit	69.39%
				TernGrad	66.90%
				Hylo	70.26%
	DFN-MR	2	64	Baseline	67.56%
				2Bit	66.72%
				TernGrad	64.36%
				Hylo	**67.62% (+0.06%)**
		6	192	Baseline	67.01%
				2Bit	64.12%
				TernGrad	63.72%
				Hylo	**67.18% (+0.17%)**

Table 4. Comparison of Top-1 validation accuracies on ImageNet

Data-set	Network	Workers	Mini-batch size	Training method	Top-1 validation accuracy
ImageNet	Inception-BN	6	768	Baseline	69.30%
				2Bit	69.41%
				Hylo	**69.74% (+0.44%)**
	ResNet-50	6	768	Baseline	73.18%
				2Bit	71.96%
				Hylo	73.04%

Table 5. Speedups of Hylo with 6 workers compared to other methods

Data-set	Network	Speedup compared to		
		Baseline	2Bit	TernGrad
CIFAR10	Inception-BN	2.02×	1.18×	1.25×
	ResNet-164	1.52×	1.17×	1.21×
CIFAR100	Inception-BN	2.10×	1.21×	1.22×
	DFN-MR	1.42×	1.08×	1.31×
ImageNet	Inception-BN	2.05×	1.08×	1.22×
	ResNet-50	1.95×	0.92×	1.07×

4.2   Comparisons of Training Speedups

Table 5 shows the speedups achieved by our proposed method. The values of $CommLT$ and $GradTN$ are set to be optimal according to experience.

Compared to the baseline, except for ResNet-164 and DFN-MR, our proposed Hylo can achieve approximately 2× speedup. For ResNet-164 and DFN-MR, suffering from the low communication-to-computation ratio, which comes from the small scale of parameters in each layer and the extremely large number of layers, Hylo only achieves speedups of 1.52× and 1.42×, respectively.

Compared to 2Bit, except for ResNet-50, our Hylo achieves about 1.08× to 1.21× speedup. For ResNet-50, the speedup of Hylo is slightly lower than the one of 2Bit. The main reason is that, there are several layers with a huge number of parameters in it. Despite of the high communication-to-computation ratios of such layers which can bring about a relatively large acceleration ratio, the top-k selection processes of Hylo consume considerable time. In the future, we will consider performing the top-k kernels selection on these layers with a sampling method similar to DGC [13].

Compared to TernGrad, our Hylo achieves about 1.07× to 1.31× speedup. Similar to 2Bit, TernGrad achieves a compression ratio of 16×, but it takes more time to quantize gradients.

4.3   Comparisons of Compression Ratios of Data Communicated at Different Networks and Different Layers

Table 6 shows the comparisons of compression ratios. Unlike the fixed compression ratio of 2Bit and TernGrad, the compression ratio of Hylo varies with networks. For small networks, the compression ratios are very small. For example, for some networks trained on CIFAR10 and CIFAR100, the compression ratios of Hylo are less than 5. However, Hylo achieves higher speedups than 2Bit and TernGrad.

In fact, larger compression ratios can be applied to diverse networks with little accuracy loss by Hylo. As shown in Table 7, $CommLT$ and $GradTN$ are set to different values to change the compression ratios. With the increase of

Table 6. Compression ratios of 2Bit, TernGrad, and Hylo

Data-set	Network	Compression ratio		
		2Bit	TernGrad	Hylo
CIFAR10	Inception-BN	16×	16×	6.42×
	ResNet-164	16×	16×	1.42×
CIFAR100	Inception-BN	16×	16×	3.85×
	DFN-MR	16×	16×	2.50×
ImageNet	Inception-BN	16×	16×	7.78×
	ResNet-50	16×	16×	16.96×

Table 7. Training results of 2Bit and Hylo with different CommLT and GradTN

Network	Data-set	Training method	CommLT	GradTN	Compression	Speedup	Top-1 accuracy
Inception-BN	CIFAR10	2Bit	–	–	16×	1.71×	90.74%
		Hylo	50000	30000	3.78×	2.01×	91.94%
			50000	10000	6.42×	2.02×	91.99%
			50000	2500	8.70×	1.99×	91.85%
			20000	5000	12.71×	1.93×	91.91%
			20000	2500	16.53×	1.97×	91.77%
			10000	2500	26.92×	1.91×	91.82%
	ImageNet	2Bit	–	–	16×	1.89×	69.41%
		Hylo	50000	20000	7.78×	2.05×	69.74%
			50000	10000	12.52×	2.04×	69.55%
			50000	5000	18.01×	2.05×	69.37%
			30000	5000	21.41×	2.05×	69.11%

the compression ratio, the speedup of Hylo even decreases to some extent (on CIFAR10) or keeps stable, while the accuracy of Hylo keeps relatively stable. This indicates that higher compression ratio is not always better. We find that for the layers with relatively small scales, it is unnecessary to compress them too much because the numbers of parameters in these layers are already small, and thus more compression can not save the communication time more. On the contrary, it may incur extra calculation overhead. Therefore, we do not optimize such layers. For example, for ResNet-164, we only make a compression ratio of 1.42×, while can get 1.17× speedup compared to 2Bit and 1.21× speedup compared to TernGrad. For networks trained on the large data-set ImageNet, due to their large parameter scales, we apply large compression ratios to them.

As aforementioned, the compression ratio of our proposed Hylo is layer-adaptive according to the number of parameters of the corresponding layer. Figure 8 shows how the compression ratio changes. We enumerate the numbers of parameters and corresponding compression ratios of some CONV layers of

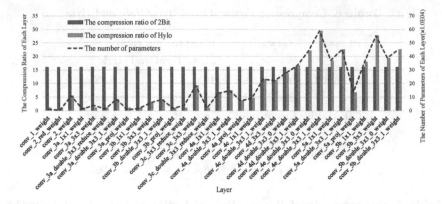

Fig. 8. The compression ratios and the numbers of parameters of some layers (Inception-BN trained on ImageNet)

Inception-BN trained on ImageNet. As shown, the more parameters of a layer, the greater the compression ratio Hylo assigns, while 2Bit and TernGrad always maintain a compression ratio of 16×. This strategy benefits the speedup more.

5   Conclusion

We propose a novel hybrid layer-based optimization approach named Hylo to reduce the communication overhead of distributed DL systems. By distinguishing and analyzing the difference of gradient matrices of different types of layers, we apply differentiated communication optimization strategies for them, respectively. For CONV layers, only some important CONV kernels are selected for gradient transmission. For FC layers, an adaptive layer-based quantization strategy is applied to the gradients. Moreover, an adaptive mechanism for deciding transmission rate according to the scales of the layers is designed for all layers to pursue high comprehensive performance. Experimental results show that Hylo achieves up to 1.31× speedup and higher accuracy compared to TernGrad. In fact, the learning curves of Hylo can match that of the baseline very well. In the future, we will consider adaptive adjustment for transmission rate based on the variation of communication bandwidth, and take model pruning into account for higher comprehensive performance of DL systems.

Acknowledgment. This work is supported by National Natural Science Foundation of China under grant No. 61672250.

References

1. Dean, J., et al.: Large scale distributed deep networks. In: Proceedings of the 25th Conference on Neural Information Processing Systems (NIPS), pp. 1223–1231. MIT Press, Cambridge (2012)

2. Chen, T., et al.: MXNet: a flexible and efficient machine learning library for heterogeneous distributed systems. In: Proceedings of the Workshop on Machine Learning Systems at the 28th Conference on Neural Information Processing Systems (LearningSys), pp. 1–6. MIT Press, Cambridge (2015)

3. Xing, E.P., et al.: Petuum: a new platform for distributed machine learning on big data. IEEE Trans. Big Data **1**(2), 49–67 (2015)

4. Mamidala, A.R., Kollias, G., Ward, C., Artico, F.: MXNET-MPI: embedding MPI parallelism in parameter server task model for scaling deep learning. arXiv preprint arXiv:1801.03855 (2018)

5. Zhang, H., et al.: Poseidon: an efficient communication architecture for distributed deep learning on GPU clusters. In: Proceedings of the 2017 USENIX Annual Technical Conference (ATC), pp. 181–193. USENIX Association, Berkeley (2017)

6. Anwar, S., Hwang, K., Sung, W.: Structured pruning of deep convolutional neural networks. ACM J. Emerg. Technol. Comput. Syst. **13**(3), 32:1–32:18 (2017)

7. Li, H., Kadav, A., Durdanovic, I., Samet, H., Graf, H.P.: Pruning filters for efficient convnets. In: Proceedings of the 5th International Conference on Learning Representations (ICLR). ICLR (2017)

8. Aji, A.F., Heafield, K.: Sparse communication for distributed gradient descent. In: Proceedings of the 2017 Conference on Empirical Methods in Natural Language Processing (EMNLP), pp. 440–445. ACL, Stroudsburg (2017)

9. Seide, F., Fu, H., Droppo, J., Li, G., Yu, D.: 1-bit stochastic gradient descent and its application to data-parallel distributed training of speech DNNs. In: Proceedings of the 15th Annual Conference of the International Speech Communication Association (INTERSPEECH), pp. 1058–1062. ISCA (2014)

10. Strom, N.: Scalable distributed DNN training using commodity GPU cloud computing. In: Proceedings of the 16th Annual Conference of the International Speech Communication Association (INTERSPEECH), pp. 1488–1492. ISCA (2015)

11. Zhou, S., Ni, Z., Zhou, X., Wen, H., Wu, Y., Zou, Y.: DoReFa-Net: training low bitwidth convolutional neural networks with low bitwidth gradients. arXiv preprint arXiv:1606.06160 (2016)

12. Dryden, N., Moon, T., Jacobs, S.A., Essen, B.V.: Communication quantization for data-parallel training of deep neural networks. In: Proceedings of the 2nd Workshop on Machine Learning in HPC Environments (MLHPC), pp. 1–8. IEEE Computer Society, Los Alamitos (2016)

13. Lin, Y., Han, S., Mao, H., Wang, Y., Dally, B.: Deep gradient compression: reducing the communication bandwidth for distributed training. In: Proceedings of the 6th International Conference on Learning Representations (ICLR), pp. 1–14. ICLR (2018)

14. Huilgol, R.: 2bit gradient compression (2017). https://github.com/apache/incubator-mxnet/pull/8662

15. Wen, W., et al.: TernGrad: ternary gradients to reduce communication in distributed deep learning. In: Proceedings of the 30th Conference on Neural Information Processing Systems (NIPS), pp. 1509–1519. MIT Press, Cambridge (2017)

Joint Reasoning of Events, Participants and Locations for Plot Relation Recognition

Shengguang Qiu[1], Botao Yu[1], Lei Qian[2], Qiang Guo[2], and Wei Hu[1,2(✉)]

[1] State Key Laboratory for Novel Software Technology, Nanjing University,
Nanjing 210023, Jiangsu, China
`sgqiu.nju@gmail.com,btyu.nju@gmail.com,whu@nju.edu.cn`
[2] State Key Laboratory of Mathematical Engineering and Advanced Computing,
Wuxi 214125, Jiangsu, China
`{qian.lei,guo.qiang}@meac-skl.cn`

Abstract. Event information is of great value, but the exploitation of it generally relies on not only extracting events from the text, but also figuring out the relations among events and organizing them accordingly. In this paper, based on a more flexible and practical type of event relation called the plot relation, we study the method of automatic event relation recognition. Specifically, we propose a local prediction method by using diversified linguistic and temporal features. Furthermore, we design a joint reasoning framework, in which we leverage the information of participants and locations, and add global constraints to further improve the performance. Finally, we transform the proposed model into integer linear programming (ILP) to obtain the global optimum. Our experiments demonstrate that our method significantly outperforms all the existing methods.

Keywords: Plot relation · Joint reasoning · Integer linear programming

1 Introduction

There exists a massive amount of event information in news, interviews and other verbal documents, recording various kinds of things about certain people or topics that happen at certain times and places. This information is of great value, as it can be used in public opinion monitoring, information analysis, emergency early-warning and more promising applications. Many of these real-world applications require the streams of events as the input, which indicates that in

This work is supported by the National Natural Science Foundation of China (No. 61872172), the Open Project Program of the State Key Laboratory of Mathematical Engineering and Advanced Computing, and the Fundamental Research Funds for the Central Universities (No. 020214380064).

X. Wang et al. (Eds.): APWeb-WAIM 2020, LNCS 12317, pp. 700–715, 2020.
https://doi.org/10.1007/978-3-030-60259-8_51

addition to extracting events from the text, figuring out the relations among events and organizing them accordingly are also indispensable.

There are several types of relation that can be used to depict the relations between a pair of events. Temporal relation means the order in time (i.e. *before* and *after*), organizing events by which leads to a timeline model [9,10,17,18]. However, the sole rule is incapable to represent the complicated event relations. Causal relation [8,11,12,14] labels one event as the cause and the other as the effect, but an explicit causal relation does not always exist between every two events. In addition, since causal relation has no absolute connection with the event development process, the event streams ordered by causal relation do not guarantee the accordance with the event development process. In a word, temporal relation and causal relation seem inadequate to depict the complex event relations in our natural languages and weak to adapt to our needs in the diverse applications.

In order to solve these problems, a novel relation type called plot relation has been proposed [19]. It regards events as plots of a story, and describes the changes between two plots with *rising* and *falling*. The value of the plot relation is determined by not only direct structural relations such as temporal relation and causal relation, but also other indirect relations such as co-occurrences, making this type of relation more general and flexible, capable to express more complex relations than the former two. Besides, its idea to link events into stories is naturally in accordance with the way human understand and organize information, thus more reasonable and practical for the various real-world applications. The plot relation between events is also named as PLOT_LINK [2], and organizing events by it leads to the storyline model, which can further facilitates event prediction, public opinion monitoring and more high-level applications. The whole process of storyline extraction includes 8 subtasks [2],[1] and in this paper, we mainly focus on one of the key parts, namely plot relation recognition.

Specifically, plot relation recognition aims to predict whether there is a PLOT_LINK between two event mentions as well as its type (if exists). There are two types of PLOT_LINKs, namely PRECONDITION and FALLING_ACTION. Consider two event mentions $e_1, e_2 \in M_e$, where M_e is the set of event mentions, the direction of the PLOT_LINK between them accords with their order in text, i.e. from the former to the latter. If e_1 is circumstantial to cause or enable e_2, then a PLOT_LINK of type PRECONDITION holds from e_1 to e_2; if e_1 is the (anticipated) outcome or the effect of e_2, then a PLOT_LINK of type FALLING_ACTION holds from e_1 to e_2 [3]. Note that although the plot relation is somewhat similar to the causal relation by definition, the former expresses weak causal relation in linguistics, and is the enhanced version of the latter in descriptive capability [1]. See the following example, where the bold words are the event mentions.

---

[1] The eight subtasks: relevant sentence selection, event detection, timex detection and normalization, event participant detection, event coreference resolution, temporal relation detection, plot relation recognition and climax event identification.

> A *reporter* doing **interview** was **killed** when the *rioters* **protesting** against the government **threw** petrol bombs at the *city hall*.

We graphically illustrate the PLOT_LINKs among the event mentions in Fig. 1 with solid arrows. Take the pair (*killed*, *threw*) as an example: since *killed* is the outcome of *threw*, the type of the PLOT_LINK is FALLING_ACTION. Consider the PLOT_LINK of type PRECONDITION from *interview* to *killed*: There is no explicit causal relation between them, but the plot relation still models it, because *interview* evolves to *killed* and this pair is valuable in event organization. This illustrates its difference from the ordinary causal relation.

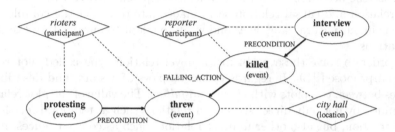

Fig. 1. A PLOT_LINK example, where solid arrows denote PLOT_LINKs and dashed lines denote associations between events and participants/locations.

Note that we also show locations participants in Fig. 1. Intuitively, the associations between event mentions and locations/participants may help the plot relation recognition. For example, *protesting* and *threw* share a common participant *rioters*, *killed* and *threw* share a common location *city hall*, then it is likely that PLOT_LINKs exist in the two pairs.

Inspired by this observation, in this paper, we propose a novel method of joint reasoning to improve plot relation recognition. Our contributions include:

- We propose a local prediction method for plot relation recognition, which leverages diversified linguistic and temporal features (Sect. 3).
- We propose a joint reasoning framework to resolve the conflicts in local prediction and leverage participants and locations associated with events. We design various constraints and convert them into integer linear programming (ILP) to achieve the global optimum (Sect. 4).
- Our experiments on the benchmark dataset, ESC, demonstrate that the proposed method significantly outperforms the baseline methods. The ablation study shows that all the defined constraints are contributory to the performance improvement (Sect. 5).

2   Related Work

Since the plot relation is proposed in [19], many efforts have been taken to improve the recognition task. Caselli and Vossen build the ESC v0.9 dataset for evaluation of the subtasks, which contains news documents on 22 topics, and each topic describes one certain news. They also propose 3 baseline models for plot relation recognition. Caselli and Inel define PLOT_LINK as weak causal relation rather than strict one in linguistics, and propose a crowdsourcing method to annotate the causal relations under their definition [1]. Besides, by comparing the results annotated by experts and crowds, they find that under the circumstance where the optimum threshold is adopted, the F1-scores just exceed 40%, which indicates that the task is very complicated even for humans. Different from [1] that uses crowdsourcing, our work does not need any manual intervention.

The current state-of-the-art performance comes from a recently proposed method in [7]. It adds various of constraints and uses ILP for global optimization just like ours. However, their method does not conduct joint reasoning with other elements, while our method implements joint reasoning with participants and locations and leverage them to further improve the performance. In addition, their method can only conduct PLOT_LINK detection, i.e. predicting if a PLOT_LINK holds between two events, while our method can further conduct PLOT_LINK classification, i.e. predicting the type of the PLOT_LINK, which, according to our experiments, is much more difficult than the former one.

Except from plot relation recognition, many works concentrates on recognition of other relations, and share some common techniques with ours. Chambers et al. propose CAEVO to recognize the temporal relations [4]. They design a global optimization framework to aggregate results from multiple classifiers while ensuring the transitivity rule. CATENA [13] extends the sieve-based architecture from CAEVO to identify temporal and causal relations between events. Some works consider the relation of different elements and propose joint reasoning frameworks to co-optimize multiple tasks. For example, Do et al. proposes a timeline construction method that predicts not only the temporal relations but also the event-interval relations, and adopts ILP to conduct joint reasoning [6]. Ning et al. design a joint framework for temporal and causal reasoning (TCR) [15,16], which refines the temporal and causal consistency by setting a number of constraints. Our method is greatly inspired by these existing methods, as we also adopt the idea of joint reasoning and ILP, but as far as we know, we are the first to introduce participant and location information into joint reasoning for event relation extraction.

3   Local Prediction

In this section, we introduce the local prediction method, in which we only make use of simple local information. Specifically, given a set of documents on the same topic, we process one document each time, and for each pair of event mentions in this document, we predict the PLOT_LINK type. We denote all the possible cases for a PLOT_LINK by R_{plot} = {PRECONDITION, FALLING_ ACTION, NONE}, where NONE means no PLOT_LINK holds for the pair. If a PLOT_LINK $r_{\text{plot}} \in R_{\text{plot}}$ holds from e_1 to e_2, where $e_1, e_2 \in M_e$ and M_e is the set of event mentions, we write it as $(e_1, e_2) \mapsto r_{\text{plot}}$. The task can be modeled as a three-class classification problem. The local features that we use include two types: linguistic features and temporal features.

Linguistic Features. Following the previous work CATENA [13], we adopt the same nine features including *sentence distance, entity distance, WordNet similarity, part-of-speech (PoS), phrase chunk, same PoS, dependency path, is main verb* and *event type.* Readers may refer to [13] for more details. Besides, let Q_e be the set of event mentions coreferent with event mention e, and by definition $e \in Q_e$. Given $e_1, e_2 \in M_e$ which are the pair we want to predict, we design two extra features as follows:

- *Intra-doc co-occurrence*: whether there exist $e'_1 \in Q_{e_1}$ and $e'_2 \in Q_{e_2}$ that appear in the same sentence, where e'_1 and e'_2 are both from the current document (which e_1 and e_2 belong to).
- *Cross-doc co-occurrence*: whether there exist $e'_1 \in Q_{e_1}$ and $e'_2 \in Q_{e_2}$ that appear in the same sentence, where e'_1 and e'_2 are both from documents except for the current one.

Since the co-occurrence of two events within one sentence generally indicates a higher possibility that some relations hold between them, these co-occurrence features should strengthen our model ability to mine the event relations.

Temporal Features. Generally, the plot relation implies the temporal relation, thus the temporal features should also be helpful. The ESC dataset defines 13 types of temporal links (abbr. TLINKs) that describe the temporal relations between events. However, under this fine-grained definition, for some types there are only a few instances. Thus, we recategorize them into six general types, namely *before, after, include, is_included, simultaneous* and *vague*, by merging some semantically similar ones.[2] We denote them by $R_{temp} = \{b, a, i, ii, s, v\}$. If a TLINK $r_{temp} \in R_{temp}$ holds from e_1 to e_2, we denote it by $(e_1, e_2) \mapsto r_{temp}$.

To further reduce the sparsity of TLINKs, we carry out a simple reasoning to supplement instances. Given $e_1, e_2, e_3 \in M_e$, the reasoning rules are as follows:

1. **Reciprocity rule.** If $(e_1, e_2) \mapsto r_{temp}$, then $(e_2, e_1) \mapsto \overline{r_{temp}}$. Semantically, we have $a = \bar{b}$, $i = \bar{ii}$, s and v are both reflexive.
2. **Transitivity rule.** If $(e_1, e_2) \mapsto r_{temp}$, and $(e_2, e_3) \mapsto r_{temp}$, then $(e_1, e_3) \mapsto r_{temp}$.

After the preprocessing, we extract the following temporal features:

- *TLINK type*: the type of the TLINK between the pair of event mentions.

---

[2] {BEFORE, BEFORE_OVERLAP, BEGINS_ON, ENDS_ON}$\mapsto$ *before*, {AFTER, AFTER_OVERLAP, BEGUN_ON, ENDED_ON}$\mapsto$ *after*, {CONTAINS}$\mapsto$ *include*, {IS_CONTAINED}$\mapsto$ *is_included*,{OVERLAP, SIMULTANEOUS}$\mapsto$ *simultaneous*, {VAGUE}$\mapsto$ *vague*.

– *Anchor mention*: whether the pair of event mentions share an anchor mention. Given $e_1, e_2, e_3 \in M_e$, we call e_3 an anchor mention for the pair of event mentions (e_1, e_2) when there exists $(e_3, e_1) \mapsto r_{\text{temp}}$ and $(e_3, e_2) \mapsto r_{\text{temp}}$. For each $r_{\text{temp}} \in R_{\text{temp}}$, we use one bit to present the existence of the anchor mention. This feature serves as the additional information, especially for those with no direct or indirect temporal relations.

We represent all the features with one-hot vectors, concatenate the vectors into a long binary vector and feed it into a softmax classifier to obtain the prediction result. The reason why we choose the softmax classifier is based on our experiment in Sect. 5.3.

4   Joint Reasoning

In local prediction, we find the following two limitations:

– Since each PLOT_LINK is predicted separately, conflicts may occur. For example, given $e_1, e_2 \in M_e$, $e'_1 \in Q_{e_1}$ and $e'_2 \in Q_{e_2}$, there may be $(e_1, e_2) \mapsto r_{\text{plot1}}$ and $(e'_1, e'_2) \mapsto r_{\text{plot2}}$ coexisting in the prediction results, where $r_{\text{plot1}}, r_{\text{plot2}} \in R_{\text{plot}}$ but $r_{\text{plot1}} \neq r_{\text{plot2}}$.
– As mentioned before, the event-participant associations and the event-location associations may be helpful for plot relation recognition, but they have not been exploited in local prediction.

To deal with the first limitation, we add several constraints to optimize the local prediction results for achieving global consistency. For the second limitation, we propose extra constraints to model the associations between events, participants and locations. We name the associations between events and participants (locations) as EP_LINKs (EL_LINKs), and denote them by r_{ptcp} (r_{loc}). The possible cases are $R_{ptcp} = R_{loc} = \{\text{RELATED}, \text{UNRELATED}\}$. If a EP_LINK r_{ptcp} holds between event mention e and participant mention p, we denote it by $(e, p) \mapsto r_{\text{ptcp}}$. And it is similar for EL_LINKs.

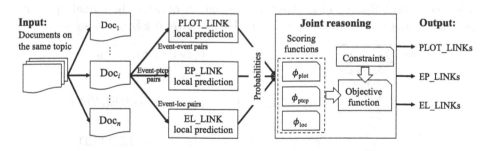

Fig. 2. Joint reasoning framework.

Figure 2 shows our joint reasoning framework. For each event mentions pair in every document, we first conduct local prediction of PLOT_LINKs, EP_LINKs and EL_LINKs. Then, we conduct joint reasoning to optimize the results. One point worth mentioning is that, in this paper, we concentrate on improving PLOT_LINK recognition and the participant/location information is merely auxiliary, thus we directly adopt the local prediction method on EP_LINK/EL_LINK similar to that of PLOT_LINK. We skip the details here and focus on the joint reasoning part.

4.1 Scoring Functions

In local prediction, for any $e_1, e_2 \in M_e$, we already have their predicted PLOT_LINK with its local probability. We define the probability function $\Pr_{\text{plot}}(r_{\text{plot}} \mid e_1, e_2)$ as

$$\Pr_{\text{plot}}(r_{\text{plot}} \mid e_1, e_2) = \begin{cases} \text{local probability for } r_{\text{plot}} & \text{if } (e_1, e_2) \mapsto r_{\text{plot}} \\ 0 & \text{otherwise} \end{cases}. \tag{1}$$

Then, we define the scoring function for r_{plot} as follows:

$$\phi_{\text{plot}}\big((e_1, e_2) \mapsto r_{\text{plot}}\big) = \max_{e_1' \in Q_{e_1}, e_2' \in Q_{e_2}} \Pr_{\text{plot}}(r_{\text{plot}} \mid e_1', e_2'). \tag{2}$$

Let M_p and M_l denote the sets of participant mentions and location mentions respectively. Likewise, we define the scoring functions for EP_LINKs and EL_LINKs:

$$\phi_{\text{ptcp}}\big((e, p) \mapsto r_{\text{ptcp}}\big) = \max_{e' \in Q_e, p' \in Q_p} \Pr_{\text{ptcp}}(r_{\text{ptcp}} \mid e', p'),$$

$$\phi_{\text{loc}}\big((e, l) \mapsto r_{\text{loc}}\big) = \max_{e' \in Q_e, l' \in Q_l} \Pr_{\text{loc}}(r_{\text{loc}} \mid e', l'), \tag{3}$$

where $p \in M_p$, $l \in M_l$, Q_p and Q_l are the sets of coreferent participant mentions and location mentions respectively. The probability functions $\Pr_{\text{ptcp}}(\cdot)$ and $\Pr_{\text{loc}}(\cdot)$ are similar to $\Pr_{\text{plot}}(\cdot)$ in Eq. (1).

4.2 Objective Function

We define the following objective function, which obtains the global optimum by maximizing the sum of PLOT_LINK, EP_LINK and EL_LINK scores:

$$\max \sum_{\substack{e_1 \in M_e \\ e_1 \neq e_2}} \sum_{e_2 \in M_e} \sum_{r_{\text{plot}} \in R_{\text{plot}}^+} x(e_1, e_2, r_{\text{plot}}) \cdot \phi_{\text{plot}}\big((e_1, e_2) \mapsto r_{\text{plot}}\big)$$

$$+ \sum_{e \in M_e} \sum_{p \in M_p} y(e, p, \text{RELATED}) \cdot \phi_{\text{ptcp}}\big((e, p) \mapsto \text{RELATED}\big) \tag{4}$$

$$+ \sum_{e \in M_e} \sum_{l \in M_l} z(e, l, \text{RELATED}) \cdot \phi_{\text{loc}}\big((e, l) \mapsto \text{RELATED}\big),$$

s.t. $x, y, z \in \{0, 1\}$,

where $R_{\text{plot}}^+ = \{\text{PRECONDITION}, \text{FALLING\_ACTION}\}$. x, y, z are indicator variables, e.g. $x(e_1, e_2, r_{\text{plot}}) = 1$ when $(e_1, e_2) \mapsto r_{\text{plot}}$.

4.3 Constraints

In this subsection, we introduce the constraints for optimization. Two motivations of adding these constraints include: (i) The constraints ensure that the prediction results conform to the plot relation definition and the real-world rules. For example, a PLOT_LINK cannot be PRECONDITION and FALLING_ACTION at the same time, and the type of the PLOT_LINK between a pair of events must be consistent regardless of the sentences they are situated in, etc. (ii) The solution space would be too large to solve if we did not limit the possible situations. Here, we introduce three groups of constraints:

PLOT_LINK Constraints. We define four basic constraints for PLOT_LINKs:

- **Equivalence.** $(e_1, e_2) \mapsto$ PRECONDITION is equivalent to $(e_2, e_1) \mapsto$ FALLING_ACTION.
- **Coreference consistency.** If $(e_1, e_2) \mapsto r_{\text{plot}}$, and $e_1' \in Q_{e_1}, e_2' \in Q_{e_2}$, then $(e_1', e_2') \mapsto r_{\text{plot}}$.
- **Uniqueness.** There must be either no PLOT_LINK or only one PLOT_LINK for a pair of event mentions.
- **Temporal consistency.** PLOT_LINK sequence should not conflict with TLINK sequence.

Moreover, we define a new constraint to avoid superfluous PLOT_LINK predictions. See the following example:

> He initially was **imprisoned** on February 1979 on three 10-year **sentences** for **rape** of a child, aggravated rape of a child, and burglary.

There exist two PLOT_LINKs in this sentence: $(imprisoned, sentences) \mapsto$ FALLING_ACTION and $(sentence, rape) \mapsto$ FALLING_ACTION, due to the immediate cause of the man's imprisonment (sentence) is sentence (rape). As for the PLOT_LINK $(imprisoned, rape) \mapsto$ FALLING_ACTION, since that the man got imprisoned is due to a sentence on him for rape, the former two imply this one, thus it is unnecessary to predict it. Based on this, the constraint is

- **Anti-transitivity.** Within a certain distance, there should be no transitive PLOT_LINKs.

Formally, if there are two directed paths (also consider the aforementioned equivalence constraint): $e_1 \to e_2$ and $e_1 \to \cdots \to e_i \to e_j \to \cdots \to e_2$ with a length of d, then the two paths cannot coexist. Let $r_{\text{plot}}^{i,j}$ be the PLOT_LINK from e_1 to e_2. The constraint is

$$x(e_1, e_2, r_{\text{plot}}^{1,2}) + \mathbb{1}\Big(\bigwedge_{(e_i, e_j, r_{\text{plot}}^{i,j}) \in \text{path}} (x(e_i, e_j, r_{\text{plot}}^{i,j}) = 1)\Big) \leq 1,$$

$$\forall \text{path} \in \text{PATHS}(e_1, e_2, d), \quad \forall r_{\text{plot}}^{1,2}, r_{\text{plot}}^{i,j} \in R_{\text{plot}}^+, \tag{5}$$

where $\mathbb{1}(\cdot)$ is the indicator function whose value equals to 1 when the condition inside the parentheses is satisfied or 0 otherwise, and $\mathrm{PATHS}(e_1, e_2, d)$ represents the set of paths from e_1 to e_2, whose length is at most d. In this paper, the length threshold is set to 4 based on our empirical experience.

EP_LINK and EL_LINK Constraints. For EP_LINKs and EL_LINKs, we define two basic constraints:

- **Coreference consistency**: If $(e, p) \mapsto r_{\mathrm{ptcp}}$, and $e' \in Q_e$, $p' \in Q_p$, then $(e', p') \mapsto r_{\mathrm{ptcp}}$. And it is similar for EL_LINKs.
- **Quantity constraints.** In most cases, there are no more than two different participants (agent and recipient) and one location in an event mention. For the sake of computation, we limit their amounts:

$$ptcp(e) = \sum_{e \in M'_e} \sum_{p \in M'_p} y(e, p, \mathrm{RELATED}), loc(e) = \sum_{e \in M'_e} \sum_{l \in M'_l} z(e, l, \mathrm{RELATED}),$$

$$ptcp \in \{0, 1, 2\}, \& loc \in \{0, 1\}. \tag{6}$$

where M'_e, M'_p, M'_l are the sets of event, participant, location mentions after coreference resolution, respectively. The functions $ptcp(e)$ and $loc(e)$ are used to calculate the number of participant mentions and location mentions associated with event mention e after coreference resolution.

Joint Reasoning Constraint. Furthermore, based on the aforementioned observation that a PLOT_LINK usually exists between event mentions which share common participants and/or location, we propose a joint reasoning constraint. For any $e_1, e_2 \in M_e$, if $(e_1, e_2) \mapsto r_{\mathrm{plot}}$, then at least one of the two conditions should be satisfied: (i) e_1 and e_2 share common participants, or at least one of them has no related participant; or (ii) e_1 and e_2 share a common location, or at least one of them has no related location. We formalize this constraint as follows:

$$x(e_1, e_2, r_{\mathrm{plot}})$$

$$\leq \mathbb{1}\Big([ptcp(e_1) = 0 \vee ptcp(e_2) = 0 \vee \sum_{p \in M_p} u(e_1, e_2, p) \geq 1]$$

$$\vee [loc(e_1) = 0 \vee loc(e_2) = 0 \vee \sum_{l \in M_l} v(e_1, e_2, l) \geq 1]\Big), \tag{7}$$

where

$$u(e_1, e_2, p) = \mathbb{1}\Big(y(e_1, p, \mathrm{RELATED}) \geq 1 \wedge y(e_2, p, \mathrm{RELATED}) \geq 1\Big),$$

$$v(e_1, e_2, l) = \mathbb{1}\Big(z(e_1, l, \mathrm{RELATED}) \geq 1 \wedge z(e_2, l, \mathrm{RELATED}) \geq 1\Big). \tag{8}$$

4.4   Converting Constraints into ILP

We rewrite the constraints into ILP and use the off-the-shelf optimization tools to solve it. Due to the space limitation, we only show some of the conversions. For example, the anti-transitivity constraint in Eq. (5) is converted to

$$x(e_1, e_2, r_{\text{plot}}^{1,2}) + \sum_{(e_i,e_j,r_{\text{plot}}^{i,j})\in\text{path}} x(e_i, e_j, r_{\text{plot}}^{i,j}) \leq \sum_{(e_i,e_j,r_{\text{plot}}^{i,j})\in\text{path}} 1, \tag{9}$$

$$\forall\text{path} \in \text{PATHS}(e_1, e_2, d), \quad \forall r_{\text{plot}}^{1,2}, r_{\text{plot}}^{i,j} \in R_{\text{plot}}^+.$$

As a more complex case, for the joint reasoning constraint, u, v in Eq. (8) are rewritten as:

$$
\begin{aligned}
2 \cdot u(e_1, e_2, p) &\leq y(e_1, p, \text{RELATED}) + y(e_2, p, \text{RELATED}), \\
u(e_1, e_2, p) &\geq y(e_1, p, \text{RELATED}) + y(e_2, p, \text{RELATED}) - 1, \\
2 \cdot v(e_1, e_2, l) &\leq z(e_1, l, \text{RELATED}) + z(e_2, l, \text{RELATED}), \\
v(e_1, e_2, l) &\geq z(e_1, l, \text{RELATED}) + z(e_2, l, \text{RELATED}) - 1.
\end{aligned}
\tag{10}
$$

Then, we use two decision variables, x_{ptcp} and x_{loc}, to represent the two cases in Eq. (7). Then we have:

$$
\begin{aligned}
x_{\text{ptcp}}(e_1, e_2) &\leq \mathbb{1}\Big(ptcp(e_1) = 0 \vee ptcp(e_2) = 0 \vee \big(\sum_{p\in M_p} u(e_1, e_2, p)\big) \geq 1\Big), \\
x_{\text{loc}}(e_1, e_2) &\leq \mathbb{1}\Big(loc(e_1) = 0 \vee loc(e_2) = 0 \vee \big(\sum_{l\in M_l} v(e_1, e_2, l)\big) \geq 1\Big).
\end{aligned}
\tag{11}
$$

Notice that $ptcp \in \{0, 1, 2\}$. In order to meet the requirement of ILP, we define $ptcp'$ as $\mathbb{1}(ptcp \geq 1)$ to transform $ptcp$ into a binary variable. Then, we have $ptcp' \in \{0, 1\}$ and $ptcp' \leq ptcp \leq 2 \cdot ptcp'$. The above equations can be further written into ILP as:

$$
\begin{aligned}
x_{\text{ptcp}}(e_1, e_2) &\leq 2 - ptcp'(e_1) - ptcp'(e_2) + \sum_{p\in M_p} u(e_1, e_2, p), \\
x_{\text{loc}}(e_1, e_2) &\leq 2 - loc(e_1) - loc(e_2) + \sum_{l\in M_l} v(e_1, e_2, l).
\end{aligned}
\tag{12}
$$

Finally, the joint reasoning constraint is

$$x(e_1, e_2, r_{\text{plot}}) \leq x_{\text{ptcp}}(e_1, e_2) + x_{\text{loc}}(e_1, e_2). \tag{13}$$

5   Experiments and Results

5.1   Dataset

We conduct experiments on the ESC v0.9 dataset [3], which contains the same documents of 22 topics as the ones in ECB+ corpus [5]. The content is about calamity events such as natural disasters and crimes. The documents on one topic describe the same series of news events, e.g. documents in topic 30 describe "Seacom operations fully restored". The dataset provides gold event mentions, participant mentions, location mentions, temporal relations and PLOT_LINKs. We also leverage some necessary annotations such as event coreferences from ECB+ that are not contained in ESC. In addition, since ESC lacks associations between participant, location and event mentions, which are required for joint reasoning, we invite three senior master students in the NLP area to manually annotate them and adopt the majority decisions for each item to reduce the annotation errors. The statistics of our annotated dataset are shown in Table 1. For comparison with the baseline methods, we use the same data split[3] [3].

Table 1. Statistics of the annotated dataset.

	Training set	Test set	Total
Articles	64	189	253
Avg. articles/topic	10.7	11.8	11.5
PLOT_LINKs	1,598	4,027	5,625
EP_LINKs	7,199	12,189	19,388
EL_LINKs	825	3,888	4,713

Table 2. Results of local prediction on different classification models.

	PLOT_LINK detection			PLOT_LINK classification			EP_LINK prediction			EL_LINK prediction		
	P	R	F1	P	R	F1	P	R	F1	P	R	F1
Softmax regr	30.9	**75.0**	**42.5**	16.6	**40.1**	**22.6**	-	-	-	-	-	-
Logistic regr	31.3	68.1	41.5	16.0	35.5	21.5	38.0	**88.6**	**51.1**	44.0	**85.7**	**56.7**
Decision tree	33.0	27.2	28.6	19.5	16.6	17.3	**42.5**	64.5	49.8	**45.9**	66.8	52.6
SVM	**52.4**	21.4	28.4	**23.1**	10.7	14.1	24.7	94.2	37.3	44.1	77.6	54.6

"-" denotes "not applicable".

5.2 Experiment Setting

We set up two tasks for the proposed method as follows:

PLOT_LINK prediction. This task contains two subtasks: (i) PLOT_LINK detection: Predict the existence of PLOT_ LINKs. In other words, predict whether $r_{plot} \in R_{plot}^{+}$. (ii) PLOT_LINK classification: In addition to detection, it further predicts the type of PLOT_LINK.

EP_LINK & EL_LINK prediction. Predict the types of EP_LINKs and EL_LINKs, i.e. RELATED or UNRELATED.

---

[3] Training set: T5, T7, T8, T32, T33, T35. Test set: T1, T3, T4, T12, T13, T14, T16, T18, T19, T20, T22, T23, T24, T30, T37, T41.

Table 3. Comparison with the existing methods.

	PLOT_LINK detection			PLOT_LINK classification			EP_LINK prediction			EL_LINK prediction		
	P	R	F1	P	R	F1	P	R	F1	P	R	F1
OP	15.6	**98.8**	26.5	7.0	**97.0**	14.0	24.7	**100.0**	37.6	28.3	**100.0**	41.6
PPMI-base	13.7	17.4	13.7	6.5	9.8	6.8	-	-	-	-	-	-
PPMI-contains	22.7	9.1	12.1	11.4	5.0	6.4	-	-	-	-	-	-
PPMI-internal	-	-	-	-	-	-	34.0	67.8	40.6	33.6	43.1	34.4
DCS	36.2	49.5	41.9	-	-	-	-	-	-	-	-	-
Local prediction	30.9	75.0	42.5	16.6	40.1	22.6	38.1	88.6	51.1	44.0	85.7	56.7
Joint reasoning	**34.2**	72.4	**45.1**	**20.0**	41.0	**26.1**	**42.7**	81.4	**54.1**	**49.5**	76.7	**59.0**

We use the PuLP modeler and the Cbc (Coin-or branch and cut) ILP solver[4] to implement the proposed method. During our experiments, the ILP solver can always return the result without timeout (even if on ESC, the current largest dataset for this task), and the computation process takes about 9 min at most. Following the previous work [3], we report average precision (P), recall (R) and F1-score (F1) over all topics in the test set.

5.3 Model Selection for Local Prediction

First of all, we evaluate several classification models for local prediction, including softmax regression, logistic regression, decision tree and SVM. All the models are implemented with scikit-learn, and the parameters are set to: class_weight = "balanced", penalty = l2, max_iter = 500. The results are shown in Table 2.

We choose the softmax regression model for PLOT_LINK local prediction, as it achieves the best recalls and F1-scores. For EP_LINK & EL_LINK prediction, since they are two-class classification, softmax regression is degraded to logistic regression. We take logistic regression also due to its optimal performance.

5.4 Comparison with Existing Methods

For PLOT_LINK prediction, we compare our method with three baseline methods proposed in [3] and a state-of-the-art method proposed in [7] as listed below. We directly use their reported results.

- **OP**, which exhaustively picks event mention pairs in terms of the textual order, and labels them as PRECONDITION.
- **PPMI-base**, which measures event mention pairs using positive pointwise mutual information (PPMI) obtained from a set of selected seed pairs and the manually-annotated pairs from the training set. The value of PPMI is normalized to [0, 1] for each topic.
- **PPMI-contains**, which uses the results from PPMI-base as candidates but restricts the event mentions to share common temporal anchor mentions (see Sect. 3).

---

[4] https://github.com/coin-or.

- **DCS** [7], which detects PLOT_LINKs at sentence-level and document-level by modeling global and fine-grained aspects of document-level causal structures and conducting optimization with ILP. However, it does not conduct joint reasoning with participants and locations like our method, and can only detect PLOT_LINKs, while our method can further classify PLOT_LINKs.

For EP_LINK and EL_LINK prediction, due to the lack of related work, we designed two alternative methods for comparison:

- **OP**, which chooses event-participant and event-location mention pairs in terms of the textual order of presentation.
- **PPMI-internal**, which is similar to the PPMI-base method in PLOT_LINK prediction, but the frequencies are obtained only from the internal corpus, while the frequencies in PPMI-base are from Google bigrams. According to the averages and standard deviations, the thresholds for EP_LINKs and EL_LINKs are set to 0.319 and 0.365, respectively.

Table 3 shows the comparison results. As we can observe, our local prediction method outperforms all the baseline models on all the tasks, and our joint reasoning method further achieves the highest precisions and F1-scores, while OP obtains the best recalls due to it contains almost all possible results. This demonstrates the superiority of our method.

Specifically, on the PLOT_LINK prediction task, we can see that the F1 scores of PLOT_LINK classification are much lower than those of PLOT_LINK detection for all methods, which indicates that the PLOT_LINK classification subtask is much more difficult than the other. In addition, all the PPMI-base/ contains/internal methods perform poorly, because they only utilize very limited information, and thus can hardly capture the characteristics of PLOT_LINKs. Furthermore, although the precisions of PPMI-contains increase compared to PPMI-base due to the common temporal anchor mentions, the recalls significantly decreased. Our local prediction method significantly outperform first four methods ($p < 0.05$), because it exploits more linguistic and temporal features. And we cannot calculate the significance with DCS because its code is not provided. Furthermore, since we couple local prediction with participant/location information and various constraints, the joint reasoning method even performs better than local prediction.

On EP_LINK & EL_LINK prediction, PPMI-internal obtained comparable results with OP, because this task is not as hard as PLOT_LINK prediction and internal corpus is appropriate for PPMI. Still, the local prediction method exceeds the two baselines, and the joint reasoning method achieves the best.

5.5   Ablation Study

To assess the newly-proposed constraints in this work, we conduct an ablation study. For abbreviation, the constraints are numbered below:

- **C1:** PLOT_LINK anti-transitivity constraint.

Table 4. Results of ablation study.

	PLOT_LINK detection			PLOT_LINK classification			EP_LINK prediction			EL_LINK prediction		
	P	R	F1	P	R	F1	P	R	F1	P	R	F1
Joint reasoning	34.2	72.4	**45.1**	20.0	41.0	**26.1**	**42.7**	81.4	**54.1**	49.5	76.7	**59.0**
Joint reasoning w/o C1	30.2	**81.0**	42.6	17.3	**45.6**	24.4	-	-	-	-	-	-
Joint reasoning w/o C2	34.2	72.4	**45.1**	18.3	37.7	23.8	24.7	**92.8**	37.2	41.5	**88.5**	54.8
Joint reasoning w/o C3	34.2	72.4	**45.1**	19.0	39.1	24.7	42.5	80.7	53.8	**50.2**	73.0	58.5

- **C2:** EP_LINK and EL_LINK constraints.
- **C3:** Joint reasoning constraint.

As we can observe from Table 4, these constraints all contributed to the performance improvement. Specifically, on the PLOT_LINK detection subtask, C1 is the key factor as it significantly improves the precision, while the other two constraints have little impact on the results. On the PLOT_ LINK classification subtask, C1, C2 and C3 all improve the results to varied degrees. Also, removing C1 leads to an increase in recall, indicating that C1 is not always satisfied.

Table 5. Constraint satisfaction ratios on the test set.

	PLOT_LINKs	EP_LINKs	EL_LINKs
C1	80.9%	-	-
C2	-	94.7%	93.2%
C3	98.0%	96.7%	97.1%

Similarly, we can observe that the F1-scores of EP_LINK & EL_LINK prediction largely decreases after removing C2, even lower than those of local prediction. According to the results, C2 has a great influence on this task.

Let us further analyze the causes of errors and discuss the difficulties in terms of the constraints. Table 5 shows the constraint satisfaction ratios on the test set: ratios of the number of event mention pairs that satisfy the constraints (according to the gold standard) over the number of all event mentions on the test set. As we can see, C1 is the most dissatisfied constraint, and the reasons may be: (i) since each conflict caused by C1 involves several PLOT_LINKs, according to our calculation, these PLOT_LINKs are all judged as not meeting the constraint; and (ii) C1 is based on a strong assumption that may not always be satisfied. As for C2, we would like to use the following example to explain:

> "There's a lot of anger here": **Riot** breaks out in *Brooklyn* following candlelight vigil for 16-year-old shot by cops. ... Anger over the death of a Brooklyn teenager shot and killed by police fueled a **riot** on the streets of *East Flatbush* Monday.

We can find that **riot** has two EL_LINKs with *Brooklyn* and *East Flatbush*, respectively, which violates C2 (the quantity constraints in C2 restrict that one event can only have one location). But obviously this is not an annotation fault, because *East Flatbush* is a residential area in *Brooklyn*, which means the two EL_LINKs can coexist. According to our statistics, most of the cases that violates the constraints are due to the same reason. Therefore, spatial reasoning is a challenging problem that need to be considered in the future.

6   Conclusion

In this paper, we study the problem of plot relation recognition between events. We firstly propose a PLOT_LINK local prediction method by using diversified linguistic and temporal features. Our experimental results show that this method outperforms the baselines including the state-of-the-art method. Furthermore, taking the associations between events, participants and locations into consideration, we present a joint reasoning framework, which gains the global optimum by leveraging various constraints and converting them into ILP. Our experiments show that joint reasoning significantly improves the performance.

In the future, we will (i) add more external knowledge to further improve the performance of plot relation recognition, and (ii) design methods with human involvement to help the model refine the prediction results.

References

1. Caselli, T., Inel, O.: Crowdsourcing storylines: harnessing the crowd for causal relation annotation. In: COLING 2018 Workshop on Events and Stories in the News. Santa Fe, NM, USA, pp. 44–54 (2018)
2. Caselli, T., Vossen, P.: The storyline annotation and representation scheme (StaR): a proposal. In: EMNLP 2016 Workshop on Computing News Storylines. Austin, TX, USA, pp. 67–72 (2016)
3. Caselli, T., Vossen, P.: The event storyline corpus: a new benchmark for causal and temporal relation extraction. In: ACL 2017 Workshop on Events and Stories in the News. Vancouver, Canada, pp. 77–86 (2017)
4. Chambers, N., Cassidy, T., McDowell, B., Bethard, S.: Dense event ordering with a multi-pass architecture. Trans. Assoc. Comput. Linguist. **2**, 273–284 (2014)
5. Cybulska, A., Vossen, P.: Guidelines for ECB+ annotation of events and their coreference. Tech. rep., Technical Report NWR-2014-1, VU University Amsterdam (2014)
6. Do, Q.X., Lu, W., Roth, D.: Joint inference for event timeline construction. In: EMNLP, pp. 677–687 (2012)
7. Gao, L., Choubey, P.K., Huang, R.: Modeling document-level causal structures for event causal relation identification. In: NAACL-HLT. Minneapolis, Minnesota, pp. 1808–1817 (2019)
8. Hanawa, K., Sasaki, A., Okazaki, N., Inui, K.: A crowdsourcing approach for annotating causal relation instances in wikipedia. In: Proceedings of the 31st Pacific Asia Conference on Language, Information and Computation, pp. 336–345 (2017)
9. Hu, P., Huang, M., Zhu, X.: Exploring the interactions of storylines from informative news events. J. Comput. Sci. Technol. **29**(3), 502–518 (2014)
10. Huang, L.: Optimized event storyline generation based on mixture-event-aspect model. In: EMNLP. Seattle, WA, USA, pp. 726–735 (2013)

11. Kruengkrai, C., Torisawa, K., Hashimoto, C., Kloetzer, J., Oh, J.H., Tanaka, M.: Improving event causality recognition with multiple background knowledge sources using multi-column convolutional neural networks. In: AAAI, pp. 3466–3473 (2017)
12. Li, P., Mao, K.: Knowledge-oriented convolutional neural network for causal relation extraction from natural language texts. Expert Syst. Appl. **115**, 512–523 (2019)
13. Mirza, P., Tonelli, S.: CATENA: CAusal and TEmporal relation extraction from NAtural language texts. In: COLING 2016. Osaka, Japan, pp. 64–75 (2016)
14. Mostafazadeh, N., Grealish, A., Chambers, N., Allen, J., Vanderwende, L.: Caters: causal and temporal relation scheme for semantic annotation of event structures. In: Proceedings of the Fourth Workshop on Events, pp. 51–61 (2016)
15. Ning, Q., Feng, Z., Roth, D.: A structured learning approach to temporal relation extraction. In: EMNLP. Copenhagen, Denmark, pp. 1027–1037 (2017)
16. Ning, Q., Feng, Z., Wu, H., Roth, D.: Joint reasoning for temporal and causal relations. In: ACL. Melbourne, Australia, pp. 2278–2288 (2018)
17. Reimers, N., Dehghani, N., Gurevych, I.: Event time extraction with a decision tree of neural classifiers. Trans. Assoc. Comput. Linguist. **6**, 77–89 (2018)
18. Shahaf, D., Yang, J., Suen, C., Jacobs, J., Wang, H., Leskovec, J.: Information cartography: creating zoomable, large-scale maps of information. In: KDD. Chicago, IL, USA, pp. 1097–1105 (2013)
19. Vossen, P., Caselli, T., Kontzopoulou, Y.: Storylines for structuring massive streams of news. In: ACL 2015 Workshop on Computing News Storylines. Beijing, China, pp. 40–49 (2015)

FedSmart: An Auto Updating Federated Learning Optimization Mechanism

Anxun He[ID], Jianzong Wang[(✉)][ID], Zhangcheng Huang[ID], and Jing Xiao

Ping An Technology (Shenzhen) Co., Ltd.,
Shenzhen 518000, People's Republic of China
jzwang@188.com

Abstract. Federated learning has made an important contribution to data privacy-preserving. Many previous works are based on the assumption that the data are independently identically distributed (IID). As a result, the model performance on non-identically independently distributed (non-IID) data is beyond expectation, which is the concrete situation. Some existing methods of ensuring the model robustness on non-IID data, like the data-sharing strategy or pre-training, may lead to privacy leaking. In addition, there exist some participants who try to poison the model with low-quality data. In this paper, a performance-based parameter return method for optimization is introduced, we term it FederatedSmart (FedSmart). It optimizes different model for each client through sharing global gradients, and it extracts the data from each client as a local validation set, and the accuracy that model achieves in round t determines the weights of the next round. The experiment results show that FedSmart enables the participants to allocate a greater weight to the ones with similar data distribution.

Keywords: Federated learning · Federated optimization · Distributed machine learning · Privacy preserving

1 Introduction

Securing high-quality machine learning models while working with different data owners is a challenge with user data security and confidentiality [15]. In the past, there have been many attempts to address user privacy issues when exchanging data. For example, Apple recommends using Differential Privacy (DP) to respond these concerns [3]. The basic idea is to add appropriately calibrated noise to data in order to eliminate the identity of any individual but still retain the statistical characteristics [2]. However, DP can only prevent user information leakage to a certain extent. In addition, it is lossy in machine learning framework because the model built with noise is injected, which can lower the model performance.

Federated Learning (FL) is a cross-distributed data modelling method proposed by [10,11]. It can establish a global model without exchanging original data among parties. Due to the exponential growth of participated data, the

© Springer Nature Switzerland AG 2020
X. Wang et al. (Eds.): APWeb-WAIM 2020, LNCS 12317, pp. 716–724, 2020.
https://doi.org/10.1007/978-3-030-60259-8_52

model naturally performs better global robustness and superiority over individual modelling.

Subsequently, [1] proposed the concept of vertical FL to update it suitable for more realistic scenarios. Since then, many scholars have started to study the application of real FL scenarios and proposed some new algorithms and frameworks, such as SplitNN [13].

[4] reveals the problem of multi-distribution between different data islands through joint clustering and FL. Through five model structure experiments on four different data-sets, [10] demonstrated that the iterative average model can be robust under both IID and non-IID data distribution patterns. However, the iterative approach is not as perfect as imagined. On non-IID data, it requires more rounds to iterate to sufficient convergence, and the final model performance trained with the same optimal parameters always slightly inferior to that obtained under IID distribution.

Almost all FL optimization algorithms are aimed at training a global model. However, in the real scenario, there exist clients who want to train a personalized model by absorbing useful information from others with similar data property. In addition, there are some dishonest participants trying to cheat with useless data to gain a high-qualified model.

Motivated by these real demands, we design a performance-based optimization algorithm, `FedSmart`, which is automatically updated. Our main contributions are as follows:

1. Demonstrate the impact and performance of using non-IID data on both FL frameworks and local training.
2. Adopt independent validation sets in each side instead of shared data sets to improve the model performance on non-IID data.
3. Propose a new parameter joint method `FedSmart` to make the multi-party joint value of the stochastic gradient descent close to the unbiased estimate of the complete gradient.

2 Related Work

In some cases, due to the advanced nature of some existing machine learning algorithm, the training results based on the non-IID data are still good. However, for some application scenarios, training with non-IID data will have unexpected negative effects based on existing frameworks, such as low model accuracy and convergence efficiency. Because the data on each device is generated independently by the device/user itself, the heterogeneous data of different devices/users have different distribution characteristics and the training data learned by each device during local learning are non-IID. Therefore, how to improve the learning efficiency of non-IID data is of great significance for FL.

2.1 Average-Based Optimization Algorithm

To improve the performance of FL and reduce the communication cost [10], a deep network algorithm `FederatedAveraging` (FedAvg) based on iterative model average is proposed for non-IID FL, which can be applied to real scenarios. Theoretical analysis and experimental results show that FedAvg is robust to unbalanced and non-IID data, and it also has a low communication cost. Compared with baseline algorithm FedSGD, FedAvg has better practicability and effectiveness. [9] theoretically clarifies the convergence of FedAvg on non-IID data. Furthermore, FedMA is aimed at settling the heterogeneity problem [14].

2.2 Performance-Based Optimization Algorithm

The proposal of FedAvg method has a great inspiration for the follow-up researches [15]. [16] proposes a data-sharing FL strategy to improve the training of non-IID Data by creating a small portion of the data globally shared between all client devices on a central server.

Local client computational complexity, communication cost, and test accuracy are three important issues addressed by [5]. It proposes a loss-based AdaBoost federated machine learning algorithm (LoAdaBoost), which further optimizes the local model with high cross-entropy loss before averaging the gradients on the central server.

FedProx, proposed by [12], lowers the potential damage to the model caused by non-IID data. It adds a near-end item to optimize the local iteration times. Similarly, SCAFFOLD introduces a new variable combined with gradients, decreasing the variance of local iteration [8].

3 Approach

In FL researches, the scholars usually focus on the algorithm framework or the improvement of the global model accuracy. However, we generally do not know the data distribution or data quality of other participants, the heterogeneous data may result in worse performance when added to the global training.

With these motivations, we propose FedSmart, a new parameter return method. In this mechanism, the FL participant is smart enough to gain information from others who have similar data property. In another aspect, FedSmart can be used to test whether the model from other clients is useful to every client's side. Furthermore, FedSmart can be treated as a kind of latent incentive mechanism, the selfish sides who provide unrealistic or unqualified data will be naturally filtered out via decreasing the weight, only the ones who provide their valuable data can benefit from the group with the similar distributions.

3.1 The Information Transfer Framework

The framework of FL is adopted. There typically exists a **server**, which controls and publishes the model and jointly deals with the parameters provided by participants. The participants who contribute parameters by doing local model training are called **clients**.

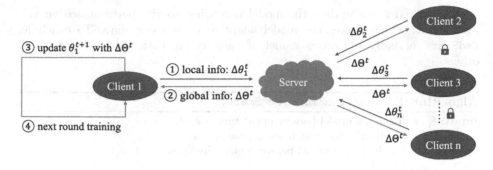

Fig. 1. Parameter update framework

All clients do the training respectively using local data. After the model is updated, each client sends the local model information to the server. Clients send the gradient training with their local data to the server; the server packs these changes and sends back, i.e. $\Delta\Theta^t(\Delta\theta_1^t, \Delta\theta_2^t, ..., \Delta\theta_n^t)$ (see Fig. 1).

3.2 The Local Model Updating Mechanism

The local model updating mechanism considers the mutual predicting ability of non-IID data. If all clients train only one global model, it will inevitably lead to distribution or sample size discrimination. **FedSmart** is designed to update the local model in the form of weights, which makes the model prefer to its self-side data. This approach actually optimizes the server model with the data from each client.

At the time of initialization, the server initializes the model. When all clients receive the initial model, they will conduct a batch-size training and then launch the information transfer as mentioned above.

3.3 Performance-Based Weight Allocation

The weight of the next moment is on the basis of the equation shown below. The performance of all the clients is taken into consideration, the principle, in brief, is that the weight of model will be smartly adjusted to the accuracy of each client.

$$||w_i^t|| = ||w_i^{t-1} + \eta(acc_i^t - acc_{median}^t)||_1 \tag{1}$$

where acc_i^t represents the accuracy of *Client i* on local validation set in round t on the validation set, acc_{median}^t is the median of the set of accuracy, and η is the learning rate. The weight in round t is allocated according to the weight in the previous round and the change of accuracy in this round. The validation set is extracted from each client with a proportion of $\alpha \in [0, 1]$, and only serves for this client.

In FedSmart, we update the model according to the performance on validation set, which makes the model adaptive to self-side data. To conclude, FedSmart actually optimizes model of each client with valuable data from others.

Algorithm 1. FederatedSmart (FedSmart)

Input: θ_i^t: i-th client's model parameters at time step t;

$\quad\quad \Delta\theta_i^t$: i-th client's model updates at time step t

Output: θ_i^{t+1}: i-th client's model parameters at time step $t+1$

1: **for** $i = 1$ to n **do**
2:     aggregate updates for validation: $\theta_i^t = \theta_i^t + aggregate(\Delta\theta_1^t, \Delta\theta_2^t, ..., \Delta\theta_n^t)$
3:     compute model validation accuracy: $acc_i^t = evaluate(\theta_i^t)$
4: **end for**
5: **for** $i = 1$ to n **do**
6:     obtain performance-based weight: $w_i^t = weight(acc_1^t, acc_2^t, ..., acc_n^t)$
7:     calculate model parameter update: $\Delta\theta_i^t = update(acc_1^t, acc_2^t, ..., acc_n^t)$
8: **end for**
9: **for** $i = 1$ to n **do**
10:     output new model parameters: $\theta_i^{t+1} = \theta_i^t + \sum_{i=1}^n w_i^t \cdot \Delta\theta_i^t$
11: **end for**

---

4 Experiment

The experiment settings will be described step by step, including how to deal with the dataset and the experimental settings of FedSmart. Also, we will explain the impact of different parameters on the model performance and demonstrate the mechanism of using validation set.

4.1 Implementation Details

The data that concerned with the performance evaluation is the simulated datasets of MIMIC-III database [6,7], which contains the health information for critical care patients at a large tertiary care hospital in the U.S. The data cleansing process is following [5].

The experimental data structure is shown in Table 1.

4.2 Experiment Settings

To illustrate the limited performance of FL on non-IID data, the data are constructed as a collective form of six heterogeneous data sets. In detail, *Client1* and *Client4*, *Client2* and *Client5*, *Client3* and *Client6* in pairs share a similar data distribution respectively.

The validation set proportion α is set to 0.25 in default all through the experiment.

Table 1. Summary of experiment dataset

Feature	Representation	Count
$SUBJECTID^a$	IDs ranging from 2 to 99,999	21000 selected from 38962
$GENDER^b$	0: female 1: male	9900/12000
AGE^b	0: age less than or equal to 65 1: age greater than 65	9903/11997
$MORTALITY^c$	0: survive 1: death	10785/11115
$DRUGS^d$	0: not prescribed to patients 1: prescribed	8 dimensions

[a] $SUBJECTID$ is the primary key.
[b] $GENDER$ and AGE indicate basic information about the patients.
[c] $MORTALITY$ indicates survival status. The original distribution of $MORTAL-ITY$ is biased, it is three-times up-sampled.
[d] $DRUGS$ represents each patient's usage of the particular drugs during the first 48 hours in the ICU.

4.3 Results

The essence of centralized training is to aggregate the data of all parties together to improve the accuracy of the model by increasing the amount of data, so the results of centralized training are often higher than the results of each client training on their datasets alone. However, when the data are non-IID, centralized training will be hard to balance the results. The model tends to favor the groups with large samples or with simple distributions, so the established global model is undoubtedly unfair to other groups.

FedSmart v.s. Local Training. The model trained with `FedSmart` outperforms the local six ones (see Fig. 2), which is in the expectation that all FL participants will gain a better model within the information sharing framework than only using their own data. Because compared to the individual, working in a team, sharing the information of data, i.e. in the framework of FL, everyone tends to gain something as a contributor.

FedSmart v.s. FedAvg v.s. LoAdaBoost. To illustrate the effectiveness of `FedSmart`, we will do a comparison among `FedSmart`, `FedAvg` and `LoAdaBoost`. In `FedAvg`, the server only receives the model parameters and returns the updated model parameters, and there is no interactive updating mechanism in `FedAvg`. `LoAdaBoost` receives the loss and parameters of the model, and combines the information of the two to update the weight of the previous iteration [5]. FedSmart adopts different parameter combinations to update the model to make it approximate to the unbiased estimate of the complete gradient. The result is shown in Fig. 3.

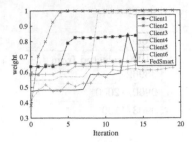

Fig. 2. FedSmart v.s. Local Training

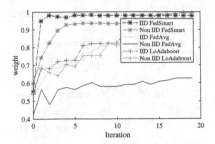

Fig. 3. FedSmart v.s. FedAvg v.s. LoAdaBoost

It can be seen that no matter what FL optimization algorithm, the performance on IID data always outperforms non-IID ones. One of the most important incentives of FL optimization algorithm is to decrease the influence of data distribution, i.e. the performance reduction on non-IID data. Also, FedSmart uses the accuracy of the validation set to measure the similarity of the distribution, establishes multiple models by adjusting the weights of different client models, and establishes multiple models on multiple clients only through the encrypted parameter exchange. The result shows that model performance is significantly better than FedAvg, and moderately better than LoAdaBoost.

FedSmart. FedSmart considers one party's distribution without repeatedly making compromises on multiple distributions. To further explain the working mechanism and performance of FedSmart, the process of the parameter joint weight changing during the training process is shown as in Fig. 4. The weight appears to change in pairs: *Client1* and *Client4*, *Client2* and *Client5*, *Client3* and *Client6*, which is in accordance with our experimental settings, indicating that FedSmart is figuring out good data.

We can observe that in the FL, there still exists the unbalanced performance improvement on some sides due to the difference in distributions. Because normally we only have one global model to be established, to reduce the global loss and improve the accuracy, there is inevitably a decrease in the performance improvement caused by the fact that one of the distributions is ignored to some extent. As long as there is only one global model, attend to one thing and lose sight of another must occur. Therefore, for the non-IID data, it is necessary to consider how to create multiple models suitable for different distributions, and then make FL more universal.

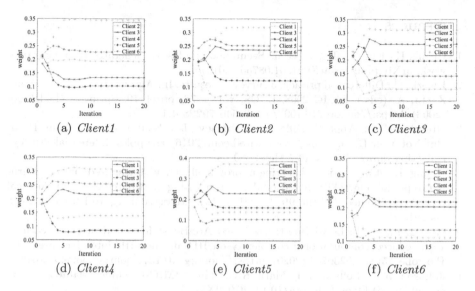

Fig. 4. The Process of Weight Allocation. The weight appears to change in pairs: *Client1* and *Client4*, *Client2* and *Client5*, *Client3* and *Client6*.

5   Conclusion

Federated Learning is raising attention in both academics and industry, as it is a way to solve the isolated island problem and a solution to privacy-preserving. We propose a performance-based parameter return method `FedSmart`. It is different from the general idea that FL shares one global model. Instead, `FedSmart` establishes multiple models by treating each client as a server to make its own model perform the best. We use the simulated MIMIC-III data and separate it into six non-IID data-sets to do the FL. The experimental result shows that `FedSmart` can have better performance than `FedAvg` and even centralized training method. `FedSmart` can be extended to the industries' data training scenarios.

In the continuation of our study, to compensate for this shortcoming and minimize the leakage of privacy caused by model delivery, `FedSmart` can use the drop-out-like mechanism to make it difficult for training participants to obtain effective information from the changes of the model. Also, we will improve and explore the `FedSmart` algorithm to make it to be generally stable and adaptable for both IID and Non-IID datasets, to tackle the root of problems for FL frameworks.

Acknowledgements. This paper is supported by National Key Research and Development Program of China under grant No.2018YFB1003500, No.2018YFB0204400 and No.2017YFB1401202.

References

1. Cheng, K., Fan, T., Jin, Y., et al.: Secureboost: a lossless federated learning framework. arXiv preprint arXiv:1901.08755 (2019)
2. Dwork, C.: Differential privacy: a survey of results. In: Agrawal, M., Du, D., Duan, Z., Li, A. (eds.) TAMC 2008. LNCS, vol. 4978, pp. 1–19. Springer, Heidelberg (2008). https://doi.org/10.1007/978-3-540-79228-4_1
3. Greenberg, A.: Apple'S 'Differential Privacy' Is About Collecting Your Data-But Not Your Data. https://www.wired.com/2016/06/apples-differential-privacy-collecting-data/. Accessed 22 May 2020
4. Huang, L., et al.: Patient clustering improves efficiency of federated machine learning to predict mortality and hospital stay time using distributed electronic medical records. J. Biomed. Inform. **99**, 103291 (2019). https://doi.org/10.1016/j.jbi.2019.103291
5. Huang, L., et al.: LoAdaBoost: loss-based AdaBoost federated machine learning with reduced computational complexity on IID and non-IID intensive care data. Plos one **15**(4), e0230706 (2020). https://doi.org/10.1371/journal.pone.0230706
6. Johnson, A.E., Pollard, T.J., Mark, R.G.: The MIMIC-III clinical database. PhysioNet (2016) https://doi.org/10.13026/C2XW26
7. Johnson, A.E., et al.: MIMIC-III, a freely accessible critical care database. Sci. Data. **3**, 1–9 (2016). https://doi.org/10.1038/sdata.2016.35
8. Karimireddy, S.P., et al.: SCAFFLOD: stochastic controlled averaging for on-device federated learning. arXiv preprint arXiv:1910.06378 (2019)
9. Li, X., et al.: On the convergence of fedavg on non-iid data. In: 2020 International Conference on Learning Representations (ICLR) (2020)
10. McMahan, B., et al.: Federated learning of deep networks using model averaging. arXiv preprint arXiv:1602.05629 (2017)
11. McMahan, B., et al.: Communication-efficient learning of deep networks from decentralized data. In: Proceedings of the 20th International Conference on Artificial Intelligence and Statistics, in PMLR. **54**, 1273–1282 (2017)
12. Sahu, A.K., et al.: Federated optimization for heterogeneous networks. arXiv preprint arXiv:1812.06127 **1**(2), p. 3 (2018)
13. Vepakomma, P., et al.: Split learning for health: distributed deep learning without sharing raw patient data. arXiv preprint arXiv:1812.00564 (2018)
14. Wang, H., et al.: Federated learning with matched averaging. In: 2020 International Conference on Learning Representations (ICLR) (2020)
15. Yang, Q., et al.: Federated machine learning: concept and applications. ACM Trans. Intell. Syst. Technol. (TIST) **10**(2), 1–19 (2019)
16. Zhao, Y., et al.: Federated learning with non-iid data. arXiv preprint arXiv:1806.00582 (2018)

Discriminative Multi-label Model Reuse for Multi-label Learning

Yi Zhang, Zhecheng Zhang, Yinlong Zhu, Lei Zhang, and Chongjun Wang$^{(\boxtimes)}$

National Key Laboratory for Novel Software Technology at Nanjing University,
Department of Computer Science and Technology,Nanjing University,
Nanjing, China
{njuzhangy,zzc,zhuyinlong}@smail.nju.edu.cn,
{zhangl,chjwang}@nju.edu.cn

Abstract. Traditional Chinese Medicine (TCM) with diagnosis scales is a holistic way for diagnosing Parkinson's Disease, where symptoms can be represented as multiple labels. To solve this problem, multi-label learning provides a framework for handling such task and has exhibited excellent performance. Besides, it is a challenging issue of how to effectively utilize label correlations in multi-label learning. In this paper, we propose a novel algorithm named Discriminative Multi-label Model Reuse (DMLMR) for multi-label learning, which exploits label correlations with model reuse, instance distribution adaptation and label distribution adaptation. Experiments on real-world dataset of Parkinson's disease demonstrate the superiority of DMLMR for diagnosing PD. To prove the effectiveness of the proposed DMLMR, extensive experiments on four benchmark multi-label datasets show that DMLMR significantly outperforms other state-of-the-art multi-label learning algorithms.

Keywords: Parkinson's disease · Multi-label learning · Label correlations · Model reuse · Distribution adaptation

1 Introduction

Tradition Chinese Medicine (TCM) is a new way for PD [13]. For one thing, *TCM scales* includes tongue phase as well as four traditional methods of diagnosis: observation, listening, interrogation and pulse-taking. For another, *syndrome types* of PD in TCM can be divided into following 5 categories: (1) stirring wind due to phlegma-heat, (2) stirring wind due to blood heat, (3) deficiency of both qi and blood, (4) insufficiency of the liver and kidney, (5) deficiency of both yin and yang. Moreover, each TCM syndrome type can be subdivided into primary and secondary *syndrome types*.

TCM scholars are supposed to collect disease information of patients, and categorize a patient into one or more *syndrome types* based on TCM theory and rich experience. This diagnostic process requires doctors equipped with extensive experience of *Syndrome Differentiation* at the time of treatment. Due to

© Springer Nature Switzerland AG 2020
X. Wang et al. (Eds.): APWeb-WAIM 2020, LNCS 12317, pp. 725–739, 2020.
https://doi.org/10.1007/978-3-030-60259-8_53

the essential characteristic of TCM, *TCM scales* appear to be overwhelmingly dependent on personal experience of doctors. The problems of diagnosing PD in TCM lie in two aspects: specialists of PD are in short supply and diagnostic levels of doctors are inconsistent. Consequently, the diagnosis of PD might be subjective, which violates the original intention of effectiveness. Therefore, it is desired to design a semi-automatic mechanism for diagnosing PD in TCM.

In this paper, we formalize the problem of diagnosing Parkinson's disease in TCM into a multi-label learning problem, where we treat *TCM scales* as features and treat *syndrome types* as multiple labels. In multi-label learning [21], each instance can be represented by multiple labels simultaneously. For example, an image may be annotated with both sea and beach. The task of multi-label learning is to learn a classification model which can predict all the relevant labels for unseen instances. Nowadays, multi-label learning has been applied to various application scenarios, such as text classification [9], image annotation [11], video annotation [14], social networks [17], music emotion categorization [18]. In addition, the exploration of label correlations has been accepted as a key component of effective multi-label learning approaches [6, 23].

The main contributions of this paper include:

- Real-world Parkinson's disease diagnosis in Traditional Chines Medicine is investigated and assessed.
- We formalize the problem of diagnosing PD in TCM as a multi-label learning problem, by treating *TCM scales* as features while treating *syndrome types* as multiple labels. Meanwhile, we apply multi-label classification technology to diagnose PD in TCM.
- We propose a novel Discriminative Multi-label Model Reuse (DMLMR) algorithm to deal with multi-label learning problem, which perform excellently in handling diagnosis of Parkinson's disease in TCM. Extensive experiments on four benchmark multi-label datasets show that DMLMR algorithm significantly outperforms the state-of-the-art multi-label learning algorithms.

The remainder of the paper is organized as follows. Section 2 briefly reviews some related work of multi-label learning. Section 3 presents formulation of the problem and our proposed DMLMR algorithm. Section 4 reports the experimental results, followed by the conclusion in Sect. 5.

2   Related Work

Generally, multi-label learning algorithms can be categorized into following three strategies based on the order of label correlations considered by the system.

First-order strategy copes with multi-label learning problem in a label-by-label manner. Binary Relevance (BR) [1] takes each label independently and decomposes it into multiple binary classification tasks. However, BR neglects the relationship among labels.

Second-order strategy introduces pairwise relations among multiple labels, such as the ranking between the relevant and irrelevant labels [5]. Calibrated

Label Ranking (CLR) [4] firstly transforms the multi-label learning problem into label ranking problem by introducing the pairwise comparison. Recently, LLSF [7] performs joint label-specific feature selection and take the label correlation matrix as prior knowledge.

High-order strategy builds more complex relations among labels for multi-label learning. Classifier Chain (CC) [15] transforms the multi-label classification problem into a chain of binary classification problems, where the quality is dependent on the label order in the chain. Ensemble Classifier Chains (ECC) [16] constructs multiple CCs by using different random label orders. Multi-modal Classifier Chains (MCC) [22] release the reliance of label order by combining predicted labels as a new modality. Multi-label k-nearest neighbour (MLkNN) [20] builds a Bayesian model by using the k-nearest neighbour method to obtain the prior and likelihood. In addition, there are also some high-order approaches that exploit label correlations on the hypothesis space. For example, a boosting approach Multi-label Hypothesis Reuse (MLHR) [8] is proposed to exploit label correlations with a hypothesis reuse mechanism. Latent Semantic Aware Multi-view Multi-label Learning (LSA-MML) [19] implicitly encodes the label correlations by the common representation based on the uncovering latent semantic bases and the relations among them. Considering the potential association between paired labels, Dual-Set Multi-Label Learning (DSML) [10] exploits pairwise inter-set label relationships for assisting multi-label learning. Most of the existing approaches take label correlations as prior knowledge, which may not correctly characterize the real relationships among labels. And then, Collaboration based Multi-Label Learning (CAMEL) [3] is proposed to learn the label correlations via sparse reconstruction in the label space.

3 Methodology

This section mainly gives the detail description of Discriminative Multi-label Model Reuse (DMLMR) algorithm after a preliminary notation explanation.

3.1 Preliminaries and Problem Formulation

Before describing the problem formulation, we begin with some notations and preliminaries.

Let $\mathcal{X} = \mathbb{R}^d$ denote the d dimensional feature space, and $\mathcal{Y} = \{-1, 1\}^L$ denote the label space with L labels.

Given the training dataset $\mathcal{D} = \{(\boldsymbol{x}_i, \boldsymbol{y}_i)\}_{i=1}^N$ with N instances, the task of multi-label learning is to learn a mapping function $\boldsymbol{H} : \mathcal{X} \rightarrow \mathcal{Y}$, which maps from feature space to label space. The i-th instance $(\boldsymbol{x}_i, \boldsymbol{y}_i)$ contains a feature vector $\boldsymbol{x}_i = [x_1, x_2, \ldots, x_d] \in \mathcal{X}$ and a label vector $\boldsymbol{y}_i = [y^1, y^2, \cdots, y^L] \in \mathcal{Y}$, where $y^k = 1$ indicating $\boldsymbol{x}_i$ is associated with the k-th label, $y^k = -1$ otherwise. $\mathcal{T} = \{(\boldsymbol{x}_i, \boldsymbol{y}_i)\}_{i=1}^M$ denotes testing dataset. In addition, $\boldsymbol{H}(\cdot) = [H^1(\cdot), H^2(\cdot), \ldots, H^L(\cdot)]$ can be used to predict labels for unseen instances in $\mathcal{T}$, where $H^k(\cdot)$ denotes the classifier of the k-th label.

For simplicity, we denote $\boldsymbol{X} = [\boldsymbol{x}_1, \boldsymbol{x}_2, \cdots, \boldsymbol{x}_N]^T \in \mathbb{R}^{N \times d}$ as the instance matrix, and $\boldsymbol{Y} = [\boldsymbol{y}_1, \boldsymbol{y}_2, \cdots, \boldsymbol{y}_N]^T \in \mathbb{R}^{N \times L}$ as the label matrix. The original training dataset can be alternatively represented by $\mathcal{D} = \{(\boldsymbol{X}, \boldsymbol{Y})\}$.

With analysis in Sect. 1, the problem of diagnosing Parkinson's disease can be modeled as multi-label learning problem.

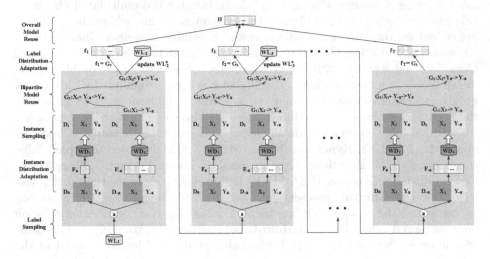

Fig. 1. The overall flowchart of DMLMR algorithm. Cylinder shadowed with orange denotes label distribution, while cylinder shadowed with blue denotes instance distribution.

3.2   Discriminative Multi-label Model Reuse

In this subsection, we introduce Discriminative Multi-label Model Reuse (DMLMR) algorithm in detail. The pseudo code of DMLMR is presented in Algorithm 1.

At first, we train on the original dataset $\mathcal{D}$ with a base multi-label algorithm (here we adopt CC algorithm) and get $\boldsymbol{F}(\cdot) = [F^1(\cdot), \cdots, F^k(\cdot), \cdots, F^L(\cdot)]$, where $F^k(\cdot)$ represents the original classifier for the k-th label. $\boldsymbol{\tau} = [\tau_1, \cdots, \tau_T]$ denotes chain of selected labels, where T denotes number of boosting round. DMLMR maintains one label distribution $\boldsymbol{WL}_t = [WL_t^1, \cdots, WL_t^k, \cdots, WL_t^L]$, where WL_t^k is the weight of the k-th label at t-th boosting round. Initially, $\boldsymbol{\tau} = \emptyset$ and $WL_1^k = \frac{1}{L}$, which means $\boldsymbol{WL}_1 = [\frac{1}{L}, \cdots, \frac{1}{L}]$.

Figure 1 illustrates an overview of our proposed DMLMR algorithm. At t-th boosting round, there are following 5 steps.

Label Sampling. We sample one label a according to the label distribution $\boldsymbol{WL}_t$, where $a \in \{1, 2, \cdots, L\}$. And then we update $\boldsymbol{\tau}$ by concatenating $\boldsymbol{\tau}$ and a, i.e., $\boldsymbol{\tau} = [\boldsymbol{\tau}, a]$.

Instance Distribution Adaptation. After getting one sampled label a, we transform the original dataset $\mathcal{D}$ into two dataset $\mathcal{D}_a = \{(\boldsymbol{X}, \boldsymbol{Y}_a)\}$ and $\boldsymbol{D}_{-a} = \{(\boldsymbol{X}, \boldsymbol{Y}_{-a})\}$.

Algorithm 1. The DMLMR algorithm

Input:

    $\mathcal{D} = \{(\boldsymbol{X}, \boldsymbol{Y})\}$: original training dataset

    λ_{intra}: intra-set reweight parameter

    λ_{inter}: inter-set reweight parameter

    T: number of boosting round

Output:

    $\boldsymbol{H}(\cdot)$: classifiers of all labels

    Initialize: $\boldsymbol{\tau} = \emptyset$, $\boldsymbol{WL}_1 = [\frac{1}{L}, \cdots, \frac{1}{L}]$

    Train on $\mathcal{D}$

    for $t = 1 : T$ **do**

        Sample one label a according to $\boldsymbol{WL}_t$

        Update $\boldsymbol{\tau} = [\boldsymbol{\tau}, a]$

        Compute $\boldsymbol{WD}_1$ and $\boldsymbol{WD}_2$ with Eq. 1

        Sample $\mathcal{D}_1$ from $\mathcal{D}$ according to $\boldsymbol{WD}_1$

        Sample $\mathcal{D}_2$ from $\mathcal{D}$ according to $\boldsymbol{WD}_2$

        Train $\boldsymbol{G}_1$, $\boldsymbol{G}_2$ and $\boldsymbol{G}_3$ with bipartite model reuse

        $\boldsymbol{f}_t(\cdot) = \boldsymbol{G}_3(\cdot)$

        Update $\boldsymbol{WL}_{t+1}$ with Eq. 6

    end for

    for $k = 1 : L$ **do**

        Compute $H^k(\cdot)$ with Eq. 7

    end for

    return $\boldsymbol{H}(\cdot)$

Here $\boldsymbol{Y}_a$ and $\boldsymbol{Y}_{-a}$ are label vectors associated with instance matrix $\boldsymbol{X}$, which is shown in Fig. 2. More specifically, $\boldsymbol{Y}_a \in \mathbb{R}^N$ denotes the a-th column vector of the matrix $\boldsymbol{Y}$ (versus $\boldsymbol{y}_i \in \mathbb{R}^L$ for the i-th row vector of $\boldsymbol{Y}$), and $\boldsymbol{Y}_{-a} = [\boldsymbol{Y}_1, \cdots, \boldsymbol{Y}_{a-1}, \boldsymbol{Y}_{a+1}, \cdots, \boldsymbol{Y}_L] \in \mathbb{R}^{N \times (L-1)}$ represents the matrix that excludes the a-th column vector of the matrix $\boldsymbol{Y}$.

And then we get $\boldsymbol{F}_a(\cdot)$ and $\boldsymbol{F}_{-a}(\cdot)$, where $\boldsymbol{F}_a(\cdot) = F^a(\cdot)$ denotes the original classifier of $\mathcal{Y}_a$ and $\boldsymbol{F}_{-a} = [F^1(\cdot), \cdots, F^{a-1}(\cdot), F^{a+1}(\cdot), \cdots, F^L(\cdot)]$ denotes the original classifiers of $\mathcal{Y}_{-a}$, where $\mathcal{Y}_a = \{-1, 1\}$ denotes label space of the a-th label and $\mathcal{Y}_{-a} = \{-1, 1\}^{L-1}$ denotes label space of all the labels exclude the a-th label.

In order to exploit label correlations, we maintain two instance distributions $\boldsymbol{WD}_1$ and $\boldsymbol{WD}_2$ adapted by Eq. 1, where WD_1^i and WD_2^i are the weight for the i-th instance with respect to $\mathcal{Y}_a$ and $\mathcal{Y}_{-a}$, respectively.

$$
\begin{aligned}
WD_1^i &= \frac{1}{N} \cdot \lambda_{intra}^{\mathbb{I}(F_a(\boldsymbol{x}_i) \neq y_{i,a})} \cdot \lambda_{inter}^{\mathbb{I}(F_{-a}(\boldsymbol{x}_i) \neq y_{i,-a})} \\
WD_2^i &= \frac{1}{N} \cdot \lambda_{intra}^{\mathbb{I}(F_{-a}(\boldsymbol{x}_i) \neq y_{i,-a})} \cdot \lambda_{inter}^{\mathbb{I}(F_a(\boldsymbol{x}_i) \neq y_{i,a})}
\end{aligned}
\tag{1}
$$

where $\mathbb{I}(\cdot)$ denotes the indicator function which outputs 1 if $\cdot$ is true, 0 otherwise. Additionally, $\boldsymbol{y}_{i,a}$ denotes ground truth of a-th label associated with $\boldsymbol{x}_i$ and $\boldsymbol{y}_{i,-a}$ denotes ground truth of all the labels excludes a-th label associated with

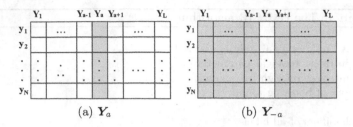

Fig. 2. Illustration of label vector $\boldsymbol{Y}_a$ and $\boldsymbol{Y}_{-a}$ in $\boldsymbol{Y}$. In the left part, matrix shadowed with orange represents $\boldsymbol{Y}_a$. In the right part, matrix shadowed with orange represents $\boldsymbol{Y}_{-a}$.

$\boldsymbol{x}_i$. λ_{intra} is the intra-set reweight parameter and λ_{inter} is the inter-set reweight parameter. Take WD_1^i as an example, item $\lambda_{intra}^{\mathbb{I}(F_a(\boldsymbol{x}_i)\neq \boldsymbol{y}_{i,a})}$ considers the mistake made by label in $\mathcal{Y}_a$, i.e, a model that has made mistake will be emphasized by assigning a higher weight. Item $\lambda_{inter}^{\mathbb{I}(F_{-a}(\boldsymbol{x}_i)\neq \boldsymbol{y}_{i,-a})}$ considers inter-set relationship between $\mathcal{Y}_a$ and $\mathcal{Y}_{-a}$, i.e., the weight of an instance on $\mathcal{Y}_a$ will be increased when misclassified on $\mathcal{Y}_{-a}$. Meaning of items in WD_2^i is similar to that in WD_1^i.

At the end of the training process, we normalize $\boldsymbol{WD}_1$ and $\boldsymbol{WD}_2$ to form a valid distribution.

Instance Sampling. We decompose the original problem into two dependent sub-problems.

And then we sample two datasets $\mathcal{D}_1 = \{(\boldsymbol{X}_1, \boldsymbol{Y}_a)\}$ and $\mathcal{D}_2 = \{(\boldsymbol{X}_2, \boldsymbol{Y}_{-a})\}$ i.i.d. according to instance distributions $\boldsymbol{WD}_1$ and $\boldsymbol{WD}_2$ respectively, where $\boldsymbol{X}_1 \in \mathbb{R}^{N\times d}$, $\boldsymbol{Y}_a \in \mathbb{R}^{N\times 1}$, $\boldsymbol{X}_2 \in \mathbb{R}^{N\times d}$, $\boldsymbol{Y}_{-a} \in \mathbb{R}^{N\times(L-1)}$.

Bipartite Model Reuse We train on two datasets $\mathcal{D}_1$ and $\mathcal{D}_2$ with model reuse and get 3 models $\boldsymbol{G}_1$, $\boldsymbol{G}_2$ and $\boldsymbol{G}_3$.

- Firstly, we train on the dataset $\mathcal{D}_2$ with basic multi-label learning algorithm (here we adopt CC algorithm), and then we get model $\boldsymbol{G}_1 : \mathcal{X} \to \mathcal{Y}_{-a}$.
- Secondly, we reuse model $\boldsymbol{G}_1$ on $\mathcal{D}_1$ and get predicted label vector $\boldsymbol{G}_1(\boldsymbol{x}_i)$. And then, we concatenate feature vector with predicted label vector, i.e, $[\boldsymbol{x}_i, \boldsymbol{G}_1(\boldsymbol{x}_i)]$. Training on dataset $\mathcal{D}_1$, we get model $\boldsymbol{G}_2 : \mathcal{X} + \mathcal{Y}_{-a} \to \mathcal{Y}_a$.
- Thirdly, we reuse model $\boldsymbol{G}_2$ on $\mathcal{D}_2$ and get predicted label vector $\boldsymbol{G}_2(\boldsymbol{x}_i)$. And then, we concatenate $\boldsymbol{x}_i$ with predicted label vector, i.e $[\boldsymbol{x}_i, \boldsymbol{G}_2([\boldsymbol{x}_i, \boldsymbol{G}_1(\boldsymbol{x}_i)])]$. Training on dataset $\mathcal{D}_2$, we get model $\boldsymbol{G}_3 : \mathcal{X} + \mathcal{Y}_a \to \mathcal{Y}_{-a}$.

It is notable that $\boldsymbol{G}_2$ reuses model $\boldsymbol{G}_1$, so $\boldsymbol{G}_3$ reuses two models $\boldsymbol{G}_1$ and $\boldsymbol{G}_2$. Model trained on one dataset is reused on the other dataset, which provides additional help for the final classification. Furthermore, we provide theoretical analysis for bipartite model reuse. $\boldsymbol{h}_a(\cdot) = \boldsymbol{G}_2(\cdot)$ and $\boldsymbol{h}_{-a}(\cdot) = \boldsymbol{G}_3(\cdot)$ in the following analysis.

Definition 1. *Generalization error of hypothesis $h(\cdot)$ mapping from $\mathcal{X}$ to $\mathcal{Y}$ based on HammingLoss:*

$$R(h) = \mathop{\mathbb{E}}_{(x,y)\sim\mathcal{D}} \left[\frac{1}{L} \sum_{k=1}^{L} \mathbb{I}(h(x) \neq y^k) \right] \tag{2}$$

where y^k is the ground-truth of the k-th label.

Definition 2. *Empirical error of hypothesis $h(\cdot)$:*

$$\hat{R}(h) = \frac{1}{m} \sum_{i=1}^{m} \left(\frac{1}{L} \sum_{k=1}^{L} \mathbb{I}(h(x) \neq y^k) \right) \tag{3}$$

Lemma 1. $R(h) \leq max\{R(h_a), R(h_{-a})\}$, *where $h(\cdot)$ is composed of $h_a(\cdot)$ and $h_{-a}(\cdot)$.*

Proof.

$$R(h) = \mathop{\mathbb{E}}_{(x,y)\sim\mathcal{D}} \left[\frac{1}{L} \sum_{k=1}^{L} \mathbb{I}(h(x) \neq y^k) \right]$$

$$= \frac{1}{L} \mathop{\mathbb{E}}_{(x,y)\sim\mathcal{D}} \left[\mathbb{I}(h_a(x) \neq y^a) \right]$$

$$+ \frac{1}{L} \mathop{\mathbb{E}}_{(x,y)\sim\mathcal{D}} \left[\sum_{k=1,k\neq a}^{L} \mathbb{I}(h_{-a}(x) \neq y^k) \right]$$

$$= \frac{1}{L} \left(R(h_a) + (L-1)R(h_{-a}) \right)$$

$$\leq \frac{1}{L} L max\{R(h_a), R(h_{-a})\}(1 + L - 1)\}$$

$$= max\{R(h_a), R(h_{-a})\}$$

$\square$

Lemma 2. $R(h_{-a}) \leq max\{R(h^k)\}_{k=1,k\neq a}^{L}$

Proof.

$$R(h_{-a}) = \mathop{\mathbb{E}}_{(x,y)\sim\mathcal{D}} \left[\frac{1}{L-1} \sum_{k=1,k\neq a}^{L} \mathbb{I}(h^k(x) \neq y^k) \right]$$

$$= \frac{1}{L-1} \mathop{\mathbb{E}}_{(x,y)\sim\mathcal{D}} \left[\sum_{k=1,k\neq a}^{L} \mathbb{I}(h^k(x) \neq y^k) \right]$$

$$= \frac{1}{L-1} \mathop{\mathbb{E}}_{(x,y)\sim\mathcal{D}} \left[\sum_{k=1,k\neq a}^{L} R(h^k) \right]$$

$$\leq \frac{1}{L-1} (L-1) max\{R(h^k)\}_{k=1,k\neq a}^{L} = R(h_m)$$

$\square$

where $\boldsymbol{h}_{-a}(\cdot) = [h^1(\cdot), \cdots, h^{a-1}(\cdot), h^{a+1}(\cdot), \cdots, h^L(\cdot)]$, and for simplicity, we denote $max\{R(h^k)\}_{k=1,k\neq a}^L$ as $R(\boldsymbol{h}_m)$.

Theorem 31. *In mono-label case, let $H \subset \mathbb{R}^{\mathcal{X} \times \mathcal{Y}}$ be a hypothesis set. Fix $\rho > 0$. Assume there exists $r > 0$ such that $k(\boldsymbol{x}, \boldsymbol{x}) \leq r^2$ for all $\boldsymbol{x} \in \mathcal{X}$. For any $\delta > 0$, with probability at least $1 - \delta$, the following holds for all $h \in H$. [12]*

$$R(h) \leq \hat{R}_\rho(h) + 2\sqrt{\frac{r^2 \wedge^2 / \rho^2}{m}} + 3\sqrt{\frac{log(2/\delta)}{m}} \tag{4}$$

Combine Lemma 1, Lemma 2 and Theorem 31, we have:

Proof.

$$R(\boldsymbol{h}) \leq max\{R(\boldsymbol{h}_a), R(\boldsymbol{h}_{-a})$$
$$\leq max\Big\{\hat{R}_\rho(\boldsymbol{h}_a) + 2\sqrt{\frac{r^2 \wedge^2 / \rho^2}{m}} + 3\sqrt{\frac{log(2/\delta)}{m}},$$
$$\hat{R}_\rho(\boldsymbol{h}_m) + 2\sqrt{\frac{r^2 \wedge^2 / \rho^2}{m}} + 3\sqrt{\frac{log(2/\delta)}{m}}\Big\}$$
$$\leq max\{\hat{R}_\rho(\boldsymbol{h}_a), \hat{R}_\rho(\boldsymbol{h}_m)\} + 2\sqrt{\frac{r^2 \wedge^2 / \rho^2}{m}} + 3\sqrt{\frac{log(2/\delta)}{m}}$$

□

The convergence rate of generalization error is standard as $O(\frac{1}{\sqrt{m}})$, which validates the effect of bipartite model reuse.

Label Distribution Adaptation. In order to select most discriminative label for bipartite model reuse, we are supposed to adapt label distribution according to the models trained by bipartite model reuse. We get prediction $\boldsymbol{f}_t(\cdot) = \boldsymbol{G}_3(\cdot)$, and $\boldsymbol{f}_t(\cdot) = [f_t^1(\cdot), \cdots, f_t^{a-1}(\cdot), f_t^{a+1}(\cdot), \cdots, f_t^L(\cdot)]$ where $f_t^k(\cdot)$ denotes the classifier of the k-th label. And then we test on dataset $\mathcal{T}$ with $\boldsymbol{f}_t(\cdot)$ and $\boldsymbol{F}_{-a}(\cdot)$ respectively. We get importance rate of the a-th label for other labels as follows:

$$\alpha_t = \frac{SubAcc(\boldsymbol{f}_t)}{SubAcc(\boldsymbol{F}_{-a})} \tag{5}$$

where $SubsetAcc_t(\boldsymbol{f}_t) = \frac{1}{M}\sum_{i=1}^M \mathbb{I}(\boldsymbol{f}_t(\boldsymbol{x}_i) = \boldsymbol{y}_{i,-a})$ and $SubsetAcc_t(\boldsymbol{F}_{-a}) = \frac{1}{M}\sum_{i=1}^M \mathbb{I}(\boldsymbol{F}_{-a}(\boldsymbol{x}_i) = \boldsymbol{y}_{i,-a})$.

On the other hand, we will increase the weight of the a-th label if $\alpha_t > 1$, i.e, the a-th label has a positive effect to other labels with bipartite model reuse. The weight of other labels exclude the a-th label remain unchanged. And then we adapt label distribution $\boldsymbol{WL}_{t+1} = [WL_{t+1}^1, \cdots, WL_{t+1}^k, \cdots, WL_{t+1}^L]$ for next boosting round.

$$WL_{t+1}^k = WL_t^k \cdot \alpha_t^{\mathbb{I}(k=a)} \tag{6}$$

where $\mathbb{I}(\cdot)$ is an indicator function and $k = \{1, \cdots, L\}$. Similar to $\boldsymbol{WD}_1$ and $\boldsymbol{WD}_2$, we then normalize $\boldsymbol{WL}_{t+1}$.

Above all, **Overall Model Reuse** is adopted. As is shown in Fig. 1, we get $f_1(\cdot), f_2(\cdot), \cdots, f_T(\cdot)$ after T number of boosting round. Finally we integrate all models together and get $\boldsymbol{H}(\cdot) = [H^1(\cdot), \cdots, H^k(\cdot), \cdots, H^L(\cdot)]$, where $H^k(\cdot)$ denotes final classifier of the k-th label. In the testing phase, labels are predicted for instance $\boldsymbol{x}$ according to:

$$H^k(\boldsymbol{x}) = \underset{l}{argmax} \sum_{t=1, k \neq \tau_t}^{T} \alpha_t \cdot \mathbb{I}(f_t^k(\boldsymbol{x}) = l) \tag{7}$$

where $l \in \{-1, 1\}$, $k = \{1, \cdots, L\}$.

4 Experiments

In this section, we validate the effectiveness of our proposed DMLMR algorithm on real-world dataset of Parkinson's disease and various benchmark multi-label datasets.

4.1 Dataset Description

Firstly, we manually collect real-world dataset of Parkinson's disease in Traditional Chinese Medicine (TCM). Furthermore, we will briefly present the feature and label generation procedure for Parkinson's disease diagnosis.

Both *Parkinson-P* and *Parkinson* have 91 *TCM scales* as features. However, *Parkinson-P* has 5 primary symptoms. *Parkinson* has 10 *syndrome types*: 5 primary *syndrome types* and 5 secondary *syndrome types*. More details with regard to *syndrome types* can be found in Sect. 1.

It is notable that DMLMR is designed for diagnosing Parkinson's disease, it is also a general multi-label learning algorithm. For comprehensive performance evaluation, we collect 4 benchmark multi-label datasets.

- *ML2000*: is an image dataset from [20], including 2000 images from 5 categories.
- *Scene*: has 2407 images and 6 possible labels [1].
- *Emotions*: is a set of 593 songs with 6 clusters of music emotions [16].
- *Genbase*: consists of 662 proteins with known structure families that belong in 27 labels [2].

Table 1 summarizes the detailed characteristics of all datasets, Given a multi-label dataset $\mathcal{D} = \{(\boldsymbol{X}, \boldsymbol{Y})\}$, we use $|\mathcal{D}|$, $dim(\mathcal{D})$, $L(\mathcal{D})$, $LCard(\mathcal{D})$, $LDen(\mathcal{D})$ and $F(\mathcal{D})$ to represent number of instances, feature dimension, number of possible labels, label cardinality, label density and feature type, respectively.

- $LCard(\mathcal{D}) = \frac{1}{N} \sum_{i=1}^{N} |\boldsymbol{y}_i|$ measures the average number of labels per instance.
- $LDen(\mathcal{D}) = \frac{LCard(\mathcal{D})}{L(\mathcal{D})}$ normalizes $LCard(\mathcal{D})$ by the number of possible labels.

Table 1. Characteristics of datasets.

Dataset	$|D|$	$dim(D)$	$L(D)$	$LCard(D)$	$LDen(D)$	$F(D)$
Parkinson-P	401	91	5	1.262	0.126	Nominal
Parkinson	401	91	10	0.798	0.160	Nominal
ML2000	2000	2000	5	1.236	0.247	Numeric
Scene	2407	294	6	1.074	0.179	Numeric
Emotions	593	72	6	1.869	0.311	Numeric
Genbase	662	1185	27	1.252	0.046	Nominal

4.2 Evaluation Metrics

To have a fair comparison, we employ five widely-used evaluation metrics, including: $HammingLoss$, $SubsetAcc$, $MacroF_1$, $MicroF_1$, $ExampleF_1$ [21].

4.3 Comparing Algorithms

We compare our proposed DMLMR algorithm with six state-of-the-art multi-label algorithms, listed as follows:

- BR [1]: first-order algorithm which transforms the multi-label learning task into multiple binary classification tasks
- CC [15]: a novel chaining method that considers the relativity between labels
- ECC [15]: state-of-the-art supervised ensemble multi-label learning method
- MLKNN [20]: is a kNN style multi-label classification algorithm, and outperforms some existing algorithms
- LLSF [7]: second-order algorithm which exploits different feature sets for the discrimination of different labels
- CAMEL [3]: a novel method to learn the label correlations via sparse reconstruction in the label space.

4.4 Experimental Results

For all these algorithms, we report the best results of the optimal parameters in terms of classification performance. 10-fold cross validation (CV) is performed on each dataset. To better characterize the comparison, we take the mean metric value as well as the standard deviation of each algorithm. Note that for all the employed multi-label evaluation metrics, their values vary within the interval [0,1]. The larger the value of them, the better the performance of the classifier for all of these evaluation metrics except $HammingLoss$.

Experimental results of our proposed DMLMR and other comparing algorithms on real-world dataset of Parkinson's disease and four benchmark multi-label datasets are listed in Table 2 and Table 3 respectively. From the results, it is obvious that DMLMR algorithm can achieve best or at least comparable performance on all datasets with different evaluation metrics, which reveals that DMLMR algorithm is a high-competitive multi-label learning algorithm.

Table 2. Performance comparison on *Parkinson-P* and *Parkinson* dataset. ↑ / ↓ indicates that the larger/smaller the better of a criterion. The best results are in bold.

Evaluation Metrics	Parkinson-P						
	BR	CC	ECC	MLKNN	LLSF	CAMEL	DMLMR
HammingLoss ↓	0.180±0.040	0.195±0.031	0.165±0.022	0.200±0.020	0.162±0.031	0.169±0.035	**0.161±0.027**
SubsetAcc ↑	0.404±0.121	0.506±0.081	0.491±0.069	0.351±0.070	0.442±0.075	0.486±0.093	**0.559±0.067**
MacroF₁ ↑	0.407±0.088	0.393±0.075	0.402±0.077	0.244±0.038	0.397±0.077	0.378±0.050	**0.410±0.050**
MicroF₁ ↑	0.541±0.104	0.512±0.082	0.549±0.061	0.411±0.068	0.553±0.093	0.565±0.088	**0.592±0.066**
ExampleF₁ ↑	0.490±0.113	0.509±0.083	0.498±0.065	0.351±0.070	0.483±0.089	0.528±0.091	**0.575±0.064**

Evaluation Metrics	Parkinson						
	BR	CC	ECC	MLKNN	LLSF	CAMEL	DMLMR
HammingLoss ↓	0.137±0.019	0.133±0.029	0.110±0.013	0.158±0.022	0.111±0.012	0.110±0.017	**0.104±0.018**
SubsetAcc ↑	0.317±0.081	0.426±0.084	0.426±0.046	0.302±0.070	0.356±0.066	0.364±0.083	**0.489±0.096**
MacroF₁ ↑	0.254±0.059	0.270±0.086	0.235±0.050	0.207±0.053	0.185±0.033	0.188±0.030	**0.273±0.012**
MicroF₁ ↑	0.443±0.064	0.475±0.098	0.479±0.052	0.363±0.077	0.462±0.059	0.454±0.063	**0.532±0.069**
ExampleF₁ ↑	0.443±0.073	0.519±0.089	0.480±0.049	0.377±0.068	0.434±0.064	0.423±0.078	**0.550±0.075**

4.5   Influence of Parameters

More experiments are conducted on one real-world *Parkinson-P* dataset and one benchmark multi-label *Scene* dataset to explore parameter sensitivity.

Inter-set Reweight Parameter. λ_{inter} is used for exploring the inter-set relationship between $\mathcal{Y}_a$ and $\mathcal{Y}_{-a}$. For *Parkinson-P* dataset, we fix $\lambda_{intra} = 1.5$, $T = 3$, and then we set λ_{inter} between 1.0 and 1.5 with an interval of 0.1. For *Scene* dataset, we fix $\lambda_{intra} = 2$, $T = 3$, and then we set λ_{inter} between 1.0 and 1.5 with an interval of 0.1.

As shown in Table 4, the performance of $\lambda_{inter} > 1.0$ is better than others when $\lambda_{inter} = 1.0$ in most cases, which validates the effectiveness of exploiting inter-set label relationship. In addition, we get optimal performance when $\lambda_{inter} = 1.7$ on *Parkinson-P* dataset and $\lambda_{inter} = 1.3$ on *Scene* dataset.

Intra-set Reweight Parameter. λ_{intra} is used for exploring the intra-set relationship on $\mathcal{Y}_a$ (or $\mathcal{Y}_{-a}$). Based on the above discussion of inter-set reweight parameter λ_{inter}, for *Parkinson-P* dataset, we fix $\lambda_{intra} = 1.7$, $T = 3$, and then we set λ_{inter} between 1.0 and 3 with an interval of 0.5. For *Scene* dataset, we fix $\lambda_{intra} = 1.3$, $T = 3$, and then we set λ_{inter} between 1.0 and 3 with an interval of 0.5. In Table 5, we find that $\lambda_{intra} = 1.25$ or $\lambda_{intra} = 1.5$ for *Parkinson-P* dataset may be a relatively proper setting, while $\lambda_{intra} = 2.0$ or $\lambda_{intra} = 2.5$ for *Scene* dataset.

Boosting Round T. We fix $\lambda_{inter} = 1.7$, $\lambda_{intra} = 1.25$ for *Parkinson-P* dataset and fix $\lambda_{inter} = 1.3$, $\lambda_{intra} = 2.0$ for *Scene* dataset. With λ_{inter} and λ_{intra} fixed, we get the optimal results when $T = 8$ on *Parkinson-P* dataset. Similarly, we get the optimal results when $T = 7$ on *Scene* dataset.

For one thing, increasing number of boosting rounds will make classifier overly complex and may lead to overfitting. We can see from Fig. 3(a) that when boosting round $T = 10$, all evaluation metrics decline slightly, which accords with our intuition since DMLMR is an approach with a boosting framework.

Table 3. Performance comparison on four benchmark multi-label datasets. ↑ / ↓ indicates that the larger/smaller the better of a criterion. The best results are in bold.

Evaluation Metrics	ML2000						
	BR	CC	ECC	MLKNN	LLSF	CAMEL	DMLMR
$HammingLoss \downarrow$	0.109±0.008	0.115±0.006	0.130±0.009	0.154±0.012	0.098±0.011	**0.098±0.011**	0.101±0.013
$SubsetAcc \uparrow$	0.586±0.034	0.636±0.022	0.521±0.029	0.488±0.036	0.626±0.045	0.633±0.036	**0.660±0.040**
$MacroF_1 \uparrow$	0.740±0.023	0.748±0.011	0.700±0.025	0.643±0.032	0.778±0.025	0.781±0.023	**0.793±0.027**
$MicroF_1 \uparrow$	0.749±0.020	0.756±0.011	0.705±0.023	0.654±0.029	0.782±0.025	0.783±0.024	**0.793±0.026**
$ExampleF_1 \uparrow$	0.690±0.026	0.758±0.011	0.646±0.028	0.607±0.030	0.740±0.031	0.739±0.029	**0.791±0.029**

Evaluation Metrics	Scene						
	BR	CC	ECC	MLKNN	LLSF	CAMEL	DMLMR
$HammingLoss \downarrow$	0.104±0.009	0.105±0.010	0.094±0.005	0.089±0.008	0.106±0.006	0.076±0.006	**0.070±0.006**
$SubsetAcc \uparrow$	0.536±0.041	0.653±0.031	0.596±0.0158	0.629±0.030	0.487±0.028	0.646±0.024	**0.733±0.020**
$MacroF_1 \uparrow$	0.692±0.025	0.713±0.028	0.710±0.012	0.743±0.022	0.644±0.027	0.772±0.021	**0.806±0.015**
$MicroF_1 \uparrow$	0.688±0.027	0.703±0.029	0.705±0.016	0.739±0.021	0.643±0.027	0.763±0.019	**0.799±0.015**
$ExampleF_1 \uparrow$	0.627±0.034	0.705±0.030	0.639±0.014	0.710±0.024	0.536±0.034	0.695±0.027	**0.787±0.015**

Evaluation Metrics	Emotions						
	BR	CC	ECC	MLKNN	LLSF	CAMEL	DMLMR
$HammingLoss \downarrow$	0.216±0.019	0.216±0.029	**0.202±0.023**	0.278±0.022	0.207±0.014	0.207±0.025	0.209±0.024
$SubsetAcc \uparrow$	0.265±0.063	0.292±0.062	0.283±0.042	0.212±0.038	0.254±0.049	0.272±0.048	**0.301±0.079**
$MacroF_1 \uparrow$	0.618±0.035	0.614±0.060	0.627±0.039	0.496±0.033	0.616±0.033	0.615±0.058	**0.631±0.035**
$MicroF_1 \uparrow$	0.638±0.043	0.649±0.053	0.647±0.038	0.529±0.030	0.641±0.033	0.637±0.048	**0.662±0.035**
$ExampleF_1 \uparrow$	0.594±0.058	0.623±0.057	0.584±0.046	0.495±0.026	0.594±0.039	0.581±0.049	**0.628±0.035**

Evaluation Metrics	Genbase						
	BR	CC	ECC	MLKNN	LLSF	CAMEL	DMLMR
$HammingLoss \downarrow$	0.001±0.001	0.001±0.001	0.001±0.001	0.003±0.001	0.001±0.001	0.001±0.001	**0.001±0.001**
$SubsetAcc \uparrow$	0.970±0.034	0.976±0.024	0.971±0.016	0.943±0.028	0.982±0.015	0.979±0.019	**0.982±0.019**
$MacroF_1 \uparrow$	0.639±0.079	0.638±0.084	0.627±0.026	0.593±0.044	0.632±0.075	0.561±0.121	**0.677±0.051**
$MicroF_1 \uparrow$	0.988±0.014	0.990±0.010	0.988±0.006	0.970±0.014	0.992±0.007	0.991±0.008	**0.993±0.007**
$ExampleF_1 \uparrow$	0.990±0.012	0.990±0.012	0.990±0.004	0.971±0.020	0.993±0.007	0.992±0.007	**0.994±0.007**

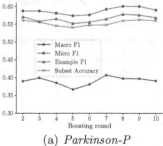

(a) *Parkinson-P*

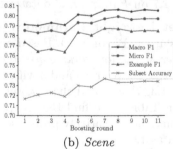

(b) *Scene*

Fig. 3. Performance of changes made by the number of boosting rounds T on *Parkinson-P* and *Scene* dataset, with λ_{inter} and λ_{intra} fixed.

For another, classifier should have low training error and a small number of boosting rounds in order to achieve good performance. As is shown in Fig. 3, with λ_{inter} and λ_{intra} fixed, the performance of DMLMR is unstable in the initial

Table 4. Performance comparison on *Parkinson-P* and *Scene* dataset when λ_{inter} increases with λ_{intra} and T fixed. ↑ / ↓ indicates that the larger/smaller the better of a criterion. The best results are in bold.

Dataset	Evaluation Metrics	$\lambda_{intra} = 1.5, T = 3$					
		$\lambda_{inter} = 1.0$	$\lambda_{inter} = 1.1$	$\lambda_{inter} = 1.3$	$\lambda_{inter} = 1.5$	$\lambda_{inter} = 1.7$	$\lambda_{inter} = 1.9$
Parkinson-P	HammingLoss ↓	0.170±0.031	0.173±0.026	0.162±0.031	0.168±0.050	**0.161±0.027**	0.167±0.024
	SubsetAcc ↑	0.544±0.065	0.524±0.072	0.546±0.082	0.546±0.118	**0.559±0.067**	0.554±0.071
	MacroF₁ ↑	0.392±0.041	0.374±0.031	0.404±0.066	0.378±0.075	**0.410±0.050**	0.398±0.048
	MicroF₁ ↑	0.571±0.073	0.559±0.062	0.586±0.083	0.580±0.122	**0.592±0.066**	0.579±0.059
	ExampleF₁ ↑	0.559±0.067	0.539±0.066	0.565±0.084	0.566±0.116	**0.575±0.064**	0.567±0.062

Dataset	Evaluation Metrics	$\lambda_{intra} = 2, T = 3$					
		$\lambda_{inter} = 1.0$	$\lambda_{inter} = 1.1$	$\lambda_{inter} = 1.2$	$\lambda_{inter} = 1.3$	$\lambda_{inter} = 1.4$	$\lambda_{inter} = 1.5$
Scene	HammingLoss ↓	0.075±0.009	0.074±0.010	0.074±0.008	**0.073±0.005**	0.074±0.009	0.075±0.005
	SubsetAcc ↑	0.719±0.030	**0.724±0.035**	0.719±0.027	0.723±0.016	0.723±0.032	0.718±0.021
	MacroF₁ ↑	0.789±0.026	0.790±0.026	0.793±0.022	**0.793±0.014**	0.790±0.023	0.789±0.011
	MicroF₁ ↑	0.780±0.029	0.782±0.027	0.783±0.023	**0.785±0.015**	0.781±0.027	0.780±0.016
	ExampleF₁ ↑	0.765±0.032	0.766±0.028	0.764±0.024	**0.767±0.016**	0.765±0.031	0.763±0.017

Table 5. Performance comparison on *Parkinson-P* and *Scene* dataset when λ_{intra} increases from 1.0 to 3.0 with λ_{inter} and T fixed. ↑ / ↓ indicates that the larger/smaller the better of a criterion. The best results are in bold.

Dataset	Evaluation Metrics	$\lambda_{inter} = 1.7, T=3$					
		$\lambda_{intra} = 1.0$	$\lambda_{intra} = 1.25$	$\lambda_{intra} = 1.5$	$\lambda_{intra} = 2$	$\lambda_{intra} = 2.5$	$\lambda_{intra} = 3.0$
Parkinson-P	HammingLoss ↓	**0.159±0.026**	0.162±0.025	0.161±0.027	0.165±0.019	0.162±0.025	0.167±0.017
	SubsetAcc ↑	0.556±0.068	**0.564±0.063**	0.559±0.067	0.544±0.050	0.551±0.068	0.534±0.048
	MacroF₁ ↑	0.407±0.052	**0.410±0.062**	0.410±0.050	0.390±0.037	0.402±0.057	0.398±0.047
	MicroF₁ ↑	0.596±0.069	0.588±0.064	**0.592±0.066**	0.579±0.048	0.586±0.063	0.573±0.043
	ExampleF₁ ↑	0.576±0.070	0.572±0.064	**0.575±0.064**	0.560±0.049	0.566±0.064	0.552±0.046

Dataset	Evaluation Metrics	$\lambda_{inter} = 1.3, T=3$					
		$\lambda_{intra} = 1.0$	$\lambda_{intra} = 1.25$	$\lambda_{intra} = 1.5$	$\lambda_{intra} = 2.0$	$\lambda_{intra} = 2.5$	$\lambda_{intra} = 3.0$
Scene	HammingLoss ↓	0.075±0.005	0.075±0.006	0.074±0.008	**0.073±0.005**	0.073±0.008	0.074±0.006
	SubsetAcc ↑	0.721±0.025	0.721±0.022	0.721±0.030	**0.723±0.016**	0.720±0.027	0.715±0.027
	MacroF₁ ↑	0.787±0.018	0.788±0.018	0.790±0.022	0.793±0.014	**0.794±0.019**	0.789±0.017
	MicroF₁ ↑	0.779±0.017	0.780±0.018	0.782±0.023	0.785±0.015	**0.785±0.023**	0.780±0.017
	ExampleF₁ ↑	0.763±0.022	0.764±0.019	0.767±0.025	0.767±0.016	**0.768±0.024**	0.761±0.017

increasing phase of T. After that, DMLMR improves remarkably. Eventually, as the number of boosting round T increases, all curves tend to be smoother, which show convergence when $T > 6$ for *Parkinson-P* and $T > 7$ for *Scene* dataset.

5 Conclusion

Traditional Chinese Medicine (TCM) is a new way for diagnosing Parkinson's disease (PD). In this paper, we apply multi-label classification technology to diagnose PD in TCM, where we treat *TCM scales* as features and treat *syndrome types* as multiple labels. Furthermore, we propose a novel Discriminative Multi-label Model Reuse (DMLMR) algorithm to advance diagnosing PD in TCM. DMLMR exploits label correlations by selecting discriminative label with label distribution adaptation, and then trains with model reuse. An assessment on the real-world dataset of PD shows that DMLMR obtains remarkable results in terms of various evaluation metrics, and DMLMR validates its ability of diagnosing PD in TCM. Extensive experiments on multi-label benchmark datasets show that DMLMR outperforms the state-of-the-art counterparts. In the future, how to extend to scenario with partial labels is a very interesting work.

Acknowledgment. This paper is supported by the National Key Research and Development Program of China (Grant No. 2018YFB1403400), the National Natural Science Foundation of China (Grant No. 61876080), the Key Research and Development Program of Jiangsu (Grant No. BE2019105), the Collaborative Innovation Center of Novel Software Technology and Industrialization at Nanjing University.

References

1. Boutell, M.R.: Learning multi-label scene classification. Pattern Recogn. **37**, 1757–1771 (2004)
2. Diplaris, S., Tsoumakas, G., Mitkas, P.A., Vlahavas, I.: Protein classification with multiple algorithms. In: Bozanis, P., Houstis, E.N. (eds.) PCI 2005. LNCS, vol. 3746, pp. 448–456. Springer, Heidelberg (2005). https://doi.org/10.1007/11573036_42
3. Feng, L., An, B., He, S.: Collaboration based multi-label learning. In: Thirty-Third AAAI Conference on Artificial Intelligence, pp. 3550–3557 (2019)
4. Fürnkranz, J., Hüllermeier, E., Mencía, E.L., Brinker, K.: Multilabel classification via calibrated label ranking. Mach. Learn. **73**(2), 133–153 (2008)
5. Ghamrawi, N., McCallum, A.: Collective multi-label classification. In: Proceedings of the 14th ACM international conference on Information and knowledge management, pp. 195–200. ACM (2005)
6. Gibaja, E., Ventura, S.: A tutorial on multilabel learning. ACM Comput. Surv. (CSUR) **47**(3), 1–38 (2015)
7. Huang, J., Li, G., Huang, Q., Wu, X.: Learning label specific features for multi-label classification. In: 2015 IEEE International Conference on Data Mining, pp. 181–190. IEEE (2015)
8. Huang, S.J., Yu, Y., Zhou, Z.H.: Multi-label hypothesis reuse. In: Proceedings of the 18th ACM SIGKDD international conference on Knowledge discovery and data mining, pp. 525–533. ACM (2012)
9. Kazawa, H., Izumitani, T., Taira, H., Maeda, E.: Maximal margin labeling for multi-topic text categorization. In: Advances in neural information processing systems, pp. 649–656 (2005)
10. Liu, C., Zhao, P., Huang, S.J., Jiang, Y., Zhou, Z.H.: Dual set multi-label learning. In: Thirty-Second AAAI Conference on Artificial Intelligence, (2018)
11. Luo, Y., Tao, D., Xu, C., Li, D., Xu, C.: Vector-valued multi-view semi-supervsed learning for multi-label image classification. In: Twenty-Seventh AAAI Conference on Artificial Intelligence, (2013)
12. Mohri, M., Rostamizadeh, A., Talwalkar, A.: Foundations of Machine Learning. MIT press (2018)

13. Peng, Y., Tang, C., Chen, G., Xie, J., Wang, C.: Multi-label learning by exploiting label correlations for tcm diagnosing parkinson's disease. In: 2017 IEEE International Conference on Bioinformatics and Biomedicine (BIBM), pp. 590–594. IEEE (2017)
14. Qi, G.J., Hua, X.S., Rui, Y., Tang, J., Mei, T., Zhang, H.J.: Correlative multi-label video annotation. In: Proceedings of the 15th ACM international conference on Multimedia, pp. 17–26. ACM (2007)
15. Read, J., Pfahringer, B., Holmes, G., Frank, E.: Classifier chains for multi-label classification. Mach. Learn. **85**(3), 333 (2011)
16. Trohidis, K., Tsoumakas, G., Kalliris, G., Vlahavas, I.P.: Multi-label classification of music into emotions. ISMIR. **8**, 325–330 (2008)
17. Wang, X., Sukthankar, G.: Multi-label relational neighbor classification using social context features. In: Proceedings of the 19th ACM SIGKDD international conference on Knowledge discovery and data mining, pp. 464–472. ACM (2013)
18. Wu, B., Zhong, E., Horner, A., Yang, Q.: Music emotion recognition by multi-label multi-layer multi-instance multi-view learning. In: Proceedings of the 22nd ACM international conference on Multimedia, pp. 117–126. ACM (2014)
19. Zhang, C., Yu, Z., Hu, Q., Zhu, P., Liu, X., Wang, X.: Latent semantic aware multi-view multi-label classification. In: Thirty-Second AAAI Conference on Artificial Intelligence, (2018)
20. Zhang, M.L., Zhou, Z.H.: Ml-knn: a lazy learning approach to multi-label learning. Pattern Recogn. **40**(7), 2038–2048 (2007)
21. Zhang, M.L., Zhou, Z.H.: A review on multi-label learning algorithms. IEEE Trans. Knowl. Data Eng. **26**(8), 1819–1837 (2013)
22. Zhang, Y., Zeng, C., Cheng, H., Wang, C., Zhang, L.: Many could be better than all: a novel instance-oriented algorithm for multi-modal multi-label problem. In: 2019 IEEE International Conference on Multimedia and Expo (ICME), pp. 838–843. IEEE (2019)
23. Zhu, Y., Kwok, J.T., Zhou, Z.H.: Multi-label learning with global and local label correlation. IEEE Trans. Knowl. Data Eng. **30**(6), 1081–1094 (2018)

Global and Local Attention Embedding Network for Few-Shot Fine-Grained Image Classification

Jiayuan Hu, Chung-Ming Own, and Wenyuan Tao[✉]

College of Intelligence and Computing, Tianjin University, Tianjin, China
{hujiayuan,chungming.own,taowenyuan}@tju.edu.cn

Abstract. Few-shot fine-grained image recognition aims to classify fine-grained images with limited training samples. Nowadays exist in a majority of few-shot fine-grained image classification methods the following problems: local information loss and ignoring pivotal parts. To solve the above problems, this paper proposes a new embedding module, called GLAE. The author designs a hierarchical structure and combines the first-order and second-order information to reduce the local information loss. Besides, this paper proposes an attention mechanism to obtain the vital parts by the attention mask. On the StanfordCars dataset, GLAE achieves an accuracy of 91.18% which is the best result in the field of few-shot fine-grained image recognition.

Keywords: Fine-grained imgae recognition · Few-shot learning · Attention mechanism · First-order and Second-order information

1 Introduction

Traditional deep neural networks (DNN) rely on large training sets to generate a possible mapping relationship through a huge amount of training. But such an approach is inefficient and leads to significant data waste. Humans, by contrast, typically need only a quite small sample of data to learn something new. Besides, with the increasingly stringent requirements of classification, the difficulty of sample collection increases. In the real environment, the number of data samples available is usually very limited [1]. Moreover, fine-grained image recognition is different from traditional image recognition tasks. There are some problems occurs in fine-grained image recognition, such as how to depart large intra-class difference from tiny inter-class difference. Therefore, it is necessary to solve the structure of fine-grained image recognition to pay more attention to the tiny but vital parts. Therefore, the traditional deep learning method is difficult to deal with the fine-grained classification problem due to the limited training set samples and strict classification requirements.

In recent years, few-shot learning has attracted extensive attention [6]. The core idea of few-shot learning is that image recognition tasks can be completed

© Springer Nature Switzerland AG 2020
X. Wang et al. (Eds.): APWeb-WAIM 2020, LNCS 12317, pp. 740–747, 2020.
https://doi.org/10.1007/978-3-030-60259-8_54

with only a few numbers of training samples just like humans. Compared with the traditional deep learning algorithm, few-shot learning is more intelligent and more in line with the idea of machine learning. Although few-shot learning shines brilliantly in the field of traditional image recognition, it is troublesome for traditional few-shot learning to recognize a fine-grained image because fine-grained image recognition requires tiny but important local information. At present, a few works focus on introducing few-shot learning into the field of fine-grained recognition, but they have the following two problems: they fail to pay attention to the local representative features and lose the local information.

The rest of this paper is organized as follows. Section 2 introduces the research progress of few-shot learning and fine-grained image recognition. Section 2.1 presents the proposed global and local attention embedding module. Experimental results and discussions are presented in Sect. 3. The conclusion is described in Sect. 4.

2   The Proposed Method

At present, the main few-shot fine-grained Classification methods rarely consider the effect of global and local features on classification effect. In addition, the current mainstream methods do not take into account the effect of attention mechanism on classification results. To solve the above problems, we proposed a network architecture based on the DenseNet structure, and used bilinear architecture to obtain the second-order information of the image and fuse it with the first-order information, to obtain the global and local features of the image. To reduce the loss of image in the pooling process, Global Average pooling (GAP) is employed instead of the traditional Global Maximum Pooling (GMP). The author adopts a new attention mask to pay more attention to the important parts to improve the results of classification.

The specific structure of this part is as follows: First, we introduce the definition of the few-shot learning problem. Next, the author explains the proposed structure in detail. The Fig. 1 illustrates the proposed method visually.

2.1   Global and Local Information

Hierarchical Structure. Most few-shot fine-grained image classification methods do not pay attention to local features with characteristics. Inspired by the DenseNet method, we propose a new feature extraction network consisting of three convolution blocks, as Fig. 1 shows, each of which is composed of two convolution layers, two pooling layers, and two Batch Normalization layers. This is the first time that both global and local features of an image have been considered in the few-shot fine-grained classification domain.

Assuming that the input can be expressed as X, then the result of the first convolution layer of the convolution block is $\Phi_1(X)$. The result is then passed through a Global Maximum Pooling (GMP) layer GMP and the Batch Normalization layer BN_1 to the next convolutional layer Φ_2, represented as

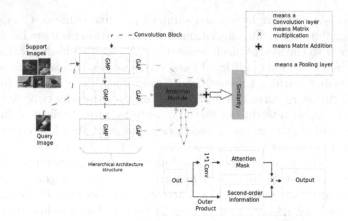

Fig. 1. Explanation of the proposed Global and Local Attention Embedding (GLAE in short) based structure for a 5-way-1-shot few shot fine-grained task on CubBird-200–2011 dataset. As shown, the proposed structure consists of a Hierarchical structure in order to reduce the information loss and an Attention Module to figure out the tiny but vital parts.

$R_1 = BN_1(GMP(\Phi_1(X)))$. Finally, via a Global Average Pooling (GAP) layer GAP and a Batch Normalization layer BN_2, The result can be showed as $Out_1 = BN_2(GAP(\Phi_2(R_1)))$.

Global Average Pooling. Here we use GAP instead of GMP. In the field of Saliency Detection, the idea of using GAP at the last layer was proposed [7]. GMP loses more image information than the GAP. However, in the process of transmission, peripheral details will be lost, leading to limited information and affecting the classification results. Although the use of GAP increases some computational complexity, the surrounding details are taken into account during the pooling process, so that these details can be further passed on, and the local features obtained from the shallow layer can be better preserved.

2.2   The Fusion of First Order and Second Order Information

Compared with traditional classification tasks, fine-grained classification requires more attention to tiny but vital parts. Second-order information can be obtained by using the network structure of the bilinear network, which can better obtain the tiny parts and improve the accuracy of fine-grained classification. However, the bilinear network structure will lose spatial information when obtaining. Meanwhile, although the first-order information does not work well when dealing with fine-grained problems, it can retain spatial information well [4]. Therefore, to better cope with few-shot fine-grained recognition, this paper fuses the first-order information and the second-order information to improve the accuracy of the final classification.

Recently, [8] has proposed a method called Bilinear pooling, which gives a sum pooling of second-order features from the outer product. The process of Bilinear pooling can be represented by a quadruple shown as Eq. (1).

$$H_{Bilinear} = (\tau_1, \tau_2, f_b, C),$$
$$\tau : F_{ij}^1 \longmapsto H \in R^{d \times (h \times w)},$$
$$f_b(F_{ij}^1, \tau_1, \tau_2) = \frac{1}{hw} \sum_{ij=1}^{hw} \tau_1(F_{ij}^1) \cdot \tau_2(F_{ij}^1)^T. \tag{1}$$

The first-order information obtained by the convolution block will be abbreviated as as Out in the rest of the paper. The information is then put into the bilinear structure to obtain the second-order information, which can be abbreviate to H_{Bi}. According to [4], the fusion of the first-order and second order information is shown as $Vec(Out, H_{Bi})$, which means the concat result between the first-order and second-order information.

2.3   Attention Mask

The difficulty of fine-grained classification lies in the dispersion within classes and compactness between classes. To better perform fine-grained classification tasks, fine-grained image recognition relies on tiny but important local parts to classification and recognition. While considering the limited amount of training data, it has trouble for the computer in learning how to find the key areas, so we hope to make the network pay attention to the key areas through the attention mechanism itself.

When humans learn about a picture, they usually divide it into the important parts that are helpful and the unimportant parts. Analogous to the cognitive process of human beings, we use the Sigmoid function to divide the acquired image features into important regions and unimportant regions. For a pixel Out_a in the image represented by the convolution block. Then the probability of the pixel $p(Out_a)$ which means the importance of the image classification. The larger the value, the more important the region is to the classification.

At the same time, it should be noted that the proposed method preserves spatial relationships between pixels. And no extra parameters are introduced in the process, so it's easy to implement.

2.4   GLAE Method

In this section, we specifically introduce how to apply the proposed GLAE method in practical applications. Assume that the input X, the results of each block can be shown as Out_1, Out_2 and Out_3. After a 1×1 convolution layer, the attention mask $X_{attention}$ is then applied to the obtained image representation, which can be noted as Eq. (2).

$$X_{attention} = Sigmoid(Conv(Out)),$$

$$= \frac{1}{1 + \exp^{-Conv(Out)}}. \tag{2}$$

According to the Eq. (3), H_{Bi}^i represents the bilinear result of each block.

$$H_{Bi}^i = X_{attention}^i (Out_i \cdot Out_i^T) \quad i \in \{1,3\}. \tag{3}$$

After that, with the help of the hierarchical structure, the fusion of the first-order and second-order information is achieved as Eq. (4) shows. α, β and γ are the hyper parameters.

$$H_{Result} = \alpha \cdot Vec(Out_1, H_{Bi}^1) + \beta \cdot Vec(Out_2, H_{Bi}^2) + \gamma \cdot Vec(Out_3, H_{Bi}^3). \tag{4}$$

As Eq. (5) shows, the corresponding category of elements in the query set is determined by calculating the cosine distance between the elements in the support set denoted by H_{Result}^S and the elements in the query set denoted by H_{Result}^Q. The cosine distance is presented by Eq. (6).

$$similarity = \sum_m^i \sum_n^j cos(H_{Result}^{s_m}, H_{Result}^{q_n}), \tag{5}$$

$$cos(H_{Result}^{s_m}, H_{Result}^{q_n}) = \frac{H_{Result}^{s_m}{}^T \cdot H_{Result}^{q_n}}{\|H_{Result}^{s_m}\|_2 \cdot \|H_{Result}^{q_n}\|_2}. \tag{6}$$

3   Experiments and Analysis

In this part, we first introduce the database of commonly used in fine-grained classification, then introduce the experimental settings and analyze the experimental results, and finally carried out ablation study on the proposed GLAE.

3.1   Experiment Settings

To meet the task requirements of few-shot learning, we arrange both 5-way-1-shot and 5-way-5-shot classification experiment in the above datasets. Specifically, in a 5-way-1-shot classification experiments, in the training process, we randomly extract five categories from the training set as a support set, and randomly extract one picture from each category. In the query set, we randomly extract 15 images from the five previously specified categories without joining into support sets. In the testing process, like the training process, we randomly select five categories from the test set or the validation set, and randomly extract one picture as the support set. Meanwhile, for the query set, we extract 15 images that are not in the support set from the same category as support set. The 5-way-5-shot experiment is basically the same as the 5-way-1-shot experiment. In addition to the production of the query set, we extract 10 pictures from each category. In the experiments, the hyper-parameters α, β and γ are set to 0.4, 0.2 and 0.4.

3.2   Few-Shot Fine-Grained Image Classification Results

Through the Table 1, we can figure that the proposed GLAE has achieved significant success in the few-shot fine-grained image classification. The proposed GLAE method carried out 5-way-5-shot experiments on CubBird-200–2011 dataset, StanfordCars dataset, and StanfordDogs dataset. The proposed method improved by 6.8%, 1.58%, and 6.21%, respectively, over the previous method. In the StanfordCars dataset, GLAE's accuracy reached 91.18%, which is the best result of the few-shot fine-grained image classification on this dataset.

Because GLAE reduces information loss and mines image information as much as possible, it is more suitable for fine-grained image recognition tasks in a few-shot learning environment. In the 5-way 1-shot experiments, GLAE improves the accuracy of CubBird-200–2011 dataset, StanfordCars dataset, and StanfordDogs dataset by 7.98%, 10.19%, and 13.82%, respectively, compared with the previous best results. The experimental results on the 5-way-1-shot proves that GLAE can still achieve excellent results with the limited training samples.

Table 1. The mean accuracies of both 5-way-1-shot and 5-way-5-shot tasks on three benchmark fine grained datasets, with 95% confidence intervals. For each setting, the best and the second best results are highlighted.

Method	Stanford Dogs		Stanford Cars		CUB Birds	
	5way1shot	5way5shot	5way1shot	5way5shot	5way1shot	5way5shot
Piecewise [9]	42.10	62.48	28.78	46.92	29.63	52.28
Matching Net [10]	35.80	47.50	34.80	44.70	45.30	59.50
Prototype Net [2]	37.59	48.19	40.90	52.93	37.36	45.28
GNN [11]	**46.98**	62.27	55.85	71.25	51.83	63.69
Relation Net [3]	44.75	58.36	56.02	66.93	**59.82**	71.83
DN4 [5]	45.73	**66.33**	**61.51**	**89.60**	53.15	**81.90**
Ours (GLAE)	**54.96**	**73.13**	**71.70**	**91.18**	**73.64**	**88.11**

3.3   Ablation Study

Attention Mask. In this paper, we use an attention mechanism based on Sigmoid. The input image area is divided into sections related to classification and sections unrelated to classification. After the training, the network will pay more attention to the important parts of classification, so as to improve the accuracy of classification. Table 2 verifes the hypothesis. In this process, no additional parameters are introduced, so the method we proposed is more suitable for coping with the few-shot fine-grained classification.

Hierarchical Structure. Relation Net introduces the convolutional layer as an encoder to map the image information to another space through a series of convolutional layers to determine the similarity between the support image and

Table 2. The effect of attention mechanism on experiment results.

Attention mask	Task	Accuracy
Without mask	CubBird 5-way-5-shot	85.14%
With mask	CubBird 5-way-5-shot	88.11%

query image. Relation Net uses a four layers network structure. However, we believe that it is difficult to extract more global information from the four layers network structure, which will lead to the loss of the information extracted from shallow layers, so we discussed the effect of encoder hierarchy on the final result. Inspired by DenseNet, this paper adopts a hierarchical structure to make full use of features gained from both shallow layers and deep layers, thus reducing information loss. On the basis of Table 3, it is obvious that the proposed hierarchical structure improves the final classification accuracy.

Table 3. Comparison of the encoder structures.

Encoder structure	Task	Accuracy
Convolutional structure	StanfordCars 5-way-5-shot	90.60%
Hierarchical structure	StanfordCars 5-way-5-shot	91.18%

Pooling Layers. In general, to better reduce the image size of the convolutional layer output, the GMP pooling method is usually used. However, because the few-shot fine-grained image classification requires tiny but significant local information, such a maximized pooling method is likely to ignore these minute local information, thus reducing the classification accuracy. According to Table 4, it is intuitive that the GAP network architecture instead of GMP achieves better accuracy results in few-shot fine-grained classification tasks.

Table 4. The effect of the pooling layer on the results.

Pooling layer	Task	Accuracy
GMP	CubBird 5-way-5-shot	85.45%
GAP	CubBird 5-way-5-shot	88.11%

4   Conclusion

In this paper, firstly, we pointed out two common problems that few-shot fine-grained image classification methods mainly exist: local information loss and the overlook of critical parts. To better adapt to few-shot fine-grained image classification, we use the hierarchical structure to reduce the lack of information, combines first-order information with second-order information, and puts forward a new but effcient attention mechanism. Experiments prove that our method outperforms the mainstream few-shot fine-grained image classification methods.

References

1. Wertheimer, D., Hariharan, B.: Few-shot learning with localization in realistic settings. In: Proceedings of the IEEE Conference on Computer Vision and Pattern Recognition, pp. 6558–6567 (2019)
2. Snell, J., Swersky, K., Zemel, R.: Prototypical networks for few-shot learning. In: Advances in Neural Information Processing Systems, pp. 4077–4087 (2017)
3. Sung, F., Yang, Y., Zhang, L., Xiang, T., Torr, P.H., Hospedales, T.M.: Learning to compare: relation network for few-shot learning. In: Proceedings of the IEEE Conference on Computer Vision and Pattern Recognition, pp. 1199–1208 (2018)
4. Zhang, Y., Tang, S., Muandet, K., Jarvers, C., Neumann, H.: Local temporal bilinear pooling for fine-grained action parsing. In: Proceedings of the IEEE Conference on Computer Vision and Pattern Recognition, pp. 12005–12015 (2019)
5. Li, W., Wang, L., Xu, J., Huo, J., Gao, Y., Luo, J.: Revisiting local descriptor based image-to-class measure for few-shot learning. In: Proceedings of the IEEE Conference on Computer Vision and Pattern Recognition, pp. 7260–7268 (2019)
6. Wang, Y., Yao, Q., Kwok, J., Ni, L.M.: Generalizing from a few examples: a survey on few-shot learning (2019). arXiv: 1904.05046
7. Peng, Y., He, X., Zhao, J.: Object-part attention model for fine-grained image classification. IEEE Trans. Image Process. **27**(3), 1487–1500 (2017)
8. Lin, T.Y., RoyChowdhury, A., Maji, S.: Bilinear CNN models for fine-grained visual recognition. In: Proceedings of the IEEE International Conference on Computer Vision, pp. 1449–1457 (2015)
9. Wei, X.S., Wang, P., Liu, L., Shen, C., Wu, J.: Piecewise classifier mappings: learning fine-grained learners for novel categories with few examples. IEEE Trans. Image Process. **28**(12), 6116–6125 (2019)
10. Vinyals, O., et al.: Matching networks for one shot learning. In: Advances in Neural Information Processing Systems, pp. 3630–3638 (2016)
11. Garcia, V., Bruna, J.: Few-shot learning with graph neural networks. arXiv preprint (2017). arXiv:1711.04043
12. Huang, G., Liu, Z., Van Der Maaten, L., Weinberger, K.Q.: Densely connected convolutional networks. In: Proceedings of the IEEE Conference on Computer Vision and Pattern Recognition, pp. 4700–4708 (2017)

Bayes Classifier Chain Based on SVM for Traditional Chinese Medical Prescription Generation

Chaohan Pei[1,4], Chunyang Ruan[2], Yanchun Zhang[3,4(✉)], and Yun Yang[5]

[1] School of Software Engineering, Fudan University, Shanghai, China
17212010027@fudan.edu.cn
[2] School of Economics and Finance Shanghai International Studies University, Shanghai, China
cyruan16@fudan.edu.cn
[3] College of Engineering and Science, Victoria University, Melbourne, Australia
[4] Cyberspace Institute of Advanced Technology, Guangzhou University, Guangzhou, China
Yanchun.Zhang@vu.edu.au
[5] Department of Oncology and Longhua Hospital, Shanghai, China

Abstract. Traditional Chinese Medicine (TCM) plays an important role in the comprehensive treatment of lung cancer. However the quality of the prescriptions from TCM doctors depends on the doctor's personal experience, which leads to the TCM prescriptions are the lack of standardization. We apply the original clinical TCM prescriptions data to train a standardized prescription generating model for TCM therapy. Our model adopts the Bayes Classifier Chain (BCC) algorithm to solve the label correlation problem, whose basic classifier is cost-sensitive SVM targeted to the class imbalance of the label. The results of experiments on the prescription dataset demonstrated the effectiveness and practicability of the proposed model for a prescription generation.

Keywords: Multi-label classification · Bayes classifier chain · Cost sensitive SVM · TCM

1 Introduction

As one of the most common malignant tumors, lung cancer is a leading cause of cancer-related death worldwide [15]. TCM is considered as an important complementary therapy with beneficial effects for lung cancer patients by reducing toxic effects, improving the quality of life [8]. It can be observed that traditional Chinese medicine has become an important part of the comprehensive treatment system for lung cancer. However, different from the normalized diagnosis and treatment standard in modern medicine, traditional Chinese medicine is more

This work is supported by the National Science Foundation of China (No. 61672161).

X. Wang et al. (Eds.): APWeb-WAIM 2020, LNCS 12317, pp. 748–763, 2020.
https://doi.org/10.1007/978-3-030-60259-8_55

individualized in the treatment of patients, and the treatment effect is closely linked to the doctor's level of clinical experience. For example, the prescription made by TCM doctors, which consists of a set of herbs, may be different from different doctors. Therefore, it is a very meaningful task to integrate the clinical prescriptions of different TCM doctors, analyze the rules, and then standardize the prescribing process. In relevant research about the TCM standardization, the prescription data were mostly from the TCM classics and pharmacopeia. There is just an obvious problem with these datasets that the prescriptions of TCM medical books are too old and simple to suit the up-to-date medical demand. Fortunately, our collaboration hospital has provided over 10000 prescriptions of TCM therapy aimed at lung cancer and we applied these data in our experiment.

Table 1 shows an example of TCM prescription excerpted from an electronic medical record. The first row is the set of symptom descriptions. The practitioner prescribes herbs shown in the second row based on the symptoms and diagnosis. In this paper, we construct a multi-label classifier, whose input is a set of symptoms and the output is a group of herbs.

Table 1. An example for a TCM prescription of lung cancer

Sympotms	Tongue reddish(舌淡红), Deficiency of both qi and yin(气阴两虚), Thin tongue fur(苔薄), Pulmonary malignant tumor(肺恶性肿瘤), Pulse fine(脉细)
Herbs	Desert cistanche(苁蓉) , Uncooked rice kernels(生米仁) ,Astragali radix(生黄芪) ,Selaginella doederleinii Hieron(石上柏) , Asparagus fern(天冬) , Hedyotis diffusa(蛇舌草) ,Lossy privet fruit(女贞子) , Raw atractylodes(生白术) ,Salvia chinensis(石见穿) , Edible tulip(山慈菇) ,Herba epimedii(仙灵脾), Akebia fruit(预知子),Radix glehniae(北沙参), Gizzard pepsin(鸡内金)

In our early experiment, we found two critical problems with the prescription dataset. The first problem is the correlation between each herb label, for example, each prescription has a fundamental prescription targeted to a specific symptom comprised of several fixed herbs. These herbs often appear together in a certain prescription. The second is the class imbalance of every label interior. In our total dataset, there are 357 herb labels, 189 symptom features, and 10000+ samples. However, there are 255 labels in total whose the number of positive samples only accounts for less than 3.3% in total samples. It can be seen in Fig. 1 that the number of positive samples with most of the labels is much less than the negative samples.

In multi-label classification algorithms, the Binary Relevance (BR) [3] is the basic algorithm, which converts the multi-label classification to single-label classification to solve. BR algorithm is simple and doesn't consider the label correlation, but the reality is complicated. Aimed to the label correlation, the label power-set approach [16] transforms the multidimensional problem into a single-class scenario by defining a new compound class variable whose possible values are all of the possible combinations of values of the original classes. It is the obvious disadvantage of this method that the computational complexity will increases exponentially with the number of labels. Based on BR, Classifier Chains (CC) algorithm [12] constructs a chain structure on labels and determines the presence/absence of the current label under the condition of previously determined

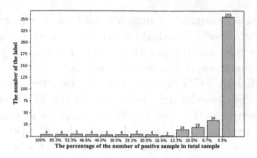

Fig. 1. We have 357 labels in our prescription dataset and we classify this label according to the percentage of the number of positive samples in the total sample. The height of every bar is the actual quantity of each category

labels. There are some problems with CC methods such as how to decide the order of the labels in the chain, and not all labels exist the correlation between each other.

Zaragoza [14] proposed a more effective method, Bayes Classifier Chain (BCC), which establishes a directed acyclic graph of the label set based on the correlation between each label. Then they train each classifier starting from the top node, the results of the parent node classifier will be added into the input feature set of the children node classifier. In our work, we built a DAG for the herb label set according to the special attribute of the prescription dataset refer to the BCC method to solve the labels correlation problem.

The solution to cope with the class imbalance can roughly be grouped into two general categories. The first is to address the problem from the respect of sampling, that is to say changing the distribution of the sample, by adopting resampling techniques such as oversampling, undersampling and synthetic sampling with data generation [1,4,6]. In our previous experiment, the performance after altering the sampling strategy was dissatisfactory because of the abnormally high false positive. Therefore we adopt the second category solution in this paper. This method is called cost-sensitive learning using different cost matrices that describe the costs for misclassifying any particular data example. In our research, we selected the SVM as the basic classifier of CC method and modified the SVM by cost-sensitive means.

We refer to the work of Masnadi-Shirazi et al. [10], in which they proposed a new cost-sensitive SVM. This new model not only can deal with the class imbalance problem but also implemented the cost-sensitive Bayes decision rule and made the model risk approximate the cost-sensitive Bayes risk. The experiment result showed that the performance of this SVM is better than others. In the following sections, we call this SVM as CS-SVM (cost-sensitive SVM). The contributions of our work are as follows:

– We improve the BCC method targeted to the unique feature about the TCM prescriptions dataset. In our BCC classifier, the DAG construction approach exhibits the fine interpretability of TCM prescriptions.

- We combine the multi-label learning algorithm with the cost-sensitive SVM and compare its performance with other different SVM algorithm. This CS-SVM exhibits excellent performance in dealing with a class imbalance of label interior in multi-label classification problems.
- We apply our multi-label classification model on the TCM prescription prediction problem and achieve better performance, which was approved by TCM doctors.

2 Related Work

2.1 TCM Knowledge Discovery

With the development of artificial intelligence, more researches pay attention to the TCM data mining using AI. The topic model has been widely applied in the analysis of the prescriptions, such as Jialin Ma et al. [9], Liang Yao et al. [19]. The graph theory model also plays an important role in TCM research. Chunyang Ruan et al. [13] adopted the graph model to find the rule between symptoms and herbs in TCM. With the development of deep learning, more and more researchers tried to adapt the neural network method into biomedical to deal with medical problems. Wei Li et al. [7] proposed a seq2seq model based on RNN to generate the herbs, which refer to the machine translation model in NLP. Qiang Xu et al. [18] chose chronic obstructive pulmonary disease as an example of investigating syndrome differentiation for TCM based on artificial neural networks.

2.2 Classifier Chain

Read et al. [12] first introduced chain classifiers as an alternative method for multi-label classification that incorporates class dependencies, while keeping the computational efficiency of the binary relevance approach. Based on the fundamental CC method, researchers have done many improvements. Dembczynski proposed [5] Probabilistic Chain Classifier (PCC) algorithm, which mainly applies a probability frame in CC. Although PCC can better consider the relativity between labels, it has very high time complexity. Goncalves et al. [14] referred to the genetic algorithm and then put forward the GACC algorithm, the purpose is to optimize the CC forecast order chain by the heuristic algorithm. J. Read et al. [11] presented the classifier trellis (CT) method for scalable multi-label classification. In recent work, we can see that many researchers pay close attention to the label order by searching for the correlation between the labels.

2.3 Cost Sensitive SVM

SVMs are based on a very solid learning-theoretic foundation and have been successfully applied to many classification problems. The cost-sensitive modification on the basic SVM algorithm can cope with the class imbalance problem and there two primary cost-sensitive modifications on SVM. The first was known as the biased penalties SVM (BP-SVM) [2,17], whose mechanism consists of applying different penalty factors C_1 and C_{-1} for the positive and negative SVM slack variables during training. It is implemented by transforming the primal SVM problem into

$$arg \min_{w,b,\xi} \frac{1}{2}||w||^2 + C \left[C_1 \sum_{\{i|y_i=1\}} \xi_i + C_{-1} \sum_{\{i|y_i=-1\}} \xi_i \right] \tag{1}$$
$$\text{s.t. } y_i(w^T x + b) \geq 1 - \xi_i$$

The BP-SVM suffers from an obvious flaw, which has limited ability to carry out a cost-sensitive strategy when the training data are separable. In the process of parametric optimization, the model intends to select large slack penalty C rather than adjust the cost-sensitive penalty C_1 and C_{-1} and then the slack variable ξ is zero-valued and the optimization degenerates into that of the standard SVM, where the separating hyperplane is placed midway between the two classes (rather than assigning a larger margin to one of them). The second is a cost-sensitive SVM model proposed by [10] and in this paper, we call it CS-SVM for simplicity. They modified the hinge loss function directly by the cost-sensitive way rather than only added penalty terms. We will elaborate on it in the following section.

3   Methodology

Our prescription predicting can be regarded as a multi-label classification mission. In the following, we use the boldface to represent a vector and the normal font is the scalar or a component of a vector. Every train sample consists of a symptom set and a herb set, which can be represented as $(\mathbf{X}_i, \mathbf{Y}_i)$. $\mathbf{X}_i$ is the input vector and $\mathbf{Y}_i$ is the output vector, in our problem, they are deemed as symptom vector and herb vector respectively. For every $\mathbf{X}_i = [x_1, x_2, \cdots, x_M] \in \{-1,1\}^M$, $\mathbf{Y}_i = [y_1, y_2, \cdots, y_L] \in \{-1,1\}^L$, the M and L are the dimension of the input vector and output vector severally. In our task, M is the number of total symptoms and the L is the number of total herbs. If the symptom set of one sample contains a symptom $s_j, (j = 1, \cdots, M)$, the jth component of the vector, x_j, will be 1, otherwise will be -1 and the herb set is like the symptom set. Our task is training a multi-label classifier $F(\cdot)$ satisfied the functional relationship $\mathbf{Y} = F(\mathbf{X})$ on the basis of training sample.

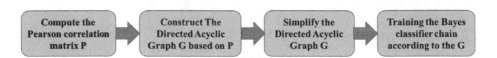

Fig. 2. The framework of our BCC training procedure

3.1 Bayes Classifier Chain Algorithm

Algorithm 1 and Fig. 2 are the framework of our BCC algorithm. The BCC in this research has two parts:

1. Constructing the order of the classifier chain, the directed acyclic graph,
2. Training the BCC classifier according to the DAG and this part is elaborated in Algorithm 3.

Construct the Directed Acyclic Graph(DAG). Ordinarily, constructing a Bayes network is an NP-hard problem. However, we can simplify this process based on the dataset feature in our prescriptions generation task.

Firstly, we count the occurrence number of every herb label in total 10000+ sample, and then sort all the labels by their occurrence numbers from large to small. We find that if a herb's occurrence frequency is higher, it will be more important and common use when doctors make a prescription. TCM doctors always consider the common herbs at first and then judge whether to use rare herbs. This fact means that we can set the direction of the herb network from the high-frequency herbs to low-frequency herbs and the most common herbs are start nodes in this network. In label sample matrix H, where $H \in \{-1, +1\}^{N \times L}$, the column vector $\mathbf{y_i}$ are arranged by the herb frequency order above.

Secondly, we compute the Pearson correlation coefficient matrix $P(L \times L)$ between every herbs label based on the label sample matrix H. Every element $p_{i,j} \in [0, 1]$ in P, after consultation with the doctor, we select the correlation coefficient threshold: 0.2 after many experiments, if $|p_{i,j}| > 0.2$, we regard the herb y_i and y_j exist correlation, and then $p_{i,j} = 1$ ortherwise $p_{i,j} = 0$ (Fig. 3).

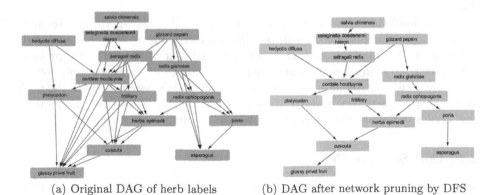

(a) Original DAG of herb labels   (b) DAG after network pruning by DFS

Fig. 3. The node-set of these two networks consists of the top 15 highest occurrence frequency herb labels in the total sample. The previous node in the topological sorting order of the network has a higher frequency than the later node.

Thirdly, we construct a DAG $G = \langle V, E \rangle$, where V is the node set and every node v_i corresponding to a herb label y_i. We stipulate that if $p_{i,j} = 1$ and $i > j$, then the directed edge$\langle y_i, y_j \rangle \in E$. At last, this DAG exists a problem

---

Algorithm 1. Framework of BCC training for our system.

Input: The sample matrix of symptom features S, where $S \in \{-1, +1\}^{N \times M}$. The sample matrix of herb labels H, where $H \in \{-1, +1\}^{N \times L}$.;

Output: The BCC classifier F;

1: Compute the Pearson correlation coefficient matrix of each label P, where $P \in \{-1, +1\}^{L \times L}$ according to S.

2: Select the threshold t, $\forall p_{i,j} \in P$, if $|p_{i,j}| > t$, $p_{i,j} \leftarrow 1$ else $p_{i,j} \leftarrow 0$. Then get the adjacent matrix G based on P.

3: Apply the **Algorithm 2**, input the DAG adjacent matrix G, get simplified DAG adjacent matrix G'.

4: Use the DAG: $G' = < V, E' >$ as the classifier chain order of BCC algorithm, then call **Algorithm 3**.

---

that if there is a path $r_{i,j}$ from v_i to v_j, we can find there are many directed edge $< v_k, v_j >$, where $\{v_k | v_k \in r_{i,j}\}$. Targeted to this problem, we apply deep first search(DFS) algorithm to remove redundant edge, which is explained in Algorithm 2.

Bayes Classifier Chain. If the DAG has been established, the training process is following Algorithm 3. We chose some special options for general training procedures. Firstly, in the training process, if we want to train a classifier for label y_i, we select the actual class value of the ancestor label node about the y_i given in the original training set instead of the prediction value in training, which will tend to produce more accurate classifiers. Secondly, we use all ancestor nodes of the label that will be training as the additional input features besides the symptoms, because this scheme conforms to the general way of thinking for TCM doctors.

Algorithm 3 shows the training procedure in detail. This algorithm references the DFS algorithm and makes some modification. We ensure that if a label node will be training, all of its ancestor nodes have been ended their training process. When we train along one path and counter a node that has more than one indegree, we will add the additional feature of this node's parent node in the path and decrease this node's in-degree by one. Then we start from other paths until this node's in-degree equal zero. If so, we can continue from this node.

3.2   Cost Sensitve SVM

The BCC can solve the label correlation problem in our prescription generation task to some degree. But there still exists the class imbalance problem, so we will improve our model in the aspect of the basic classifier. We selected the cost-sensitive SVM [10] as the basic classifier for BCC algorithm.

Bayes Consistent of Standard Binary Classifier. For binary-classify task, the goal is to predict an ubobserve value $y \in \{+1, -1\}$ based on an observed input vector $\mathbf{x}$. This requires us to train a functional relationship $y = h(\mathbf{x})$ from a set of example pairs of $(\mathbf{x}, y)$. From a statistical viewpoint, the feature vectors

Algorithm 2. Simplify the DAG of herb labels node.

Input: The adjacent matrix D of the original DAG: $G = <V, E>$,
  Sign array $Signlist = \{0\}^{num(V)}$, where $num(V)$ is the vertex number of V,
  The different connected component flag, $Sign = 0$,
  The matrix $D' = \{0\}^{num(V) \times num(V)}$.
Output: The adjacent matrix D' of the simplified DAG: $G' = <V, E'>$;
1: **function DFS**$(i, num(V))$:
2:　　**For** $j = i + 1$; $j < num(V)$; $j + +$ **do**
3:　　　**if** $D[i][j] = 1$ **and** $Signlist[j]! = Sign$ **then**
4:　　　　$D'[i][j] \leftarrow 1$ //　　　Add directed edge $e = <i, j>$ to E'
5:　　　　$Signlist[j] \leftarrow Sign$
6:　　　　**DFS**$(j, num(V))$
7:　　　**end if**
8:　　**return**
9: **end function**
10:
11: **For** $i = 0$; $i < num(V)$; $i + +$ **do**
12:　　$Sign \leftarrow Sign + 1$
13:　　**DFS**$(i, num(V))$
14: **retrun** D'

---

and class labels can be regarded as random variable possessing probability distributions $P_X(\mathbf{x})$ and $P_Y(y)$ respectively. We write the classifier function as the form that $h(\mathbf{x}) = sign[p(\mathbf{x})]$, where the function $p : \mathcal{X} \to \mathbb{R}$. A non-negative function $L(p(\mathbf{x}), y)$ be deemed as the loss function for each $(p(\mathbf{x}), y)$ pair. The classifier is considered optimal if it minimizes the expected loss $R = E_{\mathbf{X}, Y}[L(p(\mathbf{x}), y)]$, also known as the expected risk. Minimizing the expected loss also equivalent to minimizing the conditional risk

$$E_{Y|\mathbf{X}}[L(p(\mathbf{x}), y)|\mathbf{X} = \mathbf{x}] = P_{Y|\mathbf{X}}(1|\mathbf{x})L(p(\mathbf{x}), 1) + (1 - P_{Y|\mathbf{X}}(1|\mathbf{x}))L(p(\mathbf{x}), -1) \tag{2}$$

To make it easier to understand this formula in probability way, we can write the predictor function $p(\mathbf{x})$ as a composition of two functions $p(\mathbf{x}) = f(\eta(\mathbf{x}))$, where $\eta(\mathbf{x}) = P_{Y|\mathbf{X}}(1|\mathbf{x})$ is the posterior probability. $f : [0, 1] \to \mathbb{R}$ is called the link function in this paper, which establishes a connection to Bayes decision rule by this means. The Bayes error rate of the data distribution is the probability that an instance is misclassified by a classifier which knows the true class probabilities given the predictors. We hope minimized *conditional risk* closed to the Bayes error. Assuming the true probability distribution has been known, if we want to minimize the conditional risk, we can select the suited link function f when the loss function L is fixed.

The ϕ is the concrete form of the loss function L, such as the hinge loss in SVM $\phi(yf) = \lfloor 1 - yf \rfloor_+$, where $\lfloor x \rfloor = max(0, x)$. The f is the function of η, but for simplicity, we omit the η. Because the loss function ϕ may be different in a false positive and false negative, these cost-sensitive loss function can also be written as a unified form

Algorithm 3. Training BCC based on DAG.

Input: The adjacent matrix D' of the simplified DAG: $G' =< V, E' >$;
  The array of sum about every node in-degree, Sum_in;
  The additional feature sets of all herb label nodes, $T_0, T_1, T_2, \cdots = \emptyset$;
  The basic classifier $f(\cdot)$;
  The symptom feature set X.
Output: The BCC classifier F;
 1: **for** $k = 0; k < num(V); k + +$ **do**
 2:    $Sumin[k] \leftarrow sum(D[\cdot][k])//$ compute the indegree of each node
 3:
 4: **function** $\textbf{Training}(i, num(V), T')$:
 5:    $Sum\_in[i] \leftarrow Sum\_in[i] - 1$;
 6:    **if** $Sum\_in[i]! = 0$ **then**
 7:       **return**
 8:    **else**
 9:       The eventual input set X'_i for $f_i(\cdot)$: $X' \leftarrow X \cup T_i$
10:       Use the sample in input feature set X' and target set y_i train $f_i(\cdot)$
11:       **for** $j = i + 1; j < num(V); j + +$ **do**
12:          $T_i \leftarrow T_i \cup T'$;
13:          $\textbf{Training}(j, num(V), T_i)$
14:       **return**
15:    **end if**
16: **end function**
17:
18: **do**
19:    **for** $u = 0; u < num(V); u + +$ **do**
20:       **if** $Sum\_in[u] = 0$ **then**
21:          $\textbf{Training}(u, num(V), T_u)$
22:          **break**
23:       **end if**
24: **while** $u! = num(V) - 1$
25: **return** BCC classifier $F(\cdot) = \left[f_0, f_1, f_2, \ldots, f_{num(v)-1}\right]$

$$L_{\phi, C_1, C_{-1}} = \phi_{C_1, C_{-1}}(yf) = \begin{cases} \phi_1(f), & \text{if } y = 1; \\ \phi_{-1}(f), & \text{if } y = -1. \end{cases} \tag{3}$$

We get the cost-sensitive conditional risk from (2) and (3)

$$C_{\phi, C_1, C_{-1}}(\eta, f) = \eta \phi_1(f) + (1 - \eta)\phi_{-1}(-f) \tag{4}$$

There exists a suitable link function $f_\phi^*(\eta)$ and it can minimized the conditional risk $C_{\phi, C_1, C_{-1}}$.

Cost Sensitive SVM Loss Function. In this section, we will expand the hinge loss function to cost-sensitive version. The loss function of standard SVM is hinge loss, $\phi(yf) = \lfloor 1 - yf \rfloor_+$,where $\lfloor x \rfloor = max(0, x)$. Refer to [20] , the optimal link function for standard SVM is

$$f_\phi^*(\eta) = sign(2\eta - 1) \tag{5}$$

and the minimum conditional risk is

$$C_\phi^*(\eta) = 1 - -2|2\eta - 1| \tag{6}$$
$$= \eta\lfloor 1 - sign(2\eta - 1)\rfloor_+ + (1 - \eta)\lfloor 1 + sign(2\eta - 1)\rfloor_+$$

We modify the optimal link function of standard SVM by cost-sensitive parameter naturally

$$f_{\phi,C_1,C_{-1}}^*(\eta) = sign((C_1 + C_{-1})\eta - C_{-1}) \tag{7}$$

Like the conditional risk of standard SVM $C_\phi^*(\eta)$, we get the cost-sensitive counterpart

$$C_{\phi,C_1,C_{-1}}^*(\eta) = \eta\lfloor e - d \cdot sign((C_1 + C_{-1})\eta - C_{-1})\rfloor_+ + \tag{8}$$
$$(1 - \eta)\lfloor b + a \cdot sign((C_1 + C_{-1})\eta - C_{-1})\rfloor_+$$

where

$$d \geq e, \quad a \geq b, \quad \frac{C_{-1}}{C_1} = \frac{a+b}{d+e} \tag{9}$$

and the a, b, d, e are positive number. Then we can easily find that

$$sign((C_{-1} + C_1)\eta - C_{-1}) = \begin{cases} 1, & \text{if } \eta \geq \gamma \\ 0, & \text{if } \eta = \gamma \\ -1, & \text{if } \eta \leq \gamma \end{cases} \tag{10}$$

where $\gamma = \frac{C_{-1}}{C_1+C_{-1}}$. If $\eta < \gamma$, the risk is

$$C_{\phi,C_1,C_{-1}}^*(\eta) = \eta\lfloor e + d\rfloor_+ + (1 - \eta)\lfloor b - a\rfloor_+ \tag{11}$$

At last, like the form of the hinge loss about standard SVM, the loss function of cost-sensitive SVM can be deduced

$$\phi_{C_1,C_{-1}}(yf) = \begin{cases} \lfloor e - df \rfloor_+, & \text{if } y = 1; \\ \lfloor b + af \rfloor_+, & \text{if } y = -1; \end{cases} \tag{12}$$

There are four freedom degrees in this hinge loss function, which control the margin and slope of two class respectively. The positive class divide by margin $\frac{e}{d}$ and slope d of hinge loss and the negative class divide by margin $\frac{b}{a}$ and slope a of hinge loss.

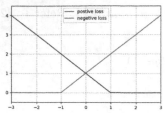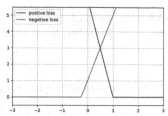

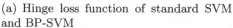

(a) Hinge loss function of standard SVM and BP-SVM

(b) Hinge loss function of CS-SVM

Fig. 4. The (a) is the hinge loss of standard SVM and BP-SVM, $\phi(yf) = max(0, 1 - yf)$. The (b) is the hinge loss of CS-SVM, where $C_{+1} = 6, C_{-1} = 2.5, \lambda = 2C_{-1} - 1 = 4$, positive loss is $\phi_{+1}(yf) = max(0, 6 - 6yf)$, negative loss is $\phi_{-1}(yf) = max(0, 1 + 4yf)$.

Cost Sensitive SVM Algorithm. In the previous section, the loss function of cost-sensitive SVM have four freedom degree but in fact, there are only two freedom degree in conditional risk function $C^*_{\phi, C_1, C_{-1}}$. We can find that we only need the proportional relation between the two class slope, $\frac{e}{d}$ and $\frac{b}{a}$. So we suppose that the positive class weight is more important, which requires the slope and margin of positive class is higher than the counterpart of negative class,

$$\frac{e}{d} \geq \frac{b}{a} \quad d \geq a \tag{13}$$

and then fix the $\frac{e}{d} = 1$ and set $e = d = C_1$ in order to specify the postive class margin. In a similar way, we only need the proportional relation between the a and b. The b can be set at 1, the accord to the third folumation of (9), $a = 2C_{-1} - 1$. At last, we bring the value of a, b, d, e into (8) and obtain the resulting cost sensitive SVM minimal conditional risk is

$$C^*_{\phi, C_1, C_{-1}}(\eta) = \eta \lfloor C_1 - C_1 \cdot sign((C_1 + C_{-1})\eta - C_{-1}) \rfloor_+ + \tag{14}$$
$$(1 - \eta) \lfloor 1 + (2C_{-1} - 1) \cdot sign((C_1 + C_{-1})\eta - C_{-1}) \rfloor_+$$

with $C_{-1} \geq 1, C_1 \geq 2C_{-1} - 1$ in order to satisfy (13). The intuitional explanation is that the positive class has a larger margin that can make the separating hyperplane deviated to negative class and have a higher slope can increase the cost risk when occurring misclassification.

There the standard SVM risk can be modified by the cost-sensitive method:

$$arg \min_{w,b} \sum_{\{i|y_i=1\}} \lfloor C_1 - C_1(w^T x_i + b) \rfloor_+ \tag{15}$$
$$+ \sum_{\{i|y_i=-1\}} \lfloor 1 + (2C_{-1} - 1)(w^T x_i + b) \rfloor_+ + \mu ||w||^2$$

then deduce to a primer optimization problem

$$arg \min_{w,b,\xi} \frac{1}{2}||w||^2 + C \left[\beta \sum_{\{i|y_i=1\}} \xi_i + \lambda \sum_{\{i|y_i=-1\}} \xi_i \right] \tag{16}$$

$$\text{s.t. } y_i(w^T x + b) \geq 1 - \xi_i, y_i = 1$$
$$y_i(w^T x + b) \geq \kappa - \xi_i, y_i = -1$$

with

$$\beta = C_1 \quad \lambda = 2C_{-1} - 1 \quad \kappa = \frac{1}{2C_{-1} - 1} \tag{17}$$

In this quadratic programming problem, the cost-sensitivity is controlled by the three parameters β, γ, κ. The β, γ decide the relative weights of margin violations and pay more attention to positive class on the constraint that $C_{-1} \geq 1, C_1 \geq 2C_{-1} - 1$. When the data are separated, the BP-SVM(1) has a defect that the optimization procedure tends to select larger the parameter C in BM-SVM(1), in that circumstances, the cost-sensitive parameter C_1, C_{-1} will be ineffective and degenerate into standard SVM. But in this model, the κ can shrink to narrow the margin rather than increase the common slack penalty C. The Fig. 4 shows that the distinction of loss function between standard SVM, BP-SVM, and CS-SVM. The SVM's margin is the X-intercept and the X-intercept of BP-SVM is 1 and -1, but the negative loss X-intercept's absolute value of CS-SVM is smaller than 1.

4 Experiment

In this section, we conduct several experiments to compare the performance of CS-SVM with BP-SVM and standard SVM with BR and BCC algorithm. We implement our method by the SVM library libsvm[1].

Table 2. The prescription dataset

Quantity of total sample	Input feature	Output labels
10052	189	357

4.1 Dataset

Our dataset consists of 10000+ TCM prescriptions targeted to lung cancer, which were provided by the cooperative hospital. Our prescription dataset D has been shown in Table 2. The quantity of the total sample is 10052, in which the dimension of input feature(the symptom) is 189 and the number of the output labels(the herbs) is 357. The proportion of training set to test set is 9:1. The data will be upload our github[2].

[1] https://www.csie.ntu.edu.tw/cjlin/libsvm/.
[2] https://github.com/xbybshd/TCM-prescription-dataset.

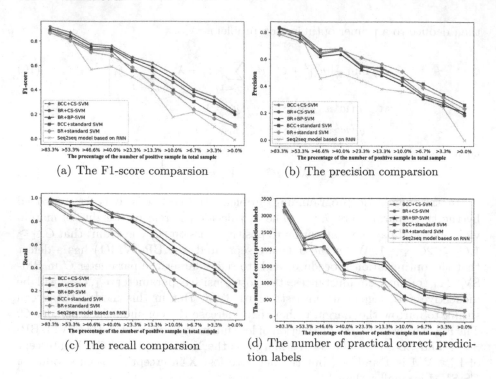

(a) The F1-score comparsion   (b) The precision comparsion

(c) The recall comparsion   (d) The number of practical correct predicition labels

Fig. 5. The multi-label evaluation of the samples which are classified by the degree of imbalance of every label, we applied BR+standard SVM, BCC+standard SVM, BR+BP−SVM, BR+CS−SVM, BCC+CS−SVM and a Seq2seq RNN model.

4.2   Multi-label Classifiy Evaluation Index

To test these three SVM models on class imbalance data, we classify these labels according to the percentage of the number of positive samples in the total sample. The percentage of a label is more deviate 50%, the data in this label are more imbalance. The evaluation indexes we adopt are the common metrics in multi-label classification, such as precision, recall, specificity, F1-score, and G-means. To test the performance in the practical application more clearly, we statistics the raw number of the label in prediction set, validation set and the intersection of prediction and validation. Besides, the total cost is also be applied to evaluate the cost sensitivity of the model, which is also the cost-sensitive zero-one risk. The $Totalcost = P_1 C_1 P_{FN} + P_{-1} C_{-1} P_{FP}$, where P_1 and P_{-1} are the class priors probability and P_{FN} and P_{FP} are the false negative and false positive rates respectively.

4.3   Result in Prescription Dataset

Table 3 is the global evaluation of three SVM methods on our test dataset and we can find that the BCC+CS−SVM exhibits the best on F1-score. Although the precision is lower than standard BR+standard SVM, it is the tradeoff for expanding the prediction scale to obtain more correct labels. We also applied a recent deep-learning model proposed by Wei Li [7] on our data, which is based on the RNN seq2seq model for a prescription generation. But the total evaluation of the RNN seq2seq model is lower than the SVM models.

Figure 5 is the comparison between five SVM methods and the Seq2seq RNN model on the labels classified by different degrees of imbalance. The 357 labels are classified by the percentage of themselves a positive sample in the total sample. Each part in the Fig. 5 doesn't have the inclusion relation, for example, that the ¿53.3% represents the part of ¡83.3% and ¿53.3%.

Table 3. The evaluation of the total sample

	F1-score	Precision	Recall	G-means	Total cost
BR+Standard-SVM	0.591	**0.644**	0.545	0.734	null
BCC+Standard-SVM	0.604	0.641	0.57	0.748	null
BR+BP-SVM	0.606	0.534	0.701	0.821	16.575
BR+CS-SVM	0.618	0.538	0.723	0.834	15.878
BCC+CS-SVM	**0.638**	0.551	**0.757**	**0.853**	**15.743**
Seq2seq model based RNN	0.533	0.551	0.516	0.711	null

In two standard SVM model, we can find the model used BCC algorithm is slightly better than the BR algorithm in Fig. 5, and the BCC model(green line) also have higher total F1-score in Table 3. The Similar situation also appears in three cost-sensitive SVM model. These phenomena prove that our BCC algorithm can improve the performance of the prescription generation model. When the doctor makes a prescription, the BCC method can consider the correlation between the herbs compared with the BR method, such as the classical rule that "The eighteen incompatible medicaments, the nineteen medicaments of mutual restraint".

In the three BR algorithm model, although the precision of BR+standard SVM is higher than others in Table 3, the BP-SVM and CS-SVM have higher recall and F1-score. It is a critical problem that the evaluation index on the total sample of the standard SVM is slightly lower than BP-SVM and CS-SVM, but if we consider the imbalance degree of every labels, in Fig. 5(a)(c)(d), we can find the three evaluation on standard SVM, the F1-score, recall and the number of practical correct prediction labels, are obviously less than counterparts of BP-SVM and CS-SVM. This phenomenon is more serious if the data of certain labels are more imbalance, which confirms the previous analysis that the standard SVM will push the separating hyperplane to the minority class and results in a few predictions. In practical application, doctors hope the model to pay attention to the minority label rather than omit them simply.

As for the comparison between BP-SVM and CS-SVM, the fifth column of Table 3 is the comparison of the total cost between the BP-SVM and CS-SVM and the cost of CS-SVM is less than BP-SVM. The total cost is also the expectable risk of the model, the lower risk indicates the error rate of this model is more close to the Bayes error rate. In other evaluation indexes, such as F1-score, the CS-SVM is also higher than the BP-SVM.

The performance of the RNN Seq2seq model is similar to the three SVM models in some class balance labels but the evaluation becomes lower and lower with the increase of the label unbalancedness, which performs worse than the standard SVM. We believe this result is because the deep learning model relies on mass data, but the number of the most unbalanced label positive sample often less than 100. In the training process, the small quantity of the sample makes the deep model overfit. But it is impossible that there is an enormous quantity of the single-disease prescriptions in the practical clinical situation so the deep learning can't exert its advantage in this situation.

5   Conclusion

TCM is one of the most significant complementary and alternative medicine and it plays an important role in the therapy of lung cancer. However, the therapeutic process of TCM lacks standardization like modern medical. Targeted to the herb correlation and class imbalance problem in clinical TCM prescription, we combined the Bayes classifier chain algorithm (BCC) and cost-sensitive SVM to process the firsthand clinical TCM prescription and construct a simple TCM prescription generating model. In detail, the BCC method was modified based on the feature of TCM prescriptions and the cost-sensitive modifications were added on standard SVM, such as bias penalty and amending the hinge loss. These modifications have obtained better performance in our clinical TCM dataset. But this model still has some room for improvement, for example, the correlations between the herbs are complex, and maybe we can try other better methods to mine these relationships to make our model adapt the more real complex clinical situation.

References

1. Akbani, R., Kwek, S., Japkowicz, N.: Applying support vector machines to imbalanced datasets. In: Boulicaut, J.-F., Esposito, F., Giannotti, F., Pedreschi, D. (eds.) ECML 2004. LNCS (LNAI), vol. 3201, pp. 39–50. Springer, Heidelberg (2004). https://doi.org/10.1007/978-3-540-30115-8_7
2. Bach, F.R., Heckerman, D., Horvitz, E.: Considering cost asymmetry in learning classifiers. J. Mach. Learn. Res. 7(Aug), 1713–1741 (2006)
3. Boutell, M.R., Luo, J., Shen, X., Brown, C.M.: Learning multi-label scene classification. Pattern Recogn. 37(9), 1757–1771 (2004)
4. Chawla, N.V., Bowyer, K.W., Hall, L.O., Kegelmeyer, W.P.: Smote: synthetic minority over-sampling technique. J. Artif. Intell. Res. 16, 321–357 (2002)
5. Cheng, W., Hüllermeier, E., Dembczynski, K.J.: Bayes optimal multilabel classification via probabilistic classifier chains. In: Proceedings of the 27th International Conference on Machine Learning (ICML-10), pp. 279–286 (2010)

6. Kubat, M., et al.: Addressing the curse of imbalanced training sets: one-sided selection. In: Icml, vol. 97, pp. 179–186. Nashville, USA (1997)
7. Li, W., Yang, Z., Sun, X.: Exploration on generating traditional Chinese medicine prescription from symptoms with an end-to-end method. arXiv preprint (2018). arXiv:1801.09030
8. Liu, R., et al.: Chinese herbal decoction based on syndrome differentiation as maintenance therapy in patients with extensive-stage small-cell lung cancer: an exploratory and small prospective cohort study. Evid. Based Complement. Altern. Med. **2015** (2015)
9. Ma, J., Wang, Z.: Discovering syndrome regularities in traditional Chinese medicine clinical by topic model. 3PGCIC 2016. LNDECT, vol. 1, pp. 157–162. Springer, Cham (2017). https://doi.org/10.1007/978-3-319-49109-7_15
10. Masnadi-Shirazi, H., Vasconcelos, N., Iranmehr, A.: Cost-sensitive support vector machines. arXiv preprint (2012). arXiv:1212.0975
11. Read, J., Martino, L., Olmos, P.M., Luengo, D.: Scalable multi-output label prediction: from classifier chains to classifier trellises. Pattern Recogn. **48**(6), 2096–2109 (2015)
12. Read, J., Pfahringer, B., Holmes, G., Frank, E.: Classifier chains for multi-label classification. Mach. Learn. **85**(3), 333 (2011)
13. Ruan, C., Wang, Y., Zhang, Y., Yang, Y.: Exploring regularity in traditional Chinese medicine clinical data using heterogeneous weighted networks embedding. In: Li, G., Yang, J., Gama, J., Natwichai, J., Tong, Y. (eds.) DASFAA 2019. LNCS, vol. 11448, pp. 310–313. Springer, Cham (2019). https://doi.org/10.1007/978-3-030-18590-9_35
14. Sucar, L.E., Bielza, C., Morales, E.F., Hernandez-Leal, P., Zaragoza, J.H., Larrañaga, P.: Multi-label classification with bayesian network-based chain classifiers. Pattern Recogn. Lett. **41**, 14–22 (2014)
15. Torre, L.A., Bray, F., Siegel, R.L., Ferlay, J., Lortet-Tieulent, J., Jemal, A.: Global cancer statistics, 2012. CA Cancer J. Clin. **65**(2), 87–108 (2015)
16. Tsoumakas, G., Vlahavas, I.: Random k-labelsets: an ensemble method for multilabel classification. In: Kok, J.N., Koronacki, J., Mantaras, R.L., Matwin, S., Mladenič, D., Skowron, A. (eds.) ECML 2007. LNCS (LNAI), vol. 4701, pp. 406–417. Springer, Heidelberg (2007). https://doi.org/10.1007/978-3-540-74958-5_38
17. Wu, G., Chang, E.Y.: Adaptive feature-space conformal transformation for imbalanced-data learning. In: Proceedings of the 20th International Conference on Machine Learning (ICML-03), pp. 816–823 (2003)
18. Xu, Q., Tang, W., Teng, F., Peng, W., Zhang, Y., Li, W., Wen, C., Guo, J.: Intelligent syndrome differentiation of traditional chinese medicine by ANN: a case study of chronic obstructive pulmonary disease. IEEE Access **7**, 76167–76175 (2019)
19. Yao, L., Zhang, Y., Wei, B., Zhang, W., Jin, Z.: A topic modeling approach for traditional chinese medicine prescriptions. IEEE Trans. Knowl. Data Eng. **30**(6), 1007–1021 (2018)
20. Zhang, T., et al.: Statistical behavior and consistency of classification methods based on convex risk minimization. Ann. Stat. **32**(1), 56–85 (2004)

A Spatial and Sequential Combined Method for Web Service Classification

Xin Wang[1], Jin Liu[1(✉)], Xiao Liu[2], Xiaohui Cui[3], and Hao Wu[4]

[1] School of Computer Science, Wuhan University, Wuhan, China
{xinwang0920,jinliu}@whu.edu.cn
[2] School of Information Technology, Deakin University, Geelong, Australia
xiao.liu@deakin.edu.au
[3] School of Cyber Science and Engineering, Wuhan University, Wuhan, China
xcui@whu.edu.cn
[4] School of Information Science and Engineering, Yunnan University,
Kunming, China
haowu@ynu.edu.cn

Abstract. With the growing prosperity of the Web service ecosystem, high-quality service classification has become an essential requirement. Web service description documents are semantic definitions of services, which is edited by service developers to include not only usage scenarios and functions of services but also a lot of prior knowledge and jargons. However, at present, existing deep learning models cannot fully extract the heterogeneous features of service description documents, resulting in unsatisfactory service classification results. In this paper, we propose a novel deep neural network which integrates the Graph Convolutional Network (GCN) with Bidirectional Long Short-Term Memory (Bi-LSTM) network to automatically extract the features of function description documents for Web services. Specifically, we first utilize a two-layer GCN to extract global spatial structure features of Web services, which serves as a pre-training word embedding process. Afterwards, the sequential features of Web services learned from the Bi-LSTM model are integrated for joint training of parameters. Experimental results demonstrate that our proposed method outperforms various state-of-the-art methods in classification performance.

Keywords: Web service classification · Graph convolutional network · Bidirectional-LSTM

1 Introduction

Web service is a new paradigm in software technology that reduces software development costs through service reuse.Web services provide application programming interfaces for Web applications to implement storage services, information services, computing services and other functions. Various assets, data and services of the enterprise can be accessed by users through the Internet, which

© Springer Nature Switzerland AG 2020
X. Wang et al. (Eds.): APWeb-WAIM 2020, LNCS 12317, pp. 764–778, 2020.
https://doi.org/10.1007/978-3-030-60259-8_56

creates huge economic benefits. In the era of big data, Web service is a kind of service resource with great value-added potential. It has become a common and central interest in both academia and industry. ProgrammableWeb is the largest online Web service registry, which includes more than 22,000 Web services by November 1, 2019. As Web services become the backbone of the Web, mobile, cloud, and software development, Web service ecosystem is emerging and growing rapidly [15]. In recent years, the Web service ecosystem has accumulated a wealth of resources that can be used to provide rich application interfaces, accelerate the software development process, search and integrate multiple services to meet software requirements.

The foundation for achieving high-quality service reuse is the accurate classification of Web services so that software developers can find the Web services they need for their specific development goals [16]. The keyword-based method is an efficient method for service discovery. Unfortunately, with the rapid growth of the Web service ecosystem, a large number of Web services have been developed and submitted to online Web service registries for sharing by service developers. The vocabulary gap between developers leads to a lack of uniform specifications for Web service descriptions and keyword representations. As a result, it is difficult for service users to efficiently find the services they need in a short time.

In recent years, researchers in the field of Web services have made significant efforts to address this issue. Existing works can be roughly divided into two categories. The first category is to use conventional machine learning methods with high-quality feature engineering to predict service categories [1,5,6,11,12,17]. Various methods such as Support Vector Machines (SVM), Naive Bayes, Random Forest (RF), AdaBoost, Topic Modeling and different features such as texts, topics and internal invocation relationships are employed to enhance the accuracy of service classification. The second category is to use various deep learning technologies to obtain representations automatically [3,8,10,19,21,22]. For example, Convolutional Neural Network (CNN), Recurrent Neural Network (RNN), also their variants and combinations (LSTM, GRU, Bi-LSTM, C-LSTM, RCNN) are used to improve classification performance. In general, most conventional machine learning based methods heavily depends on high-quality feature engineering. However, the selection of features is inherently subjective and limited, and often cannot be extended to other datasets. Meanwhile, manual feature engineering is often time-consuming, labor-intensive and costly. In addition, existing Web service classification methods based on single deep learning architecture cannot fully exploit the service information. For example, CNN focuses on capturing local spatial features of adjacent entities, while RNN only focuses on capturing sequential features. Given the large amount of heterogeneous graph structural data accumulated in the Web service ecosystem, it is difficult to take full advantage of them. For example, the implicit co-invocation relationships between Mashups (service composition) and APIs (services) in invocation history are difficult to be extracted and utilized by the general deep learning models.

In this paper, we propose a novel classification framework based on Graph Convolutional Network (GCN) and Bidirectional Long Short-Term Memory

(Bi-LSTM) Network for Web service classification on 50 categories without any manual feature engineering and extra knowledge. Firstly, we construct a large heterogeneous graph with Web service function description documents. Then, we utilize a two-layer GCN model to capture global word co-occurrence information and document-word relationships. Finally, we integrate the spatial structure features captured by GCN (as a pre-training step) with the sequential features captured by Bi-LSTM network for joint training of parameters. This method takes full account of the spatial and sequential features of Web service descriptions, and achieves robust classification performance.

The main contributions of this paper can be summarized as follows:

- We have proposed a GCN and Bi-LSTM based Web service classification method by capturing service function description information. To the best of our knowledge, this is the first study that GCN is used (as a way of pre-training) to classify Web services.
- Our proposed method can effectively integrate global spatial feature with a single sequential feature, providing a new idea for comprehensive feature extraction of service description documents.
- Through comprehensive experiments on real-world data, it is proven that our proposed method can achieve more accurate classification results than various state-of-the-art methods in Top-N accuracy and F1-macro.

The rest of the paper is structured as follows. Section II provides some backgrounds on the technologies used and analysis of Web service classification based on function description documents. Section III presents the details about our proposed method. Section IV demonstrates the experimental results. Section V reviews some recent studies. Finally, Section VI summarizes our work and point out future research directions.

2 Preliminaries

2.1 Graph Convolutional Network

Graph Convolutional Network (GCN) [9] operates directly on a graph, and obtains embedding vectors of nodes according to the adjacent features of nodes, so as to effectively learn and represent the graph structural data. Generally speaking, we define an undirected graph $G = (V, E)$, where $V(|V| = N)$ is the set of N nodes and E is the set of edges. We respectively use $A \in \mathbb{R}^{N \times N}$ and D to represent the adjacency matrix and degree matrix of G, where $Dii = \sum_j Aij$. Every node is assumed to be self-connected, so we set matrix $A = A + I$ ($I \in \mathbb{R}^{N \times N}$ is the identity matrix). $X \in \mathbb{R}^{N \times M}$ is a matrix of node feature vectors Xi, where M is the dimension of the feature vectors. A multilayer GCN has the following propagation rules:

$$L^{(l+1)} = \rho \left(D^{-\frac{1}{2}} A D^{-\frac{1}{2}} L^{(l)} W^{(l)} \right) \tag{1}$$

Where l denotes the layer number and $L^{(0)} = X$. Here, $W^{(l)}$ is the trainable weight matrix of the lth layer. $\rho(.)$ is an activation function, such as a ReLU $\rho(.) = max(0, x)$.

Figure 1 gives a simple schematic of GCN for feature learning of texts, which includes document entities, word entities as well as relationships among them. Through the semi-supervised learning by GCN, the entire corpus maps from the input channel (C) to the feature embedding (F). Labels are denoted by $Label_i$.

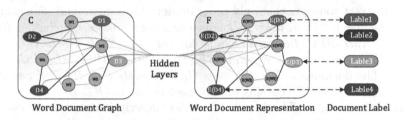

Fig. 1. A sample schema of GCN for entire corpus. Nodes begin with 'W' are word nodes, others are document nodes. Relationships between documents and words are connected with solid black lines, and word co-occurrence information is connected with solid orange lines. $E(x)$ means the embedded representation of x. Different colors for documents indicate different categories.

2.2 Long Short-Term Memory Network

Long Short-Term Memory (LSTM) [7] network is proposed to solve the gradient disappearance problem in the structure of recurrent neural networks. LSTM eliminates or adds information to the cell state through a carefully designed gate structure (input gate Γ_i, forget gate Γ_f, and output gate Γ_o), enabling LSTM to remember long-term information, forget unimportant information, and effectively avoid long-term dependencies. In terms of details, the update steps of LSTM network are defined by the following equations:

$$\widetilde{C}^{(t)} = tanh(W_{ch} * H^{(t-1)} + W_{cy} * Y^{(t)} + b_c) \tag{2}$$

$$\Gamma_i^{(t)} = \sigma(W_{ih} * H^{(t-1)} + W_{iy} * Y^{(t)} + b_i) \tag{3}$$

$$\Gamma_f^{(t)} = \sigma(W_{fh} * H^{(t-1)} + W_{fy} * Y^{(t)} + b_f) \tag{4}$$

$$\Gamma_o^{(t)} = \sigma(W_{oh} * H^{(t-1)} + W_{oy} * Y^{(t)} + b_o) \tag{5}$$

$$C^{(t)} = \Gamma_f^{(t)} \odot C^{(t-1)} + \Gamma_i^{(t)} \odot \widetilde{C}^{(t)} \tag{6}$$

$$H^{(t)} = \Gamma_o^{(t)} \odot tanh(C^{(t)}) \tag{7}$$

Here, $\Gamma_i, \Gamma_f, \Gamma_o$ correspond to input gate, forget gate and output gate, respectively. C and H each refer to the memory cell and hidden state during network update process, where $\widetilde{C}$ is the candidate memory of C. $\odot$ denotes element-wise multiplication, all W are weight matrixs, and all b are learned biases. Y is calculated as the input of LSTM layer at each time step t.

2.3   Problem Analysis

Function description documents of Web services are written and submitted by service developers to summarize the main functions, usage scenarios and precautions of services. The style of the service description documents are different from news, reviews, and Wikipedia entries. The following issues of the service description documents make service classification challenging:

- **Domain Semantics.** Service description documents often contain jargons and abstract concepts that only programmers can understand. For example, the document *"The Flickr API supports many protocols including REST, SOAP, XML-RPC. Responses can be formatted in XML, XML-RPC, JSON and PHP."* contains many terms *REST, SOAP, XML, XML-RPC, JSON, PHP*. The document *"The API uses GET requests over HTTPS and JSON for requests/returns"* contains the abstract concept *GET*.
- **Variable Length.** The length of service description document can vary widely, ranging from several words like *"For Windows Vista sidebar."*, to long sentences like *"It's about The Concepts The BeliefNetworks service is about discovering..."* including more than 1400 words. This variable-length text feature in service description document makes it difficult to achieve satisfactory classification results by using single feature extraction method.
- **Polysemy.** Polysemy is common in sentence expressions, and which is often accompanied by domain knowledge in service description document. such as *libraries, windows* in sentences mentioned above.
- **Abbreviation.** The diversity and complexity of the Web service ecosystem lead to a lack of uniform services description specifications, which make service providers often use abbreviations in description documents such as *ads(advertisements)*, *geo(geographical)*, and *DP(Developer Platform)*, etc.

These four characteristics exhibited in service description documents make single feature extraction method hard to work. Extracting potential features of different aspects in service descriptions through a combination of different feature extractors is a promising solution to address challenges mentioned above.

In this paper, given the service description documents, we first distinguish document-word relationships and word-word relationships in the entire corpus, then we construct a huge heterogeneous graph to describe intrinsic associations. Next, we utilize a two-layer GCN to extract global spatial structure information of Web services which is regarded as a pre-training step. Afterwards, we integrate the global spatial structure information with the sequential features learned from the Bi-LSTM model using pre-trained word embeddings for joint training of parameters. Finally, the classification result is obtained through a *softmax* classifier.

3   Proposed Method

In this section, we will present the details of our proposed method. The overall framework is shown in Fig. 2.

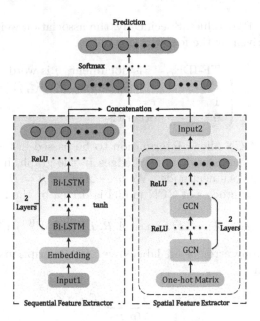

Fig. 2. A visualized architecture of our model. On the left is a sequential feature extractor that learns the sequential features through a two-layer Bi-LSTM model. On the right is a spatial feature extractor that learns global word co-occurrence information and document-word association through a two-layer GCN. "One-hot matrix" means that we use one-hot vectors to represent documents and unique words.

3.1 Spatial Feature Extractor

We use function description documents of all Web services to construct a huge heterogeneous graph. The number of nodes in the text graph is the sum of the number of documents and the number of unique words. At the beginning, we use the one-hot vector to represent each word or document. In a nutshell, we initialize the feature matrix $X = I$ (identity matrix) as the input to the GCN. We create edges for nodes in the graph based on the occurrence of words in the document and the relationship between words in the whole corpus. The weight of the edge between a word node and a document node is defined according to the term frequency-inverse document frequency (TF-IDF) value. According to the term frequency (TF) indicator, a word is more important in principle if it appears more frequently in the document. Meanwhile, if a word appears frequently in various documents, its ability to distinguish different documents will be weakened. To this end, an inverse document frequency (IDF) indicator is introduced to measure the contribution of a word to a document in the corpus. We use a fixed-size sliding window (20 words by default) on all documents to get the word co-occurrence information. We utilize point-wise mutual information (PMI) indicator to get the weight of the association between two word nodes only with positive PMI values. Specifically, the association weight between node i and node j is driven by the following formula:

$$
A_{ij} = \begin{cases}
\text{TF-IDF}_{ij} & i \text{ is document, } j \text{ is word} \\
\text{PMI}(i,j) & i,j \text{ are words, } \text{PMI}(i,j) > 0 \\
1 & i = j \\
0 & \text{otherwise}
\end{cases} \tag{8}
$$

The two-layer GCN allows information to be passed in two steps, although there is no direct document-document edges in the graph, information can be exchanged between document nodes. We pre-calculate $\hat{A} = D^{-\frac{1}{2}}AD^{-\frac{1}{2}}$, then the forward propagation process of GCN model is driven by the following equation:

$$
Z = f(X, A) = softmax\left(\hat{A}\ ReLU(\hat{A}XW^{(0)})W^{(1)}\right) \tag{9}
$$

The cross-entropy error of all labeled service descriptions is driven by the following equation:

$$
Loss = -\sum_{d \in \mathcal{T}_D} \sum_{f=1}^{F_{dim}} T_{df} \ln Z_{df} \tag{10}
$$

The weight parameters $W^{(0)}$ and $W^{(1)}$ are trained using gradient descent. Specifically, $\mathcal{T}_D$ denotes the set of document indices which have labels. F_{dim} stands for embedded dimension of the output features, which is consistent with the number of categories. T is the label indicator matrix.

3.2 Sequential Feature Extractor

LSTM network as a variant of recurrent neural networks is designed to learn the long-term dependencies of time series data. Different from using GCN to learn the spatial association between entities in the entire corpus, we use the LSTM network to learn the potential document representation of a single service description. In this paper, we use a two-layer bidirectional LSTM (Bi-LSTM) network to extract the sequential features of the service descriptions. A Bi-LSTM network can combine a forward LSTM layer and a backward LSTM layer in order to learn information from preceding as well as following tokens comprehensively. For the Web service classification task, we take the output of the hidden state of the last time step of the Bi-LSTM as its document feature representation.

Compared with GCN, recurrent neural networks generally need to use pre-trained word embeddings via the Embedding layer, which embeds words into computer-processable numeric vectors. Global Vectors for Word Representation (GloVe) [14] is a general technique for mapping words to vector representations in the field of natural language processing (NLP). We use *Glove6B* to build the embedding layer f_e, which is a neural network pre-trained with 6 billion words from Wikipedia and Gigaword. We choose the pre-trained Glove6B with 200-dimensions word vectors in the embedding layer, which converts each word into a 200-dimension vector. We fix weight values of the embedding layer and do not participate in the training. We assume that y is a Web service description and the embedding layer can be defined as:

$$e = f_e(y) \tag{11}$$

To obtain high-level features, global long-term dependencies in the description documents should be considered. Therefore, we introduce a two-layer Bi-LSTM network f_{blstm} to obtain the forward and backward sequential features of the description documents. The output h of a two-layer Bi-LSTM network is :

$$h = f_{blstm}(f_{blstm}(e)) \tag{12}$$

3.3 Learning the Proposed Model

After the above two extractors, we obtain two types of features (spatial features and sequential features) of service descriptions. Then we concatenate these two types of features and create a fully connected layer (f_{fc}) for joint training of parameters. Next, classification results of Web services are obtained by a *softmax* classifier. As shown in Fig. 2, the dotted box on the left is the sequential feature extractor, the input ($input1$) is the service description document, and the dotted box on the right is the spatial feature extractor, taking the pre-trained spatial features as input ($input2$). The joint training mode of the parameters is driven by the following equation:

$$prediction = softmax(f_{fc}(con(in\hat{p}ut1, input2))) \tag{13}$$

Where con refers to concatenating two vectors together. $in\hat{p}ut1$ is the high-level feature vector of $input1$ processed by an embedding layer and a two-layer Bi-LSTM network . The cross-entropy loss function is still used to measure the errors.

4   Experiment

In this section, we conduct comprehensive experiments aiming to answer the following two questions:

1. Q1: Whether our model of using both sequential feature extractor and spatial feature extractor performs better than models using only one of them?
2. Q2: What is the performance of our proposed method in comparison with the state-of-the-art methods in Web service classification?

4.1   Dataset Description

In our experiments, we use the dataset provided by [19], which is collected from the largest API sharing platform (ProgrammableWeb) using a Web crawler. For the fairness of comparison, we employ the data preprocessing same as [19].

Specifically, we clean up empty services and make dataset more balance by eliminating the one-shot, small size categories and keep big size categories. Finally, the service dataset contains 10184 services with 50 categories.

As the service dataset is relatively small and unbalanced, randomly partition the dataset cannot ensure the training set and testing set to follow the same distribution in small categories. After randomly selecting data by category, the dataset has been split into 8123 training and 2061 testing service description documents. In the GCN model, we delete low-frequency words that appear less than 5 times. In the LSTM model, we unify the length of the text to 100 (average length is 67). The excess part is discarded and the missing part is filled by zeros. We remove the common and meaningless words using the stopword list in the NLTK toolkit. We employ the lemmatizer packaged in the NLTK toolkit to reduce all words to their root forms. The visualized category distribution of Web services is shown in Fig. 3.

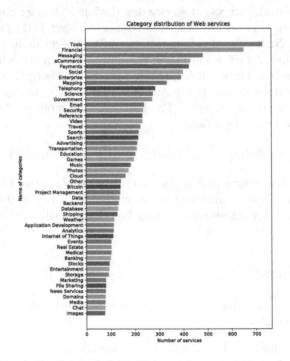

Fig. 3. A visualized distribution of 50 Web service categories, where x-axis is the number of services contained in a category and y-axis is the name of each category.

4.2   Evaluation Methods

In this section, we compare our proposed method with multiple state-of-the-art classification methods on the same dataset using Top-N accuracy, F1-macro:

Method Based on Conventional Machine Learning

- **Naive-Bayes:** A typical statistical learning method which models joint probability distribution based on bayesian inference.
- **RF:** Random forest is an algorithm that integrates multiple trees through comprehensive learning. Its basic unit is the decision tree.
- **LDA-L-SVM** [12]: A classification method integrated LDA (Latent Dirichlet Allocation) and Linear-SVM for feature extraction.

Methods Based on Deep Learning

- **CNN** [8]: At the word level, we use 1-D convolution to extract features of Web API description documents.
- **LSTM** [7]: The LSTM model uses the last hidden state as the representation of the whole text. We also use it with pre-trained word embeddings.
- **RCNN** [10]: This is a neural network that combines a recurrent neural network with a convolutional neural network to capture sequential and local features.
- **C-LSTM** [22]: A neural network structure stacks the one-dimensional (1-D) convolution layers with LSTM layers for capturing local spatial and sequential features.
- **Bi-LSTM:** A neural network combines forward and backward LSTM layers in order to learn information from preceding as well as following tokens.
- **ServeNet** [19]: A neural network which can automatically abstract low-level representations to high-level features through the stacked 2-D CNN and Bi-LSTM.
- **Text GCN** [20]: A novel text classification model using a two-layer GCN to capture global word co-occurrence information and document-word information without any external word embeddings or knowledge.

Table 1. Top-1 accuracy, Top-5 accuracy and F1-macro of our method compared with others

Model	Top-1 Accuracy	Top-5 Accuracy	F1-macro
Naive-Bayes	47.79 (+46.6%)	77.63 (+18.7%)	37.58 (+74.7%)
RF	52.61 (+33.1%)	77.88 (+18.3%)	50.13 (+31.0%)
LDA-L-SVM	55.75 (+25.7%)	84.71 (+8.8%)	53.78 (+22.1%)
CNN	59.74 (+17.3%)	86.09 (+7.0%)	56.83 (+15.5%)
LSTM	56.15 (+24.8%)	83.53 (+10.3%)	51.76 (+26.8%)
RCNN	60.08 (+16.6%)	85.64 (+7.6%)	57.00 (+15.2%)
C-LSTM	61.05 (+14.7%)	86.59 (+6.4%)	57.21 (+14.8%)
Bi-LSTM	58.70 (+19.3%)	84.56 (+9.0%)	54.75 (+19.9%)
ServeNet	62.21 (+12.6%)	88.37 (+4.3%)	59.21 (+10.9%)
Text GCN	52.75 (+32.8%)	79.01 (+16.6%)	49.58 (+32.4%)
Ours	**70.05**	**92.15**	**65.65**

4.3   Parameters and Experimental Environment

The hidden state of LSTM layers are both 64-dimension vectors. The task layer of sequential feature extractor contains 50 hidden nodes same as the dimension of $input2$, which takes into account the same importance for sequential features and spatial features. Two layers of GCN contain 512 hidden nodes and 256 hidden nodes respectively. The Adam optimizer algorithm with a learning rate of 0.001 is used in both feature extractions. To avoid overfitting, we add a dropout layer with drop probability of 0.7 between every two layers. In baseline models, we use the sklearn library to implement traditional machine learning algorithms with default parameters. We use Glove6B with 200-dimensions word vectors for all deep learning models that require pretrained word vectors. All experiments are run on a Linux system with 64GB memory and a GTX1080 GPU, implemented by leveraging the deep learning library PyTorch and conducted based on the model depicted in Fig. 2.

4.4   Experimental Results and Discussions

Top-N accuracy metric is often used in classification tasks. Specifically, in our dataset, there is only one primary category for each service, so we use the Top-1 accuracy to evaluate the precision of our model. While in the multi-category classification task (50 categories in the dataset), Top-5 accuracy is used to evaluate the accuracy of the Top-5 categories containing the actual results. In addition, we evaluate the performance of models by F1-macro, which is a harmonic mean of precision and recall. The experimental results of Top-1 accuracy, Top-5 accuracy and F1-macro are given in Table 1.

Analyses of Experimental Results for Q1. The LSTM model reaches 56.15% for Top-1 accuracy, 83.53% for Top-5 accuracy and 51.76% for F1-macro on the testing dataset. The Bi-LSTM network can learn feature information from preceding as well as following tokens. In our experiments, Bi-LSTM model has a slight performance improvement compared with the unidirectional LSTM model, reaching 58.70% for Top-1 accuracy, 84.56% for Top-5 accuracy and 54.75% for F1-macro. GCN has received increasing attention recently, which can capture larger neighborhoods information [4,13]. However, in the actual application of Web service classification, Text GCN model is not as robust as expected and it is even worse than various baseline models. This shows that it is insufficient to use the spatial feature information of the service descriptions alone for Web service classification. Our model integrates the advantages of Bi-LSTM and GCN by capturing both sequential features and spatial features of Web service descriptions obtaining the best classification performance. Specifically, our model improves Bi-LSTM by about 19.3% in Top-1 accuracy, 9.0% in Top-5 accuracy and 19.9% in F1-macro. Compared with the GCN model, our method improves the accuracy of Top-1 and Top-5 by 32.8% and 16.6%, respectively. Answer for RQ1: our method using both sequential features and spatial features can achieve better performance comparing with models using only one of them.

Analyses of Experimental Results for Q2. From Table 1, we can see that the performance of service classification is very diverse with different models. According to the experimental results, Naive Bayes is a simple but well-performed and robust method. As an emerging and highly flexible machine learning algorithm, Random Forest performs well on Web service classification tasks, and it achieves extremely competitive performance. Linear-SVM achieves optimal performance for Web service classification in all traditional machine learning algorithms and its performance significantly exceeds Naive-Bayes and RF.

For deep learning models, CNN model which considers the local feature between adjacent words has the competitive testing accuracy of 59.74% for Top-1 accuracy, 86.09% for Top-5 accuracy and 56.83%, better than either LSTM model or Bi-LSTM model. When the sequential model is combined with the 1-D CNN, the classification performance has been improved. Recurrent-CNN and C-LSTM extract the sequential and neighborhood features of service description documents and achieve superior performance than standalone CNN and LSTM models. It is evident that combining sequential features and spatial features helps to enhance service classification performance. ServeNet [19], which is a neural network stacked with 2-D CNNs and Bi-LSTM networks, can learn bidirectional sequential features and more local features in small 2-D regions inside of words. It reaches 62.21% for Top-1 accuracy, 88.37% for Top-5 accuracy and 59.21% for F1-macro. Text GCN [20] can capture global word co-occurrence and document-word information, but it ignores the order of words. In the service classification task, the service description documents are usually short texts with sparse features. Not surprisingly, Text GCN model only reaches 52.75% for Top-1 accuracy, 79.01% for Top-5 accuracy and 49.58% for F1-macro which are lower than some neural network models extracting sequential features.

Finally, our proposed method combined GCN and Bi-LSTM models (with GCN as a pre-training component) can successfully capture spatial and sequential features for Web service description documents, and achieve the highest testing accuracy of 70.05% for Top-1 accuracy, 92.15% for Top-5 accuracy and 65.65% for F1-macro. As shown in Table 1, the performance gains of our method compared with others reach at least 12.6% for Top-1 accuracy, 4.3% for Top-5 accuracy and 10.9%. With our method, the context information in a single service description is successfully extracted by the Bi-LSTM component. Meanwhile, it effectively utilizes the global word co-occurrence information and document-word relationships by a two-layer GCN component.

5   Related Work

Web service has been an active research area for many years [2,11,18]. In general, existing work can be roughly divided into two categories, one focuses on text classification based on service description documents, and the other focuses on using the various elements accumulated in the Web service ecosystem for classification. In addition, we also separately summarize the service classification methods based on different deep learning technologies.

5.1   Classification Based on Description Documents

As for the first category, Crasso et al. [5] proposed a Web service classification method based on text description vectors. The Web services are then classified using Rocchio, k-nn (k-nearest neighbor) and Naive Bayes, respectively. Bai et al. [1] proposed a naive Bayesian classification algorithm for Web service classification, which assigns more weight to each title term to reflect different degrees of importance. Wang et al. [17] proposed a Maximum entropy classification method and compared it with Naive Bayes and Support Vector Machine (SVM). The results showed that Maximum entropy has better classification performance than SVM in sparse data classification. Due to the validity of SVM in Web service classification, Liu et al. [12] utilized it as the base classifier. They also combined the probabilistic topic model to solve the sparsity problem in the generation process of service description, and reduced the dimensions to improve the efficiency.

5.2   Classification Based on Different Types of Elements

Regarding the second category, various elements and their relationships accumulated in the Web API ecosystem are used to improve classification performance. Liang et al. [11] built a heterogeneous network with multi-type relationships and employed a RWR (Random Walk with Restart) model to capture global relationships between all types of entities. Elgazzar et al. [6] selected a different set of Web service features including WSDL contents, types, messages, and ports, and obtained high precision and recall values. Boujarwah et al. [2] adopted an unsupervised machine learning technique by using concept graphs to build functional domains and divide Web services into these domains. Terms in WSDL are treated as concept nodes in a concept graph. These terms are extracted from elements, including port type, service name, operation name, and so on.

5.3   Classification Based on Deep Learning Technologies

Some emerging classification methods exploit deep learning technologies as support. For example, Yang et al. [19] presented a deep neural network *ServeNet* which integrates 2-D CNN and Bi-LSTM for Web service classification and obtained good accuracy. Cao et al. [3] proposed a topical attention based Bi-LSTM model for Web service classification. They combined feature representations of Web services using Bi-LSTM model with the topic features trained offline. They used attention mechanism to perform the topic attention strengthening processing to obtain the importance or weights of different words for Web service classification. Ye et al. [21] proposed a Web service classification method based on Wide & Bi-LSTM model. They exploit a wide learning model and a Bi-LSTM model to make breadth prediction and depth prediction of Web service description documents, respectively. Finally, the breadth and depth prediction results are combined by the linear regression algorithm to obtain the final results.

Compared with the existing work, our proposed method belongs to the classification of Web service descriptions using deep learning technologies. We propose a novel and effective framework to extract both spatial and sequential features of service descriptions in the Web service ecosystem, The experimental results demonstrate that our method can achieve the best classification accuracy compared with a variety of state-of-the-art models.

6   Conclusion

In this paper, we have proposed a novel method for Web service classification by integrating GCN and Bi-LSTM network. Specifically, considering the differences between the two methods, we use a two-layer GCN to extract the global spatial features of the Web service descriptions, which is seen as a pre-training step without any external word embeddings or prior knowledge. Next, we integrate them with the sequential features learned from the Bi-LSTM model using pre-trained word embeddings for joint training of parameters. Comprehensive experimental results based on real-world dataset demonstrated that our proposed method can achieve better classification performance compared with other SATD methods. In addition, we believe that this two-stage feature ecxtraction method can be flexibly extended to general text classification tasks, not just for Web service classification.

In the future, we plan to introduce more elements (such as invocation relationships between Mashups and APIs) of the Web service ecosystem to further improve the classification accuracy. In addition, we will try to extend our feature extraction method on other tasks.

Acknowledgment. This work was supported by National Key Research and Development Program of China (2018YFC1604000), and the grands of the National Natural Science Foundation of China (Nos.61972290, U163620068, 61562090, 61962061).

References

1. Bai, P., Li, J.: The improved naive Bayesian Web text classification algorithm. In: 2009 International Symposium on Computer Network and Multimedia Technology, pp. 1–4. IEEE (2009)
2. Boujarwah, E., Yahyaoui, H., Almulla, M.: A new unsupervised Web services classification based on conceptual graphs. In: The Eighth International Conference on Internet and Web Applications and Services (2013)
3. Cao, Y., Liu, J., Cao, B., Shi, M., Wen, Y., Peng, Z.: Web services classification with topical attention based Bi-LSTM. In: Wang, X., Gao, H., Iqbal, M., Min, G. (eds.) CollaborateCom 2019. LNICST, vol. 292, pp. 394–407. Springer, Cham (2019). https://doi.org/10.1007/978-3-030-30146-0_27
4. Cetoli, A.B., O'Harney, S., Sloan, A.D., Scout, M.C.: Graph convolutional networks for named entity recognition. Treebanks Linguist. Theor. 37
5. Crasso, M., Zunino, A., Campo, M.: Awsc: an approach to Web service classification based on machine learning techniques. Inteligencia Artificial. Revista Iberoamericana de Inteligencia Artificial **12**(37), 25–36 (2008)

6. Elgazzar, K., Hassan, A.E., Martin, P.: Clustering wsdl documents to bootstrap the discovery of Web services. In: 2010 IEEE International Conference on Web Services, pp. 147–154. IEEE (2010)
7. Hochreiter, S., Schmidhuber, J.: Long short-term memory. Neural Comput. **9**(8), 1735–1780 (1997)
8. Kim, Y.: Convolutional neural networks for sentence classification. In: Proceedings of the 2014 Conference on Empirical Methods in Natural Language Processing (EMNLP), pp. 1746–1751 (2014)
9. Kipf, T.N., Welling, M.: Semi-supervised classification with graph convolutional networks. In: International Conference on Learning Representations (ICLR) (2017)
10. Lai, S., Xu, L., Liu, K., Zhao, J.: Recurrent convolutional neural networks for text classification. In: Proceedings of the Twenty-Ninth AAAI Conference on Artificial Intelligence, pp. 2267–2273 (2015)
11. Liang, T., Chen, L., Wu, J., Bouguettaya, A.: Exploiting heterogeneous information for tag recommendation in API management. In: 2016 IEEE International Conference on Web Services (ICWS), pp. 436–443. IEEE (2016)
12. Liu, X., Agarwal, S., Ding, C., Yu, Q.: An LDA-SVM active learning framework for Web service classification. In: 2016 IEEE International Conference on Web Services (ICWS), pp. 49–56. IEEE (2016)
13. Marcheggiani, D., Titov, I.: Encoding sentences with graph convolutional networks for semantic role labeling. In: Proceedings of the 2017 Conference on Empirical Methods in Natural Language Processing, pp. 1506–1515 (2017)
14. Pennington, J., Socher, R., Manning, C.: Glove: global vectors for word representation. In: Proceedings of the 2014 Conference on Empirical Methods in Natural Language Processing (EMNLP), pp. 1532–1543 (2014)
15. Tan, W., Fan, Y., Ghoneim, A., Hossain, M.A., Dustdar, S.: From the service-oriented architecture to the Web API economy. IEEE Internet Comput. **20**(4), 64–68 (2016)
16. Verborgh, R., Dumontier, M.: A Web API ecosystem through feature-based reuse. IEEE Internet Comput. **22**(3), 29–37 (2018)
17. Wang, H., Wang, L., Yi, L.: Maximum entropy framework used in text classification. In: 2010 IEEE International Conference on Intelligent Computing and Intelligent Systems, vol. 2, pp. 828–833. IEEE (2010)
18. Wang, X., Wu, H., Hsu, C.H.: Mashup-oriented API recommendation via random walk on knowledge graph. IEEE Access **7**, 7651–7662 (2018)
19. Yang, Y., Ke, W., Wang, W., Zhao, Y.: Deep learning for Web services classification. In: 2019 IEEE International Conference on Web Services (ICWS), pp. 440–442. IEEE (2019)
20. Yao, L., Mao, C., Luo, Y.: Graph convolutional networks for text classification. In: Proceedings of the AAAI Conference on Artificial Intelligence, vol. 33, pp. 7370–7377 (2019)
21. Ye, H., Cao, B., Peng, Z., Chen, T., Wen, Y., Liu, J.: Web services classification based on wide & Bi-LSTM model. IEEE Access **7**, 43697–43706 (2019)
22. Zhou, C., Sun, C., Liu, Z., Lau, F.: A C-LSTM neural network for text classification. arXiv preprint (2015). arXiv:1511.08630

A Pruned DOM-Based Iterative Strategy for Approximate Global Optimization in Crowdsourcing Microtasks

Lizhen Cui[1,2], Jing Chen[1,2], Wei He[1,2](✉), Hui Li[1,2], and Wei Guo[1,2]

[1] School of Software, Shandong University, Jinan, China
{clz,hewei,lih,guowei}@sdu.edu.cn, 201934822@mail.sdu.edu.cn
[2] Joint SDU-NTU Centre for Artificial Intelligence Research (C-FAIR),
Shandong University, Jinan, China

Abstract. Crowdsourcing can solve many challenging problems for machines. The ability and knowledge background of employees on the Internet are unknown and different, the answers collected from the crowd are ambiguous. The choice of employee quality control strategy is really important to ensure the crowdsourcing results. In previous works, Expectation-Maximization (EM) was mainly used to estimate the real answer and quality of workers. Unfortunately, EM provides a local optimal solution, and the estimation results are often affected by the initial parameters. In this paper, an iterative optimization method based on EM local optimal results is designed to improve the quality estimation of workers for crowdsourcing micro-tasks (which has binary answers). The iterative search method works on the dominance ordering model (DOM) we proposed, which prunes the dominated task-response sequences while preserving the dominating ones, to iteratively search for the approximate global optimal estimation in a reduced space. We evaluate the proposed approach through extensive experiments on both simulated and real-world datasets, the experimental results illustrate that this strategy has higher performance than EM-based algorithm.

Keywords: Crowdsourcing · Quality management · Optimization strategy · Maximum likelihood estimation

1 Introduction

Crowdsourcing can help solve tasks that too hard for computers by leveraging the intelligence of a large group of people. Currently, there are many successful crowdsourcing platforms, such as Upwork, Crowdflow and Amazon Mechanical Turk(AMT). *Requesters* can publish *tasks* on *crowdsourcingplatforms*. *Workers* then accept and answer the tasks, and submit answers back to the platform. Crowdsourcing tasks can be divided into macro-tasks (e.g. text translation) and micro-tasks (e.g. image annotation tasks). Micro-tasks are usually simple and can be completed in seconds, while macro-tasks can take hours.

© Springer Nature Switzerland AG 2020
X. Wang et al. (Eds.): APWeb-WAIM 2020, LNCS 12317, pp. 779–793, 2020.
https://doi.org/10.1007/978-3-030-60259-8_57

This paper only focuses on micro-tasks(each is a binary task with yes/on choices), which have important application value in crowdsourcing. For example, in a query such as "Do the two videos belong to the same theme?", the expected answers of the form "yes/no" where yes is denoted by 1 and no is denoted by 0. The platforms collect responses from multiple workers on such a question and integrates them to estimate the true answer. As workers have different levels of expertise, they may provide wrong responses for tasks.

Quality management is a crucial problem for crowdsourcing platform to obtain correct answers. Based on analyzing worker responses to a set of tasks, we estimate the true answers to the tasks, as well as the quality of workers. Previous research on this problem primarily provides a local optimal solution rather than a global one. EM algorithm is a classic and effective method for estimating the true values of unknown variables. In crowdsourcing, the existing work mainly uses EM algorithm to iteratively update the parameters of worker model and the true answers of tasks until convergence. However, two limitations of EM hinder its effectiveness in this application scenario: EM-based algorithms are highly dependent on initialization parameters; Using EM to estimate the maximum likelihood can only get the local optimal results, which often get stuck in undesirable local optima [2].

Global optimization is the most ideal result, but there are difficulties in its implementation. The most intuitive method to obtain the global optimal result is to find the global maximum likelihood values of all possible mappings from tasks to answers, so as to find the most likely true answers. However, considering the large-scale operation in the context of crowdsourcing, the number of calculations required increases exponentially with the increase of tasks and workers. Therefore, it is often intractable to obtain these global optimal quality management technologies.

In this paper, we propose an iterative optimization method to obtain the approximate global optimal solution, this method is based on the dominance ordering model (DOM), which is obtained by pruning the responses of all workers to the tasks. The overall procedure of the proposed optimization method is illustrated in Fig. 1. Based on the collected worker responses to the tasks, the basic EM algorithm is used to obtain the local optimal results of task answers and worker quality. Then workers are ranked into different quality categories according to the estimation of their quality. After that, according to the known worker classification and worker response (i.e. task-response sequence), a dominance ordering model is constructed to prune the response with lower probability, which narrows the search scope and reduces the mapping space. Then a Cut-point neighbour detection algorithm is designed to iteratively search the response with the maximum likelihood based on our model until convergence.

To sum up, the main contributions of this paper include the following three points:

(1) We propose a pruning strategy-based dominance ordering model (DOM), which is composed of worker responses and worker categories

(i.e. task-response sequence), and reduces the space of potential task-response sequence while retaining the dominant sequence;

(2) We propose a Cut-point neighbour detection algorithm to find the task-response sequence with the maximum likelihood within dominance ordering model (DOM) by iterative search;

(3) We perform extensive experiments to compare our algorithm with the EM algorithm on a variety of metrics. The experimental results show that our algorithm significantly outperforms EM-based algorithms in both simulated data and real-world data.

The remains of this paper is organized as follows. Section 2 discusses the related works. Section 3 describes our concept definitions and illustrates some symbols with an example. We describe the iterative optimization method in Sect. 4, and present our experimental results in Sect. 5. Finally, we conclude our work in Sect. 6.

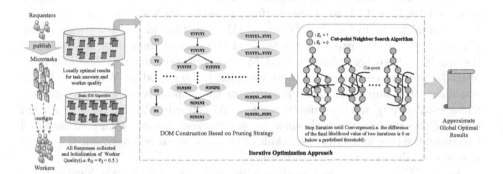

Fig. 1. Overall procedure of the proposed approach

2   Related Work

In order to guarantee the quality of the task results, existing research has proposed a variety of techniques to evaluate the true answers of tasks by managing workers' quality.

The general method is majority voting [1,9]. In addition, Wang [19] proposed a worker quality-aware model which uses workers' quality values to weigh the relative importance given to their answers. Ma [12] proposed a fine grained truth discover model to estimate both worker topical expertise and the true answers. Before the worker answers the task, the worker is required to answer the test questions with known correct answers. This method is used to evaluate the relevant ability of the worker. This can detect and eliminate some fraudsters and workers who do not have the relevant capabilities before workers answer the task. Test questions can also be randomly mixed into common tasks to test the quality of workers, so that the actual ability of workers can be more truly understood [4,8]. Liu [11] obtained the accuracy of workers' answers to tasks by adding test questions, and then used Bayesian theory to obtain the true answers of the final tasks according to the quality of the workers and the answers to the tasks.

The existing crowdsourcing quality control methods mainly use the method based on EM [9,13,15,16,20,23] to estimate the true answers of workers' quality and tasks. The EM is primarily used to make up for the lack of data through the iterative calculation of the maximum likelihood estimation of incomplete data [5]. Each iteration of the algorithm includes two steps: Expectation step and Maximization step. In crowdsourcing, the unknown variables are the task true answer and workers' quality, and incomplete data are workers' responses to tasks. Workers' quality is characterized by a worker model. The most commonly used is the static worker model, that is, the workers' quality is characterized by a single probability value [6] or a confusion matrix [7,14]. Set initial parameters for the unknown variable as input, and then iteratively update the parameters of the worker model and the true answers of tasks until convergence. The method proposed by Dawid [3] used the confusion matrix for the first time to model worker quality. Ipeirotis, P.G. [7] used EM algorithm in AMT crowdsourcing platform, and at the same time estimated the correct answer of the task and the quality of workers characterized by the confusion matrix. The effects of other factors are considered in more complex worker models. Whitehill, J. [21] considered the impact of task difficulty on the reliability of workers' answers when establishing worker quality models. Afterwards, A. Kurve [10] utilized the EM to calculate the task answers and workers quality with four latented variables: the true answer of task, skills of workers, workers' intentions (i.e. being honest or dishonest) and task difficulty.

Using EM to estimate the maximum likelihood can only get the local optimal solution. Das Sarma [2] proposed a technique for global optimal quality management, finding the maximum likelihood item ratings and worker quality estimates. They made two limiting assumptions: (1) all workers have the same quality; (2) the number of workers answering each question is fixed. These assumptions are too restrictive in reality. Snow, R. [17] used MAP to estimate parameters. Tang, W. [18] used the control problem to improve the maximum likelihood estimation. This is achieved by semi supervised learning based on the real answer of the control problem to improve the parameter estimation in DS method. Zhang, Y. [22] used the spectral method to initialize EM to search the real answer of the task and the optimal result of the estimation of the confusion matrix of the workers.

3   Problem Description

We start with the introduction of some symbols, and then combined with an example of image annotation to make a specific description of some symbols (Table 1).

Table 1. Notation table

Symbol	Explanation
t	Task
w	Worker
r_t^w	Responses from worker w to task t
z_t	The true answer of task
L	Overall likelihood
DOM	Dominance ordering model
DOG	Dominance ordering graph
d_{n*}	Distance between the nth class worker and the best worker

Task Question and Option. Consider a group of tasks $\{t\}^n$ with a total number of n. These tasks are completed by a group of workers $\{w\}^m$ with a total number of m. Work w completes task t with k options $\{1, 2, 3, \dots, k\}$. Each worker can answer multiple different tasks, and each task can be accomplished by multiple different workers. Each task has a correct answer z_t (that is, one of the k options is the true answer).

Task Response. r_t^w as the response of worker w to task t. For the binary problem studied in this paper, each r_t^w has a value of 0 or 1.

Worker Response Probability Matrix. For the binary problem studied in this paper, a worker response probability matrix of $p = \begin{bmatrix} p_{11} & p_{12} \\ p_{21} & p_{22} \end{bmatrix}$ is considered. p_{11} and p_{21} respectively represent the probability that $r_t^w = 0$ and $r_t^w = 1$ when the real answer of the task is 0. p_{12} and p_{22} respectively represent the probability that $r_t^w = 0$ and $r_t^w = 1$ when the real answer of the task is 1. The whole matrix is described by a pair of values (e_0, e_1), in which e_0 is worker false positive (FP) rates (i.e. p_{21}value) and e_1 is false negative (FN) rates (i.e. p_{12} value).

Overall Likelihood. Assuming that each worker answers the question independently. The likelihood value of t_1 is the product of the probability that the worker who answers the task t_1 makes the correct response. L is the overall likelihood value of a set of tasks. It is the product of the likelihood value of each task in the task set. Its calculation formula is $L = L(t_1) \times L(t_2) \times \dots \times L(t_n)$.

Task-Response Sequence. Task-response sequence is constructed by the combination of workers response and workers category. Worker's positive answer to binary task is 1, which is expressed by Y, and similarly, the negative answer to binary task is 0, which is expressed by N.

Distance. We calculate the distance between workers in plane rectangular coordinate system. The quality of workers is represented by his/her error rate (e_0, e_1), which is a point in the coordinate system. The distance between workers is expressed by the Euclidean distance between two points in a two-dimensional plane. The best worker quality is (0,0), which is the origin.

Table 2. Example of workers responses to t_1 and t_2

Task	Task responses			Task-answer sequence
	First class workers	Second class workers	Third class workers	
t_1	$r^{w1}_{t_1}=1, r^{w3}_{t_1}=1$	\	\	Y1Y1
	$r^{w2}_{t_1}=1$	$r^{w2}_{t_1}=1$	\	Y1Y2
	$r^{w1}_{t_1}=1$	\	$r^{w8}_{t_1}=1$	Y1Y3
	\	$r^{w5}_{t_1}=1$	$r^{w9}_{t_1}=1$	Y2Y3
	\	$r^{w6}_{t_1}=1$	$r^{w10}_{t_1}=0$	Y2N3
	\	\	$r^{w8}_{t_1}=1, r^{w10}_{t_1}=1$	Y3Y3
	$r^{w1}_{t_1}=1, r^{w2}_{t_1}=0$	\	\	Y1N1
t_2	\	$r^{w4}_{t_2}=1, r^{w7}_{t_2}=0$	\	Y2N2
	$r^{w3}_{t_2}=0$	$r^{w5}_{t_2}=1$	\	Y2N1
	\	$r^{w6}_{t_2}=0$	$r^{w9}_{t_2}=1$	Y3N2
	\	\	$r^{w8}_{t_2}=0, r^{w9}_{t_2}=0$	N3N3
	\	$r^{w7}_{t_2}=0$	$r^{w10}_{t_2}=0$	N2N3
	$r^{w1}_{t_2}=0$	\	$r^{w8}_{t_2}=0$	N1N3
	$r^{w2}_{t_2}=0$	$r^{w4}_{t_2}=0$	\	N1N2

Example 1. In this example, there are a group of image annotation tasks$\{t_1, t_2, \ldots, t_n\}$. All of which are binary task problems with two options $\{0, 1\}$. We take t_1, t_2 as an example to illustrate, we assume that $z_{t_1} = 1$, $z_{t_2} = 0$. A group of 10 workers$\{w_1, w_2, w_3, \ldots, w_{10}\}$ respond to these tasks, and the error rates of 10 workers is $(0.1, 0.3)$, $(0.2, 0.2)$, $(0.3, 0.2)$, $(0.3, 0.6)$, $(0.4, 0.4)$, $(0.5, 0.5)$, $(0.6, 0.4)$, $(0.7, 0.7)$, $(0.8, 0.6)$, $(0.9, 0.5)$. We determine the category to which each worker belongs based on the distance between the worker and the origin. In this example, We classify workers into 3 categories, which are characterized by numbers 1, 2 and 3 respectively. The workers who have high quality rank in the front. We divide the distance between the worst worker (that is, the error rate $(1,1)$) and the origin on average into three intervals. The distance between the first class workers and the origin is within $[0, \sqrt{2}/3]$ (that is $d_{1*} \in [0, \sqrt{2}/3]$). Similarly, $d_{2*} \in [\sqrt{2}/3, 2\sqrt{2}/3]$ and $d_{3*} \in [2\sqrt{2}/3, 1]$. According to the calculation, we determine the category to which each worker belongs. Workers choose tasks to answer, and different tasks will receive different numbers of answers. Here t_1 and t_2 receive 2 responses. The Table 2 shows several workers' responses received by t_1, t_2.

We take the task-response sequence of t_1 as $Y1N1$ and task-response sequence of t_2 as $Y2N2$ for example to calculate the likelihood value. From Table 2, w_1 and w_3 answer t_1, their error rate is $(0.1, 0.3)$ and $(0.2, 0.2)$ respectively, so their probability of answering the t_1 correctly is 0.7 and 0.8 respectively.

So we can get $L(t_1) = 0.7 \times 0.8 = 5.6 \times 10^{-1}$. Similarly, we can get $L(t_2) = 0.7 \times 0.4 = 2.8 \times 10^{-1}$. If $n = 2$ in task set, only t_1 and t_2 are included, then the overall likelihood of $L = L(t_1) \times L(t_2) = 1.568 \times 10^{-1}$.

4   Optimization Strategy

Overview. We first estimate the true answers for the tasks and worker quality using EM with different prior models. We can rank workers into different quality categories according to the estimates of their quality. After that, we propose a dominance ordering model (DOM) on the basis of known worker categorizations. We then design a Cut-point neighbour detection algorithm to search for the task-response sequence with the maximum likelihood in our model and prune the task-response sequence where the probability is low. The results of our search algorithm is then used as a new input to update worker categorizations and the dominance ordering model until convergence.

4.1   The Dominance Ordering Model (DOM)

We classify workers into c categories firstly, the classification method is the same as mentioned in Example 1.

After worker classification, we can construct the dominance ordering model. In this paper, we focus on the binary problem. Workers' responses are in the form of Y/N. In this way, $Y1$ denotes that a worker in the first category answered *yes* to a task; and $N1$ denotes that a worker in the first category answered *no* to the task. We observe that response sets are in dominance ordering. For the tasks with same number of responses, we sort the response sets by the level of expertise of workers. For example, there are two tasks t_1 and t_2, each with 3 responses of *yes*. Responses of t_1 are from workers belonging to the first, third and fourth categories; whereas responses of t_2 are from workers belonging to the first, third and fifth categories. Then, the response set of t_1 is ordered higher than that of t_2, $Y1Y3Y4$ dominates $Y1Y3Y5$ (i.e. $Y1Y3Y4- > Y1Y3Y5$).

Definition 1 *(Dominance Ordering). The response set for each vertex contains one or several elements from* $\{Y1...Yc, Nc...N1\}$. *Vertex* v_1 *dominates vertex* v_2 *if and only if one of the following conditions is satisfied:*

(1) v_1 *and* v_2 *contain the same number of '1' and '0' responses in total, and at least one response of '1' in* v_1 *is answered by a worker with higher quality than any worker answering '1' in* v_2; *or at least one response of '0' in* v_1 *is answered by a worker with lower quality than any worker answering '0' in* v_2.

(2) v_1 *contains more '1' responses and fewer '0' responses than* v_2.

For tasks receiving the same number of responses, the response sets of them exist in the same dominance ordering graph (DAG). In addition, in order to handle the problem that tasks receive different number of responses at the same time. We integrate the DAG with different number of responses. For the DAG where tasks receive even number of responses, we set up a central layer where response set of vertices are characterized by the same number and worker classes to responses yes and no (e.g. $Y1Y2N1N2$). However, for the DAG where tasks receive odd number of responses, we set a virtual center layer, which is composed of the edges equal to the starting point and the end point. We integrate each DAG into our model through the central layer and the vertices with the same distance from the central layer have similar dominance. Figure 2 shows an example of our model. In this example, workers are divided into 3 categories, with three workers answering tasks. DAG (a), (b) and (c) represent that tasks receiving 1, 2 and 3 responses, respectively. The red dashed line represents all the stratifed situations. As shown in the Fig. 2, the central layer exists in DAG (b), while (a) and (c) only contain a synthetic central layer.

Algorithm 1. Cut-point Neighbour Detection

Input: $data$; f;
Output: new_L(new likelihood); new_f(mapping corresponding to new_L); new_q(Worker quality corresponding to new_f);

1: Construct $V; E$ = Dominance Ordering Model(DOM);
2: **function** MAIN($f, data$)
3:   $s \leftarrow 1$;
4:   **while** $(s < \gamma)$ **do**
5:     $new\_L \leftarrow VertexSelection(s, DOM, L)$;
6:     **if** $new\_L > L$ **then**
7:       $f \leftarrow new\_f$; $L \leftarrow new\_L$; $s \leftarrow 1$;
8:     **else**
9:       $s++$;
10:    **end if**
11: **end while**
12: **return** new_L; new_f; new_q;
13: **function** VertexSelection(s, DOM, L)
14: **if** $(s = 0)$ **then**
15:    calculate new_L:
16:    **return** new_L;
17: **else**
18:    **for** $vertex$ in $vertexset$ **do**
19:      change answer of tasks in vertex;
20:      **if** $(answer = 1)$ **then**
21:        $answer \leftarrow 0$;
22:      **else**
23:        $answer \leftarrow 1$;
24:      **end if**
25:      $new\_L \leftarrow VertexSelection(s - 1, DOM, L)$
26:      **if** $new\_L > L$ **then**
27:        **return** new_L;
28:      **end if**
29:    **end for**
30: **end if**

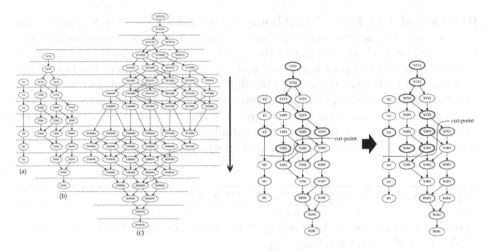

Fig. 2. An example of our model with a maximum of 3 workers

Fig. 3. An example of the proposed Cut-point neighbour detection

4.2 Cut-Point Neighbour Detection Algorithm

In this section, we describe the process of Cut-point neighbour detection as illustrated in Algorithm 1.

Definition 2 *(Cut-point). In our model, the probability that the answer to a question is 1 (Yes) decreases from top to bottom. Here, we define the Cut-point as a mapping which divides the vertices in our model into two partitions. The vertices above the Cut-point are mapped to 1, and those below the Cut-point are mapped to 0.*

After constructing the dominance ordering model (DOM), we search for the maximum likelihood mapping. The search begins from the starting Cut-point which is generated by the EM algorithm. We will constantly adjust the position of Cut-point to find sequence with maximum likelihood. First, we find the vertices closest to the Cut-point and put them into a vertex-set. We then replace the answers of the vertices in this set (that is, vertices whose answers are 1 will be changed to 0 and vice versa). In the first round of replacement, we replace the answers of the vertices one by one. Then, recalculate the overall likelihood of the task-response sequence. If the likelihood increases, the changes are retained, and these vertices are removed from the vertex-set. Otherwise, restore the answers of vertices to before the replacement operation. In the second round of replacement, we replace answers of any two vertices in the vertex set. In round s, any vertices in the vertex set are replaced. Here, we set a stop value γ for the rounds s in order to control the number of computations. This process is illustrated by the example in Fig. 3.

Iteration of Cut-Point Neighbour Detection. Our Cut-point neighbour detection algorithm eventually produces a new task-response sequence and the quality of the workers. We utilize the results as input to update the workers' classification and the position of the tasks in our model. Then, further search is performed until convergence (i.e. the difference of the final likelihood value of two iterations is 0 or below a predefined threshold). This process is illustrated in Algorithm 2. In each iteration, we increase the number of worker categories to make tasks at the same vertex more similar. In this way, we can find task-response sequence with higher likelihood effectively.

Algorithm 2. Iteration of Cut-point Neighbour Detection

Input: $data, f$ (from EM Algorithm)
Output: L^*(maximum of likelihood); f^*(mappings corresponding to likelihood*); q^*(Worker quality corresponding to f*);
1: **while** not converged **do**
2:     update c, DOM;
3:     $(new\_L, new\_f, new\_q) \leftarrow$ MAIN$(f, data)$
4: **end while**
5: **return** $L^*; f^*; q^*$

---

5   Experiments

In this section, we evaluate the performance of our iterative optimization strategy (labelled as IOS_EM) on synthetic and real rating data, and compare it against the basic EM algorithm (labelled as BAS_EM). Here, we discuss two experiments, one based on simulative data and another based on real-world data, and analyze the results to draw conclusions.

5.1   Experiment 1: Synthetic Data Experiments

In this section, we describe our experiments based on synthetic data. Here, we choose the estimation prior model of worker quality modeled by a confusion matrix. We generate the data based on this model, and compare our method against the EM algorithm in terms of overall likelihood, accuracy of answer predictions and accuracy of worker quality predictions.

Dataset. To generate the ground truth answers for a set of tasks, given a fixed selectivity u, we assign a ground truth value of 1 with a probability of u, and 0 with a probability of $(1-u)$ for each task. Then, we generate a distinct worker response probability matrix for each worker, with the only constraint that most of workers (more than 90%) are better than random (workers' error rate e_0 and e_1 are < 0.5). We then generate worker responses based on these matrices.

Experimental Process and Result. We compare our algorithm with the basic EM algorithm which is also settling maximum likelihood problem. BAS_EM takes an initial estimate or guess for worker error rates as a parameter. Here, we experiment with initialization of e_0 and $e_1 = 0.5$. We set task number $m = 500$, and we vary the selectivity u, and the number of worker responses per task k.

We perform experiments under three data settings: Setting 1, each task receives k responses and $m = k$ (m is the total number of workers); Setting 2, each task receives k responses and $m > k$; Setting 3, each task receives a different number of responses and $m > k$.

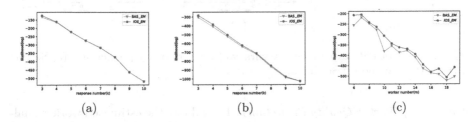

      (a)   (b)   (c)

Fig. 4. Synthetic data experiment. Overall likelihood: (a) Setting 1; (b) Setting 2; and (c) Setting 3.

Overall Likelihood. Figure 4 show the likelihoods of task-response sequence returned by our algorithm and BAS_EM instances on a varied number of workers, for three data settings. The y-axis is in log scale, with a higher value being more desirable. In Fig. 4(a), there are 3–10 workers in each data and each worker has completed all tasks (500 tasks), and in Fig. 4(b), there are 10 workers in each data and each task receives different number of responses (x-axis), so each worker completed 150–500 tasks. Contrast this to Fig. 4(c), here, each task receives different responses (less than workers) and the total number of workers (x-axis) is varying in each data. We observe that our strategy has a significant improvement in likelihood values when the information given to BAS_EM is sparser.

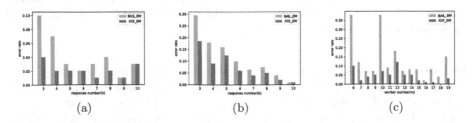

      (a)   (b)   (c)

Fig. 5. Synthetic data experiment. Accuracy of answer predictions: (a) Setting 1; (b) Setting 2; and (c) Setting 3.

Accuracy of Answer Predictions. In Fig. 5, We plot the error rate (ER) of task ground truth estimations each of the algorithms estimate task answer incorrectly (a lower score is better). Here, again, our strategy estimates true values of tasks with a higher accuracy than BAS_EM.

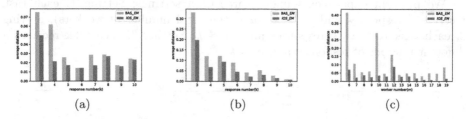

(a)   (b)   (c)

Fig. 6. Synthetic data experiment. Accuracy of worker quality predictions: (a) Setting 1; (b) Setting 2; and (c) Setting 3.

Accuracy of Worker Quality Predictions. To evaluate the estimated worker quality against the actual one, we plot the Average Euclidean Distance (AED) between our estimated matrix and the actual one (a lower score is better) in Fig. 6. We observe that our strategy's estimations are closer to the actual probability matrix than all the BAS_EM.

Summary. For all metrics, our strategy outperforms BAS_EM. It should be noted that our algorithm has more obvious advantages in the third case and is closer to the actual situation. The third set-up (i.e. each task receives a different number of responses) is common in real crowdsourcing markets.

5.2   Experiment 2: Real-World Data Experiments

In this section, we describe our results on a real-world dataset. We evaluate our method with two different estimation prior models: (a) workers' quality represented by a confusion matrix, (b) workers' quality represented by a binary parameter, and compare our method versus the BAS_EM in terms of overall likelihood and ground truth of task estimations.

Dataset. Our dataset is a sentiment analysis dataset, which corresponds to a collection of more than ten thousand sentences extracted from the movie review website *RottenTomatoes*. It contains a set of 5,000 tasks responded by 203 workers. From this collection, a random subset of 5000 sentences were selected and published on Amazon Mechanical Turk for annotation. Given the sentences, the workers were asked to provide the sentiment polarity (positive or negative). We have ground truth *yes/no* answers for each task, but we do not know the real worker quality.

Experimental Process and Result. To evaluate the performance of our strategy based on EM(IOS_EM), we vary size of data by randomly selecting a fixed number of labels from all the data, and compare the estimates of the answer (the yes/no answers) with the given ground truth.

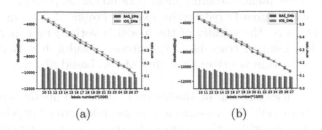

(a)   (b)

Fig. 7. Real data experiment. Likelihood and error rate of answer prediction for (a) and (b).

Overall Likelihood. Figure 7(a) and 7(b) show the likelihoods of task-response sequence returned by IOS_EM and different BAS_EM on a varied number of labels. The y-axis is on log scale, with a higher value being more desirable. And Table 3 show the difference between our method and different BAS_EM in terms of likelihood and error rate of ground truth estimations. In Fig. 7(a) and 7(b), we observe that our method can significantly improve the likelihood value with the three different estimation prior model.

Accuracy of Answer Predictions. In Fig. 7(a), and (b), we also compare error rate(ER) of label estimations with BAS_EM. We plot the error rate of task true answer estimations of each algorithm. Here, again, our method improves the accuracy of the answer estimations while improving the likelihood value.

Table 3. Difference of likelihood and error rate for (a) and (b)

Label number	D-likelihood(a)	D-ER(a)	D-likelihood(b)	D-ER(b)
10000	+138.168	−0.679%	+233.171	−1.116%
12000	+281.449	−1.200%	+247.675	−1.095%
15000	+269.892	−1.099%	+207.998	−0.753%
17000	+289.584	−0.987%	+231.146	−0.826%
20000	+297.262	−0.901%	+407.979	−1.022%
22000	+308.145	−0.880%	+205.360	−0.500%
25000	+57.137	−0.140%	+9.194	−0.040%
27000	+235.244	−0.600%	+59.636	−0.160%

6   Conclusion

This paper presents a method based on pruning and searching. A Cut-point neighborhood detection algorithm is designed to improve the estimation and work quality of the task true answers by increasing the overall likelihood value. In this paper, a dominance ordering model (DOM) is proposed as the platform of the algorithm. We greatly reduce the space of potential mappings to be considered. Furthermore, the validity of the model is verified by experiments, and the computation results is tractable. Experimental results show that the performance of this algorithm is better than that of EM based algorithm in different data settings.

This paper focuses on focus on the binary problems in microtasks. Now there are more and more multiple problems and open-ended crowdsourcing problems. In future research, we will further propose better crowdsourcing quality control research work for multiple problems and open-ended problems.

Acknowledgements. This work is partially supported by National Key R&D Program No. 2017YFB1400100, Innovation Method Fund of China No. 2018IM020200, NFSC No. 61972230, SDNFSC No. ZR2019LZH008, No. ZR2018MF014.

References

1. Cao, C.C., She, J., Tong, Y., Chen, L.: Whom to ask?: Jury selection for decision making tasks on micro-blog services. Proc. VLDB Endow. **5**(11), 1495–1506 (2012)
2. Das Sarma, A., Parameswaran, A., Widom, J.: Towards globally optimal crowdsourcing quality management: the uniform worker setting. In: Proceedings of the 2016 International Conference on Management of Data, pp. 47–62. ACM (2016)
3. Dawid, A.P., Skene, A.M.: Maximum likelihood estimation of observer error-rates using the EM algorithm. J. Roy. Stat. Soc.: Ser. C (Appl. Stat.) **28**(1), 20–28 (1979)
4. Demartini, G., Difallah, D.E., Cudré-Mauroux, P.: Zencrowd: leveraging probabilistic reasoning and crowdsourcing techniques for large-scale entity linking. In: Proceedings of the 21st International Conference on World Wide Web, pp. 469–478. ACM (2012)
5. Dempster, A.P., Laird, N.M., Rubin, D.B.: Maximum likelihood from incomplete data via the EM algorithm. J. Roy. Stat. Soc.: Ser. B (Methodol.) **39**(1), 1–22 (1977). https://doi.org/10.1111/j.2517-6161.1977.tb01600.x
6. Guo, S., Parameswaran, A., Garcia-Molina, H.: So who won?: dynamic max discovery with the crowd. In: Proceedings of the 2012 ACM SIGMOD International Conference on Management of Data, pp. 385–396. ACM (2012)
7. Ipeirotis, P.G., Provost, F., Wang, J.: Quality management on Amazon mechanical turk. In: Proceedings of the ACM SIGKDD Workshop on Human Computation, pp. 64–67. ACM (2010)
8. Khattak, F.K., Salleb-Aouissi, A.: Quality control of crowd labeling through expert evaluation. In: Proceedings of the NIPS 2nd Workshop on Computational Social Science and the Wisdom of Crowds, vol. 2, p. 5 (2011)
9. Kuncheva, L.I., Whitaker, C.J., Shipp, C.A., Duin, R.P.: Limits on the majority vote accuracy in classifier fusion. Pattern Anal. Appl. **6**(1), 22–31 (2003). https://doi.org/10.1007/s10044-002-0173-7

10. Kurve, A., Miller, D.J., Kesidis, G.: Multicategory crowdsourcing accounting for variable task difficulty, worker skill, and worker intention. IEEE Trans. Knowl. Data Eng. **27**(3), 794–809 (2014)
11. Liu, X., Lu, M., Ooi, B.C., Shen, Y., Wu, S., Zhang, M.: CDAS: a crowdsourcing data analytics system. Proc. VLDB Endow. **5**(10), 1040–1051 (2012)
12. Ma, F., et al.: Faitcrowd: fine grained truth discovery for crowdsourced data aggregation. In: Proceedings of the 21th ACM SIGKDD International Conference on Knowledge Discovery and Data Mining, pp. 745–754. ACM (2015). https://doi.org/10.1145/2783258.2783314
13. Marcus, A., Wu, E., Karger, D., Madden, S., Miller, R.: Human-powered sorts and joins. Proc. VLDB Endow. **5**(1), 13–24 (2011)
14. Raykar, V.C., et al.: Supervised learning from multiple experts: whom to trust when everyone lies a bit. In: Proceedings of the 26th Annual International Conference on Machine Learning, pp. 889–896. ACM (2009)
15. Sarawagi, S., Bhamidipaty, A.: Interactive deduplication using active learning. In: Proceedings of the Eighth ACM SIGKDD International Conference on Knowledge Discovery and Data Mining, pp. 269–278. ACM (2002)
16. Smyth, P., Fayyad, U.M., Burl, M.C., Perona, P., Baldi, P.: Inferring ground truth from subjective labelling of venus images. In: Advances in Neural Information Processing Systems, pp. 1085–1092 (1995)
17. Snow, R., O'Connor, B., Jurafsky, D., Ng, A.Y.: Cheap and fast–but is it good?: evaluating non-expert annotations for natural language tasks. In: Proceedings of the Conference on Empirical Methods in Natural Language Processing, pp. 254–263. Association for Computational Linguistics (2008)
18. Tang, W., Lease, M.: Semi-supervised consensus labeling for crowdsourcing. In: SIGIR 2011 Workshop on Crowdsourcing for Information Retrieval (CIR), pp. 1–6 (2011)
19. Wang, H., Guo, S., Cao, J., Guo, M.: Melody: a long-term dynamic quality-aware incentive mechanism for crowdsourcing. IEEE Trans. Parallel Distrib. Syst. **29**(4), 901–914 (2017). https://doi.org/10.1109/TPDS.2017.2775232
20. Wang, J., Kraska, T., Franklin, M.J., Feng, J.: Crowder: crowdsourcing entity resolution. Proc. VLDB Endow. **5**(11), 1483–1494 (2012)
21. Whitehill, J., Wu, T.F., Bergsma, J., Movellan, J.R., Ruvolo, P.L.: Whose vote should count more: optimal integration of labels from labelers of unknown expertise. In: Advances in Neural Information Processing Systems, pp. 2035–2043 (2009)
22. Zhang, Y., Chen, X., Zhou, D., Jordan, M.I.: Spectral methods meet EM: a provably optimal algorithm for crowdsourcing. In: Advances in Neural Information Processing Systems, pp. 1260–1268 (2014)
23. Zheng, Y., Wang, J., Li, G., Cheng, R., Feng, J.: QASCA: a quality-aware task assignment system for crowdsourcing applications. In: Proceedings of the 2015 ACM SIGMOD International Conference on Management of Data, pp. 1031–1046. ACM (2015). https://doi.org/10.1145/2723372.2749430

D-GHNAS for Joint Intent Classification and Slot Filling

Yanxi Tang, Jianzong Wang[✉], Xiaoyang Qu, Nan Zhang, and Jing Xiao

Ping An Technology (Shenzhen) Co., Ltd., Shenzhen, China
jzwang@188.com

Abstract. Intent classification and slot filling are two classical problems for spoken language understanding and dialog systems. The existing works, either accomplishing intent classification or slot filling separately or using a joint model, are all human-designed models with trial and error. In order to explore the variety of network architecture and to find whether there exist possible network architectures with better results, we proposed the D-GHNAS (Deep deterministic policy gradient based Graph Hypernetwork Neural Architecture Search) to accomplish intent classification and slot filling via a NAS (Neural Architecture Search) method. NAS based techniques can automatically search for network architectures without experts' trial and error. Different from early NAS methods with hundreds of GPU days to find an ideal neural architecture that takes too much computation resource, in this work, hypernetwork is used to decrease the computation cost. Experimental results demonstrate that our model improves intent classification and slot filling results on public benchmark datasets ATIS and SNIPS compared with other joint models for these tasks.

Keywords: Intent classification · Slot filling · Neural architecture search · Hyper network · Auto machine learning

1 Introduction

Spoken language understanding (SLU) system aims to automatically understand the text typed by the user or transcribed by the user voice in order to take the next proper action to satisfy user's demand. SLU is a hot research topic in natural language processing field which plays an important role in many areas like automatic customer service, automatic question answering, voice assistants, etc. Intent classification is part of NLU tasks which is to predict intent (only one label) from every input sentence. After the user intent is identified by an intent classifier, the system can make an accurate response to the user request.

The key of intent classification and slot filling lies in feature representation. Deep neural networks can learn text representations automatically without manually taking features and have achieved remarkable results in a wide range of SLU and NLP tasks. Different network structures have been explored to extract a meaningful semantic representation of the text for intent classification.

X. Wang et al. (Eds.): APWeb-WAIM 2020, LNCS 12317, pp. 794–807, 2020.
https://doi.org/10.1007/978-3-030-60259-8_58

Convolution Neural Networks (CNN), Recurrent Neural Network (RNN), and the combination of CNN and RNN have been widely used since they can capture temporal and semantic features. In order to achieve better performance, many complex structures have been applied, such as attention-based CNN [1], hierarchical attention networks [2], adversarial multi-task learning [3]. Due to the consistency of the application scenario and input text, a joint model for intent detection and slot filling [4,5] is proposed that the feature representation of one task can be shared in the other task to simplify the model and promote each other. The neural network like CNN [3], RNN [6], Long Short-Term Memory (LSTM) [7], attention-based BiRNN [4], and slot-gated attention-based model [8].

As these currently proposed models are manually designed by researchers, which is a time-consuming procedure, attention goes to NAS, which is becoming one of the hottest interests in the neural network field. Compared with conventionally manually designed architectures, NAS methods have outperformed on a lot of tasks, such as image classification [9,10] and object detection [11,12]. It will find an architecture from all possible architectures in search space by following a search strategy that will maximize the performance, usually accuracy. Early NAS approaches adopted nested optimization, which caused these search methods resource-hungry, especially for large dataset. A new paradigm was proposed recently [13] to reduce the computational complexity via a graph hypernetwork, with which NAS becomes more efficient and flexible.

For the reason to achieve better result, we proposed D-GHNAS for intent classification and slot filling task. The goal of this work is to exploit the powerful feature learning mechanism enabled by NAS and apply it to spoken language understanding tasks. The main idea is to utilize NAS technology to design good neural network architectures automatically. The main contributions of this work are as follows:

(1) We apply the reinforcement learning based GHNAS method to intent classification and slot filling task. To the best of our knowledge, it is the first study to use graph hypernetwork NAS method to deal with these problems. Experiments on the benchmark datasets demonstrate that our method show competitive results compared with other model.
(2) We proposed the DDPG search strategy to explore the search space. It takes in the network embedding as input to find next network and its network will update after numbers of searches for better searching.
(3) In order to search network effectively, We applied the cell structured network and the hypernetwork to generate weights directly.

2 Related Work

Intent Classification and Slot Filling: Accurate intent classifier helps search engines and dialog systems return a concise answer to the user's query. Intent classification is a fine-grained text classification which is a fundamental task in natural language processing. The key of text classification lies on feature representation. Deep neural networks can learn text representations automatically without human-designed features and have achieved remarkable results in a wide range of SLU and NLP tasks.

It has been a long time since the first spoken dialog understanding task merged [14]. Early approaches often use machine learning models to deal with intent classification task [15] like SVM [16] and Adaboost [17]. After that, approaches based on neural architecture have shown good performance on intent classification tasks like deep belief network (DBN) [18]. Another application is RNN [19]. RNN keeps sequence ordering information, which is beneficial to capture the long-term contextual information and correlation between non-consecutive words effectively.

For slot filling tasks, early explorations are based on Conditional Random Fields (CRF) architecture [20]. Recently, neural networks showed a great performance and outperformed CRF models. [21] used standard RNN to take in words and predict the slot labels. [22] introduced LSTM on this task and outperform RNN result. [23] applied attention-based encoder-decoder on the slot filling task without LSTM.

Recent works focus on the joint model for intent classification and slot filling tasks that user's intent and the slot labels are supposed to share features with each other. [6] applied RNN for the joint training of intent classification and slot filling task. Besides, LSTM, which is an improved variant of RNN, is applied to the joint model training and performs well [24]. LSTM can capture semantics of long sentence but the information of previous contexts will gradually lose. Attention mechanism can address this problem effectively [4]. Last year, a new language representation model BERT (Bidirectional Encoder Representations from Transformers) has created state-of-the-art models for a wide variety of natural language processing tasks after simple fine-tuning. It also showed a good performance on intent classification and slot filling task [25]. Besides, another work adopt a joint model that can use the intent information as the slot filling input through Stack-Propagation [26].

Graph Embedding: Graph embedding or network embedding is based on the idea of GNN to preserve both network topology structure and node content information, which attracts great attentions [27]. A graph neural network [28] can be described by a set of nodes and edges. Edges can be either directed or undirected, depending on whether there exist directional dependencies between nodes. Graph Neural Network is a type of Neural Network which directly operates on the graph structure. The target of GNN is to learn a state embedding $h_v \in R^s$ which contains the information of neighborhood for each node. The state embedding h_v is an s-dimension vector of node v and can be used to produce an output o_v such as the node label. Let f be a parametric function, called local transition function, that is shared among all nodes and updates the node state according to the input neighborhood. And let g be the local output function that describes how the output is produced. Then, h_v can be defined as follows:

$$h_v = f(x_v, x_{co[v]}, h_{ne[v]}, x_{ne[v]}) \tag{1}$$

Where x_v, $x_{co[v]}$, $h_{ne[v]}$, $x_{ne[v]}$ are the features of v, the edge features, states and features of v's neighborhood nodes. There are some other methods like matrix factorization [29,30] and random walks [31].

Neural Architecture Search: Neural architecture search is a method of automating architecture engineering that neural network architectures can be designed automatically. It comes to deal with the rising demand of architecture engineering and has outperformed manually designed models on some of the tasks like image classification [32], object detection [33] and semantic segmentation [34]. Moreover, neural architecture search can be a part of AutoML and it has overlap with other field like meta-learning and hyperparameter optimization. There are three main directions for the development of NAS, search space, search strategy and performance estimation strategy.

Search space defines which architectures can be represented in principle including the layer number, operation type, hyperparameters, etc. Different from early chain-structure models, recent works like [35,36] introduced some hand-crafted architectures like skip connections that allow to build more complex models with multi-branches structure. Since 2016, motivated by some hand-crafted architectures, some structures like motifs and blocks appeared.

Search strategy defines the method to find a neural network architecture from the search space, including random search, Bayesian optimization, reinforcement learning [37,38] and evolutionary methods [39]. An appropriate search strategy should be able to search the architecture from the search space while keeping the exploration.

Performance estimation strategy is the method to estimate the every step sampled architecture and the methods include lower fidelity estimates [40], learning curve extrapolation [41], network morphisms [42] and one-shot models [35]. It is important that an appropriate estimation strategy can greatly reduce the computation cost of the search procedure.

3 Graph Neural Network for Neural Architecture Search

3.1 Model Design

In order to apply NAS method on SLU task in an efficient way, we proposed a joint model of a graph hypernetwork based NAS method. Our model consists of a hypernetwork and a Deep Deterministic Policy Gradient (DDPG) [43].

Since NAS technique has been applied to many tasks, it shows a great performance on many tasks that it can go through the search space to pick the best architecture automatically, but it is based on the great cost of computation resource. In order to solve this problem, based on recent researches, hypernetwork is applied. A hypernetwork is a small network who can generate weights for large network that there is no need of training from scratched. Much time can be saved.

In our model, as shown in Fig. 1, a neural network will take in the text embedding and produce the result. The network architecture is selected from a

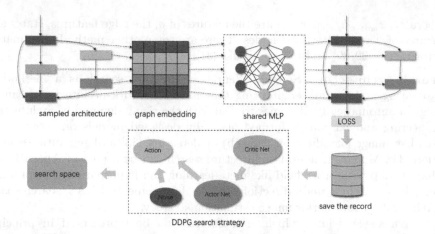

Fig. 1. D-GHNAS search procedure. First, the neural network architecture will be transformed into a directed acyclic graph embedding. Nodes represent the operations in the network and edges represent the direction of tensors. Then a hyper network will use the graph embedding as the input and produce the weights for the neural network. The record of every search result performance will be saved to train the DDPG network, which will decide the child network for the next search step.

predefined search space. In each step, a different architecture will be selected from the search space by a specific search strategy, DDPG. After selection, the architecture will be transformed to a graph embedding. A full trained hypernetwork will take in the network graph embedding and generate the weights. Then the accuracy on the validation set can be calculated through the combination of the network and generated weights. Then a step of architecture search is finished.

After steps of searching, a number of network architectures with top accuracy on the validation set will be selected to train until converge. The best model will be searched after comparisons between models on the validation set.

3.2   Architecture Embedding

The neural network architecture can be represented as a cyclic directed graph $G = (V, E)$, where each node v represents an computation operator in the neural network parameterized with weight w_v. The edges in the graph can represent tensor's flowing direction so we have edge $e_{ab} = (a, b) \in E$ stands for tensor's direction from node a to node b. So we can calculate the output activation tensor of node b by:

$$x_b = \sum_{e_{ab} \in E} f_v(x_a, w_b), \forall v \in V \tag{2}$$

3.3   Parameters Generation

A hypernetwork is used to get the weights. After transformation, a graph embedding is used to describe the neural network. Then the nodes are embedded to one-hot vectors to represent the node's computational operator and the hypernetwork will take in the network embedding to generate node weights. We define h_b as the embedding of node b and let H be the weight function. The weights generation can be described:

$$w_b = H(h_b, \delta) \tag{3}$$

Where w_b is the parameter of node b and δ is the hypernet parameter.

3.4   Search Space

The search space has to be large and representative enough or some interesting candidate architectures might be omitted. Meanwhile, the accuracy achieved by the NAS architecture on validation set should be higher than the one achieved by standalone methods. Of course, the NAS architecture must to be simple enough for training on limited memory and time.

$$A_i = f(a), a \in A^* \tag{4}$$

Early search spaces for NAS are usually a chain-structure or multi-branches structure. These search spaces are designed by experience. The chain-structure is a single path structure that former layer's output serves as the input of the next layer. The weak point is that this structure is simple that some features may lost in the forward passing. Multi-branches structure is a more complicated structure that it contains many paths between input and output. Besides, there are many paths between layers. The main feature of the structure is that the search space size has been explosively increased. On the one hand, this search space should contain the structures with affordable results. On the other hand, such a large search space makes it hard to find the best model. Most of the searches are useless while many real world tasks have constraints especially for the computation cost.

$$C_i \leq C_{max} \tag{5}$$

Instead, based on the idea of architecture motifs that the network can be seen as repeatedly stacking of small cells, the search space can be limited to a small cell.

In the experiment, the search space is reduced to a small cell $\{A_i\}_{i=1}^N$. A cell contains many operations and each operation can be one of the predefined operator. In this experiment, the operator set consists of 7 operators, 1×3 convolution, 1×5 convolution, 1×7 convolution, 1×3 convolution dilated, 1×5 convolution dilated, 1×7 convolution dilated and identity operator. A number of predefined operators will be selected to build a cell. As described before, the selected neural network will be transformed to a graph embedding. The architecture is constructed by repeatedly stacking the constructed cell.

3.5   Search Strategy

After the search space is designed where the candidate framework can be selected, the next step is to decide the search strategy to select the network architecture at each step. Some classical search policies are random search, grid search, Bayesian optimization, Reinforcement learning, Evolutionary Algorithm, etc. In order to search efficiently for a neural network with best accuracy, we use the DDPG for model selection. Compared with other network search strategy like random search or evolution algorithms, this method is efficient and stable that random search's result is not stable and convincible. On the other hand, evolution algorithms often take too much time on the selection of individuals.

In DDPG [43], the network search process can be considered as a continuous task. The network structure can be defined as the state S and each batch of input can be defined as the environment E. In the search of step n, network S_n takes in the validation dataset and get a reward r_{n-1}. The set of current network structure S_n, action a_{n-1}, reward r_{n-1} and last network structure S_{n-1} is recorded in the memory pool as $(s_{n-1}, a_{n-1}, r_{n-1}, s_n)$. A critic network σ is used to decide the next action for the neural network. In each step, the weights of the critic network will be updated by taking a batch of records from the memory pool. The function can be described as bellow:

$$L_c = argmin \frac{1}{N} \sum_i (y_i - f(s_i, a|\theta^Q))^2 \tag{6}$$

Where L_c denotes as the loss of critic network C, y_i denotes as the target value and θ^Q is the weights of the network. It is usually a multi-layer perceptron. Then an action distribution θ^μ is updated:

$$\theta^{\mu^*} = \tau\theta^\mu + (1 - \tau)\theta^{\mu^*} \tag{7}$$

The network structure is updated by sampled action a from θ^μ:

$$a_i = \mu(s_i|\theta^{\mu^*}) + \xi_i \tag{8}$$

Where ξ_i is added noise to keep the exploration of the model. The size of the memory pool equals to half of the total steps that new record will replace the oldest record in order. The network architecture will be updated based on previous architecture and the action a from $\mu(s_i|\theta^{\mu^*})$:

$$A_{n+1} = A_n + a_n \tag{9}$$

3.6   Learning

The training part can be divided into two parts. The first part is to train the hypernetworks. At the beginning, a small set of architectures will be randomly chosen as the input to train the hypernetworks and the DDPG model doesn't take part in this procedure. The hypernetwork will be trained until the architectures converge.

The next part is to find the best architecture. At step N, an architecture will be selected based on action and $N - 1$ step architecture. The critic network will be updated by sampling a batch of records from the memory pool and the critic network will update the action distribution. The weights of the architecture are generated by the hypernetwork:

$$\begin{cases} E = Y_t - (\sum w_i x_i + b_i) \\ w = h(A; \phi) \end{cases} \tag{10}$$

Where Y_t denotes as the standard label, E denotes as the difference between predicted result and the label. The next step architecture S_{N+1} can be presented as current architecture S_N with an action a:

$$S_{N+1} = S_N + a, a \in \varphi(a) \tag{11}$$

4 Experiments

In this section, the graph hypernetwork is applied to intent classification and slot filling task that two datasets are selected, Airline Travel Information System (ATIS) dataset and SNIPS dataset.

4.1 Dataset Details

Table 1. Dataset details for ATIS dataset and SNIPS dataset.

Dataset	Train utterances	Valid utterances	Test utterances	Intent types
ATIS	4478	500	893	22
SNIPS	13084	700	700	7

ATIS contains audio recordings of people making flight reservations. As shown in Table 1, the training, valid and test sets contain 4,478, 500 and 893 utterances, respectively. There are 120 slot labels and 22 intent types for the training set. SNIPS is collected from the SNIPS personal voice assistant. The training, valid and test sets contain 13,084, 700 and 700 utterances, respectively. There are 7 intent types for the training set.

4.2 Baselines

Our model is compared with following baselines:

RNN-LSTM: [7] proposed a RNN-LSTM architecture for joint modeling of slot filling, intent determination and domain classification. This model is available for multi-task deep learning where each domain's data can reinforce each other.

Attention-BiRNN: Attention-BiRNN [4] introduced a RNN based encoder decoder model, which uses attention mechanism on intent classification and slot filling tasks. Different strategies have been used to incorporate alignment information to the encoder-decoder framework. Besides, attention is introduced to the alignment-based RNN models.

Slot-Gated: Slot-Gated model [8] applied a slot gate mechanism on LSTM to improve the performance, in which the slot filling can be conditioned on the learned intent result in order to achieve better result on the joint task. For the reason that the slot-intent relations are stronger and easily modeled, the slot-gated model is more useful for a simple understanding task.

Capsule-NLU: Capsule-NLU [44] proposed a capsule based neural network model which accomplished slot filling and intent detection task via a dynamic routing-by-agreement schema. This schema can further synergize the slot filling performance by using the intent representation.

SF-ID Network: SF-ID network [45] proposed a novel bi-directional interrelated model for intent detection and slot filling. The SF-ID network can establish direct connections between these two tasks to help promote each other. Besides, an new iteration mechanism in SF-ID network can enhance the bi-directional interrelated connections.

Joint Bert: [25] introduced a Bert (Bidirectional Encoder Representations from Transformers) based model for intent classification and slot filling tasks. The model architecture of BERT is a multi-layer bidirectional transformer encoder based on the original transformer model.

4.3   Training Details

Search Space: Based on the idea of module stacking, our model searches for a cell rather than the entire network. In each cell, 7 operations are available for a single node as the maximum node number. The limit cell number for the entire network is 7. For DDPG, the memory pool size is half of the total steps. The critic networks node number is set 16. The learning rate starts at 0.01 and ends at 0.0001. The decay starts when the memory pool is full. The output of critic network is the distribution of action a, which follows the normal distribution. In order to keep the variety, a little noise has been added.

Training: A standard GRU is used as the GNN module with hidden size 32 and 2 layer multi layer perceptron. The shared hypernetwork $H(;\phi)$ is a 2 layer multi layer perceptron. 10 random sampled architectures are used to train the hypernetwork until these networks converge or reach a preset value. ADAM optimizer is chosen.

Evaluation: At the beginning, 10 random architectures are chosen as the input for hypernetworks. The hypernetwork are trained to convergence. Then DDPG is applied to the search strategy. The total architecture number is 1000 and the memory pool size is 500. In each step, a batch of 5 records will be sampled to update the critic network. The action distribution begins at uniform distribution and ends at normal distribution. The weights of selected architecture are generated by the hypernetwork. At last, 10 architectures with best accuracy will be stored.

Table 2. Comparison of intent classification and slot filling tasks on ATIS and SNIPS dataset.

Model	ATIS		SNIPS	
	Intent (Acc)	Slot (F1)	Intent (Acc)	Slot (F1)
RNN-LSTM (Hakkani-Tür)	92.6	94.3	96.9	87.3
Attention-BiRNN (Liu, Bing)	91.1	94.2	96.7	87.8
Slot-Gated (Goo, Chih-Wen)	94.1	95.2	97.0	88.8
CAPSULE-NLU (Zhang, Chenwei)	95.0	94.8	97.3	91.8
SF-ID Network (Haihong, E)	97.1	94.9	96.6	90.9
Joint Bert (Q Chen)	97.5	96.8	97.6	96.7
D-GHNAS	**97.6**	96.3	**97.8**	94.5

4.4 Results

The results is showed in Table 2. In our experiment, 1000 architectures are selected in the searching procedure. These architectures are ranked by accuracy. Then 10 architectures with top accuracy are selected and trained to converge. The final network is found by the second ranking in these 10 architectures. As we can find that the graph hypernetwork shows a very competitive result on the intent classification task. For intent classification task, it reaches 97.6% on ATIS and 97.8% on SNIPS which is better than other baseline models. For slot filling task, it reaches is 96.3% on ATIS and 94.5% on SNIPS, less than Joint Bert on both datasets.

The main reason is the trade off problem that all NAS methods should face between the search cost and performance. The search space is designed to search effectively that results in a lower result compared with other NAS methods with larger search space and search cost. The selected model is constructed by convolution operations which limit the result on this task. Another point is the network evaluation strategy. In the experiment, all networks with parameters are ordered by the accuracy and only 10 networks are selected for the consideration of efficiency. So the result should be improved if more networks can be selected. Besides, the different word embedding methods also affect the result.

Hyperparameters: In our model, the basic search unit is a cell and the architecture is constructed by stacking a number of cells. The cell structure is different

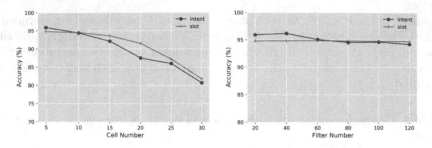

Fig. 2. The effect of cell number and filter number variation on the result.

in each search procedure. As described before, a cell can have 7 kinds of operators at most. Cells play such a significant role in our experiment that another experiment is conducted to explore the relationship between cost and the result on intent detection and slot filling with a fixed number of filters. As shown in Fig. 2, in this experiment, the cell number increases from 5 to 30 while the intent and slot results decrease from 95.9% and 94.8% to 80.7% and 81.8%. Besides, another experiment about the filter number is also conducted. As showed, the intent accuracy decreases around 2% and the clot result nearly keeps when the filter number increases from 20 to 120.

Impact of Search Strategy: In order to evaluate the performance for DDPG search strategy, another experiment has been made with different search strategies. We compared DDPG with random search and grid search. The total number of sampled architectures is 1000. The time limit is set 200 GPU hours and DDPG reaches 95.6% with much less when compared with other two other search strategies. It shows that random search method can reach a high accuracy but the performance is not stable after numbers of test. Grid search depends on the size of search space that all architectures will be sampled in order. With the increase size of search space, the computation cost also increases. It's not affordable to apply grid search on large search space and dataset. Apart from these methods, DDPG can learn from experience that critic network and action. It can be found from the result that DDPG can find a better network in less time.

Impact of Search Space: The search space is another important factor that affects the search result, so different search spaces are compared in this experiment. We picked chain-structure, multi-branches structure and cell/block structure. The max time cost is also set 200 GPU hours and the Cell/Block structure can reach 95.9% with much less time. Chain-structure is simple and has the vanishing gradient problem when depth increases. Multi-branches structure applies the skip connection and is complicated which let the search space exponentially grow up. Besides, the accuracy may increase a little. Compared with multi-branches structure, the cell/block structure is a computation saving structure that most searching cost is limited with the cell. The search space is based on cell and the search procedure can speed with hyper. From the result, it can be found that the most benefit of cell/block structure is it took the least computation cost to find the best network compared with other search spaces.

5 Conclusion

In this study, we proposed a DDPG based graph hypernetwork NAS model. It can generate the weights for architecture based on its graph embedding through a hypernetwork. DDPG is used as the search strategy to search the architecture from the search space. In the experiment, it reaches competitive results on ATIS and SNIPS datasets within a few GPU hours, which shows that the network search method can outperform some of the best manually designed architectures. Besides, another two experiments are conducted to compare other search space and search strategy that our model can accelerate the search procedure. In the future, we will keep on research of NAS application on NLP tasks.

Acknowledgements. This paper is supported by National Key Research and Development Program of China under grant No. 2018YFB1003500, No. 2018YFB0204400 and No.2017YFB-1401202.

References

1. Zhao, Z., Wu, Y.: Attention-based convolutional neural networks for sentence classification. In: Interspeech 2016 (2016)
2. Yang, Z., Yang, D., Dyer, C., He, X., Smola, A., Hovy, E.: Hierarchical attention networks for document classification. In: Proceedings of the 2016 Conference of the North American Chapter of the Association for Computational Linguistics: Human Language Technologies, pp. 1480–1489 (2016)
3. Liu, P., Qiu, X., Huang, X.: Adversarial multi-task learning for text classification. In: Proceedings of the 55th Annual Meeting of the Association for Computational Linguistics, vol. 1: Long Papers, pp. 1–10 (2017)
4. Liu, B., Lane, I.: Attention-based recurrent neural network models for joint intent detection and slot filling. In: Interspeech 2016, pp. 685–689 (2016)
5. Xu, P., Sarikaya, R.: Convolutional neural network based triangular CRF for joint intent detection and slot filling. In: 2013 IEEE Workshop on Automatic Speech Recognition and Understanding, pp. 78–83. IEEE (2013)
6. Guo, D., Tur, G., Yih, W., Zweig, G.: Joint semantic utterance classification and slot filling with recursive neural networks. In: 2014 IEEE Spoken Language Technology Workshop (SLT), pp. 554–559. IEEE (2014)
7. Hakkani-Tür, D., et al: Multi-domain joint semantic frame parsing using bi-directional RNN-LSTM. In: Interspeech, pp. 715–719 (2016)
8. Goo, C.-W., et al.: Slot-gated modeling for joint slot filling and intent prediction. In: Proceedings of the 2018 Conference of the North American Chapter of the Association for Computational Linguistics: Human Language Technologies, vol. 2 (Short Papers), pp. 753–757 (2018)
9. Pham, H., Guan, M., Zoph, B., Le, Q., Dean, J.: Efficient neural architecture search via parameter sharing. In: International Conference on Machine Learning, pp. 4092–4101 (2018)

806   Y. Tang et al.

10. Liu, C., et al.: Progressive neural architecture search. In: Ferrari, V., Hebert, M., Sminchisescu, C., Weiss, Y. (eds.) ECCV 2018. LNCS, vol. 11205, pp. 19–35. Springer, Cham (2018). https://doi.org/10.1007/978-3-030-01246-5_2
11. Ghiasi, G., Lin, T.-Y., Le, Q.V.: NAS-FPN: learning scalable feature pyramid architecture for object detection. In: Proceedings of the IEEE Conference on Computer Vision and Pattern Recognition, pp. 7036–7045 (2019)
12. Tan, M., et al.: Platform-aware neural architecture search for mobile. In: Proceedings of the IEEE Conference on Computer Vision and Pattern Recognition, pp. 2820–2828 (2019)
13. Zhang, C., Ren, M., Urtasun, R.: Graph hypernetworks for neural architecture search. arXiv preprint arXiv:1810.05749 (2018)
14. Gorin, A.L., Riccardi, G., Wright, J.H.: How may i help you? Speech Commun. 23(1–2), 113–127 (1997)
15. Young, S.: Talking to machines (statistically speaking). In: Seventh International Conference on Spoken Language Processing (2002)
16. Haffner, P., Tur, G., Wright, J.H.: Optimizing SVMS for complex call classification. In: 2003 IEEE International Conference on Acoustics, Speech, and Signal Processing, 2003, Proceedings. (ICASSP 2003), vol. 1, p. I. IEEE (2003)
17. Schapire, R.E., Singer, Y.: A boosting-based system for text categorization. Mach. Learn. 392(3), 135–168 (1999)
18. Deoras, A., Sarikaya, R.: Deep belief network based semantic taggers for spoken language understanding. In: Interspeech, pp. 2713–2717 (2013)
19. Ravuri, S., Stolcke, A.: Recurrent neural network and LSTM models for lexical utterance classification. In: Sixteenth Annual Conference of the International Speech Communication Association (2015)
20. Raymond, C., Riccardi, G.: Generative and discriminative algorithms for spoken language understanding. In: Eighth Annual Conference of the International Speech Communication Association (2007)
21. Yao, K., Zweig, G., Hwang, M.-Y., Shi, Y., Yu, D.: Recurrent neural networks for language understanding. In: Interspeech, pp. 2524–2528 (2013)
22. Yao, K., Peng, B., Zhang, Y., Yu, D., Zweig, G., Shi, Y.: Spoken language understanding using long short-term memory neural networks. In: 2014 IEEE Spoken Language Technology Workshop (SLT), pp. 189–194. IEEE (2014)
23. Simonnet, E., Camelin, N., Deléglise, P., Estéve, Y.: Exploring the use of attention-based recurrent neural networks for spoken language understanding (2015)
24. Shi, Y., Yao, K., Tian, L., Jiang, D.: Deep LSTM based feature mapping for query classification. In: Proceedings of the 2016 Conference of the North American Chapter of the Association for Computational Linguistics: Human Language Technologies, pp. 1501–1511 (2016)
25. Chen, Q., Zhuo, Z., Wang, W.: Bert for joint intent classification and slot filling. arXiv preprint arXiv:1902.10909 (2019)
26. Qin, L., Che, W., Li, Y., Wen, H., Liu, T.: A stack-propagation framework with token-level intent detection for spoken language understanding. arXiv preprint arXiv:1909.02188 (2019)
27. Hamilton, W.L., Ying, R., Leskovec, J.: Representation learning on graphs: methods and applications (2017)
28. Scarselli, F., Gori, M., Tsoi, A.C., Hagenbuchner, M., Monfardini, G.: The graph neural network model. IEEE Trans. Neural Netw. 20(1), 61–80 (2008)
29. Shen, X., Pan, S., Liu, W., Ong, Y.-S., Sun, Q.-S.: Discrete network embedding. In: Proceedings of the 27th International Joint Conference on Artificial Intelligence, pp. 3549–3555. AAAI Press (2018)

30. Yang, H., Pan, S., Zhang, P., Chen, L., Lian, D., Zhang, C.: Binarized attributed network embedding. In: 2018 IEEE International Conference on Data Mining (ICDM), pp. 1476–1481. IEEE (2018)
31. Perozzi, B., Al-Rfou, R., Skiena, S.: Deepwalk: online learning of social representations. In: Proceedings of the 20th ACM SIGKDD International Conference on Knowledge Discovery and Data Mining, pp. 701–710. ACM (2014)
32. Real, E., Aggarwal, A., Huang, Y., Le, Q.V.: Aging evolution for image classifier architecture search. In: AAAI Conference on Artificial Intelligence (2019)
33. Zoph, B., Vasudevan, V., Shlens, J., Le, Q.V.: Learning transferable architectures for scalable image recognition. In: Proceedings of the IEEE Conference on Computer Vision and Pattern Recognition, pp. 8697–8710 (2018)
34. Chen, L.-C., et al.: Searching for efficient multi-scale architectures for dense image prediction. In: Advances in Neural Information Processing Systems, pp. 8699–8710 (2018)
35. Brock, A., Lim, T., Ritchie, J.M., Weston, N.J.: Smash: one-shot model architecture search through hypernetworks. In: 6th International Conference on Learning Representations (2018)
36. Elsken, T., Metzen, J.H., Hutter, F.: Efficient multi-objective neural architecture search via Lamarckian evolution (2018)
37. Baker, B., Gupta, O., Naik, N., Raskar, R.: Designing neural network architectures using reinforcement learning (2016)
38. Zhong, Z., Yan, J., Wu, W., Shao, J., Liu, C.-L.: Practical block-wise neural network architecture generation. In: Proceedings of the IEEE Conference on Computer Vision and Pattern Recognition, pp. 2423–2432 (2018)
39. Liu, H., Simonyan, K., Vinyals, O., Fernando, C., Kavukcuoglu, K.: Hierarchical representations for efficient architecture search (2017)
40. Runge, F., Stoll, D., Falkner, S., Hutter, F.: Learning to design RNA (2018)
41. Klein, A., Falkner, S., Springenberg, J.T., Hutter, F.: Learning curve prediction with Bayesian neural networks (2016)
42. Elsken, T., Metzen, J.-H., Hutter, F.: Simple and efficient architecture search for convolutional neural networks (2017)
43. Lillicrap, T.P., et al.: Continuous control with deep reinforcement learning, US Patent App. 15/217,758, 26 January 2017
44. Zhang, C., Li, Y., Du, N., Fan, W., Yu, P.S.: Joint slot filling and intent detection via capsule neural networks. arXiv preprint arXiv:1812.09471 (2018)
45. Haihong, E., Niu, P., Chen, Z., Song, M.: A novel bi-directional interrelated model for joint intent detection and slot filling. In: Proceedings of the 57th Annual Meeting of the Association for Computational Linguistics, pp. 5467–5471 (2019)

Index-Based Scheduling for Parallel State Machine Replication

Guodong Zhao[1], Gang Wu[1,2(✉)], Yidong Song[1], Baiyou Qiao[1],
and Donghong Han[1]

[1] School of Computer Science and Engineering, Northeastern University,
Shenyang, China
{gdzhao,ydsong}@stumail.neu.edu.cn,
{wugang,qiaobaiyou,handonghong}@mail.neu.edu.cn
[2] State Key Laboratory for Novel Software Technology, Nanjing University,
Nanjing, China

Abstract. State Machine Replication is a fundamental approach to designing web services with fault tolerance. However, its requirement for the deterministic execution of transactions often results in single-threaded replicas, which cannot fully exploit the multicore capabilities of today's processors. Therefore, parallel SMR has become a hot topic of recent research. The basic idea behind it is that independent transactions can be executed in parallel, while dependent transactions must be executed in their relative order to ensure consistency among replicas. The dependency detection of existing parallel SMR methods is mainly based on pairwise transaction comparison or batch comparison. These methods cannot simultaneously guarantee both effective detection and concurrent execution. Moreover, the scheduling process cannot execute concurrently, which introduces extra scheduling overhead as well. In order to further reduce scheduling overhead and ensure the parallel execution of transactions, we propose an efficient scheduler based on a specific index structure. The index is composed of a Bloom Filter and the associated transaction queues, which provides an efficient dependency detection and preserve necessary dependency information respectively. Based on the index structure, we further devise an elaborated concurrent scheduling process. The experimental results show that the proposed scheduler is more efficient, scalable and robust than the comparison methods.

Keywords: Fault tolerance · State machine replication · High performance · Distributed systems

Gang Wu is supported by the NSFC (Grant No. 61872072), the State Key Laboratory of Computer Software New Technology Open Project Fund (Grant No. KFKT2018B05), the National Key R&D Program of China (Grant No. 2016YFC140, and the Fundamental Research Funds for the Central Universities (Grant No. N2016009).

X. Wang et al. (Eds.): APWeb-WAIM 2020, LNCS 12317, pp. 808–823, 2020.
https://doi.org/10.1007/978-3-030-60259-8_59

1   Introduction

Many large scale web applications need to ensure high availability and high efficiency of the services. State Machine Replication (SMR) [13] based on various consensus protocols, such as Paxos [9] and PBFT [3], is a common approach to designing fault-tolerate online service systems, eg. Google's Chubby and Apache Zookeeper. According to SMR model, even some of the replicas fail, the services will be kept available with the avaliable consistent replicas. SMR achieves strong consistency by regulating every replica executing the same transactions in the same order.

SMR is mainly designed to improve the system's availability rather than its performance [4]. The requirement of the sequential execution of transactions makes it difficult to take full advantage of multi-core servers. It cannot directly execute transactions concurrently because the uncertainty of thread scheduling and lock competition would result in the undeterministic execution. However, the sequential execution is not a necessary requirement for consistency [13]. In short, dependent transactions(access the same records) must be handled in the same relative order on each replica to keep consistency, while independent trans-actions(access the different records) can be executed in parallel, which can fully utilize the processor's multi-core processing ability. Thus, basing on transaction semantics, how to use the transaction independence to improve the performance of SMR has become a hot research direction [1,2,7,8,11,12].

For example, CBASE [8] is a classic parallel replication framework proposed to enhance the performance of PBFT algorithm. It sets up a scheduler for every replica which constructs a dependency graph by finding the dependencies *pair-wise* among transactions in their total order. Based on the dependency graph, the scheduler dispatches transactions to idle threads in the thread pool for exe-cution. Once a transaction is executed by one thread, the scheduler removes it from the graph and responds to clients. The scheduler of CBASE maximizes concurrency among executions while ensuring replica consistency.

However, recent research [12] has shown that, under the conditions of high workload, determining dependencies among transactions by pairwise compar-isons, is a performance bottleneck. To overcome this problem, batchCBASE [12] determine the dependencies by *batch* comparison rather than a single transac-tion comparison once a time. However, it increases the possibility of inter-batch dependencies, and as transactions in each batch are executed sequentially, it loses some of the parallelism for those transactions within a batch. Moreover, in order to promise replica consistence and operation safety, the scheduling pro-cess of CBASE and batchCBASE are in single-threaded mode, which means the scheduler and worker threads cannot access the dependency graph at the same time, it introduce more overhead to the system.

In summary, parallel SMR schedulers now face four challenges: 1) faster detection of transaction dependencies; 2) not sacrificing any parallelism of the execution; 3) concurrent scheduling process; and 4) ensuring correctness. In this paper, we propose an efficient scheduler based on a specific index structure to address the above challenges. It consists of a special Bloom filter and corresponding transaction queues for each filter element, with the Bloom filter, the dependencies among transactions can be detected within a constant time. Transaction queues can maintain the total order relations of the transactions and also simplify the representation of the transaction dependency graph. Moreover, the proposed scheduler supports record-granularity and command-granularity locks with the help of the above mentioned index structure, thereby supporting the concurrent scheduling process (specifically the *insert*, *remove*, and *get* operations) of transactions. In summary, the proposed method can efficiently solve the performance loss problem caused by the heavy scheduling overhead from the dependency graph based comparisons, and it can guarantee the execution parallelism under various workloads with different dependency rates. To show the proposed model's advantages in throughput, scalability and robustness in comparison with CBASE and batchCBASE, experiments are conducted and analyzed on a database prototype. Furthermore, the consistency among replicas and other scheduling safety propositions are proved formally.

2   System Model

We assume a general distributed service system model of SMR, which is composed of an unbounded client sets $C = \{c_1, c_2, ...\}$ and a bounded server set $S = \{s_1, s_2, ..., s_n\}$. All servers in S are replicas of each other and work together to provide highly available services to the clients where the Paxos protocol is used to ensure consistency. The message transmission among distributed replicas is in asynchronous mode, which allows arbitrary message loss and delay. We assume that replicas follow the fail-stop model and never encounter a Byzantine error, which means the state of each replica is either *correct* or *crash*, and hence the system with $2f + 1$ replicas can tolerate f replicas crashing simultaneously.

The system ensures that if a request message m is sent without failing, all the unfaulty replicas will receive it, and eventually m will be decided in the consensus instance i, which is called that the replica accepts (i, m). The Paxos protocol can promise that at least half of the replicas will accept (i, m), and no replica will accept $(i, \hat{m})$ or $(\hat{i}, m)$, where $m \neq \hat{m}$ and $i \neq \hat{i}$. Intuitively, all

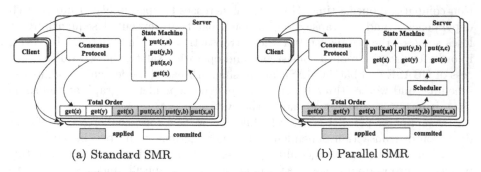

(a) Standard SMR   (b) Parallel SMR

Fig. 1. Standard versus parallel state machine replication

messages exist in most replicas or in none of them. If the messages exist, the order of messages on each replica is exactly the same, ie., *total order*.

In our system, the request messages are about transaction requests. According to the Paxos protocol, each transaction has two states in a replica *committed* and *applied* (see Fig. 1). The *committed* state represents that the transaction has been consistent with most of replicas but is not executed, and the state *applied* represents that it has been executed in this replica.

3   Parallel SMR

With the development of high-speed networks and efficient consensus protocols (eg., [10]), the CPU processing efficiency has becomes the next major performance bottleneck of SMR. It is manifested by the fact that the speed of *applied* is much slower than that of *committed*. There have been some attempts (e.g. [2,8,12]) so far to boost SMR with parallel execution by exploiting transaction dependencies. In this section, CBASE [8] and batchCBASE [12] are discussed, and conclusion of the motivation for our methods is presented in the end. More details about other related work can be found in Sect. 6.

To parallelize the execution of transactions, CBASE (see Fig. 1(b)) sets up a scheduler for each replica. The core of the scheduler is a dependency graph, which takes transactions as vertexes and the dependencies among transactions as directed edges. It keeps the partial order relationship between transactions. While accepting a transaction, the scheduler inserts it into the dependency graph. Based on the dependency graph, the scheduler dispatches free transactions to those idle threads in the thread pool for execution. Once a transaction t_i has been executed by a thread, the corresponding vertex and edges should be removed from the graph. Thus other transactions without predecessor dependencies can be executed next.

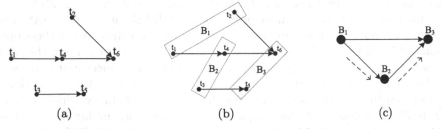

(a)   (b)   (c)

Fig. 2. CBASE and batchCBASE dependency graphs. (a) the dependency graph of CBASE. (b) and (c) show how batchCBASE works, i.e., $t_1 t_2$ becomes batch B_1, so they has to be executed sequentially though they are parallelizable; t_2 and t_3 have to be executed sequentially just because t_1 are conflict with t_4; Finally, all of them have to be executed sequentially as (c) where solid lines represents batch dependencies, and dotted lines represents execution trace.

Figure 2(a) shows how CBASE maintains the partial order of transactions based on the dependency graph. These transactions are agreed at each replica in a total order sequence $[t_1 t_2 t_3 t_4 t_5 t_6]$. Among them, $t_1 t_4 t_6$, $t_3 t_5$ and $t_2 t_6$ are dependent subsequences. For transactions in each such dependent subsequence, their position on the dependent graph path is determined by their relative order in the total order. Eg., $t_1 \rightarrow t_4 \rightarrow t_6$ represents t_6 depends on t_4, and t_4 depends on t_1, because t_1 arrives *committed* first, then t_4, and finally t_6. New transactions need to be compared to all transactions in the graph to determine the dependencies.

Intuitively, the overhead of building a dependent graph is related to the number of nodes in the graph. Specifically, the time complexity is $O(n^2)$. Experiments in batchCBASE [12] confirm that detecting conflicts (dependencies) between transactions is time consuming in heavy workloads. Therefore, batchCBASE is designed to reduce the number of comparisons by packing transactions into batches, as the example shown in Fig. 2(b). It allocates a bitmap of 1,000Kbit for each batch. If the intersection of two bitmaps is not empty, then it can be determined that the two batches have dependencies. Therefore, the time complexity of batchCBASE dependency detection is $O(l(n/m)^2)$, where l is a constant representing the time complexity of bit comparison using bitmap, n is the number of transactions, and m is the size of the batch. However, such batch-based method has a higher conflict probability between two batches. In theory, the conflict probability between two random transactions is $1/n$, while the conflict probability between two batches is $p = \sum_{i=1}^{m} \binom{n}{i} (\frac{i}{n})^m (\frac{n-i}{n})^m$. Thus, when the batch-based method is applied, the conflict probability has an exponential increase with respect to the batch size m.

Since transactions within each batch of batchCBASE is executed sequentially, the parallelism between transactions is reduced. In addition, if any two conflicting transactions from each batches conflict with each, the two batches have to be executed sequentially as well because the two batches of transactions are considered to be conflicted in this case. As shown in Fig. 2(b), when the batch size is 2, it will degenerate into a sequential execution as Fig. 2(c).

Moreover, since the scheduler operations of CBASE and batchCBASE, i.e. the *insert*, *remove*, and *get*, are mutually exclusive, the call to any of these operations will lock the whole dependency graph until it is finished. From this view, the scheduler runs in a single-threaded mode, which introduces extra overhead.

To sum up, (i) CBASE has a greater overhead of detecting dependency; in addition (ii) batchCBASE increases the conflict probability which makes it highly likely to degenerate into sequential execution, (iii)running mode of their scheduler operations is single-threaded. In next section we will describe more efficient ways to solve these problems.

4   Index-Based Scheduler Model

Our proposed method in this section dedicate to improving the performance of scheduler by designing a specific index structure and devising an elaborated concurrent scheduling scheme accordingly.

4.1   Overall Idea

The basic idea of the scheduler is as follows:

- The main part of the index structure is a simplified Bloom filter constructed from a single HashMap. Each key of the HashMap represents one record accessed by the transactions. Hence, without actually constructing and traversing the dependency graph, it can determine the dependency between transactions when they fall into the same Bloom filter bit by one hash.
- The value corresponding to each key of the HashMap is a FIFO queue containing all the transactions accessing the record of the key. Hence, any different transactions at the heads of all transaction queues of the HashMap can be executed concurrently.
- Based on the above index structure, it is easy to make the scheduler concurrently perform scheduling operations (i.e., insert, remove, get) with record-granularity and transaction-granularity lock, which can guarantee safety and correctness as well.

Transactions and Records: Transaction t_i is composed of one or couples of commands and records. We denote the total order of transaction O_T as $(T, <_T)$ where $T = \{t_i | i = 1, 2...\}$ and $<_T$ represents the total order between two transactions. Let the transaction t_i's record set $R_{t_i} = \{r_j | r_j$ is one of the record accessed by t_i's commands$\}$ and the transaction set accessing the common record r_j as $T_{r_j} = \{t_i | r_j$ is one of the records accessed by t_i's commands$\}$.

Bloom Filter: The Bloom filter is constructed from a single HashMap. Although a Bloom filter is usually composed of more than one hash functions, the only one hash used here is the one of the HashMap. The reason is that our Bloom filter is used not only for testing the existence of dependencies but also for indexing transaction queues according to the record accessed. This is achieved by letting record r be the key to be hashed and all the transactions in T_r be the corresponding value mapped. Thus, for a transaction t_i, the time complexity of finding all dependent transactions related to record r is O(1).

Transaction Queue: In order to provide efficient dependency detection and concurrent execution, all transactions in T_r is organized in a FIFO (First In First Out) queue as the value part of our Bloom filter corresponding to the key r. The transaction queue TQ_r of record r is actually a relative order $O_{T_r} = (T_r, <_T) \subseteq O_T$. Thus, for a record r, the time complexity of inserting a transaction at the end of or removing a transaction from the head of the queue is O(1). Note that a transaction may exist in different transaction queue because it usually operate on multiple records.

Simplified Dependency Graph: All transaction queues together can form a simplified dependency graph which is consistent in order $<_T$ but much simpler in structure compared with the original complete dependency graph. Since the dependency relation and relative order between transactions are all transitive, it is not necessary to explicitly establish a complete total order through pairwise

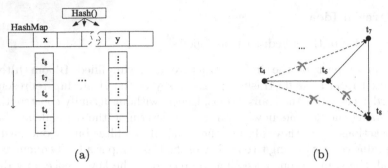

Fig. 3. Example of index structure and simplified dependency graph. (a) The index structure with four transactions having the same records x in the same FIFO transaction queue. (b) The transaction queue in (a) only keeps necessary total order between every two adjacent transactions, eg. the edge t_4 to t_7, t_4 to t_8 and others in the origin dependency graph are omitted naturally.

comparison within the transactions. Therefore, the proposed index structure can effectively reduce the overhead of detection and scheduling. Figure 3 exemplifies the basic idea of dependency graph simplifying.

Free Transaction: In our scheduler, after a transaction t_i is inserted into scheduler, it is said to be ***free***, iff $\forall r_j \in R_{t_i}, TQ_{r_j}.head = t_i$. If a transaction is free, it can be scheduled to be executed. If a transaction is still in transaction queue, it means that the transaction is under execution or not yet executed, in one word, unfinished.

Fine-Grained Lock: Two kinds of locks are set: queue lock and transaction lock. Queue lock is used for inserting and deleting transactions by the scheduler, because these two operations will modify the transaction queue. It means that when the scheduler operates transaction t_i on the above index structure, the scheduler will only lock those transaction queues corresponding to the records of R_{t_i}. The transaction lock represents the lock held by each transaction, which is only used when detecting whether the transaction can be executed. Operations in the same location (i.e. transaction queue) of HashMap are mutually exclusive, while operations in different locations are concurrent.

4.2   Detailed Algorithm of Implemention

Algorithm 1 shows how our scheduler works in detail. When the system starts, procedure $Initialization()$ initializes a HashMap (line 7), and then initializes N worker threads for waiting to execute transactions (lines 8–10). The length of HashMap does can be less than the number of records. In this case, there will be a certain probability that the hash function maps two different records to the same position. Fortunately, such false positives do not violate the consistency because those transactions that incorrectly fall into the same transaction queue will be safely executed sequentially.

Algorithm 1. Index-based scheduler

1: **data structures and variables**
2:   *Transaction t*   {transaction}
3:   *int N*   {number of worker threads}
4:   *TQueue TQ*   {transaction queue}
5:   *HashMap HM*   {HashMap}

6: **procedure** Initialization()
7:     initialize *HM*
8:     $N \leftarrow$ desired number of worker threads
9:     **for** $id = 1 \ldots N$ **do**   {initialize every worker thread}
10:         create and start a worker thread thr_{id}

11: *The scheduler executes as follows:*
12: **while** accept($t_i \in T$) **do**   {accept t_i from T}
13:     $t_i.run = true$ {used for t_i executed exactly once}
14:     dgInsertAndGet(t_i)   {scheduler inserts t_i}

15: **function** bool: free(t_i)
16:     **for** $r \in R_{t_i}$ **do**
17:         $TQ_r = HM(r)$ {Bloom Filter used as index}
18:         **if** $t_i! = TQ_r.head$ **then**
19:             return *false*
      return *true*

20: **procedure** dgInsertAndGet(t_i)
21:     **for** $r \in R_{t_i}$ **do**
22:         $TQ_r = HM(r)$
23:         Lock(TQ_r)
24:         TQ_r.insert(t_i)
25:         **if** $r == R_{t_i}.last$ **then**
26:             Lock(t_i)
27:             **if** $t_i.run \wedge free(t_i)$ **then**
28:                 $t_i.run = false$
29:                 notify worker threads to execute t_i
30:             Unlock(t_i)
31:         Unlock(TQ_r)

32: **procedure** dgRemoveAndGet(t_i)
33:     **for** $r \in R_{t_i}$ **do**
34:         $TQ_r = HM(r)$ {Bloom Filter used as index}
35:         Lock(TQ_r)
36:         TQ_r. remove(t_i)
37:         Unlock(TQ_r)
38:         $t_j = TQ_r.head$ {candidate next to be executed}
39:         Lock(t_i)
40:         **if** $t_i.run \wedge free(t_j)$ **then**
41:             $t_i.run = false$
42:             notify working threads to execute t_j
43:         Unlock(t_i)

44: *Each worker thread executes as follows:*
45: **while** $t_i \leftarrow$ *notification from the scheduler* **do**
46:     execute transaction t_i
47:     dgRemoveAndGet(t_i)

Once the scheduler accepts transactions, it will insert them into the index according to their total order (lines 12–14). As stated earlier, a transaction can be scheduled to be executed, if it does not depend on any other transactions, i.e., being *free*. There are two situations. (i) For a newly accepted transaction, if there is no dependency detected, it can be executed directly; (ii) For a transaction in the transaction queue that has not been executed yet, it must be dependent and cannot be executed until its dependent transactions are all executed and removed. Therefore unlike CBASE and batchCBASE, our scheduler does not require a separate *get* operation, but combines it with the insert operation and the remove operation to be *dgInsertAndGet* and *dgRemoveAndGet* respectively. They are detailed as follows:

dgInsertAndGet: The operation first inserts t_i into transaction queues that correspond to each record $r \in R_{t_i}$ (lines 21–24), and then determines whether t_i can be executed (lines 25–29) now. If t_i appears at the head of all corresponding transaction queues after insertion, it must be free and can be executed immediately. Otherwise, t_i can not be executed directly. Thus it will be scheduled to worker threads in *dgRemoveAndGet*(t_j). Only one transaction queue corresponding to each record in R_{t_i} is locked at a time. The process of detecting only needs to obtain it's own transaction lock(line 26 and 30) (through transaction lock table). If the transaction can be executed, it's flag run(line 28) will be set to false, and the detection process of *dgRemoveAndGet* will fail.

dgRemoveAndGet: Remove a finished transaction t_i from the index may also need to operate on multiple transaction queues. With the help of HashMap in our index, those transaction queues that correspond to each record $r \in R_{t_i}$ can be easily obtained (line 34). In our scheduler, transactions to be executed or finished transactions to be removed are kept at the head of corresponding transaction queues, which makes the remove operation more efficient. Transactions at the head of each TQ_r is checked for free after removing finished transaction t_i. Only the transaction lock (line 39 and 43) of itself needs to be obtained in the process of detecting, which can ensure that the executable transaction can be detected only once. Both *dgInsertAndGet* and *dgRemoveAndGet* achieve the goal of not having to lock all transaction queues. The operations of index-based scheduler have the maximum concurrency when it is measured by the number and granularity of the lock.

4.3   Correctness

The key to the design of the scheduler is to ensure the security of scheduling operations and the consistency of the state of the transaction execution results between replicas. In addition to a large number of tests in practice, here we highlight the validity of replica consistency and the operation safety theoretically.

Replica Consistency: conflicting transactions are processed in total order, which is guaranteed by following:

1) Safety 1 (preserve total orders of conflict transactions): All transactions are inserted into the transaction queue in the order $<_T$ they arrive (lines 12 to 14). When inserting a new transaction, all of it's conflicting transactions in the index will be calculated by hash, and it will be inserted into the tail of transaction queues. The inner sequence of queue encodes the conflicts between transactions, all transaction queues are equivalent to a DAG.

2) Safety 2 (preserve total order of transactions when getting transactions from the index): a transaction can only be scheduled when it is in the head of all corresponding transaction queues, that is, it can only be scheduled when there is no dependency edge in the DAG (lines 15 to 19). Because each edge E represents a dependency relation, no transaction will be executed regardless of the total order of the conflicting transactions.

3) Deadlock free: the first transaction does not depend on any other transactions and can be executed freely. When the executed transaction t_i is deleted, and all outgoing edges of node t_i in DAG are deleted (lines 36). Because the transaction only depends on the previous transaction, then t_j, $t_i <_T t_j$ will delete the last edge of the incoming dependency with the deletion of t_i, and it can execute freely: there is always the lowest (free) node in the graph.

4) Exactly once: all transactions will be executed and only once. Since the transaction t_i has $<_T$ order in the DAG and there is no deadlock, t_i will eventually be processed. When a transaction is detected to be executed in the process of $dgInsertandGet$ and $dgRemoveandGet$, there will be competition of transaction lock. If t_i is first preempted by $dgInsertandGet$ after inserting into the graph, then the flag $t_i.run$ will be set to false, and $dgRemoveandGet$ will not be able to detect the execution. Similarly, if the latter acquires the lock, the former will not be able to detect, so it can be guaranteed that t_i will only be executed once.

Consistency of all Replicas: All replicas deliver the same total order $<_T$, run the same algorithm, which can guarantee the order of conflicting transactions without considering the relative speed of different replicas. This is achieved by follows: Replicas may process at different speeds, so there may be different sets of transactions waiting to be executed. When transaction t_i is delivered as the same $<_T$ in two replicas Ra and Rb, t_i may belong to the pending batch in Ra, but not in Rb. In this case, Rb executes it in total order, while in Ra, if there are conflicts, it will be executed in total order, and concurrently otherwise. In any case, the total order between conflicting transactions can be guaranteed.

5   Experiments

5.1   System Prototype and Environment

To evaluate the performance of our index-based scheduler, called fastCBASE, we deployed it on a database in C/S service model, as well as CBASE/batchCBASE whose implementation follows [12]. All source code of them are published online

[5]. The whole system runs on a cluster of four HP nodes. Three of them work as servers, playing the role of proposer and acceptor in Paxos protocol, and each has 2 E5-2620 CPU, 2.10 GHz, a total of 24 threads, and 256G memory. The client is deployed in the other HP node with four-way E7-4820 CPU, 2.0 GHz, 8 cores per channel, a total of 64 threads. The clients send large number of transactions to make the servers fully loaded. All applications are implemented by go1.12.1. All communication goes through ER3200G2, a gigabit network switch.

5.2   Goals and Methods

Since our scheduler is proposed to ensure the maximum concurrency among transactions with a lower scheduler load, the main experimental purposes are:

- the speed-up achieved compared to state-of-art
- the scalability with a growing number of worker threads
- the impacts of scheduling overhead
- the false positive introduced by Bloom filter
- the impacts of conflicts on performance of scheduler

For the first point, in order to observe the most obvious speed-up ability of our scheduler and other schedulers, we evaluate each scheduler's performance under conflict-free workloads, and compare the performance under the same number of worker threads with CBASE and batchCBASE.

For the second point, we evaluate the performance improvement of our scheduler with an increasing number of threads under the conflict-free workloads, and compare it with CBASE and batchBASE.

For the third point, we can analyze with the above experimental results.

For the fourth point, since batchCBASE uses two bitmaps bitwise comparison methods in conflict detection and our scheduler uses Bloom Filter, all of them will introduce false positive conflict. We compare the false positive rate introduced by these two scheduler models under different bitmap (HashMap) sizes.

For the fifth points, we compare the performance changes of our scheduler and batchCBASE under different conflict rate workloads.

5.3   Speed-Up Analysis

Figure 4 shows the system throughput of CBASE, batchCBASE and our fastCBASE without conflict. The performance of different batch sizes are tested since the batch size of batchCBASE has a significant impact on it.

It can be seen that the traditional CBASE has a very low performance, because the scheduler has a large overhead in the dependency detection, which severely limits the throughput of the whole system. As the number of worker threads increases, its performance does not increase significantly. With 16 threads, it only achieves a throughput of about 1000 Trans/S. Even though many worker threads are available, the scheduler cannot fully utilize them.

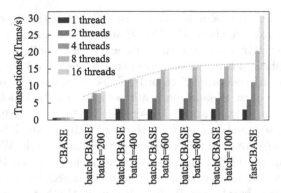

Fig. 4. Threads scalability for contention-free workloads

To improve the performance of the system, batchCBASE sacrifices scheduling freedom (transaction sequential execution within batch) for a lower number of comparisons. It can be seen that the performance of batchCBASE is more significantly improved than that of CBASE, and the performance of it increases linearly with the increase of the number of threads in 1, 2, 4, but it does not increase with batch size, which indicates that the scheduler is not a performance bottleneck, throughput is limited by the number of available worker threads.

The larger the batch of batchCBASE is, the lower the scheduler workload and the better the performance will be. The speedup of its performance gradually stabilizes gradually as the batch increases, as shown in Fig. 4. By the start of 8 threads, the performance no longer increases linearly with the number of threads in every batch. This is because although the number of comparisons is reduced by batch, the load scheduling is still relatively high compared to our scheduler.

Because of our elaborate concurrent scheduling process based on the special index structure, although our scheduler needs to manage each transaction, it is still even more efficient than batchCBASE. Figure 4 shows that the throughput of our scheduler in 8 and 16 threads is much higher than batchCBASE. And unlike batchCBASE, the performance of our method improves much near linearly with the increase of the number of threads, so it has strong scalability.

5.4 Conflict Rate Analysis

In this section, we compare the conflict rate generated by our fastCBASE scheduler with Bloom filter and compare the rate generated by batchCBASE with the bitmap of each batch through simulation.

In the simulation, unfinished transactions in the scheduler are stored in the execution queue which represents the transactions are being processed. If the new transaction conflicts with all transactions, the conflict rate is 100%. If it does not conflict with any transactions, the conflict rate is 0. Therefore, the conflict rate can be defined as: the conflict proportion of the new transaction and the unfinished transactions in the queue at a given period of time or at a specific length of the queue. In our simulation, we use a fixed length of execution queue to calculate conflict rate. For batchCBASE, if at least one common bitmap position is set as 1 in both bitmaps of the two batches, then a conflict is computed.

In our simulation, a transaction contains only one record without loss of generality. We randomly generate 10^8 records. Thus the probability of generating the same record twice in the simulation is almost zero (10^{-8}), which means conflict rate generated is mainly caused by false positive. In our scheduler, the impact on the conflict rate mainly comes from the size of HashMap. The conflict rate of batchCBASE is also affected by the size of bitmap and batch. We conducted 10^6 times simulation, the length of the execution queue is set to 10,000, ie., there are average 10,000 unfinished transactions in the scheduler. The corresponding batchCBASE has a graph size of 50 nodes when the batch size is 200, and a graph size of 25 nodes when the batch size is 400. And we set up the HashMap and bitmap size to 100 K and 1M respectively. The experimental results are show in Table 1.

Table 1. Conflict rate

HashMap size	fastCBASE conlict rate	batchCBASE conlict rate, batch = 200	batchCBASE conlict rate, batch = 400
102400	0.000984%	32.558%	79.332%
1024000	0.0000975%	3.844%	14.796%

It can be seen from Table 1 that under the same configuration, the conflict rate of batchCBASE is nearly 10,000 times of the rate of fastCBASE. As the size of HashMap or bitmap increases, the conflict rate of fastCBASE and batchCBASE will decrease, but batchCBase will amplify the conflict rate due to batch, which will also increase the false positive rate. Therefore, in reality, even if the conflict rate is very low, batchCBASE will still be greatly affected, while the false positive rate brought by our scheduler would hardly affect the performance.

5.5   Speed-Up Analysis for Conflict-Prone Workloads

Figure 5 shows that the throughput of our scheduler decreases with the increase of conflict rate. When the conflict rate is 10%, only the throughput of 16 threads decreases. This is because with the increase of the conflict rate, the parallelism of transaction execution decreases, consequently the utilization of multi-threading is reduced. For the same reason, when the conflict rate is 20%, the throughput of 8 threads begins to decrease. And as the conflict rate continuous to increase, the performance gain caused by the increase of the threads' number is significantly reduced. When the conflict rate is more than 50%, i.e. more than half of the transactions cannot be executed in parallel, the redundant threads cannot be utilized, and the performance on different threads is approximately equal.

Based on the results of Fig. 5, it can be known that our scheduler can allow a maximum parallelism among transactions. When the conflict rate reaches 20%, there is still similar performance to the batchCBASE under conflict-free workload. With the conflict rate increasing, our scheduler is more robust.

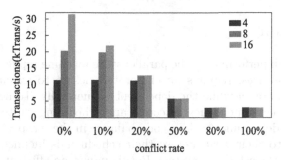

Fig. 5. Throughput under different conflict rate workloads

6   Related Work

Different from CBASE, an early schedule system model (scheduler not in replica) is proposed by [11]. By setting up a client proxy, all client transactions are grouped according to transaction's semantic. Independent transactions can be allocated to different groups, and dependent transactions must be allocated to the same group. Each group of transactions is sent to all servers by atomic broadcast. Serve-side proxy maps groups to specific threads. A transaction may conflict with transactions in multiple groups. Therefore, synchronization among groups is required to ensure that the transaction is executed only once. To optimize the process of thread scheduling in [11], a multi-objective programming model [2] is proposed to maximize parallelism and minimize execution time. To achieve the optimal scheduling results, high time complexity is required either. Therefore, the existence (or absence) of an optimization model that combines early scheduling and concurrency is still an open question.

Rex [4], an execute-agree-follow model, in which a primary machine is free to execute transactions concurrently at first, and uncertain decisions are recorded in a partial order trace, and then other secondary machines will receive the trace and executes the same trace concurrently, which keeps consistency with the primary. Eve [7] implements deterministic parallelism through a scheduler called mixer, and replicas execute transactions in parallel in a speculative manner. After the execution, the validity of the replica status is checked during the validation phase. If too many replicas are inconsistent, the replica will roll back to the previous validated state and re-execute the command sequentially. Unlike Eve, Storyboard [6] enhances SMR through a prediction mechanism that predicts the order of locks across replicas. When the prediction is correct, the transactions can be executed in parallel. If the prediction does not match the execution path of the transactions, the replica must establish a deterministic execution sequence with other replicas through consensus protocol. In this case, Storyboard stops the current execution and repredicts the execution path. All replicas will re-execute the transactions based on the new path.

7   Conclusion

To promise a high performance, the parallel state machine replication, often used in online web services, requires an elaborated design to execute independent transactions in parallel while the dependent sequentially. To achieve this goal, efficient and correct dependency detection and scheduling strategies are needed. The existing models cannot make a good balance in these aspects, whose advantages also lead to their weakness, so their scheduler is inclined to become the performance bottleneck of the system. In this paper, an efficient scheduler based on a specific index structure is designed to detect dependency, express partial order relations and to schedule transactions, which can ensure the maximum parallelism of the execution between transactions to fully exploit the advantages of multi-core processors, and also can keep consistency among replicas. To further improve the space utilization, in the future work we will try some space compression methods to cover the situation where a transaction may be inserted to multiple queues.

References

1. Alchieri, E., Dotti, F., Mendizabal, O.M., Pedone, F.: Reconfiguring parallel state machine replication. In: 2017 IEEE 36th Symposium on Reliable Distributed Systems (SRDS), pp. 104–113. IEEE (2017)
2. Alchieri, E., Dotti, F., Pedone, F.: Early scheduling in parallel state machine replication. arXiv preprint arXiv:1805.05152 (2018)
3. Castro, M., Liskov, B.: Practical Byzantine fault tolerance and proactive recovery. ACM Trans. Comput. Syst. (TOCS) **20**(4), 398–461 (2002)
4. Guo, Z., Hong, C., Yang, M., Zhou, D., Zhou, L., Zhuang, L.: Rex: replication at the speed of multi-core. In: Proceedings of the Ninth European Conference on Computer Systems, p. 11. ACM (2014)
5. The fastCBASE website (2019). https://github.com/kisisjrlly/PSMR.git
6. Kapitza, R., Schunter, M., Cachin, C., Stengel, K., Distler, T.: Storyboard: Optimistic deterministic multithreading. In: HotDep (2010)
7. Kapritsos, M., Wang, Y., Quema, V., Clement, A., Alvisi, L., Dahlin, M.: All about eve: execute-verify replication for multi-core servers. In: Presented as part of the 10th {USENIX} Symposium on Operating Systems Design and Implementation ({OSDI} 12), pp. 237–250 (2012)
8. Kotla, R., Dahlin, M.: High throughput Byzantine fault tolerance. In: International Conference on Dependable Systems and Networks, 2004, pp. 575–584. IEEE (2004)
9. Lamport, L.: The part-time parliament. ACM Trans. Comput. Syst. (TOCS) **16**(2), 133–169 (1998)

10. Lamport, L.: Fast paxos. Distrib. Comput. **19**(2), 79–103 (2006). https://doi.org/10.1007/s00446-006-0005-x
11. Marandi, P.J., Bezerra, C.E., Pedone, F.: Rethinking state-machine replication for parallelism. In: 2014 IEEE 34th International Conference on Distributed Computing Systems, pp. 368–377. IEEE (2014)
12. Mendizabal, O.M., Moura, R.S.T.D., Dotti, F.L., Pedone, F.: Efficient and deterministic scheduling for parallel state machine replication. In: 2017 IEEE International Parallel and Distributed Processing Symposium, pp. 748–757 (2017)
13. Schneider, F.B.: Implementing fault-tolerant services using the state machine approach: a tutorial. ACM Comput. Surv. (CSUR) **22**(4), 299–319 (1990)

Author Index

An, Yinan   I-319

Bao, Qing   II-360
Bi, Xin   I-154

Cai, Hui   II-45
Cai, Lei   II-529
Cao, Yifan   I-112
Chen, Chen   I-86, II-473, II-491
Chen, Enhong   I-558, II-117
Chen, Hong   I-363
Chen, Jing   I-53, I-779
Chen, Lili   II-164
Chen, Qihang   II-523
Chen, Shuo   I-639
Chen, Tianran   II-376
Chen, Tingxuan   I-145
Chen, Xiaojun   II-500
Chen, Yanmin   I-558
Chen, Yuanxu   II-545
Chen, Zhigang   I-286
Chen, Zitong   I-127
Cheng, Li   II-156
Cheng, Meng   I-424
Cheng, Ning   II-545
Cong, Qing   II-70
Cui, Bin   II-230
Cui, Dingshan   II-193
Cui, Lizhen   I-779, II-132
Cui, Xiaohui   I-764
Cui, Zhiming   I-181, I-409

Dai, Bo   II-221
Dai, Hanbo   II-351
Deng, Hongyan   II-540
Deng, Sijia   II-529
Deng, Xiaobin   I-478
Ding, Guangyao   II-523
Ding, Xiaoou   II-61
Ding, Yicheng   II-27
Dong, Sicong   I-212
Du, Guowang   I-612
Duan, Lei   II-193

Fan, Yonggang   II-3
Fang, Jiaofeng   I-639
Fang, Junhua   I-181, I-286, I-409, II-101
Fang, Lintao   I-558
Fang, Wenxiu   II-457
Feng, Dan   I-639
Feng, Zhiyong   I-102, I-212, II-70
Fu, Ada Wai-Chee   I-127
Fu, Bin   I-517
Fu, Peng   I-574

Gao, Han   I-242, I-257
Gao, Hong   I-319
Ge, Bin   I-544
Ghaleb, Taher Ahmed   II-85
Gong, Zheng   I-11
Gu, Gao   I-257
Gu, Jingzi   I-574
Gu, Yu   I-53, II-409
Guo, Qiang   I-700
Guo, Qingxing   II-529
Guo, Wei   I-779, II-132
Guo, Xintong   I-319

Han, Donghong   I-808
Han, Jingjing   II-342
Han, Lihua   II-535
Hao, Bowen   I-363
He, Anxun   I-716
He, Wei   I-779
He, Xiaofeng   II-45
He, Xin   II-294
He, Ying   I-286
Hong, Xiaoguang   I-378, I-588
Hou, Meihao   II-132
Hu, Jiayuan   I-740
Hu, Qinghua   I-69
Hu, Sen   I-302
Hu, Wei   I-700
Hu, Yong   I-603
Hu, Zhigang   I-145
Hu, Zhiqiang   II-221
Huang, Heyan   I-603
Huang, Wenjing   II-261

Huang, Xiaomei   I-478
Huang, Yongqin   II-156
Huang, Zhangcheng   I-716
Huang, Zhenya   II-117
Huang, Zhichao   I-162
Huang, Zhiqiu   II-391
Huo, Hairong   II-270
Huo, Lijun   I-544

Iwaihara, Mizuho   II-261, II-270

Ji, Genlin   II-342
Ji, Tao   I-439
Ji, Wanlin   I-352
Ji, Ye   I-242
Jia, Danping   II-317
Jiang, Cheng   II-101
Jiang, Jingang   II-117
Jiang, Wenbin   I-685
Jin, Cheqing   II-529
Jin, Hai   I-20, I-685
Jin, Jian   II-317
Jin, Yuanyuan   I-439

Kang, Xiang   I-20
Ke, Zhihui   I-424
Khaled, Afifa   II-85
Kong, Xiangnan   I-670

Lai, Yongxuan   I-470
Lan, Tian   I-603
Lee, Roy Ka-Wei   II-221
Lei, Kai   II-230
Leung, Victor   I-112
Li, Biao   II-176
Li, Bo   I-574
Li, Bohan   I-242, I-257
Li, Chao   II-141
Li, Chuanwen   I-53, II-409
Li, Cuiping   I-363
Li, FangFang   II-409
Li, Fengqi   II-3, II-18
Li, Fuxue   I-154
Li, Hui   I-11, I-779, II-351
Li, Keqiu   I-424
Li, Lin   I-655
Li, Rongrong   II-491
Li, Sizhuo   I-212

Li, Wei   II-360
Li, Xiang   I-3
Li, Xiangyu   I-302
Li, Xiao   I-3
Li, Xiaoli   II-245
Li, Xutao   I-162
Li, Ying   II-342
Li, Yukun   I-627, II-556
Li, Yusen   II-457
Li, Zhixu   I-286, I-409
Li, Zijue   II-61
Lian, Defu   II-117
Liang, Xingya   I-227
Liao, Guoqiong   I-478
Lim, Ee-peng   II-221
Lin, Chunbin   II-164
Lin, Nanzhou   II-176
Lin, Yinnian   II-517
Liu, Baozhu   I-212
Liu, Guiquan   I-558
Liu, Hongzhi   I-517
Liu, Huan   II-245
Liu, Jiaxu   I-37
Liu, Jin   I-764
Liu, Jing   II-3
Liu, Kemeng   I-455, II-3, II-18, II-309
Liu, Mingyu   II-342
Liu, Pai   I-685
Liu, Pengkai   I-212
Liu, Richen   II-342
Liu, Ruyang   I-270
Liu, Xiao   I-764
Liu, Xiaoguang   II-457
Liu, Xin   I-227
Liu, Xinyu   II-457
Liu, Xinyue   I-670
Liu, Xu   II-540
Liu, Yong   I-170
Liu, Zhenyu   II-425
Long, Cheng   I-127
Long, Jun   I-145
Lu, Haiqin   II-209
Lü, Kevin   I-612
Luo, Qianwen   II-491
Luo, Xing   I-439

Mao, Xian-Ling   I-603
Meng, Xue   II-351

Nawaz, Ásif   II-391
Ni, Jiacheng   I-409
Nie, Feiping   II-500
Nie, Yuxiang   I-603
Nummenmaa, Jyrki   II-193

Ou, Zhonghong   I-455, II-309
Own, Chung-Ming   I-740, II-85

Pan, Xiao   II-535
Pan, Yu   II-457
Pan, Zian   I-69
Pang, Xuanrong   II-500
Pei, Chaohan   I-748
Peng, Jing   I-685
Peng, Xiaoya   II-285
Peng, Yuwei   II-491
Peng, Zhaohui   I-378, I-588
Peng, Zhiyong   II-176

Qi, Jiarui   I-603
Qian, Lei   I-700
Qian, Weining   II-101, II-441, II-523
Qiang, Yang   I-286
Qiao, Baiyou   I-808
Qiao, Yongwei   I-337
Qin, Ruiqi   II-193
Qiu, Shengguang   I-700
Qiu, Tie   I-424
Qu, Xiaoyang   I-794

Rao, Guozheng   I-212, II-70
Ren, Gang   II-327
Ren, Xiaoxu   I-112
Ren, Zhuo   II-409
Rong, Chuitian   II-164
Ruan, Chunyang   I-748

Shah, Mira   II-141
Shao, Jie   I-196
Shao, Yingxia   I-37, II-230
Shen, Derong   II-327
Shen, Rujia   II-360
Shen, Yuan   II-27
Sheng, Ming   II-141
Sheng, Victor S.   I-145, I-181, I-409
Sheng, Yongpan   I-196
Shi, Bei   II-245
Shi, Yanan   II-309

Shi, Zhan   I-639
Shu, Ke   II-101, II-441
Song, Meina   I-455, II-309
Song, Wei   II-27, II-176
Song, Yang   I-517
Song, Yidong   I-808
Stones, Rebecca J.   II-457
Su, Rui   II-261
Su, Sen   I-37
Su, Tingwei   II-209
Su, Xunbin   II-517
Sun, Cihai   II-425
Sun, Leilei   I-337, I-352
Sun, Renjie   I-86

Tan, Yanxin   I-455, II-309
Tan, Zhen   II-294
Tang, Jiuyang   II-294
Tang, Yanxi   I-794
Tao, Shuo   II-117
Tao, Tianyi   I-394
Tao, Wenyuan   I-740, II-85
Tian, Peng   I-394
Tuo, Yupeng   II-376

Wan, Changxuan   I-478
Wang, Binglei   I-558
Wang, Chengyu   II-45
Wang, Chongjun   I-725
Wang, Fang   I-639
Wang, Feng   II-540
Wang, Gang   II-457
Wang, Guosen   I-394
Wang, Guowei   I-655
Wang, Hao   I-558
Wang, Hongya   II-425
Wang, Hongzhi   II-61, II-551
Wang, Jianzong   I-716, I-794, II-545
Wang, Jun   I-509
Wang, Lei   II-221
Wang, Lizhen   I-612
Wang, Lulu   I-574
Wang, Mei   II-209
Wang, Meng   I-242, I-257, I-270
Wang, Qiange   I-53
Wang, Qingqin   I-493
Wang, Senzhang   II-391
Wang, Shengfa   II-3
Wang, Shuhai   II-535

Wang, Song   II-491
Wang, Sufang   II-540
Wang, Suge   II-245
Wang, Tao   I-3
Wang, Weiguang   II-376
Wang, Weiping   I-574
Wang, Xiaofei   I-112
Wang, Xiaoling   I-439
Wang, Xiaotong   II-101
Wang, Xiaoyang   I-86
Wang, Xin   I-764
Wang, Xinao   II-193
Wang, Yijie   II-156
Wang, Yingxue   I-11, II-351
Wang, Yixuan   II-551
Wang, Zheng   I-196
Wei, Jinmao   I-509
Wei, Wenqi   II-545
Wei, Xiaochi   I-603
Wu, Gang   I-808
Wu, Hao   I-764
Wu, Haoyu   II-18
Wu, Peiyun   I-102
Wu, Yang   I-127
Wu, Yanping   I-86
Wu, Zhonghai   I-517

Xian, Xuefeng   I-181, I-409
Xiao, Chunjing   I-337, I-352
Xiao, Jing   I-716, I-794, II-545
Xiao, Shan   II-193
Xiao, Yingyuan   II-425
Xing, Chunxiao   II-141
Xiong, Anshu   I-470
Xiong, Yun   I-394, I-493, I-670
Xu, Chen   II-523
Xu, Hengpeng   I-509
Xu, Jiajie   I-181, I-409
Xu, Jian   II-360
Xu, Liang   I-535
Xu, Lixin   II-327
Xu, Ming   II-360
Xu, Tong   I-558
Xu, Wenya   II-556
Xu, Yang   I-378

Yan, Yu   II-551
Yang, Fan   I-470, II-132
Yang, Guang   I-378

Yang, Han   I-242, I-270
Yang, Jian   II-209
Yang, Lei   I-639
Yang, Liner   I-603
Yang, Liu   I-145
Yang, Peibiao   II-540
Yang, Shipeng   I-470
Yang, Shu   II-500
Yang, Wenxin   I-639
Yang, Xiandi   II-176
Yang, Yajun   I-69, I-227
Yang, Yudi   I-612
Yang, Yun   I-748
Yang, Yundan   II-535
Yang, Zhenglu   I-509
Yao, Junjie   I-535
Yao, Xin   II-535
Ye, Yunbo   I-627, II-556
Ye, Yunming   I-162
Yin, Yueshuang   I-170
Yu, Botao   I-700
Yu, Ge   I-53, II-409
Yu, Philip S.   I-493
Yu, Zheng   II-294
Yuan, Chao   II-164
Yuan, Hao   II-360
Yuan, Pingpeng   I-20

Zhang, Chuanyan   I-588
Zhang, Chuhan   I-170
Zhang, Chunxi   II-441
Zhang, Dalei   I-286
Zhang, Fuxiang   I-227
Zhang, Hengda   I-112
Zhang, Jianwei   I-655
Zhang, Jiasheng   I-196
Zhang, Jinchao   I-574
Zhang, Jing   I-154, I-363, I-627
Zhang, Jingyuan   I-270
Zhang, Juntao   II-176
Zhang, Junyu   I-145
Zhang, Le   I-558
Zhang, Lei   I-725
Zhang, Li   II-70
Zhang, Minxu   II-230
Zhang, Nan   I-794
Zhang, Peng   II-540
Zhang, Qing   I-112
Zhang, Rong   II-101, II-441
Zhang, Tao   I-517

Zhang, Xiaowang   I-102
Zhang, Xinyue   I-270
Zhang, Xu   II-18
Zhang, Yan   I-627
Zhang, Yanchun   I-748
Zhang, Yao   I-394, I-670
Zhang, Yi   I-725
Zhang, Yingjie   I-535
Zhang, Yong   II-141
Zhang, Yongzheng   II-376
Zhang, Yuxiang   II-245
Zhang, Yuxin   I-242
Zhang, Zhao   II-529
Zhang, Zhecheng   I-725
Zhang, Zhen   I-154
Zhao, Bin   II-342
Zhao, Bingchen   I-270
Zhao, Guodong   I-808
Zhao, Jun   I-86
Zhao, Kai   I-455, II-540
Zhao, Kechun   I-11
Zhao, Lei   I-181

Zhao, Pengpeng   I-181, I-409
Zhao, Shuying   II-70
Zhao, Weiliang   II-209
Zhao, Xiang   I-544, II-294
Zhao, Xiangguo   I-154
Zheng, Chu   I-102
Zheng, Jiping   II-473
Zheng, Xin   I-286
Zhou, Aoying   II-101, II-441, II-523
Zhou, Bao   II-545
Zhou, Dong   II-285
Zhou, Lihua   I-612
Zhou, Xiaobo   I-424
Zhu, Mingdong   II-327
Zhu, Xingwei   I-181
Zhu, Yanchao   II-529
Zhu, Yangyong   I-394, I-493, I-670
Zhu, Yinlong   I-725
Zhu, Yuesheng   II-230
Zou, Jian   II-551
Zou, Lei   I-302, II-517
Zou, Zhaonian   I-319

Printed in the United States
By Bookmasters